West's Law School Advisory Board

JESSE H. CHOPER
Professor of Law,
University of California, Berkeley

DAVID P. CURRIE
Professor of Law, University of Chicago

YALE KAMISAR
Professor of Law, University of Michigan

MARY KAY KANE
Dean and Professor of Law, University of California,
Hastings College of the Law

WAYNE R. LaFAVE
Professor of Law, University of Illinois

ARTHUR R. MILLER
Professor of Law, Harvard University

GRANT S. NELSON
Professor of Law,
University of California, Los Angeles

JAMES J. WHITE
Professor of Law, University of Michigan

TAX PROCEDURE AND TAX FRAUD
CASES AND MATERIALS
Third Edition

By

Marvin J. Garbis
of the Maryland and District of Columbia Bars

Ronald B. Rubin
of the Maryland and District of Columbia Bars

and

Patricia T. Morgan
Associate Dean and Associate Professor
Georgia State University, College of Law

AMERICAN CASEBOOK SERIES®

American Casebook Series, and the West Group symbol
are registered trademarks used herein under license.

COPYRIGHT © 1982, 1987 WEST PUBLISHING CO.
COPYRIGHT © 1992 By WEST PUBLISHING CO.
  610 Opperman Drive
  P.O. Box 64526
  St. Paul, MN 55164-0526
All rights reserved
Printed in the United States of America

Library of Congress Cataloging-in-Publication Data

Garbis, Marvin Joseph.
    Tax procedure and tax fraud : cases and materials / by Marvin J.
Garbis, Patricia T. Morgan, Ronald B. Rubin. — 3rd ed.
      p.   cm. — (American casebook series)
  Includes index.
  ISBN 0-314-89561-2
    1. Tax administration and procedure—United States—Cases. 2. Tax
protests and appeals—United States—Cases. 3. Tax evasion—United
States—Cases. I. Morgan, Patricia T., 1949–   II. Rubin,
Ronald B. III. Title. IV. Series.
KF6320.A7G37 1991
343.7304'2—dc20
[347.30342]
                                                91-29465
                                                    CIP

ISBN 0-314-89561-2

(G., R. & M.) Tax Proc. & Fraud 3rd ACB

For my family, Phyllis, Kendall, Jason, and Kerri and those who made Garbis, Marvel & Junghans the Camelot of law firms during our wonderful years together.

M.J.G.

To my Wife, Elisabeth, and my Daughter, Julia

R.B.R.

To Don Winslow, with gratitude

P.T.M.

*

Preface

The need for a new edition became clear in 1988 with the passage of the Omnibus Taxpayer Bill of Rights, and became even clearer in late 1989 with the passage of the Improved Penalty Administration and Compliance Tax Act, which overhauled and streamlined the civil penalties for violation of the Internal Revenue Code. Numerous significant cases and administrative pronouncements underscored the need for a new edition.

As in the previous editions, case and statute citations, as well as footnotes, of courts and commentators are omitted without so specifying. Numbered footnotes are from the original materials and retain the original numbering. Deletions from the text of cases and commentary are indicated by asterisks. The occasional use of one gender alone in the authors' text includes the other gender as well, unless the context indicates otherwise.

We are grateful to the many colleagues and students who have patiently supported this project.

MARVIN J. GARBIS
Baltimore, Maryland

RONALD B. RUBIN
Washington, D.C.

PATRICIA T. MORGAN
Atlanta, Georgia

October, 1991

Acknowledgments

The authors wish to acknowledge the generous support of numerous individuals. Foremost is Professor Donald A. Winslow of the University of Kentucky Law School, whose insights contributed significantly to the changes made in this edition. Substantial contributions were also made by the following students, among others: William Bennett, Alvin Ginsburg, Lisa Harper, and Russell Mobley (Georgia State University College of Law); and Jill Michaels and Ned Sato (both in the University of Florida Graduate Tax Program in 1990–91). Without the organizational skills and support of Melody Robinson (Assistant to the Associate Dean, GSU Law School) and Regina McNeil (research assistant), the process of converting the manuscript to its final form would have been immeasurably more difficult. The authors thank each of these individuals, and apologize for not mentioning numerous others who have provided insight and support.

The authors also wish to thank the following authors and publishers for their permission to reprint the materials listed below.

American Bar Association, A.B.A. Standing Committee on Ethics and Professional Responsibility, Formal Opinion 85–352, 39 Tax Lawyer 631 (1986). Formal Opinion 85–352 is copyrighted by the American Bar Association. All rights reserved. Reprinted with permission. The reprinted material from the American Bar Association does not constitute the full text of the opinion but rather is an excerpt from the opinion.

American Bar Association, Guidelines to Tax Practice Second, Frederic G. Corneel, 43 Tax Lawyer 297 (1990). Copyright 1990, The Tax Lawyer and the American Bar Association. All rights reserved. Reprinted with permission.

T. Gallagher, Jr., The Tax Legislative Process, 3 The Review of Taxation of Individuals 203 (1979). Reprinted with permission from the Review of Taxation of Individuals, Summer 1979, Volume 3, Number 3, Copyright 1979, Warren, Gorham and Lamont, Inc., 210 South Street, Boston, Mass. 02111. All rights reserved.

M. Garbis, P. Junghans and S. Struntz, Federal Tax Litigation—Civil Practice and Procedure (1985) and 1989 Supplement. Reprinted with permission from Federal Tax Litigation—Civil Practice and Procedure, by Marvin J. Garbis, Paula M. Junghans and Stephen C. Struntz. Copyright 1985, Warren, Gorham and Lamont, Inc., 210 South Street, Boston, Mass. 02111. All rights reserved.

M. Saltzman, IRS Practice and Procedure (1981). Reprinted with permission from IRS Practice and Procedure, by Michael I. Saltzman. Copyright 1981, Warren, Gorham and Lamont, Inc., 210 South Street, Boston, Mass. 02111. All rights reserved.

Summary of Contents

	Page
PREFACE	v
ACKNOWLEDGMENTS	vii
TABLE OF CASES	xxv
TABLE OF INTERNAL REVENUE CODE SECTIONS	xxxi

Chapter I. Introduction to the Federal Tax System 1
Sec.
1. Department of the Treasury 1
2. Department of Justice 7
3. Congress 8
4. Compliance With the Tax Laws 12

Chapter II. Responsibilities of the Tax Practitioner 16
1. Background 16
2. The Ethics of Tax Practice 17
3. Treasury Department Standards 36
4. The Multiple Representation Issue 48
5. Statutory Regulation of Income Tax Return Preparers ... 52

Chapter III. Administrative Rulemaking and Rulings 56
1. Treasury Regulations 56
2. Requests for Rulings and Determination Letters 66
3. Confidentiality and Disclosure 85

Chapter IV. Administrative Determination of Liability for Tax 121
1. Examination of Tax Returns 121
2. Administrative Appeals 131
3. Requests for Technical Advice 139
4. Settlement and Closing Agreements 140
5. The TEFRA Partnership Procedures 151

Chapter V. Statutes of Limitations on Assessment of Tax and Claims for Refund 161
1. Statute of Limitations on the Assessment of Deficiencies ... 161
2. Limitation on Filing Refund Claims and Suits 184
3. Equitable Recoupment and the Mitigation Provisions 189

Chapter VI. Civil Penalties and Interest 217
1. Historical Development 217
2. Information Reporting Penalties 220
3. The Accuracy-Related Penalties and the Civil Fraud Penalty 223

Sec.		Page
4.	Preparer, Promoter and Protester Penalties	277
5.	Delinquency Penalties	310
6.	Interest on Deficiencies and Overpayments	318

Chapter VII. Civil Tax Litigation 321
1. Taxpayers' Choice of Forum 321
2. Burden of Proof in Civil Tax Litigation 331
3. Tax Court Litigation 342
4. Tax Refund Litigation 400
5. Taxpayer's Suit on Account Stated 420
6. Special Partnership Litigation Procedures 421
7. Res Judicata and Collateral Estoppel 432
8. Suppression of Evidence in Civil Tax Cases 453
9. Recovery of Attorneys' Fees 457

Chapter VIII. The Internal Revenue Service Summons 483
1. The Formal Interview ("Q & A") 483
2. The Summons Power 486
3. Enforceability of the Summons 491
4. The Evidentiary Privileges 513
5. Third-Party Recordkeeper Summonses 526
6. The "John Doe" Summons 529

Chapter IX. Federal Tax Crimes and Methods of Proof 537
1. The Tax Crimes 537
2. Methods of Proof of Income 617

Chapter X. Criminal Tax Investigations and Prosecutions 631
1. Criminal Tax Investigations 631
2. Cash Transaction Reporting and Asset Forfeiture 663
3. Criminal Tax Prosecutions 696
4. The Fifth Amendment Claim on Tax Returns 704

Chapter XI. Collection of the Tax 717
1. Overview 717
2. Judicial and Administrative Collection Procedures 722
3. Jeopardy and Termination Assessments 753
4. Trust Fund Taxes (Withholdings) 778
5. Transferee and Fiduciary Liability 810
6. The Innocent Spouse Provisions 821
7. Restraining Tax Collection 835
8. Wrongful Levy 856
9. Bankruptcy 862

Appendices

App.
A. Power of Attorney (Form 2848) and Tax Information Authorization (Form 8821) 886

SUMMARY OF CONTENTS

App.		Page
B.	Waiver of Restrictions on Assessment and Collection of Deficiency in Tax and Acceptance of Overassessment (Form 870), Offer of Waiver of Assessment and Collection of Deficiency in Tax and Acceptance of Overassessment (Form 870–AD), Agreement as to Final Determination of Tax Liability (Form 866), Closing Agreement on Final Determination Covering Specific Matters (Form 906)	893
C.	Consent to Extend the Time to Assess Income Tax (Form 872), Special Consent to Extend the Time to Assess Tax (Form 872–A), Notice of Termination of Special Consent to Extend the Time to Assess Tax (Form 872–T)	904
D.	Tax Court Petition Forms: Form 1—Petition (Other Than in Small Tax Case) Form 2—Petition (Small Tax Case)	911
E.	Report of Cash Payments Over $10,000 Received in a Trade or Business (Form 8300)	914
INDEX		917

Table of Contents

	Page
PREFACE	v
ACKNOWLEDGMENTS	vii
TABLE OF CASES	xxv
TABLE OF INTERNAL REVENUE CODE SECTIONS	xxxi

Chapter I. Introduction to the Federal Tax System 1
Sec.
1. Department of the Treasury 1
    A. Internal Revenue Service 2
        (1) National Office 3
        (2) Office of Regional Commissioner 3
        (3) Service Centers 4
        (4) Office of District Director 4
        (5) Assistant Commissioner (International) 5
    B. Office of Chief Counsel 5
    C. Office of the Director of Practice 6
    D. Office of the Assistant Secretary for Tax Policy 7
2. Department of Justice 7
3. Congress 8
    The Tax Legislative Process 8
    Note 12
4. Compliance With the Tax Laws 12

Chapter II. Responsibilities of the Tax Practitioner 16
1. Background 16
    Question 17
2. The Ethics of Tax Practice 17
    United States v. Yorke 17
    Formal Opinion 85–352 of the American Bar Association Standing Committee on Ethics and Professional Responsibility 19
    Note 22
    Guidelines to Tax Practice Second 22
    Note 36
3. Treasury Department Standards 36
    IRS Practice and Procedure 36
    Note 42
    Treasury Department Circular 230 42
    Owrutsky v. Treasury Secretary 46
4. The Multiple Representation Issue 48
    Backer v. Commissioner 48
    Notes and Questions 51
5. Statutory Regulation of Income Tax Return Preparers 52

xiii

	Page
Chapter III. Administrative Rulemaking and Rulings	56

Sec.
1. Treasury Regulations 56
   A. Retroactive Application of Treasury Regulations 57
      Manhattan General Equipment Co. v. Commissioner 58
      Helvering v. R.J. Reynolds Tobacco Co. 59
      Notes 61
   B. Judicial Review of Treasury Regulations 62
      United States v. Vogel Fertilizer Co. 62
2. Requests for Rulings and Determination Letters 66
   A. Types of Rulings 66
   B. Revocation, Reliance and Retroactivity 71
      Lesavoy Foundation v. Commissioner 72
      Automobile Club of Michigan v. Commissioner 75
      Dixon v. United States 77
   C. Discriminatory Treatment 79
      Bookwalter v. Brecklein 79
      Question 84
3. Confidentiality and Disclosure 85
   A. The Freedom of Information Act 85
      Notes 89
      United States Department of Justice v. Tax Analysts 90
   B. The Privacy Act of 1974 102
   C. The Confidentiality Provisions of the Internal Revenue Code 103
      Calder v. IRS 104
      Barrett v. United States 107
      Mid-South Music Corp. v. United States 111
      Lampert v. United States 116
      Notes and Questions 120

Chapter IV. Administrative Determination of Liability for Tax 121

1. Examination of Tax Returns 121
   A. Selection of Returns for Examination 121
   B. Examination Procedures 123
   C. Closings, Reopenings and Second Inspections 128
      Council of British Societies in Southern California v. United States 128
      Notes 131
2. Administrative Appeals 131
   A. The "30–Day Letter" 131
   B. The Appeals Office 134
   C. Are Administrative Appeals Required? 136
      Luhring v. Glotzbach 136
3. Requests for Technical Advice 139

Sec.		Page
4.	Settlement and Closing Agreements	140
	A. Form 870 (Consent to Assessment)	140
	Maloney v. Commissioner	141
	B. Form 870–AD (Agreement to Assessment)	143
	Kretchmar v. United States	144
	C. Forms 866 and 906 (Closing Agreements)	149
	D. Collateral Agreements	150
5.	The TEFRA Partnership Procedures	151
	Notes	160

Chapter V. Statutes of Limitations on Assessment of Tax and Claims for Refund 161

1. Statute of Limitations on the Assessment of Deficiencies 161
   A. Basic Rules 161
   B. Assessment 163
      Notes 163
   C. Commencement of Running of Limitation Period 167
      Question 167
      Blount v. Commissioner 169
      Badaracco v. Commissioner 171
   D. Special Six-Year Limitations Period for 25% Omissions ... 176
      The Colony, Inc. v. Commissioner 176
      Note 178
   E. Extension of Limitations by Agreement 178
      Roszkos v. Commissioner 179
      Notes 184
2. Limitation on Filing Refund Claims and Suits 184
   A. Limitations on Filing Refund Claims 185
   B. Timely Filing of Refund Suit 188
3. Equitable Recoupment and the Mitigation Provisions 189
   A. Statutory Mitigation 190
      (1) Existence of a "Determination." 191
         Rasmussen v. United States 191
         Note 193
      (2) The "Inconsistency" Requirement 193
         Chertkof v. Commissioner of Internal Revenue 193
         Note 197
      (3) The Seven "Circumstances of Adjustment" 197
         Gardiner v. United States 197
   B. Equitable Recoupment 202
      United States v. Dalm 203
      Note 216

Chapter VI. Civil Penalties and Interest 217

1. Historical Development 217
2. Information Reporting Penalties 220
3. The Accuracy-Related Penalties and the Civil Fraud Penalty 223
   A. Background 223

Sec.			Page
3.	The Accuracy–Related Penalties and the Civil Fraud Penalty—Continued		
	B.	Uniform Reasonable Cause Exception	223
	C.	Negligence	224
		(1) Amount of the Penalty	224
		(2) Burden of Proof	225
		(3) Definition of "Negligence"	225
		Coleman v. Commissioner	225
		Druker v. Commissioner of Internal Revenue	228
		Notes	230
	D.	Substantial Understatement of Income Tax	231
		(1) Amount of the Penalty	231
		Woods II v. Commissioner	232
		Note	238
		(2) "Authority" and "Substantial Authority"	238
		Note	240
		(3) Adequate Disclosure	241
		(4) Tax Shelter Items	242
	E.	Substantial Valuation Misstatements	245
		(1) Substantial Valuation Overstatements (Section 6662(e))	245
		Todd v. Commissioner of Internal Revenue	245
		Note	251
		(2) Substantial Estate or Gift Tax Valuation Understatements (Section 6662(g))	252
		(3) Substantial Overstatements of Pension Liabilities (Section 6662(f))	252
	F.	The Civil Fraud Penalty	253
		(1) The Meaning of "Fraud"	253
		Estate of Spruill v. Commissioner	253
		Notes	271
		(2) Amount of the Penalty	276
		(3) Statute of Limitations	277
4.	Preparer, Promoter and Protester Penalties		277
	A.	Return Preparer Penalty	277
		Judisch v. United States	277
		Brockhouse v. United States	284
		Notes	292
	B.	Promoting Abusive Tax Shelters	297
		Gates v. United States	297
		Notes	302
	C.	Aiding and Abetting Understatement of Tax Liability	303
		Kuchan v. United States	303
		Notes	305
	D.	Frivolous Returns	306
		Colton v. Gibbs	306
		Note	308

Sec.		Page
4.	Preparer, Promoter and Protester Penalties—Continued	
	E. Court–Imposed Sanctions and Costs	308
	Larsen v. Commissioner	308
	Note	310
5.	Delinquency Penalties	310
	A. Failure to File a Return or Pay Tax	311
	United States v. Boyle	312
	Notes	316
6.	Interest on Deficiencies and Overpayments	318

Chapter VII. Civil Tax Litigation ... 321

1. Taxpayers' Choice of Forum ... 321
2. Burden of Proof in Civil Tax Litigation ... 331
   A. Refund Suits ... 332
      United States v. Janis ... 332
   B. Tax Court ... 334
      Anastasato v. Commissioner ... 334
      Jones v. Commissioner ... 337
      Note ... 342
3. Tax Court Litigation ... 342
   A. Jurisdictional Prerequisites ... 342
      (1) Timely Filed Petition ... 342
         McKay v. Commissioner ... 342
         Abeles v. Commissioner ... 345
         Notes ... 356
      (2) Sufficiency of Notice of Deficiency ... 357
         Scar v. Commissioner ... 357
      (3) Proper Party Petitioner ... 371
         Fletcher Plastics, Inc. v. Commissioner ... 371
         Holt v. Commissioner ... 374
         Note ... 376
      (4) Irrevocability of Tax Court Jurisdiction ... 377
         Estate of Ming, Jr. v. Commissioner ... 377
   B. Decision–Making Authority of the Tax Court ... 378
      Notes ... 379
   C. Some Aspects of Tax Court Procedure ... 384
      (1) Discovery ... 384
         HongKong and Shanghai Banking Corp. v. Commissioner ... 385
      (2) Stipulations ... 388
      (3) Sanctions ... 389
         Stringer v. Commissioner ... 390
         Note ... 392
      (4) Settlement ... 392
         Notes and Questions ... 395
      (5) Small Case Procedure ... 396
   D. Treatment of Diverse Courts of Appeals Precedents ... 396
      Golsen v. Commissioner ... 396

Sec.				Page
3.	Tax Court Litigation—Continued			
	E.	Declaratory Judgments and Disclosure Actions		397
		Note		399
4.	Tax Refund Litigation			400
	A.	Jurisdictional Prerequisites		400
	B.	The Full Payment Rule		400
		Flora v. United States		400
		Notes and Questions		408
		(1) The Divisible Tax Concept		409
			Steele v. United States	409
		(2) Payment on an Assessment		410
	C.	The Claim for Refund		410
		(1) Formal Requirements		410
			Hatter v. United States	412
		(1) Informal Refund Claims		415
		(2) New Grounds		415
			United States v. Ideal Basic Industries, Inc.	416
	D.	Timely Filing of Refund Suit		416
	E.	The Anti-Assignment Statute		418
		Wall Industries, Inc. v. United States		419
5.	Taxpayer's Suit on Account Stated			420
6.	Special Partnership Litigation Procedures			421
	Barbados # 6 Ltd. v. Commissioner			421
	Maxwell v. Commissioner			425
7.	Res Judicata and Collateral Estoppel			432
	A.	Government a Party in First Case		432
		Commissioner v. Sunnen		432
		Wright v. Commissioner		437
		Moore v. United States		441
		Notes and Questions		442
	B.	Government Not a Party in First Case		443
		Meier v. Commissioner		443
		Note		453
		Question		453
8.	Suppression of Evidence in Civil Tax Cases			453
	United States v. Janis			453
	Note			456
9.	Recovery of Attorneys' Fees			457
	Minahan v. Commissioner			459
	United States v. McPherson			468
	Bode v. United States			470

Chapter VIII. The Internal Revenue Service Summons ... 483

1.	The Formal Interview ("Q & A")	483
	Note	486
2.	The Summons Power	486
	Reisman v. Caplin	487

Sec.		Page
2.	The Summons Power—Continued	
	Notes and Questions	490
3.	Enforceability of the Summons	491
	A. The "*Powell* Standard"	491
	United States v. Powell	491
	B. Legitimate Purpose and Good Faith	494
	United States v. Abrahams	494
	United States v. Michaud	497
	Note: The TEFRA Provisions	502
	Pickel v. United States	502
	Notes and Questions	505
	C. Relevance	506
	United States v. Arthur Young & Company	506
	D. Information Not Within IRS Possession	509
	United States v. Texas Heart Institute	509
	Note	511
	E. Second Inspections	511
	United States v. Gilpin	511
	Notes and Questions	513
4.	The Evidentiary Privileges	513
	A. The Attorney–Client Privilege and the Work–Product Doctrine	513
	United States v. El Paso Company	514
	Notes and Questions	519
	B. The Privilege Against Self–Incrimination	520
	Braswell v. United States	520
	C. The Defense of Lack of Possession	525
5.	Third–Party Recordkeeper Summonses	526
	Rapp v. Commissioner	527
	Notes and Questions	529
6.	The "John Doe" Summons	529
	Tiffany Fine Arts, Inc. v. United States	529
	Notes and Questions	535
Chapter IX. Federal Tax Crimes and Methods of Proof		**537**
1.	The Tax Crimes	537
	A. The Basic Tax Offenses	540
	(1) Sections 7201, 7203 and 7207	540
	Spies v. United States	540
	Sansone v. United States	544
	Notes	548
	(2) Sections 7206(1) and 7206(2)	549
	United States v. Greenberg	549
	United States v. DiVarco	551
	United States v. Shortt Accountancy Corp.	554
	United States v. Reynolds	559
	United States v. Crum	561

Sec.		Page
1.	The Tax Crimes—Continued	
	B. The Willfulness Element	562
	(1) Willfulness Defined	562
	United States v. Bishop	562
	United States v. Pomponio	567
	(2) Willfulness Applied	568
	Cheek v. United States	568
	United States v. Jalbert	579
	Bursten v. United States	580
	Note	584
	United States v. Ausmus	584
	United States v. Garber	586
	United States v. Curtis	602
	United States v. Montalvo	605
	Notes and Questions	611
	United States v. Reynolds	611
	D. Statute of Limitations	613
	United States v. Habig	613
	United States v. Shorter	616
	Notes and Questions	617
2.	Methods of Proof of Income	617
	A. Direct Proof: The Specific Items Method	617
	B. Indirect Proof	618
	(1) The Net Worth Method	618
	Holland v. United States	618
	(2) The Cash Expenditures Method	626
	Taglianetti v. United States	626
	(3) The Bank Deposits Method	628
	United States v. Esser	628
	(4) The Percentage Mark-Up Method	629

Chapter X. Criminal Tax Investigations and Prosecutions ... 631

1.	Criminal Tax Investigations	631
	A. Defense Concerns at the Early Stages of the Investigation	633
	United States v. Richard Hebel	634
	B. Miranda-Type Warnings	639
	Mathis v. United States	639
	C. Searches and Seizures	641
	Voss v. Bergsgaard	641
	Note	644
	United States v. Caceres	645
	United States v. Payner	648
	Weiss v. Commissioner	652
	Notes and Questions	656
	D. Grand Jury Proceedings	657
	United States v. Baggot	659
	Notes and Questions	663

Sec.			Page
2.	Cash Transaction Reporting and Asset Forfeiture		663
	Questions		664
	A.	Money Laundering and Cash Transaction Reporting	664
		Notes	666
		In re Grand Jury Proceedings 88–9 (MIA)	667
	B.	Asset Forfeiture	672
		Caplin & Drysdale, Chartered v. United States	673
		Notes	695
3.	Criminal Tax Prosecutions		696
	A.	Venue	697
		United States v. United States District Court	697
		Notes and Questions	700
	B.	The Use of Summary Witnesses and Charts	701
		United States v. Citron	701
4.	The Fifth Amendment Claim on Tax Returns		704
	United States v. Sullivan		704
	Garner v. United States		705
	Question		710
	United States v. Carlson		711
	United States v. Neff		714
	Notes and Questions		716

Chapter XI. Collection of the Tax 717

Sec.			Page
1.	Overview		717
	A.	Assessment, Notice and Demand	720
	B.	The Federal Tax Lien	720
2.	Judicial and Administrative Collection Procedures		722
	United States v. Rodgers		722
	United States v. National Bank of Commerce		740
	Notes and Questions		752
3.	Jeopardy and Termination Assessments		753
	Laing v. United States		754
	Fidelity Equipment Leasing Corp. v. United States		760
	Williams v. Commissioner		764
	Notes		777
4.	Trust Fund Taxes (Withholdings)		778
	A.	Responsible Persons' Liability	778
		(1) The Basic Tests	778
		Slodov v. United States	778
		Roth v. United States	786
		Notes and Questions	798
		(2) Joint and Several Liability	800
		USLIFE Title Insurance Co. v. Harbison	800
		(3) Designation of Payments	802
	B.	Liability of Providers of Wages	803
		United States v. Fred A. Arnold, Inc.	803

Sec.		Page
4.	Trust Fund Taxes (Withholdings)—Continued	
	C. Lenders' Liability	806
	Jersey Shore State Bank v. United States	806
5.	Transferee and Fiduciary Liability	810
	Hunt v. Commissioner	810
	Grieb v. Commissioner	816
6.	The Innocent Spouse Provisions	821
	Purcell v. Commissioner	821
	Price v. Commissioner of Internal Revenue	827
	Notes and Questions	835
7.	Restraining Tax Collection	835
	Note	836
	Enochs v. Williams Packing & Navigation Co.	836
	Note	838
	Commissioner v. Shapiro	839
	Notes and Questions	842
	Flynn v. United States	842
	Notes and Questions	846
	Miklautsch v. Gibbs	847
8.	Wrongful Levy	856
	Lemaster v. United States	856
	Notes	862
9.	Bankruptcy	862
	Anglemyer v. United States	866
	Begier v. IRS	871
	United States v. Energy Resources Co.	882

Appendices

App.		
A.	Power of Attorney (Form 2848) and Tax Information Authorization (Form 8821)	886
B.	Waiver of Restrictions on Assessment and Collection of Deficiency in Tax and Acceptance of Overassessment (Form 870), Offer of Waiver of Assessment and Collection of Deficiency in Tax and Acceptance of Overassessment (Form 870–AD), Agreement as to Final Determination of Tax Liability (Form 866), Closing Agreement on Final Determination Covering Specific Matters (Form 906)	893
C.	Consent to Extend the Time to Assess Income Tax (Form 872), Special Consent to Extend the Time to Assess Tax (Form 872–A), Notice of Termination of Special Consent to Extend the Time to Assess Tax (Form 872–T)	904
D.	Tax Court Petition Forms Form 1—Petition (Other Than in Small Tax Case) Form 2—Petition (Small Tax Case)	911

App.		Page
E.	Report of Cash Payments Over $10,000 Received in a Trade or Business (Form 8300)	914

INDEX 917

Table of Cases

The principal cases are in bold type. Cases cited or discussed in the text are roman type. References are to pages. Cases cited in principal cases and within other quoted materials are not included.

Abeles v. Commissioner, 345
Abrahams, United States v., 494
Adams v. Commissioner, 395
Aetna Casua'ty & Surety Co., United States v., 418, 419
Alexander v. "Americans United" Inc., 838
American Pac. Inv. Corp. v. Nash, 862
American Radiator & Standard Sanitary Corp. v. United States, 415
American Trucking Ass'ns, United States v., 346
Anastasato v. Commissioner, 334
Anderson v. United States, 799
Anglemyer v. United States, 866
Application of (see name of party)
Ardalan v. United States, 408
Arthur Andersen & Co. v. I.R.S., 88
Arthur Young & Co., United States v., 506
Ausmus, United States v., 584
Automobile Club of Michigan v. Commissioner, 75

Backer v. Commissioner, 48, 51, 484
Badaracco v. Commissioner, 171, 277
Baggot, United States v., 659, 663
Baird v. Koerner, 666
Baker v. United States, 84
Barbados #6 Ltd. v. Commissioner, 421
Barrett v. United States, 107, 120
Barth, United States v., 525
Bast v. I.R.S., 89
Bauer v. United States, 799
Beacon Federal Sav. & Loan, United States v., 657
Begier v. I.R.S., 871
Bell v. Gray, 188, 417
Belton v. Commissioner, 862
Bishop, United States v., 562
Blount v. Commissioner, 169
Bob Jones University v. Simon, 838
Bob Jones University v. United States, 61
Bode v. United States, 470
Bokum v. Commissioner, 835
Bolich v. Rubel, 384
Bonwit Teller & Co. v. United States, 420
Bookwalter v. Brecklein, 79
Boyle, United States v., 312
Braswell v. United States, 520

Bright, Estate of v. United States, 260
Brockhouse v. United States, 284, 292
Budlong v. Commissioner, 349
Bull v. United States, 202
Bursten v. United States, 580
Busher, United States v., 540

Caceres, United States v., 62, 645, 656
Cache Valley Bank, United States v., 752
Calder v. I.R.S., 104
Campbell v. Eastland, 410
Campise v. Commissioner, 168
Caplan v. Bureau of Alcohol, Tobacco and Firearms, 89
Caplin & Drysdale, Chartered v. United States, 673, 695
Carlson, United States v., 711, 716
C.B.C. Super Markets, Inc. v. Commissioner, 443
Chamberlain v. Kurtz, 87
Cheek v. United States, 568
Chertkof v. Commissioner of Internal Revenue, 193, 197
Chertkof v. United States, 190
Chicago Golf Club, United States v., 400
Chrysler Corp. v. Brown, 88
Church of Scientology of California v. I.R.S., 108 S.Ct. 271, p. 87
Church of Scientology of California v. I.R.S., 792 F.2d 146, p. 120
Citron, United States v., 701
Clifford, Helvering v., 436
Coffey v. Commissioner, 184
Coleman v. Commissioner, 225
Colony, Inc., The v. Commissioner, 176
Colton v. Gibbs, 306
Colton v. United States, 485
Commissioner v. ___ (see opposing party)
Conway v. I.R.S., 87, 88
Copeland, United States v., 548
Cortese, United States v., 506
Council of British Societies in Southern California v. United States, 128
Cox, United States v., 584
Crouch v. Commissioner, 836
Crum, United States v., 561
Curry v. United States, 408
Curtis v. Commissioner, 131

Curtis, United States v., 602
CWT Farms, Inc. v. Commissioner, 62

Dalm, United States v., 202, 203, 216
DeMarco, United States v., 701
Detroit Trust Co. v. United States, 188, 417
DiBella v. United States, 641
Dick v. I.R.S., 88
DiVarco, United States v., 551
Dixon v. United States, 71, 77
Doe (John) No. 462, In re, 525
Druker v. Commissioner of Internal Revenue, 228, 230

18th St. Leader Stores v. United States, 189, 417
Eighty-Eight Accounts, United States v., 696
Einson-Freeman Co. v. Corwin, 189, 417
El Paso Co., United States v., 514
Energy Resources Co., Inc., United States v., 882
Enochs v. Williams Packing & Nav. Co., 836, 838
E.P.A. v. Mink, 88
Equitable Trust Co., United States v., 506
Ernst & Whinney, United States v., 535
Erwin v. United States, 419
Esser, United States v., 628
Estate of (see name of party)
Ettelson, United States v., 752
Euge, United States v., 491
Ewing v. United States, 163, 166, 167, 187, 410

Factory Storage Corp. v. United States, 410
Fairley v. United States, 216
Falcone v. I.R.S., 88
Farmer v. United States, 835
Farnsworth & Chambers Company v. Phinney, 410
Feist v. United States, 798, 799
Fidelity Equipment Leasing Corp. v. United States, 760
First Bank, United States v., 529
First Nat. State Bank of New Jersey, United States v., 511
Fletcher Plastics, Inc. v. Commissioner, 371
Flora v. United States, 332, 400, 408, 847
Flynn v. United States, 842, 846, 847
Fred A. Arnold, Inc., United States v., 803
Friend, Application of, 520
Fruehauf Corp. v. I.R.S. (Freuhauf II), 103

Garber, United States v., 586
Garbutt Oil Co., United States v., 185, 188, 417
Gardiner v. United States, 197
Gardner v. Commissioner, 395
Garman, United States v., 697
Garner v. United States, 705
Garsky, United States v., 750, 752

Gates v. United States, 297, 302
Gehl Co. v. Commissioner, 62
Gilpin, United States v., 511
Gimbel, United States v., 384, 506
Goetz, United States v., 716
Goldberger & Dubin, P.C., United States v., 664, 666
Goldstein, United States v., 632
Golsen v. Commissioner, 323, **396**
Goodyear, United States v., 548
Grabinski, United States v., 716
Grand Jury, In re, 51
Grand Jury Proceedings 88–9 (MIA), In re, 667
Grand Jury Subpoenas Served Feb. 27, 1984, In re, 525
Grand Jury Testimony of Attorney X, In re, 519
Grasso v. I.R.S., 89
Greenberg, United States v., 549
Grieb v. Commissioner, 816
Grumman Aircraft Engineering Corp. v. Renegotiation Bd., 88
Grunwald v. Commissioner, 179

Habig, United States v., 613
Harper v. United States, 102
Harris v. United States, 752
Harrison v. Commissioner, 357
Hatter v. United States, 412
Hawkes v. I.R.S., 85, 89
Hebel and Merritt, United States v., 636, 638
Heffner, United States v., 656
Helvering v. ____ (see opposing party)
Heverly v. Commissioner, 69
Hillig v. Commissioner, 392
Hodge and Zweig, United States v., 520
Holifield v. United States, 667
Holland v. United States, 618
Holt v. Commissioner, 374
Home Beneficial Life Ins. Co., Inc., United States v., 753
Hongkong and Shanghai Banking Corp. v. Commissioner, 385
Hook, United States v., 617
Horst, Helvering v., 436
Hotel Conquistador, Inc. v. United States, 415
Houser v. Commissioner, 455, 457
Huckaby, United States v., 525
Hughes Tool Co. v. Meier, 449
Hunt v. Commissioner, 810
Hunydee v. United States, 519
Hutchens Metal Products, Inc. v. Bookwalter, 185

Ideal Basic Industries, Inc., United States v., 416
Indiana Nat. Bank v. Gamble, 752
In re (see name of party)
I.N.S. v. Lopez–Mendoza, 456
Investigative Grand Jury Proceedings, Matter of, 51

Irons v. Bell, 89
Irvine, United States v., 656, 657

Jalbert, United States v., 579
Janis, United States v., 332, 453, 456
Jersey Shore State Bank v. United States, 806
John Doe Corp., In re, 520
Johnson v. Department of Treasury, 103
Jones v. Commissioner, 337, 673
Jones, Estate of v. Commissioner, 396
Jones University, Bob v. Simon, 838
Jones University, Bob v. United States, 61
Judisch v. United States, 277, 292

Kanter v. I.R.S., 89
Karras, United States v., 491
Keado v. United States, 357
Key Buick Co. v. Commissioner, 457
Kinney-Lindstrom Foundation, Inc. v. United States, 418, 419
Kirtley v. Bickerstaff, 862
Klein, United States v., 611
Kolom v. United States, 190
Kotmair v. Commissioner, 442
Kretchmar v. United States, 144
Kuchan v. United States, 303

Laing v. United States, 753, 754, 759
Lambropoulos v. United States, 408
Lampert v. United States, 116
Larsen v. Commissioner, 308
LaSalle Nat. Bank, United States v., 502, 505
Leahey, United States v., 656
LeCroy Research Systems Corp. v. Commissioner, 62
Lemaster v. United States, 855, 856
Leon, United States v., 456, 644
Lesavoy Foundation v. Commissioner, 72
Lewis, United States v., 604 F.Supp. 1169, p. 491
Lewis, United States v., 16 AFTR 2d 5244.1, p. 484
Liebman, United States v., 535
Linsteadt v. I.R.S., 89
Lipsett v. United States, 400
LTV Corp. v. Commissioner, 379, 381, 382
Luhring v. Glotzbach, 136
Luzaich v. United States, 89

Maloney v. Commissioner, 141
Malquist, United States v., 716
Manglitz, United States v., 663
Manhattan General Equipment Co. v. Commissioner, 58
Manocchio v. Commissioner, 85
Marchant, United States v., 697
Maroscia v. Levi, 89
Massachusetts v. Sheppard, 644
Mathis v. United States, 639
Matter of (see name of party)
Matut v. Commissioner, 777

Maxwell v. Commissioner, 421, 425
McEachern v. Rose, 202
McGowan v. Commissioner, 379, 381, 382
McKay v. Commissioner, 342
McMullen, United States v., 657
McPartlin, United States v., 519
McPhaul, United States v., 484
McPherson, United States v., 468
McQuade v. Commissioner, 453
Meier v. Commissioner, 271, 443, 453
Michaud, United States v., 497
Michel, United States v., 400
Mickler v. Fahs, 442
Mid-South Music Corp. v. United States, 111
Mierzwicki, United States v., 519
Miklautsch v. Commissioner, 722
Miklautsch v. Gibbs, 845, 847
Minahan v. Commissioner, 459
Ming, Jr., Estate of v. Commissioner, 377
Miranda v. State of Arizona, 633
Mistretta v. United States, 539
Mitchell, In re, 306
Mitchell, Helvering v., 442
Montalvo, United States v., 605
Moore v. United States, 360 F.2d 353, pp. 441, 442
Moore v. United States, 235 F.Supp. 387, p. 442
Morton v. Ruiz, 62, 86

National Bank of Commerce, United States v., 722, 740
National Parks and Conservation Ass'n v. Kleppe, 88
Neaderland v. Commissioner, 442
Neff, United States v., 714, 716
N.L.R.B. v. Robbins Tire & Rubber Co., 88
Noel's Estate, Commissioner v., 61
Norton, United States v., 862
Novo Trading Corp v. Commissioner, 419
Nuth, United States v., 656

O'Brien v. United States, 190
O'Henry's Film Works, Inc., United States v., 525
Omni Intern. Corp., United States v., 657
O'Neal v. United States, 862
One 1958 Plymouth Sedan v. Pennsylvania, 456
Oren, United States v., 540
Ostrer, United States v., 700
Overman, United States v., 752
Owrutsky v. Treasury Secretary, 46

Page v. Commissioner, 396
Pappas v. United States, 549
Payner, United States v., 648, 656, 657
Pettengill v. United States, 419
Philatelic Leasing Ltd., United States v., 306
Picciandra, United States v., 657
Pickel v. United States, 502

TABLE OF CASES

Pomponio, United States v., 567
Ponsford v. United States, 529
Pool v. Walsh, 836
Powell v. Commissioner, 459
Powell, United States v., 491, 511, 513, 535
Price v. Commissioner of Internal Revenue, 827, 835
Providence Journal Co. v. F.B.I., 602 F.2d 1010, p. 89
Providence Journal Co. v. F.B.I., 460 F.Supp. 762, p. 102
Provident Nat. Bank v. United States, 190
Purcell v. Commissioner, 821
Pyo v. Commissioner, 350

Quick's Trust v. Commissioner, 178

Rapp v. Commissioner, 527
Raskob v. Commissioner, 331
Rasmussen v. United States, 191, 193
Register Pub. Co. v. United States, 188, 417
Reineman v. United States, 513
Reisman v. Caplin, 485, 487
Reynolds, United States v., 919 F.2d 435, pp. 559, 611
Reynolds, United States v., 764 F.2d 1004, p. 862
Richard Hebel, United States v., 634
Rickel v. Commissioner, 240
R. J. Reynolds Tobacco Co., Helvering v., 57, 59, 61
Rochelle, United States v., 419
Rodgers, United States v., 721, 722, 752
Rogers Transp., Inc., United States v., 526
Rorex v. Traynor, 120
Roszkos v. Commissioner, 179
Roth v. United States, 786
Rothensies v. Electric Storage Battery Co., 202
Ryan v. Department of Justice, 102
Rylander, United States v., 526

Sage v. United States, 303
San Joaquin Light & Power Corporation v. McLaughlin, 185
Sansone v. United States, 544
Scar v. Commissioner, 357
Seaboard Air Line Ry. v. United States, 419
Sealed Case, In re, 663
Segura v. United States, 456
Sells Engineering, Inc., United States v., 663
Sennett v. Commissioner of Internal Revenue, 395
Shapiro, Commissioner v., 839, 842
Shea v. Commissioner, 835
Short v. Murphy, 632
Shorter, United States v., 616, 617
Shortt Accountancy Corp., United States v., 554
Sisk v. Commissioner, 663
Slodov v. United States, 778, 799

Sommer v. Commissioner, 168
Sotelo, United States v., 865
Special September 1978 Grand Jury, In re, 520
Spies v. United States, 540, 548
Spruill, Estate of v. Commissioner, 253
Steele v. United States, 409
Stenclik v. Commissioner, 184
Stevens v. Commissioner, 835
Stone v. White, 202
Stringer v. Commissioner, 390
Stringer v. United States, 529
Sullivan, United States v., 704
Sunnen, Commissioner v., 432, 442

Taglianetti v. United States, 626
Takao Ozawa v. United States, 346
Tarnopol, United States v., 540, 611
Tax Analysts and Advocates v. I.R.S., 85
Taxation with Representation Fund v. I.R.S., 85
Tax Lot 1500, United States v., 696
Teel v. United States, 799
Texas Heart Institute, United States v., 509
$38,000.00, United States v., 664
Three 'M' Investments, Inc. v. United States, 862
Tiffany Fine Arts, Inc. v. United States, 529
Time Ins. Co. v. Commissioner, 342
Todd v. Commissioner of Internal Revenue, 245
Tovar v. Jarecki, 836
Trans Mississippi Corp. v. United States, 331
Traynor, United States v., 484
Triangle Corp. v. United States, 409
Tweel, United States v., 657

Uhrig v. United States, 506
United States v. ____(see opposing party)
United States (Clemente), In re, 700
United States (Nardone), In re, 700
United States Dept. of Justice v. Tax Analysts, 90
United States Dist. Court, United States v., 697
USLIFE Title Ins. Co. v. Harbison, 800

Vanguard Intern. Mfg., Inc. v. United States, 529
Vogel Fertilizer Co., United States v., 62
Voss v. Bergsgaard, 641, 644

Wahlin, United States v., 85
Wall Industries, Inc. v. United States, 419
W.A. Schemmer Limestone Quarry, Inc. v. United States, 189, 417
Wasie v. Commissioner, 459
Weiss v. Commissioner, 652
Welch v. Schweitzer, 350

TABLE OF CASES

Western Pac R. Co. v. United States, 419
W. G. Cosby Transfer & Storage Corp. v. Froehlke, 86
White v. I.R.S., 120
Willard v. I.R.S., 89
Williams v. Commissioner, 383, **764**
Wood, Estate of v. Commissioner, 168
Woods II v. Commissioner, 218, 232, 238
Wright v. Commissioner, 437, 442

Xemas, Inc. v. United States, 856

Yorke, United States v., 17, 18, 19

Zellerbach Paper Co. v. Helvering, 168
Zolin, United States v., 518, 520
Zolla, United States v., 350

TABLE OF INTERNAL REVENUE CODE SECTIONS

Sec.	This Work Page
101(b)	17
102	17
103(a)	398
104(a)(2)	240
108	866
163	320
163(h)	224
170(c)(2)	398
332	398
351	398
354	398
355	398
356	398
361	398
367	398
367(a)(1)	398
385	57
501(a)	398
501(c)(3)	458
509(a)	398
701	152
1304(e)	190
1311—1314	190
1311(a)	190
1311(b)	191
1312	190
	197
1313	190
	193
1313(a)(4)	193
1398(d)	866
1398(d)(2)(F)	866
1463	219
	310
1491	68
1492	68
3237	700
3237(b)	700
	701
3505	865
4942(j)(3)	398
6001	231
6011	218
6011(a)	168
	170
	317
6011(e)(2)	222
6012	311
6013(e)	862

Sec.	This Work Page
6013(e)(4)	835
6031	152
6031(a)	152
6031(b)	152
6038	218
6050I	665
	666
6060	55
6091	697
6103	56
	87
	103
	120
6103(b)(2)	87
	122
6103(c)	87
	103
6103(e)(7)	87
	103
6103(h)(3)(B)	502
6109(a)(4)	54
6109(e)	222
6110	56
	67
	103
	104
	393
6110(c)	104
6110(d)(3)	398
6110(f)	67
6110(f)(3)	67
	104
	398
6110(f)(4)	103
	398
6110(f)(4)(B)	104
6110(g)(3)	104
6110(g)(4)	104
6110(i)	104
6110(i)(3)	67
6111	536
6112	536
6159	719
6161 to 6166	719
6201	163
6203	163
	720
6212	357

Sec.	This Work Page	Sec.	This Work Page
6212(a)	362	6228(a)(2)(B)	158
	835		159
6212(b)	379	6228(a)(2)(C)	159
6212(c)	835	6228(a)(2)(D)	159
6213(a)	162	6228(a)(3)	159
	835	6228(a)(4)(A)	155
	846	6228(b)	158
	864	6228(b)(2)(C)	158
6213(b)	158	6229(d)	160
6213(d)	140	6229(e)	160
6213(f)	356	6229(f)	160
	864	6230(a)	153
6214(a)	379		157
6214(b)	379	6230(c)(1)	159
6221	153	6230(c)(2)	160
6221—6232	151	6231(a)(1)(A)	152
6222	319	6231(a)(1)(B)	152
6222(a)	152	6231(a)(3)	153
6222(b)	152	6231(a)(6)	153
6222(c)	153		159
6223(a)	154	6231(a)(7)(A)	154
6223(b)(1)	154	6231(a)(7)(B)	154
6223(b)(2)	154	6231(a)(8)	154
6223(d)	154	6231(a)(11)	154
6223(d)(1)	155	6231(a)(12)	154
6223(d)(2)	157	6241—6245	160
6223(f)	157	Ch. 63	151
6224(a)	155	6303	719
6224(b)	155	6303(a)	720
6224(c)(1)	156	6321	721
6224(c)(2)	156	6322	753
6224(c)(3)(A)	156	6323(a)	721
6224(c)(3)(B)	156	6323(b)	721
6225	153	6323(c)	721
6225(a)(1)	156	6323(d)	721
	157	6323(e)	721
6225(a)(2)	157	6325	721
6225(b)	157		722
6225(c)	157	6326	722
6226(a)	156	6331	722
6226(b)	156	6331(a)	777
6226(b)(1)	157	6331(d)	719
6226(b)(2)	157		720
6226(b)(3)	157	6333	487
6226(b)(5)	157	6334	721
6226(c)	155	6334(a)	732
	157		187
6226(d)	157		188
6226(d)(1)	157	6402	187
6226(f)—6226(h)	157		410
6227(a)(1)	158		421
6227(a)(2)	158	6405(a)	136
6227(b)	158	6501	161
6227(b)(2)(A)	158		163
6227(c)	158	6501(a)	164
	159	6501(b)(1)	167
6228(a)(1)	159	6501(b)(3)	168
6228(a)(2)(A)	159	6501(c)(1)	162
			277

TABLE OF INTERNAL REVENUE CODE SECTIONS xxxiii

Sec.	This Work Page	Sec.	This Work Page
6501(c)(2)	162	6651(c)(1)	311
6501(c)(3)	162	6651(f)	311
6501(c)(4)	162		317
	178	6652 (repealed)	218
	186	6653(a)	153
6501(e)	178	6653(a) (former)	218
6501(e)(1)	162		223
6501(e)(2)	162		224
6501(h)—(j)	161	6653(a)(1)(B) (former)	224
6502	721	6653(b) (former)	276
	722	6653(g) (former)	231
	753	6654	220
6502(a)	721		317
	753	6655	220
6503(a)(1)	162	6656	219
	379		310
6503(i)	863		317
6511(a)	185	6658	317
6511(b)(2)(A)	185	6659 (former)	218
6511(b)(2)(B)	185		223
6511(c)(1)	186		251
6511(c)(2)	186		252
6511(d)	187	6659(a)	836
6513(a)	185	6659(f) (former)	252
6514(b)	189	6659A (former)	218
6531	613		223
6532(a)(1)	188		252
	411	6660 (former)	218
	416		223
6532(a)(2)	189		252
	417	6661	19
6532(a)(3)	189		231
	417	6661 (former)	19
6532(a)(4)	189		44
	417		68
6532(c)(1)	856		218
6601	318		223
6601(a)	318		231
6601(c)	141	6662	218
6611	318		223
6611(a)	318		231
6611(b)(1)	319		238
6611(b)(2)	319		251
6611(b)(3)	318		252
6621	319	6662 (former)	220
6621(a)	319	6662—6665	218
6621(a)(1)	319	6662(a)	238
6621(a)(2)	319	6662(b)	19
6621(b)	319		68
6621(c)	320	6662(b)(1)	225
6621(c) (repealed)	218		241
6651	219	6662(b)(2)	231
	220	6662(c)	225
	310		241
	311		252
	317		295
6651 (former)	218	6662(d)	19
6651(a)(2)	311		44
6651(a)(3)	311		231

xxxiv   TABLE OF INTERNAL REVENUE CODE SECTIONS

Sec.	This Work Page
6662(d) (Cont'd)	294
6662(d)(2)(A)	232
6662(d)(2)(B)(ii)	54
6662(d)(2)(D)	238
6662(f)	252
6662(g)	252
6662(h)	252
6663	223
	331
6663(b)	276
	331
6663(c)	276
	19
	223
	230
	241
6665	220
6665(b)	220
6671	836
6671(a)	220
6672	135
	219
	220
	799
	802
	865
6672(b)	799
	835
6673	133
	219
	310
6694	48
	53
	54
	219
	281
	292
	293
	296
	297
6694(a)	53
	54
	277
	292
	293
	294
	295
	296
6694(b)	53
	277
	292
	293
	295
	296
6694(b)(2)	277
6694(c)	835
6695	54
	219
	297

Sec.	This Work Page
6695(c)	836
6695(f)	41
	55
6700	219
	302
	303
	306
	308
	842
6701	52
	219
	305
	306
	308
	842
6702	219
	308
6703	308
	842
6703(c)	308
6703(c)(1)	835
6721	221
6721—6724	218
	221
6721(b)	221
6721(c)	221
	222
6721(d)	222
6722	221
	222
6724(a)	222
6724(d)(1)	221
6724(d)(2)	221
6724(d)(3)	222
6851	753
	760
	777
	842
6851(b)	759
6861	753
	760
	777
	842
6861—6867	753
6861(b)	755
6862	753
	777
	842
6863	777
6867	753
	777
6867(a)	777
6867(b)(1)	777
6867(b)(2)	777
6867(b)(3)	777
6867(c)	777
6867(d)(1)	777
6867(d)(2)	777
6867(d)(3)	777

TABLE OF INTERNAL REVENUE CODE SECTIONS

Sec.	This Work Page
6871	864
6871(b)	863
6871(c)(1)	863
7051	877
7121	69
	145
	149
	188
7122	395
	719
7201	442
	537
	540
	617
7201—7216	537
7203	442
	538
	540
	549
	617
	665
	716
7205	548
7206(1)	538
	549
	563
	665
7206(2)	54
	538
	549
	561
	700
7207	538
	540
	545
	563
7216	54
	219
7231	537
7232	537
7240	537
7261	537
7262	537
7268—7273	537
7275	537
7403	732
7407	219
7408	306
7421	835
7421(a)	837
	839
7422(a)	410
7422(e)	332
7422(h)	158
7426	856
	862
7426(a)	836
7426(a)(1)	856
7426(a)(2)	856

Sec.	This Work Page
7426(a)(3)	856
7426(b)(1)	836
7428	393
	398
7428(a)	839
7429	759
	777
	842
7429(a)	842
7429(b)	836
	842
7429(b)(2)	383
7430	133
	241
	458
	459
7432	722
7433	722
7463	396
7463(a)	396
7463(b)	396
7464	864
7476	393
	398
7477	393
	398
7478	393
	398
7481(a)	383
7481(a)(2)(A)	383
7481(c)	382
7483	383
7502	167
	168
	356
7502(b)	168
7502(c)	168
7503	168
7521	123
	486
7521(a)(1)	124
	484
	486
7521(a)(2)	486
7521(b)	123
	486
	718
7521(b)(2)	124
7521(c)	484
7601	487
7602	487
	502
	506
7602(a)	502
7602(b)	502
7602(c)	502
	633
7602(c)(1)	502
7602(c)(2)	502

Sec.	This Work Page	Sec.	This Work Page
7602(c)(3)	502	7623	122
7604(b)	487		631
7605(a)	124	7701(a)(36)	52
7605(b)	131		292
	513		293
7609	513	7701(a)(36)(B)	52
	526	7801	1
	529	7802(a)	1
	657	7805(a)	56
	659	7805(b)	58
7609(a)	529		67
7609(b)	529		69
7609(b)(2)(A)	529		72
7609(e)	527		84
7609(f)	535	7805(e)	57
7609(h)(1)	529	7811	720

TAX PROCEDURE AND TAX FRAUD
CASES AND MATERIALS
Third Edition

Chapter I

INTRODUCTION TO THE FEDERAL TAX SYSTEM

Scope Note: Representing taxpayers before revenue authorities requires a working knowledge of the internal organization of those government agencies involved in the creation and administration of the internal revenue laws. The administration of the federal tax system in the United States is focused primarily in the Internal Revenue Service, the largest component of the Treasury Department. Substantial roles are played also by senior Treasury Department officials in setting tax policy, by the congressional staff (and, of course, Congress itself) in connection with tax legislation, and by the Department of Justice in connection with litigation. The materials in this chapter are intended to provide a general description of the various components of the government which contribute to the administration of the tax laws.

SECTION 1. DEPARTMENT OF THE TREASURY

The Secretary of the Treasury possesses the ultimate authority for the administration and enforcement of the internal revenue laws.[a] Pursuant to § 7802(a) of the Code, the bulk of this authority has been delegated to the Commissioner of Internal Revenue, who directs the operations of the Internal Revenue Service. A few revenue related functions have not been delegated to the Commissioner; these relate primarily to alcohol, tobacco and firearms taxes, and to the legislation-making process. Advising the Secretary of the Treasury in legal matters are the General Counsel for the Treasury and several Assistants General Counsel. One Assistant General Counsel also serves as chief legal officer of the Internal Revenue Service in his capacity as Chief Counsel for the IRS.

---

[a] I.R.C. § 7801. The Secretary, of course, serves at the pleasure of the President and his appointment must be approved by the Senate.

A. INTERNAL REVENUE SERVICE

The Internal Revenue Service is the largest component of the Department of the Treasury. The Service consists of a National Office in Washington, D.C. and a field organization. The latter consists of seven internal revenue regions, each headed by a Regional Commissioner; sixty-two internal revenue districts, each headed by a District Director; and ten service centers. In communities where the concentration of workload requires, the Service maintains area, zone or local offices below the district level.

The IRS describes its mission and principles as follows: [b]

MISSION OF THE SERVICE

The purpose of the Internal Revenue Service is to collect the proper amount of tax revenues at the least cost to the public, and in a manner that warrants the highest degree of public confidence in our integrity, efficiency and fairness. To achieve that purpose, we will:

— Encourage and achieve the highest possible degree of voluntary compliance in accordance with the tax law and regulations;

— Advise the public of their rights and responsibilities;

— Determine the extent of compliance and the causes of noncompliance;

— Do all things needed for the proper administration and enforcement of the tax laws;

— Continually search for and implement new, more efficient and effective ways of accomplishing our Mission.

STATEMENT OF PRINCIPLES OF INTERNAL REVENUE TAX ADMINISTRATION

The function of the Internal Revenue Service is to administer the Internal Revenue Code. Tax policy for raising revenue is determined by Congress.

With this in mind, it is the duty of the Service to carry out that policy by correctly applying the laws enacted by Congress; to determine the reasonable meaning of various Code provisions in light of the Congressional purpose in enacting them; and to perform this work in a fair and impartial manner, with neither a government nor a taxpayer point of view.

At the heart of administration is interpretation of the Code. It is the responsibility of each person in the Service, charged with the duty of interpreting the law, to try to find the true meaning of the statutory provision and not to adopt a strained construction in the belief that he or she is "protecting the revenue." The revenue is properly protected only when we ascertain and apply the true meaning of the statute.

---

b. 1990–1 IRB 2.

The Service also has the responsibility of applying and administering the law in a reasonable, practical manner. Issues should only be raised by examining officers when they have merit, never arbitrarily or for trading purposes. At the same time, the examining officer should never hesitate to raise a meritorious issue. It is also important that care be exercised not to raise an issue or to ask a court to adopt a position inconsistent with an established Service position.

Administration should be both reasonable and vigorous. It should be conducted with as little delay as possible and with great courtesy and considerateness. It should never try to overreach, and should be reasonable within the bounds of law and sound administration. It should, however, be vigorous in requiring compliance with law and it should be relentless in its attack on unreal tax devices and fraud.

(1) *National Office*

The National Office, located in Washington, D.C., develops broad nationwide policies and programs to guide field personnel in administering and enforcing the internal revenue laws. At the head of the National Office is the Commissioner of Internal Revenue. As a result of a reorganization in 1982,[c] assisting the Commissioner are a Deputy Commissioner, three Associate Commissioners, eleven Assistant Commissioners and the Chief Counsel of the IRS.

The Associate Commissioners (Operations, Policy and Management, and Data Processing) report directly to the Deputy Commissioner and coordinate the activities of the Assistant Commissioners responsible for functional direction of operating programs, and participate in policy development, oversight, and control of IRS activities.

The reorganization created new positions for Assistant Commissioner (Collection), Assistant Commissioner (Examination), and Assistant Commissioner (Criminal). Along with the Assistant Commissioner (Employee Plans and Exempt Organizations), these officials report to the Associate Commissioner (Operations). The Assistant Commissioner (Inspection) functions as the internal policing unit of the Service and reports directly to the Deputy Commissioner.

(2) *Office of Regional Commissioner*

Each of the seven regional offices is headed by a Regional Commissioner. The Office of Regional Commissioner directs and coordinates the activities of the district and service center offices within the region. The Regional Commissioner also evaluates the effectiveness of Service policies and procedures, and advises the National Office as to the need for their revision.

The organization of the regional offices parallels that of the National Office. There are five Assistant Regional Commissioners: Examina-

[c.] T.D.O. 150–95, 1982–1 C.B. 510. The reorganization was effective March 21, 1982.

tion, Collection, Criminal Investigation, Resources Management and Taxpayer Service and Returns Processing.

(3) Service Centers

There are ten internal revenue service centers dispersed throughout the country. Each service center is headed by a Director who functions under the supervision of a Regional Commissioner. The service centers process the returns they receive, verify their correctness and store tax return information. They are also called upon to use their data processing capabilities to perform a variety of examination, criminal investigation and collection related functions.

In addition to the ten service centers, the IRS maintains a National Computer Center in Martinsburg, West Virginia (where some centralized returns processing functions are performed) and a Data Center in Detroit, Michigan (where statistical data are compiled for use by the Service). Both the National Computer Center and the Data Center are under the jurisdiction of the Associate Commissioner (Data Processing), in the National Office.

(4) Office of District Director

The district offices, each headed by a District Director, are charged with the responsibility for administering the internal revenue laws within an internal revenue district in conformance with the policies and programs of the National Office and the regional offices. There are sixty-two district offices, with at least one in each state. The typical district office is organized functionally into the following divisions: Examination, Collection, Criminal Investigation, Taxpayer Service and Resources Management. There is also an Employee Plans and Exempt Organizations Division in some districts. As the tax practitioner is likely to have his most frequent contacts with the Service at the district office level, the functions of the various district office personnel will be considered in some detail in the material that follows.

The Examination Division administers a district-wide program involving the selection for examination and actual examination of all types of tax returns and related documents (other than those relating to employee plans and exempt organizations) including income, estate and gift tax returns, claims for refund, offers in compromise and informants' claims for reward. Examination employees select returns for examination and perform field or office audits to determine the correctness of the taxpayer's liability for tax and penalties.

The Collection Division is responsible for the collection of delinquent accounts, the taking of distraint action, the securing of delinquent returns and the receipt and transmittal of tax returns and related documents received within the district. The Collection Division also reviews offers in compromise of 100% penalties and offers in compromise based on doubt as to the collectability of taxes. Collection personnel cause the filing of notices of tax lien and levy and provide assistance to U.S. Attorneys, District and Regional Counsel on all collection matters.

The Criminal Investigation Division enforces the criminal statutes applicable to income, estate, gift, employment and excise tax laws by developing information concerning alleged criminal violations, evaluating allegations and indications of such violations to determine whether investigations should be undertaken, and recommending prosecution when warranted. Sometimes, Criminal Investigation Division personnel will assist IRS and Justice Department attorneys in grand jury proceedings and in the trial of criminal tax cases.

The Taxpayer Service Division manages the district's disclosure, public affairs and taxpayer service activities. This division assists taxpayers in preparing returns and in responding to notice of deficiency and other communications received by the taxpayer from the Service. Through the Disclosure Officer, the Taxpayer Service Division evaluates and processes Freedom of Information, Privacy Act and other disclosure matters within the district. The district office also contains a Resources Management Division and, in some districts, an Employee Plans and Exempt Organizations Division.

Offices below the district headquarters (area, zone and local offices) perform one or more of certain Collection, Taxpayer Service, Examination and Criminal Investigation functions as the workload warrants. These offices range in size from large area offices containing all of the principal functioning elements of the district office to small, one or two person local offices set up in the town post office.

(5) *Assistant Commissioner (International)*

In 1986, a new position of Assistant Commissioner (International) was created to coordinate the Service's various international functions.[d] These functions include the administration of the internal revenue laws for foreign-based taxpayers subject to United States law whose books and records are located in another country. This office also coordinates exchanges of information with treaty partners, and participates in mutual collection assistance procedures.

The Service has promulgated separate Revenue Procedures for the issuance of rulings, closing agreements, and technical advice in the international area. Rev.Proc. 87–4, 1987–1 C.B. 529; Rev.Proc. 87–5, 1987–1 C.B. 535.

B. OFFICE OF CHIEF COUNSEL

The Chief Counsel of the Internal Revenue Service is counsel and legal advisor to the Commissioner of Internal Revenue on all matters pertaining to the administration and enforcement of the tax laws (and

---

d. Notice 86–15, 1986–2 C.B. 378.

some matters that are not strictly tax related). This includes representing the Service in connection with the formulation of tax legislation and regulations; legal review of certain proposed private letter rulings, technical advice memoranda and published rulings; preparation and review of recommendations to the Department of Justice for criminal prosecution of taxpayers; recommendations and coordination with Justice concerning refund suits in the district courts and the Claims Court; recommendations to Justice concerning certiorari and appeals of all tax litigation matters; assistance to the Department of Justice in summons enforcement, injunction, Freedom of Information Act and Privacy Act matters; legal advice to the Service in connection with assessment and collection matters; and representation of the Commissioner before the United States Tax Court.

Like the National Office, the Office of Chief Counsel was reorganized in 1982. A Deputy Chief Counsel assists the Chief Counsel by providing day-to-day executive support and ensuring the orderly functioning of the office in the Chief Counsel's absence. An Associate Chief Counsel (Technical) supervises the technical divisions, as well as the Individual Tax and Corporation Tax Divisions which were transferred from the National Office to the Office of Chief Counsel. An Associate Chief Counsel (Litigation) supervises litigation, criminal, and general legal services activities.

Organizationally, the Office of Chief Counsel is part of the Treasury Department and not subject to the authority of the Commissioner. The Commissioner, however, continues to control the rulings process, as the Chief Counsel reports to the Commissioner on these activities.

The Appeals Division (formerly the Appeals Office) was transferred from the National Office to the Office of Chief Counsel in the 1982 reorganization. Transfer of the appeals function to the Office of Chief Counsel provides a more objective review of appeals cases and produces more uniform settlement criteria.

C. OFFICE OF THE DIRECTOR OF PRACTICE

The Office of the Director of Practice was created in 1953 to replace the Committee on Practice and the Office of Attorney for the Government. Originally, the Director of Practice was under the supervision of the Commissioner, but in 1963, pursuant to T.D.O. No. 175–1 (1963–2 C.B. 731), the Office of the Director of Practice was transferred from the Internal Revenue Service to the Office of the Secretary of the Treasury.

Effective June 28, 1982, T.D.O. 150–97, the Office of the Director of Practice was transferred back to the supervision of the Commissioner. The office is now under the direct supervision of the Commissioner except for cases relating to enrollment to practice before the IRS, disbarment, or other disciplinary measures. These areas, along with appeals from recommended decisions, continue to remain under the authority of the Secretary of the Treasury.

D. OFFICE OF THE ASSISTANT SECRETARY FOR TAX POLICY

While the Internal Revenue Service is charged with the responsibility for the day-to-day administration of the tax laws, the Office of the Assistant Secretary of the Treasury for Tax Policy is concerned mainly with matters of overall tax policy. The Office of the Assistant Secretary is divided into two branches, the legal branch, headed by the Deputy Assistant Secretary for Tax Policy (Tax Legislation), and the economic branch, headed by the Deputy Assistant Secretary for Tax Policy (Tax Analysis). The legal staff, under the direction of the Tax Legislative Counsel and the International Tax Counsel, works in conjunction with the responsible officials of the Internal Revenue Service on the development of new and revised regulations; final regulations are signed by both the Commissioner of Internal Revenue and the Assistant Secretary for Tax Policy. The legal staff also reviews published rulings to determine whether the Service's interpretations of the tax laws are consistent with Treasury's overall policy direction and with developing regulations. Finally, as discussed below, the legal staff of the Office of the Assistant Secretary plays an important role in the legal aspects of the formulation of new tax legislation. The economic branch of the Office of the Assistant Secretary is staffed by economists and statisticians and is also heavily involved in the development of new legislation, through the process of "revenue estimating," the evaluation of the revenue producing potential of proposed tax legislation. The Office of Tax Analysis is also engaged in the study and analysis of the present tax system, potential changes in it, and of the tax systems of other countries.

SECTION 2. DEPARTMENT OF JUSTICE

The Tax Division of the Department of Justice, under the direction of an Assistant Attorney General, represents (or coordinates the representation of) the United States and its officers in most civil and criminal litigation arising under the internal revenue laws in the state and federal courts (with the exception of the Tax Court).

The Tax Division is divided into eight sections. The Criminal Section supervises the prosecution of criminal tax cases by United States Attorneys throughout the country. Normally, the Criminal Section's task is limited to a review of criminal tax cases referred to the Division with recommendations for prosecution by the Internal Revenue Service. However, attorneys of the Criminal Section often try a number of the more important or difficult cases, conduct grand jury investigations in some such cases, and assist United States Attorneys in the trial of others. In addition, a senior member of the Criminal Section is assigned to maintain liaison with each interdepartmental Organized Crime Strike Force which comes into existence, often participating actively in the conduct of Strike Force investigations.

The four Civil Trial Sections handle (or supervise) all refund suits in the district courts and all other civil tax litigation in federal and state trial courts, including collection and injunction matters, Freedom of Information Act suits involving the Internal Revenue Service, and other miscellaneous matters arising under the Internal Revenue Code. The Claims Court Section is responsible for all cases filed with that court.

The Appellate Section represents the government in appeals of most civil and criminal tax cases in the United States courts of appeals, and participates with the Solicitor General in proceedings taken to the Supreme Court. The Appellate Section is also charged with reviewing adverse Tax Court and district court decisions and preparing recommendations as to whether an appeal should be taken. The final decision on appeal is made by the Solicitor General, to whom the Tax Division and the Chief Counsel of the Internal Revenue Service submit recommendations.

The Review Section is responsible for coordinating the settlement policies of the Division and for conducting research on general legal matters including proposed legislation on which the Division has been asked to comment.

SECTION 3. CONGRESS

THE TAX LEGISLATIVE PROCESS
Thomas J. Gallagher, Jr.
3 The Review of Taxation of Individuals 203 (1979).

* * *

The Constitution grants Congress the power "to lay and collect Taxes, Duties, Imposts and Excises," and provides further that "all Bills for raising Revenue shall originate in the House of Representatives; but the Senate may propose or concur with Amendments * * *." Generally, this tax legislative power is limited only by the presidential veto power, which, of course, can be overridden by a two-thirds vote of each House.

The Committee on Ways and Means has primary jurisdiction over tax matters. It consists of six standing subcommittees and occasionally of various task forces assigned to examine particular problems or subjects. Members of the Committee are designated by their respective parties, and total membership may vary. The allocation of seats to the Democratic and Republican parties depends, in part, upon the ratio of party members in the House.

Although revenue raising measures must originate in the House, various executive communications frequently provide a source of legislative proposals. * * * Indeed, the Constitution requires the President to report to Congress on the state of the union, and to recommend measures considered to be necessary and expedient. Often other proposals may accompany the annual presidential message on the transmission of the budget. These, and other executive communications, are referred to the Committee which has jurisdiction over the subject matter contained in the proposal. Since only a member may introduce a bill, the chairman of the committee to which the proposal is referred usually will introduce the proposal in bill form by placing it in the "hopper." (The bill may indicate that it was introduced "by request.") However, there is no requirement that a bill be introduced to effectuate its recommendations.

Hearings by the Ways and Means Committee

Normally, the tax legislative process actually begins with hearings by the Ways and Means Committee. Generally, the committee must announce the time, place, and subject matter of any hearing at least one week in advance. Witnesses, who may be scheduled in panels, ordinarily must file a written statement of their proposed testimony with the committee in advance of the hearing, and only may summarize their argument at the oral presentation.

The House rules require that all committee hearings and business meetings, including those for the markup of legislation, be open to the public. If, however, a majority of the Committee members authorize it by roll-call vote, a one-day closed business meeting may be held. Only Committee members and authorized staff and Treasury representatives may attend a business or markup session which has been closed.

Prior to the commencement of the hearings, the Staff of the Joint Committee on Taxation [e] generally prepares a pamphlet which describes present law and the proposal on which the hearings are scheduled. It also may contain a description of the issues involved, and various factors which the Committee may wish to consider during its deliberations.

If an executive communication forms the basis of the measure under consideration, administration representatives generally will be the first witnesses to appear. Ordinarily, the Secretary of the Treasury broadly outlines the contents of, and the reasons for, the administra-

---

e. The Joint Committee on Taxation is a joint congressional committee charged with the general responsibility for overseeing the administration and operation of the Federal system of internal revenue taxation. I.R.C. §§ 8021–8023. It is composed of the five ranking members of each of the House Committee on Ways and Means and the Senate Finance Committee and is supported by a staff of experts and other assistants appointed by the Joint Committee and under the direction of its Chief of Staff. I.R.C. §§ 8001–8005.

Congress has given the Joint Committee rather wide-ranging oversight responsibilities and, by virtue of I.R.C. § 6405, requires the Joint Committee to review all claims for refunds or credits for taxes in excess of $1 million ($200,000 for refunds or credits prior to 1991). Section 6405(a) of the Code provides that no payment on such a claim may be made until after the expiration of thirty days from the date upon which a report giving the name of the person to whom the refund or credit is to be made, the amount of the refund or credit and a summary of the facts and decision of the appropriate Treasury official, is made to the Joint Committee on Taxation. The Joint Committee's review procedure is outlined in D. Alexander, New IRS Procedures for Handling Joint Committee Cases, 138 Journal of Accountancy No. 4, 93 (1974).

tion's proposals. The Assistant Secretary of the Treasury for Tax Policy normally provides a more detailed description of the proposals. * * * Witnesses from the general public normally follow these governmental spokespersons. Throughout the course of the public hearings, the Committee's staff, Treasury representatives, and members of the Staff of the Joint Committee usually are present to answer any member's questions.

Following the conclusion of the hearings, the Committee generally considers ("marks up") the proposed legislation on a conceptual basis, rather than with direct reference to a bill. Decisions made during these deliberations usually are tentative, that is, subject to reconsideration prior to final approval of a bill. The markup session generally is coordinated by the Chief of Staff of the Joint Committee. The Committee's staff, Treasury representatives, and members of the Joint Committee's Staff usually are present to state their views, respond to questions, and furnish the Committee with various data, analyses, and estimates.

The House Bill

Once the Committee's policy decisions are finalized, House Legislative Counsel, in conjunction with staff members of the Joint Committee, Ways and Means, and the Treasury, translate them into bill form. Simultaneously, the Joint Committee Staff prepares a report which accompanies and describes the bill, and which also sets forth the reasons for the legislation. * * *

* * *

Consideration on the House Floor

After the bill and report are approved and reported by the Committee, it decides upon the rule to be requested for consideration of the bill on the House floor. Generally, tax bills are considered by the House under a "closed" rule which permits amendments to be offered only by the Committee. However, the Committee may agree to seek a "modified" closed rule pursuant to which a specified amendment could be offered to the reported bill. * * *

* * *

Once a rule (together with a specified period for debate) is granted, the bill is scheduled for consideration on the House floor. The deliberation time allotted is divided evenly between the two parties, and controlled on the floor by each party's manager for the bill (generally the Committee's chairman and the ranking member of the minority). When the deliberation time has expired, opponents may move to recommit the bill to the Committee with instructions to report it back to the House with specified changes. If such a motion prevails, the bill effectively is amended; if it fails to carry, then the bill is unchanged. A complete transcript of these proceedings is reported in the *Congressional Record*.

Once the bill is approved by the House it is forwarded to the House's enrolling clerk. (At this point, the measure technically is an Act of one body of Congress rather than a bill.) The engrossed and certified bill then is delivered to the Senate, the President of which refers it to the appropriate standing committee.

Consideration by the Senate

The tax legislative process in the Senate is substantially similar to that of the House, and generally begins with hearings before the Committee on Finance. While Senate hearings invariably proceed with reference to, and focus upon, the House-passed bill, the Finance Committee may or may not call that bill from the Senate desk. In any event, the Committee's decisions may range from altering the House bill in minor detail to "stripping" the bill entirely of the House-approved provisions. The Committee, in particular, and the Senate, in general, traditionally have felt free to exercise the constitutionally granted power to "propose or concur with Amendments" to House tax bills.

Once reported by the Finance Committee, the Senate rules generally allow both unlimited debate and unrestricted amendment of the bill. * * * Since Senate floor amendments are not explained in the report of the Finance Committee, their legislative history may be contained largely in the *Congressional Record.*

Conference Committee

After approval by the Senate, the bill, and the Senate amendment, is returned for consideration by the House. (Where the Senate and House versions are identical, this procedure is not necessary.) While the House may accept the Senate changes, it generally requires a Committee of Conference of the House and Senate to reconcile the differences between the two versions. The House and Senate conferees, who are the ranking members, by party, of the Ways and Means and Finance Committees, vote separately as a unit (with a majority governing) on each of the differences between the two versions of the bill. (Provisions which are identical in both bills ordinarily are not "in conference," and therefore are not subject to adjustment by the conferees.) Conference meetings, like those of the Ways and Means and Finance Committees, are required to be open. Generally, the two versions are reconciled by compromise. * * *

* * *

The action of the Conference is contained in a Conference Report. This document explains the decision made with respect to each Senate amendment, and also contains the language of the Conference Agreement. The Report, in addition, contains a Joint Explanatory Statement of the Conference Committee by the Managers on the part of the House and the Senate, which explains the final actions taken by the conferees. This part of the document essentially functions as a committee report.

Once the Report is completed, it is submitted to the House and Senate for approval. The enrolled bill then is forwarded to the President for action. * * *

Minor Revenue Bills

While minor tax bills generally follow these same procedures, they ordinarily receive much less detailed attention. In fact, in many instances no Conference Committee action is necessary because the provisions are identical, the House simply recedes from its disagreement to Senate amendments, or the Senate recedes from its amendments to the House bill. However, minor revenue bills easily may be forgotten, and thus die, in an end-of-the-Congress rush.

Due to this general lack of public scrutiny of minor tax bills, such proposals may tend to provide substantial benefits for a limited number of persons. However, incident to an informal arrangement between the committees and the Joint Committee staff, the descriptive hearing pamphlets generally indicate whether any minor or technical bills are retroactive, or directed to any particular taxpayer(s). Thus, to the extent of the staff's information, "private-interest" tax bills can be examined, by the Committee and the public, both for their content and as to any particular potential beneficiary.

General Explanation

Ordinarily, the Staff of the Joint Committee prepares a postenactment General Explanation of major revenue measures. While this document has neither the weight nor the legislative history status of a committee report, it usually contains more detailed description and analysis of the various new or changed provisions.

Note

Upon final Congressional approval, the President has ten days to approve or veto the tax bill. During this time, various government agencies will submit their views on the legislation to the Office of Management and Budget, which then summarizes their opinions and reports to the President. Once signed, the legislation may take effect immediately, retroactively, or at some future date as specified in the legislation itself. The considerations involved in determining the effective date of tax legislation are discussed in Note, Setting Effective Dates for Tax Legislation: A Rule of Prospectivity, 84 Harv.L.Rev. 436 (1970).

SECTION 4. COMPLIANCE WITH THE TAX LAWS

A recent government report[f] explains the "tax gap" and the problems resulting from noncompliance with the federal tax laws.

f. *Overview of the Federal Tax System*, prepared for the use of the Committee on Ways and Means of the House of Representatives by its staff with the assistance of the staffs of the Joint Committee on Taxation, the Congressional Research Service, and the Congressional Budget Office, and published June 6, 1990.

OVERVIEW

The United States income tax system has one of the highest voluntary compliance levels in the world. In 1988, more than 193 million tax returns were filed and $935 billion collected by the Internal Revenue Service (IRS). Approximately 83 percent of the tax owed on income from legitimate economic activities was voluntarily reported and paid. However, the "tax gap"—an estimate of the difference between the amount of taxes voluntarily paid in a taxable year and the amount of taxes that would have been paid if all taxpayers had filed complete and accurate returns—is approaching $100 billion a year and continues to grow.

The Subcommittee on Oversight of the Committee on Ways and Means continues to study the nature and causes of taxpayer noncompliance. The objective of this study is to develop specific recommendations for improving compliance with the tax laws. A compliance rate increase of 1 percentage point would narrow the tax gap by approximately $7 billion per year.

IRS REPORT ON COMPLIANCE

On March 17, 1988, the Subcommittee on Oversight conducted a hearing on the IRS 1988 report on income tax compliance and the "tax gap" estimates and projections for 1973 through 1992. Lawrence B. Gibbs, Jr., then Commissioner of the Internal Revenue Service, testified that the "tax gap" for tax year 1987 was $84.9 billion. This figure consists of a $63.5 billion gap for individuals and $21.4 billion for corporations. According to former Commissioner Gibbs, the tax gap consists of unpaid individual and business income taxes on legally earned income; overstated deductions, credits, and exemptions; and math errors. It exists also because some persons do not file required tax returns and because some persons do not voluntarily pay reported tax liabilities.

The IRS report indicates that individual taxpayers who file returns but underreport their tax liabilities account for most tax dollars lost to noncompliance. For tax year 1987, the IRS estimates the filer tax gap to be $56.3 billion, which is almost eight times as large as the gap resulting from individuals who fail to file tax returns. Income underreported by individual filers contributes by far the largest amount to the tax gap—$48.3 billion in 1987.

The corporate tax gap estimates contained in the IRS report refer to filers of corporate returns. The IRS stated that due to the lack of specific compliance data for large corporations, unreported income and overstated expenses were estimated only for small corporations. Large corporations ($10 million or more in assets), with a tax gap of $15.8 billion, dominate the total corporate tax gap of $21.4 billion. Small corporations account for $5.2 billion of the total, split almost equally between underreported income and overstated deductions and credits.

With regard to noncompliance by large corporations, the IRS 1988 Annual Report notes that through the Coordinated Examination Program (CEP), teams of experienced examiners and specialists conducted examinations of 1,461 of the largest and most complex domestic and foreign-controlled corporations. In 1988, the examinations resulted in recommended tax deficiencies and penalties totaling $9.58 billion. In 1988, all deficiencies proposed by the Examination Division totalled $19.2 billion. In other words, approximately 50 percent of all deficiencies proposed by the Examination Division in 1988 pertained to the 1,461 corporations included in CEP.

The total tax gap (in current dollars) shows a dramatic increase from $28 billion for 1973, to $62 billion for 1979, to $85 billion for 1987. The tax gap is projected to increase for 1992 to $114 billion. The IRS states that the increase is due to "expansion in the economy and through inflation." The IRS points out, however, that its new estimates are lower than prior estimates (1979 and 1983 IRS studies) because of recent tax legislation, the availability of new compliance tools, and improvements in methodology.

The IRS has stated that the 1988 tax gap report is the first in a series of reports expected to be issued in the next few years dealing with taxpayer noncompliance. The IRS expects to issue similar reports discussing noncompliance in the areas of employment tax, excise tax, and illegal source income.

1990 GAO REPORT [g]

In response to the IRS tax gap estimate, the Subcommittee requested that the GAO compile for the Subcommittee the best detailed information available on four major components which accounted for $45 billion, or half, of the 1987 tax gap estimates: sole proprietors, informal suppliers, small corporations and large corporations. For each component, GAO compiled information on the types of taxpayers who were noncompliant, issues of noncompliance, IRS's enforcement programs to pursue noncompliance, and ways in which IRS could improve its compliance. The results of the GAO study were released at the Subcommittee hearing of April 19, 1990.

According to GAO, the components of the 1987 tax gap estimates differ in the types of noncompliance and the taxpayers who were noncompliant. For example, sole proprietors have extensive amounts of unreported income, while large corporations, for the most part, report their income but improperly allocate it among their foreign and domestic operations. Across the board, factors responsible for noncompliance have not been conclusively identified, but include the absence of third-party reporting and withholding on business transactions of small businesses and the complexity or vagueness on [of] our tax laws.

Research on Reasons for Noncompliance—Not Conclusive

Research by IRS and others has not been conclusive on the reasons that these taxpayers were noncompliant. Further, the reasons vary somewhat by component. For sole proprietors and small corporations, the tax gap was attributed to the complexity of tax laws and intentional noncompliance to survive in competitive business environments. The lack of wage

---

g. GAO is the General Accounting Office.

withholding for sole proprietors and information reporting for payments made to corporations also may contribute to the tax gap. Large corporations also may not comply because of vagueness in tax laws, such as exactly which expenses are deductible in calculating the research credit. Informal suppliers may not report income because their transactions often occur in cash, are not documented, and are not subjected to third-party controls, such as wage withholding or information reporting.

LEGISLATIVE RESPONSES

The problem of taxpayer noncompliance has resulted in a series of remedial legislative measures. Among these are the compliance provisions of the Tax Equity and Fiscal Responsibility Act (TEFRA) of 1982, the Interest and Dividend Tax Compliance Act of 1983, the Deficit Reduction Act of 1984, and the Tax Reform Act of 1986. These provisions taken together have enhanced IRS capabilities to detect and correct noncompliance with income tax laws.

As a continuation of tax reform, the Subcommittee on Oversight completed a comprehensive review of the structure, fairness, and effectiveness of the civil tax penalty provisions contained in the Internal Revenue Code.

The Subcommittee on Oversight held 4 days of hearings and a number of informal "roundtable" discussions to explore every aspect of the existing penalty structure to develop a set of legislative and administration improvements. The penalty reform package was originally set forth in H.R. 2528, the "Improved Penalty Administration and Compliance Tax Act" and was enacted into law as part of the Budget Reconciliation Act of 1989.

The Subcommittee on Oversight will continue to investigate revenue loss attributable to taxpayer noncompliance. As part of its review, the subcommittee will examine, in detail, various components of the tax gap with the objective of developing specific recommendations to enhance taxpayer compliance and fairness in tax collection. The subcommittee plans to examine noncompliance attributable to large corporations, sole proprietors, and informal suppliers (e.g., cash business operations, street vendors, etc.) These categories account for the largest share, in terms of dollars, of noncompliance as estimated by the IRS. In addition, the subcommittee will also examine the issue of money laundering.

Chapter II

RESPONSIBILITIES OF THE TAX PRACTITIONER

Scope Note: The tax practitioner operates under the constraints of several, sometimes conflicting, obligations. The most fundamental conflict is between the lawyer's obligation to serve the clients' interest to the extent permissible, and the simultaneous obligation owed by lawyers to our Government, including the IRS. The purpose of this chapter is to sensitize future practitioners to the various ethical and statutory standards governing tax practitioners.

SECTION 1. BACKGROUND

The cornerstone of our federal tax system is voluntary compliance. Each year American citizens are expected to report to the IRS their income and deductions, and to pay the appropriate tax. While the typical wage earner has little choice in reporting income from compensation (because the employer must report the information to the IRS), most people have opportunities to "fudge" on their returns. The proliferation of "tax shelters" during the 1970s and 1980s led many to believe that most people, or at least most rich people, paid less than their fair share in taxes, and that lawyers and accountants served as the well-paid architects of tax-minimizing schemes. This perception of widespread "cheating" seriously undermined voluntary compliance and led Congress, the Treasury Department, the professional bar and the accounting profession to reexamine the standards governing tax practitioners.

Just as it is difficult to articulate a bright line between tax evasion (which is illegal) and tax avoidance (which is legal), so also is it difficult to separate the lawyer's obligation of "warm zeal" in serving her clients' interests from the obligation owed by lawyers to support our system of voluntary compliance. Advising a client to take a position that is legally unsupportable, in the hope that the return will never be audited, could subject the lawyer to civil and criminal sanctions, as well as to possible disbarment from practice before the Service. On the other hand, a lawyer must attempt to minimize clients' tax liability to the extent permissible. The problem is that tax issues are often unclear, and there is frequently no clearly "wrong" or "right" position, but rather a greater or lesser likelihood that a position is correct.

When faced with an issue for which there is no clear answer, which way should the lawyer tilt? Must the advice always be in the taxpayer's favor, or must the lawyer counsel a position that resolves doubt in favor of the Government in some circumstances? Currently, the answers to these questions vary, depending on whether the answer is sought in the Internal Revenue Code, Treasury Department regulations governing practice before the Service, or ethical guidelines issued by the ABA.

Question

As you read the materials in this chapter, consider this hypothetical situation. John Jones, an officer of a medium-sized business, recently died, leaving a widow, Mary Jones, and three minor children. When his former employer realized the paucity of John's life insurance, its board of directors voted to pay John's former salary to Mary until her youngest child reached age 16, at which time Mary would resume her full-time employment with the company. Prior to the birth of their first child, Mary had been a valued employee of the company, which has tried several times to induce her to return to full-time employment. Mary agreed to return to full-time employment with the company in five years, when her youngest child reaches age 16, to demonstrate her gratitude for the company's much-needed financial help. Tipped by the company's public relations officer, the local media have covered closely the story of the company's generosity. Mary contacted you with the question whether the payments to her of her deceased husband's salary will be excludable from her income as a gift, or whether she must report the payments as income. After researching the issue, you find that the first $5,000 is excludable under I.R.C. § 101(b), that the Service generally views such payments as taxable income, and that the issue turns on several factors, including whether the employer was obligated to make the payments and whether the employer will derive economic benefit from the payments. After gathering additional facts and weighing the relevant factors, you conclude that the factors indicating the payments are income to her (and not a gift) are equally balanced by factors indicating the payments are excludable from her income as a gift under section 102. What is your advice to Mary? Does your advice depend upon whether you prepare her return? Should it?

SECTION 2. THE ETHICS OF TAX PRACTICE

UNITED STATES v. YORKE
(Unpublished Opinion, D.Md., July 19, 1976).

[YOUNG, J.:] [The taxpayer was prosecuted for failing to report as income $400 per week of advances denominated as "loans" in documents prepared by his employer's tax counsel. These advances were subject to forgiveness in the event that the taxpayer did not realize sufficient income from certain speculative stock purchases to finance the repayment from capital gains. The defendant contended that he attempted to avoid rather than evade his tax liability.]

* * *

The key to the application of the distinction [between avoidance and evasion] should be the taxpayer's state of mind. An honest belief that a particular scheme is legal negates the element of willfulness, and perforce renders the conduct non-criminal. Some authorities have gone even further and suggested that a tax practitioner need not have a genuine belief that a particular scheme will succeed. His ethical obligation is satisfied when he can find a reasonable basis in the law for the scheme, regardless of whether or not he believes it will ultimately succeed. See Opinion 314 of the A.B.A. Committee on Professional Ethics, 51 A.B.A.J. 671 (1965).

Surely, it would be unfair to judge the client's criminal liability on a stricter standard than his lawyer's ethical obligation. The question of a client's criminal liability for following such so-called "reasonable basis" advice is briefly posed by James R. Rowen in his article "When May A Lawyer Advise A Client That He May Take A Position On His Tax Return?" 29 Tax Lawyer 237 (1976). The author criticizes the A.B.A.'s position on the lawyer's duty, but his research disclosed no criminal case in which a "reasonable basis" opinion had resulted in liability.

The scheme in the instant case is a very aggressive one. The Court is somewhat shocked that it was approved by competent counsel * * *. Indeed, the literature in the entire area of tax avoidance planning, particularly the A.B.A. opinion, tends to take a rather cavalier attitude toward obviously questionable schemes.

The instant case, however, is a criminal matter. This Court's attitude toward the ethics of some tax planners should not affect its views herein. Regardless of what position is taken on the avoidance-evasion distinction, the Government has not produced a *prima facie* case of criminal liability. It is clear that the Defendant, while perhaps excessively aggressive in his planning, had both an honest belief in the legality of his plan and a reasonable basis in the law for it, as well. His implementation of that plan included full documentation, and no attempt to conceal.

Accordingly, the Defendant's motion for judgment of acquittal is this day granted.

The *Yorke* court characterizes the approach of the ABA to lawyers advising questionable positions as "cavalier." At the time *Yorke* was decided, the governing ABA policy was contained in Opinion 314, issued in 1965, which authorized attorneys to advise clients to take return positions for which there was a "reasonable basis," without any obligation to alert the IRS by disclosing or "red-flagging" the questionable position. Opinion 314 characterized the furnishing of tax advice as essentially adversarial in nature, the same as representing a client in litigation, and concluded that the same basic ethical guidelines should apply to both. Do you agree?

Spurred in part by the unfavorable publicity surrounding lawyers' opinions in tax shelters, judicial criticism of the type stated in *Yorke,* and Congressional attempts to shore up the voluntary compliance system, the ABA reexamined its position in 1985 and issued Opinion 85–352. To understand the implications of Opinion 85–352, however, it is necessary to understand the impact of legislation enacted in 1982 to plug the perceived hemorrhaging of our voluntary compliance system. As part of the Tax Equity and Fiscal Responsibility Act of 1982 ("TEFRA"), Congress enacted former section 6661, which is now codified (as amended in 1989) as section 6662(b) and (d). Former section 6661 was designed to alter taxpayer behavior, not the behavior of tax advisors. Nonetheless, there is a relationship between the two: many believe (as did the *Yorke* court) that it would be intolerable to punish a taxpayer for positions the lawyer is ethically permitted to encourage.

As enacted in 1982, I.R.C. § 6661 authorized the Service to impose a penalty on taxpayers whose return positions were disallowed and were not supported either by "substantial authority" or by a disclosure statement filed with the return notifying the Service of the questionable or uncertain position taken. Some perceived flaws in section 6661 were corrected in the Improved Penalty Administration and Compliance Tax Act of 1989 ("IMPACT," discussed in detail in Chapter 6), by the expansion of the definition of "authority" [a] and the enactment of a reasonable cause exception, in section 6664(c), which provides for greater judicial review of IRS impositions of the penalty. The taxpayer need not be negligent to be subject to this penalty; in fact, prior to enactment of section 6664(c), the Service imposed it routinely and automatically if the tax underpayment exceeded the statutory threshold of the greater of $5,000 or 10% of the total tax liability.

FORMAL OPINION 85–352 OF THE AMERICAN BAR ASSOCIATION STANDING COMMITTEE ON ETHICS AND PROFESSIONAL RESPONSIBILITY
July 7, 1985.
39 Tax Lawyer 631 (1986).

The committee has been requested by the Section of Taxation of the American Bar Association to reconsider the "reasonable basis" standard in the committee's Formal Opinion 314 governing the position a lawyer may advise a client to take on a tax return.

a. Congress directed the Treasury to expand the list of authorities upon which taxpayers may rely to include "proposed regulations, private letter rulings, technical advice memoranda," and other IRS statements of position. H.R.Rep. 101–247, 101st Cong., 1st Sess. 1389 (1989).

Opinion 314 (April 27, 1965) was issued in response to a number of specific inquiries regarding the ethical relationship between the Internal Revenue Service and lawyers practicing before it. The opinion formulated general principles governing this relationship, including the following: "[A] lawyer who is asked to advise his client in the course of the preparation of the client's tax returns may freely urge the statement of positions most favorable to the client just as long as there is a *reasonable basis* for this position." (Emphasis supplied.)

The committee is informed that the standard of "reasonable basis" has been construed by many lawyers to support the use of any colorable claim on a tax return to justify exploitation of the lottery of the tax return audit selection process. This view is not universally held, and the committee does not believe that the reasonable basis standard, properly interpreted and applied, permits this construction.

However, the committee is persuaded that as a result of serious controversy over this standard and its persistent criticism by distinguished members of the tax bar, IRS officials and members of Congress, sufficient doubt has been created regarding the validity of the standard so as to erode its effectiveness as an ethical guideline. For this reason, the committee has concluded that it should be restated.

* * *

This opinion reconsiders and revises only that part of Opinion 314 that relates to the lawyer's duty in advising a client of positions that can be taken on a tax return. It does not deal with a lawyer's opinion on tax shelter investment offerings, which is specifically addressed by this committee's Formal Opinion 346 (revised), and which involves very different considerations, including third-party reliance.

The ethical standards governing the conduct of a lawyer in advising a client on positions that can be taken in a tax return are no different from those governing a lawyer's conduct in advising or taking positions for a client in other civil matters. * * * In many cases a lawyer must realistically anticipate that the filing of the tax return may be the first step in a process that may result in an adversary relationship between the client and the IRS. This normally occurs in situations when a lawyer advises an aggressive position on a tax return, not when the position taken is a safe or conservative one that is unlikely to be challenged by the IRS.

Rule 3.1 of the Model Rules, which is in essence a restatement of DR 7–102(A)(2) of the Model Code, states in pertinent part: "A lawyer shall not bring or defend a proceeding, or assert or controvert an issue therein, unless there is a basis for doing so that is not frivolous, which includes a good faith argument for an extension, modification or reversal of existing law."

Rule 1.2(d), which applies to representation generally, states: "A lawyer shall not counsel a client to engage, or assist a client, in conduct that the lawyer knows is criminal or fraudulent, but a lawyer may discuss the legal consequences of any proposed course of conduct with a client and may counsel or assist a client to make a good faith effort to determine the validity, scope, meaning or application of the law."

On the basis of these rules and analogous provisions of the Model Code, a lawyer, in representing a client in the course of the preparation of the client's tax return, may advise the statement of positions most favorable to the client if the lawyer has a good faith belief that those positions are warranted in existing law or can be supported by a good faith argument for an extension, modification or reversal of existing law. A lawyer can have a good faith belief in this context even if the lawyer believes the client's position probably will not prevail. However, good faith requires that there be some realistic possibility of success if the matter is litigated.

* * *

Thus, where a lawyer has a good faith belief in the validity of a position in accordance with the standard stated above that a particular transaction does not result in taxable income or that certain expenditures are properly deductible as expenses, the lawyer has no duty to require as a condition of his or her continued representation that riders be attached to the client's tax return explaining the circumstances surrounding the transaction or the expenditures.

In the role of advisor, the lawyer should counsel the client as to whether the position is likely to be sustained by a court if challenged by the IRS, as well as of the potential penalty consequences to the client if the position is taken on the tax return without disclosure. Section 6661 of the Internal Revenue Code imposes a penalty for substantial understatement of tax liability, which can be avoided if the facts are adequately disclosed or if there is or was substantial authority for the position taken by the taxpayer. Competent representation of the client would require the lawyer to advise the client fully as to whether there is or was substantial authority for the position taken in the tax return. If the lawyer is unable to conclude that the position is supported by substantial authority, the lawyer should advise the client of the penalty the client may suffer and of the opportunity to avoid such penalty by adequately disclosing the facts in the return or in a statement attached to the return. If after receiving such advice the client decides to risk the penalty by making no disclosure and to take the position initially advised by the lawyer in accordance with the standard stated above, the lawyer has met his or her ethical responsibility with respect to the advice.

In all cases, however, with regard both to the preparation of returns and negotiating administrative settlements, the lawyer is under a duty not to mislead the Internal Revenue Service deliberately, either by misstatements or by silence or by permitting the client to mislead.
* * *

* * *

Note

Separate rules govern the issuance of tax opinions in tax shelter investment offerings. See Formal Opinion 346, 68 A.B.A.J. 471 (1982).

GUIDELINES TO TAX PRACTICE SECOND
Frederic G. Corneel.
43 Tax Lawyer 297 (1990).

In 1978, the ABA Tax Section Committee on Standards of Tax Practice published suggested Guidelines for Tax Practice for consideration by firms engaged in civil tax practice.[1] According to advices received at the time, scores of firms did indeed adopt the 1978 Guidelines, often with changes that evidenced thoughtful reflection.

That was more than a decade ago. Since then we have had a flood of tax shelters, and although that has now receded, it has left behind the large number of new penalties and compliance provisions which affect all tax practice, whether or not related to tax shelters. Malpractice claims arising out of tax work, which were virtually unheard of before the Seventies, have become an everyday occurrence. The growing complexity of the tax law with its pressure for ever more specialization, the increase in the fees charged for tax advice, and the growth in the size of the firms, all contribute to the "depersonalization" of the practice and thereby increase the need for a conscious effort to maintain ethical professional standards.

Therefore, a year or two ago, the author came to believe that it was time for a Guidelines for Tax Practice Second. * * *

These guidelines are in no sense official; indeed, it would be a mistake to try to develop official guidelines.

* * *

Some are concerned that the adoption of guidelines may make the defense of a malpractice claim against the firm more difficult. I do not know of any evidence to support this fear;[6] in any event, adoption and adherence to appropriate guidelines should substantially reduce the risk of actions or failures to act that are likely to give rise to such claims.

I suggest that tax firms or tax departments circulate these guidelines to their members with a view to discussing the changes that might best serve their particular needs. As revised, the guidelines should then be adopted and given to every new lawyer who joins the firm. In

---

1. Guidelines for Tax Practice, 31 Tax Lawyer 551 (1978).

6. It is true that in spite of the expressed intent of their authors, rules of professional responsibility adopted by bar associations and courts have been taken by many courts as also setting forth standards on which clients can rely in dealing with lawyers. But unlike the official disciplinary rules, the guidelines, when adopted by a particular lawyer or firm, are not intended to set forth norms of general application on which malpractice liability might be based. Indeed, as pointed out earlier in this introduction, the guidelines are expected to vary from firm to firm.

addition, every year or two a lawyer in the firm might be asked to update the authorities cited and recommend changes in light of new developments and experience.

GUIDELINES TO THE TAX PRACTICE OF _____
(name of firm)

I. INTRODUCTION

All lawyers are subject to the rules of professional ethics, requiring them to work competently and carefully for their clients, free from any prohibited conflict of interest and preserving their clients' confidences. These rules apply equally to the tax lawyer. Nevertheless, each field of practice has its own special problems which necessitate approaches specifically suited to that field.

As a result of the "self-assessment" tax system, clients must apply tax law to their own conduct. Uncertainties created by the complexities of the law, doubts as to its fairness, widespread publicity about the exploitation of loopholes, and low audit coverage which, unlike any other lottery, skew the odds of the tax lottery in favor of the client, all tend to make the average person think of a tax lawyer not so much as an expert in the law, but as an expert in what the client might get away with on the client's return.

This attitude on the part of many clients increases the need for us to adhere to the highest ethical standards in our tax practice and to make it clear to our clients that this firm insists on such adherence. Obviously, we try to do all we can to help our clients achieve their business and personal goals at the lowest tax cost, by performing our work with an understanding for their needs, competently, efficiently, and with dedication, imagination, and intelligence. But we work for tax reduction only to the extent we can do so ethically. In the long run that standard is likely to work best for most of our clients; in any event, it is essential to this firm's practice and that of each lawyer who participates in our practice.

Questions of professional responsibility should not be resolved merely on the basis of individual conscience, but on the basis of rules applicable to the entire office. With this in mind, we are publishing and circulating to every attorney in the firm guidelines to our tax practice, with the exception of criminal tax practice and tax litigation in the courts, as these involve other considerations. Familiarity with these guidelines and adherence to them should assist us in continuing the kind of practice we can enjoy and of which we can be proud. The firm expects each attorney involved in tax matters to adhere to these guidelines, accepting them not as technical rules of law to be avoided by the clever exercise of lawyerly skills, but rather as a guide to a satisfying professional life and to the building of a professional environment in which we can be comfortable in the knowledge that others in the firm bring to bear the same standards.

While the guidelines seek to reflect applicable legal authorities, they are not intended as a text of the rules governing the legal obligation of our clients to the Internal Revenue Service or of the legal obligations of lawyers either to the Service or to clients.

II. Our Relationship to Our Clients

* * *

We should do our best to justify the client's confidence, but the client does not control the ethical and legal standards by which we practice our profession. We are responsible for our actions and unethical or illegal conduct can never be justified on the basis of client pressure.

Similar considerations bear on the quality of our work. There is a clear relationship between the quality of our work and the time devoted to it. Just as clearly, there is a relationship between the time devoted to work and its cost. The client is the one who has the final word on fees and may seek to limit the scope of our work either for reasons of economy or because of time pressures. We, however, are the ones who must be satisfied with the quality of our work. Where the client does not authorize the expenditure of time necessary for a fully researched and carefully considered conclusion, we should make a conscious choice among the alternatives:

We may decline to do the work; or

We may undertake it, knowing that we will not be adequately compensated; or

We may limit the scope of our work in accordance with the limitations placed upon us.

The last alternative is generally the least desirable. Inadequate work on small jobs is likely to breed a general carelessness. * * *

Nor is the client necessarily our friend forever. Tax planning and tax reporting are complex and, although we try to do our best, mistakes and disappointments are bound to occur and malpractice claims have become common. Our best defense against such claims is doing a first class job, providing clear warnings of potential costs and risks, keeping the client fully and currently informed of the development of the case, and maintaining a complete record.[8]

---

8. For articles discussing legal malpractice and providing suggestions on how to avoid such a charge, see Burrell, Legal Malpractice of the Tax Attorney, 34 Tax Exec. 259 (1982); Mossner, Legal Malpractice—How to Avoid It, Mich.B.J. 244 (1984); Phillips, Attorneys' Personal Liabilities in Tax Counseling, 54 Wis.B.Bull. 30 (1981); Portuondo, Abusive Tax Shelters, Legal Malpractice, and Revised Formal Ethics Opinion 346: Does Revised 346 Enable Third Party Investors to Recover From Tax Attorneys Who Violate Its Standards?, 61 Notre Dame L.Rev. 220 (1986); Comment, Legal Liability of the Professional Tax Practitioner, 26 Emory L.J. 403 (1977); O'Malley, How to Avoid Legal Malpractice Suits, 33 Prac.Law. 13 (1987); Routh, Liabilities of Tax Preparers: An Overview, 13 Cap.U.L.Rev. 479 (1984); Tinsley & Pease, Guidelines for Protecting the Tax Practitioner from Criminal Liability, 40 Tax'n.Acct. 94 (1988).

To accommodate both the need to warn the client of potential risks and at the same time preserve the confidentiality of our communications, we may confine the record of warnings to our own files or mark communications that go to the client "privileged and confidential." In particular, we should be careful not to disseminate such writings to non-privileged recipients, such as accountants or investment bankers.

III. OUR RELATIONSHIP WITH THE GOVERNMENT

Our relationship with the Service, state, or local tax department should be professional and courteous. We, however, should avoid extending any kind of personal favor that might be interpreted as an effort to obtain improper favorable treatment. Furthermore, it is a violation of Internal Revenue Service rules to imply to our clients that we are in a position to obtain special treatment.[9] At times our relationship is clearly adversarial; but we are adversaries in a contest in which we observe the rules, a contest that is not a personal one between us and the government representatives.

Particularly where the client is under a legal obligation to disclose facts, as in connection with a tax return or in responding to questions on audit, we may be under pressure to compromise either our obligation to keep information received in connection with the representation of a client confidential, or our obligation to be truthful to the tax collector.[10] The following discussion suggests ways of dealing with this problem in specific situations. The basic rule which applies throughout is simple: we will not voluntarily disclose confidential information unless so authorized by the client and we will not lie to the Service.[11] We will do our best to resolve any conflict between these two principles, and if we cannot do so, we will resign.

Our obligation to the government includes an obligation to "the system." In addition to representing our clients, we should also seek to contribute to improvement of the tax laws and their administration. If in connection with such effort we take a position because it will be

---

9. Treas.Cir. 230, 31 C.F.R. § 10.51(c) (1988); see also Model Rules of Professional Conduct Rule 8.4(e) (1984) (declaring such action to be a professional misconduct).

10. Model Rules of Professional Conduct Rule 1.6 (1984), generally prohibits unauthorized disclosure of confidential information relating to the client. A number of ethics opinions also prohibit disclosure to the tax authorities of information as to tax derelictions by non-clients unless such disclosure is legally mandated or authorized by the client. See Ala.Op. 8389, ABA/BNA Lawyer's Manual on Professional Conduct [hereinafter ABA/BNA] 801:1056-57; Ariz.Op. 82-13, ABA/BNA 801:1313; N.Y.City Op. 81-100, 801:6331; N.C.Op. 374, ABA/BNA 801:6617-18.

11. Lying to the Internal Revenue Service is not only unethical but illegal. See Treas.Cir. 230, 31 C.F.R. § 10.51(b) (1988), which includes in "disreputable conduct" for which a practitioner may be disbarred from practice before the Service "giving false or misleading information, or participating in any way in giving false or misleading information * * * [whether in testimony, a return or otherwise] knowing such information to be false or misleading." See also I.R.C. § 6701 (aiding and abetting) & I.R.C. § 7206(2) (aiding or assisting in false return); 18 U.S.C. § 1001 (1982) (person making a false statement to government agency is guilty of felony).

helpful to our clients, we should make it clear that we are acting in a representative capacity.[12]

* * *

IV. Advice Concerning Tax Reporting

A. Tax Return Preparation and Advice

The tax return is the principal focus for a tax lawyer's struggles with ethical issues. This is true whether the issue arises in connection with return preparation or in planning a transaction which must eventually be reflected on a return. Indeed, giving advice on the reporting of a major item on a return may make the lawyer an "income tax preparer" for purposes of the applicable penalty regulations, even though the lawyer does not actually participate in making the entries on the return.[14] Even when our work does not fall within the statutory definition of "return preparation," for instance, when the transaction is prospective or the advice does not relate to a major item, the ethical considerations are largely the same. Therefore, most of the following discussion is applicable to advice concerning tax reporting whether or not we act as return preparers.

B. Taxpayers and Return Preparers

1. Return preparation is a two-party effort, involving the client and the return preparer. Each has responsibilities to bring to the task: knowledge of the relevant law comes from the return preparer; the relevant facts come from the client. A failure by either may occasion problems for both.

2. The preparation of returns is not the practice of law, although it may be part of such practice if performed by a lawyer.[15] Being a return preparer in a particular case may hamper us in other aspects of our role as lawyer. Information given in connection with return preparation may not be privileged.[16] Therefore, at the outset of the engagement, we should consider the relationship between our responsibility as return preparer and our role as lawyer, and consider discussing with the client any problems that we can foresee which may arise during the course of the representation.

a. We may advise a client even though his return may run the risk of incurring a penalty. As return preparers, however, we will seek

---

12. Model Rules of Professional Conduct 3.9 (1984).

14. I.R.C. § 7701(a)(36) as supplemented by Regs. § 301.7701–15(b)(2) defines who is an income tax return preparer.

15. Graves, Attorney Client Privilege in Preparation of Income Tax Returns: What Every Preparer Should Know, 42 Tax Lawyer 577, 613–17 (1989).

16. *See* United States v. Windfelder, 790 F.2d 576, 579 (7th Cir.1986); Graves, *supra* note 15; *see generally*, Spahn, Making and Breaking the Attorney–Client Privilege, 35 Prac.Law. 61 (1989) (summarizing principles of attorney-client privilege and offering suggestions for its creation and maintenance). *See also* Hartz Mountain Industries, Inc. v. Commissioner, 93 T.C. 521 (1990), where use of house counsel's affidavit was held to waive the privilege.

to avoid participation in a return likely to subject us to penalties.[17]

b. If, subsequent to our preparation of a return, it comes to our attention that there was a clear and material error on the return, we may wish to withdraw from the representation unless the error is corrected, although the client may not be under a legal obligation to make a correction.[18] We are obliged not to mislead the Service, and by continuing under the circumstances we may do so.[19] Indeed, we may from time to time be asked to assist in the defense of a client who has filed a fraudulent return. If we should ever learn, however, that a client asked us to be return preparers of a fraudulent return, we would immediately terminate all further representation.[20]

c. In return preparation, the tension between the quality service we insist on providing and the client's desire to minimize costs is particularly strong. We should not hesitate to point out to the client less expensive return preparation alternatives than we are willing to provide.

C. Diligence

We owe it to our clients and ourselves to be diligent in the preparation of returns. This duty includes making reasonable efforts to obtain all relevant information from the client, reviewing last year's income tax return for any changes, obtaining confirmation as to the client's record keeping procedures (where they are relevant to the tax result), considering the tax position of other related taxpayers (to the extent known to us), and researching any doubtful questions of law.

As return preparers, we are not under any obligation to audit our client's records; but if information given to us raises questions in our

---

17. For negligence penalties applicable to return preparers, see I.R.C. § 6694, as amended by the Omnibus Budget Reconciliation Act of 1989, Pub.L. No. 101–239, 103 Stat. 2106; *see also generally* but relating to the law prior to its 1989 amendment, Rev.Proc. 80–40, 1980–2 C.B. 774; Rev. Ruls. 80–262 through 80–266 issued in connection therewith; Arzoo, Preparer Penalties and Compliance, 18 Tax Adviser 36 (1987); Thomas, The Negligent Return Preparer: Avoiding Section 6694(a), 63 Taxes 831 (1985); Buchholz & Paley, Minimizing Your Exposure to Tax Preparer Liability: A Checklist Approach, 18 Prac. Acct. 75 (1987). In 1986, the Treasury proposed an amendment to Circular 230 under which imposition of § 6661 substantial underpayment penalties on the client would be taken as evidence of improper practice by the adviser. The ABA and AICPA opposed this proposal. See AICPA Comments on Circular 230, 18 Tax Adviser 275 (1987). *But see* Wolfman, Circular 230, 36 Tax Notes 832 (Feb. 23, 1987); Johnson, "True and Correct" Standards for Tax Return Reporting, 43 Tax Notes 1521 (June 19, 1989).

18. *See infra* parts IV.E. and V.B. (more detailed discussion of the impact of the discovery of error on a return on our relationship with the client).

19. Any withdrawal from representation must be handled in such a way as not to disclose confidences or unduly prejudice the client. ABA Comm. on Professional Ethics, Formal Op. 314 (1965); AICPA Statement on Responsibilities in Tax Practice No. 7 (rev. 1988); *see also* Model Rules of Professional Conduct Rule 1.16 comment (1984).

20. Model Rules of Professional Conduct Rule 1.16(b)(1)–(3); *see also* Model Rules of Professional Conduct Rule 1.2 comment (1983). ("A lawyer may not continue assisting a client in conduct the lawyer originally supposes is legally proper but then discovers is criminal or fraudulent.").

minds, we should ask them and not proceed further unless we are reasonably satisfied.[21]

D. Valuation

A difficult factual issue frequently arising in the preparation of returns is the value of property transferred. Most tax practitioners are not appraisers and should generally let others make the valuation. It is entirely proper, however, to assist the appraiser in preparing the report. Indeed, we should use our lawyering skills to ensure that the report is sensible and will withstand scrutiny, because thereby we serve both the system and our clients.

The Code now imposes various special penalties for overvaluation and undervaluation of property and also requires the services of a qualified appraiser in certain situations. We must advise the client of these rules so that the client can be aware of the risks involved. * * *

E. Conformity to Law

1. A tax return involves the application of law to facts. Where the law is clear, we follow the law.[24]

2. It is appropriate to assist the client in structuring a transaction and reporting it on the return in the way least likely to be subject to audit, provided we do not mislead the Service. However:

a. We will not participate in the preparation of a return containing a clear error or frivolous position merely to have "a bone to throw" to the agent on audit in the hope that the error will not be discovered, or because the client cannot afford or wants to postpone a current tax payment.

(i) We should remind the client of the exposure to penalties, interest, future audit procedures, and other potentially adverse consequences that may flow from overreaching in tax matters.

b. We will not participate in the preparation of a return where the client fails to answer a question on the return in order to save taxes.[25]

c. When it is appropriate to use estimates on a return, we may indicate that it is an estimate, and, in any event, we will not do so in a

---

21. AICPA Statement on Responsibilities in Tax Practice No. 3 (rev. 1988). This same approach also applies to relying on forms K-1, brokers' statements and similar third party information.

24. *See generally* AICPA Statement on Responsibilities in Tax Practice No. 1 (rev. 1988); ABA Comm. on Ethics and Professional Responsibility, Formal Op. 352 (1985) (lawyer's advice in regard to a tax return should be governed by good faith and the realistic possibility for success should the matter be litigated).

25. *See* AICPA Statement on Responsibilities in Tax Practice No. 2 (rev. 1988) (discussing answers to questions on returns). Our commitment to answering a question depends, of course, on our conviction that the Service is legally authorized to ask the question. At times, rather than completing a form, we may attach a statement which provides all relevant information but in a manner more helpful to the client than the official form.

manner likely to imply greater accuracy than in fact exists.[26] For instance, if we believe an amount is about $2000, we should write "$2000" or "$2000 (est'd)." We should not write "$1984.76."

3. When the application of the law to the facts is not clear, there are frequently many choices, all within permitted limits, relating both to the position to be taken and the nature of the disclosure on the return. Positions and disclosures range from the entirely safe and certain to be accepted by the Service, to aggressive positions, which may result in a lesser tax burden, but involve the risk of challenge by the Service, to interest not being deductible, and of possible civil penalties in addition to the accounting, legal and administrative costs involved in resolving a tax controversy. Within the limits indicated below, it is up to the client to make the choice; it is up to us to explain the potential benefits and hazards.

4. There have been ongoing discussion and controversy about the degree of assurance the taxpayer and the taxpayer's advisor must have in the correctness of the return. These discussions should not obscure our *general rule:* returns should be prepared carefully and should be believed to be correct. * * * In any case, no matter how urgent the client's needs, we will not participate in a return that falls below either the standards of Circular 230 or the rules set forth in applicable ABA Opinions of Ethics.[27]

a. When a client decides to take an aggressive position, we should usually explain the risks to make sure that the client is aware of what is involved. We should make a record of our warning and of the technical support for the client's position to protect this firm against possible claims from the client or the Service. We should, however, make such record in a manner that preserves the confidentiality of our communications.

b. The general view of tax return professionals is that the applicable rules of professional ethics that bar assistance to a client engaged in "violation of law" are intended solely to prohibit participation in criminal conduct. With respect to client conduct that may lead to certain lesser civil penalties—such as a penalty under section 6662 (which now includes the substantial underpayment penalty of old section 6661)—the professional's obligation is merely to warn the client.[29] Nevertheless, it would be highly unusual for this firm to participate in conduct certain to lead to civil tax penalties; indeed we will generally not participate when a civil penalty to the taxpayer would more likely than not result if the return were audited and all of

---

26. *See* AICPA Statement on Responsibilities in Tax Practice No. 4 (rev. 1988).

27. The principal current opinion is ABA Comm. on Professional Ethics, Formal Op. 314 (1965), as modified by ABA Comm. on Ethics and Professional Responsibility, Formal Op. 352 (1985). Opinion 85–352 is reproduced in 39 Tax Lawyer 613 (1988). The same volume also contains an explanation of the background, Report of the Special Task Force on Formal Opinion 85–352, 39 Tax Lawyer 613 (1988).

29. *See* Durst, The Tax Lawyer's Professional Responsibility, 39 U.Fla.L.Rev. 1027 (1987).

the facts were presented to a court. Further, we will not serve as return preparers if it appears more likely than not that we would be subject to any preparers' penalty if all the facts were known to the Service.[30]

c. Both as a matter of statutory law and as a matter of the common law of taxation, the risk of penalties resulting from aggressive positions may generally be reduced by riders or explanatory statements attached to the return.[31] No matter how complete the disclosure, however, we must in good faith believe that the taxpayer's position is not frivolous.[32]

F. Prior Years' Returns

If we discover an error in a prior year's return that is not barred by the statute of limitations, whether or not of our own creation, we must advise the client of the error.[33] We should explain that present law does not mandate the filing of an amended return, but that a tax that is owed is a debt that should be paid and, therefore, in general an

---

30. The Internal Revenue Audit Manual, Part IV, 4297.9(7)(f) (1987), instructs agents to consider imposition of preparer penalties whenever considering substantial underpayment or valuation penalties. The House Committee Report on the 1989 Civil Penalty Legislation states, however, as part of its Administrative Recommendations to the Service, in section c. 3, to instruct its employees not to threaten imposition of preparer penalties during the course of an examination, Appeals conference, or other proceeding.

The preparer penalty provisions in I.R.C. § 6694, as amended by Omnibus Budget Reconciliation Act of 1989, Pub.L. No. 101-239, 103 Stat. 2106, now follow the ethical guidelines for lawyers and accountants proposed by the ABA and the AICPA. If an understatement of tax liability on a return is due to a position of which the return preparer knew or should have known that it did not have a realistic possibility of being sustained on its merits and such position was not disclosed or was frivolous, the preparer is subject to penalty "unless it is shown that there is reasonable cause for the understatement and such person acted in good faith." For a discussion and matrix of the negligence penalty provisions for taxpayers and return preparers resulting from the 1989 revisions, see Banoff, Determining Valid Legal Authority in Advising Clients, Rendering Opinions, Preparing Tax Returns, 68 Taxes 40 (1990).

31. Substantial understatement penalties under I.R.C. § 6662(d) may be reduced by the amount attributable to "any item with respect to which the relevant facts affecting the item's tax treatment are adequately disclosed in the return or in a statement attached to the return." For relevant authority prior to the penalty provision amendments made by the Omnibus Budget Reconciliation Act of 1989, Pub.L. No. 101-239, 103 Stat. 2106, see I.R.C. § 6661(b)(2) (1986); Rev.Proc. 86-27, 1986-1 C.B. 562; Rev.Proc. 87-48, 1989-2 C.B. 645; Rev.Proc. 8837, 1988-2 C.B. 560.

32. The AICPA and the ABA formerly did not suggest the explanatory riders were ethically required, although they might be prudent. See AICPA Statement on Responsibilities in Tax Practice, No. 1[.02d] (rev.1988); ABA Comm. on Professional Ethics, Formal Op. 314 (1965). More recently, these organizations have agreed that where a position has less chance of success than the "realistic possibility of success" standard, it may nevertheless be taken on a return if adequately disclosed and not frivolous. See AICPA Comments on Circular 230, 18 Tax Adviser 275 (1987). With respect to return items not involving tax shelters, disclosure may avoid the substantial underpayment penalty. See I.R.C. § 6661(b)(2)(B)(ii); Rev.Proc. 86-22, 1986-1 C.B. 562; Rev.Proc. 87-48, 1987-2 C.B. 645; Rev.Proc. 88-37, 1988-2 C.B. 560. As a result of the Omnibus Budget Reconciliation Act of 1989, disclosure that satisfies § 6662(d)(2)(B)(ii) would also protect the preparer against penalty unless the position was frivolous. I.R.C. § 6694(a)(3).

33. 31 C.F.R. § 10.21 (1988). For planning correction of erroneous transactions, see *infra* note 49 and supporting text.

amended return should be filed to correct any clear and material errors.[34]

1. Although there is no legal obligation to file an amended return, the implications of an uncorrected error on future years' returns must be considered. An uncorrected error having an effect on future returns cannot knowingly be carried forward.

2. If correction gives rise to risk of penalty, we must describe the risk and explore ways of paying the tax due that will minimize exposure to the penalty. In any situation involving potential fraud charges, however, we should carefully explain to the taxpayer the benefits and hazards of the various options available, including any constitutional right not to cooperate with the Service. A lawyer who does not have criminal tax practice experience should consult with one who has such experience.

a. When a clear and material error was made on a return prepared by this firm or in an audit in which we acted as the client's representative, we should explain to the client our own interest in an appropriate correction, and suggest that if the client wants advice not colored by such interest, the client should consult another adviser. Indeed, we may be required to insist that the client consult another advisor, where our own interest is sufficiently disparate from that of the client.

b. When we were preparers of a return that we subsequently learned contains a clear and material error,[35] and the client decides not to amend the return, we should consider whether the circumstances are such that we should no longer represent the client either in tax matters in general or, specifically, in any audit of the return.[36]

c. As already stated, if we should ever learn that a client asked us to assist in the preparation of a fraudulent return, we would immediately terminate all further representation.[37]

3. If a client has failed to file returns for prior years and pay the taxes due, he is under a clear legal obligation to do so and usually the best advice is to report and pay. Nevertheless, this involves the same balancing of benefits and risks as described under part IV.E.1. with respect to erroneous returns.

---

34. *See generally* Ronan, Do Clients Have a Duty to File Amended Tax Returns?, 33 Prac.Law. 25 (1987); AICPA Statement on Responsibilities in Tax Practice No. 6 (rev.1988). *See also* Harris, On Requiring the Correction of Error Under the Federal Tax Law, 42 Tax Lawyer 515 (1989). A failure to correct a clear and material error in a refund claim before the refund is paid appears particularly serious.

35. The term "clear and material error" does not include a position that was appropriate under the law in effect at the time of filing the return nor one that does not have a significant effect on the tax liability. *See* AICPA Statement on Responsibilities in Tax Practice No. 1 (rev. 1988). *See also* I.R.C. § 6662(d)(2)(B)(i) which precludes substantial underpayment penalty for any underpayment due to "the tax treatment of any item by the taxpayer *if there is or was* substantial authority for such treatment." (emphasis added).

36. *See* ABA Comm. on Professional Ethics, Formal Op. 314 (1965).

37. *See supra* note 20 and supporting text.

4. When we must respond to an independent auditor's letter and know of a clear error on a prior year's return that is not barred by the period of limitations, we must carefully consider whether this is a "contingent liability" to be disclosed by the client to the auditors. In that connection, it is relevant whether we believe it more likely than not that the claim will be asserted by the Service. Nevertheless, we must be certain that, by our silence, we do not mislead the auditors as to our client's situation, particularly since our client's refusal to correct a return containing a clear and substantial error may have a bearing on the auditor's reliance on the client's statements generally.[38]

V. Audit Representation
A. *Nature of Proceeding*

1. A tax audit is the first step and often also the last step in a potentially adversarial legal proceeding.

The following recommendations address audits when either the taxpayer has the burden of proof or when the Service may reasonably infer that we do not know the taxpayer's position to be clearly wrong. Obviously, when the audit is tending toward the direction of fraud charges, the client is entitled to take a position of "prove it" toward the Service and our role becomes pretty much that of an advocate in an adversarial proceeding.

2. Some lawyers handle audits on a superficial basis, in the hope that with only a little effort they can convince the agent to drop whatever questions the agent may have raised. Our firm's general approach is to persuade the client to authorize us to do a thorough and first class job. While at times the result may be an unnecessary expenditure of time and money, far more often a thorough preparation of the client's case will permit an earlier termination of the audit and a settlement of the controversy on terms favorable to the client. * * *

Where the matter is small or the client's funds are limited, it may make sense to do less than a "full court press." Within the limits of our professional responsibility, the decision is the client's.[39]

3. The Service representatives will have substantial knowledge and experience, while the client may not be aware of all the legal aspects of his particular situation. Unlike lawyers who are usually barred from having contact with the opposing party except through the opposing party's lawyer, Service agents are not similarly restricted.[40] Clients, however, need and are entitled to the same protection as in other proceedings when the other side possesses legal expertise that they lack.

---

38. *See generally* Fuld, The Statement of Policy Regarding Lawyers' Responses to Auditors Requests for Information, 31 Bus. Law. 1709 (1976) (the impact on the attorney-client privilege by clients' responses to auditors requests).

39. *See supra* part II. (discussing the impact of costs on the work undertaken by attorneys).

40. *See* I.R.C. § 7520(b)(2) (giving taxpayers the right to consult with an attorney or other authorized representative, but this right must be specifically requested).

While a lawyer or other representative need not be present at all stages of an audit, we should at the outset seek to review with the client the legal aspects of the audit, particularly any weak spots in the client's situation.

4. Frequently we can do a better job representing a client at an appeals conference if the client is not present. When we believe this to be the case, we should point this out to the client, leaving the final decision to the client.[41]

5. Both we and the client should cooperate with the Service, where this can be done without harm to the client's situation. We must remember, however, that it is not the Service but the courts that have the last word in determining what information—including information relating to third parties—the Service has a right to obtain from the client. In a particular case, there is nothing wrong with politely informing an agent that a summons will be required or that the propriety of a summons that has been issued will be tested in court.

6. Taxpayers have a right to periodically eliminate from their files papers no longer needed under applicable record keeping requirements, including memoranda and drafts regarding tax planning. Once an audit has started, however, any destruction of potentially relevant documents is improper.[42]

B. Truthfulness in Dealings with the Service

1. We must at all times be truthful with the Service and use our best efforts to ensure that the client is also truthful.

a. To preserve our reputation for integrity and reliability we must, in communications to the Service, be clear as to the source of any facts we assert. "The corporation made all relevant elections on a timely basis" is a legitimate statement if we know it to be a fact. If we do not know it, we should say, "We are informed by John Jones, Treasurer of the corporation, that it made all relevant elections on a timely basis."[43]

b. When we become aware of a clear and material error on the client's return, we should generally urge the client to permit disclosure, particularly when the proceeding involves the general correctness of the return rather than focusing on a specific issue. See part IV.E.

---

41. The Service requires a summons to compel attendance by the taxpayer. I.R.C. § 7520(c).

42. Record retention requirements are set out in § 6001 and in Guide to Record Retention Requirements in the Code of Federal Regulations, Nat'l Archives and Rec.Ad. (rev. 1986). Model Rules of Professional Conduct Rule 3.4(a) comment (1984), bar advising the destruction or concealment of evidence once a controversy has started or can be foreseen. See also I.R.C. § 7203 (punishes the willful failure to maintain required records as a misdemeanor); I.R.C. § 7206(5) (classifies as fraud the willful withholding or destruction of certain documents); I.R.C. § 7210 (deals with the failure to obey a summons).

43. Model Rules of Professional Conduct Rule 3.3 comment (1984) (" * * * an assertion purporting to be on the lawyer's own knowledge, * * * may properly be made only when the lawyer knows the assertion is true or believes it to be true on the basis of reasonably diligent inquiry.").

above. (For instance, we should do so if we find during the course of an audit that a deduction was taken for a particular expenditure that was clearly non-deductible). Also, any mathematical mistakes whether made by ourselves, the client, or the Service, should be disclosed to the Service.[44]

c. If, in an appropriate case, the client refuses to make the necessary correction or disclosure, in general, we should withdraw from further representation; the need to withdraw is particularly strong when we were the preparers of what is now known to be an erroneous return or when we may otherwise be understood by the Service to have participated in a misrepresentation by the client.

(i) Withdrawal from the engagement must be carefully undertaken so as to balance the desire or obligation to withdraw against the requirements that confidences not be disclosed and the client's interest not be otherwise prejudiced.

(ii) It may be helpful to remind the client that, during the course of an audit, it is customary for the auditing agent to ask whether the taxpayer or taxpayer's representative is aware of any matters requiring adjustment. If there is an undisclosed problem, and we have decided to continue representation in spite of the client's refusal to authorize disclosure, we must provide a truthful answer.

2. Difficult questions occasionally arise whether, in order to avoid misleading the Service, the lawyer should disclose information not known to the Service. Generally, in an audit, as in other adversarial proceedings, our obligation to tell the truth does not require disclosure of all relevant facts and law.[45]

a. Excepting only the situations referred to in part V.B.1.b. above, we are under no legal or ethical obligation to volunteer to the Service information adverse to the client or to urge the client to do so. Nevertheless, in our dealings with the Service, we can often serve our client most effectively by frank recognition of the problems with our client's case and then explaining why, in spite of these problems, our client should prevail.

---

44. ABA Comm. on Ethics and Professional Responsibility, Informal Op. 1518 (1986), counsels disclosure of a "scrivener's error" to the opponent without consultation with the client, since raising the issue of disclosure with the client might involve the lawyer in fraud if the client refuses to authorize disclosure. *But see* Chicago Bar Ass'n Prof.Resp.Com., Op. 864, in ABA/BNA, Lawyer's Manual on Professional Conduct, Vol. 4, No. 29, 345 (1988). In a particular case, it may be preferable first to consult with the client and urge disclosure.

45. Model Rules of Professional Conduct Rule 4.1(b) (1984), requires disclosure by the lawyer when "necessary to avoid assisting a fraudulent or criminal act by a client, unless disclosure is prohibited by Rule 1.6" (which protects confidential information except to prevent crimes likely to result in death or serious bodily harm or to protect the lawyer's interest). Model Rules of Professional Conduct Rule 4.1 comment (1984), states: "A lawyer is required to be truthful when dealing with others on the client's behalf, but generally has no affirmative duty to inform an opposing party of relevant facts."

b. There is no obligation to call the attention of the Service to apparent legal or factual inconsistencies in a settlement that was arrived at fairly. A settlement is an agreement between the taxpayer and the Service relating to "the bottom line," and inconsistencies with facts or rules of law not agreed to are irrelevant.[46] Nor must the settlement agreement be followed in future years unless it specifically so provides.[47]

VII. Assuring an Ethical Tax Practice

A. Like charity, the maintenance of professional standards begins at home. We expect all who work here to comply fully with all aspects of Federal, state, and local tax law in meeting their personal tax obligations.[51]

B. We can help maintain ethical standards by wide discussion among all tax specialists of any ethical questions arising in our practice and of any court decisions, rulings, ABA opinions, AICPA statements or other developments having a bearing on professional standards in tax practice. Doubtful questions should not be resolved without such discussion based upon careful research.

C. The foregoing guidelines must be applied to all of our clients, without reference to their monetary importance to the firm. We must recognize, however, that our financial interest in a matter may affect our judgment as to whether a contemplated course is proper. Accordingly, if we have doubts as to the propriety of a particular action and the matter is material from the firm's point of view—either by risking the loss of an important client or by exposing the firm to the charge that it engaged in misconduct—it is imperative to have a full and complete discussion of the matter with one or more uninvolved partners in the firm. In some cases, it may be advisable to obtain the opinion of outside counsel.

D. We want everyone working here to feel comfortable with the standards observed in our tax practice. Suggestions for improvement are always welcome. If anyone has any questions concerning the propriety of any action or plan, involving either that person or someone else in the firm, those questions should be promptly discussed—first, with the individual involved and then with any partner or partners in whose judgment the individual reposes confidence. Remember, the ultimate responsibility for your own conduct is solely your own.

E. There is now a growing and ever-changing body of law, regulations, opinions, court decisions, and literature bearing on the conduct of

---

46. *See* ABA Comm. on Professional Ethics, Formal Op. 314 (1965). *See also* Corneel, Ethical Guidelines for Tax Practice, 28 Tax L.Rev. 1, 21–22 (1972). There is no obligation on taxpayer's counsel to educate the Service as to the Internal Revenue Code. Therefore, the Tax Court refused to set aside a settlement where the Service lost approximately $700,000 due to the ignorance of its counsel. *See* Stamm International Corp. v. Commissioner, 90 T.C. 315 (1988).

47. *See* AICPA Statement on Responsibilities in Tax Practice No. 5 (rev. 1988).

51. This is also a condition for practice before the Service. 31 C.F.R. § 10.51(d) (1985).

a tax practice. Therefore, research is essential to the proper resolution of problems that may arise. The authorities cited are intended to facilitate the beginning of such research.[52]

Note

For recent commentary on the tax lawyer's ethical responsibilities, see Durst, The Tax Lawyer's Professional Responsibility, 39 University of Florida Law Review 1027 (1987); Handelman, Constraining Aggressive Return Advice, 9 Virginia Tax Review 77 (1989); Holden, Constraining Aggressive Return Advice: A Commentary, 9 Virginia Tax Review 771 (1990); Sax, Report of the Special Task Force on Formal Opinion 85–352, 39 Tax Lawyer 635 (1986); Falk, Tax Ethics, Legal Ethics, and Real Ethics: A Critique of ABA Formal Opinion 85–352, 39 Tax Lawyer 643 (1986).

SECTION 3. TREASURY DEPARTMENT STANDARDS

IRS PRACTICE AND PROCEDURE
Michael I. Saltzman.

Introduction

Standards governing admission to practice as well as duties of those practicing before the Service are designed to protect taxpayers and the quality of representation. The Secretary of the Treasury is authorized to prescribe rules and regulations governing the recognition of persons representing claimants before his department, and he may disbar or suspend any person from practice if that person refuses to comply with those rules.[1] The Treasury Department has adopted rules governing the recognition and conduct of persons representing taxpayers before the Internal Revenue Service. These rules have been promulgated in what is commonly referred to as Treasury Department Circular No. 230.[2] Circular No. 230 is divided into four parts: (1) rules relating to authority to practice before the IRS; (2) the duties and restrictions relating to such practice; (3) rules relating to disciplinary proceedings; and (4) general rules, such as provisions relating to the availability of records. In addition, conference and practice require-

---

52. The best current general text on the subject is B. Wolfman & J. Holden, Ethical Problems in Federal Tax Practice (2d ed. 1985). The ethical requirements for practice before the Treasury Department are set forth in 31 C.F.R. §§ 10.3, 10.4. Circular 230 should be carefully reviewed because it specifies all kinds of disreputable conduct that may result in disciplinary action by the Treasury even though not directly related to dealings with the Service. *Id.* at § 10.51. *See generally* Shapiro, Professional Responsibility in the Eyes of the IRS, 17 Tax Adviser 136 (1986). The recently revised AICPA Statements on Responsibility in Tax Practice offer the best detailed discussion on the points they cover. Needless to say, tax lawyers are lawyers and the state law disciplinary rules apply to the conduct of tax practice. For bar association opinions bearing on the conduct of tax practice, see ABA/BNA, Lawyer's Manual on Professional Conduct (1988), and more generally The Restatement of The Law on Lawyers (now in preparation).

1. 31 USC § 330.

2. 31 CFR Pt. 10. Circular No. 230 was revised to incorporate amendments made through February 23, 1984, 1985–2 CB742.

ments applying to all offices of the IRS have been promulgated as Title 26, Part 601 of the Code of Federal Regulations. The Secretary has appointed a Director of Practice in his office to carry out his functions relating to admission to practice and the conduct of disciplinary proceedings.

What Constitutes "Practice" Before the Service

Every person who on behalf of a taxpayer, transferee, or fiduciary appears before the IRS must meet the practice requirement the Treasury has established in Circular No. 230, unless the person is not engaged in "practice" before the IRS. Practice occurs, in general, when a person makes an advocate's presentation of a client-taxpayer's rights, privileges, or liabilities under IRS-administered laws or regulations. A "presentation" includes the preparation and filing of necessary documents; correspondence with and communications to the Service; and the representation of a client at conferences, hearings, and meetings. But neither the preparation and signing of a tax return, claim, or election nor an appearance before the Service as a witness or the furnishing of information at its request constitutes "practice" before the IRS. Consequently, a return preparer may answer questions and supply information to an IRS agent as a witness without having to satisfy the requirements prerequisite to practice and without obtaining a power of attorney. Once a person makes an oral or written presentation that relates to a client's rights, privileges, or liabilities under the internal revenue laws (i.e., advancing the client's position in the manner of an advocate), then that person is considered to be engaged in practice before the Service and is subject to the restrictions and duties of Circular No. 230.

Who May Practice Before the Service

Three broad classes of persons may practice before the Service: attorneys, certified public accountants, and enrolled agents.[8] Enrolled actuaries and others in specific situations may engage in limited practice before the Service without enrollment.

* * *

When Powers of Attorney and Tax Information Authorizations Are Required

The Service's conference and practice regulations require an individual appearing as an advocate to file (1) an instrument authorizing the holder to perform certain acts or to receive confidential tax information (a power of attorney or tax information authorization) and (2) a declaration that the person is recognized to practice before the Service (a practice declaration).[17] Even if the person appearing is merely to act as a witness, if that person is to receive or inspect confidential tax information, a tax information authorization must be filed. * * *

---

8. Circular No. 230, note 2 supra, § 2.3.

17. 26 CFR §§ 601.502(b), 601.502(c).

* * * The power or authorization is a prerequisite to representation. Unless the representative has on file a power or authorization, he will not be heard as the taxpayer's representative and (with [only a] few exceptions) cannot receive confidential tax information, and no notice or other written communication (or copy of one) that contains confidential information about a filed tax return will be sent to the representative. The power of attorney (Form 2848) must be filed when the taxpayer's representative is to perform one or more of the following acts on behalf of the taxpayer [21]

(1) To receive (but not endorse and collect) a check in payment of any refund of internal revenue taxes, penalties, or interest. The Service does not consider itself bound to deliver any check in payment of a tax refund to a representative, despite the fact that the representative is acting under a power of attorney. But under the Service's general policy it will mail the check in care of a recognized representative who has filed a power of attorney from the taxpayer specifically authorizing him to receive but not to endorse the check. When the check is mailed to the representative it will be made payable to the taxpayer "care of" the representative.

(2) To execute a waiver of restrictions on assessment or collection of a deficiency in tax, or a waiver of notice of disallowance if a claim for credit or refund.

(3) To execute a consent to extend the statutory period for assessment or collection of a tax.

(4) To execute a closing agreement under Section 7121 of the Code.

A tax information authorization (Form 2848–D) must be used in cases where the representative will not perform one of the four enumerated acts if he wishes to receive or inspect confidential tax information in a matter. The tax information authorization is necessary for the representative to inspect the taxpayer's returns, to receive information at a conference with Service personnel of the Service's position on the taxpayer's liability, to discuss the merits of the taxpayer's request for a ruling or determination letter with the Service, and to receive such notices as a thirty-day letter and examining officer's report. But the authorization is not required to receive notices and communications that do not involve the disclosure of confidential information.

The Service has adopted a Centralized Authorization File (CAF) system for identifying taxpayers' representatives and the scope of their authority. Under this system, if a representative files a power of attorney or tax information authorization and the written practice declaration, information regarding the authorization will be reflected on the CAF, which is an automated (i.e., computerized) file. Each representative is or will be assigned an identifying number for inputting and retrieving this information, and Forms 2848 and 2848–D have

---

21. 26 CFR § 601.502(c).

been revised to accommodate use of the representative's identifying number. The stated objective of the CAF system is to enable the Service "to handle matters regarding authorizations and representatives quickly and efficiently" by, for example, identifying representatives and the scope of their authority and automatically directing copies of notices and correspondence to them. Practitioners hope that the system will enable them to communicate with IRS personnel without delays in establishing their authority because their power of attorney is on file with another IRS office.

The Practice Declaration. To act as an advocate for a taxpayer, a representative must file a practice declaration as well as a power of attorney or tax information authorization. The declaration states that the representative is (1) an attorney who is a member in good standing of the bar of the highest court of the jurisdiction in which he is admitted to practice, a CPA qualified to practice in the jurisdiction in which he practices, or an enrolled agent under Circular No. 230 and (2) not currently under suspension or disbarment from practice before the Service. This declaration is on the reverse side of the Forms 2848 and 2848-D, but the declaration need not be made on these IRS forms. The declaration must be filed when a representative presents himself for the initial meeting in the first office in the Service in which he represents the party on whose behalf he acts in connection with the matter under consideration. Once evidence of recognition is submitted, it is not necessary to submit this evidence again in any office of the Service unless a specific request is made.

A power of attorney or tax information authorization must be filed in each office of the IRS in which the representative desires to perform one of the acts enumerated above or to receive or inspect confidential information. Technically, a power or authorization is required at the district director's office, the Appeals Office, and in the district counsel's office because each of them is a separate office. Moreover, an additional copy of the power or authorization is required for each taxable period because "each taxable period constitutes a separate matter." Where, however, a power or authorization is filed in the district office that has the matter under consideration, further filing in the offices that subsequently have the matter under consideration is not required unless a ruling request is made. In that case, a copy of the power or authorization must be submitted with each request if the representative wishes to have a conference or to receive a copy of the ruling.

[5] Execution of Powers and Authorizations

Forms. The Service provides forms that representatives generally will use: Form 2848 (Power of Attorney) and Form 2848-D (Authorization and Declaration).* Use of these forms is not mandatory, but the instrument purporting to be a power or authorization must clearly express the taxpayer's intention about the scope of the representative's authority and the tax matter to which the authority relates. General-

---

* Form 2848-D has been replaced with Form 8821. See Appendix A.

ly, a power of attorney is required to be filed if the representative is to act as attorney-in-fact to perform one or more of the four specific acts listed on the Form 2848. In all other cases involving the receipt of confidential tax information, Form 2848-D is used. The Form 2848-D authorization has two parts: Part I is a tax information authorization; Part II is a practice declaration. If representation will involve the receipt of confidential tax information, both parts are filled out. If, however, representation will not involve the receipt of confidential tax information (e.g. filing a protest or executing a claim for refund), only Part II is required to be completed.

* * *

Duties and Restrictions on Practice

Circular No. 230 imposes a number of duties and restrictions on practice before the IRS. These are as follows:

(1) A person authorized to practice before the IRS may not interfere with an effort by the IRS to obtain information unless the person believes in good faith and on reasonable grounds that the information is privileged or that the effort is of doubtful legality.

(2) A person authorized to practice before the IRS must, on request, supply the Director of Practice with information about violations of the regulations and must testify in any disbarment or suspension proceeding unless the person believes in good faith and on reasonable grounds that the information is privileged or that the request is of doubtful legality.

(3) A person authorized to practice retained by a client who has not complied with the revenue laws or has made an error in or omission from a return or other document that the client is required by law to execute must advise the client promptly of the noncompliance, error, or omission. It appears that no obligation beyond this advice is necessary, and presumably the final decision to comply or correct the error or omission is the client's. * * *

* * *

(4) A person authorized to practice must exercise due diligence in preparing and filing returns, documents, and other papers relating to internal revenue matters and in determining the correctness of representations to the Treasury Department and to a client. This duty is to a substantial degree enforced by the return preparer rules and penalties provided by the Code. It has been held, however, that the regulation "suggests a principal concern with making representatives accountable for negligence" and "connotes loyalty and devotion" to the client.[50] Consequently, when a representative deceives his client in a matter before the IRS, the repre-

---

50. Harary v. Blumenthal, 555 F.2d 1113 (2d Cir.1977).

sentative violates the regulation and may be disbarred or suspended from practice.[51]

(5) A person authorized to practice must not unreasonably delay the prompt disposition of a matter before the IRS.

(6) A person authorized to practice may not knowingly and directly or indirectly (a) employ a person disbarred or suspended from practice or accept employment from such a person or (b) accept assistance from a former government employee prohibited by regulations or law from providing assistance.

(7) Special rules apply to practice by former government officials or partners of government employees.

(8) A person authorized to practice may not notarize papers in a matter in which he is also counsel, attorney, or agent.

(9) A person authorized to practice may not charge an unconscionable fee.

(10) A person authorized to practice may not represent conflicting interests, except by express consent of all directly interested parties after full disclosure has been made. * * *

(11) Persons admitted to practice may not solicit employment in matters before the IRS, except (a) from an existing or former client in a related matter or (b) by way of a mailing designed for the general public. Advertising disclosing factual data, such as a description of the services offered, membership in professional organizations, and fee information, is permitted.

(12) Persons admitted to practice may not negotiate a refund check [in violation of IRC 6695(f)].

DISCIPLINARY PROCEEDINGS: DISBARMENT AND SUSPENSION FROM PRACTICE

The Secretary of the Treasury has the power to disbar or suspend any person recognized to practice before the Service who (a) is shown to be incompetent or disreputable; (b) refuses to comply with the rules and regulations in Circular No. 230; or (c) with intent to defraud willfully and knowingly deceives, misleads, or threatens a prospective client by oral or written solicitation.

* * *

In addition, a person recognized to practice may be disbarred or suspended for willful violation of any of the regulations contained in Circular No. 230, including, presumably, the standards of and restrictions on practice.

If Service personnel have reason to believe that a person admitted to practice or any other person has information of violation of the rules of Circular No. 230, a report is made to the Director of Practice in the

---

51. In *Harary v. Blumenthal*, a CPA who was acquitted of bribing an IRS agent had told his client the agent had to be paid $2,000 but paid the agent $1,250, pocketing the $750 for himself.

Treasury Department, on the basis of which the Director may reprimand or commence disbarment or suspension proceedings. Generally, however, a proceeding will not be commenced until the person involved is notified of the facts and the conduct complained of. The Director may, but is not required to, offer the person a conference, at which he has the opportunity to convince the Director no violation has occurred, or to consent to a voluntary suspension or resignation, which the Director may, but again is not required to, accept. After the conference (if it is offered), the Director may reprimand the representative, accept the offer of consent to voluntary suspension or resignation, or proceed to file a complaint commencing the disciplinary proceedings.

Formal proceedings are heard by a hearing examiner; after the filing of an answer, motions, trial, and submission of proposed findings, the hearing examiner makes findings of fact and law and appropriate order for filing with the Director of Practice. An appeal must be filed with the Secretary of the Treasury within thirty days after the decision, but in any event the Secretary will make the agency's decision.

A disbarred or suspended person may not practice before the Service until reinstated or the period of suspension expires, and notice of disbarment or suspension is given not only to Service personnel but also to other federal and state authorities. Notices of disbarment or suspension are published in the *Internal Revenue Bulletin.*

Note

Subpart E of the Statement of Procedural Rules (Proc. Rules §§ 601.501–601.509—Conference and Practice Requirements) sets forth additional requirements concerning practice before the Internal Revenue Service. Included among these are the Service's rules regarding conferences with representatives of the IRS (§§ 601.502(a), 601.507); requirements concerning the necessity and proper execution and filing of powers of attorney and/or tax information authorizations (§§ 601.502(c), 601.503, 601.504); requirements for changing representation (§ 601.505); and regulations regarding delivery of notices and refund checks to a taxpayer's recognized representative (§ 601.506).

TREASURY DEPARTMENT CIRCULAR 230
Subpart B.
31 C.F.R. § 10.20 et seq. (1986).

§ 10.20 INFORMATION TO BE FURNISHED

(a) *To the Internal Revenue Service.* No attorney, certified public accountant, or enrolled agent shall neglect or refuse promptly to submit records or information in any matter before the Internal Revenue Service, upon proper and lawful request by a duly authorized officer or employee of the Internal Revenue Service, or shall interfere, or attempt to interfere, with any proper and lawful effort by the Internal Revenue Service or its officers or employees to obtain any such record or information, unless he believes in good faith and on reasonable grounds that such record or information is privileged or that the request for, or effort to obtain, such record or information is of doubtful legality.

(b) *To the Director of Practice.* It shall be the duty of an attorney or certified public accountant, who practices before the Internal Revenue Service, or enrolled agent, when requested by the Director of Practice, to provide the Director with any information he may have concerning violation of the regulations in this part by any person, and to testify thereto in any proceeding instituted under this part for the disbarment or suspension of an attorney, certified public accountant, or enrolled agent, unless he believes in good faith and on reasonable grounds that such information is privileged or that the request therefor is of doubtful legality.

§ 10.21   KNOWLEDGE OF CLIENT'S OMISSION

Each attorney, certified public accountant, or enrolled agent who, having been retained by a client with respect to a matter administered by the Internal Revenue Service, knows that the client has not complied with the revenue laws of the United States or has made an error in or omission from any return, document, affidavit, or other paper which the client is required by the revenue laws of the United States to execute, shall advise the client promptly of the fact of such noncompliance, error, or omission.

§ 10.22   DILIGENCE AS TO ACCURACY

Each attorney, certified public accountant, or enrolled agent shall exercise due diligence:

(a) In preparing or assisting in the preparation of, approving, and filing returns, documents, affidavits, and other papers relating to Internal Revenue Service matters;

(b) In determining the correctness of oral or written representations made by him to the Department of the Treasury; and

(c) In determining the correctness of oral or written representations made by him to clients with reference to any matter administered by the Internal Revenue Service.

§ 10.23   PROMPT DISPOSITION OF PENDING MATTERS

No attorney, certified public accountant, or enrolled agent shall unreasonably delay the prompt disposition of any matter before the Internal Revenue Service.

In 1986, the Treasury Department proposed two amendments to Circular 230. Although these proposed amendments never became final and effective, they generated considerable controversy and, even as this book goes to press in early 1991, have not been withdrawn. The first proposed amendment would have expanded the attorney's "due diligence" requirement under section 10.22 to cover advice given to clients about positions taken on returns. The other would have added a new section 10.34, which would link the lawyer's "due diligence" with the substantial understatement penalty of Code section 6662(d) (formerly section 6661). The notice of proposed rulemaking [51 Fed.Reg. 29,113 (1986)] explained the proposed amendments as follows:

BACKGROUND

This notice of proposed rulemaking is premised on the concern of the Department of the Treasury that the professional responsibility of some of those eligible to practice before the Internal Revenue Service (IRS) with respect to tax return preparation and advice relative to positions on tax returns has eroded over the years. This had led to serious problems concerning taxpayer compliance with the revenue laws, a matter which adversely affects the integrity of our voluntary self-assessment tax system.

While it is generally agreed that a practitioner owes a client competence, loyalty and confidentiality, it also is recognized that a practitioner has responsibilities to the tax system as well.

* * *

DUE DILIGENCE

The regulations in Circular 230 impose at section 10.22, a "due diligence" requirement on practitioners concerning oral and written representations made to clients and the IRS relative to tax matters. Such requirement addresses both advice on positions to be taken on tax returns and tax return preparation itself.

* * *

The Treasury Department takes the position that, as a standard of professional responsibility in the area of tax return preparation, due diligence requires the practitioner to be assured that any reporting position is in compliance with and supportable by the revenue laws. Unless the position is reasonable, meritorious and made in good faith, a practitioner has not exercised the necessary diligence imposed upon him or her. The due diligence standard cannot be met by a position advanced principally to exploit the audit selection process, a position that serves as a mere "arguing" position advanced solely to obtain leverage in the bargaining process of settlement negotiation within the IRS, a position that would serve merely to avert a successful charge that the return is false or fraudulent, or a position that has no practical and realistic possibility of being sustained in the courts.

* * *

§ 10.22 DILIGENCE AS TO ACCURACY

Each person eligible to practice before the Internal Revenue Service shall exercise due diligence with respect to the following activities:

(a) In advising clients about positions taken with respect to the tax treatment of all items and returns;

* * *

4. Section 10.34 is added to read as follows:

§ 10.34 ADVICE REGARDING POSITIONS ON TAX MATTERS WHERE INTERNAL REVENUE CODE SECTION 6661 MAY BE APPLICABLE

In advising a taxpayer about the tax treatment of any item on a return, a practitioner must comply with the following requirements:

(a) A practitioner must advise a client fully about the addition to tax provisions of section 6661 of the Internal Revenue Code with respect to any return if, [in] the exercise of due diligence, the practitioner determines that the taxpayer filing the return may be liable for an addition to tax under section [6661] as a result of a position taken with respect to the tax treatment of any item on the return.

(b) A practitioner may not advise or recommend to a client that a position be taken with respect to the tax treatment of any [item] on a return unless in the exercise of due diligence the practitioner determines that the taxpayer filing the return will not be liable for an addition to tax under section 6661 of the Internal Revenue Code as a result of the position.

(c) A practitioner may not prepare or sign a return unless in the exercise of due diligence the practitioner determines that the taxpayer filing the return will not be liable for an addition to tax under section 6661 of the Internal Revenue Code as a result of a position taken with respect to the tax treatment of any item on the return.

(d) For purposes of this section, the term "tax shelter" has the same meaning as the term "tax shelter" in section 6661(b)(2)(C)(ii) of the Internal Revenue Code.

The 1986 proposed amendments to Circular 230 sparked heated debate and were never put into effect. In 1987, the ABA proposed the following substitute section 10.34, with which the American Institute of Certified Public Accountants ("AICPA") concurred (with minor differences):

§ 10.34 STANDARDS FOR ADVISING OR RECOMMENDING TAX RETURN POSITIONS AND PREPARING OR SIGNING RETURNS

With respect to tax return positions, practitioners must comply with the following standards:

(a) A practitioner may not advise or recommend to a client that a position be taken with respect to the tax treatment of any item on a return unless the practitioner has a good faith belief that the position has a realistic possibility of being sustained administratively or judicially on its merits if challenged.

(b) A practitioner may not prepare or sign a return if that return takes a position that the practitioner could not advise or recommend under the standard expressed in paragraph (a).

(c) Notwithstanding paragraphs (a) and (b), the practitioner may advise or recommend that a position be presented in the context of either: (1) a return on which the position is adequately disclosed as such, or (2) an amended return that serves as a claim for refund (e.g., a Form 1040X or 1120X), in either case so long as the practitioner concludes that there is a basis for doing so that is not frivolous.

(d) In advising or recommending a return position where there is or may not be substantial authority for the position, or in preparing or signing a return on which such a position is taken, a practitioner must advise the client fully as to the potential penalty consequences under section 6661 of the Internal Revenue Code and, if relevant, the opportunity to avoid the penalty through disclosure or other means.

(e) In preparing or signing a return, a practitioner may in good faith rely without verification upon information furnished by the client or by third parties. However, the practitioner may not ignore the implications of information furnished and must make reasonable inquiries if the information furnished appears to be incorrect, incomplete, or inconsistent, either on its face or on the basis of other known facts.

OWRUTSKY v. TREASURY SECRETARY
United States Court of Appeals, Fourth Circuit, 1991.
952 F.2d 1457.

The Secretary of the Treasury appeals an order of the district court reversing the Secretary's decision to disbar Morton J. Owrutsky from practice before the Internal Revenue Service for failure to timely file income tax returns. We reverse.

I.

Owrutsky is an attorney admitted to practice law in the State of Maryland. He had sufficient income to require him to file personal federal income tax returns for the tax years 1974 through 1979. He received an extension to August 25, 1975 for filing his 1974 tax return, but did not file it until May 4, 1976. He filed his 1975 tax return, due April 15, 1976, more than two years late on April 24, 1978. Although he was granted an extension to June 15, 1977 for his 1976 return, he did not file it until September 18, 1978. His 1977 return, due April 15, 1978, was not filed until June 4, 1980. He filed his 1978 return on July 12, 1980, which was more than one year after the extended deadline of April 30, 1979. After receiving an extension to June 15, 1980 for filing his 1979 tax return, he finally filed that return on June 26, 1981. Owrutsky received refunds for the years 1974, 1975, and 1976 and reported no tax liability for 1977, 1978, and 1979. During these years he represented clients in both civil and criminal tax matters in Internal Revenue Service proceedings.

On February 23, 1984, the Director of Practice for the Department of the Treasury initiated proceedings to have Owrutsky disbarred from practice before the Internal Revenue Service for willfully failing to file timely returns for the tax years 1974 through 1979. At a hearing before an administrative law judge, Owrutsky stated that he had not timely filed his tax returns because a partner in a real estate venture did not maintain adequate records to provide him the information needed to complete the returns in a timely manner. Rejecting this explanation, the ALJ found that the specific testimony given by Owrutsky and other witnesses who testified on his behalf concerning the partnership was not truthful and that in general Owrutsky's testimony was not worthy of belief.

The ALJ concluded that Owrutsky knew he was required to file returns, knew when they were required to be filed, and knew they were required to be timely filed. He held that Owrutsky's failure to timely file tax returns for six consecutive years was "clearly a voluntary, intentional violation of a known legal duty." Accordingly, he ordered Owrutsky disbarred from further practice before the Internal Revenue Service. In affirming the decision of the ALJ, the Secretary concluded that Owrutsky was aware of his obligations to timely file and "consciously, intentionally, and voluntarily chose not to file his returns when they were due."

II.

The Secretary of the Treasury is authorized to "disbar from practice before the Internal Revenue Service any attorney * * * shown to be * * * disreputable." 31 C.F.R. § 10.50 (1990). Disreputable conduct includes "[w]illfully failing to make Federal tax return[s] in violation of the revenue laws of the United States." 31 C.F.R. § 10.51(d) (1990). The Internal Revenue Code provides that individuals are required to file income tax returns before the April 15 deadline or within a period of time granted by an extension. *See* I.R.C. §§ 6012(a), 6072(a), 6081(a) (West 1989). In the context of the felony and misdemeanor sections of the Revenue Code, the term "willfully" is defined as "a voluntary, intentional violation of a known legal duty." *United States v. Pomponio,* 429 U.S. 10, 12 (1976).

The district court held that Owrutsky's eligibility for refunds and his lack of any tax liability precluded a willful motive. The court overlooked the important finding by the ALJ that Owrutsky, an experienced practicing attorney, was fully aware that he had a legal duty to timely file returns regardless of his tax liability. *See Spies v. United States,* 317 U.S. 492 (1943). Under the *Pomponio* standard, willfulness does not require proof of any motive other than an intentional violation of a known legal duty. *Cheek v. United States,* 59 U.S.L.W. 4049 (U.S. Jan. 8, 1991); *see also United States v. Sullivan,* 369 F.Supp. 568, 569 (D.Mont.1974) ("If by congressional fiat it is bad to fail to file an income tax return," then willfulness may be found when "the obligation to act is fully known and consciously disregarded.").

In determining whether the ALJ properly found that Owrutsky's failure to timely file the tax returns was willful, we review his findings, as did the district court, under the substantial evidence standard. 5

U.S.C.A. § 706(2)(E) (West 1977). As this court has emphasized, our scope of review of the ALJ's factual findings is limited and deference must be given to the factfinder's inferences and credibility determinations. *Newport News Shipbuilding & Dry Dock Co. v. Tann*, 841 F.2d 540 (4th Cir.1988). We hold that these facts, coupled with the ALJ's findings of the lack of credibility on the part of Owrutsky and his witnesses, provide substantial evidence to support a determination of willfulness.

Reversed

WIDENER, CIRCUIT JUDGE, concurring:

I concur in the result.

In late 1989, Congress entered the skirmish by amending the return preparer penalty provision (section 6694, discussed at pp. 52–55) and making the following "administrative recommendations" to the IRS:

(1) Disciplinary sanctions by the Director of Practice should not be viewed as an adjunct to the civil penalty system as it applies to tax return preparers. In matters involving non-willful conduct, the IRS should only refer cases to the Director of Practice in instances where the IRS can establish a pattern of failing to meet the required standards. An isolated instance in which a penalty may apply should not, in and of itself, require a referral unless willful conduct is involved.

* * *

(4) The Director of Practice should publish more information about the basis for being disciplined and warnings in appropriate cases. Questions and Answers prepared in conjunction with input from practitioners would be helpful to the tax practitioner community. [H.R.Rep. 101–247, 101st Cong., 1st Sess. 1406 (1989).]

SECTION 4. THE MULTIPLE REPRESENTATION ISSUE

BACKER v. COMMISSIONER
United States Court of Appeals, Fifth Circuit, 1960.
275 F.2d 141.

TUTTLE, CIRCUIT JUDGE.

This action covers a very narrow compass. Appellant is a Certified Public Accountant who had been employed in connection with preparation of the tax returns of one Walter D. Williams, Jr. In the course of investigation of Williams' tax affairs for five years numerous consultations were had between the Internal Revenue agents and special agents and appellant. Appellant fully answered all questions asked, produced all papers requested during the many interviews conducted both with and without the presence of an attorney for taxpayer.

In this posture of affairs, after appellant had disclosed all the information sought from him touching on Williams' tax affairs, he was subpoenaed to appear and testify under oath before the Special Agent at a prescribed time and place. He did appear, accompanied by counsel, Cubbedge Snow, Esquire. Mr. Snow had previously filed a power of attorney to represent the taxpayer, Williams, in the investigation of his tax matters. The Special Agent stated that Mr. Snow could not be present at the investigation of appellant, whereupon appellant, on the advice of his counsel, declined to submit to the interrogation; counsel based this action on the provisions of the Administrative Procedure Act which says:

"Any person compelled to appear in person before any agency or representative thereof shall be accorded the right to be accompanied, represented, and advised by counsel * * * " 5 U.S.C.A. § 1005.

Thereupon the Commissioner of Internal Revenue filed his petition with the United States District Court to require the attendance of Backer "without the presence of counsel retained by or connected with the said Walter D. Williams, Jr."

The trial court expressly found that counsel was employed by Backer at his own expense and without any suggestion from the taxpayer. It also found that both appellant and his counsel were "of unquestioned and unquestionable character" and that neither of them had attempted in any manner to impede the investigation.

Nevertheless, the court held that Backer must appear to give his testimony without being represented by Mr. Snow. The trial court said:

" * * * Whether or not the Commissioner is correct in contending that the mere presence of taxpayer's counsel at the investigation while taxpayer's accountant is being questioned serves as a damper upon the voluntary testimony of taxpayer's accountant, I think the correct solution to this problem was pointed out in United States v. Smith, D.C.Conn.1949, 87 F.Supp. 293, 294, where the Court said:

" 'While no harm seems likely from such a situation in this case, since the knowledge of these witnesses is necessarily also the knowledge of the taxpayer, any possibility of prejudice to the investigation should be obviated by requiring that counsel be not connected with, or retained by, the taxpayer.' "

The Commissioner does not base his right to exclude any particular counsel from such representation of the appellant on any Regulations of the Internal Revenue Service. He acts under a policy established by him prior to the adoption of the Administrative Procedure Act. The policy is stated in a Manual of Instructions for Special Agents, Intelligence Unit, July 10, 1945, which gave a witness the right stated as follows:

> "The right to have an attorney present at the time of his questioning for the purpose of advising the witness relevant to his right to refuse to give any answers which might incriminate him under the laws of the United States. Under this policy, however, a third party witness is entitled to the attendance of his own counsel, but not the counsel for taxpayer."

It is clear that the right to counsel guaranteed under the Administrative Procedure Act is much broader than the right to have an attorney to advise him relative to his rights under the Fifth Amendment. The Act says such counsel may accompany, represent and advise the witness, without any limitation. Moreover, it seems quite doubtful that the policy statement itself, even if it were valid under the new act, covers the situation where the counsel is in fact counsel for the witness, even though he is also counsel for the taxpayer. It draws the distinction between counsel for the witness and counsel for the taxpayer. It does not seem to deal with the situation where one lawyer is both.

In any event, we are not here dealing with an attempted limitation on the generality of the right guaranteed under the Administrative Procedure Act by a formally adopted department regulation. We, therefore, do not come to the question whether, if under formal rulemaking procedures the Treasury Department had adopted regulations purporting to qualify the right of a witness to be represented by a lawyer who is also counsel for the person under investigation, such regulation would warrant the ruling of the court below. Certain it is that in the absence of any such regulation the Commissioner cannot put limitations on the general authority to have counsel as granted by the statute by saying that the witness's choice cannot include one who also represents the taxpayer.

We recognize that what is in issue here is not the constitutional right to counsel. It is, however, a statutory right. The term "right to counsel" has always been construed to mean counsel of one's choice. We think this is the plain and necessary meaning of this provision of the law. When Congress used the terms "right to be accompanied, represented, and advised by counsel," it must have used the language in the regularly accepted connotation, even though the language of the courts in using it was in connection with the right to counsel guaranteed by the Sixth Amendment to the Constitution.

Nor do we have a case in which the Commissioner is complaining to a trial court that counsel is in fact obstructing the orderly inquiry process by improper conduct or tactics.

None of the harm which the Commissioner here apprehends will result from letting taxpayer's counsel represent a witness as his own selected counsel will result except upon the failure of counsel to conduct himself in accord with his sworn duty to the court. If he does so fail then is the time for remedial action to be taken. Such action is not permissible when, as here, the trial court and government counsel reject any suggestion that either the witness or counsel will violate either the law or the ethics of their profession in the proposed investigation.

We hold that under the circumstances of this case the action of the District Court was not authorized.

The order of the District Court is reversed and vacated and the case remanded for further proceedings not inconsistent with this opinion.

Notes and Questions

1. Treasury Department Circular 230, § 10.29, provides that no attorney "shall represent conflicting interests in his practice before the Internal Revenue Service, except by express consent of all directly interested parties after full disclosure has been made." In view of the *Backer* decision, under what circumstances might the IRS attempt to prevent an attorney from representing both targets and witnesses in an investigation. See IRS Handbook for Special Agents, § 343.6, which states: "the mere existence of a dual representation situation which may potentially have an adverse impact on the investigation will not, without some action by the attorney to impede or obstruct the investigation, provide a sufficient basis for seeking a disqualification. However, where an attorney's representation has substantially prejudiced the questioning of a third-party witness and, as a result, has significantly impaired the progress of the investigation, the Service will request the Department of Justice to seek a court order, as part of the summons enforcement proceeding, to disqualify that attorney as counsel for that witness. In view of the well-established principle granting a person the right to counsel of one's choice, this disqualification procedure will only be used in extreme circumstances, such as where an attorney has taken some action to improperly or unlawfully impede or obstruct the investigation. It is essential that the interviewing officer have sufficient facts to support such allegations."

2. The multiple representation issue is often raised in grand jury proceedings by a motion to disqualify the attorney who seeks to represent both the target of the investigation and witnesses in the matter. There can be serious questions of conflict of interest. For example, when the witness pleads the fifth amendment it could be to protect the witness, but it could also be to protect the target. The temptation for the attorney to coach the witness is very great. On the other hand, there is strong bias toward allowing a witness to have the attorney of the witness' choice. The right to select counsel of one's choice is not absolute in grand jury proceedings. The court may find it necessary to regulate the professional conduct of attorneys. Compare In re Grand Jury, 446 F.Supp. 1132 (N.D.Tex.1978) (where there was no actual conflict of interest between employees and their employer corporation which was under investigation, and each witness had clearly waived any potential conflict of interest, the court denied a motion to disqualify an attorney from multiple representation); with In the Matter of Investigative Grand Jury Proceedings, 480 F.Supp. 162 (N.D.Ohio 1979) (joint representation of individual and organizational clients presents a

substantial danger that an attorney cannot provide zealous representation and fidelity both to clients who are witnesses, and to clients who are targets of an investigation. Judicial remedy is disqualification where evaluation of alternatives to protect fifth amendment rights of witnesses must be balanced against the validity of the clients' waiver of the right to conflict-free counsel.).

SECTION 5. STATUTORY REGULATION OF INCOME TAX RETURN PREPARERS

The tax return preparer provisions of the Code impose obligations upon persons who participate in the preparation of income tax returns and claims for refunds. The return preparer provisions are discussed in detail in chapter 6. This is a brief introduction to the return preparer rules. These provisions impose disclosure and record-keeping requirements and provide penalties for the negligent and willful understatement of the taxpayer's tax liability. Moreover, in appropriate circumstances the preparer can be enjoined from engaging in practice before the IRS and from the preparation of tax returns. These provisions were added to the Code by the Tax Reform Act of 1976 in order to improve the accountability of commercial tax return preparers and to upgrade the quality of their work. Unfortunately for tax professionals, these requirements were made applicable to attorneys and accountants who prepare their clients' returns as well as to commercial tax return preparers. Although generally regarded as a nuisance by professional tax advisers, the preparer regulations are accompanied by significant penalty provisions which require strict internal office controls to ensure compliance with their requirements.[b]

Who is an "income tax return preparer"? The income tax return preparer regulations are applicable to any person who prepares, for compensation, all or a substantial portion of an income tax return or claim for refund.[c] Only a person who prepares a substantial portion of a return or claim for refund will be considered an income tax return preparer. The regulations state that "[w]hether a schedule, entry, or other portion of a return or claim for refund is a substantial portion is determined by comparing the length and complexity of, and tax liability or refund involved in, that portion to the length and complexity of, and tax liability or refund involved in, the return or claim for refund as a whole."[d] Reg. § 301.7701–15(b)(2) establishes a safe harbor—an objective means of determining when the preparation of only a portion of a return or claim for refund will be considered insubstantial and the

b. Tax return preparers may also be subject to penalty under § 6701, discussed in chapter 6.

c. I.R.C. § 7701(a)(36). A person who prepares an income tax return or a claim for refund as a fiduciary for another, or for his regular employer, or in response to any notice of deficiency issued to a taxpayer, is not deemed to be an income tax return preparer subject to the tax preparer regulations. I.R.C. § 7701(a)(36)(B). Neither is a person who furnishes merely typing, reproducing, or mechanical assistance a tax return preparer. Id.

d. Reg. § 301.7701–15(b)(1).

preparer need not, therefore, comply with the recordkeeping and disclosure requirements of the preparer regulations. Generally, if the portion prepared for compensation by someone other than the taxpayer involves amounts of gross income, deductions, or amounts determining credits which are either less than $2,000 in the absolute, or less than $100,000 *and* also less than 20 percent of the taxpayer's adjusted gross income, then the portion prepared will not be considered "substantial". A person who does not physically prepare the return but who furnishes the taxpayer or other preparer with sufficient advice so that completion of the return is largely a mechanical or clerical matter is deemed to be a tax return preparer. Under the regulations, both the physical preparer of the return and off-return advisers may be income tax return preparers; a single return may subject several persons to the income tax return preparer requirements.

A tax adviser who provides his client with advice on a specific issue subjects himself to the preparer regulations if the advice is given with respect to a completed transaction and if the advice is directly relevant to the existence, characterization, or amount of an entry on a return or claim for refund.[e] Of course, the entry must also constitute a substantial portion of the return. A preparer of an income tax return may be deemed to be an income tax return preparer of a related income tax return where the entries reported in the first return are directly reported in the second return. Thus, an accountant who prepares a partnership's income tax return will be considered to be a preparer of the individual partners' returns where the entries from the partnership return constitute substantial portions of the partners' returns. Note that the preparer regulations are not applicable to preparers of excise, estate and gift tax returns; nor are they applicable to applications for tentative carrybacks.

Penalty provisions. Sections 6694(a) and (b) of the Code authorize monetary penalties against preparers who understate the taxpayer's tax liability intentionally (section 6694(b)) or knowing that there was not a realistic possibility that the position taken would be sustained (section 6694(a)). Prior to amendment of section 6694 as part of the 1989 IMPACT legislation, section 6694(a) imposed a penalty of $100 for tax understatements attributable to the preparer's negligence or intentional disregard of rules and regulations, and section 6694(b) imposed a $500 penalty for a preparer's willful understatement of tax liability. The 1989 IMPACT legislation increased the penalty amounts to $250 and $1,000, respectively, and changed the standard of conduct that would trigger a section 6694(a) penalty. The new standard authorizes a $250 penalty if all of the following occur:

(1) any part of any understatement of liability with respect to any return or claim for refund is due to a position for which there was not a realistic possibility of being sustained on its merits,

---

e. Reg. § 301.7701-15(a)(2).

(2) any person who is an income tax return preparer with respect to such return or claim knew (or reasonably should have known) of such position, and

(3) such position was not disclosed as provided in section 6662(d)(2)(B)(ii) or was frivolous.

The preparer is not required to verify information provided by the taxpayer, but the preparer may not ignore the implications of the information furnished. For example, if the taxpayer tells the preparer that he incurred substantial deductible expenses, but has no records or receipts, the preparer could be liable for the section 6694(a) penalty for entering the unsubstantiated deductions on the taxpayer's return. To contest preparer penalties assessed under § 6694 for the willful or negligent understatement of tax liability, the preparer must pay 15% of the penalty assessed, file a claim for refund, and seek review of the Service's decision in the district court.[f]

Tax return preparers are also subject to the general criminal provisions of the Code. Especially relevant is IRC § 7206(2), dealing with willfully assisting in the preparation or presentation of a false document to revenue authorities. Additionally, IRC § 7216 makes it a misdemeanor for any preparer to use or disclose tax return information without authorization from the taxpayer except as specifically provided in the statute.

Disclosure and recordkeeping requirements. An income tax return preparer must personally sign the completed return,[g] note the preparer's place of business, and include his identification or social security number on the return.[h] The failure to satisfy these requirements subjects the preparer to immediate assessment of a penalty through the Service Center computers. After receiving the assessment notice, the preparer may seek abatement of the penalty by providing the Service with a written explanation of why he believes there was reasonable cause for his noncompliance.[i]

Preparers also must provide the taxpayer with a copy of the return or claim for refund, and retain a completed copy of the return or of a listing of the taxpayer's name and identification number. These records must be retained for three years after the close of the return period to which the return relates. Violations of preparer regulations which are not apparent from the face of the return are assessed through the district office. The penalty provisions will not be applied if the preparer can prove that the violations were due to reasonable cause and not willful neglect.

Employers of tax return preparers, and self-employed preparers, are required to file an annual information return, setting forth the

f. Reg. § 1.6696–1.
g. Reg. § 1.6695–1(b).
h. I.R.C. § 6109(a)(4).
i. See Reg. § 1.6695–1(b)(5); see also Reg. § 1.6696–1 (relating to claims for credit or refund by tax return preparers of penalties assessed under I.R.C. §§ 6694, 6695).

name, identification number and principal place of business of each preparer under their employ.[j] The regulations also contain a prohibition against the negotiation, by tax return preparers, of refund checks issued to a taxpayer.[k]

j. I.R.C. § 6060.

k. I.R.C. § 6695(f).

Chapter III

ADMINISTRATIVE RULEMAKING AND RULINGS

Scope Note: In order to provide taxpayers with an understanding of the meaning and application of the internal revenue laws, the Treasury Department promulgates Treasury Regulations and the IRS responds to taxpayer requests for rulings interpreting the tax laws and applying them to specific factual situations. The regulations are accorded substantial weight by the courts in applying the Code to a specific set of facts. This chapter discusses the factors that influence a court to give more or less weight to the applicable Treasury Regulations and to limit the retroactive application of regulations and other rulings. This chapter also outlines the nature of the Service's rulings program. The section on Confidentiality and Disclosure considers the usefulness of the Freedom of Information Act, the Privacy Act and sections 6103 and 6110 of the Code in obtaining access to agency records and in protecting taxpayers from damaging disclosure of confidential information by revenue authorities.

SECTION 1. TREASURY REGULATIONS

Legislative and Interpretive Regulations

The regulations issued by the Treasury Department constitute the single most authoritative source of guidance in interpreting the Internal Revenue Code. There are several types of regulations promulgated by the Treasury Department and the IRS, and the amount of judicial deference accorded a regulation will depend upon the source of authority for the regulation. Section 7805(a) of the Code provides that the Treasury Secretary "shall prescribe all needful rules and regulations for the enforcement of" the Code. Regulations issued pursuant to this blanket grant of authority are known as "interpretive" (or "interpretative") regulations. Interpretive regulations are given less judicial deference than so-called "legislative regulations," which are issued under a specific Congressional delegation of rulemaking power. An example of a Congressional delegation of rulemaking power is section 385, which directs the Treasury to issue regulations to determine whether an interest in a corporation is to be treated for tax purposes as debt or equity.

The courts have developed several rationales to buttress the force and effect of interpretive regulations. First, if the underlying statute was reenacted by Congress while the regulation was in effect, the court may deem such reenactment as tacit approval of the regulation. *Helvering v. R.J. Reynolds Tobacco Co.* below is an example of the application of this theory. In addition, regulations that have been in effect for a long period of time are often accorded greater weight than newly-enacted regulations. Finally, an interpretive regulation is accorded greater weight if it was developed simultaneously with the statute it interprets.

Legislative regulations must be issued in compliance with the requirements of the Administrative Procedure Act ("APA").[a] Generally, the APA requires that the public be given notice and an opportunity to comment on proposed regulations. Notice is published in the *Federal Register,* and regulations become effective 30 days after the date of final publication.

In certain circumstances, the usual notice-and-comment requirements of the APA need not be followed. For example, when immediate interpretation of a newly-enacted statute is required, the Treasury may issue temporary regulations, which are effective until superseded by permanent regulations. Under section 7805(e), temporary regulations remain effective for no more than three years from the date of their enactment. Particularly in the recent past, the Treasury Department has issued temporary regulations in "Question & Answer" format following enactment of significant tax legislation. A second exception to the notice-and-comment requirements is that when a revision of an existing regulation only serves to benefit taxpayers, the Treasury need not follow APA procedures for notice and comment. Both of these exceptions are based on 5 U.S.C.A. § 553(b)(3)(B), which allows an agency to dispense with the notice and comment procedures when the rulemaking agency "for good cause finds * * * that notice and public procedure thereon are impracticable, unnecessary, or contrary to the public interest."

A. RETROACTIVE APPLICATION OF TREASURY REGULATIONS

Although the Treasury Department is subject to the APA, Treasury Regulations differ from most other regulations in one very significant way. The APA defines "rule" (which is synonymous with "regulation")

---

a. Although interpretive regulations are not technically subject to the APA notice-and-comment requirements, the Treasury Department complies with these procedures in issuing interpretive regulations. *See* M. Saltzman, IRS Practice and Procedure, ¶ 3.02[3] (1981).

as having future or prospective effect.[b] By contrast, the Treasury Department's regulations are presumptively retroactive in effect. Section 7805(b), enacted more than 25 years prior to enactment of the APA, provides as follows:

> The Secretary may prescribe the extent, if any, to which any ruling or regulation, relating to the internal revenue laws, shall be applied without retroactive effect.

Particularly when the Treasury amends a regulation, and applies the amendment retroactively, taxpayers have challenged the retroactive application of the amended regulation.

MANHATTAN GENERAL EQUIPMENT CO. v. COMMISSIONER
Supreme Court of the United States, 1936.
297 U.S. 129, 56 S.Ct. 397, 80 L.Ed. 528.

[By the Editors: Taxpayers had sold certain shares of stock they acquired in a reorganization at a loss, the amount of which they had determined under a regulation in effect in the tax year involved, 1926. The regulation in question was a legislative regulation. In 1928 the Treasury amended this regulation and applied the amended regulation retroactively to the taxpayer's 1926 transaction. The Supreme Court upheld the application of the amended regulation.]

The power of an administrative officer or board to administer a federal statute and to prescribe rules and regulations to that end is not the power to make law, for no such power can be delegated by Congress, but the power to adopt regulations to carry into effect the will of Congress as expressed by the statute. A regulation which does not do this, but operates to create a rule out of harmony with the statute, is a mere nullity. * * * The original regulation as applied to a situation like that under review is both inconsistent with the statute and unreasonable.

The contention that the new regulation is retroactive is without merit. Since the original regulation could not be applied, the amended regulation in effect became the primary and controlling rule in respect of the situation presented. It pointed the way for the first time, for correctly applying the antecedent statute to a situation which arose under the statute. The statute defines the rights of the taxpayer and fixes the standard by which such rights are to be measured. The regulation constitutes only a step in the administrative process. It does not, and could not alter the statute. It is no more retroactive in its operation than is a judicial determination construing and applying a statute to a case in hand.

---

b. On October 5, 1990, a bill entitled the "Taxpayer Regulatory Relief Act," S.3161, 101st Cong., 2d Sess. (1990) was introduced. If enacted, this bill will require that all regulations issued by the Treasury or the IRS have prospective effect only.

HELVERING v. R.J. REYNOLDS TOBACCO CO.
Supreme Court of the United States, 1939.
306 U.S. 110, 59 S.Ct. 423, 83 L.Ed. 536.

MR. JUSTICE ROBERTS delivered the opinion of the Court.

The sole question for decision is whether gain accruing to a corporation consequent on the purchase and resale of its own shares constitutes gross income within the meaning of Section 22(a) of the Revenue Act of 1928.

* * *

The Commissioner determined a deficiency in the tax paid * * *. He based his claim upon Treasury Regulation 74, Article 66, as amended by a Treasury decision of May 2, 1934, which states "where a corporation deals in its own shares as it might in the shares of another corporation, the resulting gain or loss is to be computed in the same manner as though the corporation were dealing in the shares of another."

The Board, after finding the facts in detail, sustained the Commissioner. The Circuit Court of Appeals reversed the Board's ruling. * * *

Section 22(a) is: "General definition. 'Gross income' includes gains, profits, and income derived from salaries, wages, or compensation for personal service, of whatever kind and in whatever form paid, or from professions, vocations, trades, businesses, commerce, or sales, or dealings in property, whether real or personal, growing out of the ownership or use of or interest in such property; also from interest, rent, dividends, securities, or the transaction of any business carried on for gain or profit, or gains or profits and income derived from any source whatever." Section 62 [c] directs the Commissioner, "with the approval of the Secretary" of the Treasury, to "prescribe and publish all needful rules and regulations for the enforcement of this title [chapter]." Article 66 of Treasury Regulations 74, promulgated under the Act of 1928, so far as material, is: "If * * * the corporation purchases any of its stock and holds it as treasury stock, the sale of such stock will be considered a capital transaction and the proceeds of such sale will be treated as capital and will not constitute income of the corporation. A corporation realizes no gain or loss from the purchase or sale of its own stock."

Petitioner contends that, as Congress must be taken to have exercised its constitutional power to the fullest extent in laying the tax, Section 22(a) should be held to include the gain realized from sales of a corporation's own stock, and the quoted regulation cannot restrict the scope of the statutory definition. The respondent replies that such gain is capital gain and not income, as is demonstrated by the theory and

---

c. The predecessor to § 7805(a) of the 1986 Code.

practice of accounting and by court decisions. The court below found it unnecessary to decide this issue, holding that whether the increment is income is at least a debatable question and the regulation was, therefore, proper as an interpretation of the meaning of the section. We agree that Section 22(a) is so general in its terms as to render an interpretative regulation appropriate.

The administrative construction embodied in the regulation has, since at least 1920, been uniform with respect to each of the revenue acts from that of 1913 to that of 1932, as evidenced by Treasury rulings and regulations, and decisions of the Board of Tax Appeals. In the meantime successive revenue acts have reenacted, without alteration, the definition of gross income as it stood in the Acts of 1913, 1916, and 1918. Under the established rule Congress must be taken to have approved the administrative construction and thereby to have given it the force of law.

The petitioner concedes that if nothing further appeared he would be bound to apply the statute in conformity to the regulation. He asserts, however, that the amendment adopted by the Treasury May 2, 1934, while this cause was pending before the Board, is controlling. By the amendment Article 66 is made to read: "Whether the acquisition or disposition by a corporation of shares of its own capital stock gives rise to taxable gain or deductible loss depends upon the real nature of the transaction, which is to be ascertained from all its facts and circumstances. * * *

"But where a corporation deals in its own shares as it might in the shares of another corporation, the resulting gain or loss is to be computed in the same manner as though the corporation were dealing in the shares of another. * * * Any gain derived from such transactions is subject to tax, and any loss sustained is allowable as a deduction where permitted by the provisions of applicable statutes."

Petitioner urges that the amendment operates retroactively and governs the ascertainment of gross income for taxable periods prior to the date of its promulgation, and, further, since Congress has reenacted Section 22(a) in the Revenue Acts of 1936 and 1938 it has approved the regulation as amended. We hold that the respondent's tax liability for the year 1929 is to be determined in conformity to the regulation then in force.

Section 605 of the Revenue Act of 1928 [d] provides that "In case a regulation or Treasury decision relating to the internal revenue laws is amended by a subsequent regulation or Treasury decision, made by the Secretary or by the Commissioner with the approval of the Secretary, such subsequent regulation or Treasury decision may, with the approval of the Secretary, be applied without retroactive effect." It is clear from this provision that Congress intended to give to the Treasury power to correct misinterpretations, inaccuracies, or omissions in the

d. The predecessor to § 7805(b) of the 1986 Code.

regulations and thereby to affect cases in which the taxpayer's liability had not been finally determined, unless, in the judgment of the Treasury, some good reason required that such alterations operate only prospectively. The question is whether the granted power may be exercised in an instance where, by repeated reenactment of the statute, Congress has given its sanction to the existing regulation.

Since the legislative approval of existing regulations by reenactment of the statutory provision to which they appertain gives such regulations the force of law, we think that Congress did not intend to authorize the Treasury to repeal the rule of law that existed during the period for which the tax is imposed. We need not now determine whether, as has been suggested, the alteration of the existing rule, even for the future, requires a legislative declaration or may be shown by reenactment of the statutory provision unaltered after a change in the applicable regulation. As the petitioner points out, Congress has, in the Revenue Acts of 1936 and 1938, retained Section 22(a) of the 1928 Act in haec verba. From this it is argued that Congress has approved the amended regulation. It may be that by the passage of the Revenue Act of 1936 the Treasury was authorized thereafter to apply the regulation in its amended form. But we have no occasion to decide this question since we are of opinion that the reenactment of the section, without more, does not amount to sanction of retroactive enforcement of the amendment, in the teeth of the former regulation which received Congressional approval, by the passage of successive Revenue Acts including that of 1928.

The judgment is affirmed.

Notes

1. Can the decisions in the two principal cases be reconciled?

2. The doctrine of legislative reenactment, relied upon in *R.J. Reynolds,* is based on the dubious assumption that Congress is actually aware of the regulation and intends to affirm it by not changing the statute upon which it is based. In a 1983 case involving the denial of tax-exempt status to a private university that discriminated on the basis of race, the Supreme Court applied the legislative reenactment theory, despite its observation that "nonaction on the part of Congress is not often a useful guide," and that "[o]rdinarily, and quite appropriately, courts are slow to attribute significance to the failure of Congress to act on particular legislation." Bob Jones University v. United States, 461 U.S. 574, 103 S.Ct. 2017, 76 L.Ed.2d 157 (1983). The Court relied on the existence of Congressional studies and committee debates as an indication that Congress was in fact aware of the IRS position.

3. Although typically invoked to uphold a regulation, the doctrine of legislative reenactment has been applied to a longstanding administrative practice and uniform judicial construction of the underlying Code provision. Commissioner v. Estate of Noel, 380 U.S. 678, 85 S.Ct. 1238, 14 L.Ed.2d 159 (1965) ("We have held in many cases that such a longstanding administrative interpretation, applying to a substantially re-enacted stat-

ute, is deemed to have received congressional approval and has the effect of law.")

4. Generally, the IRS is not bound by its "unofficial" publications, such as pamphlets and handbooks. Because these publications are not promulgated pursuant to APA procedures and are not the official position of the Service, taxpayers generally have not succeeded in challenging the retroactive application of regulations that differ from the pre-regulation unofficial publications. In three cases involving identical facts, the Circuits split on the permissibility of retroactive application of a regulation that differed from the position stated in an IRS pamphlet. The pamphlet contained the following promises: the "Service will follow the rules and procedures set forth in this [pamphlet] until such time as they may be modified in regulations or Treasury publications," and "[a]ny such modifications which may be adverse to taxpayers will apply prospectively only." The Second and Seventh Circuits held it an abuse of discretion to apply the regulation retroactively. Gehl Co. v. Commissioner, 795 F.2d 1324 (7th Cir.1986); LeCroy Research Systems Corp. v. Commissioner, 751 F.2d 123 (2d Cir.1984). The Eleventh Circuit, however, upheld the retroactive application of the regulation. CWT Farms, Inc. v. Commissioner, 755 F.2d 790 (11th Cir.1985).

5. In addition to legislative and interpretive regulations, there exists a species of regulations known as "procedural regulations." Procedural regulations are issued by the IRS, rather than the Treasury Department, and are not subject to APA notice-and-comment requirements. Procedural regulations generally pertain to the organization of the IRS and its own internal rules. The IRS procedural rules are contained in the IRS Statement of Procedural Rules, 26 CFR Part 601. Some regulations that pertain to "procedural" matters are interpretive regulations found either under the general Treasury regulations interpreting specific "substantive" Code sections or under the regulations interpreting administrative and procedural Code sections, found at 26 CFR Part 301. The Supreme Court has held that an agency will be bound by its procedural rules that affect individuals' rights, even if the procedural rules are stricter than the law otherwise requires. Morton v. Ruiz, 415 U.S. 199, 94 S.Ct. 1055, 39 L.Ed.2d 270 (1974). However, in a case involving the failure of IRS agents to follow a procedural rule, Supreme Court held that the evidence obtained in violation of the procedural rule need not be suppressed, finding that the individual had not relied on the rule and it had no effect on his conduct. United States v. Caceres, 440 U.S. 741, 99 S.Ct. 1465, 59 L.Ed.2d 733 (1979).

B. JUDICIAL REVIEW OF TREASURY REGULATIONS
UNITED STATES v. VOGEL FERTILIZER CO.
Supreme Court of the United States, 1982.
455 U.S. 16, 102 S.Ct. 821, 70 L.Ed.2d 792.

JUSTICE BRENNAN delivered the opinion of the Court.

Section 1561(a) of the Internal Revenue Code of 1954, limits a "controlled group of corporations" to a single corporate surtax exemption. Section 1563(a)(2) provides that a "controlled group of corporations" includes a "brother-sister controlled group," defined as "[t]wo or more corporations if 5 or fewer persons * * * own * * * stock possessing (A) at least 80 percent of the total combined voting power * * * or at least 80 percent of the total value * * * of each corporation, and (B) more than 50 percent of the total combined voting power * * * or more than 50 percent of the total value * * * of each corporation, taking into account the stock ownership of each such person only to the extent such stock ownership is identical with respect to each such corporation." The interpretation of the statutory provision by Treas.Reg. § 1.1563–1(a)(3) is that the "term 'brother-sister controlled group' means two or more corporations if the same five or fewer persons * * * own * * * *singly or in combination* " the two prescribed percentages of voting power or total value. The question presented is whether the regulatory interpretation—that the statutory definition is met by the ownership of the prescribed stock by five or fewer persons "singly or in combination"—is a reasonable implementation of the statute or whether Congress intended the statute to apply only where each person whose stock is taken into account owns stock in each corporation of the group.

* * *

Our role is limited to determining the validity of Treas.Reg. § 1.1563–1(a)(3). Deference is ordinarily owing to the agency construction if we can conclude that the regulation "implement[s] the congressional mandate in some reasonable manner." *United States v. Correll*, 389 U.S. 299, 307, 88 S.Ct. 445, 450, 19 L.Ed.2d 537 (1967). But this general principle of deference, while fundamental, only sets "the framework for judicial analysis; it does not displace it." *United States v. Cartwright*, 411 U.S. 546, 550, 93 S.Ct. 1713, 1716, 36 L.Ed.2d 528 (1973).

The framework for analysis is refined by consideration of the source of the authority to promulgate the regulation at issue. The Commissioner has promulgated Treas.Reg. § 1.1563–1(a)(3) interpreting this statute only under his general authority to "prescribe all needful rules and regulations." 26 U.S.C. § 7805(a). Accordingly, "we owe the interpretation less deference than a regulation issued under a specific grant of authority to define a statutory term or prescribe a method of executing a statutory provision." *Rowan Cos. v. United States*, 452 U.S. 247, 253, 101 S.Ct. 2288, 2292, 68 L.Ed.2d 814 (1981). In addition, Treas.Reg. § 1.1563–1(a)(3) purports to do no more than add a clarifying gloss on a term—"brother-sister controlled group"—that has already been defined with considerable specificity by Congress. The Commissioner's authority is consequently more circumscribed than would be the case if Congress had used a term " 'so general * * * as to render an interpretive regulation appropriate.' " *National Muffler Dealers Assn., Inc., v. United States*, 440 U.S. 472, 476, 99 S.Ct. 1304, 1306, 59 L.Ed.2d 519 (1979), quoting *Helvering v. R.J. Reynolds Co.*, 306 U.S. 110, 114, 59 S.Ct. 423, 425, 83 L.Ed. 536 (1939).

We consider first whether the Regulation harmonizes with the statutory language. *National Muffler Dealers Assn., Inc. v. United States, supra,* 440 U.S., at 477, 99 S.Ct., at 1307. That language, while not completely unambiguous, is in closer harmony with the taxpayer's interpretation than with the Commissioner's Regulation. The term that the statute defines—"brother-sister controlled group"—connotes a close horizontal relationship *between* two or more corporations, suggesting that the same indivisible group of five or fewer persons must represent 80 percent of the ownership of each corporation.

This interpretation is strengthened by the structure of the statute.
* * *

* * *

Of course, a Treasury Regulation is not invalid simply because the statutory language will support a contrary interpretation. But the mere fact that there are no words in Part (A) explicitly requiring that each shareholder own stock in each corporation does not mean that the Regulation's interpretation, "singly or in combination," must be accepted as reasonable. This Court has firmly rejected the suggestion that a regulation is to be sustained simply because it is not "technically inconsistent" with the statutory language, when that regulation is fundamentally at odds with the manifest congressional design. *United States v. Cartwright, supra,* at 557, 93 S.Ct., at 1719. The challenged Regulation is not a reasonable statutory interpretation unless it harmonizes with the statute's "origin and purpose." *National Muffler Dealers Assn., Inc. v. United States, supra,* 440 U.S., at 477, 99 S.Ct., at 1307.

The legislative history of § 1563(a)(2) resolves any ambiguity in the statutory language and makes it plain that Treas.Reg. § 1.1563–1(a)(3) is not a reasonable statutory interpretation. Through the controlled-group test, Congress intended to curb the abuse of multiple incorporation—large organizations subdividing into smaller corporations and receiving unintended tax benefits from the multiple use of surtax exemptions, accumulated earnings credits, and various other tax provisions designed to aid small businesses. S.Rep. No. 91–552, p. 134 (1969), U.S.Code Cong. & Admin.News 1969, p. 1645. * * *

* * *

Until 1964, the method prescribed by the Code to curb the abuse of multiple incorporation was subjective: Multiple exemptions or benefits were allowed or disallowed depending on the reasons for the taxpayer's actions. The Revenue Act of 1964 changed this approach, adding §§ 1561–1563 to the Code. Pub.L. 88–272, § 235(a), 78 Stat. 116–125. These sections prescribed the application of mechanical, objective tests for determining whether two corporations were a "controlled group" and thereby restricted to one surtax exemption. * * *

* * *

In 1969 Congress adopted the present two-part percentage test codified in § 1563(a)(2). Pub.L. 91–172, § 401(c), 83 Stat. 602. This change was proposed by the Treasury Department as part of an extensive package of tax reform proposals. * * * In setting forth the "Technical Explanation" for this new definition of brother-sister controlled groups, the Treasury Department was most explicit that the 80-percent requirement, like the 50-percent requirement, included common ownership: * * *

* * *

The Treasury Department's "General Explanation" of the amendment to § 1563(a)(2) defined a brother-sister controlled group as one "in which five or fewer persons own, to a large extent in identical proportions, at least 80 percent of the stock of each of the corporations." Hearings, at 5394 (footnote omitted). * * *

* * *

The General Explanation made it clear that, under the 1969 amendment to § 1563(a)(2), the 80-percent requirement would remain the primary basis for determining whether two or more corporations represent the *same* financial interests. Part (A) of the 1969 test was simply an expansion of the 1964 test, which considered the two or more corporations to be a brother-sister controlled group only when one person owned 80 percent of all of the corporations. * * *

* * *

The "singly or in combination" provision of Treas.Reg. § 1.1563–1(a)(3) is clearly incompatible with the explanation offered by the Treasury Department when it proposed the statute. * * *

* * *

The Treasury Department's explanations of the proposed statute are not, as the dissent in the Court of Claims suggested, a mere "admission against interest" by the Commissioner. 225 Ct.Cl., at 44, 634 F.2d, at 514. The expanded definition of "brother-sister controlled group" was proposed by the Treasury Department and adopted in the same form in which it was presented. Of course, it is Congress' understanding of what it was enacting that ultimately controls. But we necessarily attach "great weight" to agency representations to Congress when the administrators "participated in drafting and directly made known their views to Congress in committee hearings." *Zuber v. Allen,* 396 U.S. 168, 192, 90 S.Ct. 314, 327, 24 L.Ed.2d 345 (1969). The subsequent legislative history of § 1563(a)(2) confirms that Congress adopted not only the proposal of the Treasury Department, but also the Department's explanation and interpretation which are wholly incompatible with the "singly or in combination" interpretation of the Regulation. * * *

* * *

The Commissioner's further reasons for sustaining his interpretation are unpersuasive.

The Commissioner relies on the fact that, in expanding the coverage of § 1563(a)(2), Congress expressly adopted part of the language used in § 1551(b)(2) of the Code to describe a transfer from one corporation to another "controlled" by the same "five or fewer" individuals. The Commissioner contends that Congress thereby approved the interpretation the Commissioner had placed on § 1551(b)(2). Even if we could assume that Congress was aware of Treasury Regulations interpreting § 1551, promulgated only two years before § 1563 was enacted, see 32 Fed.Reg. 3214–3216 (1967), the promulgated regulations do not support the Commissioner's present interpretation of the statutory language in § 1563(a)(2). The Regulations defining control under § 1551 contain no language similar to the words "singly or in combination" found in Treas.Reg. § 1.1563–1(a)(3) and they contain no suggestion that the Treasury Department had interpreted § 1551(b)(2) as *not* having a common-ownership requirement.

Also unpersuasive is the Commissioner's reliance on the fact that § 1563(a)(2) is referred to in § 1015 of the Employee Retirement Income Security Act of 1974, 26 U.S.C. § 414. From this the Commissioner infers congressional approval of all the Regulations promulgated under § 1563(a)(2), including the Regulation at issue in this case. But it is the intent of the Congress that amended § 1563(a), not the views of the subsequent Congress that enacted § 414, that are controlling. See *Teamsters v. United States*, 431 U.S. 324, 354, n. 39, 97 S.Ct. 1843, 1864, n. 39, 52 L.Ed.2d 396 (1977). In any event, this passing reference in 26 U.S.C. § 414(b), enacted only two years after Treas.Reg. § 1.1563–1(a)(3) was promulgated, 37 Fed.Reg. 8068–8070 (1972), hardly constitutes legislative approval of a longstanding administrative interpretation, from which we could infer any congressional acceptance. Cf. *United States v. Correll*, 389 U.S., at 305–306, 88 S.Ct., at 448–449.

* * *

Affirmed.

SECTION 2. REQUESTS FOR RULINGS AND DETERMINATION LETTERS

A. TYPES OF RULINGS

In the recent past, the IRS rulings program has become increasingly important and seriously understaffed. When considering a transaction whose tax consequences are important but unclear, tax lawyers seek the advice of the Service concerning its view of the proper tax treatment. The Service issues many types of rulings in response to such requests.

1. *Revenue rulings.* If the IRS believes a particular issue may apply to numerous taxpayers, it may issue a revenue ruling, which is

its official interpretation of the issue involved. Revenue rulings are issued by the IRS National Office, not the Treasury Department, and APA notice and comment procedures are not followed. Revenue rulings are published in the *Internal Revenue Bulletin* and collected in bound form in the *Cumulative Bulletin.* Revenue rulings bind both the IRS and taxpayers. Applicability of revenue rulings is limited, however, by the specific fact situations to which they are addressed. Thus, a taxpayer may rely on a revenue ruling only if "the facts and circumstances are substantially the same" as those in the revenue ruling.[e] Like regulations, revenue rulings can apply retroactively under the authority of section 7805(b).

2. *Revenue procedures.* The Service issues revenue procedures to inform the public of procedural rules that affect taxpayers' rights and duties. Like revenue rulings, revenue procedures are published in the *Internal Revenue Bulletin* and collected in bound volumes of the *Cumulative Bulletin.*

3. *Letter rulings.* Also known as "private letter rulings" or "PLRs," letter rulings are issued by the IRS National Office to specific (but unidentified)[f] taxpayers in response to their written requests. Unlike revenue rulings, which bind all taxpayers, letter rulings may not be relied upon by another taxpayer. Letter rulings are not officially published by the Government and were not available to the public until 1976, when courts ruled that they were subject to disclosure under the Freedom of Information Act (discussed in Section 3). Congress promptly enacted section 6110 of the Code, which removed applicability of the Freedom of Information Act to IRS rulings and determinations and established rules for their disclosure. Although section 6110(i)(3) specifically provides that "a written determination may not be used or cited as precedent," letter rulings are widely relied upon in practice as affording valuable insight into the Service's position on many issues. Congress recently recognized this fact when it directed the Service to expand the list of authorities upon which taxpayers may rely for purposes of avoiding the substantial understatement of income tax

---

e. The following precautionary statement appears in each issue of the *Internal Revenue Bulletin:*

Revenue rulings represent the conclusions of the Service on the application of the law to the pivotal facts stated in the revenue ruling. * * * Rulings and procedures published in the Bulletins do not have the force and effect of Treasury Regulations, but they may be used as precedents. * * * In applying published rulings and procedures, the effect of subsequent legislation, regulations, court decisions, rulings, and procedures must be considered, and Service personnel and others concerned are cautioned against reaching the same conclusions in other cases unless the facts and circumstances are substantially the same.

f. I.R.C. § 6110(f) requires the Service to mail a "notice of intention to disclose" to any person whose ruling or determination letter is subject to disclosure to the public. The taxpayer has the burden of supplying a statement identifying and supporting the desired deletions. Section 6110(f) also directs the Service to prescribe regulations establishing administrative remedies to restrain disclosure and to process requests for additional information. See Rev.Proc. 90–1, §§ 3.23, 3.24, 1990–1 C.B. 367, for a description of these administrative remedies. If the matter cannot be settled administratively, the person affected may petition the Tax Court to restrain disclosure pursuant to § 6110(f)(3).

penalty of section 6662(b) (former § 6661) to include "proposed regulations, *private letter rulings,* technical advice memoranda, actions on decisions, general counsel memoranda, information or press releases, notices and any other similar documents published by the IRS in the *Internal Revenue Bulletin.*" [g]

Because the number of requests for rulings exploded in the 1970s and 1980s, seriously taxing the ability of the Service to provide timely guidance, Congress passed legislation in late 1987 directing the Treasury Department to implement a "user fee" program imposing a charge on requests for letter rulings, determination letters and other types of IRS determinations. The amount of the fee depends on the type of request and ranges from $50 to $3,000. Rev.Proc. 90–17, 1990–12 IRB 13. In late 1990, Congress extended the user fee program to October 1, 1995.

In 1989, the Service tried to stem further the unrelenting number of ruling requests by announcing that it would no longer issue so-called "comfort rulings." [h] The Service defined "comfort rulings" as those issued "with respect to an issue that is clearly and adequately addressed by a statute, regulation, decision of the Supreme Court, tax treaty, revenue ruling, revenue procedure, notice or other authority published in the Internal Revenue Bulletin." Following vocal criticism of the proposed policy, the Service announced that it would replace the proposed no-comfort-ruling policy with a variety of measures, including "specific no rule areas, model documents, published ruling checklists and automatic action revenue procedures, among others." [i]

In some circumstances (for example, in the case of a transfer to a foreign entity under Code sections 1491 and 1492), a ruling is required as a legal matter. Conversely, the Service refuses to rule on completed transactions for which a return has been filed and on issues identified annually as being on its "no-ruling" list.[j] In most circumstances, however, taxpayers are free to choose whether to submit a proposed transaction for an advance ruling. A number of factors influence the decision whether to seek a ruling. Perhaps most important is the likelihood of obtaining a favorable ruling. If the tax lawyer's research indicates that the Service is likely to rule against the taxpayer, then a ruling should not be sought. If it becomes apparent through discussions with personnel in the National Office that a requested ruling will not be favorable, the request may be withdrawn at any time before the ruling is issued. Significantly, if the taxpayer is adamant about proceeding with the proposed transaction, requesting a ruling and later

g. H.R.Rep. 101–247, 101st Cong., 1st Sess. 1389 (1989) (emphasis added).

h. Rev.Proc. 89–34, 1989–1 C.B. 197, *superseded by* Announcement 90–65, 1990–20 IRB 23.

i. Announcement 90–65, 1990–20 IRB 23.

j. *See, e.g.,* Rev.Proc. 90–3, 1990–1 IRB 54, 55, explaining that the no-rulings list is comprised of areas involving "inherently factual" questions. The annual revenue procedures also identify areas in which the Service will "not ordinarily" issue a ruling and areas in which the Service has temporarily suspended rulings.

withdrawing the request could be disastrous since the National Office can forward information concerning the withdrawn request to the District where the taxpayer's return will be filed, thus possibly triggering an audit.[k]

Another factor that influences the decision whether to request a ruling is timing. If the transaction must be completed by a certain date, it may not be possible to obtain a timely ruling. The Service must contact the taxpayer within 21 days of its receipt of the ruling request to discuss the request and often to request additional information, but processing of requests is done only "in regular order and as expeditiously as possible."[l] Expedited treatment may be requested, but it will only be granted if the Service believes there is a "compelling need" for expedition. Examples of circumstances the IRS does not believe present a "compelling need" include the existence of a scheduled closing date and the possible effect of market fluctuation in price.[m]

To minimize delay, the ruling request should contain all the information required under the annual revenue procedure outlining requirements for ruling and other requests. Among the required documents are an executed power of attorney (on either Form 2848 or 8821),[n] and a "perjury declaration," signed by the taxpayer, declaring under penalty of perjury that the facts presented in the request "are true, correct, and complete." A ruling or determination letter is only as valid as the statement of facts upon which it is based. Hence, the factual assertions in the request are subject to verification on audit, and the ruling can be withdrawn if the Service discovers factual inaccuracies.[o] Except to the extent it is incorporated in a closing agreement under section 7121, a ruling may be revoked or modified at any time under appropriate circumstances.[p] Although letter rulings can be revoked retroactively under the authority of section 7805(b), the Service actually applies the revocation or modification of a letter ruling to a specific taxpayer retroactively only "in rare or unusual circumstances."[q] To forestall possible retroactive application of a revocation or modification of a ruling, however, a taxpayer may request and receive assurance that any modification or revocation of a ruling will not be applied retroactively.[r]

k. According to the Service: "in such a case, the National Office may furnish its views to the District Director in whose office the return * * * will be filed. The District Director will consider the information submitted in a subsequent audit or examination * * *." Rev.Proc. 90–1, 1990–1 C.B. 356, 374, § 7.

l. Rev.Proc. 90–1, 1990–1 C.B. 356, 366 (§ 3.21).

m. *Id.*

n. See Appendix A for copies of these forms.

o. *See, e.g.,* Heverly v. Commissioner, 621 F.2d 1227 (3d Cir.1980) (involving retroactive revocation of favorable ruling issued to International Telephone and Telegraph Corp. in connection with its acquisition of Hartford Insurance Company).

p. See Rev.Proc. 90–1, 1990–1 C.B. 356, 374 (§ 8.04).

q. *Id.* § 8.05.

r. *Id.* at 28, § 9.

4. *Determination letters.* These are written statements issued by District Directors (not the National Office) to taxpayers requesting advice, but determination letters are issued "only if the question presented is specifically answered by statute or regulation, or by a position stated in a ruling, opinion, or court decision published in the Internal Revenue Bulletin."[s] Determination letters have the same effect as letter rulings (binding the Service and the taxpayer to whom issued), but they differ from letter rulings in that they apply only to completed transactions, rather than contemplated transactions. Like letter rulings, determination letters can be revoked or modified retroactively, and taxpayers may request and receive assurance that a determination letter will not be revoked or modified retroactively. Most determination letters involve the "qualification" of employee benefit plans and the tax-exempt status of organizations.[t]

5. *Technical advice.* The National Office issues technical advice memoranda ("TAMs") to District or Appeals Offices in response either to a request from IRS personnel or from the taxpayer. Although technical advice is usually sought by IRS personnel during the examination or appeals process to resolve technical or procedural questions, taxpayers may initiate the request if they believe the IRS has dealt with the issue inconsistently or that the issue is so complex or novel that National Office consideration of it is warranted.[u] Like letter rulings and determination letters, TAMs are available to the public after identifying information has been deleted. Unlike letter rulings, which generally are issued prospectively, TAMs that are favorable to the taxpayer are applied retroactively "[e]xcept in rare and unusual circumstances."[v] Taxpayers who fear an adverse TAM may request that the Service limit its authority to apply the TAM retroactively.[w]

6. *Acquiscence or nonacquiescence.* The following statement, published in each volume of the Cumulative Bulletin, sets forth the Service's policy regarding acquiescence or nonacquiescence in decisions of the Tax Court:

> It is the policy of the Internal Revenue Service to announce in the Internal Revenue Bulletin at the earliest practicable date the determination of the Commissioner to acquiesce or not acquiesce in a decision

---

s. *Id.* at 28, § 10.01.

t. M. SALTZMAN, IRS PRACTICE AND PROCEDURE, ¶ 3.04[3][e] (1981).

u. Rev.Proc. 90-2, 1990-1 C.B. 386, § 3.01 provides in part as follows:

> The District Director or Chief, Appeals Office, is responsible for determining whether to request technical advice on any issue being considered. Each request must be submitted through channels and signed by a person who is authorized to sign for the District Director or Chief, Appeals Office * * *. However, while the case is under the jurisdiction of the District Director or the Chief, Appeals Office, a taxpayer may request that an issue be referred to the National Office for technical advice.
>
> * * * The grounds for a request are that a lack of uniformity exists on the disposition of the issue or that the issue is unusual or complex enough to warrant consideration by the National Office.

v. Rev.Proc. 90-2, 1990-1 C.B. 386, § 9.01.

w. *Id.,* § 10.01.

of the Tax Court which disallows a deficiency in tax determined by the Commissioner to be due.

Notice that the Commissioner has acquiesced or nonacquiesced in a decision of the Tax Court applies only to the issue or issues decided adversely to the Government.

Actions of acquiescences in adverse decisions shall be relied on by revenue officers and others concerned as conclusions of the Service only to the application of the law to the facts in the particular case. Caution should be exercised in extending the application of the decision to a similar case unless the facts and circumstances are substantially the same, and consideration should be given to the effect of new legislation, regulations, and rulings as well as subsequent court decisions and actions thereon.

Acquiescence in a decision means acceptance by the Service of the conclusion reached, and does not necessarily mean acceptance and approval of any or all of the reasons assigned by the court for its conclusions.

No announcements are made in the Bulletin with respect to memorandum opinions of the Tax Court.

The announcements published in the weekly Internal Revenue Bulletins are consolidated semiannually and annually. The semiannual consolidation appears in the first Bulletin for July and in the Cumulative Bulletin for the first half of the year and the annual consolidation appears in the first Bulletin for the following January and in the Cumulative Bulletin for the last half of the year.

Suspend your view of the reliability of published acquiescences pending your consideration of *Dixon v. United States,* at page 76.

7. *Actions on decisions.* Rulings adverse to the Government on tax issues in any federal court, including the Tax Court, trigger the preparation of an "action on decision" ("AOD") memorandum by a lawyer in the Office of the Associate Chief Counsel (Litigation), which is a division of the Office of Chief Counsel. The purpose of an AOD is to explain why the Government should or should not appeal the adverse decision. AODs are available to the public under the Freedom of Information Act and are published, like letter rulings, by commercial publishers.

8. *IRS pamphlets and booklets.* The IRS is not bound by its statements or positions in its unofficial publications. However, some courts have found it an abuse of discretion to retroactively apply regulations that contradict earlier unofficial statements of position. See Note 4, page 61 *supra.*

B. REVOCATION, RELIANCE AND RETROACTIVITY

The IRS, in the course of issuing rulings and determination letters, necessarily causes reliance to be placed upon its statements as to the interpretation and application of the tax law. All taxpayers may rely upon published rulings. The particular taxpayers receiving private letter rulings or determination letters may rely upon such rulings to the extent that the facts upon which they are issued are correct. However, the tax law is highly volatile. New legislation, court decisions and other developments can cause the Service in perfectly good faith to change a position set forth in a ruling. The following cases discuss the extent to which the Service is able to change a position set forth in a ruling or determination letter, and the limits upon the Commissioner's exercise of the discretionary authority contained in IRC § 7805(b) to prescribe the extent to which such a change may be applied without retroactive effect.

LESAVOY FOUNDATION v. COMMISSIONER
United States Court of Appeals, Third Circuit, 1956.
238 F.2d 589.

GOODRICH, CIRCUIT JUDGE.

This case raises the question of (1) the liability to taxation of a corporation organized for charitable, educational and philanthropic purposes,[1] which the Commissioner claims departed from its exempt purpose and was used in part as a means of furthering business enterprises in which the donor of the foundation of the charitable trust was interested and (2) the limits, if any, of the power of the Commissioner to make a revocation of an exemption retroactive.

The foundation on July 31, 1945, upon application was granted a certificate of exemption from taxation under the statute just referred to. Six years later, on December 19, 1951, the Commissioner revoked the certificate of exemption alleging the reason just mentioned and assessed a deficiency against the petitioner along with penalties. The revocation was made retroactive to 1946 during which year the foundation acquired Clover Spinning Mills, an enterprise which manufactured cotton yarn and cloth. This imposed a deficiency on the taxpayer for the years 1946 to 1948 and 1950. The taxpayer claims the resulting deficiency thus assessed will completely wipe out the assets of the foundation. This statement seems to be borne out by the last report we have for the year ending December 31, 1949 * * *.

* * *

* * * [W]e think the Commissioner went beyond his authority in revoking the certificate of exemption retroactively. We quite realize that the Commissioner may change his mind when he believes he has made a mistake in a matter of fact or law. Our own decision in Keystone Automobile Club v. Commissioner, 3 Cir.1950, 181 F.2d 420, recognizes this point fully and that point is sustained by abundant authority. But it is quite a different matter to say that having once changed his mind the Commissioner may arbitrarily and without limit

---

1. Int.Rev.Code of 1939, § 101(6) (now Int.Rev.Code of 1986, § 501(c)(3)) exempts organizations for "religious, charitable, scientific, literary or educational purposes."

have the effect of that change go back over previous years during which the taxpayer operated under the previous ruling.

Although there is ample authority that the Commissioner may change retroactively a ruling of general application, there is a dearth of cases involving individualized taxpayer's rulings. This is so because the Commissioner has almost invariably followed a policy of honoring his rulings and making changes prospective only * * *. Indeed, this policy has been codified by one of the Commissioner's own rulings.[6]

The few authorities that there are concerning individualized rulings are not unanimous. The point has had the most attention in the Sixth Circuit. The latest decision of that Court in Automobile Club of Michigan v. Commissioner, 6 Cir., 1956, 230 F.2d 585, certiorari granted, 352 U.S. 817, 77 S.Ct. 32, discusses previous rulings and comes out with elaborate opinions both supporting and against the Commissioner's action. The result of that case, another one concerning an automobile club, was to permit a two-year retroactive effect to a revocation of the certificate under which the club was exempt as a social club. Note, however, that the majority found, 230 F.2d at pages 588 and 590, that the ruling was not arbitrary or oppressive since the retroactive effect was limited to two years though it could have been extended back eleven, and there was no element of estoppel since the taxpayer did not assert that it acted in reliance on the certificate. On the other hand, there is respectable authority that the Commissioner may not retroactively change an individualized taxpayer's ruling, unless the taxpayer is himself estopped from relying on the ruling in good faith because he has concealed the facts, or because of some other fraud or misrepresentation.

We, therefore, turn our attention to the question of whether this taxpayer has done anything to estop itself from relying on the certificate. In arguing that it has, the government urges that the taxpayer was not frank in the manner in which it filled out its 1946 information return. The income tax form asks: "Have you any sources of income or engaged in any activities which have not previously been reported to the Bureau? If so, attach detailed statement." Taxpayer answered, "Yes" in the blank provided after the question. In the margin directly under the question was typed, "Purchased Clover Spinning Mills Co., Clover, So. Carolina, March 18, 1946." A balance sheet attached to the 1946 return listed such assets as mill buildings, machinery and equip-

---

6. Rev.Rul. 54–146, 1954–1 Cum.Bull. 88, 91 provides:

"It is the general policy of the Internal Revenue Service to limit the revocation of a ruling with respect to an organization previously held to qualify under section 101 to a prospective application only, if the organization has acted in good faith in reliance upon the ruling issued to it and a retroactive revocation of such ruling would be to its detriment. Any ruling issued as to the exempt status of an organization will not be considered controlling where there has been a misstatement or omission of a material fact or where the operations of the organization are conducted in a manner materially different from that represented. A revocation may be effected by a notice to the organization or by a ruling or other statement published in the Internal Revenue Bulletin applicable to the type of organization involved. * * *"

[Compare § 16 of Rev.Proc. 87–1, supra.]

ment, accounts receivable and under inventory listed cotton, work in progress, finished yarn and manufacturing supplies. Under liabilities were items for accounts payable and payroll. Another question on the form asked for gross receipts from business activities and the taxpayer reported substantial sales of yarn and cloth. Taken as a whole, we think that the return fully and fairly disclosed that taxpayer was engaged in an active textile spinning enterprise. We see nothing more that the form called for. The taxpayer did not misstate anything it told the Commissioner, nor did it omit to disclose anything it should have told him. In fact, a schedule attached to the 1946 return indicated a close connection between the foundation and other textile enterprises by listing as contributors Fabrics Corporation of America, Rayon Corporation of America and two other businesses which contain "Mills" as part of their names.

The taxpayer fully disclosed the information required by the informational return. The original exemption certificate imposed upon the foundation a duty to inform the Commissioner of any relevant changes in the facts and, as already stated, taxpayer gave the information. The taxpayer did not bring to the Commissioner's attention the fact that Clover sold yarn to the donor's mills. We do not find this fact any evidence of lack of frankness for the information would have been irrelevant at the time the return was made. The Commissioner's theory is a debatable one at best even today and some of the cases he relies on most heavily were not decided until the end of the taxable years involved.

The statutory section on retroactivity is found in section 3791(b) of the 1939 Code (now Int.Rev.Code of 1954, § 7805(b)). The section reads as follows:

> "Retroactivity of regulations or rulings. The Secretary, or the Commissioner with the approval of the Secretary, may prescribe the extent, if any, to which any ruling, regulation, or Treasury Decision, relating to the internal revenue laws, shall be applied without retroactive effect."

As the Sixth Circuit points out, the provision gives the Commissioner discretionary power to determine the extent of retroactivity in a given case. The usual rule in such case is that an official vested with discretionary power is not to be interfered with unless it can be found that his action in a given case goes beyond the bounds of discretion. We think that usual rule should be applicable here.

We think further that the bounds of permissible discretion were exceeded when the Commissioner changed his mind as to the exemption to be granted this foundation and made it liable for a tax bill so large as to wipe it out of existence. As already indicated the people in charge of it committed no fraud and made no misstatement. Whether there was any basis for holding that it departed from the facts which would entitle it to a charitable exemption is at least an arguable question of law. We, therefore, see no grounds for sustaining such a harsh result as the ruling of the Commissioner, if enforced, would involve.

The judgment of the Tax Court will be reversed.

AUTOMOBILE CLUB OF MICHIGAN v. COMMISSIONER
Supreme Court of the United States, 1957.
353 U.S. 180, 77 S.Ct. 707, 1 L.Ed.2d 746.

MR. JUSTICE BRENNAN delivered the opinion of the Court.

In 1945, the Commissioner of Internal Revenue revoked his 1934 and 1938 rulings exempting the petitioner from federal income taxes, and retroactively applied the revocation to 1943 and 1944. The Commissioner also determined that prepaid membership dues received by the petitioner should be taken into income in the year received, rejecting the petitioner's method of reporting as income only that part of the dues as was recorded on petitioner's books as earned in the tax year. The Tax Court sustained the Commissioner's determinations, and the Court of Appeals for the Sixth Circuit affirmed. * * *

The Commissioner had determined in 1934 that the petitioner was a "club" entitled to exemption under provisions of the internal revenue laws corresponding to § 101(9) of the Internal Revenue Code of 1939, notifying the petitioner that " * * * future returns, under the provisions of section 101(9) * * * will not be required so long as there is no change in your organization, your purposes or methods of doing business." In 1938, the Commissioner confirmed this ruling in a letter stating: " * * * as it appears that there has been no change in your form of organization or activities which would affect your status the previous ruling of the Bureau holding you to be exempt from filing returns of income is affirmed * * *." Accordingly the petitioner did not pay federal taxes from 1933 to 1945. The Commissioner revoked these rulings in 1945, however, and directed the petitioner to file returns for 1943 and subsequent years.[5] Pursuant to this direction, the petitioner filed, under protest, corporate income and excess profits tax returns for 1943, 1944 and 1945.

The Commissioner's earlier rulings were grounded upon an erroneous interpretation of the term "club" in § 101(9) and thus were based upon a mistake of law. It is conceded that in 1943 and 1944 petitioner was not, in fact or in law, a "club" entitled to exemption within the meaning of § 101(9), and also that petitioner is subject to taxation for 1945 and subsequent years. It is nevertheless contended that the

---

5. The letter of revocation stated that in order to qualify as a club under § 101(9), the " * * * organization should be so composed and its activities be such that fellowship among the members plays a material part in the life of the organization * * *." It was then stated that the previous rulings were revoked because "[t]he evidence submitted shows that fellowship does not constitute a material part of the life of * * * [petitioner's] organization and that * * * [petitioner's] principal activity is the rendering of commercial services to * * * [its] members."

Commissioner had no power to apply the revocation retroactively to 1943 and 1944 * * *.

The petitioner argues that, in light of the 1934 and 1938 rulings, the Commissioner was equitably estopped from applying the revocation retroactively. This argument is without merit. The doctrine of equitable estoppel is not a bar to the correction by the Commissioner of a mistake of law. * * *

Petitioner's reliance on H.S.D. Co. v. Kavanagh, 6 Cir., 191 F.2d 831, and Woodworth v. Kales, 6 Cir., 26 F.2d 178, is misplaced because those cases did not involve correction of an erroneous ruling of law. Reliance on Lesavoy Foundation v. Commissioner, 3 Cir., 238 F.2d 589, is also misplaced because there the court recognized the power in the Commissioner to correct a mistake of law, but held that in the circumstances of the case the Commissioner had exceeded the bounds of the discretion vested in him under § 3791(b) of the 1939 Code.

The Commissioner's action may not be disturbed unless, in the circumstances of this case, the Commissioner abused the discretion vested in him by § 3791(b) of the 1939 Code. * * * The petitioner contends that this section forbids the Commissioner taking retroactive action. On the contrary, it is clear from the language of the section and its legislative history that Congress thereby confirmed the authority of the Commissioner to correct any ruling, regulation or Treasury decision retroactively, but empowered him, in his discretion, to limit retroactive application to the extent necessary to avoid inequitable results.

The petitioner, citing Helvering v. R.J. Reynolds Tobacco Co., 306 U.S. 110, 59 S.Ct. 423, 83 L.Ed. 536, argues that resort by the Commissioner to § 3791(b) was precluded in this case because the repeated reenactments of § 101(9) gave the force of law to the provision of the Treasury regulations relating to that section. These regulations provided that when an organization had established its right to exemption it need not thereafter make a return of income or any further showing with respect to its status unless it changed the character of its operations or the purpose for which it was originally created. Helvering v. R.J. Reynolds Tobacco Co. is inapplicable to this case. As stated by the Tax Court: "The regulations involved there [Helvering v. R.J. Reynolds Tobacco Co.] * * * purported to determine what did or did not constitute gain or loss. The regulations here * * * in no wise purported to determine whether any organization was or was not exempt."[11] These regulations did not provide the exemption or interpret § 101(9), but merely specified the necessary information required to be filed in order that the Commissioner might rule whether or not the taxpayer was entitled to exemption. This is thus not a case of " * * * administrative construction embodied in the regulation[s] * * * " which, by repeated re-enactment of § 101(9), " * * * Congress must be taken to have approved * * * and thereby to have given * * * the force of law."

11. 20 T.C. at page 1041.

Helvering v. R.J. Reynolds Tobacco Co., 306 U.S. at pages 114, 115, 59 S.Ct. at page 425.

We must, then, determine whether the retroactive action of the Commissioner was an abuse of discretion in the circumstances of this case. The action was the consequence of the reconsideration by the Commissioner, in 1943, of the correctness of the prior rulings exempting automobile clubs, initiated by a General Counsel Memorandum interpreting § 101(9) to be inapplicable to such organizations. The Commissioner adopted the General Counsel's interpretation and proceeded to apply it, effective from 1943, indiscriminately to automobile clubs. We thus find no basis for disagreeing with the conclusion, reached by both the Tax Court and the Court of Appeals, that the Commissioner, having dealt with petitioner upon the same basis as other automobile clubs, did not abuse his discretion. Nor did the two-year delay in proceeding with the petitioner's case, in these circumstances, vitiate the Commissioner's action.

* * *

Affirmed.

DIXON v. UNITED STATES
Supreme Court of the United States, 1965.
381 U.S. 68, 85 S.Ct. 1301, 14 L.Ed.2d 223.

MR. JUSTICE BRENNAN delivered the opinion of the Court.

* * *

In Automobile Club of Michigan v. Commissioner of Internal Revenue, 353 U.S. at 183–184, 77 S.Ct. at 709, we held that the Commissioner is empowered retroactively to correct mistakes of law in the application of the tax laws to particular transactions. He may do so even where a taxpayer may have relied to his detriment on the Commissioner's mistake. This principle is no more than a reflection of the fact that Congress, not the Commissioner, prescribes the tax laws. The Commissioner's rulings have only such force as Congress chooses to give them, and Congress has not given them the force of law. Consequently it would appear that the Commissioner's acquiescence in an erroneous decision, published as a ruling, cannot in and of itself bar the United States from collecting a tax otherwise lawfully due.

But petitioners point to prefatory statements in the Internal Revenue Bulletins for 1952 and other years stating that Tax Court decisions acquiesced in "should be relied upon by officers and employees of the Bureau of Internal Revenue as precedents in the disposition of other cases." These are merely guidelines for Bureau personnel, however, and hardly help the petitioners here. The title pages of the same Revenue Bulletins give taxpayers explicit warning that rulings

"* * * are for the information of taxpayers and their counsel as showing the trend of official opinion in * * * the Bureau of Internal

Revenue; the rulings other than Treasury Decisions have none of the force or effect of Treasury Decisions and *do not commit the Department to any interpretation of the law which has not been formally approved and promulgated by the Secretary of the Treasury.*" [6]
(Emphasis added.)

This admonition, together with the language of § 7805(b)'s predecessor, § 3791(b) of the 1939 Code, gave ample notice that the Commissioner's acquiescence * * * was not immune from subsequent retroactive correction to eliminate a mistake of law.

* * *

We cannot agree with petitioners that Automobile Club of Michigan v. Commissioner of Internal Revenue, supra, supports a finding that the Commissioner abused his discretion in giving retroactive effect to the withdrawal of the acquiescence. In that case the Commissioner had issued general pronouncements according exempt status to all automobile clubs similarly situated, following letter rulings to that effect in favor of the taxpayer. The Commissioner then corrected his erroneous view and, in 1945, specifically revoked the taxpayer's exemption for 1943 and subsequent years. We rejected the taxpayer's claim that the Commissioner had abused the discretion given him by § 7805(b)'s predecessor. The Commissioner's action had been forecast in a General Counsel Memorandum in 1943, and the corrected ruling had been applied to all automobile clubs for tax years back to 1943. 353 U.S., at 185–186, 77 S.Ct. at 710–711.

* * *

Although we mentioned certain facts in support of our conclusion in Automobile Club that there had not been an abuse of discretion in that case, it does not follow that the absence of one or more of these facts in another case wherein a ruling or regulation is applied retroactively establishes an abuse of discretion. Automobile Club merely examined all the circumstances of the particular case to determine whether the Commissioner had there abused his discretion. 353 U.S., at 185, 77 S.Ct. at 711. In the present case it cannot be said that the Commissioner abused his discretion in either of the respects urged by petitioners. The absence of notice does not prove an abuse, since, for

---

6. Compare the current Internal Revenue Bulletins, wherein, with specific regard to acquiescences, it is stated:

"Actions of acquiescences in adverse decisions shall be relied on by Revenue officers and others concerned as conclusions of the Service only to the application of the law to the facts in the particular case. Caution should be exercised in extending the application of the decision to a similar case unless the facts and circumstances are substantially the same * * *." And the introduction to Revenue Rulings now expressly warns that "Except where otherwise indicated, published rulings and procedures apply retroactively." See also Rev.Proc. 62–28, 1962–2 Cum.Bull. 496, which states at 504:

"A ruling * * * may be revoked or modified at any time in the wise administration of the taxing statutes. * * * If a ruling is revoked or modified, the revocation or modification applies to all open years under the statutes, unless the Commissioner exercises the discretionary powers given to him under section 7805(b) of the Code to limit the retroactive effect of the ruling."

the reasons we have stated, the petitioners were not justified in relying on the acquiescence as precluding correction of the underlying mistake of law and the retroactive application of the correct law to their case. Since no reliance was warranted, no notice was required.

* * *

Insofar as petitioners' arguments question the policy of empowering the Commissioner to correct mistakes of law retroactively when a taxpayer acts to his detriment in reliance upon the Commissioner's acquiescence in an erroneous Tax Court decision, their arguments are more appropriately addressed to Congress. Congress has seen fit to allow the Commissioner to correct mistakes of law, and in § 7805(b) has given him a large measure of discretion in determining when to apply his corrections retroactively. In the circumstances of this case we cannot say that this discretion was abused.

Affirmed.

C. DISCRIMINATORY TREATMENT

It would appear to be axiomatic that all taxpayers should receive equal treatment from the Internal Revenue Service. Certainly, one would expect that all taxpayers similarly situated would have the tax law interpreted by the Internal Revenue Service in the same manner. Yet, for valid reasons, one taxpayer generally is not permitted to rely upon a private letter ruling issued to another taxpayer regardless of the identity of the circumstances of the two taxpayers. The following case considers the ability of one taxpayer to obtain the favorable tax treatment afforded another by virtue of a private letter ruling.

BOOKWALTER v. BRECKLEIN
United States Court of Appeals, Eighth Circuit, 1966.
357 F.2d 78.

VOGEL, CIRCUIT JUDGE.

The question in this case is whether the taxpayer, plaintiff-appellee herein, is entitled to refunds for tax deductions not previously taken by him in 1957 [for certain special assessments paid to the city of Kansas City, Missouri for the construction of parking facilities] on the grounds that private letter rulings issued to other taxpayers in 1958 erroneously allowed such other taxpayers to take similar deductions. The said letter rulings were eventually revoked but were revoked prospectively rather than retroactively. The District Court * * * allowed appellee to recover for years prior to the time the private letter rulings were revoked. We reverse.

* * *

In 1958 the City of Bismarck, North Dakota, sought a ruling relating to the deductibility for income tax purposes of special assessments levied by that city against some 500 property owners with land located in and benefitted by parking improvement districts in Bismarck's central business area. Such deductions were made permissible in a May 21, 1958, letter sent to the Commissioners of the City of Bismarck by Dan J. Ferris, the Acting Director of the Tax Rulings Division (this will hereafter be referred to as the Bismarck letter). * * * The Bismarck letter was never published in the Internal Revenue Bulletin but it was picked up and published by the Commerce Clearing House, a private tax service. The Bismarck letter was revoked prospectively in an April 4, 1960, letter from Dana Latham, the Commissioner of Internal Revenue, to the Bismarck Commissioners. * * * The revocation of the Bismarck letter was published in the Internal Revenue Bulletin as Rev.Rul. 60–327, 1960–2, Cum.Bull. 65.

After the issuance, but before the revocation, of the Bismarck letter, a Bismarck type of ruling was sought by a partnership owning business rental property known as the Wirthman Building in Kansas City, Missouri. * * * In response to their request, the Wirthman partners were informed in a letter dated June 18, 1959, * * * (hereafter this will be referred to as the Wirthman determination letter) that in the future a deduction for the assessment payments would be allowed. * * * For the fiscal years ending in 1959 and 1960, the Wirthman partners deducted the installments paid as ordinary and necessary business expenses pursuant to the Wirthman determination letter. However, the Wirthman determination letter was revoked "henceforth" in a letter, dated January 12, 1961, sent to the Wirthman partners * * *.

Following the prospective repudiations of the Bismarck letter and the Wirthman determination letter, appellee, on March 23, 1961, filed suit to recover an overpayment of taxes for 1957 resulting from a failure to deduct the benefit district assessments paid by him in one lump sum in 1957. After an evidentiary hearing, the District Court entered judgment for appellee, holding that the taxpayer was

> " * * * entitled as a matter of law to equality of treatment with the 500 Bismarck taxpayers, the Wirthman partners, and any others who were accorded the benefit of the Commissioner's modification provision of no retroactive application of the modification ruling of April 4, 1960."

The authority for making the revocation of the Bismarck and Wirthman letters prospective only is derived from 26 U.S.C.A. § 7805(b) * * *.

Appellee argues that:

"The Unlawful Discrimination Between Similarly–Situated Taxpayers, As Found by the District Court, Was Such That the Judgment of the District Court Was Not Erroneous."

We do not agree. Ordinarily, the Commissioner of Internal Revenue or his duly authorized subordinates act within their power when revoking an erroneous private ruling with or without retroactive effect. The evidence does not show that the appellee herein is being treated any worse or any differently from other taxpayers in his position who did not request or receive private letter rulings. Taxpayers without rulings are entitled only to be taxed the same as other taxpayers without rulings. See, e.g., Bornstein v. United States, Ct.Cl., 1965, 345 F.2d 558, 563–564; Goodstein v. Commissioner, 1 Cir., 1959, 267 F.2d 127, 132.

The fact that the private Bismarck letter was published by the Commerce Clearing House is not of decisive consequence. In *Goodstein*, supra, the taxpayer had seen other private but officially unpublished rulings and this factor was not enough to allow him (and, inferentially, all other taxpayers in his position) to rely on the said private rulings. As a practical matter, officials of the Internal Revenue Service are themselves not bound for precedent purposes by rulings or decisions not officially published. This fact is not unknown to the public since the policy of the Internal Revenue Service is set out in the introduction to the Internal Revenue Bulletins. In any event, the appellee did not rely either on the Bismarck letter or the Wirthman determination letter for he had paid his taxes on the assessment prior to when those letters were issued. There is no showing that appellee ever incurred expense or arranged his affairs in reliance on the Bismarck or Wirthman determinations. Even if such reliance had been shown, this is not necessarily decisive.

Certain cases relied on by the court below and by the appellee in his brief are inapposite to the instant situation. Each case must be viewed on its facts to determine if the Commissioner has abused his discretion under 26 U.S.C.A. § 7805(b). We will deal with these cases individually below.

International Business Machines Corp. v. United States, Ct.Cl., 1965, 343 F.2d 914, certiorari denied, 86 S.Ct. 647, (hereafter referred to as the *I.B.M.* case), a three to one decision, involved two competitors, I.B.M. and Remington Rand, in the manufacturing, selling and leasing of large electronic computer systems. On April 13, 1955, Remington requested a ruling from the Commissioner of Internal Revenue to permit it to avoid existing tax liabilities arising out of the sale and rental of its computers. A favorable ruling was issued by the Commissioner in a telegram sent to Remington on April 15, 1955. On July 13, 1955, I.B.M., having learned of the Remington ruling, sought a similar ruling on its sale and leasing of comparable computers. I.B.M.'s letter to the Commissioner was marked "Urgent! Please Expedite" and closed as follows:

> "In view of the extreme urgency of this matter, your immediate ruling, wire collect, is respectfully requested."

I.B.M.'s request was not acted upon for over two years, and then in a negative manner. Both I.B.M. (on July 29, 1955) and Remington (in September 1955) also sought refunds for taxes paid on the sale and leasing of computers in the past. I.B.M.'s claim covered the period from June 1, 1951, to May 31, 1955, and Remington's from January 1, 1952, to April 30, 1955. Remington's refund was allowed in July of

1956. I.B.M.'s refund claim, however, was rejected. The favorable tax ruling as to Remington was finally revoked prospectively as of February 1, 1958. In other words, Remington enjoyed six years of paying no tax on the selling and leasing of its computers, while I.B.M. did not share in such advantages for the selling and leasing of an almost identical product, even though both companies made similar requests of the Commissioner. This amounted to a comparative loss of over $13,000,000 to I.B.M. The Court of Claims allowed I.B.M. to recover the taxes paid by it on income derived from the rental and sale of computers for the period that Remington was not subjected to the tax.

Clearly, the facts of the *I.B.M.* case are entirely different from those in the instant situation. In *I.B.M.* there are clear and uncontradicted indications that the Commissioner abused his discretion in granting Remington tax-free treatment to the detriment of I.B.M. Unlike the instant appeal, the *I.B.M.* case involved a situation where one competitor was being favored unjustifiably over the only other competitor in the computer industry. Thus, the only members of the only logical class therein—the computer industry—were being treated in exactly opposite ways to the great detriment of I.B.M. Herein the situation is entirely different since appellee was treated no differently from many other similarly situated taxpayers who also had not sought rulings. In *I.B.M.* no reason was shown as to why Remington was not taxed retroactively. Here rational explanations were set forth as to why the Wirthman partners were not taxed retroactively—e.g., Mr. Jack U. Hiatt, a group supervisor for the Field Audit Branch of the Internal Revenue Service, testified that it was not feasible to collect a relatively small tax liability from a large number of taxpayers (the 22 members of the Wirthman partnership) located in different collection districts. There is a great contrast between the relatively small amounts involved herein and the $13,000,000 involved in *I.B.M.* Furthermore, there was a much greater reliance factor in *I.B.M.* since I.B.M. was, at the time it was paying the disputed taxes, aware of the ruling made to Remington and within three months after the private ruling to Remington had made an urgent request for a similar ruling. Herein appellee paid his assessment *before* either the Bismarck or Wirthman determination letters were issued.

In *I.B.M.* Judge Davis, writing for the three-man majority, stated:

"Implicit, too, in the Congressional award of discretion to the [Internal Revenue] Service, through Section 7805(b), is the power as well as the *obligation to consider the totality of the circumstances surrounding the handing down of a ruling—including the comparative or differential effect on the other taxpayers in the same class. 'The Commissioner cannot tax one and not tax another without some rational basis for the difference.'* United States v. Kaiser, 363 U.S. 299, 308, 80 S.Ct. 1204, 1210, 4 L.Ed.2d 1233 (1960) (Frankfurter, J., concurring). This factor has come to be recognized as central to the administration of the section. Equality of treatment is so dominant in our understanding of justice that discretion, where it is allowed a role, must pay the strictest heed.

* * *

"* * * *When we examine the agreed facts,* we cannot escape holding that there was a clear abuse, that the circumstances compelled the Service to confine its ruling (when it was finally given) to the future period for which Remington Rand's computers were to be held taxable. * * *

* * *

"*This history* exposes a manifest and unjustifiable discrimination against the taxpayer." (Emphasis supplied.)

As is apparent from the italicized portions of the above quotation, the Court of Claims was limiting itself in *I.B.M.* to the "totality of the circumstances" there involved. That *I.B.M.* was not intended to be a blanket ruling is clearly evidenced in two later cases decided by the Court of Claims. Those decisions are Knetsch v. United States, Ct.Cl., 1965, 348 F.2d 932, certiorari denied 86 S.Ct. 1221, and Bornstein v. United States, supra. In *Knetsch*, that court stated:

"As the court pointed out in *Bornstein,* supra, *our decision in International Business Machines Corp. v. United States,* Ct.Cl., 343 F.2d 914, decided April 16, 1965, rested in section 7805(b) of the Internal Revenue Code, of 1954, and *was based on the court's evaluation of the particular circumstances in that case.*" (Emphasis supplied.)

In *Bornstein* the Court of Claims stated:

"There are also controlling factual differences between these cases [*Bornstein*] and International Business Machines Corp. v. United States. In that case the court applied Section 7805(b) of the Internal Revenue Code of 1954 in behalf of a taxpayer who had made prompt application to obtain a private ruling to the same effect as a ruling issued to another taxpayer, which manufactured and sold business machines that were similar in all material respects to the machines manufactured by plaintiff. *In these cases, none of the taxpayers nor the corporations in which they are shareholders asked for rulings.*" (Emphasis supplied.)

Herein, as in *Bornstein,* the appellee had not requested a ruling prior to paying his assessment and was clearly not discriminated against in the manner that I.B.M. was in the *I.B.M.* case. In *I.B.M.* the evidence was very strong that the Commissioner abused his discretion under 26 U.S.C.A. § 7805(b) but, under the facts of the instant case, the evidence is at least just as strong that there was no abuse of administrative discretion in prospectively withdrawing the Bismarck and Wirthman letters.

The other authorities relied on by appellees i.e., City Loan & Savings Co. v. United States, N.D.Ohio, 1959, 177 F.Supp. 843, aff'd 6 Cir., 1961, 287 F.2d 612; Exchange Parts Co. of Fort Worth v. United States, 1960, 279 F.2d 251, 150 Ct.Cl. 538; Connecticut Ry. & Lighting Co. v. United States, 1956, 142 F.Supp. 907, 135 Ct.Cl. 538—are also of no avail to the appellee herein. In *Exchange Parts Co.* and *Connecticut Ry. & Lighting Co.*, as pointed out in *Bornstein,* supra, "* * * This court [the Court of Claims] held that it was an abuse of discretion for the Commissioner to apply his ruling retroactively, *solely* on the basis that plaintiffs had paid the taxes in question." (Emphasis supplied.) Herein, as we have already noted and as the record clearly indicates, the Commissioner's decision was based on rational administrative considerations and was not intended to be nor actually was discriminatory to appellee in regard to others in his situation—i.e., those who had not desired to nor actually did not receive private rulings prior to paying taxes on the assessments. In the *City Loan & Savings Co.* case there was a strong reliance factor not present herein since there the Commissioner, after some fourteen years, had attempted to retroactively revoke as to the taxpayer there involved his (the Commissioner's) official published acquiescence in a certain Tax Court case previously relied on by the taxpayer.

We would not be remiss to point out that a favorable ruling to appellee herein could open the proverbial floodgates of litigation as suits could feasibly be brought by all other similarly situated taxpayers who did not deduct special assessments from their returns during the years in question. Not allowing the Commissioner some proper discretion in prospectively or retroactively revoking private rulings could cause the elimination of private letter rulings and any and all benefits to be derived therefrom. Private letter rulings are issued to certain private parties and are not intended to be relied on by the general public as a whole. It is only when the Commissioner abuses his discretion under 26 U.S.C.A. § 7805(b) that remedial action should be taken. The instant case is no such situation.

We also note that to allow appellee to recover herein would arguably prejudice other taxpayers—e.g., the Wirthman partners—since appellee could deduct his entire assessment, whereas other taxpayers could deduct only that portion paid prior to the revocation of the private letter rulings. The shoe would then be on the other foot and appellee would have a windfall merely because he chose to pay his entire assessment in one lump sum. This could give rise to even more undesirable litigation. In the absence of cogent reasons to the contrary, no court should overturn a discretionary ruling by the Commissioner under 26 U.S.C.A. § 7805(b) which could lead to wholesale and time-consuming litigation. As already noted, such cogent reasons are not present herein.

We reverse and remand for further proceedings not inconsistent with the foregoing.

Question

Can the "discriminatory treatment" principle be used to circumscribe the Commissioner's authority under § 7805(b) to apply a revenue ruling retroactively? Compare Baker v. United States, 748 F.2d 1465 (11th Cir.1984) (holding that it was an abuse of discretion to deny retroactively the deduction of flight training benefits that were subsidized by the taxpayer's veterans benefits, while denying only prospectively the deductibility of other educational expenses subsidized by veterans benefits) with Manocchio v. Commissioner, 710 F.2d 1400 (9th Cir.1983) (ruling on the identical issue and finding no abuse of discretion).

SECTION 3. CONFIDENTIALITY AND DISCLOSURE

A. THE FREEDOM OF INFORMATION ACT

The Freedom of Information Act, 5 U.S.C.A. § 552, enacted in 1966 as an amendment to the public disclosure section of the Administrative Procedure Act, provides the public with an effective means of access to a broad spectrum of government information and records. By opening up vast stores of agency information to the public, the Freedom of Information Act has become a valuable resource tool for individuals and businesses who find themselves subject to government regulation. Not surprisingly, the Act has had a significant impact upon tax practice. FOIA suits have triggered the disclosure of private letter rulings,[x] large portions of the Internal Revenue Manual,[y] and numerous other types of internal IRS memoranda.[z]

Disclosed material provides tax practitioners with valuable insights into IRS positions and policies. Agency records obtained through FOIA disclosures may be utilized in subsequent tax proceedings in a variety of ways. Inconsistent rulings by the IRS can show an abuse of discretion by the Service in the retroactive revocation of rulings or the good faith of a taxpayer's position in a penalty or criminal context.[a] Differential treatment of similarly situated taxpayers may also tend to indicate intentionally discriminatory conduct on the part of the IRS.[b]

INFORMATION SUBJECT TO DISCLOSURE

The FOIA requires each federal agency to make various categories of official information available to the public. Disclosable material is classified into three broad categories according to the manner in which the information is to be made available to the public:

> 1. Materials that must be published in the Federal Register, including substantive rules of general applicability, statements of

---

x. Tax Analysts and Advocates v. IRS, 362 F.Supp. 1298 (D.D.C.1973), affirmed in pertinent part, 505 F.2d 350 (D.C.Cir.1974).

y. Hawkes v. IRS, 467 F.2d 787 (6th Cir.1972), appeal after remand, 507 F.2d 481 (6th Cir.1974).

z. See, e.g., Taxation with Representation Fund v. IRS, 485 F.Supp. 263 (D.D.C.1980); affirmed in part and remanded in part, 646 F.2d 666 (D.C.Cir.1981).

a. In United States v. Wahlin, 384 F.Supp. 43 (W.D.Wis.1974), a defendant charged with evasion of manufacturer's excise taxes used FOIA procedures to obtain access to private letter rulings (and correspondence relating thereto) in order to construct his defense that the taxing provision which he allegedly violated was unduly vague, confusing, indefinite and inconsistent.

b. See discussion in Walter, *The Battle for Information: Strategies of Taxpayers and the IRS to Compel (or Resist) Disclosure*, 56 TAXES 740 (1978).

general policy, and interpretations of general applicability which have been formulated and adopted by the agency. 5 U.S.C.A. § 552(a)(1).

2. Material that must be made available for public inspection and copying, including final orders and opinions resulting from agency adjudications, statements of policies and interpretations which have been adopted by the agency but not published in the Federal Register, and administrative staff manuals and agency instructions that affect the public. 5 U.S.C.A. § 552(a)(2).

3. Other information, not subject to disclosure by the above-described methods, and not specifically exempted from disclosure, must be made available upon a request "reasonably describing" the desired records. 5 U.S.C.A. § 552(a)(3).

In an attempt to balance the public's right to know about the function and operation of its government against the government's legitimate need for secrecy, the Act specifically exempts nine categories of information from public disclosure.[c] The presence of some exempt material in a document does not justify the withholding of the entire document. When exempt and non-exempt material are present in the same record, the Act requires the agency to disclose any "reasonably segregable" portion of the requested records. 5 U.S.C.A. § 552(b).[d]

In addition to the segregation requirement, the Act contains several incentives to ensure the agency's voluntary compliance with the Act's disclosure provisions. First, the FOIA provides that no person shall be "adversely affected" by material required to be published in the Federal Register but not so published. 5 U.S.C.A. § 552(a)(1). Failure to comply with the publication requirement may estop the agency from invoking an unpublished "rule of general applicability" against an individual.[e] A further incentive to disclose is found in § 552(a)(2), which provides that no agency can rely on or cite as precedent any final order, opinion, or statement of policy which has not previously been made available to the public. Finally, the Act authorizes the allowance of attorneys' fees and other costs in actions in which the complainant "substantially prevails". 5 U.S.C.A. § 552(a)(4)(E).

SCOPE OF THE ACT'S EXEMPTIONS

Litigation under the FOIA generally has focused upon the scope of the nine exemptions. The exemptions of particular relevance to the tax practitioner are discussed below.

---

c. 5 U.S.C.A. § 552(b)(1)–(9).

d. Treasury regulations define "reasonably segregable portions" to be those portions released when "the meaning is not distorted by deletion of the denied portions and when it reasonably can be assumed that a skillful and knowledgeable person could not reconstruct the deleted information." 31 C.F.R. § 1.2(c)(4) (1990).

e. See, e.g., Morton v. Ruiz, 415 U.S. 199, 232–236, 94 S.Ct. 1055, 1073–1074, 39 L.Ed.2d 270, 292–295 (1974); W.G. Cosby Transfer & Storage Corp. v. Froehlke, 480 F.2d 498 (4th Cir.1973).

Exemption 3: Information Specifically Exempted By Other Statutes. Exemption 3 permits the withholding of information the confidentiality of which is assured by some other (non-FOIA) statute. To qualify as an Exemption 3 statute, the statute which purportedly requires nondisclosure must either: (1) leave no discretion to the agency as to its duty to withhold, or (2) establish particular criteria for agency guidance in determining which material is to be withheld. 5 U.S.C.A. § 552(b)(3)(A) and (B). Section 6103 of the Internal Revenue Code, relating to the confidentiality of returns and return information, has been held to be an Exemption 3 statute.[f]

Under § 6103, tax returns and "tax return information" (defined so as to include all information collected to determine a taxpayer's tax liability) may not be disclosed to persons other than the taxpayer about whom the information was compiled.[g] Tax return information may be released to the individual about whom the information pertains unless the Secretary of the Treasury determines that the disclosure would "seriously impair Federal tax administration."[h]

Exemption 4: Trade Secrets and Certain Commercial or Financial Information. Exemption 4 prohibits the disclosure of "trade secrets and commercial or financial information obtained from a person and privileged or confidential." This exemption has been narrowly construed by the courts. Information is not exempted from disclosure merely because the information is not customarily provided to the public by the person from whom it was obtained. Rather, the courts

---

f. Chamberlain v. Kurtz, 589 F.2d 827 (5th Cir.1979), cert. denied, 444 U.S. 842, 100 S.Ct. 82, 62 L.Ed.2d 54 (1979); *see* Church of Scientology of California v. IRS, 484 U.S. 9, 108 S.Ct. 271, 98 L.Ed.2d 228 (1987) (parties agreed section 6103 is an Exemption 3 statute).

g. In Conway v. IRS, 447 F.Supp. 1128 (D.D.C.1978), a taxpayer seeking disclosure of IRS memoranda regarding third parties' attempts to obtain tax credits for foreign tax payments was unable to view the relevant documents until all identifying information had been excised.

It should be noted that § 6103(b)(2) excepts from the definition of "return information" "data in a form which cannot be associated with, or otherwise identify, directly or indirectly, a particular taxpayer." This exception known as the Haskell Amendment, allows the IRS to perform statistical studies and to release the results of those studies.

The Supreme Court resolved a split in the Circuits concerning the Haskell Amendment in Church of Scientology of California v. IRS, 484 U.S. 9, 108 S.Ct. 271, 98 L.Ed.2d 228 (1987). The Court rejected the notion that the Haskell Amendment requires the Service, in response to a FOIA request, to delete identifying material from documents and release what would otherwise have been nondiscloseable return information. The Court held that "as with a return itself, removal of identification from return information would not deprive it of protection under § 6103(b). Since such deletion would not make otherwise protected return information discloseable, [the IRS] has no duty under the FOIA to undertake such reduction." Instead, the data must have been reformulated by the IRS into a composite study or report for it to lose its protection from disclosure.

h. I.R.C. § 6103(c) and (e)(7). In Chamberlain v. Kurtz, supra, a taxpayer was denied access to various investigatory files compiled in the course of an audit and fraud inquiry concerning him on the grounds that disclosure would "seriously impair Federal tax administration." The Fifth Circuit sustained the Secretary's determination that the documents were not subject to release, as disclosure was likely to impair the federal government in collecting back taxes and penalties from the plaintiff and would tend to assist the taxpayer in defending himself from those claims currently being leveled against him by the government.

generally require the agency to demonstrate that disclosure is likely to impair the government's ability to obtain necessary information in the future, or to cause substantial competitive harm to the person from whom the information was obtained.[i] The Trade Secrets Act, 18 U.S.C.A. § 1905, which imposes criminal penalties for the unauthorized disclosure of trade secrets by federal employees, appears to afford no independent basis to withhold information; neither does it qualify as an Exemption 3 statute.[j]

Exemption 5: Certain Inter-Agency and Intra-Agency Memoranda. Exemption 5 permits the withholding of internal memoranda which would not be available to a party in litigation with an agency under the rules of discovery. This exemption preserves the traditional common law evidentiary privileges including the attorney-client and governmental privileges, as well as material unavailable under the attorney work-product doctrine.[k] This exemption is routinely raised by the IRS to justify the withholding of internal agency memoranda.

The pertinent inquiry in determining the scope of Exemption 5 is whether the disclosure sought would be injurious to the consultative and decision-making processes of government.[l] Generally, agency memoranda must be both predecisional and of a deliberative nature to be subject to withholding under Exemption 5.[m] The courts have held that the disclosure of intra-agency memoranda containing purely factual material does not threaten the deliberative and consultative functions of government.[n]

Exemption 7: Certain Investigatory Records Compiled for Law Enforcement Purposes. Exemption 7, relating to investigatory records compiled for law enforcement purposes, is frequently important in tax practice. The Supreme Court, in NLRB v. Robbins Tire & Rubber Co., 437 U.S. 214, 98 S.Ct. 2311, 57 L.Ed.2d 159 (1978) adopted a broad construction of Exemption 7. In *Robbins,* an employer sought to obtain statements of potential witnesses collected by the NLRB for use in a pending labor practices dispute. The NLRB resisted disclosure on the

---

i. National Parks & Conservation Ass'n v. Kleppe, 547 F.2d 673 (D.C.Cir.1976).

j. See National Parks & Conservation Ass'n v. Kleppe, supra, at 686; Grumman Aircraft Engineering Corp. v. Renegotiation Bd., 425 F.2d 578, 580, n. 5 (D.C.Cir. 1970), reversed on other grounds, 421 U.S. 168, 95 S.Ct. 1491, 44 L.Ed.2d 57 (1975). See also Chrysler Corp. v. Brown, 441 U.S. 281, 99 S.Ct. 1705, 60 L.Ed.2d 208 (1979).

k. See generally E.P.A. v. Mink, 410 U.S. 73, 93 S.Ct. 827, 35 L.Ed.2d 119 (1973).

l. See Arthur Andersen & Co. v. IRS, 679 F.2d 254 (D.C.Cir.1982) (denying access to drafts of revenue rulings and background notes under Exemption 5).

m. Falcone v. IRS, 479 F.Supp. 985 (E.D.Mich.1979); Dick v. IRS, 41 AFTR2d 78–639 (D.D.C.1978). In *Dick*, a taxpayer sought disclosure of an IRS memorandum which allegedly recommended that IRS agents discontinue accepting intelligence information from Bahamian banks. Reasoning that disclosure of this type of recommendation would discourage frank discussions between IRS officials and their superiors on matters of sensitive investigative policy, the court held the memorandum to be within the ambit of Exemption 5.

n. E.P.A. v. Mink, supra, 410 U.S. at 89–92, 93 S.Ct. at 836–838, 35 L.Ed.2d 119, at 133–35. See also Conway v. IRS, supra (IRS may delete emphasis remarks and other indications of its deliberative process from documents otherwise subject to disclosure).

grounds that release of these statements would interfere with pending enforcement proceedings. The district court ordered disclosure of the statements upon the NLRB's failure to make a particularized showing that the requested disclosures were likely to interfere with administrative enforcement proceedings. In reversing the lower court's decision, the Supreme Court held that an agency's claim of interference with a pending enforcement proceeding need not be shown on a case-by-case basis. A sufficient showing of interference is made when disclosure would give the requestor "earlier and greater" access to the agency's case than it otherwise would have.

Exemption 7 has been invoked successfully by the IRS to prevent disclosure of IRS files to the subject of an ongoing tax fraud investigation.º Information gathered for law enforcement purposes is protected from disclosure even before there is an actual prosecution. Exemptions 7(C) and 7(D) are typically raised to shield from disclosure the identity of informants and other individuals who have provided the Service with information in the course of a tax investigation.ᵖ

Exemption 7 also applies even though the records were compiled in the course of a law enforcement investigation with little or no possibility of eventual enforcement.ᑫ However, there is respectable authority that Exemption 7 is inapplicable where the underlying investigation was unauthorized or illegal.ʳ

Exemption 7, by its own terms does not prevent the disclosure of administrative staff manuals, the disclosure of which would significantly impede the law enforcement process, as such materials are not investigatory records compiled for law enforcement purposes. However, the courts need not require disclosure of such documents when the government demonstrates that disclosure would "significantly impede" the law enforcement process.ˢ

Notes

1. Any person may request disclosure of records which have not been published in the Federal Register or made available for public inspection

---

o. See Willard v. IRS, 776 F.2d 100 (4th Cir.1985); Linsteadt v. IRS, 729 F.2d 998 (5th Cir.1984). But see Grasso v. IRS, 785 F.2d 70 (3d Cir.1986) (taxpayer's own statements ordered disclosed).

p. See Maroscia v. Levi, 569 F.2d 1000 (7th Cir.1977) (reports of interviews and the names of interviewees resulting from FBI investigation not subject to disclosure). See also Luzaich v. United States, 435 F.Supp. 31 (D.Minn.1977), affirmed without opinion, 564 F.2d 101 (8th Cir.1977); Bast v. IRS, 42 AFTR2d 78–5078 (D.D.C.1978).

q. Irons v. Bell, 596 F.2d 468 (1st Cir. 1979).

r. Kanter v. IRS, 433 F.Supp. 812, 822 (N.D.Ill.1977). However, in Providence Journal Co. v. FBI, 602 F.2d 1010 (1st Cir. 1979), cert. denied, 444 U.S. 1071, 100 S.Ct. 1015, 62 L.Ed.2d 752 (1980), the First Circuit held that information gathered as a result of illegal electronic surveillance, in violation of Title III of the Omnibus Crime Control and Safe Streets Act of 1968, 18 U.S.C.A. §§ 2510–2520, was exempt from disclosure as an unwarranted invasion of personal privacy, 5 U.S.C.A. § 552(b)(7)(C).

s. Hawkes v. IRS, supra. Similarly, in Caplan v. Bureau of Alcohol, Tobacco and Firearms, 445 F.Supp. 699 (S.D.N.Y.1978), the court exercised its equitable discretion in declining to order the disclosure of a government manual on "Raids and Searches".

and copying. However, strict compliance with the agency's published rules relating to FOIA disclosure is required. The IRS regulations relating to FOIA requests are contained in Proc.Rules §§ 601.701 and 601.702. These sections also set forth internal IRS rules for processing requests for information.

2. After pursuing one's administrative remedies, an unsuccessful requestor may apply to a district court for an order enjoining the agency from withholding agency records and to order the production of records improperly withheld. For details as to the procedure to be followed in the district court action, see 5 U.S.C.A. § 552(a)(4).

UNITED STATES DEPARTMENT OF JUSTICE v. TAX ANALYSTS

Supreme Court of the United States, 1989.
492 U.S. 136, 109 S.Ct. 2841, 106 L.Ed.2d 112.

JUSTICE MARSHALL delivered the opinion of the Court.

The question presented is whether the Freedom of Information Act (FOIA or Act), 5 U.S.C. § 552 (1982 ed. and Supp. V), requires the United States Department of Justice (Department) to make available copies of district court decisions that it receives in the course of litigating tax cases on behalf of the Federal Government. We hold that it does.

I

The Department's Tax Division represents the Federal Government in nearly all civil tax cases in the district courts, the courts of appeals, and the Claims Court. Because it represents a party in litigation, the Tax Division receives copies of all opinions and orders issued by these courts in such cases. Copies of these decisions are made for the Tax Division's staff attorneys. The original documents are sent to the official files kept by the Department.

If the Government has won a district court case, the Tax Division must prepare a bill of costs and collect any money judgment indicated in the decision. If the Government has lost, the Tax Division must decide whether to file a motion to alter or amend the judgment or whether to recommend filing an appeal. The decision whether to appeal involves not only the Tax Division but also the Internal Revenue Service (IRS) and the Solicitor General. A division of the IRS reviews the district court's decision and prepares an appeal recommendation known as an "action on decision" (AOD). The court decision and the accompanying AOD are circulated to the Tax Division, which formulates its own recommendation, and then to the Solicitor General, who reviews the district court decision in light of the IRS and Tax Division's recommendations. If the Solicitor General ultimately approves an appeal, the Tax Division prepares a record and joint appendix, both of which must contain a copy of the district court decision, for transmittal to the court of appeals. If no appeal is taken, the Tax Division is responsible for ensuring the payment of any court-ordered refund and for defending against any claim of attorney's fees.

Respondent Tax Analysts publishes a weekly magazine, Tax Notes, which reports on legislative, judicial, and regulatory developments in the field of federal taxation to a readership largely composed of tax attorneys, accountants, and economists. As one of its regular features, Tax Notes provides summaries of recent federal court decisions on tax issues. To supplement the magazine, Tax Analysts provides full texts of these decisions in microfiche form. Tax Analysts also publishes Tax Notes Today, a daily electronic data base that includes summaries and full texts of recent federal court tax decisions.

In late July 1979, Tax Analysts filed a FOIA request in which it asked the Department to make available all district court tax opinions and final orders received by the Tax Division earlier that month. The Department denied the request on the ground that these decisions were not Tax Division records. Tax Analysts then appealed this denial administratively. While the appeal was pending, Tax Analysts agreed to withdraw its request in return for access to the Tax Division's weekly log of tax cases decided by the federal courts. These logs list the name and date of a case, the docket number, the names of counsel, the nature of the case, and its disposition.

Since gaining access to the weekly logs, Tax Analysts' practice has been to examine the logs and to request copies of the decisions noted therein from the clerks of the 90 or so district courts around the country and from participating attorneys. In most instances, Tax Analysts procures copies reasonably promptly, but this method of acquisition has proven unsatisfactory approximately 25% of the time. Some court clerks ignore Tax Analysts' requests for copies of decisions, and others respond slowly, sometimes only after Tax Analysts has forwarded postage and copying fees. Because the Federal Government is required to appeal tax cases within 60 days, Tax Analysts frequently fails to obtain copies of district court decisions before appeals are taken.

Frustrated with this process, Tax Analysts initiated a series of new FOIA requests in 1984. Beginning in November 1984, and continuing approximately once a week until May 1985, Tax Analysts asked the Department to make available copies of all district court tax opinions and final orders identified in the Tax Division's weekly logs. The Department denied these requests and Tax Analysts appealed administratively. When the Department sustained the denial, Tax Analysts filed the instant suit in the District Court for the District of Columbia, seeking to compel the Department to provide it with access to district court decisions received by the Tax Division.

The District Court granted the Department's motion to dismiss the complaint, holding that 5 U.S.C. § 552(a)(4)(B), which confers jurisdiction in the district courts when "agency records" have been "improperly withheld,"[2] had not been satisfied. 643 F.Supp. 740, 742 (1986). The court reasoned that the district court decisions at issue had not been "improperly withheld" because they "already are available from their primary sources, the District Courts," *id.*, at 743, and thus were "on the public record." *Id.*, at 744. The court did not address whether the district court decisions are "agency records." *Id.*, at 742.

The Court of Appeals for the District of Columbia Circuit reversed. 269 U.S.App.D.C. 315, 845 F.2d 1060 (1988). It first held that the district court decisions were "improperly withheld." An agency ordinarily may refuse to make available documents in its control only if it proves that the documents fall within one of the nine disclosure exemptions set forth in § 552(b), the court noted, and in this instance, "[n]o exemption applies to the district court opinions." *Id.*, at 319, 845 F.2d, at 1064. As for the Department's contention that the district court decisions are publicly available at their source, the court observed that "no court * * * has denied access to * * * documents on the ground that they are available elsewhere, and several have assumed that such documents must still be produced by the agency unless expressly exempted by the Act." *Id.*, at 321, 845 F.2d, at 1066.

The Court of Appeals next held that the district court decisions sought by Tax Analysts are "agency records" for purposes of the FOIA. The court acknowledged that the district court decisions had originated in a part of the Government not covered by the FOIA, but concluded that the documents nonetheless constituted "agency records" because the Department has the discretion to use the decisions as it sees fit, because the Department routinely uses the decisions in performing its official duties, and because the decisions are integrated into the Department's official case files. *Id.*, at 323–324, 845 F.2d, at 1068–1069. The court therefore remanded the case to the District Court with instructions to enter an order directing the Department "to provide some reasonable form of access" to the decisions sought by Tax Analysts. *Id.*, at 317, 845 F.2d, at 1062.

We granted certiorari, 488 U.S. [1003], 109 S.Ct. 781, 102 L.Ed.2d 773 (1989), and now affirm.

II

In enacting the FOIA 23 years ago, Congress sought " 'to open agency action to the light of public scrutiny.' " *United States Dept. of Justice v. Reporters Committee for Freedom of Press*, 489 U.S. [749, 772],

---

2. Section 552(a)(4)(B) provides:

"On complaint, the district court of the United States in the district in which the complainant resides, or has his principal place of business, or in which the agency records are situated, or in the District of Columbia, has jurisdiction to enjoin the agency from withholding agency records and to order the production of any agency records improperly withheld from the complainant. In such a case the court shall determine the matter de novo, and may examine the contents of such agency records in camera to determine whether such records or any part thereof shall be withheld under any of the exemptions set forth in subsection (b) of this section, and the burden is on the agency to sustain its action."

109 S.Ct. 1468, 1481, 103 L.Ed.2d 774 (1989), quoting *Department of Air Force v. Rose,* 425 U.S. 352, 372, 96 S.Ct. 1592, 1604, 48 L.Ed.2d 11 (1976). Congress did so by requiring agencies to adhere to " 'a general philosophy of full agency disclosure.' " *Id.,* at 360, 96 S.Ct., at 1599, quoting S.Rep. No. 813, 89th Cong., 2nd Sess., 3 (1965). Congress believed that this philosophy, put into practice, would help "ensure an informed citizenry, vital to the functioning of a democratic society." *NLRB v. Robbins Tire & Rubber Co.,* 437 U.S. 214, 242, 98 S.Ct. 2311, 2327, 57 L.Ed.2d 159 (1978).

The FOIA confers jurisdiction on the district courts "to enjoin the agency from withholding agency records and to order the production of any agency records improperly withheld." § 552(a)(4)(B). Under this provision, "federal jurisdiction is dependent on a showing that an agency has (1) 'improperly' (2) 'withheld' (3) 'agency records.' " *Kissinger v. Reporters Committee for Freedom of Press,* 445 U.S. 136, 150, 100 S.Ct. 960, 968, 63 L.Ed.2d 267 (1980). Unless each of these criteria is met, a district court lacks jurisdiction to devise remedies to force an agency to comply with the FOIA's disclosure requirements.[3]

In this case, all three jurisdictional terms are at issue. Although these terms are defined neither in the Act nor in its legislative history, we do not write on a clean slate. Nine Terms ago we decided three cases that explicated the meanings of these partially overlapping terms. *Kissinger v. Reporters Committee for Freedom of Press, supra; Forsham v. Harris,* 445 U.S. 169, 100 S.Ct. 977, 63 L.Ed.2d 293 (1980); *GTE Sylvania, Inc. v. Consumers Union of United States, Inc.,* 445 U.S. 375, 100 S.Ct. 1194, 63 L.Ed.2d 467 (1980). These decisions form the basis of our analysis of Tax Analysts' requests.

A

We consider first whether the district court decisions at issue are "agency records," a term elaborated upon both in *Kissinger* and in *Forsham.*

Two requirements emerge from *Kissinger* and *Forsham,* each of which must be satisfied for requested materials to qualify as "agency records." First, an agency must "either create or obtain" the requested materials "as a prerequisite to its becoming an 'agency record' within the meaning of the FOIA." *Id.,* at 182, 100 S.Ct., at 985. In performing their official duties, agencies routinely avail themselves of studies, trade journal reports, and other materials produced outside the agencies both by private and governmental organizations. See *Chrysler Corp. v. Brown,* 441 U.S. 281, 292, 99 S.Ct. 1705, 1712, 60 L.Ed.2d 208 (1979). To restrict the term "agency records" to materials generated

---

3. The burden is on the agency to demonstrate, not the requester to disprove, that the materials sought are not "agency records" or have not been "improperly" "withheld." See S.Rep. No. 813, 89th Cong., 2nd Sess., 8 (1965) ("Placing the burden of proof upon the agency puts the task of justifying the withholding on the only party able to explain it"); H.R.Rep. No. 1497, 89th Cong., 2d Sess., 9 (1966), U.S.Code Cong. & Admin.News 1966, pp. 2418, 2426 (same); cf. *Federal Open Market Committee v. Merrill,* 443 U.S. 340, 352, 99 S.Ct. 2800, 2808, 61 L.Ed.2d 587 (1979).

internally would frustrate Congress' desire to put within public reach the information available to an agency in its decision-making processes. See *id.,* at 290, n. 10, 99 S.Ct., at 1712, n. 10. As we noted in *Forsham,* "[t]he legislative history of the FOIA abounds with * * * references to records *acquired* by an agency." 445 U.S., at 184, 100 S.Ct., at 986 (emphasis added).[4]

Second, the agency must be in control of the requested materials at the time the FOIA request is made. By control we mean that the materials have come into the agency's possession in the legitimate conduct of its official duties. This requirement accords with *Kissinger's* teaching that the term "agency records" is not so broad as to include personal materials in an employee's possession, even though the materials may be physically located at the agency. See 445 U.S., at 157, 100 S.Ct., at 972. This requirement is suggested by *Forsham* as well, 445 U.S., at 183, 100 S.Ct., at 985, where we looked to the definition of agency records in the Records Disposal Act, 44 U.S.C. § 3301. Under that definition, agency records include "all books, papers, maps, photographs, machine readable materials, or other documentary materials, regardless of physical form or characteristics, made or received by an agency of the United States Government *under Federal law or in connection with the transaction of public business * * *." Ibid.* (emphasis added).[5] Furthermore, the requirement that the materials be in the agency's control at the time the request is made accords with our statement in *Forsham* that the FOIA does not cover "information in the abstract." 445 U.S., at 185, 100 S.Ct., at 987.[6]

---

4. Title 5 U.S.C. § 552(b)(4), which exempts from disclosure trade secrets and commercial or financial information "obtained from a person," provides further support for the principle that the term "agency records" includes materials received by an agency. See *Forsham v. Harris,* 445 U.S. 169, 184–185, 100 S.Ct. 977, 986–987, 63 L.Ed.2d 293 (1980); see also *id.,* at 183–184, 100 S.Ct., at 985–986 (noting that the definition of "records" in the Records Disposal Act, 44 U.S.C. § 3301, and in the Presidential Records Act of 1978, 44 U.S.C. § 2201(2), encompassed materials "received" by an agency).

5. In *GTE Sylvania, Inc. v. Consumers Union of United States, Inc.,* 445 U.S. 375, 385, 100 S.Ct. 1194, 1201, 63 L.Ed.2d 467 (1980), we noted that Congress intended the FOIA to prevent agencies from refusing to disclose, among other things, agency telephone directories and the names of agency employees. We are confident, however, that requests for documents of this type will be relatively infrequent. Common sense suggests that a person seeking such documents or materials housed in an agency library typically will find it easier to repair to the Library of Congress, or to the nearest public library, rather than to invoke the FOIA's disclosure mechanisms. Cf. *United States Dept. of Justice v. Reporters Committee for Freedom of Press,* 489 U.S. ___, ___, 109 S.Ct. 1468, 1477, 103 L.Ed.2d 774 (1989) ("if the [requested materials] were 'freely available,' there would be no reason to invoke the FOIA to obtain access"). To the extent such requests are made, the fact that the FOIA allows agencies to recoup the costs of processing requests from the requester may discouarge recourse to the FOIA where materials are readily available elsewhere. See 5 U.S.C. § 552(a)(4)(A).

6. Because requested materials ordinarily will be in the agency's possession at the time the FOIA request is made, disputes over control should be infrequent. In some circumstances, however, requested materials might be on loan to another agency, "purposefully routed ... out of agency possession in order to circumvent [an impending] FOIA request," or "wrongfully removed by an individual after a request is filed." *Kissinger v. Reporters Committee for Freedom of Press,* 445 U.S. 136, 155, n. 9, 100 S.Ct. 960, 971, n. 9, 63 L.Ed.2d 267 (1980). We leave consideration of these issues to another day.

Applying these requirements here, we conclude that the requested district court decisions constitute "agency records." First, it is undisputed that the Department has obtained these documents from the district courts. This is not a case like *Forsham,* where the materials never in fact had been received by the agency. The Department contends that a district court is not an "agency" under the FOIA, but this truism is beside the point. The relevant issue is whether an agency covered by the FOIA has "create[d] or obtaine[d]" the materials sought, *Forsham,* 445 U.S., at 182, 100 S.Ct., at 985, not whether the organization from which the documents originated is itself covered by the FOIA.[7]

Second, the Department clearly controls the district court decisions that Tax Analysts seeks. Each of Tax Analysts' FOIA requests referred to district court decisions in the agency's possession at the time the requests were made. This is evident from the fact that Tax Analysts based its weekly requests on the Tax Division's logs, which compile information on decisions the Tax Division recently had received and placed in official case files. Furthermore, the court decisions at issue are obviously not personal papers of agency employees. The Department counters that it does not control these decisions because the district courts retain authority to modify the decisions even after they are released, but this argument, too, is beside the point. The control inquiry focuses on an agency's possession of the requested materials, not on its power to alter the content of the materials it receives. Agencies generally are not at liberty to alter the content of the materials that they receive from outside parties. An authorship-control requirement thus would sharply limit "agency records" essentially to documents generated by the agencies themselves. This result is incompatible with the FOIA's goal of giving the public access to all non-exempted information received by an agency as it carries out its mandate.

The Department also urges us to limit "agency records," at least where materials originating outside the agency are concerned, "to those documents 'prepared substantially to be relied upon in agency decisionmaking.'" Brief for Petitioner 21, quoting *Berry v. Department of Justice,* 733 F.2d 1343, 1349 (CA9 1984). This limitation disposes of Tax Analysts' requests, the Department argues, because district court judges do not write their decisions primarily with an eye toward agency decisionmaking. This argument, however, makes the determination of "agency records" turn on the intent of the creator of a document relied upon by an agency. Such a *mens rea* requirement is nowhere to be found in the Act.[8] Moreover, discerning the intent of the drafters of a

---

7. This point is implicit in *United States Dept. of Justice v. Julian,* 486 U.S. 1, ___, and n. 6, 108 S.Ct. 1606, 1610, and n. 6, 100 L.Ed.2d 1 (1988), where it was uncontroverted that presentence reports, which had been prepared under district court auspices and turned over to the Department and the Parole Commission, constituted "agency records."

8. Nonpersonal materials in an agency's possession may be subject to certain disclosure restrictions. This fact, however,

document may often prove an elusive endeavor, particularly if the document was created years earlier or by a large number of people for whom it is difficult to divine a common intent.

B

We turn next to the term "withheld," which we discussed in *Kissinger*. Two of the requests in that case—for summaries of all the telephone conversations in which Kissinger had engaged while serving as National Security Adviser and as Secretary of State—implicated that term. These summaries were initially stored in Kissinger's personal files at the State Department. Near the end of his tenure as Secretary of State, Kissinger transferred the summaries first to a private residence and then to the Library of Congress. Significantly, the two requests for these summaries were made only after the summaries had been physically delivered to the Library. We found this fact dispositive, concluding that Congress did not believe that an agency "withholds a document which has been removed from the possession of the agency prior to the filing of the FOIA request. In such a case, the agency has neither the custody nor control necessary to enable it to withhold." 445 U.S., at 150–151, 100 S.Ct., at 968–969.[9] We accordingly refused to order the State Department to institute a retrieval action against the Library. As we explained, such a course "would have us read the 'hold' out of 'withhold * * *. A refusal to resort to legal remedies to obtain possession is simply not conduct subsumed by the verb withhold.'" *Id.*, at 151, 100 S.Ct., at 969.[10]

The construction of "withholding" adopted in *Kissinger* readily encompasses Tax Analysts' requests. There is no claim here that Tax Analysts filed its requests for copies of recent district court tax decisions received by the Tax Division after these decisions had been transferred out of the Department. On the contrary, the decisions were on the Department's premises and otherwise in the Department's control, *supra*, at 10, when the requests were made. See *supra*, n. 6. Thus, when the Department refused to comply with Tax Analysts'

does not bear on whether the materials are in the agency's control, but rather on the subsequent question of whether they are exempted from disclosure under § 552(b)(3).

9. Although a control inquiry for "withheld" replicates part of the test for "agency records," the FOIA's structure and legislative history make clear that agency control over requested materials is a "prerequisite to triggering *any* duties under the FOIA." *Kissinger*, 445 U.S., at 151, 100 S.Ct., at 969 (emphasis added); see also *id.*, at 152–153, 100 S.Ct., at 969–970; *Forsham*, 445 U.S., at 185, 100 S.Ct., at 986.

10. *Kissinger's* focus on the agency's present control of a requested document was based in part on the Act's purposes and structure. With respect to the former, we noted that because Congress had not intended to "obligate agencies to create or retain documents," an agency should not be "required to retrieve documents which have escaped its possession, but which it has not endeavored to recover." 445 U.S., at 152, 100 S.Ct., at 969 (citations omitted). As for the Act's structure, we noted that, among other provisions, § 552(a)(6)(B) gives agencies a 10-day extension of the normal 10-day period for responding to FOIA requests if there is a need to search and collect the requested materials from facilities separate from the office processing the request. The brevity of this extension period indicates that Congress did not expect agencies to resort to lawsuits to retrieve documents within that period. See *id.*, at 153, 100 S.Ct., at 970.

requests, it "withheld" the district court decisions for purposes of § 552(a)(4)(B).

The Department's counterargument is that, because the district court decisions sought by Tax Analysts are publicly available as soon as they are issued and thus may be inspected and copied by the public at any time, the Department cannot be said to have "withheld" them. The Department notes that the weekly logs it provides to Tax Analysts contain sufficient information to direct Tax Analysts to the "original source of the requested documents." Brief for Petitioners 23. It is not clear from the Department's brief whether this argument is based on the term "withheld" or the term "improperly." [11] But, to the extent the Department relies on the former term, its argument is without merit. Congress used the word "withheld" only "in its usual sense." *Kissinger,* 445 U.S., at 151, 100 S.Ct., at 969. When the Department refused to grant Tax Analysts' requests for the district court decisions in its files, it undoubtedly "withheld" these decisions in any reasonable sense of that term. Nothing in the history or purposes of the FOIA counsels contorting this word beyond its usual meaning. We therefore reject the Department's argument that an agency has not "withheld" a document under its control when, in denying an otherwise valid request, it directs the requester to a place outside of the agency where the document may be publicly available.

C

The Department is left to argue, finally, that the district court decisions were not "improperly" withheld because of their public availability. The term "improperly," like "agency records" and "withheld," is not defined by the Act. We explained in *GTE Sylvania,* however, that Congress' use of the word "improperly" reflected its dissatisfaction with § 3 of the Administrative Procedure Act, 5 U.S.C. § 1002 (1964 ed.), which "had failed to provide the desired access to information relied upon in Government decisionmaking, and in fact had become 'the major statutory excuse for withholding Government records from public view.'" 445 U.S., at 384, 100 S.Ct., at 1200, quoting H.R.Rep. No. 1497, 89th Cong., 2d Sess., 3 (1966), U.S.Code Cong. & Admin.News 1966, p. 2420. Under § 3, we explained, agencies had "broad discretion * * * in deciding what information to disclose, and that discretion was often abused." 445 U.S., at 385, 100 S.Ct., at 1201.

* * * Congress formulated a system of clearly defined exemptions to the FOIA's otherwise mandatory disclosure requirements. An agency must disclose agency records to any person under § 552(a), "unless they may be withheld pursuant to one of the nine enumerated exemptions listed in § 552(b)." *United States Dept. of Justice v. Julian,* 486 U.S. 1, 8, 108 S.Ct. 1606, 1611, 100 L.Ed.2d 1 (1988). Consistent with

11. The Court of Appeals believed that the Department was arguing "that it need not affirmatively make [the district court decisions] available to Tax Analysts because the documents have not been *withheld* to begin with." 269 U.S.App.D.C. 315, 319–320, 845 F.2d 1060, 1064–1065 (1988) (emphasis in original).

the Act's goal of broad disclosure, these exemptions have been consistently given a narrow compass. See, *e.g., ibid.; FBI v. Abramson,* 456 U.S. 615, 630, 102 S.Ct. 2054, 2063, 72 L.Ed.2d 376 (1982). More important for present purposes, the exemptions are "explicitly exclusive." *FAA Administrator v. Robertson,* 422 U.S. 255, 262, 95 S.Ct. 2140, 2146, 45 L.Ed.2d 164 (1975); see also *Rose,* 425 U.S., at 361, 96 S.Ct., at 1599; *Robbins Tire & Rubber Co.,* 437 U.S., at 221, 98 S.Ct., at 2316; *Mink, supra,* 410 U.S., at 79, 93 S.Ct., at 832. As Justice O'CONNOR has explained, Congress sought "to insulate its product from judicial tampering and to preserve the emphasis on disclosure by admonishing that the 'availability of records to the public' is not limited, 'except as *specifically* stated.'" *Abramson, supra,* 456 U.S., at 642, 102 S.Ct., at 2070 (dissenting opinion) (emphasis in original), quoting § 552(c) (now codified at § 552(d)); see also 456 U.S., at 637, n. 5, 102 S.Ct., at 2067, n. 5; H.R.Rep. No. 1497, *supra,* at 1. It follows from the exclusive nature of the § 552(b) exemption scheme that agency records which do not fall within one of the exemptions are "improperly" withheld.[12]

The Department does not contend here that any exemption enumerated in § 552(b) protects the district court decisions sought by Tax Analysts. The Department claims nonetheless that there is nothing "improper" in directing a requester "to the principal, public source of records." Brief for Petitioners 26. The Department advances three somewhat related arguments in support of this proposition. We consider them in turn.

First, the Department contends that the structure of the Act evinces Congress' desire to avoid redundant disclosures. An understanding of this argument requires a brief survey of the disclosure provisions of § 552(a). Under subsection (a)(1), an agency must "currently publish in the Federal Register" specific materials, such as descriptions of the agency, statements of its general functions, and the agency's rules of procedure. Under subsection (a)(2), an agency must "make available for public inspection and copying" its final opinions, policy statements, and administrative staff manuals, "unless the materials are promptly published and copies offered for sale." Under subsection (a)(3), the general provision covering the disclosure of agency records, an agency need not make available those materials that have already been disclosed under subsections (a)(1) and (a)(2). Taken together, the Department argues, these provisions demonstrate the inapplicability of the FOIA's disclosure requirements to previously dis-

---

12. Even when an agency does not deny a FOIA request outright, the requesting party may still be able to claim "improper" withholding by alleging that the agency has responded in an inadequate manner. Cf. § 552(a)(6)(C); *Kissinger v. Reporters Committee for Freedom of Press,* 445 U.S., at 166, 100 S.Ct., at 976 (STEVENS, J., concurring in part and dissenting in part). No such claim is made in this case. Indeed, Tax Analysts does not dispute the Court of Appeals' conclusion that the Department could satisfy its duty of disclosure simply by making the relevant district court opinions available for copying in the public reference facility that it maintains. See 269 U.S.App.D.C., at 321–322, and n. 15, 845 F.2d, at 1066–1067, and n. 15.

closed, publicly available materials. "*A fortiori,* a judicial record that is a public document should not be subject to a FOIA request." *Id.,* at 29.

The Department's argument proves too much. The disclosure requirements set out in subsections (a)(1) and (a)(2) are carefully limited to situations in which the requested materials have been previously published or made available by the *agency itself.* It is one thing to say that an agency need not disclose materials that it has previously released; it is quite another to say that an agency need not disclose materials that some other person or group may have previously released. Congress undoubtedly was aware of the redundancies that might exist when requested materials have been previously made available. It chose to deal with that problem by crafting only narrow categories of materials which need not be, in effect, disclosed twice *by the agency.* If Congress had wished to codify an exemption for all publicly available materials, it knew perfectly well how to do so. It is not for us to add or detract from Congress' comprehensive scheme, which already "balances, and protects all interests" implicated by Executive Branch disclosure. *Mink, supra,* 410 U.S., at 80, 93 S.Ct., at 832 quoting S.Rep. 813, 89th Congress, 2nd Sess., 3 (1965).[13]

It is not surprising, moreover, that Congress declined to exempt all publicly available materials from the FOIA's disclosure requirements. In the first place, such an exemption would engender intractable fights over precisely what constitutes public availability, unless the term were defined with precision. In some sense, nearly all of the information that comes within an agency's control can be characterized as publicly available. Although the form in which this material comes to an agency—*i.e.,* a report or testimony—may not be generally available, the information included in that report or testimony may very well be. Even if there were some agreement over what constitutes publicly available materials, Congress surely did not envision agencies satisfying their disclosure obligations under the FOIA simply by handing requesters a map and sending them on scavenger expeditions throughout the Nation. Without some express indication in the Act's text or legislative history that Congress intended such a result, we decline to adopt this reading of the statute.

The Department's next argument rests on the fact that the disclosure of district court decisions is partially governed by other statutes, in particular 28 U.S.C. § 1914, and by rules set by the Judicial Conference of the United States. The FOIA does not compel disclosure of district court decisions, the Department contends, because these other provi-

---

13. The obligations imposed under subsections (a)(1) and (a)(2) are not properly viewed as additions to the disclosure exemptions set out in subsection (b). If an agency refuses to disclose agency records that indisputably fall within one of the subsection (b) exemptions, the agency has "withheld" the records, albeit not "improperly" given the legislative authorization to do so. By contrast, once an agency has complied with the (a)(1) and (a)(2) obligations, it can no longer be charged with "withholding" the relevant records.

sions are "more precisely drawn to govern the provision of court records to the general public." Brief for Petitioners 30. We disagree. As with the Department's first argument, this theory requires us to read into the FOIA a disclosure exemption that Congress did not itself provide. This we decline to do. That Congress knew that other statutes created overlapping disclosure requirements is evident from § 552(b)(3), which authorizes an agency to refuse a FOIA request when the materials sought are expressly exempted from disclosure by another statute. If Congress had intended to enact the converse proposition—that an agency may refuse to provide disclosure of materials whose disclosure is *mandated* by another statute—it was free to do so. Congress, however, did not take such a step.[14]

The Department's last argument is derived from *GTE Sylvania*, where we held that agency records sought from the Consumer Products Safety Commission were not "improperly" withheld even though the records did not fall within one of subsection (b)'s enumerated exemptions. The Commission had not released the records in question because a district court, in the course of an unrelated lawsuit, had enjoined the Commission from doing so. In these circumstances, we held, "[t]he concerns underlying the Freedom of Information Act [were] inapplicable, for the agency * * * made no effort to avoid disclosure." 445 U.S., at 386, 100 S.Ct., at 1201. We therefore approved the Commission's compliance with the injunction, noting that when Congress passed the FOIA, it had not "intended to require an agency to commit contempt of court in order to release documents. Indeed, Congress viewed the federal courts as the necessary protectors of the public's right to know." *Id.*, at 387, 100 S.Ct., at 1202.

Although the Department is correct in asserting that *GTE Sylvania* represents a departure from the FOIA's self-contained exemption scheme, this departure was a slight one at best, and was necessary in order to serve a critical goal independent of the FOIA—the enforcement of a court order. As we emphasized, *GTE Sylvania* arose in "a distinctly different context" than the typical FOIA case, *id.*, at 386, 100 S.Ct., at 1201, where the agency decides for itself whether to comply with a request for agency records. In such a case, the agency cannot contend that that it has "no discretion * * * to exercise." *Ibid.*

The present dispute is clearly akin to those typical FOIA cases. No claim has been made that the Department was powerless to comply with Tax Analysts' requests. On the contrary, it was the Department's decision, and the Department's decision alone, not to make the court decisions available. We reject the Department's suggestion that *GTE Sylvania* invites courts in every case to engage in balancing, based on public availability and other factors, to determine whether there has been an unjustified denial of information. The FOIA invests courts neither with the authority nor the tools to make such determinations.

---

14. It is unclear, moreover, whether 28 U.S.C. § 1914 permits a private cause of action to compel disclosure of a court decision.

III

For the reasons stated, the Department improperly withheld agency records when it refused Tax Analysts' requests for copies of the district court tax decisions in its files.[15] Accordingly, the judgment of the Court of Appeals is

Affirmed.

JUSTICE WHITE concurs in the judgment.

JUSTICE BLACKMUN, dissenting.

The Court in this case has examined once again the Freedom of Information Act (FOIA), 5 U.S.C. § 552. It now determines that under the Act the Department of Justice on request must make available copies of federal district court orders and opinions it receives in the course of its litigation of tax cases on behalf of the Federal Government. The majority holds that these qualify as agency records, within the meaning of § 552(a)(4)(B), and that they were improperly withheld by the Department when respondent asked for their production. The Court's analysis, I suppose, could be regarded as a fairly routine one.

I do not join the Court's opinion, however, because it seems to me that the language of the statute is not that clear or conclusive on the issue and, more important, because the result the Court reaches cannot be one that was within the intent of Congress when the FOIA was enacted.

Respondent Tax Analysts, although apparently a nonprofit organization for federal income tax purposes, is in business and in that sense is a commercial enterprise. It sells summaries of these opinions and supplies full texts to major electronic databases. The result of its now-successful effort in this litigation is to impose the cost of obtaining the court orders and opinions upon the Government and thus upon taxpayers generally. There is no question that this material is available elsewhere. But it is quicker and more convenient, and less "frustrating," see *ante,* at 2845, for respondent to have the Department do the work and search its files and produce the items than it is to apply to the respective court clerks.

This, I feel, is almost a gross misuse of the FOIA. What respondent demands, and what the Court permits, adds nothing whatsoever to public knowledge of government operations. That, I had thought, and the majority acknowledges, see *ante,* at 2846, was the real purpose of the FOIA and the spirit in which the statute has been interpreted thus far. See, *e.g., Forsham v. Harris,* 445 U.S. 169, 178, 100 S.Ct. 977, 983, 63 L.Ed.2d 293 (1980); *NLRB v. Robbins Tire & Rubber Co.,* 437 U.S. 214, 242–243, 98 S.Ct. 2311, 2326–2327, 57 L.Ed.2d 159 (1978). I also

---

15. On appeal, Tax Analysts limited its requests to the approximately 25% of the district court decisions that it was unable to procure from court clerks or other sources. See 269 U.S.App.D.C., at 318, n. 5, 845 F.2d, at 1063, n. 5; Brief for Respondent 8, n. 7. The Court of Appeals' remand thus was limited to these decisions, as is our affirmance. However, the reasoning we have employed applies equally to all of the district court decisions initially sought by Tax Analysts.

sense, I believe not unwarrantedly, a distinct lack of enthusiasm on the part of the majority for the result it reaches in this case.

If, as I surmise, the Court's decision today is outside the intent of Congress in enacting the statute, Congress perhaps will rectify the decision forthwith and will give everyone concerned needed guidelines for the administration and interpretation of this somewhat opaque statute.

B. THE PRIVACY ACT OF 1974

The Privacy Act of 1974, codified at 5 U.S.C.A. § 552a (1976), provides individuals with a right of access to agency records concerning them. The Privacy Act also contains various restrictions on the collection and dissemination of personal information by federal agencies. It is important to note, however, that the Act's provisions apply only to information compiled concerning *individuals,* and not information relating to corporations or other artificial entities. 5 U.S.C.A. § 552a(a)(2).

The Privacy Act protects individuals against the unauthorized disclosure of personal information by administrative agencies. The Act forbids the disclosure of personal records by an agency unless the agency has obtained the prior consent of the individual to whom the records relate. 5 U.S.C.A. § 552a(b). The Act's general proscription against unauthorized disclosures is subject to several exceptions that are of interest to the tax practitioner. Agency records may be disclosed, upon request, to federal, state and local law enforcement authorities without the prior consent of the individual whose records are at issue. 5 U.S.C.A. § 552a(b)(7). Personal information may also be disclosed without prior consent pursuant to a court order. 5 U.S.C.A. § 552a(b)(11). Disclosure is also permitted for routine agency uses, provided that notice of such uses has been furnished by publication in the Federal Register. 5 U.S.C.A. § 552a(a)(7).[t] An example of a routine agency use is when the IRS discloses information pursuant to its policy of providing notice to interested parties of the Service's referral of cases to the Justice Department for criminal prosecution.[u]

Agency records which are subject to mandatory disclosure under the FOIA are also exempted from the Privacy Act's consent requirement. 5 U.S.C.A. § 552a(b)(2). Material which is not subject to mandatory disclosure under the FOIA, but which the agency nevertheless chooses to disclose, would appear to implicate the consent requirements of § 552a(b).[v] The difficulty in determining when FOIA disclosures are mandatory as opposed to permissive, combined with the potential liability of agency officials for improper disclosure, is likely to inhibit

---

t. See Ryan v. Department of Justice, 595 F.2d 954 (4th Cir.1979).

u. Harper v. United States, 423 F.Supp. 192 (D.S.C.1976).

v. See Providence Journal Co. v. IRS, 460 F.Supp. 762, 767–768 (D.R.I.1978), reversed on other grounds, 602 F.2d 1010 (1st Cir.1979), cert. denied, 444 U.S. 1071, 100 S.Ct. 1015, 62 L.Ed.2d 752 (1980).

agency officials from exercising their discretionary authority to disclose material exempted from the mandatory disclosure requirements of the FOIA.

An individual's rights under the Privacy Act are enforceable in the district courts in proceedings closely resembling FOIA suits. After exhausting one's administrative remedies, an individual seeking access to agency records concerning him, or seeking damages for unauthorized disclosure of private information, may apply to the district court for relief. 5 U.S.C.A. § 552a(g).[w]

C. THE CONFIDENTIALITY PROVISIONS OF THE INTERNAL REVENUE CODE

In response to the strongly felt need to protect the confidentiality of tax returns and tax return information, Congress enacted §§ 1201(a) and 1202(a) of the Tax Reform Act of 1976, extensively amending section 6103 of the Code and adding a new section 6110. The amendments to § 6103 created a comprehensive regulatory scheme for the release of tax returns and "tax return information." Section 6110 created a separate category of records (written determinations and background file documents relating to such written determinations), and established a special set of rules for disclosure of such records. Section 6110 has been held to provide the exclusive means of public access to records falling within the definition of "written determination" or "background file document", ruling out resort to the regular FOIA procedures.[x]

Section 6103 establishes the general rule that tax returns and tax return information shall be confidential. The section then goes on to identify those requesting parties to whom tax return information may be released, including particular government officials, presidential designees, taxpayers or their representatives, and others with a material interest. The statute also vests in the Secretary of the Treasury the discretion to withhold information from the taxpayer whose records are at issue, where the Secretary determines that such disclosure "would seriously impair Federal tax administration". IRC § 6103(c) and (e)(7).

In contrast to the general obligation of secrecy imposed by § 6103, section 6110 provides that all written determinations, including rulings, determination letters, technical advice memoranda, and background file documents relating thereto, shall be made available to the public. In the case of rulings, determination letters and technical advice memoranda, disclosure is an automatic procedure. Background file documents, however, are disclosed only upon a written request.[y] The

---

w. Johnson v. Department of Treasury, 700 F.2d 971 (5th Cir.1983).

x. Fruehauf Corp. v. IRS, 566 F.2d 574 (6th Cir.1977) (Fruehauf II).

y. I.R.C. § 6110(f)(4) vests the Tax Court and the District Court for the District of Columbia with jurisdiction to entertain suits to compel the disclosure of written determinations and background file

routine disclosure of written determinations generally occurs within 75 to 90 days after their issuance. The statute allows for the postponement of disclosure when the transaction which is the subject of the determination has not yet been completed. IRC § 6110(g)(3) and (4).

Several mechanisms are provided by § 6110 to protect the privacy interests of taxpayers who apply to the IRS for written determinations. Most significantly, the statute requires the IRS to delete identifying details from written determinations prior to their disclosure. IRC § 6110(c). To facilitate this process, the Service has promulgated regulations which require taxpayers who make requests for written determinations to provide the IRS with redacted versions of their requests.[z] Section 6110 also requires the Service to notify any persons to whom a written determination pertains of its intention to disclose. Should disputes arise regarding the proper scope of the Service's proposed deletions, any person to whom the determination pertains may apply to the Tax Court for relief after exhausting his administrative remedies. IRC § 6110(f)(3). In situations where the Service fails to make deletions required by law, or to follow the statutorily prescribed procedure, an injured party may vindicate his rights in the Claims Court, where he is entitled to actual damages (not less than $1,000) and attorney's fees.[a]

CALDER v. IRS

United States Court of Appeals, Fifth Circuit, 1989.
890 F.2d 781.

JOHNSON, CIRCUIT JUDGE:

While researching the development of federal crime control policies, University of Texas at San Antonio Professor James Calder requested certain documents from the Internal Revenue Service (hereinafter IRS) pertaining to tax investigations of Al Capone. The IRS, determining that the request sought nondisclosable "return information," denied Calder's request. 26 U.S.C. § 6103.[1]

documents (or portions thereof). The procedure is analogous to an FOIA action, except that § 6110(f)(4)(B) allows intervention by any person to whom the determination or background file document at issue pertains. The right to intervene is very important, since these documents are often extremely valuable for planning purposes, and may contain copies of the contracts and other papers which are the subject of the written determination as well as trade secrets and other confidential financial information.

z. See, e.g., Rev.Proc. 87–1, 1987–1 C.B. 509, § 8.09.

a. I.R.C. § 6110(i).

1. This section, effective January 1, 1977, provides that the term "return information" includes

a taxpayer's identity, the nature, source, or amount of his income, payments, receipts, deductions, exemptions, credits, assets, liabilities, net worth, tax liability, tax withheld, deficiencies, overassessments, or tax payments, whether the taxpayer's return was, is being, or will be examined or subject to other investigation or processing, or any other data, received by, recorded by, prepared by, furnished to, or collected by the Secretary with respect to a return or with respect to the determination of the existence, or possible existence, of liability (or the amount thereof) of any person under this title for any tax, penalty, interest,

Calder, after exhausting his administrative remedies, brought suit under the Freedom of Information Act (FOIA) and the first and fifth amendments to the Constitution. Calder later dropped the FOIA claim and proceeded solely on the constitutional issues. Specifically, Calder argued that the IRS's denial of access to the materials violated his asserted constitutional right of access to government information as well as his fifth amendment right to equal protection under the laws. The equal protection claim was based on the pre–1977 access to the files granted several individuals.

The district court granted the IRS's motion for summary judgment on the ground that Calder has no constitutional or statutory right of access to Capone's IRS records. Calder has timely appealed the judgment to this Court. We affirm.

Discussion

In his brief to this Court, Calder argues that the first amendment creates a right of access to records in the hands of an administrative agency which have historically been available for public perusal.[2] Calder argues that section 6103 is unconstitutional as applied to him because it limits this alleged right of access to information held by an administrative agency, specifically, the records of Al Capone. Calder bases this argument on *Richmond Newspapers, Inc. v. Virginia,* 448 U.S. 555, 100 S.Ct. 2814, 65 L.Ed.2d 973 (1980), and its progeny.[3]

Calder acknowledges that the cases in the *Richmond* line establish and define the scope of the first amendment right of access to criminal trials and certain criminal proceedings. *See, e.g., Gannett Co., Inc. v. De Pasquale,* 443 U.S. 368, 99 S.Ct. 2898, 61 L.Ed.2d 608 (1979) (pretrial suppression hearing); *Richmond, supra* (criminal trial); *Globe, supra* (criminal trial involving sex offenses and minors); *Press–Enterprise I* and *Press–Enterprise II, supra* (transcripts of preliminary hearings). Calder acknowledges that the Supreme Court has not specifically addressed the question of a right of access to records which are in the hands of an administrative agency. Calder urges this Court to conclude that the reasoning behind the *Richmond* line mandates the conclusion that the right of access is not limited to criminal proceedings, but extends to other governmentally held information. We decline to do so, and hold that Calder has not established the existence of a constitution-

---

fine, forfeiture, or other imposition, or offense * * *.

Section 6103(b)(2)(A).

Prior to the 1977 effective date of this section, the information on Capone was made available on several occasions. Several researchers took advantage of this availability and gained access to the records; these researchers then incorporated the information in books and other documents. Interestingly, the IRS promoted access to these records during the fiftieth anniversary of its Intelligence Division.

2. Calder has not briefed his fifth amendment argument, and we do not address that issue. *See Morrison v. City of Baton Rouge,* 761 F.2d 242, 244 (5th Cir. 1985).

3. *Globe Newspaper Co. v. Superior Court,* 457 U.S. 596, 102 S.Ct. 2613, 73 L.Ed.2d 248 (1982); *Press–Enterprise Co. v. Superior Court,* 464 U.S. 501, 104 S.Ct. 819, 78 L.Ed.2d 629 (1984) (*Press–Enterprise I*); *Press Enterprise Co. v. Superior Court,* 478 U.S. 1, 106 S.Ct. 2735, 92 L.Ed.2d 1 (1986) (*Press–Enterprise II*).

al right of access to the IRS records of Al Capone. The district court did not err in granting summary judgment in favor of the IRS.

In *Richmond*, the Supreme Court held that in the context of criminal trials, the first amendment prohibits the government from summarily closing the courthouse doors which stood open to the public prior to the adoption of the amendment. Chief Justice Burger traced the public character of criminal trials back to the time of the Norman conquest. He pointed out that "a presumption of openness inheres in the very nature of a criminal trial under our system of justice." *Richmond* at 573, 100 S.Ct. at 2825. In *Globe*, the Supreme Court articulated the features of criminal proceedings which implicate the first amendment right of access. Specifically, the Court pointed to the history of openness in criminal proceedings as well as to the significant role that access plays in the functioning of the judicial process. The Court also noted that openness in the context of criminal proceedings acts as a check on the judicial process while providing an appearance of fairness and providing therapeutic value to the community. It is questionable whether these reasons apply in other contexts.

Although the dicta in *Richmond* does indicate that the first amendment "prohibit[s] government from limiting the stock of information from which members of the public may draw.", *id.* at 576, 100 S.Ct. at 2827, Justice O'Connor has indicated that she "interpret[s] neither *Richmond Newspapers* nor the Court's decision [in *Globe*] to carry any implications outside the context of criminal trials." *Globe* at 611, 102 S.Ct. at 2622 (O'Connor, J., concurring). In fact, no Supreme Court case has applied the two-tier analysis which looks for a history of openness and examines the significant role access plays in the judicial process to areas other than criminal proceedings.

In *Capital Cities Media, Inc. v. Chester*, 797 F.2d 1164 (3d Cir.1986), a newspaper challenged, on first amendment grounds, its denial of access to records of a state agency. The Third Circuit, citing *Houchins v. KQED, Inc.*, 438 U.S. 1, 98 S.Ct. 2588, 57 L.Ed.2d 553 (1978), stated that such access was a matter for legislative determination and noted the complete absence of guidelines for the judiciary. Justice Stewart, quoted by the Court in *Houchins*, has noted that

> There is no constitutional right to have access to particular government information, or to require openness from the bureaucracy ... The public's interest in knowing about its government is protected by the guarantee of a Free Press, but the protection is indirect. The Constitution itself is neither a Freedom of Information Act nor an Official Secrets Act.

Id. at 14, 98 S.Ct. at 2596 (quoting Justice Stewart, "Or of the Press," 26 Hastings L.J. 631, 636 (1975)). Quite simply, the right to speak and publish does not carry with it an unrestricted license to gather information. *See Zemel v. Rusk*, 381 U.S. 1, 85 S.Ct. 1271, 14 L.Ed.2d 179 (1965).

Section 6103 creates the type of comprehensive legislative scheme discussed by the courts in *Houchins* and *Capital Media*. The determination of who should have access to particular government held information and what constitutes a legitimate use of such information is "clearly a legislative task which the Constitution has left to the political processes." *Houchins* at 12, 98 S.Ct. at 2595. The pre–1977 access to the files does not change this determination.

Even assuming that the two-tier analysis applies to the information and agency involved in the instant case, Calder has failed to demonstrate the requisite history of access. Calder points to persons who were allowed access to the specific file of Al Capone. This focus is much too narrow. The historic practice referred to in *Richmond* and its progeny "looked not to the practice of the specific public institution involved, but rather to whether the particular type of government proceeding had historically been open in our free society." *Capital Media* at 1175.

Calder cites to eight individuals who were allowed access to Capone's records prior to 1977. The record does not indicate, however, that these records were available for casual scrutiny, or that the access allowed those eight individuals was unlimited. In fact, the type of IRS records at issue was not routinely available even prior to 1977. The legislative history of section 6103 indicates that Congress was concerned about interagency availability of such records; there is little mention of availability to individuals, presumably because such a practice was rare and sporadic. Such inconsistent government practice does not satisfy the "historical openness" prong of the *Richmond* analysis. The district court correctly concluded that Calder failed to demonstrate that there was a history of access to the files.

CONCLUSION

Calder has failed to demonstrate that he has been denied a constitutional right of access to the IRS records of Al Capone. The district court did not err in granting summary judgment in favor of the IRS. Consequently, we affirm.

Affirmed.

BARRETT v. UNITED STATES
United States Court of Appeals, Fifth Circuit, 1986.
795 F.2d 446.

E. GRADY JOLLY, CIRCUIT JUDGE:

Dr. Barrett seeks damages against the United States under 26 U.S.C. § 7431 for unlawful disclosures of tax return information during a civil and criminal investigation. The Internal Revenue Service mailed letters to Dr. Barrett's patients that were designed to determine whether cash payments had been made to him. Dr. Barrett argues that the letters were unnecessary to the IRS's investigation, and therefore improperly disclosed the fact that he was under investigation, in violation of 26 U.S.C. §§ 7431, 6103.

* * *

* * * The IRS began auditing Dr. Barrett's tax returns on July 27, 1979. It is still investigating him. The investigation began as a civil audit, but was later transferred to the criminal investigation division.

* * *

The IRS sent summonses to Dr. Barrett and all the hospitals in which he practiced. The hospital summonses were designed to obtain the names of Dr. Barrett's patients, so that the IRS could compare the patients' payment information with Dr. Barrett's to determine whether he was failing to report cash payments of fees he received.

Some of the hospitals cooperated voluntarily, and provided the names. Others resisted, and the IRS filed the petition in [United States v.] Texas Heart [Institute, 755 F.2d 469 (5th Cir.1985)] to enforce the summons. * * *

* * *

In the meantime, in March 1983, the IRS, through Agent Hanson, sent letters to between 350 and 400 of Barrett's patients whose names were obtained from the cooperative hospitals. Hanson did not use standard IRS letter forms. Instead, he sent specially prepared letters that informed each patient that Dr. Barrett was under investigation by the Criminal Investigation Division of the IRS, stated the years under investigation, and requested documents concerning the patients' payments to Dr. Barrett and insurance claim information. Only eighty-one patients responded to the letters. At the time the letters were sent, the IRS had free access to Dr. Barrett's bank records, which contained much of the same information.

In November 1983, Dr. Barrett filed an action for damages under 26 U.S.C. § 7431 against the United States and the IRS. The district court held that, although the disclosures in the letters undoubtedly constituted return information, the IRS was authorized to disclose this information because of its strong interest in choosing the source of information it sought, and because the bank records were not a source of information "otherwise reasonably available" pursuant to section 6103(k)(6). Dr. Barrett appeals.

* * *

The primary issue we face on appeal is whether the disclosures in the letters to Dr. Barrett's patients were necessary to obtain information that was not otherwise reasonably available, and in particular, whether summary judgment should have been granted on this issue.

* * *

Section 6103(a) states the general rule that returns and return information shall be confidential, and section 6103(b) defines the terms "return" and "return information" broadly, to include, *inter alia,* the taxpayer's identity, the nature, source and amount of his income, and whether his return is, was or may be subject to examination or other investigation. Section 6103(k)(6) provides an exception to the general rule of confidentiality permitting disclosures in limited circumstances: the disclosure must be "necessary" to obtain the information the IRS seeks, and the information must not be "otherwise reasonably available."[2] Section 6103(k)(6) also allows the Secretary of the Treasury to limit the situations and conditions under which disclosures can be made.[3]

The district court found as a fact that Hanson disclosed return information. The district court found, however, that the disclosures fell within the exception provided by section 6103(k)(6), because the information Hanson sought was "not otherwise reasonably available."

We turn then to consider whether the disclosures were necessary, and whether the information sought was otherwise reasonably available. In the case before us, these two questions are interdependent, and we therefore consider them together. * * *

Dr. Barrett provided an affidavit from a former IRS agent who stated that it was not standard IRS procedure to contact first the customers of a service business, such as a medical practice, when attempting to locate unreported income. Instead, the former agent stated that the first step was usually to obtain copies of all deposit items, and that this procedure eliminated the necessity of contacting the customers in most instances. Dr. Barrett also presented an affidavit from the vice president of a bank, which stated that all deposit information concerning Dr. Barrett's account, including 900 to 1,000 patient checks per year for a five-year period, was at all times available to the IRS agent. * * *

---

2. Section 6103(k)(6) provides:

An internal revenue officer or employee may, in connection with his official duties relating to any audit, collection activity, or civil or criminal tax investigation or any other offense under the internal revenue laws, disclose return information to the extent that such disclosure is necessary in obtaining information, which is not otherwise reasonably available, with respect to the correct determination of tax, liability for tax, or the amount to be collected or with respect to the enforcement of any other provision of this title. Such disclosures shall be made only in such situations and under such conditions as the Secretary may prescribe by regulation.

3. The IRS has argued that the following regulation, quoted in relevant part, authorized the disclosures in the letters:

In connection with the performance of official duties relating to any * * * civil or criminal investigation, * * * an officer or employee of the Internal Revenue Service * * * is authorized to disclose taxpayer identity information (as defined in section 6103(b)(6)), *the fact that the inquiry pertains to the performance of official duties, and the nature of the official duties* in order to obtain necessary information relating to performance of such official duties. * * * (Emphasis added.)

Treas.Reg. § 301.6103(k)(6)-1(a). This regulation obviously does not create additional exceptions that are not provided in the statute or issue authorizations that conflict with the statute. Thus, the regulation can only be interpreted to authorize disclosures that are "necessary" to obtain information "not otherwise reasonably available" in a given case.

These affidavits, if accepted as true, create a genuine issue of material fact as to whether it was necessary for Hanson to disclose return information to each, or any, of Dr. Barrett's patients; some disclosures, perhaps all, might have been avoided by reviewing and analyzing the bank records. On the other hand, this possibility may not prove true; we do not know. Whether it is true or untrue is a factual dispute making the grant of summary judgment inappropriate.

Hanson's affidavit, which denies that the information he sought could have been obtained from bank records, only contradicts, in conclusory terms, the former agent's affidavit, and does not eliminate the material issue of fact raised. Indeed, Hanson's affidavit itself may be read to say that some of these disclosures might have been avoided if he had carefully analyzed the bank records: Hanson stated that it was necessary for him to go to the patients, rather than bank records, to determine whether payments were made in cash, because "the basis of the investigation was that payments made in cash by patients were not being deposited by Barrett." To the extent, therefore, that a patient's payments were deposited, they were not unreported cash payments. Thus, if Hanson had examined the patients' checks in the bank records and other deposit information, he might or might not have eliminated disclosures to many of the 350 to 400 patients. Again, a dispute of fact is raised that the district court should properly resolve.

We therefore find it necessary to remand to allow the district court to consider the evidence "otherwise reasonably available," and to consider whether, in the light of the evidence available, it was necessary to send the letters. We note that the letters ask for cancelled checks, insurance information, and receipts for cash payments. Of course, there is no evidence that insurance information would have been available from the bank records. This information might or might not have been reasonably available from another source that would have made unnecessary disclosure to between 350 and 400 persons. * * * Similarly, there is no evidence that proof of cash payments was reasonably available from sources other than the taxpayer. In some instances, however, the disclosures may not have been necessary once all the information available to the IRS was reviewed and analyzed. We leave the resolution of this question to the district court, based on its analysis of the evidence and the arguments of the parties.

Even if, however, the district court should determine that any or all of these three items were not reasonably available from another source, the district court will still have to determine whether it was necessary to disclose the return information contained in the letters to Dr. Barrett's patients to obtain the requested items of information. Although disclosure of the taxpayer's name was clearly necessary if the letter had to be sent at all, a genuine issue of material fact has been raised as to whether disclosure of the return information that the taxpayer was under investigation, particularly criminal investigation, was "necessary." We recognize that this may be a mixed question of law and fact; that is, the district court must interpret section 6103(k)(6) and the relevant IRS regulations in the light of the facts developed. Nevertheless, to the extent that a factual dispute is presented, it will have to be resolved by the district court on remand.

We should make clear that our holding today is not an attempt to provide a set of instructions that the IRS must follow to conduct an investigation. We emphasize that in a section 7431 action the court does *not* inquire whether the information sought is necessary: the questions are whether the *disclosures* are "necessary" to obtain the information sought and whether the information sought is "otherwise reasonably available." Stated differently, in a section 7431 action, we do not question the right, wisdom, or necessity of a particular IRS investigation. We do question, however, the means of investigation, but only to the limited extent consistent with section 7431.

In conclusion, we hold that the evidence presented by Dr. Barrett creates a genuine issue of material fact whether it was necessary to contact some or all of Dr. Barrett's patients, whether it was necessary to disclose each of the items of return information included in the letter mailed to Dr. Barrett's patients, and whether at least some of the information the IRS sought from the patients was otherwise reasonably available from bank records.[5]

* * *

This case is remanded for proceedings not inconsistent with this opinion.

Reversed and remanded.

MID–SOUTH MUSIC CORP. v. UNITED STATES
United States Court of Appeals, Sixth Circuit, 1987.
818 F.2d 536.

ALAN E. NORRIS, CIRCUIT JUDGE.

Defendant, the United States, appeals from a judgment rendered against it by the district court for $174,000 in compensatory damages, and $1,000 in punitive damages, as the result of its having found, after a trial to the court, that employees of the Internal Revenue Service (IRS) had made unauthorized disclosures of information from plaintiff's 1981 income tax return, in violation of 26 U.S.C. § 6103.

This litigation has been the subject of two previously published opinions. In *Mid–South Music Corp. v. United States Dep't of the Treasury,* 579 F.Supp. 481 (M.D.Tenn.1983), the district court sustained defendant's Fed.R.Civ.P. 12(b)(6) motion to dismiss plaintiff's complaint for failure to state a claim upon which relief could be granted. In going beyond the face of the complaint, the district court examined a "prefiling letter" sent by IRS to persons who had invested in plaintiff's tax

---

5. Since the district court did not reach the issue of a possible good-faith interpretation of section 6103, we leave that issue to the district court on remand. *See Huckaby v. United States,* [794 F.2d 1041 (5th Cir.1986)].

shelter, advising them that, if they claimed a deduction on their income tax returns, the deduction would be disallowed. That letter follows:

Re: Tax Shelter Promotion: Mid–South Music Corporation

Dear Taxpayer:

Our information indicates that you invested in the above-named tax shelter in 1982. Based upon our review of that promotion, the indications are that the purported tax deductions are not allowable.

If you claim such deductions on your income tax return, your return will be examined and the deductions disallowed. With respect to the tax shelter deductions, you may be subjecting yourself to a negligence penalty under Section 6653(a) and/or the overvaluation penalty under Section 6659 of the Internal Revenue Code.

Sincerely,
/s/
Alvin H. Kolak
District Director

In relevant part, 26 U.S.C. § 6103 provides:

(a) **General Rule.**—Returns and return information shall be confidential, and except as authorized by this title—

(1) no officer or employee of the United States

* * *

shall disclose any return or return information obtained by him * * *.

(b) **Definitions.**—For purposes of this section—

* * *

(2) **Return information.**—The term "return information" means—

(A) a taxpayer's identity, the nature, source, or amount of his income, payments, receipts, deductions, exemptions, credits, assets, liabilities, net worth, tax liability, tax withheld, deficiencies, overassessments, or tax payments, whether the taxpayer's return was, is being, or will be examined or subject to other investigation or processing, or any other data, received by, recorded by, prepared by, furnished to, or collected by the Secretary with respect to a return or with respect to the determination of the existence, or possible existence, of liability (or the amount thereof) of any person under this title for any tax, penalty, interest, fine, forfeiture, or other imposition, or offense * * *.

In referring to the letter, the district court concluded:

Here, the letter did not disclose whether *the plaintiff's* return " * * * was, is being, or will be examined or subject to other investigation or processing. * * * " Instead, the letter disclosed that, if the third-party recipients of the letter claimed the questioned deductions on *their* tax-returns, *their tax-returns*—not that of the plaintiff—would be examined. This Court is simply unpersuaded by the argument of

Mid–South that this letter disclosed that its own return was, is being, or will be examined; the letter made no allusion whatever to the plaintiff's tax-return.

Neither does the Court believe that the letter disclosed improperly " * * * a taxpayer's identity * * *." The letter stated the name of the plaintiff, however; it referred to Mid–South in its status as a business entity which had promoted the venture in which the addresses of the subject-letter had invested. The letter did not identify Mid–South in its capacity as a taxpayer, rather as a business establishment. That Mid–South was a taxpayer also was but coincidental.

Here, the disclosure of the plaintiff's name merely specified the venture with which the affected taxpayers had transacted business and particularized to them the particular deductions with which the IRS was concerned; there is no suggestion that the name of the plaintiff was derived by IRS from its tax return.

579 F.Supp. at 485.

On appeal, we reversed on the basis that plaintiff's complaint had stated a colorable claim, and that dismissal in response to a Fed. R.Civ.P. 12(b)(6) motion was premature. Indeed, this conclusion was inescapable when we considered plaintiff's allegation that "[t]he actions of the individual Defendants, as officers and employees of the United States, knowingly, or by reason of negligence, disclosed return information with respect to the Plaintiff in violation of Section 6103 of the Internal Revenue Code of 1954 (26 U.S.C.A.)."

We therefore remanded the case to the trial court for consideration of plaintiff's claim and the defenses raised by defendant. *Mid–South Music Corp. v. Kolak,* 756 F.2d 23 (6th Cir.1984).

At the trial of plaintiff's cause, upon remand, plaintiff relied solely upon the letter quoted above, as its evidence to support the allegation that it had been the victim of unlawful disclosure.

This time the trial court concluded that the letter did amount to an unlawful disclosure of return information, and explained its about-face in this manner:

13. In commenting upon the language of the foregoing letter in its memorandum opinion and order of November 2, 1983 herein, this Court noted *inter alia:* "there is no suggestion that the name of the plaintiff [Mid–South] was derived by the IRS from its tax return"; in addition, Mid–South was not claiming at that time that there was bad faith on the part of personnel of the IRS. Subsequent evidence reflected that Mr. Weissand had indeed obtained information concerning the tax shelter implicated from the 1981 income-tax return of Mid–South in the process of his examination thereof, and that personnel of the IRS acted in bad faith in sending such letter for the intended purpose of destroying the tax-shelter promotion of Mid–South before its abusiveness was established as a matter of law.

14. Exhibit no. 1 (the above letter) disclosed "knowingly" that Mid-South's tax return for 1981 "was * * * examined" by IRS,[1] and that Mid-South's promotion was "subject to other investigation or proceeding." As is obvious, that personnel of the IRS could have altered the receiving taxpayers of their forebodings without revealing the name of the taxpayer, Mid-South, proves that the unlawful disclosures were "willfull" and made with the bad-faith intention to put Mid-South's promotion "out of business."

Once it became clear, upon remand, that the only evidence of disclosure relied upon by plaintiff was the letter, the focus of the issue presented to the trial court was whether the letter amounted to an improper disclosure of plaintiff's return information, as contemplated by 26 U.S.C. § 6103. If it did not, then concerns about motive and attitude, while perhaps relevant to damages, were irrelevant to the issue of liability. When the letter is parsed, one is led to the inescapable conclusion that the district court had correctly characterized its contents, when it earlier went beyond the complaint to examine it in the course of deciding the Fed.R.Civ.P. 12(b)(6) motion. The letter identifies plaintiff as a promoter of tax shelters, and advises investors that IRS has reviewed plaintiff's promotion of tax shelters and will disallow deductions taken in reliance upon plaintiff's tax shelter promotion. There is no indication that plaintiff's tax returns were being examined or subjected to investigation. *See In re Grand Jury Investigation,* 688 F.2d 1068, 1071 (6th Cir.1982).

The letter is not subject to the criticism that it is simply a cleverly worded attempt to evade the "spirit" of the disclosure prohibition. Under the circumstances of this case, we are hard-pressed to discern the evil to be guarded against by resorting to Section 6103. We are unable to divine a public policy undergirding the statute which would prevent the IRS from advising a taxpayer-investor, in advance of his filing of his income tax return, that a deduction will be disallowed, as opposed to advising him of the disallowance after he has filed his return and claimed the deduction. Nor is Section 6103(a) the proper remedy available to a tax shelter promoter who complains that the IRS, prior to any formal proceedings declaring its shelter abusive, disallows deductions claimed by taxpayers who invest in its shelter.

Section 6103 contemplates that the IRS be able to disclose to taxpayers information with respect to their own returns. *See* 26 U.S.C. §§ 6103(e)(1) and (7). In essence, that is precisely what occurred here.

The judgment of the district court is reversed, and this cause is remanded to the district court with instructions to enter judgment for defendant.

MERRITT, CIRCUIT JUDGE, concurring in the judgment.

---

1. Such return could hardly have been the subject of a "review" by IRS without its having been examined, and "indications" that the tax shelter provided for disallowable deductions implied that "other investigation or proceeding" would ensue in the wake of those "indications."

Although I disagree with the reasoning of the court in this case, I agree with the result it reaches. Accordingly, I write separately to explain the narrow basis on which I would uphold the prefiling notification program at issue in this case.

The information disclosed by the IRS to Mid–South's individual investors was plainly the "return information" of Mid–South as that term is used in 26 U.S.C. § 6103(b)(3) (1982). In *In re Grand Jury Investigation,* 688 F.2d 1068 (6th Cir.), *reh. denied,* 696 F.2d 449 (1982), we held that "[a] taxpayer's name and the fact that he is, or will be subject to an investigation regarding Title 26 obligation, does constitute return information." 688 F.2d at 1071. The letter at issue in this case identified Mid–South as a taxpayer and the fact that Mid–South was under investigation by the IRS. This clearly falls within the definition of tax return information given in *In re Grand Jury Investigation, id.* The IRS is thus subject to liability for this disclosure unless it falls within one of the statutory exceptions which permit disclosure in certain limited circumstances.

Section 6103 permits the IRS to disclose the tax return information of a taxpayer to the taxpayer himself unless such disclosure would seriously impair federal tax administration. 26 U.S.C. §§ 6103(e)(1)(A)(i), (e)(7) (1982). Thus, if the information contained in the prefiling notification letter is deemed to be the "return information" of the investors to whom the letters were sent, the disclosure is proper.

The definition of return information in § 6103 includes, among other things, all data collected by the IRS with respect to the tax liability of an individual. 26 U.S.C. § 6103(b)(2) (1982). The information revealed by the IRS to the Mid–South investors-lessees in the prefiling notification letter was compiled from the "pass through documents" that Mid–South was to file with its tax return. The pass through document is a form whereby parties to a lease elect to permit the investment tax credit to be passed from the lessor to the lessee, and a copy of the form must be filed with the lessor's and the lessee's income tax return. As such, the pass through documents contained data collected by the IRS concerning the tax liability of *both* Mid–South and the individual lessees. Consequently, the information contained in the pass through documents, and compiled into the prefiling notification letters, is the "return information" of both Mid–South and the lessees as that term is defined by § 6103(b)(2).

The prefiling notification letters were only sent to the lessees themselves. The letter contained the "return information" of the lessees. Therefore, as the letters merely disclosed the "return information" of the lessees *to the lessees,* disclosure was permissible under § 6103. 26 U.S.C. §§ 6103(e)(1)(A)(i), (e)(7) (1982). This is the only basis on which I concur in the result reached by the court.

WELLFORD, CIRCUIT JUDGE, concurring.

I concur in the decision of Judge Norris, and would add an additional basis for reversing the district court.

In *First Western Government Securities, Inc. v. United States*, 796 F.2d 356, 357 (10th Cir.1986) the investors of the abusive tax shelter *were* under investigation by the IRS when they received a revenue agent report containing alleged return information of First Western Government Securities, Inc. The court held 26 U.S.C. § 6103(h)(4)(C) applicable because "the information is directly related to a transactional relationship between the investors and plaintiffs and directly affected the resolution of an issue in the proceeding, that being the disallowance of deductions related to plaintiffs' tax shelters." *Id.* at 360. The court also noted that the "term 'tax administration' is to be interpreted broadly." *Id.* I believe the rationale of *First Western* is applicable in this situation even if the investors in Mid–South may not themselves have been under investigation when they received the prefiling notification letter. Section 6103 "cannot be read to provide a general right of privacy to anyone called upon to submit information to the IRS," particularly under the circumstances of the IRS investigation in this case. *Id.* at 359.

The information here directly relates to a "transactional relationship" between Mid–South Music and the recipients of the letter in question.

I agree that the judgment of the district court must be reversed.

LAMPERT v. UNITED STATES
United States Court of Appeals, Ninth Circuit, 1988.
854 F.2d 335.

SKOPIL, CIRCUIT JUDGE:

We must decide in these consolidated appeals whether press releases by government officials, relating to public judicial proceedings, constitute unauthorized disclosures of "tax return information" in violation of 26 U.S.C. § 6103 (1982) of the Internal Revenue Code. We agree with the district courts that the press releases here do not violate section 6103. We need not reach the government's alternative theory that the "good faith" exception of 26 U.S.C. § 7431 (1982) would nevertheless preclude liability in these cases.

FACTS AND PRIOR PROCEEDINGS

There are no disputed facts in these cases. In *Figur*, the U.S. Attorney's Office issued a press release summarizing tax evasion charges against Figur. The same U.S. Attorney issued two press releases in *Peinado*, one announcing that Peinado pleaded guilty to tax evasion and another when he was sentenced for the crime. In *Lampert*, the government filed an action seeking a permanent injunction against the defendants' promotion and sale of abusive tax shelters. The U.S. Attorney and the Internal Revenue Service issued separate press releases relating the filing of that action and the investigation of the defendants.

In each instance, the taxpayer brought an action alleging that the respective press release was an unauthorized disclosures of "return information" as defined by 26 U.S.C. § 6103. The government responded that (1) a press release based solely on information contained in a public court record is not an unauthorized disclosure; and (2) even if the disclosure was unauthorized, the government acted in good faith, thereby precluding liability.

The government prevailed on motions for summary judgments. In *Figur*, the district court held that a "governmental press release disseminating return information contained in the public record does not violate § 6103." *Figur v. United States*, 662 F.Supp. 515, 518 (N.D.Cal. 1987). Similarly, the court in *Peinado* concluded that "[i]t was not the intent of Congress in enacting § 6103 to penalize the government for issuing a press release repeating information that is already a matter of public record. A press release that simply announces or broadcasts what is already known from court proceedings is not a disclosure as that term is defined in § 6103." *Peinado v. United States*, 669 F.Supp. 953, 954 (N.D.Cal.1987). Finally, the trial judge in *Lampert* stated that a violation had occurred but held that the government was protected by its good faith interpretation of section 6103. *Lampert v. United States*, unpublished opinion, slip op. 5–11 (N.D.Cal. April 8, 1987).

DISCUSSION

Section 6103(a), 26 U.S.C. § 6103(a), of the Internal Revenue Code "lays down a general rule that 'returns' and 'return information' * * * shall be confidential." *Church of Scientology of California v. I.R.S.*, [484] U.S. [9, 10], 108 S.Ct. 271, 272, 98 L.Ed.2d 228 (1987). The statute is designed to protect the flow of information between taxpayers and the Internal Revenue Service by controlling the disclosure of tax information by government employees. *See Stokwitz v. United States*, 831 F.2d 893, 894 (9th Cir.1987), *cert. denied*, [485] U.S. [1033], 108 S.Ct. 1592, 99 L.Ed.2d 907 (1988). The Act creates a private cause of action by taxpayers against the United States and provides for damages. 26 U.S.C. § 7431(c).

There is no dispute here that the press releases disclosed "return information" as defined by section 6103(b). *See, e.g., Barrett v. United States*, 795 F.2d 446, 449 (5th Cir.1986) (statute broadly defines term to include taxpayer's identity, the nature, source or amount of income, and whether there is an investigation). There is also no dispute that 26 U.S.C. § 6103(h)(4)(A) authorizes the disclosure of return information in judicial proceedings involving a taxpayer's civil or criminal tax liability. The government argues that once such information is lawfully disclosed in judicial proceedings, it loses its confidentiality and is no longer subject to the restrictions of section 6103. *See Nixon v. Warner Communications, Inc.*, 435 U.S. 589, 597, 98 S.Ct. 1306, 1311, 55 L.Ed.2d 570 (1978) (court proceedings are public record).

Taxpayers argue, however that section 6103(h)(4)(A) on its face applies only to disclosures *in* judicial proceedings. The disclosures at issue occurred not in court but to the press through the issuance of press releases. The taxpayers therefore contend that while the contested information could lawfully be disclosed in court, the act forecloses further dissemination of even "public record" return information.[1]

In *Rodgers v. Hyatt*, 697 F.2d 899, 904 (10th Cir.1983), the court accepted the taxpayers' position. There an IRS agent disclosed to others certain return information that had been the subject of his testimony in a prior court proceeding. The court held that "[e]ven assuming the loss of confidentiality in the content of the statements * * * the [later] disclosure was clearly unauthorized." *Id.* at 906; *see also Malis v. United States*, 87–1 U.S.T.C. ¶ 9212 (C.D.Cal.1986) [available on WESTLAW, 1986 WL 15721] (citing *Rodgers* for proposition that disclosure of return information that has been made public does not preclude liability for later unauthorized disclosures of the identical return information).

Similarly, *Johnson v. Sawyer*, 640 F.Supp. 1126 (S.D.Tex.1986), supports the taxpayers' argument. There the IRS issued a press release following Johnson's plea of tax evasion. The government argued that there was no violation of section 6103 because Johnson had no reasonable expectation of privacy concerning information already disclosed in the public record of his criminal prosecution. *Id.* at 1132. The court rejected that argument, concluding that "Congress made the language of § 6103 quite clear: any disclosure of return information is illegal 'except as authorized * * *.'" *Id.* The court, citing *Rodgers*, refused to create an additional exception to section 6103. *Id.* at 1133. In so doing, the court recognized that by strictly enforcing section 6103, the government's ability to publicize the prosecution of tax evaders is greatly hampered. *Id.* at 1133 n. 18. Nevertheless, "[i]f that result is poor public policy, it is for Congress—not the Courts—to amend § 6103 to allow the issuing of such releases." *Id.*

In contrast to *Rodgers* and *Johnson,* several district courts have concluded that once return information is disclosed in court, such information is no longer confidential, the taxpayer loses any privacy interests in that information, and there is no violation of section 6103 for subsequent disclosures. *See Thomas v. United States*, 671 F.Supp. 15, 16 (E.D.Wis.1987) (IRS press release summarizing the results of tax court proceedings is not unlawful disclosure); *United States v. Posner*, 594 F.Supp. 930, 936 (S.D.Fla.1984) (no right of privacy for information that has already been placed in public court file); *Cooper v. I.R.S.*, 450

---

1. The taxpayers also contend that the press releases here contained return information that was not disclosed in the judicial proceedings. *See e.g., Husby v. United States,* 672 F.Supp. 442, 444 (N.D.Cal.1987) (limiting the right of subsequent disclosure to only that information actually disclosed in the judicial proceedings). The district courts here found that the information disclosed in the press releases were restatements of the allegations in the indictments or of the events that took place in open court at trial, plea hearing, or sentencing. Our review of the record convinces us that the courts' findings on this point are not clearly erroneous.

F.Supp. 752, 755 (D.D.C.1977) (tax return information is never again confidential once disclosed by use in a public trial). These courts reason that trial proceedings are public events and "[o]nce tax return information enters the public domain, the taxpayer no longer has any privacy interests in that information." *Thomas,* 671 F.Supp. at 16. Thus if a taxpayer's return information is lawfully disclosed in a judicial proceeding pursuant to section 6103(h)(4)(C), the information is no longer confidential and may be disclosed again without regard to section 6103. *See United Energy Corp. v. United States,* 622 F.Supp. 43, 46 (N.D.Cal.1985) (U.S. Attorney's disclosure to newspaper reporter of information disclosed in court proceeding did not violate section 6103).

We have observed that section 6103 does not create a general prohibition against public disclosure of tax information. *Stokwitz,* 831 F.2d at 896; *but see Wiemerslage v. United States,* 838 F.2d 899, 902 (7th Cir.1988) (describing section 6103 as a "general prohibition against the disclosure of tax return information"). The taxpayers admit that anyone is free to obtain return information from public court records. They acknowledge that court records are public domain and that "[t]hose who see and hear what transpired can report it with impunity." *Craig v. Harney,* 331 U.S. 367, 374, 67 S.Ct. 1249, 1254, 91 L.Ed. 1546 (1947). Nevertheless, they insist that for a government employee to disclose any return information, confidential or not, there must exist an applicable exception to section 6103(a).

Only a strict, technical reading of the statute supports the taxpayers' position. *See Johnson,* 640 F.Supp. at 1132. While generally our duty is to give effect to the literal language of a statute, we are not obligated to do so when reliance on that language would defeat the purposes of the statute. *Brothers v. First Leasing,* 724 F.2d 789, 793 (9th Cir.), *cert. denied,* 469 U.S. 832, 105 S.Ct. 121, 83 L.Ed.2d 63 (1984). We believe that Congress sought to prohibit only the disclosure of confidential tax return information. Once tax return information is made a part of the public domain, the taxpayer may no longer claim a right of privacy in that information. *See Thomas,* 671 F.Supp. at 16; *United Energy,* 622 F.Supp. at 46. We agree when once information is lawfully disclosed in court proceedings, "§ 6103(a)'s directive to keep return information confidential is moot." *Figur,* 662 F.Supp. at 517. Therefore we hold that once return information is lawfully disclosed in a judicial forum, its subsequent disclosure by press release does not violate the Act.

Affirmed.[2]

2. We may affirm *Lampert* on this ground even though Judge Peckham did not reach the issue. *See United States v. Washington,* 641 F.2d 1368, 1371 (9th Cir. 1981) (appellate court may affirm on any basis supported by the record), *cert. denied,* 454 U.S. 1143, 102 S.Ct. 1001, 71 L.Ed.2d 294 (1982); *see also Rueckert v. I.R.S.,* 775 F.2d 208, 212 (7th Cir.1985) (affirming the district court on alternative ground that disclosure at issue did not violate section 6103).

Notes and Questions

1. There is a split of authority over whether Congress intended § 6103 to be the sole standard governing the disclosure of return information or whether the standards applicable to the FOIA apply. The distinction is not without significance because if § 6103 supercedes the FOIA, the IRS' decision may only be reversed if it is arbitrary and capricious. However, if the FOIA applies to requests for disclosure of "return information" there is de novo review of the IRS' decision. Which way should the Supreme Court rule if ultimately presented with this question? Compare Church of Scientology of California v. IRS, 792 F.2d 146 (D.C.Cir.1986) with White v. IRS, 707 F.2d 897 (6th Cir.1983).

2. The *Barrett* case deals with the improper disclosure of return information during an IRS investigation. Can you think of any improper disclosures that could be made during the collection process? See Rorex v. Traynor, 771 F.2d 383 (8th Cir.1985).

Chapter IV

ADMINISTRATIVE DETERMINATION OF LIABILITY FOR TAX

Scope Note: Chapter IV traces the path of a tax dispute from the selection of a return for audit through the administrative appeals. Besides describing agency practice at the examination and appeal stages, and the many related legal issues, this chapter discusses such topics as requests for technical advice, reopening of closed cases by the Service, and the various settlement forms and their effect on subsequent attempts to litigate the correctness of an asserted deficiency. A final section discusses the TEFRA partnership procedures.

SECTION 1. EXAMINATION OF TAX RETURNS

A. SELECTION OF RETURNS FOR EXAMINATION

A tax controversy begins when a tax return is selected for examination or when the absence of a required return is detected by the Internal Revenue Service. If the return is not selected for examination there will be no adjustment to the tax liability reported by the taxpayer. In practical terms, a taxpayer wins the audit lottery when his ticket is not pulled from the barrel. The Service cannot examine every taxpayer's liability; hence, there will always be winners in the audit lottery. However, the IRS tries to ensure that no taxpayer can be certain that he will escape examination. Moreover, the Service can, and does, select returns for examination based upon the probability of finding tax deficiencies and thereby encouraging voluntary compliance.

The IRS does not publicize the standards it employs to select returns for examination, which may vary from year to year and, sometimes, from area to area. In addition, in every selection process some factor of randomness is introduced so that there is at least some chance that any given return will be the subject of an examination. Probably the majority of those returns selected are chosen through the DIF (discriminant function) system. In essence, the IRS computers analyze each return in terms of various formulas [a] designed to detect variations from normal relationships among items on the return and between return information and other data (perhaps including industry standards, specific information items, or prior returns and audit results).

Due in part to budgetary restrictions and allocations, the percentage of returns audited has declined significantly in recent years. Only about 1% of all individual returns were audited in 1988, as compared to a 2% rate for 1978 and a 6% rate in 1965.[b] Although the audit rate for high-income individual returns is more than double (at 2⅓% for 1988) the overall rate for individual returns, it too has decreased dramatically from over 10% in 1978.[c] Audit rates for corporations have also declined in the recent past, from about 8% in 1978 to 1⅓% in 1988.[d] While most very large corporations are audited regularly, the audit rates of small and medium sized corporations have plunged in the recent past.

Returns may be selected for examination by a process of "infection." Thus, the audit of a corporation may trigger the audit of its principal shareholders. The examination of a partnership may result not only in adjustments to the partnership return, but also to those of the individual partners.

An examination may be caused by an inconsistent position being taken by another taxpayer (for example, two taxpayers claiming the same dependents), or perhaps even due to actions taken by the taxpayer which attract attention to the subject return. An audit will often result from the filing of a refund claim, a request for ruling or determination letter, or some other special action requested from the Service. Almost certainly, the discovery of a substantial deficiency on one audit will lead to another.

Examinations can also be triggered by informants seeking bounty or revenge. Ex-spouses and former employees with detailed knowledge of the taxpayer's financial affairs frequently supply leads to the Service, sometimes anonymously. Section 7623 of the Code authorizes the Service to pay a reward or "bounty" to an informant for tax collected as a result of the "tips." Only a small percentage of informants actually receive a reward, however, and the rewards are often minimal. The maximum reward is 10% of the total tax, fines and penalties paid to the government as a result of the tip. Furthermore, no reward is made unless two conditions are met: the informant must have provided

---

a. DIF formulas are revised from time to time, based upon the results of TCMP (Taxpayer Compliance Measurement Program) audits, which are in-depth, random audits of a statistical sample of all classes of taxpayers.

DIF formulas are secret and cannot be obtained pursuant to a request under the Freedom of Information Act. I.R.C. § 6103(b)(2).

b. Dubin, Graetz & Wilde, The Changing Face of Tax Enforcement, 43 Tax Lawyer 893, 896 (1990).

c. *Id.* at 898. "High income" individual returns are those reflecting total positive income (*i.e.*, no offset for deductions) of $50,000 or more.

d. *Id.* at 902.

specific and responsible information that caused the examination and resulted in the recovery, and the information must have led to the collection of taxes that would not ordinarily be collected. The reward program has been very successful for the Service. For example, in 1988 there were 7,853 claims for rewards filed, of which only 8% of the informants received rewards. While total rewards paid in 1986 totalled $1.3 million ($1,600 being the average reward), the amount collected from the informants' leads was over $258 million.

There cannot be a comprehensive list or precise statement of the criteria used for the selection of returns for audit. Moreover, assuming honest reporting, a taxpayer can do little (if anything) to shape his return to avoid an audit selection profile. Should there be less than honest reporting, the taxpayer still must be concerned with the inevitable random selection component of the process.

B. EXAMINATION PROCEDURES

The examination of returns is normally the function of Revenue Agents in the Examination Division of the office of each District Director, although some individual income tax return adjustments are handled entirely by correspondence between the taxpayer and the Examination Division of regional service centers. There are two general types of district office examinations, commonly called "office examinations" (conducted in the IRS office) and "field examinations" (conducted in the field).

The examination is the primary (but not exclusive) issue raising stage of a tax controversy. Should the examination conclude with an agreement as to the taxpayer's liability, the case will be closed with a "no change" letter, an agreed deficiency assessment or even an agreed refund. However, should there be no agreement as to liability, the case will proceed to administrative and judicial procedures for the resolution of tax disputes.

TAXPAYER SAFEGUARDS

The Taxpayer Bill of Rights Act, enacted as part of the Technical and Miscellaneous Revenue Act of 1988, provides significant new procedural safeguards for taxpayers involved in audits and other dealings with the IRS. Section 7521 establishes several new safeguards in connection with taxpayer "interviews," which includes any in-person interview between a taxpayer and an officer or employee of the Service, in connection with the determination or collection of any tax. Excluded from section 7521's reach, however, are criminal investigations, discussed in Chapter IX.

Explanations. Section 7521(b) requires the IRS to furnish a statement to the taxpayer, prior to or at the *initial* interview, describing in detail the audit process and the taxpayer's rights in the process. Although the Service's prior practice involved furnishing IRS publications describing the audit process, Section 7521 now provides a statutory requirement for furnishing an explanation of rights to the taxpayer for any "interview" occurring on or after February 8, 1989.

If a taxpayer clearly states during an interview that she wishes to consult with an attorney or other authorized representative, the IRS agent must suspend the interview, even if the taxpayer already has answered some questions. IRC § 7521(b)(2). This right does not apply to interviews conducted pursuant to an IRS summons.

Taxpayer Not Required To Attend Interview. If the taxpayer is represented by an authorized representative who is not disbarred or suspended from practice before the IRS,[e] and if that representative has an executed power of attorney from the taxpayer,[f] then the taxpayer may elect not to attend the interview and to be represented at the interview by his authorized representative. This right of a taxpayer to forego the interview and send an authorized representative does not apply to interviews pursuant to an IRS summons.

Recording. Taxpayers (or their authorized representatives) may make audio recordings of interviews with IRS personnel if they request to do so in writing and the recording is at the taxpayers' expense and on their equipment. IRC § 7521(a)(1). The Service requires that the written notice of intent to record must be addressed to the IRS employee who will conduct the interview and must be received by the Service ten calendar days before the interview.[g] Similarly, the IRS may record any taxpayer interview, at its expense and using its equipment, if it notifies the taxpayer (or the taxpayer's authorized representative) at least ten calendar days in advance of the interview.[h] If the IRS records an interview, the taxpayer may request and receive a copy or transcript of the recording, but must pay the costs of duplication or transcription.[i]

Time and Place of Interviews. Section 7605(a) requires that examinations be conducted at a reasonable time and place. As part of the Taxpayer Bill of Rights Act, Congress directed the Treasury Secretary to issue regulations defining or identifying times and places that are reasonable. On April 2, 1990, the Treasury issued Temporary Regulation § 301.7605–1T, which establishes criteria for determining whether a designated time and place are reasonable under all the circumstances. The Temporary Regulation directs IRS employees to "balance convenience of the taxpayer with the requirements of sound and efficient tax administration."[j] In general, it will be reasonable to schedule an examination on any normal workday of the IRS[k] and, in the case of an "office audit," at the IRS office closest to the taxpayer's residence.[l]

---

e. See Chapter 2, § 3 for an explanation of authorized representatives and suspension or disbarment from practice before the IRS.

f. See appendix A for copies of the IRS power of attorney forms.

g. Notice 89–51, 1989–1 C.B. 691 (1989).

h. *Id.*

i. *Id.*

j. Temp.Reg. § 301.7605–1T(a)(1).

k. Temp.Reg. § 301.7605–1T(b)(1).

l. Temp.Reg. § 301.7605–1T(d)(2).

CONDUCT OF THE EXAMINATION

Office Examination. In the examination of most nonbusiness returns, where the records to be examined are not extensive or only minor adjustments are necessary, a form letter will be forwarded to the taxpayer requesting that he furnish additional information by mail or that he appear at an office interview. Generally, the letter requesting an office conference also will request proof to support certain items on the return. In these instances the taxpayer's representative will be able to prepare thoroughly for the interview. Proof as to any of the questioned items and favorable legal authority should be organized for effective presentation. Generally, the objective should be to dispose of the matter in a single interview.

Field Examination. Field examinations generally are performed in connection with a return filed by a business with extensive records to be examined. In these instances the taxpayer will not know which issues will be raised until the examination is completed. Accordingly, preparation of evidence and legal authority relevant to potential issues will be less extensive than in the case of an office examination. Some effort, however, should be made to anticipate the issues and to gather the necessary information and, where necessary, favorable legal authority, before the field examination.

Generally, notification of a field examination will be received by a phone call or letter from the agent. The appointment will then be arranged. When the agent arrives, his credentials should be requested. The taxpayer should ascertain whether the agent is from the Examination Division or a special agent from the Criminal Investigation Division. If there are two agents, the taxpayer should be sure that neither is a special agent from the Criminal Investigation Division. The presence of a special agent indicates that a criminal investigation is being made. In these cases the examination should not proceed until counsel has been consulted and the advisability of permitting an examination is considered in light of the taxpayer's right not to incriminate himself. Where it is ascertained that the examination is routine, it should proceed.

In conducting the examination the agent should be given a comfortable place to work—preferably a private office or semi-private work area. Only one person should be assigned to work with the agent. The agent should be provided with the information and records he requests. Answers to his questions should be candid and complete and be given by someone qualified to answer. If the agent detects an attempt to be devious or evasive or to conceal something, he is apt to extend his examination to be certain he is getting the full story. In providing the agent with the information he requests the taxpayer should, however, be mindful of the fact that it is neither necessary nor desirable to volunteer more than the information requested. After the agent has completed his examination of the taxpayer's records, the first phase of the examination is complete.

It is desirable to use this first phase to determine what items on the return the agent is questioning, to provide the agent with the information he needs, and to avoid any detailed discussion of the issues. From the taxpayer's standpoint it is desirable to discuss the issues in detail at a second conference. This generally will prevent the agent from extending his examination to find added issues or at least make it inconvenient for him to do so, although he may find at the second conference that certain issues are seriously disputed or that most issues are being resolved in the taxpayer's favor.

The taxpayer's representative may use the time between the first and second conferences and his knowledge of the items questioned by the agent to gather and organize additional proof and to research any technical legal questions involved.

Working with the Agent. Obviously, an important element in arriving at a successful disposition of the issues raised during an examination is the development of a sound relationship with the agent. Perhaps the first step in establishing this relationship is the adoption of the attitude that both the taxpayer's representative and the agent are professionals, and that neither of them is personally or emotionally involved in the case. Toward this end the taxpayer's representative should start with the assumption that the agent is doing a job and will be fair and open-minded. It is important also that the taxpayer's representative have the respect of the agent—respect not only for his knowledgeability but more significantly for his integrity. The acknowledgment of the validity of the agent's points when they are clearly valid, as well as the volunteering of information as to obvious errors or omissions, will help establish this respect. Of course general friendliness, cordiality and consideration will help create the desired relationship with the agent. The creation of this relationship will also be fostered by providing the agent with favorable working conditions, assisting him effectively, and facilitating his conduct of the examination.

PRESENTING PROOF TO THE SERVICE

Establishing a case before the Service is much like presenting a case to any other fact-finding forum. Evidence is introduced by means of testimony or documents that support the taxpayer's conclusions. The major distinction between administrative proof and judicial proof is that the rules of evidence are not applicable before the Service, and the proceedings themselves are informal.

The degree of formality increases as the taxpayer proceeds up the administrative ladder, but requirements as to evidence and admissible proof are flexible. Accordingly, the Service will accept as proof not only the taxpayer's business records, but also documents, letters, contemporaneous memoranda, diaries, and similar items. Unlike a judicial proceeding, these items need not be sworn to or formally authenticated.[m]

AGREEMENT WITH THE AGENT

When the examination is concluded, the taxpayer will have the opportunity to reach an agreement with the agent as to the amount of tax due. Agreement at this point may be the simplest and most desirable means of disposing of the dispute, particularly if the agent's approach indicates that he is willing to recognize the validity of the taxpayer's position to some extent and a compromise seems possible. Once the examination has been completed, the agent will prepare what is known as the Revenue Agent's Report. If the agent and the taxpayer have reached a tentative agreement, the report will outline the nature of the agreement and the reasons for making the agreement, and will indicate the proposed computations. The taxpayer eventually will receive a copy of portions of this report. When the tentative agreement is reached, the taxpayer will be asked to sign a settlement form, Form 870.

If no agreement has been reached with the taxpayer, the agent's report will serve as a summary of the case and will be passed on for use by the agent's superiors at the next administrative level. If such is the case, the report will include a statement of the arguments advanced, the settlements proposed, the reasons for rejecting them, all facts, documents and chronological events relating to the case, and a summary of the agent's own opinion of the case.

Review of the Agreement. An agent's agreement with a taxpayer is only tentative pending a number of steps of review. When the agent submits his report, it will be reviewed first by his group supervisor and then forwarded to the Quality Review Staff in the office of the Examination Division.[n] At either point the report may be returned to the agent with the request that he supply additional information or ask the taxpayer to supply additional information, or with instructions to continue the examination in order to resolve newly raised legal issues. If the Quality Review Staff accepts the report, the settlement may proceed. If the report is not accepted, the taxpayer is left with the alternative of making a settlement satisfactory to the reviewers or proceeding to the next administrative level for further negotiations.

Processing the Settlement. Assuming that there is agreement between the taxpayer and the agent, and that the agreement has not been disturbed upon review, the settlement will be forwarded for processing. The Accounting Branch will perform a thorough check of the mathe-

---

m. See, however, Proc.Rules § 601.507, which states, in part: "All evidence, except that of a supplementary or incidental character, may be required to be submitted over the signed declaration of the taxpayer, made under penalties of perjury, that such evidence is true."

n. For the procedures involved in cases where the settlement calls for a refund in excess of $1 million, see page 9, note e, above.

matics of the computations and will investigate whether any other taxes are owed or refunds are due, and what effect the settlement may have on any other matters affecting the taxpayer that are still pending. All deficiencies and overassessments will be offset against one another, and the Collection Division finally will issue a bill for a deficiency, or a refund for overassessment will be made from Washington or through the local office. The above procedure may take anywhere from two months to over a year, depending on the complexity of the issues involved in the case. There may be an additional delay if the taxpayer's case has come up for post examination review.

Post Examination Review Procedure. Each year, certain cases selected at random are subjected to what is known as a post examination review. The standards for choosing cases for such a review are established in Washington, but there is much discretion on the part of the Regional Commissioner, who carries out the review. Generally, the post examination review functions merely as a psychological deterrent to inappropriate activity by the agent as well as to insure uniformity in application of the provisions of the Code.

C. CLOSINGS, REOPENINGS AND SECOND INSPECTIONS

COUNCIL OF BRITISH SOCIETIES IN SOUTHERN CALIFORNIA v. UNITED STATES
42 AFTR 2d 78–6014 (C.D.Cal.1978).

KELLEHER, DISTRICT JUDGE:

* * *

Plaintiff [hereinafter cited as "CBSSC"] was formed as an incorporated association in 1932 for the primary purpose of incorporating the activities of various British organizations in Southern California. The IRS granted CBSSC tax exempt status in 1966 as a social and recreational club pursuant to 26 U.S.C. § 501(c)(7). Since 1958, CBSSC has sponsored charter air flights to and from Europe for its members, for whom annual membership fees are $1.00 per person. In December 1972, IRS Agent Nyberg issued a report recommending retroactive revocation of CBSSC's tax exempt status. That report concluded:

> Your nominal membership fee ($1.00 annually), your fluctuating membership (6,000 to 15,000) and the limited number of other social activities (5 to 6 annual dances) indicates [sic] that most individuals are members of your Council for the primary purpose of enjoying reduced rates on your charter flights. It has been concluded that in substance you are a federation of clubs whose primary activity is the operation of charter flights and in accordance with Revenue Ruling 67–428, you do not qualify for exemption from Federal income tax as an organization described in section 501(c)(7) of the Code.

Notwithstanding this recommendation, upon filing of an appeal with the District Director and hearing with District Conferee Lacher of the

District Director's Office, the Conferee did not sustain the revocation so proposed:

> It is the opinion of the conferee based on the information in the case file and from the information secured from the National Office and from other information that any form of revocation is improper on the grounds that CBSSC was always a social club organized and operated exclusively within the intendment of Section 501(c)(7).

Despite this rejection of the recommendation to revoke tax exempt status, the IRS determined that CBSSC was liable for filing certain tax forms:

> * * * Accordingly, under the 1969 Tax reform act, it was determined that the organization was liable for filling [sic] forms 990–T on its interest income for the years 1970 and 1971. (* * * Liability for filing forms 990–T was not an issue which was determined at the district conference.)

* * *

On February 14, 1974, the IRS sent a "thirty-day letter" to plaintiff proposing deficiencies for unrelated business income received in 1970 and 1971. * * * The IRS made the determination that CBSSC's interest income for 1970 and 1971 was "unrelated business income."

On March 12, 1974, Thomas Barrett, CBSSC President, sent a letter to the IRS District Director objecting to the February 14, 1974 report:

> On January 8, 1974, a determination letter L–251 Code 421 covering tax years 1971 and 1972 for the Council of British Societies in Southern California, Inc, [sic] was issued by the District Director, in which the tax returns were accepted as filed * * *.
>
> As we understand it, the acceptance by the District Director of the tax returns for said years indicates that the returns are no longer in question. Therefore, we believe the report by Agent Robbins [dated February 14, 1974] is not applicable at this time.

On March 14, 1974, the IRS sent a statutory notice of deficiency (Form L–21) for the years 1970 and 1971. * * *

Hence, as framed by the parties, this action presents two issues: (1) Did the IRS erroneously reopen an audit involving plaintiff's tax obligations for 1970 and 1971? (2) Did plaintiff realize unrelated business income during the calendar years 1970 and 1971, and if so, were the assessments of tax for such income valid?

A. *Reopening Issue.* Plaintiff contends that the District Director reopened the return without using the proper reopening procedure. 26 U.S.C. § 7605(b) is cited by plaintiff and provides:

> No taxpayer shall be subject to unnecessary examination or investigations, and only one inspection of a taxpayer's books of account shall be made for each taxable year unless the taxpayer requests otherwise or unless the Secretary or his delegate, after investigation, notifies the taxpayer in writing that an additional inspection is necessary.

Each party refers to Rev.Proc. 72–40, 1972–2 Int.Rev.Cum.Bull. 819, which sets forth the rules governing the reopening of cases closed after examination in the office of a District Director. Section 3.01(1) of Rev.Proc. 72–40, 1972–2 Int.Rev.Cum.Bull. at 820 provides the applicable definition of "closed case:"

> A case agreed at the district level is considered closed when the taxpayer is notified in writing, after district conference, if any, of adjustments to tax liability or acceptance of his return without change.

Plaintiff contends that it was notified in writing that the returns for 1970 and 1971 were "accepted as filed," which would mean that the interest reported on the Form 990 had been so accepted. In section 4.02 of Rev.Proc. 72–40, supra, it is provided:

> All reopenings must be approved by the District Director or by the Director of International Operations for cased [sic] under his jurisdiction. If an additional inspection of the taxpayer's books of account is necessary, the notice to the taxpayer required by section 7605(b) of the Code must be signed by the District Director, or by the Director of International Operations for cases under his jurisdiction.

Plaintiff contends that this case was reopened because Statutory Notices of Deficiency were issued without approval or authorization of the District Director of Internal Revenue, as required in this section. Because the returns were accepted as filed, plaintiff contends that all income, including all interest income, reported on Form 990–T, "should be closed by the closing letter of the District Director."

* * *

The government contends (1) the audit involving the 990–T liabilities was never closed so that a reopening never occurred, thus rendering Rev.Proc. 72–40 inapplicable, and (2) even if Rev.Proc. 72–40 is applicable, failure to adhere to the procedures for reopening the case would not invalidate the assessments. As the government points out, the revenue procedure is inapplicable in this case because there had been no prior closing of the audit of taxpayer's unrelated business income under section 512(a)(3), and no reopening therefore occurred. Plaintiff's argument ignores the fact that two distinct aspects of the audit were involved: a Form 990 audit (dealing with qualification for exemption under section 501(c)(7)) and a Form 990–T audit (dealing with the section 512(a)(3) issue). The prior audit, which was closed by the January 8, 1974 letter, dealt only with the exemption issue, and taxpayer was aware of this. The subsequent Form 990–T audit did not constitute a reopening.

Even if Rev.Proc. 72–40 were applicable, the assessments would not be invalid. Tax determinations are not invalidated because they involve a violation of an internal procedural rule. Brown v. Comm'r, T.C.M. 1968–29, aff'd per curiam, 418 F.2d 574 (9th Cir.1969). See also, Collins v. Comm'r, 61 T.C. 693, 701 (1974):

It is too well settled for discussion that procedural rules, such as Rev.Proc. 68–28, [superseded by Rev.Proc. 72–40] are merely directory, not mandatory, "and compliance with them is not essential to the validity of a notice of deficiency." Luhring v. Glotzbach, 304 F.2d 560, 563 (C.A.4).

The Court finds that the IRS did not erroneously reopen the audit involved herein.

* * *

Accordingly, judgment is entered for defendant and against plaintiff on all issues.

Notes

1. Rev.Proc. 85–13, 1985–1 C.B. 514, which superseded Rev.Proc. 72–40, referred to in the CBSSC case, states that the IRS will not reopen any case closed after examination by a district office to make an adjustment unfavorable to the taxpayer unless: (1) there is evidence of fraud, malfeasance, collusion, concealment or misrepresentation of a material fact; or (2) the prior closing involved a clearly defined substantial error based on an established Service position existing at the time of the previous examination; or (3) other circumstances exist which indicate failure to reopen would be a serious administrative omission. See also Proc.Rules § 601.-105(j)(1).

2. The prohibition against second inspections contained in § 7605(b) was designed to prevent abusive and unnecessary inspections of a taxpayer's *books and records*. The reexamination of a taxpayer's *return,* or the books and records of another taxpayer or entity, does not generally constitute a second inspection within the meaning of § 7605(b). See Curtis v. Commissioner, 84 T.C. 1349 (1985).

SECTION 2. ADMINISTRATIVE APPEALS

A. THE "30–DAY LETTER"

At the conclusion of Examination Division consideration of a return the taxpayer normally will be issued a "30–day letter"—so denominated because the document provides thirty days in which the taxpayer must respond. There are a number of different forms of 30–day letters for use in cases concerning various types of taxes and various procedural and substantive situations. However, in essence, the 30–day letter puts the taxpayer on notice that there has been a conclusion of the Examination Division consideration of the return at issue, and that there are proposed adjustments to the return. The taxpayer may, at that point, agree with the adjustments or take one of a number of alternative routes to obtain administrative and/or judicial review of the issues.

ALTERNATIVE RESPONSES TO THE 30–DAY LETTER

When a 30–day letter is received, the taxpayer has four alternatives: he can pay the deficiency asserted, make partial payment, ignore the letter, or protest it and request further administrative proceedings in the hope of settling the case.°

Payment. If payment of the deficiency asserted in the 30–day letter is made, such payment will be assessed and will waive, in effect, the taxpayer's right to petition the Tax Court. He will be able, however, to file a claim for refund and institute suit in a United States District Court or the Claims Court for recovery of the taxes paid, if he wishes to contest the issues raised by the 30–day letter in one of those tribunals.

Partial Payment. Some taxpayers will make partial payment of the deficiency asserted in order to stop the running of interest. Yet, they will still be hopeful of using further administrative procedures with respect to the balance of the asserted deficiency, or they may wish to file a petition in the Tax Court to contest all issues relative to the year in question. Payment with respect to some issues generally will impede subsequent administrative proceedings because the taxpayer, by such payment, gives up in advance concessions that might be of value in the give-and-take of a settlement conference. Unless the interest that can be saved is significant, partial payment is inadvisable because it may result in a waiver of the taxpayer's right to petition the Tax Court.ᵖ This waiver may occur because a Tax Court petition may be filed only during the 90 days following the issuance of a deficiency notice. If the Service accepts the taxpayer's payment and does not issue a deficiency notice, the taxpayer will not be able to petition the Tax Court. If, however, a deficiency notice is issued with respect to the unpaid portion of the deficiency, the taxpayer can allege overpayment and collect any sums erroneously paid.

No Protest. If the taxpayer chooses to ignore the 30–day letter, a statutory notice of deficiency ("90–day letter") will be issued. The taxpayer will then have 90 days to file a petition in the Tax Court. If a petition is filed, the deficiency may not be assessed or collected until the litigation is completed. If a petition is not filed, the deficiency asserted may be assessed and collected. However, the taxpayer is not foreclosed from pursuing post-payment administrative and judicial review via a claim for refund.

Protest. If the taxpayer believes he can dispose of the case administratively, he can respond to the 30–day letter by filing a protest (when required) and requesting a conference with the Appeals Office.

o. No written protest is required to obtain an Appeals Office conference in an office examination case. However, in a field examination case, a written protest is required to obtain an Appeals Office conference if the total amount of proposed additional tax, proposed overassessment, or claimed refund (or, in the case of an offer in compromise, the total amount of assessed tax, penalty, and interest sought to be compromised) exceeds $2,500 for any taxable period. If the total exceeds $2,500 but is less than $10,000, then a written protest is optional, but the taxpayer must submit a brief written statement of the disputed issues. Proc.Rules §§ 601.-105(c)(2)(iii), 601.105(d)(2).

p. In order to avoid the issues raised by partial payment the taxpayer can make a deposit in the nature of a cash bond. See the discussion at pages 327–328, below.

FACTORS INFLUENCING RESPONSE TO THE 30-DAY LETTER

If the taxpayer does not wish to concede that the agent's determinations set forth in the 30-day letter are correct, his basic decision is whether to litigate the issues or make further attempts to resolve them administratively by filing a protest. If the decision to litigate is made, the taxpayer must decide whether to (1) ignore the 30-day letter or request a deficiency notice and litigate in the Tax Court, or (2) pay the asserted deficiency, file a claim for refund, and litigate in the appropriate United States District Court or the Claims Court. If the decision is to continue efforts to resolve the issues with the Service, the taxpayer must protest the 30-day letter, usually in writing, and request a meeting with the Appeals Office.

In deciding how to proceed, at least three important factors must be considered. First is the impact of the disposition on years not involved in the examination. An issue resolved by litigation or in certain settlements (depending on the settlement form used) will be binding in other years. Second, the taxpayer's representative must be mindful of his client's vulnerability on doubtful items on the return that have not been raised by the agent or in the review of his report. While the Service professes that no intensive effort is made to find additional issues once the examination is completed, if an issue that has not been raised previously is evident to the Appeals Office conferee, it will of course be explored. If the vulnerability on these issues is substantial, it may dictate an early payment of the asserted deficiency, foregoing all post-examination procedures. If the taxpayer wishes, he may reopen the conceded issues without vulnerability on undiscovered issues by making a claim for refund after the statute of limitations on assessment has expired. He may then sue for a refund on the claim if the likelihood of recovery and the amounts involved warrant the suit. The government in this case will then be able to raise new issues only to offset the claim. However, the government will not be able to create additional liability.

The third significant factor is the possibility that the taxpayer can recover attorneys' fees under Code section 7430. If the taxpayer substantially prevails in civil tax litigation, and if the government's position was not substantially justified, then the taxpayer may recover reasonable litigation costs (and certain reasonable administrative costs). No recovery is permitted, however, unless the taxpayer exhausted all available administrative remedies, which requires that the taxpayer request an Appeal Office conference and, if granted, participate in the conference. Reg. § 301.7430-1. Thus, a decision not to file a protest and request an Appeals Office conference will preclude recovery of litigation costs if the taxpayer ultimately prevails. Recovery of litigation costs under section 7430 is discussed in detail in Chapter 6. Finally, failure to pursue administrative remedies (such as an Appeals Office conference) can result in a penalty under Code section 6673 for frivolous cases or cases brought principally for delay.

THE PROTEST

Contents of the Protest. If the taxpayer decides that additional administrative proceedings probably will result in a desirable disposition of the dispute, he must file a protest in response to the 30-day letter.[q] No particular form is required for the protest that must be filed, but certain information is essential to presenting a clear and precise statement of the taxpayer's arguments. These requirements are set out in Publication No. 5, which accompanies the 30-day letter. Basically, the protest should include:

1. The name and address of the taxpayer.

2. Designation of the year or years involved and the type and amount of tax in dispute for each year.

3. A detailed list of each finding in the Revenue Agent's Report to which an exception is taken. Each exception should be followed by the taxpayer's own contentions. Excessive length should be avoided, but the material facts should be presented and, if unfavorable, explained, not deleted.

4. In conclusion, a request for an Appeals Office conference.

All protests must be executed by the taxpayer. The execution must contain a statement that the taxpayer is subject to the penalties for perjury for any false statement in the protest.[r]

B. THE APPEALS OFFICE

The Appeals Office, formerly known as the Appeals Division, has "exclusive and final authority" to settle tax disputes administratively and thereby avoid litigation. The mission of the Appeals Office is "to resolve tax controversies, without litigation, on a basis which is fair and impartial to both the government and the taxpayer and in a manner that will enhance voluntary compliance and public confidence in the integrity and efficiency of the Service."[s] Review by the Appeals Office is an opportunity to frankly and candidly review the merits of the case with individuals whose goal is to resolve the matter fairly. In evaluating cases, the Appeals Office is guided by a "hazards of litigation" standard, under which it must review the entire case (including the credibility of witnesses and the probative value of the taxpayer's

---

q. Except in the cases described in note o above.

r. See Proc.Rules § 601.507. That section also provides as follows:

* * * In lieu of a declaration of the taxpayer made under penalties of perjury, every claim, written argument, brief, or recitation of the facts, prepared or filed by the taxpayer's representative in any matter pending before the Revenue Service, should have endorsed thereon a declaration signed by such representative as to whether or not he prepared such document and whether or not he knows of his own knowledge that the facts contained therein are true and correct. In any case in which the taxpayer's representative is unable or unwilling to declare of his own knowledge that the facts are true and correct, the Revenue Service may request the taxpayer to make such a declaration under penalties of perjury.

s. *Internal Revenue Manual* § 8711.

evidence) to determine how a court would likely rule.[t] Prior to this stage, the taxpayer has been involved with IRS employees whose goal was to find additional tax liability.

Jurisdiction. The Appeals Office has jurisdiction over two principal types of cases, so-called "docketed" cases and "nondocketed" cases. "Nondocketed" cases are those initiated by the taxpayer's submission of a protest, if required,[u] following receipt of the "30-day letter." "Docketed" cases are those in which the taxpayer has received a statutory notice of deficiency (the "90-day letter") and filed a petition in the Tax Court seeking redetermination of the deficiency. Thus, even if an initial decision is made to skip the protest and go directly to the Tax Court, the Appeals Office will nonetheless be involved after the Tax Court petition is filed. The Appeals Office also has jurisdiction to review claims for refund that have been rejected by the District Office and proposed rejections of offers in compromise in collection cases.[v] In addition, the Appeals Office will occasionally review a so-called "90-day case," in which the taxpayer has received the statutory notice of deficiency but has not yet filed a Tax Court petition and the 90-day period has not expired.[w] Special rules apply to appeals of the "100% penalty" imposed on "responsible persons" under section 6672.[x]

Settlement Rates. The overwhelming majority of all federal tax controversies are settled administratively. In fiscal year 1988, 94% of all nondocketed cases not invoking tax shelters that were received by the Appeals Office were settled, and 99.9% of all docketed cases not involving tax shelters were settled.[y] If no settlement is reached in nondocketed cases, the Appeals Office will issue the statutory notice of deficiency and, if a Tax Court petition is filed, the District Counsel (rather than the Appeals Office) will normally have exclusive settlement authority.[z]

Restrictions. While the authority of the Appeals Office is extensive, some limitations exist. For example, the Appeals Office must secure agreement of District Counsel to abate an asserted civil fraud penalty in any case in which the IRS has recommended criminal prosecution, even though the Justice Department may have declined to prosecute or the taxpayer was acquitted.[a] In addition, if an IRS recommendation of prosecution is pending with the Justice Department, the Appeals Office must obtain the consent of the District

t. *Id.* § 8711(2).

u. See note o for a description of circumstances in which a protest need not be filed to obtain Appeals Office review.

v. Proc.Rules § 601.106(a)(1)(ii).

w. *Internal Revenue Manual* § 8482.

x. For these rules, see Rev.Proc. 84-78, 1984-2 C.B. 754. The section 6672 penalty is discussed in Chapter 10.

y. *IRS 1988 Annual Report* at pp. 55-56.

z. Rev.Proc. 82-42, 1982-2 C.B. 761. Note, however, that District Counsel may return a case to the Appeals Office that has already considered it if District Counsel believes the referral would promote efficiency in disposing of the case. *Id.* § 3.05.

a. Proc.Reg. § 601.106(a)(2)(v).

Counsel before taking any action on the case.[b] Furthermore, in so-called "whipsaw cases," in which taxpayers take inconsistent positions on the same transaction, the Appeals Office must reach settlement with all involved parties to avoid potential double loss by the government. For example, if the issue is whether certain payments constituted alimony or support, both the payor and the payee must agree to the settlement to avoid a possible deduction of the payment by the payor with the payee not being taxed on the payment as income.

In very large refund cases involving refunds or overpayments in excess of $200,000, the Appeals Office must report its decision to make the refund to the Joint Committee on Internal Revenue Taxation of the Congress.[c] If the committee does not object within 30 days from its receipt of the report, the refund may be made.[d]

Finally, the Appeals Office must turn over to the District Director for immediate assessment of tax any income, estate or gift tax cases under its review (docketed or nondocketed) in which the taxpayer files a bankruptcy proceeding or a receiver is appointed for the taxpayer's property.[e]

C. ARE ADMINISTRATIVE APPEALS REQUIRED?
LUHRING v. GLOTZBACH
United States Court of Appeals, Fourth Circuit, 1962.
304 F.2d 560.

SOPER, CIRCUIT JUDGE.

Separate suits were filed August 9, 1961 in the District Court against the District Director of Internal Revenue at Richmond, Virginia, by Henry G. Luhring, Jr., and wife, and by Lawrence R. Luhring and wife, and on August 10th by Henry G. Luhring, Sr. and wife, seeking to enjoin the collection of income taxes assessed against them in excess of the taxes reported by them on their several joint income tax returns for the taxable years 1957, 1958 and 1959. * * *

The gravamen of the complaints is that the deficiencies claimed for the taxable years were illegally assessed because the District Director, before sending deficiency notices to the taxpayers, failed to follow certain general procedural rules set forth in 26 C.F.R.—Internal Revenue Part 601 of Subchapter H, Internal Revenue Practice, prescribing the actions to be followed by agents of the Internal Revenue Service under the direction of the Commissioner of Internal Revenue, unless the procedure is interrupted by the imminent expiration of the statutory period for the assessment of the tax. * * *

* * *

The taxpayers complain that the agents of the District Director ignored and violated the procedural rules set out in § 601.105 which

b. *Id.*
c. I.R.C. § 6405(a); Proc.Reg. § 601.108.
d. *Id.*
e. Proc.Reg. § 601.109(c).

were promulgated under the authority of 5 U.S.C.A. § 22.[f] Particularly, it is charged that the taxing authorities failed to comply with the provisions set forth in Subsection (b)(1), (3) and (4), and in Subsections (c) and (d) of § 601.105, as follows:

    1. The agents did not examine, at the taxpayers' premises, the taxpayers' returns for the years 1957, 1958 and 1959, or their books and papers bearing on the matters required to be included in the returns, and did not afford the taxpayers an opportunity to agree with the findings of the examining agents.

    2. The taxpayers were deprived of the right to an informal conference in the Auditing Department of the District Director, as provided by Subsection (c), which a taxpayer may have if he applies for it within 10 days after he is advised in writing that he may present his objections to the findings of the examining agent.

    3. The taxpayer was deprived of the benefit of the provisions of Subsection (d) which directs the District Director to send to the taxpayer a 30-day letter setting out the agent's determination and advising the taxpayer of his right to file a written protest within 30 days and to have a hearing in the Appellate Division of the region.

The taxpayers contend that these procedural rules were promulgated under the authority of Section 7805(a) of the Internal Revenue Code of 1954 and the Administrative Procedure Act, 5 U.S.C.A. § 1011,[g] and were published in the Federal Register in accordance with 5 U.S.C.A. § 1002(a)[h] of the latter act. They contend in effect that the rules have the force and effect of law and are mandatory in their operation and unless they are observed no valid assessment and collection of taxes can be made.

In our view the procedural rules do not have this weight; and compliance with them is not essential to the validity of a notice of deficiency. The Statement of Procedural Rules, part of which is pertinent here, was promulgated and published in the Federal Register of June 30, 1955, 20 F.R. 4621, now 26 C.F.R., part 600, et seq. It was signed only by the Commissioner, Internal Revenue, and purports to be issued under R.S. § 161; 5 U.S.C.A. § 22, which reads: "The head of each department is authorized to prescribe regulations, not inconsistent with law, for the government of his department, the conduct of its officers and clerks, the distribution and performance of its business, and the custody, use, and preservation of the records, papers, and property appertaining to it." This statute was originally passed in 1789 and codified in 1875 as section 161 of the Revised Statutes. Its purpose was to enable General Washington to get his administration under way by spelling out the authority of Government officers to set up offices and to file Government documents.

    f. The predecessor to 5 U.S.C.A. § 301.
    g. The predecessor to 5 U.S.C.A. § 559.
    h. The predecessor to 5 U.S.C.A. § 553(b).

The significance of the promulgation of the rules without the approval of the Secretary should not be overlooked. Section 7805, I.R.C., gave to the Secretary, or his delegate, authority to prescribe needful rules and regulations for the enforcement of the statute. Section 7802 provides for the appointment of a Commissioner of Internal Revenue by the President with such duties and powers as may be prescribed by the Secretary. Section 301.7085-1 of Part 301, Procedure and Administration, 26 C.F.R.—Internal Revenue, empowers the Commissioner, with the approval of the Secretary, to prescribe all rules and regulations for the enforcement of the Code. Since the procedural rules now under examination were promulgated without the approval of the Secretary they constitute rules laid down by the Commissioner for the regulation of the affairs of his office rather than formal regulations with the force and effect of law; and they have no added authority by reason of the terms of the Administrative Procedure Act, 5 U.S.C.A. § 1001 et seq.,[i] as the taxpayers contend. Section 1002 of that statute requires the publication of the rules of an agency adopted according to law for guidance of the public, and Section 1011 grants every agency the authority to comply with the requirements of the statutes through the issuance of rules or otherwise. It is obvious, however, that the latter provision merely enables the agencies to comply with the statute and does not take the place of or modify Section 7805 from which the Secretary of the Treasury or his delegate derives authority to prescribe needful rules for the enforcement of the Internal Revenue laws.

Even if it should be supposed that the procedural rules have the same authority as if they had been issued by the Commissioner with the approval of the Secretary in strict conformity to Section 7805, their directory character would still be apparent. Obviously, they are rules to govern the conduct of the agents of the Internal Revenue Service in the performance of their duty to determine the correctness of the income tax returns of the taxpayers. They are carefully devised to avoid litigation in disputed cases by affording an opportunity to the taxpayer to agree with examining agents in adjustments of the tax shown on the return and by authorizing the representatives of the Commissioner to enter into compromises and settlements when complete agreement cannot be had. To this end, if a return has been audited and found to be incorrect the taxpayer is notified and given an opportunity to agree to the changes suggested by the agent and, if no agreement is reached, further informal conferences between the taxpayer and the Government agents may be had in the auditing office of the District Director and later with the Appellate Board of the District. Obviously, this pretrial procedure is of great value both to the taxpayer and to the Government in composing disputed questions of fact and law and avoiding the delay and expense of litigation; and it is so much to the interest of the parties that it is customarily employed. We think, however, that the rules are directory and not mandatory in legal effect,

---

i. The predecessor to 5 U.S.C.A. § 551 et seq.

and they do not curtail the power conferred upon the Secretary of the Treasury or his delegate by § 6212, I.R.C. to send a notice of deficiency if he determines that there is a deficiency in the tax shown on the taxpayer's return.

* * *

Affirmed.

SECTION 3. REQUESTS FOR TECHNICAL ADVICE

As explained in Chapter 3, "technical advice" means advice or guidance furnished by the National Office of the IRS upon request of a District Director or the Appeals Office in response to any technical or procedural question that develops during any stage of administrative proceedings on the interpretation and proper application of the tax laws to a specific set of facts. The Assistant Commissioner (Technical) and the Assistant Commissioner (Employee Plans and Exempt Organizations) act as the primary assistants to the Commissioner in the rendering of technical advice to field personnel.

The proceedings with respect to which technical advice may be requested include the examination of a taxpayer's return, claim for refund or credit, and any other matter involving a specific taxpayer under the jurisdiction of the Chief, Examination Division of any district office. They also include processing and consideration of nondocketed cases in any Appeals Office. Technical advice is furnished as a way of helping Service personnel close cases and establish and maintain consistent holdings throughout the Internal Revenue Service. To justify a request for technical advice it must be demonstrated that a lack of uniformity exists on the disposition of the issue or that the issue is unusual or complex enough to warrant consideration by the National Office. Obviously, a request for technical advice is desirable only in extraordinary cases. It is of little effect when there is simply a disagreement as to interpretation of legal principles. It is most useful when the Service concedes that there is a substantial doubt as to the existing law.

The District Director or Chief, Appeals Office is responsible for determining whether to request technical advice on any issue being considered. However, while the case is under the consideration of the District Director or the Chief, Appeals Office, a taxpayer may request that an examining agent or Appeals conferee refer an issue to the National Office for technical advice. Regardless of who initiates the request, the taxpayer is given an opportunity to present his version of the statement of facts and specific points at issue. If the examining agent or Appeals conferee declines the taxpayer's request to submit the issue for technical advice, the taxpayer may protest the refusal to the appropriate district or Appeals Office officials. Where the referral is made, but it appears that advice adverse to the taxpayer will be given, the taxpayer is entitled to a conference in the National Office.

Rev.Proc. 90–2, 1990–1 C.B. 386 governs most situations in which requests for technical advice are made. It sets forth the taxpayer's rights and the procedures to be followed by the taxpayer, the internal IRS procedures, the effect of technical advice and various other matters relating to the processing of requests.

SECTION 4. SETTLEMENT AND CLOSING AGREEMENTS

The form that the taxpayer executes in connection with the settlement of the case at the administrative level determines the effect of the settlement on possible future litigation of the issues. The principal forms, Form 870, Form 870–AD, Form 866 and Form 906 are reproduced in Appendix B and are discussed in sections A, B and C of this section. Collateral agreements are discussed in section D.

A. FORM 870 (CONSENT TO ASSESSMENT)

If the taxpayer and the Service reach an agreement at a stage in the examination process prior to an Appeals Office conference, the taxpayer will execute a consent to assessment without deficiency notice on Form 870 (income tax), Form 890 (estate or gift tax) or a similar form for other tax liabilities.[j] Form 870 (or 890) may also be used when the government makes no concession in reaching agreement as to the tax due at an Appeals Office conference.

By executing Form 870 (or 890), the taxpayer waives the statutory notice requirement that the Service formally notify him that it has determined, and intends to assess, a deficiency at least 90 days prior to the actual assessment.[k] Since a petition may be filed in the Tax Court only after a formal notice has been received by the taxpayer, the execution of either form results in relinquishment of the taxpayer's right to petition the Tax Court for a redetermination of the deficiency.

---

j. The operative language of Form 870 is as follows:

I consent to the immediate assessment and collection of any deficiencies (increase in tax and penalties) and accept any overassessments (decrease in tax and penalties) shown below, plus any interest allowed by law. I understand that by signing this waiver, I will not be able to contest these years in the United States Tax Court, unless additional deficiencies are determined for these years.

In a note on the form, it is provided further:

* * * Your consent will not prevent you from filing a claim for refund (after you have paid the tax) if you later believe you are so entitled; nor prevent us from later determining, if necessary, that you owe additional tax; nor extend the time allowed by law for either action.

If you later file a claim and the Service disallows it, you may file suit for refund in a district court or in the United States Court of Claims, but you may not file a petition with the United States Tax Court.

We will consider this waiver a valid claim for refund or credit of any overpayment due you resulting from any decrease in tax and penalties determined by the Internal Revenue Service, shown above, provided you sign and file it within the period established by law for making such a claim.

k. See I.R.C. § 6213(d).

Filing the waiver, in addition to allowing immediate assessment, suspends the running of interest for the period beginning on the 31st day after such filing and ending on the date the Service makes notice and demand on the taxpayer for payment of the deficiency.[1]

Although the execution of Form 870 (or 890) usually results in final disposition of the case, it does not (as the form itself indicates) prevent the assertion of an additional deficiency by the government, nor does it prevent a suit for refund by the taxpayer. Therefore, Form 870 (or 890) is often used by taxpayers to consent to immediate assessment at the conclusion of an examination with a view to the later filing of a claim for refund and the possible prosecution of a tax refund suit.

MALONEY v. COMMISSIONER
Tax Court of the United States, 1986.
86 P–H Memo TC ¶ 86,091.

PARR, JUDGE:

* * *

Petitioner timely filed his 1976 Federal income tax return on July 15, 1977, pursuant to an extension of time requested by petitioner. Petitioner's 1973, 1975 and 1976 returns were subsequently selected for audit. Respondent submitted an examination report explaining proposed adjustments to these returns on May 3, 1979. The report proposed a disallowance of $87,062 of petitioner's 1976 partnership loss of $131,386 from Sunshine Associates. Petitioner's 1976 loss from Gibraltar Associates, in the amount of $24,073, was not included in the report as a proposed disallowance.

On June 29, 1979, petitioner executed a Form 870, Waiver of Restrictions on Assessment and Collection, agreeing to the proposed deficiencies for 1973, 1975, and 1976 in the amounts of $2,736, $3,555, and $27,625, respectively. He remitted the amount of taxes and interest due. By letter dated September 25, 1979, respondent notified petitioner that the revenue agent's examination report had been reviewed and accepted.

By letter dated February 4, 1980, respondent informed petitioner that Sunshine Associates and Gibraltar Associates were under audit by a second revenue agent, and that adjustments might be proposed to the partnerships' returns which might affect petitioner's 1976 return. The revenue agent requested that petitioner sign a Form 872, Consent to Extend the Time to Assess Tax, since it was unlikely the partnership audit would be completed before petitioner's statute of limitations expired. Petitioner refused to extend the statute of limitations for his 1976 income tax return, stating that respondent was estopped from determining additional deficiencies since petitioner had agreed to the prior adjustments.

1. I.R.C. § 6601(c).

The revenue agent conducting the examination of the partnerships then initiated a request to reopen petitioner's 1976 tax year. The request was made on March 4, 1980, on a Form 4505, Reopening Memorandum. The reason for the request was marked as "serious administrative omission resulting in criticism, undesirable precedent, or inconsistent treatment." The agent's request was subsequently approved by the District Director on March 19, 1980, after three intermediary levels of review.

On July 15, 1980, respondent timely mailed a notice of deficiency to petitioner relating to his 1976 return. The notice stated that petitioner's loss from Gibraltar Associates and the remainder of his loss from Sunshine Associates were disallowed in the absence of verification and substantiation of the partnership items. * * * The deficiency determined was $184,655.

Petitioner contends that the examination of his 1976 income tax return was closed pursuant to an agreement with respondent. This contention appears to be based on his execution of a Form 870 agreeing to respondent's deficiency for that year, and on respondent's subsequent letter stating that the examination report was accepted. Petitioner does not allege, nor do the facts indicate, that these documents constitute a formal written closing agreement, as provided in section 7121. That section sets forth the exclusive procedure under which a final closing agreement as to the tax liability of any person can be executed. Estate of Meyer v. Commissioner, 58 T.C. 69, 70 (1972). See also Botany Worsted Mills v. United States, 278 U.S. 282, 288 (1929).

The form signed by petitioner, entitled Waiver of Restrictions on Assessment and Collection of Deficiency in Tax and Acceptance of Overassessment, does not constitute a binding closing agreement under section 7121. The Form 870 is merely a waiver by petitioner of the statutory notice requirements imposed upon respondent by section 6213(a).

The very language of the Form 870 executed by the parties in this case indicates an intent not to be bound. Joyce v. Gentsch, 141 F.2d 891. The form expressly states that petitioner may later file a claim for refund and the respondent is not prevented from later determining that additional tax is owed. By its own terms, therefore, the Form 870 did not purport to be a final closing agreement, and did not prevent respondent from determining additional deficiencies relating to the same tax years.

The September 25, 1979, letter sent to petitioner informing him that his examination report was accepted likewise was not a closing agreement, and did not bar a subsequent notice of deficiency. Such letter merely indicated that for administrative purposes, the examination was closed. Petitioner concedes that respondent has procedures which allow for the reopening of such cases where necessary.

As a corollary to this argument, petitioner maintains that because he agreed to the deficiencies and paid the tax due, he has been prejudiced, and respondent is therefore estopped from issuing the notice of deficiency. We cannot find any grounds for equitable estoppel here. Petitioner has not established the existence of the traditional elements of equitable estoppel, particularly a binding representation on which petitioner relied to his detriment. See Consolidated Freightways, Inc. v. Commissioner, 74 T.C. 768, 791 (1980), affd. on other issues 708 F.2d 1385 (9th Cir.1983). Respondent made no representation that he would not issue an additional notice of deficiency. Furthermore, petitioner's position was in no way prejudiced as a result of his execution of the Form 870 as he could sue for a refund at any time.

We therefore hold that there was no binding closing agreement, and respondent was not estopped from issuing his notice of deficiency.

* * *

B. FORM 870–AD (AGREEMENT TO ASSESSMENT)

If the taxpayer and the IRS reach a settlement at the Appeals Office level, the settlement usually is documented by an agreement to assessment on Form 870–AD (income tax), 890–AD (estate tax) or a similar form for other taxes.^m These forms are often used rather than the statutory closing agreements (Forms 866 and 906), discussed in the next section.

In effect, the Form 870–AD (or 890–AD) is an offer by the taxpayer to waive the restrictions on assessments and collection in return for concessions by the Service. The Forms indicate that, if the offer is accepted by the IRS, " * * * the case shall not be reopened in the absence of fraud * * *." In keeping with this language, the government does not assert additional deficiencies (absent fraud or other malfeasance by the taxpayer) once the Form 870–AD (or 890–AD) "settlement" has been consummated. In a number of instances, how-

---

m. The operative language of the Form 870–AD is as follows:

Pursuant to the provisions of section 6213(d) * * * the undersigned offers to waive the restrictions provided in section 6213(a) * * * and to consent to the assessment and collection of the following deficiencies with interest as provided by law. The undersigned offers also to accept the following overassessments as correct * * *.

This offer is subject to acceptance for the Commissioner of Internal Revenue. It shall take effect as a waiver of restrictions on the date it is accepted. Unless and until it is accepted, it shall have no force or effect.

If this offer is accepted for the Commissioner, the case shall not be reopened in the absence of fraud, malfeasance, concealment or misrepresentation of material fact, an important mistake in mathematical calculation, or excessive tentative allowances of carrybacks provided by law; and no claim for refund or credit shall be filed or prosecuted for the year(s) stated above other than for amounts attributed to carrybacks provided by law.

In a note on the form, it is provided further:

The execution and filing of this offer will expedite the above adjustment of tax liability. This offer, when executed and timely submitted, will be considered a claim for refund for the above overassessments, as provided in Revenue Ruling 68–65, 1968–1 C.B. 555. It will not, however, constitute a closing agreement under section 7121 of the Internal Revenue Code.

ever, taxpayers have sought to violate the Form 870–AD agreement, typically, but not always, by waiting until the statute of limitations on further assessments has expired and then filing claims for refunds for years covered by the agreement. The circuits are split concerning whether the Form 870–AD agreement precludes a later refund suit. The following case explains the issues involved.

KRETCHMAR v. UNITED STATES
United States Claims Court, 1985.
9 Cl.Ct. 191.

GIBSON, JUDGE:

In this tax refund action, plaintiffs, Frank R. and Bertha M. Kretchmar, jointly seek a refund of federal income taxes, interest, and penalties in the amounts of $19,006.05, $27,404.64, and $24,250.02 for the taxable years 1976, 1977, and 1978, respectively. * * *

* * *

Defendant has moved for summary judgment on plaintiffs' refund claims (the taxable years 1976–1977) on the ground that their previous execution of IRS Form 870–AD equitably estops plaintiffs from litigating these now compromised and settled claims. * * *

Research discloses that the application of the doctrine of equitable estoppel, to bar the prosecution of tax refund claims settled and concluded by the execution of a Form 870–AD, has provoked not only controversy but outright inconsistency among various federal circuits. On the one hand, there are those courts which strictly hold, according to the Supreme Court in Botany Worsted Mills v. United States, 278 U.S. 282, 49 S.Ct. 129, 73 L.Ed. 379 (1929), that the only binding form of tax settlement is one which conforms to the finality prescribed through a settlement agreement pursuant to 26 U.S.C. § 7121 (1982). The justification for this conclusion is apparently premised on the fact that Form 870–AD specifically states that it is not such an agreement. Absent strict adherence to the formality envisioned in § 7121, these courts, therefore, reject the application of the doctrine of equitable estoppel relying instead on the Supreme Court's admonishment that "[w]hen a statute limits a thing to be done in a particular mode, it includes the negative of any other mode." Botany, 278 U.S. at 289, 49 S.Ct. at 132. Cf. Uinta Livestock Corp. v. United States, 355 F.2d 761 (10th Cir.1966); Associated Mutuals, Inc. v. Delaney, 176 F.2d 179, 181 n. 1 (1st Cir.1949); and Bank of New York v. United States, 170 F.2d 20 (3d Cir.1948).

On the other hand, there are also those courts which have a tradition of affirmatively applying the doctrine of equitable estoppel to bar the litigation of claims previously concluded through the taxpayer's execution of a settlement Form 870–AD. * * * In support of this position, they refer to the following often cited dicta in Botany, to wit:

It is plain that no compromise is authorized by this statute which is not assented to by the Secretary of the Treasury. For this reason, if for no other, the informal agreement made in this case did not constitute a settlement which in itself was binding upon the Government or the Mills. *And, without determining whether such an agreement, though not binding in itself, may when executed become, under some circumstances, binding on the parties by estoppel, it suffices to say that here the findings disclose no adequate ground for any claim of estoppel by the United States.*

Botany, 278 U.S. at 289, 49 S.Ct. at 132 (emphasis added, citations omitted). Since the Supreme Court has expressly reserved the issue of what circumstances might ultimately raise the execution of a Form 870–AD to a binding settlement, certain courts have consequently held that Botany does not estop the courts from developing their own law on the subject. Thus, it is on the foregoing premises that a properly executed Form 870–AD has become a recognized impediment, in certain circuits, to estop taxpayers from litigating the merits of tax refund claims settled therein. Cf. Stair v. United States, 516 F.2d 560 (2d Cir.1975); * * * Elbo Coals, Inc. v. United States, 763 F.2d 818 (6th Cir.1985).

* * * [T]he predecessor Court of Claims saw fit on a number of occasions to apply the doctrine of equitable estoppel on facts arising out of a taxpayer's previous execution of a Form 870–AD. See Guggenheim v. United States, 77 F.Supp. 186 (Ct.Cl.1948). In so doing, said Court of Claims made particular mention of the language cited from Botany, supra. For example, in the seminal case adopting the doctrine in the predecessor Court of Claims, Guggenheim v. United States, all of the formalities required for executing an efficacious Form 870–AD were present. Guggenheim, 77 F.Supp. at 196. Both parties had signed, and the form was properly accepted by the Commissioner on the same day. Id. at 194. There, the court noted in contradistinction to Botany that:

> Many of the elements in the formal agreement involved in this case [Guggenheim] were lacking in that case [Botany]. Moreover, we do not understand that case to hold, as plaintiff contends, that under no circumstances will a closing agreement be held binding unless executed in accordance with Section [7121] * * *

Guggenheim, 77 F.Supp. at 196. Having effectively distinguished Botany, the Court of Claims in Guggenheim went on to dismiss the tax refund action therein holding that cause of action to be equitably barred due solely to the plaintiff's previous execution of Form 870. Id. at 197.

* * *

In general terms, binding precedent teaches that the doctrine of equitable estoppel, arising out of the execution of a Form 870–AD, may be applied to hold a taxpayer to his bargain if the following three criteria are established: (1) the execution of the Form 870–AD was the result of mutual concession or compromise; (2) there was a meeting of the minds that the claims be extinguished; and (3) that to allow the plaintiff to reopen the case would be prejudicial given the defendant's reliance on the extinguishment thereof. Guggenheim, 77 F.Supp. at 196. As the pleading of the doctrine raises an affirmative defense, the burden is on the defendant to establish these criteria by the requisite quantum of proof.

A. Mutual Concession and Compromise

With respect to the first criterion, mutual concession or compromise, the defendant's documentary evidence clearly establishes this fact for all taxable years with striking similarity to the facts in Guggenheim. * * * Indeed, as in Guggenheim, it is clear beyond cavil, and we so find, that plaintiffs' settlement, manifested by the execution of Form 870–AD in this case, was a bilateral process driven by mutual concession and compromise.

* * * [W]e also stress that plaintiffs' proof regarding their contrary assertion was thoroughly insufficient to raise, even by their contentions, a genuine issue of material fact. While we acknowledge plaintiffs' attempt to raise such genuine issues of material fact based on the holding in Lignos v. United States, 439 F.2d 1365 (2d Cir.1971), we find that case to be clearly distinguishable from the case at bar. In Lignos, the Second Circuit refused to affirm the district court's grant of summary judgment on the grounds of equitable estoppel because there *plaintiffs* had adduced sufficient proof to raise a *factual issue* regarding whether defendant had in truth "conceded" its position in arriving at the settlement recorded on the Form 870–AD. Id. * * * In the case at bar, however, plaintiffs have neither apprised this court of any *specific facts* illustrating that there exists genuine issues for trial, nor have they proffered an affidavit averring such. Because of the foregoing, plaintiffs are entitled to no comfort from Lignos. * * *

* * *

B. Meeting of the Minds

The second criterion * * * requires that there must also be a meeting of the minds to the effect that the right to raise any prospective claims or to otherwise reopen the case, for such years, be extinguished (save exceptions not here relevant). In Guggenheim, the court added substance to the evaluation of this concept by examining two additional factors: (1) the parties' course of conduct; and (2) the express language adopted by the parties on the Form 870–AD. Guggenheim, 77 F.Supp. at 195. * * *

* * * [O]n this issue the documentary evidence is thoroughly supportive of defendant's position, particularly when we examine defendant's Form 5278, Statement–Income Tax Changes, prepared by the Appeals Office of the IRS which contains a box plainly checked "settlement computation." Similarly, in the Appeals Transmittal Memorandum and Supporting Statement, supra, the words "Proposal of Settlement" are used consistently throughout to characterize the nature of

the procedural posture of plaintiffs' appeal. While plaintiffs may, as an afterthought, *now* contend otherwise, the evidence is wanting and it strains credulity to contend that the lengthy and detailed negotiations, which led to the preparation and execution of Form 870–AD, were conducted with any purpose other than that they were aimed at a definitive settlement.

* * *

C. Detrimental Reliance

* * *

* * * The degree of detrimental reliance sufficient to support the application of the doctrine of equitable estoppel has been characterized by the courts in various ways. In McGraw–Hill, for example, the court stated that "equitable estoppel [is to be applied] whenever the IRS cannot be placed in the same position it was when the agreement was executed" (emphasis added). McGraw–Hill, 623 F.2d at 706. More specifically, perhaps, is the definition given in D.D.I. wherein the court states that detrimental reliance is the result which obtains "where the statute of limitations has run on the collection of further deficiencies between the time an informal compromise agreement was executed and the time the refund claim was filed * * *." D.D.I., 467 F.2d at 500.

Quite logically, the predecessor Court of Claims has also, by implication, suggested the necessity for the defendant's reliance to have been reasonable under the circumstances. In this regard, the key variable is the timing of the defendant's knowledge regarding the plaintiff's decision to change its position, i.e., whether the repudiation of the Form 870–AD occurs at a time when the statute of limitations on assessment has expired. Or, on the other hand, the question is whether such knowledge preceded the running of the statute of limitations to the extent that the Service could be restored to the "same position," i.e., by expeditiously effecting an additional assessment within the general three-year period of limitations (§ 6501(a)). * * *

* * * [T]he cut-off date for the defendant to claim detrimental reliance is certainly the date the Form 870–AD is "formally repudiated in writing." Thus, the prejudice to defendant emanating from detrimental reliance because of the running of the three-year limitations period, must have accrued at the date just prior to the time the claim for refund was filed with the IRS, or just prior to the date when any other written notice of repudiation was served on defendant, whichever occurs first. For defendant to proceed in allowing the three-year statute to run, after having received such written notice of repudiation, would clearly not be reasonable, nor indicative of the requisite prejudice required to be *caused* by the plaintiff. In other words, equity will only estop a plaintiff based on that prejudice which is traceable to its *own* action or inaction, not for that which is self-imposed by the defendant.

* * *

* * * [A]s of the critical date of notice, May 23, 1983, we note that at that date, the three-year statutory period (inclusive of plaintiffs' extensions) had clearly run for both taxable years 1976 and 1977. For each of these two years, plaintiffs' consent to an extension of the three-year statutory period on assessment was effective up to December 31, 1982. The three-year period of limitations on assessments as extended for each year, therefore, expired approximately five months *before* plaintiffs filed their May 23, 1983 claims with the IRS. Consequently, on these facts, we find the * * *. Defendant cannot be put back in the "same position" today (or at any time after December 31, 1982) as it held before the Form 870–AD was signed simply because the *general statute* of limitations on additional assessments (§ 6501(a)), extended by § 6501(c)(4), which had *not* then run on February 9, 1982, had in fact expired at the date plaintiffs' claims for refund were filed.

* * *

Plaintiffs' first argue that there would be no prejudice to defendant upon a reopening of the deficiency assessment and considering their claims for refund because defendant continues to be free to assess additional income tax deficiencies upon proof of fraud (§ 6501(c)(1)). * * *

* * *

Plaintiffs' attempt to rely on the § 6501(c)(1) fraud exception to claim that defendant is in as good a position *now* to assess a tax deficiency as it was in *prior* to the execution of the Form 870–AD, is clearly erroneous. Because the three-year statute has run as to all years, the power to make additional assessments for each year arises *only* upon an initial showing of fraud. This is obviously *not* the most favorable position defendant was in prior to the approval of the Form 870–AD early in 1982. At that time, defendant had *no* initial burden on the tax deficiency assessment (only on the fraud penalty). The initial burden to prove that the *tax* deficiency was in error was on the plaintiffs, * * *. Now, upon proceeding to assess under § 6501(c)(1), defendant would have the burden as to *both* the tax deficiency as well as the fraud penalty. And upon a failure to prove fraud, it would lose both the tax and the penalty. * * *

Secondly, plaintiffs' reliance on § 6501(e), which permits a *six*-year limitations period for assessment based upon a showing of a 25 percent understatement relative to the taxpayer's originally reported gross income, is also ineffective to negate the prejudice to defendant based upon a running of the three-year statute. * * * [D]efendant would have the affirmative burden to *prove* a 25 percent understatement in order to effect an assessment. We stress that *prior* to the running of the three-year statute, defendant would have had *no* such burden as was true on the date the 870–AD was executed. Thus, like the results under § 6501(c)(1) discussed supra, the power to assess a deficiency, after the three-year limitations period had expired, would become *contingent* upon defendant's initial proof of a 25 percent gross income understatement after the statutory three-year period had expired. We also view this added burden as the precise prejudice defendant would encounter, due to the running of the general three-year limitations period on assessments, if it proceeded under § 6501(e).

* * *

* * * [W]e believe that where the three-year limitation period has run as to even *one* year of a unified multi-year settlement, significant prejudice would result to defendant to allow a reopening of any included year whereas here said statute on assessment for that year has run. This is so because we do not view the "trade-offs" embodied in a multi-year Form 870–AD compromise to be reasonably and *unprejudicially* severable. Rather, such "trade-offs," in our view, are inextricably intertwined and contingent *across* all years in issue to the extent that, if the formula is involuntarily and/or unilaterally modified for any year, the benefit to one party may be transformed into a detriment to the other. For example, if the 1976 assessment were to stand—a year in which *defendant* conceded $6,000 in income—and 1977 were to be modified favorably to plaintiffs—a year in which *plaintiffs* conceded their position—the result would be that only defendant would be held to its Form 870–AD concession, while plaintiffs would have the benefit of renouncing their concession. Under such a scenario, plaintiffs would be guaranteed the benefit of their bargain, while the defendant would be deprived of its bargain.

* * *

Notwithstanding the fact that some courts may permit a taxpayer to sue for a refund even though a Form 870–AD "settlement" has been reached, a practitioner should not advise a client to execute the form with an intent to file a claim for refund. As a practical matter, one cannot be sure that the taxpayer will not be held to be estopped from pursuing the refund claim. More important, perhaps, is the fact that the execution of a Form 870–AD in this situation may be perceived as an implicit misrepresentation to the Appeals Office of the IRS, because of the agency's view that refund claims are forbidden once the agreement is accepted. It is perfectly acceptable, and far better practice, to provide on the Form 870–AD itself that the taxpayer expressly reserves the right to file and pursue refund claims with respect to specified issues.

C. FORMS 866 AND 906 (CLOSING AGREEMENTS)

Forms 866 and 906 are the closing agreements that comply with § 7121 of the Internal Revenue Code. The Code states, with respect to the finality of these agreements:

>   (b) FINALITY—If such agreement is approved by the Secretary (within such time as may be stated in such agreement, or later agreed

to) such agreement shall be final and conclusive, and, except upon a showing of fraud or malfeasance, or misrepresentation of a material fact—

>(1) the case shall not be reopened as to the matters agreed upon or the agreement modified by any officer, employee, or agent of the United States, and

>(2) in any suit, action, or proceeding, such agreement, or any determination, assessment, collection, payment, abatement, refund, or credit made in accordance therewith, shall not be annulled, modified, set aside or disregarded.

Thus, execution of these forms results in a final settlement or closing which may not be disturbed by the government or the taxpayer.

Form 866 (Agreement as to Final Determination of Tax Liability) is used to effect the final closing of the total tax liability of the taxpayer. Form 906 (Closing Agreement as to Final Determination Covering Specific Matters) is used to effect the final closing as to one or more separate issues affecting the tax liability of a taxpayer.

Thus, Form 866 is used to close conclusively the total tax liability for a period ending prior to the date of the agreement. This form is not only useful in resolving disputes, but may also be desirable for a fiduciary seeking discharge of his obligations, or in making final distributions, or in the case of a corporate liquidation or sale of a corporate business. Form 906 may be used not only as to prior years, but also with respect to subsequent taxable periods. With regard to prior years' items, such as the amount of gross income, a particular deduction or valuation may be agreed upon; and with respect to future years, matters such as basis and depreciation may be agreed upon.

D. COLLATERAL AGREEMENTS

The term "collateral agreement" can be defined as an agreement secured from a taxpayer under examination (or related parties) to clarify or resolve a matter other than the particular tax liability at issue, but corollary to the disposition of the pending case.

A typical example of the use of a collateral agreement is found in the context of the settlement of the valuation, for estate tax purposes, of an item of property. Assume that the estate under examination reported the property in question at $100,000 and that the agent proposes a value of $200,000. The Appeals Office conferee and the estate's representative reach accord on a $150,000 valuation for estate tax purposes, and the estate's deficiency is computed using that figure. The Appeals conferee will often condition settlement with the estate upon the obtaining of a collateral agreement with the heirs, binding them to use the estate tax valuation as their basis in the asset.

Collateral agreements also are used frequently to bind a taxpayer with respect to a matter for future years, or to prevent a taxpayer whose tax liability is not currently at issue from placing the Service in a "whipsaw" situation by taking a position inconsistent with that of the taxpayer whose liability is at issue.

A collateral agreement is an administrative device which is not expressly provided for in the Code. It is, therefore, distinctly different from a closing agreement, which binds both the IRS and the taxpayer. Thus, at least in a theoretical sense, a collateral agreement does not bind the Service to the terms of the collateral agreement. Hence, in the estate tax example discussed above, the basic substantive agreement as to the estate tax deficiency would be effected on a Form 890-AD, which binds the Service vis-a-vis the estate, absent specified exceptions for fraud, etc. The collateral agreement would bind the heirs and require them to value their basis in the property at $150,000, but might not be binding on the IRS. As a practical matter, the likelihood that the Service, having finally accepted an estate tax valuation of $150,000, would subsequently contend that the valuation (hence the heirs' basis) was excessive, is remote indeed. Moreover, in most cases, the effect of the collateral agreement is to restrict the nongovernmental parties from claiming tax treatment of an item which would be more favorable to them than treatment consistent with the settlement embodied in the underlying agreement. Nevertheless, in circumstances in which the terms of the collateral agreement are favorable to the nongovernmental parties, the possibility of a statutorily authorized closing agreement in lieu of a collateral agreement should be considered.

The term "collateral agreement" is also used to describe the agreement customarily required by the Service when compromising an assessed tax liability based upon considerations of collectibility. This type of collateral agreement, which is connected to the settlement of a tax liability for payment of less than 100 cents on the dollar, requires the taxpayer to make payments in excess of the compromised amount if his income (and certain other receipts) exceed specified levels during the term of the agreement.

SECTION 5. THE TEFRA PARTNERSHIP PROCEDURES

Special rules apply to audits and administrative proceedings involving partnerships and S corporations. These rules are described in the following excerpt.[n]

In Title IV of TEFRA [enacted in 1982], Congress added Subchapter C (Sections 6221–6232) to Chapter 63 of the Code, which covers assessments. The subchapter has revolutionized the procedures used for examining partnership returns, adjusting partnership items on the return, and resolving disputes arising over partnership items. The principal impetus for enacting the new rules were the procedural and

n. From Garbis, Junghans & Struntz, Federal Tax Litigation (1985).

logistical problems encountered in examining large tax shelter partnerships. Under the old system, too much time was consumed in examining too few returns. The Service was unable to examine enough returns with tax shelter issues to create a likelihood that unreasonable reporting would be detected, and, ultimately, it failed to deter the proliferation of abusive tax shelters. However, the new rules apply to most investment and professional partnerships as well as to tax shelter partnerships. Moreover, the examination procedures adopted for Subchapter S corporations incorporate most of the features of the new partnership rules.

Under the tax law, a partnership is not a taxable entity subject to income tax. Instead, the individual partners report their respective shares of partnership profits and losses on their returns.[79] However, in each taxable year, every partnership must file a partnership return stating the partnership's income, allowable deductions, and other tax information relating to the partnership.[80] The partnership is also required to provide information schedules (Form K-1) to the partners,[81] which the partners must file in conjunction with their income tax returns. In other words, the returns of each partner are the operative tax returns upon which tax liabilities are assessed, refunds are claimed, and so forth, whereas the partnership return is an information return only.

* * *

Partnerships Subject to the Subchapter C Procedures

The general rule is that all partnerships required to file a partnership return under Section 6031 of the Code are subject to the TEFRA rules on the tax treatment of partnership items.[82] There is one notable exception: a partnership with ten or fewer partners, each of whom is a natural person or an estate, and each of whom has a proportionate interest in the profits, losses, credits, deductions, and all other partnership items, is not subject to the revised rules[83] unless it so elects. However, once such an election is made, it is binding on all subsequent tax years, unless the Commissioner (as a delegate of the Secretary) permits the election to be withdrawn.[84]

Uniform Reporting, or Consistency, Requirement

The general rule is that a partner must treat partnership items on his return in a manner consistent with the treatment of those items on the partnership return.[85] Where a partner chooses to treat a partnership item on his income tax return in a manner inconsistent with its treatment on the partnership return, he must clearly disclose the inconsistency on his return or an accompanying supplement.[86] Upon

---

79. I.R.C. § 701.
80. I.R.C. § 6031(a).
81. I.R.C. § 6031(b).
82. I.R.C. § 6231(a)(1)(A).
83. I.R.C. § 6231(a)(1)(B).
84. Id.
85. I.R.C. § 6222(a).
86. I.R.C. § 6222(b).

failure to properly identify an inconsistency, the Service may treat the item on the partner's tax return in a manner consistent with its treatment on the partnership return, determine any resulting tax liability, and assess any computational adjustment.[87] Any tax so assessed may be collected immediately and without notice to the partner and is not subject to the restrictions against adjustment contained in Section 6225.[88] In other words, such an assessment is not governed by the normal procedures for assessment as treated in the following discussion, since it arises from the reporting of a partnership item.[89] In addition, a partner who negligently or intentionally reports an item inconsistently may be subject to the penalty under Section 6653(a) of the Code for failure to pay tax. In a tax shelter case, even when a partner red flags (i.e., clearly identifies and discloses) an inconsistently treated partnership item, he may be subject to the substantial underpayment penalty * * *

* * *

TAX TREATMENT DETERMINED AT PARTNERSHIP LEVEL

At the heart of the new processing rules for partnership returns is the basic requirement that the treatment of all partnership items be determined at the partnership level.[91] The legislative history indicates that the purpose for this requirement is to ensure that the tax treatment of each partnership item is resolved in unified administrative and judicial proceedings rather than in separate proceedings with the partners.[92] Thus, with certain exceptions, a single administrative proceeding and a single judicial proceeding determine the tax treatment of partnership items. * * *

ADJUSTMENTS PERMITTED UNDER SUBCHAPTER C PROCEDURES

The requirement of a partnership resolution of partnership issues applies only to partnership items.[93] Under the Subchapter C procedures, no adjustments may be made to the nonpartnership items on a partner's income tax return. Therefore, it is important to determine the meaning of partnership items. The Code provides that the Commissioner may, by regulation, define partnership items to include any item that is more appropriately determined at the partnership level than at the partner level.[94] The regulations contain a comprehensive definition of partnership items and includes within that definition everything from items of income, gain, loss, deduction, and credit to information concerning contributions to and distributions from the partnership.[95]

* * *

---

87. I.R.C. § 6231(a)(6). An assessment of a computational adjustment is equivalent to the assessment of a deficiency. * * *
88. I.R.C. § 6222(c).
89. I.R.C. § 6230(a).
91. I.R.C. § 6221.

92. Palmer III, 58 *Journal of Taxation* 34, 35 (1983), citing HR Rep. No. 760, 97th Cong., 2d Sess. 600 (1982).
93. I.R.C. § 6221.
94. I.R.C. § 6231(a)(3).
95. Reg. § 301.6231(a)(3)–1.

Tax Matters Partner

A central figure in the new partnership procedures is the tax matters partner (TMP). One general partner from every partnership that is subject to the new procedures is to be designated as the TMP in accordance with regulations yet to be promulgated.[97] Presumably, the parties will be permitted to name the partner of their choice as the TMP in the partnership agreement. In the absence of any designation, the general partner having the largest share of partnership profits at the close of the taxable year involved is designated as the TMP, and, if there is more than one such partner, the partner among those with the largest share of partnership profits whose name appears first in an alphabetical list is the designated TMP.[98] If no TMP is designated, and it is impractical to apply the largest-share method, the Service may select the TMP. * * *

* * *

Administrative Proceedings

Partnership administrative proceedings begin when the Service mails notice to the partnership (or the TMP, if known to the Service) of its intention to conduct an examination at the partnership level.[106] The Service must also notify each partner who has submitted his name, address, and information that identifies him as a partner in the partnership being examined to the Commissioner at least thirty days prior to the date notice of commencement of the examination was mailed[107] (such partners are called notice partners).[108] The Service is not required to notify any partner who has less than a one-percent interest in a partnership's profits if that partnership has more than 100 partners.[109] Similarly, the Service need not notify any partner who fails to identify himself to the Commissioner at least thirty days prior to issuance of the notice.[110] Determining who is a notice partner, and thus entitled to notice, is important, because it affects which partners will be bound by any subsequent adjustments assessed or settlements agreed upon should such partners never receive notice of the commencement of partnership proceedings until after the proceedings are concluded. In effect, the notice rules relieve the Service of the burden of identifying a partner. Now the partner must supply identifying

---

97. I.R.C. § 6231(a)(7)(A).
98. I.R.C. § 6231(a)(7)(B).
106. I.R.C. § 6223(a).
107. Id.
108. I.R.C. § 6231(a)(8).
109. I.R.C. § 6223(b)(1). For purposes of determining who is at least a one-percent partner, a husband and wife having a joint interest in a partnership shall be treated as one person. I.R.C. § 6231(a)(12). Less than one percent partners can combine with any other partners to form a 5 percent group. A 5 percent group is a group of partners who, for the partnership taxable year, have, in the aggregate, at least a 5 percent interest in partnership profits. I.R.C. § 6231(a)(11). A 5 percent group can designate a notice partner. Such partner is then entitled to receive notice of the commencement of administrative proceedings and of issuance of a final partnership administrative adjustment (FPAA). I.R.C. §§ 6223(b)(2), 6223(d).
110. I.R.C. § 6223(a).

information to the Service or risk being bound by any adverse administrative or judicial determinations of which the partner was uninformed.

The notice of commencement of administrative proceedings must be mailed to every notice partner at least 120 days before the date on which a final partnership administrative adjustment (FPAA) is issued.[111] This is one point at which the Subchapter C procedures diverge from normal examination and assessment procedures. Under the normal procedures, if the limitations period for assessment is about to expire and the Service is just beginning to examine the return in question, it may issue a deficiency notice, which would provide the taxpayer with the first indication that he was under investigation. Under the Subchapter C procedures, a taxpayer must receive notice of the commencement of administrative proceedings before an FPAA (which is the equivalent of a deficiency notice) can be issued. In effect, the provision requiring this 120–day notice period serves to shorten the limitations period for the assessment of adjustments to partnership items. It is believed that, if the Service fails to issue a timely notice of commencement of administrative proceedings, it will declare partnership items to be nonpartnership items and assess adjustments under the normal deficiency procedures. It is uncertain whether the validity of an FPAA may be challenged on the grounds that it was issued less than 120 days after a notice of commencement of administrative proceeding was issued.

As of this writing, neither the Code nor the Procedural Rules mention anything about the conduct of partnership administrative proceedings. The Service contemplates that the partners will choose to have the TMP represent them in all administrative and judicial proceedings, thus keeping all proceedings less time-consuming and more manageable than they have been in the past. However, Congress has enacted some provisions that appear to be at odds with its overall desire to fulfill the Service's expectations. In protection of the taxpayer, Congress has provided that each partner has a right to participate in every administrative [112] or judicial [113] proceeding relating to the determination of a partnership item. * * * Congress has included a provision that allows a partner to execute a waiver of his rights to participate in any administrative or judicial proceedings and allows a partner to waive any restrictions placed on the Commissioner's ability to take any action during the course of such proceedings.[115]

Presumably, partnership administrative proceedings will progress in a manner similar to standard administrative proceedings: first a revenue agent conducts a field examination and conveys proposed adjustments to the TMP and any other partner wishing to become involved in the proceedings; next, absent an agreeable resolution, a thirty-day letter is issued; finally, if a protest is filed, an Appeals

---

111. I.R.C. § 6223(d)(1).
112. I.R.C. § 6224(a).
113. I.R.C. §§ 6226(c), 6228(a)(4)(A).
115. I.R.C. § 6224(b).

conference is scheduled. Under the Subchapter C rules, a settlement is generally binding only upon those partners who are parties to the agreement.[116] However, there is a major exception to this rule. A TMP may enter into a settlement agreement on behalf of and binding upon all partners who are not notice partners, provided the agreement specifically states that it is binding on all such partners.[117] A nonnotice partner can avoid being bound by such a settlement agreement only by filing a timely statement with the Commissioner denying the TMP authority to settle on his behalf.[118] When the Commissioner enters into a settlement agreement with any partner with respect to partnership items prior to the issuance of an FPAA, the terms of the settlement must be offered to every partner requesting them within the 150-day period following the date on which the FPAA was mailed to the TMP.[119] It is unclear whether the terms of a settlement agreement executed by the Commissioner after a notice of an FPAA is mailed must be offered to every partner desirous of settling.[120]

JUDICIAL REVIEW OF FINAL PARTNERSHIP ADMINISTRATIVE ADJUSTMENT

An FPAA is the equivalent of a statutory notice of deficiency at the partnership level. * * * Generally, an FPAA is issued to the TMP when a case cannot be settled at the administrative level or when the limitations period for assessment is about to expire. During the ninety days following the date on which the FPAA is mailed, the TMP has the exclusive power to challenge the proposed adjustments, and he can do so by filing a petition for readjustment.[121] A petition for readjustment may be filed in the Tax Court, the district court in which the partnership's principal place of business is located, or the Claims Court.[122] Thus, the TMP has the exclusive power to choose the forum in which partnership adjustments will be litigated. If the TMP chooses to file a petition for readjustment in a refund tribunal (i.e., the district court or the Claims Court), the Service may commence assessment and collection at the close of the 150th day following the issuance of the FPAA.[123] This can have a devastating effect on a nonliquid partner who is unable, or would be hard-pressed, to pay the asserted computational adjustments should the TMP chose to litigate in one of the refund tribunals.

If the TMP fails to file a petition for readjustment within the ninety-day period following the date on which the FPAA is mailed, any

---

116. I.R.C. § 6224(c)(1).
117. I.R.C. § 6224(c)(3)(A).
118. I.R.C. § 6224(c)(3)(B).
119. I.R.C. § 6224(c)(2).
120. I.R.C. § 6224(c)(2) is written ambiguously. It expressly addresses only settlements entered into prior to the issuance of an FPAA. Leading authorities who participated in drafting the new partnership procedures feel that the IRS need not offer the terms of a settlement entered into after the issuance of an FPAA to the other partners. This will enable the IRS to settle out partners who are not affected by the proposed adjustments.

121. I.R.C. §§ 6226(a), 6226(b), by negative implication.
122. I.R.C. § 6226(a).
123. I.R.C. § 6225(a)(1).

notice partner (or 5 percent group) [124] with an interest in the outcome of the case may file a petition for readjustment during the sixty days following the expiration of the ninety-day period.[125] If more than one petition is filed by a qualified partner, only one of the cases may go forward. The first petition filed in the Tax Court during the sixty-day period will go forward, even if an earlier petition is filed in one of the refund tribunals.[126] If no petition is filed in the Tax Court, the first petition filed in either of the two refund tribunals, the district court or the Claims Court, will go forward.[127] Finally, the TMP may intervene in any action brought by another partner, notwithstanding the fact that the TMP failed to file a petition within the ninety-day period.[128] No matter which action goes forward, every partner who was a member of the partnership at any time during the year involved is a party to the litigation and has a right to join in the action,[129] provided he has an interest in the outcome of the case.[130] * * *

* * *

Where no partner files a petition for readjustment in the Tax Court within 150 days after the FPAA is issued, the Service may make computational adjustments (i.e., compute the change in the tax liability) for each partner and assess a deficiency thereon without issuing a statutory notice of deficiency to each partner.[134] If a proceeding is begun in the Tax Court within the 150-day period after the issuance of the FPAA, no deficiency may be assessed until the decision of the Tax Court in such proceeding has become final.[135] An assessment made in violation of these rules may be enjoined in the proper court.[136] If no partner files a petition for readjustment in any of the three tribunals, the deficiency assessed against any partner with respect to which a computational adjustment relates may not exceed the amount determined in accordance with the FPAA.[137]

* * * Under the Subchapter C procedures, in the absence of a showing of fraud, malfeasance, or misrepresentation of a material fact, the Service may issue only one notice of an FPAA.[139] Similarly, all disputes over the tax liability resulting from the treatment of partnership items must be resolved in any judicial proceeding arising from the commencement of administrative proceedings and the issuance of an FPAA.[140] A taxpayer may not file a refund claim, or a request for administrative adjustment (RAA) for the refund of an overpayment of

124. See supra note 109.
125. I.R.C. §§ 6226(b)(1), 6226(d).
126. I.R.C. § 6226(b)(2). Note that notice of the FPAA must be mailed to the notice partners and any 5 percent group no later than sixty days after notice of the FPAA is mailed to the tax management partner (TMP). I.R.C. § 6223(d)(2).
127. I.R.C. § 6226(b)(3).
128. I.R.C. § 6226(b)(5).
129. I.R.C. § 6226(c).
130. I.R.C. § 6226(d)(1).
134. I.R.C. §§ 6225(a)(1), 6230(a).
135. I.R.C. § 6225(a)(2).
136. I.R.C. § 6225(b).
137. I.R.C. § 6225(c).
139. I.R.C. § 6223(f).
140. I.R.C. §§ 6226(f)–6226(h).

taxes with regard to a partnership item covered in a year for which an FPAA was issued.[141]

REQUESTS FOR ADMINISTRATIVE ADJUSTMENTS

Under the Subchapter C procedures, a partner may not file a refund claim attributable to partnership items unless the Service declares the partnership items on his return to be nonpartnership items and is reviewing his return independently from the partnership return.[142] The new partnership procedures replace the refund claim with the RAA. Basically, an RAA is an amended return and acts as a formal request that the Service either allow the requested adjustments (and any refund resulting therefrom) or commence a partnership-level administrative proceeding to resolve how to treat partnership items.

Any partner may file an RAA, provided it is filed within three years from the later of the date upon which the partnership return is due to be filed (in the case of a return filed early or on time) or the date upon which the partnership return actually is filed[143] and before the Service issues an FPAA.[144] Once an FPAA is issued, any adjustments sought by a partner must be asserted in court during litigation over the adjustments proposed in the FPAA. In such cases, a partner should protect his right to litigate new issues by filing a timely petition for readjustment. Failure to do so will forever preclude a partner from asserting his refund claim. Assuming no FPAA has been issued, an RAA must be filed.

The Service may respond in a variety of ways to an RAA, depending upon whether it was made by a TMP on the partnership's behalf or by any individual partner (including the TMP) on his own behalf. Where a TMP files an RAA on behalf of the partnership and requests that it be treated as a substitute return, the Service may treat the changes as mathematical errors[145] and either assess any resulting deficiency immediately[146] or make any appropriate refund. Where such an RAA is not treated as a substitute return, the Service may either allow or make any requested refunds or credits to all the partners, commence a partnership administrative proceeding to resolve the issues raised, or take no action on the request (in which case the TMP can seek judicial intervention).[147] Where a partner files an RAA on his own behalf, the Service may notify the partner that it intends to treat the partnership items on his return as nonpartnership items. In such cases, the request is treated as an ordinary refund claim, and the partner may seek judicial review of his claim, provided the Service refuses to allow the claim or takes no action during the first six-month period following the filing of the claim.[148] The Service may also decide to conduct a partnership-level administrative proceeding.[149]

141. I.R.C. §§ 6228(a)(2)(B), 6228(b)(2)(C).
142. I.R.C. §§ 6228(b), 7422(h).
143. I.R.C. § 6227(a)(1).
144. I.R.C. § 6227(a)(2).
145. I.R.C. § 6227(b).
146. See I.R.C. § 6213(b).
147. I.R.C. § 6227(b)(2)(A).
148. I.R.C. §§ 6227(c), 6228(b).
149. I.R.C. § 6227(c).

In the event that the Service takes no action on an RAA filed by a TMP, the TMP may file a petition for readjustment either in the Tax Court, the district court in which the partnership's principal place of business is located, or the Claims Court.[150] Generally, the petition for readjustment must be filed in the period beginning six months after the TMP files the RAA and ending two years from that date, although this period may be extended by agreement with the Commissioner.[151] In any event, no petition may be filed after the Service has mailed notice of the beginning of a partnership administrative proceeding to the partnership.[152] If the TMP fails to file a petition for readjustment, it is as though no RAA were filed by him. The Code contains no provision allowing a partner to file a petition for readjustment where the TMP fails to file a petition within the two-year period provided.[153] To protect himself, a partner should file his own RAA.

There is a series of detailed rules explaining which proceeding will go forward where a petition for readjustment seeking judicial review of an RAA is filed and, subsequently, the Service begins a partnership-level administrative proceeding.[154] * * *

* * *

Erroneous Computational Adjustments

What, in ordinary proceedings, is called an assessment of a deficiency is, in partnership proceedings, called an assessment of computational adjustments. Thus, a computational adjustment reflects any tax liability applied to a partner as the result of an inconsistent reporting of partnership items that was not red-flagged, a binding settlement agreement, an adjustment asserted in any FPAA once it is finally litigated or goes unchallenged for 150 days, or an adjustment made after review of an RAA.[155]

No partner may challenge the grounds for assessing a computational adjustment. Any challenge should have been made by filing a petition for readjustment following either the issuance of an FPAA or the refusal of the Service to take the action requested in an RAA. However, a refund claim may be filed by any partner on the grounds that a computational adjustment has been erroneously computed.[156] Thus, a partner may challenge a computational adjustment where the Service has made a mathematical error in assessing an adjustment or has failed to make a full refund after a settlement agreement is executed or after an FPAA is issued and all resulting litigation termi-

---

150. I.R.C. § 6228(a)(1).

151. I.R.C. §§ 6228(a)(2)(A), 6228(a)(2)(D).

152. I.R.C. § 6228(a)(2)(B).

153. This is in contrast to the sixty-day period provided to a partner to file a petition for readjustment when the TMP fails to do so within the ninety-day period following issuance of an FPAA.

154. I.R.C. §§ 6228(a)(2)(C), 6228(a)(3).

155. I.R.C. § 6231(a)(6).

156. I.R.C. § 6230(c)(1).

nated. Any refund claim must be filed within six months from the date on which the notice of a computational adjustment is mailed to the partner or within two years after a settlement agreement is executed, the time for filing a petition for readjustment to challenge an FPAA has expired, or any judicial decision becomes final.[157]

LIMITATIONS PERIOD FOR MAKING ASSESSMENTS

In keeping with the decision to shift the examination of partnership returns to the partnership level, the statute of limitations for assessment of computational adjustments with respect to partnership items is now determined at the partnership level. The limitations periods are basically identical to the limitations periods for assessment of a deficiency under the ordinary procedures. * * *

In any case, where an FPAA has been issued to the TMP, the limitations period for assessment is suspended until one year after the expiration of the period during which a petition for judicial review may be filed by any partner or any judgment resulting from litigation over an FPAA becomes final.[165] Similarly, where the Service declares a partnership item to be a nonpartnership item, the limitations period for assessment with respect to such partner is extended to one year after the date on which the item becomes a nonpartnership item.[166] Finally, the statute of limitations for assessment is extended to one year after the name, address, and taxpayer identification number of any partner is furnished to the Service where such information does not appear on the partnership return, if the Service has issued an FPAA or if the partner has failed to identify the inconsistent treatment of a partnership item on his return.[167]

* * *

Notes

1. The Subchapter S Revision Act of 1982 applied the TEFRA partnership procedures to Subchapter S corporations and their shareholders. I.R.C. §§ 6241 through 6245.

2. The Tax Court has adopted special rules to govern actions for adjustment and readjustment of partnership items. See Tax Court Rules 240 through 247 (Title XXIV). These rules are similar to the Tax Court rules governing ordinary deficiency actions but they do contain a number of provisions peculiar to partnership proceedings.

157. I.R.C. § 6230(c)(2).
165. I.R.C. § 6229(d).
166. I.R.C. § 6229(f).
167. I.R.C. § 6229(e).

Chapter V

STATUTES OF LIMITATIONS ON ASSESSMENT OF TAX AND CLAIMS FOR REFUND

Scope Note: The rules governing the time in which tax assessments must be made by the IRS, or refund claims filed by taxpayers, are quite technical and complex. This Chapter will explain and illustrate these rules and the often huge stakes involved. Section 1 examines the general 3–year statute of limitation on assessments of deficiencies and the exceptions to that general rule. Section 2 addresses the time limits on refund claims. Finally, Section 3 explores the highly technical rules (both statutory and judge-made) governing mitigation of the statute of limitations in federal tax cases.

SECTION 1. STATUTE OF LIMITATIONS ON THE ASSESSMENT OF DEFICIENCIES

A. BASIC RULES

The following is a discussion of the *basic* rules governing limitations on assessments of taxes under the Internal Revenue Code. It does not cover the many circumstances in which special limitations rules may be applicable in the case of a particular type of tax or of a particular type of adjustment.[a]

The Basic Three–Year Period. The IRS is given a three-year period to make assessments against taxpayers absent circumstances deemed (under § 6501 of the Code) sufficient to justify additional time. The limitations period begins with the later of the date the subject tax return is due or is filed. Thus, if a 1985 federal income tax return which is due on April 15, 1986 is filed timely (or early) and there are no

---

a. For example, certain carryback adjustments receive special treatment under I.R.C. § 6501(h)–(j).

special circumstances causing an extension of the period, limitations expire on April 15, 1989. If the return was filed June 15, 1986 (regardless of whether it was timely because of an extension obtained by the taxpayer) limitations would run June 15, 1989. Where no tax return is ever filed, the period of limitations never commences and, hence, never expires.[b]

The Double (Six-Year) Period for 25% Omissions. The basic three-year period is doubled to six years if there has been a 25% omission (defined below) from the subject return. The policy of the law is to provide a longer period for assessment if the omitted amount is above the statutorily set proportion. The requisite omission is specifically defined as gross income in excess of 25% of the amount stated in the return for income taxes, and total gifts or gross estate assets in excess of 25% of the amount stated in the return for gift or estate tax purposes.[c]

The Open-Ended Period for Fraud. If the taxpayer has engaged in a willful attempt in any manner to evade tax or has filed a false or fraudulent return with the intent to evade tax, an assessment may be made at any time.[d] Hence, in many cases, the basic tax liability is not debated but the deficiency stands or falls on the existence of an attempt to evade.

Extended Period by Consent. Except in the case of estate taxes, the taxpayer may enter into an agreement with the IRS to extend the period of limitations for assessment.[e]

Suspension of Period by Deficiency Notice. Certain taxes, particularly income, estate and gift taxes, cannot be assessed prior to the issuance of a statutory notice of deficiency [f] and, if a timely petition is filed, the conclusion of Tax Court proceedings in which the liability is determined.[g] Therefore, the running of the period of limitations on assessments is suspended once a deficiency notice is issued. The suspension is in effect during the period assessment is prohibited and for 60 days thereafter.[h] Hence, if a deficiency notice (providing 90 days to petition the Tax Court) is ignored, limitations are suspended for a total of 150 days. But, if a timely petition is filed, limitations are suspended until 60 days after the decision of the Tax Court becomes final—which might not occur until years after the deficiency notice is issued.

Reopening of Closed Periods. In the tax law there are situations in which periods of limitations long closed may be reopened for a particular purpose. As discussed more fully below in some circumstances the

---

b. I.R.C. § 6501(c)(3), perhaps superfluously, states expressly that where there is a failure to file a return, an assessment may be made at any time.

c. I.R.C. § 6501(e)(1) and (2).

d. I.R.C. § 6501(c)(1) and (2).

e. I.R.C. § 6501(c)(4).

f. However, in a jeopardy situation, the IRS may assess any tax without first issuing a notice of deficiency.

g. I.R.C. § 6213(a).

h. I.R.C. § 6503(a)(1).

doctrine of equitable recoupment or the statutory mitigation provisions will permit a closed period to be reopened to avoid an inequitable result of a party's taking inconsistent positions for closed and opened years.

B. ASSESSMENT

The statutory periods of section 6501 all refer to the time in which a tax may be "assessed." "Assessment" of a tax is simply the recording of the tax liability, together with the taxpayer's name and address and the date of assessment, in the office of the District Director. I.R.C. § 6203. Section 6201 authorizes the Commissioner to assess all taxes imposed by the Code, and the Commissioner has delegated this authority to the District Directors. District Directors, in turn, appoint assessment officers who sign summary records of assessment (Forms 23C) that can cover thousands of taxpayers. The summary records, through supporting records, identify the taxpayer, the nature of the liability assessed, the taxable period and the amount of the assessment.[i] The date of the assessment is the date the assessment officer signs the summary record.[j]

Notes

1. Although the assessment procedure described immediately above appears simple enough, costly bureaucratic errors occasionally occur. For example, on September 13, 1990, the IRS acknowledged that because IRS employees had failed to sign up to 31 summary assessment record forms, the IRS could lose as much as $22.6 million. The IRS said the 31 unsigned forms affected 10,854 tax returns with total assessments of $46 million. New assessments were made in the 7,673 cases (involving $23.4 million in assessments) in which the statute of limitations had not expired. The $22.6 million loss is from the remaining 3,181 cases in which the statute of limitations on assessment expired before the forms were executed. The IRS also announced that it is considering amending Reg. § 301.6203-1 to permit computer-generated signatures on summary assessment record forms.

2. As part of its September 13, 1990 announcement discussed in Note 1, the Service indicated it would refund any taxes paid pursuant to the invalid assessments within two years from date of payment. The two-year period refers to the time limit on refunds of overpayments, discussed in Section 2 below. The IRS spokesman is quoted as saying "there's no question that the amount of tax owed was correct. But if we expect taxpayers to comply with technical requirements, we should do the same." (*USA Today* Friday, September 14, 1990, at p. 2B)

3. On September 17, 1990, the Fourth Circuit issued its opinion in Ewing v. United States, 914 F.2d 499 (4th Cir.1990). Taxpayers in *Ewing* had entered into closing agreements (Forms 906) for tax years 1976–1979 in 1984, after having consented to an extension of the statute of limitations. (See Chapter 4, Section 4 for a discussion of closing agreements.) The day

---

i. Reg. § 301.6203-1.   j. *Id.*

after the closing agreements were executed, taxpayers sent a check for $258,956.18 to the IRS. Notations on the check indicated how the sum was to be apportioned among the tax years, and the year-by-year amounts were identical to the deficiency amounts agreed to in the closing agreements. Taxpayers later sent checks for the interest on the deficiencies. After sending these checks, taxpayers became aware that the IRS had not formally assessed the deficiencies within the statutory time limit. Taxpayers then filed a claim for refund (discussed in Section 2 of this Chapter) and filed suit when the refund claim was denied. The trial court granted taxpayers summary judgment and awarded them all taxes and interest paid pursuant to the closing agreements, finding that the IRS had failed to comply with the Code, as the closing agreements required it to do. Because it failed to assess the deficiencies within the time limit established by Section 6501(a), the court reasoned, the IRS must return the "deposits" made by the taxpayers. On appeal, the IRS argued that the checks were "payments" of tax, not "deposits," which it was entitled to retain regardless of whether the deficiency was timely assessed. The Fourth Circuit agreed with the IRS:

> [T]axpayers are not contending they initially paid the correct amount of tax when they filed their returns for tax years 1976–1979. By executing the Closing Agreements and associated forms, they acknowledged they owed taxes for those years, and they do not now contend that those Closing Agreements were invalid. Rather, they seek to gain advantage from the IRS's error of not making timely assessment.
>
> Taxpayers point out correctly that the appellate courts' task in tax cases such as this is not that of weighing equities, but of determining technical application of the law. We agree with the well-established view that tax laws are technical and, for the most part, are to be accordingly interpreted. Even given technical interpretation and application, however, we conclude that the 1984 remittances of the Ewings were payments of principal and interest on their tax deficiencies (as agreed to by them) properly collected by the IRS, and that the failure of the government to comply with the requirements of 26 U.S.C. § 6501 does not entitle taxpayers to return of those monies.

* * *

> The taxpayers contend that their remittances to the IRS were not payments of tax, but deposits, and that they are entitled to their return because the IRS did not comply with the conditions on which it was to be permitted to apply the deposit to their tax liabilities—i.e., making formal assessments within the appropriate time period. Their argument is that, prior to assessment, there can be no tax liability and thus no "payment" of tax. They suggest that, once the statutory period for assessment is past, it is impossible for the government to create a tax liability, and therefore any "deposits" made in anticipation of assessment must be returned. Although taxpayers have cited to cases in which the reasoning infers support of their position, we believe the weight of authority and the plain meaning of the statute compel a different conclusion.

There has been no firm resolution of the question of whether a taxpayer is entitled to return of monies remitted in accordance with their admitted tax deficiencies simply because the IRS failed to assess within the time requirements of § 6501. Several cases from the 1930's support the government's position that it may retain such payments, but those holdings arguably were brought into question by the Supreme Court case of Rosenman v. United States, 323 U.S. 658 (1945). That case and subsequent decisions by several of our sister circuits have entertained questions necessarily implicating the issue of the necessity of assessment, but the outcomes in each of those cases hinged on distinct issues relating to "payment."

Rosenman, on which taxpayers rely heavily, decided whether estate taxes had been "paid" when remitted by the taxpayer or when later assessed by the IRS. After receiving an extension of time for filing the estate tax return, the Rosenman estate delivered a check to the IRS, noting "This payment is made under protest and duress, and solely for the purpose of avoiding penalties and interest, since it is contended by the executors that not all of this sum is legally or lawfully due." *Id.* at 660. The check was delivered on December 24, 1934. The IRS placed the delivered funds in a suspense account to the credit of the estate. Later, the estate filed its return. The IRS audited the return and assessed a deficiency, and the estate paid additional taxes.

In 1940, six years after the original check had been remitted, the estate filed a claim for refund, which was rejected. The estate then filed suit in the Court of Claims, which held that recovery was barred by the three-year statute of limitations running from the date the taxpayer's remittance was forwarded. The Supreme Court, reversing, held that the statute of limitations commenced running only when the Commissioner assessed the delinquency [*sic*—deficiency] after the audit. *Id.* at 661. In support of that conclusion, the Court stated:

> [O]n December 24, 1934, the taxpayer did not discharge what he deemed a liability nor pay one that was asserted. There was merely an interim arrangement to cover whatever contingencies the future might define. *Id.* at 662.

The Circuit courts have divided in their application of *Rosenman*. The Fifth Circuit has created a per se rule that there simply can be no payment of taxes prior to assessment. Thomas v. Mercantile National Bank, 204 F.2d 943 (5th Cir.1953); see also Ford v. United States, 618 F.2d 357, 361 (5th Cir.1980) (following *Thomas* as precedential, but opining that *Thomas* should be overruled). The Eighth Circuit also took this approach in United States v. Dubuque Packing Co., 233 F.2d 453 (8th Cir.1956), holding that until assessment there is no tax liability defined and thus there can be no payment of tax. See also Plankinton v. United States, 267 F.2d 278, 280 (7th Cir.1959) (generally remittances prior to the time liability is defined are not payments).

In *Rosenman*, however, the fact that the IRS had not assessed the estate taxes prior to the estate's initial transmittal was only one factor discussed by Justice Frankfurter. More dramatic was the estate's notation of paying under protest and duress with the intention of contesting the tax amount. The reasoning of *Rosenman* hardly supports the *Thomas/Dubuque* conclusion that there never can be tax liability without a previous tax assessment. To the contrary, it gives weight to the notion that assessment is but one factor in consideration of whether and when a remittance becomes a payment of a valid tax liability.

A number of courts have disagreed with *Thomas* and *Dubuque,* concluding that *Rosenman* does not foreclose the possibility that a remittance made prior to assessment can be a payment of tax. * * *

These cases (and the dicta in *Ford*) reason that, for purposes of deciding whether a remittance was a payment of tax, formal assessment is only one factor to be considered. Other factors deemed relevant have included when the tax liability is defined, the taxpayer's intent in remitting the money, and how the IRS treats the remittance upon receipt. In our view, the rule that tax liability is not premised on a per se requirement of previous assessment is the better reasoned one and represents the clear weight of authority.

We are also of the view that § 6501(a) plainly and fully describes the consequence of the IRS's failure to comply with its terms. To reiterate, it states: "The amount of any tax * * * shall be assessed within three years after the return was filed ... and no proceeding in court without assessment for the collection of such tax shall be begun after the expiration of such period." This section simply mandates that the United States has no authority to collect a tax forcibly after the applicable period for assessment has expired. It does not forbid the government from collecting and retaining taxes voluntarily paid without assessment and which do not constitute an overpayment.

We are persuaded by the views expressed in [several cases] (which are supported by our reading of *Rosenman*), and by the language of 26 U.S.C. § 6501(a) that a payment results from the remittance by a taxpayer concomitant with the recognition of a tax obligation whether by filing with a return, resolution of a dispute by an agreement, as in this case, or otherwise. The documents executed by the IRS and the Ewings were unadorned agreements recognizing and settling a tax dispute. We see no indication of, nor for that matter purpose in, the Ewings conditioning their agreement on a timely assessment. We thus find that the Ewings' remittances made in accordance with their Closing Agreements and related documents and received by the government prior to the closing of the assessment period were payments of tax which the government is entitled to retain.

* * *

In view of the above, the judgment of the district court is reversed and remanded for appropriate actions consistent with the views expressed in this opinion.

4. Although the courts are split concerning the "payment" versus "deposit" issue addressed in *Ewing,* the Service took the position in a 1985 revenue ruling that the advance payment of a deficiency and interest, when

Sec. 1   **DEFICIENCY ASSESSMENTS**   167

the deficiency is never properly assessed and the statute of limitations has expired, does *not* constitute an overpayment of the tax that would entitle the taxpayer to a refund. Rev.Rul. 85–67, 1985–1 C.B.364. See also Rev.Proc. 84–58, 1984–2 C.B.501, which explains procedures for making deposits in the nature of a cash bond to terminate the running of interest on potential deficiencies that have not yet been assessed. That Revenue Procedure states: "A remittance not specifically designated as a deposit in the nature of a cash bond will be treated as a payment of tax if it is made in response to a proposed liability * * * and remittance in full of the proposed liability is made." Can you reconcile these rulings with the IRS's stated position in the September 1990 invalid assessment fiasco? Do you find it curious that the *Ewing* decision does not even mention these rulings?

C. COMMENCEMENT OF RUNNING OF LIMITATION PERIOD

Of course, to determine when a limitation period will expire, you must first establish when that period begins. One aspect of this question is the angle most of us confront more frequently: when will my return be treated as having been filed?

Question

As you read the following materials, consider that you are vacationing abroad when you remember the April 15 deadline for filing your individual income tax return. Unable to find a form for extending the due date, you hurriedly fill out a Form 1040, with all required attachments. In your haste, you forget to sign the return. You send the return via Federal Express on Friday, April 14. Two years later the IRS notifies you that it never received the return. Are you in trouble? What if they received the return on Monday, April 16? What if they received it on Tuesday, April 17?

The period of limitations on assessments begins to run on the later of the date the return is due or filed. Returns filed early are treated as having been filed on the due date. I.R.C. § 6501(b)(1). Section 7502 establishes a "timely filed if timely mailed" rule. Section 7502 provides in part:

(a) *General Rule.*

   (1) *Date of delivery.* If any return, claim, statement or other document required to be filed, or payment required to be made within a prescribed period or on or before a prescribed date * * * is, after such period or date, delivered by United States mail to the agency, officer or office with which such return * * * is required to be filed, * * * the date of the United States postmark stamped on the cover in which such return * * * is mailed shall be deemed to be the date of delivery or the date of payment, as the case may be.

   (2) *Mailing requirements.* This subsection shall apply only if—

   (A) The postmark date falls within the prescribed date [for filing or for making payment], and

(B) The return, claim, statement or other document, or payment was, within the time prescribed in subparagraph (A), deposited in the mail in the United States in an envelope or other appropriate wrapper, postage prepaid, properly addressed to the agency, officer, or office with which the return * * * is required to be filed * * *.

(b) *Postmark.* This section shall apply in the case of postmarks not made by the United States Postal Service only if and to the extent provided by regulations * * *.

The "timely filed if timely mailed" rule established by § 7502 does not apply to delinquent returns or payments. Thus, a return due on April 15 but mailed on April 20 is treated as filed on the date the IRS receives it.[k] Pursuant to § 7502(b) the Service announced that it will treat as timely filed tax returns mailed in a foreign country, so long as they bear an official postmark dated on or before midnight of the last date prescribed for the filing.[l]

Under § 7503, when the last day for filing falls on a Saturday, Sunday or legal holiday, then filing is timely if performed on the next succeeding day that is not a Saturday, Sunday or legal holiday. For example, if the last day for filing is April 15 and April 15 falls on a Saturday, the return is timely filed if mailed on Monday, April 17.

The safest course is to send a return by registered or certified mail, in which case the postal receipt is prima facie evidence of mailing.[m] According to the Regulation, "the risk that the document or payment will not be postmarked on the day that it is deposited in the mail may be overcome by the use of registered or certified mail."[n] Obviously, the postal receipt should be retained in case a question arises. In one recent case, however, proof of mailing was established by testimony of the postmistress, who remembered weighing and mailing the return.[o]

If no return is filed, the statute of limitations never begins to run and there is no time limit on assessing and collecting the tax. I.R.C. § 6501(b)(3). Section 6011(a) requires that tax returns be made "according to forms and regulations prescribed by" the IRS and that "the information required by such forms or regulations" must be furnished. In an early case considering what constitutes a "return" for purposes of commencing the limitations period, the Supreme Court stated that "perfect accuracy or completeness is not necessary to rescue a return from nullity."[p] Some errors or omissions can be fatal, however. For example, a return that is not signed by the taxpayer under penalties of perjury is not a "return" and thus does not start the statute of limitations.[q]

k. Rev.Rul. 73–133, 1973–1 C.B. 605.
l. Rev.Rul. 80–218, 1980–2 C.B. 386.
m. I.R.C. § 7502(c) (registered mail); Reg. § 301.7502–1(c)(iii)(B)(2) (certified mail).
n. Reg. § 301.7502–1(c)(iii)(B)(2).
o. Estate of Wood v. Commissioner, 909 F.2d 1155 (8th Cir.1990).

p. Zellerbach Paper Co. v. Helvering, 293 U.S. 172, 55 S.Ct. 127, 79 L.Ed. 264 (1934).
q. Campise v. Commissioner, T.C. Memo. 1980–130; Sommer v. Commissioner, T.C.Memo. 1983–196.

BLOUNT v. COMMISSIONER

Tax Court of the United States, 1986.
86 T.C. 383.

JACOBS, JUDGE: This case is before us on petitioners' motion for summary judgment under Rule 121(a). * * *

The sole issue involved is whether the period for assessing a deficiency against the petitioners for 1980 expired prior to the date (July 5, 1984) on which respondent issued his notice of deficiency. Resolution of this issue depends upon whether the omission of Form W-2 with the return filed by petitioners on or before June 15, 1981 rendered the return incomplete.

* * *

Petitioners requested and obtained an extension to file their income tax return for 1980 until June 15, 1981. They mailed their joint 1980 income tax return within the extended time period (the June 15 return) to the Internal Revenue Service Center at Austin, Texas. The return was received at the Service Center on June 17, 1981.

The June 15 return was prepared by a certified public accountant and consisted of 30 pages, * * *. Among the items of income reported was $36,000 of salary income received by Mr. Blount from Sherwood Blount & Co., Realtors. * * *

The Wage and Tax Statement (Form W-2) relating to Mr. Blount's 1980 salary income from Sherwood Blount & Co., Realtors was not attached to the June 15 return. On June 30, 1981, the Service Center returned the June 15 return to petitioners for resubmission with a Form W-2. On July 7, 1981, petitioners' 1980 return was resubmitted (the resubmitted return) with the requested Form W-2. The resubmitted return and Form W-2 were received by the Service Center on July 9, 1981. Respondent mailed a notice of deficiency to petitioners on July 5, 1984, determining a $210,132 deficiency in their 1980 income tax.

* * *

Section 6011(a), in general, requires any person who is liable for tax to:

> make a return or statement according to the forms and regulations prescribed by the Secretary. Every person required to make a return or statement shall include therein the information required by such forms or regulations.

Section 6501(a) generally prescribes a 3 year period of limitations "after the return was filed" in which an assessment of tax can be made.

Pursuant to section 6011(a), respondent has mandated in section 1.6011–1(a), Income Tax Regs., that a return shall contain the information required by the appropriate forms. Because the income tax return for individuals (Form 1040) provides that a Form W-2 be attached thereto, respondent argues that the June 15 return is not in compliance with section 1.6011–1(a), Income Tax Regs; thus, he concludes that the June 15 return was not a return for purposes of section 6501(a).

* * *

In Beard v. Commissioner, 82 T.C. 766 (1984) [aff'd, 793 F.2d 139 (6th Cir.1986)], we held that a tampered form filed by a tax protestor was not a return for purposes of section 6651(a)(1). We determined that the inquiry into the sufficiency of a return for section 6651(a)(1) purposes is the same as the inquiry into the sufficiency of the return for section [6011(a)] purposes. Relying on the relevant Supreme Court cases regarding the statute of limitations for assessments, we stated:

> The Supreme Court test to determine whether a document is sufficient for statute of limitations purposes has several elements: First, there must be sufficient data to calculate tax liability; second, the document must purport to be a return; third, there must be an honest and reasonable attempt to satisfy the requirements of the tax law; and fourth, the taxpayer must execute the return under penalties of perjury. [82 T.C. at 777]

The document which petitioners filed on June 15, 1981 was an unaltered Form 1040 that set forth the items of gross income, deductions, and credits from which petitioners' 1980 tax liability could be calculated. It purported to be a return; it was an honest and reasonable attempt to report the taxable income which petitioners believed they had received during 1980; it reported the tax petitioners believed was due; and it was signed under penalties of perjury. We therefore find that the June 15 return satisfies the four-pronged test laid down by the Supreme Court.

The omission of a Form W-2 does not prevent the calculation of tax liability. Even if the return is considered incomplete solely due to the omission of a Form W-2, the subsequent resubmission of the return with a Form W-2 operates to supply the omitted information or correct inaccurate information.

Respondent makes an additional argument on the grounds of policy and administrative convenience. Essentially, respondent claims that it is logistically impossible for him to retain a return filed without a Form W-2 while he notifies the taxpayer of the omission and awaits the taxpayer's response. Therefore, he argues, efficient operation of the tax collection system requires that returns filed without Forms W-2 be returned to taxpayers and that the filing then be considered a nullity for purposes of computing the period of limitations. To treat such incomplete returns as sufficient for the purpose of starting the limitations period, respondent contends, would put him at a disadvantage because the clock would be running against him during such time period when he has no return in his possession.

We recognize that respondent's task of processing tax returns is formidable and is more difficult when a Form W-2 is not attached to Form 1040. However, once a return has been filed (or is deemed filed), the period of limitations on assessment begins to run. Respondent cannot extend the period of limitations by returning a return simply because it does not include a Form W-2.

Accordingly,

Petitioners' motion for summary judgment will be granted.

BADARACCO v. COMMISSIONER
Supreme Court of the United States, 1984.
464 U.S. 386, 104 S.Ct. 756, 78 L.Ed.2d 549.

JUSTICE BLACKMUN delivered the opinion of the Court.

These cases focus upon § 6501 of the Internal Revenue Code of 1954, 26 U.S.C. § 6501. Subsection (a) of that statute establishes a general three-year period of limitations "after the return was filed" for the assessment of income and certain other federal taxes. Subsection (c)(1) of § 6501, however, provides an exception to the three-year period when there is "a false or fraudulent return with the intent to evade tax." The tax then may be assessed "at any time."

The issue before us is the proper application of §§ 6501(a) and (c)(1) to the situation where a taxpayer files a false or fraudulent return but later files a nonfraudulent amended return. May a tax then be assessed more than three years after the filing of the amended return?

* * *

II

Our task here is to determine the proper construction of the statute of limitations Congress has written for tax assessments. This Court long ago pronounced the standard: "Statutes of limitation sought to be applied to bar rights of the Government, must receive a strict construction in favor of the Government." *E.I. Dupont de Nemours & Co. v. Davis,* 264 U.S. 456, 44 S.Ct. 364, 366, 68 L.Ed. 788 (1924). * * *

We naturally turn first to the language of the statute. Section 6501(a) sets forth the general rule: a three-year period of limitations on the assessment of tax. Section 6501(e)(1)(A) (first introduced as § 275(c) of the Revenue Act of 1934, 48 Stat. 745) provides an extended limitations period for the situation where the taxpayer's return nonfraudulently omits more than 25% of his gross income; in a situation of that kind, assessment now is permitted "at any time within 6 years after the return was filed."

Both the three-year rule and the six-year rule, however, explicitly are made inapplicable in circumstances covered by § 6501(c). This subsection identifies three situations in which the Commissioner is allowed an unlimited period within which to assess tax. Subsection (c)(1) relates to "a false or fraudulent return with the intent to evade tax" and provides that the tax then may be assessed "at any time." Subsection (c)(3) covers the case of a failure to file a return at all (whether or not due to fraud) and provides that an assessment then also may be made "at any time." Subsection (c)(2) sets forth a similar rule for the case of a "willful attempt in any manner to defeat or evade tax" other than income, estate, and gift taxes.

All these provisions appear to be unambiguous on their face, and it therefore would seem to follow that the present cases are squarely controlled by the clear language of § 6501(c)(1). Petitioners Badaracco concede that they filed initial returns that were "false or fraudulent with the intent to evade tax." Petitioner Deleet, for present purposes, upon this review of its motion for summary judgment, is deemed to have filed false or fraudulent returns with the intent to evade tax. Section 6501(c)(1), with its unqualified language, then allows the tax to be assessed "at any time." Nothing is present in the statute that can be construed to suspend its operation in the light of a fraudulent filer's subsequent repentant conduct.[7] Neither is there anything in the wording of § 6501(a) that itself enables a taxpayer to reinstate the section's general three-year limitations period by filing an amended return. Indeed, as this Court recently has noted, *Hillsboro National Bank v. Commissioner,* [460] U.S. [370], [378], n. 10, 103 S.Ct. 1134, 1140, n. 10, 75 L.Ed.2d 130 (1983), the Internal Revenue Code does not explicitly provide either for a taxpayer's filing, or for the Commissioner's acceptance, of an amended return; instead, an amended return is a creature of administrative origin and grace. Thus, when Congress provided for assessment at any time in the case of a false or fraudulent "return," it plainly included by this language a false or fraudulent *original* return. In this connection, we note that until the decision of the Tenth Circuit in *Dowell v. Commissioner,* 614 F.2d 1263 (1980), cert. pending, No. 82–1873, courts consistently had held that the operation of § 6501 and its predecessors turned on the nature of the taxpayer's original, and not his amended, return.[8]

The substantive operation of the fraud provisions of the Code itself confirms the conclusion that § 6501(c)(1) permits assessment at any time in fraud cases regardless of a taxpayer's later repentance. It is established that a taxpayer who submits a fraudulent return does not purge the fraud by subsequent voluntary disclosure; the fraud was committed, and the offense completed, when the original return was prepared and filed. See, *e.g., United States v. Habig,* 390 U.S. 222, 88 S.Ct. 926, 19 L.Ed.2d 1055 (1968). * * *

---

7. Under every general income tax statute since 1918, the filing of a false or fraudulent return has indefinitely extended the period of limitations for assessment of tax.

8. The significance of the original, and not the amended, return has been stressed in other, but related, contexts. It thus has been held consistently that the filing of an amended return in a nonfraudulent situation does not serve to extend the period within which the Commissioner may assess a deficiency. See, *e.g., Zellerbach Paper Co. v. Helvering,* 293 U.S. 172, 55 S.Ct. 127, 79 L.Ed. 264 (1934). It also has been held that the filing of an amended return does not serve to reduce the period within which the Commissioner may assess taxes where the original return omitted enough income to trigger the operation of the extended limitations period provided by § 6501(e) or its predecessors. See, *e.g., Houston v. Commissioner,* 38 T.C. 486 (1962); *Goldring v. Commissioner,* 20 T.C. 79 (1953). And the period of limitations for filing a refund claim under the predecessor of § 6511(a) begins to run on the filing of the original, not the amended, return.

* * *

We are not persuaded by Deleet's suggestion, that § 6501(c)(1) should be read merely to suspend the commencement of the limitations period while the fraud remains uncorrected. The Tenth Circuit, in *Dowell v. Commissioner, supra,* made an observation to that effect, stating that the three-year limitations period was "put in limbo" pending further taxpayer action. 614 F.2d, at 1266. The language of the statute, however, is contrary to this suggestion. Section 6501(c)(1) does not "suspend" the operation of § 6501(a) until a fraudulent filer makes a voluntary disclosure. Section 6501(c)(1) makes no reference at all to § 6501(a); it simply provides that the tax may be assessed "at any time." And § 6501(a) itself contains no mechanism for its operation when a fraudulent filer repents. By its very terms, it does not apply to a case, such as one of "a false or fraudulent return," that is "otherwise provided" for in § 6501. When Congress intends only a temporary suspension of the running of a limitations period, it knows how unambiguously to accomplish that result. See, *e.g.,* §§ 6503(a)(1), (a)(2), (b), (c), and (d).

The weakness of petitioners' proposed statutory construction is demonstrated further by its impact on § 6501(e)(1)(A), which provides an extended limitations period whenever a taxpayer's return nonfraudulently omits more than 25% of his gross income.

Under petitioners' reasoning, a taxpayer who *fraudulently* omits 25% of his gross income gains the benefit of the three-year limitations period by filing an amended return. Yet a taxpayer who *nonfraudulently* omits 25% of his gross income cannot gain that benefit by filing an amended return; instead, he must live with the six-year period specified in § 6501(e)(1)(A). We agree with the conclusion of the Court of Appeals in the instant cases that Congress could not have intended to "create a situation in which persons who committed willful, deliberate fraud would be in a better position" than those who understated their income inadvertently and without fraud. 693 F.2d, at 302.

We therefore conclude that the plain and unambiguous language of § 6501(c)(1) would permit the Commissioner to assess "at any time" the tax for a year in which the taxpayer has filed "a false or fraudulent return," despite any subsequent disclosure the taxpayer might make.
* * *

III

Petitioners argue that their original returns, to the extent they were fraudulent, were "nullities" for statute of limitations purposes. Inasmuch as the original return is a nullity, it is said, the amended return is necessarily "the return" referred to in § 6501(a). And if that return is nonfraudulent, § 6501(c)(1) is inoperative and the normal three-year limitations period applies. * * *

Petitioners do not contend that their fraudulent original returns were nullities for purposes of the Code generally. There are numerous provisions in the Code that relate to civil and criminal penalties for submitting or assisting in the preparation of false or fraudulent returns; their presence makes clear that a document which on its face plausibly purports to be in compliance, and which is signed by the taxpayer, is a return despite its inaccuracies. See, *e.g.*, §§ 7207, 6531(3), 6653(b). Neither do petitioners contend that their original returns were nullities for all purposes of § 6501. They contend, instead, that a fraudulent return is a nullity only for the limited purpose of applying § 6501(a). The word "return," however, appears no less than 64 times in § 6501. Surely, Congress cannot rationally be thought to have given that word one meaning in § 6501(a), and a totally different meaning in §§ 6501(b) through (q).

* * *

We conclude, therefore, that nothing in the statutory language, the structure of the Code, or the decided cases supports the contention that a fraudulent return is a nullity for statute of limitations purposes.

IV

Petitioners contend that a nonliteral reading should be accorded the statute on grounds of equity to the repentant taxpayer and tax policy. * * *

The cases before us, however, concern the construction of existing statutes. The relevant question is not whether, as an abstract matter, the rule advocated by petitioners accords with good policy. The question we must consider is whether the policy petitioners favor is that which Congress effectuated by its enactment of § 6501. * * *

We conclude that, even were we free to do so, there is no need to twist § 6501(c)(1) beyond the contours of its plain and unambiguous language in order to comport with good policy, for substantial policy considerations support its literal language. First, fraud cases ordinarily are more difficult to investigate than cases marked for routine tax audits. Where fraud has been practiced, there is a distinct possibility that the taxpayer's underlying records will have been falsified or even destroyed. The filing of an amended return, then, may not diminish the amount of effort required to verify the correct tax liability. * * *

Second, the filing of a document styled "amended return" does not fundamentally change the nature of a tax fraud investigation. An amended return, however accurate it ultimately may prove to be, comes with no greater guarantee of trustworthiness than any other submission. It comes carrying no special or significant imprimatur; instead, it comes from a taxpayer who already has made false statements under penalty of perjury. * * * We see no "tax policy" justification for holding that an amended return has the singular effect of shortening the unlimited assessment period specified in § 6501(c)(1) to the usual three years. * * *

Third, the difficulties that attend a civil fraud investigation are compounded where * * * the Commissioner's initial findings lead him to conclude that the case should be referred to the Department of Justice for criminal prosecution. The period of limitations for prosectuting criminal tax fraud is generally six years. See § 6531. Once a criminal referral has been made, the Commissioner is under well-known restraints on the civil side and often will find it difficult to complete his civil investigation within the normal three-year period; the taxpayer's filing of an amended return will not make any difference in this respect. As a practical matter, therefore, the Commissioner frequently is forced to place a civil audit in abeyance when a criminal prosecution is recommended.

* * *

Neither are we persuaded by Deleet's argument that a literal reading of the statute "punishes" the taxpayer who repentantly files an amended return. The amended return does not change the status of the taxpayer; he is left in precisely the same position he was in before. It might be argued that Congress should provide incentives to taxpayers to disclose their fraud voluntarily. Congress, however, has not done so in § 6501. That legislative judgment is controlling here.

V

Petitioners contend, finally, that a literal reading of § 6501(c) produces a disparity in treatment between a taxpayer who in the first instance files a fraudulent return and one who fraudulently fails to file any return at all. * * *

The argument centers in § 6501(c)(3), which provides that in a case of failure to file a return, the tax may be assessed "at any time." It is settled that this section ceases to apply once a return has been filed for a particular year, regardless of whether that return is filed late and even though the failure to file a timely return in the first instance was due to fraud. See *Bennett v. Commissioner,* 30 T.C. 114 (1958), acq., 1958–2 Cum.Bull. 3. This, however, does not mean that § 6501 should be read to produce the same result in each of the two situations. From the language employed in the respective subsections of § 6501, we conclude that Congress intended different limitations results. Section 6501(c)(3) applies to a "failure to file a return." It makes no reference to a failure to file a timely return (cf. §§ 6651(a)(1) and 7203), nor does it speak of a fraudulent failure to file. The section literally becomes inapplicable once a return has been filed. Section 6501(c)(1), in contrast, applies in the case of "a false or fraudulent return." The fact that a fraudulent filer subsequently submits an amended return does not make the case any less one of a false or fraudulent return. Thus, although there may be some initial superficial plausibility to this argument on the part of petitioners, we conclude that the argument cannot prevail. If the result contended for by petitioners is to be the rule, Congress must make it so in clear and unmistakable language.

The judgment of the Court of Appeals in each of these cases is affirmed.

It is so ordered.

JUSTICE STEVENS, dissenting.

The plain language of § 6501(c)(1) of the Internal Revenue Code conveys a different message to me than it does to the Court. * * *

In both cases before the Court, the Commissioner assessed deficiencies based on concededly nonfraudulent returns. The taxpayers' alleged prior fraud was not the basis for the Commissioner's action. Indeed, whether or not the Commissioner was obligated to accept petitioners' amended returns, he in fact elected to do so and to use them as the basis for his assessment. When the Commissioner initiates a deficiency proceeding on the basis of a nonfraudulent return, I do not believe that the resulting case is one "of a false or fraudulent return."

* * *

If anything, considerations of tax policy argue against the result reached by the Court today. In a system based on voluntary compliance, it is crucial that some incentive be given to persons to reveal and correct past fraud. Yet the rule announced by the Court today creates no such incentive; a taxpayer gets no advantage at all by filing an honest return. Not only does the taxpayer fail to gain the benefit of a limitations period, but at the same time he gives the Commissioner additional information which can be used against him at any time. Since the amended return will not give the taxpayer a defense in a criminal or civil fraud action, there is no reason at all for a taxpayer to correct a fraudulent return. Apparently the Court believes that taxpayers should be advised to remain silent, hoping the fraud will go undetected, rather than to make full disclosure in a proper return. I cannot believe that Congress intended such a result.

I respectfully dissent.

D. SPECIAL SIX-YEAR LIMITATIONS PERIOD FOR 25% OMISSIONS

THE COLONY, INC. v. COMMISSIONER

Supreme Court of the United States, 1958.
357 U.S. 28, 78 S.Ct. 1033, 2 L.Ed.2d 1119.

MR. JUSTICE HARLAN delivered the opinion of the Court.

The sole question in this case is whether assessments by the Commissioner of two asserted tax deficiencies were barred by the three-year statute of limitations provided in the Internal Revenue Code of 1939.

* * * A special five-year [now six-year] period of limitations is provided when a taxpayer, even though acting in good faith, "omits from gross income an amount properly includible therein which is in excess of 25 per centum of the amount of gross income stated in the

return * * *." § 275(c).ʳ * * *

[In this case there was a nonfraudulent overstatement of the basis of certain lots which were sold, resulting in a greater than 25% understatement of gross income. The assessments were made more than three but less than five years after the subject returns were filed. The Commissioner argued that the extended statute was applicable because of the 25% understatement of gross income. The taxpayer argued that the extended statute was available only where there was a *complete* omission of *specific items* of gross income.]

Although we are inclined to think that the statute on its face lends itself more plausibly to the taxpayer's interpretation, it cannot be said that the language is unambiguous. In these circumstances we turn to the legislative history of § 275(c). We find in that history persuasive evidence that Congress was addressing itself to the specific situation where a taxpayer actually omitted some income receipt or accrual in his computation of gross income, and not more generally to errors in that computation arising from other causes.

* * *

The Commissioner also suggests that in enacting § 275(c) Congress was primarily concerned with providing for a longer period of limitations where returns contained relatively large errors adversely affecting the Treasury, and that effect can be given this purpose only by adopting the Government's broad construction of the statute. But this theory does not persuade us. For if the mere size of the error had been the principal concern of Congress, one might have expected to find the statute cast in terms of errors in the total tax due or in total taxable net income. We have been unable to find any solid support for the Government's theory in the legislative history. Instead, * * * this history shows to our satisfaction that the Congress intended an exception to the usual three-year statute of limitations only in the restricted type of situation already described.

We think that in enacting § 275(c) Congress manifested no broader purpose than to give the Commissioner an additional two years to investigate tax returns in cases where, because of a taxpayer's omission to report some taxable item, the Commissioner is at a special disadvantage in detecting errors. In such instances the return on its face provides no clue to the existence of the omitted item. On the other hand, when, as here, the understatement of a tax arises from an error in reporting an item disclosed on the face of the return the Commissioner is at no such disadvantage. And this would seem to be so whether the error be one affecting "gross income" or one, such as overstated deductions, affecting other parts of the return. To accept the Commissioner's interpretation and to impose a five-year limitation when such errors affect "gross income," but a three-year limitation when they do not, not only would be to read § 275(c) more broadly than is justified by

r. The predecessor to § 6501(e) of the 1986 Code.

the evident reason for its enactment, but also to create a patent incongruity in the tax law.

Finally, our construction of § 275(c) * * * is in harmony with the unambiguous language of § 6501(e)(1)(A) of the Internal Revenue Code of 1954.³

We hold that both tax assessments before us were barred by the statute of limitations.

Reversed.

Note

The Tax Court has stated that, to avoid the special 6-year limitations period of § 6501(e), taxpayers need not make "a detailed revelation of each and every underlying fact," but they must disclose more than a clue that might "intrigue a Sherlock Holmes." Quick's Trust v. Commissioner, 54 T.C. 1336, 1347 (1970), aff'd, 444 F.2d 90 (8th Cir.1971).

E. EXTENSION OF LIMITATIONS BY AGREEMENT

Under normal circumstances the IRS must assess a tax deficiency within three years of the date the subject tax return was filed. Frequently, three years are not sufficient for the Service to commence and complete an examination and provide internal reviews and administrative appeal. The Code permits taxpayers and the Service to agree to extend limitations except as to estate taxes.ˢ These agreements, commonly referred to as "Consents," usually are solicited by the Service sufficiently in advance of the expiration of limitations to permit the issuance of a deficiency notice ᵗ if the taxpayer declines to execute the Consent.

The agreement to extend limitations is entered into on a Form 872—Consent to Extend the Time to Assess Tax—or its equivalent.

---

3. "§ 6501. Limitations on assessment and collection.

* * *

"(e) Omission from gross income—Except as otherwise provided in subsection (c)—

"(1) Income taxes.—In the case of any tax imposed by subtitle A—

"(A) General rule.—If the taxpayer omits from gross income an amount properly includible therein which is in excess of 25 percent of the amount of gross income stated in the return, the tax may be assessed, or a proceeding in court for the collection of such tax may be begun without assessment, at any time within 6 years after the return was filed. For purposes of this subparagraph—

"(i) In the case of a trade or business, the term 'gross income' means the total of the amounts received or accrued from the sale of goods or services (if such amounts are required to be shown on the return) prior to diminution by the cost of such sales or services; and

"(ii) In determining the amount omitted from gross income, there shall not be taken into account any amount which is omitted from gross income stated in the return if such amount is disclosed in the return, or in a statement attached to the return, in a manner adequate to apprise the Secretary or his delegate of the nature and amount of such item."

s. I.R.C. § 6501(c)(4).

t. Or the making of an assessment in the case of certain taxes for which no deficiency notice is required.

There are two types of Consents utilized. The "regular" Consent (Form 872) extends limitations to the earlier of a specified date or the assessment date of an increase in tax reflecting the final IRS determination of tax. The Special Consent (Form 872-A) keeps the period of limitations open until 90 days after either the taxpayer or the Service decides to end activity on the case in the Examination, Appeals, or Employee Plans and Exempt Organizations Division.[u] Appendix C contains copies of Forms 872 and 872-A.

It is not essential that a Consent keep limitations open for all purposes. Subject, of course, to IRS agreement, a Consent can be restricted to a specified matter. The effect of a restricted Consent is to allow limitations to expire except for assessments arising from specific adjustments. The Service may balk at entering into a restricted Consent for fear of getting involved in a future controversy over precisely what is the scope of the extension of limitations. However, in some circumstances, for example a Consent in which the only unsettled issue relates to the taxpayer's reporting of a share of a partnership loss, a restricted Consent may be acceptable.

The taxpayer always has the option to refuse to provide a requested Consent altogether, or to refuse to execute a Consent unless it has the expiration date or other terms the taxpayer wishes. However, the Service can always reject the taxpayer's proposal and issue a deficiency notice. Therefore, the duration and the restrictions (if any) on a Consent are very much negotiable items. The taxpayer's representative should consider carefully whether some variation from the solicited Consent is appropriate, particularly with regard to the length of time given the Service. Hence, it often will be advisable at the examination level to give extensions of three or six months rather than the year or more usually requested by the Service. The three or six month extension will give the taxpayer a chance to reconsider how long he wishes the examination to continue. On the other hand, at the Appeals Office level the effect of failing to provide a reasonable time for administrative review will mean the abandonment of the opportunity for an administrative resolution of the controversy.

ROSZKOS v. COMMISSIONER
United States Court of Appeals, Ninth Circuit, 1988.
850 F.2d 514.

BRUNETTI, CIRCUIT JUDGE:

Louis and Vivian Roszkos ("the Roszkos") filed joint federal tax returns for the years 1973 through 1976, reflecting losses incurred and investment credits for various partnerships in which they participated. The Internal Revenue Service ("IRS") initiated an investigation of those returns. In connection with that investigation, the Roszkos executed

---

u. Rev.Proc. 79-22, 1979-1 C.B. 563 sets out the procedures for using the Form 872-A. See Grunwald v. Commissioner, 86 T.C. 85 (1986).

periodic Forms 872, consenting to a limited extension of the ordinary three-year statute of limitations for assessment of tax deficiencies. *See* IRC § 6501(a). Eventually, in late 1981, the Roszkos executed Forms 872–A for tax years 1973 and 1974, consenting to an unlimited extension of the statute of limitations. The unlimited waiver in Form 872–A can be terminated by either the IRS or the taxpayer. The taxpayer can only terminate the waiver by mailing a Form 872–T to the IRS office "considering the case," and termination is not effective until the IRS has received the Form 872–T. The IRS can terminate the waiver by mailing either a Form 872–T or a notice of deficiency to the taxpayer, and termination is effective upon mailing. Upon termination, the IRS has ninety days within which to assess a tax deficiency, if any.

On December 31, 1981, the IRS issued, by certified mail to two former (but not last known) addresses of the Roszkos, duplicate notices of deficiency for tax years 1973 through 1976. It is clear that the IRS had been notified of the Roszkos' then current address when the 1981 notices of deficiency were sent to the Roszkos' former addresses. The alleged deficiency totaled approximately $75,000, primarily relating to tax years 1973 and 1974. Both notices were returned to the IRS undelivered, the Roszkos never having received them. Thereafter, on May 24, 1982, the IRS assessed the entire deficiency, with interest.

Through subsequent IRS collection activity, the Roszkos first learned of the unsuccessfully mailed notices. They paid the assessed tax and interest in late 1982 and early 1983. More than a year later, on June 11, 1984, the Roszkos petitioned the Tax Court to declare the assessment invalid for insufficient notice pursuant to IRC § 6212(b)(1), and to dismiss their case for lack of jurisdiction. The Commissioner of Internal Revenue ("Commissioner") filed a notice of no objection to the Roszkos' petition; and on November 9, 1984, the Tax Court dismissed the case for lack of jurisdiction, having found insufficient notice to support the assessment.

On September 16, 1985, more than ten months after the dismissal, the Roszkos mailed a Form 872–T to the IRS. The Roszkos assert that they mailed this Form 872–T in order to prompt the IRS to refund the taxes they had paid relative to the now invalid assessment for tax years 1973 and 1974. They included on the Form the following additional language:

> This Notice of Termination is filed without a waiver of the taxpayers' position that the time to assess tax for the years in question has expired, based on the Services' mailing of a notice of deficiency on December 31, 1981.

The Roszkos maintain that this language was included to emphasize that they considered their Form 872–A waiver of the statute of limitations to have been terminated more than three years earlier. In response, the IRS issued, on October 28, 1985, by certified mail to the Roszkos' current address, a new notice of deficiency for tax years 1973 and 1974. The new notice of deficiency covered tax years 1973 and

1974 because the IRS believed the Forms 872–A, which the Roszkos had executed for those years, remained effective to waive the statute of limitations. The new notice did not cover tax years 1975 and 1976 because the Roszkos had never executed Forms 872–A for those years, and the Commissioner concedes that the statute of limitations had expired for tax years 1975 and 1976. On November 25, 1985, the IRS refunded to the Roszkos all payments they had made relating to the invalid 1982 assessment.

The Roszkos reacted to the new notice of deficiency by once again petitioning the Tax Court, on December 23, 1985, to dismiss their case for lack of jurisdiction, this time on the ground that the statute of limitations had expired prior to the issuance of the new notice. One week later, the Roszkos paid the IRS the amount of the alleged deficiency.

On December 4, 1986, the Tax Court held that the statute of limitations had expired prior to the issuance of the new notice.[1] The Court reasoned that the IRS had terminated the Form 872–A waivers of the statute of limitations by mailing the first notices of deficiency, albeit unsuccessfully, almost five years earlier. As a result, the Court dismissed the case for lack of jurisdiction.

The Commissioner appeals the Tax Court decision. We review decisions of the Tax Court on the same basis as District Court decisions in civil bench trials. *Mayors v. C.I.R.*, 785 F.2d 757, 759 (9th Cir.1986). The issue on appeal is whether the mailing of a concededly invalid notice of deficiency terminates a Form 872–A waiver of the statute of limitations for assessment of tax deficiencies. Interpretation of these waiver agreements is subject to the rules governing interpretation of contracts, *see Pursell v. Commissioner,* 38 T.C. 263, 278 (1962), *aff'd per curiam,* 315 F.2d 629 (3d Cir.1963); and when, as in this case, the lower court based its decision on the language of the agreement and principles of contract interpretation, the decision is one of law which we review de novo. *See Miller v. Safeco Title Insurance Co.,* 758 F.2d 364, 367 (9th Cir.1985).

DISCUSSION

The critical language of the Form 872–A waiver agreement is as follows:

> *The amount of any federal income tax due on any return(s) made by or for the above taxpayer(s) for the period ended December 31, 19[xx], may be assessed on or before the 90th (nineitieth) day after:* (a) the Internal Revenue Service office considering the case receives Form 872–T, Notice of Termination of Special Consent to Extend the Time to Assess Tax, from the taxpayer(s), or (b) *the Internal Revenue Service mails a Notice of Deficiency for such period(s).* However, if a Notice of

---

1. Judge Gerber's Tax Court opinion, *Roszkos v. C.I.R.*, 87 T.C. 1255 (1986), was joined by twelve other judges. Judge Cohen concurred in the result only, Judge Parker joined Judge Simpson's dissent, and Judges Koerner and Swift did not participate.

Deficiency is sent to the taxpayer(s), the time for assessing the tax for the period(s) stated in the Notice of Deficiency will be further extended by the number of days the assessment was previously prohibited, plus 60 days.

(Emphasis added). The Commissioner argues that mailing a notice of deficiency which does not satisfy the statutory requirements for notice set forth in IRC § 6212 was not an act which the parties contemplated would terminate the above agreement.

In rejecting the Commissioner's position, the Tax Court looked to the literal terms of the agreement, resolving doubtful terms against the drafting party, namely the IRS. The Tax Court also looked to case law governing notices of deficiency in general. Its holding rests on two central conclusions. First, in drafting Form 872–A, the Commissioner has enabled the IRS to terminate the agreement by the simple act of mailing, thereby rendering irrelevant the accuracy of the address. *See Roszkos*, 87 T.C. at 1260–61. Second, although a misaddressed notice is a "nullity" for assessment purposes, it is still a notice of deficiency for purposes of the waiver. *See id.* at 1263. Although we agree with the method of the Tax Court's analysis, we are compelled to reject its conclusions.

To focus on the distinction between a "mailing" standard and a "receipt" standard is to ignore the basic function of the notice of deficiency. As provided in IRC § 6212, the notice of deficiency has a distinct and unambiguous purpose. Its very name denotes that it was intended to serve as a vehicle of notification. Indeed, it follows that a notice of deficiency which does not satisfy the minimum statutory requirement for notice cannot reasonably be considered a notice of deficiency.

In *Clodfelter v. C.I.R.*, 527 F.2d 754 (9th Cir.1975), *cert. denied*, 425 U.S. 979, 96 S.Ct. 2184, 48 L.Ed.2d 805 (1976), we discussed the interplay between the mailing standard and the function of the notice of deficiency. We stated "that the legislative plan contemplates that actual notice of the deficiency should be given where such can reasonably be achieved and that the mailing authorized by § 6212(a) is a means to that end." Thus, even though § 6212(b)(1) provides for a mailing standard, which removes a great burden from the IRS, that standard has built-in features which give the notice great potential to reach the taxpayer—certified or registered mail, and last known address.

Apparently recognizing that the mailing standard for a notice of deficiency is founded in the principle of actual notice, the Tax Court stated: "[W]e believe that an improperly addressed notice of deficiency or Form 872–T which does not have the potential to advise a taxpayer of the intended termination by [the IRS], would not suffice to terminate the parties' agreement." *Roszkos*, 87 T.C. 1255, 1261 (1986). However, in the face of this accurate analysis of the law, the Tax Court proceeded to misapply its own principle. It concluded that the ill-fated notices of deficiency in this case became cloaked with the necesary "potential to advise" when, at some unspecified time after the mailing, the Roszkos became aware of the mailing. This conclusion, the court believed, was "conceptually analogous to the case law governing notices of deficiency * * *." *Id.* at 1261–62.

Whatever tenuous analogy can be drawn between the Tax Court's position and case law governing notices of deficiency is wholly contrary to the clear precedent of this court. In *Mulvania v. C.I.R.*, 769 F.2d 1376 (9th Cir.1985), we confronted the question of whether the notice requirement of § 6212 was satisfied when a taxpayer learned of, but did not receive, the misaddressed notice of deficiency. We held that a misaddressed notice of deficiency, which is returned to the IRS undelivered, is "null and void." The only exception to this scenario that we noted is if the taxpayer acknowledges notice by timely petitioning the Tax Court for a redetermination of deficiency, thereby rendering harmless the IRS' error in mailing.* *Id.* at 1379–81.

In the present case, the purported notices of deficiency were misaddressed and returned to the IRS undelivered. The Roszkos did not render harmless the IRS' error because they did not *timely* petition the Tax Court for a determination of deficiency. In fact, there is nothing in the record to indicate that the Roszkos discovered, within ninety days, *see* IRC § 6213, that notices of deficiency had been mailed to their former addresses. As a result, the notices which were mailed on December 31, 1981, were null and void. "Regardless of the coincidence by which [the taxpayer] later came to know of its existence, the taxpayer's actual knowledge did not transform the void notice into a valid one." *Mulvania,* 769 F.2d at 1380–81.

We see no reason to conclude that the Form 872-A reference to mailing a notice of deficiency was intended to include a misaddressed, undelivered, and unacknowledged letter which would not qualify as a notice of deficiency in any other context. Rather, interpreting the reference to include only valid notices gives meaning to the entire excerpt of the waiver form which we have set out above. That excerpt is devoted to the topic of when the IRS may assess a tax deficiency for the period covered by the waiver. In most cases a deficiency shall not be assessed until after a notice in compliance with § 6212 is mailed, *see* IRC § 6213(a).

The Tax Court rationalizes its decision to give effect to a statutorily invalid notice of deficiency by comparing the notice to a Form 872-T. The Court notes that the waiver agreement enables the IRS to terminate the waiver simply by mailing either a notice of deficiency or a Form 872-T. The Court reasons that because there is no statutory requirement that a Form 872-T be properly addressed, the statutory requirements for the notice of deficiency should be disregarded for purposes of the waiver agreement. *See Roszkos,* 87 T.C. at 1261.

---

* *Mulvania* has been severely limited by *McKay v. Commissioner*, page 342 below.

Although we express no opinion relative to Form 872-T, we reject the Tax Court's rationale. Form 872-T exists for a fundamentally different purpose than the notice of deficiency. The former was created for the narrow purpose of terminating the Form 872-A waiver agreement, and may be sent by either party. The latter, which may also be used by the IRS as a vehicle of termination, was designed for the broader purpose of notifying the taxpayer of a tax deficiency so that the taxpayer may have an opportunity to litigate the merits of the deficiency before it is assessed. That Form 872-A subjects both of these documents to a mailing standard sheds no light on the analysis. As discussed earlier, however, we find the statutory requirements surrounding the notice of deficiency to be quite illuminating, and we choose not to disregard them.

We therefore hold that a notice of deficiency must comply with § 6212 in order to terminate a Form 872-A waiver. The Roszkos' contention that such a holding will deny them due process of law is both unfathomable and without merit. Because the notices mailed on December 31, 1981 did not comply with § 6212, the May 24, 1982 assessment was invalid, the Form 872-A waiver did not terminate, and the statute of limitations for assessing a deficiency for the Roszkos' 1973 and 1974 tax years did not expire.

Accordingly, the Tax Court order entered June 11, 1987 is vacated, and the case is remanded to the Tax Court for further proceedings not inconsistent with this opinion.

Notes

1. The Tax Court subsequently adopted the reasoning of the Ninth Circuit. Coffey v. Commissioner, 96 T.C. No. 7 (Jan. 28, 1991) (reviewed).

2. Assume that in 1980 a taxpayer and the Service entered into a Special Consent (Form 872-A) agreement to extend the statute of limitation on his 1976 and 1977 income tax. Through oversight, the Service neglected to take any action on the open tax years until 1992, when it issued a notice of deficiency for the open years. Should the 1992 notice of deficiency be time-barred on equitable grounds of estoppel or laches? In Stenclik v. Commissioner, 907 F.2d 25 (2d Cir.1990), the court held that there is no "reasonable time" requirement for terminating a Form 872-A and that the taxpayers could not rely on estoppel or laches because the taxpayer also failed to terminate the consent. The consent in *Stenclik* was executed in 1980, and the notice of deficiency was issued in 1988.

SECTION 2. LIMITATION ON FILING REFUND CLAIMS AND SUITS

To recover overpayments of tax, a taxpayer must first file a claim for refund. If the claim is disallowed by the Service, the taxpayer may then file a "refund suit" in either the United States District Court or the Claims Court. Litigation procedures in these courts are discussed in Chapter 7. This section discusses the time limits on filing refund claims and refund suits.

Sec. 2   **LIMITATION ON FILING REFUND CLAIMS & SUITS**   185

Refund claims for overpaid income tax should be made on Form 1040X (individuals) or Form 1120X (corporations). Form 843 should be used for refunds of taxes other than income taxes. The contents of refund claims and amendments thereto are discussed in Chapter 7.

A. LIMITATIONS ON FILING REFUND CLAIMS

GENERAL RULES

A claim for refund is timely filed if filing occurs within whichever of the following periods expires later:

1. Three years from the date the return in question was filed.

2. Two years from the date the payments were made that are sought to be refunded.[w]

In the event that no tax return was filed, the period for filing a claim expires two years after the payment in question was made.[x]

The limitations period applicable to the filing of claims for refund are statutorily imposed and cannot be waived by the government.[y] Therefore, where a claim is not filed within three years of the time the subject return is filed but is filed within two years of the date some of the payments in question are made, the refund allowable on the claim is limited to the amount paid during the two years immediately preceding the filing of the claim.[z] Where the claim is filed within three years of the date the return was filed, the claim is effective only as to payments made during a period immediately preceding the filing of the claim for refund equal to three years plus the period of any extension or extensions of time granted for the filing of the subject return.[a] It should be noted that where a claim for refund is timely as to only a part of the payments made on the subject assessment it is not invalid. A refund suit can be based upon the claim. However, the taxpayer's recovery in the suit will be limited to the payments with respect to which the claim for refund was timely.[b]

The limitation on recovery relates only to the amount recoverable, not the grounds for refunds that can be asserted. Therefore, if the only payment "covered" by a claim was made on an assessment based upon the disallowance of travel expenses, a refund could still be claimed on the ground, for instance, that the taxpayer was entitled to a depreciation deduction larger than had been taken on the originally filed

---

w. I.R.C. § 6511(a). For a stamp tax, the statute of limitations expires 3 years after the tax is paid. Id.

x. Id.

y. United States v. Garbutt Oil Co., 302 U.S. 528, 58 S.Ct. 320, 82 L.Ed. 405 (1938).

z. I.R.C. § 6511(b)(2)(B).

a. I.R.C. § 6511(b)(2)(A). Note that advance payments of taxes are considered to have been paid on the date the return was due. I.R.C. § 6513(a).

b. Hutchens Metal Products, Inc. v. Bookwalter, 174 F.Supp. 338 (W.D.Mo. 1959), reversed on other grounds, 281 F.2d 174 (8th Cir.1960); San Joaquin Light & Power Corp. v. McLaughlin, 65 F.2d 677 (9th Cir.1933).

return. The following example illustrates operation within the limitation rules:

April 15, 1990	Return filed and reported taxes paid ($10,000) by prepaid estimated taxes.
May 3, 1992	Deficiency assessed ($5,000 plus interest).
June 1, 1992	First payment ($2,000 plus interest).
September 1, 1992	Second payment ($2,000 plus interest).
December 1, 1992	Final payment ($1,000 plus interest).

A claim filed before April 16, 1993 would be filed within three years of the date the return was filed. Thus, it would be timely and effective to support a claim for all payments made including a claim for a refund of a portion of the taxes shown due on the original return.

A claim filed on April 20, 1993 would be outside the three year period. However, it would be timely with regard to all deficiency payments made. Hence, it would be effective only to the extent of the $5,000 plus interest paid within two years of the date it was filed.

A claim filed in August, 1994 would be timely only as to the second and final payments; the maximum allowable refund would be the $3,000 plus interest paid two years prior to the claim.

Finally, a claim filed after December 1, 1994 would be too late as to all payments and completely ineffective.

EFFECT OF EXTENDING STATUTE OF LIMITATIONS ON ASSESSMENTS

The IRS sometimes requests a taxpayer to agree to extend the period during which assessments may be made, as discussed in Section 1D. above. Section 6511(c)(1) of the Code provides that where such a § 6501(c)(4) agreement has been made, the period for filing a claim for refund (and the period within which the Service can make a refund or credit without a claim) shall not expire prior to six months after the expiration of the period within which an assessment could have been made pursuant to the agreement and any extensions thereof. Furthermore, as to any claim filed after the § 6501(c)(4) agreement is made and prior to six months after the end of the extended assessment period, the normal rules limiting the amount of refundable pursuant to the claim are also extended. Finally, § 6511(c)(2) provides that the claim will be effective to obtain a refund of all amounts paid between the date the agreement is executed and the date the claim is filed, plus all amounts that would be refundable under the normal rules if a claim had been filed on the date the agreement was executed.

The limitations benefits given to a taxpayer who agrees to extend the assessment period do not shorten any longer period otherwise available to him. Section 6511(c)(1) states that where an agreement is made, the limitation period for filing claims "shall not expire prior to" the end of the extended period. Therefore, the normal rule permitting a claim to be filed within two years after payment is made is still

Sec. 2 LIMITATION ON FILING REFUND CLAIMS & SUITS 187

applicable. The following example illustrates operation within the extension rules:

April 15, 1990	Return filed and reported taxes paid by prepaid estimated taxes.
April 1, 1993	Form 872 agreement executed, extending statute of limitations for assessment to April 15, 1989.
April 1, 1994	Deficiency assessment made.
August 1, 1994	Deficiency assessment paid.

By virtue of the Form 872 agreement a claim for refund filed not later than October 15, 1994 would be timely since it would have been filed within six months after the extended period for assessments expired. Moreover, the October 15, 1994 claim would be valid even if it sought a refund of all taxes paid by the taxpayer on the subject return, since a claim filed on the date the agreement was made would have been filed within three years of the date the return was filed. A claim filed on or before August 1, 1996 but after October 15, 1994 would still be valid insofar as it sought a refund of the amount paid on August 1, 1994. That is, the claim, which would be filed within two years of the date of the payment in question, would be timely (as to that payment only) under the normally applied limitations rules.

SPECIAL CIRCUMSTANCES

Recognizing that there are circumstances in which it would be difficult, or impossible, for a taxpayer to file a claim for refund within the normal limitations period, the Code provides lengthened periods for filing claims based upon certain specified grounds enumerated in § 6511(d) of the Code, such as claims based on bad debt losses, worthless securities and various carrybacks. Whereas the general rule requires a claim to be filed within three years after the return in question was filed or within two years after the taxes in question were paid, the special rules set out in § 6511(d) lengthen the three-year period. In other words, the taxpayer retains the ability to file a claim within two years of a tax payment and also receives the right to file a timely claim within a period greater than three years after the subject tax return was filed. Where a claim is filed within the lengthened period, the amount recoverable is not limited by the normally applicable rules to the extent the claim is based upon the special grounds for which the lengthened period is provided.

OVERPAYMENTS

Section 6402 authorizes the IRS to refund an "overpayment," which is defined in section 6401(a) as including "that part of the amount of the payment of any internal revenue tax which is assessed or collected after the expiration of the period of limitation properly applicable thereto." Consider again Ewing v. United States, discussed in Notes 3 and 4 at pages 163–167 above. Recall that the Fourth Circuit held that payments of tax deficiencies and interest made pursuant to a closing agreement should not be refunded simply because proper assessment of the tax was not made within the statutory time limit. Some payments, however, were made after the statutory limitation period had expired. The court ordered refund of these amounts under authority of section 6401(a), holding that section 6401(a) overrides section 7121, which makes closing agreements binding on both the taxpayer and the government. See Chapter 4, Section 4 for a discussion of closing agreements.

B. TIMELY FILING OF REFUND SUIT

Premature Filing. After all other administrative prerequisites have been met, a taxpayer must still refrain from filing his tax refund suit until either (1) six months have elapsed from the date he filed his refund claim or (2) his claim has been disallowed by the Internal Revenue Service.[c]

A suit brought prematurely is properly subject to a motion to dismiss for lack of jurisdiction. A dismissal due to premature filing would be without prejudice, thus enabling the taxpayer to file a new action as soon as the administrative prerequisites have been met.

Late Filing. Section 6532(a)(1) of the Code provides that a tax refund suit may not be commenced:

> * * * before the expiration of 6 months from the date of filing the claim [for refund] unless the Secretary renders a decision thereon within that time, nor after the expiration of 2 years from the date of mailing by certified mail or registered mail by the Secretary to the taxpayer of a notice of the disallowance of the part of the claim to which the suit or proceeding relates.

This statute prescribes a condition under which the United States has consented to suit by taxpayers for a refund of taxes. Commencing suits within the statutory period, therefore, is a jurisdictional prerequisite to a tax refund suit.[d]

The two-year limitation period commences on the date of mailing of the formal notice of disallowance of the subject claim.[e] If a claim is never formally rejected, the statutory period may never commence running. Hence, the cause of action could theoretically remain alive indefinitely.[f]

The two-year limitation period may begin without the issuance of a formal notice of disallowance where the taxpayer has filed a written waiver of the requirement of a formal notice (Form 2297). On the day

---

c. I.R.C. § 6532(a)(1); Regs. § 301.6532–1(a).

d. United States v. Garbutt Oil Co., 302 U.S. 528, 58 S.Ct. 320, 82 L.Ed. 405 (1938); Bell v. Gray, 287 F.2d 410 (6th Cir.1960), affirming on the decision of the district court, 191 F.Supp. 328 (E.D.Ky.1960).

e. One court has alluded to the possibility that a 30–day letter referring to the claim for refund could constitute a statutory notice of rejection. Register Pub. Co. v. United States, 189 F.Supp. 626 (D.Conn. 1960).

f. See Detroit Trust Co. v. United States, 130 F.Supp. 815 (Ct.Cl.1955), where suit was timely, though filed almost thirty years after the original claim.

a written waiver of the formal notice requirement is filed, the two-year limitation period for commencing a tax refund suit begins to run.[g]

The two-year statutory period may be extended by agreement between the taxpayer and the IRS.[h] Such an agreement (Form 907) must be signed by the taxpayer and is not effective until signed by a District Director, an Assistant Regional Commissioner, or a Regional Director of Appeals.

The statutory period for filing a refund suit cannot be enlarged except by the aforementioned specific agreement. Thus, once a formal notice of disallowance has been mailed, further action (such as reconsideration) by the IRS on the claim for refund will not extend the period within which suit may be begun.[i] Therefore, the period of limitations for filing a refund suit cannot be extended by the device of filing a second or further timely claim for refund raising the same grounds as an earlier filed claim. A notice of disallowance (or a waiver of notice of disallowance) of the first filed claim raising the grounds on which the suit is based will commence the statutory period of limitations. Later rejection, or consideration without rejection, of the second or later filed claim will not operate to enlarge the time within which the suit may be brought.[j]

SECTION 3. EQUITABLE RECOUPMENT AND THE MITIGATION PROVISIONS

Statutes of limitations, designed to provide finality and avoid surprise, are applied strictly in tax controversies. In the specific context of tax refunds, the Internal Revenue Code provides that the government may not offset against a taxpayer's overpayment of taxes for a given taxable period his underpayment for another period as to which collection or assessment is barred by the statute of limitations. That is, a credit of an overpayment against an asserted tax liability for a period for which assessment or collection is barred by the statute of limitations is void.[k] Thus, for example, a taxpayer who has established a $25,000 overpayment of his income taxes for 1985 normally is entitled to a full refund even though he may, in fact, have underpaid his income taxes for 1975 (a year as to which assessment and collection is barred) by $50,000. However, in very limited situations, where the strict application of the statutes of limitations would enable a party to gain an unfair advantage by assuming inconsistent positions for closed and

---

g. I.R.C. § 6532(a)(3). Note, however, that the taxpayer must still wait 6 months before filing the refund suit. Reg. § 301.-6532–1(c).

h. I.R.C. § 6532(a)(2). See Regs. § 301.-6532–1(b), stating the formal requirements for such an agreement.

i. I.R.C. § 6532(a)(4).

j. 18th Street Leader Stores v. United States, 142 F.2d 113 (7th Cir.1944); Einson–Freeman Co. v. Corwin, 112 F.2d 683 (2d Cir.1940); Cf. W.A. Schemmer Limestone Quarry, Inc. v. United States, 240 F.Supp. 356 (S.D.Iowa 1964) (if the later claim raises new grounds, the date of its disallowance will commence the statutory period).

k. I.R.C. § 6514(b).

open taxable periods, an inequitable result will not be permitted. In effect, the law sometimes permits the opening of a closed taxable period in order to make corrections normally barred by the statute of limitations. There are two sources of relief: the judge-made doctrine of equitable recoupment, and the statutory mitigation provisions, I.R.C. §§ 1311–1314.

A. STATUTORY MITIGATION

The intricate mitigation provisions of the Code, sections 1311–1314, were first enacted in 1938 to codify and supplement the emerging but ill-defined doctrine of equitable recoupment, discussed below. According to the legislative history, Congress believed that "[l]egislation has long been needed to supplement the equitable principles and to check the growing volume of litigation by taking the profit out of inconsistency, whether exhibited by taxpayers or revenue officials whether fortuitous or the result of design."[l] The statutory mitigation provisions permit relief from the bar of the statute of limitations only in limited circumstances; unless all their conditions are met, no relief will be granted, unless equitable recoupment is available.[m] Importantly, the mitigation provisions do not apply to all types of taxes. They apply to income tax, but do not apply to "trust fund" (employment) taxes.[n] The courts are split regarding applicability of statutory mitigation to estate taxes.[o]

The following conditions must be met in order to obtain relief under the statutory mitigation scheme:[p]

1. There must be a "determination" (as defined in section 1313) that an error was made concerning the proper treatment of an item.

2. The "operation of any law or rule of law" (*i.e.*, the statute of limitation or the doctrine of res judicata) prevents correction of the error. I.R.C. § 1311(a).

3. The "determination," coupled with the erroneous inconsistent treatment, must result in one of seven "circumstances of adjustment" listed in section 1312.

---

l. S.Rep. No. 1567, 75th Cong.3d Sess. 48 (1938), as quoted in M. SALTZMAN, IRS PRACTICE AND PROCEDURE ¶ 5.07 (1981).

m. *See, e.g.,* Kolom v. United States, 791 F.2d 762 (9th Cir.1986) (holding no relief permitted under statutory mitigation provisions, but granting relief under doctrine of equitable recoupment).

n. I.R.C. § 1304(e).

o. *Compare* Chertkof v. United States, 676 F.2d 984 (4th Cir.1982) (can apply to estate tax) *with* Provident Nat. Bank v. United States, 507 F.Supp. 1197 (E.D.Pa. 1981) (do not apply to estate tax).

p. Courts and commentators differ in their descriptions the number and contents of the conditions. *See, e.g.,* O'Brien v. United States, 766 F.2d 1038, 1042 (7th Cir.1985) (three conditions); M. Saltzman, IRS Practice and Procedure ¶ 5.07 (1981) (four conditions); Willis, Some Limits of Equitable Recoupment, Tax Mitigation, and Res Judicata: Reflections Prompted by Chertkof v. United States, 38 Tax Lawyer 625, 630 (1985) (at least five and sometimes seven).

4. The party in whose favor the "determination" is made must have maintained an inconsistent position with the "determination" in a year now barred from litigation. I.R.C. § 1311(b).

These conditions and other issues are discussed in the cases that follow.

(1) Existence of a "Determination."
RASMUSSEN v. UNITED STATES
United States Court of Appeals, Fifth Circuit, 1987.
811 F.2d 949.

THORNBERRY, CIRCUIT JUDGE:

The United States appeals the district court's judgment in favor of taxpayer Hans Rasmussen on Rasmussen's claim for refund of overpaid federal income tax. We agree with the United States that Rasmussen did not satisfy the mitigation provisions of the Internal Revenue Code, and the statute of limitations therefore bars his claim.

On October 23, 1984, Hans Rasmussen, as sole shareholder and liquidator of Canal Marine Repairs, Inc. ("Canal"), filed this action to recover $84,235 in corporate income taxes paid by Canal for its taxable year ended April 30, 1978. Canal sold all its assets and adopted a plan of liquidation in May 1977, and received a certificate of liquidation from the State of Louisiana in December 1977. On July 10, 1978, Canal filed its federal income tax return for its taxable year ended April 30, 1978. On that return, it reported the sale of the assets and paid $84,504 in tax.

Rasmussen did not report any gain or loss from the liquidation of Canal on his individual return. As the result of an audit, the Internal Revenue Service ("Service") alleged that Rasmussen, individually, owed capital gains tax on Canal's liquidation because he had actually or constructively received the proceeds of the liquidation. In November 1981, Rasmussen consented to the adjustments to his tax liability and paid the additional individual income tax due.

On October 13, 1982, Rasmussen filed a claim for refund on behalf of Canal seeking to recover the corporate income tax paid on the sale of Canal's assets. Rasmussen argued that because the Service had determined that Canal had distributed the proceeds of the liquidation to him, I.R.C. § 337 applied to the liquidation. Under I.R.C. § 337, Canal did not owe tax on the liquidation and therefore, it overpaid its federal income tax for the taxable year ended April 30, 1978. The Service denied the claim because Rasmussen filed it more than three years after he had filed the return for Canal's taxable year ended April 30, 1978. *See* I.R.C. § 6511(a).

On October 23, 1984, Rasmussen filed suit in the U.S. District Court to recover the tax that Canal paid on its liquidation. The complaint alleged that his claim for refund fell within the mitigation provisions of the Code. I.R.C. §§ 1311–1314. The complaint also alleged that I.R.C. § 337 applied to Canal's liquidation and that as a result, Canal had overpaid its corporate income tax.

The government moved to dismiss the complaint because Rasmussen's claim was not timely and therefore did not confer jurisdiction on the district court. The government contended that the mitigation provisions were inapplicable because Rasmussen did not satisfy the specific statutory requirements. The district court denied the government's motion to dismiss and held that I.R.C. § 337 applied to the transaction.

In certain narrowly tailored situations the mitigation provisions of the Internal Revenue Code provide relief from the application of the general three-year statute of limitations:

> (a) GENERAL RULE.—If a determination (as defined in section 1313) is described in one or more of the paragraphs of section 1312 and, on the date of the determination, correction of the effect of the error referred to in the applicable paragraph of section 1312 is prevented by the operation of any law or rule of law, other than this part and other than section 7122 (relating to compromises), then the effect of the error shall be corrected by an adjustment made in the amount and in the manner specified in section 1314.

I.R.C. § 1311. * * *

Section 1313 defines the word "determination" to include four things:

> (1) a decision by the Tax Court or a judgment, decree, or other order by any court of competent jurisdiction, which has become final;
>
> (2) a closing agreement made under section 7121;
>
> (3) a final disposition by the Secretary of a claim for refund * * *;
>
> (4) under regulations prescribed by the Secretary, an agreement for purposes of this part, signed by the Secretary and by a person, relating to the liability of such person (or the person for whom he acts) in respect of a tax under this subtitle for any taxable period.

I.R.C. § 1313(a). Rasmussen argues that, "Form 870, evidencing [his] personal tax liability, and his subsequent payment of the deficiency, constituted a final determination by the Commissioner. In making this final determination as to Rasmussen's personal tax liability based on the corporation's liquidation status, the Government made a final determination respecting the corporation's tax liability as well." The district court accepted Rasmussen's argument.

Both Rasmussen and the district court ignore the statutory definition of "determination" in I.R.C. § 1313. Rasmussen stipulated that there was neither a Tax Court decision, nor a judgment of any other court, nor a closing agreement, nor a final disposition of a refund claim, nor an agreement between Rasmussen and the Secretary as defined in § 1313(a)(4).

Rasmussen cites cases for the proposition that the mitigation provisions are remedial in nature and should be construed to do equity. The government cites cases for the proposition that the provisions should be strictly construed. In any case,

> [t]his Circuit has held that when applying the mitigation statutes the facts of each case must fit "into the concrete, detailed requirements set out in the statute." *United States v. Rachal*, 312 F.2d 376, 383 (5th Cir.1962). Moreover, taxpayer has the burden of proving that the mitigation statutes apply. *United States v. Rushlight*, 291 F.2d 508, 514 (9th Cir.1961).

Cocchiara v. United States, 779 F.2d 1108, 1112 (5th Cir.1986). Because neither the district court nor Rasmussen can fit the facts of this case into the statutory definition of "determination," we reverse the district court's judgment in favor of Rasmussen and remand the case with instructions to dismiss. * * *

Reversed and remanded.

Note

Informal determinations are specifically provided for in section 1313. Closing agreements (Forms 866 and 906) qualify, as do agreements pursuant to § 1313(a)(4). The latter type of agreement is entered into between the taxpayer and the IRS on Form 2259 and must contain the statements listed in Reg. § 1.1313(a)–4(b), including a statement that it is made pursuant to § 1313(a)(4). The result in *Rasmussen* would have been different if the taxpayer had not signed the Form 870 and instead had insisted on an agreement under § 1313(a)(4).

(2) The "Inconsistency" Requirement.

CHERTKOF v. COMMISSIONER OF INTERNAL REVENUE

United States Court of Appeals, Fourth Circuit, 1981.
649 F.2d 264.

[*Editor's Note.* Jack Chertkof and his father owned E & T Realty Company, with Jack owning one-third of its stock and his father the remaining two-thirds. Following a disagreement, Jack and the corporation executed an agreement in July of 1965 pursuant to which the corporation agreed to redeem Jack's stock in exchange for a one-third interest in the corporation's assets. Jack received a private letter ruling that this distribution would qualify for capital gain treatment. In February of 1966, Jack surrendered his stock in the corporation and received one-third of its assets. Later that year, when his father became ill, Jack agreed to manage certain assets of the corporation.

On his 1966 return, Jack reported the redemption distribution as a capital gain, and filed a statement that he would not acquire any interest in the corporation—including as an officer—for 10 years. After an audit, the Service ruled that the distribution was taxable in 1965, not 1966, and that it did not qualify for capital gain treatment. Jack paid the assessed deficiency and the IRS voluntarily refunded to him the capital gain tax he had paid for 1966. Meanwhile, Jack filed a suit for refund of the tax he had paid pursuant to the assessed deficiency for 1965. In 1973, a federal district court held for Jack, finding that 1966 was the proper year for inclusion of the distribution. In 1974, the IRS issued a deficiency notice for 1966, again asserting that the distribution did not qualify for capital gain treatment. Jack petitioned the Tax Court and moved for summary judgment, claiming the statute of limitations had expired for 1966. The Tax Court held for the IRS, finding that the statutory mitigation provisions permitted reopening of the 1966 tax year.]

SPROUSE, CIRCUIT JUDGE.

I.

Taxpayers' first contention is that, since it was the Commissioner and not they who erroneously determined the tax was due in 1965, and since their position has never been inconsistent with the conclusion reached in *Perma-Rock* that 1966 was the proper tax year, the mitigation provisions do not apply and the deficiency assessed in 1974 for the taxable year 1966 is barred by the statute of limitations. Taxpayers correctly assert that the deficiency assessment for 1966 would have been time-barred after April 15, 1970, unless kept alive by the mitigation provisions of 26 U.S.C. §§ 1311–1314. We agree with the Tax Court, however, that the mitigation provisions do apply and, therefore, that the Commissioner's action is not barred by the normal statute of limitations.

As the Tax Court rightly concluded, application of the mitigation provisions is conditioned on the following:

1. There must have been an error in a tax year now closed (i.e., 1966). Section 1311(a).

2. There must have been a "determination" under section 1313(a) with respect to the item giving rise to the error for some other year (i.e., 1965).

3. The error must have been of a kind specified in section 1312; i.e., one of the "circumstances of adjustment" enumerated in section 1312 must have occurred.

4. The party who prevailed in said "determination" must have maintained a position inconsistent with the erroneous treatment. Section 1311(b).

It is undisputed that the first two conditions have been satisfied. The refund by the Commissioner of the tax payment tendered for 1966 erroneously excluded the redemption payment from Taxpayers' income for that year. The judgment of the district court holding the payment to have been income in 1966 and not in 1965 was a "determination" within the meaning of 1313(a)(1). The Commissioner relies on 1312(3)(A) as outlining the "circumstances of adjustment" required to satisfy the third condition; this requires a previous erroneous exclusion of the item involved in the determination from Taxpayers' income in another taxable year. It is Taxpayers' position that 1312(3)(A) requires the error to have been committed by the party who seeks to avoid the application of the mitigation provisions. Taxpayers also contend it was the Commissioner, not they, who took the inconsistent position. They point out that their initial position that the tax was payable in 1966 was consistent with the holding of the district court and was inconsistent with the initial determination of the IRS.

Taxpayers misconceive the meaning of both aspects of the statute. It was not congressional intent, in enacting the mitigation provisions, to benefit either the Commissioner or the taxpayer to the exclusion of the other. The basic purpose of the mitigation provisions is to permit the correction of an earlier decision which is determined to be erroneous in a subsequent administrative or judicial action; the intent is that the correct tax be paid or the correct deductions be allowed, not that a windfall be provided to either the taxpayer or the government on a gamesmanship theory of "fault."

We cannot read into section 1312(3)(A) a requirement that Taxpayers must have erred; not only does the statutory language indicate otherwise but legislative history points to a contrary congressional intent. Likewise, there is no requirement that the party who benefits from the application of the statute of limitations must have maintained a position inconsistent with that which it initially advanced. It is only necessary that the position adopted in the determination be inconsistent with the exclusion or deduction in another year.

The Senate Report accompanying the Revenue Bill of 1938 stated with respect to section 819:

> In each [of the examples], under existing law, an unfair benefit would have been obtained by assuming an inconsistent position and then taking shelter behind the protective barrier of the statute of limitations. Such resort to the statute of limitations is a plain misuse of its fundamental purpose. The purpose of the statute of limitations to prevent the litigation of stale claims is fully recognized and approved. But it was never intended to sanction active exploitation, by the beneficiary of the statutory bar, of opportunities only open to him if he assumes a position diametrically opposed to that taken prior to the running of the statute * * *. Legislation has long been needed to supplement the equitable principles applied by the courts and to check the growing volume of litigation by taking the profit out of inconsistency, whether exhibited by taxpayers or revenue officials *and whether fortuitous or the result of design.*
>
> The legislation here proposed is based upon the following principles:

(1) To preserve unimpaired the essential function of the statute of limitations, corrective adjustments should (a) never modify the application of the statute except when the party or parties in whose favor it applies shall have justified such modification by active inconsistency, and (b) under no circumstances affect the tax save with respect to the influence of the particular items involved in the adjustment.

(2) Subject to the foregoing principles, disputes as to the year in which income or deductions belong, or as to the person who should have the tax burden of income or the tax benefit of deductions, should never result in a double tax or a double reduction of tax, or an inequitable avoidance of tax.

* * *.

(4) Corrective adjustments should produce the effect of attributing income or deductions to the right year and the right taxpayer, and of establishing the proper basis.

S.Rep. No. 1567, 75th Cong., 3d Sess. 49–50 (1938) (emphasis added).

Case law also supports the Commissioner's position that the mitigation provisions can apply regardless of who erroneously excluded the taxable item and who took inconsistent positions. * * *

In *Albert W. Priest Trust v. Commissioner,* 6 T.C. 221 (1946), the Tax Court considered and rejected the argument made by the taxpayers therein that the mitigation provisions should not apply to their disadvantage unless *they* had maintained inconsistent positions.

The sole requirement of the statute is that the position so adopted be inconsistent with the prior erroneous allowance of the deduction. It does not seem important to us who proposed the allowance of the deduction, or upon what theory. The important fact is that it was allowed, that a tax was paid pursuant to the allowance of the deduction, and that the action was erroneous.

Id. at 226.[4]

The case *sub judice* illustrates the inequities which would result if Taxpayers' arguments were adopted. Concededly, Taxpayers owed some tax on the stock redemption in either 1965 or 1966. They initially included this item in their 1966 tax return. The Commissioner then ruled the proper tax year was 1965; Taxpayers paid a deficiency judgment for 1965 and received a refund for 1966. After years of administrative and judicial litigation, the correct taxable year was finally determined to be 1966 and the deficiency paid for 1965 was refunded. In the meantime, the statute of limitations ran on April 15, 1970, and absent application of the mitigation provisions, Taxpayers would pay no tax on their profits from the stock redemption. Applying

---

4. Taxpayers rely heavily on *Kappel v. Commissioner,* 615 F.2d 91 (3d Cir.1980), for the proposition that they must have maintained an active inconsistency which misled the Commissioner in order for the mitigation provisions to apply. *Kappel* is distinguishable, however, since it involved an attempt by the Commissioner to collect a tax for a year on which the statute of limitations had run before a statutory notice was first issued.

the Taxpayers' argument to a hypothetical case, a taxpayer could be the victim of a parallel inequity. If, for example, a future taxpayer belatedly claimed that a refund should be allowed by virtue of sections 1311(b)(1)(A) and 1312(1) or (4), he would be barred under Taxpayers' theory unless it was the Commissioner who had erroneously included income, disallowed deductions or maintained an inconsistent position rather than the taxpayer.

Affirmed.

Note

The position adopted by the *Chertkof* court is sometimes referred to as "passive inconsistency" and contrasted with the view espoused by the taxpayer (and adopted by some courts) requiring "active inconsistency," by which is meant a conscious exploitation of the statute of limitations. For an in-depth discussion of this issue, see M. Saltzman, IRS Practice and Procedure ¶ 5.07 (2d ed. 1991).

(3) The Seven "Circumstances of Adjustment"

Section 1312 lists seven "circumstances of adjustment." If the determination does not result in one of those circumstances, relief will not be available under the statutory mitigation scheme.

1. Double inclusion of an item of gross income.
2. Double allowance of deduction or credit.
3. Double exclusion of an item of gross income.
4. Double disallowance of a deduction or credit.
5. Correlative deductions and inclusions for trusts or estates and legatees, beneficiaries, or heirs.
6. Correlative deductions and credits for certain related corporations.
7. Basis of property after erroneous treatment of a prior transaction.

GARDINER v. UNITED STATES
United States Court of Appeals, Tenth Circuit, 1976.
536 F.2d 903.

DOYLE, CIRCUIT JUDGE.

This is a so-called income tax refund action in which the plaintiff-taxpayer sought recovery of allegedly erroneously or illegally paid taxes. The claim involves the tax years 1964, 1965 and 1966, and the amount in controversy is $7,846 together with interest. The claim was filed on September 6, 1973, and on April 15, 1974, the action in district court was filed. Thereafter, on March 7, 1975, the district court entered judgment in favor of the government. 391 F.Supp. 1202 (D.Utah 1975). Thereupon, a notice of appeal was filed and the appeal has now been perfected.

The problem arises out of the taxpayer's failure to deduct allowable depreciation for the years 1964, 1965 and 1966.

In the year 1963 the taxpayer purchased property which was subject to depreciation under Section 167 of the Internal Revenue Code of 1954. Notwithstanding that depreciation was allowable, plaintiff, in the tax years 1964, 1965 and 1966, did not claim depreciation deductions with respect to the property. (In subsequent years she did claim depreciation.) She filed her income tax returns for these years and paid taxes amounting to $2,661 for 1964; $4,858 for 1965; and $4,966 for 1966. When she sold the property in 1971 she did not reduce the basis by the depreciation which was allowed but not claimed for the years 1964, 1965 and 1966. As she figured it, she had a loss in the amount of $3,346.84. In the recomputation of the transaction the IRS determined that the sale of the property produced a taxable gain rather than a loss. It reached this conclusion by adding depreciation allowance of $7,586.79 for each of the years 1964, 1965 and 1966. As a result of the reduction of the basis by the inclusion of depreciation for these years, there resulted a taxable gain in the amount of $19,413.53. Appellant paid additional income tax as a result of the adjustment by the Internal Revenue Service.

When appellant discovered that she had failed to claim depreciation for the mentioned years, she filed a claim for refund of federal income taxes paid for those years in the amounts of $2,182, $2,828 and $2,836. The position of the Internal Revenue Service is that the statute of limitations, Section 6511(a) of the Internal Revenue Code of 1954, bars claims filed by a taxpayer after three years from the time the return was filed or two years from the time the tax was paid. The claim in question was not made until September 6, 1973, which is outside the statute of limitations.

Appellant argues that Sections 1311–1314 of the Internal Revenue Code are available to allow the case to be reopened even though such years would be otherwise barred by the statute of limitations. The procedural requirements for the application of the mentioned mitigation sections are met. Therefore, the sole issue for determination is whether or not the sections relied on by the plaintiff for relief, namely Sections 1311–1314, but, particularly, Section 1312(1) or (7), apply.

The trial court gave full consideration to the appellant's contention and in a fully reasoned opinion gave judgment to the government. In essence, the court determined that the failure to take allowable depreciation did not constitute a "transaction which was erroneously treated as affecting basis."

The contentions of appellant on this appeal are:

1. That the fact situation here qualifies as a circumstance of adjustment as described in Section 1312(1), and

2. As an adjustment of the basis of property after erroneous treatment of a prior transaction within the meaning of Section 1312(7).

Sec. 3   RECOUPMENT & MITIGATION PROVISIONS   199

Appellant would then give a broad interpretation to Sections 1311-1315, an interpretation which would broadly allow correction of an error made in the inclusion of income or in the allowance or disallowance of a deduction or in the tax treatment "of a transaction affecting the basis of property, whereby such error can be corrected notwithstanding the ordinary period of limitations is run."

I.

THE ARGUMENT IN SUPPORT OF APPLICABILITY OF SECTION 1312(1)

Section 1312(1)[1] defines a circumstance in which adjustment is to be made and that is where there has been double inclusion of an item of gross income resulting from a determination by the IRS or a court requiring the inclusion in gross income of an item which was earlier erroneously included in the gross income of the taxpayer for another year. E.g., *M. Fine & Sons Mfg. Co. v. United States,* 168 F.Supp. 769, 144 Ct.Cl. 46 (1958). In *Fine* the taxpayer was given a factory by the local Chamber of Commerce. A few years later the factory was sold. IRS policy was that the donated factory had a zero basis and, therefore, no deductions for depreciation were allowed. When the factory was sold, the Fine Company computed its gain and paid the tax using the zero basis. Subsequently, the Supreme Court held in *Brown Shoe Co. v. Commissioner,* 339 U.S. 583, 70 S.Ct. 820, 94 L.Ed. 1081 (1950), that a taxpayer which received property from a community as an inducement to locate or expand its operations in the area was entitled to deductions for depreciation; that the basis in the hands of the taxpayer was the cost to the donating community. Thereupon, the Fine Company filed a claim for refund for the year of the sale, contending that its basis for the factory had been the cost to the Chamber of Commerce. The Commissioner agreed in part with the Fine Company and allowed the Company to use the donating community's cost basis, reduced by the previously disallowed annual depreciation, in computing the gain from the sale. He rejected the company's claim for refund for the prior years' disallowed depreciation. A suit was thereupon filed in the Court of Claims, relying on Section 1312(1). That court ruled that the disallowance of depreciation resulted in an erroneous inclusion in gross income, thus making the mitigation provisions applicable. Our case differs factually from *Fine*.

The Internal Revenue Service argues that Section 1312(1) is inapplicable. The section is activiated by inclusion of an item of gross income required by the Commissioner to be included, notwithstanding that it was erroneously included in gross income in a previous year. The IRS says that this is not present here. The failure to take

---

1. The provision reads:
"The circumstances under which the adjustment provided in Section 1311 is authorized are as follows:
(1) *Double inclusion of an item of gross income.*—The determination requires the inclusion in gross income of an item which was erroneously included in the gross income of the taxpayer for another taxable year or in the gross income of a related taxpayer."

deductions for allowable depreciation does not constitute an erroneous inclusion in the taxpayer's gross income in another tax year.

The meaning of an *item* of gross income is, under Section 61 of the 1954 Code, limited to specific items and does not include everything that results in an increase in tax. It is restricted to positive items and does not include negative elements such as deductions (like depreciation), the omission of which results in increased taxes.

The *Fine* case does not support appellant's position. The Court of Claims there considered that factory depreciation was a constituent element of the taxpayer's cost of goods in determining its gross income and was not a simple deduction. Such an analysis would not apply here because our case is not concerned with the computation of gross income based upon cost of goods sold.

In our view depreciation is not part of the computation of gross income. Rather, it represents a deduction applicable to gross income.

In addition to this difference, it is to be conceded that our general approach to the issue differs from that which was followed by the Court of Claims in *Fine*.

II.

Whether the Failure to Claim Allowable Depreciation Deductions for the Years 1964, 1965 and 1966 Qualifies as a Circumstance of Adjustment Under Section 1312(7)

The alternative contention of the taxpayer is that Subsection (7) of Section 1312 of the Revenue Act of 1954, which is entitled "Basis of property after erroneous treatment of a prior transaction", applies in the instant case to relieve the taxpayer by permitting reopening (notwithstanding the statute of limitations) the returns for the taxable years 1964, 1965 and 1966.[2]

Subsection (7) provides for an adjustment in a situation where the determination of the taxpayer's later year tax liability establishes the basis of property and in respect of any transaction on which such basis depends or in respect of any transaction which was erroneously treated

---

2. The provision reads:

(A) General rule.—The determination determines the basis of property, and in respect of any transaction on which such basis depends, or in respect of any transaction which was erroneously treated, as affecting such basis, there occurred, with respect to a taxpayer described in subparagraph (B) of this paragraph, any of the errors described in subparagraph (C) of this paragraph.

(B) Taxpayers with respect to whom the erroneous treatment occurred.—The taxpayer with respect to whom the erroneous treatment occurred must be—

(i) the taxpayer with respect to whom the determination is made.

* * *

(C) Prior erroneous treatment.—With respect to a taxpayer described in subparagraph (B) of this paragraph—

(i) there was an erroneous inclusion in, or omission from, gross income,

(ii) there was an erroneous recognition, or nonrecognition, of gain or loss, or

(iii) there was an erroneous deduction of an item properly chargeable to capital account or an erroneous charge to capital account of an item properly deductible.

Sec. 3 RECOUPMENT & MITIGATION PROVISIONS 201

as affecting such basis, there occurred with respect to the taxpayer any of the type of errors described in Paragraph (C) of that subsection, such as an erroneous inclusion or omission from gross income under Subparagraph (i); or an erroneous recognition or non-recognition of gain or loss under Subparagraph (ii); an erroneous deduction of an item properly chargeable to a capital account; or an erroneous charge to a capital account of an item properly deductible, under Subparagraph (iii).

Section 1312(7) deals then with a capital transaction and relief available in connection with such a transaction where certain errors have taken place affecting the basis of property or in respect of any transaction which was erroneously treated as affecting such basis. The aforementioned errors contained in Subparagraph (C) are summarized above.

The district court here ruled that the failure to take an allowable deduction for depreciation, which is the situation here, did not constitute a transaction within the meaning of the section. The court explained that the word transaction contemplates a business transaction in the ordinary sense. For example, a sale, purchase, acquisition or exchange. The court's reasoning was that the failure to take an allowable deduction for depreciation does not qualify under the definition of transaction.

The cases of *United States v. Rushlight,* 291 F.2d 508 (9th Cir.1961) and *Granger v. United States,* 3 A.F.T.R.2d 361 (S.D.Cal.1958), recognize that the neglect of the taxpayer to claim depreciation does not constitute a transaction within the meaning of Section 1312(7)(A).

The court was correct then in construing the term "transaction" as meaning business transaction in the ordinary sense of the term such as distributions, sales, purchases, dispositions, acquisitions or exchanges. The failure to make a particular entry falls far short of being a sale, an exchange or transfer, and hence it cannot be considered in and of itself a transaction. At most it is one small element of an entire or whole transaction.

There is another reason why the appellant does not qualify under Section 1312(7). None of the errors which are set forth in (C) of Section 1312(7) are present here. There is no erroneous inclusion or omission of gross income (*see* the discussion in Part I above), (C)(i); nor is there an erroneous recognition or non-recognition of gain o[r] loss, (C)(ii); nor is there an erroneous deduction of an item which should have been capitalized or vice versa, (C)(iii).

Appellant argues that the failure to claim allowable depreciation constitutes an erroneous deduction of an item properly chargeable to capital account or is an erroneous charge to a capital account of an item properly deductible, (C)(iii). We do not see failure to claim allowable depreciation as a circumstance in which the cost of property was initially erroneously added at the time of purchase to a capital account instead of being currently deducted in full in the year of said purchase. The cost of the property here at issue is not deductible in full in the year of purchase. Where there is an erroneous charge to capital account of property depreciable or subject to amortization, the taxpayer then simply recovers the cost of the property through depreciation allowance for the useful life of the property. He does not fully deduct it in the year of purchase. The instant case, in which the taxpayer failed by oversight to claim an allowable depreciation allowance on a capital item, just does not fall within the deduction/capitalization dichotomy of Section 1312(7)(C)(iii).

Appellant relies on our decision in *Oklahoma Gas and Electric Company v. United States,* 464 F.2d 1188 (10th Cir.1972), *aff'g* 333 F.Supp. 1178 (W.D.Okla.1971). In *Oklahoma Gas,* the taxpayer was accorded relief under the mitigation provisions for the erroneous capitalization of sales and use taxes paid in the acquisition of certain machinery, subparagraph (7)(C)(iii) of Section 1312. (Federal Power Commission regulations required the capitalization of such expenses on the utility's books; until Oklahoma Gas changed accounting firms in 1957 it capitalized such expenditures for tax accounting purposes as well.) Unlike the depreciation involved in the instant case, Oklahoma Gas' sales and use tax expenses were fully deductible in the year incurred, and, thus, appellant's reliance on that decision is misplaced.

Contrary to the appellant's contention, the Ninth Circuit's opinion in *United States v. Rushlight, supra,* does not support her contention that the failure to claim depreciation allowance constitutes an erroneous charge to the capital account. What was said in *Rushlight* is dictum and it is not shown in the opinion how the failure to claim depreciation constitutes an erroneous charge to capital account of an item that was fully deductible.

We have carefully examined the examples described in the regulations promulgated under Section 1312, and the examples given in the Congressional Committee reports on the predecessor provision to Section 1312 in the 1939 Code, Section 3801(b). These we find to be of no help to appellant's case.

The judgment of the district court is affirmed.

B. EQUITABLE RECOUPMENT

The doctrine of equitable recoupment in federal tax cases was articulated in the 1935 case *Bull v. United States,* 295 U.S. 247, 55 S.Ct. 695, 79 L.Ed. 1421 (1935). The Supreme Court revisited the doctrine twice in 1937,[p] then again in 1946.[q] Perhaps because the statutory mitigation provisions "preempted" so much of the litigation concerning unfairness of the bar of the statute of limitations, the Supreme Court did not again address the doctrine of equitable recoupment until its 1990 decision in *Dalm.*

p. McEachern v. Rose, 302 U.S. 56, 58 S.Ct. 84, 82 L.Ed. 46 (1937); Stone v. White, 301 U.S. 532, 57 S.Ct. 851, 81 L.Ed. 1265 (1937).

q. Rothensies v. Electric Storage Battery Co., 329 U.S. 296, 67 S.Ct. 271, 91 L.Ed. 296 (1946).

UNITED STATES v. DALM
Supreme Court of the United States, 1990.
494 U.S. 596, 110 S.Ct. 1361, 108 L.Ed.2d 548.

JUSTICE KENNEDY delivered the opinion of the Court.

Single transactions, it is well known, may be susceptible to different, and inconsistent, theories of taxation. In the case before us, the taxpayer treated moneys derived from her deceased employer's estate as a gift, and paid gift tax on the transfer. Some years later, the Government contended that the money the taxpayer had received from the transaction was income. The taxpayer disagreed, and the Government's assertion of an income tax deficiency was the subject of proceedings in the United States Tax Court. The question presented is whether, the statute of limitations long since having run, the doctrine of equitable recoupment supports a separate suit for refund of the earlier paid gift tax after the taxpayer settled the Tax Court deficiency proceeding and agreed to pay income tax on the transaction. We hold that it does not.

I

The taxpayer, Frances Dalm, is the respondent here. Dalm was appointed administratrix of the estate of Harold Schrier in May 1975, at the request of Schrier's surviving brother, Clarence. It appears Dalm had been the decedent's loyal secretary for many years and that Clarence wanted her to take charge of the affairs of the estate and receive some of the moneys that otherwise would belong to him.

Dalm received fees from the estate, approved by the probate court, of $30,000 in 1976 and $7,000 in 1977. She also received from Clarence two payments, $180,000 in 1976 and $133,813 in 1977. Clarence and his wife filed a gift tax return in December 1976 reporting the $180,000 payment as a gift to Dalm, and in that same month Dalm paid the gift tax of $18,675. The Internal Revenue Service (IRS) later assessed an additional $1,587 in penalties and interest with respect to the transfer. The Schriers paid the penalties and interest in 1977, and were reimbursed by Dalm. But no gift tax return was filed with respect to the 1977 payment of $133,813.

After auditing Dalm's 1976 and 1977 income tax returns, the IRS determined that the payments from Clarence represented additional fees for Dalm's services as administratrix of the estate and should have been reported as income. The IRS asserted deficiencies in her income tax of $91,471 in 1976, and $70,639 in 1977, along with additions to the taxes under § 6653(a) of the Internal Revenue Code of 1954 (IRC), 26 U.S.C. § 6653(a) (1982 ed.).[1]

1. Unless otherwise noted, all statutory references are to the Internal Revenue Code of 1954 (26 U.S.C.), as amended.

Dalm petitioned the Tax Court for a redetermination of the asserted deficiencies, as was her right under § 6213(a). In her petition, she argued that the 1976 and 1977 payments from Clarence were gifts to carry out the wish of the decedent that she share in the estate. After two days of trial, Dalm and the IRS settled the case, with the parties agreeing to a stipulated decision that respondent owed income tax deficiencies of $10,416 for 1976 and $70,639 for 1977. No claim for a credit or recoupment of the gift tax paid by Dalm was raised in the Tax Court proceedings, although there is some dispute whether the gift tax was one of the factors considered in arriving at the terms of the settlement. See n. 2, *infra.*

Immediately after agreeing to the settlement, Dalm filed an administrative claim for refund of the $20,262 in gift tax, interest, and penalties paid with respect to the $180,000 transfer in 1976. The claim was filed in November 1984, even though the IRC required Dalm to file any claim for a refund of the gift tax by December 1979. See § 6511(a). When the IRS failed to act upon her claim within six months, Dalm filed suit in the United States District Court for the Western District of Michigan, seeking what in her complaint she denominated a refund of "overpaid gift tax." Her complaint alleged that the District Court had jurisdiction under 28 U.S.C. § 1346(a)(1) (1982 ed.).

The Government moved to dismiss the suit for lack of jurisdiction and for summary judgment, arguing that the suit was untimely under the applicable statute of limitations. The District Court granted the Government's motions, rejecting Dalm's contention that her suit was timely under the doctrine of equitable recoupment as set forth in our opinion in Bull v. United States, 295 U.S. 247, 55 S.Ct. 695, 79 L.Ed. 1421 (1935), a case we shall discuss. The court held that equitable recoupment did not authorize it to exercise jurisdiction over "an independent lawsuit, such as this suit, * * * maintained for a refund for a year in which the statute of limitations has expired." App. to Pet. for Cert. 19a.

On appeal, the Court of Appeals for the Sixth Circuit reversed. 867 F.2d 305 (1989). The court found Dalm's claim satisfied all of the requirements for equitable recoupment expressed in our cases. It rejected the District Court's characterization of Dalm's action as an independent lawsuit barred by the statute of limitations, reasoning that she could maintain an otherwise barred action for refund of gift tax because the Government had made a timely claim of a deficiency in her income tax based upon an inconsistent legal theory. *Id.*, at 311–312 (citing *Kolom v. United States,* 791 F.2d 762 (CA9 1986)).[2]

2. In its opinion granting summary judgment to the Government, the District Court had suggested that an alternative ground for decision was that the only plausible explanation for the allocation of the agreed income tax liability between 1976 and 1977 in the Tax Court settlement was that the allocation reflected the previously paid gift tax on the 1976 transfer. The Sixth Circuit held that the District Court had erred in granting summary judgment on this issue giving the taxpayer an opportunity to show the parties' intent in effecting the settlement. Accordingly, it re-

Because the approach taken by the Sixth and Ninth Circuits is in conflict with that adopted by Seventh Circuit, see *O'Brien v. United States,* 766 F.2d 1038 (1985), we granted certiorari, 493 U.S. ___, 110 S.Ct. 46, 107 L.Ed.2d 15 (1989), and now reverse.

II

The ultimate question in the case is whether the District Court had jurisdiction over Dalm's suit seeking a refund of the gift tax, interest, and penalties paid on the 1976 transfer. We hold that it did not.

A

In her complaint, Dalm invoked 28 U.S.C. § 1346(a)(1) (1982 ed.), under which a district court has jurisdiction over a "civil action against the United States for the recovery of any internal-revenue tax alleged to have been erroneously or illegally assessed or collected, or any penalty claimed to have been collected without authority or any sum alleged to have been excessive or in any manner wrongfully collected under the internal-revenue laws." Despite its spacious terms, § 1346(a)(1) must be read in conformity with other statutory provisions which qualify a taxpayer's right to bring a refund suit upon compliance with certain conditions. First is § 7422(a), which, tracking the language of § 1346(a)(1), limits a taxpayer's right to bring a refund suit by providing that

> "[n]o suit or proceeding shall be maintained in any court for the recovery of any internal revenue tax alleged to have been erroneously or illegally assessed or collected, or of any penalty claimed to have been collected without authority, or of any sum alleged to have been excessive or in any manner wrongfully collected, until a claim for refund or credit has been duly filed with the Secretary, according to the provisions of law in that regard, and the regulations of the Secretary established in pursuance thereof."

Second, § 6511(a) provides that if a taxpayer is required to file a return with respect to a tax, such as the gift tax, the taxpayer must file any claim for refund within three years from the time the return was filed or two years from the time the tax was paid, whichever period expires later. Read together, the import of these sections is clear: unless a claim for refund of a tax has been filed within the time limits imposed by § 6511(a), a suit for refund, regardless of whether the tax is alleged to have been "erroneously," "illegally," or "wrongfully collected," §§ 1346(a)(1), 7422(a), may not be maintained in any court. See *United States v. Kales,* 314 U.S. 186, 193, 62 S.Ct. 214, 217, 86 L.Ed. 132 (1941).

There is no doubt that Dalm failed to comply with these statutory requirements. The Schriers filed their gift tax return and Dalm paid the gift tax on the 1976 transfer in December 1976. She paid the penalties and interest on that tax in March 1977. Dalm did not file her claim for refund of the gift tax until November 1984, long after the limitations period expired. Under the plain language of §§ 6511(a) and

manded the case for further proceedings on this issue. 867 F.2d, at 312.

7422(a), the District Court was barred from entertaining her suit for a refund of the tax.

B

The Court of Appeals did not contest this analysis; indeed, it recognized that "[t]here is no statutory basis for permitting the recovery of a tax overpayment after the statute of limitations has expired." 867 F.2d, at 308. Despite the lack of a statutory basis for recovery, the court concluded that the doctrine of equitable recoupment permits Dalm to maintain an action to recover the overpaid gift tax. We disagree.

The doctrine of equitable recoupment was first addressed by us in our opinion in *Bull v. United States, supra*. There, the dispute centered on whether partnership distributions received by a decedent's estate after his death were subject to estate tax or income tax. After an audit, the executor of the estate included the sums in the estate tax return, and paid the estate tax in 1920 and 1921. In 1925, the Commissioner of Internal Revenue notified the estate of a deficiency in the estate's income tax for the 1920 tax year, contending that the same distributions upon which estate tax had been paid should have been treated as income. The Commissioner, however, did not give credit for the estate tax earlier paid on the value of the distributions.

That same year, the estate petitioned to the Board of Tax Appeals for a redetermination of the deficiency.[3] After the Board sustained the Commissioner's deficiency determination, the estate paid the additional income tax, and filed a claim for refund of the income tax paid. The Commissioner rejected the claim, and, in September 1930, the executor sued in the Court of Claims for a refund of the income tax.[4] In his

---

3. The Board of Tax Appeals, the forerunner to the United States Tax Court, was established by the Revenue Act of 1924 as "an independent agency in the executive branch of the Government." Revenue Act of 1924, Pub.L. 176, § 900(k), 43 Stat. 338. Under the Act, a taxpayer was permitted to challenge an income tax deficiency asserted by the Commissioner, prior to paying the deficiency, by way of petition to the Board. See *id.*, §§ 274, 900; *Old Colony Trust Co. v. Commissioner*, 279 U.S. 716, 721, 49 S.Ct. 499, 501, 73 L.Ed. 918 (1929).

4. Before the enactment of the Revenue Act of 1926, there was no direct review of Board of Tax Appeals decisions. As a result, a taxpayer who lost in proceedings before the Board was permitted to sue in district court or the Court of Claims for a refund after payment of the deficiency. In effect, the refund suit, although nominally a separate proceeding, was a mechanism by which taxpayers could obtain review of Board decisions. See *Old Colony Trust Co.*, *supra*, at 721–722, 49 S.Ct., at 501; Ferguson, Jurisdictional Problems in Federal Tax Controversies, 48 Iowa L.Rev. 312, 350–351 (1963). The Revenue Act of 1926 put an end to this circuitous process. First, it provided for direct judicial review of Board decisions in the courts of appeals. Revenue Act of 1926, ch. 27, § 1001(a), 44 Stat. 109. Second, the Act provided that, once a taxpayer had filed a timely petition with the Board, the taxpayer generally could not institute a new suit in another court for refund of the same tax. *Id.*, § 284(d), 44 Stat. 67. Under our decision in *Old Colony Trust Co., supra*, at 725–728, 49 S.Ct., at 502–03, the Act did not apply to cases where, as in *Bull*, the taxpayer filed his or her petition with the Board and the Board had not issued a decision prior to the enactment of the Act in 1926. See generally Andrews, Modern–Day Equitable Recoupment and the "Two Tax Effect:" Avoidance of the Statutes of Limitation in Federal Tax Controversies, 28 Ariz.L.Rev. 595, 599, n. 20 (1986).

petition to the Court of Claims, the executor argued (1) that the amount taxed was not income, so that the estate was entitled to a refund of the entire amount of income tax paid; and (2) alternatively, if the amount taxed was income, the Government should credit against the income tax due the overpayment of estate tax, plus interest, attributable to the inclusion of the amount in the taxable estate. The Court of Claims rejected both arguments.

We reversed, holding that the executor was entitled to a credit against the income tax deficiency in the amount of the overpayment of estate tax, with interest. 295 U.S., at 263, 55 S.Ct., at 701. We began by acknowledging that the executor had not filed a claim for refund of the estate tax within the limitations period, and that any action for refund of the tax was now barred. *Id.*, at 259, 260–261, 55 S.Ct., at 699, 699–700. "If nothing further had occurred Congressional action would have been the sole avenue of redress." *Id.*, at 261, 55 S.Ct., at 700.

What did occur, however, was that after the limitations period on the estate tax had run, the Government assessed a deficiency in the estate's income tax based upon the same taxable event, and the deficiency became the subject of litigation between the estate and the Government. We reasoned that a tax assessment is in essence an assertion by the sovereign that the taxpayer owes a debt to it; but that, because "taxes are the life-blood of government," it was necessary for the tax assessed to be collected prior to adjudication of whether the assessment was erroneous or unlawful. As a result,

> "the usual procedure for the recovery of debts is reversed in the field of taxation. Payment precedes defense, and the burden of proof, normally on the claimant, is shifted to the taxpayer * * *. But these reversals of the normal process of collecting a claim cannot obscure the fact that after all what is being accomplished is the recovery of a just debt owed the sovereign." *Id.*, at 260, 55 S.Ct., at 699.

Under our reasoning, the proceeding between the executor and the Government was in substance an attempt by the Government to recover a debt from the estate. The debt was the income tax that was owed, even though in fact it already had been paid. Had the Government followed the "usual procedure" of recovering debts by instituting an action at law for the income tax owed, the executor would have been able to defend against the suit by "demanding recoupment of the amount mistakenly collected as estate tax and wrongfully retained." *Id.*, at 261, 55 S.Ct., at 700 (citing *United States v. State Bank*, 96 U.S. 30, 24 L.Ed. 647 (1878)).

> "If the claim for income tax deficiency had been the subject of a suit, any counter demand for recoupment of the overpayment of estate tax could have been asserted by way of defense and credit obtained notwithstanding the statute of limitations had barred an independent suit against the Government therefor. This is because recoupment is in the nature of a defense arising out of some feature of the transaction upon which the plaintiff's action is grounded. Such a defense is never

barred by the statute of limitations so long as the main action itself is timely." 295 U.S., at 262, 55 S.Ct., at 700.

We found it immaterial that, rather than the Government having to sue to collect the income tax, the executor was required first to pay it and then seek a refund. "This procedural requirement does not obliterate his substantial right to rely on his cross-demand for credit of the amount which if the United States had sued him for income tax he could have recouped against his liability on that score." *Id.,* at 263, 55 S.Ct., at 701.[5]

Dalm contends that the only distinction between her case and *Bull* is the "meaningless procedural distinction" that her claim of equitable recoupment is raised in a separate suit for refund of gift tax, after she had litigated the income tax deficiency, while in *Bull* the claim of equitable recoupment of the estate tax was litigated as part of a suit for refund of that tax alleged to be inconsistent with the estate tax. A distinction that has jurisdiction as its central concept is not meaningless. In *Bull,* the executor sought equitable recoupment of the estate tax in an action for refund of income tax, over which it was undisputed that the Court of Claims had jurisdiction. See n. 4, *supra.* All that was at issue was whether the Court of Claims, in the interests of equity, could adjust the income tax owed to the Government to take account of an estate tax paid in error but which the executor could not recover in a separate refund action. Here, Dalm does not seek to invoke equitable recoupment in determining her income tax liability; she has already litigated that liability without raising a claim of equitable recoupment, and is foreclosed from relitigating it now. See § 6512(a). She seeks to invoke equitable recoupment only in a separate action for refund of gift tax, an action for which there is no statutory authorization by reason of the bar of the limitations statute.

It is instructive to consider what the facts in *Bull* would have to be if Dalm's contention is correct that her case is identical to *Bull* in all material respects. The executor in *Bull* would have litigated the income tax liability, without raising a claim of equitable recoupment, in the Board of Tax Appeals and/or in the Court of Claims, with the Government winning in each forum. Then, having exhausted his avenues of litigating the income tax liability and paid the tax, the executor would have filed a claim for refund of the estate tax with the Commissioner, asserting equitable recoupment as the basis for the refund, with the Commissioner rejecting it as untimely. At that point, the executor would have brought suit for refund of the estate tax in the

---

5. Since *Bull,* we have emphasized that a claim of equitable recoupment will lie only where the Government has taxed a single transaction, item, or taxable event under two inconsistent theories. See *Rothensies v. Electric Storage Battery Co.,* 329 U.S. 296, 299–300, 67 S.Ct. 271, 272, 91 L.Ed. 296 (1946); cf. *Stone v. White,* 301 U.S. 532, 57 S.Ct. 851, 81 L.Ed. 1265 (1937) (permitting the Government to invoke equitable recoupment as a defense against a claim for refund of income tax paid by a trust where there was a complete identity of interest between the trust and the beneficiary who had received the income, and a claim against the beneficiary for the income tax was then barred).

Court of Claims after the statute of limitations had run. Had the case come to us with those facts, we would have faced the issue presented here: whether the court in which the taxpayer was seeking a refund was barred from entertaining the suit. We can say with assurance that we were not presented with this issue in *Bull*, and did not consider it. Even had the issue been raised, *Bull* itself suggests that we would have rejected Dalm's argument out-of-hand. See *Bull*, 295 U.S., at 259, 55 S.Ct., at 699 ("The fact that the petitioner relied on the Commissioner's assessment for estate tax, and believed the inconsistent claim of deficiency of income tax was of no force, cannot avail to toll the statute of limitations, which forbade the bringing of any action in 1930 for refund of estate tax payments made in 1921").

The only other decision in which we have upheld a claim or defense premised upon the doctrine of equitable recoupment is consistent with our analysis today. In *Stone v. White*, 301 U.S. 532, 57 S.Ct. 851, 81 L.Ed. 1265 (1937), a trust had paid the income it received from the corpus to its sole beneficiary, and also paid the tax due on the income. After the statute of limitations governing the Government's right to collect the income tax from the beneficiary had run, the trust filed a timely suit seeking a refund of the income tax paid on the theory that the beneficiary, not the trust, was liable for the tax. We held that, given the identity of interest between the beneficiary and the trust, the Government could invoke equitable recoupment to assert its now-barred claim against the beneficiary as a defense to the trust's timely claim for a refund. *Id.*, at 537–539, 57 S.Ct., at 853–54. As in *Bull*, there was no dispute that the court in which we allowed the doctrine of equitable recoupment to be raised had jurisdiction over the underlying action: the trust's timely action for a refund of income tax.

In sum, our decisions in *Bull* and *Stone* stand only for the proposition that a party litigating a tax claim in a timely proceeding may, in that proceeding, seek recoupment of a related, and inconsistent, but now time-barred tax claim relating to the same transaction. In both cases, there was no question but that the courts in which the refund actions were brought had jurisdiction. To date, we have not allowed equitable recoupment to be the sole basis for jurisdiction.

C

Under settled principles of sovereign immunity, "the United States, as sovereign, 'is immune from suit, save as it consents to be sued * * * and the terms of its consent to be sued in any court define that court's jurisdiction to entertain the suit.'" A statute of limitations requiring that a suit against the Government be brought within a certain time period is one of those terms. "[A]lthough we should not construe such a time-bar provision unduly restrictively, we must be careful not to interpret it in a manner that would 'extend the waiver beyond that which Congress intended.'"

As we have determined, our previous equitable recoupment cases have not suspended rules of jurisdiction and so have not deviated from these principles. We likewise refuse Dalm's invitation to do so here. She seeks a refund not of income tax but of gift tax on which the return was filed and the tax paid in December 1976. For the District Court to have jurisdiction over her suit for refund, Dalm was required to file a claim for refund of the tax within three years of the time the gift tax return was filed or two years of the time the tax was paid, whichever period expires later. See §§ 6511(a), 7422(a).[6] There is no question but that she failed to do so.[7] Having failed to comply with the statutory requirements for seeking a refund, she asks us to go beyond the authority Congress has given us in permitting suits against the Government. If any principle is central to our understanding of sovereign immunity, it is that the power to consent to such suits is reserved to Congress.

Our conclusion is reinforced by the fact that Congress has legislated a set of exceptions to the limitations period prescribed by §§ 7422 and 6511(a). In 1938, Congress adopted what are known as the mitigation provisions, now codified at §§ 1311–1314. These statutes, in specified circumstances, permit a taxpayer who has been required to pay inconsistent taxes to seek a refund of a tax the recovery of which is otherwise barred by §§ 7422(a) and 6511(a). It is undisputed that Dalm's action does not come within these provisions; were we to allow

---

6. Justice Stevens calls it a fiction to cast Dalm's action as a suit for refund. He creates instead a distinction between refund actions and suits for funds wrongfully retained. See *post*, at 1374–1375. Neither the IRC nor our authorities support the distinction. Section 6511(a) applies to claims for refund of a tax "overpayment." The common sense interpretation is that a tax is overpaid when a taxpayer pays more than is owed, for whatever reason or no reason at all. Even in *Bull*, the case upon which the dissent relies to assert that retention of the gift tax is unjust or fraudulent, we described the inconsistent tax as being an "overpayment." See, *e.g.*, 295 U.S., at 258, 262, 263, 55 S.Ct., at 699, 700, 701. The word encompasses "erroneously," "illegally," or "wrongfully" collected taxes, as those terms are used in 28 U.S.C. § 1346(a)(1) (1982 ed.) and § 7422(a).

There is a further statutory point. By its express language, § 7422(a) conditions a district court's authority to hear a refund suit, regardless of whether the tax is alleged to have been erroneously, illegally, or wrongfully collected, upon the filing of a claim for refund. If, as even Justice Stevens appears to concede, see *post*, at 1374, the term "overpayment" as used in § 6511(a) encompasses erroneous or illegal collection, there is no reason to conclude that it does not also encompass wrongful collection.

As a final matter, we note that both Dalm and the Court of Appeals must have been misled by what Justice Stevens now thinks a fiction. Dalm's complaint sought a "refund" of "overpaid gift taxes"; and the Court of Appeals treated the claim as one for "recovery of a tax overpayment." See Complaint, 2–3; 867 F.2d 305, 308 (CA6 1989). We have no doubt that these characterizations were correct.

7. In a final attempt to bring her refund suit within the statute, Dalm contends that her suit was timely. She argues that the gift tax was not paid for the purposes of § 6511(a) until 1984, when it was determined that she owed income tax on the same transaction under an inconsistent theory. So, she asserts, her cause of action for refund of gift tax did not arise until that time. We disagree. The most sensible interpretation of § 6511(a) is that a tax is paid when the taxpayer tenders payment of the tax to the IRS, not when the taxpayer discovers that the payment was erroneous. The very purpose of statutes of limitation in the tax context is to bar the assertion of a refund claim after a certain period of time has passed, without regard to whether the claim would otherwise be meritorious. That a taxpayer does not learn until after the limitations period has run that a tax was paid in error, and that he or she has a ground upon which to claim a refund, does not operate to lift the statutory bar.

her to maintain a suit for refund on the basis of equitable recoupment, we would be doing little more than overriding Congress's judgment as to when equity requires that there be an exception to the limitations bar.

Our holding today does not leave taxpayers in Dalm's position powerless to invoke the doctrine of equitable recoupment. Both the Secretary, at the administrative level, see Rev.Rul. 71–56, 1971–1 Cum.Bull. 404 (revoking Rev.Rul. 55–226, 1955–1 Cum.Bull. 469), and a court which has jurisdiction over a timely suit for refund may consider an equitable recoupment claim for an earlier tax paid under an inconsistent theory on the same transaction.

III

The Court of Appeals reasoned that recoupment should be permitted because it effected, with respect to a single transaction, the recovery of a tax based upon a theory inconsistent with the theory upon which a later tax was paid. But to permit an independent action for recoupment because there is but one transaction is to mistake the threshold requirement for its rationale. It is true that our precedents allowing recoupment pertain to cases where a single transaction is subjected to inconsistent taxation, but the reason the statute of limitations is not a bar in those cases is that the court has uncontested jurisdiction to adjudicate one of the taxes in question. In such cases, a court has the equitable power to examine and consider the entire transaction:

"The essence of the doctrine of recoupment is stated in the *Bull* case: 'recoupment is in the nature of a defense arising out of some feature of the transaction upon which the plaintiff's action is grounded.' 295 U.S. 247, 262 [55 S.Ct. 695, 700]. It has never been thought to allow one transaction to be offset against another, but only to permit a transaction which is made the subject of suit by plaintiff to be examined in all its aspects, and judgment to be rendered that does justice in view of the one transaction as a whole." *Rothensies v. Electric Storage Battery Co.*, 329 U.S. 296, 67 S.Ct. 271, 272, 91 L.Ed. 296 (1946).

Here the Government asserted an income tax deficiency on a theory inconsistent with the theory upon which Dalm relied in paying gift tax. She chose to litigate the deficiency in the Tax Court, where she did not attempt to raise a recoupment claim.[8] She cannot choose this avenue to adjudicate the income tax consequences of the transaction, and then seek to reopen the matter and override the statute of limitations for the sole purpose of seeking recoupment. The controlling jurisdictional statutes do not permit her to do so.

The judgment of the Court of Appeals is therefore reversed.

It is so ordered.

JUSTICE STEVENS, with whom JUSTICE BRENNAN and JUSTICE MARSHALL join, dissenting.

8. We have no occasion to pass upon the question whether Dalm could have raised a recoupment claim in the Tax Court.

This is not a decision that will be much celebrated or often cited. Few cases are affected, and not a single brief *amicus curiae* was filed. The Court reserves in a footnote an issue that would render obsolete its holding. The case casts a shadow on the Executive—and on this Court—but otherwise has no apparent importance.

Indeed, the Court's opinion is remarkable not at all for what it says but rather for what it leaves unsaid. The majority's passing of sovereign immunity and jurisdiction masks what is the ultimate question before us: whether a statute of limitations otherwise barring a refund of federal income tax is tolled by government conduct that this Court has censured as "immoral" and tantamount to "a fraud on the taxpayer's rights." See *Bull v. United States*, 295 U.S. 247, 261, 55 S.Ct. 695, 700, 79 L.Ed. 1421 (1935). The Court today offers a jurisdictional apology when it could—and should—follow the just rule of the *Bull* case.

I

This case is remarkably similar to its 55 year-old precursor. The *Bull* case involved an attempt by the Government to collect income tax on partnership distributions received by the estate of a deceased partner. This Court rejected the Commissioner's first argument, and characterized as follows his claim that the Government could retain the estate tax while collecting a second tax on the same transaction pursuant to an inconsistent theory:

> "The United States, we have held, cannot, as against the claim of an innocent party, hold his money which has gone into its treasury by means of the fraud of its agent. *United States v. State Bank*, 96 U.S. 30 [24 L.Ed. 647]. While here the money was taken through mistake without any element of fraud, the unjust retention is immoral and amounts in law to a fraud on the taxpayer's rights." 295 U.S., at 261, 55 S.Ct., at 700.

This case involves an equally unjust retention of a previously paid tax. The Government has collected an income tax on a transfer of $180,000 to respondent while retaining the gift tax previously paid on the same transfer. The Court's decision assumes, as the summary judgment record requires, that when the Government compromised its claim for an income tax deficiency, it allowed respondent no credit for the gift tax that had previously been paid. Thus, the critical fact that made the Government's position in *Bull* immoral is present here: a single taxable event has been subjected to two taxes on mutually inconsistent theories.[1]

---

1. Arguably the Government's position in this case is even more outrageous than the position it took in *Bull* because its income tax assessment in that case was perfectly sound. In this case, however, its income tax claim was based on the remarkable theory that payments aggregating $313,813 constituted compensation for respondent's services as administratrix of her former employer's estate when the probate court had approved a total of $37,000 as compensation for those services. I do not, however, place any reliance on this aspect of the case, just as the Court correctly abstains from suggesting that the harshness of its holding is mitigated by the unre-

II

Even with the parallel between *Bull* and this case clearly in mind, most readers of the majority's opinion must wonder how this case ever came before our Court, and why the majority must recite so much law to decide it. According to the majority, respondent chose to litigate in Tax Court the deficiency assessed against her, and, having made this choice, cannot "then seek to reopen the matter and override the statute of limitations for the sole purpose of seeking recoupment." *Ante,* at 1370. This may seem fair enough, but also plain enough: a legal claim that might have been settled in an earlier proceeding is usually barred by rules of claim preclusion. If the claim is not barred by the settlement agreement in this case, then surely the Government can— without any help from this Court—avoid such problems in the future by drafting its settlement agreements more carefully. There is accordingly no justification for the Court's exercise of certiorari jurisdiction in this case, a discretionary act which has done nothing more useful than deprive the twice-taxed respondent *in this case* of a remedy for a wrong done by the Government.[2]

Two facts explain why the Government does not rely on principles of claim preclusion as a defense in this case. The first is this: it is undisputed by the parties to this case that the Tax Court lacked jurisdiction to consider recoupment of the gift tax payment against the income tax deficiency.[3] According to the Government, respondent

solved factual dispute about whether the Tax Court settlement took into account the prior gift tax payment. See *ante,* at 1364, n. 2.

2. The majority states that certiorari was granted in this case to resolve a conflict among the Courts of Appeal. If there were such a conflict it would not be of sufficient importance to merit our attention, but in fact no relevant conflict exists. The majority correctly observes that the decision of the Court of Appeals for the Sixth Circuit in this case agrees with that of the Court of Appeals for the Ninth Circuit in *Kolom v. United States,* 791 F.2d 762 (1986). The Court erroneously suggests that these decisions are contrary to *O'Brien v. United States,* 766 F.2d 1038 (CA7 1985). *O'Brien* was not a case in which a taxpayer sought to litigate an equitable recoupment claim in district court after litigating in Tax Court the assessment which generated the recoupment claim. In *O'Brien,* the beneficiary of an estate sought to litigate a recoupment claim after a deficiency was assessed against, and litigated in Tax Court by, the estate itself. The Court of Appeals for the Seventh Circuit held that only the estate, not the beneficiary, could assert any available recoupment claim. 766 F.2d, at 1050–1051. I do not believe the Court of Appeals for the Seventh Circuit spoke to the question at issue here, see 766 F.2d, at 1050, n. 15, but to the extent it did so, its remarks were obviously dicta. The Court thus today endorses a rule which no Court of Appeals has ever adopted.

3. See Rev.Rul. 71–56, 1971–1 Cum. Bull. 404, 405 ("the Tax Court lacks jurisdiction to consider a plea of equitable recoupment"); see also *Estate of Schneider v. Commissioner,* 93 T.C. No. 47, p. __ (Nov. 6, 1989). In *Rothensies v. Electric Storage Battery Co.,* 329 U.S. 296, 303, 67 S.Ct. 271, 274, 91 L.Ed. 296 (1946), we cited *Commissioner v. Gooch Milling & Elevator Co.,* 320 U.S. 418, 64 S.Ct. 184, 88 L.Ed. 139 (1943), for the proposition that the Tax Court has no jurisdiction to consider recoupment. A careful reading of the *Gooch Milling* opinion, and of the relevant statute, however, will show that it actually considered only the question of recoupment based on an overpayment in a year other than the year in dispute. I therefore commend the Court for its careful reservation of this issue, see *ante,* at 1370, n. 8. It is nevertheless appropriate to assume for purposes of deciding the jurisdictional issue in this case that respondent's counsel correctly believed that no recoupment could be had in the Tax Court.

cannot, and for that reason did not, raise her equitable recoupment claim in Tax Court: "respondent's choice of the Tax Court forum precluded her from claiming equitable recoupment against the income tax deficiency." Reply Brief for United States at 6. The Government acknowledges that respondent may have had a sound claim for recoupment, but insists that to pursue this claim she should have "paid the 1976 and 1977 income tax deficiencies and then brought a timely refund suit in district court or the Claims Court." *Id.*, at 3–4.

The second fact is this: an affluent taxpayer, but not a less fortunate one, can pay a deficiency assessment and file suit for a refund. It is undisputed that if respondent had the means to do so, she could have recovered the gift tax that had been paid in 1976 by a refund action filed after she received the notice of income tax deficiency in 1983, even though the statute of limitations had long since run. One might infer from the posture of this case—as respondent's counsel represented to the Court—that respondent's limited means foreclosed this avenue of relief for her. She therefore challenged the deficiency in the Tax Court.

These two facts explain what the majority does not: why we are not addressing a simple case of res judicata. It is clear that the basis for respondent's equitable recoupment claim did not exist until it was determined that the payment made in 1976 was taxable as income. Thus, respondent could apparently obtain a forum to hear her equitable recoupment claim only by seeking a refund of the previously paid gift tax—an action which all agree was barred by limitations when respondent received the notice of deficiency in 1983.

When that determination was made—that is to say, when the income tax case was settled—respondent promptly asserted her recoupment claim in the only forum available. Indeed, she filed her claim for a gift tax refund even *before* the settlement agreement was consummated. In view of the fact that the character of the 1976 transaction remained in dispute until the claim was filed, none of the policy reasons that normally support the application of a statute of limitations is implicated by this case.

III

The Court nevertheless denies respondent the relief devised by the *Bull* Court. Ignoring both the policies underlying the statute of limitations and the principles of just conduct underlying *Bull*, the Court confronts respondent with the majestic voices of "jurisdiction" and "sovereign immunity"—voices that seem to have a haunting charm for this Court's current majority.

Of course, if this Court were eventually to decide the reserved issue by holding that the Tax Court has jurisdiction to hear an equitable recoupment claim, today's decision would become a complete dead letter. No taxpayer would have any reason to litigate the deficiency and the recoupment issues separately, and in any event a judgment upon the former would bar a subsequent suit upon the latter under the doctrine of res judicata.

The Court that decided the *Bull* case reasoned not in obeisance to these siren-like voices but rather under the reliable guidance of a bright star in our jurisprudence: the presumption that for every right there should be a remedy. See *Marbury v. Madison,* 5 U.S. (1 Cranch) 137, 162–163, 2 L.Ed. 60 (1803). * * *

I would adopt the same course in this case. By initiating a proceeding to recover income tax based on the 1976 payment, the Government waived the time bar that would otherwise have precluded a claim for refund of the gift tax. Had respondent paid the deficiency and asserted the claim for a gift tax refund as a second count in one action, even this Court would agree that the claim was timely. If we adopt the Court's reasoning in *Bull*, it is proper to treat the second count of the refund action as timely even when the income tax issues are litigated before the Tax Court, because the deficiency assessment was sufficient to put in issue the right to recoupment and to justify treating the taxpayer as a defendant, rather than a plaintiff. If it was not too late for the Government to litigate the tax consequences of the 1976 payment, it should not be too late for the taxpayer to do so. "A different result here [is] a reproach to our jurisprudence." *United States v. State Bank,* 96 U.S. 30, 36, 24 L.Ed. 647 (1878).

* * *

The majority is able to complete its argument only by inventing a small, but blatant, fiction: that respondent is bringing a suit for the refund of overpaid gift tax within the meaning of 26 U.S.C. § 6511(a). This minor fiction is then conscripted by the majority's strategy to serve the vainest of all legal fictions, the doctrine of sovereign immunity. The doctrine has its origin in the ancient myth that the "King can do no wrong." See 1 W. Blackstone, Commentaries *238. Whatever might be said in favor of this polite falsehood in English law, the doctrine is an anomalous import within our own. See *Nevada v. Hall,* 440 U.S. 410, 414–415, 99 S.Ct. 1182, 1185, 59 L.Ed.2d 416 (1979); see also *Will v. Michigan Dept. of State Police,* 491 U.S. ___, ___, 109 S.Ct. 2304, ___, 105 L.Ed.2d 45 (1989) (Stevens, J., dissenting). Its persistence cannot be denied but ought not to be celebrated. Nor should its fictive origin ever be forgotten. There is no cause to expand the doctrine, and we do better to interpret § 1346(a)(1) by the light of equity and with due regard for the practicalities of revenue collection discussed in *Bull*.

To be useful, legal concepts must accommodate most disputes without the dissonance accompanying blended categories, but must also permit such flexibility when judgment demands it. It is not surprising that our concepts should be stressed when the Government taxes a citizen twice upon inconsistent theories and then subjects the citizen to a Hobson's choice among competing fora, each of which provides only half a remedy. It is equally unsurprising, and in fact encouraging, that such problems occur so rarely that Congress has not made any explicit provision for them.[10]

10. The majority supposes that its "con- clusion is reinforced by the fact that Con-

What is surprising is that this Court believes the equitable decision of the Court of Appeals in need of correction. The Court today has taken discretionary jurisdiction over a case of no broad import, and has undone equity by rendering an opinion true to neither the spirit nor the letter of American law. The Court takes its stand upon the grave declaration that a "distinction that has jurisdiction as its central concept is not meaningless." *Ante,* at 1367. I am not sure what this solemn truism means, but I do know that it does not decide this case.

Because I am unable to discover any just reason for distinguishing this case from *Bull,* I respectfully dissent.

Note

Immediately after the *Dalm* decision, several cases involving equitable recoupment were dismissed for lack of jurisdiction, citing *Dalm. See, e.g., Fairley v. United States,* 901 F.2d 691 (8th Cir.1990).

gress has legislated a set of exceptions to the limitations period" which "permit a taxpayer who has been required to pay inconsistent taxes to seek a refund of a tax the recovery of which is otherwise barred." See *ante,* at 1369. The exceptions were enacted two years after *Bull* was decided. It is undisputed that these exceptions do not apply in this case. Unlike the majority, I am not persuaded that because Congress took special steps to ensure that twice-taxed citizens were treated equitably under some circumstances, Congress must have intended to gut judicially created doctrines which ensured equitable treatment for twice-taxed citizens under other circumstances. The contrary inference seems more plausible. See Andrews, Modern-Day Equitable Recoupment and the "Two Tax Effect:" Avoidance of the Statutes of Limitation in Federal Tax Controversies, 28 Ariz.L.Rev. 595, 619–623 (1986).

Chapter VI

CIVIL PENALTIES AND INTEREST

Scope Note: Before the decade of the 1980's the consequences of losing in the "audit lottery" were minimal. The civil penalties contained in the Internal Revenue Code provided little downside risk for the taxpayer who was willing to gamble that his return would not be examined, and the interest rates on tax deficiencies were much lower than market rates. That is no longer the case. Since 1980, Congress has acted to strengthen the traditional civil penalties, to add new ones, and to bring interest rates more in line with market rates. As the number of new penalties increased, however, the system was increasingly perceived as unfair and too complex. In late 1989, Congress responded to several years of study of the system by enacting sweeping legislation to overhaul the civil penalty system. Litigation concerning the post–1990 rules will begin in the mid–1990's; meanwhile, the pre–1990 rules will continue to dominate the litigated cases. Both regimes are explored in this chapter, which will examine the most commonly encountered of the traditional penalties (such as the delinquency, negligence and fraud penalties) as well as the more important of the relatively newer penalties (such as the valuation penalties and the penalty for substantial understatements of income tax liability). This chapter also addresses the return preparer penalties and three penalties designed to deter specific types of abuse (promoting abusive tax shelters; aiding and abetting an understatement; and filing frivolous income tax returns). The chapter concludes with a discussion of the rules applicable to the payment of interest on deficiencies and overpayments.

SECTION 1. HISTORICAL DEVELOPMENT

Civil penalties for noncompliance with tax laws have existed since the 1800's. In recent years, however, both the number of penalty provisions in the Code and the number of penalties actually assessed have increased dramatically. For example, in 1954, there were 13 penalty provisions in the Code, in 1967 there were 25, and in 1987 there were 150.[a] As mentioned in the *Scope Note,* much of this staggering increase occurred during the 1980's. During that same approximate time, the *number* of penalties assessed by the Service almost doubled (from 15.4 million in 1978 to 27 million in 1987), while the *dollar amounts* increased tenfold (from $1.4 million in 1978 to $14 million in 1987.)[b]

In the late 1980's, the civil penalty system was the subject of several studies, including one by the Tax Section of the American Bar Association and one by the Commissioner's Executive Task Force on Civil Penalties. The basic conclusion of these studies was that the civil penalty system had become unfair, unduly harsh and complex, and ineffective in its principal purpose of promoting voluntary compliance. Congress reacted by enacting the Improved Penalty Administration and Compliance Tax Act ("IMPACT") in late 1989, which applies to all returns due after December 31, 1989. Because the pre-IMPACT penalties will continue to be assessed to returns due prior to 1990, and issues pertaining thereto will be litigated during the 1990's, familiarity with both regimes is essential.

(a) IMPACT eliminated "stacking" of penalties

One of the most significant changes made by IMPACT was the elimination of "stacking" of penalties for a single act or omission. A typical example of "stacking" penalties is the imposition of the following three penalties for failure to file a return: the delinquency penalty under former section 6651, the negligence penalty under former section 6653(a), and the substantial understatement penalty of former section 6661.[c] Under the IMPACT rules, only a single penalty (the delinquency penalty of section 6651) could be imposed in this situation because section 6662 requires that a return have been filed as a precondition to imposition of any of the accuracy-related penalties (such as negligence and substantial understatement of income) contained in section 6662.

(b) IMPACT streamlined four categories of penalties

IMPACT overhauled and streamlined four broad categories of penalties, which are discussed in this Chapter in the following order:

1. *Information reporting penalties* (sections 6011, 6038, and 6721 through 6724 were amended). These rules are discussed briefly in Section 2 of this Chapter.
2. *Accuracy-related penalties* (sections 6621(c), 6659, 6659A, 6660 and 6661 were repealed, most of section 6652 was repealed, and all were replaced by new sections 6662–6665). These rules are

---

a. Internal Revenue Commissioner's Study of Civil Tax Penalties, February 1989, at V–1.

b. *Id.*

c. This example is drawn from Woods II v. Commissioner, 91 T.C. 88 (1988) (reviewed), in which all three penalties were sustained by the court. The *Woods II* opinion is at p. 232, *infra.*

discussed at length in Section 3 of this Chapter, which also discusses the *civil fraud penalty.*

3. *Preparer, promoter and protester penalties* (sections 6672, 6673, 6694, 6695, 6700, 6701, 6702, 7216, and 7407 were amended). These rules are discussed in Section 4 of this Chapter.

4. *Delinquency penalties* (section 1463 and 6651 were amended and new § 6656 was added). These rules are discussed in Section 5 of this Chapter.

(c) "Administrative recommendations" of Congress

To reflect its concern that merely amending the law would not cure all of the problems with the civil penalty system, Congress made a series of "Administrative Recommendations" as part of IMPACT. Some of these Administrative Recommendations are discussed in the sections of this Chapter that address the various categories of penalties. Others, labelled by Congress as "general administrative recommendations," reflect Congress' concern that the civil penalty system is not understood either by the general public or by many IRS employees, and that penalties are sometimes imposed arbitrarily. These "general administrative recommendations" are as follows:

(1) The IRS should develop a policy statement emphasizing that civil tax penalties exist for the purpose of encouraging voluntary compliance.

(2) The IRS should develop a handbook on penalties for all employees. This handbook should be sufficiently detailed to serve as a practical guide for most issues of penalty administration.

(3) The IRS should provide clear guidance to its employees on how to compute penalties. This guidance should be incorporated into the penalty handbook.

(4) The IRS should revise existing training programs to reflect the purpose for penalties and their administration.

(5) The IRS should examine its communications with taxpayers (including penalty notices and publications) to determine whether these communications do the best possible job of explaining to taxpayers why the penalty was imposed and how taxpayers can avoid the penalty in the future. Penalty notices should also provide the telephone number of contact offices which taxpayers may call with questions and which have the authority to address disputed penalties.

(6) The IRS should finalize its review and analysis of the quality and clarity of machine-generated letters and notices used in the Adjustments and Correspondence Branches of the IRS service centers and report to Congress by July 1, 1990.

(7) The IRS should consider ways to develop better information concerning the administration and effects of penalties. The IRS

should develop a master file data base to provide statistical information regarding the administration of penalties. The IRS should continuously review information for the purpose of suggesting changes in compliance programs, educational programs, penalty design and penalty administration.

(8) In the application of penalties, the IRS should make a correct substantive decision in the first instance rather than mechanically assert penalties with the idea that they will be corrected later.[d]

(d) Comparison of civil and criminal tax penalties

Civil tax penalties are assessed and collected in the same manner as the underlying tax (with a few minor exceptions),[e] and are subject to the same statute of limitations.[f] The civil penalty system coexists with the criminal sanctions for noncompliance with the Code. The same act or omission can trigger *both* a criminal prosecution and imposition of civil penalties. The principal purpose of the civil penalty system differs from the purposes for criminal sanctions, however. The principal purpose of civil penalties is to encourage voluntary compliance with the tax laws, not punishment for noncompliance, raising revenues, or reimbursing the government for the cost of maintaining compliance programs.[g] On the other hand, criminal penalties are designed to punish and deter noncompliant behavior.[h]

(e) Section 6672 penalty

While this Chapter discusses many of the principal civil tax penalties, discussion of the section 6672 penalty imposed on "responsible persons" for failure to collect, account for and pay over so-called "trust fund taxes" is deferred until Chapter XI.

SECTION 2. INFORMATION REPORTING PENALTIES

The Service's ability to "match" tax return information with certain information filed by taxpayers' employers and financial institutions, among others, converts our voluntary compliance system to one of coerced compliance. To illustrate, the Service announced in January of 1991 that 7 million dependents claimed in 1986 "disappeared" in

---

d. H.R.Rep. No. 101-247, 101st Cong., 1st Sess. 1404-05 (1989).

e. I.R.C. §§ 6671(a), 6665 (as recodified by IMPACT) (formerly section 6662). Because civil penalties are assessed and collected in the same manner as taxes, the Service must issue a statutory notice of deficiency ("90-day letter") prior to assessment and collection. Exceptions to this requirement are contained in section 6665(b), which exempts penalties under section 6651 for failure to file a return, as well as those under sections 6654 and 6655 (for failure to pay estimated tax) from the requirement of following deficiency procedures.

f. *See* I.R.C. § 6671(a).

g. Commissioner's Study of Civil Tax Penalties, by Commissioner's Executive Task Force at II-1 (February 1989).

h. See *id.* at II-3.

Sec. 2 INFORMATION REPORTING PENALTIES 221

1987, when the requirement that the return list the Social Security number for dependents over age 5 went into effect. The IRS estimated that 80% of the "children" claimed in 1986 but not mentioned in 1987 never existed.[i] Similarly, few taxpayers should be tempted to understate interest income that has been reported to the IRS by the payor on a Form 1099, or compensation income reported by the employer on a Form W-2. Of course, the "matching" system depends on timely and accurate information from banks, employers, etc. that can be electronically compared to the information reported on tax returns. To encourage those responsible for furnishing "information returns"[j] and "payee statements"[k] to do so in a timely manner (and with complete and correct information), the Code (sections 6721-6724) authorizes penalties for the failure to file such returns timely or with complete and correct information.

Under pre-1990 rules, failure to file an information return triggered a penalty of $50 per return, up to a maximum total annual penalty per reporting person of $100,000,[l] and failure to furnish payee statements triggered identical penalties.[m] Filing incomplete or incorrect information return or payee statements triggered a penalty of $5 per error, up to an annual maximum per reporting person of $20,000.[n] IMPACT altered these rules by creating a three-tiered penalty that keys the amount of the penalty to the length of the delay in furnishing correct and complete information. The sooner the error or omission is corrected, the smaller the penalty, as the following summary of section 6721(b) reflects.

When correct information return filed	*Penalty/return*	*Annual maximum*
Within 30 days of due date	$15	$ 75,000
Between 31 days after due date and August 1	$30	$150,000
After August 1	$50	$250,000

Because most information returns must be filed by February 28, the practical effect of § 6721(b) is to make March 30 the deadline date for the first tier of the penalty.

These penalty amounts can be avoided or reduced in certain circumstances. Section 6721(c) provides a *de minimis* exception for the filing of incomplete or inaccurate information returns if the error is

i. *The Tampa Tribune*, Mon. Jan. 7, 1991 p. 3.

j. As defined in I.R.C. § 6724(d)(1). The principal information returns are the 1099 series for the payment of dividends, interest, etc., and Forms W-2, W-2P and W-3.

k. As defined in I.R.C. § 6724(d)(2). Payee statements are copies of information returns required to be furnished to the affected taxpayer.

l. Information returns relating to interest and dividends were subject to the $50 per return penalty with no maximum annual penalty amount, prior to the 1989 amendments of section 6721.

m. I.R.C. § 6722.

n. Stricter penalties could be imposed with respect to dividend or interest information returns or payee statements, or for intentional failure to comply.

corrected before August 1 of the calendar year the return is required to be filed and if the failure is due to reasonable cause. The section 6721(c) exception applies only to the greater of ten returns or .05% of all information returns required to be filed by the person for the calendar year. Section 6721(d) provides for lower maximum annual penalties for "small businesses," defined as those with annual gross receipts for the preceding three years not exceeding $5 million. For such "small businesses," the maximum annual penalties are reduced to $25,000, $50,000 and $100,000 respectively. The pre–1990 penalty amounts for failure to furnish correct payee statements were retained.[o]

For errors due to intentional disregard of the law, both pre–1990 and post–1990, the penalty is $100 per information return. In addition, for post–1990 payee statement errors, the penalty is $100 per payee statement for errors due to intentional disregard of the payee statement rules.[p]

The 1989 legislation established a uniform "reasonable cause" exception for all information reporting penalties in section 6724(a), which provides for a waiver of the penalty if the "failure is due to reasonable cause and not to willful neglect." According to the legislative history, this waiver should be applied "if significant mitigating factors are present, such as the fact that a person has an established history of complying with the information reporting requirements."[q] The higher waiver standard for errors in returns relating to interest and dividends was repealed by the 1989 amendments, as was the criminal sanction applicable to payors of interest and dividends for failure to reflect a payee's taxpayer identification number ("TIN").

Additional penalties for other types of information reporting were also enacted as part of IMPACT. Section 6724(d)(3) lists the "specified information reporting requirement[s]" to which the post–1990 penalty of $50 per failure (up to an annual maximum of $100,000 per person) is applicable. Included are the failure to furnish one's TIN to another person to include on his return, or the failure to include the TIN of another person on one's return, in the case of alimony payments; the failure to include the TIN of a dependent on one's return, as required by section 6109(e); and the failure to include one's TIN on any return, statement, or document other than an information return or payee statement.

Finally, the 1989 legislation amended the requirement that certain information returns (such as Forms W–2 and the 1099 series) be filed on "magnetic media or in other machine-readable form." IRC § 6011(e)(2). That section now specifies that the regulations required to be promulgated thereunder shall not require filing via magnetic media by any person required to file 250 or fewer returns per calendar year.

o. I.R.C. § 6722.
p. I.R.C. § 6722.
q. H.R.Rep. No. 101–247, 101st Cong., 1st Sess. (1989).

SECTION 3. THE ACCURACY-RELATED PENALTIES AND THE CIVIL FRAUD PENALTY

A. BACKGROUND

Prior to IMPACT, the Code contained numerous accuracy-related penalties that imposed monetary sanctions of varying amounts and that were frequently "stacked" or "pyramided" by the simultaneous imposition of several penalties for the same act or omission. IMPACT consolidated these penalties in section 6662, repealed their predecessors, provides for a uniform 20% penalty, provides a uniform reasonable cause exception for all accuracy-related and civil fraud penalties, and prohibits "stacking." The penalties consolidated in section 6662 are the negligence penalty of former section 6653(a), the substantial understatement of income tax penalty of former § 6661, and the valuation penalties of former sections 6659, 6659A, and 6660. The civil fraud penalty is contained in section 6663.

B. UNIFORM REASONABLE CAUSE EXCEPTION

For returns due after 1989, section 6664(c) prohibits imposition of a penalty under section 6662 or 6663 if there is "reasonable cause" for the error and the taxpayer acted in good faith. The legislative history explains the purpose of this provision:

> The enactment of this standardized exception criterion is designed to permit courts to review the assertion of penalties under the same standards that apply in reviewing additional tax that the Internal Revenue Service asserts is due. By applying this unified exception criterion to all accuracy-related penalties, the committee believes that taxpayers will more easily understand the standard of behavior that is required. The committee also believes that this unified exception criterion will simplify the administration of these penalties by the IRS.
>
> The committee is concerned that the present-law accuracy-related penalties (particularly the penalty for substantial understatements of tax liability) have been determined too routinely and automatically by the IRS. The committee expects that the enactment of standardized exception criterion will lead the IRS to consider fully whether imposition of these penalties is appropriate before determining these penalties.
>
> In addition, the committee has designed this standardized exception criterion to provide greater scope for judicial review of IRS determinations of these penalties. Under the waiver provision contained in present law, the Tax Court has held that it can overturn an IRS determination of the substantial understatement penalty on reasonable cause and good faith grounds only if the Tax Court finds that the IRS abused its discretion in asserting the penalty. The committee

believes that it is appropriate for the courts to review the determination of the accuracy-related penalties by the same general standard applicable to their review of the additional taxes the IRS determines are owed. The committee believes that providing greater scope for judicial review of IRS determinations of these penalties will lead to greater fairness of the penalty structure and minimize inappropriate determinations of these penalties.[r]

C. NEGLIGENCE

(1) Amount of the Penalty

Prior to 1990, the negligence penalty of former section 6653(a) was 5% of the total underpayment of tax,[s] if any portion of the underpayment was attributable to negligence. To illustrate, if the total understatement was $1,000 and the portion due to negligence was $200, the penalty was $50 (5% of $1,000). In addition, for returns due from 1982 through 1988, there is a second component of the negligence penalty tied to the interest that has accrued on the underpayment. This time-sensitive portion of the negligence penalty is 50% of the interest payable on the portion of the underpayment attributable to negligence.[t] For individuals, this "add-on" portion of the negligence penalty, like the interest on the deficiency, is not fully deductible for years after 1986.[u] The interest "add-on" portion of the penalty was repealed for years after 1988.

For returns due after 1989, the amount of the negligence penalty is 20% of the portion of the underpayment attributable to negligence. Thus, while IMPACT increased the percentage amount of the penalty from 5% to 20%, it restricted the scope of the penalty by making it applicable only to the portion of the underpayment attributable to negligence. According to the legislative history, Congress viewed the prior law as unfair:

> Thus, under present law, a taxpayer who has an underpayment, only a small portion of which was attributable to negligence, is subject to the same penalty as a taxpayer with the same underpayment, all of which is attributable to negligence, even though the behavior of the first taxpayer is arguably less culpable than the behavior of the second taxpayer. The bill rectifies this inequity by applying the negligence penalty only to the portion of the underpayment attributable to negligence.[v]

---

[r]. H.R.Rep. No. 101-247, 101st Cong., 1st Sess. 1392.

[s]. Prior to 1986, the negligence penalty applied only to income, gift, and windfall profits taxes. As part of the Tax Reform Act of 1986, the negligence penalty was made applicable to the underpayment of any tax.

[t]. Former section 6653(a)(1)(B).

[u]. I.R.C. § 163(h); Temp. Reg. § 1.163-8T(b)(2).

[v]. H.R.Rep. No. 101-247, 101st Cong., 1st Sess. 1389.

(2) Burden of Proof

Unlike the civil fraud penalty, as to which the Commissioner bears the burden of proof of fraud, the imposition of the negligence penalty is presumptively correct, and the taxpayer has the burden of proving the absence of negligence.

(3) Definition of "Negligence"

Section 6662(b)(1) authorizes the 20% penalty for "[n]egligence or disregard of rules or regulations." Section 6662(c) retains the prior law's definitions of "negligence" and "disregard": negligence "includes any failure to make a reasonable attempt to comply with" the Code, and disregard "includes any careless, reckless or intentional disregard."

COLEMAN v. COMMISSIONER
United States Tax Court
T.C.Memo. 1990–511.

OPINION BY: JUDGE WELLS

OPINION: SUPPLEMENTAL MEMORANDUM OPINION

The instant case [1] is before us on petitioners' motion for reconsideration of our opinion in Coleman v. Commissioner, T.C.Memo. 1990–357, filed on July 16, 1990 (prior opinion).

Petitioners contend, among other things, that the addition to tax for negligence was imposed erroneously against petitioners Edward and Margaret Maher. Upon reconsideration, however, after reviewing petitioners' contentions, we adhere to our conclusion in our prior opinion that the negligence addition was appropriately determined.

In our prior opinion, we found petitioner Edward Maher's reliance on the tax opinion prepared by his law firm, the K–1 he received from the Partnership, and Mr. Beningson's business reputation insufficient to satisfy the Mahers' burden of proof with respect to the negligence addition. Petitioners argue that, in refusing to accept Mr. Maher's reliance on the tax opinion as sufficient to defeat a finding of negligence, we have "created a conflict" with three of our prior decisions; namely, Ewing v. Commissioner, 91 T.C. 396 (1988) (on appeal, 9th Cir., June 7, 1990; on appeal 5th Cir., June 12, 1990); Gralnek v. Commissioner, T.C.Memo. 1989–433; and Davis v. Commissioner, T.C.Memo. 1989–607, and have disregarded the Supreme Court's decision in United States v. Boyle, 469 U.S. 241 (1985). We disagree.

While the Ewing and Gralnek cases cited by petitioners do attach significance to the taxpayers' reliance on tax opinions included in promotional materials, the cases do not establish a blanket rule that such reliance defeats imposition of the negligence addition. As we

---

1. The cases consolidated herein are collectively referred to as "the instant case."

stated in Freytag v. Commissioner, 89 T.C. 849, 888 (1987), affd. 904 F.2d 1011 (5th Cir.1990), "Reliance on professional advice, standing alone, is not an absolute defense to negligence, but rather a factor to be considered. First, it must be established that the reliance was reasonable." Negligence is defined as a "lack of due care or failure to do what a reasonable and ordinarily prudent person would do under the circumstances." Neely v. Commissioner, 85 T.C. 934, 947 (1985) (quoting Marcello v. Commissioner, 380 F.2d 499, 506 (5th Cir.1967)) (emphasis supplied).

In Ewing v. Commissioner, supra, we found that the taxpayers' "good faith" reliance on a law firm to formulate the straddle program in issue (including reliance on the firm's tax opinion included in promotional materials) was not unreasonable "under the circumstances of this record." 91 T.C. at 423. We specifically noted in Ewing that the tax opinion "described in detail, with citations to case law and statutes, the tax consequences which, in the opinion of the author, could be expected by investors from different methods of closing positions in straddles." 91 T.C. at 406. Unlike in Ewing, we found in our prior opinion that "The content of the tax opinion allegedly relied upon by Mr. Maher should * * * have alerted him as to the necessity of seeking independent advice on the availability of the promised tax benefits." Coleman v. Commissioner, 60 T.C.M. 123, 135, 59 P–H Memo.T.C. par. 90,357 at 1704. Our reference to "the content of the tax opinion," was meant to encompass not only its warning to investors not to construe the opinion as advice but also its lack of reasoning in the section of the opinion dealing with profit objective.

At the time that Mr. Maher decided to invest in the Partnership, he had been an attorney at Townley & Updike, the firm that prepared the tax opinion, for 37 years; he specialized in corporate and commercial work, including securities offerings. (Mr. Maher's name appeared fourth on the Townley & Updike letterhead used for the first page of the tax opinion.) A person of Mr. Maher's experience should have heard "warning bells" in view of the tax opinion's reliance on a profit objective representation from the general partner and lack of meaningful analyses of the profit objective issue. See Freytag v. Commissioner, 89 T.C. at 889.

The Davis case cited by petitioners is also distinguishable in that it focuses primarily on the taxpayers' reliance on their own attorney, who recommended the investment at issue. We believe that there is a distinction between relying on "a trusted and long-term adviser," as in Davis; and relying on a tax opinion that specifically warns the investor not to regard it as advice but to consult independent tax counsel. While petitioners criticize our reference to such disclaimers on the grounds that they are well known as "Boiler Plate provisions," petitioners characterize such provisions as "included to protect the attorneys from being in privity with the reader and thereby shield the attorneys from any claims of malpractice," a characterization that reinforces our reasoning. It also should be noted that our prior opinion is not unique

Sec. 3   ACCURACY-RELATED & CIVIL FRAUD PENALTY   227

in referring to such disclaimers in support of a finding of negligence. See Owen v. Commissioner, T.C.Memo. 1990–172;[4] Foerstel v. Commissioner, T.C.Memo. 1987–546; Bowman v. Commissioner, T.C.Memo. 1987–545. None of the cases cited in petitioners' motion mention such disclaimers.

For similar reasons, petitioners' reference to the Supreme Court's decision in United States v. Boyle, 469 U.S. 241 (1985) is unpersuasive. In Boyle, the Supreme Court held that an executor was not excused from the late filing addition under section 6651(a)(1) although such late filing resulted from an oversight by the attorney he retained to handle the estate. In reaching that conclusion, the Court distinguished a taxpayer's failure to meet a statutory filing deadline—which cannot be excused by reason of reliance on an attorney—from a situation in which "an accountant or attorney advises a taxpayer on a matter of tax law," 469 U.S. at 251 (emphasis in original). In the latter situation, the Supreme Court stated that:

> When an accountant or attorney advises a taxpayer on a matter of tax law, such as whether a liability exists, it is reasonable for the taxpayer to rely on that advice. Most taxpayers are not competent to discern error in the substantive advice of an accountant or attorney. To require the taxpayer to challenge the attorney, to seek a "second opinion," or to try to monitor counsel on the provisions of the Code himself would nullify the very purpose of seeking the advice of a presumed expert in the first place. "Ordinary business care and prudence" do not demand such actions. [469 U.S. at 251; emphasis in original and citation omitted.]

The foregoing language in no way suggests that a taxpayer may be excused from the negligence addition based on his reliance on a tax opinion and prospectus that specifically disavow such reliance. Requiring the taxpayer to seek independent advice in circumstances such as those present herein is not equivalent to requiring him to seek a "second opinion," rather, it is merely requiring him to seek "advice" for the first time. Cf. Heasley v. Commissioner, 902 F.2d 380 (5th Cir.1990) (unsophisticated investors not liable for negligence addition where they relied on the expertise of their financial advisor and accountant and monitored their investment).

We have considered all of petitioners' other arguments and find them without merit.

To reflect the foregoing, an appropriate order will be issued.

---

4. In Owen v. Commissioner, T.C.Memo. 1990–172, we stated:

Petitioners also argue that the additions to tax for negligence are avoided because they relied on the prospectuses provided by the promoters as would be expected of a reasonable, prudent person. We disagree. Each prospectus included several caveats with respect to the Federal income tax consequences of the transactions and included the warning, "Accordingly, each prospective Limited Partner is urged to consult his own tax advisor with respect to the Federal * * * income tax consequences to him of his investment in the Partnership." 59 T.C.M. 290, 302, 59 P–H Memo T.C. par. 90,172 at 786.

DRUKER v. COMMISSIONER OF INTERNAL REVENUE

United States Court of Appeals, Second Circuit, 1982.
697 F.2d 46.

OPINION:

Before: FEINBERG, CHIEF JUDGE, and FRIENDLY and KAUFMAN, CIRCUIT JUDGES.

FRIENDLY, CIRCUIT JUDGE:

We have here an appeal by taxpayers and a cross-appeal by the Commissioner from a judgment after trial before Chief Judge Tannenwald of the Tax Court, 77 T.C. 867 (1981).

I.

The principal issue on the taxpayers' appeal is the alleged unconstitutionality of the so-called "marriage penalty". The issue relates to the 1975 and 1976 income tax returns of James O. Druker and his wife Joan. During the tax years in question James was employed as a lawyer, first by the United States Attorney for the Eastern District of New York and later by the District Attorney of Nassau County, New York, and Joan was employed as a computer programmer. For each of the two years they filed separate income tax returns, checking the status box entitled "married filing separately". In computing their respective tax liabilities, however, they applied the rates in I.R.C. § 1(c) for "Unmarried individuals" rather than the higher rates prescribed by § 1(d) for "Married individuals filing separate returns". Prior to undertaking this course of action, James consulted with the United States Attorney for the Eastern District and with members of the Intelligence Division of the IRS, explaining that he and his wife wanted to challenge the 697 F.2d 46; 83–1 U.S. Tax Cas. (CCH) P9116; 51 A.F.T.R.2d constitutionality of the "marriage penalty" without incurring liability for fraud or willfulness. Following these conversations they filed their returns as described, attaching to each return a letter explaining that, although married, they were applying the tax tables for single persons because they believed that the "income tax structure unfairly discriminates against working married couples" in violation of the equal protection clause of the fourteenth amendment. The Tax Court rejected this constitutional challenge, sustaining the Commissioner's determination that the Drukers were subject to tax at the rates provided in § 1(d) for married persons filing separately.

Determination of the proper method for federal taxation of the incomes of married and single persons has had a long and stormy history.

We do not doubt that the "marriage penalty" has some adverse effect on marriage; indeed, James Druker stated at argument that, having failed thus far in the courts, he and his wife had solved their tax problem by divorcing but continuing to live together.

IV.

We come finally to the Commissioner's cross-appeal from the Tax Court's refusal to impose a 5% addition for "intentional disregard of rules and regulations" under I.R.C. § 6653(a). This section provides:

> Negligence or intentional disregard of rules and regulations with respect to income or gift taxes.—If any part of any underpayment (as defined in subsection (c)(1)) of any tax imposed by subtitle A or by chapter 12 of subtitle B (relating to income taxes and gift taxes) is due to negligence or intentional disregard of rules and regulations (but without intent to defraud), there shall be added to the tax an amount equal to 5 percent of the underpayment.

See also Treas.Reg. § 301.6653–1(a) (incorporating the statutory language).

In computing their respective tax liabilities the Drukers applied the rates in I.R.C. § 1(c) for "Unmarried individuals" instead of the higher rates prescribed by § 1(d) for "Married individuals filing separate returns" as the regulations required. There was, to be sure, nothing furtive or fraudulent in this; they checked the "married filing separately" status box on their returns, cross-referenced the returns by providing each other's Social Security number, and attached to each return a letter explaining what they were doing and why. Nevertheless, the record leaves no doubt that in using rate schedules applicable only to unmarried persons, they intentionally violated Section 1 of the Code and the rules and regulations promulgated thereunder, see Treas. Reg. § 1.1–1(a).

While conceding that the Drukers acted "deliberately and in open disregard of the requirements of the statute", the Tax Court nonetheless disallowed the 5% addition on the ground that the Drukers' "position herein is not so frivolous and meritless as to fall within the ambit of numerous cases involving even sincere taxpayers where the addition to the tax under section 6653(a) has been imposed", that "it is common knowledge that the 'marriage penalty' has been the subject of widespread comment and discussion, including extensive legislative consideration",[5] and that "[a]ccordingly [the Drukers] should not be

---

5. We do not grasp the force of this. Many tax issues, e.g., whether capital gains should be taxed and, if so, what the rate and the holding period should be; the alleged "double taxation" of so much of corporate profits as is declared as dividends; indexing of income to avoid "bracket creep" due to inflation, etc., have likewise been and doubtless will continue to be discussed for years. The Tax Court could hardly have meant that persons sincerely entertaining views on such matters differing from the legislators' could resort to self-help without incurring the 5% addition to the tax. If the distinction is thought to be that the Drukers raised constitutional and not mere policy objections, there is no showing of widespread discussion of that. Moreover the generous attitude of the Tax Court presumably would have to carry over to persons who sincerely dispute the legality of their being subjected to income taxation to support activities such as the Vietnam war or nuclear armament of which they strongly disapprove and who make fully disclosed deductions from their taxes on that account.

penalized for seeking to litigate the issue." 77 T.C. at 875. We think the Tax Court took unto itself a dispensing power not granted by Congress.

The statutory language, "there shall be added", could hardly be clearer. The reasonableness of a taxpayer's action may indeed be relevant when he is charged with negligence but not when he admittedly has flouted applicable rules and regulations which he fully understood. Departure from the natural and ordinary meaning of the words, whose literal application does not result in any manifestly absurd or unfair result, could be justified only if there were other evidence that the over-all purpose of Congress would be better served by such a reading. We find no sufficient evidence of this.

Notes

1. Would the result in *Druker* be different under the post–1989 reasonable cause exception of § 6664(c)? Consider the following excerpt from the legislative history and the temporary guidance provided by the Service in Notice 90–20:

> The committee believes that the application of the standardized exception criteria to the negligence component of the accuracy-related penalty will result in several consequences that are beneficial to taxpayers. First, the complete, item-specific disclosure of a non-frivolous position may generally be considered to permit an exception from the negligence penalty insofar as such disclosure would tend to demonstate that there was no intentional disregard of rules or regulations. Disclosure must be full and substantive, parallel to the disclosure required under the substantial understatement component of the accuracy-related penalty; completing and filling in a tax form is by itself insufficient disclosure for this purpose. In addition, the disclosure must be clearly identified as being made to avoid the accuracy-related penalty. Imposition of the negligence component of the accuracy-related penalty would not be eligible for exception due to disclosure where the taxpayer fails to keep proper books and records or to substantiate items properly. Second, the application of the standardized exception criteria to the negligence component of the accuracy-related penalty may also permit a taxpayer to avoid imposition of that penalty where the taxpayer makes a good-faith challenge to the validity of an IRS regulation, if the taxpayer discloses (in the manner just described) that the taxpayer is taking the position and makes specific reference to the regulation being challenged. As under present law, frivolous challenges to IRS regulations would be subject to penalty. The committee intends that the terms "reasonable cause" and "good faith" be interpreted under the bill as those terms are interpreted under present law. [H.R.Rep. 101–247, 101st Cong., 1st Sess. 1393 (1989).]

In Notice 90–20, 1990–1 C.B. 328, the Service provided temporary guidance concerning the manner of disclosing items to avoid the negligence penalty pending adoption of regulations. Significantly, although the substantial understatement of income tax penalty can be avoided in some circumstances merely by completing certain forms and schedules of a tax return, the negligence penalty cannot be so avoided. Instead, the taxpayer must either complete and file a Form 8275 Disclosure Statement under Section 6661 (or its equivalent after the Form is updated to reflect IMPACT) or make the disclosure on the return itself. In the latter case, the return must contain the following caption at the top left-hand corner of the first page: "DISCLOSURE MADE UNDER SECTION 6662," and must refer to the line(s) of the return or schedules that contain the uncertain position. In addition, the line(s) of the return or schedule referenced in the caption must contain "the additional information necessary to make full disclosure."

2. Under former § 6653(g), enacted in 1986, failure to report interest or dividends shown on any information return was automatically considered negligence, and the taxpayer could avoid the penalty only by "clear and convincing evidence to the contrary." A 1988 amendment made the automatic negligence penalty of section 6653(g) applicable only to the portion of the underpayment attributable to the interest or dividend omission. IMPACT repealed this provision (for returns due after December 31, 1989). Nonetheless, the legislative history recognizes that "even in the absence of a statutory presumption, evidence of such a failure is still strong evidence of negligence." H.R.Rep. 101–247, 101st Cong., 1st Sess. 1389 (1989).

3. Section 6001 requires taxpayers to keep adequate records to determine taxable income. See Reg. § 1.6001–1(a). Failure to keep adequate records may constitute both negligence and disregard of the recordkeeping requirement.

D. SUBSTANTIAL UNDERSTATEMENT OF INCOME TAX

The Tax Equity and Fiscal Responsibility Act of 1982 created numerous new civil penalties, but none has generated as much controversy as the substantial understatement of income tax penalty of section 6662(b)(2) and (d) (formerly section 6661). The controversy stems principally from the fact that the penalty requires no culpable conduct by the taxpayer, but is imposed in the absence of fraud or negligence if its technical requirements are met. Another target of criticism of former section 6661 was that the definition of "authority" for purposes of determining whether the penalty could be avoided because "substantial authority" for the return position exists was too narrow. As discussed below, IMPACT addressed this aspect of the provision.

(1) Amount of the Penalty

As originally enacted, section 6661 imposed a penalty of 10% of the underpayment of tax, if the understatement was "substantial." The penalty amount was raised twice in 1986, to 20% then to 25%. When this penalty was incorporated into new section 6662 as part of IMPACT, the amount was reduced to 20%, the penalty rate applicable to all accuracy-related penalties. There is a "substantial understatement" of income tax liability if the correct tax liability exceeds the reported liability by the greater of 10% of the correct tax or $5,000 ($10,000 for corporations). I.R.C. § 6662(d)(2)(A). To illustrate: if an individual's correct tax liability for 1992 is $25,000, but she reports a total tax liability of $15,000, a "substantial understatement" exists because the understatement ($10,000) exceeds the greater of 10% of the correct tax liability ($2,500) or $5,000. Had the understatement been only $4,000, no penalty could be imposed under this provision, because the minimum understatement that will trigger the penalty for individuals is $5,000.

WOODS II v. COMMISSIONER
Tax Court of the United States, 1988.
91 T.C. 88.

OPINION BY: Chabot

OPINION: Chabot, Judge: This case was assigned to Special Trial Judge Pate pursuant to the provisions of section 7456(d) (redesignated as section 7443A(b) by the Tax Reform Act of 1986, Pub.L. 99–514, 100 Stat. 2775) and Rules 180 and 181. The Court agrees with and adopts her opinion which is set forth below.

Opinion of the Special Trial Judge

Pate, Special Trial Judge: This case is before the Court on respondent's Motion for Judgment on the Pleadings, pursuant to Rule 120(a). Petitioner filed an opposition thereto. Subsequently, this Court issued an order asking respondent to file a supplemental motion together with a memorandum of legal authorities addressing certain allegations made in the petition. Respondent filed such supplemental motion and petitioner filed an opposition thereto. At oral argument, respondent moved that this Court award damages to the United States under section 6673.

William A. Woods, II (petitioner) was single during 1983, the year in issue. He did not file a Federal income tax return despite receiving $32,844 in wages and $53 in interest income during that year. On September 13, 1985, respondent determined a deficiency in petitioner's federal income tax in the amount of $7,152 and additions to tax under section 6651(a)(1) of $834.75, section 6653(a)(1)[2] of $357.60, section 6653(a)(2)[3] of fifty percent of the interest due on the underpayment, and section 6661(a) of $715.20. Petitioner timely filed his petition alleging that respondent erred in asserting all of the additions to tax,[5]

---

2. Redesignated as section 6653(a)(1)(A) by section 1503(a) of the Tax Reform Act of 1986, Pub.L. 99–514, 100 Stat. 2742.

3. Redesignated as section 6653(a)(1)(B) by section 1503(a) of the Tax Reform Act of 1986, Pub.L. 99–514, 100 Stat. 2742.

5. Petitioner also protested an addition to tax under section 6654. Although such addition apparently was proposed (as it is discussed in one of the schedules attached to the notice of deficiency) it does not appear on the face of the notice of deficiency and respondent has not mentioned it in his

and alternatively, that he had not been given credit for withholding taxes of $3,813.77 [6] in the calculation of such additions.

Deficiency in Income Tax

In the petition and the various objections filed thereafter, petitioner raised numerous "tax protester" type arguments. He maintains that his wages do not constitute gross income; that reporting and paying income taxes is strictly voluntary and, therefore, the filing of an income tax return was not required; that the Fifth Amendment to the Constitution of the United States prevents respondent from requiring him to provide the information called for on an income tax return; that the Sixteenth Amendment to the Constitution was not properly ratified; and, at least impliedly, that he was wrongfully denied a jury trial.

Since no other issues were raised by petitioner with regard to his income tax for 1983, and petitioner bears the burden of proving that respondent's determinations are incorrect, we find that petitioner is liable for the amount of income tax shown on the notice of deficiency. Welch v. Helvering, 290 U.S. 111 (1933); Rule 142(a).

Section 6651

We now turn our attention to the various additions to tax as determined by respondent. The first, section 6651(a)(1), imposes an addition to tax for failure to file a timely income tax return. It is uncontested that petitioner failed to file a Federal income tax return for the year in issue. Further, as we previously stated, requiring petitioner to report the requisite financial information on his income tax return does not violate petitioner's Fifth Amendment privilege against self-incrimination. The computation of the addition to tax does take into consideration petitioner's withholding tax credits, as is required by section 6651(b)(1). See section 301.6651–1(d)(1), Proced. and Admin.Regs. Accordingly, we find that petitioner is liable for the addition to tax under 6651(a)(1) as shown on the notice of deficiency.

Section 6653

Petitioner also questions whether he is liable for the addition to tax under section 6653(a)(1) and (2) for negligence or intentional disregard of rules and regulations. Since petitioner presented no objection to respondent's determination of negligence other than his timeworn tax protestor arguments, we find that he is liable for the additions to tax under 6653(a)(1) and (2).

Section 6661

Finally, we consider respondent's determination under section 6661. In the notice of deficiency, respondent determined that petition-

---

Motion for Judgment on the Pleadings. Consequently, no addition to tax under section 6644 is at issue in this case.

6. In his petition, petitioner alleged that $3,813.77 was withheld from his wages. This amount was not contested by respondent during the course of these proceedings.

er was liable for an addition under this section in the amount of $715.20, based on ten percent of the total amount of the deficiency in income tax of $7,152. Respondent moved to increase the addition to tax under section 6661 from $715.20 to $1,788 in his Supplemental Motion for Judgment on the Pleadings, based on the Omnibus Budget Reconciliation Act of 1986 (hereinafter OBRA 86). OBRA 86, sec. 8002, Pub.L. 99–509, 100 Stat.1987, 1951. Petitioner opposed this increase at the hearing of this case. Because respondent asserted his claim for the increased amount prior to the hearing, and the issue has been heard by the consent of the parties, we have jurisdiction to make a determination thereon. Sec. 6214(a); Rule 41(a)(1); Pallottini v. Commissioner, 90 T.C. 498 (1988).

Section 6661(a) originally provided for an addition to tax equal to 10 percent. In 1986, Congress passed two acts, each of which amended section 6661(a). One of the acts called for the increase to a 20–percent rate and the other (OBRA 86) called for an increase to a 25–percent rate. In a decision reviewed by this Court, we decided that OBRA 86 controlled and, therefore, that the correct rate was 25 percent. Pallottini v. Commissioner, supra. Accordingly, respondent was correct in asserting the 25–percent rate in this case.[8]

We must now decide whether respondent correctly computed the increased addition to tax by applying 25 percent to the entire deficiency of $7,152. He maintains that because petitioner did not file any return for 1983, the percentage is properly applied to the total amount of the income tax determined in the notice of deficiency. On the other hand, petitioner maintains that the percentage applies only to the difference between the deficiency and the amount of Federal taxes withheld from his wages.[9]

Section 6661(a) provides that:

> If there is a substantial *understatement* of income tax for any taxable year, there shall be added to the tax an amount equal to 25 percent of the amount of any *underpayment* attributable to such *understatement*. [Emphasis added.]

Since the statute provides that the 25–percent rate shall be applied to "the amount of any underpayment," our determination turns on the meaning of the term "underpayment" in the context of section 6661.

To put our discussion into perspective, we must first consider the meaning of some of the other terms used in that section. The term

---

8. Petitioner argues that since he was assessed on September 13, 1985 and the 25–percent rate is only applicable to section 6661 additions assessed after October 13, 1986, it does not apply to him. However, assessment is not allowed until after our decision became final. Sec. 6213(a). Since the assessment of this addition to tax will necessarily occur after October 13, 1986, we find that the increased rate is applicable.

9. Respondent asserts that in Du Bose v. Commissioner, T.C. Memo. 1986–288, this Court already has found that the section 6661 addition to tax is to be applied to the total deficiency before applying credits for income tax withheld. We have carefully examined that opinion and fail to find any mention withholding tax or prepayment credits.

"understatement" is expressly defined by section 6661(b)(2) as the excess of the amount of the tax required to be shown on the return over the amount of the tax imposed which is shown on the return.[10] Due to the fact that petitioner failed to report any of his income, the entire amount of the tax required to be shown on the return is equal to the total deficiency of $7,152.[11] Further, since no return was filed by petitioner, the amount of tax which is shown on the return is considered to be zero. Sec. 1.6661–2(d)(2), Income Tax Regs. Therefore, the "understatement" is $7,152.[12]

The term "substantial understatement" is defined in section 6661(b)(1) as an "understatement" which exceeds the greater of 10 percent of the tax required to be shown on the return or $5,000 * * * If a "substantial understatement" is present, it triggers the application of the addition to tax provided for in section 6661(a). We already have determined that the "understatement" is the entire amount of the tax deficiency in this case. Thus, the "understatement" is necessarily greater than 10 percent of the tax required to be shown. Further, the understatement of $7,152 is greater than $5,000. Therefore, the "understatement" of petitioner's tax is a "substantial understatement" as defined by section 6661(b)(1). Consequently, respondent correctly determined that the addition to tax under section 6661(a) applied in this case.

However, section 6661(a) states the amount of the addition to tax is equal to 25 percent of the "underpayment" attributable to the "understatement." Unlike the terms "understatement" or "substantial understatement," the term "underpayment" is not defined in section 6661. Respondent urges us to construe "underpayment" to be synonymous with "understatement." In fact, that is what the Regulations attempt to do, inasmuch as section 1.6661–2(a), Income Tax Regs., states that:

> If there is a *substantial understatement* of income tax for a taxable year (as defined in paragraph (b) of this section), section 6661 imposes a penalty equal to [25] percent of the *understatement* of tax liability. [Emphasis added.]

In justifying his position, respondent first argues that we should use the definition of the term "underpayment" that is contained in

---

10. The various exceptions provided for in the balance of section 6661 are not applicable in this case.

11. Petitioner argues that section 6661 should not be applied in his case since he did not file an income tax return and therefore, could not have had an "understatement" of tax. However, section 1.6661–2(d)(2), Income Tax Regs., provides that "if no return was filed for the taxable year * * * the amount of tax shown on the return is considered to be zero." This regulation is not plainly inconsistent with the statute, and petitioner has not presented any "weighty reasons" why we should invalidate it. Accordingly, his argument fails. Fulman v. United States, 434 U.S. 528, 533 (1978), and cases cited therein. See also Allen v. Commissioner, T.C. Memo. 1987–242, where we previously have found this section applicable where no income tax return was filed.

12. We note that the regulations rightfully disregard withheld taxes in determining "the amount of tax shown on the return" and "the amount of tax required to be shown on the return" in computing the "understatement." Sec. 1.6661–2(d)(5)(i), Income Tax Regs.

section 6659(g)(1) because section 6661 is coordinated with section 6659.[13] The coordination of these two sections is provided for in section 6661(b)(3) which states:

> Coordination with penalty imposed by section 6659.—For purposes of determining the amount of the addition to tax assessed under subsection (a), there shall not be taken into account that portion of the substantial understatement on which a penalty is imposed under section 6659 (relating to additions to tax in the case of valuation overstatements).

In turn, section 6659(g)(1) defines "underpayment" by reference to section 6653(c)(1).[14] Section 6653(c)(1) defines "underpayment" as a deficiency (as defined in section 6211), except that only the tax shown on a timely filed return is to be used to reduce the amount of the deficiency to arrive at the "underpayment" under section 6653. In other words, where no income tax return is filed, the term "underpayment" under section 6653(c)(1) is equal to the entire amount of the tax that should have been shown on the return if one had been filed.

There is no real merit to this argument. Upon close examination we find that the reason section 6661 is coordinated with section 6659 is to eliminate the overlap which would result when an "underpayment" caused by a valuation overstatement covered in section 6659 was also a part of the "understatement" covered in section 6661. See section 6661(b)(3). Consequently, the reason for coordinating sections 6659 and 6661 is totally unrelated to the meaning of "underpayment" for purposes of section 6661.[15]

Generally, to glean the meaning of the words used by Congress in a statute, we first look to the ordinary or settled meaning of the words used to convey its intent. Lynch v. Alworth–Stephens Co., 267 U.S. 364, 370 (1925); Mountain Water Co. of La Crescenta v. Commissioner, 35 T.C. 418, 424 (1960). In so doing, we find that "pay" means to satisfy a demand or obligation by "transfer of money" and the term "underpayment" means "insufficient payment."[16] As applied to this case, petitioner made payment of his money to the United States to satisfy his tax liability through payroll deductions. Petitioner's "underpayment" occurred only because he paid less than he was supposed to pay; that is, his payment was insufficient.[17] Petitioner's "underpayment"

---

13. Section 6659 provides for an addition to tax in the case of valuation overstatements.

14. Section 6659(g)(1) reads:
Underpayment.—The term "underpayment" has the meaning given to such term by section 6653(c)(1).

15. The term "underpayment" in section 6659 and the term "understatement" in section 6661 are parallel concepts (i.e., differences in tax resulting from adjustments made by the Internal Revenue Service). This is all the more reason that "underpayment" in section 6659 cannot be equated with "underpayment" in section 6661.

16. Webster's Third New World International Dictionary (1981). In determining the ordinary usage of words, it is appropriate to consult dictionaries. National Muffler Dealers Ass'n., Inc. v. United States, 440 U.S. 472, 480 n. 10 (1979).

17. This interpretation of "underpayment" conforms to the meaning given that term in sections 6654, 6655 and 6656. See sections 6654(b) and 6656(a).

Sec. 3   ACCURACY-RELATED & CIVIL FRAUD PENALTY   237

was not caused by his failure to report his income on an income tax return as respondent would have us hold, but rather by his failure to pay all of the tax that he owed. A reporting error is taken into account only in computing the "understatement" under section 6661. Therefore, the plain reading of the statute clearly means that the 25 percent rate is applied only to the unpaid amount rather than to the entire understatement.[18]

Congress modified the ordinary and regular meaning of the term "underpayment" for purposes of section 6653 and 6659 by including specific definitional sections. Sections 6653(c)(1) and 6659(g)(1). These definitional sections were needed because credits for taxes withheld and otherwise paid were not to be taken into account in making computations under those sections. Since there is no such modification in section 6661, it follows that the term "underpayment" takes such credits into account.

Finally, we observe that, if we would construe the terms "understatement" and "underpayment" as basically synonymous, the phrase "of the amount of any underpayment attributable to" in section 6661(a) would be superfluous and totally without meaning or significance. Stated another way, using respondent's interpretation, the statute could merely read "an amount equal to 25 percent of such understatement." In fact, this abbreviated version is essentially what the Regulations say in section 1.661-2(a), Income Tax Regs.

However, it is a cardinal rule of statutory construction that "effect shall be given to every clause and part of statutes." Ginsberg & Sons v. Popkin, 285 U.S. 204, 208 (1932). Therefore, we find that giving "underpayment" its ordinary meaning in the context of section 6661 is proper, since this gives full effect to every clause and part of the statute and does not ignore the phrase "of the amount of any underpayment attributable to."[19]

To summarize, we do not accept respondent's position (or the regulation) because (1) it would render part of the statutory language of

18. Wage earners who file proper W-4 Forms frequently overpay their tax by their withholding, yet many fail to file income tax returns to claim rightful refunds. See Hearings on S. 2198 before the Subcomm. on Oversight of the Internal Revenue Service of the Senate Comm. on Finance, 97th Cong., 2d Sess. 99 (1982). Respondent's interpretation would subject these wage earners to an addition to tax equal to 25% of their entire tax even though it all had been paid. We believe Congress did not intend this result when it enacted section 6661. See 111 Cong.Rec. S 8791, 8811 (1982) (Remarks by Senator Grassley, cosponsor of S. 2198 Taxpayer Compliance Improvement Act of 1982). See also the minimum addition for extended failure to file a return in section 6651(a) that was enacted concurrently with section 6661.

19. Where, as here, a statute is clear on its face, we require unequivocal evidence of legislative purpose before construing the statute so as to override the plain meaning of the words used therein. Hirasuna v. Commissioner, 89 T.C. 1216 (1987); Huntsberry v. Commissioner, 83 T.C. 742, 747-748 (1984); see Rubin v. United States, 449 U.S. 424, 430 (1981); TVA v. Hill, 437 U.S. 153, 187 n. 33 (1978). Section 6661 was enacted on September 3, 1982, as part of the Tax Equity and Fiscal Responsibility Act of 1982, sec. 323, Pub.L. 97-428, 96 Stat. 324, 613 (TEFRA). There is nothing in the legislative history of this bill to refute our definition of "underpayment."

section 6661 superfluous, (2) it ignores the limiting language of the definition of "underpayment" in sections 6653(c)(1) and 6659(g)(1), and (3) it conflicts with the ordinary and settled meaning of "underpayment" (i.e., the amount by which the payment was insufficient). For these reasons, we hold that the amount of petitioner's withholding credits must be subtracted from the "understatement" to arrive at the "amount of any underpayment" for the calculation of the addition to tax under section 6661.

Section 6673

We have held that petitioner's position on section 6661(a) has merit. Exercising our discretion, we deny respondent's motion for damages under section 6673.

CONCLUSION

We are mindful of the fact that our holding invalidates a portion of the Regulations under section 6661. Sec. 1.6661-2(a), Income Tax Regs. We arrived at such holding only after taking into account that regulations are to be accorded the highest standard of judicial deference. Estate of Bullard v. Commissioner, 87 T.C. 261, 281 (1986). If this regulation had constituted a reasonable interpretation of section 6661(a), we would have upheld it. But where, as here, all of the words of the statute are not given effect, and as a result the addition is substantially higher, the regulation must fail.

Decision will be entered under Rule 155.

Reviewed by the Court.

Note

Congress endorsed the *Woods II* reasoning in section 6662(a), which provides that the 20% penalty applies only to the portion of the underpayment attributable to conduct (such as negligence, etc.) to which section 6662 applies.

(2) "Authority" and "Substantial Authority"

(a) Annual list of positions. Section 6662(d)(2)(D) requires the Service to publish not less frequently than annually a list of positions for which the Service believes substantial authority does not exist and that affect a significant number of taxpayers. Congress explained the purpose of this list as follows:

> The purpose of this list is to assist taxpayers in determining whether a position should be disclosed in order to avoid the substantial understatement penalty. Thus, if a taxpayer takes a position that is enumerated on this list, the taxpayer could choose to disclose that position to avoid the imposition of the substantial understatement penalty. However, inclusion of a position on this list is not conclusive as to whether or not substantial authority exists with respect to that position. If, however, there is litigation as to whether there is substantial

Sec. 3   ACCURACY-RELATED & CIVIL FRAUD PENALTY   239

authority, and the court concludes that the IRS is correct in its belief that there is not substantial authority for the position, then this penalty would apply. The committee believes that this list will be useful to taxpayers, in that it will assist taxpayers in determining whether substantial authority exists with respect to a particular issue on the list. Although the list is not exclusive, the committee intends that the IRS make the list as comprehensive as practical, which will make it more useful to taxpayers and their advisors. The committee intends that there should be no inference that substantial authority exists with respect to positions that are not included on this list. Disclosure of a position for purposes of this penalty does not necessarily prevent imposition of the negligence penalty. Thus, for example, if a taxpayer discloses a frivolous position, the imposition of the negligence penalty could be appropriate. [H.R. Rep. 101-247, 101st Cong., 1st Sess. 1390 (1989).]

(b) Expanded definition of "authority." Section 1.6662-4(d)(3)(iii) of the proposed accuracy-related penalty regulations provides an expanded definition of "authority."

(iii) *Types of authority.* Except in cases described in paragraph (d)(3)(iv) of this section concerning written determinations, only the following are authority for purposes of determining whether there is substantial authority for the tax treatment of an item: applicable provisions of the Internal Revenue Code and other statutory provisions; proposed, temporary and final regulations construing such statutes; revenue rulings and revenue procedures; tax treaties and regulations thereunder, and Treasury Department and other official explanations of such treaties; Federal court cases interpreting such statutes; congressional intent as reflected in committee reports, joint explanatory statements of managers included in conference committee reports, and floor statements made prior to enactment by one of a bill's managers; General Explanations of tax legislation prepared by the Joint Committee on Taxation (the Blue Book); private letter rulings and technical advice memoranda issued after October 31, 1976; actions on decisions and general counsel memoranda issued after March 12, 1981; Internal Revenue Service information or press releases; and notices, announcements and other administrative pronouncements published by the Service in the Internal Revenue Bulletin. Conclusions reached in treatises, legal periodicals, legal opinions or opinions rendered by other tax professionals are not authority. The authorities underlying such expressions of opinion where applicable to the facts of a particular case, however, may give rise to substantial authority for the tax treatment of an item. Notwithstanding the preceding list of authorities, an authority does not continue to be an authority once it is overruled or modified, implicitly or explicitly, by an authority of the same or higher source. For example, a district court opinion on an issue is not an authority if overruled or reversed. Similarly, a private letter ruling is not authority if revoked or if inconsistent with a subsequent proposed regulation, revenue ruling or other administrative pronouncement published in the Internal Revenue Bulletin.

(c) "Substantial authority." Section 1.6662–4(d)(3) of the proposed accuracy-related penalty regulations explains how to determine if there is substantial authority for a position:

> There is substantial authority for the tax treatment of an item only if the weight of the authorities supporting the treatment is substantial in relation to the weight of authorities supporting contrary treatment. All authorities relevant to the tax treatment of an item, including the authorities contrary to the treatment, are taken into account in determining whether substantial authority exists.
>
> * * *
>
> The weight accorded an authority depends on its relevance and persuasiveness, and the type of document providing the authority.... An authority that merely states a conclusion ordinarily is less persuasive than one that reaches its conclusion by cogently relating the applicable law to pertinent facts * * *. The type of document also must be considered. For example, a revenue ruling is accorded greater weight than a private letter ruling addressing the issue. An older private letter ruling, technical advice memorandum, general counsel memorandum or action on decision generally must be accorded less weight than a more recent one. Any document described in the preceding sentence that is more than 10 years old generally is accorded very little weight.

Note

Prior to IMPACT, the Service's imposition of the substantial understatement penalty was reviewable by the courts only under the "abuse of discretion" standard, according to the Tax Court. That is, the court could not waive the penalty unless it found that the Commissioner had abused his discretion in imposing it. Rickel v. Commissioner, 92 T.C. 510 (1989) (reviewed), affirmed in part and reversed in part, 900 F.2d 655 (3d Cir. 1990), illustrates the difficulty in avoiding the penalty if the questioned return position was not disclosed. In that case the taxpayer excluded from income amounts received from a former employer in settlement of a suit brought under the Age Discrimination in Employment Act. The Tax Court, in a reviewed opinion, held that only half the amount received was properly excludable under section 104(a)(2) and upheld the imposition of the substantial understatement penalty. The Tax Court reasoned as follows:

> Petitioners did not disclose the unreported income on their 1983 return. Petitioners argue, however, that their position with respect to this unreported income was supported by substantial authority.
>
> In evaluating whether a taxpayer's position regarding the tax treatment of an item is supported by substantial authority, the weight of authorities in support of the taxpayer's position must be substantial in relation to the weight of authorities supporting contrary positions. Sec. 1.6661–3(b)(1), Income Tax Regs. Petitioners argue that they relied on Internal Revenue Service Publication 17 in determining whether the settlement damages were taxable income. That publication, however, quoted above, is not authority for the characterization of

the amounts petitioner received as damages for personal injury rather than as back pay.

* * *

Finally, petitioners argue that they are entitled to a waiver of the addition to tax under section 6661(c). We are not persuaded, however, that petitioners qualify for a waiver and cannot conclude that a failure to provide a waiver is an abuse of respondent's discretion. We believe that this is the type of case where Congress intended doubts about taxability to be the subject of a disclosure on the return if the taxpayer is to avoid the addition to tax. [92 T.C. at 523–524.]

On appeal, the Third Circuit Court of Appeals reversed on the issue of excludability of the amount from income. The court stated: "[The taxpayer] argues that under our decision in *Byrne* the entire settlement amount should be excludable as compensation for personal injury. We agree and find that the Tax Court failed to properly apply the analysis adopted by this Court—and, indeed, the analysis the full Tax Court itself has adopted in *Threlkeld*—to determine whether settlement proceeds are excludable from income under § 104(a)(2)." Because the amount was properly excluded from the taxpayer's income, no understatement existed and the penalty could not be imposed. The taxpayer petitioned for an award of litigation costs under section 7430, but the court affirmed the Tax Court's refusal to award litigation costs on the basis that the inconsistent treatment of the underlying issue by the courts precluded a finding that the Commissioner's position was "not substantially justified." Thus, while the Tax Court had found the taxpayer's position justified the substantial understatement penalty, the Third Circuit upheld the taxpayer's position and carefully considered whether the taxpayer might be entitled to litigation costs because of the potential unreasonableness of the Commissioner's position.

As discussed in section B above, the reasonable cause exception of section 6664(c), applicable to returns filed after 1989, is designed to permit greater judicial scrutiny of the accuracy-related penalties. The courts are to review impositions of the penalty under the same standards employed in reviewing the Commissioner's assertion of additional tax liability, rather than the "abuse of discretion" standard.

(3) Adequate Disclosure

The substantial understatement penalty can be avoided by either adequately disclosing the questionable return position or by the existence of substantial authority for the position. Guidance concerning adequate disclosure for purposes of this penalty is contained in Rev. Proc. 90–16, 1990–1 C.B. 477. Unlike the disclosure requirements for avoiding the negligence penalty of sections 6662(b)(1) and (c), discussed at pages 230–31, it is possible to avoid the substantial understatement penalty merely by completing certain forms and schedules of an income tax return. Thus, a taxpayer who wishes to avoid both penalties should follow the more rigorous procedures for avoiding the negligence penalty.

(4) Tax Shelter Items

REV.RUL. 89-74

ISSUE

Are "churches" such as those described in Rev.Rul. 78-232, 1978-1 C.B. 69, and Rev.Rul. 81-94, 1981-1 C.B. 330, "tax shelters" within the meaning of section 6661 of the Internal Revenue Code?

FACTS

In Rev.Rul 78-232, the taxpayer, claiming to be a duly ordained minister, formed a "church." The original members of the church consisted of the taxpayer, the taxpayer's spouse and two minor children, and a few family friends. The taxpayer was employed full-time by a state government, and continued in this employment after the church was formed. The taxpayer's salary checks were received by the taxpayer and deposited into the church's bank account. The funds from the church bank account, however, were primarily used to furnish the taxpayer with lodging, food, clothing, and other living expenses in a manner comparable to that which the taxpayer previously enjoyed.

In Rev.Rul. 81-94, a professional nurse formed a "church" and became its minister by purchasing a "certificate of ordination" and a church charter from an organization selling such certificates and charters. Pursuant to a vow of poverty, all the nurse's assets, including a house and an automobile, were transferred to the church. In addition, the nurse's wage income was deposited into the church bank account. In return, the church assumed all the nurse's existing liabilities, such as the home mortgage and all outstanding credit card balances. The church also provided the nurse with a full living allowance sufficient to maintain or improve the nurse's standard of living and permitted the nurse to use the house and automobile for personal purposes.

LAW AND ANALYSIS

Section 501(c)(3) of the Code provides for the exemption from federal income tax of organizations organized and operated exclusively for religious or charitable purposes, no part of the net earnings of which inures to the benefit of any private shareholder or individual. Section 1.501(c)(3)-1(d)(1)(ii) of the Income Tax Regulations provides that an organization described in section 501(c)(3) must serve a public rather than a private interest. For example, such an organization cannot be organized or operated for the purpose of benefiting certain designated individuals or the creator or the creator's family.

Sections 170(a)(1) and 170(c) of the Code provide a deduction for any "charitable contribution." A "charitable contribution" is defined to include a contribution or a gift to or for the use of an organization organized and operated exclusively for religious or charitable purposes,

Sec. 3 ACCURACY-RELATED & CIVIL FRAUD PENALTY   243

no part of the net earnings of which inures to the benefit of any private shareholder or individual.

Section 262 of the Code provides, in general, that no deduction shall be allowed for personal, living, or family expenses.

Section 6661(a) of the Code imposes a penalty if there is a substantial understatement of income tax. The penalty is equal to 25 percent of the underpayment attributable to such understatement.

Section 6661(b)(1) of the Code provides that a substantial understatement exists if the understatement exceeds the greater of 10 percent of the tax required to be shown on the return or $5,000 ($10,000 in the case of certain corporations).

Section 6661(b)(2)(B) of the Code provides that the amount of the understatement shall be reduced by the portion of the understatement which is attributable to (i) the tax treatment of any item by the taxpayer if there is or was substantial authority for such treatment, or (ii) any item with respect to which the relevant facts affecting the item's tax treatment are adequately disclosed in the return or in a statement attached to the return.

In the case of any understatement attributable to a tax shelter, section 6661(b)(2)(C)(i) of the Code provides that the taxpayer must be able to show that there is or was substantial authority for the tax treatment taken *and* that the taxpayer reasonably believed that the tax treatment was more likely than not the proper tax treatment. That section further provides that the adequate disclosure exception in section 6661(b)(2)(B)(ii) does not apply to any item attributable to a tax shelter.

Section 6661(b)(2)(C)(ii) of the Code and the underlying regulations define the term "tax shelter," for purposes of section 6661, to mean a partnership or other entity (such as a corporation or trust), any investment plan or arrangement, or any other plan or arrangement, if the principal purpose of such partnership, entity, plan, or arrangement is the avoidance or evasion of federal income tax.

Section 1.6661–5(c) of the regulations provides that an item of income, gain, loss, deduction or credit will be considered a "tax shelter item" if the item is directly or indirectly attributable to the principal purpose of a tax shelter to avoid or evade federal income tax.

Rev.Proc. 89–11, page 797, this Bulletin, provides, in section 4(a)(4), that merely disclosing "the name of an organization to which the taxpayer makes a donation and the amount of the donation (for which a charitable contribution deduction is claimed) will not constitute adequate disclosure for purposes of section 6661 of the Code if the taxpayer receives a substantial benefit from the donation shown." This revenue procedure has no applicability, however, if the organization to which the donation is being made is a "tax shelter" under section 6661(b)(2)(C)(ii), since the adequate disclosure exception does not apply in such cases.

In *Tweeddale v. Commissioner*, 92 T.C. No. 31 (March 22, 1989), the petitioner claimed on his individual income tax return that his income was exempt from tax because he was a "minister" in the Basic Bible Church of America. For the purchase price of $1200, the petitioner received a letter certifying him to be a minister of the Basic Bible Church, a certificate of ordination, a certificate of Doctor of Divinity, a letter from the "Archbishop" of the Church outlining the minister's obligations and duties, and a vow of poverty. Petitioner attached the documents to his individual income tax return for 1983. The court concluded that the principal purpose for establishing the ministry was tax avoidance and that the ministry was a tax shelter for purposes of section 6661 of the Code. Accordingly, the adequate disclosure exception to the penalty did not apply.

Rev.Rul. 78-232 holds that the amount of the salary checks deposited by the taxpayer in the church bank account is not deductible as a charitable contribution under section 170 of the Code on two alternative grounds. First, the contribution is not a "charitable contribution" within the meaning of section 170 because the transfer was made with the expectation of procuring a benefit in return. Second, the church is not an organization described in section 170(c) because it was operated for the private purposes of the taxpayer and not exclusively for religious or other charitable purposes.

Rev.Rul. 81-94 holds that the church is not an exempt organization under section 501(c)(3) of the Code because it was operated to serve the private interests of the taxpayer rather than a public interest and therefore was not operated exclusively for religious or charitable purposes. The church was merely a vehicle for handling the taxpayer's personal financial transactions.

The churches in Rev.Rul. 78-232 and Rev.Rul. 81-94 were formed for the principal purpose of avoiding federal income taxes. These churches thus come within the definition of "tax shelter" under section 6661 of the Code.

HOLDING

"Churches" such as those described in Rev.Rul. 78-232 and Rev.Rul. 81-94 are "tax shelters" within the meaning of section 6661 of the Code. Therefore, in the case of any understatement of income tax attributable to such a church, the adequate disclosure exception in section 6661(b)(2)(B)(ii) is not available to reduce such a taxpayer's understatement of income tax for purposes of applying the substantial understatement penalty.

EFFECT ON OTHER REVENUE RULINGS

Rev.Rul. 78-232 and Rev.Rul. 81-94 are amplified.

E. SUBSTANTIAL VALUATION MISSTATEMENTS

(1) Substantial Valuation Overstatements (Section 6662(e)

TODD v. COMMISSIONER OF INTERNAL REVENUE

United States Court of Appeals, Fifth Circuit, 1988.
862 F.2d 540.

Before THORNBERRY, RUBIN and HIGGINBOTHAM, CIRCUIT JUDGES.

PATRICK E. HIGGINBOTHAM, CIRCUIT JUDGE:

Taxpayers Richard and Denese Todd appealed deficiencies and penalties assessed by the Commissioner of Internal Revenue. The Tax Court denied the taxpayers' claimed depreciation deductions and investment tax credits. In a later opinion, the Tax Court refused to impose the Commissioner's requested penalties under Internal Revenue Code § 6659 for tax underpayments attributable to valuation overstatements. The Commissioner appeals that determination. We affirm.

I

Beginning in 1980, FoodSource, Inc. sold investors interests in refrigerated food containers. The containers were designed to preserve perishable agricultural products during shipment to foreign and domestic markets. Each investor paid a fraction of the alleged purchase price of part or all of a refrigerated unit, signing a promissory note for the balance. FoodSource managed the containers, renting them to food transporters and regularly reporting profits supposedly earned by each investor.

Appellees Richard and Denese Todd purchased two FoodSource containers on December 8, 1981, and a third on October 14, 1982. The Todds paid $52,000 to FoodSource for each unit, signing notes to raise the "purchase price" of each container to $260,000. Using the $260,000 figure as the basis of each unit, the Todds claimed investment tax credits and depreciation deductions for the 1981 and 1982 tax years, carrying unused portions of the investment tax credits back to 1979 and 1980. However, due to a payment dispute with FoodSource, the manufacturer retained control of all three containers purchased by the Todds until 1983.

The Internal Revenue Service assessed deficiencies and penalties against many investors in the FoodSource program, including the Todds. The Todds participated with various other "test case petitioners" in litigation before the Tax Court, challenging the IRS actions. In *Noonan v. Commissioner of Internal Revenue*,[1] the Tax Court determined that the Todds were not entitled to their claimed deductions and credits for 1979–82, since none of their containers had been placed in service until 1983. Other investors, such as the Hillendahls and the Hendricks, did have containers placed in service during the years for

---

1. T.C.Memo. 1986–449 (1986).

which they claimed tax benefits. Finding the obligations represented by the promissory notes illusory, the Tax Court limited the maximum adjusted basis taxpayers could claim in each FoodSource container to the lesser of its $60,000 fair market value or the actual cash payments made by the investor. Consequently, investors like the Hendricks and Hillendahls, though purchasing their containers with an actual profit motive, still received substantially smaller deductions and tax credits due to their reduced basis in their assets. These investors were also found liable under IRC § 6659 for a 30% addition to tax on portions of their tax deficiencies "attributable to [ ] valuation overstatement[s]."

Upon remand for calculation of deficiencies, the Commissioner assessed a § 6659 penalty against the Todds. The Todds appealed once again to the Tax Court. In *Todd v. Commissioner of Internal Revenue*,[2] the Tax Court refused to allow the § 6659 addition to tax. It reasoned that the Todds' deductions and credits were disallowed on the Commissioner's alternative ground that the food storage units had not been placed in service during the tax years in issue. Consequently, the Tax Court decided, the taxpayers' underpayments of tax could not be "attributable to" the valuation overstatements contained in their tax returns. The court refused to read § 6659 as imposing a penalty anytime a tax underpayment had been accompanied by a valuation overstatement. The Commissioner now asks us to reverse the Tax Court's decision.

II

The statute we must construe, IRC § 6659(a), provides:

(a) Addition to the tax.—If—

(1) an individual, or

(2) a closely held corporation or a personal service corporation,

has an underpayment of the tax imposed by chapter 1 for the taxable year which is attributable to a valuation overstatement, then there shall be added to the tax an amount equal to the applicable percentage of the underpayment so attributable.

The penalty only applies if the tax underpayment attributable to the overstated valuation equals at least $1000 and the claimed property value or adjusted basis is at least 150 percent of the actual value or basis.[3] The parties agree that, under the Tax Court ruling in *Noonan*, the Todds overstated the value of their FoodSource containers by 500%. If § 6659 applies, the Todds will be liable for an addition to tax of 30% of underpayments attributable to the valuation overstatements.[4]

The parties divide only over the meaning of the words "attributable to" in the statute. The Commissioner asks us to hold the Todds liable under § 6659, basing his arguments on the statute's language, its legislative history, its underlying policy, and the Commissioner's per-

---

2. 89 T.C. 912 (1987).
3. IRC § 6659(c), (d).
4. IRC § 6659(a), (b).

ception of inequity in the Tax Court's result. First, the government argues that "attributable" ordinarily means "capable of being attributed." Thus, it contends that § 6659 applies anytime a taxpayer's underpayment is "capable of being attributed" to a valuation overstatement, regardless of the actual ground relied on to uphold the deficiency. Unfortunately, the Commissioner's formulation merely substitutes one ambiguity for another. Whether a given underpayment is "capable of being attributed" to a valuation overstatement depends on the meaning of "capable." In one sense, that urged by the government, there can be several problems with a particular deduction and the resulting tax deficiency is, then, capable of being attributed to any of them. In this case, however, the Commissioner asserted and the Tax Court found that the Todds' FoodSource units had not been placed in service until after the 1982 tax year. Given those circumstances, no deductions or credits could legally be taken with respect to these food containers on the Todds' 1981 and 1982 tax returns. Thus, the value claimed for the containers became irrelevant to the Todds' tax liability, since it played no part in calculating the tax they actually owed. One can certainly argue the position that a tax underpayment is not "capable of being attributed" to an irrelevant figure on the income tax return. While a client might be "capable" of kicking the bottom of her lethargic lawyer in an abstract sense, one might still say she was "incapable" of doing so at a time when the two were a thousand miles apart. Thus, we find the language of the statute ambiguous, and look instead to the legislative history.[5]

Congress initially enacted § 6659 as part of the Economic Recovery Tax Act of 1981. The House Ways and Means Committee recognized the large number of property valuation disputes clogging the tax collection system, and added the overvaluation penalty to discourage those taxpayers who would inflate the value of property on their tax returns in hopes of "dividing the difference" with the IRS.[6] Unfortunately, none of the formal legislative history provides a method for calculating whether a given tax underpayment is attributable to a valuation overstatement.

Such a formula is found, however, in the *General Explanation of the Economic Recovery Tax Act of 1981,* or "blue book," prepared by the

---

5. The Commissioner also argues that if Congress wanted to reach the Tax Court's result, it should have used the phrase "solely attributed" to a valuation overstatement. He points out that in some code sections, Congress modified the "attributable to" language to narrow its meaning. *See, e.g.,* IRC § 6697(a) ("attributable solely to"). We find more helpful, however, code sections using the identical language we must construe. For instance, in § 6653, Congress clearly intended the phrase "attributable to" as synonymous with "due to." *Compare* IRC § 6653(b)(1) ("due to fraud") *with* IRC § 6653(a)(2), (b)(1)(A), (b)(2) ("attributable to fraud"). If we substituted this language into § 6659, the penalty would apply to "an underpayment of * * * tax * * * which is [due to] a valuation overstatement." This formulation seems more suggestive of the concrete causation approach applied by the Tax Court rather than the hypothetical causation theory advocated by the Commissioner.

6. H.R.Rep. No. 201, 97th Cong., 1st Sess. 243 (1981) *reprinted in* 1981-2 C.B. 352, 398.

staff of the Joint Committee on Taxation. Though not technically legislative history, the Supreme Court relied on a similar blue book in construing part of the Tax Reform Act of 1969, calling the document a "compelling contemporary indication" of the intended effect of the statute.[7] The committee staff explained § 6659's operation as follows:

> *The portion of a tax underpayment that is attributable to a valuation overstatement will be determined after taking into account any other proper adjustments to tax liability.* Thus, the underpayment resulting from a valuation overstatement will be determined by comparing the taxpayer's (1) actual tax liability (i.e., the tax liability that results from a proper valuation and which takes into account any other proper adjustments) with (2) actual tax liability as reduced by taking into account the valuation overstatement. The difference between these two amounts will be the underpayment that is attributable to the valuation overstatement.[2]
>
> 2. The determination of the portion of a tax underpayment that is attributable to a valuation overstatement may be illustrated by the following example. Assume that in 1982 an individual files a joint return showing taxable income of $40,000 and tax liability of $9,195. Assume, further, that a $30,000 deduction which was claimed by the taxpayer as the result of a valuation overstatement is adjusted down to $10,000, and that another deduction of $20,000 is disallowed totally for reasons apart from the valuation overstatement. These adjustments result in correct taxable income of $80,000 and correct tax liability of $27,505. Accordingly, the underpayment due to the valuation overstatement is the difference between the tax on $80,000 ($27,505) and the tax on $60,000 ($17,505) (i.e., actual tax liability reduced by taking into account the deductions disallowed because of the valuation overstatement), or $9,800 [sic].[8]

Applying this formula, the Tax Court determined that no portion of the Todds' tax underpayment was attributable to their valuation overstatements. The Todds' actual tax liability, after adjusting for the failure to place the food containers in service before 1983, did not differ from their actual tax liability adjusted for the valuation overstatements. In other words, where the deductions and credits for these refrigeration units were inappropriate altogether, the Todds' valuation of the property supposedly generating the tax benefits had no impact whatsoever on the amount of tax actually owed. Since the legislative history of § 6659 provides no alternative method of applying the statute, we are persuaded that the formula contained in the committee staff's explanation evidences congressional intent with respect to calculating underpayments subject to the penalty.

Our conclusion that Congress intended this formula to be applied in determining liability for the § 6659 addition to tax is fortified by the legislative history of a closely related tax provision. In the Tax Reform Act of 1986, Congress added § 6659A providing, in statutory language and structure almost identical to § 6659, for an addition to tax where a tax underpayment "is attributable to an overstatement of pension liabilities."[9] This time, the House Ways and Means Committee report explained the provision:

---

7. *Federal Power Commission v. Memphis Light, Gas & Water Division,* 411 U.S. 458, 471–72, 93 S.Ct. 1723, 1731, 36 L.Ed.2d 426, 437 (1973).

8. Staff of the Joint Committee on Taxation, General Explanation of the Economic Recovery Tax Act of 1981, at 333 (Comm. Print 1981).

9. *See* IRC § 6659A.

The bill provides a new penalty in the form of a graduated addition to tax applicable to certain income tax overstatements of deductions for pension liabilities. As an addition to tax, this penalty is to be assessed, collected, and paid in the same manner as a tax. This addition to tax applies only to the extent of any income tax underpayment that is attributable to such an overstatement.

The portion of a tax underpayment that is attributable to a valuation overstatement is to be determined after taking into account any other proper adjustments to tax liability. Thus, the underpayment resulting from a valuation overstatement is the excess of the taxpayer's (1) actual tax liability (i.e., the tax liability that results from a proper valuation of deductions for pension liabilities and takes into account any other proper adjustments) over (2) actual tax liability as reduced by taking into account the valuation overstatement.[10]

Obviously, the second paragraph repeats, almost word for word, the test contained in the committee staff's explanation of § 6659. Given that Congress modelled § 6659A after § 6659, we conclude that the same formula should be applied under each statute—the formula contained in the legislative history of § 6659A and in the committee staff's explanation of § 6659.[11]

The Commissioner asserts, however, that the formula was only meant to apply "in the simple case where there are separate, unrelated adjustments to an individual's tax, one of which is concededly attributable to a valuation overstatement."[12] He contends that this case is more complex because all of the adjustments to the Todds' tax liability "stem from their participation in the FoodSource shelter."[13] The Commissioner's attempted distinction finds no support in the language of the statute, its legislative history, or in the description of the committee staff's formula. The formula instructs us to determine § 6659 liability "*after*" taking account of "*any* other proper adjustment to tax liability." It does not distinguish among other tax adjustments based on their degree of relationship to the valuation overstatement.

Finding no explicit support for his position, the Commissioner argues that the policies underlying § 6659 mandate imposition of the addition to tax in this instance. He notes that Congress wanted to make tax shelters based on property overvaluations less attractive. To allow the Todds to significantly overvalue the adjusted basis of these food containers on their tax returns without suffering an addition to tax would supposedly frustrate the policies behind § 6659. We point

---

10. H.R.Rep. No. 426, 99th Cong., 1st Sess. 763 (1985); *see also* Staff of the Joint Committee on Taxation, General Explanation of the Tax Reform Act of 1986, at 770 (Comm.Print 1987).

11. The Tax Court also relied on a similar formula, achieving the same outcome, contained in the temporary Treasury Regulations for applying the § 6621(c) interest penalty on tax underpayments "attributable to tax motivated transactions." *See Todd*, 89 T.C. at 917–18; 26 C.F.R. § 301.-6621–2T, at A–5. One of the tax motivated transactions subject to the interest penalty is "any valuation overstatement (within the meaning of section 6659(c))." IRC § 6621(c)(3)(A)(i).

12. Appellant's Brief, at 16 n. 11.

13. *Id.*

out, of course, that the Todds did not benefit from their tax shelter, since their depreciation deductions and investment tax credits were denied in full. Further, it is probable that Congress was balancing competing policies when it determined how to apply § 6659. First, Congress may not have wanted to burden the Tax Court with deciding difficult valuation issues where a case could be easily decided on other grounds.[14] Second, Congress may have wanted to moderate the application of the § 6659 penalty so that it would not be imposed on taxpayers whose overvaluation was irrelevant to the determination of their actual tax liability.[15] We cannot say for certain why Congress chose this test to measure § 6659 liability, rather than modifying the formula to address the Commissioner's concerns. However, we remain convinced that the formula set out above represents Congress' intent for determining whether to impose the § 6659 addition to tax in any given case.

Finally, appellant argues that the Tax Court decision leads to anomalous results. He points out that some investors in the FoodSource program, like the Hillendahls and Hendricks, were found liable for the § 6659 penalty since their FoodSource units had been placed in service. Yet, arguably, the only difference between the Todds on the one hand and the Hendricks and Hillendahls on the other is that the

---

14. Congress saw § 6659 as a measure to help the Tax Court control its docket:

The conferees note that a number of the provisions of recent legislation have been designed, in whole or in part, to deal with the Tax Court backlog. Examples of these provisions are the increased damages assessable for instituting or maintaining Tax Court proceedings primarily for delay or that are frivolous or groundless (sec. 6673), the adjustment of interest rates (sec. 6621), the valuation overstatement and substantial understatement penalties (secs. 6659 and 6661)....

The conferees believe that, with this amendment, the Congress has given the Tax Court sufficient tools to manage its docket, and that the responsibility for effectively managing that docket and reducing the backlog now lies with the Tax Court * * *. The Court should * * * assert, without hesitancy in appropriate instances, the penalties that the Congress has provided.

H.R.Conf.Rep. No. 861, 98th Cong., 2d Sess. 985 (1984), U.S.Code Cong. & Admin.News 1984, p. 1673, *reprinted in* 1984–3 C.B. 1, 239. While Congress desired the penalties to be applied in "appropriate" cases, it may not have wanted the Tax Court to have to decide difficult valuation questions for no reason other than the application of penalties. Though judicial economy is not a factor in this case, where the Tax Court had already determined the correct value of the property in issue, the rule we adopt will determine whether the Commissioner can force the Tax Court to decide valuation issues in the future for the sole purpose of imposing a § 6659 addition to tax.

15. Congress knows how to adjust penalties to achieve deterrent effect. For instance, § 6653(a)(1) adds a five percent penalty to the entire tax underpayment if any portion of it "is due to negligence or disregard of rules or regulations." *Commissioner of Internal Revenue v. Asphalt Products Co.*, 482 U.S. 117, 107 S.Ct. 2275, 96 L.Ed.2d 97 (1987) (per curiam). By contrast, the seventy-five percent penalty on tax underpayments due to fraud applies only to the portion of the underpayment attributable to fraud. IRC § 6653(b)(1)(A).

Congress recognized that valuation questions involve difficult factual determinations. For this reason, it applied § 6659 only to significant overvaluations. *See* Staff of the Joint Committee on Taxation, General Explanation of the Economic Recovery Tax Act of 1981, at 332 (Comm. Print 1981). The same concerns may have led Congress to develop a test which would not penalize overvaluations having no effect on the taxpayer's tax liability. Further, Congress may have concluded that with significant penalties for fraud, negligence and tax motivated transactions, the Commissioner possessed sufficient weapons to deter tax shelter schemes without making § 6659 too draconian.

deductions and credits claimed by the Todds suffer from greater infirmities. The Commissioner also raises the spectre that under the Tax Court ruling, taxpayers might avoid § 6659 penalties by denying they had a profit motivation in entering the transactions in issue.

We admittedly hesitate to ascribe an intent to Congress which might, at first blush, seem inequitable. However, though incongruous results can be considered in construing statutes, once a court knows Congressional intent, it may not vary the rules to avoid what it considers an undesirable outcome.[16] Having set forth the reasons for believing Congress intended to impose the committee staff's formula as the method for determining the application of § 6659, the results appellant complains of do not persuade us to reverse the Tax Court.

We note, however, that the results the Commissioner deplores may not be as inequitable as he argues. First, while the Hendricks and Hillendahls had to pay a § 6659 penalty, they were also allowed to retain a portion of their claimed depreciation deductions and investment tax credits. The Todds, on the other hand, while escaping the § 6659 penalty, were denied any of their claimed deductions and credits for the years in question. Further, to say that the Todds' claimed tax benefits were subject to greater infirmities than those claimed by the Hillendahls and Hendricks does not mean that the Todds were more at fault. As the Tax Court noted, "the failure to place the containers in service during the years of purchase was due to circumstances beyond the control of the Todds and may not have been known to the Todds."[17]

Finally, the fear that taxpayers will deny profit motivation to avoid § 6659 penalties is unimpressive. Significant penalties attach to tax underpayments attributable to fraud, negligence, or tax motivated transactions. To the extent a taxpayer took the position that he entered a transaction without profit motive, but still claimed tax benefits relating to the transaction, he might well win a Pyrrhic victory, escaping § 6659 penalties only to subject himself to a much larger seventy-five percent penalty for fraud.

III

We hold that the Tax Court applied the correct formula for determining when to impose penalties under § 6659. The Commissioner has failed to persuade us that an alternative test was intended by Congress. The Tax Court decision is AFFIRMED.

Note

IMPACT abandoned the three-tiered penalty of former section 6659 in favor of the uniform 20% amount for the accuracy-related penalties of § 6662. The 20% penalty applies only to valuation overstatements of 200% or more. Under pre-IMPACT rules, valuation overstatements of

---

16. *See Asphalt Products Co.,* 107 S.Ct. at 2278 ("Judicial perception that a particular result would be unreasonable may enter into the construction of ambiguous provisions, but cannot justify disregard of what Congress has plainly and intentionally provided.").

17. *Todd,* 89 T.C. at 921.

150% to 200% triggered a 10% penalty, those of 200% to 250% triggered a 20% penalty and those exceeding 250% triggered a 30% penalty. For "gross" valuation overstatements (those exceeding 400% of the correct value or adjusted basis), § 6662(h) provides for a 40% penalty. IMPACT also increased the threshold underpayment that justifies the penalty from $1,000 to $5,000 for individuals and to $10,000 for corporations other than S corporations and personal holding companies. No penalty under § 6662(e) may be imposed unless the underpayment attributable to the valuation overstatement exceeds these threshold amounts. Section 6662(e) is applicable to all taxpayers, unlike former § 6659, which applied only to individual, closely-held corporations and personal service corporations. IMPACT also repealed the special 30% penalty of former § 6659(f) for substantial valuation overstatements of property donated to charity. Such valuation overstatements are now subject to the 20% penalty of § 6662, except for "gross" valuation overstatements, which are subject to the 40% penalty of § 6662(h).

(2) Substantial Estate or Gift Tax Valuation Understatements (Section 6662(g))

IMPACT repealed section 6660 and modified the penalty in ways similar to the changes made to the valuation understatement penalty. For returns due after 1989, the threshold underpayment that will trigger the penalty has been increased from $1,000 to $5,000. Section 6662(g) also raised the minimum percentage error in valuation understatements that will justify the penalty from $66\frac{2}{3}\%$ to 50%. Thus, property valued by the taxpayer at $50,000, but ultimately determined to have a value of $90,000 will not subject the taxpayer to a penalty under section 6662(g), but could have triggered a penalty under former section 6660. The legislative history explains the purpose of these changes. "The committee believes that raising both the threshold and the minimum percentage will eliminate from the penalty's scope a number of instances of good-faith valuation disputes that may be subject to penalty under present law." [w] "Gross" valuation understatements (those representing only 25% of the correct amount) are subject to the 40% penalty of section 6662(h).

(3) Substantial Overstatements of Pension Liabilities (Section 6662(f))

IMPACT repealed the three-tiered penalty of former section 6659A for understatements of pension liabilities and replaced it with the uniform 20% accuracy-related penalty (or 40% for "gross" overstatements under section 6662(h)). Under section 6662(f), the penalty will be imposed only if the overstatement exceeds 200% of the correct amount. Under former section 6659A, a penalty could be imposed for overstatements that exceeded 150% of the correct amount. IMPACT

---

w. H.R.Rep. 101-247, 101st Cong., 1st Sess. 1390 (1989).

did not alter the threshold underpayment resulting from the overstatement of liabilities. It remains at $1,000.

F. THE CIVIL FRAUD PENALTY

(1) The Meaning of "Fraud"

ESTATE OF SPRUILL v. COMMISSIONER
Tax Court of the United States, 1987.
88 T.C. 1197.

FEATHERSTON, JUDGE: Respondent determined a deficiency in the amount of $13,570,174.98 in the estate tax for the Estate of Euil S. Spruill and an addition to tax under section 6653(b)[2] in the amount of $6,785,087.49. Also, respondent determined deficiencies in the individual petitioners' 1981 Federal income taxes as follows:

Petitioner	Deficiency
Weyman E. and Jennie Spruill	$2,600,815.56
Lewis J. Miers, Jr., and Kathleen S. Miers	2,616,954.34

The issues for decision are:

(1) Whether the Ashford–Dunwoody Farm (exclusive of two homesites thereon) is includable in decedent's gross estate under section 2033; the answer depends on whether a resulting trust arose in 1956 in favor of decedent's two adult children, who had remainder interests in the property, when they executed quitclaim deeds conveying their interests to decedent.

(2) Whether the homesite where decedent's daughter lived on the Ashford–Dunwoody Farm is includable in decedent's gross estate under section 2033; the answer depends on whether decedent's daughter and her husband retained their beneficial interest in the homesite when they conveyed it to decedent in 1961 in order to obtain a loan with which to pay decedent for the homesite.[3]

(3) Whether the homesite on which decedent's son lived on the Ashford–Dunwoody Farm is includable in decedent's gross estate under section 2033; the answer depends on whether decedent, within the meaning of section 2036(a)(1), retained the right to possession or enjoyment of the homesite for a period which did not, in fact, end before his death when he conveyed the homesite to his son in 1961.

---

2. All section references are to the Internal Revenue Code of 1954 as amended, unless otherwise noted.

3. Respondent issued "protective" notices of deficiency to the individual petitioners determining that the gain from the sale of the Ashford–Dunwoody Farm was not reported on their Federal income tax returns for 1981. The individual petitioners' liability for the income tax deficiencies depends on our conclusions as to whether or not the Ashford–Dunwoody Farm and Kathleen's homesite (issues 1 and 2, above) are includable in decedent's gross estate for purposes of the estate tax and the valuation of the farm (issue 4, above). All adjustments to the individual petitioners' income tax may be addressed in a computation pursuant to Rule 155.

(4) What was the fair market value of the Ashford-Dunwoody Farm includable in decedent's gross estate on October 5, 1980, the date of decedent's death.

(5) What was the fair market value of the River Farm, another piece of real estate includable in decedent's gross estate, on October 5, 1980, the date of decedent's death.

(6) Whether any part of the underpayment of estate tax of decedent's estate was due to fraud within the meaning of section 6653(b).

FINDINGS OF FACT

1. Background

Euil S. Spruill (decedent) died on October 5, 1980. Under decedent's will, his two children, Weyman E. Spruill (Weyman) and Kathleen Spruill Miers (Kathleen), residents of Georgia, are the coexecutors of decedent's estate. A Federal estate tax return was timely filed on July 6, 1981, with the Internal Revenue Service Center, Atlanta, Georgia.

Until his retirement, Weyman had been a farmer all his life. After graduating from high school, with the exception of military service in World War II, Weyman worked full time for his father in farming and in a grading and landscaping business that decedent had begun in the mid-1930's to supplement the farm income.

After receiving her high school education, Kathleen began working as a bank teller. For 18 years prior to her retirement in 1978, Kathleen was employed at Citizens & Southern Bank first as a proof operator, then as a teller, and finally as a loan officer.

5. Valuation and Fraud Issue [8]

(A) Ashford-Dunwoody Farm

(1) *Background.*—On October 5, 1980, the date of decedent's death, the Ashford-Dunwoody Farm (exclusive of the homesites) consisted of a 38.4456-acre [9] tract of undeveloped farmland, roughly rectangular in shape, located at the northeast corner of the intersection of Ashford-Dunwoody Road and I-285 in DeKalb County, Georgia. The farm is situated in an unincorporated area of DeKalb County known as Perimeter Center, approximately 12 miles from downtown Atlanta. Perimeter Center has undergone extensive development since the late 1960's, and provides premium accommodations for office and retail-based commercial enterprises. At the time of decedent's death, it was

---

8. The trial of this case consumed 9 days and the record consists of the testimony of 35 witnesses and approximately 660 exhibits. To avoid repetition, we have included some factual material in the opinion portion and excluded it from our findings.

9. The Ashford-Dunwoody Farm, including the homesites, consisted of 41.7572 acres. Because we conclude *infra* that the homesites are not part of decedent's gross estate, the term Ashford-Dunwoody Farm excludes the homesites for purposes of placing a value on the property and consists of the remaining 38.4456 acres. The sale to the Hines Interests, described *infra*, covered the entire 41.7572 acres.

considered by some to be equal or superior in this regard to any similar location in the metropolitan Atlanta area. Located in close proximity to the developed areas in Perimeter Center are some of the most desirable and economically stable neighborhoods in metropolitan Atlanta.

At the time of decedent's death, the Ashford–Dunwoody Farm was bordered on the east and north by a major suburban office park. Across Ashford–Dunwoody Road, which forms the eastern border of the property, lay Perimeter Mall, a major regional shopping center. Additional office parks and major freestanding buildings, including two multi-story hotels, were located in the immediate vicinity of the Ashford–Dunwoody Farm. On October 5, 1980, the Ashford–Dunwoody Farm was zoned for residential use. Attached to this opinion as an appendix is a map of the Ashford–Dunwoody Farm, showing its boundaries as well as the homesites of Weyman and Kathleen.

Historically, applications for rezoning from residential to office-institutional (O–I) in the Perimeter Center area have been met with staunch opposition from the area residents and homeowners associations. Many opponents of rezoning applications in the area were concerned with density, which refers to the ratio of building floor area (expressed in square feet) to land area, and height restrictions. Their concerns related to the visual obstruction caused by higher buildings, increased traffic, congestion, and a desire to maintain the residential character of the neighborhood to the extent possible. At the time of decedent's death, the average density obtained in zoning actions in DeKalb County was approximately 30 percent (or 12,600 square feet of building floor area per acre) and zoning ordinances required building height to be limited to 5 stories without a variance. The zoning application process, itself, would normally last anywhere from 2 months to 2 years, and some applicants were required to resort to litigation to resolve zoning disputes.

(2) *Estate Advisors.*—Shortly after decedent's death, the executors engaged Thomas O. Davis (Davis) and Ralph H. Birdsong, C.P.A. (Birdsong), as lawyer and accountant, respectively, for the estate. Davis had previously represented decedent, Stephen's estate, and other Spruill family members. Birdsong had prepared decedent's tax returns for approximately 15 years. Both Davis and Birdsong had extensive experience in estate administration, including the preparation and filing of estate tax returns. The executors relied on Davis to advise them on legal matters pertaining to decedent's estate and on Birdsong to prepare the estate tax return, and consistently followed their advice.

Davis recommended that the executors employ William P. Kenyon (Kenyon) to appraise the value of the four parcels of real estate in decedent's estate, including the Ashford–Dunwoody Farm, as of the date of decedent's death, and upon Davis' advice, the executors did so. Davis had previously engaged Kenyon to make a number of appraisals on behalf of other clients. During the course of his appraisal, Kenyon contacted Davis and Weyman to get accurate descriptions of the properties and have the property lines pointed out to him. Kenyon did not at any time discuss with Davis, Birdsong, or the executors any matter concerning the value of the properties.

In his appraisal report dated March 17, 1981, Kenyon appraised the value of the Ashford–Dunwoody Farm at $50,000 per acre ($1,975,000 for 39.5 acres).[10] Both Davis and Birdsong at all relevant times considered Kenyon's appraisal of the Ashford–Dunwoody Farm to be a good and fair appraisal of the property, and Davis told the executors his opinion of the appraisal.

In February 1981, the executors met with William H. Woodward (Woodward), a real estate broker who had previously been acquainted with decedent and involved in the Gearon sale. After discussion, the executors orally agreed to engage Woodward as a real estate advisor to assist them in marketing the Ashford–Dunwoody Farm for a consulting fee of 2.5 percent of the sales price of any property sold. An employment contract was later drawn up and backdated to February 4, 1981.

(3) *Inquiries From Brokers and Developers.*—After decedent's death, the executors began to receive inquiries from brokers and other interested parties about their interest in selling all or a part of the Ashford–Dunwoody Farm. Weyman and Kathleen told one another about the inquiries each had received, and Kathleen kept a list of the contacts. They agreed between themselves to give all inquirers the same response, namely, that they had not yet decided what they were going to do about selling the land but would advise them when and if a decision was made. Davis informed the executors of the inquiries he received about selling the Ashford–Dunwoody Farm.

On March 10, 1981, Malcolm Powell, a land developer and personal friend of the executors, presented to the executors a written offer to buy the Ashford–Dunwoody Farm, including the two homesites, for $5,950,000 ($140,000 per acre for 42.5 acres). The contract to purchase was conditioned on the property's being rezoned O–I at the purchaser's application. The executors returned the contract to Powell and explained that they were not accepting contracts on the property at that time.[11]

In May or early June 1981, after Woodward had fulfilled a prior commitment and could turn his attention to the executors, Kathleen provided Woodward with her list of contacts that had been made with

---

10. Kenyon's report also contained appraisals of the River Farm and two additional properties included in decedent's estate tax return.

11. In an interview with the Government's special agent on Mar. 31, 1982, Weyman stated that he did not recall having received an offer on the Ashford–Dunwoody Farm, and when asked specifically about the Powell offer, replied that it was for $45,000 to $50,000 per acre. Kathleen stated in the interview that she recalled the Powell offer at a price of $37,000 per acre but recalled at trial the price of $140,000. At trial, neither Weyman nor Kathleen denied making these statements to the special agent and testified that because the offer had been made prematurely, neither executor had read the offer word for word.

her and Weyman regarding the sale of the Ashford–Dunwoody Farm and correspondence they had received from interested parties. At this time Woodward reviewed with both Weyman and Kathleen the results of his studies of the sales of properties comparable to the Ashford–Dunwoody Farm. The results were prepared for the purpose of advising the executors as to the price they might expect to get for their land contingent on rezoning, and revealed land sales prices ranging up to $190,000 per acre, subject to zoning in the Perimeter Center area, and higher, in other areas north of Atlanta, for property already zoned. (See note 26 *infra.*) In response to this information, Kathleen advised Woodward that they would not be willing to take less than $235,000 per acre subject to zoning.

(4) *The "Party Line."*—Woodward and the executors met with Davis and Birdsong on June 3, 1981 (June 3 meeting), where it was agreed that Woodward would begin making personal contacts with brokers and prospective purchasers who had previously contacted them. Woodward was to issue the following statement (the so-called party line) to all interested parties:

> Property not for sale. There has been continuous heavy pressure from brokers and qualified institutional investors. Tax considerations dictate heirs may be able to look at an unsolicited offer to purchase around 7/10/81,[12] however they will not seek an offer nor name a price. Heirs fully aware of land values, are not compelled to sell. Subject to counsel may be in position to sign contract late Oct. or early Nov. 81.

Woodward was to first contact Taylor and Mathis, a real estate development and brokerage firm, at least in part because the executors initially believed that Taylor and Mathis had a right of first refusal on the Ashford–Dunwoody Farm.[13]

Also at the June 3 meeting, Birdsong advised the executors of the approximate amount of the estate tax liability, and the final decision to sell the Ashford–Dunwoody Farm was made.

On June 8, 1981, Woodward sent Davis a list of potential purchasers and those individuals who had contacted him, the executors, or Davis expressing interest in the Ashford–Dunwoody Farm. On June

[12]. Later changed to 8/10/81.

My personal judgment of value ranges between $200,000/ac. recent sales in area and $350,000 to $400,000/ac. Piedmont Road and Peachtree Road area. Terms would most likely be cash. (Obvious need of institutional investor) If subject to rezoning there should be a stiff penalty for failure. In event of several equal acceptable offers, acceptance would probably be made based on a. past track record of development and quality, b. ability to achieve zoning, c. heirs want development they would be proud of and an asset to the community. This is homeplace.

13. In 1967, decedent had given Michael Gearon a letter of first refusal on the Ashford–Dunwoody Farm pursuant to the Gearon sale. Taylor and Mathis bought out Michael Gearon in 1973, and thereafter owned the approximately 150 acres bordering the Ashford–Dunwoody Farm on the north and east. Although the executors initially thought that Taylor and Mathis had a legal right of first refusal on the property, Davis later advised them that the right was not a binding one.

15, 1981, Woodward met with representatives of Taylor and Mathis and presented the party line. Between that time and July 6, 1981 (the date the estate tax return was filed), Woodward contacted at least 25 to 30 potential purchasers and repeated the party line. Woodward kept detailed notes of these contacts and gave the executors copies of all his notes regarding various contacts and communications on the Ashford-Dunwoody Farm.

By mid-July 1981, following negotiations, the executors had decided that they would accept an offer from Taylor and Mathis for $275,000 per acre, contingent on acceptable terms on rezoning. An offer at that price was submitted but in late July, before the terms were agreed upon, the parties received a report from a responsible buyer of an interest at a higher price.

(5) *Sale of the Ashford-Dunwoody Farm.*—In late September 1981, the executors, acting with the advice of their advisors, invited the responsible prospects to submit sealed bids for the purchase of the property, including the two homesites. Enclosed with the invitation for bids was a fully prepared contract with provisions for the bidder to enter only the price per acre, not to be less than $350,000, and sign its name. The contract provided for a sale of the property "as is" (no contingency for zoning) and a substantial portion of the purchase price to be paid into escrow to ensure sufficient funds to pay estate taxes.

Four contracts were received in response to the invitation. One of those was submitted subject to conditions and was withdrawn before the day set for opening bids. The second bid, made by a partnership acting for W.B. Johnson Properties, was at a price of $350,000 per acre or an escalating price from $375,000 to $450,000 per acre, conditioned on the density obtaining in rezoning. This bidder modified several provisions of the proposed contract, including an added provision for payment on terms not meeting the requirements of the invitation. The third bid was for a price of $366,404 per acre, but included numerous modifications to the contract, including a closing date 9 months later than that specified in the invitation. Gerald D. Hines Interests of Houston, Texas (Hines Interests), entered an unconditional bid of $505,000 per acre, which was accepted on November 3, 1981. The sale of the Ashford-Dunwoody Farm to the Hines Interests was closed on December 1, 1981.

The first hearing before the DeKalb County Board of Commissioners (board) on the rezoning application filed by the Hines Interests with respect to the Ashford-Dunwoody Farm was held on May 25, 1982. Members of the community appeared at the meeting and expressed concern about the density levels requested by the Hines Interests. The Hines Interests had applied for rezoning to O–I and requested a density level in excess of 40,000 square feet per acre, more than 3 times the then prevailing average density of 12,600 square feet per acre. Although the DeKalb County Planning Department had recommended that the Hines Interests' rezoning application be granted, the board granted the requested rezoning to O–I but not at the requested density. Before their application was approved for a density in excess of 40,000 square feet per acre in August 1982, the Hines Interests filed suit to obtain the desired zoning and incurred unforeseen costs as a result of the delay.

(6) *Examination of the Estate Tax Return.*—The executors filed decedent's estate tax return on July 6, 1981, and reported the value of the Ashford–Dunwoody Farm in the return as $50,000 per acre ($1,975,-000 for 39.5 acres)[14] based on Kenyon's appraisal whose report was attached to the return. The executors applied for an extension of time to pay estate taxes based on insufficient cash funds in the estate with which to pay the tax, and their application was approved. Both Davis and Birdsong anticipated that the estate tax return would be examined by the Internal Revenue Service and, before the return was filed, Davis so advised the executors.

Following the acceptance of the Hines Interests' contract, Davis recommended that the sale be reported immediately to the IRS to obtain an early determination. Birdsong responded that he did not believe such a report to be necessary as he understood that the examination had already begun. Davis and Birdsong agreed that if the examination had not begun by January 1, 1982, Davis would contact the IRS gift and estate tax office in Atlanta.

The executors and their advisors became aware that an examination had begun when Woodward was visited by examining agents on December 10, 1981. During the IRS examination of the estate tax return, Davis made his files available to the examining agents, with the executors' approval, and advised Woodward and Birdsong to do the same. Following Davis' advice, Birdsong and Woodward turned over to the examining agent all their papers relating to decedent's estate.

Upon referral from the estate and gift tax division which was conducting the examination of decedent's estate tax return, the IRS special agent began a criminal investigation of Woodward, Kenyon, Birdsong, Davis, and the executors. Following his investigation, the special agent recommended criminal prosecution of Weyman and Kathleen for submitting a false and fraudulent estate tax return under section 7206(1) and prosecution of Davis and Birdsong for aiding and assisting in the preparation of a false and fraudulent estate tax return under section 7206(2). The special agent also recommended prosecution of Davis, Birdsong, and the executors for conspiracy to defraud the IRS by submitting a false and fraudulent estate tax return; however, the Department of Justice declined to prosecute the executors and their advisors on any charge.[15]

14. The Kathleen Miers Homesite was included with the Ashford–Dunwoody Farm in decedent's gross estate, and the parcels were valued together for purposes of the estate tax return. The acreage of the two parcels was approximated at 39.5 acres.

15. Although they were originally subjects of the special agent's criminal investigation, Woodward and Kenyon were not

Respondent determined that the value of the Ashford–Dunwoody Farm on the date of decedent's death was $505,000 per acre ($19,854,125.50 for 39.3151 acres).[16]

ULTIMATE FINDINGS OF FACT

* * *

(4) A successful rezoning of the Ashford–Dunwoody Farm to O–I with a density of 30 percent (or 12,600 square feet per acre) was reasonably foreseeable on October 5, 1980, the date of decedent's death.

(5) Neither the purchase of the Ashford–Dunwoody Farm by the Hines Interests or any other purchases for a price approaching $505,000 per acre "as is" nor its rezoning to the density ultimately obtained by the Hines Interests was reasonably foreseeable on October 5, 1980.

(6) On October 5, 1980, the fair market value of the Ashford–Dunwoody Farm was $7,304,664 ($190,000 per acre × 38.4456 acres).

(7) On October 5, 1980, the fair market value of the River Farm was $668,000.

(8) The record does not clearly and convincingly show that any part of the estate tax was due to fraud within the meaning of section 6653(b).

3. Valuation Issues

Section 2031(a) provides that the value of decedent's gross estate includes "the value at the time of his death of all property, real or personal, tangible or intangible, wherever situated." For purposes of section 2031(a), "value" means "fair market value," defined by the regulations as (sec. 20.2031–1(b), Estate Tax Regs.):

> the price at which the property would change hands between a willing buyer and a willing seller, neither being under any compulsion to buy or to sell and both having reasonable knowledge of relevant facts.
> * * *

The willing buyer and willing seller referred to in the above regulation are necessarily a "hypothetical buyer and seller having a reasonable knowledge of relevant facts." *United States v. Simmons,* 346 F.2d 213, 217 (5th Cir.1965).

> The notion of the "willing seller" as being hypothetical is also supported by the theory that the estate tax is an excise tax on the transfer of property at death and accordingly that the valuation is to be made as of the moment of death and is to be measured by the interest that passes, as contrasted with the interest held by the decedent before death or the interest held by the legatee after death. * * * [*Estate of Bright v. United States,* 658 F.2d 999, 1006 (5th Cir.1981).]

---

recommended to the Department of Justice for criminal prosecution.

16. 39.3151 acres represents the exact combined acreage of the Ashford–Dunwoody Farm (38.4456 acres) and the Kathleen Miers Homesite (.8695 acres).

With respect to the Ashford-Dunwoody Farm, our task is to determine the fair market value on the date of decedent's death of the property without the Weyman Spruill and Kathleen Miers Homesites which we have concluded were not owned by decedent when he died. We may not assume, as respondent urges, that all three parcels would be marketed and sold as one 41-acre parcel, but must determine the includable property's value as if the homesites were owned by strangers. *Estate of Bright v. United States, supra* at 1002–1006.

Valuation is not an exact science and each case necessarily turns on its own particular facts. *Messing v. Commissioner,* 48 T.C. 502, 512 (1967). It is well settled that, in examining all the relevant facts and circumstances, events occurring subsequent to the valuation date are not considered in determining fair market value, except to the extent that such events were reasonably foreseeable on the valuation date—in estate tax cases, the date of the decedent's death. *Ithaca Trust Co. v. United States,* 279 U.S. 151, 155 (1929); *First National Bank of Kenosha v. United States,* 763 F.2d 891, 894 (7th Cir.1985); *Estate of Van Horne v. Commissioner,* 720 F.2d 1114, 1116 (9th Cir.1983), affg. 78 T.C. 728 (1982).

(A) Ashford-Dunwoody Farm

Based on the documents and the testimony of the experts and other witnesses, and relying on that evidence which we deem most persuasive, we have concluded and found as an ultimate fact that the Ashford-Dunwoody Farm had a fair market value of $7,304,664 ($190,000 per acre × 38.4456 acres) on October 5, 1980, the date of decedent's death.

(1) *Kenyon's Report.*—Petitioners' first expert witness, Kenyon, appraised the fair market value of the Ashford-Dunwoody Farm including the Kathleen Miers Homesite at $1,975,000 ($50,000 per acre × 39.5 acres). Kenyon's appraisal report dated March 17, 1981, had been attached to the estate tax return filed in that year; Kenyon reaffirmed his opinion at trial that the value of the property was $50,000 per acre on the date of death. Kenyon holds the designation of senior residential appraiser, was formerly an appraiser with the DeKalb County Board of Tax Assessors, and since 1972 has been in private practice appraising real estate in DeKalb and Gwinnett Counties.

In appraising the value of the Ashford-Dunwoody Farm, Kenyon used the "comparable sales" method [24] and concluded that the highest and best use of the property was "intensive office-institutional use" although such use would require rezoning. Kenyon's comparable sales

---

24. The "comparable sales" or "market data" approach involves gathering information on sales of property similar to the subject property, then comparing and weighing them to reach a value for the land being appraised. In the case of vacant, unimproved property (such as the Ashford-Dunwoody Farm) the comparable sales approach is "generally the most reliable method of valuation, the rationale being that the market place is the best indicator of value, based on the conflicting interests of many buyers and sellers." *Estate of Rabe v. Commissioner,* T.C. Memo. 1975–26, affd. without published opinion 566 F.2d 1183 (9th Cir.1977).

consisted of six tracts of land varying in size from approximately 8.5 acres to approximately 54 acres, in price from $28,500 [25] to $128,300 per acre and in date of sale from June 28, 1979, to January 28, 1981. Like the Ashford-Dunwoody Farm, five of Kenyon's six comparables required rezoning to meet the purchaser's needs and all five were sold subject to rezoning.[26] The rezoning of these five parcels from single family residential to office-institutional (O-I) and multifamily residential required lengthy and expensive litigation to obtain the change. The remaining comparable sale (at $128,300 per acre) consisted of property already zoned O-I and substantially developed.

We have found little to criticize about Kenyon's expert opinion. His testimony at trial was credible and respondent failed on cross-examination to effectively challenge any aspect of Kenyon's report. We think, however, that Kenyon neglected to take into account the reasonable probability that the Ashford-Dunwoody Farm could be rezoned to O-I with relatively little difficulty.[27] Every other witness who testified as to rezoning possibilities, including real estate brokers, developers, appraisal and zoning experts, and the assistant director of the DeKalb County Planning Department, stated that on the date of decedent's death a reasonable probability existed that the property would be rezoned O-I to at least the prevailing density.

(2) *Ward's Report.*—Petitioners' second expert, V. Stuart Ward (Ward), appraised the fair market value of the Ashford-Dunwoody Farm excluding both the Weyman Spruill and the Kathleen Miers Homesites, at $6,120,000. Ward has been self-employed as a real estate appraiser since 1973, is a member of the American Institute of Real Estate Appraisers, and appraised the value of several properties in the vicinity of the Ashford-Dunwoody Farm between 1980 and 1983.

Ward incorporated by reference in his report the report of Dillard, Greer, Westmoreland, and Wilson (Dillard report), a firm experienced in zoning litigation, which concluded that as of the date of decedent's death a reasonable probability existed that the Ashford-Dunwoody Farm could be rezoned from residential to O-I at a 30-percent density level (12,600 square feet per acre). Ward concluded that the highest and best use of the property would be for a "comprehensively planned

---

25. Kenyon testified that when he learned of the sale to the Hines Interests at $505,000 per acre, he questioned his appraisal and reviewed his research with a "fine tooth comb." Although he found nothing that would lead him to believe that $50,000 per acre was not a fair appraisal, he noted that the contract for one of his comparable sales listed in his report at $28,500 was eventually sold for about $62,500.

26. A sale subject to rezoning generally refers to a sale contingent on successful rezoning by the purchaser. If the purchaser fails to obtain the required zoning, his obligation to buy the property ceases and he may or may not be required to pay a penalty to the seller. Thus, the price of property sold subject to rezoning is likely to be higher than a sales price for the property "as is."

27. His report states:

"While in my opinion, a zoning change can eventually be obtained for the subject Spruill property, it will be done so only after lengthy and costly litigation as was the case in all sales. Therefore, the present value of the Spruill land is adversely affected by this prospect."

multi-use complex including office, retail commercial, motor hotel and/or multi-family accommodations."

We have found Ward's expert opinion particularly helpful in our analysis. While we realize that he had the benefit of considerable hindsight in preparing his appraisal, Ward's conclusion that the Ashford–Dunwoody Farm could be rezoned to O–I at the prevailing rate of 30 percent was well supported by the Dillard report and several witnesses. In addition, Ward chose comparable sales which occurred prior to or a few months after the valuation date (October 5, 1980). Just as with Kenyon's testimony, respondent failed to discredit Ward's appraisal on cross-examination.

We think, however, that Ward exaggerated the negative effects of the exclusion of the homesites in arriving at his final figure.

Ward further discounted the value of the Ashford–Dunwoody Farm by 5 percent to reflect the shift in costs and risk of rezoning from the seller (property sold subject to rezoning) to the purchaser (property sold "as is"). While we agree that, in general, property sold subject to rezoning would command a higher price than property sold "as is," we accept Dillard's report that on October 5, 1980, a reasonable probability existed that the subject property could be rezoned to O–I at the then prevailing density.

For the adverse effects of both the homesites and the necessity of obtaining rezoning at the prevailing 30 percent density, we think a 5–percent discount is appropriate. Therefore, based on all the relevant facts and circumstances, we conclude that $200,000 per acre, discounted 5 percent to reflect the negative effect of the exclusion of the two homesites and the zoning problem ($190,000), represents the fair market value of the Ashford–Dunwoody Farm on October 5, 1980, the date of decedent's death.[32]

(3) *Sale to Hines Interests as Fair Market Value.*—Respondent argues, however, that the price at which the Ashford–Dunwoody Farm sold to the Hines Interests on December 1, 1981 ($505,000 per acre), is the best evidence of the fair market value of the property on October 5, 1980. While subsequent events are generally not relevant in fixing a property's fair market value on a given date, the price set by a freely negotiated agreement made reasonably close to the valuation date is persuasive evidence of fair market value (*Ambassador Apartments, Inc. v. Commissioner,* 50 T.C. 236, 244 (1968), affd. per curiam 406 F.2d 288 (2d Cir.1969); *Estate of Schroeder v. Commissioner,* 13 T.C. 259, 263 (1949)), except where a material change in circumstances occurs between the valuation date (herein the date of decedent's death) and the date of sale which renders the subsequent sale unforeseeable. See *Georgia Ketteman Trust v. Commissioner,* 86 T.C. 91, 101 (1986); *Estate*

---

32. The fair market value for the entire 38.4456–acre tract is $7,304,664 ($190,000 × 38.4456).

of *Loewenstein v. Commissioner,* 17 T.C. 60, 63–64 (1951); *Estate of Ridgely v. United States,* 180 Ct.Cl. 1220 (1967).[33]

We do not think that the sale to the Hines Interests at $505,000 per acre on December 1, 1981, represents the fair market value of the Ashford–Dunwoody Farm on October 5, 1980. The changes which occurred both nationally and locally in the real estate market during the 14 months following decedent's death could not have been reasonably foreseen at the time of decedent's death. In those months, land prices escalated rapidly in the Perimeter Center area due at least in part to national trends such as the legislative changes in the Economic Recovery Tax Act of 1981 (including liberalized depreciation allowances and the Accelerated Cost Recovery System) which favored real estate transactions and the increased use of limited partnership syndications to finance real estate ventures. Locally, improvements to the major thoroughfares in the Perimeter Center area and an increased demand for more intense use of land (higher density rezoning) contributed to the abrupt rise in land prices in 1981.

Moreover, although rezoning the Ashford–Dunwoody Farm to O–I use at the prevailing density rate was a probable occurrence at the time of decedent's death, no prudent investor could have foreseen that the property would be rezoned to the high level of density eventually obtained by the Hines Interests, a level essential for the price paid by the Hines Interests. In October 1980, no developer had achieved or even approached a density level of 40,000 square feet; the prevailing average density level was 12,600 square feet per acre at the time.

Indeed, the pervasive attitude among real estate developers and brokers was one of caution where rezoning, and density level in particular, were concerned. * * * Other Atlanta brokers and developers agreed that purchasing unzoned real estate at that time with the hope of obtaining rezoning at the level of density required to construct an intensive commercial development, such as that planned and built by the Hines Interests, involved taking an unacceptable risk.

Nor do the facts in the record describe the Hines Interests as representative of a hypothetical willing buyer with reasonable knowledge of all the relevant facts. First, because we have concluded that the Weyman Spruill and Kathleen Miers Homesites are not included in decedent's gross estate, the issue is the price at which the Ashford–Dunwoody Farm would have changed hands between a willing buyer or seller assuming that the homesites were not for sale. The homesites would have seriously complicated development as well as rezoning at the needed density level. The Hines Interests paid $505,000 per acre for the farm with both homesites included and, according to a repre-

---

33. Cf. *Estate of Shlensky v. Commissioner,* T.C. Memo. 1977–148 (parties agreed that no material change in circumstances had occurred between date of death and date of sale); *Estate of Ballas v. Commissioner,* T.C. Memo. 1975–103 (subsequent sale foreseeable under the circumstances).

sentative, might not have even considered purchasing the property had the homesites not been part of the bargain.

Second, the Hines Interests, a Houston-based developer which initially learned of the property's availability in July 1980, underestimated the community opposition to rezoning in the Perimeter Center area, and in particular, to requests for high density O–I rezoning, as well as the time and expense necessary to obtain such rezoning. Charles Davidson (Davidson), then project manager with the Hines Interests, testified that the developer had been "a little undereducated in * * * [its] assumptions about the achievable zoning," explaining that the interest cost alone caused by the rezoning delay between May 1982 and August 1982 was approximately $1 million.

Third, Davidson testified that the Hines Interests did not arrive at a bid price of $505,000 per acre by assessing or appraising the fair market value of the Ashford–Dunwoody Farm, but through a process of valuing the planned development as constructed, as leased, and as financed, with particular emphasis on the intrinsic value that the Hines Interests brings to a project as a result of its expertise as a developer. This method of valuation makes sense from the point of view of the Hines Interests. However, the concept of a hypothetical willing buyer is not restricted to a particular developer or even a particular type of purchaser (*Estate of Bright v. United States*, 658 F.2d 999, 1006 (5th Cir.1981)), and the method of valuation employed by the Hines Interests reflected factors peculiar to that developer.[35]

(4) *Dr. Wendt's Report.*—Respondent's argument that the sales price of the Ashford–Dunwoody Farm on December 1, 1981 ($505,000 per acre), represents the fair market value of the property on October 5, 1980, is based in part on the report and testimony of the Government's expert, Dr. Paul F. Wendt (Dr. Wendt). Dr. Wendt appraised the value of the property including both the Weyman Spruill and Kathleen Miers Homesites at $21 million ($503,597 per acre × 41.7 acres).

Dr. Wendt's appraisal of the Ashford–Dunwoody Farm was based entirely on information obtained during the course of his employment with the Government, from March to June 1984 when his report was completed. Dr. Wendt spent a total of 7 days in May of that year in Atlanta conducting the field work for his appraisal. Dr. Wendt employed two valuation methods in appraising the value of the Ashford–Dunwoody Farm: the comparable sales method and the land residual value method.

We found Dr. Wendt's analysis under the comparable sales approach to be of little probative value in making our determination. Dr.

---

35. The facts also indicate that the closed bids process itself may have induced the Hines Interests to pay more for the Ashford–Dunwoody Farm than necessary. The Hines Interests' unconditional bid of $505,000 per acre exceeded the minimum bid specified in the offering by $155,000 per acre and exceeded the next highest bid, subject to several conditions, by $138,596 per acre. Only one of numerous individuals or companies identified by respondent as potential purchasers submitted a final bid and it was subject to a variety of conditions.

Wendt's selection of comparable sales included only one sale prior to the valuation date, while two of his selected sales occurred as late as 1983, more than 2 years after the valuation date.[37] Dr. Wendt testified that he selected the later transactions in preference to earlier sales of the same properties [38] because the earlier sales were "not relevant to the computations that I wanted to make which illustrate the relationship of density to value." Dr. Wendt admittedly selected as comparable sales only those properties which were already zoned for development and had been granted permission for development to a particular level of density. His inclusion of the Ashford–Dunwoody Farm itself as a comparable is unprecedented.

Despite his reliance on the comparable sales approach as the preferred valuation method, Dr. Wendt ultimately concluded that no property comparable to the Ashford–Dunwoody Farm existed on the valuation date and that the sales price of the property on December 1, 1981, represented the best evidence of its fair market value on October 5, 1980.

Dr. Wendt based his opinion largely on information obtained directly from respondent's examining agent, much of which was reproduced verbatim in Dr. Wendt's report. He relied heavily on a schedule, provided by the examining agent and included in his expert report, listing offers allegedly made on the Ashford–Dunwoody Farm, and which was shown through testimony and documentary evidence to contain numerous errors and misstatements. Dr. Wendt also relied on, and quoted without verification in his report, statements attributed to prospective purchasers and Woodward, all of which were shown to have been provided by the examining agent. Dr. Wendt's unquestioning reliance on information provided by respondent tends to reveal his lack of preparation and independence in making his appraisal. We are not surprised that, despite evidence to the contrary, Dr. Wendt came to exactly the same conclusions with respect to the fair market value of the property as did respondent.

In summary, Dr. Wendt's analysis was based on biased, unsubstantiated, and erroneous information, as well as several basic assumptions contrary to the overwhelming evidence presented in this case. We find his opinion to be of little probative value in our determination.

(5) *Conclusion.*—Based on the relevant facts and circumstances, we find that the fair market value of the Ashford–Dunwoody Farm on

---

37. Eliminating the 1983 transactions and the sale of the Ashford–Dunwoody Farm itself, which clearly does not qualify as a "comparable" sale, reveals a range of sales prices among the remaining properties of $117,216 to $283,018 per acre.

38. Dr. Wendt selected as one of his comparable sales the January 1982 sale of a portion of the Brunette Spruill property for $283,018 per acre without mentioning that the same tract sold for $28,500 per acre in June 1980 or that the contract to purchase another part of the same Brunette Spruill property sold for $62,209 per acre in June 1980 only 4 months before

October 5, 1980, was $7,304,664 ($190,000 per acre × 38.4456 acres).[42]

4. *The Fraud Issue*

Section 6653(b), in the form in which it was in effect when decedent's estate tax return was filed, calls for the imposition of a 50-percent addition to tax if any part of an underpayment is "due to fraud." For purposes of this section, fraud is the intentional commission of an act or acts for the specific purpose of evading a tax believed to be owing. Fraud implies bad faith, intentional wrongdoing, and a sinister motive. It is never imputed or presumed. Whether fraud has been committed is a question of fact to be determined from the entire record.

By statute, the burden rests with the Commissioner to prove affirmatively by clear and convincing evidence actual and intentional wrongdoing on the part of the taxpayer. Sec. 7454. This burden may be met by showing that the taxpayer intended to evade taxes known to be owing by conduct designed to conceal, mislead, or otherwise prevent the collection of such taxes. *Stoltzfus v. United States*, 398 F.2d 1002, 1004 (3d Cir.1968); *Rowlee v. Commissioner*, 80 T.C. 1111, 1123 (1983).

We find that respondent has failed to carry his burden. Respondent's whole fraud case is based on the proposition that the executors knowingly undervalued the Ashford–Dunwoody Farm with the specific intent of evading estate taxes. As we have discussed in deciding the valuation issue, the executors in filing the estate tax return were required to place a value on the Ashford–Dunwoody tract as of the date of decedent's death, the "exact moment of death," on October 5, 1980. *United States v. Simmons*, 346 F.2d 213, 218 n. 2 (5th Cir.1965). In arriving at that value, they could appropriately take into account subsequent events, such as real estate developers' escalating interest in purchasing their property, only if those events and the changing conditions could have been reasonably foreseen on the date of decedent's death. *Georgia Ketteman Trust v. Commissioner*, 86 T.C. 91, 101 (1986); *Estate of Ridgely v. United States*, 180 Ct.Cl. 1220 (1967).

We do not think respondent has shown that the executors knew that the Kenyon report did not reflect a reasonable appraisal of the property as of October 5, 1980, or that they used the valuation in the Kenyon report rather than some higher valuation with the specific intent of evading estate taxes.

---

decedent's death. See note 34 and related text.

42. Petitioners argue that we must discount the fair market value of the Ashford–Dunwoody Farm to reflect a hypothetical cloud on the title resulting from the physical presence of Weyman and Kathleen on the property. We disagree. First, the presence of Weyman and Kathleen within the boundaries of the Ashford–Dunwoody Farm would not put a purchaser on notice of their claim to the property adverse to decedent's record ownership, as both Weyman and Kathleen owned and occupied their own homesites within those boundaries. Second, we have found above that on the date of decedent's death, Weyman and Kathleen did not claim ownership of the Ashford–Dunwoody Farm under the 1931 deed, but treated the land then and at all times prior, as belonging solely to their father.

(A) The Kenyon Report Attached to the Estate Tax Return

Although we have found that the value reported in the estate tax return was substantially less than the property's fair market value at decedent's death, there is no evidence of any effort to conceal from, or mislead, the IRS as to what the reported value reflected. The returned value reflected the written well-documented opinion of a widely experienced appraiser recommended to the executors by Davis, their attorney. A copy of Kenyon's report was attached to the estate tax return and it spelled out in detail the basis of his appraisal. It is difficult to believe that one committing fraud would attach to his return a full and complete explanation of what he was doing, especially where, as here, the value of a highly publicized piece of property was the issue. Cf. *Delone v. Commissioner,* 100 F.2d 507, 509 (3d Cir.1938), revg. an order of this Court.

There is not a syllable of testimony suggesting that there was any connivance between Kenyon and the executors or any of their representatives on the preparation of his report or impugning in any way his integrity. Although we have found that the property had greater value than the reported amount, it is relevant that "There is no question upon which all persons, reasonable or otherwise, are so apt to differ as upon a question of value." *Penn v. Commissioner,* 219 F.2d 18, 20 (9th Cir.1955), affg. a Memorandum Opinion of this Court.[45] By attaching Kenyon's report to the estate tax return, the executors explicitly and openly informed the IRS of the facts relied upon and the reasoning employed in arriving at the value of the Ashford–Dunwoody property. Nothing was concealed and no one could have been misled in this respect.

(B) Reliance on Advisors

The record clearly shows, moreover, contrary to respondent's arguments, that Weyman and Kathleen had no reliable knowledge of land appraisals or the preparation of estate tax returns. In filing the estate tax return, they initiated nothing except the engagement of the lawyer and the accountant who had represented their father. They relied completely upon their advisors in valuing the Ashford–Dunwoody property on decedent's estate tax return.

Weyman had little business education or experience. He was employed most of his life by his father, running landscaping equipment and working on the family farm. Kathleen had spent her career working as a bank employee. Neither one of them had handled substantial land transactions or done any work involving the estate tax laws. Neither of them considered themselves competent to place a value on the Ashford–Dunwoody tract or to handle its sale.[46]

---

45. Congress has addressed the issue of valuation understatements for purposes of the estate or gift taxes and has provided for additions to tax in sec. 6660.

46. Respondent makes the point that Weyman and Kathleen had seen their father become a millionaire by selling his land. This assertion overlooks the fact that most of decedent's land in the Ash-

Upon their father's death, Weyman and Kathleen, as executors, turned to Davis, a lawyer who had served as attorney for their grandfather's estate, had revised their father's will, and had previously served as an attorney for the Spruill family for years, to handle the legal work required for the administration of decedent's estate. Davis was an experienced, respected lawyer. Pursuant to Davis' advice, the executors retained Kenyon to make an appraisal of the estate's real estate for use in filing the estate tax return. For the preparation of the estate tax return, they retained Birdsong, who had prepared decedent's and Weyman's tax returns for many years. In addition, they later employed Woodward to advise them on the handling of the sale of the Ashford–Dunwoody property.

The record is explicitly clear that the executors relied upon the advice they received from Davis, Kenyon, and Birdsong in reporting the value of the Ashford–Dunwoody property. Davis testified that "They were looking to me for the legal validity of their actions[,] in my judgment." Birdsong testified they "were relying on Mr. Davis and me" and that they followed their advice. Birdsong testified that he reviewed the Kenyon report, "accepted" it as "being well-founded, well-grounded," "a good appraisal." Although Davis advised the executors that the estate tax return would be examined by the IRS, he also told them Kenyon's appraisal "was a good appraisal." Neither Davis nor Birdsong ever considered not using the Kenyon report as a basis for the valuation in the estate tax return.

In *United States v. Boyle,* 469 U.S. 241 (1985), an executor argued that, because he relied on his attorney to file a timely return for the estate, the executor's failure to file a return on time was due to reasonable cause and that the estate was not, therefore, liable for the section 6651(a)(1) addition to tax for failure to file a return. The Supreme Court held that reliance on an agent does not excuse the failure to make a return but distinguished the failure to file a return from a taxpayer's reliance on the advice of his attorney on whether a return was necessary at all. As stated by the Supreme Court (469 U.S. at 251):

> When an accountant or attorney *advises* a taxpayer on a matter of tax law, such as whether a liability exists, it is reasonable for the taxpayer to rely on that advice. Most taxpayers are not competent to discern error in the substantive advice of an accountant or attorney. To require the taxpayer to challenge the attorney, to seek a "second opinion," * * * would nullify the very purpose of seeking the advice of a presumed expert in the first place. * * * "Ordinary business care and prudence" does not demand such actions.

Although that case involved the addition to tax imposed under section 6651(a)(1) for failure to file a timely return, the principle is, in our

ford–Dunwoody Road area was sold in the Gearon sale for $14,500 per acre, approximately one-third of the value reported for the Ashford–Dunwoody Farm on the estate tax return.

judgment, equally applicable under section 6653(b) where fraud on the part of the taxpayer must be shown by clear and convincing evidence.

According to respondent, however, the executors "failed to make a complete disclosure to their advisors" and misled them as to the value of the Ashford–Dunwoody property. At one point, respondent asserts that "Weyman and Kathleen deliberately insulated themselves from potential purchasers and discussions of value." Even so, respondent contends elsewhere in his brief, the executors "withheld pertinent information and knowledge from the appraiser and from the preparer of the estate tax return" and "chose not to disclose the offers they had received to their attorney or real estate broker."

This argument that the executors' return preparer and attorney were victims of the executors' deceit hardly comes with good grace. The record shows that the IRS recommended that the executors be prosecuted for filing an estate tax return containing a false statement (the value of the Ashford–Dunwoody Farm) in violation of section 7206(1) and that Davis and Birdsong be prosecuted on a charge of aiding and abetting and conspiring with the executors in filing such return in violation of section 7206(2). The Department of Justice declined to prosecute any of these individuals. Now, in the wake of damaged reputations, untold expense, and months of anguish, we are asked to accept the view that Weyman and Kathleen are the villains and that they misled the professionals, Davis, Birdsong, Kenyon, and Woodward, on the value of the Ashford–Dunwoody tract.

The facts do not bear out respondent's new theory. The Davis legal file shows that he received numerous telephone calls or held frequent conferences regarding the purchase of the property beginning on November 12, 1980, and continuing up to the date the estate tax return was filed. Davis knew of the intense interest in the property and, as he described developments, "prices exploded" in the Perimeter Center area between October 1980 and October 1981. In addition, Davis testified as to conversations with Weyman and Kathleen and with Woodward on the interest expressed by the several brokers on behalf of potential purchasers. We think it inconceivable that Weyman and Kathleen misled either Davis or Woodward as to the value of the property or that they could have done so if they had tried. Indeed, in May or early June 1981, before the estate tax return was filed, Kathleen provided Woodward with her file showing contacts made with her and Weyman by possible purchasers of the property.

Birdsong, who actually prepared the estate tax return, relied upon the Kenyon appraisal—consistent with his practice of using a professional appraiser's values in completing estate tax returns during his entire accountancy career. Respondent contends that the executors should have informed Kenyon of the inquiries about purchasing the land that they had received and the Malcolm Powell offer. The executors would have been subject to adverse criticism, however, if they had attempted to influence Kenyon's views during the course of the preparation of his professional report. The courts have stated repeatedly that the best evidence of value is like and comparable sales within a reasonable time preceding the valuation date.

(C) Cooperation During the Investigation

When the estate tax return investigation started, Davis advised the executors, Kenyon, Birdsong, and Woodward to cooperate fully with the IRS and give the agents the information they requested. Instead of relying on the attorney-client privilege, Davis, with the executors' consent, opened his file on the estate to the IRS agents; he kept meticulous records on conversations regarding the estate, and he was examined in court on practically every scrap of paper in his file. Birdsong opened his files and furnished the IRS agents with previous income and gift tax returns for decedent and Weyman that he had prepared over a period of approximately 15 years prior to decedent's death. Weyman and Kathleen submitted to interviews. This is not the kind of conduct that characterizes tax defrauders or reflects a feeling of guilt for having knowingly attempted to conceal facts or mislead the IRS.

(D) Conclusion.

In summary, we conclude that the record does not show that Weyman and Kathleen as executors attempted, or intended, to defraud the Government. To the estate tax return they attached the Kenyon appraisal report showing openly and fully how the value used in the estate tax return was determined. They attempted to conceal neither the factual basis of the returned value nor the reasoning on which it was founded. Both their attorney and their accountant regarded the appraisal as a good one and advised its use in filing the return. The executors acted on that advice. They expected the return to be examined, and throughout the investigation they freely made available the testimony and the files of their advisors as well as the information that they had. The record simply does not show that any part of the underpayment was due to fraud within the meaning of section 6653(b).[47]

To reflect the foregoing,

Decisions will be entered under Rule 155.

Notes

1. As discussed in Chapter 7, it is possible for the Commissioner to use the doctrine of collateral estoppel to carry his burden of proving fraud. In Meier v. Commissioner, page 443 of Chapter 7, the Tax Court held that the taxpayer was collaterally estopped to deny diversion of his employer's funds to his own use, based on a judgment against him in an accounting action to recover the diverted amounts. The Commissioner sought to use

---

47. Respondent contends that the attorneys' fees and executors' commissions incurred by the estate are not deductible on the ground that the executors fraudulently undervalued the Ashford–Dunwoody Farm. Because fraud has not been established, the attorneys' fees and executors' commissions are allowable. The amount thereof will be determined under a Rule 155 computation.

that same earlier judgment to help carry his burden of proving that the taxpayer's failure to report this income was fraudulent. The Tax Court (in a reviewed opinion with no dissents) ruled in favor of the Commissioner, reasoning as follows:

Fraud/Section 6653(b) Addition

Respondent argues that petitioner's failure to report diverted funds and other income on his tax returns for 1968, 1969, and 1970 is fraudulent. If any part of any underpayment for the taxable years is due to fraud, the addition under section 6653(b) will apply, not only to the underpayment attributable to fraud, but to the entire underpayment. Fraud must be proved by clear and convincing evidence. Sec. 7454; Rule 142(b). The existence of fraud is a question of fact to be resolved upon consideration of the entire record. Fraud is never presumed, but rather must be established by some independent evidence. Fraud may be proven by circumstantial evidence and reasonable inferences drawn from the facts because direct proof of the taxpayer's intent is rarely available. *Spies v. United States,* 317 U.S. 492 (1943); *Rowlee v. Commissioner,* 80 T.C. 1111 (1983); *Stephenson v. Commissioner,* 79 T.C. 995 (1982), affd. 748 F.2d 331 (6th Cir.1984). The taxpayer's entire course of conduct may establish the requisite fraudulent intent. *Rowlee v. Commissioner, supra; Stone v. Commissioner,* 56 T.C. 213 (1971).

In a recently decided case, *Bradford v. Commissioner,* 796 F.2d 303 (9th Cir.1986), affg. T.C. Memo. 1984–601 (*Bradford*), the Court of Appeals for the Ninth Circuit reaffirmed that it is appropriate to infer fraudulent intent from various kinds of circumstantial evidence and set forth a nonexclusive list of the "badges of fraud" that demonstrate fraudulent intent. These include: (1) The understatement of income; (2) inadequate records; (3) failure to file tax returns; (4) implausible or inconsistent explanations of behavior; (5) concealment of assets; and (6) failure to cooperate with tax authorities. The following are additional indicia of fraud: (1) Engaging in illegal activities; (2) attempting to conceal these activities; (3) dealing in cash; and (4) failing to make estimated tax payments. *Bradford v. Commissioner, supra* at 307–308.

Respondent has established that Meier's returns for the years involving the mining transactions were fraudulent. The first indicia of fraud in *Bradford* is understating income. We have already found that petitioner diverted funds of Hughes to his own use and control and that said funds constituted substantial income from the mining transactions during the 1969 and 1970 taxable years. Through introducing petitioners' returns into evidence, respondent has shown the failure to report any of this income. The failure to report said income resulted in large understatements of income on petitioners' 1969 and 1970 joint returns.

Part of the evidence relied upon by respondent to carry his burden of establishing fraud has been established through the offensive use of collateral estoppel. Accordingly, we must consider the burden of proof required in both proceedings. Civil tax fraud must be proven by clear and convincing evidence. Sec. 7454; Rule 142(b). Section 27, Restatement, Judgments 2d (1982), and the holding in *Synanon Church v. United States,* 820 F.2d 421 (D.C.Cir.1987), state the general rule that a fact found in a first case may be established by means of collateral estoppel either as an evidentiary or ultimate fact in the second case. Subsection (4) of section 28, Restatement, Judgments 2d (1982), recommends an exception in the following circumstances where "The party against whom preclusion is sought had a significantly heavier burden of persuasion with respect to the issue in the initial action than in the subsequent action; the burden has shifted to his adversary; or the adversary has a significantly heavier burden than he had in the first action." [30] Accordingly, we consider the standard of proof for an accounting action brought in a Federal District Court in Utah.

As previously indicated, plaintiff in an accounting action must show that through fraud or breach of a fiduciary duty, or both, he is entitled to money or property held by the defendant. There is no explicit burden of proof for accounting actions in Utah. However, where fraud is alleged it must be proven by clear and convincing evidence. *Holland v. Moreton,* 10 Utah 2d 390, 353 P.2d 989 (1960); *Lynch v. MacDonald,* 12 Utah 2d 427, 367 P.2d 464 (1962).

Fraud and breach of fiduciary duty can be separate bases for instituting an accounting action. An agent commits a breach of his fiduciary duty if he sells property to or buys property from his principal without full disclosure to his principal. *Tatsuno v. Kasai,* 70 Utah 203, 259 P. 318 (1927).[31] See also Restatement, Agency 2d, secs. 387–389 (1957). It would appear that such a breach becomes fraudulent when accompanied by intentional nondisclosure and bad faith. See comment "a" to Restatement, Agency 2d, section 389 (1957). Conduct similar to that of petitioner's has been found to be fraudulent by Utah courts in several cases.

The trial court in the Hughes case did not state with acuity the standard of proof it used. Although fraud was not expressly alleged, Hughes contended that Meier was its agent in the acquisition of mining claims, that Meier abandoned his fiduciary duty to Hughes and, together with others, sold the mining claims to Hughes at inflated prices and secretly participated in the redistribution of money to and for the benefit of defendant Meier and others. *Hughes Tool Co. v. Meier,* 489 F.Supp. 354, 359 (D.Utah 1977).

All of the classic indicia of fraud are present in the Hughes case; a misrepresentation by Meier about the price and/or value of the mining claims, in addition to concealing his role on both sides of the transaction, reliance on his representations by Hughes, and damage to Hughes. See *Pace v. Parrish,* 122 Utah 141, 247 P.2d 273 (1952). The facts of this case

---

30. We are not certain whether the Restatement's recommended exception would apply equally to facts which are established as "evidentiary" in the second case. Where an evidentiary or ultimate fact from the first case is used as an ultimate fact in the second (without further evidence) a comparison of the degree of the burden of proof would be necessary. In a setting where a collaterally estopped fact is merely a part of the evidence considered to determine whether a party has met his burden of proof, the need for an equal or higher burden of proof in the first case is less obvious. We do not have to address this nuance because the burden of proof in both cases under consideration is by "clear and convincing evidence."

31. Comment "a" to sec. 389 of the Restatement, Agency 2d (1957), indicates that "an agent who is appointed to sell or give advice concerning sales violates his duty if, without the principal's knowledge, he sells to himself or purchases from the principal through the medium of a 'straw.'"

are strikingly similar to those in *Tatsuno v. Kasai, supra; Holland v. Moreton, supra;* and *Lynch v. MacDonald, supra.* The District Court in *Hughes Tool Co. v. Meier, supra,* found that Meier held a fiduciary position, that he breached such position by secretly diverting funds from the sales for his own use and benefit and to the damage of his principal, and that there was no basis upon which he could keep the funds. Under these circumstances, plaintiff (Hughes) established fraud through the breach of Meier's fiduciary duty.

The District Court in *Hughes Tool Co.* used language in its opinion indicating that the quantum of proof would have, at a minimum, met a clear and convincing standard. The Court held as follows: "In view of the foregoing findings, the court concludes as a *matter of law* defendant Meier must * * * render an accounting." *Hughes Tool Co. v. Meier, supra* at 369. Emphasis supplied.

> Defendant Meier appears to misapprehend the quantity and quality of the evidence which has been presented in this case to date * * *. As the court rehearsed in great detail * * * there is substantial evidence in the record upon which to base a ruling fixing liability on defendant * * *. That is, plaintiff established [the sales transactions and that the funds were the responsibility of Meier]. [*Hughes Tool Co. v. Meier, supra* at 373.]

"The court is of the opinion that *all* of the evidence in this matter shows that the sum of * * * is due the plaintiff." *Hughes Tool Co. v. Meier, supra* at 374. Although not entirely clear, we conclude that the standard of proof required in this type proceeding in Utah is "clear and convincing." Based upon our review of Judge Anderson's opinion and the record[33] in the District Court proceeding, we believe that Hughes Tool was held to a "clear and convincing" standard of proof in establishing that Meier, through a breach of his fiduciary duty, secretly diverted Hughes' funds for his own use and control.

Another indicia of fraud in *Bradford* is the failure to keep records or keeping inadequate records. In this case, many of the documents were back-dated or dated "as of" a certain date, to retroactively reflect the transactions in the light petitioner wanted them to appear, i.e., making the foreign corporations the owners of the claims. Additionally, Meier's role on both sides of these transactions is not reflected in the records (of necessity, to conceal his involvement). In the context of this case, the records of the transactions are inadequate and were intended, at the very least, to conceal information from petitioner's employer and likely from the taxing authorities, including respondent.

Another indicia noted in *Bradford* is the concealment of assets. This is a highly probative factor here. The sales proceeds were almost immediately transferred overseas after the execution of the transactions. In addition, the documentation makes it appear that the foreign corporations were the owners of the funds, while the funds were under the control of and for the benefit of petitioner. We find it highly indicative of fraudulent intent that

---

33. Most of the documents and testimony received in the District Court were offered and received in this case.

the funds, after being channeled through two different foreign corporations, ended up in a trust for the benefit of petitioner. This conduct, calculated to mislead and conceal, is indicative of fraud. *Spies v. United States*, 317 U.S. 492 (1943). *Gajewski v. Commissioner*, 67 T.C. 181 (1976), affd. without published opinion 578 F.2d 1383 (8th Cir.1978).

Petitioner contends that his so-called "fraudulent intent," because of the transfer of funds, was merely "tax planning" by a group of knowledgeable advisers. We find that the use of the foreign entities, in the context of this case, was a sham or subterfuge to disguise the real owner, avoid identification of petitioner, and to evade Federal income taxes.

A final factor relevant here is whether the activity was illegal. While we know of no State criminal charges filed in connection with this case, petitioner rather egregiously breached his fiduciary duty to his employer, to the extent of benefiting by several million dollars. We find that this situation is not significantly different than a case involving embezzlement or other kind of theft. The lack of potential for criminal punishment or penalty seems to be a distinction without a difference in this setting; petitioner's activities are no less illegal or improper.

Respondent need not prove the precise amount of the underpayment resulting from fraud. *Otsuki v. Commissioner*, 53 T.C. 96, 105 (1969). In any event, some amount of underpayment has been established for the years 1969 and 1970. We conclude, therefore, based on the facts in the record, that petitioner intended not only to conceal his activities from his employer, Hughes, but also fraudulently intended to evade Federal income tax.[34]

Respondent has determined that petitioner underreported his income for 1968 because petitioner's bank deposits exceeded his reported income by approximately $29,000.[35] In addition, petitioner engaged in large numbers of cash transactions during 1968, 1969, and 1970. *Bradford v. Commissioner*, 796 F.2d 303 (9th Cir.1986), affg. T.C. Memo. 1984–601. However, for taxable year 1968, respondent has not established the quantum of evidence sufficient to prove fraud and thereby lift the bar of the statute of limitations. While the Hughes episode provided highly probative evidence of fraudulent intent for 1969 and 1970, this does not flow to years unrelated to those transactions. This finding renders moot respondent's determina-

---

34. Although neither party brought this matter to our attention, it is obvious that respondent has only proven that petitioner-husband fraudulently intended to evade Federal income tax. Sec. 6653(b), in part, provides: "In the case of a joint return under sec. 6013, this subsection shall not apply with respect to the tax of a spouse unless some part of the underpayment is due to the fraud of such spouse." Respondent has not shown that any part of the underpayment is due to fraud on the part of petitioner-wife (Jennie E. Meier). The addition to tax under sec. 6653(b) is not applicable to petitioner-wife for any of the 3 taxable years in issue. However, petitioner-wife has not otherwise alleged or proven that she is an "innocent spouse" within the meaning of sec. 6013 for any of the 3 taxable years in issue. Thus, petitioner-wife is jointly and severally liable with petitioner-husband for the income tax deficiency, but she is not liable for any addition to tax under sec. 6653(b). *Stone v. Commissioner*, 56 T.C. 213 (1971).

35. Respondent also included other amounts in petitioner's income, a $9,000 cash insurance premium payment, $137.25 of interest income, and approximately $7,000 without a designated origin.

tion that petitioner omitted interest income and other items of income for 1968.

To reflect the foregoing,

> *Decision will be entered for the respondent in part and the petitioners in part.*

Reviewed by the Court.

NIMS, CHABOT, PARKER, WHITAKER, KORNER, SHIELDS, HAMBLEN, CLAPP, SWIFT, JACOBS, WRIGHT, PARR, WILLIAMS, WELLS, RUWE, and WHALEN, JJ., agree with this opinion.

2. Section 6663(b) clarifies the parties' burden of proof in cases involving the civil fraud penalty. If the IRS establishes by clear and convincing evidence that any portion of the underpayment is attributable to fraud, then the entire underpayment is deemed attributable to fraud, except any portion of the underpayment that the taxpayer establishes is not attributable to fraud. Under § 6663(b) it is clear that the taxpayer may satisfy the burden of disproving fraud by a preponderance of the evidence, and need not meet the higher "clear and convincing evidence" standard. The legislative history of IMPACT explains that Congress "believes that it is appropriate that the burden imposed on the IRS be higher than the burden imposed on a taxpayer in these circumstances."[w]

3. Section 6663(c) continues the spousal rule of former § 6653(b), under which the fraud of one spouse is not to be attributed to the other spouse simply because a joint return was filed.

(2) Amount of the Penalty

For returns due after 1989, the civil fraud penalty is 75% of the portion of the underpayment of tax that is attributable to fraud. Recall, however, that under section 6663(b) if the Commissioner establishes that any portion of the underpayment is attributable to fraud, then the entire underpayment is deemed attributable to fraud, unless the taxpayer can disprove fraud with respect to some portion of the underpayment.

For returns due on or before December 31, 1989 and after December 31, 1988, the penalty amount is the same as that of section 6663: 75% of the portion of the underpayment attributable to fraud. For returns due in 1987 and 1988, the fraud penalty contained two parts: the 75% penalty plus an "add-on" interest component of 50% of the interest on the portion of the underpayment attributable to fraud. Congress repealed the add-on interest component of the fraud penalty in 1988, at the same time it repealed the similar component of the negligence penalty. For returns due in 1983 through 1986, the penalty was 50% of the entire underpayment plus the add-on interest penalty of 50% of the interest on the underpayment. 1986 legislation increased the penalty amount from 50% to 75%, but narrowed the scope of the

---

w. H.R.Rep. 101-247, 101st Cong., 1st Sess. 1392 (1989).

penalty by making it applicable only to the portion of the underpayment attributable to fraud.

(3) *Statute of Limitations*

As discussed in Chapter 5, there is no time limit on assessing tax deficiencies or the civil fraud penalty if the return is fraudulent. IRC § 6501(c)(1). This is true regardless of the fact that the return is 99% nonfraudulent: if any portion of an underpayment is attributable to fraud, then additional tax and the fraud penalty can be assessed at any time. Recall also from Chapter 5 that the Supreme Court has held that this rule applies even if the taxpayer later files a correct, nonfraudulent amended return. *Badaracco v. Commissioner*, 464 U.S. 386, 104 S.Ct. 756, 78 L.Ed.2d 549 (1984).

SECTION 4. PREPARER, PROMOTER AND PROTESTER PENALTIES

A. RETURN PREPARER PENALTY

As discussed in Chapter 2, IMPACT changed the standard for judging understatements of tax liability caused by return preparers. Prior to its amendment in 1989, section 6694(a) authorized a $100 penalty for understatements due to the return preparer's negligent or intentional disregard of "rules and regulations." For returns prepared after December 31, 1989, the penalty amount is $250 per return, and the standard is that the understatement resulted from "a position for which there was not a realistic possibility of being sustained on its merits," the position was not disclosed or, even if disclosed, was frivolous, and the preparer cannot establish reasonable cause and good faith. According to the legislative history, Congress "believes that this standard of behavior is stricter than present law, so that negligent behavior subject to penalty under present law will continue to be subject to penalty under this new standard."[x]

Section 6694(b) formerly imposed a penalty of $500 for willful understatements of liability by return preparers. IMPACT increased the amount of the penalty to $1,000 and added recklessness as a basis for imposing the penalty. IRC § 6694(b)(2) ("any reckless or intentional disregard of rules or regulations").

JUDISCH v. UNITED STATES
United States Court of Appeals, Eleventh Circuit, 1985.
755 F.2d 823.

TJOFLAT, CIRCUIT JUDGE:

Section 6694(a) of the Internal Revenue Code, 26 U.S.C. § 6694(a) (1982),[1] imposes a penalty on an income tax preparer [2] who understates

---

x. H.R.Rep. 101-247, 101st Cong., 1st Sess., 1396 (1989).

1. 26 U.S.C. § 6694(a) (1982) provides:

2. See note 2 on page 278.

a taxpayer's liability on an income tax return by negligently or intentionally disregarding revenue rules and regulations. Section 6694(b) of the Code, 26 U.S.C. § 6694(b) (1982),[3] penalizes a tax preparer who willfully understates a taxpayer's liability on a return. The principal question presented in this appeal is whether a tax preparer can be penalized under section 6694(b) if the understatement of taxpayer liabilities is caused by the tax preparer's willful disregard of revenue rules and regulations.

I.

Clara Mann Judisch, the appellee here, is a federal income tax return preparer in Sarasota, Florida. She has been preparing income tax returns since 1952, when she began practicing law in Ames, Iowa. Judisch practiced law in Ames until she moved to Sarasota in 1968. Thereafter, she limited her professional work to the preparation of income tax returns.

Most of Judisch's taxpayer clients were individuals; some were sole proprietors of small businesses. Judisch's first step in preparing a client's tax return would be to mail the client a four-page questionnaire. On receipt of the filled-out questionnaire, Judisch would prepare the return and send it to the client for his signature. The client would then mail the return to the Internal Revenue Service. Usually, Judisch would prepare a client's return without communicating with him except through the questionnaire. In a few instances, she would call the client to inquire about information disclosed in his answers to her questionnaire.

In 1976 Congress amended the Internal Revenue Code, adding section 280A, 26 U.S.C. § 280A (1976), to limit the type of taxpayer eligible to take a "home office" deduction; to be eligible for such a deduction, the taxpayer must use the portion of his residence employed as a "home office" exclusively, and on a regular basis, as his principal place of business or as a place of business used by patients, clients, or customers in meeting or dealing with the taxpayer in the normal course

(a) **Negligent or Intentional Disregard of Rules and Regulations**

If any part of any understatement of liability with respect to any return ... is due to the negligent or intentional disregard of rules and regulations by any person who is an income tax return preparer with respect to such return or claim, such person shall pay a penalty of $100 with respect to such return or claim.

2. An "income tax return preparer" is defined by section 7701(a)(36)(A) of the Internal Revenue Code as a person who prepares for compensation, or who employs one or more persons to prepare for compensation, any income tax return. 26 U.S.C. § 7701(a)(36)(A) (1982).

3. 26 U.S.C. § 6694(b) provides:

(b) **Willful Understatement of Liability**

If any part of any understatement of liability with respect to any return * * * is due to a willful attempt in any manner to understate the liability for a tax by a person who is an income tax return preparer with respect to such return or claim, such person shall pay a penalty of $500 with respect to such return or claim. With respect to any return or claim, the amount of the penalty payable by any person by reason of this subsection shall be reduced by the amount of the penalty paid by such person by reason of [26 U.S.C. § 6694](a).

of business. The amount of the deduction is limited to the gross income derived from the use of the home office. This amendment to the Code was effective for the tax years relevant to this suit, 1976 and 1977, and Judisch had knowledge of this fact.

In mailing her questionnaire to her clients for these two tax years, Judisch did not elicit the information necessary to enable her to determine whether a given client was entitled to a home office deduction. Judisch did ask the client to indicate whether a part of his home was "used for production of income," and, if so, the percentage of the home so used, and to list expenditures the client incurred in carrying out such business activity. She did not, however, seek the critical information necessary to determine the client's eligibility for a home office deduction: whether the portion of the client's home used for the production of income was used exclusively, and on a regular basis, for that purpose; whether it was the principal place of the client's trade or business; and the gross income derived therefrom. Nevertheless, Judisch routinely claimed a home office deduction on her clients' 1976 and 1977 income tax returns. She did so even when it was clear that the client either had no earnings from a trade or business or had no home office used exclusively as his principal place of business. Moreover, Judisch claimed as business expenses, items, such as cable television, the home telephone, and the home newspaper, that could not qualify as business expense. She also claimed investment tax credits for property, such as personal property that the client decided to use in his home office, that was ineligible for such a credit. The IRS discovered Judisch's home office deduction practice while auditing some of her clients' tax returns, and, after a full investigation, assessed fifty-eight penalties against her under sections 6694(a) and (b) of the Internal Revenue Code [5] for understating tax liability with respect to tax returns prepared by her for the 1976 and 1977 tax years.

Judisch thereafter brought this action in the district court, as authorized by section 6694(c) of the Internal Revenue Code, 26 U.S.C. § 6694(c) (1982), seeking a determination of her liability for these penalties. She demanded a trial by jury. After the parties joined issue, they agreed, for reasons unimportant to this appeal, to limit the trial of the case to the penalties assessed in connection with five tax returns, Wotring's 1977 return,[6] the Roates' 1976 and 1977 returns, and the Joneses' 1976 and 1977 returns. The parties also agreed that the order of proof at trial would require the government to put on its evidence first.

The government produced the only witnesses called at trial, Judisch and Priscilla A. Quina, the IRS agent who audited Judisch's clients' tax returns. Judisch called no witnesses. All that she present-

---

5. *See supra* notes 1 and 3.

6. The district court granted a directed verdict on both penalties assessed in connection with the 1977 Wotring return because Judisch testified that she did not prepare the return. The government does not appeal this ruling. Therefore, the issue is not before us.

ed to the jury was a copy of a 1980 Joint Congressional Resolution, Act of Oct. 1, 1980, Pub.L. No. 96–369, 1980 U.S.Code Cong. & Ad.News (94 Stat.) § 123, which prohibited the IRS from using any funds to enforce the rules or regulations it had promulgated to implement section 280A of the Code relating to "the determination of the principal place of business of the taxpayer."

At the close of all the evidence, Judisch moved for a directed verdict as to the section 6694(b) penalties for willfully understating her clients' tax liability. She contended that a finding of "willfulness" under section 6694(b) required that the tax return preparer purposely disregard "information furnished by the taxpayer" and that the evidence failed to show that she had done so. In response, the government argued that a section 6694(b) penalty for willful understatement of liability may be based on the tax preparer's intentional disregard of applicable rules and regulations and that there was ample evidence for the jury to conclude that Judisch had intentionally disregarded such rules and regulations in preparing the five returns in question. The district court directed a verdict in Judisch's favor as to the section 6694(b) penalties, because, as Judisch contended, the evidence did not demonstrate that she had intentionally disregarded information furnished by the taxpayer. The court also concluded that the evidence was insufficient to sustain the penalties under the government's theory. The court submitted the question of Judisch's liability for the section 6694(a) penalties to the jury, and the jury found for Judisch.

The government appeals, contending that the district court erred as a matter of law in removing the section 6694(b) penalties from the jury. The government also contends that, with respect to the section 6694(a) penalties that were submitted to the jury, the jury's verdict must be set aside, and a new trial ordered, because the court committed prejudicial error in admitting into evidence the 1980 Joint Congressional Resolution concerning the IRS' enforcement of section 280A of the Code. We consider these contentions in turn.[8]

II.

A.

1.

The district court directed verdicts as to the section 6694(b) penalties, relying, in part, on the assumption that an income tax preparer's intentional disregard of the Internal Revenue Code or treasury rules

---

8. The government also contends that the district court committed reversible error in refusing to allow the government to call a rebuttal witness. The court stated that the rebuttal witness had not been listed as a witness ahead of time, that she had been sitting in the courtroom during the trial, and that, if it had known she was going to testify, it would have invoked Fed. R.Evid. 615, which allows the court to sequester witnesses so that they cannot hear the testimony of other witnesses. Whether to sequester the witness was clearly within the sound discretion of the trial court, especially in view of the limited use of the witness' testimony and the lack of prejudice to the government. *United States v. Nash*, 649 F.2d 369, 371 (5th Cir.1981). There was no error.

and regulations cannot constitute a violation of section 6694(b). The court reasoned that Congress did not intend to proscribe the same conduct in both sections 6694(a) and (b). As to the former, the court reasoned, Congress intended to proscribe the negligent or intentional disregard of the rules and regulations; as to the latter, it intended to proscribe the willful disregard of information furnished by the taxpayer for the purpose of understating the amount of taxes owed. As an alternative holding, the court found the evidence insufficient to show that Judisch had willfully understated the tax liability on any of the returns before the court.

Section 6694(b), on its face, proscribes "a willful attempt in any manner to understate the [taxpayer's] liability." The willful disregard of rules and regulations for the purpose of understating tax liability constitutes a manner of willful attempt under the section; accordingly, Judisch violated section 6694(b) if she willfully disregarded the Code or treasury rules and regulations to understate tax liability.

A tax return preparer's willful disregard of the tax code or regulations, for the purpose of understating a client's tax liability, violates both sections 6694(a) *and* (b). The text of the latter suggests this result: "the amount of the penalty payable by any person by reason of this [section] shall be reduced by the amount of the penalty paid by such person by reason of [section 6694] (a)." The treasury regulations and the legislative history also support this position. Treas.Reg. § 1.6694–1(b)(2)(iv) (1984) provides as follows:

> In certain situations, a preparer shall be subject both to a penalty under [section 6694] (a) * * * for intentional disregard of rules and regulations and to a penalty under [section 6694] (b) for willful understatement of liability. A penalty for willful understatement of liability may be based on an intentional disregard of rules and regulations. For example, a preparer who claims a personal exemption deduction for the taxpayer's mother with knowledge that the taxpayer is not entitled to the deduction will have both intentionally disregarded rules and regulations within the meaning of [section 6694] (a) * * * and willfully understated liability for tax within the meaning of [section 6694] (b).[10]

The legislative history directly supports this regulation. H.R.Rep. No. 94–658, 94th Cong. 1st Sess., at 279 (1975), *reprinted in* 1976 U.S.Code Cong. & Ad.News 2897, 3175, states in pertinent part:

> A willful understatement of tax liability can also include an intentional disregard of Internal Revenue Code rules and regulations.

---

10. Treasury regulations must be sustained unless unreasonable or plainly inconsistent with the Internal Revenue Code. *National Muffler Dealers Ass'n, Inc. v. United States*, 440 U.S. 472, 476–77, 99 S.Ct. 1304, 1307, 59 L.Ed.2d 519 (1979); *Thor Power Tool Co. v. Comm.*, 439 U.S. 522, 533 n. 11, 99 S.Ct. 773, 781 n. 11, 58 L.Ed.2d 785 (1979). Furthermore, the regulation we quote, proposed nine months after sections 6694(a) and (b) became effective, has particular force because it represents a substantially contemporaneous construction by those presumed to have been aware of the congressional intent. *National Muffler Dealers*, 440 U.S. at 477, 99 S.Ct. at 1307; *Comm. v. South Texas Lumber Company*, 333 U.S. 496, 501, 68 S.Ct. 695, 698, 92 L.Ed. 831 (1948).

For example, an income tax return preparer who deducts all of a taxpayer's medical expenses, intentionally disregarding the percent of adjusted gross income limitation, may have both intentionally disregarded Internal Revenue Code rules and regulations and willfully understated tax liability. In such a case, the Internal Revenue Service can assess either or both penalties against the income tax return preparer.

See also S.Rep. No. 94–938, 94th Cong.2d Sess., at 356 (1976), *reprinted in* 1976 U.S.Code Cong. & Ad.News 3439, 3785. In light of the regulations and the legislative history, we conclude that an income tax preparer's willful disregard of the Code or the rules and regulations for the purpose of understating a client's tax liability violates section 6694(b) and section 6694(a) as well.

The district court erred in concluding that Judisch could not have violated both sections 6694(a) and (b). The Congress plainly contemplated that an income tax preparer could transgress both sections simultaneously. Every violation of section (b), based on evidence that the taxpayer willfully disregarded IRS rules and regulations, is also a violation of section (a); a violation of section (a) is a violation of section (b) only where the government proves willfulness.

2.

The district court directed a verdict for Judisch on all of the section 6694(b) willfulness penalties on the ground that there was insufficient evidence in the record from which a jury could find that Judisch had intentionally disregarded the applicable rules and regulations. The sufficiency of the evidence presents a nettlesome question on review [11] in this case because of the government's trial strategy. Inexplicably, the government decided not to establish the information Judisch's clients provided her to enable her to prepare the tax returns under scrutiny. That is, the government neither introduced the questionnaires those clients filled out and mailed to Judisch [12] nor called the clients to testify as to the information they provided her. In short, the government did not prove the amount of tax liability understatement that resulted from the home office deduction, and, as to the Wotring return for 1977, the government even failed to establish that Judisch prepared it. *See supra* note 6. A directed verdict with respect to the Wotring return was therefore in order. A directed verdict was also in

---

11. In ruling on a motion for directed verdict, the district court must consider all the evidence in the case, in the light and with all reasonable inferences most favorable to the party opposed to the motion. A directed verdict should be granted only "[i]f the facts and inferences point so strongly and overwhelmingly in favor of one party that the Court believes that reasonable men could not arrive at a contrary verdict * * *." *Boeing Co. v. Shipman,* 411 F.2d 365, 374 (5th Cir.1969) (en banc). The motion must be denied if there is "evidence of such quality and weight that reasonable and fair-minded men in the exercise of impartial judgment might reach different conclusions * * *." *Id. See also Federal Kemper Life Assurance Co. v. First Nat. Bank of Birmingham,* 712 F.2d 459, 464 (11th Cir.1983); *Neff v. Kehoe,* 708 F.2d 639, 641–42 (11th Cir.1983).

12. The government did introduce the Joneses' 1976 questionnaire into evidence.

order as to the Joneses' returns for 1976 and 1977. The government, after auditing those returns, allowed the Joneses' home office deduction. Under these circumstances, it could not be said that Judisch intentionally disregarded the section 280A home office deduction requirements.

The government did manage, however, to present sufficient evidence to withstand a motion for directed verdict with respect to the Roates' 1976 and 1977 tax returns. Judisch admitted that she knew of the requirements for a home office deduction at the time she prepared these returns. She knew, for example, that section 280A(c)(5) of the Code specified that a home office deduction could not exceed the portion of the gross income from the taxpayers' business attributable to business activity in the home office. The Roates had no income from a trade or business, whether conducted out of the home or elsewhere, in 1976 or 1977, and Judisch reported no such income on the Roates' tax returns for those years.[13] Nevertheless, she had the Roates take a home office deduction in both years. These deductions were false for two reasons. First, the Roates had no income from a trade or business against which a home office deduction could be taken. Second, the Roates had no "home office" as defined in section 280A. All they had was a family room where they watched television and listened to the stereo. On these facts, the jury could readily have found that Judisch intentionally disregarded section 280A for the purpose of understating the Roates' tax liability for the 1976 and 1977 tax years. The district court therefore erred in directing a verdict with respect to the section 6694(b) penalties on the Roates' returns.

B.

The government's second contention in this appeal is that the district court committed reversible error by admitting into evidence the 1980 Joint Congressional Resolution concerning the IRS' enforcement of section 280A of the Code because it was irrelevant. Judisch argues, in response, that the Joint Resolution, passed three years after she prepared the returns in question, demonstrated that Congress disagreed with the IRS position on home office deductions.[14] Judisch contends

---

13. In the Roates' 1977 return, Judisch did attempt to show that the Roates had earned income from a trade or business by labeling salary income of $5,200, received from their employer, as self-employment income on schedule C. This was patently improper, and Judisch knew it.

14. The background of the resolution indicates that Congress was dissatisfied with certain portions of the proposed regulations, not Code section 280A itself. In proposed treasury regulation § 1.280A–2(b) (Aug. 7, 1980), the IRS stated that a taxpayer may have only one principal place of business for purposes of section 280A and that, if the home office is not his principal place of business, no deduction is allowable. Proposed Treas.Reg. § 1.280A–2(b), 8 Stand.Fed.Tax Rep. (CCH) ¶ 229740 (1981). In late December 1981, Congress passed legislation to allow a taxpayer to have a different principal place of business for each of his separate trades or businesses. Black Lung Benefits Revenue Act of 1981, Pub.L. No. 97–119, 1981 U.S.Code Cong. & Ad.News (95 Stat.) 113. Nevertheless, it declared that the pertinent portion of the dwelling unit must still be exclusively used on a regular basis as the principal situs for some recognized trade or business carried on by the taxpayer, and the amount of the

that the congressional resolution was relevant in her situation, proving her good faith and reasonableness in disregarding the statute and claiming the deductions on behalf of her clients. We are not persuaded.

An income tax preparer's "good faith" and the reasonableness of a position he takes must be judged at the time the work is done. Therefore, only the information available to and considered by the income tax preparer in preparing a tax return is relevant to this good faith issue. It was pure coincidence that the Congress passed the resolution in question two years after the events in issue here. We will not permit a litigant in these circumstances to prove his good faith or a reasonable basis for his action by subsequent developments in the law.

Judisch argued to the jury that the congressional resolution indicated that the IRS was wrong in challenging the tax returns she prepared on behalf of her clients. As we indicate in the margin, *see supra* note 14, Congress did not intend to approve home office deductions for the vast majority of individual taxpayers who do not operate a trade or business from their residence. Furthermore, several of her clients had no legitimate trade or business income which the Code required to offset the deductions. In this context, the challenged evidence was highly misleading and prejudicial to the jury. In summary, we reverse and remand for a new trial, with respect to the Roates' returns, on the section 6694(a) issue of negligent understatement of liability. *See Perry v. State Farm Fire & Casualty Co.,* 734 F.2d 1441, 1446 (11th Cir.1984); Fed.R.Evid. 103.

For the foregoing reasons, we reverse the district court's judgment with respect to the section 6694(a) and (b) penalties on the Roates' 1976 and 1977 returns and remand the case for a new trial. In all other respects, the court's judgment is affirmed.

Affirmed in part, Reversed in part, and Remanded.

BROCKHOUSE v. UNITED STATES

United States Court of Appeals, Seventh Circuit, 1984.
749 F.2d 1248.

Flaum, Circuit Judge.

This appeal raises the issue of whether the tax return preparer negligence penalty, section 6694(a) of the Internal Revenue Code,[1] can be assessed against a preparer who understates income tax liability because he relied solely on information supplied to him by the taxpay-

---

deduction cannot exceed the income from that trade or business.

1. Section 6694(a) provides:

    (a) Negligent or Intentional Disregard of Rules and Regulations.—If any part of any understatment of liability with respect to any return or claim for refund is due to the negligent or intentional disregard of rules and regulations by any person who is an income tax return preparer with respect to such return or claim, such person shall pay a penalty of $100 with respect to such return or claim.

ers. The Internal Revenue Service ("IRS") assessed a penalty against appellant John Brockhouse. Pursuant to section 6694(c), the appellant paid 15% of the penalty and sued for a refund.[2] The district court, 577 F.Supp. 55, denied the refund. For the reasons stated below, we affirm.

I.

The appellant is a certified public accountant. In January 1979, he was hired by the CPA firm of Goldman, Weiss, Gelman & Sered ("Goldman, Weiss"). For several years Goldman, Weiss had prepared the income tax returns of Rubert–Busch, M.D., S.C., an Illinois professional corporation, and those of Dr. Robert Busch, the corporation's sole shareholder. The appellant's first contact with the tax affairs of Rubert–Busch and Dr. Busch was in March 1979.

The appellant prepared Rubert–Busch's corporate income tax return for its fiscal year ended February 28, 1979. He used a trial balance sheet prepared by the corporation's bookkeeper. The trial balance sheet showed loans to the corporation from Dr. Busch and from a bank. It also showed that the corporation had made payments for interest expense; however, it did not show whether any of the interest had been paid to Dr. Busch.

The appellant also prepared the 1978 income tax return for Dr. and Mrs. Busch. Goldman, Weiss had adopted a procedure of sending a data questionnaire to its individual income tax clients. The client was either to complete and return the questionnaire or to use it as a guide in collecting the information necessary to prepare the return. The Busches chose not to complete a questionnaire. Rather, the information was supplied by the corporation's business manager or bookkeeper. The information was then entered on input sheets of an outside computer service. The appellant reviewed the sheets and compared them with the information supplied and the information shown on the Busches' 1977 return. There were no items shown on the 1977 return that were not accounted for in the 1978 return. The appellant signed

---

2. Section 6694(c) provides in pertinent part:

(c) Extension of Period of Collection Where Preparer Pays 15 Percent of Penalty.—

(1) In general.—If, within 30 days after the day on which notice and demand of any penalty under subsection (a) or (b) is made against any person who is an income tax return preparer, such person pays an amount which is not less than 15 percent of the amount of such penalty and files a claim for refund of the amount so paid, no levy or proceeding in court for the collection of the remainder of such penalty shall be made, begun, or prosecuted until the final resolution of a proceeding begun as provided in paragraph (2)....

(2) Preparer must bring suit in district court to determine his liability for penalty.—If, within 30 days after the day on which his claim for refund of any partial payment of any penalty under subsection (a) or (b) is denied (or, if earlier, within 30 days after the expiration of 6 months after the day on which he filed the claim for refund), the income tax return preparer fails to begin a proceeding in the appropriate United States district court for the determination of his liability for such penalty, paragraph (1) shall cease to apply with respect to such penalty, effective on the day following the close of the applicable 30-day period referred to in this paragraph.

the 1978 return and sent it to the Busches for signature and filing. The appellant never inquired whether any of the interest expense shown on the corporate trial balance sheet had been paid to the Busches.

In May 1980, an IRS agent began an examination of the corporate return. The agent requested an analysis of the corporation's interest expense account. The appellant went to the corporation's offices and examined the general ledger and disbursements journal. From this, he learned that the corporation had paid interest to Dr. Busch. The appellant promptly brought the omission to the attention of the IRS agent.

The corporation had paid Dr. Busch interest income in the amount of $15,291.20. The Busches had not reported the income on their 1978 return. This resulted in an underpayment of federal income taxes in the amount of $10,538.76.

The IRS assessed a $100 tax preparer penalty against the appellant. Pursuant to section 6694(c), the appellant paid $15 and filed a claim for refund. The refund was disallowed, and he filed suit in district court.

The district court denied the refund. It found that the appellant was negligent in omitting interest income from the return. The court found that he knew that the corporation had borrowed money from Dr. Busch and also that it had made interest payments. The court held that under these circumstances, a reasonable, prudent person would have made inquiries to determine whether any interest was paid to Dr. Busch. The court held that appellant was negligent in failing to obtain a completed data questionnaire from the Busches. Finally, the court relied on the factors listed in Revenue Procedure 80-40, which deals with liability under section 6694(a), to hold that the appellant had negligently disregarded a tax rule or regulation and thus was liable.

On appeal, the appellant argues that section 6694(a) does not apply to a tax return preparer's negligence in gathering facts from the taxpayer. He contends that section 6694(a) only applies where a preparer negligently misapplies a rule or regulation to a known item, and that where the preparer does not know of an item, he is not required to make inquiries or verify data. The appellant maintains that even if section 6694(a) does apply to a negligent failure to gather facts, his actions in this case were not negligent.

II.

Section 6694(a) allows a penalty of $100 to be assessed against an income tax return preparer whose negligent disregard of rules or regulations results in an understatement of tax liability.[3] The preparer

---

3. Section 6694(a) also applies to intentional disregard of rules or regulations. There is no claim that the appellant's actions were intentional, and thus we limit our discussion to negligent disregard.

has the burden of proving the absence of negligence. Treas.Reg. § 1.6694–1(a)(5).

Section 6694 was one of several provisions added by the Tax Reform Act of 1976 to regulate income tax return preparers. Congress generally was concerned with deterring abusive practices by preparers. Prior to 1976, preparers were subject only to criminal penalties for willfully aiding or assisting in the preparation of a fraudulent return. Congress found that these criminal penalties were inadequate. *See* H.R.Rep. No. 658, 94th Cong., 2d Sess. 273–76, *reprinted in* 1976 U.S.Code Cong. & Ad.News 2897 at 3169–71. Although Congress was concerned with abuses by "commercial" preparers—those who are not accountants or lawyers—it determined that regulation of all preparers was appropriate. *Id.* at 274–75, 1976 U.S.Code Cong. & Ad.News at 3169–70. Section 6694 was added primarily to deter preparers from engaging in negligent or fraudulent practices designed to understate tax liability. *Id.* at 278, 1976 U.S.Code Cong. & Ad.News at 3174. However, Congress did not limit the applicability of section 6694(a) to situations involving disregard of rules or regulations applicable to the facts as provided by the taxpayer. Rather, section 6694(a) applies generally to "negligent disregard." We therefore hold that a tax preparer negligently disregards a rule or regulation under section 6694(a) if his or her negligent failure to inquire into information provided by the taxpayer results in the filing of a return that violates a rule or regulation.

To determine whether a tax preparer's actions constitute negligence under section 6694(a), we must first determine the applicable standard of care. Negligence in this context is defined generally as a "lack of due care or failure to do what a reasonable and ordinarily prudent person would do under the circumstances." *Marcello v. Commissioner*, 380 F.2d 499, 506 (5th Cir.1967), *cert. denied*, 389 U.S. 1044, 88 S.Ct. 787, 19 L.Ed.2d 835 (1968); *see also Zmuda v. Commissioner*, 731 F.2d 1417, 1422 (9th Cir.1984).[4] The regulation under section 6694(b), relating to willful disregard of rules or regulations, expressly provides that a preparer may not rely without verification on information supplied by the taxpayer if that information appears incomplete or incorrect. Treas.Reg. § 1.6694–1(b)(2)(ii). The regulation under section 6694(a) does not contain such an express provision, but it does provide that a preparer is not negligent if he or she "exercises due diligence in an effort to apply the rules and regulations to the information given" to him or her. Treas.Reg. § 1.6694–1(a)(1). This due diligence requirement means that a preparer must act as a reasonable, prudent person with respect to the information supplied to the preparer. We hold that if the information supplied would lead a reasonable, prudent preparer

---

4. These cases were decided under § 6653(a), relating to disregard of rules or regulations by taxpayers on their own returns. Congress has indicated that § 6694(a) is to be interpreted in a manner similar to § 6653(a). *See* H.R.Rep. No. 658, 94th Cong., 2d Sess. 278, *reprinted in* 1976 U.S.Code Cong. & Ad.News at 3174.

to seek additional information, it is negligent not to do so. A reasonable, prudent preparer would inquire as to additional information where it is apparent that the information supplied was incorrect or incomplete and it is simple to collect the necessary additional information.

We find this standard of care to be consistent with the congressional purpose behind section 6694(a). Congress passed section 6694 as part of an attempt to curb abusive practices by preparers. For a preparer to ignore the implications of information furnished where the error is apparent and simple to correct would be an abusive practice. We note that the IRS has interpreted section 6694(a) to apply to situations where the preparer has reason to know that the information supplied is incomplete or incorrect. *See* Rev.Rul. 80–265, 1980–2 C.B. 378 (under section 6694(a), although the preparer is not required to audit information, "the preparer may not ignore the implications of information furnished to the preparer") (citing guidelines set forth in Rev.Proc. 80–40, 1980–2 C.B. 774–75).

Applying the standard of care outlined above to the facts in this case, we agree with the district court that the appellant was negligent in failing to inquire whether any of the interest paid by the corporation had been paid to Dr. Busch. The error involved was relatively apparent. The appellant was aware that Dr. Busch had made loans to the corporation and that the corporation had made interest payments.[5] This should have alerted him to the possibility that interest had been paid to Dr. Busch. The appellant also was aware that the Busches did not report any interest paid on the loans made to the corporation. This should have alerted him to the possibility that the information supplied to him was not complete. The fact that a loan from a shareholder to a corporation could bear interest and that such interest would be income to the shareholder is not uncommon. Moreover, the appellant could have discovered the error merely by asking the corporation or the Busches whether any of the interest paid by the corporation had been paid to the Busches or by requesting and examining the corporate ledger. A prudent preparer would have inquired about interest payments on the loans rather than ignoring the implications of the information furnished.[6] Appellant's negligent failure to inquire led him to disregard the applicability of section 61, which provides that gross

---

5. The appellant contends that there is no proof that he received the corporate trial balance sheet before he prepared the individual return. We do not regard the order in which he prepared the returns as significant. Even if he prepared the individual return first, the corporate trial balance sheet should have alerted him to the possibility of interest payments to Dr. Busch. At that time, he should have made the appropriate inquiries, recognizing that an amended individual return might be necessary.

6. We do not regard the appellant's failure to obtain a completed data questionnaire from the Busches as significant in determining whether he was negligent. The parties stipulated that a client did not have to fill out the questionnaire but rather could use it as a guide. Stipulation of Facts ¶ 10.

income includes interest income.⁷ Thus, appellant is liable under section 6694(a).

Affirmed.

WILLIAM J. CAMPBELL, SENIOR DISTRICT JUDGE, dissenting.

I regret that I cannot agree with the majority either in its construction of the statute or in its application to this case. The majority utilizes a general negligence analysis which is not justified by the language of the statute or the legislative history. In doing so it has given a broad interpretation to the statute in contravention of the principle that penal statutes are to be strictly construed. Furthermore, the majority has failed to present all the material facts and thus does not properly analyze the appellant's conduct. While the penalty assessed is quite modest, the sanction is important to the professional standing of the appellant. Moreover, this is the first published case involving this aspect of 26 U.S.C. § 6694(a). For these reasons, it is important that this case receive careful consideration.

The facts were presented to the district court in the form of a lengthy written stipulation. As noted by the majority, it is undisputed that the trial balance sheet indicated loans to the corporation from Dr. Busch and included entries for interest expense.¹ However, the balance sheet also noted that Rubert-Busch, M.D., S.C. borrowed money from the Michigan Avenue National Bank. The data submitted to Brockhouse did not indicate to whom the interest was paid as that information was irrelevant to the preparation of the corporate tax returns. Furthermore, the Busches' 1977 income tax return, which the appellant compared with the data for the 1978 return, accurately reflected no income from interest on loans to the corporation. These facts are crucial to an evaluation of appellant's conduct because they indicate that the information presented to him did not create the implication that Dr. Busch received interest income from the corporation in 1978. It is a common business practice for sole shareholders to make interest-free loans to their corporations. Such transactions can be compared to taking money out of one pocket and putting it in the other pocket. The data presented to Brockhouse was entirely consistent with this scenario. Therefore, I believe it is overstating the case to say that appellant ignored the implications of the information provided to him.

The majority notes that the appellant prepared the income tax return of Dr. and Mrs. Busch without requiring them to comply with

---

7. The appellant argues that § 7216, providing sanctions for unauthorized disclosure of information by tax return preparers, prohibited him from using information obtained from the corporate trial balance sheet in attempting to prepare the individual return. However, it appears that the regulations permit such disclosure. Treas.Reg. § 301.7216-2.

1. The stipulation of the parties reads:

This trial balance sheet contained an item showing loans made by the Corporation to its sole shareholder. Stip. ¶ 14.

This is apparently an error as it is undisputed that Dr. Busch made the loans to the corporation.

the Goldman, Weiss data questionnaire procedure.[2] The district judge relied heavily on this fact as evidence of Brockhouse's lack of due diligence. However, the information was given to the appellant by Robert Eubank, the corporation's business manager and Dr. Busch's personal financial consultant. The data was prepared by the corporation's part-time bookkeeper who had a degree in law and business and was employed on a full-time basis by a national firm of certified public accountants. The fact that Brockhouse did not require compliance with the questionnaire procedure is not compelling, or even persuasive, evidence of negligence where the information was gathered by experienced specialists and not laypersons.

Turning to the statute in issue, the majority utilizes a general negligence analysis in determining the applicability of the penalty. They state:

> Congress did not limit the applicability of section 6694 to situations involving disregard of rules or regulations applicable to the facts as provided by the taxpayer. Rather, it applies generally to "negligent disregard." p. 1251

I do not understand what "negligent disregard" in the abstract is, but I do know that such a selective editing of the statute is not supported by the legislative history. The majority relies on *Marcello v. Commissioner*, 380 F.2d 499 (5th Cir.1967), *cert. den.*, 389 U.S. 1044, 88 S.Ct. 787, 19 L.Ed.2d 835 (1968), a case applying 26 U.S.C. § 6653(a), as authority for the application of a general negligence standard. The justification for such reliance is provided in a footnote:

> Congress has indicated that § 6694(a) is to be interpreted in a manner similar to § 6653(a). *See* H.R.Rep. No. 658, 94th Cong., 2d Sess. 278, *reprinted in* 1976 U.S.Code Cong. & Ad.News at 3174. fn. 4.

This statement is an oversimplification. The penalty provision in § 6653 applies to taxpayers for under-payments "due to *negligence* or intentional disregard of rules or regulations" [Emphasis supplied]. The penalty provision in § 6694 applies to "*negligent* or intentional disregard of rules or regulations" [Emphasis supplied]. Thus, under § 6653 two discrete standards of conduct are involved: general negligence and intentional disregard of rules or regulations, *see discussion Marcello, supra*, 380 F.2d at 505–507. However, under § 6694 there must be a disregard of rules or regulations (either negligent or intentional) in order to impose the penalty.

* * *

In summary, the language of the statute does not provide that the penalty applies to all acts of negligence by an income tax preparer. While clearly § 6694(a) is modelled after § 6653(a) there is a significant difference in the terms of the statutes and we must assume that that distinction was intended by Congress. * * *

---

2. The majority indicates in footnote 6 that it did not consider this fact to be significant in evaluating Brockhouse's conduct. I agree with them on that point and I discuss the issue only because the district court found that evidence to be persuasive.

Sec. 4   PREPARER, PROMOTER & PROTESTER   291

* * *

Thus, we are strictly limited to determining whether Brockhouse "disregarded a rule or regulation" either negligently or intentionally. The standard provided in the IRS's regulations is:

> A preparer is not considered to have negligently or intentionally disregarded a rule or regulation if the preparer exercises due diligence in an effort to apply the rules and regulations to the information given to the preparer to determine the taxpayer's correct liability for tax. 26 C.F.R. § 1.6694–1(a).

In this case, there is no question that Brockhouse properly applied the rules and regulations to the information he received. The underpayment of tax occurred because he was not informed that Dr. Busch received interest on his loans to the corporation. The issue then becomes whether he was justified in relying on the information provided. Rev.Proc. 80–40 provides:

> .03 The penalty under section 6694(a) of the Code generally will not apply where a preparer in good faith relies without verification upon information furnished by the taxpayer. Thus, the preparer is not required to audit, examine or review books and records, business operations, or documents or other evidence in order to verify independently the taxpayer's information.

This language further exculpates the appellant. There is a caveat, however:

> [T]he preparer may not ignore the implications of information furnished to the preparer or which was actually known by the preparer. The preparer shall make reasonable inquiries if the information as furnished appears to be incorrect or incomplete. Rev.Proc. 80–40.

I have no quarrel with this standard of conduct, but I do not think the appellant violated it in this case. It is undisputed that Brockhouse did not have any personal knowledge of the financial operations of Rubert-Busch, M.D., S.C. Furthermore, I do not believe we can find that the information provided to him appeared incorrect or incomplete. The corporation's trial balance sheet, the Busches' income data, and their 1977 income tax return are all consistent with a situation in which a sole shareholder made interest-free loans to his corporation. There was no data presented to Brockhouse which contradicted that common scenario. Thus, I do not believe that we can find that the appellant ignored the implication of the information provided to him.[4]

---

4. Revenue Ruling 80–265 presents two factual situations similar to ours with slight, but significant, differences. In Situation 1, the income tax preparer had no knowledge of any loans by the sole shareholder to the corporation, although he did deduct an interest expense on the corporate return. Subsequently, it was determined by the IRS that the shareholder had loaned money to the corporation and received interest income on it. The Revenue Ruling concludes that the penalty provision of § 6694(a) does not apply to the income tax preparer in that situation. In Situation 2 the information relating to the corporation indicated that the shareholder had received interest on loans to the corporation. However, the data provided the income tax preparer with respect to the shareholder's individual return did not reflect the interest income. The failure to

In conclusion, I believe there is no basis for finding that Brockhouse disregarded any rule or regulation of the IRS. That is the conduct described in the statute and that is the conduct that Congress intended to penalize. If Congress had intended to sanction all negligence by income tax preparers, it would have said so. But it did not and we should not redraft the legislation. We are duty bound to apply the plain language of the statute and to construe it narrowly. Under those guidelines I believe it is clear that the imposition of the penalty in this case is in error and the District Court should be reversed.

Notes

1. On February 28, 1991, the Service issued Proposed Regulations under § 6694. Prop.Reg. §§ 1.6694-1—1.6694-4. Under these Proposed Regulations, would the results in *Judisch* and *Brockhouse* be the same?

The following overview of the Proposed Regulations may be helpful.

Overview of the 1991 Proposed Return Preparer Regulations

I. Section 1.6694-1: Section 6694 Penalties Applicable to Income Tax Return Preparer

A. Section 1.6694-1(a): Overview.

Section 6694 imposes penalties on return preparers for certain understatements of liability on a return or a claim for refund. Section 6694(a) imposes a penalty where the understatement of income tax liability is due to a position for which there was not a realistic possibility of being sustained on the merits. Section 6694(b) imposes a penalty where the understatement is due to a willful attempt to understate the liability or due to a reckless or intentional disregard of rules or regulations.

B. Section 1.6694-1(b)(1) and (2): Income Tax Return Preparer Definitions.

The regulation provides that a "return preparer" means any person who is an income tax return preparer within the meaning of § 7701(a)(36) and Reg. § 301.7701-15. According to the proposed regulation, only one individual associated with a firm is treated as a preparer for the same return or claim for refund.

The proposed regulation distinguishes between a "signing preparer" and a "nonsigning preparer." A "signing preparer" is any preparer who signs a return or claim for refund as a preparer. A "nonsigning preparer" is a preparer who is not a signing preparer. A "nonsigning preparer," for example, is a preparer who provides advice (written or oral) to a taxpayer or to a preparer who is not associated with the same firm as the preparer who provides the advice.

If a signing preparer is associated with a firm, that individual is a preparer for purposes of section 6694. If two or more individuals associat-

report that item of income on the shareholder's tax return was determined to justify imposition of the penalty under § 6694(a). The reasoning was that in Situation 2 the income tax preparer had reason to believe that the information provided to him was incomplete, while in Situation 1 he did not. Our case falls in between those two situations and, utilizing the same analysis, the penalty should not apply.

ed with a firm are preparers within the meaning of § 7701(a)(36), and none of them is a signing preparer, then for purposes of § 6694, the preparer is the individual with direct supervisory responsibility for the matter. The principle is that only one person in the firm will be liable for the penalty.

C. Example.

Attorney A provides advice to Client C concerning the proper treatment of a significant item on C's income tax return. The advice constitutes preparation of a substantial portion of the return. In preparation for providing that advice, A discusses the matter with Attorney B, who is associated with the same firm as A, but A is the attorney with direct supervisory responsibility for the matter. For purposes of the regulations under § 6694, A is a preparer with respect to C's return and is subject to penalty under § 6694 with respect to C's return. B is not a preparer with respect to C's return and, therefore, is not subject to penalty under § 6694 with respect to a position taken on C's return. This would be true even if B recommends that A advise C to take an undisclosed position that did not satisfy the realistic possibility standard. In addition, since B is not a preparer for purposes of the regulations under § 6694, A may not avoid a penalty under § 6694 with respect to C's return by claiming he relied on the advice of B. See Prop.Reg. § 1.6694-2(d)(5).

D. Section 1.6694-1(c): Understatement of Liability.

For purposes of § 6694 and the regulations, an "understatement of liability" exists if, viewing the return or claim for refund as a whole, there is an understatement of the net amount payable with respect to any tax imposed or an overstatement of the net amount creditably or refundable with respect to any tax imposed.

E. Section 1.6694-1(e): Verification of Information Furnished by Taxpayer.

For purposes of § 6694(a) and (b), a preparer may generally rely in good faith without verification upon information furnished by a taxpayer. However, the preparer may not ignore the implications of information furnished or actually known by the preparer. The preparer must make reasonable inquiries if the information as furnished appears to be incorrect or incomplete.

F. Section 1.6694-1(f): Effective Date.

Sections 1.6694-1 through 1.6694-3 are effective for documents prepared and advice given after December 31, 1991. Section 6694 and the existing rules and regulations thereunder (to the extent not inconsistent with the statute) and Notice 90-20, 1990-1 C.B. 328, apply to documents prepared and advice given on or before December 31, 1991.

II. Section 1.6694-2: Penalty for Understatement Due to an Unrealistic Position

A. Section 1.6694-2(a): In General.

If any part of an understatement of liability relating to a return or claim for refund of tax is due to a position for which there was not a realistic possibility of being sustained on its merits, any person who is a preparer with respect to such return or claim for refund who knew or reasonably should have known of such position is subject to a penalty of $250. An employer or partnership of a preparer subject to this penalty is also subject to the penalty if the employer or partnership also knew or reasonably should have known of the position.

B. Section 1.6694-2(b)(1): Realistic Possibility of Being Sustained on its Merits

A position is considered to have a realistic possibility of being sustained on its merits if a reasonable and well-informed analysis by a person knowledgeable in the tax law would lead such a person to conclude that the position has approximately a one in three, or greater, likelihood of being sustained on its merits. One may not take into account the chance that a return will not be audited by the Service. The regulations give nine examples of the realistic possibility standard in § 1.6694-2(b)(3).

C. Section 1.6694-2(b)(5)(i) and (ii): When "Realistic Possibility" is Determined.

In the case of a signing preparer, the relevant date to determine the realistic possibility requirement is the date the preparer signs and dates the return or claim for refund. If the preparer did not date the return or claim for refund, the relevant date is the date the taxpayer signed and dated the return. If the taxpayer did not date the document, the relevant date is the date the form was filed.

In the case of a nonsigning preparer, the relevant date is the date the preparer provides the advice.

D. Section 1.6694-2(c)(1)-(3): Exception for Adequate Disclosure of Nonfrivolous Positions.

The § 6694(a) penalty will not be imposed if the position taken is not frivolous and is adequately disclosed. A "frivolous" position with respect to an item is one that is patently improper.

For a signing preparer, there is adequate disclosure only if the disclosure is made in accordance with § 1.6662-4(f) which permits disclosure on a properly completed and filed Form 8275 or on the return in accordance with revenue procedure.

For a nonsigning preparer, there are two additional means to satisfy adequate disclosure. If a nonsigning preparer provides advice with respect to a position that does not satisfy the realistic possibility standard, disclosure is adequate if the advice includes a statement that the position lacks substantial authority and, therefore, may be subject to penalty under § 6662(d) unless adequately disclosed in the manner provided in § 1.6662-4(f). If the advice is in writing, the statement concerning disclosure should also be in writing. If the advice is oral, the statement concerning the need to disclose may also be oral.

E. Section 1.6694-2(d)(1)-(5): Exception for Reasonable Cause and Good Faith and Factors Considered.

If, after considering all the facts and circumstances, it can be established that the preparer acted reasonably and in good faith, the penalty under § 6694(a) will not be imposed. Factors taken into account include the nature of the error causing the understatement, the frequency of errors, the materiality of the errors, the preparer's normal office practice and reliance on the advice of another preparer.

F. Section 1.6694–2(e)(1)–(3): Burden of Proof.

The preparer bears the burden of proof that he neither knew nor reasonably should have known that the questioned position was taken on the return; that there is reasonable cause and good faith with respect to such position; and that the position was disclosed adequately.

III. Section 1.6694–3: Penalty for Understatement Due to Willful, Reckless or Intentional Conduct

    A. Section 1.6694–3(a)(1) and (2): In General.

If any part of an understatement or claim for refund is due to a willful attempt in any manner, any reckless or intentional disregard of rules or regulations, such preparer is subject to a penalty of $1,000. An employer or partnership of a preparer is also subject to penalty if they also participated in the willful attempt or participated in or knew of the reckless or intentional disregard of a rule or regulation.

    B. Section 1.6694–3(b) and (c)(1)–(3): Willful Attempt and Reckless or Intentional Disregard.

A preparer has willfully attempted to understate liability if he disregards, in an attempt wrongfully to reduce the tax liability of the taxpayer, information furnished by the taxpayer or other persons.

A preparer is considered to have recklessly or intentionally disregarded a rule or regulation if the preparer takes a position on the return or claim for refund that is contrary to a rule or regulation and the preparer knows of, or is reckless in not knowing of, the rule or regulation. A preparer is reckless if he makes little or no effort to determine whether a rule or regulation exists.

A preparer is not considered to have recklessly or intentionally disregarded a rule or regulation if a position contrary to a revenue ruling has a realistic possibility of being sustained on its merits.

    C. Section 1.6694–3(e)(1) and (2): Adequate Disclosure.

For a signing and nonsigning preparer, disclosure of a position that is contrary to a rule or regulation is adequate if the position is disclosed on a properly completed and filed form 8275. The disclosure must adequately identify the rule or regulation being challenged.

Additionally, for a nonsigning preparer who provides advice to a taxpayer with respect to a position contrary to a rule or regulation, disclosure is adequate if the advice includes a statement that the position is contrary to a specific rule or regulation and, therefore, is subject to a penalty under § 6662(c) unless adequately disclosed. If the advice was in writing, the statement must be in writing. If the advice was oral, the statement may be made orally. If the advice was to another preparer, disclosure is adequate if that advice includes a statement that disclosure under § 6694(b) is required.

    D. Section 1.6694–3(g): Section 6694(b) Penalty Reduced by 6694(a) Penalty.

The amount of any penalty imposed under § 6694(b) is $1,000 minus any amount assessed and collected against the preparer under § 6694(a) for the same return or claim for refund.

E. Section 1.6694–3(h): Burden of Proof

With respect to a penalty imposed under § 6694(b), the Government bears the burden of proof on the issue of whether the preparer willfully attempted to understate the liability for tax. The preparer bears the burden of proof on the issues of whether the preparer recklessly or intentionally disregarded a rule or regulation and whether disclosure was adequate.

IV. Section 1.6694–4: Extension of Period of Collection Where Preparer Pays 15% of a Penalty for Understatement of Taxpayer's Liability and Certain Other Procedural Matters.

A. Section 1.6694–4(a)(1)–(4): In General.

The IRS will investigate the preparation by a preparer of a return or claim for refund and send a report of the examination to the preparer before the assessment of either a penalty under § 6694(a) or (b). If either of these two penalties is assessed, the IRS will send a statement of notice and demand to the preparer, separate from any notice of tax deficiency.

Within 30 days after the day on which notice and demand of either of the two penalties is made against the preparer, he must either pay the entire amount assessed or pay an amount which is not less than 15% of the entire amount assessed with respect to each return or claim for refund. If the preparer pays the entire amount, he may file a claim for refund at any time not later than three years after the date of payment. If the preparer pays at least 15%, he is entitled to file a claim for refund of the amount paid and the IRS may not make, begin or prosecute a levy for collection of the unpaid remainder until a later determined time. See § 1.6694–4(a)(4).

B. Section 1.6694–4(b): Effective Date.

The provisions of § 1.6694–4 are effective as of December 19, 1989.

2. *Unrealistic positions.* Recall from Chapter 2 that tax practitioners have been subject to various standards of conduct imposed by the Code (in § 6694), by professional organizations (such as the ABA), and by the Treasury Department (in Circular 230). In changing the standard of § 6694(a) from "negligent or intentional disregard of rules or regulations" to taking "a position for which there was not a realistic possibility of being sustained on its merits," Congress closely tracked the standard that had been recommended by lawyers' and accountants' professional organizations. While some standards might be fairly easy to quantify, this new standard was not. For example, if the standard is "more likely than not to be correct," then the position must have a greater than 50% chance of being correct. How sure must the preparer be of the position to avoid the post-1989 penalty under section 6694(a)? See Prop.Reg. § 1.6694–2(b), which provides:

A position is considered to have a realistic possibility of being sustained on its merits if a reasonable and well-informed analysis by a person knowledgeable in the tax law would lead such a person to conclude that the position has approximately a one-in-three, or greater, likelihood of being sustained on its merits (realistic possibility standard).

3. Given the stakes involved, how do you determine whether you are an income tax return preparer with respect to a return or claim for refund? Consult Reg. § 301.7701-15 and Rev.Rul. 81-246, 1981-2 C.B. 249.

4. Firms that prepare computer programs and sell them to tax practitioners can be income tax return preparers subject to penalty under section 6694 and 6695 if the program goes beyond mere mechanical assistance, as can companies that prepare computer programs and sell them directly to taxpayers for use in preparing their own returns. Rev.Rul. 85-187, 1985-2 C.B. 338; Rev.Rul 85-189, 1985-2 C.B. 341.

5. Congress expressed its concern that the stricter standard of § 6694 as amended in 1989 not lead to massive referrals of return preparers to the IRS Director of Practice for possible sanctions under Circular 230. According to the legislative history: "The committee intends that imposition of this penalty not lead to an automatic referral to the Internal Revenue Service Director of Practice. The committee believes that the IRS should exercise discretion in referring specific cases to the Director of Practice. The committee also intends that, in exercising this discretion in response to this provision, the IRS not generally expand its investigations of preparer penalty cases." H.R.Rep. 101-247, 101st Cong., 1st Sess. 1396 (1989).

One of the "administrative recommendations" made by Congress as part of IMPACT was as follows: "The IRS should instruct its employees that they cannot threaten the use of preparer penalties during an examination, Appeals conference, or other proceedings involving a tax advisor." H.R.Rep. 101-247, 101st Cong., 1st Sess. 1406 (1989).

B. PROMOTING ABUSIVE TAX SHELTERS

GATES v. UNITED STATES
United States Court of Appeals, Eighth Circuit, 1989.
874 F.2d 584.

PER CURIAM: Bill Gates appeals from the district court's order granting summary judgment against him in his suit contesting a $69,000 penalty assessed against him by the Internal Revenue Service (IRS) for promoting abusive tax shelters. On appeal Gates challenges the district court's determination of liability and its assessment of penalties. We affirm on the issue of liability and reverse as to the assessment of penalties.

In 1982 and 1983 Gates became involved with the promotion of two tax shelter schemes established by H & L Schwartz, Inc. (Schwartz, Inc.). Gates encouraged people to invest in American Educational Leasing (AEL) and American Videogame Leasing (AVL), by leasing recordings and video programs for a stated price. AEL or AVL would then pass through to each investor/lessee an investment tax credit calculated at 10% of the program's stated purchase price, which Schwartz, Inc. stated was equivalent to the program's fair market value. Section 48(d) of the Internal Revenue Code of 1954 permitted a lessor to pass the investment tax credit through to a lessee, provided the lessee "acquired" the property for an amount equal to its fair market value.

Gates, as a representative for AEL and AVL solicited tax preparers by presenting promotional material containing projections of the tax benefits to be derived by the investors. These presentations included slide/videotape shows detailing how the audio and video programs were manufactured and how they were to be reproduced and distributed, and referred to various appraisals to answer questions concerning the programs' purported fair market value. Gates received a percentage of the money on every lease completed by tax preparers he recruited. Eventually, Gates received fees on 132 leases, totaling $79,791.

In an earlier proceeding, a United States district court in California, after hearing testimony that the audio programs were essentially worthless and the video programs were overvalued by at least 2000% found that Schwartz, Inc. and its chief operating officer had been promoting a fraudulent tax scheme in violation of 26 U.S.C. § 6700[1] (amended 1984). Subsequently, the IRS established that Gates had participated in the sale of sixty-nine interests in the Schwartz, Inc. tax shelters, and under section 67 assessed a penalty of $1000 per sale, for a total of $69,000.

Gates paid a portion of the penalty and filed an administrative claim for refund, which was denied by the IRS. He then filed this refund suit in the Eastern District Court of Arkansas claiming that (1) he had never assisted in the organization of the scheme, nor furnished a gross valuation overstatement; and, alternatively, (2) the penalty should have been assessed at 10% of the gross income derived from his alleged participation ($7971), instead of $1000 per sale ($69,000).

The district court granted the government's motion for summary judgment, finding that the evidence that Gates had solicited, trained, and equipped salesmen for the AEL and AVL programs was sufficient to establish that he "assisted in the organization" within the meaning

---

1. Section 6700 provides as follows: Promoting abusive tax shelters, *etc.*

    (a) Imposition of penalty.—Any person who—

    (1)(A) organizes (or assists in the organization of)—

    (i) a partnership or other entity,

    (ii) any investment plan or arrangement, or

    (iii) any other plan or arrangement, or

    (B) participates in the sale of any interest in an entity or plan or arrangement referred to in sub-paragraph (A), and

    (2) makes or furnishes (in connection with such organization or sale)—

    (A) a statement with respect to the allowability of any deduction or credit, the excludability of any income, or the securing of any other tax benefit by reason of holding an interest in the entity or participating in the plan or arrangement which the person knows or has reason to know is false or fraudulent as to any material matter, or

    (B) a gross valuation overstatement as to any material matter,

    shall pay a penalty equal to the greater of $1,000 or 10 percent of the gross income derived or to be derived by such person from such activity.

of section 6700(a)(1)(A)(ii), and that his admission that he had furnished the offering materials containing the valuation overstatements was sufficient to establish he "furnished" such statements within the meaning of section 6700(a)(2)(B). Because the section imposed strict liability, the court concluded that Gates' alleged ignorance of the overvaluation was no defense. Finally, the court granted summary judgment on the issue of the proper calculation of the penalty, finding that "the plain language of the statute and the weight of authority favors the government's position."

A. LIABILITY

Gates acknowledged he recruited tax preparers to market AEL and AVL business opportunities to their clients, recruited sales people to solicit tax preparers and to sell interests in AEL and AVL, "strongly pointed out" to those he recruited that they were not to give tax advice, and "made clear" they were to enlist tax preparers in the same way he did. He also admitted that in responding to questions about the valuation, he would refer individuals to the valuation statements contained in the promotional offering materials. This conduct is sufficient to satisfy the requirements of section 6700.

Gates also seeks to avoid liability on the ground that he did not know that the valuations were gross overstatements. When read in its entirety, however, section 6700(a)(2) indicates that the government can establish liability by showing that a person made or furnished either a tax-related statement he knew or had reason to know was false *or* a gross valuation overstatement. Accordingly, knowledge is relevant only when a promoter furnishes a false tax-related statement.

B. PENALTY CALCULATION

Under section 6700, the penalty for organizing or promoting abusive tax shelters is assessed as "the greater of $1,000 or 10 percent [now 20 percent] of the gross income derived or to be derived by such person *from such activity.*" 26 U.S.C. § 6700(a) (emphasis added).

Gates argues that section 6700 mandates a minimum penalty equal to the greater of $1000 per year or 10% (now 20%) of the total amount of income earned from the sale of such shelters in any one year and that the assessment should be on an annual tax-year basis.

The IRS argues that the statute's use of singular terms—organization, sale, penalty, activity—clearly indicates congressional intent to impose a separate penalty of $1000, or 10% of the income derived from each organization of an abusive tax shelter or each sale of an interest therein. Accordingly, it argues that the penalty should be calculated on a transactional basis, *i.e.,* a minimum $1000 penalty for each prohibited sale. It also argues that the penalty should be assessed once for the overall activity.

1. *Standard of Review*

We are mindful that an interpretation given a statute by the administering agency is entitled to considerable deference. *Groseclose*

v. Bowen, 809 F.2d 502, 505 (8th Cir.1987). This deference, however, "is constrained by our obligation to honor the clear meaning of the statute, as revealed by its language, purpose, and history." *International Bhd. of Teamsters v. Daniel,* 439 U.S. 551, 566 n. 20 (1979). We also recognize that although the section 6700 penalty is an important weapon in the IRS's efforts to eliminate abusive shelters, the penalty must be assessed fairly. Furthermore, principles of statutory interpretation require resolution of ambiguities in penalty statutes in favor of lenity. See *United States v. Anderson,* 626 F.2d 1358, 1370 (8th Cir. 1980), *cert. denied,* 450 U.S. 912 (1981). Accordingly, we conclude that a transactional "per sale" assessment is not supported by a reasoned analysis of the statute or legislative history and that such interpretation would lead to inequitable results. We agree with the IRS, however, that the assessment should be made on a one-time basis rather than annually.

2. Calculation of Penalty on Non-Transactional Basis

Lower court decisions that have addressed the meaning of "such activity" in the context of section 6700 penalties have reached different results. Of the reported decisions, we find the analysis in *Spriggs v. United States* [87-2 USTC ¶ 9392], 660 F.Supp. 789, 791 (E.D.Va.1987), *Aff'd without published opinion,* 850 F.2d 690 (4th Cir.1988), and *In re Bowen* [88-1 USTC ¶ 9373], 84 Bankr. 214 (Bankr.D. Utah 1988), to be most persuasive.[2] As noted in *Spriggs,* the term "activity" stands in contrast to the use of "organization or sale" in the previous subsection. Had Congress intended the penalty to apply to each separate sale, it could have repeated the phrase "such organization or sale" or used explicit language to that effect, as it did in other penalty provisions.[3]

Gates' reading of the statute is further bolstered by the legislative history. In 1982 Congress enacted section 6700 to attack the source of abusive tax shelters by penalizing the "promoters." See S.Rep. No. 494, 97th Cong., 2d Sess. 1, *reprinted in* 1982 U.S.Code Cong. & Admin.News 781, 1014. In 1984 Congress concluded that the existing section 6700 did not effectively deter abusive tax shelter promoters, and it raised the penalty from 10% to 20% of income derived from the activity. The House Committee Report on the 1984 Act states:

> The bill increases the penalty for promoting abusive tax shelters to the greater of 20 percent of the gross income derived, or to be derived, from the activity, or $1,000. The committee did not increase the $1,000 penalty because, as originally enacted, the $1,000 was intended to be a

---

2. But see *Popkin v. United States,* 88-2 USTC (CCH) ¶ 9461 (N.D.Ga.1988) (penalty assessed per transaction); *Johnson v. United States* [88-1 USTC ¶ 9149], 677 F.Supp. 529, 531 (E.D.Mich.1988) (same); *Waltman v. United States* [86-1 USTC ¶ 9222], 618 F.Supp. 718, 720 (M.D.Fla.1985) (same).

3. Individuals who aid and abet in the understatement of tax liability must pay a penalty "with respect to each such document" (26 U.S.C. § 6701(a) (1982)). Similarly, a penalty for failure to supply a taxpayer identification number (26 U.S.C. § 6676(e)), or to supply information on a place of residence (26 U.S.C. § 6687), or a tax shelter identification number (26 U.S.C. § 6707(b) (Supp. IV 1986)) applies to "each such failure."

minimum penalty on small promoters who derive little income from the deals they promote.

H.R.Rep. No. 432, 98th Cong., 2d Sess., 1357–58, *reprinted in* 1984 U.S.Code Cong. & Admin.News 697, 1009.

This comment indicates that the $1,000 amount was not to be compounded as a means of punishing high-volume tax shelter promoters, but rather established a minimum penalty to be applied when 20% of the gross income from the activity of promoting abusive tax shelters fell below $1000. Although the government argues that the opinion of a Congress subsequent to the Congress that enacted section 6700 deserves little weight, views of a subsequent Congress are entitled to significant weight when the precise intent of the enacting Congress is obscure. See *Seatrain Shipbuilding Corp. v. Shell Oil Co.*, 444 U.S. 572, 596 (1980).

The IRS also argues that Congress intended the penalty to be a means of reimbursing the IRS for the cost of auditing individual returns of persons involved in tax shelter schemes, thereby making it entirely appropriate to impose a penalty based on each sale. We disagree. A close reading of the legislative history reveals that Congress was concerned with the IRS's limited resources and determined that they could be used more economically by focusing on the prevention of tax shelters instead of enforcement actions. "[T]he Internal Revenue Service can be expected to approach the problem with vigor since prevention * * * will require less manpower than enforcement action against numerous investors-taxpayers." H.R.Rep. No. 494, 97th Cong.2d Sess. 1, *reprinted in* 1982 U.S.Code Cong. & Admin.News 781, 1014.

In addition, as noted in *In re Bowen,* 84 Bankr. at 218, the scope of section 6700 covers both organizers and sellers. Under the IRS's reading, organizers who retain several individual sellers would likely be subjected to a 10% penalty for the creation of the overall shelter, whereas the sellers would likely be penalized $1000 per sale. We find no legislative support for punishing sellers more severely than organizers, and we conclude that such an inconsistent application would not aid in achieving the goal of discouraging abusive tax shelters.

Moreover, as noted in *Spriggs,* 660 F.Supp. at 792, the IRS's reading could result in inequitable penalty assessments between two promoters: one who earns a 10% commission on the sale of one shelter for $10,000; the other who earns a 10% commission on the sale of ten shelters for $1000 each. Although each seller earned $1000 in commission, the first would be penalized $1000, the second $10,000. Although the IRS argues that a larger penalty is justified in the second instance because of the increased administrative work generated by multiple proscribed sales, we have already concluded that Congress did not intend the penalty provision to be a means of reimbursing the IRS for the cost of auditing returns.

Finally, the IRS argues that Gates' reading of the statute would result in his paying a penalty of approximately $7900 on three years' gross income totaling approximately $79,000, a penalty that hardly furthers the legislative goal of deterring the organization of abusive tax shelters. Nevertheless, Congress chose a percentage penalty instead of opting for a complete forfeiture of all income derived from abusive tax shelter schemes, and we are bound by that choice.

3. Assessment Period

The assessment of section 6700 penalties is governed by 26 U.S.C. § 6671 which reads in relevant part:

(a) **Penalty assessed as tax.—**

The penalties and liabilities provided by this subchapter shall be paid upon notice and demand by the Secretary, and shall be assessed and collected in the same manner as taxes. Except as otherwise provided, any reference in this title to 'tax' imposed by this title shall be deemed also to refer to the penalties and liabilities provided by this subchapter.

The IRS argues that the penalty should be assessed once. Gates argues the penalty should be assessed annually, and urges us to adopt the analysis of the *Spriggs* court which focused on the language directing that penalties "be assessed * * * in the same manner as taxes," and concluded that an annual basis determination was proper because taxes are assessed on an annual basis. *Spriggs,* 660 F.Supp. at 791 n. 2.

We do not find this conclusory statement persuasive. Indeed, it does not appear that section 6671 dictates any particular assessment period for section 6700 penalties, which do not relate to any specific tax. Accordingly, we find the IRS's assessment based on all tax-shelter income, actually received or reasonably expected to be received at the time of the assessment, to be reasonable, as it makes computation of the penalty administratively easier.

Accordingly, we affirm in part, reverse in part, and remand for further proceedings consistent with this opinion.

Notes

1. IMPACT made several changes to § 6700. First, it clarified the amount of the penalty. As *Gates* explains, prior to 1989, the penalty was the greater of $1,000 or 20% of the gross income from the activity, and the courts had split on the issue of how to calculate the penalty. IMPACT clarified that the penalty (now the greater of $1,000 or 100% of the gross income from the activity) applies to each separate sale of an interest in an abusive tax shelter.

2. IMPACT also broadened the scope of § 6700, which now applies to anyone who participates directly or indirectly in the sale of interests in abusive tax shelters. The legislative history describes the section's potential applicability to those involved in issuing state or municipal bonds:

[T]he penalty may apply to bond counsel, investment bankers and their counsel, issuers (and beneficiaries of "conduit" bonds) and their counsel, financial advisors, feasibility consultants and engineers, and other persons, who (1) are involved in the organization or sale of such State or local government bonds and (2) know or have reason to know that their opinions, offering documents, reports, or other statements (or material on which they relied in making such statements) are false or fraudulent as to any matter material to the tax exemption of the interest on the bonds. A person who makes a statement facilitating the issuance or sale of State or local government bonds (including a sale subsequent to the issuance of the bonds) is involved in the organization or sale of such bonds. [H.R.Rep. 101–247, 101st Cong., 1st Sess. 1391.]

3. Should the general 3–year statute of limitations apply to assessment of the section 6700 penalty? The Fifth Circuit has held that it does not apply and that there is no limitation period on assessment of the penalty. Sage v. United States, 908 F.2d 18 (5th Cir.1990).

C. AIDING AND ABETTING UNDERSTATEMENT OF TAX LIABILITY

KUCHAN v. UNITED STATES

United States District Court, Northern District of Illinois, 1988.
679 F.Supp. 764.

MEMORANDUM OPINION

KOCORAS, DISTRICT JUDGE: This dispute concerns the interpretation and application of § 6701 of the Internal Revenue Code of 1954, as amended (the "Code"). 26 U.S.C.A. It is presently before the court on defendant's motion for partial summary judgment and plaintiff's motion for summary judgment. For the reasons contained herein, defendant's motion is granted and plaintiff's motion is denied.

FACTS

Plaintiff, William T. Kuchan, is a certified public accountant who provides tax and financial advice and reviews and prepares tax returns for his clients. He has been an accountant since 1952. On May 5, 1986, the Internal Revenue Service ("IRS") assessed penalties against plaintiff in the following amounts and for the following years: $95,000.00 for the taxable period ending December 31, 1983; $67,000.00 for the taxable period ending December 31, 1984; and $29,000.00 for the taxable period ending December 31, 1985.

Each penalty was based on plaintiff's activities involving an investment plan offered by Price Coal & Energy, Inc. ("Price Coal"). The investment plan involved coal mining leases entered into by investors. This plan had been offered by Price Coal over a period of years, between 1977 and 1985. The IRS determined that the investment plan was an abusive tax shelter.

In May of 1981, Kuchan began to provide services to Rodman G. Price, individually, and Price Coal. Kuchan prepared Price's personal income tax returns and corporate tax returns for Price Coal. Plaintiff also prepared tax returns and, in 1983 and 1984, financial statements for Coal Funding Corporation, a corporation involved in the investment plan with Price Coal.

In 1983, 1984 and 1985, plaintiff prepared a "transmittal letter" that was to be sent to each of the investors in the Price Coal coal mining plan. Plaintiff prepared these transmittal letters at the request of, and as a service to, Rodman Price, the president of Price Coal. Plaintiff was paid for preparing these transmittal letters.

Plaintiff knew that the transmittal letters were to be attached to "Schedule C's" which Price Coal sent to each of the investors in their investment plan. Schedule C's are tax return documents that are to be filed by persons who claim profits or losses from business activities on their tax returns. Kuchan did not prepare any of the Schedule C's or income tax returns for any investor.

Kuchan's letter dated January 28, 1983, with respect to the 1982 Schedule C's prepared on Kuchan's letterhead, is reproduced below:

"Dear Price Coal & Energy Lessee:

Enclosed please find a copy of Schedule C, Form 1040, Profit or (Loss) from Business or Profession. This indicates the amount of coal mining royalties for use as a deductible business expense in connection with the filing of your Federal Income Tax Return for the year ended December 31, 1982.

This is being transmitted to you in accordance with the information which has been provided by Price Coal & Energy, Inc.

Very truly yours,

William T. Kuchan"

With the exception of adding language that the Schedule C also related to "mine development expenses," the substance of the letters for tax years 1983 and 1984 were identical.

§ 6701, which plaintiff is alleged to have violated, provides in relevant part:

(a) Imposition of penalty.—Any person—

(1) who aids or assists in, procures, or advises with respect to, the preparation or presentation of any portion of a return, affidavit, claim, or other document in connection with any matter arising under the internal revenue laws,

(2) who knows that such portion will be used in connection with any material matter arising under the internal revenue laws, and

(3) who knows that such portion (if so used) will result in an understatement of the liability for tax of another person, shall pay

a penalty with respect to each such document in the amount determined under subsection (b).

(b) Amount of penalty.—

(1) In general.—... the amount of the penalty imposed by subsection (a) shall be $1,000.

26 U.S.C. § 6701. In determining the amount of the § 6701 penalty ultimately imposed on plaintiff, the IRS used listings of Price Coal's investors for 1982, 1983, and 1984, showing to whom the Schedule C's were to be sent. Over the three year period, there were 191 investors to whom the Schedule C's, with the accompanying transmittal letter, were sent.

Defendant's Motion for Partial Summary Judgment

Defendant's motion is limited to a single issue: assuming plaintiff violated § 6701 by preparing the three transmittal letters to accompany the Schedule C's which were sent to 191 investors, was it proper to compute the penalty based on the number of Schedule C's to which the transmittal letter was attached and sent out? Without expressing any opinion as to whether plaintiff is liable for *any* penalty under § 6701, we find that the method of computation which the IRS used in this case is proper.

Although plaintiff prepared only three letters, he knew that each letter was to be duplicated and sent to each investor as a cover letter for the Schedule C's which Price Coal prepared. Under § 6701, if plaintiff is subject to the imposition of a penalty at all, he is so subject "with respect to each such document in the amount of * * * $1,000." 26 U.S.C. § 6701(a) and (b). The "document" to which this language refers is "any portion of a return, affidavit, claim, or other document in connection with any matter arising under the internal revenue laws. * * * " 26 U.S.C. § 6701(a)(1). Thus, assuming that plaintiff violated § 6701, he did so with respect to each Schedule C to which his letter referred and was attached. Therefore, the IRS properly calculated the amount of penalty for which plaintiff may be liable based on the number of investors to whom a Schedule C and plaintiff's transmittal letter were sent. Accordingly, defendant's motion for partial summary judgment on this single, narrow issue is granted.

Notes

1. Prior to its amendment as part of IMPACT, § 6701 applied only if the person who aided or assisted in the preparation or presentation of any document *knew* that the document would be used in connection with any material federal tax matter and *knew* that, if used, it would result in an understatement of tax liability. As amended in 1989, the penalty now applies if the person has *reason to believe* both of these elements.

2. IMPACT did not alter the amount of the penalty. It remains $1,000 for noncorporate returns and $10,000 for corporate returns. In a case involving an S corporation return that affected each of the corporation's 34 shareholders, the court held the preparer of the false return

subject to the $10,000 corporate return penalty, rather than a $34,000 penalty ($1,000 multiplied by the 34 shareholders), and distinguished Kuchan. *In re Mitchell* 90–2 USTC ¶ 50,495.

3. Section 7408 authorizes the Service to bring an action to enjoin any person from continuing to engage in conduct subject to penalty under § 6700 or 6701. The injunction action can be brought in any district in which the defendant resides, has a principal place of business, or has engaged in conduct that is subject to the penalties. If the court finds that the defendant has engaged in the prohibited conduct and that an injunction is appropriate to prevent recurrence, the court can enter an injunction. See United States v. Philatelic Leasing Ltd., 794 F.2d 781 (2d Cir.1986).

D. FRIVOLOUS RETURNS

COLTON v. GIBBS
United States Court of Appeals, Ninth Circuit, 1990.
902 F.2d 1462.

OPINION

NELSON, CIRCUIT JUDGE: Appellant Ernest Colton appeals the district court's dismissal of this action, in which Colton is seeking the return of a penalty assessed by the Internal Revenue Service (IRS) under 26 U.S.C. section 6702. Since the IRS was acting within its statutory authority when it imposed the penalty, Colton is entitled to none of the relief sought. The district court correctly dismissed the complaint and we affirm.

I. Facts

Ernest Colton filed a Form 1040X (Amended U.S. Individual Income Tax Return) with the IRS on April 11, 1986. The form was filed as an amendment to Colton's original 1984 tax return, which had shown a total tax liability of $2,206.90. On the amended return, Colton changed this amount to zero and demanded a refund of all taxes paid in 1984. In a statement attached to the form, he cited "crimes" allegedly committed by the government and claimed a right not to become an accomplice in those crimes by paying taxes.

The IRS denied Colton's refund and assessed a $500 penalty against him for filing a frivolous income tax return in violation of 26 U.S.C. section 6702.[1] Colton paid $75 toward the penalty and then filed a claim for a refund of the $75.[2] The IRS denied this claim.

Colton subsequently filed a complaint against the Commissioner of Internal Revenue and unknown government officials, seeking, *inter*

---

[1]. This section authorizes the IRS to collect a $500 civil penalty from any individual who files a return containing "information that on its face indicates that the self-assessment is substantially incorrect" when such filing is based on "a position which is frivolous." 26 U.S.C. § 6702.

[2]. By paying 15% of the total amount of the penalty and filing a claim for a refund of that payment, a taxpayer can stay collection proceedings long enough to obtain a determination of liability from a district court. 26 U.S.C. § 6703(c).

alia, the return of his $75, a refund of his 1984 taxes, and $1,000 in damages. He also sought "[a] determination if income taxes are voluntary or not" and "[a] clarification why payment must be made to the Internal Revenue Service instead of the U.S. Treasury."

The government filed a motion to dismiss. The district court granted the motion in a minute order, but reserved judgment on the questions of whether 26 U.S.C. section 6702 applies to amended tax returns and whether notice is required prior to imposition of section 6702 penalties. After the parties filed supplemental authorities on these issues, the court entered an order of dismissal which confirmed its earlier minute order and specifically found that section 6702 does apply to amended tax returns and that no notice is required prior to imposition of a section 6702 penalty.

Appellant filed a timely notice of appeal.

II. Standard of Review

The district court dismissed Colton's complaint for failure to state a claim pursuant to Fed.R.Civ.P. 12(b)(6). This is a question of law and is reviewed de novo. *Kruso v. International Tel. & Tel. Corp.*, 872 F.2d 1416, 1421 (9th Cir.1989).

III. Merits of the Complaint

The district court was correct in dismissing this entirely frivolous complaint; we accordingly reject this entirely frivolous appeal.

Colton's assertion that payment of taxes would implicate him in crimes is without foundation. Paying income taxes is not a crime; it is an obligation. 26 U.S.C. § 6151. The amended tax return which bore this assertion was therefore frivolous and incorrect under the meaning of 26 U.S.C. section 6702. See *Bradley v. United States* [87–1 USTC ¶ 9336], 817 F.2d 1400, 1403–04 (9th Cir.1987).

Section 6702 applies to all tax returns, including amended returns. See *Branch v. IRS* [88–1 USTC ¶ 9317], 846 F.2d 36, 37 (8th Cir.1988) (per curiam); *Sisemore v. United States* [86–2 USTC ¶ 9576], 797 F.2d 268, 270 (6th Cir.), *cert. denied*, 479 U.S. 849, 107 S.Ct. 173, 93 L.Ed.2d 110 (1986). The IRS was justified in imposing the $500 penalty, and was not required to give notice before doing so. 26 U.S.C. § 6703(b). Colton is not entitled to the relief sought.[3]

IV. Sanctions and Costs

Since we find this appeal to be frivolous, we are authorized to award appellees "just damages * * * and single or double costs." 28 U.S.C. § 1912; Fed.R.App.P. 38; see *Olson v. United States* [85–1 USTC ¶ 9401], 760 F.2d 1003, 1005 (9th Cir.1985) (per curiam). We note that

---

3. Colton's claim that the IRS did not follow purely internal procedures of the Internal Revenue Manual, specifying, for example, that "tax examiners [must] underline [certain] entries on form 8278 in brown pencil [to] provide easy identification for the remote terminal operators," is as frivolous as the rest of this action. See *Bradley*, 817 F.2d at 1405 n. 7.

Colton has a long history of tax-related litigation (including three unsuccessful appeals to this court), most of which has been dilatory and abusive. We therefore award appellees the sum of $500 to offset the expenses of this appeal.

Affirmed.

Note

IMPACT repealed the provision in § 6703(c) that permitted taxpayers to pay 15% of the § 6702 penalty and file a claim for refund. For section 6702 penalties imposed after December 31, 1989, the taxpayer must pay the entire penalty and then file a refund claim. The special 15% rule continues to apply to penalties imposed under §§ 6700 and 6701, however. Section 6703 also provides that the penalties of §§ 6700, 6701 and 6702 are immediately assessable, upon notice and demand, and that the deficiency procedures do not apply. As a result, the Tax Court lacks jurisdiction over these penalties, which must be contested in a refund action in the federal district court or the Claims Court.

E. COURT-IMPOSED SANCTIONS AND COSTS

LARSEN v. COMMISSIONER
United States Court of Appeals, Ninth Circuit, 1985.
765 F.2d 939.

PER CURIAM.

Taxpayer appeals from an order of the Tax Court which dismissed his petition for redetermination of a tax deficiency. We affirm and impose sanctions.

Taxpayer filed a petition in the Tax Court challenging the Commissioner's disallowance of taxpayer's claimed charitable contributions to the Universal Life Church, Inc., a qualified donee organization under the Internal Revenue Code. 26 U.S.C. § 170. The Commissioner claimed that the alleged contributions were a tax avoidance scheme designed to insulate taxpayer's income from tax while using the income allegedly contributed to the Church for personal living expenses. The Commissioner further sought damages of $5,000 pursuant to 26 U.S.C. § 6673, asserting that taxpayer's petition was frivolous and filed for the purpose of delay.

In the Tax Court proceeding, the taxpayer refused to sign a stipulation, to specify his objections to the Commissioner's proposed stipulation, or to offer his own proposed stipulation, as required by Tax Court Rule 91. After taxpayer also refused to comply with a subpoena duces tecum for documents supporting the alleged contribution, the Commissioner moved for dismissal for failure to prosecute. In a brief oral hearing, the Tax Court granted the Commissioner's motion, sustained the tax deficiency and additions to tax determined by the Commissioner, *see* 26 U.S.C. § 6651, and imposed the maximum statutory damages against the taxpayer of $5,000 pursuant to § 6673. *See* Tax Court Rule 123.

Tax Court Rule 91 requires the parties to stipulate, to the fullest extent possible, to all nonprivileged matters which are relevant to a pending case. Tax Court Rule 147(b) authorizes the issuance of a subpoena duces tecum. Taxpayer's refusal to comply with a subpoena for documentary evidence is a violation of Rule 147(e). Because the taxpayer refused to comply with its rules, the Tax Court properly exercised its discretion in dismissing the petition under Rule 123. *See McCoy v. C.I.R.*, 696 F.2d 1234, 1236 (9th Cir.1983).

The Tax Court may impose a penalty on a taxpayer for maintaining a proceeding primarily for delay or for bringing an action which is frivolous and groundless. 26 U.S.C. § 6673. Taxpayer argues that the penalty provision is unconstitutional because it infringes upon his right to petition the government for redress of grievances. This argument is frivolous. The right to petition protected by the First Amendment does not include the right to maintain groundless proceedings. *See Bill Johnson's Restaurants, Inc. v. NLRB*, 461 U.S. 731, 103 S.Ct. 2161, 2170, 76 L.Ed.2d 277 (1983). The taxpayer was warned, both in this proceeding and in earlier disputes with the Commissioner, that a penalty would be assessed for bringing frivolous challenges. Given taxpayer's refusal to prosecute his petition properly and the consistency with which courts have rejected similar legal challenges, the Tax Court did not abuse its discretion in assessing a penalty. *See Hall v. C.I.R.*, 729 F.2d 632, 635 (9th Cir.1984).

Once the Commissioner has determined that additions to tax should be imposed, those additions are presumptively correct. The taxpayer has the burden of proving his lack of negligence under 26 U.S.C. § 6673. *See Hall v. C.I.R.*, 729 F.2d at 635. This court has routinely affirmed the placing of this burden on the taxpayer. *Id.*, and cases cited therein.

Taxpayer argues that, because it is not an Article III court, the Tax Court cannot have jurisdiction over constitutional questions. Because the Tax Court did not rule on the substance of taxpayer's petition but dismissed his petition for failure to prosecute, that court did not reach any constitutional questions. Furthermore, taxpayer's argument that Article I courts cannot consider constitutional issues is groundless; we have often upheld Tax Court decisions which were based on a constitutional inquiry. *See, e.g., McCoy*, 696 F.2d at 1236; *Edwards v. C.I.R.*, 680 F.2d 1268, 1270 (9th Cir.1982).

This court finds taxpayer's arguments and appeal to be frivolous. *See Kalgaard v. C.I.R.*, 764 F.2d 1322, at 1324 (9th Cir.1985). Under Fed.R.App.P. 38, this court has frequently imposed sanctions for frivolous appeals. *See Gattuso v. Pecorella*, 733 F.2d 709, 710 (9th Cir. 1984); *McCoy*, 696 F.2d at 1237; *Edwards*, 680 F.2d at 1271. Both the taxpayer and his attorney should have known this case to be frivolous. As in *Kalgaard*, therefore, we impose double costs and award the

Commissioner $1,000 in attorney's fees, taxpayer and his counsel being jointly and severally liable.

Affirmed.

Note

Changes to § 6673 made by IMPACT are summarized and explained in the legislative history as follows:

The bill authorizes the Tax Court to impose a penalty not to exceed $25,000 if a taxpayer (1) institutes or maintains a proceeding primarily for delay, (2) takes a position that is frivolous, or (3) unreasonably fails to pursue available administrative remedies. The committee intends that the increased penalty (above $5,000) apply primarily (but not exclusively) to tax shelter cases, where the $5,000 maximum provided under present law appears to be ineffective in deterring taxpayers from taking frivolous positions.

The committee has explicitly chosen to call these awards "penalties", rather than "damages" (as under present law), so that it is clear that specific damages incurred by the United States need not be proved before the court may impose this penalty. The committee believes that dealing with these frivolous lawsuits wastes scarce judicial resources and delays the resolution of legitimate disputes. The committee expects that its modifications to this provision will further decrease frivolous lawsuits. * * * The committee has also called these awards "penalties" rather than "damages" in the parallel provisions applicable to other courts. The committee has provided that any monetary sanctions, penalties, or costs awarded in a tax case by one of these other courts may be assessed and collected in the same manner as a tax. This permits these sanctions, penalties, and costs, when awarded by one of these other courts, to be collected in the same manner as if they were awarded by the Tax Court.

* * *

The bill also authorizes the Tax Court to require any attorney or other person permitted to practice before the Tax Court to pay excess costs, expenses, and attorney's fees that are incurred because the attorney or other person unreasonably and vexatiously multiplied any proceeding before the Court. If the attorney is appearing on behalf of the Commissioner of Internal Revenue, the United States is to pay these costs in the same manner as an award of these costs by a district court. This provision is comparable to the authority already provided to district courts under 28 U.S.C. section 1927. * * *

SECTION 5. DELINQUENCY PENALTIES

IMPACT amended three delinquency penalties: the penalty for failure to file a return (section 6651), the penalty for failure to make timely deposits of withheld taxes (section 6656), and the penalty for failure to withhold on the income of a foreign person (section 1463). Only the first two of these provisions will be discussed.

A. FAILURE TO FILE A RETURN OR PAY TAX   §6651

Section 6651 imposes penalties for failure to file a timely return, failure to pay timely the amount shown as tax due on any return, and failure to pay any amount in respect of any tax required to be shown on a return which is not so shown (*i.e.*, failure to pay a deficiency on time).

IMPACT removed the opportunity to "stack" the delinquency penalty of section 6651 with other penalties (such as negligence or fraud) by requiring that a return have been filed as a condition for application of the accuracy-related or fraud penalties. IMPACT also added new section 6651(f), which triples the penalty amount (to 15% per month, up to a maximum of 75%, of the net tax due) for fraudulent failure to file a return.

The failure to file penalty of 5% per month of the net amount of tax due (up to a maximum of 25%) is imposed if a return is not timely filed, unless it is shown that the failure to file timely was due to reasonable cause and not willful neglect. Where the return is more than 60 days late there is a minimum penalty of the lesser of $100 or 100% of the tax due. Where a return is filed late and the tax is not paid, both the failure to file penalty and the section 6651(a)(2) failure to pay penalty can be imposed. However, under section 6651(c)(1), the failure to file penalty is reduced by the amount of the failure to pay penalty for any month as to which both are imposed, except that the failure to file penalty cannot be reduced to less than the minimum penalty where the return was filed more than 60 days late.

The late payment penalties of ½% per month (up to a maximum of 25%) are imposed for the late payment of tax shown due on a return or assessed, unless the failure to pay on time was due to reasonable cause and not willful neglect. The section 6651(a)(2) penalty is imposed on the net amount of tax due, and if the amount required to be shown as tax on a return is less than the amount shown as tax on the return, the lesser amount is used to calculate the penalty. The section 6651(a)(3) penalty is imposed where a taxpayer fails to pay a deficiency within 10 days of notice and demand, and also is imposed on the net amount due.

The failure to file penalty essentially involves two basic issues. First, was there in fact a failure to timely file a required tax return? Second, if there was a failure to file a timely return, was the failure due to reasonable cause and not willful neglect?

The first of the two issues most frequently involves the question of whether for a given year the taxpayer was required to file an income tax return under the provisions of § 6012 of the Code (or whether some other type of return was required to be filed by some other section of the Code). However, this issue can also turn upon the question of whether a document which was filed timely will be held to be a tax return. See pages 167–176 above for a discussion of this matter in the context of the commencement of the period of limitations on assessments.

The second of the issues, whether the failure to file timely returns was due to reasonable cause and not willful neglect, is discussed in the following case.

UNITED STATES v. BOYLE
Supreme Court of the United States, 1985.
469 U.S. 241, 105 S.Ct. 687, 83 L.Ed.2d 622.

CHIEF JUSTICE BURGER delivered the opinion of the Court.

We granted certiorari to resolve a conflict among the Circuits on whether a taxpayer's reliance on an attorney to prepare and file a tax return constitutes "reasonable cause" under § 6651(a)(1) of the Internal Revenue Code, so as to defeat a statutory penalty incurred because of a late filing.

I

A

Respondent, Robert W. Boyle, was appointed executor of the will of his mother, Myra Boyle, who died on September 14, 1978; respondent retained Ronald Keyser to serve as attorney for the estate. Keyser informed respondent that the estate must file a federal estate tax return, but he did not mention the deadline for filing this return. Under 26 U.S.C. § 6075(a), the return was due within nine months of the decedent's death, *i.e.,* not later than June 14, 1979.

Although a businessman, respondent was not experienced in the field of federal estate taxation, other than having been executor of his father's will 20 years earlier. It is undisputed that he relied on Keyser for instruction and guidance. He cooperated fully with his attorney and provided Keyser with all relevant information and records. Respondent and his wife contacted Keyser a number of times during the spring and summer of 1979 to inquire about the progress of the proceedings and the preparation of the tax return; they were assured that they would be notified when the return was due and that the return would be filed "in plenty of time." When respondent called Keyser on September 6, 1979, he learned for the first time that the return was by then overdue. Apparently, Keyser had overlooked the matter because of a clerical oversight in omitting the filing date from Keyser's master calendar. Respondent met with Keyser on September 11, and the return was filed on September 13, three months late.

B

Acting pursuant to 26 U.S.C. § 6651(a)(1), the Internal Revenue Service assessed against the estate an additional tax of $17,124.45 as a penalty for the late filing, with $1326.56 in interest. Section 6651(a)(1) reads in pertinent part:

"In case of failure * * * to file any return * * * on the date prescribed therefor * * * *unless it is shown that such failure is due to reasonable cause and not due to willful neglect,* there shall be added to the amount required to be shown as tax on such return 5 percent of the amount of such tax if the failure is for not more than 1 month, with an additional 5 percent for each additional month or fraction thereof during which such failure continues, not exceeding 25 percent in the aggregate * * *." (Emphasis added.)

A Treasury Regulation provides that, to demonstrate "reasonable cause," a taxpayer filing a late return must show that he "exercised ordinary business care and prudence and was nevertheless unable to file the return within the prescribed time." 26 CFR § 301.6651–1(c)(1) (1984).[1]

Respondent paid the penalty and filed a claim for a refund. He conceded that the assessment for interest was proper, but contended that the penalty was unjustified because his failure to file the return on time was "due to reasonable cause," *i.e.,* reliance on his attorney. Respondent brought suit in the United States District Court, which * * * granted summary judgment for respondent and ordered refund of the penalty. A divided panel of the Seventh Circuit, with three opinions, affirmed.

II

A

Congress' purpose in the prescribed civil penalty was to ensure timely filing of tax returns to the end that tax liability will be ascertained and paid promptly. The relevant statutory deadline provision is clear; it mandates that all federal estate tax returns be filed within nine months from the decedent's death, 26 U.S.C. § 6075(a). Failure to comply incurs a penalty of 5 percent of the ultimately determined tax for each month the return is late, with a maximum of 25 percent of the base tax. To escape the penalty, the taxpayer bears the heavy burden of proving both (1) that the failure did not result from "willful neglect," and (2) that the failure was "due to reasonable cause."

---

1. The Internal Revenue Service has articulated eight reasons for a late filing that it considers to constitute "reasonable cause." These reasons include unavoidable postal delays, the taxpayer's timely filing of a return with the wrong IRS office, the taxpayer's reliance on the erroneous advice of an IRS officer or employee, the death or serious illness of the taxpayer or a member of his immediate family, the taxpayer's unavoidable absence, destruction by casualty of the taxpayer's records or place of business, failure of the IRS to furnish the taxpayer with the necessary forms in a timely fashion, and the inability of an IRS representative to meet with the taxpayer when the taxpayer makes a timely visit to an IRS office in an attempt to secure information or aid in the preparation of a return. Internal Revenue Manual (CCH) § 4350, (24) ¶ 22.2(2) (Mar. 20, 1980) (Audit Technique Manual for Estate Tax Examiners). If the cause asserted by the taxpayer does not implicate any of these eight reasons, the district director determines whether the asserted cause is reasonable. "A cause for delinquency which appears to a person of ordinary prudence and intelligence as a reasonable cause for delay in filing a return and which clearly negatives willful neglect will be accepted as reasonable." *Id.,* at ¶ 22.-2(3).

The meaning of these two standards has become clear over the near-70 years of their presence in the statutes. As used here, the term "willful neglect" may be read as meaning a conscious, intentional failure or reckless indifference. Like "willful neglect," the term "reasonable cause" is not defined in the Code, but the relevant Treasury Regulation calls on the taxpayer to demonstrate that he exercised "ordinary business care and prudence" but nevertheless was "unable to file the return within the prescribed time." 26 CFR § 301.6651(c)(1) (1984). The Commissioner does not contend that respondent's failure to file the estate tax return on time was willful or reckless. The question to be resolved is whether, under the statute, reliance on an attorney in the instant circumstances is a "reasonable cause" for failure to meet the deadline.

B

In affirming the District Court, the Court of Appeals placed great importance on the fact that respondent engaged the services of an experienced attorney specializing in probate matters and that he duly inquired from time to time as to the progress of the proceedings. The court stressed that the question of "reasonable cause" was an issue to be determined on a case-by-case basis.

Other Courts of Appeals have dealt with the issue of "reasonable cause" for a late filing and reached contrary conclusions. In *Ferrando v. United States*, 245 F.2d 582 (CA9 1957), the court held that taxpayers have a personal and nondelegable duty to file a return on time, and that reliance on an attorney to fulfill this obligation does not constitute "reasonable cause" for a tardy filing. The Fifth Circuit has similarly held that the responsibility for ensuring a timely filing is the taxpayer's alone, and that the taxpayer's reliance on his tax advisors—accountants or attorneys—is not a "reasonable cause." The Eighth Circuit also has concluded that reliance on counsel does not constitute "reasonable cause."

III

We need not dwell on the similarities or differences in the facts presented by the conflicting holdings. The time has come for a rule with as "bright" a line as can be drawn consistent with the statute and implementing regulations. * * *

Congress has placed the burden of prompt filing on the executor, not on some agent or employee of the executor. The duty is fixed and clear; Congress intended to place upon the taxpayer an obligation to ascertain the statutory deadline and then to meet that deadline, except in a very narrow range of situations. Engaging an attorney to assist in the probate proceedings is plainly an exercise of the "ordinary business care and prudence" prescribed by the regulations, but that does not provide an answer to the question we face here. To say that it was "reasonable" for the executor to *assume* that the attorney would comply with the statute may resolve the matter as between them, but not with respect to the executor's obligations under the statute. Congress has charged the executor with an unambiguous, precisely defined duty to file the return within nine months; extensions are granted fairly routinely. That the attorney, as the executor's agent, was expected to attend to the matter does not relieve the principal of his duty to comply with the statute.

This case is not one in which a taxpayer has relied on the erroneous advice of counsel concerning a question of law. Courts have frequently held that "reasonable cause" is established when a taxpayer shows that he reasonably relied on the advice of an accountant or attorney that it was unnecessary to file a return, even when such advice turned out to have been mistaken. This Court also has implied that, in such a situation, reliance on the opinion of a tax advisor may constitute reasonable cause for failure to file a return. See *Commissioner v. Lane–Wells Co.*, 321 U.S. 219, 64 S.Ct. 511, 88 L.Ed. 684 (1944) (remanding for determination whether failure to file return was due to reasonable cause, when taxpayer was advised that filing was not required).⁹

When an accountant or attorney *advises* a taxpayer on a matter of tax law, such as whether a liability exists, it is reasonable for the taxpayer to rely on that advice. Most taxpayers are not competent to discern error in the substantive advice of an accountant or attorney. To require the taxpayer to challenge the attorney, to seek a "second opinion," or to try to monitor counsel on the provisions of the Code himself would nullify the very purpose of seeking the advice of a presumed expert in the first place. "Ordinary business care and prudence" does not demand such actions.

By contrast, one does not have to be a tax expert to know that tax returns have fixed filing dates and that taxes must be paid when they are due. In short, tax returns imply deadlines. Reliance by a lay person on a lawyer is of course common; but that reliance cannot function as a substitute for compliance with an unambiguous statute. Among the first duties of the representative of a decedent's estate is to identify and assemble the assets of the decedent and to ascertain tax obligations. Although it is common practice for an executor to engage a professional to prepare and file an estate tax return, a person experienced in business matters can perform that task personally. It is not unknown for an executor to prepare tax returns, take inventories, and carry out other significant steps in the probate of an estate. It is even not uncommon for an executor to conduct probate proceedings without counsel.

It requires no special training or effort to ascertain a deadline and make sure that it is met. The failure to make a timely filing of a tax

---

9. Courts have differed over whether a taxpayer demonstrates "reasonable cause" when, in reliance on the advice of his accountant or attorney, the taxpayer files a return after the actual due date but within the time the advisor erroneously told him was available. We need not and do not address ourselves to this issue.

return is not excused by the taxpayer's reliance on an agent, and such reliance is not "reasonable cause" for a late filing under § 6651(a)(1). The judgment of the Court of Appeals is reversed.

It is so ordered.

JUSTICE BRENNAN, with whom JUSTICE MARSHALL, JUSTICE POWELL, and JUSTICE O'CONNOR join, concurring.

I concur that the judgment must be reversed. * * *

* * *

I write separately, however, to underscore the importance of an issue that the Court expressly leaves open. Specifically, I believe there is a substantial argument that the "ordinary business care and prudence" standard is applicable only to the "ordinary person"—namely, one who is physically and mentally capable of knowing, remembering, and complying with a filing deadline. In the instant case, there is no question that the respondent not only failed to exercise ordinary business care in monitoring the progress of his mother's estate, but also made no showing that he was *unable* to exercise the usual care and diligence required of an executor. The outcome could be different if a taxpayer were able to demonstrate that, for reasons of incompetence or infirmity, he understandably was unable to meet the standard of ordinary business care and prudence. In such circumstances, there might well be no good reason for imposing the harsh penalty of § 6651(a)(1) over and above the prescribed statutory interest penalty. See 26 U.S.C. §§ 6601(a), 6621(b).

* * *

Notes

1. Suppose that the taxpayer was an investment banker on Wall Street during the boom days of the 1980's, but lost her job, at which she had been earning more than $200,000 annually, took another job that pays only $50,000 annually, and simply cannot afford to pay the income taxes due in the year following the loss of her high-paying job. If she files her return in timely fashion, but pays only a portion of the tax due, should she be subject to the failure to pay penalty? Would it matter if she were living in a $4,000/month condo and driving a $50,000 car? Consult Reg. § 301.-6651–1(c)(1), which requires a taxpayer to make an affirmative showing of reasonable cause to avoid either the failure to file penalty or the failure to pay penalty. According to the Regulation: "A failure to pay will be considered to be due to reasonable cause to the extent that the taxpayer has made a satisfactory showing that he exercised ordinary business care and prudence in providing for payment of his tax liability and was nevertheless either unable to pay the tax or would suffer an undue hardship (as described in § 1.6161–1(b) of this chapter) if he paid on the due date. In determining whether the taxpayer was unable to pay the tax in spite of the exercise of ordinary business care and prudence in providing for payment of his tax liability, consideration will be given to all the facts and circumstances of the taxpayer's financial situation, including the amount and

nature of the taxpayer's expenditures in light of the income (or other amounts) he could, at the time of such expenditures, reasonably expect to receive prior to the date prescribed for the payment of the tax. Thus, for example, a taxpayer who incurs lavish or extravagant living expenses in an amount such that the remainder of his assets and anticipated income will be insufficient to pay his tax, has not exercised ordinary business care and prudence in providing for the payment of his tax liability."

Section 8(11)[13] of the *Internal Revenue Manual* lists circumstances the IRS will recognize as satisfying the reasonable cause standard. These include death or serious illness of the taxpayer or a member of his immediate family and destruction by fire or other casualty of the taxpayer's residence, business premises or business records.

2. Section 6651 penalties are frequently assessed against tax protestors who file incomplete returns. Returns that are incomplete are not "returns" and their filing does not prevent a section 6651 penalty. Section 6011(a) requires that returns contain the information required by the forms or regulations. See the discussion of § 6011(a) in Chapter 5.

3. Section 6651(f), added by IMPACT, triples the § 6651 penalty for fraudulent failure to file a return. The burden of proof of fraud is on the Commissioner. If the deficiency notice asserts only the fraudulent failure to file penalty of § 6651(f), and the Commissioner fails to carry the burden of establishing fraud, then no § 6651 penalty can be imposed. This situation can be avoided by the Commissioner's assertion of the basic § 6651 penalty in his answer or other pleading filed in the case, but the burden of proof on the basic penalty would be on the Commissioner. Normally the burden of proof on the basic § 6651 penalty is on the taxpayer. If, however, the basic failure to file penalty is asserted in the deficiency notice as an alternative to the § 6651(f) penalty, then failure by the Commissioner to carry the burden of proving fraud does not result in the burden of proof on the regular § 6651 penalty remaining with the Commissioner. In that case, the taxpayer will have the burden of proof.

4. Section 6658 prohibits imposition of the § 6651 penalty (as well as those under §§ 6654 and 6656 relating to failure to pay estimated taxes) in cases in which the taxpayer is involved in a bankruptcy proceeding.

2. Prior to IMPACT, § 6656 imposed a 10% tax on employers that failed to make timely deposits of tax withheld from their employees' compensation. The penalty could be abated if the failure was due to reasonable cause and not to willful neglect. IMPACT amended § 6656 by creating a four-tiered penalty, with the amount of the penalty increasing as the length of the delinquency increases.

For deposits required to be made after December 31, 1989, the § 6656 penalty structure is as follows:

—the penalty is 2% of the underpayment if full payment is made within 5 days of the due date;

—the penalty is 5% of the underpayment if full payment is made within 6 to 15 days of the due date;

—the penalty is 10% of the underpayment if full payment is made more than 15 days after the due date but within 10 days of the first delinquency notice sent to the employer;

—the penalty is 15% of the underpayment if full payment is not made within 10 days after the first delinquency notice.

SECTION 6. INTEREST ON DEFICIENCIES AND OVERPAYMENTS

Absent an agreement or a specific prohibition, interest must be paid to the IRS on underpayments of tax (§ 6601(a)) and to the taxpayer on overpayments of tax (§ 6611(a)). As stated in Rev.Proc. 60–17, 1960–2 C.B. 942:

> Under the general rule, interest is paid on a tax overpayment for the time the government has the use of the taxpayer's money. Interest is collected, similarly, for the time the taxpayer has the use of the government's money. The underlying objective is to determine in a given situation whose money it is and for how long the other party had the use of it.

Interest on Underpayments. As to tax deficiencies, the taxpayer is considered to have the use of the government's money starting with the due date of the subject tax return. Therefore, for a 1991 income tax return due April 15, 1992, interest on an underpayment of tax shown on the return or on a deficiency in tax assessed many years later commences running on April 15, 1992. Prior to amendments to section 6601 in 1984, 1988 and 1989, interest on most penalties accrued only after assessment, notice and demand, and then only if the penalties were not paid within ten days of the notice and demand. However, TRA '84 changed the rules with respect to interest on the late filing penalty, the valuation penalties, and the substantial understatement penalty. If any of those penalties are assessed on or after July 18, 1984, interest accrues on them from the later of the due date (including extensions) of the subject return or July 18, 1984. In 1988 and 1989, the TRA '84 rules were extended to the accuracy-related and fraud penalties, interest on which begins accruing on the due date (including extensions) of the return.

Interest on amounts due to the IRS ceases running on the date the underlying liability is paid. However, if a deficiency is assessed and payment is made within ten days of notice and demand, the interest termination date is the date of the notice and demand.

Interest on Overpayments. Under § 6611, interest on overpayments, whether refunded or credited, generally starts running on the date of the overpayment. Payments made early (including withholdings and estimated payments) are deemed paid on the due date of the return. However, in the case of a late return (i.e., one filed after the due date, including extensions) interest on an overpayment starts running on the date the return is filed. IRC § 6611(b)(3).

Interest on amounts refunded to taxpayers ceases running on a date preceding the issuance of a refund check by not more than thirty days.[y] If the overpayment is credited against a tax debt due from the taxpayer, interest runs to the due date of the amount against which the credit is taken.[z] Note that when an overpayment is applied to an amount with a due date earlier than the overpayment date, no interest is payable on the credited overpayment.[a]

Rates of Interest. Prior to TRA '86, the rate of interest on underpayments and overpayments was the same. Until July 1, 1975, that rate had remained constant at 6% simple interest per annum. However, the interest rate fluctuated from July 1, 1975 through December 31, 1986 under a series of amendments to IRC § 6621 that permitted the IRS to adjust the rate periodically based on a formula tied to the prime rate. At first, the rate could be adjusted not more frequently than once every two years. Later, ERTA permitted an annual adjustment, and TEFRA permitted a semiannual adjustment. A further and perhaps more significant change to interest rates made by TEFRA was the introduction of daily compounding,[b] effective for interest accruing after December 31, 1982.

Under TRA '86 a differential interest rate for overpayments and underpayments was created, and both rates are adjusted quarterly.[c] The rates are determined during the first month of a calendar quarter, and become effective for the following calendar quarter.[d] Thus, for example, the rates that are determined during January are effective for the following April through June. Interest on overpayments is the short-term Federal rate plus *two* percentage points,[e] and interest on underpayments is the short-term Federal rate plus *three* percentage points.[f]

Special Rate for Tax Motivated Transactions. Under a provision added by TRA '84 (effective with respect to interest accruing after December 31, 1984), interest payable with respect to any substantial underpayment attributable to "tax motivated transactions" accrues at 120% of the normally applicable rate. For purposes of this interest provision, a "substantial underpayment attributable to tax motivated transactions" means any underpayment in excess of $1,000 for any taxable year which is attributable to one or more tax motivated transactions. The term "tax motivated transactions," in turn, includes any valuation overstatement; any loss or credit disallowed by virtue of the at-risk rules; any tax straddle; any use of an accounting method specified in regulations as potentially resulting in a substantial distortion of income; any sham or fraudulent transaction; and any other type of transaction specified in regulations as being tax motivated. The

y. I.R.C. § 6611(b)(2).

z. I.R.C. § 6611(b)(1). See Reg. § 301.-6611-1(h)(2) for the definition of the term "due date" for purposes of I.R.C. § 6611(b)(1).

a. See I.R.C. § 6611(b)(1).

b. See I.R.C. § 6222.

c. I.R.C. § 6621(a), (b).

d. I.R.C. § 6621(b).

e. I.R.C. § 6621(a)(1).

f. I.R.C. § 6621(a)(2).

Tax Court is given jurisdiction to determine the applicability of this provision to any deficiency determined by the Tax Court. In 1989 IMPACT repealed this special rate for returns due after December 31, 1989. Thus, this special rate applies only to returns filed between January 1, 1985 and December 31, 1989.

Special Rate for Large Deficiencies of C Corporations. The Omnibus Budget Reconciliation Act of 1990 established new interest rate amounts for certain large deficiencies of C corporations. For deficiencies over $100,000 the interest rate is the short-term federal rate plus five percentage points. This special rate applies beginning after the 30th day following the earlier of the IRS's furnishing to the taxpayer of a proposed deficiency (the so-called "30-day letter") or of a statutory notice of deficiency (the so-called "90-day letter"). For deficiencies in taxes other than income taxes, the special rate begins accruing when the IRS issues a similar notice to the taxpayer. The increased rate is effective for periods after December 31, 1990, regardless of the taxable period to which the underlying tax deficiency applies. IRC § 6621(c).

Deductibility of interest. Individuals may not deduct interest paid on tax deficiencies, because such interest is "personal interest" under § 163. Corporations are generally permitted to deduct all interest, including interest on tax deficiencies. The Senate in 1990 recommended denying an interest deduction to corporations for interest on deficiencies that accrued after the 30th day after the corporation received a 30-day letter or a 90-day letter, but the compromise provision described above (imposing a special higher rate on large deficiencies of C corporations) was adopted instead.

Chapter VII

CIVIL TAX LITIGATION

Scope Note: This chapter discusses those factors which must be taken into account by the tax practitioner in making an intelligent decision as to the most favorable forum in which to litigate a civil tax dispute. Considered below are the subject matter jurisdiction, applicable precedent, trial and settlement procedures, burden of proof considerations and the jurisdictional prerequisites of each of the tax litigation forums. Collateral topics which frequently arise in civil tax litigation are also discussed, including: the application of the doctrines of res judicata and collateral estoppel, the suppression of evidence in civil tax controversies and the recovery of attorney's fees. Brief consideration is also given to the action for recovery of taxes paid based upon the theory of an account stated.

SECTION 1. TAXPAYERS' CHOICE OF FORUM

The following excerpt from a treatise entitled "Federal Tax Litigation"[a] describes the importance of the proper choice of forum in civil tax litigation.

IMPORTANCE OF FORUM SELECTION

Perhaps the greatest oddity of the federal system for the adjudication of tax disputes lies in the area of forum selection. In the United States, a taxpayer engaged in a [Federal] tax dispute, subject to certain practical and legal restrictions, actually has the opportunity to select the forum that will determine the case from among three different courts. Each court has a different procedure, each provides judges of different backgrounds, and each may be governed by a different body of precedent. [The governing precedents in the various courts is often the most important factor in the selection of the proper forum.] * * *

AVAILABLE FORUMS

A civil tax case may be heard in any one of three courts: the U.S. Tax Court, a U.S. district court, and, effective October 1, 1982, the * * *

---

a. By Garbis, Junghans and Struntz (1985).

U.S. Claims Court, which assumed the trial jurisdiction of the U.S. Court of Claims. In determining, in a given case, which forum is best for the taxpayer, it is necessary to consider the specific characteristics and procedures in each of these courts as applied to the particular nature of the taxpayer's case. A number of factors must be weighed and, in each instance, a judgment made—generally on all the factors together, as only rarely does one factor so predominate as to make the decision obvious or easy. * * *

* * *

U.S. Tax Court

The U.S. Tax Court is a Washington, D.C.-based tribunal that hears only tax cases. The Tax Court's jurisdiction includes income, estate, gift, and windfall profits taxes (Chapter 45 of the Internal Revenue Code), as well as certain excise tax matters arising under Chapters 41, 42, 43, or 44 of the Code.

The Tax Court also has been given jurisdiction over declaratory judgment actions with regard to the initial or continuing qualification of certain retirement plans, the initial or continuing qualification of certain exempt organizations, and the initial or continuing classification of certain private foundations; with regard to exchanges described in Section 367(a)(1) of the Code; with regard to the status of certain government obligations; and with regard to certain public disclosure matters arising under the Code.

Created to provide a forum in which a taxpayer could contest tax liability before payment, the Tax Court is the only one of the three tax forums that does not make payment of the taxes in question a prerequisite to filing suit.

The Tax Court consists of nineteen judges who hear cases and motions in most of the major cities of the United States. Its jurisdiction is nationwide. Tax Court judges hear only tax cases and thus are well-versed in the complexities of the Code. If the legal issue is highly technical and intricate, and the taxpayer wishes to have the matter decided by a court accustomed to winding its way through the labyrinthian maze of the tax law, the Tax Court is the forum in which to obtain consideration of the case by a tax specialist.

Although the Tax Court maintains its headquarters in Washington, D.C., individual judges travel at regularly scheduled intervals to most of the principal cities in the United States to hear tax dockets. Consequently, the trial of the case is likely to be as geographically convenient in the Tax Court as it would be in the district court for the taxpayer's home district.

Trial by jury is not available in the Tax Court. Accordingly, trial proceedings are conducted before a single judge of the court who determines the facts and the law and they are subject to possible internal review and, indeed, reversal by the Tax Court as a whole. In small tax cases, and in some regular cases, trials are conducted by a special trial judge.

The Tax Court Rules adopted in 1974 departed from the prior procedures by virtue of the introduction of discovery procedures. * * * In practice, discovery procedures are usually used less frequently and less burdensomely than in the other tax litigation forums.

* * *

Trial procedure in the Tax Court is much the same as trial procedure in the district court in nonjury cases. Enforcement of the rules of evidence in the Tax Court sometimes is more lenient than in the district courts and the Claims Court. If the taxpayer's case rests on a piece of evidence the admissibility of which may be doubtful, the chances of getting it in before the Tax Court are better than elsewhere (although the Claims Court may also be less than technical in this respect). Needless to say, if the taxpayer's case rests on keeping certain government evidence out, it may not be the best court.

* * *

Unlike the district court and the Claims Court, the Tax Court permits the representation of taxpayers by individuals who are not attorneys. Accountants and others can qualify to practice before the Tax Court by passing an examination. * * *

The Commissioner of Internal Revenue is always the defendant (called the "respondent") in a Tax Court case. In most Tax Court cases, the Commissioner is represented by a staff attorney from the Service's District Counsel, who functions autonomously to a great degree and is located convenient to the taxpayer's counsel. * * *

The Tax Court's decisional process is unique. The Tax Court judge who hears a case, after considering the evidence and submissions of the parties, writes an opinion that is then referred to the Chief Judge for consideration. The Chief Judge either permits the trial judge's opinion to constitute the decision of the Tax Court or refers the case to the full court, which then decides the suit en banc (resulting in a decision "reviewed by the court").

The losing party in this court has the right to appeal the decision to a U.S. court of appeals. [Governing precedent in Tax Court decisions is that of the Court of Appeals to which an appeal will lie, based on the taxpayer's residence. See *Golsen v. Commissioner* at page 396 below].

U.S. District Courts

* * * In contrast to the Tax Court and the Claims Court, which hear cases from all over the country, the district court's geographical scope is that of a single federal district the size of no more than a single state. Therefore, the district court is well aware of local conditions and circumstances that may bear upon a tax case. Similarly, the local district judge, being close to the local business and professional commu-

nity, may be in a better position to judge the credibility of local lay and expert witnesses than a judge from Washington, D.C.

The district courts are bound by the decisions of the U.S. Supreme Court and of the court of appeals for the circuit in which the district is located.

The district court is a refund tribunal, which means that, to maintain a refund suit, the taxpayer must pay any deficiency assessed by the Service and file a claim for refund before the district court will have jurisdiction to hear the case. Thus, a taxpayer who is unable to make full payment of any tax assessed is precluded from litigating in the district court.

The district court is the only tax trial court in which a jury trial is available and, thus, the only tax tribunal in which the facts of a case may be determined by the commonsense approach of a lay person.

* * * [G]enerally speaking, it is reasonable to expect a broader approach to a tax case heard in a district court than to one heard in the Tax Court or even in the Claims Court. In the district courts, the technical niceties of the Code are frequently tempered with a view toward practicality and equity, particularly in jury cases. On the other hand, the rules of evidence are most strictly construed in the district courts, especially in jury trials.

The district court handles tax-refund litigation in much the same manner as any other civil action. Both parties have available to them all the extensive discovery tools found in the Federal Rules of Civil Procedure. There are occasions when these discovery provisions can be most helpful in the preparation of a tax case. However, it is important to note that the government can, and almost always does, use the discovery provisions fully. Therefore, the taxpayer will make ample pretrial disclosures in the district courts and may be put to substantial expense to comply with the government's request for discovery. On the other hand, when it is needed, access to the government's evidence before trial is equally available to the taxpayer.

The proper defendant in a district court tax refund suit is the United States. Attorneys from the Tax Division of the Justice Department represent the government in district court tax refund cases, except in the Southern District of New York and in two California districts, where assistant U.S. attorneys handle tax cases. This fact may influence the choice of forum if settlement is desired. Tax Division attorneys are principally trial lawyers, and their primary interest is litigation rather than taxes. Therefore, their approach to a case is likely to be the traditional one of the advocate: What are the chances of success in court? Moreover, neither they nor their agency has passed upon the case prior to litigation. A taxpayer who desires a compromise but has reached a stalemate at the administrative level may have more luck at settling the case with the Tax Division in a refund suit than with the District Counsel and the Appeals Division of the Service in a Tax Court case.

A factor that influences the decision on where to litigate, but which varies from district to district, is the length of time it takes the case to reach the trial list. In some larger cities, the dockets in the district courts may be so clogged that years can pass before a case comes up for trial. * * *

* * *

As far as comparative time is concerned, a district court tax-refund case (in most districts) will probably reach decision faster than a Claims Court tax suit. The specific comparison can only be made, however, in the light of the situation in the particular district court under consideration.

Appeals from district court decisions in tax-refund suits lie to the respective courts of appeals.

U.S. CLAIMS COURT

On October 1, 1982, the U.S. Court of Claims was abolished and the U.S. Claims Court and the U.S. Court of Appeals for the Federal Circuit were created. The tax-refund suit trial jurisdiction (together with substantially all other trial jurisdiction) of the former Court of Claims was assumed by the Claims Court. Like the Court of Claims, the Claims Court is a Washington, D.C.-based tribunal. However, it is authorized to hold sessions throughout the United States at such locations as it chooses to designate by rule. The new Federal Circuit Court resulted from a merger of the U.S. Court of Claims and the U.S. Court of Customs and Patent Appeals. The Federal Circuit has jurisdiction over appeals from the Claims Court as well as appeals from certain other court and agency decisions.

The Claims Court is an Article I "legislative" court, not an Article III court as was the Court of Claims. * * *

* * *

One noteworthy aspect of trial procedure in the Claims Court is the attention that can be paid to the convenience of the parties and the witnesses. Sometimes, the judge will hear evidence at several locations if the circumstances warrant. Moreover, where appropriate, the judge may schedule several trial sessions in the same case, permitting a significant interval between witnesses. In the Tax Court or in a district court, the trial of a case is much more likely to be continuous. In a complex case, the spacing of witnesses can afford essentially needed time for reflection and further preparation during the course of a trial. In addition, where the transportation of widely scattered witnesses to one trial location at one time can present serious logistic problems, Claims Court procedures can ease the way. Since the judge will travel to a location convenient for the witnesses, testimony that otherwise might have to be presented through an evidentiary deposition can often be given by the witness in person.

The Claims Court considers itself bound by precedents of the Court of Claims, its own precedents, decisions of the Federal Circuit Court, and decisions of the U.S. Supreme Court.

Although many tax-refund suits are docketed in the Claims Court, it is considerably less specialized than the Tax Court. However, its judges may be presumed to have more expertise in the tax field than the average district judge.

The discovery procedures available in the Claims Court are almost identical to those in the district courts, as the Claims Court Rules were patterned after the Federal Rules of Civil Procedure. In addition, attorneys from the Tax Division of the Justice Department, with their traditional penchant for taking the greatest possible advantage of discovery techniques, are the government's advocates before the Claims Court. * * * As in district courts, the defendant in a Claims Court tax-refund action is the United States.

Unlike the district court, however, the Claims Court does not afford a local forum for the taxpayer, despite the fact that the trial may be held in the taxpayer's home city. The judges are based in Washington and cannot be as familiar with local conditions as a district judge. In addition, there is no trial by jury in the Claims Court. * * *

* * *

Legal Restrictions on Choice of Forum

Not every tax case necessarily provides the taxpayer with a choice among all three tax tribunals. The courts have jurisdictional requirements that can legally and practically narrow the selection available in a given case.

In the first place, the Tax Court, as noted, only has jurisdiction over income, estate, gift, and windfall profits taxes and over certain excise taxes arising under Chapters 41, 42, 43, or 44 of the Code. In a controversy involving any other type of tax (e.g., ordinary excise taxes or employer's taxes), this forum is not available. Second, the Tax Court's jurisdiction generally begins only after the Commissioner determines that a deficiency exists, or a computational adjustment is required (with respect to partnership returns), and has issued a statutory notice of deficiency or a final partnership administrative adjustment (FPAA).[b] Usually, the Tax Court is unavailable in cases arising from the taxpayer's discovery of a right to a refund (e.g., where the taxpayer erred in the government's favor on a tax return). There is one exception to this general rule in the new partnership procedures. A tax matters partner (TMP) may file a petition for readjustment in the Tax Court if a request for administrative adjustment (RAA), the equivalent of a refund claim, is disallowed by the Commissioner. A third limitation on suits in the Tax Court is the jurisdictional prerequisite of

b. See Section 5 of Chapter 4 for a discussion of the TEFRA partnership procedures.

a timely petition. A taxpayer who misses the court's deadline for filing the petition has no choice but to pay the tax assessed and to seek a refund.

The Claims Court and the U.S. district courts have jurisdiction over suits for refund of all internal revenue taxes. Therefore, regardless of the type of tax in question, the refund forums are available. * * *

* * *

The U.S. Tax Court has exclusive jurisdiction with regard to certain types of declaratory judgment actions involving tax matters. Only the Tax Court may hear declaratory judgment actions with regard to the initial or continuing qualification of retirement plans, with regard to the reasonableness of the Commissioner's determinations concerning Section 367(a)(1) exchanges, and with regard to the status of certain governmental obligations. However, each of the tax forums—the Tax Court, the Claims Court, and the U.S. district courts—has concurrent jurisdiction over declaratory judgment actions concerning the initial or continuing qualification of certain exempt organizations, the initial or continuing classification of certain private foundations, and revocation of the status of such organizations. Also, both the Tax Court and the U.S. District Court for the District of Columbia have jurisdiction over certain public disclosure matters arising under the Code. * * *

* * *

Ability to Pay as Factor in Forum Selection

Unfortunately, the taxpayer's financial condition can be an important aspect of forum selection. The jurisdictional prerequisites for a tax-refund suit (in a district court or the Claims Court) require that before bringing an action in these courts, the taxpayer make full payment of the deficiency asserted for each taxable year (in the case of income and gift taxes) or for each taxable estate (in the case of estate taxes) in which there is a dispute. Some taxpayers simply are unable to raise the money needed to make the required payments and are forced to litigate in the Tax Court. Others, although theoretically able to make the payment, may feel that the difficulty of payment makes the Tax Court, with its free admission, a more desirable forum. Still other taxpayers may prefer to litigate in the Tax Court and use the money that would have been spent to make full payment of the tax assessed, if litigating in a refund forum, for other purposes. Today, however, many taxpayers who elect to litigate in the Tax Court decide to make a payment in the nature of a cash bond because of the high rate at which interest accrues on any tax finally determined to be due.

* * *

Effect of Payment on Interest

A taxpayer who wants to pay the tax assessed and thereby stop the running of interest is not compelled to litigate in one of the refund forums.[10] Payment of the deficiency after the filing of a petition in the Tax Court does not deprive that court of jurisdiction. Neither does payment of the deficiency before the filing of a petition in the Tax Court, provided the proper procedures are followed.

The taxpayer who elects to pay the tax and sue for a refund in either a district court or the Claims Court, or who elects to pay the deficiency after filing a Tax Court petition, usually is entitled to receive interest on account of tax, penalty, and assessed (paid) interest ultimately refunded as a result of a compromise or a judicial determination. * * * However, where a partial payment is made prior to the filing of a petition in the Tax Court and is designated as a "deposit," a taxpayer is not entitled to receive any interest on the amount of any deposit ultimately refunded.

PRECEDENTS

Legal Issues

The most significant single factor in selecting the forum for a tax case is a determination of which tribunal is governed by the most favorable body of precedents. * * *

Of course, where the U.S. Supreme Court has spoken on a particular issue, all courts are bound to treat the decision as the law of the land.

The U.S. Claims Court, established October 1, 1982, adopted [13] all published decisions of the U.S. Court of Claims as binding precedents unless and until modified by decisions of the U.S. Court of Appeals for the Federal Circuit or the U.S. Supreme Court. Therefore, in the Claims Court, the relevant body of precedents includes Claims Court decisions, decisions of the formerly existing Court of Claims and of its successor court, the Federal Circuit, as well as decisions of the U.S. Supreme Court.

The district courts are bound by precedents in the court of appeals for the circuit in which they are located as well as by decisions of the U.S. Supreme Court. The decisions of other circuits, including the Federal Circuit (established October 1, 1982), will be given weight but will not necessarily be followed.

In determining which precedents to consider binding, the Tax Court has had the difficult task of reconciling its role as a national tribunal with the practical fact that its decisions are subject to review by the courts of appeals in the various circuits. The Tax Court initially rejected the idea that it was bound by the decisions of the courts of appeals, but this led to certain jurisdictional problems. For example, it was possible for two taxpayers in different circuits, having cases involving identical issues, to appeal identical Tax Court decisions to the courts of appeals in their respective circuits and to receive completely

---

10. I.R.C. § 6213(b)(4).

13. General Order No. 1, (U.S. Claims Court, Oct. 7, 1982).

opposite results if their circuits held opposing views. For this reason, the Tax Court changed its position in 1970 and agreed to follow decisions of the appellate circuit to which an appeal would lie.[14] By so doing, the Tax Court has eliminated the possibility of unnecessary appeals in those cases where the Tax Court disagrees with the view of the law pronounced by the court of appeals to which venue for an appeal would lie.

However, it is still possible for two taxpayers in identical cases to receive inconsistent results from the same tribunal by virtue of appellate venue. For example, in the identical cases of *Doehring v. Comm'r*[15] and *Puckett v. Comm'r*,[16] interest income from the same loan company was deemed passive investment income as to *Puckett* (Fourth Circuit appellate venue) but not as to *Doehring* (Fifth Circuit appellate venue). These inconsistent decisions are an inevitable consequence of the regional appellate system and would presumably have occurred if each taxpayer had proceeded in his home federal district court. However, had they both proceeded in the Court of Claims, then, by virtue of their both being before the same court and subject to the same precedents, they would have obtained consistent results.

Therefore, the following guidelines should be kept in mind.

1. If the taxpayer's home circuit has spoken on an issue, then, at least as to that issue, both the Tax Court and the district courts will apply the law as pronounced by that circuit.

2. If the taxpayer's home circuit has decided an issue one way and the Claims Court has reached a contrary result, the Claims Court will follow its own precedents and Federal Circuit Court precedents, and not the precedents of the other courts of appeals.

3. If the taxpayer's home circuit has not ruled on the issue involved, then the Tax Court will be guided by its own precedents, the Claims Court will follow its previous decisions and any precedents of the Federal Circuit, but the district courts will tend to give the heaviest weight to decisions in other circuits.

* * *

GOVERNMENT'S POWER TO ASSERT NEW ISSUES

One hazard of litigating a tax dispute is the possibility that the Service will, at some point, assert issues in addition to those presented at the administrative level. The taxpayer's choice of forum has a definite effect upon the Service's ability to assert tax deficiencies during the course of litigation.

---

14. Golsen v. Comm'r, 54 T.C. 70 (1970). The Tax Court will not, however, consider itself bound to follow actions of the court of appellate venue that do not have precedential value. Reugsegger v. Comm'r, 68 T.C. 463 (1977) (affirmance of prior case in open court without opinion is not precedent in Second Circuit and not binding on Tax Court).

15. T.C. Memo. 74,234 (1974), rev'd, 527 F.2d 945 (8th Cir.1975).

16. T.C. Memo. 74,235 (1974), aff'd, 522 F.2d 1385 (5th Cir.1975).

The basic principles are relatively simple. Filing a Tax Court petition suspends the running statute of limitations on assessments for the duration of the litigation and for sixty days thereafter [19] (or for one year thereafter in the case of a partnership proceeding).[20] Therefore, a taxpayer who proceeds to the Tax Court is vulnerable to an additional deficiency (over and above that proposed by the deficiency notice) if the Service should raise the new issues in the course of litigation. Although the Service must sustain the burden of proof on these issues, this burden is often surmountable. An illustration of the effect of this principle of law is provided by the *Raskob* case,[21] in which the taxpayer decided to litigate a $16,000 deficiency. The government raised a new issue and was sustained. The result was a final deficiency in the amount of $1,026,000.

The statute of limitations is not suspended by suit in a refund forum, and the government cannot assess any deficiency more than three years after the filing of the relevant tax return unless the assessment is for fraud or one of the other events that extends the normal limitations period. Since the taxpayer almost always can delay the commencement of a refund suit until after the expiration of the limitations period on assessments, this shield is usually available to any taxpayer in the refund forums. The government, of course, can raise new issues in tax-refund suits. However, if the statute of limitations on assessments has run, these new issues may only be used to offset the taxpayer's eventual recovery.[22] The new (postlimitations) issues cannot result in a net recovery for the government against the taxpayer. If the taxpayer in *Raskob* had taken advantage of this feature of refund litigation, he could not have lost more than the original $16,000 assessment. As the case turned out, his error in choosing a forum was a $1 million mistake.

Choice of Forum Under the New Partnership Procedures

The same factors are important to consider when choosing the best forum in which to litigate during a partnership proceeding. However, under the new partnership procedures, a partner must take precautions to protect his right to choice of forum. It must be remembered that the TMP has the exclusive right to choose the forum in which to litigate an FPAA for the first ninety days after it is issued. If the TMP chooses to litigate in one of the refund tribunals (i.e., either the district court or the Claims Court), a partner may find himself in a financial pinch, since the Service can immediately assess and collect any computational adjustment set forth in the FPAA. To protect himself, a partner should have a contractual right to control the TMP's forum selection.

---

19. I.R.C. § 6503(a).
20. I.R.C. § 6229(d).
21. Raskob v. Comm'r, 37 B.T.A. 1283 (1938), aff'd sub nom. Dupont v. Comm'r, 118 F.2d 544 (3d Cir.), cert. denied, 314 U.S. 623 (1941).
22. Lewis v. Reynolds, 284 U.S. 281 (1932), aff'g 48 F.2d 515 (10th Cir. 1931).

Under the Subchapter C procedures, an RAA, which is the equivalent of a refund claim, may be litigated in the Tax Court as well as in the traditional refund forums, provided the TMP files the RAA. Prior to the Subchapter C partnership procedures, all refund claims arising from erroneous reporting of partnership items had to be brought either in a district court or in the Claims Court.

The disastrous result in *Raskob*, described above, cannot be avoided by selecting a refund tribunal after passage of the statute of limitations on assessment of deficiencies if fraud is involved. An infamous example is Trans Mississippi Corp. v. United States, 494 F.2d 770 (5th Cir.1974). Judge Gee, writing for the court, stated:

> In this case, appellant taxpayer kicked the sleeping revenue service and lost an arm and a leg in the ensuing process. We affirm.
>
> Appellant * * * sought over $78,000 in tax refunds for claimed embezzlement losses * * *. The United States denied that the mishandling of corporate funds was an embezzlement, claimed the funds were unreported corporate income which went for clandestine corporate purposes, and counterclaimed for some $247,000 in unpaid taxes, fraud penalties of $123,000 and $82,000 interest, bridging a limitations gap with assertions of fraud.

SECTION 2. BURDEN OF PROOF IN CIVIL TAX LITIGATION

The taxpayer generally bears the burden of proof in any tax controversy, regardless of forum. The Commissioner's determination of a deficiency is presumptively correct, and the taxpayer must present competent and convincing evidence to overcome this presumption. Burden of proof contains two elements: the burden of persuasion and the burden of production. The party who bears the burden of persuasion must persuade the trier of fact, for if he fails he will lose on that issue. The burden of production requires the party bearing the burden to produce the necessary quantum of evidence on the issue to create an issue for the trier of fact. Failure to carry the burden of production results in the withholding of the issue from the jury (or the judge in a non-jury trial). Although the burden of persuasion remains fixed, the burden of production may shift.

The principal exception to the presumption of correctness of the Commissioner's determination is the imposition of the civil fraud penalty of section 6663. Section 6663(b), as amended in 1989, provides that the IRS must prove by "clear and convincing evidence" that some portion of the underpayment is attributable to fraud. If it does so, the entire underpayment is treated as attributable to fraud, unless the taxpayer establishes that some portion or portions are *not* attributable to fraud. The taxpayer meets her burden in disproving fraud as the cause of part of the underpayment if she establishes the absence of fraud by a preponderance of the evidence, a lesser standard than the "clear and convincing" evidence standard the IRS must satisfy to establish fraud.

A. REFUND SUITS

As described above in connection with Trans Mississippi Corp. v. United States, the taxpayer's filing of a refund suit can prompt the government to file a counterclaim for collection of additional taxes if the statute of limitations has not expired on the years involved. Under section 7422(e), if the IRS decides, after the filing of a refund suit, that additional taxes are due for the years in question, it must issue a notice of deficiency ("90–day letter"). The taxpayer may then file a Tax Court petition contesting the asserted deficiency, in which case the refund tribunal loses jurisdiction of the issues pending in the Tax Court. If the taxpayer does not file a Tax Court petition, the government may counterclaim for the amount of the asserted deficiency in the refund proceeding. The taxpayer, not the government, bears the burden of proof on issues raised in the government counterclaim.

UNITED STATES v. JANIS
Supreme Court of the United States, 1976.
428 U.S. 433, 96 S.Ct. 3021, 49 L.Ed.2d 1046.

MR. JUSTICE BLACKMUN delivered the opinion of the Court.

[In this case there was an unconstitutional seizure of evidence upon which an assessment of wagering excise taxes was based. The taxpayer effected a partial payment on the assessment and brought a refund suit in which the government filed a counterclaim for the unpaid balance of the assessment. Because excise taxes are not subject to the *Flora* "full payment" rule, discussed *infra*, partial payment was sufficient. The following discussion of burden of proof considerations arose in the context of a decision as to the applicability of the exclusionary rule to civil tax litigation. See pages 453–456, below, for the exclusionary rule aspect of the *Janis* case.]

* * *

Some initial observations about the procedural posture of the case in the District Court are indicated. If there is to be no limit to the burden of proof the respondent, as "taxpayer," must carry, then, even though he were to obtain a favorable decision on the inadmissibility-of-evidence issue, the respondent on this record could not possibly defeat the Government's counterclaim. The Government notes, properly we think, that the litigation is composed of two separate elements: the refund suit instituted by the respondent, and the collection suit instituted by the United States through its counterclaim. In a refund suit the taxpayer bears the burden of proving the amount he is entitled to recover. Lewis v. Reynolds, 284 U.S. 281, 52 S.Ct. 145, 76 L.Ed. 293

(1932). It is not enough for him to demonstrate that the assessment of the tax for which refund is sought was erroneous in some respects.

This Court has not spoken with respect to the burden of proof in a tax collection suit. The Government argues here that the presumption of correctness that attaches to the assessment in a refund suit must also apply in a civil collection suit instituted by the United States under the authority granted by §§ 7401 and 7403 of the Code. Thus, it is said, the defendant in a collection suit has the same burden of proving that he paid the correct amount of his tax liability.

The policy behind the presumption of correctness and the burden of proof, see Bull v. United States, 295 U.S. 247, 259–260, 55 S.Ct. 695, 699–700, 79 L.Ed. 1421 (1935), would appear to be applicable in each situation. It accords, furthermore, with the burden-of-proof rule which prevails in the usual preassessment proceeding in the United States Tax Court. In any event, for purposes of this case, we assume that this is so and that the burden of proof may be said technically to rest with respondent Janis.

Respondent, however, submitted no evidence tending either to demonstrate that the assessment was incorrect or to show the correct amount of wagering tax liability, if any, on his part. In the usual situation one might well argue, as the Government does, that the District Court then could not properly grant judgment for the respondent on either aspect of the suit. But the present case may well not be the usual situation. What we have is a "naked" assessment without *any* foundation whatsoever if what was seized by the Los Angeles police cannot be used in the formulation of the assessment. The determination of tax due then may be one "without rational foundation and excessive," and not properly subject to the usual rule with respect to the burden of proof in tax cases. Helvering v. Taylor, 293 U.S. 507, 514–515, 55 S.Ct. 287, 290–291, 79 L.Ed. 623 (1935).[8]

There appears, indeed, to be some debate among the Federal Courts of Appeals, in different factual contexts, as to the effect upon the burden of proof in a tax case when there is positive evidence that an assessment is incorrect. Some courts indicate that the burden of showing the amount of the deficiency then shifts to the Commissioner. Others hold that the burden of showing the correct amount of the tax remains with the taxpayer. However that may be, the debate does not extend to the situation where the assessment is shown to be naked and without *any* foundation. The courts then appear to apply the rule of the *Taylor* case. See Pizzarello v. United States, 408 F.2d 579 (CA2), cert. denied, 396 U.S. 986, 90 S.Ct. 481, 24 L.Ed.2d 450 (1969); Suarez v. Commissioner of Internal Revenue, 58 T.C. 792, 814–815 (1972). But cf. Compton v. United States, 334 F.2d 212, 216 (CA4 1964).

8. *Taylor*, although decided more than 40 years ago, has never been cited by this Court on the burden-of-proof issue. The Courts of Appeals, the Court of Claims, the Tax Court, and the Federal District Courts, however, frequently have referred to that aspect of the case.

Certainly, proof that an assessment is utterly without foundation is proof that it is arbitrary and erroneous. For purposes of this case, we need not go so far as to accept the Government's argument that the exclusion of the evidence in issue here is insufficient to require judgment for the respondent or even to shift the burden to the Government. We are willing to assume that if the District Court was correct in ruling that the evidence seized by the Los Angeles police may not be used in formulating the assessment (on which both the levy and the counterclaim were based), then the District Court was also correct in granting judgment for Janis in both aspects of the present suit. * * *

* * *

B. TAX COURT

Tax Court Rule 142(a) provides in part that

[t]he burden of proof shall be upon the petitioner, except as otherwise provided by statute or determined by the court; and except that, in respect of any new matter, increases in deficiency, and affirmative defenses, pleaded in his answer, it shall be upon the respondent.

The presumption of correctness of the Commissioner's deficiency determination, and the resulting burden on the taxpayer to prove the incorrectness of that determination, have been questioned and eroded in recent cases involving alleged illegal income.

ANASTASATO v. COMMISSIONER
United States Court of Appeals, Third Circuit, 1986.
794 F.2d 884.

HUNTER, CIRCUIT JUDGE.

Pano Anastasato, the taxpayer, has been involved in the travel business since 1954. In 1960, he established his own travel agency, Panmarc, Inc. ("Panmarc"), and a tour operation business, Wholesale Tours International ("WTI"). During the years 1974 through 1976, both companies were wholly owned by the taxpayer.

* * *

Panmarc did a large volume of business with KLM Royal Dutch Airlines ("KLM"). On April 15, 1981, the Commissioner issued statutory notices of deficiency to Anastasato totaling $633,468.00 for the years 1974, 1975, and 1976. * * * The Commissioner alleged that KLM had paid override commissions to the taxpayer by making payments into a Swiss bank account identified by the code name "GIGE." This account contains over one million dollars.

The Tax Court heard the testimony of revenue agents, employees of Panmarc, and employees of KLM. * * *

* * *

The taxpayer claims that the Commissioner's deficiency determination was arbitrary and unreasonable. In addressing this contention, we first note that the government's deficiency assessment is generally afforded a presumption of correctness. *See United States v. Janis*, 428 U.S. 433, 441, 96 S.Ct. 3021, 3025, 49 L.Ed.2d 1046 (1976). This presumption is a procedural device that places the burden of producing evidence to rebut the presumption on the taxpayer. *See Janis*, 428 U.S. at 441, 96 S.Ct. at 3025. A court usually will not look behind the Commissioner's determination, even though it may be based on hearsay or other evidence inadmissible at trial. *See Dellacroce v. Commissioner*, 83 T.C. 269, 280 (1984).

Several courts, including this one, have noted an exception to the general rule that they will not examine the basis of the deficiency determination before recognizing the Commissioner's presumption of correctness. Under this exception, a court must not give effect to the presumption of correctness in a case involving unreported income if the Commissioner cannot present "some predicate evidence connecting the taxpayer to the charged activity." *Gerardo v. Commissioner*, 552 F.2d 549, 554 (3d Cir.1977). Most of the cases stating that the Commissioner is not entitled to the presumption based on a naked assessment without factual foundation have involved illegal income. *See Weimerskirch v. Commissioner*, 596 F.2d 358 (9th Cir.1979) (drugs); *Gerardo v. Commissioner*, 552 F.2d 549 (3d Cir.1977) (gambling); *Pizzarello v. U.S.*, 408 F.2d 579 (2d Cir.), *cert. denied*, 396 U.S. 986, 90 S.Ct. 481, 24 L.Ed.2d 450 (1969) (gambling); *Dellacroce v. Commissioner*, 83 T.C. 269 (1984) (racketeering payoff); *Llorente v. Commissioner*, 74 T.C. 260 (1980), *aff'd in part and rev'd in part*, 649 F.2d 152 (2d Cir.1981) (drugs). Given the obvious difficulties in proving the nonreceipt of income, we believe the Commissioner should have to provide evidence linking the taxpayer to the tax-generating activity in cases involving unreported income, whether legal or illegal.

Along with other courts, we have recognized that the Commissioner's deficiency determination is entitled to a presumption of correctness and that the burden of production as well as the ultimate burden of persuasion is placed on the taxpayer. *See Sullivan v. United States*, 618 F.2d 1001, 1008 (3d Cir.1980). The government meets its initial burden of proof in an action to collect tax merely by introducing its deficiency determination. The presumption of correctness establishes a prima facie case, but it arises only if supported by foundational evidence connecting the taxpayer with the tax-generating activity. The presumption shifts the burden of proof to the taxpayer.

If the taxpayer rebuts the presumption by showing that it is arbitrary and erroneous, *see Helvering v. Taylor*, 293 U.S. at 515, 55 S.Ct. at 290, the presumption disappears. Courts differ on whether the burdens of production and persuasion can be shifted to the Commissioner. Most agree that if the presumption drops out the burden of going forward shifts to the Commissioner. However, some courts have stated that at this point the ultimate burden of persuasion, or risk of nonpersuasion, remains on the taxpayer. *See Higginbotham v. United States,* 556 F.2d 1173, 1176 (4th Cir.1977). Other courts, however, have indicated that in unreported income cases the ultimate burden shifts to the Commissioner. *See Keogh v. Commissioner,* 713 F.2d 496, 501 (9th Cir.1983). In 1976, the Supreme Court noted, but did not reconcile, this conflict in the circuits. *See United States v. Janis,* 428 U.S. at 442, 96 S.Ct. at 3026.

In *Sullivan,* we stated that if the taxpayer rebuts the presumption with credible and relevant evidence sufficient to establish that the determination was erroneous, the procedural burden of going forward with the evidence shifts to the Commissioner. We further held, however, that the ultimate burden of proof or persuasion remains with the taxpayer. If the taxpayer offers evidence that the determination was incorrect and the Commissioner offers no evidence to support the assessment, the taxpayer will have met his ultimate burden "unless such evidence is specifically rejected as improbable, unreasonable, or questionable." *Id.* at 1009. * * *

In the case before us, the Commissioner was entitled to the presumption of correctness because he introduced evidence linking the taxpayer to the tax-generating activity. * * * The taxpayer has not shown that the deficiency determination was arbitrary and without factual foundation and he therefore cannot rely on *Gerardo* to dispel the presumption.

* * * the Tax Court properly concluded that the deficiency determination was entitled to its usual presumption of correctness. The court then should have determined whether the taxpayer had at trial, nevertheless, met his burden of ultimate persuasion and shown that the determination was incorrect. The court noted only that "petitioners herein (the taxpayer) presented no affirmative evidence to demonstrate any error in respondent's said determinations, having contented themselves throughout this trial with attacking only the *basis* for respondent's determinations, rather than the accuracy thereof." This statement indicates that the court believed that, once the Commissioner was granted the usual presumption of correctness, the question whether the taxpayer received the allegedly unreported income no longer remained at issue and only the amount of the assessment could be considered.

Even if the Commissioner is entitled to the initial presumption of correctness, the taxpayer must be given the opportunity to prove that the determination was incorrect. In this case, the taxpayer's evidence consisted of denials that he ever received the income in question. A general denial of liability is insufficient to meet the taxpayer's burden of nonpersuasion. We are "not bound to accept taxpayer's testimony at face even when it is uncontradicted if it is improbable, unreasonable, or questionable." *Baird,* 438 F.2d at 493. The Tax Court apparently rejected the taxpayer's testimony on nonreceipt of income not as "improbable, questionable, or unreasonable," but as irrelevant once the Commissioner provided a factual foundation for the assessment and the presumption of correctness arose. The court erred since it was possible that the taxpayer could ultimately prevail by proving that while he engaged in the activity in question he never received the income in question.

It is possible that the Tax Court, on proper consideration of the taxpayer's denial of receipt of the income, will find such denials improbable. Nevertheless, because the court did not explicitly or implicitly reject the taxpayer's testimony, we will remand the case for consideration of this point.

* * *

JONES v. COMMISSIONER
United States Court of Appeals, Tenth Circuit, 1990.
903 F.2d 1301.

STEPHEN H. ANDERSON, CIRCUIT JUDGE.

Cornell Jones appeals a decision of the United States Tax Court sustaining an income tax deficiency for the calendar year 1985 in the amount of $16,490,402 together with additions to tax under 26 U.S.C. §§ 6651(a)(1), 6653(a)(1), 6654, and 6661 totalling $4,125,107. *Jones v. Commissioner,* No. 36601–86 (T.C. Aug. 18, 1988) (Decision); R.Vol. I, Tab 27.[1] The Tax Court made no mention in its opinion of the Commissioner's asserted addition to Jones' 1985 tax under 26 U.S.C. § 6653(a)(2), and only partially sustained the asserted addition under § 6661. *Jones v. Commissioner,* 55 T.C.M. (CCH) 1556 (1988). The Commissioner cross-appeals as to these two items. We affirm the Tax Court's decision concerning the tax deficiency, and remand for further proceedings to determine the correct amount of additions to the tax.

BACKGROUND

Jones was arrested on October 29, 1985 by the Washington, D.C. Metropolitan Police Department after having participated in the purchase of what he then believed to be one kilogram of cocaine from undercover police officers. Jones pled guilty to conspiracy to possess with intent to distribute cocaine in violation of 21 U.S.C. § 846 (1982) and he was sentenced to a term of 9 to 27 years imprisonment.

Jones' arrest was the result of a lengthy investigation of large scale drug trafficking taking place at a small area known as Hanover Place in the District of Columbia. Searches of Jones' residence and of several

---

1. On October 18, 1988 the Tax Court issued an "Order" *sua sponte* which purported to amend its decision by increasing the addition to tax under 26 U.S.C. § 6651(a)(1) and by assessing a final addition to tax related to interest on the deficiency pursuant to 26 U.S.C. § 6653(a)(2). Jones filed his notice of appeal on September 8, 1988; after that date the Tax Court lacked jurisdiction to issue its "Order." It therefore has no effect on the Tax Court's decision dated August 18, 1988. *See, e.g., United States v. 397.51 Acres of Land,* 692 F.2d 688, 693 (10th Cir.1982) (with two recognized exceptions, "[t]he filing of a notice of appeal divests the district court of jurisdiction * * *."); *SEC v. Investors Security Corp.,* 560 F.2d 561, 568 (3d Cir. 1977).

apartments in and around D.C. produced assets worth millions of dollars, including $870,000 cash at his residence and $643,900 cash in bank deposit boxes; three gold ingots; two Mercedes Benz automobiles; jewelry; furs; 28 airline tickets from Washington, D.C. to Las Vegas, Nevada; tickets to a championship fight in Las Vegas; five handguns; over 10.5 kilograms of cocaine; drug packaging paraphernalia; a bill counting machine; communications equipment; and a drug identification kit; all of which convincingly linked Jones to the cocaine trade at Hanover Place. Furthermore, statements by certain individuals to police officers investigating the Hanover Place operation identified Jones as the organizer behind the significant drug activity taking place.

In January 1986 the IRS made a termination assessment against Jones of $33,990,402 based on $68 million in unreported income from drug related activities which the IRS estimated Jones received in the first ten months of 1985 prior to his arrest. The government later modified its estimate of Jones' drug related income, asserting in its statutory notice of deficiency that Jones received unreported income of $33 million in 1985. Jones kept no records of income from drug sales, and he did not file an income tax return for 1985.

Jones petitioned the Tax Court which upheld the deficiency based on the asserted $33 million income for 1985 and certain additions to tax based on the amount of the resulting deficiency. Jones now appeals the Tax Court's ruling on several grounds, the most relevant of which is that the assessment based on $33 million income is unreasonable and arbitrary.[2]

Discussion

Ordinarily, the statutory notice of deficiency is presumed correct; the burden rests on the taxpayer to establish that the determination of income is erroneous. *Zell v. Commissioner,* 763 F.2d 1139, 1141 (10th Cir.1985).[3] As a taxpayer, Jones has the duty to maintain adequate and accurate records to enable him to file a tax return. *See* 26 U.S.C. § 6001; *Anson v. Commissioner,* 328 F.2d 703, 705 (10th Cir.1964)

---

2. Jones' other contentions relate to hearsay evidence which the Tax Court admitted at trial. Although much of the government's evidence consisted of numerous layers of hearsay evidence, most of these otherwise hearsay statements were admitted for very limited purposes, not to prove their truth. Hearsay is admissible to support the methodology used by the Commissioner in arriving at his deficiency assessment. *See DiMauro v. Commissioner,* 706 F.2d 882, 885 (8th Cir.1983); *Avery v. Commissioner,* 574 F.2d 467, 468 (9th Cir.1978). Furthermore, Jones waived most of his objections to the admissibility of evidence by failing to properly object at trial. The fact that he chose to represent himself at trial in no way excuses this waiver. *Wallis v. Commissioner,* 357 F.2d 313, 314 (10th Cir.1966) (*pro se* appearance before Tax Court, "whether by choice or circumstance, does not lessen the impact of applicable rules").

3. At trial, Jones disclaimed any involvement with the drug trade other than the single purchase for which he was arrested. He now claims that the Commissioner's assertion that he received unreported income from illegal drug sales lacks any foundation in fact, thereby making any assessment for such income improper. The evidence produced at trial supports the Tax Court's determination that Jones was in fact involved in drug sales and that he did receive substantial income from sales which he did not report.

("[T]he privilege of original self-assessment accorded the taxpayer carries with it the burden of support through the maintenance of records which clearly and accurately reflect income."). Where, as here, the taxpayer keeps inadequate records or no records at all the Commissioner is entitled to reconstruct the taxpayer's gross receipts and costs to arrive at an assessment for the unreported income. *See Anson,* 328 F.2d at 705–06; *Adamson v. Commissioner,* 745 F.2d 541, 548 (9th Cir.1984) ("The absence of tax records cannot automatically deprive the Commissioner of a rational foundation for the income determination."). Thus a taxpayer who has abandoned the advantage of mathematical precision by failing to keep adequate records cannot complain that the Commissioner's assessment is based on estimates rather than proven amounts of unreported income. *See Anson,* 328 F.2d at 707 (calculation of unreported tip income by use of arithmetic formula acceptable even though such a method "cannot produce exactness").

Jones offered almost no real evidence to prove that the Commissioner's assessment was erroneous except his weak attempts to distance himself from all drug sales. He made no attempt to suggest a more appropriate or more accurate estimate of his drug related income, nor did he suggest who, if not he, was receiving the majority of income arising from drug trafficking at Hanover Place in 1985. Where no such evidence of error is produced, we might ordinarily rely solely on the presumptive correctness of the deficiency notice and dispose of the case without further discussion. As we stated in *Ruidoso Racing Ass'n, Inc. v. Commissioner,* 476 F.2d 502, 507–08 (10th Cir.1973), "With regard to unreported income, the taxpayer must prove that the determination is arbitrary and erroneous * * *."

We pause, however, to discuss Jones' contention that the sheer magnitude of the government's assessment is itself sufficient to demonstrate that it is arbitrary and erroneous. The $33 million income which the government assigned to Jones over a ten-month period is indeed a figure which almost defies credibility. This court has never directly addressed the outer boundary of reasonableness at which point the bare presumption afforded the Commissioner's assessment must ultimately give way; nevertheless, we believe that such a point probably does exist. The Fifth Circuit has concluded that "[T]he absence of adequate tax records does not give the Commissioner carte blanche for imposing Draconian absolutes * * * [even though] such absence does weaken any critique of the Commissioner's methodology." *Webb v. Commissioner,* 394 F.2d 366, 373 (5th Cir.1968); *see Bradford v. Commissioner,* 796 F.2d 303, 306 (9th Cir.1986); *Walker v. Commissioner,* 757 F.2d 36, 37 (3d Cir.1985) ("The Internal Revenue Service has sometimes overreacted [to unreported income from illegal sources] by imposing arbitrary assessments."); *United States v. Carson,* 560 F.2d 693, 698 (5th Cir.1977) (unlimited reliance entirely on a bare presumption of correctness is a position "which would support the most arbitrary of assessments" and "does not become the government's agents * * *.").

Jones has not satisfied any evidentiary burden in contesting the Commissioner's assessment. Had he met such a burden, the presumption of correctness afforded the Commissioner's assessment would disappear and the government would be required to prove the accuracy of its determination. *Cf. Ruidoso Racing Ass'n, Inc. v. Commissioner,* 476 F.2d at 508 (where the government's determination is demonstrably arbitrary * * * "the Commissioner must satisfy the court as to the existence and amount of unreported income."). Rather than offering any explanation or other evidence concerning the amount of drug-related income he received, Jones merely attempted to prove that he received no income from drug sales. His attempt to distance himself from illegal income failed miserably. He therefore has not demonstrated that the government's estimate is exaggerated or arbitrary, nor has he proved that the government lacks factual basis for its assessment. *See United States v. Janis,* 428 U.S. 433, 442, 96 S.Ct. 3021, 3026, 49 L.Ed.2d 1046 (1976) ("Certainly, proof that an assessment is utterly without foundation is proof that it is arbitrary and erroneous.").

After reviewing the entire record before us, we cannot conclude that the government's assessment lacks any reasonable foundation. The formula used to estimate Jones' income from drug sales is sufficiently related to the amount of drug activity taking place at Hanover Place to withstand review. As we stated in *Anson v. Commissioner,* 328 F.2d at 707:

> "Although assessment by formula cannot produce exactness, it can, when adapted and adjusted to particular facts, be expected to reach substantial correctness * * *. We agree with the Tax Court that the Commissioner * * * adopted a reasonable method to compute [the unreported] income."

The record clearly demonstrates that Jones was involved in the cocaine trade taking place at Hanover Place for some indeterminate period of time prior to his arrest in October 1985. At trial, a Metropolitan Police Department sergeant testified that in the one-block area known as Hanover Place, "there were several locations * * * being used for the distribution of the drugs." R.Vol. I, Tab 22 at p. 83. The sergeant stated further: "[t]here was hundreds of people lining the street selling drugs." [4]

As to Jones' involvement in this massive operation, the police sergeant testified that beginning in mid to late 1984,

> "What we did was, we were making arrests. Officers out of my unit were making arrests in the area of the people who were selling right there on the street. The people were brought in and they were

---

4. The testimony of the Metropolitan Police sergeant includes descriptions of the drug trade at Hanover Place as "operating 24 hours a day," with "hundreds" of people working three eight-hour shifts. Money and drugs were located in various apartments along the dead end street making up Hanover Place, and the officer testified that "during 1985 the vehicle traffic was so bad [near Hanover Place] that the traffic couldn't get through the block and they would often times double park for blocks away to get into Hanover Place to purchase drugs." R.Vol. I, Tab 22, pp. 78–99.

interviewed, and they were interrogated as to who was behind the operation on Hanover Place. Several of the individuals that were arrested informed the investigating officers and myself that the person behind the drugs on Hanover Place was Mr. Cornell Jones."

R.Vol. I, Tab 22 at p. 81. In setting up the undercover sale of cocaine substitute to Jones, the police gained further knowledge of his role:

"Q. How did the police department, in its reverse sale operation with Mr. Jones, how did it initially make contact with Mr. Jones?

A. We did not know that we were actually making contact with Mr. Jones. We had a cooperating individual who said that it had been selling drugs to an individual who identified himself as the Czar of Hanover Place. This individual, to us, was believed to be Mr. Cronell Jones [sic]."

Id. at p. 90.

The government originally estimated Jones' unreported income based on an assumption that drug sales at Hanover Place totalled 20 kilograms per week, or 20,000 weekly sales of one-gram bags at the street price of $100 each. The government's revenue agent testified that in preparing the statutory notice of deficiency he had halved the original sales volume "in an effort to come up with what I thought was a more reasonable and conservative estimate * * *." *Id.* at 57.

* * *

It is almost certain that the Commissioner's assessment of unreported income is inaccurate. The inaccuracy results, however, not from uncertainty concerning Jones' significant involvement in this massive drug scheme, but from his failure to maintain any records whatsoever reflecting drug related income, and his refusal to even suggest a more accurate amount or more reasonable basis to compute his income. There is simply too much evidence supporting the government's assessment of enormous income derived from illegal sources to sustain Jones' attack which in turn is totally devoid of any evidentiary foundation. We conclude that the government's assessment is entitled to a presumption of correctness; therefore, we affirm the Tax Court's decision as to the income tax deficiency for the calendar year 1985.

* * *

CONCLUSION

The government has no burden of proof as to its notice of deficiency in the face of Jones' silence at trial except that the assessment it makes must be reasonably based on facts appearing in the record. The record before us amply demonstrates that Jones was significantly involved in a massive drug selling operation for some period preceding his arrest in 1985. The evidence produced at trial supports the Tax Court's conclusion that the assessment of unreported income was reasonable in light of the enormous proceeds which were generated by the Hanover Place drug operation. We therefore affirm the Tax Court's decision sustaining the income tax deficiency.

Note

Would the burden shift to the IRS if the alleged arbitrary deficiency resulted from the disallowance of deductions rather than omissions from income? See Time Insurance Co. v. Commissioner, 86 T.C. 298 (1986), in which the court held that the taxpayer always bears the burden of proving the allowability of deductions.

SECTION 3. TAX COURT LITIGATION

A. JURISDICTIONAL PREREQUISITES

(1) Timely Filed Petition

McKAY v. COMMISSIONER
United States Court of Appeals, Ninth Circuit, 1989.
886 F.2d 1237.

JAMES R. BROWNING, CIRCUIT JUDGE:

On April 7, 1977 the IRS issued a notice of deficiencies and fraud penalties with respect to appellant's 1972 and 1973 income tax returns. Some eight years later, appellant filed a pro se petition for redetermination. The tax court dismissed the petition as untimely under 26 U.S.C. § 6213(a), which requires that such a petition be filed "[w]ithin 90 days * * * after the notice of deficiency authorized in section 6212 is mailed."

Appellant claims he did not receive the notice of deficiency. The tax court found appellant received a copy of the notice from his attorney, Herbert D. Sturman, in ample time to file a timely petition for review in the tax court. That factual finding is not clearly erroneous. Although IRS records of mailing and receipt of such notices were destroyed after 5 years, appellant's attorney testified he received the notice and it was and remained his normal practice to personally deliver such notices to his clients within a few days of receipt. The tax court credited Sturman's testimony, noting that he was a credible and forthright witness, and that his testimony was uncontroverted. Such credibility determinations are for the tax court. Moreover, petitioner declined to testify and since the fact at issue was peculiarly within his knowledge, the court properly concluded his testimony would be unfavorable to him. * * *.

As the government points out, the finding was confirmed by contemporaneous documentary evidence—including Sturman's letter of April 13, 1977 to the government acknowledging receipt of the deficiency notice—and by the fact that although appellant denied receipt of the notice, he attached a copy to his petition for review.

* * *

Appellant contends the notice of deficiency was ineffective because it was not addressed to his "last known address" within the meaning of section 6212(b)(1). "Actual notice" is the central goal of this section.

Clodfelter v. Commissioner, 527 F.2d 754, 756 (9th Cir.1975). "[I]f mailing results in actual notice without prejudicial delay * * * it meets the conditions of § 6212(a) no matter to what address the notice successfully was sent." *Id.* at 757. For the same reason it is irrelevant that actual notice is conveyed by a copy of the notice of deficiency rather than the original. Either is sufficient to provide the taxpayer with the information he requires to obtain pre-payment review by filing a timely petition in the tax court.

Mulvania v. Commissioner, 769 F.2d 1376 (9th Cir.1985), is not to the contrary. There the taxpayer's accountant informed the taxpayer of the receipt of a copy of a misaddressed notice of deficiency. There was "no evidence in the record that [the accountant] discussed the contents of the notice with Mulvania," *id.* at 1377, and Mulvania "never physically received a notice of deficiency." *Id.* at 1379. The IRS argued that it was sufficient that the taxpayer "had actual knowledge of the notice even if not its contents." *Id.* at 1380. We held to the contrary, distinguishing *Clodfelter* as a case in which a notice of deficiency was "actually, physically received by a taxpayer." *Id.* at 1378.

Since appellant, unlike the taxpayer in *Mulvania*, had "actual notice without prejudicial delay" of the contents of the 1977 notice, through timely receipt of an exact copy of that notice, his petition filed eight years later was properly dismissed. *Clodfelter*, 527 F.2d at 756; 26 U.S.C. § 6213(a); *see also Tenzer v. Commissioner*, 285 F.2d 956, 958 (9th Cir.1960) (copy of notice personally delivered to taxpayer by agent of Commissioner). We confine our ruling to cases in which it is beyond contention that the taxpayer has received all of the information that would be furnished by receipt of the notice of deficiency itself—that is, cases in which the taxpayer has received a duplicate of the notice of deficiency.

Affirmed.

SCHROEDER, CIRCUIT JUDGE, dissenting:

The majority's decision in this case will make the administration of the law for the future more burdensome.

Congress has declared that when the IRS, by appropriate means, sends a notice of deficiency to the taxpayer's last known address, the notice is effective regardless of whether the taxpayer actually receives it. An IRS mailing of a notice to an attorney can be as effective as a mailing to the taxpayer's "last known address," but only when the taxpayer requests that all communications be mailed directly to the attorney. A limited power of attorney, requesting that copies of correspondence be sent to the taxpayer's attorney or other agent, does not effect a change of the taxpayer's last known address, and notice to the attorney does not constitute valid notice to the taxpayer.

In our court's prior decisions, we have recognized that the IRS may provide valid notice to the taxpayer by personally delivering a copy of the notice to the taxpayer, or by mailing the notice to an address other than the taxpayer's last known address if the notice actually reaches the taxpayer through the mail. But we have squarely, and correctly, held that the agent of the taxpayer cannot provide notice by informing the taxpayer that the agent has received a copy of a misaddressed notice. *Mulvania v. CIR*, 769 F.2d 1376, 1380–81 (9th Cir.1985).

In this case, the IRS did not mail the notice to the taxpayer's last known address. The taxpayer did not designate his attorney to be the recipient of all communications from the IRS. In this case, as in *Mulvania*, the only notice the taxpayer received was from his agent, not from the IRS. Yet the majority holds that the notice was as valid as if the IRS had correctly addressed the original mailing. It distinguishes *Mulvania* on the ground that here the agent provided the taxpayer with an actual physical copy of the notice, whereas in *Mulvania* the agent did not.

Until today's decision, the lines were drawn with clarity; if the IRS did not itself provide actual notice to the taxpayer or mail the notice to the taxpayer's last known address, the notice was invalid. We now depart from that line, and hold that in some circumstances notice can be provided by the taxpayer's own attorney, rather than the IRS. The inquiry now must shift from what IRS records show, to the nature of communications between tax advisors and clients. This decision opens up the prospect of costly and time-consuming litigation probing sensitive relationships. It provides a disincentive for accurate record keeping on the part of the IRS, and will impede communication between tax advisors and their clients.

The benefit from salvaging a few misdirected notices is not worth this high price. In my view, Chief Judge Goodwin aptly summarized the relevant policy concerns in his opinion in *Mulvania*:

> It is better for the government to lose some revenue as the result of its clerical error than to create uncertainty. If [the taxpayer's agent], either intentionally or unintentionally, had not informed Mulvania of the receipt of the copy of the notice of deficiency, then Mulvania would not have received any notification of the deficiency. Tax law requires more solid footings than the happenstance of a tax adviser telephoning a client to tell him of a letter from the IRS.

> We conclude that, where a notice of deficiency has been misaddressed to the taxpayer or sent only to an adviser who is merely authorized to receive a copy of such a notice, actual notice is necessary but not sufficient to make the notice valid. The IRS is not forgiven for its clerical errors or for mailing notice to the wrong party unless the taxpayer, through his own actions, renders the Commissioner's errors harmless.

769 F.2d at 1380–81.

Today's decision is contrary to the spirit, if not the letter, of that decision and of the law as Congress intended it to operate. I therefore respectfully dissent.

ABELES v. COMMISSIONER
Tax Court of the United States, 1988.
91 T.C. 1019.

[Editors' note: Barbara and Harold Abeles filed joint federal income tax returns for their 1975, 1976, and 1977 tax years. The IRS issued a joint notice of deficiency to them in 1980 for the tax year 1976. Barbara Abeles filed her 1981 return on June 15, 1982, indicating her status as married, filing separately, and showing a new address for her. On November 15, 1982, the IRS issued a joint notice of deficiency for the couple's 1975 and 1977 tax years. This notice was sent only to Harold Abeles's address. Barbara never received actual notice of the 1982 deficiency notice until 1986, when the IRS levied on her bank accounts and placed a lien against her house. She then filed an untimely petition for redetermination in the Tax Court.]

* * *

In order to determine whether this Court has jurisdiction over the subject matter of petitioner's 1975 and 1977 taxable years, we must first determine whether respondent was required, pursuant to section 6212(b)(2), to send duplicate originals of the joint statutory notice of deficiency concerning such taxable years to each of the Abeles' last known addresses. Under section 6212(b)(2), respondent is required to send duplicate originals, rather than a single joint notice, "if the Secretary has been notified by either spouse that separate residences have been established." Thus, the question is: What constitutes sufficient notice that "separate residences have been established?"

Respondent focuses upon the literal wording of the statute, and contends that the statutory language "notified * * * that separate residences have been established" should be interpreted as: "notified that the spouses no longer cohabit." From this, respondent argues that duplicate originals of the joint notice are required to be sent only where respondent has been notified that the joint filers have discontinued living together.

Petitioner contends that such statutory language should be interpreted as: "notified that each spouse maintains separate last known addresses." Based on this interpretation, petitioner argues that duplicate originals of the joint notice of deficiency are required to be sent to each spouse's last known address whenever respondent has been notified that each joint filer maintains a last known address different from the other joint filer's.

While we recognize that, in general, the plain language of a statute controls, we do not accept respondent's interpretation or application of the statute, as it is one which exalts the statute's form at the demise of its substance. As the Supreme Court has stated:

> There is, of course, no more persuasive evidence of the purpose of a statute than the words by which the legislature undertook to give

expression to its wishes. Often these words are sufficient in and of themselves to determine the purpose of the legislation. In such cases we have followed their plain meaning. When that meaning has led to absurd or futile results, however, this Court has looked beyond the words to the purpose of the act. Frequently, however, even when the plain meaning did not produce absurd results but merely an unreasonable one "plainly at variance with the policy of the legislation as a whole" this Court has followed that purpose, rather than the literal words. * * * [*United States v. American Trucking Associations, Inc.*, 310 U.S. 534, 543 (1940), quoting *Ozawa v. United States*, 260 U.S. 178, 194 (1922). (Fn. refs. omitted.)]

We shall do the same in this instance.

By enacting sections 6212 and 6213, Congress intended to provide a means by which a taxpayer is provided notice of a tax deficiency determination made by respondent such that the taxpayer is afforded an opportunity to avail himself or herself, if desired, to a forum in which such determination of deficiency could be litigated prior to the taxpayer's having to make payment of the tax liability. See *Dolan v. Commissioner*, 44 T.C. 420, 433 (1965). Congress' focus, when it considered what type of notice should be required to be sent in connection with a joint return, was upon the type of relationship which is presumed to exist as between two joint filers. Congress believed that most marital relationships maintain open and frequent communication between the spouses such "that receipt of the notice by either spouse would be well calculated to equal notice to both." *Cohen v. United States*, 297 F.2d 760, 773 (9th Cir.1962). Thus, Congress provided that respondent must send a single joint notice to the joint filers as the general rule. Congress also recognized, however, that not all marital relationships continued to deserve such a presumption of open communication. It is for this reason that Congress provided for the issuance of a duplicate original of the joint notice to each of the joint filers. That is, Congress provided that duplicate originals of the joint notice of deficiency should be sent to each spouse's last known address when, by reason of communications the Commissioner has received from the taxpayer, it is evident that a single joint notice could not reasonably be expected to constitute notice to both joint filers. See *Dolan v. Commissioner, supra* at 434, where we said that "The provision relating to the sending of duplicate originals of the joint notices where respondent has been notified that the spouses have *separate addresses* clearly was intended to assure that each spouse received actual notice, if respondent chose to send a joint notice of deficiency." [8]

If we were to adopt respondent's interpretation of section 6212(b)(2)—that the focus is upon whether notice had been given that the spouses no longer cohabited—we would not be giving proper deference to Congress' intent. Such an interpretation would, as it did in this case, lead to respondent's sending a statutory notice to only one of the joint filers' last known addresses, i.e., the primary taxpayer's last

---

8. See also *Reno v. Commissioner*, T.C. Memo. 1980–255.

known address, despite the spousal taxpayer's having previously indicated to respondent that he or she was using a separate address to which respondent should have reasonably believed the spousal taxpayer wanted all communications sent. It would make no sense to say that the notice required of the taxpayer to cause duplicate originals of the joint notice to be issued is one which relates to the taxpayer's living arrangements, when it has long been the law that the validity of a notice of deficiency under section 6212 depends upon that notice's being mailed to the taxpayer's last known address, and when it has long been recognized that one's last known address is not necessarily one's residence.

In addition, and more importantly, respondent's interpretation would also lead to respondent's discordant conclusion that it is possible for a spousal taxpayer to have *two* last known addresses. Respondent argues that, without notice that the joint filers no longer cohabit, it would be appropriate to continue to use the spousal taxpayer's last known *joint* address, as such was determined from an examination of the joint tax account records maintained under the primary TIN, for communications concerning that taxpayer's jointly filed returns. Further, respondent contends that it would only be appropriate to use the spousal taxpayer's *separate* last known address, as determined from a reference to the computer records maintained under the spousal TIN, for communications concerning that person's subsequently filed separate returns.

We have consistently held that a taxpayer's last known address is defined as "the last known permanent address or legal residence of the taxpayer, or the last known temporary address of a definite duration or period to which *all* communications during such period should be sent." *Weinroth v. Commissioner*, 74 T.C. 430, 435 (1980) (emphasis in original); *McCormick v. Commissioner*, 55 T.C. 138, 141 (1970). From such a definition, it is clear that respondent can have, with respect to any one taxpayer, only one last known address on the date that a notice of deficiency is issued.[9] To argue that it is reasonable to assume that a taxpayer wishes communications from the IRS to be sent to one of several addresses, depending upon the filing status utilized in those years, is absurd. A "last known" address is precisely that; if respondent knows of one address for a taxpayer and is then notified of another address for the same taxpayer, such other address supersedes the previous address and becomes, as far as respondent is concerned, that taxpayer's "last known address," regardless of the filing status used by the taxpayer when using the different addresses.

To give effect to the policy behind section 6212(b)(2), and to avoid the incongruous results another interpretation of the statute would provide, we hold that compliance with such section requires respondent

---

9. See *Karosen v. Commissioner*, T.C. Memo. 1983–540, for an explanation of how respondent should proceed when confronted with what appears to be multiple last known addresses for a lone taxpayer.

to send duplicate originals of the joint notice of deficiency to each spouse's last known address whenever respondent has been notified, prior to the time that the notice of deficiency is to be issued, that the joint filers maintain separate last known addresses. Further, this rule shall apply so long as respondent is given notice that the two spouses do not share the same last known address, even if respondent is given notice of only one of such spouses' last known addresses.

Thus, to determine whether respondent was required to send duplicate originals of the joint notice to each of the Abeles' last known addresses, we must determine whether petitioner had, prior to the date the notice of deficiency was mailed, given respondent notice of a new last known address different from that of Mr. Abeles. This is because, if petitioner had not so given respondent notice of a new last known address, she could not be said to have taken the action which would require respondent to send such duplicate originals of the joint notice to each of the Abeles.

In addition to our definition of a last known address, as such was expressed in *Weinroth v. Commissioner, supra*, we have held that, as a general proposition, a taxpayer's "last known address" is that address to which, in light of all surrounding facts and circumstances, respondent reasonably believed the taxpayer wished the notice of deficiency to be sent. *Looper v. Commissioner*, 73 T.C. 690 (1980). Further, it has heretofore been our position that respondent is entitled to treat the address of the taxpayer, appearing on the return under examination, as the taxpayer's last known address, within the meaning of section 6212, absent "clear and concise notification" of an address change. *Alta Sierra Vista, Inc. v. Commissioner*, 62 T.C. 367, 374 (1974), affd. 538 F.2d 334 (9th Cir.1976).

If respondent is notified of a change of address, however, respondent must exercise reasonable care and diligence in ascertaining, and mailing the notice of deficiency to, the correct address. *Keeton v. Commissioner, supra* at 382; *Alta Sierra Vista, Inc. v. Commissioner, supra* at 374; *O'Brien's v. Commissioner*, 62 T.C. 543, 550 (1974).[10] When attempting to reasonably determine a taxpayer's last known address, respondent is then entitled to rely upon those documents submitted to him by the taxpayer. *Brown v. Commissioner*, 78 T.C. 215, 219 (1982). However, in connection with whether the taxpayer has given the requisite notice of a change in address, we have heretofore taken the position that the filing of a return, which is more recent than, and which bears an address different from that appearing on, the return under examination, does not constitute, for purposes of mailing a notice of deficiency with respect to that return under examination,

---

10. See Borison, "The Evolving Due Diligence Requirement of the Service in Determining a Taxpayer's Last Known Address," 41 Tax Law Rev. 111 (1985), for an in-depth discussion of what has previously been considered, by this and other courts, to be: (1) "Clear and concise notification" of a change of address; and, (2) an exercise of due diligence by the Internal Revenue Service in determining a taxpayer's last known address.

the necessary notice of an address change. *Weinroth v. Commissioner, supra* at 436–437; *Budlong v. Commissioner,* 58 T.C. 850, 852–853 (1972).

This Court's position with respect to the effect to be given a more recently filed return for purposes of determining a taxpayer's last known address was initially set forth in *Budlong v. Commissioner, supra.* In that case, the taxable year at issue was 1968, and the subsequently filed return was for the 1969 taxable year. The 1969 return had been filed only 20 days prior to the date the notice of deficiency concerning 1968 was mailed. In determining whether the 1969 return was sufficient notice of an address change, we held:

> Petitioners' filing of their 1969 return with the North-Atlantic Service Center is not sufficient notification to respondent. The service center does not have any responsibility with respect to the auditing of returns or the issuing of statutory notices of deficiency. The service center provides the means for handling in an effective, administrative fashion the millions of returns to be filed with the district directors within its realm. The Code does not require a check with a service center for verification of the "last known address" of a taxpayer prior to the issuance of a statutory notice. *At best, petitioners' filing of their 1969 return would, upon final processing, indicate to respondent that for their 1969 taxable year correspondence to petitioners should be directed to the address thereon.* [*Budlong v. Commissioner, supra* at 852–853; emphasis added.]

Although not expressly stated in the *Budlong* opinion, our holding that a more recently filed return was not notice of a change of address was based, in part, upon to whom we were willing to attribute knowledge of the information contained in a recently filed return. At the time of the *Budlong* opinion, in 1972, the computer capabilities of the IRS were such that an agent of respondent responsible for issuing a notice of deficiency did not have the ability to conduct, within a reasonable time, a search of the IRS's computer files for a more recent address for the taxpayer. Today, however, the state of the IRS's computer capabilities is such that a computer search of the information retained with respect to a certain taxpayer, including his or her last known address, may be performed by respondent's agent without unreasonable effort or delay. See *Crum v. Commissioner,* 635 F.2d 895, 900 (D.C.Cir.1980), revg. an unreported order of this Court, wherein the District of Columbia Circuit Court of Appeals recognized that "a search of the computer files for a taxpayer's most recent address would take less than a minute today, [whereas] that same task would have taken approximately six weeks in 1972."

In contrast to our position, the U.S. Court of Appeals for the Ninth Circuit has held:

> A taxpayer's last known address is that on his most recent return, unless the taxpayer communicates to the IRS "clear and concise" notice of a change of address. See *McPartlin v. Commissioner,* 653 F.2d 1185, 1189 (7th Cir.1981); *Alta Sierra Vista, Inc. v. Commissioner,* 62

T.C. 367 (1974), *aff'd mem*, 538 F.2d 334 (9th Cir.1976). [*United States v. Zolla*, 724 F.2d 808, 810 (9th Cir.1984).]

The Ninth Circuit has adopted this standard partly because it has recognized the advancements made in the computer capabilities of the IRS, and partly because it has consistently applied ordinary agency principles to governmental departments for purposes of determining to whom knowledge should be attributed. See *Cool Fuel, Inc. v. Connett*, 685 F.2d 309 (1982), citing *Welch v. Schweitzer*, 106 F.2d 885 (9th Cir.1939), and *Crum v. Commissioner, supra*. As early as 1939, the Ninth Circuit said:

> This recognized continued relationship of the taxpayer to the Treasury created by statute * * * made available in this case to the Commissioner the true residence address of the taxpayer *as shown in his later returns*. The application of ordinary business principles to the tax business of the government would seem to require the Commissioner to avail himself of the facilities of his business organization in the performance of his duty to mail the notice of deficiency. [*Welch v. Schweitzer*, 106 F.2d 885, 887 (9th Cir.1939); emphasis added.]

This Court has previously intimated that we may, at some point, attribute knowledge of an address on a more recently filed return to the agent responsible for mailing a notice of deficiency. In *Pyo v. Commissioner, supra*, we were faced with a factual pattern in which the taxpayers had filed a Federal income tax return for the years at issue which reflected an "F" Street address with the Fresno, California, Service Center. The taxpayers subsequently moved to a "C" Street address and filed Federal income tax returns reflecting such address with the Fresno Service Center. Subsequently, the Commissioner's Los Angeles District Director's Office sent a notice of deficiency to the taxpayers, for the years at issue, to the taxpayers' F Street address. With respect to such facts, we stated:

> It is * * * relevant to observe that at the time the notice of deficiency was first mailed to [the taxpayers] at their [F Street] address, the Los Angeles District Director's Office employees who mailed this document to petitioners had access to the Fresno Service Center computer system which, at that time, contained their [C Street] address. Although, at this juncture, we will not attribute the information contained in this computer system to such employees and require them to consult this system in order to satisfy the "last known address" investigative responsibilities, the time may come when this is appropriate. See *Weinroth v. Commissioner*, 74 T.C. 430, 437 n. 7 (1980). * * * [*Pyo v. Commissioner, supra* at 637 n. 10.]

In *Weinroth v. Commissioner, supra* at 437 n. 7, we said:

> Although petitioners adduced some evidence that the Internal Revenue Service now employs a computerized system to update its files from the filing of subsequent returns, this evidence was by no means sufficient for us to reconsider our holding in *Budlong [v. Commissioner, supra]*. Petitioners did not show whether this system was in use when the notice of deficiency was issued nor the efficacy of the system.

To the contrary, in the case at hand the evidence shows that the IRS's computer system was available to respondent's agent responsible for mailing the notice of deficiency, and that the system would have reflected the address from petitioner's most recently filed return had such agent caused a computer search of petitioner's TIN. Considering the technological advancement respondent's computer system has undergone, and the efficacy such system has achieved, we hold that the time has come for us to adopt a new rule with respect to whether a more recently filed return should be considered notice of a change of address.

For purposes of determining whether a notice of deficiency has been properly mailed to the taxpayer's last known address, we now hold that a taxpayer's last known address is that address which appears on the taxpayer's most recently filed return, unless respondent has been given clear and concise notification of a different address. For these purposes, however, we hold that a taxpayer's "most recently filed return" is that return which has been properly processed by an IRS service center [11] such that the address appearing on such return was available to respondent's agent when that agent prepared to send a notice of deficiency in connection with an examination of a previously filed return. Further, we hold that the address from the more recently filed return is *available* to the agent issuing a notice of deficiency with respect to a previously filed return, if such address could be obtained by a computer generation of an IRS computer transcript using the taxpayer's TIN in the case of a separately filed return, or *both* taxpayers' TINs in the case of a previously filed joint return.

In so holding, we are merely reiterating our position that what is of significance is what respondent knew at the time the statutory notice was issued (*Alta Sierra Vista, Inc. v. Commissioner, supra*), and attributing to respondent information which respondent knows, or should know, with respect to a taxpayer's last known address, through the use of its computer system.

* * *

We thus conclude that: (1) Petitioner's motion to dismiss for lack of jurisdiction, based upon the invalidity of the notice of deficiency concerning petitioner's 1975 and 1977 taxable years, will be granted; (2) respondent's motion to dismiss for lack of jurisdiction, based upon the untimeliness of the petition herein as such related to petitioner's 1976 taxable year, will be granted; and, (3) respondent's motion to dismiss for lack of jurisdiction, based upon the lack of a notice of deficiency concerning petitioner's 1978 taxable year, will be granted.

To reflect the foregoing,

---

11. We express no opinion with respect to the situation where respondent fails to exercise reasonable diligence in the processing of a return, and where, had reasonable diligence been exercised, such return would have been the taxpayer's "most recently filed return." Because such facts are not now before us, we leave that case for consideration at another time.

An appropriate order will be entered.

Reviewed by the Court.

NIMS, CHABOT, WHITAKER, KÖRNER, SHIELDS, COHEN, CLAPP, SWIFT, JACOBS, WRIGHT, PARR, WELLS, WHALEN, and COLVIN, JJ., agree with the majority opinion.

* * *

RUWE, J., dissenting: Today the majority announces that it is overruling nearly 16 years of precedent in this Court. The principles of these prior opinions still appear to be generally supported by a majority of the courts of appeals. See *King v. Commissioner,* 857 F.2d 676, 679 n. 5 (9th Cir.1988) (noting that the Tax Court and a majority of the courts of appeals have ruled that a subsequent return is not wholly determinative of a taxpayer's last known address). The majority, while continuing to adhere to a rationale requiring respondent to "exercise reasonable diligence in ascertaining the taxpayer's correct address" (see *Alta Sierra Vista, Inc. v. Commissioner, supra* at 374), nevertheless finds that respondent was unreasonable on November 30, 1982 (the date the notice of deficiency was mailed) in determining petitioner's last known address in conformity with the very rules we have prescribed prior to today. Exacerbating this situation is the fact that both the old and new rules for determining a taxpayer's last known address are largely procedural in nature, making it of utmost importance that the controlling rules provide a "bright line" so that respondent has "clear guidance as to what information it must examine in determining a taxpayer's last known address."

I do not disagree with the trial judge's fact finding regarding the technological advances in respondent's computer capabilities nor do I advocate unswerving adherence to past precedent for its own sake. Although the majority's new rule will require respondent to increase significantly his use of computer resources, I do not find anything in the record indicating that these new requirements are unreasonable if they are *prospective* requirements. However, invalidation of the notice of deficiency in issue, which was mailed 6 years ago in accordance with procedures we upheld until today, is inequitable and inconsistent with any rule whose foundation is based upon the required exercise of reasonable diligence.

Proper resolution of this case and implementation of the majority's new rule requires a consideration of competing objectives. On the one hand, the rules for determining a taxpayer's last known address are designed to provide "petitioner with prompt and fair notice of the deficiencies." *Alta Sierra Vista, Inc. v. Commissioner, supra* at 377. The best methods for achieving this objective will necessarily change with technological advancements. Competing with the objective of giving actual notice is the recognition that respondent should not be required to exhaust all possibilities in ascertaining a last known address. The very structure of section 6212(b)(1) recognizes that actual notice is not always reasonably possible and that actual receipt of the notice is not a prerequisite to validity. *King v. Commissioner, supra* at 679. Finally, given the numerous possible methods that might be used to determine a last known address, the rules for ascertaining a taxpayer's last known address should be clear and serve as a reliable guide to the respondent. *King v. Commissioner, supra* at 680. The application of new and different rules to notices of deficiency mailed in prior years, in accordance with our then-outstanding precedents, totally ignores these last two considerations and makes our opinions an unreliable source of guidance. Following the majority's approach, it is possible that 6 years from now we might invalidate a notice issued this year in conformity with the majority's new rule by finding that there existed even better methods for determining a last known address.

A solution is to apply the majority's new rules for determining a taxpayer's last known address prospectively only. The primary authority for limiting the retroactive application of judicial decisions is *Chevron Oil Co. v. Huson*, 404 U.S. 97 (1971).[1] * * *

* * *

Chevron sets forth three separate factors to be considered when evaluating the extent to which a new rule will not be applied retroactively. "First, the decision to be applied nonretroactively must establish a new principle of law, either by overruling clear past precedent on which litigants may have relied, * * * or by deciding an issue of first impression whose resolution was not clearly foreshadowed." *Chevron Oil Co. v. Huson, supra* at 106. There is no doubt that we are overruling "clear past precedent" in this Court. Presently, most courts have said that respondent is required to consult computer records for the address on the taxpayer's most recent return *only* when he knows, or should know, based on all the facts and circumstances, that the taxpayer has moved. While the majority cites cases indicating that we might at some point consider new requirements for determining a taxpayer's last known address, none of our opinions clearly foreshadow the specific rules laid down in the majority opinion.

The majority holds that the address appearing on a taxpayer's most recently filed return is his or her last known address *and* that this address "is *available* to the agent issuing a notice of deficiency with respect to a previously filed return, if such address could be obtained by a computer generation of an IRS computer transcript using the taxpayer's TIN [social security number] in the case of a separately filed return, or *both* taxpayers' TINs in the case of a previously filed joint return." The majority does not cite, and I am unaware of, any cases from other courts requiring respondent to ascertain joint filers' last known addresses by not only searching for subsequently filed returns using the primary taxpayer's social security number, but also by conducting an independent search for subsequent separate returns that

---

1. A very recent application of the *Chevron* case by the Court which has appellate jurisdiction over this case is contained in *Austin v. City of Bisbee, Arizona*, 855 F.2d 1429 (9th Cir.1988).

might possibly have been filed by the spouse even though the spouse gave no other indication that he/she was maintaining a separate residence. Indeed, the majority's new rule also goes beyond any decision previously rendered by the one court that has consistently differed with the Tax Court in this area, the Ninth Circuit Court of Appeals.

* * *

Aside from overruling clear past precedent, the majority opinion also decides an issue that is before this Court for the first time. Respondent argued that a literal interpretation of section 6212(b)(2) supports his decision in this case to not conduct an independent search absent specific notice to him "by either spouse that separate *residences* have been established." Sec. 6212(b)(2); emphasis added. Petitioner's most recent return shows the address of her accountants and does not purport to indicate that it was her residential address. The majority opinion cites no precedent rejecting (or even discussing) respondent's literal application of the statute nor any opinion "clearly foreshadowing" the result reached by the majority. Indeed, I think even the majority would concede respondent is "literally" correct. Under these circumstances, the majority's ruling was not clearly foreseeable nor could respondent's approach to the "last known address" determination be branded unreasonable.

The second factor considered in *Chevron* requires "looking to the prior history of the rule in question, its purpose and effect, and whether retrospective operation will further or retard its operation." *Chevron Oil Co. v. Huson, supra* at 107. The purpose of the rule announced by the majority is to enhance the likelihood of actual notice by requiring respondent to use his present computer capabilities when determining the taxpayer's last known address. At the same time, one of the concepts behind the statutory provision is that actual notice is not required so long as respondent's method for determining a taxpayer's last known address is reasonable. Nothing can now be done to improve past determinations of last known addresses. The issue is whether respondent was reasonable. Retroactive application as a sanction is inappropriate where respondent adhered to procedures which we had previously found sufficient. The legislative purpose of prohibiting the assessment of a deficiency prior to giving notice of a deficiency could arguably be served by retroactive application, but then we would have to ignore the legislative intent, that it is not actual notice, but only the exercise of reasonable diligence by respondent that is required.

The third factor to be considered in a retroactivity determination is the weighing of the inequities that would result. *Chevron Oil Co. v. Huson, supra* at 107. The majority's opinion will invalidate an unknown number of notices of deficiency issued in conformity with our prior opinions and will result in the wholesale dismissal of an unknown number of cases on jurisdictional grounds without ever considering the underlying facts and law determinative of the actual tax liability. It is also likely that the statute of limitations will prevent respondent from reissuing notices in the vast majority of such cases.[2] Respondent conformed his conduct to the requirements set forth in our prior opinions, and it is inequitable to conclude that he should be barred from the opportunity of ever obtaining a correct determination of tax based upon the individual merits of these cases.[3] This result is particularly inequitable considering the procedural nature of the majority's new rule. It is true that taxpayers such as petitioner also suffer a disadvantage if the rule is not applied retroactively because nonretroactive application will result in loss of a prepayment forum. Taxpayers, however, may still obtain a resolution of their cases on the merits, in that they still have an opportunity for an administrative disposition with respondent and, if that proves unsuccessful, the merits can be adjudicated in a refund suit.

Another equitable factor to consider is the significant increase in the burdens being placed on respondent. The majority's broad based rule will require computer searches using social security numbers of all taxpayers in all situations. The majority and the Ninth Circuit in *Wallin v. Commissioner, supra,* recognized that it was respondent's long-standing practice normally to restrict his search for later filed returns to one looking for primary taxpayers' social security numbers. If the taxpayer appeared as the spousal taxpayer on a subsequent return, this type of search would not reveal it. This general practice has never previously been criticized in the absence of other factors putting respondent on notice that the taxpayer has moved. Under the new rule, it seems clear that whenever a notice of deficiency is to be mailed regarding a joint liability, the respondent will be required, in all cases, to search for subsequently filed returns using both the primary and spousal social security number. It will also be necessary for the search to cover the possibility that either of the prior spouses might have remarried and been listed as either primary or spousal taxpayers on their subsequent joint returns. Notices of deficiency regarding individual returns will also require similar searches for subsequently filed joint returns where the individual's name may have changed and/or the individual is listed as the spousal taxpayer, rather than the primary taxpayer. It is likely that all of the possible search variations will frequently be necessary since taxpayers can, but frequently do not, file early. For example, a computer search for a primary taxpayer made on April 1, that fails to show a return for the prior year, may mean that no return has yet been filed or processed, but may also mean that the taxpayer is listed as a spouse on a recently filed joint return.

---

2. A notice of deficiency incorrectly addressed and not received by a taxpayer prior to the 90th day after its mailing does not toll the running of the statute of limitations. *Boren v. Riddell,* 241 F.2d 670, 671 (9th Cir.1957); *Welch v. Schweitzer,* 106 F.2d 885 (9th Cir.1939); *Reddock v. Commissioner,* 72 T.C. 21, 26 (1979); *Rodgers v. Commissioner,* 57 T.C. 711, 713 (1972).

3. As previously noted, it is far from clear how the Ninth Circuit will rule if this case is appealed. In any event, the opinions definitively setting forth the Ninth Circuit rule were decided subsequent to issuance of the notice of deficiency in this case. *Wallin v. Commissioner,* 744 F.2d 674 (9th Cir.1984), revg. a Memorandum Opinion of this Court; *United States v. Zolla,* 724 F.2d 808 (9th Cir.1984).

Considering that over one hundred million individual income tax returns are filed each year (see Internal Revenue Service Annual Report 1987), the increased obligations imposed by the majority's rule, and the possibility that significant system changes are necessary, it is inequitable to invalidate notices of deficiency issued prior to today's ruling in conformity with our prior opinions.

A final equitable consideration that applies to all taxpayers is that retroactive application of the majority's new rule will result in disparate treatment of similarly situated taxpayers depending upon whether their case was disposed of before or after the announcement of our new standards.

Regarding the equities in this particular case, the facts do not support special consideration for petitioner. Petitioner apparently relied totally upon her ex-husband to handle her tax matters, even to the extent of being ignorant about whether returns were ever filed. When petitioner separated from her husband, she apparently made no provisions for ascertaining the status of her tax obligations for prior years and failed to notify respondent that she had changed residences. The fact that she filed a subsequent return using the filing status of married filing separately and giving her address as "c/o: Segal, Goldman & Macnow, Inc.," her accountants, gave no notice that petitioner was separated or had changed her residence, nor, in my opinion did it constitute "clear and concise notification from the taxpayer directing the Commissioner to use a different address" with respect to correspondence involving prior years. It is only after the majority's establishment of a "bright line" test that petitioner's subsequent return in this case can be said to constitute sufficient notification of a change in her last known address for the years in issue.

For the reasons set forth above, I dissent from that portion of the majority's opinion which would apply its newly announced rules for determining a taxpayer's last known address to notices of deficiency mailed prior to the date of the opinion in this case.

PARKER, GERBER, and WILLIAMS, JJ., agree with this dissent.

Notes

1. The "timely filed if timely mailed" rule of § 7502 applies to Tax Court petitions. Thus, a petition mailed on the 90th day after the notice of deficiency is sent is timely filed, so long as it is properly addressed and the postage is prepaid. Reg. § 301.7502–1(b)(ii).

2. Section 6213(f) provides a "bankruptcy exception" to the 90-day period in which a Tax Court petition must be filed. If the taxpayer-debtor cannot file a Tax Court petition because of the bankruptcy court's automatic stay, the running of the 90 days is suspended during the period of the stay and for 60 days thereafter.

3. The legions of cases dealing with the "last known address" issue defy summarization. Illustrative examples include:

(a) *Change of status of taxpayer.* A notice sent to the taxpayer's last known address is valid even though the taxpayer has died, been incarcerated, become incompetent, or been shipped overseas due to military duty.

(b) *Notice never received.* One unlucky taxpayer, who claimed he never received the notice of deficiency and presented evidence of a fire in his local post office, was barred from Tax Court because the notice was found valid because it was sent to his last known address. Harrison v. Commissioner, T.C. Memo. 1979–045. Taxpayers who never receive the statutory notice of deficiency (and thus, like Ms. Abeles, learn about the problem when the Service begins collection activity) stand little chance of winning a challenge to the validity of the notice. The *Internal Revenue Manual* requires IRS employees to follow certain procedures in mailing deficiency notices, and compliance with these procedures in mailing the notice to the last known address is proof of mailing. Keado v. United States, 853 F.2d 1209 (5th Cir.1988).

4. Congress amended section 6212 in 1986 and 1988 to permit rescission of deficiency notices and to clarify the effect of rescission on the statute of limitations. Procedures for rescinding a statutory notice of deficiency are outlined in Rev.Proc. 88–17, 1988–2, C.B. 486. Generally, the IRS will agree to rescind a statutory notice of deficiency if it was issued due to administrative error and if the taxpayer submits information indicating that the asserted deficiency is wrong and requests an Appeals Office conference. Under the 1988 amendment (effective for deficiency notices mailed after November 10, 1988), rescission of the deficiency notice will cause the statute of limitations on assessment (which was suspended by the issuance of the deficiency notice) to begin running again at the point where it was suspended. Thus, although the rescinded notice is treated for most purposes as if it had never been issued, it will have suspended the limitations period while it was outstanding. To illustrate: if a deficiency notice is issued when five months remain on the statute of limitations, and the notice is later rescinded, the statute of limitations will begin to run on the date of rescission, with five months still remaining.

(2) Sufficiency of Notice of Deficiency
SCAR v. COMMISSIONER
United States Court of Appeals, Ninth Circuit, 1987.
814 F.2d 1363.

FLETCHER, CIRCUIT JUDGE:

Taxpayers Howard and Ethel Scar petition for review of the Tax Court's denial of their motion to dismiss for lack of jurisdiction and denial of their two summary judgment motions. Taxpayers argue that the Tax Court lacked jurisdiction because the Commissioner of the Internal Revenue Service (IRS) issued an invalid notice of deficiency. Alternatively, they argue that the Tax Court incorrectly denied their motions for summary judgment and should not have granted the Commissioner's request to amend his answer. We reverse.

Background

On September 3, 1979, petitioners Howard and Ethel Scar filed a joint return for tax year 1978.[1] The Scars claimed business deductions totaling $26,966 in connection with a videotape tax shelter, and reported total taxes due of $3,269.

On June 14, 1982, the Commissioner mailed to the Scars a letter (Form 892); it listed taxpayers' names and address, the taxable year at issue (the year ending December 31, 1978), and specified a deficiency amount ($96,600). The body of the letter stated in part:

> We have determined that there is a deficiency (increase) in your income tax as shown above. This letter is a NOTICE OF DEFICIENCY sent to you as required by the law.

It informed the taxpayers that if they wished to contest the deficiency they must file a petition with the United States Tax Court within 90 days.

Attached to the letter was a Form 5278 ("Statement—Income Tax Changes") purporting to explain how the deficiency had been determined. It showed an adjustment to income in the amount of $138,000 designated as "Partnership—Nevada Mining Project." The Form 5278 had no information in the space on the form for taxable income as shown on petitioners' return as filed. It showed as the "total corrected income tax liability" the sum of $96,600 and indicated that this sum was arrived at by multiplying 70 percent times $138,000.

Another attached document, designated as "Statement Schedule 2," with the heading "Nevada Mining Project, Explanation of Adjustments," stated as follows:

> In order to protect the government's interest and since your original income tax return is unavailable at this time, the income tax is being assessed at the maximum tax rate of 70%.
>
> The tax assessment will be corrected when we receive the original return or when you send a copy of the return to us.
>
> The increase in tax may also reflect investment credit or new jobs credit which has been disallowed.

Also attached to the letter was a document, designated as "Statement Schedule 3," with the heading "Nevada Mining Project, Explanation of Adjustments." This document explained why the Nevada Mining Project deductions were being disallowed.

On July 7, 1982, the taxpayers filed a timely petition with the Tax Court to redetermine the deficiency asserted. In their petition, they alleged that they had never been associated with the "Nevada Mining Project Partnership" and had not claimed on their 1978 return any expenses or losses related to that venture. The Commissioner, on

---

1. The return was timely, the Scars having received an extension of time to file.

August 30, 1982, filed an answer denying the substantive allegations of the petition.

Sometime in September 1982, the Commissioner conceded in a telephone conversation with the taxpayers that the June 14 notice of deficiency was incorrect because it overstated the amount of disallowed deductions and wrongly connected taxpayers with a mining partnership. Nevertheless, the Commissioner maintained that the notice of deficiency was valid. The Commissioner confirmed his position in a letter dated November 29, 1982, stating "the taxpayers should not be surprised by the fact that the Commissioner means to disallow the deductions claimed in 1978 for Executive Productions, Inc." because similar objections had been made to the deductions claimed for the same tax shelter on taxpayers' 1977 return. The Commissioner enclosed with this letter a revised Form 5278, which contained the appropriate shelter explanation and decreased the amount of tax due to $10,374, and notified the taxpayers that he intended to request leave from the Tax Court to amend his answer.

On December 6, 1982 the taxpayers filed a motion to dismiss for lack of jurisdiction, claiming that the June 14 notice of deficiency was invalid because the Commissioner failed to make a "determination" of additional tax owed before issuing the notice of deficiency. The Commissioner filed a response which conceded the inaccuracy of the notice of deficiency but maintained that it was sufficient to give the Tax Court jurisdiction. On March 21, 1983, the Tax Court held a hearing on the taxpayers' motion to dismiss. At the hearing, counsel for the Commissioner attempted to explain why the Form 5278 sent to the taxpayers contained a description of the wrong tax shelter. He stated that an IRS employee transposed a code number which caused the IRS to assert the deficiency on the basis of the Nevada mining project instead of the videotape tax shelter. No witness, however, testified to this fact at the hearing,[3] and no explanation was ever offered for the discrepancy of over $80,000 between the deficiency notice assessment and that later conceded to be the correct amount.

Following the March 21 hearing, the taxpayers filed a motion for summary judgment based on the Commissioner's concession that they had not been involved in any mining partnerships. The Commissioner shortly thereafter filed his motion to amend his answer to correct the error made in the notice of deficiency and accompanying documents. On November 17, 1983 the Tax Court, in an opinion reviewed by the full court, ruled on these various motions. The Tax Court majority upheld the validity of the June 14 notice of deficiency, finding that it satisfied section 6212(a), which states the formal requirements for a deficiency notice. The Tax Court further ruled that the Commissioner could amend his answer as requested, and denied taxpayers' motion for

3. The Commissioner argues that a witness was present at the hearing, but since taxpayers failed to object to counsel's explanation of the IRS's mistake, the witness was never called.

summary judgment. The reviewed opinion contained several concurring and dissenting opinions. Five dissenting judges would have denied jurisdiction on the basis that the deficiency notice was invalid and four dissenting judges would not have permitted the Commissioner to amend his answer.

The Commissioner amended his answer and asserted in it, despite the patent incorrectness of the notice of deficiency and the acknowledgment of error by the Service, that the taxpayer had the burden of disproving the correctness of the Commissioner's revised determinations. The taxpayers renewed their motion for summary judgment. The Tax Court denied this second motion for summary judgment on the ground that triable issues of fact remained concerning whether the taxpayers' primary motivation for entering the videotape venture was the prospect of earning a profit or avoiding tax. On February 22, 1985, the Tax Court entered a decision, pursuant to a stipulation, that taxpayers owed $10,377 in additional tax.[5] The stipulation afforded the taxpayers the right to file a petition for review of the Tax Court's adverse rulings.

Discussion

In order to decide whether the Tax Court had jurisdiction we review *de novo* the Tax Court's interpretation of section 6212(a).

Section 6212(a) states in part: "If the Secretary determines that there is a deficiency in respect of any tax imposed * * * he is authorized to send notice of such deficiency to the taxpayer by certified mail or registered mail." Section 6213(a) provides in part: "Within 90 days * * * after the notice of deficiency authorized in section 6212 is mailed * * * taxpayer may file a petition with the Tax Court for a redetermination of the deficiency." The Tax Court has jurisdiction only when the Commissioner issues a valid deficiency notice, and the taxpayer files a timely petition for redetermination. "A valid petition is the basis of the Tax Court's jurisdiction. To be valid, a petition must be filed from a valid statutory notice." *Stamm International Corp. v. Commissioner*, 84 T.C. 248, 252 (1985).

The taxpayers correctly note that section 6212(a) authorizes the Commissioner to send a notice of deficiency only if he first "determines that there is a deficiency." Because the deficiency notice mailed to the taxpayers contained an explanation of a tax shelter completely unrelated to their return, contained no adjustments to tax based on their return as filed, and stated affirmatively that the taxpayers's return is "unavailable at this time," taxpayers maintain that the Commissioner could not have "determined" a deficiency with respect to them. The taxpayers assert that, in the absence of a determination, the deficiency notice was invalid and therefore the Tax Court lacked jurisdiction.

---

5. This amount is inexplicably $3.00 higher than the amount claimed by the Commissioner in his amended answer.

The Tax Court rejected this argument, finding that "[t]he requirements of section 6212(a) are met if the notice of deficiency sets forth the amount of the deficiency and the taxable year involved." *Scar v. Commissioner,* 81 T.C. 855, 860–61 (1983).

We agree with the Tax Court that no particular form is required for a valid notice of deficiency, and the Commissioner need not explain how the deficiencies were determined. The notice must, however, "meet certain substantial requirements." *Abrams,* 787 F.2d at 941. "The notice must at a minimum indicate that the IRS has determined the amount of the deficiency." *Benzvi,* 787 F.2d at 1542. The question confronting us is whether a form letter that asserts that a deficiency has been determined, which letter and its attachments make it patently obvious that no determination has in fact been made, satisfies the statutory mandate.[6]

In none of the cases on which the Tax Court relied was the notice challenged on the basis that there was no determination. *See Abatti v. Commissioner,* 644 F.2d 1385, 1389 (9th Cir.1981) (notice valid although it did not advise the taxpayer under which code section the IRS would proceed because fair warning was given before trial); *Barnes,* 408 F.2d at 68 (notice need not state the basis for the deficiency determination nor contain particulars of explanations concerning how alleged deficiencies were determined); *Foster v. Commissioner,* 80 T.C. 34, 229–30 ((1983) (notice must advise taxpayer that Commissioner has, in fact, determined a deficiency, and must specify the year and amount), *aff'd in part and vacated in part,* 756 F.2d 1430 (9th Cir.1985), *cert. denied,* [474] U.S. [1055], 106 S.Ct. 793, 88 L.Ed.2d 770 (1986); *Hannan v. Commissioner,* 52 T.C. 787 (1969) (deficiency notice valid where record did not show that Commissioner had not assessed a deficiency even though Commissioner asserted that no deficiency existed and that the notice had been issued in error).[7] The cases assume that the deficiency

---

6. The dissent misstates this case in complaining that the majority is requiring the Commissioner "to prove that he has reviewed specific data before making a determination." Under normal circumstances it would be presumed that a determination had been made prior to notification. In this case, the *taxpayers* proved that a determination of their deficiency had not been made. Not only was there no relationship between the Scars and the tax shelter or the amount of the "deficiency," but also the attachment to the notice entitled "Nevada Mining Project, Explanation of Adjustments" stated: "In order to protect the government's interest and since your original income tax return is unavailable at this time, the income tax is being assessed at the maximum tax rate of 70%." *Scar v. Commissioner,* 81 T.C. 855, 856 (1983). The Scars demonstrated that the Commissioner had *not,* as the dissent argues, "clearly determined that the taxpayers had invested in a tax shelter" for the tax year 1978. Furthermore, even if the Commissioner had adduced proof through the "stand-by" witness, *see supra* note 3, that the Commissioner had examined the 1978 tax return of Executive Productions, Inc., a tax shelter, and that it reported an investment by the Scars, the Commissioner could not determine a deficiency for the Scars without examining their return for 1978 to see whether they had claimed a deduction for such an investment.

7. In *Hannan,* the IRS attempted to avoid a Tax Court redetermination by asserting that the deficiency notice had been sent in error and that the taxpayers were liable for an addition in tax not attributable to a deficiency. Such additions can be assessed and collected immediately under § 6662 (formerly § 6659) without resort to the statutory deficiency procedures. The

determination was made. With the exception of *Hannan*, they deal instead with the question of whether the notice imparted enough information to provide the taxpayer with fair notice.

The Tax Court asserts that it is following long-established policy not to look behind a deficiency notice to question the Commissioner's motives and procedures leading to a determination. *See, e.g., Riland v. Commissioner,* 79 T.C. 185, 201 (1982) (notice valid, even though IRS agents violated procedures set forth in internal manual and failed to forward relevant documents to agents handling the case); *Estate of Brimm v. Commissioner,* 70 T.C. 15, 23 (1978) (notice valid despite taxpayer's argument that procedures followed were not valid, the amount of time spent evaluating a case and the extent to which review functions were perfunctorily performed are irrelevant; even if Commissioner's procedures are flawed, the proper remedy would not be dismissal); *Greenberg's Express, Inc. v. Commissioner,* 62 T.C. 324, 327 (1974) (court will not look behind notice to examine whether Commissioner discriminatorily selected taxpayer for audit; even if his actions are discriminatory, notice not void).

We agree that courts should avoid oversight of the Commissioner's internal operations and the adequacy of procedures employed. This does not mean, however, that the courts cannot or should not decide the validity of a notice that can be determined solely by references to applicable statutes and review of the notice itself.

In this case, we need not look behind the notice sent to the taxpayers to determine its invalidity. The Commissioner acknowledges in the notice that the deficiency is not based on a determination of deficiency of tax reported on the taxpayers' return and that it refers to a tax shelter the Commissioner concedes has no connection to the taxpayers or their return.

Section 6212(a) "authorize[s]" the sending of a deficiency notice "[i]f the Secretary *determines* that there is a deficiency." (emphasis added). We agree with Judge Goffe's statement in this case that "[e]ven a cursory review of this provision [section 6212(a)] discloses that Congress did not grant the Secretary unlimited and unfettered authority to issue notices of deficiency." *Scar,* 81 T.C. at 872 (Goffe, J., dissenting). In *Appeal of Terminal Wine Co.,* 1 B.T.A. 697, 701 (1925), the Board of Tax

---

issue in *Hannan* was not whether a determination had occurred, but rather whether the Commissioner's contention that no deficiency actually existed deprived the Tax Court of jurisdiction.

In *Hannan*, the IRS clearly had made a determination of a deficiency in tax owed by taxpayers who were petitioning the tax court; the question was whether it was a determination of deficiency entitling the taxpayers to appeal before payment. The *Hannan* court found that the act of sending the notice constituted a determination of deficiency. 52 T.C. at 7981. That finding must, however, be read in the context of the case: The IRS *had* examined the taxpayers returns and made a determination that money was owing *and* the record did not show that the type of assessment requiring deficiency procedures had not been made. We do not read *Hannan* to stand for the proposition that the existence of a deficiency letter establishes the existence of a determination. To the extent that the *Hannan* court intended such a reading, we disagree with its interpretation of the tax code.

Appeals construed the meaning of the term "determine" as applied to deficiency determinations: "By its very definition and etymology the word 'determination' irresistibly connotes consideration, resolution, conclusion, and judgment."

The term "deficiency" is defined in section 6211(a) as the amount by which tax due exceeds "the amount shown as the tax by the taxpayer upon his return" (provided that a return showing an amount has been filed), plus previously assessed deficiencies over rebates made. A literal reading of relevant code sections, and the absence of evidence of contrary legislative intent, leads us to conclude that the Commissioner must consider information that relates to a particular taxpayer before it can be said that the Commissioner has "determined" a "deficiency" in respect to that taxpayer.[8] To hold otherwise would entail ignoring or judicially rewriting the plain language of the Internal Revenue Code.[9]

This reading of the Code is not a new one. Almost sixty years ago, the Board of Tax Appeals, while refusing to examine the intent, motive or reasoning of the Commissioner, emphasized that

> the statute clearly contemplates that before notifying a taxpayer of a deficiency and hence before the Board can be concerned, a determination must be made by the Commissioner. This must mean a thoughtful and considered determination that the United States is entitled to an amount not yet paid. If the notice of deficiency were other than the expression of a *bona fide* official determination, and were, say, a mere

---

8. In construing section 6212(a), we follow some basic, yet fundamental, rules:

As in all cases including statutory construction, "our starting point must be the language employed by Congress," *Reiter v. Sonotone Corp.*, 442 U.S. 330, 337 [99 S.Ct. 2326, 2330, 60 L.Ed.2d 931] (1979), and we assume "that the legislative purpose is expressed by the ordinary meaning of the words used." *Richards v. United States*, 369 U.S. 1, 9 [82 S.Ct. 585, 591, 7 L.Ed.2d 492] (1962). Thus, "[a]bsent a clearly expressed legislative intention to the contrary, that language must ordinarily be regarded as conclusive." *Consumer Product Safety Comm'n v. GTE Sylvania, Inc.*, 447 U.S. 102, 108 [100 S.Ct. 2051, 2056, 64 L.Ed.2d 766 (1980).

American Tobacco Co. v. Patterson, 456 U.S. 63, 68, 102 S.Ct. 1534, 1537, 71 L.Ed.2d 748 (1982).

The dissent complains that we are "overload[ing] the statutory requirement of a 'determination' of a deficiency with burdensome substantive content." Dissent at 1372. On the contrary, we work on the premise that Congress does not use words idly, and that "determination" is not devoid of content. If, in fact, that which is required by the unambiguous terms of the statute is more burdensome than Congress envisioned or intended, it is Congress, not the courts, that must remedy the problem.

9. The dissent, characterizing the deficiency notice as a "'ticket' to the tax court" suggests that the majority fails "to grasp the function of the deficiency notice." *Dissent* at 1372. What the dissent fails to grasp, however, is that processes that may "serve their intended purposes" nonetheless may be legally insufficient. For example, notice by telephone would not suffice if written notice were required. Here, the statute requires that the Commissioner make a determination. None was made. The fact that the taxpayers received a deficiency notice does not cure the failure to make a determination.

The dissent in looking only to the fact that notice was sent skips over the Commissioner's failure to make the statutorily required determination. We readily agree with the dissent that in the usual case the sending of the notice of deficiency presumes a determination. *See supra* note 6. Where, however, the notice belies that presumption, it is both reasonable and necessary that the Commissioner demonstrate his compliance with the statute.

formal demand for an arbitrary amount as to which there were substantial doubt, the Board might easily become merely an expensive tribunal to determine moot questions and a burden might be imposed on taxpayers of litigating issues and disproving allegations for which there had never been any substantial foundation.

Couzens v. Commissioner, 11 B.T.A. 1040, 1159–60 (1928).

Recently, taxpayers who had invested in a "tax shelter" known as the "Liberty Financial 1983 Government Securities Trading Strategy" argued that so-called pre-filing notifications (PFNs) sent to them by the IRS were in fact deficiency notices entitling them to a Tax Court redetermination. The notices, which in most if not all cases were received after filing, informed the taxpayers that the IRS believed that deductions or credits claimed pursuant to Liberty Financial were not allowable; that the IRS would review the taxpayers' deductions and reduce returns or adjust the returns as required; that various penalties could be assessed; and that the taxpayers might wish to amend previously filed returns. *Abrams v. Commissioner,* 787 F.2d 939, 940–41 (4th Cir.), *cert. denied,* [479] U.S. [882], 107 S.Ct. 271, 93 L.Ed.2d 248 (1986). In agreeing with the IRS that the PFNs did not qualify as deficiency notices, the Fourth Circuit found the obvious lack of an actual determination of deficiency crucial:

> As the letter * * * made pellucidly clear, examination of the returns of each individual taxpayer had not as yet been made. The most important observation to be made about the letter is that it left no doubt that, as yet, there had been no general review of any return, no computation of any deficiency nor reduction in refunds to which the taxpayers might otherwise be entitled. It was in essence only fair warning of what the taxpayers * * * might expect.

Abrams, 787 F.2d at 941. Similarly, the Eleventh Circuit found the lack of a determination dispositive: "We cannot conclude that a PFN is a notice of deficiency absent a clear indication that the IRS has reviewed the PFN recipient's return and determined that a deficiency of a stated amount exists." *Benzvi v. Commissioner,* 787 F.2d 1541, 1543 (11th Cir.), *cert. denied,* [479] U.S. [883], 107 S.Ct. 273, 93 L.Ed.2d 250 (1986).

These cases inform our judgment here. They support the view that the "determination" requirement of section 6212(a) has substantive content.[10] The Commissioner's and the dissent's contention that the issuance of a formally proper notice of deficiency[11] of itself establishes

---

10. It is, of course true, as the dissent points out, that Tax Court jurisdiction does not depend on the existence of an actual deficiency. Dissent at 1372 (quoting *Stevens v. Commissioner,* 709 F.2d 12, 13 (5th Cir.1983)). It is the purpose of the Tax Court to determine whether the Commissioner's determination is correct. *Stevens,* 709 F.2d at 13. We agree more fully, however, with the passage quoted in the dissent when that passage is quoted in full: "'[I]t is not the *existence* of a deficiency but the Commissioner's *determination* of a deficiency that provides a predicate for Tax Court jurisdiction.'" *Id.* (quoting *Hannan,* 52 T.C. at 791).

11. In the case before us the Commissioner argues that, because the notice contained the Taxpayers' names, social securi-

that the Commissioner has determined a deficiency must be rejected. To hold otherwise, would read the determination requirement out of section 6212(a).[12]

Finally, the Commissioner asserts that the proper remedy in this case is to eliminate the presumption of correctness that normally attaches to deficiency determinations, *see, e.g., Dix v. Commissioner*, 392 F.2d 313 (4th Cir.1968), not to dismiss for lack of jurisdiction. He relies, however, on cases that challenge the correctness of the determination, and not its existence. The Commissioner's belated willingness to assume the burden of proof before the Tax Court cannot cure his failure to determine a deficiency before imposing on taxpayers the obligation to defend themselves in potentially costly litigation in Tax Court. Jurisdiction is at issue here. Failure to comply with statutory requirements renders the deficiency notice null and void and leaves nothing on which Tax Court jurisdiction can rest.

Section 6212(a) of the Internal Revenue Code requires the Commissioner to determine that a deficiency exists before issuing a notice of deficiency. Because the Commissioner's purported notice of deficiency revealed on its face that no determination of tax deficiency had been made in respect to the Scars for the 1978 tax year, it did not meet the requirements of section 6212(a). Accordingly, the Tax Court should have dismissed the action for want of jurisdiction.[13]

Petition for review granted.

CYNTHIA HOLCOMB HALL, CIRCUIT JUDGE, dissenting:

---

ty number, the tax year in question, and "the" amount of deficiency, it was "clearly sufficient." It is quite clear, however, that the notice did not contain *the* amount of deficiency, but rather contained *an* amount unrelated to any deficiency for which the Scars were responsible.

12. Judge Sterrett, in dissenting, offered a sample of a valid deficiency letter under the statutory construction urged by the IRS and accepted by the Tax Court:

Dear Taxpayer:

There is a rumor afoot that you were a participant in the Amalgamated Hairpin Partnership during the year 1980. Due to the press of work we have been unable to investigate the accuracy of the rumor or to determine whether you filed a tax return for that year. However, we are concerned that the statute of limitations may be about to expire with respect to your tax liability for 1980.

Our experience has shown that, as a general matter, taxpayers tend to take, on the average, excessive (unallowable) deductions, arising out of investments in partnerships comparable to Amalgamated that aggregate some $10,000. Our experience has further shown that the average investor in such partnerships has substantial taxable income and consequently has attained the top marginal tax rate.

Accordingly, you are hereby notified that there is a deficiency in tax in the amount of $7,000 due from you for the year 1980 in addition to whatever amount, if any, you may have previously paid.

Sincerely yours,

Commissioner of Internal Revenue

Scar, 81 T.C. at 869 (Sterrett, J., dissenting).

13. *Cf. United States v. Lehigh*, 201 F.Supp. 224, 234 (W.D.Ark.1961) ("The procedures set forth in the Internal Revenue Code were prescribed for the protection of both Government and taxpayer. Neglect to comply with those procedures may entail consequences which the neglecting party must be prepared to face, whether such party be the taxpayer or the Government.")

Today, the majority fortifies the impediments to tax collection on behalf of errant taxpayers seeking "no taxation without litigation." R. Jackson, *Struggle for Judicial Supremacy* 141 (1941). I believe the majority undermines the jurisdiction of the Tax Court by constructing a superfluous yet substantial hurdle to its jurisdiction. In reaching the conclusion that section 6212(a) of the Internal Revenue Code imposes a substantive requirement on the Commissioner of the Internal Revenue Service to prove that he has reviewed specific data before making a determination, the majority eagerly expands jurisdictional requirements while discarding the carefully-honed and expedient jurisdictional rules that exist.

I

The majority first turns a blind eye to reality when it finds that the incorrect explanation for the deficiency "[makes] it patently obvious that no determination has in fact been made." The 1978 tax return of taxpayers Howard and Ethel Scar was hardly an unlikely object of the Commissioner's suspicion. In 1977 the taxpayers participated in a videotape tax shelter, investing $6,500 in cash, signing a promissory note for $93,500, and then deducting over $15,000 in depreciation and other expenses from their 1977 tax return based on their "investment." The Commissioner audited this 1977 return and determined a deficiency of $15,875, finding that the taxpayers' "purchase of the film was lacking in profit motive and economic substance other than the avoidance of tax." The Commissioner mailed a notice of deficiency to the taxpayers, who responded by filing a petition for redetermination of the deficiency with the Tax Court on June 30, 1981.

The taxpayers' 1978 return included additional deductions totaling $27,040 based upon the now suspect videotape shelter. In all likelihood, the Commissioner's decision to issue a second deficiency notice regarding this 1978 return resulted from the continuation of the audit process which began with the previous year's tax return. This second deficiency notice, however, incorrectly explained the deficiency in terms of a Nevada mining venture in which the taxpayers had never participated. At the Tax Court hearing on March 21, 1983, counsel for the Commissioner explained that this misdescription resulted from a technical error: an IRS employee had transposed a code number, resulting in the incorrect identification of the basis of the deficiency as being the Nevada mining project instead of the videotape tax shelter. The Commissioner argues that a witness able to testify to this numerical error was present at the hearing, but was not called since the taxpayers did not object to this explanation of the IRS' mistake.

The procedural history of the taxpayers' efforts to challenge the 1978 deficiency consists largely of motions attempting to exploit this apparent mishap. These motions evince the tactics of delay employed by "every litigious man or every embarrassed man, to whom delay [is] more important than the payment of costs." *Tennessee v. Sneed*, 96 U.S. (6 Otto) 69, 75, 24 L.Ed. 610 (1877).

II

The majority correctly recognizes that section 6212(a) authorizes the Commissioner to send a notice of deficiency only if he first determines that there is a deficiency. The taxpayers themselves concede that the notice of deficiency in this case satisfied section 6212(a)'s formal requirements of stating the amount of the deficiency and the taxable year involved.

The majority then proceeds to overload the statutory requirement of a "determination" of a deficiency with burdensome substantive content. First, the majority ignores the rule that a deficiency notice need not contain any explanation whatsoever.

Second, the majority fails to grasp the function of the deficiency notice. It is nothing more than "a jurisdictional prerequisite to a taxpayer's suit seeking the Tax Court's redetermination of [the Commissioner's] determination of the tax liability." *Stamm*, 84 T.C. at 252. "[T]he notice is only to advise the person who is to pay the deficiency that the Commissioner means to assess him; anything that does this unequivocally is good enough." *Olsen v. Helvering*, 88 F.2d 650, 651 (2nd Cir.1937).[1] Nothing more is required as a predicate to Tax Court jurisdiction.[2] In fact, this Circuit has recognized that " 'it is not the *existence* of a deficiency that provides a predicate for Tax Court jurisdiction.' " *Stevens v. Commissioner*, 709 F.2d 12, 13 (5th Cir.1983) (quoting *Hannan v. Commissioner*, 52 T.C. 787, 791 (1969) (emphasis in original)). The *Stevens* court lucidly commented:

> That seems obvious: the very purpose of the Tax Court is to adjudicate contests to deficiency notices. If the existence of an error in the determination giving rise to the notice deprived the Court of jurisdiction, the Court would lack power to perform its function.

---

1. The notice of deficiency mailed to the taxpayers included two forms: Form 892 and Form 5278. Form 892 is the basic deficiency notice. It includes the taxpayer's name, social security number, amount of the deficiency for the taxable year, and a short explanation of the taxpayer's options. Here, the Commissioner properly completed the Form 892. If the Commissioner had mailed only the Form 892, and nothing else, it is clear that this would have been a valid deficiency notice. *Abatti*, 644 F.2d at 1389; *Barnes*, 408 F.2d at 69; *Stevenson*, 43 T.C.M. (CCH) at 290. The Tax Court's jurisdiction would have been established, even though the Commissioner relied on the wrong tax shelter in making the determination.

2. "It may well be true that the [Commissioner] erred in his determination that a deficiency existed for this period. But when he once determined that there was a deficiency, that fact gives us jurisdiction to determine whether or not it was correctly arrived at." *H. Milgrim & Bros. v. Commissioner*, 24 B.T.A. 853, 854 (1931).

The key question is whether the inclusion of an erroneous Form 5278, which purports to explain the deficiency in terms of an unrelated tax shelter, invalidates the deficiency notice. I believe the inclusion of the wrong Form 5278 constitutes a preparation error which does not invalidate the deficiency notice. "An error in a notice of deficiency, which otherwise fulfills its purpose, will be ignored where the taxpayer is not misled thereby and is provided by it with information sufficient for the preparation of his case for trial." *Meyers v. Commissioner*, 81 T.C.M. (P–H) 276, 278 (1981). Here, the taxpayers were not misled by the stray Form 5278 because they had notice from the IRS that a mistake had been made before the Tax Court had set a trial date for either the 1977 or 1978 disputes concerning the videotape tax shelter.

709 F.2d at 13.

Therefore, the deficiency notice is effectively the taxpayer's "ticket" to the Tax Court. This "ticket" gives the taxpayer access to the only forum where he can litigate the relevant tax issue without first paying the tax assessed. If a properly-addressed deficiency notice states the amount of the deficiency, the taxable year involved, and notifies the taxpayer that he has 90 days from the date of mailing in which to file a petition for redetermination, then the notice is valid. The merits of the Commissioner's deficiency should not be litigated in the form of a motion to dismiss for lack of jurisdiction; once jurisdiction has been established, both sides will have the opportunity to press their views before the Tax Court.

The majority escapes from under the undesirable weight of authority requiring that the validity of a deficiency notice be determined primarily by its form by distinguishing these cases as not addressing the challenge that no determination was made by the Commissioner. In light of the emphasis of this authority on the *form* of the deficiency notice, I cannot agree with such a strained interpretation of these cases. *See* B. Bittker, *Federal Taxation* ¶ 115.2.2 at 115–12 ("[t]he requirement of an IRS *determination* coalesces with the requirement of a *notice* of deficiency, since the usual evidence that a deficiency has been 'determined' is the notice") (emphasis in original).

For example, in *Hannan v. Commissioner*, 52 T.C. 787 (1969), the Tax Court concluded that there was a valid notice of deficiency, despite the Commissioner's contentions that he neither determined a deficiency nor sought to collect one.[3] The Tax Court rejected the Commissioner's position and found it had jurisdiction:

> Here petitioners were sent a letter which admittedly meets all the formal requirements of a statutory notice of deficiency, notifying them that "We [respondent] have determined the income tax deficiencies shown above" and listing tax deficiencies and additions to tax under section 6651(a). This was a determination of a deficiency in tax, even though, as respondent argues, on trial it may develop that there is in fact no deficiency.

---

3. In *Hannan*, the Commissioner assessed additions to tax for late filing. Under 26 U.S.C. § 6662 (formerly section 6659), if additions to tax are not attributable to a deficiency, the Commissioner can immediately assess and collect the additions. On the other hand, if the additions are attributable to a deficiency the Commissioner is required to follow statutory deficiency procedures. In *Hannan*, the Commissioner sent taxpayers a letter, on the form used for deficiency notices, setting forth amounts referred to as "deficiencies" in one column, together with the "additions to tax" in the next column.

The Commissioner argued in the Tax Court that no deficiency actually existed and therefore the Tax Court lacked jurisdiction. The Commissioner's attorney stated that the notice of deficiency was issued in error. The figures listed in the "deficiency" column correspond to the figures that the taxpayers had reported as tax due on their returns. The Commissioner presumably was contending that he had used the notice of deficiency form in order to collect additions to tax, and not to notify taxpayers of the existence of deficiencies. Because the Commissioner was not imposing taxes in excess of what taxpayers showed on their returns (i.e., he used the wrong form), he argued there was no deficiency.

Id. at 791 (footnotes omitted).

The majority misreads *Hannan* in denying that *Hannan* stands for the proposition that deficiency notices are to be judged on their face, rather than on the substance of the Commissioner's determination. *See ante* at n. 7. It is true that the Tax Court partly explained its decision by stating that there was no proof that the Commissioner was not in fact asserting a deficiency and that the taxpayers could only protect their interests by filing a petition. Although one might read this statement as implying that the Tax Court based its decision on more than a facial examination of the deficiency notice, I understand the Tax Court to mean that because the notice was ambiguous, the taxpayers had no alternative but to file a petition. This concern does not detract from the court's emphasis on the *form* of the deficiency notice.

Judging the deficiency notice in this case by the standards discussed above, I believe that the notice warned the taxpayers that the Commissioner had, rightly or wrongly, determined a deficiency and that the notice complied with the formal requirements of section 6212(a). The Commissioner clearly determined that the taxpayers had invested in a tax shelter without economic substance in order to avoid taxes. The inclusion of an erroneous explanation of the basis of the deficiency should not in itself deprive the Tax Court of jurisdiction to decide the question of whether the Commissioner can sustain the asserted deficiency.

The majority contends that here, it "need not look beyond the notice sent to the taxpayers to determine its invalidity." *See ante* at 1368. This, however, is exactly what the majority requires when it concludes that the "determination" requirement is only satisfied where the Commissioner shows he has determined a deficiency with respect to a particular taxpayer beyond the notice itself.[4]

---

4. The majority in footnote 6 makes much of the government's statement that, "In order to protect the government's interest and since your original income tax return is unavailable at this time, the income tax is being assessed at the maximum rate of 70%." The majority points to this statement as evidence supporting their conclusion that the Commissioner did not make a determination. I disagree.

Although the "unavailability" of the Scars' return may indicate that the Scars' original paper return was not before the Commissioner, it does not show that specific data on that return or relating to the video-tape tax shelter was not considered. Due to the computerization of the IRS, the Commissioner no longer operates from original paper returns. *See, e.g.,* Murphy, *Glitches and Crashes at the IRS,* TIME, Apr. 29, 1985, at 71; *New Machines Helping IRS,* Dun's Business Month, Jan. 1984, at 24; IRS, *1980 Annual Report,* 9, 14, 42–43 (1981). With well over 100 million income tax returns plus an even larger number of information returns, such as Forms W–2's and 1099's, being filed annually, it is no wonder the Commissioner has turned to the computer. *See* Klott, *Fewer IRS Workers to Process Tax Returns,* N.Y. Times, Dec. 24, 1986, at 30, col. 3; IRS, *1981 Annual Report* 5, 42–43 (Table 6) (1982). When a return is filed in a Service Center, pertinent summary data is entered into the computer system. *1980 Report* at 14; Quaglietta, *How IRS Service Centers Process Returns,* 16 Prac.Acct. 63 (1983). Such summary data includes the fact that a return was filed, whether the tax was paid or a refund check was mailed, and other data needed to match information returns with the taxpayer's return. *See 1980 Report* at 4, 14; Cloonan, *Compliance Programs,* 16 Prac.Acct. 67 (1983). This matching is done by computer. *1980 Report* at 4, 14; Walbert, *A Net Too Wide,* FORBES, Mar.

As a matter of tax policy, the rule against looking behind the deficiency notice appears to be well-grounded in the administrative necessities of the Commissioner's job. The Commissioner must administer tens of thousands of deficiency notices per year. A requirement that he prove the basis of his determination before the Tax Court can assert jurisdiction would unduly burden both the Commissioner and the Tax Court.

In addition, the majority's ruling that the inclusion of an erroneous explanation invalidates a deficiency notice creates an incentive for the Commissioner not to disclose his theory for asserting a deficiency when he sends the deficiency notice. If the Commissioner discloses his theory at this stage, the majority's rule invites every taxpayer to litigate whether the Commissioner has made a determination before litigating the merits.[5] Because it is to the taxpayer's advantage that the Commissioner disclose his theory when the notice is sent, I believe it is undesirable to establish a rule which would discourage him from doing so.

I view this case as presenting two related policy goals. One goal is to ensure that early in the assessment procedure each individual taxpayer receives fair notice as to the theory on which the Commissioner based his deficiency. The other goal is to encourage the Commissioner to disclose the theory on which he intends to rely in the deficiency notice whenever possible. However, because the Commissioner is not required to disclose his theory in the notice, the majority's rule that invalidates a deficiency notice accompanied with an erroneous description encourages the Commissioner to issue deficiency notices without *any* explanation. Such a rule detracts from the goal of early notice and taxpayers, on the whole, will suffer because the Commissioner is likely to use the deficiency notice solely for jurisdictional purposes and only thereafter reveal his reasons for issuing the notice. I believe that

12, 1984, at 154. It is conceivable that the Commissioner had enough information on the computer to match information regarding both the tax shelter promoted by Executive Productions, Inc. and the Scars' suspect 1977 return to their 1978 income tax taxpayer's return, but not enough to determine the exact amount of a deficiency without calling up from storage the actual return. Thus, the Commissioner assessed the Scars at the 70% rate.

As of 1980, the Commissioner had identified approximately 27,000 abusive tax shelters. *1980 Report* at 3. In light of this number, the punching of the wrong computer key during an audit at the partnership level is a viable explanation for the unfortunate error of one of the 26,999 inapplicable tax shelters popping up and then being entered on the Scars' Form 5278.

So, as a result of the need to computerize information regarding the millions of filed returns and the huge number of tax shelters, we have a reasonable explanation for the two errors on the gratuitously prepared Form 5278 (the wrong shelter and the wrong tax rate of 70%). The taxpayer could have contested these errors and probably would have settled the amount of the tax due promptly. The importance of these errors is further undermined by the fact that they are found in Form 5278, which the Commissioner is not required to send with the basic deficiency notice, Form 892. *See ante* n. 1.

5. This "invitation to litigation" represents a major step backward for those of us who believe that litigation should be streamlined, attorneys' fees should be kept within reasonable bounds, and courts should not be further over-burdened.

preserving the Tax Court tradition of not looking behind the deficiency notice promotes the goal of ensuring early notice to the taxpayer.

Finally, alternative remedies exist to protect the taxpayer's interests besides dismissal of the case for lack of jurisdiction. If the taxpayers are confused by the Commissioner's theory or explanation supporting the deficiency, they may seek clarification prior to trial. The Tax Court Rules "contemplate that after the case is at issue the parties will informally confer in order to exchange necessary facts, documents, and other data with a view towards defining and narrowing the areas of dispute. Rules 38, 70(a)(1), 91(a)." *Foster*, 80 T.C. at 230. Here, the informal contacts between the parties resulted in the Commissioner's disclosure of his mistake within two months of when the taxpayers filed their petition for redetermination in the Tax Court.

Furthermore, the presumed correctness of the Commissioner's deficiency notice disappears if the deficiency is arbitrary or capricious, since the burden of proof then shifts to the Commissioner.

These measures are more than adequate to prevent the Commissioner from littering the country with baseless deficiency notices. *Scar*, 81 T.C. at 869 (Sterrett, J., dissenting). The precedent holding that the validity of the deficiency notice is to be determined on its face was effective in furthering policy goals which benefit the taxpayer and the public. The majority's opinion sabotages the machinery of tax collection, thereby portending injury to the taxpayer and to the public. I therefore dissent.

(3) Proper Party Petitioner
FLETCHER PLASTICS, INC. v. COMMISSIONER
Tax Court of the United States, 1975.
64 T.C. 35.

DAWSON, CHIEF JUDGE.

This matter is before the Court on respondent's motion to dismiss for lack of jurisdiction on the ground that the petition in this case was not filed by a proper party.

In a notice of deficiency dated June 20, 1974, respondent determined * * * Federal income tax deficiencies * * *. This notice of deficiency was addressed to "Atlas Tool Co. Inc., Successor to Fletcher Plastics, Inc." * * *

* * *

There is no dispute that the petition captioned "Fletcher Plastics, Inc., Stephan Schaffan, Transferee, Petitioner" was timely filed. However, respondent asserts in his motion that neither Fletcher Plastics, Inc., nor Stephan Schaffan is the party to whom a notice of deficiency was sent nor are they legally entitled to institute a case on behalf of Atlas Tool Co., Successor to Fletcher Plastics, Inc., based on the notice of deficiency mailed in this case.

The only issue for our decision is whether Atlas Tool Co., Inc., the taxpayer to whom the notice of deficiency was sent, can ratify and amend, after the 90-day statutory period has expired, a petition filed on its behalf and signed by its counsel which was intended to contest the deficiencies determined in that notice, but incorrectly captioned.

The jurisdiction of the Tax Court is specifically limited by statute, section 7442, and the statutory requirements must be satisfied for us to acquire jurisdiction.

To invoke our jurisdiction, section 6213(a) requires that "the taxpayer" to whom a notice of deficiency is addressed must file a timely petition with this Court for a redetermination of the deficiency determined in such notice.

A review of the cases decided prior to the adoption of our new Rules of Practice and Procedure on January 1, 1974, indicates that the general rule is that a petition must be filed by the taxpayer against whom the deficiency was determined or his duly authorized representative, except in cases of transferee liability, and except where a party is permitted to ratify an imperfect petition, after proving that the original filing was made on his behalf by one authorized to do so.

Section 7453 provides that proceedings in this Court "shall be conducted in accordance with such rules of practice and procedure * * * as the Tax Court may prescribe." The conflict here arises because respondent believes that language in selected portions of the Notes accompanying the new Rules reflects a change in our attitude toward amendments to pleadings, even though the Note to Rule 41(a), which deals with amendments to pleadings, expressly states that the new Rule does "not represent a change in present practice."

Respondent notes that Rule 60(a) provides that a petition should be filed by and in the name of the person against whom the Commissioner determined a deficiency. He contends that since that was not done here, Rule 41(a) bars amendment of the petition. The pertinent part of that Rule reads as follows:

> No amendment shall be allowed after expiration of the time for filing the petition, however, which would involve conferring jurisdiction on the Court over a matter which otherwise would not come within its jurisdiction under the petition as then on file * * *

* * *

To the contrary, petitioner argues that this is a procedural, not a jurisdictional problem. After noting that Rules 23(a)(1) and 32(a) require that a proper caption be placed on all pleadings filed with this Court, petitioner cites Rule 41(a) which provides, in relevant part, that a party may amend his pleadings either "by leave of court or by written consent of the adverse party; *and leave shall be given freely when justice so requires.*" (Emphasis added.) Petitioner argues that this reflects a liberal attitude toward amendment of pleadings.

In further support of his position, petitioner refers to Rule 60(a) which provides, in relevant part, that:

> A case timely brought shall not be dismissed on the ground that it is not properly brought on behalf of a party until a reasonable time has been allowed after objection for ratification by such party of the bringing of the case; and such ratification shall have the same effect as if the case had been properly brought by such party.

The Note following this Rule further shows a liberal attitude toward amendment and/or correction of pleadings in a case like that presently before us:

> Where the intention is to file a petition on behalf of a party, the scope of this provision permits correction of errors as to the proper party or his identity made in a petition otherwise timely and correct. * * *

After careful examination of the record and the law, we will deny respondent's motion to dismiss and grant petitioner's motion to amend the caption and the pleadings. Atlas Tool clearly intended to file a petition to contest the deficiencies determined in a notice of deficiency sent to it and this petition was signed by its duly authorized counsel, as permitted by Rule 34(b)(7). Rule 60(a) expressly permits a party to timely ratify a defective petition filed on its behalf. The Note states that this Rule permits the correction of errors as to the proper party to be made where there was an intent to file a petition on behalf of a party.

Our holding here is consistent with Rule 34(a) which provides that "Failure of the petition to satisfy applicable requirements *may* be ground for dismissal of the case." (Emphasis added.) The Note to this Rule explains the emphasized language as follows:

> The dismissal of a petition, for failure to satisfy applicable requirements, depends on the nature of the defect, and therefore is put in the contingent "may" rather than the mandatory "shall" of present T.C.Rule 7(a)(2). * * *

In so acting, we are not taking jurisdiction of a matter which is outside our jurisdiction as determined by the petition originally filed. See Rule 41(a). A review of the cases cited in the Note to that Rule shows that most deal with untimely amendments relating to taxable years or categories of taxes different than those contained in the original petition.

* * *

This situation is also distinguishable from those cases where a petition has been brought by a nonexistent party, see Great Falls Bonding Agency, Inc., 63 T.C. 304 (1974), since Atlas Tool was in existence when the petition and amendment were filed. Finally, this case is to be distinguished from [cases in which] a party to whom a statutory notice of deficiency was not sent attempts to join, as a party-petitioner, the taxpayer to whom the notice of deficiency was sent. Here the statutory notice was sent to Atlas Tool on whose behalf a petition was filed. Atlas Tool has ratified that filing and seeks to amend that petition here.

Accordingly, we conclude that although the original defective petition was not filed in the name of a proper party as required by Rule 60, and did not have a proper caption as required by Rules 23(a)(1) and 32(a), the clear language of Rule 60(a) bars dismissal under these particular facts. We hold that this is a proper case for amendment of the pleadings under Rule 41(a); and under Rule 41(d) the amendment will relate back to the date of the filing of the original petition.

HOLT v. COMMISSIONER
Tax Court of the United States, 1977.
67 T.C. 829.

DAWSON, CHIEF JUDGE.

* * *

Ernest B. Holt and Lessie L. Holt filed joint Federal income tax returns for 1971, 1972, and 1973. On October 17, 1975, a joint statutory notice of deficiency was mailed to them by the Commissioner determining deficiencies for those years * * *.

On January 15, 1976, this Court received the following handwritten letter in an envelope postmarked January 13, 1976:

1/13/76

U.S. TAX COURT
400 Second St. N.W.
Wash. D.C. 20217

DEAR SIR:

I would like to file a petition to the U.S. Tax Court, as I do not agree with the findings of I.R.S. Commissioner, Donald C. Alexander. Inclosed is a letter dated Oct. 17, 1975. I am also enclosing 10.00 check for your consideration of this case.

> Sincerely Yours,
> ERNEST B. HOLT
> RT. ONE
> ASHER, OKLA. 74826

The joint notice of deficiency was attached to the letter which was filed as a "petition" in the name of Ernest B. Holt, and an "Order for Proper Petition" was sent to him on January 16, 1976. That order required him to file a proper amended petition by March 16, 1976.

On March 17, 1976, the Court received a petition in an envelope postmarked March 15, 1976. The petition was captioned in the names of both Ernest B. and Lessie L. Holt and was signed by both of them. On March 26, 1976, the Court ordered that the latter petition be filed as an amended petition and that the caption of the case be amended to include both names.

After filing an answer to the amended petition, the Commissioner filed a motion to dismiss as to Lessie L. Holt on the grounds that the January 13 letter did not purport to be an appeal on behalf of Lessie L. Holt, and that the amended petition filed 152 days after the statutory notice of deficiency was mailed cannot confer jurisdiction as to her.

In response to such motion to dismiss, the Court received an affidavit which provides in part:

> Ernest B. Holt and Lessie L. Holt, being duly sworn upon oath depose and state:
>
>> That since Ernest B. Holt and his wife, Lessie L. Holt filed a joint return, Mr. Holt considers that anything filed by him is filed by both; that by Mrs. Holt signing this Memorandum, she indicates that she wants to be embraced therein; that since they wish to represent themselves and have the matter heard in a more convenient location other than Washington, D.C., they are asking the Court to give them a chance to have the matter heard on substance and merit rather than on form.

Such affidavit was signed by both parties.

In John L. Brooks, 63 T.C. 709 (1975), the facts were essentially the same, with one exception. In *Brooks,* the original document which was filed as a petition bore a caption in the joint names of the parties. The *Brooks* opinion discussed and analyzed the applicable portions of the Tax Court Rules of Practice and Procedure, particularly Rule 34(a), Rule 34(b)(7), Rule 41(a), and Rule 60(a). We do not think it necessary here to repeat that analysis. The essence of the *Brooks* opinion is the statement that "in the light of the explanatory Notes to such Rules, we think the 'intent test' should continue to be applied to cases such as this under the new Rules." The "intent" which we seek to ascertain in this particular type of case is whether the nonsigning spouse (typically the wife) intended that the signing spouse (typically the husband) act on her behalf and with her approval when he filed a timely imperfect petition with this Court.

In determining this Court's jurisdiction we think a distinction which turns upon the presence or absence of a caption in an imperfect petition could deservedly be labeled as a "captious distinction." We do not believe that the intent which the *Brooks* opinion directs us to ascertain can, in any realistic sense, be gleaned so mechanically. Certainly, lack of knowledge should not be equated with lack of intent, and Ernest Holt obviously was not sophisticated enough to place a caption on his letter which we accepted and filed as an imperfect petition. That letter was a response, in the best way he knew how to respond, to a notice of deficiency addressed to both spouses. The realistic presumption of intent, based upon the letter and the attached joint notice of deficiency and upon the totality of circumstances herein, is that the petitioner-husband was acting as agent for his wife as well as for himself in filing such imperfect petition in response to the joint notice of deficiency.

Accordingly, in situations where there is a joint notice of deficiency, a timely filed imperfect petition, the Court's "Order for Proper Petition," and the filing of a timely amended petition signed by both spouses, it is our view that the spouse who did not sign the imperfect petition should be given the opportunity to confirm the correctness of that presumption of intent. In this case the presumed intent was confirmed by filing, within the time specified in our "Order for Proper Petition," the amended petition captioned in the names of both spouses and signed by both. To rule otherwise would be wholly inconsistent with the liberal and salutary policy which we followed in accepting and filing as an imperfect petition the original and inartfully drawn letter which is quoted above. Such a shifting between realism and hypertechnicality cannot be justified in these circumstances.

Since the facts of this case sufficiently establish to our satisfaction that Ernest B. Holt was acting both for himself and Lessie L. Holt in sending the letter which was filed herein as the timely imperfect petition, we will deny the Commissioner's motion to dismiss for lack of jurisdiction as to Lessie L. Holt and to change the caption.

An appropriate order will be entered.

Reviewed by the Court.

STERRETT, J., dissenting: It is an article of faith of this Court that a taxpayer shall be given an opportunity to have his tax liability judicially determined before paying any portion thereof if the statute granting jurisdiction can be reasonably interpreted to permit it. In the instant case the majority has, in my opinion, gone beyond the bounds of statutory reason to reach a desired result.

* * *

I would go no further than the doctrine laid down in John L. Brooks, 63 T.C. 709 (1975). There must be some objective indication within the four corners of the documents timely filed that fairly raises the question as to whether the filing spouse was authorized to speak for the other. Once fairly raised we should accept a subsequent ratification of the intent.

I respectfully submit that, rather than establishing any rule, the majority has in fact, in any joint notice situation, established an open-end situation where only one spouse need file a timely petition, and the other spouse can have such additional time to determine whether to join in the petition as the Court in its sole discretion decides. No matter how nobly motivated, judicial legislation remains just that.

DRENNEN, QUEALY, and GOFFE, JJ., agree with this dissent.

Note

The Tax Court has prescribed forms for petitions to the Tax Court for redetermination of a deficiency. There are two basic forms: one for a "regular" Tax Court petition (Form 1), and the other for a "small tax" case

(Form 2). Copies of these Forms are in Appendix D. The filing fee for all Tax Court petitions is $60.

(4) Irrevocability of Tax Court Jurisdiction
ESTATE OF MING, JR. v. COMMISSIONER
Tax Court of the United States, 1974.
62 T.C. 519.

DRENNEN, JUDGE.

Respondent, by notice of deficiency dated October 8, 1970, determined deficiencies in petitioners' income taxes for the years 1964, 1965, and 1966 in the total amount of $2,714.07, and additions to tax under section 6653(b) in the total amount of $8,992.17. Petitioners filed a timely petition in the Tax Court for redetermination of those deficiencies on January 6, 1971. The case was set for trial on a trial calendar of the Tax Court starting February 4, 1974, in Chicago, Ill. On January 25, 1974, petitioners filed a motion to continue the case and a motion for leave to withdraw the petition without prejudice. * * *

* * *

* * * We assume the motion means that petitioners may withdraw their petition in the Tax Court, pay the deficiencies, and sue for refund in the United States District Court.

In the recent case of Emma R. Dorl, 57 T.C. 720, 721–722 (1972), this Court held that a taxpayer's motion for removal of her case to the United States District Court, after issuance of a notice of deficiency and filing a petition in the Tax Court, must be denied; and also that the taxpayer was not entitled to a jury trial in the Tax Court. In our opinion in that case, we said:

> Where, as here, a taxpayer receives a notice of an income tax deficiency and filed a timely petition with the United States Tax Court, he gives the Tax Court exclusive jurisdiction. See sec. 6512(a). Thereafter, a refund suit in the U.S. District Court for the same tax and the same taxable year is barred. The mere filing of the petition in the Tax Court is enough to deprive a U.S. District Court of jurisdiction for years as to which the petition was filed. This is the rule even where the Tax Court petition was dismissed, or the issue sought to be litigated was not presented in the Tax Court. It is significant that it is the taxpayer's action in filing a valid petition in the Tax Court, under circumstances which give the Tax Court jurisdiction, and not any action taken by the Court, that bars a subsequent refund suit in the U.S. District Court.
>
> It is now a settled principle that a taxpayer may not unilaterally oust the Tax Court from jurisdiction which, once invoked, remains unimpaired until it decides the controversy.

Our opinion in the *Dorl* case is supported not only by the cases cited therein, but also by the legislative history of sections 6512(a) and 7459(d), which had their origins in sections 284(d) and 906(c) of the Revenue Act of 1926, respectively. The significance of those provisions is explained in the Senate Finance Committee Report (S.Rept. No. 52, 69th Cong., 1st Sess., 1939-1 C.B. (Part 2) 351), as follows:

> But if he [the taxpayer] does elect to file a petition with the Board his entire tax liability for the year in question (except in case of fraud) is finally and completely settled by the decision of the Board when it has become final, whether the decision is by findings of fact and opinion, *or by dismissal,* as in case of lack of prosecution, insufficiency of evidence to sustain the petition, *or on the taxpayer's own motion.* The duty of the Commissioner to assess the deficiency thus determined is mandatory, and no matter how meritorious a claim * * * for refund he cannot entertain it, nor can suit be maintained against the United States * * *. Finality is the end sought to be attained by these provisions of the bill, and the committee is convinced that to allow the reopening of the question of the tax for the year involved either by the taxpayer or by the Commissioner (save in the sole case of fraud) would be highly undesirable. [Emphasis added.]

While we were concerned in the Dorl case with petitioner's motion to remove the case to the District Court, and here we have petitioners' motion to withdraw without prejudice, the reasoning in the Dorl opinion applies with equal force to require us to deny petitioners' motion in this case. Under section 7459(d), if a petition has been filed by the taxpayer in the Tax Court and the Court dismisses the case for any reason other than lack of jurisdiction, the Court must enter an order finding the deficiency in tax to be the amount determined by the Commissioner in his notice of deficiency, unless the Commissioner reduces the amount of his claim. See also Rule 123(d) of the Tax Court Rules. Thus, if we were to grant petitioners' motion, we would be required to enter a decision finding deficiencies in petitioners' taxes for the years involved in the amounts determined by respondent in the notice of deficiency. This would clearly negate the objective of petitioners' motion to withdraw without prejudice and would preclude petitioners' efforts to litigate this case on its merits in a District Court.

* * *

Furthermore, respondent has been prejudiced by the filing of a petition in this Court in that he has been precluded from assessing and collecting the additional taxes he claims to be owing by petitioners. See sec. 6212. We do not believe the law intended to permit a taxpayer to avoid payment of deficiencies determined by the Commissioner by filing a petition in this Court and then later withdrawing it without prejudice to his right to litigate the merits of his case by the refund route in the District Court or the Court of Claims. Accordingly, the motion will be denied.

B. DECISION-MAKING AUTHORITY OF THE TAX COURT

As discussed in Section 1 of this Chapter, one danger of litigating a tax controversy in the Tax Court is the possibility that the government will discover and raise new issues and assert additional deficiencies.

This is possible because the statute of limitation on asserting additional deficiencies is suspended by the mailing of the deficiency notice and further suspended by the filing of the Tax Court petition. I.R.C. § 6503(a)(1). These same rules can also benefit the taxpayer, however.

Once Tax Court jurisdiction is properly invoked by the timely filing of a petition following a valid notice of deficiency, the Tax Court is authorized to determine the correct tax for the year or years involved. The correct tax may be a deficiency, no deficiency (the liability is exactly what was paid), or an overpayment (entitling the taxpayer to a refund). If the court determines that a deficiency exists, the amount of the deficiency may be exactly that asserted by the Commissioner or less. It can also be *more* than the amount stated in the deficiency notice, if the government asserts the additional deficiency "at or before the hearing or a rehearing." IRC § 6214(a). To determine the correct tax, the court is authorized to consider tax years and types of tax not before it. For example, the court in deciding an income tax issue for 1989 can consider facts relating to a 1987 gift tax. IRC § 6214(b). The court lacks jurisdiction to determine underpayments or overpayments for the years not properly before it, however.

Based on its consideration of all the facts, the court may determine that the taxpayer has overpaid his tax. Prior to 1989, the Tax Court lacked authority to order a refund of any overpayment it determined. As part of the Technical and Miscellaneous Revenue Act of 1988, Congress amended section 6212(b) to give the Tax Court authority to order the refund of any overpayment it determines, plus interest, if the IRS fails or refuses to make the refund within 120 days of the Tax Court decision.

Notes

1. Assume that your client, whose case is pending before the Tax Court, has huge (but disputed) net operating losses incurred in tax years not at issue in the litigation. Before trial, the government lawyer offers to enter into a stipulated agreement of "no deficiency." Should you advise your client to accept this offer? Consider LTV Corp. v. Commissioner, 64 T.C. 589 (1975), and McGowan v. Commissioner, 67 T.C. 599 (1976). In *LTV* the taxpayer agreed to the government's offer of "no deficiency." The government then argued that the court lacked jurisdiction to consider facts relating to years not at issue in the case. The taxpayer pleaded for the court's consideration of facts relating to the years in which the loss at issue had occurred. Although the court rejected the government's jurisdiction argument, it nonetheless decided to terminate the case:

> We agree with petitioner that respondent's concession of no deficiency does not deprive us of jurisdiction over the subject matter. It would be anomalous in the extreme if respondent's concession on the merits deprived the Court of jurisdiction to enter a decision in favor of petitioner. As we said in Daniel E. Hannan, 52 T.C. 787, 791 (1969):
>
>> it is not the *existence* of a deficiency but the Commissioner's *determination* of a deficiency that provides a predicate for Tax

Court jurisdiction. * * * Indeed, were this not true, then the absurd result would be that in every case in which this Court determined that no deficiency existed, our jurisdiction would be lost.

Having acquired jurisdiction, this Court has the authority and responsibility to enter a decision on the merits.

It is true that section 6214, after directing us to redetermine the deficiency before us by referring, to the extent necessary, to facts relating to other years, specifically denies us "jurisdiction to determine whether or not the tax for any other year * * * has been overpaid or underpaid." But section 6214(b) simply makes unmistakably clear what is contemplated by the jurisdiction conferred in section 6214(a) and the two preceding sections: that this Court's jurisdiction is limited to a redetermination of the correct amount of the deficiency, if any, for the years for which the deficiency notice specified in section 6212 has determined a deficiency as defined in section 6211.

We must look at the facts relevant to the years before us even if these facts relate to taxes for other taxable years. Respondent's concession as to the facts bearing on the correct amount of the tax liability does not diminish our jurisdiction, but goes only to the merits of the controversy, even where the facts involved relate to the taxes of other taxable years. In this, as in other instances involving concessions by either party, the Court retains jurisdiction to redetermine the correct amount of the deficiency.

Having decided that our jurisdiction is unimpaired by respondent's concession of no deficiency (which we accept), we must decide whether we should simply enter a decision for petitioner, or whether we should nevertheless determine the correct amount of the pre-carryback deficiencies, if any, for 1965 and 1966, the precise amount of the consolidated net operating losses attributable to 1968 and 1969, and the amount of the 1968 and 1969 losses that must be used to eliminate any such deficiencies.

Petitioner argues that the 1968 and 1969 losses, not absorbed by the 1965 and 1966 deficiencies, will be carried to the years 1973 and 1974, thus requiring a determination of all the issues currently before the Court at some future date. Petitioner emphasizes the convenience of resolving these issues now when witnesses are available and memories fresh, rather than in connection with 1973 and 1974, which (given the complexity of the returns involved) may not reach the litigation stage until 1980. Petitioner urges that the parties have a real stake in a concrete controversy in view of the impact any decision is likely to have on future years, and also because of the substantial interest associated with any pre-carryback deficiency for 1965 and 1966. Petitioner notes that if we do not resolve the issues for 1965 and 1966, they will be resolved in a refund suit over restricted interest, resulting in a multiplicity of litigation in different forums. Finally, petitioner points out that the failure to resolve the issues now is inconsistent with the mechanical steps for computing a net operating loss carryover and will impose substantial uncertainties undermining corporate financial planning.

Respondent argues that in view of his concession of no deficiency, resolution of these issues will have no impact on the years before the Court, but will be merely an advisory opinion concerning the amount of a deduction (that may or may not be needed) for future years over which the Court has no present jurisdiction. He argues that any existing controversy over the pre-carryback deficiencies or the size of the losses for 1968 and 1969 has been mooted by his concession. While he acknowledges that interest computations are predicated on the deficiency redetermined by the Court, he points out that this is an indirect consequence of the exercise of our jurisdiction over deficiencies, and that we clearly do not have jurisdiction over interest.

Although the issue is not as free from doubt as it at first appears, we have determined that we should enter a decision in favor of petitioner rather than continue these proceedings. Our responsibility is limited to redetermining the deficiency asserted for the years before us.

* * * It is unnecessary to determine which of the parties is correct as to specific deduction and income items making up their respective computations. The result is the same in either case: the deficiency as redetermined for the years before us is zero.

* * *

We recognize that this may be far from a perfect solution to the problems confronting petitioner. * * * We are not without sympathy relative to the practical problems petitioner has so ably detailed in its brief, but we take the statute as we find it.

Decision will be entered for the petitioner.

---

2. On the other hand, taxpayer in *McGowan* refused to accept the government's concession, hoping to obtain a favorable decision on the merits. The court distinguished *LTV* and issued an opinion on the merits:

* * * Respondent's position is that the Court must honor his tendered concession and cannot thereafter act upon the case in any fashion other than to enter a decision of no deficiency in accordance with the terms of that concession.

* * *

[In LTV Corp., 64 T.C. 589 (1975),] we ruled that a concession by the Commissioner did not impair our ability to *enter decision* for the taxpayer because we retained jurisdiction over the subject matter of the controversy, but that the existence of an *accepted, bilateral* agreement of no deficiency covering the years in issue rendered the factual controversies moot. Therefore, we declined to proceed further and entered decision for the taxpayer.

The most salient distinguishing feature between *LTV Corp.* and the instant case is the type of judicial discretion in issue. We are concerned with the question whether judicial discretion to accept or reject an offered concession exists, while in *LTV Corp.* we had to decide whether judicial discretion could be exercised during the postacceptance period to give the Court jurisdiction over nonessential matters. *LTV Corp.* provides us with no guidance concerning whether we must accept a tendered concession.

Respondent's contentions predicated upon the Court's lack of general declaratory judgment powers and our admitted policy of declining to rule on years not before us or our refusal to consider issues that may never be litigated are not persuasive. By virtue of our failure to accept this tendered concession we have a bona fide question before us arising out of a taxable year properly placed in issue. Only our acceptance of either the concession or an agreed joint stipulated decision would remove the matter from issue.

* * * Neither party can forcibly remove a case from the Court's jurisdiction through the mere act of filing a concession once our jurisdiction has been properly invoked. All concessions, including stipulated settlement agreements, are subject to the Court's discretionary review. Only through this process can the interests of justice be protected. If we were to adopt respondent's position as our own, the Court's role as a viable, independent arbiter of Federal Tax disputes would be undermined. * * *

* * *

* * * Many taxpayers in Rhode Island will be affected by the outcome herein and the time for filing another year's return is rapidly approaching for most of them. We continuously have emphasized our desire to reach a speedy determination from the moment petitioner's motion for summary judgment was filed on October 15, 1976. * * * Therefore, we conclude that our rejection of respondent's Notice of Concession represents a valid exercise of judicial discretion.

* * *

All in all, we perceive no sound or rational legal basis for sustaining the validity of [respondent's position, as stated in] Rev.Rul. 75–148, 1975–1 C.B. 64. In our judgment the ruling is invalid and, in fairness to thousands of Rhode Island employees, it should be revoked immediately. To let linger the uncertainty created by respondent's inaction would show a careless and callous disregard of the rights of these individuals. They seek a definitive answer. They are entitled to have it.

* * *

3. For a discussion of stipulations (such as the one entered into in *LTV* but rejected in *McGowan*), see section C.(2) of this Chapter, below.

4. The 1988 legislation that authorized the Tax Court to order refunds in cases in which it determined overpayments also expanded the court's jurisdiction to redetermine interest on deficiencies. Section 7481(c) grants the Tax Court jurisdiction to reopen a proceeding if a dispute arises over

the proper computation of interest on the deficiency determined by the court in an earlier proceeding. To re-invoke the Court's jurisdiction, the taxpayer must pay the deficiency determined by the Tax Court plus the disputed interest as computed by the IRS and, within one year from the date the Tax Court decision becomes final, move to reopen the proceeding.

5. The 1988 Taxpayer Bill of Rights Act expanded the Tax Court's jurisdiction over certain disputes concerning IRS collection activities. Under § 7429(b)(2), applicable to IRS assessments and levies made on or after July 1, 1989, the Tax Court now has concurrent jurisdiction with U.S. district courts in these disputes, so long as the Tax Court's jurisdiction has already been properly invoked by a timely filed petition. The types of disputes include:

(a) Taxpayer challenges to jeopardy assessments or levies if the assessment or levy relates to a matter or issue pending before the court.

(b) Taxpayer challenges to an IRS attempt to assess and collect tax that is the subject of a Tax Court proceeding.

(c) Taxpayer challenges to an IRS decision to sell seized property.

Jeopardy assessments and levies and other IRS collection procedures are discussed in Chapter 9. For the appropriate procedures to follow to obtain Tax Court review of the IRS actions described above, see Tax Court Rules 55, 56 and 57. A thorough discussion of these procedures is contained in the first Tax Court consideration of them, Williams v. Commissioner, 92 T.C. 920 (1989) (reviewed) at p. 764 in Chapter 11.

6. Section 7481(a) establishes rules for determining when a Tax Court decision becomes final. Under those rules:

(a) If the decision is not appealed, it becomes final 90 days after it is entered. (Under section 7483, a Tax Court decision must be appealed within 90 days of its entry.)

(b) If the decision is appealed and the appellate court either dismisses the appeal or affirms the Tax Court decision, and neither party takes further action, the decision becomes final 90 days after entry of the appellate court decision. (Under section 7481(a)(2)(A), a petition for certiorari to the U.S. Supreme Court must be filed within 90 days of the appellate court's decision.)

(c) If a certiorari petition is filed but is not granted, the decision becomes final upon the denial of certiorari.

(d) If a certiorari petition is granted, and the decision is affirmed, the decision becomes final 30 days after the Supreme Court's decision.

(e) If the Supreme Court modifies or reverses the Tax Court's decision, the decision becomes final 30 days after the Tax Court's modified decision is entered.

C. SOME ASPECTS OF TAX COURT PROCEDURE

(1) Discovery [c]

As a result of the 1974 revision of the Tax Court Rules, formal discovery procedures became available for the first time in the Tax Court. This is not to say that, before the adoption of these Rules, there was no "discovery" in the sense that neither party had the opportunity to obtain information from the other. Indeed, under prior practice, such procedures as settlement conferences, required stipulation sessions, and occasional pretrial conferences did tend to open channels of communication between the parties. However, to a large degree, these communications were voluntary. Rarely was a party required to divulge information to the adversary except in furtherance of his own purposes—for example, to obtain a more favorable settlement.

It should be noted that the administrative summons power [discussed in Chapter 8] of the Internal Revenue Service (the Service) in effect provides it with a form of compulsory discovery. The Service can make use of the administrative summons to obtain a taxpayer's books and records or to obtain documents and testimony from third persons during the examination of a taxpayer's return. Indeed, it has even been held that a summons from the Service can be used to gather evidence during the pendency of a Tax Court case.[2] However, it must be noted that the often stated policy of the Chief Counsel is to eschew the use of the administrative summons for purposes of discovery in Tax Court litigation.[d] Nevertheless, at least in the examination stage, the Service, under prior practice, did have the power in the course of a tax controversy to compel the adversary to produce evidence. However, at no point—save perhaps in an unusual case in which a Tax Court judge might issue an anomalous order—could the taxpayer compel the Service to produce evidence prior to the trial of a case in the Tax Court.

The Tax Court was designed to be an inexpensive forum in which to litigate tax determinations. In keeping with this design, Tax Court Rule 70(a)(1) provides that both the taxpayer and the Commissioner of Internal Revenue must make every attempt to "obtain the objectives of discovery through informal consultation or communication before utilizing the discovery procedures provided [by the] Rules." In other words, in a Tax Court case, proceedings will progress smoothly and according to design if none of the discovery rules is ever utilized. Although the discovery provisions are available and should be used whenever necessary for the development of a case, the discovery provisions should not be used to delay proceedings, to burden the opposition, or to increase the expense of litigation.

---

c. This discussion is excerpted from Garbis, Junghans & Struntz, Federal Tax Litigation, Ch. 6 (1985).

2. Bolich v. Rubel, 67 F.2d 894 (2d Cir. 1933).

d. But see United States v. Gimbel, 782 F.2d 89 (7th Cir.1986).

* * *

[The specific discovery devices available in the Tax Court include interrogatories,[e] requests for production of documents or entry on property,[f] depositions [g] requests for admissions [h] (which are not, strictly speaking, discovery devices) and, in transferee cases, the examination of the records of a nonparty.[i]]

HONGKONG AND SHANGHAI BANKING CORP. v. COMMISSIONER
Tax Court of the United States, 1985.
85 T.C. 701.

NIMS, JUDGE: This matter is before the Court on respondent's motion for an order under section 7456(b) to require petitioner to produce in Court certain books and records located in its home office in Hong Kong. * * *

* * *

Petitioner is a Hong Kong corporation primarily engaged in the banking business, worldwide. During the years in issue, petitioner had U.S. branch offices in New York, Chicago, and Seattle. It also had assets and operations in most western nations throughout the world. Foreign corporations which earn income which is effectively connected with the conduct of a trade or business within the United States must report annually on Form 1120F, U.S. Income Tax Return of a Foreign Corporation. Petitioner timely filed Forms 1120F for its taxable years 1974, 1975, and 1976.

* * *

Section 7456(b) was new with the 1954 Code and has remained unchanged since the date of enactment. It provides:

> SEC. 7456(b). PRODUCTION OF RECORDS IN THE CASE OF FOREIGN CORPORATIONS, FOREIGN TRUSTS OR ESTATES AND NONRESIDENT ALIEN INDIVIDUALS.—The Tax Court or any division thereof, upon motion and notice by the Secretary, and upon good cause shown therefor, shall order any foreign corporation, foreign trust or estate, or nonresident alien individual, who has filed a petition with the Tax Court, to produce, or, upon satisfactory proof to the Tax Court or any of its divisions, that the petitioner is unable to produce, to make available to the Secretary, and, in either case, to permit the inspection, copying, or photographing of such books, records, documents, memoranda, correspondence and other papers, wherever situated, as the Tax Court or any division thereof, may deem relevant to the proceedings and which are in the possession, custody or control of the petitioner, or of any person directly or indirectly under his control or having control over him or subject to the same common control. If the petitioner fails or refuses

---

e. T.C.R. 71.
f. T.C.R. 72.
g. T.C.R. 74, 75.

h. T.C.R. 90.
i. T.C.R. 73.

to comply with any of the provisions of such order, after reasonable time for compliance has been afforded to him, the Tax Court or any division thereof, upon motion, shall make an order striking out pleadings or parts thereof, or dismissing the proceeding or any part thereof, or rendering a judgment by default against the petitioner. For the purpose of this subsection, the term "foreign trust or estate" includes an estate or trust, any fiduciary of which is a foreign corporation or nonresident alien individual; and the term "control" is not limited to legal control.

The regulations promulgated under section 7456(b) simply paraphrase the Code section. Neither our own research nor the written submissions by the parties have disclosed any prior case law under section 7456(b), and there is a paucity of legislative history. * * * Consequently, we are left on our own to discern the parameters of section 7456(b). Fortunately, the statutory language is straightforward and relatively unambiguous.

In his motion, respondent asks that petitioner be ordered to produce in Court books and records from petitioner's home office in Hong Kong. * * *

* * *

[The Commissioner sought access to the bank's original records maintained in Hong Kong in order to substantiate an interest expense deduction and the allocation of indirect expenses of the Hong Kong office to the U.S. branches.]

For the reasons above stated by respondent, we think he has shown "good cause" for some form of order under section 7456(b).

We turn now to the type of order to be granted. We agree with petitioner that it would be wholly impractical for petitioner to produce in Court the books and records specified in the [Commissioner's motion]. Section 7456(b) deals with this kind of contingency, however, by directing the Tax Court to order the foreign entity—petitioner—to make the relevant "books, records, documents, memoranda, correspondence and other papers" (herein called books and records), *wherever situated,* available to the Commissioner for inspection, copying, or photographing. Since the books and records are located in Hong Kong, an appropriate order under section 7456(b) will direct petitioner to make relevant books and records available to respondent in Hong Kong.

We cannot agree that respondent should be forced to speculate, as petitioner seems to be urging, as to what books and records might be material and relevant in this case, based simply upon a perusal of the Peat, Marwick, Mitchell & Co. and Price Waterhouse & Co. reports * * *

* * *

On the other hand, we agree with petitioner that any order fashioned in response to respondent's motion should not mandate to respondent's agents a general rummaging through all of petitioner's books and records, without limitation.

We think the basic criteria for the scope of a section 7456(b) order should be patterned after those for judicial enforcement of an administrative summons set forth in *United States v. Powell,* 379 U.S. 48, 57–58 (1964). Based upon *Powell,* we formulate the following guidelines, namely, (1) that the investigation is to be conducted pursuant to a legitimate purpose, (2) that the inquiry must be relevant to the purpose, (3) that the information sought is not already within the Commissioner's possession, and (4) that the procedural steps required by section 7456(b) have been followed.

First applying the third and fourth of the above criteria to the case before us, we observe that the information sought is not already within the Commissioner's possession because he has yet to see the books and records, and he has complied with the requisite procedural steps by duly filing and serving the motion and notice required by section 7456(b). This leaves the criteria of "legitimate purpose" and "relevant to the purpose" to be dealt with. We agree with respondent that he must be permitted to examine petitioner's books and records in Hong Kong, but legitimacy and relevance require that the scope of the examination be limited to the challenged deductions, namely, the deduction for the indirect general and administrative expenses charged to petitioner's U.S. branches and petitioner's interest expense allocable to its U.S. operations.

* * * Therefore, notwithstanding the Commissioner's legitimate interest in inspecting petitioner's books and records located in Hong Kong insofar as they relate to petitioner's U.S. operations, we think it would be highly inappropriate for this Court to apply section 7456(b) in a manner which might encourage a tax examination by the Commissioner of petitioner's operations worldwide.

Consideration of principles of international law and comity are undoubtedly involved as a preliminary to the promulgation of any section 7456(b) order. But at the hearing on the section 7456(b) motion, respondent's counsel agreed that the scope of the order should be limited to inspection in Hong Kong of books and records relevant to the challenged deductions, and petitioner's counsel stated (contrary to the position taken in petitioner's pre-hearing brief) that the Hong Kong Bank Secrecy Act is not involved here. Without further exploration of the ramifications of that act, we deem this to be a waiver by petitioner of any privilege thereunder. Thus, the problem of resolving conflicting interests of foreign nations and the United States * * * is not presented here.

* * *

A final word. Respondent's section 7456(b) motion was filed on August 16, 1985, only 19 days before the trial of this case was scheduled to commence. Under other circumstances, we might have been disposed to deny the motion summarily as being untimely, since any order under the motion would necessarily cause a postponement of the trial. Respondent represents, however, that since the two issues to which the motion relates are essentially questions of substantiation, a lengthy trial on these issues will in all probability be avoided if respondent can be assured through inspection that petitioner's books and records in Hong Kong support the deductions claimed. Petitioner does not strenuously challenge this representation, and we have accordingly entertained the motion. We would observe, nevertheless, that section 7456(b) being substantially analogous to discovery, we would expect the parties in future cases to comply with the time constraints relating to discovery contained in Rule 70(a)(2).

* * *

An appropriate order will be entered.

(2) *Stipulations* [j]

The use of extensive stipulations is characteristic of Tax Court litigation. Indeed, as stated by the court in one of the first decisions issued after the 1974 Rules revision, when Rule 91 first appeared: "For many years the bedrock of Tax Court practice has been the stipulation process, now embodied in Rule 91. * * * The recently adopted discovery procedures were not intended in any way to weaken the stipulation process." [2]

The parties to a Tax Court case may not themselves decide whether they want to enter into a stipulation regarding undisputed areas of the case. Tax Court Rule 91(a)(1) requires them "to stipulate, to the fullest extent to which complete or qualified agreement can or fairly should be reached, all matters not privileged which are relevant to the pending case, regardless of whether such matters involve fact or opinion or the application of law to fact."

In case any Tax Court practitioners are left in doubt as to the required content of stipulations, the Rule further explains its intent, stating that stipulations should include "all facts, all documents and papers or contents or aspects thereof, and all evidence which fairly should not be in dispute." [3] The Rule is drafted in broad terms so that it is clear that stipulations should be made to more than mere facts or evidence admissible at trial. Stipulations should be made to any matter upon which the parties agree that has a bearing on the disposition of an issue in the case.

Rule 91 leaves the process of stipulation largely to the parties. However, there should be early meetings between opposing counsel to work out the exchanges of information and views requisite to the formalization of a stipulation. Certainly, it is expected that the parties

---

[j] This discussion is excerpted from Garbis, Junghans & Struntz, Federal Tax Litigation, Ch. 8 (1985).

[2] Branerton Corp. v. Comm'r, 61 T.C. 691, 692 (1974), later proceeding, 64 T.C. 191 (1975).

[3] T.C.R. 91(a)(1).

will make every effort to stipulate and to exchange data informally before any resort to the formal discovery procedures or to the formal procedures attendant to the process of stipulation. In addition, the establishment of candid communications between opposing counsel and a mutual consideration of the facts of the case may be of material assistance in settlement efforts.

(3) Sanctions

A combination of a flood of cases involving tax shelters and a constant stream of so-called "tax protestor" cases during the 1980's seriously overburdened the Tax Court. Congress responded by amending § 6673, which authorizes the Tax Court to impose monetary penalties for instituting or maintaining a Tax Court proceeding primarily for delay. In the early 1980's, the maximum penalty was established at $5,000, and the penalty was made applicable to situations in which the taxpayer's position was frivolous or groundless. In 1986, the provision was amended again to make it applicable when a taxpayer fails to pursue available administrative remedies.

In response to testimony of the Chief Judge of the Tax Court that stiffer sanctions were necessary, Congress again amended section 6673 in 1989 as part of the Improved Penalty Administration and Compliance Tax Act ("IMPACT"). As discussed in Chapter 6, the IMPACT legislation increased the maximum penalty to $25,000, effective for positions taken after December 31, 1989, regardless of whether the action was commenced prior to that date. IMPACT also changed the description of the monetary amount from "damages" to "penalty," to clarify that the government need not prove actual damages to support the penalty.

Recognizing the need to restrain taxpayers' lawyers, as well as the taxpayers themselves, Congress in 1989 also added a new provision to section 6673 to deter delay tactics by lawyers. Under § 6673(a)(2), the Tax Court may require the taxpayer's attorney (or other authorized representative) to pay personally the excess costs, expenses and attorney's fees caused by the attorney's "multipl[ying] the proceedings in any case unreasonably and vexatiously." Congress did not overlook the possibility of such misconduct by government lawyers. If the Tax Court finds that a government lawyer has engaged in such conduct, it can order the government to pay the additional costs, expenses and fees resulting from the misconduct. IRC § 6673(a)(2)(B).

As the following case illustrates, the Tax Court has substantial authority beyond section 6673 to deal with uncooperative taxpayers (and presumably—but indirectly—their counsel).

STRINGER v. COMMISSIONER
Tax Court of the United States, 1985.
84 T.C. 693 (affirmed, 789 F.2d 917 (4th Cir.1985)).

STERRETT, JUDGE:

* * *

We think it appropriate to stress at the outset, * * * that the record in this case borders on being totally unintelligible. We have before us a 598–page transcript, literally scores of exhibits, altered 1978 Forms 1040 announcing frivolous constitutional objections, a delinquent 1978 return filed on December 30, 1981, unsigned Forms 1040 for the years 1978 through 1981, and a final set of Forms 1040 for the years 1978 through 1981 filed 1 day before trial of this case. We place the blame for the confusion squarely with petitioners and their counsel. Without the aid of a brief on petitioners' behalf containing "detailed findings of fact" based upon "specific, detailed, easily found and legible evidence," as directed by the Court, we are hard pressed to state with anything approaching remote certainty the final of countless inconsistent positions advanced by petitioners. We are absolutely convinced that the tactics employed by petitioners and their counsel were carefully calculated to prevent any meaningful resolution of their case. To the extent that we deal harshly with petitioners, petitioners have only themselves and their counsel to blame.

* * *

Rule 151(a) provides, in part, that "Briefs *shall be filed* after trial or submission of a case, except as otherwise directed by the presiding Judge." (Emphasis added.)

Rule 123 provides, in part, as follows:

(a) Default: When any party has failed to plead or otherwise proceed as provided by these Rules or as required by the Court, he may be held in default by the Court either on motion of another party or on the initiative of the Court. Thereafter, the Court may enter a decision against the defaulting party, upon such terms and conditions as the Court may deem proper * * *

(b) Dismissal: For failure of a petitioner properly to prosecute or to comply with these Rules or any order of the Court or for other cause which the Court deems sufficient, the Court may dismiss a case at any time and enter a decision against the petitioner. The Court may, for similar reasons, decide against any party any issue as to which he has the burden of proof; and such decision shall be treated as a dismissal * * *

* * *

(d) Effect of Decision on Default or Dismissal: A decision rendered upon a default or in consequence of a dismissal, other than a dismissal for lack of jurisdiction, shall operate as an adjudication on the merits.

Our Rule 151 *requires* that briefs be filed, except as otherwise directed by the presiding Judge. Thus, from the standpoint of the parties, the Rule is not couched in permissive language.

* * *

By the end of the rather lengthy trial, the Court was well aware that it would need specific clarification of the deductions and credits petitioners were claiming. To that end, the Court did not rely solely on the existence of Rule 151. It issued an oral directive to petitioners' counsel specifying the type of findings of fact the Court would need to understand petitioners' legal positions. Thus, by failing to file a brief in this case petitioners not only have violated a Rule of this Court but also have disregarded a specific and easily understandable oral directive of the Court. Under the circumstances, we believe that petitioners' inexcusable conduct not only warrants some sanctioning but, in fact, requires it. Petitioners have attempted to shift to the Court the burden of sifting through a 598-page transcript and a large number of exhibits, many of which are suspect in appearance, in order to ferret out petitioners' legal positions and whatever facts may support those positions. We will not accept this burden, nor should we. Our pending docket is well documented, and we can ill afford the time or the manpower to perform duties that properly rest with petitioners.

With respect to the proper means of sanctioning petitioners, respondent has requested that we render a default judgment pursuant to Rule 123(a) or dismiss petitioners' case pursuant to Rule 123(b) to the extent of those issues upon which petitioners bear the burden of proof. We entertain no reservations but that Rule 123 is broad enough to cover respondent's motion, and we can think of no persuasive reason why we, under the circumstances of this case and in the exercise of our discretion, should decline to grant that motion. The failure of petitioners and their counsel to comply with the dictates of Rule 151 and the specific directions of the Court, can be said to constitute a default under Rule 123(a), since they have "failed to * * * proceed as provided by these Rules or as required by the Court." Furthermore, the inactivity of petitioners and their counsel can be said to constitute a failure to properly prosecute pursuant to Rule 123(b), since there has been a "failure * * * to comply with these Rules or any order of the Court."

Although we have located no reported Tax Court case defaulting or dismissing a party for failure to file a brief, we consistently have given Rule 123 broad applicability. Thus, for example, Rule 123 has been applied when a party has refused to appear at trial, to stipulate, or to comply with Court-ordered discovery. See, e.g., *Long v. Commissioner,* 742 F.2d 1141 (8th Cir.1984), affg. per curiam an order of dismissal by this Court for failure to stipulate; *Miller v. Commissioner,* 654 F.2d 519 (8th Cir.1981), affg. per curiam an unpublished order of this Court dismissing for failure to stipulate; *Rechtzigel v. Commissioner,* 79 T.C. 132 (1982), affd. per curiam 703 F.2d 1063 (8th Cir.1983) (refusal to comply with Court-ordered discovery); *Ritchie v. Commissioner,* 72 T.C. 126 (1979) (failure to appear at trial).

There is no question but that Rule 123 may be invoked after, as well as before, a trial has been held. In fact, Rule 123(b) by its very terms authorizes a dismissal "at any time." On numerous occasions, we in essence have defaulted or dismissed issues for failure to brief them. Generally, we have accomplished this result by considering the issue waived or conceded.

* * *

We conclude that petitioners' failure to file a brief, under the circumstances of this case, fully justifies the dismissal of all issues as to which petitioners have the burden of proof. Accordingly, respondent's motion to dismiss those issues pursuant to Rule 123(b) will be granted.

* * *

Note

The Tax Court has significant sanctions power to remedy failures to comply with discovery, including the power of dismissal. Tax Court Rule 104. See Hillig v. Commissioner, 916 F.2d 171 (4th Cir.1990), for a discussion of when the power of dismissal may properly be invoked. In *Hillig,* the Fourth Circuit vacated the Tax Court's dismissal, finding it inappropriate to punish the taxpayer for the lawyer's failure to comply with an order compelling production of documents.

(4) *Settlement*

Failure to reach a settlement at the administrative level does not mean that a tax dispute will not be settled prior to trial. Quite the contrary, in fact, is true. As overwhelming majority of all docketed Tax Court cases are settled.[k] The following excerpt [l] describes the settlement procedures.

SETTLEMENT PROCEDURES

During 1982, the Service adopted a new settlement procedure applicable to all cases docketed in the Tax Court.[1] In essence, sole settlement authority will pass between District Counsel and the Appeals Division as a case is transferred between the two Service offices.

The Appeals Division

All docketed cases in which the statutory notice of deficiency was not issued by the Appeals Division will be referred initially to the Appeals Division for consideration of settlement. Cases in which the deficiency notice was issued by the Appeals Division may be referred to

---

k. *1988 IRS Annual Report* at pp. 55–56 (greater than 99% settlement rate, excluding tax-shelter cases).

l. From Garbis, Junghans & Struntz, Federal Tax Litigation, Ch. 10 (1985).

1. Rev.Proc. 82–42, 1982–2 CB 761, superseding Rev.Proc. 79–59, 1979–2 CB 573.

the Appeals Division, unless District Counsel determines that a settlement of all or part of the case is not likely to be achieved within a reasonable time.[2]

The time during which the Appeals Division will have settlement authority will vary from case to case. Cases involving deficiencies of tax and penalty (per taxable period) of more than $10,000 will be returned promptly when the case appears on the Tax Court's Trial Status Report, or earlier if it appears that no progress toward total or partial settlement is being made. District Counsel may, however, agree to extend the period of Appeals Division jurisdiction.

Smaller cases (i.e., those involving deficiencies of less than $10,000, including small tax cases) will be referred to the Appeals Division for a period of six months or, if earlier, until receipt of the notice of trial in regular cases or fifteen days prior to the trial calendar in small tax cases. At the conclusion of the period, if Appeals determines that the case is not susceptible of total or partial settlement, it will be returned to District Counsel. If, however, the Appeals Division believes settlement is likely and District Counsel agrees, the period of the Appeals Division's jurisdiction may be extended.

When a case is referred to Appeals, the taxpayer will be given notice that the Appeals Division has sole authority to settle the case and will be provided with the opportunity to discuss the case, submit appropriate information, and seek to arrive at a mutually acceptable settlement. In view of the limited time of Appeals Division jurisdiction and the need to demonstrate progress toward a settlement, it is important for the taxpayer to act expeditiously to explore settlement with Appeals. Of course, there are those cases (especially those in which there have been Appeals Division proceedings prior to the statutory notice of deficiency) in which it may be best to have the case referred to Counsel as early as possible.

District Counsel

Following the period, if any, during which the Appeals Division has exclusive settlement jurisdiction, the authority to settle the Tax Court case passes to District Counsel. It is important to be aware that the Service usually views this phase as a new look at the case. It is the normal position of the Service that settlement offers and counteroffers made between Appeals and the taxpayer are not binding on District Counsel.

When District Counsel obtains sole jurisdiction of the case, it will take steps to develop fully all of the relevant facts and legal positions before determining whether to proceed with settlement negotiations.

---

2. Rev.Proc. 82–42 is not applicable to cases (or issues in cases) involving qualification of employee plans or the tax-exempt or foundation status of an organization. Nor is it applicable to cases docketed pursuant to IRC §§ 6110 (disclosures), 7428 (status and classification of organizations), 7476 (qualification of retirement plans), 7477 (transfer of property from the United States), or 7478 (status of government obligations). Id. § 4.

Conferences will be set to request informally any additional information thought to be needed; and if any requested information is not forthcoming within a reasonable period of time, the Tax Court's discovery procedures will be utilized as appropriate.

The ultimate aim of the new Service procedure is to encourage taxpayers to settle those matters susceptible of settlement while a case is within Appeals Division jurisdiction. Thus, it is intended that District Counsel's efforts be devoted toward the preparation for trial of those cases (or issues) that must be tried.

* * *

BASIS FOR SETTLEMENT

Tax Court settlements are somewhat more complex than settlements in the typical civil suit, where the settlement agreement usually results in a flat reduction of the plaintiff's claim for damages. A tax settlement may take this form, with the government settling for a reduced liability across the board. However, where several issues are involved, the settlement may take the form of an agreement that each party concede totally on certain issues or that some issues be conceded and others be settled by means of an adjustment. For example, in a situation where the Service claims that a taxpayer was not entitled to use an accelerated form of depreciation on certain property, that certain expenses claimed as business deductions were really personal, and that the taxpayer should have been taxed on certain receipts received by a family member, the Service might abandon the claim with reference to depreciation, the taxpayer might concede that the income was really taxable to him, and the parties might agree that some of the claimed business deductions were really for business purposes and make a partial adjustment of this issue. Settlement of some tax claims may also affect other issues that are not in dispute. For example, a settlement with regard to depreciation will affect previous and future years' tax liabilities. The parties should include in the settlement an agreement regarding the effect the resolution of disputed items will have on items or periods not currently at issue.

The question of the basis for settlement of a Tax Court case should be approached with an attitude of flexibility. It is, of course, necessary that the settlement provide for some agreed resolution of the Tax Court case itself. However, the settlement need not be limited to the mere agreement upon a Tax Court judgment. Rather, it is possible, and sometimes necessary, to agree upon various matters that are not included on the face of the Tax Court judgment. For example, in a gift tax case, it may be appropriate or required, in valuing the gift, to establish the basis that the subject matter will have in the hands of donees who are not parties to the Tax Court case. In such a situation, it may be appropriate to have a collateral agreement between the Service and the donees regarding the basis of the property.

Although the Service may not settle a Tax Court case because of the effort that will be involved in defending its position, it is specifically authorized to compromise a case, in certain limited circumstances, based upon doubt as to collectibility.[4] Nevertheless, except in extremely rare circumstances, it has been the practice of the Service not to consider collectibility in the process of settlement of a Tax Court case. * * *

* * *

ENFORCEMENT OF SETTLEMENT AGREEMENTS

Once a basis for settlement of a case has been reached by the parties, the Appeals Officer or the District Counsel attorney who participated in the settlement negotiations on behalf of the Commissioner will prepare a set of computations reflecting the agreement. In addition, he or she will prepare a document bearing the caption of the case and usually entitled "DECISION," setting forth only the "bottom line" of the settlement agreement in terms of the deficiency in tax (if any) due from the petitioner, plus any additions to tax as may have been agreed upon by the parties. The decision document takes the form of an order of the Tax Court and contains a line for the judge's signature and a stipulation at the bottom with spaces for signing by the petitioner and on behalf of the Chief Counsel.

Occasionally, one of the parties to a settlement agreement attempts to withdraw from it, either before or after the decision document has been executed by both parties and submitted to the Tax Court. The Tax Court has held uniformly that where a settlement stipulation has been filed or a partial settlement orally stipulated into the record, it will enforce the parties' agreement unless, for reasons of justice, one party or the other should be relieved from the stipulation.[7] On the other hand, the Tax Court has held consistently that when a "purported settlement stipulation was never signed or approved by, or even submitted to, any IRS official authorized to do so," the proposed stipulation will not be given binding effect.[8]

The Tax Court also has made it clear that it will not enforce an offer of settlement made by the Service that goes unaccepted by the taxpayer. * * *

* * *

Notes and Questions

1. Should a taxpayer be bound by a settlement agreement entered into by his attorney? See Adams v. Commissioner, 85 T.C. 359 (1985), which held that taxpayers were bound by the actions of their former attorney who acted within the scope of an executed power of attorney. On behalf of the taxpayers, the attorney agreed that the taxpayers would be bound by the result in other cases involving an issue in the taxpayers' case.

---

4. I.R.C. § 7122; Reg. § 301.7122–1(a).
7. See, e.g., Sennett v. Comm'r, 69 T.C. 694 (1978). * * *
8. Gardner v. Comm'r, 75 T.C. 475, 479 (1980); * * *

2. Should the Commissioner be able to reject a settlement reached between the taxpayer and the Appeals Division? See Estate of Jones v. Commissioner, 795 F.2d 566 (6th Cir.1986), which held that the settlement agreement was not validly executed and not enforceable.

(5) *Small Case Procedure*

Special informal rules and procedures are available for cases involving deficiencies of $10,000 or less for any taxable year. These rules are contained in Code section 7463 and in Tax Court Rules 170–179 and are designed to provide a less expensive and technical route for settlement of relatively small disputes. As noted in Section 1 of this Chapter, a taxpayer may represent himself in any Tax Court proceedings. The availability of the small case procedures makes exercise of that right more advisable than in a normal proceeding. Tax Court Rule 177 requires that "[t]rials of small tax cases [must] be conducted as informally as possible consistent with orderly procedure, and any evidence deemed by the court to have probative value shall be admissible."

Small tax cases are heard by special trial judges, rather than regular Tax Court judges.[m] For the taxpayer's convenience, the trial will be scheduled at the place selected by the taxpayer, if suitable facilities are available.[n] One price paid by the taxpayer for selecting small tax case procedures is that the decision of the trial judge is final and non-appealable. I.R.C. § 7463(b). Small case procedures must be requested by the taxpayer, and the Tax Court must concur. I.R.C. § 7463(a). Because decisions in small tax cases are not treated as precedent for any other case, the Tax Court has refused to permit taxpayers to use the procedures when the issues involved were identical to the issues in other cases pending before the court. See, e.g., Page v. Commissioner, 86 T.C. 1 (1986). Refusal to permit the small case procedure is especially likely in tax shelter cases (like *Page*) in which numerous taxpayers are litigating identical issues and one or more seeks the small case route to avoid the decision having precedential effect for the related cases.

D. TREATMENT OF DIVERSE COURTS OF APPEALS PRECEDENTS

GOLSEN v. COMMISSIONER
Tax Court of the United States, 1970.
54 T.C. 742.

RAUM, JUDGE.

* * *

The precise question relating to the deductibility of "interest" like that involved herein has been adjudicated by two Courts of Appeals. In

---

m. Tax Court Rule 182.   n. Tax Court Rule 177.

one case, Campbell v. Cen–Tex., Inc., 377 F.2d 688 (C.A.5), decision went for the taxpayer; in the other, Goldman v. United States, 403 F.2d 776 (C.A.10), affirming 273 F.Supp. 137 (W.D.Okla.), the Government prevailed. *Goldman* involved the same insurance company, the same type of policies, and the same financial arrangements as are before us in the present case. *Cen–Tex.* involved a different insurance company but dealt with comparable financing arrangements. Despite some rather feeble attempts on the part of each side herein to distinguish the case adverse to it, we think that both cases are in point. It is our view that the Government's position is correct.

Moreover, we think that we are in any event bound by *Goldman* since it was decided by the Court of Appeals for the same circuit within which the present case arises. In thus concluding that we must follow *Goldman,* we recognize the contrary thrust of the oft-criticized case of Arthur L. Lawrence, 27 T.C. 713. Notwithstanding a number of the considerations which originally led us to that decision, it is our best judgment that better judicial administration requires us to follow a Court of Appeals decision which is squarely in point where appeal from our decision lies to that Court of Appeals and to that court alone.

Section 7482(a), I.R.C.1954, charges the Courts of Appeals with the primary responsibility for review of our decisions, and we think that where the Court of Appeals to which appeal lies has already passed upon the issue before us, efficient and harmonious judicial administration calls for us to follow the decision of that court. Moreover, the practice we are adopting does not jeopardize the Federal interest in uniform application of the internal revenue laws which we emphasized in *Lawrence.* We shall remain able to foster uniformity by giving effect to our own views in cases appealable to courts whose views have not yet been expressed, and, even where the relevant Court of Appeals has already made its views known, by explaining why we agree or disagree with the precedent that we feel constrained to follow.

To the extent that *Lawrence* is inconsistent with the views expressed herein it is hereby overruled. We note, however, that some of our decisions, because they involve two or more taxpayers, may be appealable to more than one circuit. This case presents no such problem, and accordingly we need not decide now what course to take in the event that we are faced with it.

* * *

E. DECLARATORY JUDGMENTS AND DISCLOSURE ACTIONS

The vast majority of cases in the Tax Court are those brought by taxpayers for a redetermination of deficiencies determined by the Commissioner of Internal Revenue. However, since 1975 the Tax Court also has exercised jurisdiction over several types of tax-related declaratory judgment and disclosure actions.

Initially, the Tax Court was authorized to render declaratory judgments as to the initial or continuing qualification of employer (and self-employed) retirement plans.º The Tax Reform Act of 1976 added to the declaratory judgment jurisdiction of the Tax Court, authorizing the rendition of judgments as to the following:

(a) The initial or continuing qualification of an organization as exempt under section 501(a) or as a qualified charitable gift recipient under section 170(c)(2).ᵖ

(b) The initial or continuing classification of an organization as a private foundation under section 509(a) or as a private operating foundation under section 4942(j)(3).ᑫ

(c) Determinations under section 367,ʳ concerning transfers of property to foreign corporations in connection with certain types of exchanges.ˢ

In 1978, the Congress added once more to the declaratory judgment jurisdiction of the Tax Court. For determinations made after 1978, the Tax Court was authorized to issue declaratory judgments regarding the tax exempt status of interest on certain governmental obligations under section 103(a).ᵗ

The Tax Reform Act of 1976 also added to the Tax Court's jurisdiction several types of disclosure actions. These are actions:

(a) To restrain disclosure by the Internal Revenue Service of information contained in written determinations and background file documents relating thereto.ᵘ

(b) To require additional disclosure from the Internal Revenue Service of information contained in written determinations and background file documents relating thereto.ᵛ

(c) To obtain the identity of certain third-parties making contact with the Internal Revenue Service regarding pending requests for written determinations.ʷ

The Tax Court procedures in declaratory judgment and disclosure actions are governed largely by special rules designed for these types of

o. I.R.C. § 7476.
p. I.R.C. § 7428.
q. Id.
r. Section 367 of the Code provides that where a United States person transfers property to a foreign corporation, in connection with an exchange described in section 332, 351, 354, 355, 356 or 361, the foreign corporation shall not be recognized as a corporation for purposes of determining recognition of gain on the transfer, unless there has been a determination that the exchange is not part of a plan to avoid federal income taxes. I.R.C. § 367(a)(1).

s. I.R.C. § 7477.
t. I.R.C. § 7478.
u. I.R.C. § 6110(f)(3).
v. I.R.C. § 6110(f)(4). Jurisdiction is concurrent with the United States District Court for the District of Columbia.
w. I.R.C. § 6110(d)(3). This provision enables taxpayers to investigate allegations of undue influence or other improprieties relating to the issuance of a written determination. Jurisdiction is concurrent with the United States District Court for the District of Columbia.

cases.[x] Those actions which involve solely a review of an Internal Revenue Service determination made upon materials submitted by a taxpayer, such as the initial qualification of a retirement plan or of an alleged charitable organization, normally would be decided upon the administrative record. Other actions, for example, whether revocation of an organization's tax exempt status was proper in light of events occurring subsequent to the organization's initial qualification, may require pre-trial and trial procedures similar to those in a tax deficiency case. In any event, these declaratory judgment and disclosure actions can raise procedural and practical problems. The potential existence of multiple parties, the possibility that the taxpayer and the Internal Revenue Service may be aligned against a third party (protesting qualification, for example), the possibility of the Labor Department and/or the Pension Benefit Guaranty Corporation as a litigant (and possibly as a litigant opposed to the IRS) and other complexities can be features of these types of actions.

Note

Although the wisdom of declaratory judgments in tax matters can be debated, there was a sound rationale for each type of action currently permitted. In each case there was concern that the inability to obtain judicial review of an adverse IRS determination would prevent taxpayers from undertaking legitimate and socially useful activities. An organization cannot operate effectively or solicit contributions if it has not been determined exempt, even if it, or its contributors, could receive vindication (in litigation occurring years after the fact) as to the deductibility and tax exempt status of the contributions. An employer would be most unwise to proceed to make substantial contributions to a retirement plan which, at the administrative level, has been determined to be unqualified. A township can hardly sell bonds if it must represent to investors that, although the IRS takes the position that the interest is taxable, counsel for the township feels strongly that, if the investor will take the matter to court, it is more likely than not that the interest will be declared exempt.

Persuasive arguments can thus be made for providing declaratory judgment jurisdiction with respect to the qualification of exempt organizations and retirement plans, and of the taxability of interest on government obligations as well as with respect to determinations involving transfers to foreign corporations. However, apparently equally effective arguments can be made in other contexts in which taxpayers are required to accept IRS dictates and forego transactions or take substantial tax risks. It could be argued that in every case of denial of a private ruling request the taxpayer should be able to obtain a declaratory judgment. However, this would overwhelm the resources of the Tax Court. Obviously, Congress cannot overload the Tax Court or the other tax litigation forums with declaratory judgment cases. In all but the most essential areas taxpayers must perform their own analyses of tax effects and bear the risk if they choose to

---

x. T.C.R. 210 et seq. (declaratory judgment actions), 220 et seq. (disclosure actions).

take steps which will be challenged by the IRS. Further expansion of the declaratory judgment jurisdiction of the Tax Court should be undertaken, if at all, most carefully.

SECTION 4. TAX REFUND LITIGATION

A. JURISDICTIONAL PREREQUISITES

Tax refund suits are actions in which the sovereign has waived immunity and consented to be sued by taxpayers who wish to contest their tax liability.[y] This waiver of sovereign immunity has been conditioned upon the taxpayer's complying with a number of prerequisites to the bringing of his or her suit.[z]

In order to bring a tax refund suit before a court, a taxpayer must take all of the required steps in the required order. He must:

1. Pay the tax of which refund is sought;
2. File a proper and timely claim for refund;
3. Wait until six months pass or the claim for refund is denied; and
4. File a timely and proper complaint with the court.

The time limits on the filing of refund claims and suits are discussed in Chapter 5.

B. THE FULL PAYMENT RULE

The case of Flora v. United States, excerpted below, should be read not only for its holding espousing what has come to be known as the "full payment rule," but also for its detailed discussion of the history and structure of our system for the resolution of civil tax controversies.

FLORA v. UNITED STATES
Supreme Court of the United States, 1960.
362 U.S. 145, 80 S.Ct. 630, 4 L.Ed.2d 623, affirming on rehearing,
357 U.S. 63, 78 S.Ct. 1079, 2 L.Ed.2d 1165 (1958).

MR. CHIEF JUSTICE WARREN delivered the opinion of the Court.

The question presented is whether a Federal District Court has jurisdiction under 28 U.S.C.A. § 1346(a)(1) of a suit by a taxpayer for the refund of income tax payments which did not discharge the entire amount of his assessment.

THE FACTS

[The IRS assessed a deficiency of $28,908.60 against the taxpayer. The taxpayer paid $5,058.54 and then filed a claim for refund of that

---

y. United States v. Michel, 282 U.S. 656, 51 S.Ct. 284, 75 L.Ed. 598 (1931).

z. United States v. Chicago Golf Club, 84 F.2d 914 (7th Cir.1936); Lipsett v. United States, 37 F.R.D. 549 (S.D.N.Y.1965), appeal dismissed, 359 F.2d 956 (2d Cir. 1966).

amount. The lower court dismissed the refund claim for lack of jurisdiction due to the absence of a full payment on the amount assessed. The Court of Appeals for the Tenth Circuit affirmed the decision of the district court, and the Supreme Court granted certiorari to resolve a conflict among the Courts of Appeals.]

* * *

THE STATUTE

* * *

Section 1346(a)(1) provides that the District Courts shall have jurisdiction, concurrent with the Court of Claims, of

"(1) Any civil action against the United States for the recovery of *any internal-revenue tax* alleged to have been erroneously or illegally assessed or collected, or *any penalty* claimed to have been collected without authority or *any sum* alleged to have been excessive or in any manner wrongfully collected under the internal-revenue laws * * *." (Emphasis added.)

It is clear enough that the phrase "any internal-revenue tax" can readily be construed to refer to payment of the entire amount of an assessment. Such an interpretation is suggested by the nature of the income tax, which is "*A* tax * * * imposed for each taxable year," with the "amount of *the* tax" determined in accordance with prescribed schedules. (Emphasis added.) But it is argued that this reading of the statute is foreclosed by the presence in § 1346(a)(1) of the phrase "any sum." This contention appears to be based upon the notion that "any sum" is a catchall which confers jurisdiction to adjudicate suits for refund of part of a tax. A catchall the phrase surely is; but to say this is not to define what it catches. The sweeping role which petitioner assigns these words is based upon a conjunctive reading of "any internal-revenue tax," "any penalty," and "any sum." But we believe that the statute more readily lends itself to the disjunctive reading which is suggested by the connective "or." That is, "any sum," instead of being related to "any internal-revenue tax" and "any penalty," may refer to amounts which are neither taxes nor penalties. Under this interpretation, the function of the phrase is to permit suit for recovery of items which might not be designated as either "taxes" or "penalties" by Congress or the courts. One obvious example of such a "sum" is interest. And it is significant that many old tax statutes described the amount which was to be assessed under certain circumstances as a "sum" to be added to the tax, simply as a "sum," as a "percentum," or as "costs." Such a rendition of the statute, which is supported by precedent, frees the phrase "any internal-revenue tax" from the qualifications imposed upon it by petitioner and permits it to be given what we regard as its more natural reading—the full tax. Moreover, this construction, under which each phrase is assigned a distinct meaning, imputes to Congress a surer grammatical touch than does the alternative interpretation, under which the "any sum" phrase completely assimilates the other two. Surely a much clearer statute could have been written to authorize suits for refund of any part of a tax merely by use of the phrase "a tax or any portion thereof," or simply "any sum paid under the internal revenue laws." This Court naturally does not review congressional enactments as a panel of grammarians; but neither do we regard ordinary principles of English prose as irrelevant to a construction of those enactments.

We conclude that the language of § 1346(a)(1) can be more readily construed to require payment of the full tax before suit than to permit suit for recovery of a part payment. But * * * the statutory language is not absolutely controlling, and consequently resort must be had to whatever other materials might be relevant.

LEGISLATIVE HISTORY AND HISTORICAL BACKGROUND

Although frequently the legislative history of a statute is the most fruitful source of instruction as to its proper interpretation, in this case that history is barren of any clue to congressional intent.

* * *

Thus there is presented a vexing situation—statutory language which is inconclusive and legislative history which is irrelevant. This, of course, does not necessarily mean that § 1346(a)(1) expresses no congressional intent with respect to the issue before the Court; but it does make that intent uncommonly difficult to divine.

It is argued, however, that the puzzle may be solved through consideration of the historical basis of a suit to recover a tax illegally assessed. The argument proceeds as follows: A suit to recover taxes could, before the Tucker Act,[a] be brought only against the Collector. Such a suit was based upon the common-law count of assumpsit for money had and received, and the nature of that count requires the inference that a suit for recovery of part payment of a tax could have been maintained. Neither the Tucker Act nor the 1921 amendment indicates an intent to change the nature of the refund action in any pertinent respect. Consequently, there is no warrant for importing into § 1346(a)(1) a full-payment requirement.

For reasons which will appear later, we believe that the conclusion would not follow even if the premises were clearly sound. But in addition we have substantial doubt about the validity of the premises. As we have already indicated, the language of the 1921 amendment does in fact tend to indicate a congressional purpose to require full payment as a jurisdictional prerequisite to suit for refund. Moreover, we are not satisfied that the suit against the Collector was identical to the common-law action of assumpsit for money had and received. One difficulty is that, because of the Act of February 26, 1845, which restored the right of action against the Collector after this Court had held that it had been implicitly eliminated by other legislation, the Court no longer regarded the suit as a common-law action, but rather as a statutory remedy which "in its nature [was] a remedy against the

a. 49 P.L. 359, 24 Stat. 505 (1887), as amended, 28 U.S.C.A. §§ 1346, 1491.

Government." On the other hand, it is true that none of the statutes relating to this type of suit clearly indicate a congressional intention to require full payment of the assessed tax before suit. Nevertheless, the opinion of this Court in Cheatham v. United States, 92 U.S. 85, 23 L Ed. 561, prevents us from accepting the analogy between the statutory action against the Collector and the common-law count. In this 1875 opinion, the Court described the remedies available to taxpayers as follows:

> "So also, in the internal-revenue department, the statute which we have copied allows appeals from the assessor to the commissioner of internal revenue; and, if dissatisfied with his decision, *on paying the tax* the party can sue the collector; and, if the money was wrongfully exacted, the courts will give him relief by a judgment, which the United States pledges herself to pay.
>
> * * *
>
> "* * * While a free course of remonstrance and appeal is allowed within the departments before the money is finally exacted, the general government has wisely made *the payment of the tax claimed,* whether of customs or of internal revenue, a condition precedent to a resort to the courts by the party against whom the tax is assessed. * * * If the compliance with this condition [that appeal must be made to the Commissioner and suit brought within six months of his decision] requires the party aggrieved to pay the money, he must do it. He cannot, after the decision is rendered against him, protract the time within which he can contest that decision in the courts by his own delay in paying the money. It is essential to the honor and orderly conduct of the government that its taxes should be promptly paid, and drawbacks speedily adjusted; and the rule prescribed in this class of cases is neither arbitrary nor unreasonable. * * *
>
> "The objecting party can take his appeal. He can, if the decision is delayed beyond twelve months, rest his case on that decision; or he can *pay the amount claimed,* and commence his suit at any time within that period. So, after the decision, he can pay at once, and commence suit within the six months * * *." 92 U.S. at pages 88–89, 23 L.Ed. 561. (Emphasis added.)

Reargument has not changed our view that this language reflects an understanding that full payment of the tax was a prerequisite to suit. Of course * * * the *Cheatham* statement is dictum; but we reiterate that it appears to us to be "carefully considered dictum." 357 U.S. at page 68, 78 S.Ct. at page 1083. Equally important is the fact that the Court was construing the claim-for-refund statute from which, as amended, the language of § 1346(a)(1) was presumably taken. Thus it seems that in *Cheatham* the Supreme Court interpreted this language not only to specify which claims for refund must first be presented for administrative reconsideration, but also to constitute an additional qualification upon the statutory right to sue the Collector. It is true that the version of the provision involved in *Cheatham* contained only the phrase "any tax." But the phrases "any penalty" and "any sum" were added well before the decision in *Cheatham;* the history of these amendments makes it quite clear that they were not designed to effect any change relevant to the *Cheatham* rule; language in opinions of this Court after *Cheatham* is consistent with the *Cheatham* statement; and in any event, as we have indicated, we can see nothing in these additional words which would negate the full-payment requirement.

If this were all the material relevant to a construction of § 1346(a)(1), determination of the issue at bar would be inordinately difficult. Favoring petitioner would be the theory that, in the early nineteenth century, a suit for recovery of part payment of an assessment could be maintained against the Collector, together with the absence of any conclusive evidence that Congress has ever intended to inaugurate a new rule; favoring respondent would be the *Cheatham* statement and the language of the 1921 statute. There are, however, additional factors which are dispositive.

We are not here concerned with a single sentence in an isolated statute, but rather with a jurisdictional provision which is a keystone in a carefully articulated and quite complicated structure of tax laws. From these related statutes, all of which were passed after 1921, it is apparent that Congress has several times acted upon the assumption that § 1346(a)(1) requires full payment before suit. * * * The laws which we consider especially pertinent are the statute establishing the Board of Tax Appeals (now the Tax Court), the Declaratory Judgment Act, 28 U.S.C.A. § 2201 et seq., and § 7422(e) of the Internal Revenue Code of 1954.

The Board of Tax Appeals

The Board of Tax Appeals was established by Congress in 1924 to permit taxpayers to secure a determination of tax liability before payment of the deficiency. The Government argues that the Congress which passed this 1924 legislation thought full payment of the tax assessed was a condition for bringing suit in a District Court; that Congress believed this sometimes caused hardship; and that Congress set up the Board to alleviate that hardship. Petitioner denies this, and contends that Congress' sole purpose was to enable taxpayers to prevent the Government from collecting taxes by exercise of its power of distraint.

We believe that the legislative history surrounding both the creation of the Board and the subsequent revisions of the basic statute supports the Government. The House Committee Report, for example, explained the purpose of the bill as follows:

> "The committee recommends the establishment of a Board of Tax Appeals to which a taxpayer may appeal *prior to the payment* of an additional assessment of income, excess-profits, war-profits, or estate taxes. *Although a taxpayer may, after payment of his tax, bring suit for the recovery thereof* and thus secure a judicial determination on the questions involved, he can not, in view of section 3224 of the Revised Statutes, which prohibits suits to enjoin the collection of taxes, secure

such a determination prior to the payment of the tax. The right of appeal after payment of the tax is an incomplete remedy, and does little to remove the hardship occasioned by an incorrect assessment. The payment of a large additional tax on income received several years previous and which may have, since its receipt, been either wiped out by subsequent losses, invested in non-liquid assets, or spent, sometimes forces taxpayers into bankruptcy, and often causes great financial hardship and sacrifice. These results are not remedied by permitting the taxpayer *to sue for the recovery of the tax after this payment.* He is entitled to an appeal and to a determination of his liability for the tax prior to its payment." (Emphasis added.)

Moreover, throughout the congressional debates are to be found frequent expressions of the principle that payment of the full tax was a precondition to suit * * *.

Petitioner's argument falls under the weight of this evidence. It is true, of course, that the Board of Tax Appeals procedure has the effect of staying collection, and it may well be that Congress so provided in order to alleviate hardships caused by the long-standing bar against suits to enjoin the collection of taxes. But it is a considerable leap to the further conclusion that amelioration of the hardship of prelitigation payment as a jurisdictional requirement was not another important motivation for Congress' action. To reconcile the legislative history with this conclusion seems to require the presumption that all the Congressmen who spoke of payment of the assessment before suit as a hardship understood—without saying—that suit could be brought for whatever part of the assessment had been paid, but believed that, as a practical matter, hardship would nonetheless arise because the Government would require payment of the balance of the tax by exercising its power of distraint. But if this was in fact the view of these legislators, it is indeed extraordinary that they did not say so. Moreover, if Congress' only concern was to prevent distraint, it is somewhat difficult to understand why Congress did not simply authorize injunction suits. It is interesting to note in this connection that bills to permit the same type of prepayment litigation in the District Courts as is possible in the Tax Court have been introduced several times, but none has ever been adopted.

In sum, even assuming that one purpose of Congress in establishing the Board was to permit taxpayers to avoid distraint, it seems evident that another purpose was to furnish a forum where full payment of the assessment would not be a condition precedent to suit. The result is a system in which there is one tribunal for prepayment litigation and another for post-payment litigation, with no room contemplated for a hybrid of the type proposed by petitioner.

THE DECLARATORY JUDGMENT ACT

The Federal Declaratory Judgment Act of 1934 was amended by § 405 of the Revenue Act of 1935 expressly to except disputes "with respect to Federal taxes." The Senate Report explained the purpose of the amendment as follows:

> "Your committee has added an amendment making it clear that the Federal Declaratory Judgments Act of June 14, 1934, has no application to Federal taxes. The application of the Declaratory Judgments Act to taxes would constitute a *radical departure* from the long-continued policy of Congress (as expressed in Rev.Stat. 3224 and other provisions) with respect to the determination, assessment, and collection of Federal taxes. Your committee believes that the orderly and prompt determination and collection of Federal taxes should not be interfered with by a procedure designed to facilitate the settlement of private controversies, and that existing procedure both in the Board of Tax Appeals and the courts affords ample remedies for the correction of tax errors." (Emphasis added.)

It is clear enough that one "radical departure" which was averted by the amendment was the potential circumvention of the "pay first and litigate later" rule by way of suits for declaratory judgments in tax cases. Petitioner would have us give this Court's imprimatur to precisely the same type of "radical departure," since a suit for recovery of but a part of an assessment would determine the legality of the balance by operation of the principle of collateral estoppel. With respect to this unpaid portion, the taxpayer would be securing what is in effect—even though not technically—a declaratory judgment. The frustration of congressional intent which petitioner asks us to endorse could hardly be more glaring, for he has conceded that his argument leads logically to the conclusion that payment of even $1 on a large assessment entitles the taxpayer to sue—a concession amply warranted by the obvious impracticality of any judicially created jurisdictional standard midway between *full* payment and *any* payment.

SECTION 7422(E) OF THE 1954 CODE

One distinct possibility which would emerge from a decision in favor of petitioner would be that a taxpayer might be able to split his cause of action, bringing suit for refund of part of the tax in a Federal District Court and litigating in the Tax Court with respect to the remainder. In such a situation the first decision would, of course, control. Thus if for any reason a litigant would prefer a District Court adjudication, he might sue for a small portion of the tax in that tribunal while at the same time protecting the balance from distraint by invoking the protection of the Tax Court procedure. On the other hand, different questions would arise if this device were not employed. For example, would the Government be required to file a compulsory counterclaim for the unpaid balance in District Court under Rule 13 of the Federal Rules of Civil Procedure, 28 U.S.C.A.? If so, which party would have the burden of proof?

Section 7422(e) of the 1954 Internal Revenue Code makes it apparent that Congress has assumed these problems are nonexistent except in the rare case where the taxpayer brings suit in a District Court and the Commissioner then notifies him of an additional deficiency. Under § 7422(e) such a claimant is given the option of pursuing his suit in the District Court or in the Tax Court, *but he cannot litigate in both.* Moreover, if he decides to remain in the District Court, the Government may—but seemingly is not required to—bring a counterclaim; and if it does, the taxpayer has the burden of proof. If we were to overturn the assumption upon which Congress has acted, we would generate upon a broad scale the very problems Congress believed it had solved.

* * *

[The Court noted that of the approximately 40,000 tax refund suits litigated between 1900 and 1940, the full payment issue was present only 9 times. In 6 cases it was the basis for a government objection to jurisdiction; the failure of the government to contest the issue in 3 cases was held not significant. The small number of cases presenting the issue reinforced the Court's conclusion that there was a uniform pre-1940 belief that full payment was required prior to suit.]

A word should also be said about the argument that requiring taxpayers to pay the full assessments before bringing suits will subject some of them to great hardship. This contention seems to ignore entirely the right of the taxpayer to appeal the deficiency to the Tax Court without paying a cent. If he permits his time for filing such an appeal to expire, he can hardly complain that he has been unjustly treated, for he is in precisely the same position as any other person who is barred by a statute of limitations. On the other hand, the Government has a substantial interest in protecting the public purse, an interest which would be substantially impaired if a taxpayer could sue in a District Court without paying his tax in full. * * * It is quite true that the filing of an appeal to the Tax Court normally precludes the Government from requiring payment of the tax, but a decision in petitioner's favor could be expected to throw a great portion of the Tax Court litigation into the District Courts. Of course, the Government can collect the tax from a District Court suitor by exercising its power of distraint—if he does not split his cause of action—but we cannot believe that compelling resort to this extraordinary procedure is either wise or in accord with congressional intent. Our system of taxation is based upon voluntary assessment and payment, not upon distraint. A full-payment requirement will promote the smooth functioning of this system; a part-payment rule would work at cross-purposes with it.

In sum, if we were to accept petitioner's argument, we would sacrifice the harmony of our carefully structured twentieth century system of tax litigation, and all that would be achieved would be a supposed harmony of § 1346(a)(1) with what might have been the nineteenth century law had the issue ever been raised. Reargument has but fortified our view that § 1346(a)(1), correctly construed, requires full payment of the assessment before an income tax refund suit can be maintained in a Federal District Court.

Affirmed.

Notes and Questions

1. Although the dissenting opinions are omitted here, the *Flora* Court split 5-4. One of the four dissenters, Justice Frankfurter, wrote separately about the difficulty presented by tax cases:

> *   *   *   For one not a specialist in this field to examine every tax question that comes before the Court independently would involve in most cases an inquiry into the course of tax legislation and litigation far beyond the facts of the immediate case. Such an inquiry entails weeks of study and reflection. Therefore, in construing a tax law it has been my rule to follow almost blindly accepted understanding of the meaning of tax legislation, when that is manifested by long-continued, uniform practice, unless a statute leaves no admissible opening for administrative construction.
>
> Therefore, when advised in connection with the disposition of this case after its first argument that "there does not appear to be a single case before 1940 in which a taxpayer attempted a suit for refund of income taxes without paying the full amount the Government alleged to be due," (357 U.S. 63, at 69), I deemed such a long-continued, unbroken practical construction of of the statute controlling as to the meaning of the Revenue Act of 1921, now 28 U.S.C. § 1346(a)(1). Once the basis which for me governed the disposition of the case was no longer available, I was thrown back to an independent inquiry of the course of tax legislation and litigation for more than a hundred years, for all of that was relevant to a true understanding of the problem presented by this case. This involved many weeks of study during what is called the summer vacation. Such a study led to the conclusion set forth in detail in the opinion of my Brother Whittaker.

2. The inevitable effect of the full payment rule is to make a jury trial (in the district courts) or a different body of precedent (for example, in the Claims Court) available only to those taxpayers with sufficient funds to make a full payment of the tax asserted to be due before litigation. Do the reasons outlined by the Supreme Court in *Flora* adequately support this discrimination?

3. Can you think of any circumstances under which the courts should create an exception to the full payment rule? Suppose a taxpayer has waived his right to challenge a deficiency in the Tax Court and consented to assessment in reliance upon erroneous representations of a Revenue Agent? See Ardalan v. United States, 748 F.2d 1411 (10th Cir.1984), in which the court held that such circumstances did not justify creating an exception to the *Flora* rule. What if the Tax Court is unavailable, because there is no deficiency, and the taxpayer is clearly due a "refund" which he cannot afford to prepay? See Curry v. United States, 774 F.2d 852 (7th Cir.1985), in which the court (citing *Ardalan* and similar decisions) refused to create a "hardship" exception to *Flora*.

4. Does the "full tax" required to be paid under *Flora* include interest and penalties? Numerous decisions hold that "full payment" includes interest and penalties. See, e.g., Lambropoulos v. United States, 64 A.F.T.R.2d 89–5620 (Cl.Ct.1989).

5. Does the refund jurisdiction of the district courts encompass suits only to recover interest? See Triangle Corp. v. United States, 592 F.Supp. 1316 (D.Conn.1984), clarified, 597 F.Supp. 507 (1984), holding that the district courts do have jurisdiction to consider suits to recover only interest.

(1) The Divisible Tax Concept

STEELE v. UNITED STATES
United States Court of Appeals, Eighth Circuit, 1960.
280 F.2d 89.

PER CURIAM.

Penalties were assessed administratively against the president and the secretary of Davidson–Steele, Inc., in the amount of $5,186.47 as to each officer for willfully failing to pay over to the Internal Revenue Service the withholdings of income taxes and social security taxes made by the corporation from the wages of its employees.

Each officer made a payment of $50 to the Internal Revenue Service on the amount of the assessment against him, and they thereafter brought suit in the District Court for refund of these payments, on the ground that the penalties were erroneously and illegally assessed against them.

The Government moved to dismiss the action, contending that, under the holding in Flora v. United States, 357 U.S. 63, 78 S.Ct. 1079, 2 L.Ed.2d 1165, no right to sue for refund could exist, because the entire penalty had not been paid.

The District Court dismissed the action on this basis, 172 F.Supp. 793, and the plaintiffs have appealed.

The Government now in effect concedes that it was in error in the position which it took in the District Court; that the withholdings involved constituted separate taxes as to the individual employees of the corporation; and that the penalties imposed similarly would be entitled to be regarded as divisible assessments made in relation to the individual withholdings.

A stipulation has been presented to us in which the parties agree that the situation is subject to the recognition made in footnotes 37 and 38 of the Flora opinion, 362 U.S. 145, at pages 171 and 175, 80 S.Ct. 630, at pages 644 and 646, 4 L.Ed.2d 623, that the full-payment rule is not applicable to an assessment of divisible taxes; and that on this basis the judgments herein should be reversed and the case remanded to the District Court for further proceedings on the merits.

We are in accord with and accept the view and implication of the stipulation that the penalties imposed amounted legally, under §§ 6671 and 6672 of the Internal Revenue Code of 1954, 26 U.S.C.A., to divisible assessments or taxes against the officers, in their relationship to and predication upon the separate taxes of the individual employees. Thus, the officers would be legally entitled to make payment of the amount of the penalty applicable to the withheld taxes of any individual employee, to make claim for refund, and to institute suit for recovery, as a means of settling the question of the right of the Government to have made penalty assessment against them personally in the circumstances of the situation.

The judgment as to each appellant is accordingly reversed, and the case is remanded for further proceedings on the merits.

(2) Payment on an Assessment

The payment jurisdictionally required is one made on a tax assessment.[b] It is not enough for a taxpayer voluntarily to advance a payment in the amount of an anticipated assessment.[c] Hence, an attempt to create a tax refund suit in court prior to assessment will not succeed. This procedure is sometimes attempted by taxpayers seeking to obtain the benefits of civil discovery against the Government during the pendency of a criminal investigation or prosecution.[d]

Should a taxpayer wish to make an advance remittance prior to assessment in order to stop the running of interest against him, he may do so without relinquishing his right ultimately to sue for a refund. He should wait until after the anticipated assessment is made, however, before he files his claim for refund with respect to the advance remittance.[e]

C. THE CLAIM FOR REFUND

(1) Formal Requirements

Section 7422(a) of the Code provides that no tax refund suit may be brought in any court until a claim for refund has been filed with the IRS in accordance with the applicable law and regulations. The regulations are those promulgated pursuant to § 6402 of the Code,[f] which authorize the Service to credit the amount of any overpayment (including interest) against "any outstanding tax liability for any tax [including interest and penalties] owed by the person making the overpayment," and mandates the refund of any balance to the person who made the overpayment.

As a general rule, claims for refund are to be filed with the Service Center serving the internal revenue district in which the tax was paid. The claim must set forth in detail each ground upon which a credit or

---

b. Farnsworth & Chambers Co. v. Phinney, 279 F.2d 538 (5th Cir.1960), affirming, 178 F.Supp. 330 (S.D.Tex.1959).

c. See Factory Storage Corp. v. United States, 611 F.Supp. 433 (E.D.N.C.1985). But see Ewing v. United States, 914 F.2d 499 (4th Cir.1990), discussed in chapter 5 at pages 163–67, which permitted refunds of payments made after the statute of limitations on assessments had expired and no assessment was made.

d. E.g., Campbell v. Eastland, 307 F.2d 478 (5th Cir.1962), cert. denied, 371 U.S. 955, 83 S.Ct. 502, 9 L.Ed.2d 502 (1963).

e. See Rev.Proc. 84–58, 1984–2 C.B. 501.

f. Regs. § 301.6402–1 et seq.

refund is claimed and facts sufficient to apprise the Commissioner of the exact basis thereof. The statement of the grounds and facts must be verified by a written declaration that it is made under the penalties of perjury. A claim which does not comply with the foregoing requirements will not be considered. In the case of income, gift and Federal unemployment taxes, a separate claim must be made for each type of tax for each taxable year or period. If a return is filed by an individual and, after his death, a refund claim is filed by his or her legal representative, certified copies of the letters testamentary or other similar evidence must be annexed to the claim, to show the authority of the legal representative to file the claim.

All claims except those for the refund of overpaid income taxes must be made on Form 843. In the case of income taxes the claim for refund or credit is made on the appropriate income tax return. A great number of taxpayers, of course, automatically claim the excess of estimated taxes paid or taxes withheld by employers over actual tax liability when they file their yearly return. In this situation the Service Center will credit or refund the overpayment as a matter of course, without awaiting examination of the completed return and without awaiting filing of a separate claim for refund. Where a claim is made with respect to income tax overpaid in a prior year, however, a separate amended return must be filed. In the case of individuals who have filed either a Form 1040 or 1040A, the claim is made on Form 1040X. Corporations make claims for refund on Form 1120X and all other claims (for example for taxes overpaid by a fiduciary or an exempt organization) must be made on the appropriate tax return, which should be clearly marked to indicate that it is an amended return.

After the claim is filed with the Service Center, it will be forwarded to the appropriate district office for examination. When claims are examined by the Examination Division of the district office, substantially the same procedure is followed (including appeal rights afforded to taxpayers) as when taxpayers' returns are originally examined. If the claim is allowed, a refund will be made or a credit given by the Service Center. If it is disallowed, a statutory notice of claim disallowance will be issued pursuant to § 6532(a)(1) of the Code, and the stage will be set for the filing of a refund suit.[g] If the Service fails to take any action with respect to the claim, the taxpayer may bring suit at any time after the expiration of six months from the date of filing the claim.[h]

g. As discussed in chapter 5 at p. 188, the taxpayer may waive the statutory notice of claim disallowance. The taxpayer must still wait six months before filing the refund suit, however.

h. Apparently, if the Service never acts on the claim, the statute of limitation on filing the refund suit remains open.

HATTER v. UNITED STATES
United States Claims Court, 1990.
21 Cl.Ct. 786.

Plaintiffs are ten Article III* federal judges serving on various United States district courts and on one United States court of appeals. They bring this action pursuant to U.S. Const. art. III, § 1 (Compensation Clause) claiming that their compensation has been diminished by reason of the Social Security Amendments of 1983, Pub.L. 98–21, § 101, 97 Stat. 65, 68 (codified as amended in scattered sections of 26 U.S.C. and 42 U.S.C.). Plaintiffs seek damages in the amount of the Social Security taxes withheld from their salaries from January 1, 1984 to the present.

Defendant filed a motion to dismiss the complaint pursuant *inter alia,* to RUSCC 12(b)(1). It alleges that this is a tax refund suit over which the Claims Court currently lacks subject matter jurisdiction because the plaintiffs failed to file an administrative claim for refund with the Internal Revenue Service as required by 26 U.S.C. § 7422(a). Hearing concerning defendant's motion was conducted on November 9, 1990 in Washington, D.C.

For reasons stated below, we conclude that the Claims Court lacks subject matter jurisdiction over the complaint at this time. Although plaintiffs characterize their claims as ones for damages other than a tax refund, we conclude that, in essence, their claims are for tax refunds which must be brought first before the IRS. 26 U.S.C. § 7422(a).

I

Prior to January 1, 1984, the salaries of Article III judges were not subject to withholding for Social Security taxes. Effective January 1, 1984, Congress amended the Social Security Act, 42 U.S.C. § 410(a)(5)(E) (1988), and the Internal Revenue Code of 1954, 26 U.S.C. § 3121(b)(5)(E) (1988), extending Social Security coverage to many previously exempt civilian government employees, including judges of the United States district courts and courts of appeals. Pursuant to this statute, the plaintiffs in this case had the following amounts withheld from their salaries during the years 1984 through 1989:

Year	Amount Withheld
1984	$2,532.60
1985	$2,791.80
1986	$3,003.00
1987	$3,131.70
1988	$3,379.50
1989	$3,604.80

All of the plaintiffs were appointed and took office prior to January 1, 1984, the effective date of the amendments. At the time of their

---

* The designation stems from Article III, Section 1, of the United States Constitution which provides:

The judicial Power of the United States, shall be vested in one supreme Court, and in such inferior Courts as the Congress may from time to time ordain and establish. The Judges, both of the supreme and inferior Courts, shall hold their Offices during good Behaviour, and shall, at stated Times, *receive for their Services a Compensation, which shall not be diminished during their Continuance in Office.* [Emphasis added.]

respective appointments, the only mandatory deductions from their salaries were for federal and state income taxes. No mandatory deductions were made for retirement or for Social Security benefits. Plaintiffs now seek to recover as damages the amounts withheld for Social Security taxes.

II

Title 26 U.S.C. § 7422(a) provides in pertinent part:

No suit or proceeding shall be maintained in any court for the recovery of any internal revenue tax alleged to have been erroneously or *illegally* assessed or *collected * * * or of any sum alleged to have been* excessive or *in any manner wrongfully collected, until a claim for refund or credit has been duly filed with the Secretary,* according to the provisions of law in that regard, and the regulations of the Secretary established in pursuance thereof. [emphasis added.]

Plaintiffs conceded that if the court determines that their claims are for tax refunds, then they must file an administrative refund claim with the IRS before suit may be brought in this court. See 26 U.S.C. § 7422(a). They argue, however, that this is not a tax refund suit but rather a claim for damages based on the diminution in compensation caused by withholding the Social Security tax from their salaries. To support their position, plaintiffs rely on the Court of Claims opinion in *Atkins v. United States,* 556 F.2d 1028 (Ct.Cl.1977), *cert. denied,* 434 U.S. 1009 (1978). They argue that since, according to *Atkins,* the court would have great flexibility in fashioning a remedy for a violation of the Compensation Clause, their claim is somehow distinguished from an ordinary tax refund suit. Plaintiffs argue that the court could provide a remedy by awarding damages or by ordering an appropriate increase in their salaries to counteract the effect of the Social Securities deductions. The possibility of alternative relief, according to plaintiffs, demonstrates that defendant's characterization of their claim as one for a tax refund is mistaken.

Defendant argues that this is a tax refund suit, relying primarily on the Court of Claims opinion in *United States v. King,* 182 Ct.Cl. 631, 633–34, 390 F.2d 894, 896 (1968), *rev'd on other grounds,* 395 U.S. 1, 2, (1969). In *King,* the plaintiff was a retired Army colonel who claimed that by misclassifying his armed services retirement status, the government caused him to pay federal income taxes which he was not legally obligated to pay. King asserted that he should be allowed to maintain his claim even though he had not filed a refund claim with the IRS. The Court of Claims held that his monetary claim was barred because he did not file an administrative refund claim but granted him relief in the form of a declaratory judgment and was later reversed on this ground. 395 U.S. at 5.

Although *King* did not involve a diminution claim based on the Compensation Clause, we conclude that it is more analogous to the present case than *Atkins.* Plaintiffs attempt to distinguish their case from *King* on the ground that, unlike *King,* they do not challenge the government's authority to deduct Social Security contributions from their wages. Plaintiffs argue that if they are legally obligated to pay the Social Security taxes, then the diminution which results must be rectified. Putting aside semantics, we find that this is a tax refund suit. Like the plaintiff in *King,* plaintiffs here are asserting that they should be allowed to maintain their claim in this court even though they have not filed a refund claim with the IRS. For jurisdictional purposes, plaintiffs' position is identical to the plaintiff in *King* and we find it controlling.

The fact that the plaintiffs in *Atkins* brought a claim for damages is of no help to the plaintiffs in this case. The claim in *Atkins* was for a violation of the Compensation Clause based on alleged diminution in salary caused by inflation and by the failure of Congress to raise judicial salaries. Since *Atkins* did not involve alleged diminution by taxation, it did not present a jurisdictional problem for the court similar to the one addressed in *King.*

The issue of whether taxes withheld from Article III judicial salaries constitute a diminution in violation of the Compensation Clause is not new. It was first brought before the United States Supreme Court in 1920 in a case involving income taxes. *Evans v. Gore,* 253 U.S. 245 (1920). Thereafter, each time the "diminution" issue has arisen in the context of income taxes, the claim originated as one against the IRS. *See Miles v. Graham,* 268 U.S. 501 (1925), *overruled by O'Malley v. Woodrough,* 307 U.S. 277 (1939). In *O'Malley,* the Supreme Court described the suit below as "an action at law to recover a tax on income claimed to have been illegally exacted." 307 U.S. at 278. The Court further noted that the suit had been brought against the Collector of Internal Revenue and the plaintiff's claim for refund had been rejected. 307 U.S. at 279.

None of the claims for violation of the Compensation Clause brought after *O'Malley* was based on taxes. *See United States v. Will,* 449 U.S. 200 (1980); *Duplantier v. United States,* 606 F.2d 654 (5th Cir.1979), *cert. denied,* 449 U.S. 1076 (1981); *Atkins v. United States,* 556 F.2d 1028 (Ct.Cl.1977), *cert. denied,* 434 U.S. 1009 (1978).

We conclude that there is no logical reason to view a claim for diminution based on Social Security taxes differently from one based on income taxes. In order to obtain a refund of either, the claim must be brought before the IRS prior to filing a complaint in this court. Manifestly, however artfully characterized, plaintiffs seek recovery of Social Security taxes which have been deducted from their salaries since January 1, 1984. Based on the Supreme Court's interpretation of diminution claims involving income taxes as claims for a tax refund rather than damages, the Court of Claims opinion in *King,* and the face of 26 U.S.C. § 7422(a), we conclude that plaintiffs' claims are for tax refunds over which this court lacks subject matter jurisdiction at this time.

III

Defendant's motion to dismiss filed on May 15, 1990, to the extent that it asserts this court's current lack of jurisdiction, *see* RUSCC 12(b)(1), is GRANTED. It is ORDERED that judgment be entered dismissing the complaint for lack of jurisdiction.

Each party shall bear its own costs. *See Johns–Manville Corp. v. United States,* 893 F.2d 324, 328 (Fed.Cir.1989) ("the Claims Court has no power to award costs in cases over which it has no * * * jurisdiction").

(1) Informal Refund Claims

In some circumstances, the taxpayer need not file a formal refund claim. For example, if a taxpayer is audited and the Service determines that he has overpaid his taxes, then the Form 870 will serve as the refund claim and a separate claim need not be filed. Rev.Rul. 68–65, 1968–1 C.B. 555 Recall, however, from Chapter 4 that the courts are split on the question whether a refund suit may be maintained after execution of a Form 870–AD. Thus, if there was an agreed overpayment of tax and no concessions were made by the Appeals Office, Form 870 should be used instead of the Form 870–AD. Other types of "informal" claims that have been recognized by the courts include a protest filed with the Appeals Office that informs the IRS that the taxpayer contends he overpaid his taxes. Hotel Conquistador, Inc. v. United States, 597 F.2d 1348 (Ct.Cl.1979), cert. denied 444 U.S. 1032, 100 S.Ct. 702, 62 L.Ed.2d 668 (1980). At a minimum, an informal refund claim must have a written component. American Radiator & Standard Sanitary Corp. v. United States, 318 F.2d 915 (Ct.Cl.1963). Because a timely filed refund claim is a jurisdictional prerequisite to a refund suit, a formal refund claim should be filed if there is any doubt about whether one is required.

Because informal refund claims can satisfy the jurisdictional requirement of a timely filed refund claim, when no formal refund claim has been filed all written communications between the taxpayer (or his representative) and the IRS should be carefully scrutinized. It is possible that correspondence clearly identifying the grounds for a claimed overpayment will be held sufficient. Even if the informal claim is not itself sufficient (for example, because it lacks specificity), it can toll the statute of limitation to permit the taxpayer time to correct or complete the claim. *American Radiator, supra.*

(2) New Grounds

After a refund claim is filed, it may be amended to add new grounds for the alleged overpayment. New grounds may not be added, however, after the statute of limitations on filing refund claims has expired.

UNITED STATES v. IDEAL BASIC INDUSTRIES, INC.
United States Court of Appeals, Tenth Circuit, 1968.
404 F.2d 122.

HICKEY, CIRCUIT JUDGE.

[The taxpayer initially filed timely refund claims for the years 1951 through 1954 contending that it was entitled to greater deductions for percentage depletion than it had claimed on its original returns for the reason that gross income from mining should be computed on the basis of the sales price of the finished cement. After the running of the limitations period, the taxpayer determined that materials previously identified as calcium carbonate and shale, subject to depletion percentages of 10% and 5%, respectively, were in reality chemical grade limestone and clay, both subject to a 15% depletion percentage. On this basis the taxpayer submitted amended claims for refund.]

The test applied to determine, "[w]hether a new ground of recovery may be introduced after the statute has run by amending a pending claim filed in time depends upon the facts which an investigation of the original claim would disclose. Where the facts upon which the amendment is based would necessarily have been ascertained by the Commissioner in determining the merits of the original claim, the amendment is proper." Pink v. United States, 105 F.2d 183, 187 (2d Cir.1939). "The test is one which affords the government ample protection against the filing of stale claims * * * while at the same time providing no arbitrary limit on the amendment of claims previously filed." St. Joseph Lead Co. v. United States, 299 F.2d 348, 350 (2d Cir.1962).

The trial court found the contested mineral identification issues in favor of the taxpayer. When the initial claim was filed it was incumbent upon the Commissioner to identify the minerals upon which depletion was claimed. The findings clearly indicated the identity of the minerals as limestone and clay, entitled to the 15% depletion rate. Therefore, the Commissioner could not have been misled nor did the amendment introduce a new ground for recovery.

* * *

D. TIMELY FILING OF REFUND SUIT

See Chapter 5, pages 185–189 for the rules governing the time limits on filing refund suits. The following discussion is a brief synopsis of the earlier discussion.

Section 6532(a)(1) of the Code provides that a tax refund suit may not be commenced:

> * * * before the expiration of 6 months from the date of filing the claim [for refund] unless the Secretary renders a decision thereon within that time, nor after the expiration of 2 years from the date of mailing by certified mail or registered mail by the Secretary to the taxpayer of a notice of the disallowance of the part of the claim to which the suit or proceeding relates.

This statute prescribes a condition under which the United States has consented to suit by taxpayers for a refund of taxes. Commencing suits within the statutory period, therefore, is a jurisdictional prerequisite to a tax refund suit.[i]

The two-year limitation period commences on the date of mailing of the formal notice of disallowance of the subject claim.[j] If a claim is never formally rejected, the statutory period may never commence running. Hence, the cause of action could theoretically remain alive indefinitely.[k]

The two-year limitation period may begin without the issuance of a formal notice of disallowance where the taxpayer has filed a written waiver of the requirement of a formal notice (Form 2297). On the day a written waiver of the formal notice requirement is filed, the two-year limitation period for commencing a tax refund suit begins to run.[l]

The two-year statutory period may be extended by agreement between the taxpayer and the IRS.[m] Such an agreement (Form 907) must be signed by the taxpayer and is not effective until signed by a District Director, an Assistant Regional Commissioner, or a Regional Director of Appeals.

The statutory period for filing a refund suit cannot be enlarged except by the aforementioned specific agreement. Thus, once a formal notice of disallowance has been mailed, further action (such as reconsideration) by the IRS on the claim for refund will not extend the period within which suit may be begun.[n] Therefore, the period of limitations for filing a refund suit cannot be extended by the device of filing a second or further timely claim for refund raising the same grounds as an earlier filed claim. A notice of disallowance (or a waiver of notice of disallowance) of the first filed claim raising the grounds on which the suit is based will commence the statutory period of limitations. Later rejection, or consideration without rejection, of the second or later filed claim will not operate to enlarge the time within which the suit may be brought.[o]

---

i. United States v. Garbutt Oil Co., 302 U.S. 528, 58 S.Ct. 320, 82 L.Ed. 405 (1938); Bell v. Gray, 287 F.2d 410 (6th Cir.1960), affirming the decision of the district court, 191 F.Supp. 328 (E.D.Ky.1960).

j. One court has alluded to the possibility that a 30-day letter referring to the claim for refund could constitute a statutory notice of rejection. Register Pub. Co. v. United States, 189 F.Supp. 626 (D.Conn. 1960).

k. See Detroit Trust Co. v. United States, 130 F.Supp. 815 (Ct.Cl.1955), where suit was timely, though filed almost thirty years after the original claim.

l. I.R.C. § 6532(a)(3).

m. I.R.C. § 6532(a)(2). See Regs. § 301.6532–1(b), stating the formal requirements for such an agreement.

n. I.R.C. § 6532(a)(4).

o. 18th Street Leader Stores v. United States, 142 F.2d 113 (7th Cir.1944); Einson–Freeman Co. v. Corwin, 112 F.2d 683 (2d Cir.1940); Cf. W.A. Schemmer Limestone Quarry, Inc. v. United States, 240 F.Supp. 356 (S.D.Iowa 1964) (if the later claim raises new grounds, the date of its disallowance will commence the statutory period).

E. THE ANTI-ASSIGNMENT STATUTE

Assignments of claims against the United States, including tax refund claims, are limited by the "Anti-assignment" Statute.[p] This statute provides, in pertinent part:

> All transfers and assignments made of any claim upon the United States, or of any part or share thereof, or interest therein, whether absolute or conditional, and whatever may be the consideration therefor, and all powers of attorney, orders, or other authorities for receiving payment of any such claim, or of any part of share thereof * * * shall be absolutely null and void, unless they are freely made and executed in the presence of at least two attesting witnesses, after the allowance of such a claim, the ascertainment of the amount due, and the issuing of a warrant for the payment thereof.

The statutory ban on assignment of claims does not apply to assignments that take place "by operation of law." [q]

Tax refund suits are, of course, actions to recover on claims against the United States. The tax refund claims on which the suits are based have not been allowed by the government. Accordingly, their assignment, other than by operation of law, is prohibited by the Anti-assignment Statute. Where suit on a claim for refund is brought by an assignee, if the assignment should be held void, the action is subject to dismissal for want of the proper plaintiff. For example, consider the situation of an individual who sells all his stock in his wholly owned corporation at a time when it had a claim for refund pending before the IRS. If, as part of the deal, the corporation transferred the pending claim for refund to the seller, the Anti-assignment Statute would be violated. Therefore, a tax refund suit by the seller (transferee) based on the claim for refund that had been transferred to him would be subject to dismissal.[r]

The exemption from the Anti-assignment Statute of assignments or transfers of claims that take place by operation of law was read into the statute by the courts to prevent manifest unfairness. As noted by Judge Graven:

> Where a just claim against the United States passes by operation of law from the party to whom the claim accrued to another, if the Anti-assignment Statute were to be held to interdict such assignee from bringing action on the claim, then the result would be that a just claim would go unpaid since the party to whom the claim accrued could not bring an action on it because he was no longer the owner of it. The exception was based on the necessity.[s]

The judicially created exception allows transferees to bring actions on claims for refund where they became the owner of the claim by

---

p. 31 U.S.C.A. § 203.

q. United States v. Aetna Casualty & Sur. Co., 338 U.S. 366, 70 S.Ct. 207, 94 L.Ed. 171 (1949).

r. Lane, Assignment of Claims for Refund, 19 J.Tax. 362 (1963).

s. Kinney-Lindstrom Foundation, Inc. v. United States, 186 F.Supp. 133, 138 (N.D.Iowa 1960).

"devolutions of title by force of law."[t] Thus, the personal representative of a deceased taxpayer may pursue the decedent's claims for refund,[u] and the trustee of a bankrupt may prosecute the bankrupt's claims.[v] The claims of estate are considered to pass by operation of law to the beneficiaries upon the final distribution of the assets of the estate.[w] However, an attempt to assign claims owned by an estate prior to final distribution will violate the Anti-assignment Statute.[x] Similarly, transfers of claims from a corporation to its shareholders in connection with the complete liquidation of the business,[y] or assignments by virtue of corporate merger, dissolution, or consolidation are considered to occur by operation of law and do not violate the Anti-assignment Statute.[z]

WALL INDUSTRIES, INC. v. UNITED STATES
United States Claims Court, 1986.
10 Cl.Ct. 82.

GIBSON, JUDGE:

* * *

Defendant's argument that the AAA is a bar to the assertion of the plaintiff's claim appears not to be well founded. It avers that the AAA should operate in this case to not only preclude the assignment of plaintiff's claim, but to preclude an action brought by Wall, the assignor, because Wall's otherwise invalid assignment makes the assignee, Arthur Young & Co., the real party in interest. Defendant claims this is a form of "procedural contrivance" that is a "variation of a type of evil sought to be avoided by the Act." Quite simply, defendant is literally arguing that tails I win and heads you lose. Either the AAA bars any assignment, thus leaving the claim with Wall, or the AAA does not bar the assignment, in which case Arthur Young, depending on the substance of the agreement, might be the real party in interest. However, the AAA cannot be seen to essentially vitiate the claim and concomitantly *void* the assignment, with the result that the remaining claim is *unenforceable* by the assignor as well.

Plaintiff's citation of authority in this regard is on point. In this connection, we believe our predecessor court, as far back as 1960,

---

t. Id.

u. United States v. Aetna Casualty & Sur. Co., supra note q, at 375; Erwin v. United States, 97 U.S. (7 Otto) 392, 397, 24 L.Ed. 1065 (1878); Kinney-Lindstrom Foundation, Inc. v. United States, supra note s.

v. Erwin v. United States, supra note u, at 397. Cf. United States v. Rochelle, 363 F.2d 225, 233 (5th Cir.1966).

w. Pettengill v. United States, 253 F.Supp. 321 (N.D.Ill.1966).

x. Kinney-Lindstrom Foundation, Inc. v. United States, supra note s.

y. Novo Trading Corp. v. Commissioner, 113 F.2d 320 (2d Cir.1940).

z. Seaboard Air Line Ry. v. United States, 256 U.S. 655, 41 S.Ct. 611, 65 L.Ed. 1149 (1921). Cf. Western Pac. R. Co. v. United States, 268 U.S. 271, 45 S.Ct. 503, 69 L.Ed. 951 (1925).

settled this issue when it stated in the case of Colonial Navigation Co. v. United States, 181 F.Supp. 237 (Ct.Cl.1960) that:

> [A]n attempted assignment of a claim against the United States does not forfeit the claim. *It leaves the claim where it was before the purported assignment [i.e., with the assignor].*

Id. at 247. Similarly on point is the case of K & R Service Co. v. United States, 568 F.Supp. 38 (D.Mass.1983), where the identical argument of the defendant was rejected by the U.S. District Court:

> "The effect of the statute is upon the assignment, not upon the claim. The assignor can still bring suit." [citations omitted] The government's position would create the untenable situation in which the assignment of a tax claim against the United States would effectively preclude all parties from seeking enforcement thereof.

Id. at 40. What this statute means in the context of this case is that whether Wall did, or did not, attempt an assignment, only Wall has the right to bring suit against the United States to recover such taxes as it alleges that it erroneously paid. That is precisely what it did.

* * *

SECTION 5. TAXPAYER'S SUIT ON ACCOUNT STATED

A consideration of civil tax litigation would not be complete without some reference to the taxpayer's action on the theory of an account stated. This theory, in essence, is that there exists an implied contract between the government and the taxpayer whereby a stipulated refund is to be made to the taxpayer.[a]

Usually, a suit on an account stated arises in a context in which a taxpayer has not met the jurisdictional prerequisites to a tax refund suit but can contend that the government has agreed to make a refund to him. The courts require all three of the following to have occurred:

1. The government and the taxpayer have agreed that the taxpayer has overpaid his taxes for a given taxable period.

2. Accord has been reached with regard to the amount of the overpayment.

3. The government has proposed, and the taxpayer has agreed, that a refund of the stated amount will be made and accepted to close the account.

If there was, in fact, an account stated the taxpayer would be able to recover on contractual grounds without having to satisfy the stringent prerequisites to the bringing of a tax refund suit.

   a. Bonwit Teller & Co. v. United States, (1931). 283 U.S. 258, 51 S.Ct. 395, 75 L.Ed. 1018

Jurisdiction over account stated suits is based solely upon the statutes by means of which the United States has consented to be sued on contractual claims.[b] The pertinent statute of limitations provisions, 28 U.S.C.A. §§ 2401 and 2501, require account stated suits to be commenced within six years after the cause of action "first accrues." The cause of action "first accrues" when the implied contract first comes into existence. This generally occurs when the critical document, the District Director's Notice of Adjustment[c] (advising the taxpayer that an overassessment has been determined with regard to his tax liability), is delivered to the taxpayer and he accepts it.

SECTION 6. SPECIAL PARTNERSHIP LITIGATION PROCEDURES

As noted at pages 151–160 above, the 1982 TEFRA legislation created special administrative and litigation procedures for cases involving partnerships. The decisions in the *Barbados* and *Maxwell* cases, below, illustrate some of the many procedural issues the courts are confronting as TEFRA partnership cases wind their way through either the Tax Court or the refund courts.

BARBADOS # 6 LTD. v. COMMISSIONER
Tax Court of the United States, 1985.
85 T.C. 900.

CANTREL, SPECIAL TRIAL JUDGE:

* * *

On June 18, 1984, respondent issued notices of final partnership administrative adjustment (sometimes referred to as FPAA) for Barbados # 5 Ltd., and Barbados # 6 Ltd., to Mr. Wally Jensen, president of Bajan Services, Inc., in Salt Lake City, Utah pursuant to section 6223(a)(2). Subsequently, on June 25, 1984, identical notices of final partnership administrative adjustment for each of the limited partnerships were issued to Bajan Services, Inc., in Salt Lake City. In each of the two sets of notices the following notation appeared in the heading information: "Date FPAA Mailed to Tax Matters Partner: June 18, 1984." The two sets of notices were respectively date-stamped June 18, 1984, and June 25, 1984, * * *

* * *

In the case of Barbados # 6 Ltd., respondent disallowed a partnership interest expense in the amount of $1,832,000 and increased the

---

b. 28 U.S.C.A. §§ 1346(a)(2) and 1491. The United States district courts and the Claims Court have concurrent jurisdiction over these actions.

c. The Notice of Adjustment, issued pursuant to I.R.C. § 6402, discloses to the taxpayer the amount of the overassessment determined by the District Director and his disposition of it, i.e., the amount to be credited to the outstanding tax liabilities of the taxpayer and the amount to be refunded.

partnership's income by $10,000 for the tax year ending December 31, 1982.[4] In the case of Barbados # 5 Ltd., respondent disallowed a partnership interest expense of $5,335,000 and increased the partnership's income by $48,500 for the tax year ending December 31, 1982.

Petitioner mailed its petition in each case to the Tax Court on September 21, 1984, which was 95 days after respondent issued the June 18 FPAA and 88 days after he issued the June 25 FPAA. Petitioner attached only the June 25, 1984, notice of FPAA to each petition.

Respondent filed the motions to dismiss that we consider herein challenging the Court's jurisdiction over these cases on the theory that petitioner, as tax matters partner, failed to file a timely petition in each case. * * * Thus, respondent alleges, to be timely filed the petitions must have been filed on or before September 17, 1984, the 90th day, as extended,[6] after the FPAA notice was mailed pursuant to section 6226(a).

* * *

* * * we hold that petitioner is both a tax matters partner and a notice partner as defined in section 6231(a)(7) and (8), respectively, and thus is qualified to file a petition in the Tax Court within the 90–day period provided in section 6226(a) or within the 60–day period provided in section 6226(b).

In the Tax Equity and Fiscal Responsibility Act of 1982 (TEFRA), Pub.L. 97–248, 96 Stat. 324, Congress introduced a system whereby the tax treatment of items of partnership income, loss, deductions, and credits would be determined at the partnership level in a unified partnership proceeding at both the administrative and judicial levels. Under this system, each partner generally must treat a partnership item in a manner consistent with the treatment of that item on the partnership return. Sec. 6222(a). In addition, this Court has jurisdiction to determine the partnership items and the proper allocation of such items among the partners for the partnership taxable year to which the notice of FPAA relates (sec. 6226(f));[8] and all the partners in a partnership are bound by such determination.

4. The new partnership provisions of subch. C of ch. 63, I.R.C. 1954 as amended, are generally effective for partnership taxable years beginning after Sept. 3, 1982. For partnership taxable years beginning before and ending after Sept. 3, 1982, the new partnership provisions apply only if the partnership, with the consent of each partner, requests to have the new provisions apply and the Secretary of the Treasury consents to such application. The partnerships in these cases, Barbados # 5 Ltd. and Barbados # 6 Ltd., commenced business on Nov. 18, 1982, and Nov. 19, 1982, respectively. Because the partnerships' taxable years begin and end after Sept. 3, 1982, the new provisions apply irrespective of a request and consent.

6. The 90th day was Sunday, Sept. 16, 1984. Thus, the filing period was extended to Monday, Sept. 17, 1984. See sec. 7503.

8. As in a deficiency case, a proceeding in the Tax Court provides a prepayment forum, while a petition may be filed in a Federal District Court or the Claims Court only if the partner filing the petition pays the amount of his allotted share of the increase in tax liability determined in the FPAA.

To commence judicial review of a FPAA, a timely petition for readjustment of the partnership items must be filed pursuant to section 6226. With[in] 90 days after the Internal Revenue Service has mailed a notice of FPAA to the tax matters partner, the tax matters partner may file a petition for readjustment of the partnership items in the Tax Court. Sec. 6226(a). The tax matters partner is the general partner designated as such or if there is no designation, the general partner having the largest profits interest in the partnership (sec. 6231(a)(7)). Here, because petitioner is the only general partner in each partnership, it is the tax matters partner in each partnership. Thus, petitioner has 90 days from June 18, 1984, in which to file each petition as a tax matters partner. Sec. 6226(a).

If the tax matters partner does not file a petition within 90 days, "*any* notice partner" may file a petition within 60 days after the close of the 90–day period. Sec. 6226(b). (Emphasis supplied.) Section 6231(a)(8) defines a notice partner as one who is entitled to notice under section 6223(a), that is any partner in a partnership with 100 or fewer partners, and a partner with a 1–percent or greater profits interest in a partnership with more than 100 partners. Petitioner also satisfies the requirements for being a notice partner in both Barbados # 6 Ltd., a partnership with fewer than 100 partners, and in Barbados # 5 Ltd., which has more than 100 partners. * * *

* * * Respondent would have us create two distinct time periods for filing and separate the eligibility of petitioner from other notice partners for filing a petition during the later period. While we agree that the statute creates a two-tiered system for filing, we do not think the TEFRA provisions preclude a notice partner who is also the tax matters partner from filing as a notice partner. As such, we hold that petitioner as a notice partner, timely filed the petitions within the 60–day period provided in section 6226(b)(1).

* * *

We agree with respondent that as the tax matters partner, petitioner failed to timely file a petition since a petition was not filed within the 90–day period. However, respondent overlooks the fact that a notice partner may file a petition within 60 days after the 90–day period has expired in those cases where the tax matters partner fails to file a petition under section 6226(a). Sec. 6226(b)(1). Also, respondent ignores the fact that an entity or an individual may be both a tax matters partner and a notice partner. To follow respondent's reasoning, a notice partner would forfeit his right to file a petition on his own behalf if he was also the tax matters partner. We find no statutory support for such reasoning.

The scheme of the statute is designed to make certain all partners have an opportunity to litigate a dispute with the Internal Revenue Service including a notice partner who may also happen to be the tax matters partner. It is true that since petitioner is the only general partner, the statute provides that it be the tax matters partner.

However, we do not conceive that this particular factual situation requires that its rights as a notice partner be forfeited and we do not think the statute intended such a result. Consider the factual situation where the tax matters partner, who also is a notice partner, is precluded from filing a petition by those controlling the partnership. If we follow respondent's reasoning, such individual would be precluded from filing a petition to protect his own rights as a notice partner. In essence, we are simply saying here that petitioner wore two hats—one as the tax matters partner and another as a notice partner. Since a timely petition was not filed by petitioner as the tax matters partner, we see no statutory prohibition which precludes petitioner from proceeding on its own behalf by filing a petition as a notice partner.

* * *

The thrust of the statutory scheme is to get the partnership and all interested partners into court in one proceeding so that time and resources will not be wasted in needless, repetitive litigation. Although this scheme allows extra leeway in those situations such as the present one where the tax matters partner is also a notice partner, it insures that the partnership will have its prepayment day in the Tax Court.[12] * * * We wish to point out, however, that a petition filed under section 6226(b) by the notice partner/tax matters partner would be entitled to no more priority under section 6226(b)(2) and (3) than a petition filed by any other notice partner.

Having drawn a conclusion in favor of petitioner, we hasten to reject most of the contentions petitioner puts forward in support of its position. First, we cannot agree that the June 25 notice of FPAA sent to the notice partners, including petitioner, superseded the June 18 notice of FPAA sent to the tax matters partner. Although the June 18 notice was sent to Mr. Jensen, it is clear that the notice was intended for him as president of the general (tax matters) partner. * * * Also, because the Internal Revenue Service is precluded from sending a second notice of FPAA without a showing of fraud, malfeasance, or misrepresentation of a material fact, it would gut the limitations period if we were to find that the second notice superseded the first.[13]

Nor do we agree with petitioner's argument that, because the Internal Revenue Service sent out the second notice, which contains the exact wording as the first notice, the two notices somehow contradict each other, and only the second notice is operative. * * *

* * *

12. Indeed to hold otherwise would verge on the unconscionable in these circumstances for it would effectively deny any judicial review at the partnership level in these cases since a subsequent petition filed with the United States District Court or Claims Court would not be timely. Sec. 6226(a) and (b).

13. Sec. 6223(f). The two notices mailed to petitioner were identical albeit one was directed to petitioner as the tax matters partner on June 18, 1984, and the other was directed to petitioner as a notice partner on June 25, 1984. Because of the identical language, it is our opinion that the notice mailed on June 25, 1984, does not constitute a second notice proscribed by sec. 6223(f).

Petitioner also asserts that the filing of the petitions in these cases tolled the 60-day period in which a notice partner could file a petition under section 6226(b)(1). Thus, petitioner argues, any notice partner should be able to come into the case as a named party to cure defects in the originally filed petition. It is true that an amended petition relates back to the time of filing of the original petition. *Derksen v. Commissioner,* 84 T.C. 355, 359 (1985); see also Rule 41(d). It is also true that in certain circumstances we have allowed a third party to file a petition in the Court on behalf of the taxpayer. These are not cases in which either of these issues need be considered, however, because we have found that petitioner filed timely petitions as a notice partner.

* * *

* * * Moreover, we direct petitioner's attention to section 6226(c) and (d) which provides that each partner that has an interest in the outcome of an action brought under section 6226(a) or (b) shall be treated as a party to the action and be allowed to participate in the action. Pursuant to our Rules, a partner may participate in the action by filing with the Court a notice of election to participate setting forth facts establishing that such partner satisfies the requirements of section 6226(d). Rule 244(b). The notice of election to participate is required to be filed with the Court within 210 days from the date of mailing of the FPAA to the tax matters partner; however, with leave of this Court *upon a showing of sufficient cause,* a notice of election to participate in the proceeding may be filed out of time. Rule 244(b) and (c). Should C. Martin Unterreiner, Kenneth R. Haley, and Marilyn R. Haley or any other notice partner want to participate in these cases, appropriate notices of election that comply with the directives of these Rules should be filed.[16] * * *

* * *

Appropriate orders will be issued.

Reviewed by the Court.

MAXWELL v. COMMISSIONER
Tax Court of the United States, 1986.
87 T.C. 783

WILLIAMS, JUDGE. Respondent has filed a motion to strike certain items at issue in this case from the petition for lack of jurisdiction. This Court must decide whether we have jurisdiction over the portion of the deficiencies and the additions to tax determined by respondent for petitioners' 1979, 1980, 1981 and 1982 taxable years that arise out of certain adjustments of partnership items of income, deduction or credit for the partnership taxable year ended December 31, 1982.

* * *

---

16. Of course, any such notice must be accompanied by a motion for leave to file same out of time which sets forth a showing of sufficient cause.

On April 4, 1985, respondent mailed a statutory notice of deficiency to petitioners determining deficiencies and additions to tax for their 1979, 1980, 1981 and 1982 taxable years. The deficiency for 1982 resulted, in part, from a disallowance of petitioners' distributive share of VIMAS, LTD.'s claimed loss and investment tax credit for the partnership's taxable year ended December 31, 1982. The deficiencies determined in petitioners' 1979 and 1980 taxable years result from the disallowance of investment tax carryback claimed by petitioners in 1982 as partners in VIMAS, LTD. It is unclear from the record what, if any, portion of the deficiency determined for 1981 results from petitioners' interest in VIMAS, LTD. An addition to tax pursuant to section 6659 was determined for 1979, 1980 and 1982 relating to the alleged overvaluation or overstated basis of VIMAS, LTD.'s partnership property. An addition to tax pursuant to section 6653(a)(2) determined for 1982 is identified in the statutory notice of deficiency as being attributable to petitioners' claimed tax benefits resulting from their interest in VIMAS, LTD. An addition to tax pursuant to section 6653(a)(2) was determined for 1981. An addition to tax was determined pursuant to section 6653(a) for 1979 and 1980 and pursuant to section 6653(a)(1) for 1981 and 1982.

VIMAS, LTD. was formed as a limited partnership under the laws of Texas on December 10, 1982. Petitioner Larry Maxwell was the general partner and 13 individuals, including Larry and petitioner Vickey Maxwell, were limited partners.

VIMAS, LTD. was formed to acquire, market and exploit video game masters. The earliest that VIMAS, LTD. acquired video game master recordings and cassettes was December 10, 1982, when it executed leases pertaining to such properties. VIMAS, LTD.'s partnership information return (Form 1065) for 1982 states that it commenced operations on December 27, 1982.

Respondent commenced an administrative proceeding within the meaning of section 6224 and mailed to Larry notice of the beginning of the administrative proceedings on February 28, 1985. Larry is, within the meaning of section 6231(a)(7), the tax matters partner of VIMAS, LTD. On May 2, 1985, the required notice of the beginning of an administrative proceeding was mailed to each VIMAS, LTD. partner whose name and address had been furnished to respondent. No notice of final partnership administrative adjustment ("FPAA") resulting from the administrative proceeding has, as yet, been mailed. On November 14, 1985, Larry executed a Consent to Extend the Time to Assess Tax Attributable to Items of a Partnership (Form 872–P) on behalf of VIMAS, LTD.

This case presents an issue of first impression arising from the application of the partnership audit and litigation provisions of Subchapter C of Chapter 63 of Subtitle F of the Internal Revenue Code of 1954, as amended. Respondent argues that certain adjustments that resulted in his determination of a portion of the deficiency for 1982 were "partnership items" within the meaning of section 6231(a)(3).[2] In respondent's view, this Court has jurisdiction over these items only if they are raised in a petition filed subsequent to the issuance of the FPAA pursuant to the procedures of section 6226 and Rules 240 et seq.[3] Petitioners counter that dismissal of their claims for redetermination of the portions of the deficiencies attributable to their interest in VIMAS, LTD. and related additions to tax would be prejudicial to them. Petitioners claim that they had reached a basis for settlement of all issues in their case and that the dismissal urged by respondent adversely affects this settlement.

This case presents the dichotomy between, on the one hand, the procedures applicable to the determination and redetermination of *deficiencies* and, on the other hand, the procedures applicable to the administrative adjustment and judicial readjustment of *partnership items*. Prior to the enactment of the partnership audit and litigation provisions, no dichotomy existed. Any deficiency determination that involved items of income, loss, deduction or credit of a partnership was made for each partner in conjunction with determining the proper tax treatment of all other items on his individual Federal income tax return. Judicial review of respondent's deficiency determination considered only the case of the particular partner before the court. Each partner's tax liability was determined independently of what any other partner's tax liability in respect of identical items might have been. * * *

* * *

By enacting the partnership audit and litigation procedures, Congress provided a method for uniformly adjusting items of partnership income, loss, deduction or credit that affect each partner. Congress decided that no longer would a partner's tax liability be determined uniquely but "the tax treatment of any partnership item [would] be determined at the partnership level." Section 6221.

In drawing the line between those matters which may be the subject of a partnership proceeding and those which may not be, the statute divides disputes arising from "partnership items" from disputes arising from "nonpartnership items." Compare paragraphs (3) and (4) of section 6231(a). If the tax treatment of a "partnership item" is at issue, the statute requires the matter to be resolved at the partnership level. Section 6221. Respondent has no authority to assess a deficiency attributable to a partnership item until after the close of a partner-

---

2. SEC. 6231. DEFINITIONS AND SPECIAL RULES.
    (a) DEFINITIONS.—For purposes of this subchapter—

    * * *

    (3) PARTNERSHIP ITEM.—The term "partnership item" means, with respect to a partnership, any item required to be taken into account for the partnership's taxable year under any provision of subtitle A to the extent regulations prescribed by the Secretary provide that, for purposes of this subtitle, such item is more appropriately determined at the partnership level than at the partner level.

3. All Rule references are to the Tax Court Rules of Practice and Procedure.

ship proceeding, section 6225(a), and may be enjoined from making premature assessments. Section 6225(b). Special rules apply to settlement agreements. Section 6224(c). Special statutes of limitations apply to assessment of deficiencies attributable to partnership items. Section 6229. In separating partnership adjustments from the deficiency procedures applicable in all other income tax matters, Congress intended that all nonpartnership matters on a partner's Federal income tax return continue to be subject to the existing rules for administrative and judicial resolution of the partner's tax liability. As reported by the Conference Report, H.Rept. No. 97-760 at 611:

> Existing rules relating to administrative and judicial proceedings, statutes of limitations, settlements, etc., will continue to govern the determination of a partner's tax liability attributable to nonpartnership income, loss, deductions, and credits. Neither the Secretary nor the taxpayer will be permitted to raise nonpartnership items in the course of a partnership proceeding nor may partnership items, except to the extent they become nonpartnership items under the rules, be raised in proceedings relating to nonpartnership items of a partner.

It is evident both from the statutory pattern and from the Conference Report that Congress intended administrative and judicial resolution of disputes involving partnership items to be separate from and independent of disputes involving nonpartnership items. Consequently, the portion of any deficiency attributable to a "partnership item" cannot be considered in the partner's personal case involving other matters that may affect his income tax liability. The "partnership items" must be separated from the partner's personal case and considered solely in the partnership proceeding.

This Court's Rules follow this statutory pattern. Rule 240(b)(2) defines "partnership action," in part, as "an 'action for adjustment of partnership items' under Code Section 6228." Rule 240(c) states that [this] "Court does not have jurisdiction of a partnership action" if no FPAA has been issued.

It is certain on this record that the partnership audit and litigation provisions apply to this case. Sections 6221 et seq. are "applicable to partnership taxable years beginning after September 3, 1982" and "to any partnership taxable year ending after September 3, 1982, if the partnership, each partner, and each indirect partner requests such application and the Secretary or his delegate consents to such application." Section 402(a), Tax Equity and Fiscal Responsibility Act of 1982, Pub.L. 97-248, 96 Stat. 648. The consent provision of this effective date rule is not applicable in this case because VIMAS, LTD.'s first partnership taxable year commenced after September 3, 1982.[4] VIMAS, LTD.,

---

4. While it is true that VIMAS, LTD.'s first taxable year ended after September 3, 1982, it is also true that every one of its taxable years will end after September 3, 1982. To construe the effective date rule as applying the consent requirement to all taxable years ending after September 3, 1982 without limiting it to those years that began before September 4, 1982, would result in applying the consent requirement to all future years of all partnerships. The Conference Report states that the partner-

a partnership of more than 10 partners that was formed on December 10, 1982, was a partnership within the meaning of section 6231(a)(1). VIMAS, LTD. acquired its operating partnership property on December 10, 1982 and commenced operations in December, 1982. As a result, adjustments to VIMAS, LTD.'s items of partnership income, loss, deduction or credit, such as those at issue in this case, are subject to the partnership audit and litigation provisions.

In this case, no FPAA has been issued to VIMAS, LTD. Because the issuance of an FPAA is a condition precedent to the exercise of our jurisdiction over a partnership action, it follows that we have no jurisdiction in this case to redetermine any portion of a deficiency attributable to a "partnership item." We must, therefore, decide whether any of the items giving rise to any part of the deficiencies in this case are "partnership items."

Section 6231(a)(3) provides that a "partnership item" means any item required to be taken into account for the partnership's taxable year to the extent prescribed by respondent's regulations as an item that "is more appropriately determined at the partnership level than at the partner level." Partnership losses or credits are items taken into account by VIMAS, LTD. for the 1982 partnership taxable year. Cf. *Southern v. Commissioner*, 87 T.C. 49 (1986); section 301.6231(a)(3)-1(a)(1)(i), Proced. and Admin.Regs., provides that "[i]tems of * * * loss, deduction, or credit of the partnership" are more appropriately determined at the partnership level. VIMAS, LTD.'s partnership loss for 1982 and VIMAS, LTD.'s investment tax credit for 1982 are, therefore, "partnership items" unless some provision of the statute transmutes them into "nonpartnership items."

On this record it is clear that respondent has given notice of the beginning of the administrative proceeding. Consequently, section 6223(a)(1) has been satisfied and none of the other events that could cause a transmutation of "partnership items" into "nonpartnership items" has occurred. Section 6231(b)(1).[5] It follows that the VIMAS, LTD. loss and investment tax credit are "partnership items" and that we lack jurisdiction over deficiencies attributable to those partnership items.

---

ship audit and litigation provisions are mandatory except for that narrow class of partnership years that do not begin after September 3, 1982.

5. SEC. 6231. DEFINITIONS AND SPECIAL RULES.

(b) ITEMS CEASE TO BE PARTNERSHIP ITEMS IN CERTAIN CASES.—

(1) IN GENERAL.—For purposes of this subchapter, the partnership items of a partner for a partnership taxable year shall become nonpartnership items as of the date—

(A) the Secretary mails to such partner a notice that such items shall be treated as nonpartnership items,

(B) the partner files suit under section 6228(b) after the Secretary fails to allow an administrative adjustment request with respect to any of such items,

(C) the Secretary enters into a settlement agreement with the partner with respect to such items, or

(D) such change occurs under subsection (e) of section 6223 (relating to effect of Secretary's failure to provide notice) or under subsection (c) of this section.

The carryback of VIMAS, LTD.'s investment tax credit that results in the deficiencies for petitioners' 1979 and 1980 taxable years is not a "partnership item." Although the existence or amount of the carryback cannot be determined without reference to the VIMAS, LTD. investment tax credit to which VIMAS, LTD. partners were entitled for 1982, the amount of credit to be carried back is not a "partnership item" because a partnership does not take into account any carryback for any taxable year. Rather, the carryback is peculiar to each partner's own tax posture. The carryback is, however, an "affected item" since its existence or amount is "affected by" the investment tax credit that is a partnership item. Section 6231(a)(5). An item whose existence or amount is dependent on any partnership item is an affected item. See Conference Report, H.Rept. No. 97-760 at 609, 1982-2 C.B. 667. As an affected item, however, the carryback gives rise to deficiencies for petitioners' 1979 and 1980 years that are attributable to the partnership item which is the claimed investment tax credit for 1982. Because the carrybacks are the only items giving rise to the deficiencies at issue for 1979 and 1980, we lack jurisdiction over the deficiencies determined for those years.[6]

An addition to tax has been determined for 1979, 1980 and 1982 pursuant to section 6659 which, in this case, relates solely to VIMAS, LTD.'s partnership property. Although the basis or value of partnership property is a partnership item, the section 6659 addition to tax is not an item "required to be taken into account for the partnership's taxable year." It is, therefore, not a partnership item. The existence or amount of this addition to tax, however, depends on a finding of proper basis or value of VIMAS, LTD.'s property. Consequently, it is an affected item.

The addition to tax for negligence in 1979, 1980, 1981 or 1982 may have been determined because of either the partnership's tax reporting positions or the partner's own tax reporting positions. The partnership's reporting positions will be exclusively the subject of the partnership action while the partner's reporting positions, except for positions consistent with the partnership's, section 6222(b), will be the subject of the partner's personal case. A finding of negligence in either the partnership action or the partner's personal case will affect the other. The five percent addition (whether pursuant to section 6653(a) for 1979 and 1980 or pursuant to section 6653(a)(1) for 1981 and 1982) is applied to the entire deficiency for the year. Consequently, if the partner was negligent in his own reporting positions, any deficiency attributable to partnership items will also bear that five percent addition. Likewise, if the partnership's reporting positions resulted from negligence, the five

---

6. See section 6229(a) which extends the period of limitations for assessments of tax "attributable to any partnership item (or affected item)." As discussed *infra*, a deficiency attributable to an affected item such as a partner's carryback of a partnership's investment tax credit is also a "deficiency attributable to a partnership item." Assessments of such deficiencies can be made only at the conclusion of the partnership proceeding in which readjustments to the partnership items giving rise to the deficiencies are determined. Section 6225(a).

percent addition would apply also to the portion of any deficiency attributable to nonpartnership items.

Certain complications in applying section 6653 to the entire deficiency for a year result, however, from following the separate partnership audit and litigation procedures. As discussed above, Congress intended that partnership tax issues be resolved without hindering, and without hindrance from, the resolution of nonpartnership tax issues. If a decision of deficiency in tax is entered in a partner's personal tax case without a finding of negligence while the partnership action is pending, any five percent addition due to the negligence of the partnership cannot be part of that decision. Similarly if a finding of negligence is made in the partner's personal case, the addition to tax will increase if an additional deficiency results for the partnership action. It appears that the resolution of this complication is found in treating as an "affected item" (1) any addition to tax for negligence found in the partnership action or (2) where negligence is found in the personal case, any increased addition to tax on a deficiency resulting from partnership adjustments.

Affected items depend on partnership level determinations, cannot be tried as part of the personal tax case and must await the outcome of the partnership proceeding.[7] Apparently, in these circumstances respondent may issue a second notice of deficiency to the partner determining an additional deficiency attributable to "affected items."[8] In other circumstances a computational adjustment is made.[9]

As an "affected item," the addition to tax for negligence resulting from partnership reporting positions cannot be an issue joined in a partner's personal tax case because a deficiency determined by reference to such an affected item requires a partnership level determination—*i.e.*, whether the partnership reported partnership items negligently. Such affected items cannot be considered in the course of deciding petitioners' personal case without trespassing the line of demarcation drawn by Congress between the audit and litigation of partnership tax matters and the resolution of all other tax items of the

---

7. An item, such as a medical expense deduction, the deductibility of which depends on adjusted gross income, may or may not be affected by partnership adjustments. A medical expense deduction would be a nonpartnership item, the partner's entitlement to which would be litigated in the partner's personal case. The deduction may be limited (or increased) by a partnership adjustment and to that extent only it would be an affected item. The proper tax liability attributable to such a[n] affected item would be the subject of a computational adjustment (see note 9 below).

8. Section 1875(d), Tax Reform Act of 1986, Pub.L. 99–514; see also Proposed Income Tax Regs. sec. 301.6231(a)(6)–1(c), 51 Fed.Reg. 13245 (Apr. 18, 1986).

9. SEC. 6231. DEFINITIONS AND SPECIAL RULES.

(a) Definitions.—For purposes of this subchapter—

(6) COMPUTATIONAL ADJUSTMENT.—The term "computational adjustment" means the change in the tax liability of a partner which properly reflects the treatment under this subchapter of a partnership item. All adjustments required to apply the results of a proceeding with respect to a partnership under this subchapter to an indirect partner shall be treated as computational adjustments.

partner. Any other principle would inextricably tie the two together and remove the statutory dichotomy whenever an addition to tax affected by partnership items were determined by respondent.

Consequently, the VIMAS, LTD. partnership items and affected items that are presently raised in the petition in this case will be struck from the petition for lack of jurisdiction. Nevertheless, respondent is barred from assessing the deficiencies and additions to tax for 1979 and 1980 and those portions of the deficiencies for 1981 and 1982 and related additions to tax attributable to partnership items (including any portion calculated by reference to affected items) prior to the termination of the partnership proceeding. The statute of limitations, of course, does not run on the deficiencies attributable to partnership items (including affected items). Section 6229(a).

The collapse of the settlement that petitioners believed they had constructed is unfortunate, but we may not take jurisdiction except where the statute mandates it.

An appropriate order will be entered.

Reviewed by the Court.

STERRETT, SIMPSON, GOFFE, CHABOT, NIMS, PARKER, WHITAKER, KÖRNER, SHIELDS, HAMBLEN, COHEN, CLAPP, SWIFT, JACOBS, GERBER, WRIGHT, and PARR, JJ., agree with this opinion.

SECTION 7. RES JUDICATA AND COLLATERAL ESTOPPEL

A. GOVERNMENT A PARTY IN FIRST CASE

COMMISSIONER v. SUNNEN
Supreme Court of the United States, 1948.
333 U.S. 591, 68 S.Ct. 715, 92 L.Ed. 898.

MR. JUSTICE MURPHY delivered the opinion of the Court.

* * *

The respondent taxpayer was an inventor-patentee and the president of the Sunnen Products Company, a corporation engaged in the manufacturer and sale of patented grinding machines and other tools. * * *

The taxpayer had entered into several non-exclusive agreements whereby the corporation was licensed to manufacture and sell various devices on which he had applied for patents. In return, the corporation agreed to pay to the taxpayer a royalty equal to 10% of the gross sales price of the devices. * * *

The taxpayer at various times assigned to his wife all his right, title and interest in the various license contracts. She was given exclusive title and power over the royalties accruing under these contracts. All the assignments were without consideration and were made as gifts to the wife, those occurring after 1932 being reported by the taxpayer for gift tax purposes. The corporation was notified of each assignment.

In 1937 the corporation, pursuant to this arrangement, paid the wife royalties in the amount of $4,881.35 on the license contract made in 1928; no other royalties on that contract were paid during the taxable years in question. The wife received royalties from other contracts totaling $15,518.68 in 1937, $17,318.80 in 1938, $25,243.77 in 1939, $50,492.50 in 1940, and $149,002.78 in 1941. She included all these payments in her income tax returns for those years, and the taxes she paid thereon have not been refunded.

Relying upon its own prior decision in Estate of Dodson v. Commissioner, 1 T.C. 416, the Tax Court held that, with one exception, all the royalties paid to the wife from 1937 to 1941 were part of the taxable income of the taxpayer. The one exception concerned the royalties of $4,881.35 paid in 1937 under the 1928 agreement. In an earlier proceeding in 1935, the Board of Tax Appeals dealt with the taxpayer's income tax liability for the years 1929–1931; it concluded that he was not taxable on the royalties paid to his wife during those years under the 1928 license agreement. This prior determination by the Board caused the Tax Court to apply the principle of *res judicata* to bar a different result as to the royalties paid pursuant to the same agreement during 1937.

* * *

We * * * brought the case here on certiorari, the Commissioner alleging that the result below conflicts with prior decisions of this Court.

If the doctrine of *res judicata* is properly applicable so that all the royalty payments made during 1937–1941 are governed by the prior decision of the Board of Tax Appeals, the case may be disposed of without reaching the merits of the controversy. We accordingly cast our attention initially on that possibility, * * *.

It is first necessary to understand something of the recognized meaning and scope of *res judicata*, a doctrine judicial in origin. The general rule of *res judicata* applies to repetitious suits involving the same cause of action. It rests upon considerations of economy of judicial time and public policy favoring the establishment of certainty in legal relations. The rule provides that when a court of competent jurisdiction has entered a final judgment on the merits of a cause of action, the parties to the suit and their privies are thereafter bound "not only as to every matter which was offered and received to sustain or defeat the claim or demand, but as to any other admissible matter which might have been offered for that purpose." Cromwell v. County of Sac, 94 U.S. 351, 352, 24 L.Ed. 195. The judgment puts an end to the cause of action, which cannot again be brought into litigation between the parties upon any ground whatever, absent fraud or some other factor invalidating the judgment.

But where the second action between the same parties is upon a different cause or demand, the principle of *res judicata* is applied much more narrowly. In this situation, the judgment in the prior action operates as an estoppel, not as to matters which might have been litigated and determined, but "only as to those matters in issue or points controverted, upon the determination of which the finding or verdict was rendered." Cromwell v. County of Sac, supra, 353 of 94 U.S. Since the cause of action involved in the second proceeding is not swallowed by the judgment in the prior suit, the parties are free to litigate points which were not at issue in the first proceeding, even though such points might have been tendered and decided at that time. But matters which were actually litigated and determined in the first proceeding cannot later be relitigated. Once a party has fought out a matter in litigation with the other party, he cannot later renew that duel. In this sense, *res judicata* is usually and more accurately referred to as estoppel by judgment, or collateral estoppel.

These same concepts are applicable in the federal income tax field. Income taxes are levied on an annual basis. Each year is the origin of a new liability and of a separate cause of action. Thus if a claim of liability or non-liability relating to a particular tax year is litigated, a judgment on the merits is *res judicata* as to any subsequent proceeding involving the same claim and the same tax year. But if the later proceeding is concerned with a similar or unlike claim relating to a different tax year, the prior judgment acts as a collateral estoppel only as to those matters in the second proceeding which were actually presented and determined in the first suit. Collateral estoppel operates, in other words, to relieve the government and the taxpayer of "redundant litigation of the identical question of the statute's application to the taxpayer's status." Tait v. Western Md. R. Co., 289 U.S. 620, 624, 53 S.Ct. 706, 707, 77 L.Ed. 1405.

But collateral estoppel is a doctrine capable of being applied so as to avoid an undue disparity in the impact of income tax liability. A taxpayer may secure a judicial determination of a particular tax matter, a matter which may recur without substantial variation for some years thereafter. But a subsequent modification of the significant facts or a change or development in the controlling legal principles may make that determination obsolete or erroneous, at least for future purposes. If such a determination is then perpetuated each succeeding year as to the taxpayer involved in the original litigation, he is accorded a tax treatment different from that given to other taxpayers of the same class. As a result, there are inequalities in the administration of the revenue laws, discriminatory distinctions in tax liability, and a fertile basis for litigious confusion. Such consequences, however, are neither necessitated nor justified by the principle of collateral estoppel. That principle is designed to prevent repetitious lawsuits over matters which have once been decided and which have remained substantially static, factually and legally. It is not meant to create vested rights in decisions that have become obsolete or erroneous with time, thereby causing inequities among taxpayers.

And so where two cases involve income taxes in different taxable years, collateral estoppel must be used with its limitations carefully in mind so as to avoid injustice. It must be confined to situations where the matter raised in the second suit is identical in all respects with that decided in the first proceeding and where the controlling facts and applicable legal rules remain unchanged. If the legal matters determined in the earlier case differ from those raised in the second case, collateral estoppel has no bearing on the situation. And where the situation is vitally altered between the time of the first judgment and the second, the prior determination is not conclusive. As demonstrated by Blair v. Commissioner, 300 U.S. 5, 9, 57 S.Ct. 330, 331, 81 L.Ed. 465, a judicial declaration intervening between the two proceedings may so change the legal atmosphere as to render the rule of collateral estoppel inapplicable. But the intervening decision need not necessarily be that of a state court, as it was in the *Blair* case. While such a state court decision may be considered as having changed the facts for federal tax litigation purposes, a modification or growth in legal principles as enunciated in intervening decisions of this Court may also effect a significant change in the situation. Tax inequality can result as readily from neglecting legal modulations by this Court as from disregarding factual changes wrought by state courts. In either event, the supervening decision cannot justly be ignored by blind reliance upon the rule of collateral estoppel. It naturally follows that an interposed alteration in the pertinent statutory provisions or Treasury regulations can make the use of that rule unwarranted. Tait v. Western Md. R. Co., supra, 625.

Of course, where a question of fact essential to the judgment is actually litigated and determined in the first tax proceeding, the parties are bound by that determination in a subsequent proceeding even though the cause of action is different. And if the very same facts and no others are involved in the second case, a case relating to a different tax year, the prior judgment will be conclusive as to the same legal issues which appear, assuming no intervening doctrinal change. But if the relevant facts in the two cases are separable, even though they be similar or identical, collateral estoppel does not govern the legal issues which recur in the second case. Thus the second proceeding may involve an instrument or transaction identical with, but in a form separable from, the one dealt with in the first proceeding. In that situation, a court is free in the second proceeding to make an independent examination of the legal matters at issue. It may then reach a different result or, if consistency in decision is considered just and desirable, reliance may be placed upon the ordinary rule of *stare decisis*. Before a party can invoke the collateral estoppel doctrine in these circumstances, the legal matter raised in the second proceeding must involve the same set of events or documents and the same bundle of legal principles that contributed to the rendering of the first judgment.

It is readily apparent in this case that the royalty payments growing out of the license contracts which were not involved in the earlier action before the Board of Tax Appeals and which concerned different tax years are free from the effects of the collateral estoppel doctrine. That is true even though those contracts are identical in all important respects with the 1928 contract, the only one that was before the Board, and even though the issue as to those contracts is the same as that raised by the 1928 contract. For income tax purposes, what is decided as to one contract is not conclusive as to any other contract which is not then in issue, however similar or identical it may be. In this respect, the instant case thus differs vitally from Tait v. Western Md. R. Co., supra, where the two proceedings involved the same instruments and the same surrounding facts.

A more difficult problem is posed as to the $4,881.35 in royalties paid to the taxpayer's wife in 1937 under the 1928 contract. Here there is complete identity of facts, issues and parties as between the earlier Board proceeding and the instant one. The Commissioner claims, however, that legal principles developed in various intervening decisions of this Court have made plain the error of the Board's conclusion in the earlier proceeding, thus creating a situation like that involved in Blair v. Commissioner, supra. This change in the legal picture is said to have been brought about by such cases as Helvering v. Clifford, 309 U.S. 331, 60 S.Ct. 554, 84 L.Ed. 788; Helvering v. Horst, 311 U.S. 112, 61 S.Ct. 144, 85 L.Ed. 75, 131 A.L.R. 655. These cases all imposed income tax liability on transferors who had assigned or transferred various forms of income to others within their family groups, although none specifically related to the assignment of patent license contracts between members of the same family. It must therefore be determined whether this *Clifford–Horst* line of cases represents an intervening legal development which is pertinent to the problem raised by the assignment of the 1928 agreement and which makes manifest the error of the result reached in 1935 by the Board. If that is the situation, the doctrine of collateral estoppel becomes inapplicable. A different result is then permissible as to the royalties paid in 1937 under the agreement in question. But to determine whether the *Clifford–Horst* series of cases has such an effect on the instant proceeding necessarily requires inquiry into the merits of the controversy growing out of the various contract assignments from the taxpayer to his wife. To that controversy we now turn.

[After reviewing the *Clifford–Horst* line of cases, the Court concluded:] The principles which have thus been recognized and developed by the *Clifford* and *Horst* cases, and those following them, are directly applicable to the transfer of patent license contracts between members of the same family. They are guideposts for those who seek to determine in a particular instance whether such an assignor retains sufficient control over the assigned contracts or over the receipt of income by the assignee to make it fair to impose income tax liability on him.

Moreover, the clarification and growth of these principles through the *Clifford–Horst* line of cases constitute, in our opinion, a sufficient change in the legal climate to render inapplicable in the instant proceeding, the doctrine of collateral estoppel relative to the assignment of the 1928 contract. True, these cases did not originate the concept that an assignor is taxable if he retains control over the assigned property or power to defeat the receipt of income by the assignee. But they gave much added emphasis and substance to that concept, making it more suited to meet the "attenuated subtleties" created by taxpayers. So substantial was the amplification of this concept as to justify a reconsideration of earlier Tax Court decisions reached without the benefit of the expanded notions, decisions which are now sought to be perpetuated regardless of their present correctness. Thus in the earlier litigation in 1935, the Board of Tax Appeals was unable to bring to bear on the assignment of the 1928 contract the full breadth of the ideas enunciated in the *Clifford–Horst* series of cases. And, as we shall see, a proper application of the principles as there developed might well have produced a different result, such as was reached by the Tax Court in this case in regard to the assignments of the other contracts. Under those circumstances collateral estoppel should not have been used by the Tax Court in the instant proceeding to perpetuate the 1935 viewpoint of the assignment.

* * *

The judgment below must therefore be reversed and the case remanded for such further proceedings as may be necessary in light of this opinion.

Reversed.

One of the most important uses of collateral estoppel (or "issue preclusion") in the tax area involves civil penalties imposed after criminal prosecutions. Although it may surprise some individuals, the same act or omission by a citizen can subject her to both criminal and civil penalties.

WRIGHT v. COMMISSIONER
Tax Court of the United States, 1985.
84 T.C. 636.

TANNENWALD, JUDGE:

* * *

* * * The sole issue for our decision is whether petitioner John T. Wright's conviction under section 7206(1) collaterally estops petitioners from denying, for purposes of section 6653(b), that part of their underpayment for 1978 was due to fraud.

* * *

Petitioner was indicted in the U.S. District Court, Central District of Illinois, Springfield Division, on March 22, 1982, on two counts of violation of section 7206(1) and two counts of violation of section 7201, one of each of the counts relating to the taxable year 1977 and one of each of the counts relating to the taxable year 1978. On June 15, 1982, that court, based on petitioner's guilty plea, entered a finding of guilty for "the offense(s) of subscribing to a false income tax return as charged in Count 3 of the Indictment, in violation of title 26, U.S.C. sec. 7206(1). Counts 1, 2, and 4 dismissed upon Government Motion." * * *

* * *

Respondent bases his motion on the allegedly preclusive effect of petitioner's conviction under section 7206(1) upon the issue of fraud under section 6653(b). Respondent contends that our opinions in *Goodwin v. Commissioner*, 73 T.C. 215 (1979), and *Considine v. Commissioner*, 68 T.C. 52 (1977), compel the conclusion that petitioner's conviction establishes as a matter of law that the underpayment for 1978 was "due to fraud," for purposes of section 6653(b), and thus that respondent's motion should be granted. Petitioners contend that petitioner's lack of business acumen raises a genuine issue as to a material fact, and that respondent's motion should thus be denied. For the reasons hereinafter stated, we agree with petitioners.

The doctrine of collateral estoppel precludes relitigation of any issue of fact or law that is actually litigated and necessarily determined by a valid and final judgment. *Montana v. United States*, 440 U.S. 147, 153 (1979). Its purpose is to avoid repetitious litigation of issues between the same parties or their privies. The doctrine, however, "must be confined to situations where the matter raised in the second suit is identical in all respects with that decided in the first proceeding and where the controlling facts and applicable legal rules remain unchanged." *Commissioner v. Sunnen*, 333 U.S. 591, 599–600 (1948). Thus, the question is whether the issue under section 6653(b) is "identical in all respects" to that decided under section 7206(1).

* * *

In *Considine v. Commissioner*, 68 T.C. 52 (1977), a case in which the taxpayer had been convicted under section 7206(1) and was disputing the addition to tax under section 6653(b), we held that "a conviction under section 7206(1) for 'willfully' making a return which the taxpayer does not believe to be true and correct is proof that the return is fraudulent," and that the taxpayer was thus "collaterally estopped to deny that he willfully filed a false and fraudulent return." *Considine v. Commissioner, supra* at 61, 68.

Our reasoning in *Considine* was as follows: (1) This Court, in *Amos v. Commissioner*, 43 T.C. 50, 55 (1964), affd. 360 F.2d 358 (4th Cir.1965), had held that "the term 'willfully' as used in section 7201 has authoritatively been defined in prior judicial decisions to encompass all of the elements of fraud which are envisioned by the civil penalty described in section 6653(b)"; (2) the Supreme Court, in *United States v. Bishop*, 412

U.S. 346, 356–361 (1973), had held that "willfully" has the same meaning in each of sections 7201, 7202, 7203, 7204, 7205, 7206, and 7207; therefore, (3) a conviction under section 7206(1) actually and necessarily determined that there was, for purposes of section 6653(b), a specific intention to evade tax. *Considine v. Commissioner, supra* at 59–60. Our opinion in *Considine* and the rationale upon which it was predicated were followed in the Court-reviewed opinion in *Goodwin v. Commissioner*, 73 T.C. 215, 224 (1979), with six Judges dissenting.

Subsequent to our opinions in *Considine v. Commissioner, supra*, and *Goodwin v. Commissioner, supra*, the Court of Appeals for the Ninth Circuit had occasion, in *Considine v. United States*, 683 F.2d 1285, 1287 (9th Cir.1982), to review the imposition of the addition to tax for fraud on the Considines for the taxable year 1965 [8] by the United States District Court on the ground that Mr. Considine's conviction of a violation of section 7206(1) for that year collaterally estopped him from contesting the fraud element of the addition to tax for that year under section 6653(b). The Ninth Circuit disagreed with the District Court's application of collateral estoppel, and, in so doing, stated flatly that they believed that our opinion in *Considine v. Commissioner, supra*, was incorrect. See 683 F.2d at 1287.[9] Beyond the Ninth Circuit's criticism of our opinion in *Considine v. Commissioner, supra*, it has been held on numerous occasions, both before and after *Considine*, although not in the context of the issue of collateral estoppel, that the intent to evade taxes is not an element of the crime covered by section 7206(1). * * *

Against this background, we have reexamined our opinions in *Goodwin v. Commissioner, supra*, and *Considine v. Commissioner, supra*, and have concluded that they should no longer be followed to the extent that they hold that a conviction under section 7206(1) is equated by way of collateral estoppel with the existence of fraud within the meaning of section 6653(b).

---

8. The interplay between the criminal and civil phases of the Considines' liability for Federal income taxes for the taxable years 1965–67 and 1969 has had the attention of the courts on several occasions. Mr. Considine was convicted under sec. 7206(1) as to his returns for 1965–67 and 1969 (*United States v. Considine*, an unreported case (S.D.Cal.1973, 34 AFTR 2d 74–5412, 74-2 USTC par. 9639), affd. 502 F.2d 246 (9th Cir.1973)), and brought three separate actions challenging respondent's subsequent imposition of the additions to tax under sec. 6653(b). *Considine v. Commissioner*, 68 T.C. 52 (1977), concerned the addition for 1969; *Considine v. United States*, 645 F.2d 925 (Ct.Cl.1981), concerned the additions for 1966 and 1967; and *Considine v. United States*, 683 F.2d 1285 (9th Cir.1982), concerned the addition for 1965.

9. The District Court was nevertheless affirmed on the ground that the Government had in fact carried its burden of proof on the fraud issue under sec. 6653(b) with respect to both Mr. and Mrs. Considine. In *Considine v. United States*, 645 F.2d 925, 928–931 (Ct.Cl.1981), which involved the Considines' taxable years 1966 and 1967, the Government contended only that the issue of knowing falsification as to the amount of income and deductions should be disposed of on the basis of collateral estoppel, and did not claim that collateral estoppel applied to the issues of intent to evade or existence of an underpayment. See 645 F.2d at 928. The Court of Claims was thus not required to reach the issue which was the fulcrum of our opinions in *Considine* and *Goodwin*. It sustained the Government's limited contention and, like the Court of Appeals for the Ninth Circuit, went on to hold that the Government had in fact carried its burden of proof as to fraud.

We begin our analysis in support of our conclusion with the word "willfully," as used in section 7206(1). In *United States v. Pomponio*, 429 U.S. 10 (1976), the Supreme Court held that, for purposes of sections 7201–7207, "willfully" "simply means a voluntary, intentional violation of a known legal duty." 429 U.S. at 12. This definition says nothing about fraud, and requires nothing more than a specific intention to violate the law. *United States v. Pomponio*, 412 U.S. at 11–13; * * *

* * *

In *Amos v. Commissioner, supra,* we equated the element necessary for conviction under section 7201 (i.e., an "attempt to evade") with that essential for the imposition of the civil penalty under section 6653(b) (i.e., an "underpayment * * * due to fraud"). *Amos v. Commissioner, supra* at 55. Because the attempt to evade tax is the gravamen of fraud we concluded in *Amos* that a taxpayer convicted under section 7201 of having attempted to evade or defeat a tax for a taxable year is collaterally estopped from denying under section 6653(b) that part of his underpayment for the same year was "due to fraud." Such identity of criminal tax evasion and civil tax fraud for purposes of collateral estoppel has been repeatedly sustained by the courts. See *Gray v. Commissioner*, 708 F.2d 243, 246 (6th Cir.1983). However, to have held, as we did in *Considine v. Commissioner, supra,* and *Goodwin v. Commissioner, supra,* that a conviction for "willfully" making a false statement in an income tax return within the meaning of section 7206(1) estops a taxpayer from denying that any underpayment made for the year of the return was "due to fraud" misapplies the principle of collateral estoppel and creates the semantic confusion warned against in *United States v. Bishop, supra.*

In a criminal action under section 7206(1), the issue actually litigated and necessarily determined is whether the taxpayer voluntarily and intentionally violated his or her known legal duty not to make a false statement as to any material matter on a return. The purpose of section 7206(1) is to facilitate the carrying out of respondent's proper functions by punishing those who intentionally falsify their Federal income tax returns and the penalty for such perjury is imposed irrespective of the tax consequences of the falsification. (*United States v. DiVarco*, 343 F.Supp. 101, 103 (N.D.Ill.1972), affd. 484 F.2d 670 (7th Cir.1973)). As noted above, the intent to evade taxes is not an element of the crime charged under section 7206(1). Thus, the crime is complete with the knowing, material falsification, and a conviction under section 7206(1) does not establish as a matter of law that the taxpayer violated the legal duty with an intent, or in an attempt, to evade taxes.

In short, it cannot be said that the combined effect of the Supreme Court's opinions in *United States v. Pomponio, supra,* and *United States v. Bishop, supra,* and our opinion in *Amos v. Commissioner, supra,* is to equate the standards under section 7206(1) with those under section 6653(b); the Supreme Court simply did not engraft the "attempt to evade" language from section 7201 into section 7206(1) by holding that "willfully" has a uniform meaning in sections 7201–7207. Thus, to the extent that they give collateral estoppel effect to a conviction under section 7206(1) on the issue of intent to evade tax under section 6653(b), *Considine v. Commissioner, supra,* and *Goodwin v. Commissioner, supra,* are overruled. Of course, a conviction for willful falsification, under section 7206(1), while not dispositive, will be one of the facts to be considered in a trial on the merits.

In the instant case, petitioners argue that we should deny respondent's motion for partial summary judgment because petitioner's lack of business acumen, and not an attempt to evade taxes, was the reason for the underpayments in question, and the factual issue thus raised is a "genuine issue as to any material fact" under Rule 121(b). We agree. The issue of intent, adequately raised by petitioners herein, is clearly one requiring a trial on the merits. Cf. *Considine v. United States,* 683 F.2d at 1288 (intent to evade is "natural inference" from willful underpayment by sophisticated, knowledgeable taxpayer).[12] Thus, on the sole issue before us, i.e., the addition to tax for 1978, respondent's motion for partial summary judgment will be denied.

An appropriate order will be entered.

Reviewed by the Court.

MOORE v. UNITED STATES

United States Court of Appeals, Fourth Circuit, 1965.
360 F.2d 353.

SOBELOFF, CIRCUIT JUDGE:

* * *

Jerome H. Moore and his wife, Mildred V. Moore, filed joint income tax returns for the years 1955–1958. In 1961 the husband was convicted after trial, pursuant to 26 U.S.C.A. § 7201, for willful evasion of taxes in those years. Subsequently a fraud assessment was made against both taxpayers pursuant to 26 U.S.C.A. § 6653(b), and when they sued in the District Court for a refund of certain taxes paid, the Government counter-claimed for the unpaid fraud penalties. In our original opinion, issued December 7, 1965, we agreed with the Government's contention that the existence of fraud on Mr. Moore's part was necessarily determined in his prior criminal trial and that as to him the issue of fraud was therefore foreclosed in the civil proceeding. * * *

[The taxpayer * * * contended in the District Court that the Government itself was collaterally estopped from redetermining the amount of taxes owed for the years in question, since it had stipulated

---

12. We do not have a sufficient factual foundation in the moving papers to determine that no material issue of fact exists as to the fraud, as the Court of Appeals for the Ninth Circuit and the Court of Claims were able to do in the *Considine* cases before them.

in the earlier criminal proceeding the exact amount owed. The District Judge ruled that the Government was not estopped because the determination of an exact liability was not "essential to the judgment," a prerequisite to the application of the doctrine of collateral estoppel. Commissioner of Internal Revenue v. Sunnen, 333 U.S. 591, 601, 68 S.Ct. 715, 92 L.Ed. 898 (1948). With this ruling we agree. As stated by the District Judge, "a conviction under 26 U.S.C.A. § 7201 does not require the proving of any definite sum of taxable income beyond a substantial amount." Moore v. United States, 235 F.Supp. 387, 391 (W.D.Va.1964). There is therefore no basis here for the application of the estoppel doctrine against the Government in respect to the amount of taxes due.] [d]

* * *

Notes and Questions

1. The *Wright* case discusses the collateral estoppel effects of a conviction or guilty plea. In contrast, the taxpayer obtains no collateral estoppel benefits when there is an acquittal. Helvering v. Mitchell, 303 U.S. 391, 58 S.Ct. 630, 82 L.Ed. 917 (1938) (acquittal on jury verdict); Neaderland v. Commissioner, 52 T.C. 532 (1969), affirmed, 424 F.2d 639 (2d Cir.1970), cert. denied, 400 U.S. 827, 91 S.Ct. 53, 27 L.Ed.2d 56 (1970) (acquittal on motion). "The difference in the legal rules relating to the burden of proof prevents estoppel from applying because the acquittal is merely an adjudication that the proof was not sufficient to overcome all reasonable doubt of the guilt of the defendant-taxpayer." M. Saltzman, IRS Practice and Procedure ¶ 7.08[2][b] (1981). What should be the collateral estoppel effects flowing from a plea of *nolo contendere*? A plea of *nolo contendere* to criminal fraud does *not* estop the taxpayer from contesting a civil fraud penalty. See Mickler v. Fahs, 243 F.2d 515 (5th Cir.1957) (forbidding use of taxpayer's *nolo contendere* plea for the limited purpose of impeaching the taxpayer).

2. The court in *Moore* held that the government was not estopped to vary in a subsequent civil tax case the amount of the deficiency established in the criminal prosecution for evasion. This conclusion results from the principle that the amount of the deficiency (as long as it is not insubstantial) is not essential to a successful prosecution under § 7201. Should the defendant-taxpayer likewise be able to contest the amount of the deficiency in a civil tax case following a conviction for attempted evasion? In any event, a taxpayer who pleads guilty to criminal tax charges should avoid inadvertant admissions regarding the amount of tax deficiencies by noting on the record in the criminal case that the precise amounts charged in the indictment are not (if it is true) conceded.

3. Would a conviction for willfully failing to file a return under § 7203 bar the taxpayer from contesting the civil negligence penalty? See Kotmair v. Commissioner, 86 T.C. 1253 (1986), in which a conviction for willful failure to file tax returns collaterally estopped the taxpayer from denying that the failure to file was due to willful neglect.

d. From text of original opinion of December 7, 1965.

4. What should be the result if the majority shareholder of a corporation is convicted of causing the corporation to file fraudulent returns? Would the outcome turn on whether the corporation was a party to the criminal case? See C.B.C. Super Markets, Inc. v. Commissioner, 54 T.C. 882 (1970), in which the majority shareholder was estopped from denying fraud, but the corporation was not estopped from denying fraud since it was not a party to the criminal proceeding in which the majority shareholder was convicted.

B. GOVERNMENT NOT A PARTY IN FIRST CASE

The following case illustrates not only the emerging "offensive" use by the IRS of collateral estoppel, but also the interrelationship of many principles already covered, such as the statute of limitations and burden of proof.

MEIER v. COMMISSIONER
Tax Court of the United States, 1988.
91 T.C. 273.

GERBER, JUDGE: Respondent, in a statutory notice dated May 24, 1977, determined deficiencies and additions to petitioners' income tax as follows:

Year	Deficiency	Sec. 6653(b) addition [1]
1968	$ 26,141.28	$ 13,070.64
1969	1,504,622.39	752,311.20
1970	379,230.45	189,615.23

The issues for our consideration are: (1) Whether petitioners are collaterally estopped from relitigating certain facts found by the Federal District Court in an action for an accounting brought by Hughes Tool Co. against petitioner John Meier;[2] (2) whether petitioners failed to report income from the sale of mining claims to Hughes Tool Co. during taxable years 1969 and 1970; (3) whether deposits to bank accounts and cash investments made by petitioners during 1968 and 1969 constituted taxable income in those years; (4) whether any part of any underpayment of tax for the years 1968, 1969, and 1970 is due to fraud; and (5) whether the statute of limitations bars the assessment and collection of the deficiencies and additions to tax for the years 1968, 1969, and 1970.

FINDINGS OF FACT

At the time of filing their petition in this case, petitioners resided in British Columbia, Canada.

---

1. All section references are to the Internal Revenue Code of 1954 as amended and in effect during the years at issue. All Rule references are to the Tax Court Rules of Practice and Procedure

2. *Hughes Tool Co. v. Meier*, 489 F.Supp. 354 (D.Utah 1977), affd. per curiam No. 78–1565 (10th Cir., Apr. 24, 1980). "Petitioner," when referred to in the singular, refers to petitioner John Meier.

The factual predicate for this case, at least as to the mining claim transactions, is relatively simple. However, for a number of reasons, drawing the facts from the record has been an unnecessarily complicated and arduous task.[3] For purposes of clarity, a simplified macroscopic factual picture is presented prior to our detailed findings.

Factual Summary

Petitioner John Meier (Meier) was employed by Hughes Tool Co. (Hughes). In that capacity, he was apparently directed to acquire silver mining claims. In derogation of his duty to his employer, Meier, through agents or co-conspirators, purchased such claims for nominal amounts, and then sold them to Hughes at immensely inflated prices. The sales proceeds were then channeled overseas, at petitioner's direction and for his benefit, to avoid detection by his employer and to avoid the incidence of the U.S. income tax.

Detailed Findings of Fact [4]

* * *

OPINION

Use of Collateral Estoppel

Respondent seeks to offensively utilize the doctrine of collateral estoppel to estop petitioner from denying the diversion of funds from Hughes for his own use. Once the diversion of these funds for petitioner's use and control is established, the failure to report said amounts for Federal tax purposes may be readily shown. Respondent also attempts to utilize the diversion of funds and substantial understatement of income along with other findings from our record to, in toto, carry his

---

3. The complication and arduousness were due mainly to the parties' practical failure to stipulate to anything; respondent's almost exclusive reliance on collateral estoppel, testimony, and depositions taken in the prior Hughes Tool action which was also protracted and complex; petitioners' failure to submit proposed findings of fact on brief as required by Rule 151(e); and the convoluted manner in which the transactions took place.

4. Prior to and at the beginning of the trial in this case, respondent moved for summary judgment based solely upon the use of collateral estoppel derived from *Hughes Tool Co. v. Meier*, 489 F.Supp. 354 (D.Utah 1977). Respondent sought to satisfy his burden with respect to the additions to tax under sec. 6653(b) for all 3 taxable years. We were not disposed to grant the motion, but chose to take it under consideration in rendering this opinion. With regard to the mining transactions, the ultimate factual findings from *Hughes Tool Co. v. Meier, supra*, are sufficient to establish that petitioner diverted his employer's funds for his own use and control during petitioners' 1969 and 1970 taxable years. However, the factual findings from that proceeding are not sufficient, standing alone, to satisfy respondent's burden of proving fraud.

The record in our case is comprised of the testimony of numerous witnesses and more than 100 documentary exhibits. Respondent offered an extensive amount of testimony in the alternative if no part of their collateral estoppel position was approved or to supplement any effective use of collateral estoppel. The testimony and documentary evidence received in this case was used in our consideration of whether respondent satisfied the burden of showing that petitioner was subject to an addition to tax under sec. 6653(b). The only findings established by means of collateral estoppel are the quoted ultimate findings from the Hughes accounting action, which appear at the end of our findings in this case. The remainder of our findings are supported by the evidence in this case.

burden of showing that the understatement was fraudulent. In addition to relying on the doctrine of collateral estoppel, respondent offered a substantial amount of documentary evidence and testimony.[9]

In an effort to achieve "judicial economy" we first consider whether petitioner is collaterally estopped from relitigating certain facts found by the District Court in *Hughes Tool Co. v. Meier,* 489 F.Supp. 354 (D.Utah 1977), affd. per curiam No. 78–1565 (10th Cir., Apr. 24, 1980). Collateral estoppel and the related doctrine of res judicata have the dual purpose of protecting litigants from the burden of relitigating an identical issue and of promoting judicial economy by preventing unnecessary or redundant litigation. Under the doctrine of res judicata, or claim preclusion, a judgment on the merits in a prior suit bars a second suit which involves the same parties or their privies and is based on the same cause of action. On the other hand, under the doctrine of collateral estoppel, or issue preclusion, the judgment in the prior suit precludes, in the second cause of action, litigation of issues actually litigated and necessary to the outcome of the first action.[10] *Parklane Hosiery Co. v. Shore,* 439 U.S. 322, 326 (1979) (*Parklane*).

Thus, collateral estoppel is used to foreclose an adversary from relitigating an issue the adversary previously litigated unsuccessfully in a different action. Until recently, however, the scope of collateral estoppel was limited by the doctrine of mutuality of parties—neither party could use the judgment as an estoppel against the other unless both parties were bound by the judgment. *Parklane* at 326–327. In *Parklane,* the Supreme Court abandoned the requirement of mutuality and sanctioned the use of collateral estoppel both offensively and defensively. Offensive use occurs when a party asserting a claim[11] (respondent herein) relies upon collateral estoppel to estop a "defendant" (petitioner herein) from denying the findings of a prior proceeding. Defensive use occurs when estoppel is interposed as a defense to "plaintiff's" claim. *Parklane* at 326 n. 4. Trial courts are given broad discretion to determine when collateral estoppel should be applied offensively. *Parklane* at 331.

In *Montana v. United States,* 440 U.S. 147 (1979) (*Montana*), the Supreme Court refined the *Parklane* parameters for use of collateral estoppel. In *Montana,* the Court used a three-prong test. First, wheth-

---

9. Respondent advanced three alternative approaches to prove a fraudulent understatement, as follows: (1) Petitioner is estopped to deny that the District Court's findings establish fraud; or (2) fraud is established based upon collateral estoppel supplemented by the documentary evidence and testimony evidence in our record; or (3) the documentary evidence and testimony evidence in our record alone support a finding of fraud. Respondent would not prevail upon the first alternative and the second alternative was utilized to realize judicial economy.

10. The Restatement defines the doctrine in the following manner: When an issue of fact or law is actually litigated and determined by a valid and final judgment, and the determination is essential to the judgment, the determination is conclusive in a subsequent action between the parties, whether on the same or a different claim. 1 Restatement, Judgments 2d, sec. 27 (1982).

11. In the setting of this case, "asserting a claim" is the equivalent of respondent's attempting to carry his burden of proof.

er the issues presented in the subsequent litigation are in substance the same as those in the first case; second, whether controlling facts or legal principles have changed significantly since the first judgment; and third, whether other special circumstances warrant an exception to the normal rules of preclusion. *Montana* at 155. See *Estate of Best v. Commissioner*, 76 T.C. 122, 134 (1981). Application of the doctrine in this manner "preclude[s] parties from contesting matters that they have had a full and fair opportunity to litigate [and] protects their adversaries from the expense and vexation attending multiple lawsuits, conserves judicial resources, and fosters reliance on judicial action by minimizing the possibility of inconsistent decisions." *Montana* at 153–154.

Collateral estoppel may be utilized in connection with matters of law, matters of fact, and mixed matters of law and fact. Historically, with regard to factual matters, a distinction was made between (1) "ultimate" and (2) "evidentiary" or "intermediate" facts.[12] This distinction was made with respect to the first proceeding (in which the fact is initially found) and the second proceeding (in which one of the parties attempts to establish the same fact by means of collateral estoppel). Early case law differed over whether the facts found in the first proceeding were limited to those which were "ultimate" or included both "ultimate" and "intermediate" facts. See *The Evergreens v. Nunan*, 141 F.2d 927, 928–929 (2d Cir.1944) (*Evergreens*).[13] In *Evergreens* at 929–931, the Circuit Court of Appeals for the Second Circuit considered, for the first time, whether the fact to be established by means of collateral estoppel in the second proceeding was likewise limited to ultimate facts in the context of the second proceeding. Although the Circuit Court did not express a preference as to whether the facts had to be found as ultimate in the context of the first proceeding, they held that the fact established must be an ultimate fact in the context of the second proceeding. *Evergreens* at 930–931. We adopted this rule in *Amos v. Commissioner*, 43 T.C. 50, 54 (1964), affd. 360 F.2d 358 (4th Cir.1965).[14]

Contemporary case law and commentary have been critical of the *Evergreens* approach and the limitation of collateral estoppel to ulti-

---

12. Ultimate facts are "those facts upon whose combined occurrence the law raises the duty or right in question," while evidentiary facts are "those facts from whose existence may be rationally inferred the existence of an ultimate fact." *Amos v. Commissioner*, 43 T.C. 50, 54 (1964), affd. 360 F.2d 358 (4th Cir.1965), citing *The Evergreens v. Nunan*, 141 F.2d 927 (2d Cir. 1944).

13. One commentator saw this more strict interpretation as an attempt to differentiate which facts were actually litigated and necessary to the first judgment and which were not. See C. Wright, A. Miller & E. Cooper, Federal Practice and Procedure, sec. 4424 (1981 & Supp.1987). We do not have to address this distinction because the use of collateral estoppel in this case is limited to facts which were ultimate facts from the "first case."

14. Although we adopted the *Evergreens* approach requiring the establishment of ultimate facts by means of collateral estoppel, our stated standard for the facts found in the first proceeding was that they be "necessary or essential to the result." We made no distinction between ultimate and intermediate facts in the first proceeding.

mate facts, either as taken from the first proceeding or as applied in the second proceeding. Comment j to Restatement, Judgments 2d, section 27 (1982), is especially instructive on the difficulties resulting from applying the *Evergreens* rule.

> *Determinations essential to the judgment.* It is sometimes stated that when a determination is a necessary step in the formulation of a decision and judgment, the determination will not be conclusive between the parties if it relates only to a "mediate datum" or "evidentiary fact" rather than to an "ultimate fact" or issue of law. It has also been stated than [sic] even a determination of "ultimate fact" will not be conclusive in a later action if it constitutes only an "evidentiary fact" or "mediate datum" in that action. Such a formulation is occasionally used to support a refusal to apply the rule of issue preclusion when the refusal could more appropriately be based on the lack of similarity between the issues in the two proceedings. If applied more broadly, the formulation causes great difficulty, and is at odds with the rationale on which the rule of issue preclusion is based. The line between ultimate and evidentiary facts is often impossible to draw. Moreover, even if a fact is categorized as evidentiary, great effort may have been expended by both parties in seeking to persuade the adjudicator of its existence or nonexistence and it may well have been regarded as the key issue in the dispute. In these circumstances the determination of the issue should be conclusive whether or not other links in the chain had to be forged before the question of liability could be determined in the first or second action.
>
> The appropriate question, then, is whether the issue was actually recognized by the parties as important and by the trier as necessary to the first judgment. * * *

[Restatement, Judgments 2d, sec. 27 (1982). Emphasis added.]

Most recently, the Court of Appeals for the District of Columbia expressed its preference for the Restatement test over the *Evergreens* rule. *Synanon Church v. United States*, 820 F.2d 421 (D.C.Cir.1987).[15] The court noted "many courts, including the Second Circuit itself, have ignored the *Evergreens* rule, and they have measured the scope of preclusion, not by a distinction between ultimate and mediate facts, but rather by focusing more directly on the quality and extensiveness of litigation in the first action." (Fn. ref. omitted.) Also, recent opinions of this Court have questioned the vitality and correctness of the *Evergreens* rule. See *Peck v. Commissioner*, 90 T.C. 162, 169 (1988).

We find the reasoning in the Restatement to be the better view. Thus, we will no longer follow *Amos v. Commissioner, supra*, to the

---

15. Petitioners (Meiers) resided in British Columbia (outside of the United States) at the time of filing of their petition. Accordingly, their appeal, if any, would lie in the Court of Appeals for the District of Columbia. See sec. 7482(b)(1)(E). Further, we consider opinions of the circuit to which a case is appealable to be controlling. See *Golsen v. Commissioner*, 54 T.C. 742 (1970), affd. 445 F.2d 985 (10th Cir.1971), cert. denied 404 U.S. 940 (1971). With respect to the *Evergreens* rule only, we will no longer follow *Amos v. Commissioner*, 43 T.C. 50, 54 (1964), affd. 360 F.2d 358 (4th Cir.1965), irrespective of the "Golsen rule."

extent it prescribes a test based on "ultimate" versus "evidentiary" facts in applying the doctrine of collateral estoppel or issue preclusion.

We now consider the extent to which the doctrine of collateral estoppel may apply in this case. We first focus on the first prong of the *Montana* test, i.e., the issues decided and necessary to the decision in the Hughes accounting proceeding. *Montana v. United States*, 440 U.S. 147 (1979); *Commissioner v. Sunnen*, 333 U.S. 591 (1948). Collateral estoppel cannot apply if the party against whom it is asserted did not have a full and fair opportunity to litigate [16] the issue for which the doctrine is being asserted in the earlier proceeding. *Allen v. McCurry*, 449 U.S. 90 (1980).

Petitioner is correct in pointing out that his tax liability was not in issue in the earlier proceeding, and neither did the District Court decide whether he fraudulently omitted income. However, collateral estoppel applies to issues of *fact* or law previously litigated. *Parklane Hosiery Co. v. Shore*, 439 U.S. 322 (1979); *Montana v. United States*, *supra*. It is clear that the factual predicate for petitioner's diversion of funds for his own use and control and the accounting action are identical, even though the resulting legal and tax consequences might differ. Both causes of action are based on petitioner's sale of mining claims at inflated prices to Hughes. Every significant fact considered in the Hughes litigation is at issue in this case.

To better evaluate whether petitioner had a full and fair opportunity to litigate this issue in the earlier accounting action we must consider the nature and purposes of such an action. An accounting is essentially an equitable remedy which is civil in nature. It is designed to prevent unjust enrichment by requiring the disgorgement of any benefits or profits received as a result of a breach of fiduciary duty. The right to an equitable accounting arises generally from defendant's possession of money or property which, because of some particular relationship between himself and plaintiff, he is obliged to surrender.

* * *

Generally, there are two parts to an accounting proceeding.[17] First, the party seeking an accounting must establish a right to an accounting. Plaintiff must show an inadequate legal remedy, fiduciary relationship, and the other prerequisites noted above. If this is shown, the court will order an accounting. After this order, the second part of the action proceeds. "After the order for an accounting, interlocutory in character, is entered, the burden shifts to defendant to show that the plaintiff, in fact, is not entitled to the money or property." *Hughes Tool Co. v. Meier, supra* at 374.

---

16. *Commissioner v. Sunnen*, 333 U.S. 591 (1948), requires that a question of fact be "actually litigated" and "essential" to the judgment.

17. Some court opinions and treatise material reflect that both parts may be addressed either in a single proceeding or opinion, or both. In the Hughes action, Judge Anderson first ordered that Meier was to account to Hughes and required him to do so within 30 days. Upon Meier's failure to come forward to account within 30 days, Judge Anderson entered final judgment against Meier.

The District Court found that Meier had breached his fiduciary duty to Hughes by converting Hughes' funds to his own use and control. The court ordered Meier to account to Hughes for such funds. The key element in both cases is the diversion of Hughes' funds to Meier's use and control. It is clear that Meier's motivation and purposes in defending against the allegations in the accounting action are identical to his need to show that respondent's determination that he derived income from these same transactions is in error.

The extent of the controversy here is largely due to petitioners' failure to stipulate facts as required by Rule 91.[18] Making our task even more difficult, petitioners omitted any proposed findings of fact in their brief. Moreover, petitioners filed a 15-page reply brief which did not specifically respond to nearly 80 pages of proposed factual findings set forth in respondent's 124-page opening brief. The District Court in the *Hughes* case found—

> that the defendant Meier occupied a trusted fiduciary position with the plaintiff for the acquisition of mining properties; that the defendant Meier breached that duty by secretly diverting funds from the five sales *to his own use and benefit* and to the damage of his principal; that there is no legal basis under which defendant Meier could have properly received for his own use and benefit any of such money; and that the defendant Meier must account for the funds entrusted to his care in relation to these transactions. * * *. [*Hughes Tool Co. v. Meier, supra* at 369. [Emphasis added.]]

There is a complete identity of factual issues in this case. Respondent must prove an underpayment exists of which some portion is due to fraud. Rule 142(b). However, as to the underlying deficiency, petitioner has the burden of showing that he did not receive the additional amounts of income determined by respondent. Also, petitioner bears the burden of proof with respect to the amount of the underpayment of his tax liability determined in the notice of deficiency. *Welch v. Helvering*, 290 U.S. 111 (1933); Rule 142(a).

Our analysis here is largely an application of familiar principles of taxation to the facts as found by the District Court. Gross income includes gains derived from dealings in property. Sec. 61(a)(3). The District Court found that Meier's agents diverted proceeds from the sale of mining claims for Meier's benefit. Because income is taxed to the true owner (*Lucas v. Earl*, 281 U.S. 111 (1930)), and the funds were handled for petitioner's benefit and control, such funds constitute

---

18. Petitioners offered to stipulate to facts found by the District Court, but withdrew their offer when respondent continued to offer into evidence exhibits and depositions from the prior trial. The District Court had the onerous task of unraveling this complicated set of facts. Petitioners have not set forth any convincing reason why we should have to go through the same process again. Most of respondent's presentation in this case consisted of testimony and depositions from the prior action. Petitioner made exactly the same objections as in the prior case, urging that the District Court's evidentiary rulings were erroneous. Petitioners' actions in making the same objections is another indicator that the issues and petitioner's motivations herein are either identical or substantially the same as those in the prior action.

income to petitioner. See *Warren v. United States,* 613 F.2d 591 (5th Cir.1980); United States v. Pfister, 205 F.2d 538 (8th Cir.1953); *Huntington National Bank v. Commissioner,* 90 F.2d 876 (6th Cir.1937). Respondent, by introducing petitioners' returns, has established that petitioners failed to report this income.

Also, petitioner argues that because he validly claimed the Fifth Amendment privilege in the Hughes Tool case, he did not receive a full and fair opportunity to litigate in that action. Thus, he argues, collateral estoppel should not apply. See *Allen v. McCurry, supra.* We believe, however, despite petitioner's self-imposed testimonial incapacity, he was afforded a full and fair opportunity to litigate.

Despite invoking the Fifth Amendment, petitioner was able to vigorously defend in the District Court action. He thoroughly cross-examined witnesses, either in depositions or at trial. He made numerous objections to the testimony offered by Hughes. He moved, on various occasions, to dismiss for lack of jurisdiction, for a stay pending an outcome in the criminal case, and for the trial judge to recuse himself. He appealed to the Court of Appeals for the 10th Circuit based on alleged errors in the holding of the District Court. In short, he used all the legal and procedural means available to him to defend in the accounting action.[19] Petitioner was unsuccessful in the District Court accounting action not for lack of an opportunity, but on the substantial weight of the factual evidence presented against him. Indeed, the question of whether petitioner had diverted the funds to his own use and control was an essential issue in the accounting action, as well as in the criminal indictment for evasion and the issues in this civil tax case. Moreover, petitioner's loss in defending the accounting action or this proceeding would not collaterally estop him in a criminal proceeding. In the context of discussing collateral estoppel, we must also assume, as the District Court did when petitioner raised the Fifth Amendment issue in *Hughes Tool Co. v. Meier, supra* at 374, that " 'the prevailing rule' in *Baxter v. Palmigiano,* 425 U.S. 308 (1976), [is] that 'the Fifth Amendment does not forbid adverse inferences against parties to civil actions when they refuse to testify in response to probative evidence offered against them.' " See also *Singleton v. Commissioner,* 606 F.2d 50, 52 n. 3 (3d Cir.1979), affg. a Memorandum Opinion of this Court.[20]

---

19. The Court of Appeals for the Tenth Circuit went so far as to describe petitioner's tactics as "dilatory." *Hughes Tool Co. v. Meier,* No. 78–1565 (10th Cir., Apr. 24, 1980) (slip op. p. 2). In addition, it has come to the Court's attention that petitioner was convicted of obstruction of justice by knowingly submitting false documents to the District Court in the Hughes action. See *United States v. Meier,* 484 F.Supp. 1129 (D. Utah 1980).

20. Petitioner has not referred us to any cases which hold that simultaneous civil and criminal actions deprive an individual of a full and fair opportunity to litigate in either case. Additionally, the District Court and Circuit Court of Appeals for the 10th Circuit refused to stay the accounting action on the same Fifth Amendment grounds.

Petitioner's position seems to be that there can never be a full and fair opportunity to litigate in a civil case so long as there is a related criminal action pending. Petitioner misapprehends the scope of the Fifth Amendment privilege. The Fifth Amendment protects against *compulsory* self-incrimination. *Fisher v. United States,* 425 U.S. 391 (1976). However, it does not prevent an accused from testifying, and the privilege may be waived. *Raffel v. United States,* 271 U.S. 494 (1926). In both civil and criminal actions, a party having the privilege must weigh the benefits of his testimony against the possibility of giving incriminating evidence in discovery, or on direct or cross-examination. See *Barnes v. United States,* 412 U.S. 837 (1973); *Raffel v. United States, supra.* Thus, as part of a party's litigating strategy, there is a choice of whether or not to testify. It was petitioner's choice whether or not to avail himself of this opportunity. Petitioner asserted the privilege and must bear the consequences of such action. Moreover, while the amendment prevents self-incrimination, it does not prevent testimony by others. See *California Bankers Association v. Shultz,* 416 U.S. 21 (1974); *Couch v. United States,* 409 U.S. 322 (1973).

It appears that petitioner may have benefited from asserting the privilege, rather than it impairing his opportunity to litigate. Petitioner, in the Hughes accounting action, could validly refuse to answer interrogatories and deposition requests, and would not be compelled to produce documents. Hughes had to obtain materials and testimony from third parties.

Petitioner also refused to testify in the present case, based on the Fifth Amendment privilege. In the absence of new facts that might have been brought to light had petitioner testified in this case, there is nothing to suggest a different factual result. In addition, petitioner was afforded the opportunity in this case to bring in testimony by others supporting a theory that Hughes consented to the sales, or any other admissible evidence he wished to offer. In short, petitioner's asserting the Fifth Amendment privilege did not impair his ability to litigate in the District Court or in this Court. The adverse result in the prior action was based upon the overwhelming evidence presented against petitioner.

The second prong of the *Montana* test is whether the controlling facts and legal principles have changed significantly since the first action. We find that there have been no such changes. As previously discussed, collateral estoppel in this case relates primarily to factual issues, thus the legal principles are largely unaffected. The factual underpinnings of the earlier action are identical to the present proceeding. The only factual matter that may differ is a claimed defense of petitioner in this case. Petitioner alleges that Howard Hughes authorized such transactions at the behest of the Central Intelligence Agency. We left the record open for the deposition testimony of respondent's former agent Kaminski, whom petitioner contends would substantiate his claim.[21] Petitioner failed to advance any testimony or other evidence in support of such claims during the trial or within the extended time that the record was left open. Thus, the second prong of the test has been met.

The third prong of the *Montana* test is whether there are any special circumstances that would warrant exception to the normal rules of preclusion. Petitioner has not presented any such circumstances. Petitioner had ample incentive to litigate, both here and in the District Court, because of the large amounts of money involved. In addition, the waste of judicial resources occasioned by the retrial of identical factual issues mitigates against petitioner.

Petitioners rely upon two Memorandum Opinions of this Court in further support of their contention that collateral estoppel should not apply. In *Cipparone v. Commissioner,* T.C. Memo. 1985–234, it was held that a conviction in State Court for bribery did not collaterally estop the taxpayer from litigating the amount of money received, because mere benefit, not receipt of any specific amount of money, was all that was necessary to a conviction under the statute.[22] Because respondent failed to prove that the taxpayer *actually* received any money, we declined to sustain the fraud addition. Petitioner's reliance on this opinion is misplaced. In the instant case, the District Court clearly found that petitioner, through his agents, diverted substantial amounts of money for his own benefit and control. In addition, the crux of an accounting action is that plaintiff is entitled to a specific amount of money that has come into the defendant's hands. *Hughes Tool Co. v. Meier,* 489 F.Supp. 354, 374 (D. Utah 1977).

Petitioners' reliance on *Mosteller v. Commissioner,* T.C. Memo. 1986–505, also is misplaced. In that case, we declined to sustain the fraud addition based upon the taxpayer's conviction of larceny by false pretenses in a bid-rigging scheme. There we stated "Mere evidentiary facts in the criminal case, as opposed to ultimate facts, would not be established in this case under the principle of collateral estoppel by judgment." Because we have declined to place emphasis on the ultimate/evidentiary distinction in applying collateral estoppel, this rationale is not controlling in the instant case. In any event, Meier has chosen to put every fact in issue. Considerations of judicial economy should preclude petitioner from relitigating those issues of fact previously found. In addition, in *Mosteller,* respondent failed to establish by clear and convincing evidence that amounts received in the bid-rigging scheme were not in fact reported. In this case, it has been established that the items creating the underpayments were not reported on petitioners' income tax returns.

---

21. In the District Court case, Meier also attempted to show that his activities were not on behalf of Hughes but instead that he was acting on behalf of a Mr. Maheu. That claim was summarily rejected by the District Court judge and did not meet with any success in diverting the Court's attention from the facts proven by Hughes.

22. The taxpayer was collaterally estopped from denying participation in the bribery scheme.

We accordingly hold that petitioner is collaterally estopped from denying the facts which support the finding that he had diverted funds from Hughes to his own use and control, as found by the District Court.

* * *

Note

As discussed in Chapter 6 at page 271, the Tax Court in *Meier* also upheld the imposition of the civil fraud penalty against the taxpayer.

Question

Can a taxpayer who was not a formal party in a prior case assert collateral estoppel against the IRS to prevent the relitigation of an issue that the IRS lost in the prior case? See McQuade v. Commissioner, 84 T.C. 137 (1985), in which the IRS was collaterally estopped due to prior determinations in Bankruptcy Court. The taxpayer who took part in the prior action was an interested party and was financially affected by its outcome.

SECTION 8. SUPPRESSION OF EVIDENCE IN CIVIL TAX CASES

UNITED STATES v. JANIS

Supreme Court of the United States, 1976.
428 U.S. 433, 96 S.Ct. 3021, 49 L.Ed.2d 1046.

MR. JUSTICE BLACKMUN delivered the opinion of the Court.

This case presents an issue of the appropriateness of an extension of the judicially created exclusionary rule: Is evidence seized by a state criminal law enforcement officer in good faith, but nonetheless unconstitutionally, inadmissible in a civil proceeding by or against the United States?

[Based upon the affidavit of a police officer, a Los Angeles judge issued a search warrant, pursuant to which the police seized from Janis $4,940 in cash and certain wagering records. The officer advised the IRS that Janis had been arrested for bookmaking activity. Using a calculation based upon the seized evidence, the IRS assessed Janis for wagering excise taxes and levied upon the $4,940 in partial satisfaction. In the subsequent state criminal proceedings against Janis the trial court found the police officer's affidavit defective, granted a motion to quash the warrant, and ordered the seized items returned to Janis, except for the $4,940. Janis later filed a claim for refund and, after it was denied, a civil action in the United States District Court for return of the $4,940. The United States answered, and counterclaimed for a substantial unpaid balance of the assessment. In the civil action, Janis moved to suppress the evidence seized and all copies thereof, and to quash the assessment. The District Court concluded that Janis was entitled to a refund because the assessment "was based in substantial part, if not completely, on illegally procured evidence," and that under the circumstances Janis was not required to prove the extent of the claimed refund. The assessment was quashed and the Government's counterclaim was dismissed with prejudice. The Court of Appeals for the Ninth Circuit affirmed.]

The debate within the Court on the exclusionary rule has always been a warm one. It has been unaided, unhappily, by any convincing empirical evidence on the effects of the rule. The Court, however, has established that the "prime purpose" of the rule, if not the sole one, "is to deter future unlawful police conduct." United States v. Calandra, 414 U.S. 338, 347, 94 S.Ct. 613, 619, 38 L.Ed.2d 561 (1974). * * *

In the complex and turbulent history of the rule, the Court never has applied it to exclude evidence from a civil proceeding, federal or state.

In the present case we are asked to create judicially a deterrent sanction by holding that evidence obtained by a state criminal law enforcement officer in good faith reliance on a warrant that later proved to be defective shall be inadmissible in a federal civil tax proceeding. Clearly, the enforcement of admittedly valid laws would be hampered by so extending the exclusionary rule, and, as is nearly always the case with the rule, concededly relevant and reliable evidence would be rendered unavailable.

* * *

If the exclusionary rule is the "strong medicine" that its proponents claim it to be, then its use in the situations in which it is now applied (resulting, for example, in this case in frustration of the Los Angeles police officers' good-faith duties as enforcers of the criminal laws) must be assumed to be a substantial and efficient deterrent. Assuming this efficacy, the additional marginal deterrence provided by forbidding a different sovereign from using the evidence in a civil proceeding surely does not outweigh the cost to society of extending the rule to that situation. If, on the other hand, the exclusionary rule does not result in appreciable deterrence, then, clearly, its use in the instant situation is unwarranted. Under either assumption, therefore, the extension of the rule is unjustified.

In short, we conclude that exclusion from federal civil proceedings of evidence unlawfully seized by a state criminal enforcement officer has not been shown to have a sufficient likelihood of deterring the conduct of the state police so that it outweighs the societal costs imposed by the exclusion. This Court, therefore, is not justified in so extending the exclusionary rule.

Respondent argues, however, that the application of the exclusionary rule to civil proceedings long has been recognized in the federal courts. He cites a number of cases. But respondent does not critically distinguish between those cases in which the officer committing the unconstitutional search or seizure was an agent of the sovereign that sought to use the evidence, on the one hand, and those cases, such as the present one, on the other hand, where the officer has no responsibility or duty to, or agreement with, the sovereign seeking to use the evidence.[31]

* * * Only one case cited by the respondent squarely holds that there must be an exclusionary rule barring use in a civil proceeding by one sovereign of material seized in violation of the Fourth Amendment by an officer of another sovereign. In Suarez v. Commissioner, 58 T.C. 792 (1972) (reviewed by the court, with two judges dissenting), the Tax Court determined that the exclusionary rule should be applied in a situation similar to the one that confronts us here. The court concluded that

> "any competing consideration based upon the need for effective enforcement of civil tax liabilities * * * must give way to the higher goal of protection of the individual and the necessity for preserving confidence in, rather than encouraging contempt for, the processes of Government." Id., at 805.

No appeal was taken.

We disagree with the broad implications of this statement of the Tax Court for two reasons. To the extent that the court did not focus on the deterrent purpose of the exclusionary rule, the law has since been clarified. Moreover, the court did not distinguish between intersovereign and intrasovereign uses of unconstitutionally seized material. Working, as we must, with the absence of convincing empirical data, common sense dictates that the deterrent effect of the exclusion of relevant evidence is highly attenuated when the "punishment" imposed upon the offending criminal enforcement officer is the removal of that evidence from a civil suit by or against a different sovereign. In Elkins [v. United States, 364 U.S. 206, 80 S.Ct. 1437, 4 L.Ed.2d 1669 (1960),] the Court indicated that the assumed interest of criminal law enforcement officers in the criminal proceedings of another sovereign counterbalanced this attenuation sufficiently to justify an exclusionary rule. Here, however, the attenuation is further augmented by the fact that the proceeding is one to enforce only the civil law of the other sovereign.

This attenuation, coupled with the existing deterrence effected by the denial of use of the evidence by either sovereign in the criminal trials with which the searching officer is concerned, creates a situation in which the imposition of the exclusionary rule sought in this case is unlikely to provide significant, much less substantial, additional deterrence. It falls outside the offending officer's zone of primary interest. The extension of the exclusionary rule, in our view, would be an

31. * * * Respondent remains free on remand to attempt to prove that there was federal participation in fact. If he succeeds in that proof, he raises the question, not presented by this case, whether the exclusionary rule is to be applied in a civil proceeding involving an intrasovereign violation.

* * *

unjustifiably drastic action by the courts in the pursuit of what is an undesired and undesirable supervisory role over police officers.

In the past this Court has opted for exclusion in the anticipation that law enforcement officers would be deterred from violating Fourth Amendment rights. Then, as now, the Court acted in the absence of convincing empirical evidence and relied, instead, on its own assumptions of human nature and the interrelationship of the various components of the law enforcement system. In the situation before us, we do not find sufficient justification for the drastic measure of an exclusionary rule. There comes a point at which courts, consistent with their duty to administer the law, cannot continue to create barriers to law enforcement in the pursuit of a supervisory role that is properly the duty of the Executive and Legislative Branches. We find ourselves at that point in this case. We therefore hold that the judicially created exclusionary rule should not be extended to forbid the use in the civil proceeding of one sovereign of evidence seized by a criminal law enforcement agent of another sovereign.

The judgment of the Court of Appeals is reversed, and the case is remanded for further proceedings consistent with this opinion.

MR. JUSTICE STEWART, dissenting.

* * *

If state police officials can effectively crack down on gambling law violators by the simple expedient of violating their constitutional rights and turning the illegally seized evidence over to Internal Revenue Service agents on the proverbial "silver platter," then the deterrent purpose of the exclusionary rule is wholly frustrated. "If, on the other hand, it is understood that the fruit of an unlawful search by state agents will be inadmissible in a federal trial, there can be no inducement to subterfuge and evasion with respect to federal-state cooperation in criminal investigation." Elkins v. United States, supra, 364 U.S., at 222, 80 S.Ct., at 1446.

Note

The application of the exclusionary rule to criminal, much less civil, proceedings has recently undergone substantial modification. E.g., United States v. Leon, 468 U.S. 897, 104 S.Ct. 3405, 82 L.Ed.2d 677 (1984) (recognizing "good faith" exception to exclusionary rule where warrant subsequently determined to be invalid); Segura v. United States, 468 U.S. 796, 104 S.Ct. 3380, 82 L.Ed.2d 599 (1984) (initial illegal entry of premises does not taint evidence discovered in subsequent search under valid warrant). Thus, one can only speculate as to the outcome if the Supreme Court were today presented with the question reserved in *Janis*—whether exclusion would apply in a civil tax proceeding where there was an intrasovereign violation. Compare I.N.S. v. Lopez–Mendoza, 468 U.S. 1032, 104 S.Ct. 3479, 82 L.Ed.2d 778 (1984) (exclusionary rule does not apply in civil deportation hearing) with One 1958 Plymouth Sedan v. Pennsylvania, 380 U.S. 693, 85 S.Ct. 1246, 14 L.Ed.2d 170 (1965) (exclusionary rule applies in quasi-criminal forfeiture proceeding).

The Tax Court recently considered the application of the exclusionary rule to a civil case involving a warrantless search of a physician's office and residence. In Houser v. Commissioner, 96 T.C. 184 (1991), state officers began the search and called in IRS agents after discovering a laundry bag full of cash. The court noted: "There is no clear definition of the level or nature of Federal involvement to constitute Federal participation which would result in an *intra*sovereign violation (suppression undecided by *Janis*) rather than an *inter*sovereign violation (suppression denied by *Janis*). There appears to be a continuum, as to both type and extent of Federal activity, with few opinions to mark the permissible margins."

SECTION 9. RECOVERY OF ATTORNEYS' FEES

The problem of providing for the award of attorneys' fees to taxpayers successful in tax litigation has long vexed the tax bar and Congress. A somewhat illusory solution to the problem was reached as a result of the enactment of the Civil Rights Attorneys' Fees Awards Act of 1976.[f] While this statute clearly provided for the awarding of attorneys' fees in civil tax litigation under appropriate circumstances, it was held inapplicable to the vast majority of civil tax cases. The reason was that in both Tax Court and tax refund litigation the action was not considered to have been brought "by or on behalf of" the United States—it is the taxpayer who was the plaintiff in the case. The fact that in virtually every civil tax case the government was the moving party by virtue of its action in issuing a notice of deficiency or initiating an audit was not sufficient for purposes of the statute. As noted in Key Buick Co. v. Commissioner, 613 F.2d 1306, 1308 (5th Cir.1980), "if it were the intent of Congress to provide attorneys' fees in practically every instance involving government review of tax returns, we are convinced Congress would have done so in much more specific terms."

Just four years after the passage of the Civil Rights Attorneys' Fees Awards Act of 1976, Congress again considered the subject of the awarding of attorneys' fees in litigation involving the United States, and, on October 21, 1980, the Equal Access to Justice Act (EAJA), was signed into law. The Act amended 42 U.S.C.A. § 1988 and 28 U.S.C.A. § 2412 and added a new section 504 to title 5 of the United States Code. Title II of the Act, which was opposed by the Treasury Department and other administrative agencies, provided for the awarding of attorneys' fees and other expenses to the prevailing party (other than the United States) in administrative "adversary adjudications" (defined as those in which the United States is represented by counsel) as well as actions brought in "courts of the United States" as defined in 28 U.S.C.A. § 451. In addition to the Supreme Court, courts of appeals, district courts and certain specified courts, § 451 included "any court created by Act of Congress the judges of which are entitled to hold office during good behavior." The Tax Court, whose judges are appointed for fifteen

---

f. 42 U.S.C.A. § 1988.

year terms, was not covered by the Act. However, suits initiated in district courts or the Court of Claims were subject to the attorneys' fees provisions of the Act. The new law contained no restrictions relating to whether the United States initiated the action; nor did it require the party seeking the award to show bad faith on the part of the government. Under the Act, fees and certain other expenses of a "prevailing party" are to be awarded upon application to the court or agency involved unless the *government* shows that its action was "substantially justified" (i.e., that there was a reasonable basis in law and fact for the action) or that special circumstances exist which would make the award unjust.

In 1982, Congress wrote a new chapter in the continuing saga of attorneys' fees awards in civil tax litigation by adding new section 7430 to the Internal Revenue Code and revising 28 U.S.C.A. § 2412 to provide that the new Code section will apply (rather than 28 U.S.C.A. § 2412) to the award of costs, fees and expenses in civil tax cases.

Under § 7430, the "prevailing party" in any civil proceeding commenced against the United States after February 28, 1983 in connection with the determination, collection or refund of any tax, penalty or interest may be awarded a judgment for "reasonable litigation costs" incurred in such proceeding. The proceeding must be brought in a court of the United States (including the Tax Court); the award may not be made unless the prevailing party has exhausted the administrative remedies available within the IRS; and only costs allocable to the United States and not to any other party may be awarded. Awards may not be made in declaratory judgment actions, except those relating to the revocation of the tax-exempt status of a section 501(c)(3) organization.

The term "prevailing party" was originally defined to mean any party other than the United States which established that the position of the United States was "unreasonable," and either substantially prevailed with respect to the amount in controversy or with respect to the most significant issue or set of issues presented. The Tax Reform Act of 1986 amended the definition of prevailing party to mean the party which shows that the position of the United States was not "substantially justified," thus bringing the language of § 7430 more closely in line with that of the EAJA. However, in contrast to the EAJA, under § 7430 it is the taxpayer and not the government which bears the burden of proof on the issue of whether the government's conduct was "substantially justified". As originally enacted, § 7430 imposed a $25,000 cap on the amount of attorneys' fees that could be awarded. The 1986 amendment eliminated that cap, but imposed a $75 per hour limit, subject to increases for cost of living and to waiver in the case of extraordinary circumstances. The 1986 amendments also incorporated the net worth limitations of the EAJA in section 7430. Certain "wealthy" taxpayers (such as individuals with net worth of more than $1 million) may not recover costs and fees regardless of the circumstances.

There was substantial controversy under the original version of § 7430 over whether the IRS' prelitigation position should be considered in determining whether the position of the United States was unreasonable.[a] Similar controversy had arisen in EAJA cases until that act was amended by Congress to specifically provide that the position of the United States was intended to include the government's prelitigation conduct.[b] In the Tax Reform Act of 1986, Congress settled this controversy as applied to § 7430 by providing that the term "position of the United States" means not only the position taken in the civil action but also "any administrative action or inaction by the District Counsel of the Internal Revenue Service (and all subsequent administrative action or inaction) upon which such proceeding is based."[c] Finally, the sunset provision enacted as part of the TEFRA legislation was removed by the 1986 amendment.

In 1988 Congress again amended section 7430, applicable to proceedings begun after November 11, 1988. The definition of "prevailing party" was amended to permit fee recovery prior to litigation, if the taxpayer prevails at the administrative level. Thus, the taxpayer and the Service can agree that the taxpayer is entitled to recover "reasonable administrative costs" (basically the same as "litigation costs," but incurred at the administrative level). Recoverable administrative costs include only those incurred after the first to occur of: (a) issuance of the statutory notice of deficiency, or (b) notification of the taxpayer by the Appeals Office of its decision. In practice, the two events often occur simultaneously—*i.e.,* the taxpayer learns of the final decision of the Appeals Office by receiving a statutory notice of deficiency. The definition of "position of the United States" was amended again in 1988. The amended definition tracks the rule for recovering administrative costs. Thus, the position of the United States is the position stated in the first to occur of issuance of the notice of deficiency or rendering of the Appeals Office decision. This restriction on recoverable administrative costs could have the unfortunate effect of discouraging vigorous efforts to settle with the Appeals Office, as costs incurred in drafting the protest and negotiating with Appeals will not be recoverable, whether the taxpayer prevails at the administrative or judicial level.

MINAHAN v. COMMISSIONER
Tax Court of the United States, 1987.
88 T.C. 492.

* * *

Exhaustion of Administrative Remedies

Respondent asserts that petitioners failed to exhaust administrative remedies available within the Internal Revenue Service as required by section 7430(b)(2). Respondent relies on section 301.7430–1(b)(1),

a. Compare Powell v. Commissioner, 791 F.2d 385 (5th Cir.1986) with Wasie v. Commissioner, 86 T.C. 962 (1986).

b. Act of Aug. 5, 1986, Pub.L. No. 99–80, § 2(c)(2), 99 Stat. 183, 185.

c. Pub.L. No. 99–514, § 1551(e)(1)(B) 100 Stat. 2085 (1986).

Proced. & Admin.Regs.,[10] and section 301.7430–1(f), Proced. & Admin.Regs.[11] Respondent asserts that petitioners failed to exhaust administrative remedies available within the Internal Revenue Service in that petitioners did not participate in an Appeals Office conference before filing their petitions in the Tax Court, and in that petitioners refused to agree under section 6501(c)(4) to extend the time for an assessment of tax so as to provide the Appeals Office with reasonable time to consider the matter. Respondent further asserts that the exceptions to the requirement that a party pursue administrative remedies, in section 301.7430–1(f), Proced. & Admin.Regs., where a party did not receive a 30–day letter before the notice of deficiency was issued, do not apply because the failure to receive the 30–day letter was due to petitioners' refusal to consent to extend the period for assessment. Sec. 301.7430–1(f)(2)(i), Proced. & Admin.Regs.

Petitioners assert that section 6501 provides them with a statutory right to receive notice of any assessment of tax within the prescribed 3–year period and that the refusal to extend the statute of limitations does not constitute a failure to exhaust administrative remedies so as to preclude an award of litigation costs under section 7430(b)(2). Petition-

---

10. Sec. 301.7430–1. Exhaustion of administrative remedies.—* * *

(b) *Tax, penalty and addition to tax—(1) In general.* A party has not exhausted its administrative remedies available within the Internal Revenue Service with respect to any tax matter for which an Appeals office conference is available under secs. 601.105 and 601.106 of the Statement of Procedural Rules (26 CFR Part 601) * * * unless—

(i) The party, prior to filing a petition in the Tax Court or a civil action for refund in a court of the United States—

(A) Participates, either in person or through a qualified representative * * * in an Appeals office conference; and

(B) Agrees under section 6501(c)(4) to extend the time for an assessment of tax if necessary to provide the Appeals office with a reasonable time period to consider the tax matter; or

(ii) If no Appeals office conference is granted, the party, prior to the issuance of a statutory notice of deficiency in the case of a petition in the Tax Court or the issuance of a statutory notice of disallowance in the case of a civil action for refund in a court of the United States—

(A) Requests an Appeals office conference * * *;

(B) Files a written protest if a written protest is required to obtain an Appeals office conference; and

(C) Agrees under section 6501(c)(4) to extend the time for an assessment of tax if necessary to provide the Appeals office with a reasonable time period to consider the tax matter.

11. Sec. 301.7430–1. Exhaustion of administrative remedies.—* * *

(f) *Exception to requirement that party pursue administrative remedies.* A party's administrative remedies within the Internal Revenue Service are considered exhausted for purposes of section 7430 if—

(1) The Internal Revenue Service notifies the party in writing that the pursuit of administrative remedies in accordance with paragraphs (b), (c), and (d) is unnecessary.

(2) In the case of a petition in the Tax Court—

(i) The party did not receive a preliminary notice of proposed deficiency (30–day letter) prior to the issuance of the statutory notice of deficiency and the failure to receive such notice was not due to actions of the party (such as a refusal to sign an extension of time for assessment * * *); and

(ii) The party does not refuse to participate in an Appeals office conference while the case is in docketed status.

ers further assert that the exemption in section 301.7430–1(f)(2)(i), Proced. & Admin.Regs., does apply because petitioners' failure to receive 30–day letters was not due to their actions but, rather, due to respondent's nonaction at the administrative level.

We agree with petitioners' conclusion.

Although the parties direct us to respondent's procedural and administrative regulations, we believe that the focus of our attention should be, at least initially, the statute that the Congress wrote.

In section 7430(b)(2),[12] the Congress provided as follows:

> (2) REQUIREMENT THAT ADMINISTRATIVE REMEDIES BE EXHAUSTED.—A judgment for reasonable litigation costs shall not be awarded under subsection (a) unless the court determines that the prevailing party has exhausted the administrative remedies available to such party within the Internal Revenue Service.

In the instant cases, respondent claims petitioners failed to exhaust their administrative remedies in that (1) they failed to participate in an Appeals Office conference, and (2) they refused to extend the time for assessment of tax.

Firstly, the controlling statute does not speak in terms of administrative remedies in the abstract, but rather focuses on "the administrative remedies available to *such party* [the prevailing party] within the Internal Revenue Service." (Emphasis added.) Respondent did not make an Appeals Office conference available to petitioners. Consequently, an Appeals Office conference was not an administrative remedy available to *these* petitioners within the Internal Revenue Service. Consequently, an Appeals Office conference was not an administrative remedy that these petitioners failed to exhaust.

Secondly, an extension of time for assessment is not an administrative remedy at all; consequently it is not an administrative remedy that these petitioners failed to exhaust.

Respondent does not assert that petitioners failed to respond promptly and sufficiently to any request for information or discussion. The record does not reveal any such failure on the part of any petitioner. Respondent does not assert, and the record does not reveal, any other administrative remedy which petitioners failed to exhaust.

We conclude that petitioners have carried their burden of proving that they exhausted the administrative remedies available to them within the Internal Revenue Service.

Since respondent relies entirely on his regulations in this matter, we examine those regulations to which he directs us.

---

12. As a result of sec. 1551(a) of the Tax Reform Act of 1986, the same language appears as sec. 7430(b)(1), effective in general for proceedings commenced after Dec. 31, 1985. See sec. 1551(h)(1) of the Tax Reform Act of 1986, *supra*.

In our unanimous opinion in *Durbin Paper Stock Co. v. Commissioner*, 80 T.C. 252, 256–257 (1983), we set down the following standards for examining the validity of respondent's regulations:

> The Commissioner has broad authority to promulgate all needful regulations. Sec. 7805(a); *United States v. Correll*, 389 U.S. 299, 306–307 (1967). It is well settled that Treasury regulations "must be sustained unless unreasonable and plainly inconsistent with the revenue statutes." *Commissioner v. South Texas Lumber Co.*, 333 U.S. 496, 501 (1948); accord *Commissioner v. Portland Cement Co. of Utah*, 450 U.S. 156, 169 (1981). Because they constitute contemporaneous constructions by those charged with administration of these statutes, they "should not be overruled except for weighty reasons." *Bingler v. Johnson*, 394 U.S. 741, 750 (1969); *Commissioner v. South Texas Lumber Co., supra* at 501.
>
> It is equally clear, however, that, although regulations are entitled to considerable weight, "respondent may not usurp the authority of Congress by adding restrictions to a statute which are not there." *Estate of Boeshore v. Commissioner*, 78 T.C. 523, 527 (1982). See *United States v. Marvett*, 325 F.2d 28, 30 (5th Cir.1963); *Coady v. Commissioner*, 33 T.C. 771, 779 (1960), affd. 289 F.2d 490 (6th Cir.1961). A regulation is not a reasonable statutory interpretation unless it harmonizes with the plain language of the statute, its origins, and its purpose. *United States v. Vogel Fertilizer Co.*, 455 U.S. 16 (1982); *National Muffler Dealers Association v. United States*, 440 U.S. 472, 477 (1979).
>
> A regulation which is in conflict with the statute is invalid to that extent. *Citizen's National Bank of Waco v. United States*, 417 F.2d 675, 679 (5th Cir.1969); *Arrow Fastener Co. v. Commissioner*, 76 T.C. 423, 430 (1981). Where the provisions of the statute are unambiguous and its directive specific, there is no power to amend it by regulation. *Koshland v. Helvering*, 298 U.S. 441, 447 (1936); *Arrow Fastener Co. v. Commissioner, supra.*[5]
>
> ----
> 5. The regulation in issue is an "interpretative" regulation issued under general authority vested in respondent under sec. 7805 and is to be accorded less weight than "legislative" regulations issued pursuant to a specific congressional delegation of lawmaking authority. *Estate of Boeshore v. Commissioner*, 78 T.C. 523, 527 n. 5 (1982).

In the instant cases, the legislative history presents us with another consideration. In the description of the reasons for enacting section 7430 in the Tax Equity and Fiscal Responsibility Act of 1982, the first reason given is as follows:

> Fee awards in such tax cases [i.e., "when the United States has acted unreasonably in pursuing the case"] will deter abusive actions or overreaching by the Internal Revenue Service and will enable individual taxpayers to vindicate their rights regardless of their economic circumstances. [H.Rept. 97–404 (1981), at 11; Staff of the Joint Committee on Taxation, General Explanation of the Revenue Provisions of the Tax Equity and Fiscal Responsibility Act of 1982, at 445.]

When the regulation interpreting a statute is written by the very agency whose "abusive actions or overreaching" were intended to be deterred by that statute, we must be especially vigilant to insure that the regulation "harmonizes with the plain language of the statute, its origins, and its purpose." *Durbin Paper Stock Co. v. Commissioner,* 80 T.C. at 257.

In the instant cases, respondent relies on paragraphs (b)(1)(i)(B) and (f)(2)(i) of section 301.7430–1, Proced. and Admin.Regs.

Paragraph (b)(1)(i)(B) *requires* a taxpayer "to extend the time for an assessment of tax if necessary to provide the Appeals Office with a reasonable time period to consider the tax matter". The sanction for a taxpayer who refuses to grant the waiver is loss of litigation costs—even though the taxpayer substantially prevails in the litigation and the taxpayer establishes that respondent's position was unreasonable.

Paragraph (f)(2)(i) *requires* a taxpayer "to sign an extension of time for assessment", that is necessary in order to permit respondent to issue a 30-day letter, which might lead to an Appeals Office conference. Note that paragraph (f)(2)(i) does not include any reasonableness limitation. Here, too, the sanction for failure to comply is loss of litigation costs—even though the taxpayer substantially prevails in the litigation and the taxpayer establishes that respondent's position was unreasonable.

There is no statutory authority to impose a condition of extending the period of limitations on assessment in order to qualify for litigation costs. The statute of limitations, section 6501 and its many subsections, is an elaborate and complex set of rules applicable to numerous situations.[13] When the Congress has seen fit to amend section 6501, it has done so explicitly and meticulously.[14] The importance of the statute of limitations is demonstrated by the fact that it is one of the few areas of the tax law where the burden of proof is imposed on respondent. (E.g., *Stratton v. Commissioner,* 54 T.C. 255, 289 (1970), and cases there cited.) It is not treated lightly by the courts. The clear language of paragraphs (b)(1)(i)(B) and (f)(2)(i) forces consent to extend the period of limitations by a taxpayer who contemplates claiming litigation costs where respondent's position is unreasonable. This gives radical control of the statute of limitations to respondent.

In granting taxpayers the right to collect litigation costs, the Congress did not suggest that taxpayers should be required to consent

---

13. Other statutes of limitations appear elsewhere in the statute. For example, special partnership limitations had been contained in sec. 6501(q), then modified and redesignated sec. 6501(*o*), and then substantially revised by the Tax Treatment of Partnership Items Act of 1982 (title IV of the Tax Equity and Fiscal Responsibility Act of 1982) and placed in sec. 6229. Also, a special statute of limitations appears in sec. 183(e)(4), in the case of elections made under sec. 183(e)(1).

14. The Congress amended sec. 6501 in 1958 (Pub.Laws 85–859 and 866); 1959 (Pub.L. 86–69); 1960 (Pub.L. 86–780); 1962 (Pub.Laws 87–794, 834, and 858); 1964 (Pub.Laws 88–272 and 571), 1965 (Pub.L. 89–44); 1966 (Pub.Laws 89–721 and 809); 1967 (Pub.L. 90–225); 1969 (Pub.L. 91–172); 1970 (Pub.L. 91–614); 1971 (Pub.L. 92–178); 1974 (Pub.L. 93–406); 1976 (Pub.L. 94–455); 1977 (Pub.L. 95–30); 1978 (Pub.Laws 95–227, 600, and 628); 1980 (Pub.Laws 96–222 and 223); 1982 (Pub.L. 97–248); 1984 (Pub.L. 98–369); and 1986 (Pub.L. 99–514, the Tax Reform Act of 1986).

to extend the period of limitations. The Congress could have, but did not, amend section 6501. Nothing in the legislative history of section 7430 suggests that the Congress intended to alter the provisions of section 6501, and the Congress did not provide for extensions of time in section 7430.

The Congress previously expressed itself on the statute of limitations when respondent attempted to alter the application of section 6501 in the provisions involving hobby losses. Section 183(e) was added to the Code in 1971 to provide an election to the taxpayer to postpone a determination as to whether the taxpayer could benefit from a presumption that an activity was conducted for profit if the activity produced gross income for 2 of 5 years (2 of 7 years for horses). The Senate Finance Committee, which originated the provision, expressed an intent that a taxpayer who made such an election should be required to waive the statute of limitations for that 5-year (or 7-year) period and a reasonable time thereafter. The purpose was to prevent the running of the period of limitations for any year in that period. S.Rept. 92–437 (1971), at 74; Staff of the Joint Committee on Internal Revenue Taxation, General Explanation of the Revenue Act of 1971, at 72. The Treasury Department issued temporary regulations which required the taxpayer making such an election to waive the period of limitations for all years within the 5-year (or 7-year) presumption period and for 18 months after the last year in the presumption period. The temporary regulations further provided that the waiver applied not only to the potential section 183 issue but to *all* potential issues on the tax returns.

This provision was included in the temporary regulations because respondent is precluded from mailing more than one notice of deficiency to a taxpayer for a given taxable year. If respondent examined a year for a nonsection 183 issue and mailed a statutory notice and later determined that the hobby loss provisions applied for that year, then respondent would be forbidden to mail a second notice of deficiency. The Congress amended the Code by adding section 183(e)(4) which changes the period of limitations on assessment and permits mailing a second notice of deficiency. In so doing, the Congress emphasized the importance of the statute of limitations as a right of the taxpayer, as follows:

> [The Congress] believes that a taxpayer should be able to take full advantage of a statutory presumption which was intended for his benefit, without unnecessarily extending the statute of limitations for items on his return which are unrelated to deductions which might be disallowed under section 183. [S.Rept. 94–938 (1976), at 67–68, 1976–3 C.B. (Vol. 3) 49, 105–106; H.Rept. 94–658 (1975), at 128, 1976–3 C.B. (Vol. 2) 695, 820; Staff of the Joint Committee on Taxation, General Explanation of the Tax Reform Act of 1976, at 61, 1976–3 C.B. (Vol. 2) 1, 73.]

In that situation, the legislative history of the 1971 Act specifically suggested a waiver of the statute of limitations as a requirement for making elections under section 183(e). The Treasury Department's temporary regulation appears to have been no more extensive than it had to be, considering the state of the law at that time. Nevertheless, the Congress determined that required waivers should not be so broad and overrode the temporary regulation to provide by statute a far more limited waiver.

The situation we face in the instant cases is that respondent's regulations seek to coerce waivers broadly and without any authority in either the statute or the legislative history. The history of the 1976 Act indicates a congressional policy that such waivers should not be coerced except to the extent that the Congress has specifically authorized.

We conclude that paragraphs (b)(1)(i)(B) and (f)(2)(i) of section 301.7430–1, Proced. & Admin.Regs., are invalid insofar as they provide that a taxpayer's failure to extend the statute of limitations is to be taken into account in determining whether the taxpayer has exhausted administrative remedies under section 7430(b).

In reaching our conclusion, we have taken into account the Congress' admonition that the condition of section 7430(b)(2) that taxpayers exhaust the administrative remedies available within the Internal Revenue Service is "intended to preserve the role that the administrative appeals process plays in the resolution of tax disputes by requiring taxpayers to pursue such remedies prior to litigation." H.Rept. 97–404, *supra* at 13. The House report further states that a taxpayer who actively participates in and discloses all relevant information during the administrative stages of the case will be considered to have exhausted the administrative remedies available within the Internal Revenue Service. Failure to so participate and disclose all relevant information may be sufficient grounds to determine that such taxpayer has not exhausted administrative remedies and, therefore, is ineligible for an award of litigation costs. H.Rept. 97–404, *supra* at 13.

Accordingly, we note that we do not disturb the provisions in the regulations that require a taxpayer to participate in an Appeals Office conference if that administrative remedy is made available to that taxpayer within the Internal Revenue Service. We note also, that requests for information at the audit level may properly be viewed as administrative remedies in that they may result in the parties reaching informed agreements which avoid the necessity of litigation. We note, finally, that a taxpayer's failure to respond in a full and timely manner to requests for information may constitute a failure to exhaust administrative remedies made available to that taxpayer within the Internal Revenue Service.

We hold for petitioners on this issue.

Appropriate orders will be issued.

Reviewed by the Court.

STERRETT, NIMS, PARKER, WHITAKER, KÖRNER, CLAPP, SWIFT, JACOBS, WRIGHT, PARR, and WELLS, JJ., agree with the majority opinion.

SIMPSON and COHEN, JJ., concur in the result only.

GERBER and WILLIAMS, JJ., did not participate in the consideration of this opinion.

* * *

SIMPSON, J., concurring: I accept the conclusions of the majority that the petitioners have exhausted their administrative remedies in this case and that the regulations are invalid insofar as they appear to require a taxpayer to consent to an extension of the statute of limitations in all cases in order to be entitled to recover litigation costs. However, I respectfully suggest that the majority goes too far. Suppose that the Commissioner's agents commence a timely examination of a taxpayer's return, but the complexity or the multitude of legal or factual issues make it impossible to complete the examination within the 3–year period. In such circumstances, there is insufficient time to issue a 30–day letter and to provide the taxpayer with an opportunity for an appeals hearing before the running of the statute. In such circumstances, I believe that it would be reasonable for the Commissioner to request the taxpayer to consent to an extension and that if the taxpayer refuses, we should hold that he has failed to exhaust his administrative remedies. In my opinion, the statute should be construed to include a test of reasonableness; that is, when the circumstances reveal that there was a reasonable need for the Commissioner to request an extension, the failure to grant one will constitute a failure to exhaust administrative remedies.

STERRETT, COHEN, and SWIFT, JJ., agree with this concurring opinion.

* * *

HAMBLEN, J., concurring and dissenting: I respectfully dissent from the portion of the majority opinion which invalidates section 301.7430–1(b)(1)(i)(B) and section 301.7430–1(f)(2)(i), Proced. & Admin. Regs., insofar as such regulations provide that a taxpayer's failure to extend the statute of limitations is relevant to our determination as to whether a taxpayer has exhausted administrative remedies available within the Internal Revenue Service as required by section 7430(b)(2). Courts should defer to interpretive regulations if the regulations are "found to 'implement the congressional mandate in some reasonable manner.'" *National Muffler Dealers Association v. United States,* 440 U.S. 472, 476 (1979). As recently suggested, "It follows from this principle of deference to Treasury regulations that the existence of an interpretive regulation should be decisive in a case in which an interpretive regulation is appropriate and in which reasonable arguments can be made both for a literal interpretation and for a nonliteral contextual interpretation" of the statutory provisions of the Internal Revenue Code. Zelenak, "Thinking About Nonliteral Interpretations of the Internal Revenue Code," 64 N.C.L.Rev. 623, 673–674 (1986). "The choice among reasonable interpretations is for the Commissioner, not the courts." *National Muffler Dealers Association v. United States, supra* at 488. And we have appropriately announced that we prefer to interpret regulations "so as to uphold their validity." *Graves v. Commissioner,* 88 T.C. 28 (1987), and cases cited.

I submit that it is not proper for this Court to strike down interpretative regulations such as these which can be applied without regard to whether the consequences benefit the Government or the taxpayer but which carry out the purpose, indeed the mandate, of the legislation before us. In this respect, I note the majority's reliance on "our unanimous opinion in *Durbin Paper Stock Co. v. Commissioner,* 80 T.C. 252, 256–257 (1983)," as the absolute canon of judicial statutory construction in this case. See 88 T.C. at 32–33. However, as I read the quoted section from *Durbin Paper Stock Co.* in the majority opinion, it merely confirms that rules of statutory construction may be applied to obtain the objective or result intended. In this respect, I cite *National Muffler Dealers Association v. United States, supra,* to reach what I believe is the correct standard. It seems, perhaps, that such precepts, like passages from the Bible, can be cited to support diverse propositions or platforms, and it has been observed that such rules are mutually contradictory and may be considered neither generally accepted nor consistently applied by American courts. Zelenak, *supra* at 630–633. "There are no talismanic words that can avoid the process of judgment." *Universal Camera Corp. v. Labor Bd.,* 340 U.S. 474, 489 (1951). As the courts of old held, rather pragmatically it seems to me, a statute which provides that a prisoner who escapes commits a felony "does not extend to a prisoner who breaks out when the prison is on fire—'for he is not to be hanged because he would not stay to be burnt.'" Zelenak, *supra* at 632, quoting *United States v. Kirby,* 74 U.S. (7 Wall.) 482, 487 (1868). I fear that here the majority condemns innocent regulations because they will not submit them to the test of reasonableness.

In the instant case, I would reach the same result as the majority without the inappropriate and unnecessary invalidation of the pertinent regulation. My view is that respondent's regulations are reasonable and capable of application in a manner consistent with the intent of Congress, as evidenced within the statute and gleaned from the legislative history. Consequently, the invalidation of paragraphs (b)(1)(i)(B) and (f)(2)(i) of section 301.7430–1, Proced. & Admin.Regs., is neither appropriate nor necessary. In the context of the entitlement to an award of litigation costs, the majority opinion does a great disservice to the entire administrative process of the Internal Revenue Service and obscures a clear congressional preference that cases be resolved in the administrative process rather than the legal forum.

I would determine that petitioners exhausted administrative remedies made available within the Internal Revenue Service for purposes of section 7430(b)(2) notwithstanding the refusal to extend the period for assessment. I submit that respondent's interpretive regulation, in general, establishes "the circumstances in which the Internal Revenue Service *normally will consider* such administrative remedies exhausted." Sec. 301.7430–1(a), Proced. & Admin.Regs. (Emphasis added.) In this context, respondent's regulation sets forth the standard that a party's entitlement to an award of litigation costs is dependent upon such party's agreement "to extend the time for an assessment of tax *if necessary to provide the Appeals office with a reasonable time period to consider the tax matter."* Sec. 301.7430–1(b)(1)(i)(B), Proced. & Admin.Regs. (Emphasis added.)

My stated view is that the request to extend the period for assessment should be a relevant consideration in the context of the exhaustion of administrative remedies requirement. The majority opinion obviates any role which the request to extend the period for assessment could have played to resolve tax matters at the administrative level.

In the context of the exhaustion of administrative remedies requirement, the majority ignores congressional preference for settlement of tax matters at the administrative level. I find troublesome the prospect that a taxpayer may now opt for the preliminary notice of deficiency and file a protest with the appellate section, but if a consent to extend the period for assessment is necessary to provide for Appeals Office review, the taxpayer may compel the issuance of the statutory notice of deficiency. We must now determine that such a taxpayer has complied with the exhaustion of administrative remedies requirement.

I am concerned that in voiding these regulations we have forsaken judicial discretion for the sake of pure judicial casuistry.

UNITED STATES v. McPHERSON
United States Court of Appeals, Fourth Circuit, 1988.
840 F.2d 244.

BUTZNER, SENIOR CIRCUIT JUDGE:

The United States appeals the district court's award of attorney's fees under 26 U.S.C. § 7430 to an attorney who appeared *pro se* in a tax case in which the government's position was determined to be unreasonable. The district court found that William V. McPherson, Jr., an attorney, reasonably spent 97.8 hours representing himself and that a rate of $90 an hour was appropriate. Based on these figures, it awarded a fee of $8,202, reasoning that McPherson "paid" for his own services by foregoing other opportunities to earn income.[1] We reverse because section 7430 restricts the allowance of attorney's fees to those actually "paid or incurred."

The facts of the case are not in dispute and need not be reviewed in detail. The government in 1984 brought a collection action against McPherson in which he substantially prevailed. The government con-

---

1. The district court's opinion is reported as *United States v. McPherson*, 660 F.Supp. 298 (M.D.N.C.1987).

cedes, for the purposes of this appeal, that its position in that litigation was unreasonable. The sole issue is whether, in this situation, an attorney who appeared *pro se* is entitled to collect reasonable fees for the time spent in his own defense.

I

At times pertinent to this case, section 7430 authorized awards of reasonable litigation costs to taxpayers who substantially prevailed in civil tax litigation in which the government's position was unreasonable. Reasonable litigation costs are defined by section 7430(c)(1)(A)(ii)(III) to include "reasonable fees paid or incurred for the services of attorneys in connection with the civil proceeding * * *."[2] Therefore, McPherson's services to himself can only be compensable if they can fairly be described as "fees paid or incurred for the services of attorneys."

Prior to the district court's decision in this case, the only authority interpreting section 7430 in the case of an attorney acting *pro se* was that of the Tax Court, which held in *Frisch v. Commissioner,* 87 T.C. 838 (1986), that such self-help was not compensable. *See also Minahan v. Commissioner,* 88 T.C. 516 (1987) (applying *Frisch*). The Tax Court concluded that neither the text nor the legislative history of the statute justified compensation for "lost opportunity costs." 87 T.C. at 845-46. The court noted that the fee shifting provision of the Equal Access to Justice Act, 28 U.S.C. § 2412, which has been construed by some courts to allow awards to *pro se* attorneys, speaks merely of "reasonable fees and expenses of attorneys," without the limiting requirement that those fees be "paid or incurred."[3] The court reasoned that section 7430, by contrast, was drafted specifically to compensate only actual out-of-pocket expenses or debts which would have to be paid. 87 T.C. at 843-46.[4]

We believe the Tax Court's interpretation of the phrase "paid or incurred" is the correct one. McPherson did not pay any fees for legal services nor incur any debts which remain outstanding. While the government might have chosen to compensate him and other litigants for the time its unreasonable lawsuit costs them, this statute does not do so. It is not improbable, for instance, that an accountant with tax expertise could adequately and successfully represent himself in a tax dispute with the IRS. Just like the lawyer, the accountant acting *pro se* faces real opportunity costs in devoting his time to his own defense

---

2. Section 7430 was amended by the Tax Reform Act of 1986, Pub.L. No. 99-514, by minor changes that do not affect the issue presented by this case.

3. We have denied fees to a *pro se* attorney under the Truth in Lending Act, 15 U.S.C. § 1640, which makes provision for "a reasonable attorney's fee." *White v. Arlen Realty & Development Corp.,* 614 F.2d 387 (4th Cir.1980).

4. The Tax Court also held that a lawyer acting on his own account is not acting as, or providing the services of, an attorney, a role which by its very definition involves the representation of another. We find it unnecessary to address this alternative ground.

rather than profitably working for others. Indeed, even a taxpayer in an unreasonable suit who does retain counsel may often be required to devote substantial time to the case, organizing records, attending depositions, and conferring with an attorney. All these are costs imposed on a citizen by the government's misguided action. Yet this statute cannot possibly be stretched to pay the accountant acting *pro se* or the represented layman for his lost time. In agreement with the Tax Court, we adhere to the plain text of the statute, which requires proof that the taxpayer "paid or incurred fees for the services of an attorney."

II

McPherson also requested fees under the Equal Access to Justice Act, 28 U.S.C. § 2412. In light of its award under § 7430 of the Internal Revenue Code, the district court considered McPherson's EAJA request moot, observing in dicta that it also lacked merit. 660 F.Supp. at 300–01.

It is apparent that McPherson cannot recover fees under the EAJA. As the district court noted, the EAJA expressly excludes from its coverage "any costs, fees, and other expenses in connection with any proceeding to which section 7430 of the Internal Revenue Code * * * applies." 28 U.S.C. § 2412(e).

McPherson offered Rule 11 as a third basis for an award of attorney fees. The district court did not rule on his Rule 11 motion, considering it, like the EAJA claim, moot in light of its award under section 7430.

Section 7430(a) by its terms governs the availability of costs and fees in "any civil proceeding * * * brought by or against the United States * * * [for the] collection of any tax," a category clearly encompassing the present case. This section prescribes in detail how and under what circumstances fees may be allowed in litigation over federal taxes. This precision would be pointless if fees could also be awarded in such cases under Rule 11 standards. For this reason, section 7430 must be considered the only waiver of sovereign immunity in this context, and the exclusive authority for an award of attorney's fees in the class of cases described by § 7430. Rule 11 does not afford McPherson a basis for recovery.

The judgment of the district court is reversed, and the case is remanded with directions to deny the application for attorney fees.

BODE v. UNITED STATES
United States Court of Appeals, Fifth Circuit, 1990.
919 F.2d 1044.

Before JONES, DUHÉ, and WIENER, CIRCUIT JUDGES.

PER CURIAM:

After an audit, the Internal Revenue Service (Service) assessed a deficiency against John and Toni Bode, plaintiffs-appellees (Taxpayers).

The Taxpayers paid the deficiency and filed a refund suit in the district court against the defendant-appellant, the United States. The district court ruled for the Taxpayers on the merits and in addition, awarded attorneys' fees under 26 U.S.C. § 7430 for 600 hours at $150 per hour. The United States appeals, contesting both the number of hours and the hourly rate awarded, and the Taxpayers request an award of attorneys' fees for defending this appeal. We affirm in part, reverse in part, and remand in part.

I.

The Taxpayers owned and operated a ranch prior to and during the years in question, 1982, 1983, and 1984. Their ranching activities included farming, auctioneering, horse breeding, and horse racing. The horse breeding and racing operation, by itself, had never generated a profit.

In April of 1985, the Service initiated an audit of the Taxpayers' joint tax returns for the years in question. The Service, as a result of that audit, disallowed deductions that the Taxpayers took for horse breeding and racing activities, claiming that those activities were not engaged in for profit. The Taxpayers paid the resulting deficiencies and filed the instant suit for refund.

The district court held that all of the ranch activities, including the horse-related activities, should be viewed together as one business, and that, as such, the Taxpayers' ranching business was profitable overall. Because the business had been profitable during each of the years in question, the district court ruled that the Taxpayers were entitled to deduct the losses generated by the horse-related activities from the gross income generated by the ranching business as a whole. The United States does not appeal that decision.

The district court also determined that the Taxpayers were eligible for an award of attorneys' fees under 26 U.S.C. § 7430. The United States does not appeal that holding either, but does appeal the quantum of the award. On the issue of attorneys' fees, the Taxpayers did not submit any documentary evidence showing the number of attorney hours billed, the rates at which the hours were billed, or the tasks performed. Instead, the Taxpayers introduced only expert testimony. Their expert, Bill Rosch, testified about (1) the total dollar amount of the invoice for the services rendered by one set of the Taxpayers' attorneys, (2) the billing rates for some of the Taxpayers' attorneys, (3) the qualifications and abilities of the Taxpayers' attorneys, and (4) the hourly rate that the court should award for reimbursement under section 7430. He did not testify about the total number of hours billed to the Taxpayers. Rather, he testified that the fee of one of the firms—Mr. Urquardt's firm—was "in the neighborhood of $119,000"; and that the estimated fee of the other firm—Mr. Alexander's firm—was $50,-000.

The Taxpayers' expert also did not testify about the precise hourly rate charged by each attorney who rendered services to the Taxpayers. Instead, he testified that, at one time, one of the Taxpayers' attorneys may have been billing at $175 per hour, and that at some point, that rate changed to $250 per hour. The evidence also indicated that one of the Taxpayer's attorneys billed the time of an associate to the Taxpayers. The Taxpayers did not offer any evidence, however, about how many hours that associate billed or at what rate that associate was billed.

Because the expert based his testimony, in part, on his examination of the invoices that the attorneys sent to the Taxpayers, he was unsure what rate was used by each attorney at the firm. And, although he testified that the total fees were reasonable for a case of this type, he did not testify that the hours were reasonably expended.

The Service made no attempt to controvert the expert's testimony. Neither did it adduce any affirmative evidence of reasonable hourly rates for the geographic area of the trial, the reasonable number of hours for preparation and trial, or the relative complexity of the case.

The district court, without articulating its reasons, awarded 600 hours of attorney time at an hourly rate of $150. Both the number of hours and the hourly rate were substantially less than invoiced to the Taxpayers and testified to by their expert.

II.

Section 7430 of the Internal Revenue Code provides:

(a) In any administrative or court proceeding which is brought by or against the United States in connection with the * * * refund of any tax, * * * the prevailing party may be awarded a judgment or settlement for—

(2) reasonable litigation costs incurred in connection with such court proceeding.

26 U.S.C. § 7430(a)(2) (1988).

The United States contends that the district court's attorney fee award was excessive in two respects: (1) the number of hours—600; and (2) The hourly rate—$150. We review the overall amount of a prevailing party's attorney fee award under the abuse of discretion standard, see *Hensley v. Eckerhart*, 461 U.S. 424, 437, 103 S.Ct. 1933, 1941, 76 L.Ed.2d 40 (1983), and we review the district court's subsidiary findings of fact for clear error, see *Creske v. Commissioner*, 896 F.2d 250, 252 (7th Cir.1990).

A. THE NUMBER OF HOURS AWARDED

The Taxpayers' evidence on the issue of the number of compensable hours is insufficient to support an award of 600 hours of attorney time for several reasons. First, the Supreme Court held that the party seeking reimbursement of attorneys' fees pursuant to 42 U.S.C. § 1988 in the context of civil rights litigation under 42 U.S.C. § 1983 has the burden of establishing the number of attorney hours expended, and can meet that burden only by presenting evidence that is adequate for the court to determine what hours should be included in the reimbursement.[1] *See Hensley,* 461 U.S. at 437, 103 S.Ct. at 1941. In determining the amount of an attorney fee award, courts customarily require the applicant to produce contemporaneous billing records or other sufficient documentation so that the district court can fulfill its duty to examine the application for non-compensable hours. *See, e.g., White v. City of Richmond,* 713 F.2d 458, 461 (9th Cir.1983) (noting that courts may exclude hours that are insufficiently documented and "should not award attorneys' fees unless the prevailing party presents sufficiently detailed records that the time expended and the need for services are clearly established"); *National Ass'n of Concerned Veterans v. Secretary of Defense,* 675 F.2d 1319, 1327 (D.C.Cir.1982) (holding that "it is insufficient to provide the district court with broad summaries of work done and hours logged"). Although this Circuit held in *Alberti v. Klevenhagen,* 896 F.2d 927 (5th Cir.1990), that an application for attorneys' fees can succeed even if it is unsupported by the preferred method of contemporaneous time records, their absence was excused in that case by "an abundance of other evidence" supporting the number of hours claimed. *Id.* at 931. Even assuming that billing statements are not *required* under section 7430, we cannot overlook the insufficiency of the Taxpayers' evidence on the number of attorney hours.

Second, section 7430 does not permit recovery of fees for services performed prior to the preparation of the complaint. *See, e.g., Sliwa v. Commissioner,* 839 F.2d 602, 607 (9th Cir.1988); *Baker v. Commissioner,* 787 F.2d 637, 641 (D.C.Cir.1986). The Taxpayers produced absolutely no evidence from which the district court could have determined how many hours were devoted to compensable activities under *Sliwa* and *Baker.*

Third, the expert's testimony contains no statement on which the court could have relied in determining, as courts are required to do in setting attorneys' fees under 42 U.S.C. § 1988, that the total number of hours claimed were not only reasonable, but also that particular hours were reasonably expended. *See Alberti,* 896 F.2d at 932. Because the expert had not examined the billing records or any other document showing the tasks and services performed, he did not testify, and could not have testified, that the hours billed to the Taxpayers were reasonably expended.

Fourth, the expert's testimony did not provide any basis from which the district judge could have arrived at even a "ball park" figure of the actual number of hours billed. The expert testified that Mr. Urquardt's firm charged in the neighborhood of $119,000. The expert did not testify as to the total number of hours billed or as to the precise

---

[1]. While not directly applicable to an attorney fee award under section 7430, section 1988 cases are at least instructive.

hourly rate charged by each attorney who worked on the Taxpayers' case. Instead, he testified that at one time Mr. Urquardt's firm charged an hourly rate of $175 per hour, but the expert was unsure what rate was used by each attorney at that firm. We also know that Mr. Urquardt and his associate, Mr. Pacquette, worked on the case. We do not know, however, who else in his firm, if anyone, may have worked on it. We do not know how many hours anyone put in. We do not know what hourly rates are commonly billed by any of the persons who worked on the file.

Neither do we know whether anyone from Mr. Alexander's firm, other than Mr. Alexander, worked on the case. We have no idea how much time that firm put into the case or what its hourly rates are. We only have the expert's testimony that Mr. Alexander charges $5,000 a day for trial.

The Taxpayers suggest that their expert's testimony establishes that 680 hours were expended by Mr. Urquardt's firm on their case ($119,000 divided by $175 per hour). Even if the district judge arrived at the 600 hour figure that way, we cannot affirm the number of hours awarded because the evidence does not establish that all of the attorneys at Mr. Urquardt's firm were charging $175 per hour at all relevant times. In fact, the expert's testimony indicates that some of the attorneys may have been billing at $250 per hour (dividing by $250 per hour would yield a much smaller number of hours). Additionally, an associate who may have billed at a lower rate also worked on the case, yet the imputed calculation does not reflect a different rate for the associate's time. Neither does the calculation reflect the possibility that much of the time may have been billed at $250 per hour. Finally, the calculation offered by the Taxpayers does not take into account how many hours were billed by partners as opposed to associates.

The Taxpayers argue, citing *Blum v. Stenson*, 465 U.S. 886, 104 S.Ct. 1541, 79 L.Ed.2d 891 (1984), that the Service has waived the right to complain about the quantum of attorneys' fees by failing to controvert the Taxpayers' evidence on the issue of attorneys' fees. *Blum*, in a footnote, declined to reach the merits of the petitioner's argument that the hours charged by the respondent's counsel were unreasonable because the "petitioner failed to submit to the district court any evidence challenging the accuracy and reasonableness of the hours charged. * * * She therefore waived her right to an evidentiary hearing [and] to challenge in this Court the district court's determination that the number of hours billed were reasonable for cases of similar complexity." *Id.* at 892 n. 5, 104 S.Ct. at 1545 n. 5.

Blum is distinguishable from this case because here the Taxpayers failed to produce evidence in the first instance sufficient to establish the number of compensable hours of attorney time expended on this case. The United States was not required to put on any evidence challenging the reasonableness of the hours expended because the

Taxpayers had failed to meet their initial burden of establishing the actual number of attorney hours.

The Taxpayers also rely on language in the opinion of this Court in *Powell v. Commissioner* (*Powell II*), 891 F.2d 1167 (5th Cir.1990). In that case, we held that a district court erred in disregarding evidence of prevailing market rates that was uncontroverted by the Service. *See id.* at 1173. Our holding in *Powell II* is likewise distinguishable because there was no indication in that case that there was any problem with the sufficiency of the Taxpayer's evidence.

The Taxpayers argue that if this court cannot affirm the district court's award, we should remand for the district court to articulate its reasons for arriving at 600 hours of attorney time. *See Blanchard v. Bergeron*, 893 F.2d 87, 90 (5th Cir.1990) (rejecting a wholly conclusory decision by the district court because the appellate court had "no inkling why the court awarded about 100 hours of legal time, as opposed to 200 hours or 50 hours. On remand, the court should provide some explication for its choice of the reasonably necessary amount of hours."). We disagree. Because the only evidence which the district court could have used to calculate the number of attorney hours did not provide a reasonable basis from which to make this calculation, we must reverse the district court's award of 600 hours.

Although the district court erred in awarding 600 hours based on the evidence before it, that court may make an award of fees for the number of hours that it observed the Taxpayers' attorneys before it during the trial of the case. That court was, after all, its own "eye witness" of those hours. Thus, on remand, the district court should articulate on the record its reasons for the number of hours that it awards.

B. THE HOURLY RATE AWARDED

Section 7430 provides that "reasonable litigation costs" include:

reasonable fees paid or incurred for the services of attorneys in connection with the court proceeding, except that such fees *shall not be in excess of $75 per hour unless* the court determines that an increase in the cost of living or a special factor, such as the limited availability of qualified attorneys for such proceeding, justifies a higher rate.

26 U.S.C. § 7430(c)(1)(B)(iii) (1988) (emphasis added).

Because we are reversing the award of 600 hours and remanding that issue for reconsideration in the district court, we also must address whether the district court's award of an hourly rate above the $75 per hour presumed statutory cap was proper. The United States argues that the Taxpayers failed to present any evidence of a "special factor." The Taxpayers counter that they established the existence of several "special factors" justifying the district court's award of an hourly rate in excess of $75 per hour: (1) they could not obtain skilled counsel qualified to handle their refund suit at $75 per hour because theirs was not a routine tax case but rather a complex and unusual, if not unique, tax case; (2) their counsel possessed special skills and expertise in the subject matter that formed the basis of their refund suit; and (3) their counsel obtained exceptional results.

1. The Unavailability of Qualified Counsel at $75 per hour

The Taxpayers posit that because they could not obtain qualified counsel at the $75 per hour presumed statutory rate, they are entitled to an attorney fee award above that rate. The Supreme Court explained that the similarly worded exception for limited availability of qualified attorneys in the Equal Access to Justice Act, 28 U.S.C. § 2412(d)(2)(A)(ii),[2] cannot mean simply that lawyers skilled and experienced enough to try a particular case are in short supply and cannot be hired at $75 per hour. *See Pierce v. Underwood,* 487 U.S. 552, 571, 108 S.Ct. 2541, 2553, 101 L.Ed.2d 490 (1988). Also Congress did not intend that the market-minimum rate should govern instead of the presumed statutory rate if the national or local market rate was above the statutory cap. *See id.* at 572, 108 S.Ct. at 2553. The statutory exception for the limited availability of qualified attorneys for the proceedings involved "refers to attorneys having some distinctive knowledge or specialized skill *needful for the litigation in question*—as opposed to an extraordinary level of the generally lawyerly knowledge and ability useful in all litigation." *Id.* (emphasis added). Because the test for limited availability is couched in terms of a special expertise needful for the litigation in question, the Taxpayers' arguments under this issue are inexorably intertwined with their separately asserted argument that their counsel possessed special skills and expertise in the basic subject matter of their refund suit.

2. Special Skill and Expertise

One of the Taxpayers' attorneys, Mr. Urquardt, was a specialist in the field of taxation. The Taxpayers urge that his specialty in tax law enabled him skillfully to coordinate with the other attorney on the cross-examination of the United States' lone witness, and to conduct with like skill the direct examination of another expert witness who testified about matters concerning both the Internal Revenue laws and certain principles of tax accounting. The United States contends that if a special expertise in tax law qualifies as a "special factor" under section 7430, which applies only to proceedings against the United States "in connection with the determination, collection, or refund of any tax," 26 U.S.C. § 7430(a), the exception would wholly swallow the rule because almost all attorneys seeking compensation under section 7430 possess an expertise in tax law.

---

2. The EAJA provides that attorneys' fees "shall be based upon prevailing market rates for the kind and quality of the services furnished," but "shall not be awarded in excess of $75 per hour unless the court determines that an increase in the cost of living or a special factor, such as the limited availability of qualified attorneys for the proceedings involved, justifies a higher fee." 28 U.S.C. § 2412(d)(2)(A)(ii).

The United States argues persuasively that Congress probably did not intend for a specialty in tax law to be a special factor [3] meriting an increase in the section 7430 statutory rate unless the particular nature of the litigation required a tax specialist. Applying the *Pierce* test, however, we note that the underlying merits of this case did require a distinctive knowledge of tax, a specialized tax litigation skill, and perhaps even a special knowledge of the quarterhorse industry.[4]

The record reflects that the judge was familiar with the $75 per hour statutory cap and with the necessity of finding a special factor to award fees above the cap. On the issue of a "special factor" within the meaning of section 7430, the Taxpayers' expert testified that "there would be a limited opportunity to hire qualified lawyers to handle a case of this nature for $75.00 an hour." He also testified that it is not possible to hire competent tax litigators in the Houston area for less than $5,000 per day of trial. The United States did not controvert this evidence.

The district court did not articulate the section 7430 special factors upon which it relied. Nevertheless, the inference from the record is inescapable that the judge found, based on the uncontroverted testimony of the limited availability of qualified counsel, and, presumably, on his own experience and knowledge, that special factors under section 7430 existed and that they were sufficient to justify a departure from the $75 per hour cap. Clearly, counsel's expertise in tax law, in and of itself, is not a special factor warranting a fee award in excess of $75 per hour under section 7430. *See Mattingly v. United States*, 711 F.Supp. 1535, 1542 (D.Nev.1989); *accord Kim v. United States*, 709 F.Supp. 932,

---

3. Very few cases have been decided under the current version of section 7430. The previous version of the statute did not have a recommended cap of $75 per hour, and instead, provided a cap of $25,000 for the total amount recoverable. 26 U.S.C. § 7430(b)(1) (1982). Thus, courts deciding cases under the previous version were not bound to determine whether a "special factor" existed meriting a rate above $75 per hour, but instead, merely had to determine whether the requested hourly rate was *reasonable*. This Court's decision in *Powell v. Commissioner* (*Powell II*), 891 F.2d 1167 (5th Cir.1990), is distinguishable on this basis. *Powell II* held that the tax court erred in limiting the hourly rate to $75. The tax court indicated that it reduced the requested hourly rate to $75 because the case involved a rather routine tax shelter settlement. This court, in rejecting that reasoning, said that "routine" services of that nature are not provided at "routine" legal rates. *Powell II*, 891 F.2d at 1173. Although this Court observed in *Powell II* that "[t]ax practice is a specialty area in which relatively few attorneys participate," *id.*, that case does not stand for the proposition that an expertise in tax would qualify as a "special factor" under the current version of 7430. *See id.* at 1173 n. 6. Thus, other cases decided under the previous version of 7430 indicating that a specialty in tax law merits an upward adjustment in the hourly rate, *see, e.g., Harding v. Manners*, 646 F.Supp. 277, 280 (N.D.Ga.1986), are inapplicable both because those cases merely indicated that a specialty in tax could be considered in determining a *reasonable* hourly rate, and because those cases did not apply the current statutory test.

4. The Taxpayers argue that because their other attorney, Mr. Alexander, possessed knowledge, familiarity, and experience with the Texas quarterhorse industry, his expertise qualifies as a special factor under section 7430. They argue that this knowledge was essential for Mr. Alexander to effectively present what the Taxpayers' horse program was trying to accomplish. We do not reach this issue because the taxpayers failed to present any evidence to establish that attorneys with an expertise in the horse business were unavailable for the $75 per hour rate.

933 (N.D.Cal.1989) (rejecting an hourly rate of $150 under the current version of section 7430 for an attorney with a tax specialty in a case that contested the tax-deferred status of an exchange of property and noting that "[w]e presume that Congress was aware that the prevailing rates for tax attorneys in metropolitan areas normally exceed $75.00 per hour"). The district court in this case, however, could have found that a special skill and expertise in tax were, under *Pierce,* "needful for the litigation in question." *Pierce,* 487 U.S. at 572, 108 S.Ct. at 2554.

Our decision today is distinguishable from *Mattingly* and *Kim* because we are not holding that a specialty in tax law, whether or not the underlying merits of the tax case actually require a tax specialist, automatically constitutes a special factor under section 7430. We do find, however, that the uncontroverted evidence is sufficient to establish that the Taxpayers could not have obtained qualified attorneys who could handle the complex nature of the underlying merits *in this case*—attorneys with a special expertise in tax law—for substantially less than the hourly rate of $150 awarded by the district court, and certainly not for $75 per hour. We do not find that the district court erred in departing from the statutory cap of $75 per hour for Mr. Urquardt's time.[5]

Moreover, because the United States did not controvert the expert's opinion on the unavailability of qualified counsel for this type of case, the United States, under *Blum v. Stenson,* has waived this factual issue and cannot now contend that the taxpayers could have obtained qualified legal counsel for less. 465 U.S. 886, 892 n. 5, 104 S.Ct. 1541, 1545 n. 5, 79 L.Ed.2d 891 (1984); *see also Powell v. Commissioner (Powell II),* 891 F.2d 1167, 1173 (5th Cir.1990). Based on the record, we find that this conclusion was not clearly erroneous. Because section 7430 specifically identifies limited availability of qualified counsel as a special factor justifying a departure from the statutory rate, the district judge on remand may award an hourly rate above the statutory cap for the hours that Mr. Urquardt spent during trial.[6]

Additionally, the Taxpayers suggest that Mr. Alexander's special knowledge about the quarterhorse industry qualifies as a special factor meriting an hourly rate above the $75 per hour statutory rate. Special legal expertise about the quarterhorse industry may well have qualified as a special factor, but the Taxpayers not only failed to present any evidence to establish that they could not have hired an attorney with

---

5. On remand, however, the district court should articulate the special factor upon which it relied in departing from the statutory cap. *See Baker v. Bowen,* 839 F.2d 1075, 1082 (5th Cir.1988) (holding that increases over the statutory cap should be allowed only after the court makes a "particularized and careful analysis of the individual facts of the case").

6. The record before this court does not disclose if any of Mr. Urquardt's associates participated at trial. If any attorneys from Mr. Urquardt's firm, other than Mr. Urquardt, did participate during the trial, their time should be reimbursed at the presumed statutory rate of $75 per hour since the Taxpayers produced no evidence that anyone other than Mr. Urquardt had a special knowledge in the field of tax that was needful for the litigation in question.

quarterhorse industry expertise for $75 per hour, but they also failed to present any evidence to establish that Mr. Alexander possessed such special knowledge. The only evidence about Mr. Alexander's special skill indicated that he was a trial specialist and that an attorney with his skill could not have been hired for less than $5,000 per day of trial. We find the evidence inadequate to support findings that Mr. Alexander possessed a special knowledge of the Texas quarterhorse industry and that his special knowledge of the quarterhorse industry qualified as a special factor, and we hold that a general expertise in trial work is not a special factor under section 7430. *See Pierce,* 487 U.S. at 572, 108 S.Ct. at 2554.

3. *Exceptional Results*

To the extent that exceptional results can be a special factor in a section 7430 case, the district court could find, without committing reversible error, that the results obtained in this case meet that definition. Not only did the Taxpayers' attorneys achieve a total victory on the merits in the trial court, they also were able to convince the district court that the Service's position was "not substantially justified." If, on remand, the district court does find that the results obtained in the case were exceptional, and that the services of Mr. Alexander were instrumental and necessary in obtaining those results, the court in its discretion may depart from the statutory cap and articulate its reasons for doing so, as in the case of Mr. Urquardt, in awarding fees for the time that Mr. Alexander spent before the court.

C. ATTORNEYS' FEES FOR THIS APPEAL

The Taxpayers ask for an additional award of attorneys' fees for this appeal, arguing that the United States' unreasonable position in the underlying litigation forced them to incur the additional cost of defending this appeal. When the government's underlying position is "not substantially justified," the Taxpayer is entitled "to recover *all* attorney's fees and expenses reasonably incurred in connection with the vindication of its rights, including those related to any litigation over fees on appeal." *See Powell II,* 891 F.2d at 1172 (emphasis added). *Powell II* has been modified by the Supreme Court's holding in *Commissioner, INS v. Jean,* 495 U.S. ___ n. 10, 110 S.Ct. 2316, 2321 n. 10, 110 L.Ed.2d 134, 145 n. 10 (1990): although attorneys' fees may be awarded for all aspects of litigation, including appeal, fees for defending an appeal "should be excluded to the extent that the applicant ultimately fails to prevail in such litigation."

To award attorneys' fees for this appeal, this court need only be satisfied that the district court's determination that the United States' position in the underlying litigation was "not substantially justified," which was a prerequisite to its award of attorneys' fees for the litigation below, was not an abuse of discretion. *See Powell II,* 891 F.2d at 1172. We need not make our own determination that the government's appellate position was not substantially justified once the threshold finding has been made at the trial court. *See Jean,* 495 U.S. at ___, 110 S.Ct. at 2315–16, 110 L.Ed.2d at 143–45.

In light of the failure of the United States to appeal on the merits, we find that the district court did not abuse its discretion in determining that the United States' position was not substantially justified. We must, however, make our own determination whether the Taxpayers are "a prevailing party" on appeal. *See id.* And we do so find. Although the Taxpayers have not prevailed on every issue on this appeal, these losses are "not of such magnitude as to deprive [them] of prevailing party status." *Leroy v. City of Houston (Leroy V),* 906 F.2d 1068, 1082 n. 24 (5th Cir.1990). Nonetheless, because the Taxpayers are only partly successful on appeal, it is not proper to reimburse them for 100% of their appellate fees. *See Jean,* 495 U.S. at ___, 110 S.Ct. at 2321 n. 10, 110 L.Ed.2d at 145 n. 10. On remand, the district court should take limited evidence on this issue to determine how much of the time billed to the Taxpayers for the appellate work was devoted to those issues on which the Taxpayers prevailed.[7] Because the entirety of the remand proceedings will be devoted to matters on which the Taxpayers prevailed, there need be no such allocation of the attorneys' fees which the district court awards to the Taxpayers for the reasonable costs of their attorneys' services therein.

Under different circumstances this court would set the appellate attorney fee award, as we did in *Davis v. Board of School Commissioners,* 526 F.2d 865, 868 (5th Cir.1976) and in *Leroy V,* 906 F.2d at 1806. We decline to set them here, however, because we do not have before us sufficient evidence upon which to determine such an award.

We therefore remand on that issue for the district court to set attorneys' fees for defending this appeal. In determining the appropriate attorneys' fees to award the Taxpayers for defending this appeal, as well as for participating in the proceedings on remand, the district court will be limited to the $75 per hour statutory rate. We can envision no reason why the Taxpayers would require either a tax, quarterhorse, or trial specialist to defend an appeal or participate in the remand proceedings on the sole issue of the quantum of attorneys' fees.

If on remand, the district court determines that no special factor exists justifying a departure from the $75 hourly cap for some attorney hours, it should also consider whether, for those hours for which it makes an award of $75 per hour, an "increase in the cost of living * * * justifies a higher rate."[8] 26 U.S.C. § 7430(c)(1)(A)(ii)(III) (1988). In

---

7. Because the issues that the Taxpayers won and those that they lost are so intertwined, a good faith allocation by the Taxpayers' attorneys as to the number of compensable hours may suffice.

8. The Internal Revenue Code, the Treasury Regulations, and the Committee Reports are silent as to which particular index should be used in making such an adjustment, so the district court has some flexibility in that regard. Certainly the district court could not be faulted if it should select an appropriate inflation index, such as the United States Department of Labor's Consumer Price Index for All Urban Consumers (CPI–U) published by

saying that the district court should consider a cost of living adjustment, we do not decide that any such adjustment must be awarded or what amount, if any, is ultimately appropriate.

III.

On remand, the district court should award attorneys' fees to the Taxpayers based solely on the time that the district court observed the attorneys spend during trial before it, and should explicate special factors justifying its departure from the statutory hourly rate. That court should also determine how many billable hours the Taxpayers' attorneys devoted to the issues on which the Taxpayers prevailed on appeal, and likewise how many billable hours they devoted to proceed-

the Bureau of Labor Statistics. *See, e.g., Johnson v. Sullivan*, 1990 WL 180588 (8th Cir.1990) ("We believe that the Consumer Price Index constitutes "proper proof" of the increased cost of living since the EAJA's enactment and justifies an award of attorney's fees greater than $75 per hour in these cases."); *Allen v. Bowen*, 821 F.2d 963, 967 (3d Cir.1987) (expressly approving the use of the Consumer Price Index in determining EAJA cost-of-living adjustment (citing *Natural Resources Defense Council v. EPA*, 703 F.2d 700, 713 (3d Cir.1983))); *Ramon-Sepulveda v. INS*, 863 F.2d 1458, 1463, 1464 n. 6 (9th Cir.1988) (using the CPI-U to calculate increase in the cost of living in an EAJA case).

Since oral argument, the government has invited our attention to a recent decision on the issue of the appropriate date that a court should use as the *base date* for determining a cost-of-living increase under section 7430. *Buchanan v. United States*, No. 89-969-PA (D.Ore. Nov. 11, 1990). In *Buchanan*, the court adjusted the $75 per hour cap for an increase in the cost of living and used March 1, 1983 as the base date. That court reasoned that March 1, 1983 was appropriate because it was the effective date of the original version of section 7430. Tax Equity and Fiscal Responsibility Act of 1982, Pub.L. No. 97-248, § 292, 96 Stat. 324, 572 (1982). We disagree. The original version of section 7430 simply set a $25,000 limit on the amount that could be awarded for all litigation costs—no hourly cap and no cost-of-living adjustment. The amended version of section 7430, which for the first time provided a $75 per hour cap and a cost-of-living factor, and which deleted the aggregate limit of $25,000, became effective on January 1, 1986. Tax Reform Act of 1986, Pub.L. No. 99-514, § 1551, 100 Stat. 2085, 2752 (1986). Although the original version of section 7430 did not provide for an adjustment for an increase in the cost of living, the *Buchanan* court held that a cost-of-living increase should be measured from the effective date of the original version "[b]ecause Congress always intended that taxpayers receive awards of reasonable attorneys fees [and because] only the method guaranteeing such reasonableness has changed." *Id.*

We decline to follow the *Buchanan* court's choice of March 1, 1983 as the base date for determining a cost-of-living increase under section 7430. Congress amended the current version of the statute, which contains the $75 hourly cap, to be effective in 1986, not in 1983. Just as the *Buchanan* court rejected using October 1, 1981, the effective date of the similarly-worded EAJA, as the base date "because section 7430 did not even exist on October 1, 1981," *id.*, we reject using the effective date of the older version of the statute to increase the $75 hourly cap because that version of the statute contained no cap in 1982 when it was drafted or in 1983 when it became effective. Rather, Congress set the hourly rate in 1985 when it drafted the current version of section 7430 to become effective on January 1, 1986. Therefore, the effective date of the current version of the statute is the appropriate base date for a cost-of-living adjustment, should the district court on remand determine that an increase in the cost of living justifies a higher rate for those hours that otherwise would be compensated at $75 per hour. Were we to follow *Buchanan*, we would produce the anomalous result of applying a two years and 10 months cost-of-living increase to the maximum statutory rate on the very first day that the $75 hourly rate became effective. If Congress had intended that result, it certainly would have specified the greater hourly rate produced by applying such an inflation adjustment to $75 per hour, not by specifying $75 as the rate as of January 1, 1986.

ings on remand. In awarding those fees, the district court should also articulate its reasons for the award at each stage. For the foregoing reasons, this case is

Affirmed in Part, Reversed in Part, and Remanded in Part.

Chapter VIII

THE INTERNAL REVENUE SERVICE SUMMONS

Scope Note: The power to issue summonses to compel the production of documents and testimony constitutes the single most important investigative tool of the Internal Revenue Service. Although the power is a broad one, certain limitations have been placed upon it. The materials that follow discuss these limitations and consider the procedures used in raising objections to improper summonses. Included in this context is a discussion of the evidentiary privileges, particularly the attorney-client privilege and the privilege against self-incrimination. Also treated below are the special requirements applicable to "John Doe" and third-party recordkeeper summonses.

SECTION 1. THE FORMAL INTERVIEW ("Q & A")

The Internal Revenue Service summons literally calls for the summoned party to appear to produce documents and to give testimony. In situations in which the summons is used solely to obtain documents (for example, in most cases in which a summons is issued for bank records) the formality of an appearance and testimony is dispensed with. Compliance is accomplished by the summoned party making available the documents (originals or copies) for the Service.

In those cases in which information in addition to documents is desired, the agents frequently will seek to have an informal conversation with the summoned party in lieu of, or prior to, a formal interview. A number of considerations (including the relationship between the summoned party and the subject of the investigation, the status of the summoned party as a potential subject, and the existence of possible objections to providing information) enter into the decision whether to agree to an informal interview. In the majority of instances the summoned party, either through ignorance of his options, lack of concern, or perhaps even due to an informed decision, will consent to an informal interview. However, there is no legal duty to provide information to the Service on an informal basis. Moreover, there can be circumstances in which it is unwise for the summoned party to discuss (except in a formal context) matters with the investigating agents.

The formal interview, commonly referred to as a "Q & A",[a] is essentially a deposition conducted by the agent. The witness must provide the answers to questions under oath.[b] The IRS normally will have the interview recorded by a reporter or electronically. The witness should always make his own recording of the interview for several reasons. When the witness has his own recording he can review it (or have it transcribed) and correct any inadvertent errors or omissions personally without waiting for the Service to prepare the transcript and disclose it to him. Moreover, the witness can, if he wishes, make the recording available to the taxpayer's representative for such assistance as it may provide in defending the case. A witness now has a statutory right to record the interview, so long as he first notifies the Service of his intent to record it.[c] The witness also must be given a chance to read and correct the transcript of the interview and provide any necessary explanation of his statements.[d]

There is no specific authority holding that the taxpayer under investigation has the right to insist upon being present (personally or through counsel) at the formal interview of third-party witnesses.[e] Normally, however, the witness (as distinct from the taxpayer under investigation) can insist upon the presence of an authorized representative of the taxpayer during the formal interview.[f]

The witness is entitled to be represented by counsel at the formal interview.[g] Absent a conflict of interest, the witness can be represented by the same attorney who represents the taxpayer under investigation.[h] However, there are circumstances in which it may not be wise for an attorney to represent both the subject of the investigation and a witness. Unforeseen future developments could create a situation in which the attorney might be disqualified from further representation of either (or both). However, in many instances there is no realistic chance of a conflict of interest; in fact, there may be a common interest on the part of the witness and the subject, or other practical reasons (for example, the cost of "educating" independent counsel) for one attorney to represent both the subject and a witness. In such circum-

a. This name derives from the standard "Q & A" (i.e. question and answer) format of the transcripts produced by the Internal Revenue Service.

b. United States v. Lewis, 16 AFTR 2d 5244.1 (W.D.Tenn.1965).

c. I.R.C. § 7521(a)(1).

d. United States v. Lewis, 16 AFTR 2d 5244.1 (W.D.Tenn.1965).

e. See United States v. Traynor, 611 F.2d 809 (10th Cir.1979).

f. See IRS Special Agents Handbook, § 343.6.

g. I.R.C. § 7521(c). 5 U.S.C.A. § 555(b). This right applies even when the witness is only producing documents. United States v. McPhaul, 617 F.Supp. 58 (W.D.N.C.1985). However, the summoned person must personally appear and cannot simply send his authorized representative. I.R.C. § 7521(c).

h. Backer v. Commissioner, 275 F.2d 141 (5th Cir.1960).

stances, dual representation is common. However, where the witness is going to assert his own privilege against self-incrimination (as distinct from a privilege effectively on behalf of the taxpayer—for example the attorney-client privilege) it is advisable for the witness to be represented separately.

The formal interview itself is roughly equivalent to a deposition. The summons requires the witness to appear and to have available (actually or constructively) the summoned documents in his possession or control. However, as held in Reisman v. Caplin,[i] the summons *per se* does not require the witness to answer questions or to produce documents if there is a good faith objection asserted. Hence, the witness (preferably through counsel) should place on the record objections to the production of documents which are in his possession or control and not produced. As to testimony, the witness should not simply state "blanket" objections (absent an agreement with the agent). The witness must respond to specific questions with appropriate objections so that a record can be made as to the validity of the objections in the event a summons enforcement action is brought.[j] Of course if the witness has some objections which, if sustained, would invalidate the entire formal interview, then such an objection should be stated at the commencement of the interview as the ground for refusing to answer any questions at all. Thus, where there is a bona fide contention that the summons was issued in bad faith such an objection would justify (pending a ruling on the objection in a summons enforcement action) a good faith declination to produce any documents or to respond to any questions at all. Even where there is an overall objection, the witness should permit the agent to make whatever record he wishes, and should invite the agent to place on the record any specific questions upon which the agent wishes a ruling.

The formal interview will conclude with a standardized series of questions designed to establish that the witness testified freely, without being threatened or coerced by the agents. In appropriate circumstances it may be noted on the record that the witness testified under legal compulsion and not voluntarily. The witness will also be given the opportunity to make any further statement that he wishes to have on the record. The witness, or his counsel, should be alert to the fact that the purpose of the formal interview is for the Service to make a formal record tying down the testimony of the witness. In this regard, some agents might omit from the formal interview subjects upon which testimony favorable to the taxpayer under investigation would be given. Similarly, the agents might fail to ask questions which would permit explanations of answers given during the course of the questioning. The witness (preferably through questions asked by his attorney) should consider clarifying the record if the agent's questioning might otherwise leave an incorrect or incomplete impression.

i. 375 U.S. 440, 84 S.Ct. 508, 11 L.Ed.2d 459 (1964).

j. Colton v. United States, 306 F.2d 633 (2d Cir.1962).

Following the formal interview (sometimes many months thereafter) the Internal Revenue Service will prepare a transcript and, eventually, present it to the witness for review and signing. The IRS transcript should be reviewed carefully before signing. Where there are errors (either due to transcription or due to mistakes made by the witness in responses to questions) they should be noted. Errors in transcription should be corrected on the transcript itself. If there is any doubt as to what actually was said, the witness should compare the transcript with a tape recording (hopefully, the one that he made) of the interview. If the agent refuses to permit such corrections then the witness should decline to sign the transcript but should submit, in writing, a statement of the changes which would have to be made to provide a correct transcript. Errors in statements made by the witness should be corrected by an addendum to the transcript submitted by the witness. It may be that the witness will have to undergo a further session in light of the necessary corrections. However, it is essential that any material mistake made by the witness be corrected so that no incorrect statement of the witness (even though inadvertently made) becomes a part of the formal record. Where there has been a mistake by the witness, the transcript can properly be signed, but the signature should be followed by a statement indicating that the transcript is acknowledged as correct subject to the addendum correcting inadvertent errors.

Note

Section 7521, added to the Code by the Omnibus Taxpayer Bill of Rights Act of 1988, defines a taxpayer's rights in interviews with the IRS not involving criminal investigations. A summoned person is entitled to be accompanied by counsel or other representative with a power of attorney. However, a summoned person not so represented is *not* entitled to the protection of § 7521(b), which provides that a taxpayer who expresses a desire to consult with an attorney, at any time during the interview, be permitted to do so. In interviews not pursuant to a summons, the interview must be immediately suspended, regardless of whether the taxpayer has already answered one or more questions, if the taxpayer requests an opportunity, to consult.

Another major change resulting from the Taxpayer Bill of Rights pertains to the taxpayer's right to record the interview, which is now codified in § 7521. Pursuant to § 7521(a)(1) a summoned person wishing to record the interview may, upon advance request, record the interview at her own expense and with her own equipment. If the IRS intends to record the interview, § 7521(a)(2) requires that the taxpayer be informed of the recording prior to the interview. Additionally, the taxpayer may request a transcript of the interview provided the taxpayer assumes the expense of copying.

SECTION 2. THE SUMMONS POWER

The IRS has the duty to enforce compliance with the federal tax laws—in the words of the statute, to "inquire after and concerning all persons * * * who may be liable to pay any internal revenue tax * * *."[k] Although, perhaps, one can look to taxpayers for voluntary compliance [l] in terms of reporting their liability, one can hardly expect taxpayers voluntarily to assist the Service in its audits and investigations. Hence, the duty to inquire can be carried out only if the means to enforce responses to inquiries is available. The means provided by the Internal Revenue Code is the power to examine relevant data and to issue the IRS summons for documents and testimony.[m]

Every tax audit, however informally conducted, is performed pursuant to the summons authority. In the vast majority of cases audits are conducted without the use, or even mention, of an administrative summons. Informal requests for documents and for answers to questions often suffice. However, behind every request for documents or information lies the power to issue a summons.

The IRS summons clearly imposes a legal obligation upon the summoned party. However, until the decision in Reisman v. Caplin, below, the extent of that duty was not resolved. In the face of a Code provision permitting the Service to seek the arrest of anyone who "neglects or refuses to obey" a summons,[n] there was considerable concern as to the correct course of action to take if one wished to resist compliance.

REISMAN v. CAPLIN
Supreme Court of the United States, 1964.
375 U.S. 440, 84 S.Ct. 508, 11 L.Ed.2d 459.

MR. JUSTICE CLARK delivered the opinion of the Court.

[Reisman, an attorney representing the Bromleys in a tax investigation, had hired accountants to assist in the representation. The IRS issued a summons demanding that the accountants produce their workpapers and appear to provide testimony. Reisman, alleging that the accountants intended to comply with the summons in spite of what he contended were valid objections to compliance, filed an injunction action against the Commissioner and the accountants, in an attempt to restrain compliance.]

* * *

The case reaches us at a stage when the only affirmative action taken by the Commissioner is the issuance of the summonses for the accountants to appear before a hearing officer, i.e., a special agent of the Internal Revenue Service, to testify and produce records. The

---

k. I.R.C. § 7601.

l. Inasmuch as the failure to comply with reporting requirements subjects a taxpayer to a wide range of civil and criminal penalties, the term "voluntary compliance" may not be precisely accurate in describing the process by which most taxpayers report their liabilities.

m. I.R.C. § 7602. See also I.R.C. § 6333, which provides the Service with the right to demand access to books and records relating to property rights in connection with a levy to collect taxes.

n. I.R.C. § 7604(b).

accountants have not yet refused to do so. It is therefore necessary that we first consider the statutory scheme which Congress has provided for the issuance and enforcement of the summonses.

II.

Section 7602 authorizes the Secretary of the Treasury, or his delegate, for "the purpose of ascertaining the correctness of any return * * *, determining the liability of any person for any internal revenue tax * * *, or collecting any such liability * * * [t]o summon the person liable for tax * * *, or any person having possession, custody, or care of books of account containing entries relating to the business of the person liable for tax * * *, or any other person the Secretary or his delegate may deem proper, to appear * * * and to produce such books, papers, records, or other data, and to give such testimony, under oath, as may be relevant or material to such inquiry * * *." The petitioners make no claim that this provision suffers any constitutional infirmity on its face. This Court has never passed upon the rights of a party summoned to appear before a hearing officer under § 7602. However, the Government concedes that a witness or any interested party may attack the summons before the hearing officer. There are cases among the circuits which hold that both parties summoned and those affected by a disclosure may appear or intervene before the District Court and challenge the summons by asserting their constitutional or other claims. We agree with that view and see no reason why the same rule would not apply before the hearing officer. Should the challenge to the summons be rejected by the hearing examiner and the witness still refuse to testify or produce, the examiner is given no power to enforce compliance or to impose sanctions for noncompliance.

If the Secretary or his delegate wishes to enforce the summons, he must proceed under § 7402(b), which grants the District Courts of the United States jurisdiction "by appropriate process to compel such attendance, testimony, or production of books, papers, or other data."[4]

Any enforcement action under this section would be an adversary proceeding affording a judicial determination of the challenges to the summons and giving complete protection to the witness. In such a proceeding only a refusal to comply with an order of the district judge subjects the witness to contempt proceedings.

III.

It is urged that the penalties of contempt risked by a refusal to comply with the summonses are so severe that the statutory procedure amounts to a denial of judicial review. The leading cases on this question are Ex parte Young, 209 U.S. 123, 28 S.Ct. 441, 52 L.Ed. 714 (1908), and Oklahoma Operating Co. v. Love, 252 U.S. 331, 40 S.Ct. 338, 64 L.Ed. 596 (1920). However, we do not believe that this point is well

---

4. Section 7604(a) and (b) gives an additional remedy which is considered hereafter.

taken here. In *Young* certain railroad rates could be tested only by a failure to comply, which occasioned a risk of both imprisonment and large fines, regardless of the willfulness of the refusal to comply. And in *Oklahoma Operating Co.* the laundry rate fixed by the Oklahoma Corporation Commission could be tested only by contempt with a penalty of $500 per day, each day being a separate violation.

On the other hand, in tax enforcement proceedings the hearing officer has no power of enforcement or right to levy any sanctions. It is true that any person summoned who "neglects to appear or to produce" may be prosecuted under § 7210 [5] and is subject to a fine not exceeding $1,000, or imprisonment for not more than a year, or both. However, this statute on its face does not apply where the witness appears and interposes good faith challenges to the summons. It only prescribes punishment where the witness "neglects" either to appear or to produce. We need not pass upon the coverage of this provision in light of the facts here. It is sufficient to say that noncompliance is not subject to prosecution thereunder when the summons is attacked in good faith.[6]

Petitioners also point to § 7604(b) as posing the risk of arrest should the Commissioner proceed under that section for an "attachment * * * as for a contempt." Arguably, such a sanction, even though temporary, might be a penalty severe enough to bring the section within the rationale of *Young*, supra, but we do not so read § 7604(b). This section provides that where "any person summoned * * * neglects or refuses to obey such summons" the Commissioner may proceed before the United States Commissioner or the judge of the District Court "for an attachment against him as for a contempt." Upon a showing of "satisfactory proof," an attachment for the person so refusing is issued and he is brought before the United States Commissioner or the district judge who proceeds "to a hearing of the case." Upon the hearing the United States Commissioner or the district judge may "make such order as he shall deem proper, not inconsistent with the law for the punishment of contempts * * *." The predecessor of § 7604(b) was adopted by the Congress in 1864 at a time when Congress was greatly concerned with tax collection delay. The proponents of the bill emphasized that after arrest the witness could assert his objections to the summons. It appears to us that the provision was intended only to cover persons who were summoned and wholly made default or contumaciously refused to comply. Section 7402(b) came into the

---

5. Internal Revenue Code of 1954 § 7210:

"Any person who, being duly summoned to appear to testify, or to appear and produce books, accounts, records, memoranda, or other papers, as required under sections 6420(e)(2), 6421(f)(2), 7602, 7603, and 7604(b), neglects to appear or to produce such books, accounts, records, memoranda, or other papers, shall, upon conviction thereof, be fined not more than $1,000, or imprisoned not more than 1 year, or both, together with costs of prosecution."

6. The only prosecution under § 7210 is United States v. Becker, 2 Cir., 259 F.2d 869. There the word "neglect" was equated with willfulness. The Government admits that the section is inapplicable to persons who appear and in good faith interpose defenses as a basis for noncompliance.

statute in 1913 and has been uniformly used since that time.[8] As we read the legislative history, § 7604(b) remains in this comprehensive procedure provided by Congress to cover only a default or contumacious refusal to honor a summons before a hearing officer. But even in such cases, just as in a criminal prosecution under § 7210, the witness may assert his objections at the hearing before the court which is authorized to make such order as it "shall deem proper." § 7604(b).

Furthermore, we hold that in any of these procedures before either the district judge or United States Commissioner, the witness may challenge the summons on any appropriate ground. This would include, as the circuits have held, the defenses that the material is sought for the improper purpose of obtaining evidence for use in a criminal prosecution, Boren v. Tucker, 9 Cir., 239 F.2d 767, 772–773, as well as that it is protected by the attorney-client privilege. In addition, third parties might intervene to protect their interests, or in the event the taxpayer is not a party to the summons before the hearing officer, he, too, may intervene. And this would be true whether the contempt be of a civil or criminal nature. Finally, we hold that such orders are appealable. It follows that with a stay order a witness would suffer no injury while testing the summons.

Nor would there be a difference should the witness indicate—as has Peat, Marwick, Mitchell & Co.—that he would voluntarily turn the papers over to the Commissioner. If this be true, either the taxpayer or any affected party might restrain compliance, as the Commissioner suggests, until compliance is ordered by a court of competent jurisdiction. This relief was not sought here. Had it been, the Commissioner would have had to proceed for compliance, in which event the petitioners or the Bromleys might have intervened and asserted their claims.

Finding that the remedy specified by Congress works no injustice and suffers no constitutional invalidity, we remit the parties to the comprehensive procedure of the Code, which provides full opportunity for judicial review before any coercive sanctions may be imposed.

Affirmed.

Notes and Questions

1. Is the following description of summoned documents sufficiently definite?

> All information which would be necessary to enable a representative of the Internal Revenue Service to properly determine total income earned or sources of funds received for the period January 1, 1981, through December 31, 1982.

---

8. It is true that the attachment procedure of § 7604(b) has been occasionally used even where the person summoned refused to testify because of a claimed privilege. We believe that the use of § 7604(b) in that context is inappropriate. Attachment of a witness who has neither defaulted nor contumaciously refused to comply would raise constitutional considerations, which need not be considered at this time under our reading of the statute.

This same description was held to be overbroad in United States v. Lewis because it requests all relevant documents. Since the person summoned is forced to determine whether documents are relevant, it would be impossible to enforce the summons by a contempt proceeding. Further the IRS would not be able to establish that a document is relevant by simply requesting all relevant information. United States v. Lewis, 604 F.Supp. 1169 (E.D.La.1985).

2. If the summoned party does not possess the records, he cannot be compelled to obtain them from a third party from whom the IRS could also obtain them by using a third-party recordkeeper summons. The court in United States v. Karras, 57 AFTR 2d 86–881 (D.S.D.1985), held that lack of possession or control of records are appropriate grounds for contesting a summons. The Government's failure to make a showing of hardship to examine the records, in the possession of taxpayer's bank, strengthened taxpayer's argument that the records could have been obtained by the third-party recordkeeper summons.

3. The Supreme Court has settled the question of whether a summons requiring a witness to appear and execute a handwriting exemplar is enforceable. In United States v. Euge, 444 U.S. 707, 100 S.Ct. 874, 63 L.Ed.2d 141 (1980), the Court held that Congress empowered the Service to seek handwriting exemplars relevant to the investigation and the witness is obligated to oblige. The Court further held that the compulsion of handwriting exemplars is neither a search and seizure subject to Fourth Amendment protections, nor testimonial evidence protected by the Fifth Amendment privilege against self-incrimination.

SECTION 3. ENFORCEABILITY OF THE SUMMONS

A. THE "*POWELL* STANDARD"

UNITED STATES v. POWELL
Supreme Court of the United States, 1964.
379 U.S. 48, 85 S.Ct. 248, 13 L.Ed.2d 112.

Mr. Justice Harlan delivered the opinion of the Court.

In March 1963, the Internal Revenue Service, pursuant to powers afforded the Commissioner by § 7602(2) of the Internal Revenue Code of 1954, summoned respondent Powell to appear before Special Agent Tiberino to give testimony and produce records relating to the 1958 and 1959 returns of the William Penn Laundry (the taxpayer), of which Powell was president. Powell appeared before the agent but refused to produce the records. Because the taxpayer's returns had been once previously examined, and because the three-year statute of limitations barred assessment of additional deficiencies for those years except in cases of fraud (the asserted basis for this summons),[2] Powell contended

---

2. I.R.C. § 6501(c)(1), which in relevant part provides:

"In the case of a false or fraudulent return with the intent to evade tax, the tax may be assessed, or a proceeding in

that before he could be forced to produce the records the Service had to indicate some grounds for its belief that a fraud had been committed. The agent declined to give any such indication and the meeting terminated.

Thereafter the Service petitioned the District Court for the Eastern District of Pennsylvania for enforcement of the administrative summons. With this petition the agent filed an affidavit stating that he had been investigating the taxpayer's returns for 1958 and 1959; that based on this investigation the Regional Commissioner of the Service had determined an additional examination of the taxpayer's records for those years to be necessary and had sent Powell a letter to that effect; and that the agent had reason to suspect that the taxpayer had fraudulently falsified its 1958 and 1959 returns by overstating expenses. At the court hearing Powell again stated his objections to producing the records and asked the Service to show some basis for its suspicion of fraud. The Service chose to stand on the petition and the agent's affidavit, and, after argument, the District Court ruled that the agent be [allowed] to re-examine the records.

The Court of Appeals reversed. It reasoned that since the returns in question could only be reopened for fraud, re-examination of the taxpayer's records must be barred by the prohibition of § 7605(b) of the Code against "unnecessary examination" unless the Service possessed information "which might cause a reasonable man to suspect that there has been fraud in the return for the otherwise closed year"; and whether this standard has been met is to be decided "on the basis of the showing made in the normal course of an adversary proceeding * * *." The court concluded that the affidavit in itself was not sufficient to satisfy its test of probable cause. Consequently, enforcement of the summons was withheld.

* * *

We reverse, and hold that the Government need make no showing of probable cause to suspect fraud unless the taxpayer raises a substantial question that judicial enforcement of the administrative summons would be an abusive use of the court's process, predicated on more than the fact of re-examination and the running of the statute of limitations on ordinary tax liability.

* * *

Respondent primarily relies on § 7605(b) to show that the Government must establish probable cause for suspecting fraud, and that the existence of probable cause is subject to challenge by the taxpayer at the hearing. That section provides:

> "No taxpayer shall be subjected to unnecessary examination or investigations, and only one inspection of a taxpayer's books of account shall be made for each taxable year unless the taxpayer requests otherwise or unless the Secretary or his delegate, after investigation,

court for collection of such tax may be begun without assessment, at any time."

notifies the taxpayer in writing that an additional inspection is necessary."

We do not equate necessity as contemplated by this provision with probable cause or any like notion. If a taxpayer has filed fraudulent returns, a tax liability exists without regard to any period of limitations. Section 7602 authorizes the Commissioner to investigate any such liability. If, in order to determine the existence or nonexistence of fraud in the taxpayer's returns, information in the taxpayer's records is needed which is not already in the Commissioner's possession, we think the examination is not "unnecessary" within the meaning of § 7605(b). Although a more stringent interpretation is possible, one which would require some showing of cause for suspecting fraud, we reject such an interpretation because it might seriously hamper the Commissioner in carrying out investigations he thinks warranted, forcing him to litigate and prosecute appeals on the very subject which he desires to investigate, and because the legislative history of § 7605(b) indicates that no severe restriction was intended.

* * *

Congress recognized a need for a curb on the investigating powers of low-echelon revenue agents, and considered that it met this need simply and fully by requiring such agents to clear any repetitive examination with a superior. For us to import a probable cause standard to be enforced by the courts would substantially overshoot the goal which the legislators sought to attain. There is no intimation in the legislative history that Congress intended the courts to oversee the Commissioner's determinations to investigate. No mention was made of the statute of limitations and the exception for fraud.

We are asked to read § 7605(b) together with the limitations sections in such a way as to impose a probable cause standard upon the Commissioner from the expiration date of the ordinary limitations period forward. Without some solid indication in the legislative history that such a gloss was intended, we find it unacceptable. Our reading of the statute is said to render the first clause of § 7605(b) surplusage to a large extent, for, as interpreted, the clause adds little beyond the relevance and materiality requirements of § 7602. That clause does appear to require that the information sought is not already within the Commissioner's possession, but we think its primary purpose was no more than to emphasize the responsibility of agents to exercise prudent judgment in wielding the extensive powers granted to them by the Internal Revenue Code.

* * *

Reading the statutes as we do, the Commissioner need not meet any standard of probable cause to obtain enforcement of his summons, either before or after the three-year statute of limitations on ordinary tax liabilities has expired. He must show that (1) the investigation will be conducted pursuant to a legitimate purpose, that (2) the inquiry may be relevant to the purpose, that (3) the information sought is not already within the Commissioner's possession, and that the administrative steps required by the Code have been followed—in particular that the "Secretary or his delegate," after investigation, has determined the further examination to be necessary and has notified the taxpayer in writing to that effect. This does not make meaningless the adversary hearing to which the taxpayer is entitled before enforcement is ordered.[18] At the hearing he "may challenge the summons on any appropriate ground," Reisman v. Caplin, 375 U.S. 440, at 449, 84 S.Ct. at 513. Nor does our reading of the statutes mean that under no circumstances may the court inquire into the underlying reasons for the examination. It is the court's process which is invoked to enforce the administrative summons and a court may not permit its process to be abused. Such an abuse would take place if the summons had been issued for an improper purpose, such as to harass the taxpayer or to put pressure on him to settle a collateral dispute, or for any other purpose reflecting on the good faith of the particular investigation. The burden of showing an abuse of the court's process is on the taxpayer, and it is not met by a mere showing, as was made in this case, that the statute of limitations for ordinary deficiencies has run or that the records in question have already been once examined.

The judgment of the Court of Appeals is reversed, and the case is remanded for further proceedings consistent with this opinion.

B. LEGITIMATE PURPOSE AND GOOD FAITH

UNITED STATES v. ABRAHAMS
United States Court of Appeals, Ninth Circuit, 1990.
905 F.2d 1276.

I. Facts

Abrahams is an attorney who prepares income tax returns for his clients, and also represents many of them in disputes with the Internal Revenue Service before the Tax and Claims Courts. As a preparer, Abrahams' routine practice has been to file amended client returns, which claim new deductions, just before the close of the statutory three-year period for assessing tax liability. The IRS is investigating this conduct.

Acting pursuant to 26 U.S.C. § 7602, the IRS issued a summons directing Abrahams to produce material relevant to his preparation of client returns from 1978 to 1984. Abrahams objected that the summons called for virtually all of his files and that it allowed only twelve days for compliance. The IRS responded by limiting its request to

---

18. Because § 7604(a) contains no provision specifying the procedure to be followed in invoking the court's jurisdiction, the Federal Rules of Civil Procedure apply, Martin v. Chandis Securities Co., 9 Cir., 128 F.2d 731. The proceedings are instituted by filing a complaint, followed by answer and hearing. If the taxpayer has contumaciously refused to comply with the administrative summons and the Service fears he may flee the jurisdiction, application for the sanctions available under § 7604(b) might be made simultaneously with the filing of the complaint.

documents used in preparing returns for thirty-nine named clients, extending the deadline fifteen days, and offering clerical assistance. Abrahams refused to comply.

As authorized by 26 U.S.C. § 7604(b), the IRS filed a petition in district court to compel compliance with the summons. The IRS presented a declaration by the special agent conducting the Abrahams investigation, who stated that his purpose was "to determine whether [Abrahams] wilfully aided or assisted or procured, counseled or advised the preparation of federal income tax returns which are fraudulent or false," particularly with respect to deductions claimed on amended returns. Henderson Declaration at 2–3. Abrahams responded by alleging that the summons had been issued "solely to unearth evidence of criminal conduct"; to gather information for the Justice Department to use against him and for the IRS Audit Division to use against his clients.

Following a hearing, the court ordered partial compliance: Abrahams was to produce documentation used in his preparation of twenty "representative" returns (of Abrahams' choosing) for each of the years in question. The court also ordered that the IRS, in pursuing its investigation of Abrahams, was not to interview any of Abrahams' clients unless Abrahams was present in his capacity as counsel.

The United States and Abrahams appealed to this court, which (in an unpublished disposition) reversed and remanded for a limited evidentiary hearing on Abrahams' allegations of bad faith and harassment. *See United States v. Abrahams,* 833 F.2d 1017 (9th Cir.1987). At that hearing, Abrahams examined the special agent investigating him and three other agents involved in his clients' cases. The district court then concluded that Abrahams had not substantiated his charges. The court again ordered enforcement, with the same restrictions imposed previously.

Both parties now appeal once more.

II. Abrahams' Appeal

Abrahams contends that the lower court erred (1) in finding that the summons had been issued in "good faith," as required for enforcement. We disagree, and affirm the district court's decisions on these issues.

A. *The Good Faith Elements*

Contrary to Abrahams' contention, the summons satisfied the requirements for enforcement. In order to establish a *prima facie* case, the IRS had only to make a "minimal" showing that it issued the summons for a legitimate purpose, and that the information sought in the summons was relevant to that purpose. *Stuart v. United States,* 813 F.2d 243, 248 (9th Cir.1987) (citing *United States v. Powell,* 379 U.S. 48, 57–58, 85 S.Ct. 248, 254–55, 13 L.Ed.2d 112 (1964)). Declarations by the special agent that he was investigating Abrahams for possible improper conduct in preparing clients' returns and that the summoned material was necessary for the investigation satisfied the minimal standard. *Liberty Financial Services v. United States*, 778 F.2d 1390, 1392 (9th Cir.1985). The *prima facie* case having been made, a "heavy" burden fell upon Abrahams to disprove the IRS assertions. *Id.* The record developed below indicates that the district court committed no "clear error" in concluding that Abrahams had failed to carry that burden. *Ponsford v. United States*, 771 F.2d 1305, 1308 (9th Cir.1985).

1. Purpose.

Abrahams' objection to the district court's finding of legitimate purpose raises two distinct issues, one a question of law and the other a question of fact. First, Abrahams argues that the summons is invalid because tax collection was not the IRS' objective in issuing it. Abrahams is right that the investigation is not aimed at collecting taxes from him, but he is plainly wrong that the summons power may be used only for that purpose. The IRS may issue a summons in order to "inquir[e] into any offense connected with the administration or enforcement of the internal revenue laws." 26 U.S.C. § 7602(b). Improper conduct in the preparation of clients' returns clearly constitutes "an offense connected with the administration and enforcement" of the tax laws, and therefore falls within the scope of the summons power.

Secondly, Abrahams argues that, despite its claims to the contrary, the IRS issued the summons in order to gain information for use in the Tax and Claims Court cases and to harass him because he represents clients against the IRS. More specifically, Abrahams offered two factual circumstances as evidence of that allegation: (1) the name of an IRS lawyer handling Tax Court litigation involving Abrahams' clients appeared as part of an intra-office reference code in the margin of a letter to Abrahams from the special agent handling his investigation; (2) when leaving the District Counsel's office after an unsuccessful effort to have the Counsel stipulate to an agreement in his clients' cases, Abrahams encountered the special agent who issued the summons.[5]

Under extended questioning by Abrahams' counsel at the hearing, the special agent directing the Abrahams investigation held fast to his assertion that he issued the summons to inquire into possible improper conduct by Abrahams as a preparer of his clients' returns. None of the witnesses testified that anyone involved in the client cases suggested, encouraged or participated in issuing the summons to Abrahams. Hence, as the district court found, Abrahams was not able to show that the purpose stated by the IRS was "merely camouflage for an ulterior non-tax motive." *United States v. Zolin*, 809 F.2d 1411, 1416 (9th Cir.1987), *aff'd in part and vac'd in part on other grounds*, [491] U.S. [554], 109 S.Ct. 2619, 105 L.Ed.2d 469 (1989).

5. Abrahams further urges that, by demanding documents respecting deductions whose validity is at issue in, and to be determined by, the Tax and Claims Court actions, the IRS betrayed its lack of a legitimate purpose in issuing the summons. This argument misses the point that the focus of the inquiry is *Abrahams' conduct as a preparer*, not the tax liability of his clients.

2. *Relevance.*

Abrahams' argument that the summons demands documents that are not relevant to the IRS purpose is meritless. The IRS is investigating Abrahams' conduct in preparing his clients' tax returns; nothing is more likely to "throw light" on that subject than the documents supplied to him by his clients or generated by him for the purpose of filing those returns. *Zolin*, 809 F.2d at 1414 (defining standard of relevance for IRS summons).

IV. Conclusion

We affirm the district court's conclusion that the summons satisfies the requirements of *Powell* and is not violative of the fourth amendment or the attorney-client privilege.

Affirmed in Part; Vacated in Part; Remanded.

UNITED STATES v. MICHAUD
United States Court of Appeals, Seventh Circuit, 1990.
907 F.2d 750.

BAUER, CHIEF JUDGE, joined by CUMMINGS, HARLINGTON WOOD, JR., CUDAHY, COFFEY, FLAUM and KANNE, CIRCUIT JUDGES.

In this case we reconsider *United States v. Michaud* ("*Michaud I*"), in which a panel of this court reversed an order by District Judge Terence T. Evans. Judge Evans quashed several summonses issued by the Internal Revenue Service ("the Service") which directed the Michauds to submit to fingerprinting and to provide handwriting exemplars. The Service claimed (and still claims) that this information is relevant to its civil investigation into the employment and unemployment tax liabilities of Superior Engineering, Inc., a Green Bay corporation of which the Michauds were shareholders and officers. In the order at issue here, Judge Evans appeared to reject this claim and denied enforcement based in some part on that reason. The panel in *Michaud I* found reversible error in that decision, holding that Judge Evans had no basis for quashing the summonses. Because Judge Evans' order is ambiguous on several potentially dispositive points, we depart from the tack taken by the panel and remand to Judge Evans for additional findings.

At the heart of this controversy lie important questions of when and how the Service can, in the course of a civil investigation, bring to bear against a taxpayer the full weight of federal enforcement mechanisms. Primary responsibility over these questions has been entrusted to the federal district courts, which have the power and duty to monitor these investigations through the enforcement (and non-enforcement) of the Service's demands on taxpayers. 26 U.S.C. §§ 7402, 7604 & 7605. *See also United States v. Bisceglia*, 420 U.S. 141, 146–47, 95 S.Ct. 915, 918–19, 43 L.Ed.2d 88 (1974) and the cases cited there. "Congress has provided protection from arbitrary or capricious action by placing the federal courts between the Government and the person summoned." *Id.* at 151, 95 S.Ct. at 921.

The above-cited sections of the Internal Revenue Code give district courts the authority to "render such judgments and decrees as may be necessary or appropriate for the enforcement of the internal revenue laws," § 7402(a), and to "make such order[s] as [they] deem proper, not inconsistent with the law for the punishment of contempts, to enforce obedience to the requirements of the [Service's] summons...." § 7604(b).[1] Under this authority, district courts deny enforcement of the Service's demands when they find that the Service is acting in bad faith or attempting to abuse the court's process. "Such an abuse would take place if the summons had been issued for an improper purpose, such as to harass the taxpayer or put pressure on him to settle a collateral dispute, or for any purpose reflecting on the good faith of the particular investigation." *United States v. Powell,* 379 U.S. 48, 58, 85 S.Ct. 248, 255, 13 L.Ed.2d 112 (1964).

Along with this power and duty to check for abuse, district courts hold the Service to the burden of making a *prima facie* showing of "good faith." As established in *Powell,* the *prima facie* case must include the following elements:

> [The Service] must show [1] that the investigation will be conducted pursuant to a legitimate purpose, [2] that the inquiry may be relevant to the purpose, [3] that the information sought is not already within the [Service's] possession, and [4] that the administrative steps required by the Code have been followed * * *.

379 U.S. at 57–58. Thus, a district court can deny the Service's demands on a taxpayer if it finds that the Service has fallen short of establishing these four elements, or if the taxpayer otherwise establishes that the Service's request is in bad faith.

Beyond this "good faith" requirement, the Code has long prohibited enforcement of a Service summons after the matter has been referred to the Justice Department for criminal prosecution. *See* 26 U.S.C. § 7602(c) and its predecessors. The Supreme Court, in *United States v. LaSalle National Bank,* 437 U.S. 298, 98 S.Ct. 2357, 57 L.Ed.2d 221 (1978), read § 7602 to include a prohibition against the Service's use of an administrative summons solely for criminal investigatory purposes.

---

1. *See also* 26 U.S.C. § 7402(b):

   If any person is summoned under the internal revenue laws to appear, to testify, or to produce books, papers, or other data, the district court of the United States for the district in which the person resides or may be found shall have jurisdiction by appropriate process to compel such attendance, testimony, or production of books, papers, or other data.

   The district courts also enforce the Code's restrictions on the time, place and manner of the Service's examinations of taxpayers contained in § 7605:

   No taxpayer shall be subjected to unnecessary examination or investigations, and only one inspection of a taxpayer's books of account shall be made for each taxable year unless the taxpayer requests otherwise or unless the [Service], after investigation, notifies the taxpayer in writing that an additional inspection is necessary.

   26 U.S.C. § 7605(b).

In *LaSalle*, the Court reviewed a decision of this court in which we held that enforcement can also be denied in certain cases short of a formal referral to the Justice Department: "[T]he use of an administrative summons solely for criminal purposes is a quintessential example of bad faith." The Supreme Court agreed that enforcement can and should be denied when the Service is attempting to exploit its civil investigatory powers as a *de facto* grand jury: "We shall not countenance delay in submitting a recommendation to the Justice Department when there is an institutional commitment to make the referral and the Service merely would like to gather additional evidence for the prosecution." *LaSalle*, 437 U.S. at 316–17, 98 S.Ct. at 2367–68. (The Court reversed our decision on the outcome, however, because it found insufficient evidence of such an institutional commitment. *Id.*, at 318–19, 98 S.Ct. at 2368.) Thus, under § 7602 and *LaSalle*, a summons issued by the Service after it has referred the matter to the Justice Department, or after it, in an institutional sense, has abandoned any proper civil purpose, should not be enforced.

In this case, it is impossible to tell from Judge Evans' order whether and to what extent his decision to quash the summonses rested on any one of (or perhaps all of) these grounds. The operative passage from his brief order merits quotation in full.

> Although I believe the failure to provide me with the full story of what occurred * * * in and of itself justifies denying enforcement to the summonses, a more fundamental reason for denying enforcement exists. The purpose of the investigation by the [Service] is "to investigate the federal employment and unemployment tax liabilities of Superior Engineering * * * for the taxable years 1983 through 1986" [quoting government submissions]. I do not think the handwriting or the fingerprints of the Michauds are necessary to establish the tax liabilities of Superior Engineering. Furthermore, requiring them to appear at a police station to be fingerprinted appears to be a little heavy-handed and perhaps violative of 26 U.S.C. § 7605(b) * * *.
>
> Also, it should be noted that assessments have been issued against Superior Engineering alleging that its taxes were not properly stated and that the correct amount (higher, of course) has been determined by the [Service]. Implicit in this action is the assumption that the [Service] knows the tax liabilities of Superior Engineering. Therefore, the reason, if there ever was a good one, for wanting the Michauds' handwriting and fingerprints seems to have evaporated. And lastly, it appears that the aroma of a criminal proceeding is emanating from this investigation, and the government should not be allowed to use these civil proceedings to arm itself for that fight should it eventually occur.

Unfortunately, this passage raises at least as many questions as it answers. First, does the court's decision actually rely on the omission in the agent's affidavit, and/or the "heavy-handedness" of requiring the Michauds to appear at a police station to be fingerprinted? As the panel in *Michaud I* noted, these factors, at least as they are currently developed in the record, do not qualify as the kind of "abuse of process" or harassment that trigger the court's power under either *Powell* or § 7604(b), nor do they appear to make the Service's demand "unnecessary" as described in § 7605(b). The misleading statement was found by Judge Evans to be unintentional, and merely choosing a police station for the fingerprinting, assuming it was reasonably convenient and was not chosen for some improper purpose, does not appear to constitute harassment. Because the record is inadequate to confirm or deny such dispositive assumptions, however, this issue must be remanded to Judge Evans, who has dealt first-hand with these parties and is in a much better position to assess their conduct, before it can be resolved by this court.

Second, how are we to interpret the court's discussion of the purpose(s) of the investigation and the relevance of the requested information thereto? Judge Evans states that "*I do not think* the handwriting or the fingerprints of the Michauds are *necessary* * * *," and that "the reason, if there ever was a good one, for wanting the Michauds' handwriting and fingerprints *seems* to have evaporated" (emphasis added). He also speaks of an "assumption" that is "implicit" in the fact that assessments have issued against Superior Engineering. By these statements, does Judge Evans mean to say that, from his review of the facts and the testimony and behavior of the parties, the purpose of the investigation was limited to the corporation's tax liabilities, and that, because this purpose has been exhausted, the requested information is no longer relevant? Or is it that the requested information was never relevant to the sole, legitimate purpose of the investigation, making the government's request unenforceable *ab initio*? Explicit findings along these lines could result in the conclusion that the government has not met the four-part "good faith" predicate established in *Powell*, 379 U.S. 48, 85 S.Ct. 248, that the sole remaining purpose is to harass the Michauds, or that enforcement of the summonses would otherwise be an abuse of process. The statements in Judge Evans' order, however, though sufficient to raise these troubling concerns, do not constitute the findings necessary to resolve them.

Third, and finally, by expressing concern that "the aroma of a criminal proceeding is emanating from this investigation, and the government should not be allowed to use these civil proceedings to arm itself for that fight," was the court's intent to invoke the *de facto* grand jury concerns discussed in *LaSalle*, 437 U.S. 298, 98 S.Ct. 2357? By its terms, *LaSalle* requires the court to find evidence that the Service has made an "institutional commitment" to refer the matter to the Justice Department, *id.*, and this court has held that, to successfully raise the "sole criminal purpose" defense, a taxpayer must come forward with specific facts that establish that the summons has "*no* civil purpose whatsoever," and that the Service "has abandoned any institutional pursuit of a civil tax determination." *United States v. Kis*, 658 F.2d 526, 538–42 (7th Cir.1981) (emphasis in original), *cert. denied sub nom. Salkin v. United States*, 455 U.S. 1018, 102 S.Ct. 1712, 72 L.Ed.2d 135

(1982). Judge Evans' one-sentence statement showing concern over an "aroma," without more, does not constitute a sufficient finding to raise the *LaSalle* issue.

Because of these ambiguities, we remand this case to Judge Evans for additional findings. Specifically, the court should develop further whether the Service is harassing the Michauds for some improper purpose; whether it is attempting to abuse the court's process; whether it has failed to establish its *Powell* good faith predicate; whether it has made an "institutional commitment" to refer the Michauds to the Justice Department for criminal prosecution; and, importantly, which of these grounds (if any) it finds dispositive. Only then can this court assess and resolve the issues discussed in this opinion; issues that a majority of this court found sufficient to merit this *en banc* rehearing.

POSNER, CIRCUIT JUDGE, with whom EASTERBROOK, RIPPLE, and MANION, CIRCUIT JUDGES, join, dissenting.

There is neither material ambiguity in the district court's opinion nor any possible ground on which to deny enforcement of the government's summons. We should, as the panel did, reverse outright. The remand throws a monkey wrench into the machinery for the investigation of tax violations and in the course of doing so commits a serious error in the interpretation of the tax-summons statute. A fishing expedition into the government's motives, such as the court invites the district judge to conduct, is inconsistent with the summary nature of proceedings to enforce tax summonses. Worse, the court allows the district judge to troll for fish in an area that Congress has placed beyond judicial authority.

To refuse to enforce a summons because the government has made an immaterial mistake (saying the Michauds had failed to appear, rather than that they had failed to cooperate) violates the principle that courts do not punish governmental misconduct by dismissing valid cases. *United States v. Hasting,* 461 U.S. 499, 103 S.Ct. 1974, 76 L.Ed.2d 96 (1983).

Finally and most important, the fact that the government may have wanted to use the summons procedure to obtain evidence for use in a criminal proceeding against the Michauds is not an authorized ground for refusing to enforce the summons. The statute could not be clearer. "The purposes for which [the IRS may issue and execute a tax-investigation summons] include the purpose of inquiring into any offense connected with the administration or enforcement of the internal revenue laws." 26 U.S.C. § 7602(b). The only exception is "if a Justice Department referral is in effect with respect to such person," §§ 7602(c)(1), (2)(A)(i). Since no such recommendation has yet been made, no referral is in effect and the IRS is entitled to use the summons to investigate the potential criminal liability of the Michauds.

Since the government's entitlement to enforcement of the summons is plain, *United States v. Abrahams, supra,* no purpose can be served by remanding the case to the district judge for further findings or the taking of evidence. We should reverse with directions to enforce the summons.

APPENDIX TO DISSENT: THE PANEL'S OPINION

Note: The TEFRA Provisions

Under *LaSalle National Bank,* an administrative summons could not be used once the IRS had referred a case to the Department of Justice for prosecution or had made an "institutional commitment" to abandon the pursuit of civil tax determination or collection. Congress believed that the *LaSalle* standard had "spawned protracted litigation without any meaningful results for taxpayers," and that a clear definition of when the power to issue a summons exists and when it does not exist in cases with a criminal content would simplify administration of the laws without prejudicing the rights of taxpayers. Accordingly, to permit the drawing of a clear distinction, section 333 of TEFRA revised Code § 7602 (effective September 4, 1982) to expand the purposes for which a summons may be issued and to define clearly what is meant by a "Justice Department referral."

Subsection (b) of § 7602 provides that the purposes for which any action authorized by subsection (a) of § 7602 (including the issuance of a summons) may be taken *include* "the purpose of inquiring into any offense connected with the administration or enforcement of the internal revenue laws." However, under § 7602(c)(1), no summons may be issued and no summons enforcement action may be commenced with respect to any person if a "Justice Department referral" is in effect with respect to such person.

A "Justice Department referral" is in effect if there has been an IRS recommendation to Justice for a grand jury investigation or for a prosecution, or if Justice has made a request under Code § 6103(h)(3)(B) for a tax return or return information. A "Justice Department referral" is terminated when the Justice Department declines or discontinues a grand jury investigation or declines prosecution (including a decision not to prosecute on tax charges one as to whom a request for return or return information was made), or after final disposition of any criminal prosecution pertaining to the tax laws. I.R.C. § 7602(c)(2). For purposes of § 7602(c), each taxable period (or, if there is no taxable period, each taxable event) and each type of tax imposed by the Internal Revenue Code is to be treated separately. I.R.C. § 7602(c)(3).

PICKEL v. UNITED STATES
United States Court of Appeals, Third Circuit, 1984.
746 F.2d 176.

OPINION OF THE COURT

BECKER, CIRCUIT JUDGE.

The government appeals from an order of the United States District Court for the Western District of Pennsylvania quashing two summonses issued, pursuant to 26 U.S.C. § 7602 (1983), by the Internal Revenue Service. The district court refused to enforce the summonses because of the violation of a sequestration order by a government agent, the refusal of the government to identify an FBI informant, and the court's conclusion that the IRS was acting in "bad faith" by using its civil arm to develop a criminal case. We reverse and remand for further proceedings.

I. FACTS AND PROCEDURAL HISTORY

Bruce Pickel is the major shareholder and officer of two corporations, Gardner Steel Corporation and H. Wolfe Iron and Metal Company. In September 1981, IRS Revenue Agent William Manolis conducted an audit of the income tax returns of Pickel, his wife, and the two corporations. During the investigation, Pickel informed Manolis that he had sold a number of securities from a pension fund of one of the corporations to pay off a gambling debt. Pickel also told Manolis that he had since repaid the fund. Thereafter, Manolis independently uncovered other information which, in his mind, indicated the existence of fraud in one or more of the returns under examination. Following established procedures, Manolis referred the case to the IRS's Criminal Investigation Division (CID) for an investigation into possible tax fraud.

In July 1982, the Pittsburgh office of the FBI was told by an informant that Pickel was embezzling money from one of the corporate pension funds. The FBI initiated an investigation into the allegations, headed by Agent Peter McCann. In November 1982, the IRS and the FBI each discovered that the other was investigating Pickel. FBI Agent McCann then deferred his investigation until the IRS investigation was terminated, because both inquiries would require access to the same pension records. Shortly thereafter, IRS Special Agent Ruggiero issued the summonses that are the subject of this case.

The Pickels filed a petition to quash each summons in the district court, pursuant to 26 U.S.C. § 7609(b). In their petitions the Pickels asserted, *inter alia*, that the purpose of the summonses was to gather information for the conduct of an FBI investigation rather than for a valid IRS investigation, and therefore that they were not issued in good faith, and further that the IRS was already in possession of the information it sought.

Orders granting the petitions to quash were filed. The government appeals.

II. DISCUSSION

The precise basis of the court's decision to grant the petitions to quash the summonses is unclear. It appears to be based in relatively equal measure on three factors: (1) the court's displeasure over the violation of its sequestration order; (2) the court's conclusion that the government acted in bad faith by using civil processes to aid a criminal investigation; and (3) the government's failure to disclose the identity of the FBI's source.

* * *

C. The Government's Alleged Bad Faith

26 U.S.C. § 7602 empowers the IRS to summon taxpayers for inquiry into their tax liability, to examine "any books, papers, records, or other data" relevant to the inquiry, and to take the testimony of the taxpayer. The Tax Equity and Fiscal Responsibility Act of 1982 (TEFRA) Pub.L. No. 97–248, 96 Stat. 324 (1982), amended § 7602 in two ways. First it expanded the purposes for which the summons power could be used, to include criminal as well as civil tax investigations. *Moutevelis v. United States*, 727 F.2d 313 (3d Cir.1984). Second, it drew a "bright line" delineating where the summons power ended: at the point where an investigation was referred to the Justice Department for prosecution. By this change, Congress intended to establish a mechanical test for determining the validity of the summons.

The sections of TEFRA that deal with administrative summonses were, in part, a response to *United States v. LaSalle National Bank*, 437 U.S. 298, 98 S.Ct. 2357, 57 L.Ed.2d 221 (1978). *LaSalle National Bank* dealt with the application of the "good faith" requirement for the enforcement of administrative summonses to cases in which a summons was being used to investigate a criminal violation of the tax laws. Prior to TEFRA, the good faith requirement limited the use of summonses to civil investigations; a summons issued as part of a criminal investigation was considered to be improper, because it fell beyond the scope of congressional authorization and thus was held to be unenforceable. In *LaSalle National Bank*, the agent who issued the summons was found to be conducting his investigation "solely for the purpose of unearthing evidence of criminal conduct." 437 U.S. 299, 98 S.Ct. 2359. Nevertheless, the summonses were ordered enforced. The court determined that the criminal and civil elements of tax enforcement were inherently intertwined. "When an investigation examines the possibility of criminal misconduct, it also necessarily inquires about the appropriateness of the 50% civil tax penalty." *Id.* at 309, 98 S.Ct. 2363.

The four dissenters, in an opinion by Justice Stewart, argued against an examination of the "institutional good faith" of the IRS as the yardstick for summons enforcement. They preferred a bright line test: to enforce a summons it must be issued in good faith and prior to a recommendation for criminal prosecution. 437 U.S. at 320, 98 S.Ct. at 2369, quoting *Donaldson v. United States*, 400 U.S. 517 at 536, 91 S.Ct. at 545. Section 7602, according to the dissenters, did not prohibit the issuance of a summons for a purely criminal investigation, and the civil/criminal distinction embodied in the good faith requirement was "unjustified, unworkable and unwise." 437 U.S. at 321, 98 S.Ct. at 2369. Congress codified the position of the dissenters in *LaSalle National Bank* by enacting the TEFRA amendments to section 7602. *Moutevelis v. United States*, 727 F.2d at 315. A summons is now enforceable if it is issued in good faith, i.e., if it is for the purpose of inquiring into any offense connected with the administration or enforcement of the internal revenue laws, and if it is issued before there is a Justice Department referral.

The IRS advanced uncontradicted evidence that the summonses in controversy here were issued because Pickel had admitted to the revenue agent that he had "borrowed" funds from one of the corporate pension funds, and because the revenue agent discovered other indications of fraud in the tax returns of Pickel and his wife, in possible violation of 26 U.S.C. § 7206(1). The Pickels, as the parties opposing the summonses, bore the burden of showing either (1) that the summonses were not issued for a congressionally authorized purpose under § 7602, i.e., were not issued as part of a legitimate investigation into a violation of the tax laws, but were instead issued to gather evidence for another agency or to harrass or pressure taxpayers in connection with another matter, or (2) that a Justice Department referral had taken place. This burden has been characterized as a heavy one, *LaSalle National Bank,* 437 U.S. 298, 98 S.Ct. 2357, and as "almost insurmountable." *United States v. Garden State National Bank,* 607 F.2d 61, 69 (3d Cir.1979).

The district court based its decision to quash the summons in part on the fact that the IRS was using its "civil arm in order to develop a criminal case" against the taxpayer. Investigation of criminal violations of the Internal Revenue Code, however, is a valid purpose for issuance of a summons under § 7602. *Moutevelis,* 727 F.2d at 315. We do not doubt that portions of the *Powell* and *LaSalle* discussions of bad faith retain vitality and that where the taxpayer can prove that the summons is issued solely to harass him, or to force him to settle a collateral dispute, *Powell,* 379 U.S. at 58, 85 S.Ct. at 255, or that the IRS is acting solely as an information-gathering agency for other departments, such as the Department of Justice, *LaSalle,* 437 U.S. at 317, 98 S.Ct. at 2367, or the FBI, the summons will be unenforceable because of the IRS's bad faith. Congress has not authorized the IRS to pursue these ends.[13] But the Pickels have not come forward with any evidence that would justify such a conclusion.

III. Conclusion

We have examined the three factors on which the district court relied in quashing the summons, and have concluded that none of them justifies the district court's action in this case, nor would they taken together. The judgment of the District Court will be reversed, and the case remanded for proceedings consistent with this opinion.

Notes and Questions

1. Do the TEFRA provisions adequately address the following comment made by the Supreme Court in *LaSalle:*

> * * * We shall not countenance delay in submitting a recommendation to the Justice Department when there is an institutional com-

---

13. It is also quite clear that Congress did not intend for the TEFRA amendments to IRC § 7602 to broaden the right of criminal discovery, or infringe on the grand jury's domain. Joint Comm. on Taxation, *supra,* at 236; Sen.Rep. No. 494, 97th Cong., 2d Sess., 286.

mitment to make the referral and the Service merely would like to gather additional evidence for the prosecution. Such a delay would be tantamount to the use of the summons authority after the recommendation and would permit the Government to expand its criminal discovery rights. * * *

437 U.S. 298, at 316–317, 98 S.Ct. 2357, at 2367?

2. Under TEFRA, a Justice Department referral which occurs after both the issuance of the summons and the commencement of an enforcement action does not invalidate the summons or bar the enforcement action. See Uhrig v. United States, 601 F.Supp. 881 (D.Md.1985).

3. The motive of an informant is not a relevant consideration in determining whether a summons was issued in good faith. In United States v. Cortese, 614 F.2d 914 (3d Cir.1980), the court held that the motive of an informant does not taint the motive of the IRS. The court did warn that a different result could be reached if it were found that either the Service or the investigating agent was motivated by the same force that motivated the informant.

4. A summons issued with regard to taxpayer A's liability for the purpose of obtaining A's cooperation in connection with an investigation of taxpayer B is enforceable. United States v. Equitable Trust Co., 611 F.2d 492 (4th Cir.1979). According to the court, there was no bad faith on the part of the IRS resulting from the discussion of immunity with taxpayer A. The court held that the IRS is expressly provided with the authority to allow both criminal and civil immunity in return for testimony against another.

5. The court in United States v. Gimbel held that the IRS does not act in "bad faith" when it seeks to enforce a summons after it has issued a notice of deficiency and the taxpayer has filed a petition in the Tax Court. See United States v. Gimbel, 782 F.2d 89 (7th Cir.1986). Even though there was a pending Tax Court proceeding, the Government still had a legitimate interest in properly determining a taxpayer's liability and the documents it seeks are relevant to that determination. In such a case, the court believed it could not be said that the Government's attempt to enforce the summons was in "bad faith."

C. RELEVANCE

UNITED STATES v. ARTHUR YOUNG & COMPANY

Supreme Court of the United States, 1984.
465 U.S. 805, 104 S.Ct. 1495, 79 L.Ed.2d 826.

CHIEF JUSTICE BURGER delivered the opinion of the Court:

[The Supreme Court granted certiorari to consider whether tax accrual workpapers prepared by an independent certified public accountant in the course of a regular financial audit were protected from disclosure in response to a summons issued under Code § 7602. The following discussion of relevance thus arose in the context of whether the workpapers were privileged from disclosure.]

* * *

I

A

Respondent Arthur Young & Co. is a firm of certified public accountants. As the independent auditor for respondent Amerada Hess Corp., Young is responsible for reviewing the financial statements prepared by Amerada as required by the federal securities laws. In the course of its review of these financial statements, Young verified Amerada's statement of its contingent tax liabilities, and, in so doing, prepared the tax accrual workpapers at issue in this case. Tax accrual workpapers are documents and memoranda relating to Young's evaluation of Amerada's reserves for contingent tax liabilities. Such workpapers sometimes contain information pertaining to Amerada's financial transactions, identify questionable positions Amerada may have taken on its tax returns, and reflect Young's opinions regarding the validity of such positions.

In 1975 the Internal Revenue Service began a routine audit to determine Amerada's corporate income tax liability for the tax years 1972 through 1974. When the audit revealed that Amerada had made questionable payments of $7830 from a "special disbursement account," the IRS instituted a criminal investigation of Amerada's tax returns as well. In that process, pursuant to Code § 7602, the IRS issued an administrative summons to Young, which required Young to make available to the IRS all its Amerada files, including its tax accrual workpapers. Amerada instructed Young not to comply with the summons.

The IRS then commenced this enforcement action against Young in the United States District Court for the Southern District of New York. Amerada intervened. * * * The District Court found that Young's tax accrual workpapers were relevant to the IRS investigation within the meaning of § 7602 and refused to recognize an accountant-client privilege that would protect the workpapers. Accordingly, the District Court ordered the summons enforced.

B

A divided United States Court of Appeals for the Second Circuit affirmed in part and reversed in part. The Court of Appeals majority agreed with the District Court that the tax accrual workpapers were relevant to the IRS investigation of Amerada, but held that the public interest in promoting full disclosure to public accountants, and in turn ensuring the integrity of the securities markets, required protection for the work that such independent auditors perform for publicly owned companies. * * *

* * *

We granted certiorari, [459] U.S. [1199], 103 S.Ct. 1180, 75 L.Ed.2d 429 (1983). We affirm in part and reverse in part.

* * *

In seeking access to Young's tax accrual workpapers, the IRS exercised the summons power conferred by Code § 7602, which authorizes the Secretary of the Treasury to summon and "examine any books, papers, records, or other data which may be relevant or material" to a particular tax inquiry. The District Court and the Court of Appeals determined that the tax accrual workpapers at issue in this case satisfied the relevance requirement of § 7602, because they "might have thrown light upon" the correctness of Amerada's tax return.[11] * * * We agree that such workpapers are relevant within the meaning of § 7602.

As the language of § 7602 clearly indicates, an IRS summons is not to be judged by the relevance standards used in deciding whether to admit evidence in federal court. Cf.Fed.Rule Evid. 401. The language "may be" reflects Congress' express intention to allow the IRS to obtain items of even *potential* relevance to an ongoing investigation, without reference to its admissibility. The purpose of Congress is obvious: the Service can hardly be expected to know whether such data will in fact be relevant until it is procured and scrutinized. As a tool of discovery, the § 7602 summons is critical to the investigative and enforcement functions of the IRS, the Service therefore should not be required to establish that the documents it seeks are actually relevant in any technical, evidentiary sense.

That tax accrual workpapers are not actually used in the preparation of tax returns by the taxpayer or its own accountants does not bar a finding of relevance within the meaning of § 7602. The filing of a corporate tax return entails much more than filling in the blanks on an IRS form in accordance with undisputed tax principles; more likely than not, the return is a composite interpretation of corporate transactions made by corporate officers in the light most favorable to the taxpayer. It is the responsibility of the IRS to determine whether the corporate taxpayer in completing its return has stretched a particular tax concept beyond what is allowed. Records that illuminate any aspect of the return—such as the tax accrual workpapers at issue in this case—are therefore highly relevant to legitimate IRS inquiry. The Court of Appeals acknowledged this: "It is difficult to say that the assessment by the independent auditor of the correctness of positions taken by the taxpayer in his return would not throw 'light upon' the correctness of the return." 677 F.2d, at 219. We accordingly affirm the Court of Appeals' holding that Young's tax accrual workpapers are relevant to the IRS investigation of Amerada's tax liability.

---

11. The relevance standard employed by the Second Circuit—whether the documents at issue "might have thrown light upon the correctness of the return"—appears to be widely accepted among the Courts of Appeals. See, *e.g., United States v. Wyatt*, 637 F.2d 293, 300 (CA5 1981). In *United States v. Harrington*, 388 F.2d 520, 524 (1968), the Second Circuit amplified this test by stating that "the 'might' in the articulated standard, 'might throw light upon the correctness of the return,' is * * * an indication of a realistic expectation rather than an idle hope that something may be discovered."

D. INFORMATION NOT WITHIN IRS POSSESSION

UNITED STATES v. TEXAS HEART INSTITUTE
United States Court of Appeals, Fifth Circuit, 1985.
755 F.2d 469.

JOHNSON, CIRCUIT JUDGE:

* * *

In 1979, the IRS began an income tax audit of Dr. Barrett. Initially, Dr. Barrett gave the IRS agents involved complete access to all his records. * * *

* * *

In 1981, the case was referred to the Criminal Investigation Division (CID) of the IRS to determine whether criminal violations of the Internal Revenue Code had occurred. * * * Special Agent * * * Hanson determined it was necessary to verify the sums each of Dr. Barrett's patients had paid Dr. Barrett in order to determine whether Dr. Barrett had reported all his income for the years at issue. In order to obtain the names and addresses of some of Dr. Barrett's patients, Agent Hanson issued summonses to all the hospitals at which Dr. Barrett practiced. The summonses requested each hospital to provide the names and addresses of Dr. Barrett's patients, as well as any information regarding amounts and method of payment for Dr. Barrett's services. The summonses also requested the names of the patients' insurance companies. The summonses asked for this information for all of Dr. Barrett's patients admitted, treated, or tested at that hospital during the period 1976 through 1980.

* * *

Upon refusal by the four named hospitals to comply with the summonses, the Government filed petitions to enforce the summonses. Dr. Barrett intervened. The district court conducted a hearing where Agent Hanson and Dr. Barrett testified, along with other witnesses. At the conclusion of the hearing, the district court ruled that it would not enforce the summonses.

* * *

As one of its reasons for denying enforcement of the instant summonses, the district court stated that the IRS had all the records they needed in Dr. Barrett's office. This finding is relevant to the *Powell* requirement that "the information sought is not already within the Commissioner's possession." This "already possessed" exception to the enforcement of IRS summonses has been narrowly construed by this Court. Once the IRS has denied possession of the summonsed information, as here by affidavit and testimony, then the burden of showing "at a minimum, 'actual possession of the information by the IRS'" shifts to the parties resisting the summonses. *Davis,* 636 F.2d at

1037 (quoting *United States v. Garrett,* 571 F.2d 1323, 1328 (5th Cir. 1978)).

In *Davis,* the Court construed the "already possessed" exception as follows:

> Read in context, we construe the "already possessed" principle enunciated by *Powell* as a gloss on [26 U.S.C.] § 7605(b)'s prohibition of "unnecessary" summonses, rather than an absolute prohibition against the enforcement of any summons to the extent that it requests the production of information already in the possession of the IRS.

636 F.2d at 1037.

Dr. Barrett and the hospitals argue that the Government "already possessed" the information summonsed because IRS agents had reviewed Dr. Barrett's records prior to assigning the case to the Criminal Investigation Division. They cite *United States v. Pritchard,* 438 F.2d 969 (5th Cir.1971), for the proposition that once the IRS has examined the taxpayer's files, the information in those files is in the Government's possession. The argument is simple: once the Government has seen the documents, the Government "possesses" the documents.

That proposition does not state the law in this Circuit. In *Garrett,* this Court limited the import of *Pritchard:*

> *Pritchard* does not bar the enforcement of the summons issued to Garrett. In *Pritchard,* the IRS never made reference to whether the commissioner already possessed the information sought in the summons. Therefore, we agreed with the district court that the government had not shown the requisites for enforcement. *See Powell, supra.* The case at bar differs from *Pritchard,* because here the government alleged and set about to prove that it did not possess the information sought. To defeat the summons under these circumstances, Garrett had to show actual possession of the information by the IRS.

571 F.2d at 1328. We view the requirement in this Circuit to be that the taxpayer must show that the Government *actually possesses* the information summonsed, such that enforcement of a summons is "unnecessary" as that term is used in section 7605(b) of the Code.

Dr. Barrett and the hospitals have failed to meet their burden in the instant case. All parties agree that the IRS conducted an audit of Dr. Barrett, and at that time Dr. Barrett made all his records available to the IRS. The IRS asserts that Dr. Barrett's accounts could not be reconciled. Dr. Barrett's accountant also testified to that fact. The IRS now seeks to discover why the accounts do not reconcile by contacting patients, perhaps to add the total amounts paid to the doctor to arrive at total income, as Dr. Barrett suggests, or perhaps, as the Government asserts, to find patients not recorded or sums not recorded in Dr. Barrett's records. As to any patients' names and addresses not appearing in Dr. Barrett's records, the IRS clearly is not in actual possession of that information. As to names and addresses that appeared in Dr. Barrett's files, the IRS agents testified that only some surnames and no addresses were copied by the IRS auditors. Thus, those names and addresses are not actually in the IRS's possession.

* * *

Thus, this Court concludes that a mere showing by the taxpayer that the IRS has previously examined the taxpayer's own records is not sufficient to show either that the IRS *possesses* that information or that it *possesses* information in the custody of parties other than the taxpayer. We conclude that the IRS is not already in possession of the summonsed information in the instant appeal; consequently, the enforcement of these summonses is not "unnecessary." [7]

* * *

Note

In order for the Service to make a *prima facie* showing of "good faith," the Service must establish the four elements already studied in *Powell*. One of those four necessary elements is that the Service not already be in possession of the information sought in the summons. In United States v. First National State Bank of New Jersey, 616 F.2d 668 (3d Cir.1980), the Third Circuit resolved the issue of whether the IRS may obtain by summons the copies of Forms 1099 and 1087 retained by third-party recordkeepers.

The bank argued that the 1099 and 1087 forms were already in the Service's possession and, therefore, the summons should not be enforced. The court held that while the forms at issue may technically be deemed within the physical proprietary control of the Government, it is clear that the information sought is, as a practical matter, neither accessible to nor readily available to the IRS.

E. SECOND INSPECTIONS

UNITED STATES v. GILPIN
United States Court of Appeals, Third Circuit, 1976.
542 F.2d 38.

PER CURIAM:

Appellees, United States of America and Internal Revenue Special Agent Patrick W. McDermott, filed a petition on 25 September 1975 in the United States District Court for the Northern District of Illinois, Eastern Division, to enforce compliance with an Internal Revenue Service summons. The summons sought the production of designated books and records of Appellant Gilpin for the years 1969 through 1972 and Gilpin's testimony relating to the tax liability of Illinois Office Supply Company, the corporation of which Gilpin is president.

---

7. The hospitals and doctor argue that this information could be obtained from sources other than Dr. Barrett's patients, such as Dr. Barrett's own records or his bank records. When information is obtainable from more than one source, the IRS has great discretion to choose the source it prefers. The test is not whether the IRS *might be* able to obtain the information from some other source, but whether the information is *presently* in the possession of the IRS. * * *

[The district court ordered that the summons be enforced.]

* * *

Appellants contend that § 7605(b) of the Internal Revenue Code of 1954 authorizes only one inspection of a taxpayer's books of account for each taxable year unless, after investigation, the Commissioner notifies the taxpayer that an additional inspection is necessary. In this regard, appellants assert that the Revenue Agent who conducted the investigation in this case, Robert Chejlava, had completed his examination and that the summons issued herein was in aid of a second examination for which the statutory notice requirement was not fulfilled. * * * With respect to this Section of the Code, it is clear in this Circuit that no second inspection notice is required if it is factually established that the Agent involved had not completed his examination when he referred the case to a Special Agent for further investigation. In this regard, it is established procedure that when, during his investigation, a Revenue Agent discovers an indication of fraud, he is required to cease his examination and refer the case to the Intelligence Division. * * *

In the present case, Agent Chejlava testified in the district court that he had not completed the audit and had not closed out any of the years in question when he made his referral to the Intelligence Division in August of 1974. He went on to state that the referral was prompted by the realization that there existed a possibility of fraud. The only evidence to the contrary was that of appellants' bookkeeper, Verna Irwin, who testified that Agent Chejlava stated at a summons hearing on 29 January 1975 that he had completed the corporate auditing some time in early 1974. The trial court, as it is empowered to do as the trier of fact, elected to give more weight to the testimony of Agent Chejlava and the other evidence relating thereto than that of the witness Irwin; * * * Based on our review of the facts and circumstances of the instant case, there was ample evidence upon which the district court could have concluded, as it did, that the summons herein was part of an ongoing investigation that had commenced with Agent Chejlava's audit in July of 1972; that the audit had not been completed when the matter was referred to Special Agent McDermott of the Intelligence Division; and that, therefore, the "second inspection" provisions of 26 U.S.C. § 7605(b) were not applicable.

Finally, we do not consider appellants' contention that Agent Chejlava had substantially understated the amount of his audit time in connection with his examination of the taxpayer as being dispositive of the instant appeal. Although we recognize the discrepancy that exists in the record as to the actual time spent by Agent Chejlava in this investigation, and that an investigation of this type should not be prolonged beyond any reasonable need, we will not exercise our supervisory power and intervene in an agent's decision to engage in further examination unless it is shown by the taxpayer that the agent has abused his discretion in wielding the extensive powers granted to him by the Internal Revenue Code. Appellants have failed to show, and we can find no such abuse of discretion in the instant case.

For many years, we and other courts have been plagued with second investigation notice cases. To save the Internal Revenue Service, Department of Justice, private counsel's and the courts' valuable time, the I.R.S. should more commonly notify taxpayers "in writing that an additional investigation is necessary" under 26 U.S.C. § 7605(b).

* * *

Notes and Questions

1. In those cases in which there is a reasonable debate as to whether there is a continuing, or new, investigation, what reasons (if any) are there for the Service's frequent refusal to issue the second inspection notice?

2. In Reineman v. United States, 301 F.2d 267 (7th Cir.1962), the taxpayers objected to a second inspection of their 1954 records during an examination of their 1955 return. The agent, without advising that he was doing so, inspected the 1954 records and discovered a potential adjustment to the 1954 return. What remedy, if any, should have been provided to the taxpayer? The court held that in this situation the deficiency assessment had to be set aside as a result of the agent's actions.

3. Although the only "administrative step" mentioned in *Powell* relates to the second inspection notice required in certain cases under § 7605(b), some additional administrative steps must now be complied with under § 7609 (added to the Code by the Tax Reform Act of 1976) in cases involving "third-party recordkeeper" summonses. What remedies are (or should be) available to taxpayers where the IRS fails to follow the § 7609 requirements? See pages 526–529 below, for a discussion of the third-party recordkeeper summons procedure.

SECTION 4. THE EVIDENTIARY PRIVILEGES

Any privilege that may be asserted to prevent the compulsory production of testimony or documents is potentially pertinent to a consideration of the enforceability of an IRS summons. This section covers the two privileges that are most commonly invoked in tax investigations—the attorney-client privilege and the privilege against self-incrimination.

A. THE ATTORNEY–CLIENT PRIVILEGE AND THE WORK–PRODUCT DOCTRINE

The attorney-client privilege, deeply rooted in the common law, provides absolute protection from the compulsory production to the Internal Revenue Service (or any adversary) of those communications which fall within the scope of the privilege. The work-product doctrine, by comparison, is not a privilege. This doctrine provides qualified protection from production to those materials which fall within the definition of attorney's work-product. The protection afforded by the doctrine is overcome upon an adequate showing of necessity and unavailability by the party seeking production. In many cases, the same documents must be analyzed in the context of both the attorney-client and the work-product doctrine before it can be determined whether production should be ordered.

UNITED STATES v. EL PASO COMPANY
United States Court of Appeals, Fifth Circuit, 1982.
682 F.2d 530.

JERRE S. WILLIAMS, CIRCUIT JUDGE:

The United States and two agents of the Internal Revenue Service (IRS) petitioned the district court to enforce two summonses issued to the El Paso Company (El Paso) with regard to a tax audit. One summons sought El Paso's "tax-pool analysis"—a summary of El Paso's contingent liability for additional taxes should it ultimately be determined that El Paso owed more taxes than indicated on its return. After a hearing, the district court enforced the tax pool analysis summons and El Paso brought this appeal. We affirm.

I.

The audit of El Paso that triggered the summons in this case was not conducted on suspicion of fraud; rather, it was a routine audit occasioned by the amount of taxes at stake.

Each audit of El Paso covers several years of tax returns. The relevant cycle in this case includes the years 1976, 1977, and 1978. Early in the audit of the 1976–1978 cycle, the IRS team coordinator delivered a document request to El Paso for "all analyses prepared by the El Paso Company regarding potential tax liabilities and tax problems" for the years covered by the cycle. Five days later, Jack McCarthy, the head of El Paso's tax department, returned the request form marked "refused".

Shortly after receiving El Paso's refusal to respond to the potential tax-liabilities document request, the IRS issued a summons to McCarthy covering "any document, memorandum, letter, or work papers which identify potential tax liabilities or tax problems for the period beginning January 1, 1976 and ending December 31, 1978, inclusive." McCarthy also declined to comply with the summons, stating his reasons in a letter written to the case manager of the El Paso audit.

On May 27, 1981, the IRS filed its petition to enforce the summons under 26 U.S.C. § 7604. El Paso defended against enforcement on grounds of burdensomeness, relevance, attorney-client privilege, and work product doctrine. After a hearing at which both sides were permitted to call and cross-examine witnesses, the district court rejected El Paso's defenses and concluded that El Paso must comply with the summons.

El Paso appealed and sought a stay of the district court's judgment from this Court.

II.

This appeal is centrally concerned with documents known to the accounting profession under various names—the noncurrent tax account, the tax accrual work papers, and the tax pool analysis.

Business reality compels corporations to recognize on their financial sheets that the return as filed is not the last word in determining the taxes owed. To demonstrate to the accountant that a balance sheet does not portray an overly-rosy view of a corporation's financial health, the balance sheet must provide for contingent future tax liabilities. In short, the corporation must set aside an account to cover additional taxes that it may become liable to pay above and beyond the amount indicated on the initial return.

* * * The tax pool analysis is undertaken solely to insure that the corporation sets aside on its balance sheet a sufficient amount to cover contingent tax liability.

III.

* * *

V.

We now turn to El Paso's contention that the tax pool analysis is shielded by the attorney-client privilege. El Paso carries the burden of establishing this defense to the enforcement of the summons.

The scope of the attorney-client privilege is shaped by its purposes. *United States v. Pipkins,* 528 F.2d 559, 563 (5th Cir.1976), *cert. denied,* 426 U.S. 952, 96 S.Ct. 3177, 49 L.Ed.2d 1191 (1976). While the elements of the privilege have been comprehensively restated elsewhere, it is sufficient here to note that "[w]hat is vital to the privilege is that the communication be made *in confidence* for the purpose of obtaining *legal* advice *from the lawyer.*" *United States v. Kovel,* 296 F.2d 918, 922 (2d Cir.1961) (emphasis in original). Moreover, "disclosure of any significant portion of a confidential communication waives the privilege as to the whole." *United States v. Davis,* 636 F.2d at 1043 n. 18. Finally, we have made clear that the attorney-client privilege may not be tossed as a blanket over an undifferentiated group of documents. *United States v. Davis,* 636 F.2d at 1044 n. 20; *United States v. Roundtree,* 420 F.2d 845, 852 (5th Cir.1969). The privilege must be specifically asserted with respect to particular documents.

The IRS argues that El Paso has failed to prove any of the elements of the attorney-client privilege. In its broadest theory, the IRS urges that preparing the tax pool analysis is not legal work and that El Paso's attorneys in performing it are not giving legal advice. In the IRS's view the tax pool analysis is a business document, drawn up solely to bring the company's financial statements in line with generally accepted auditing principles. Because the tax pool analysis simply supports a record of the corporation's finances, the IRS sees it as business work rather than legal work.

The line between accounting work and legal work in the giving of tax advice is extremely difficult to draw. We have held that the preparation of tax returns is generally not legal advice within the scope of the privilege. *United States v. Davis,* 636 F.2d at 1043. *Davis* withheld the privilege from communications made to an attorney to prepare a tax return because such work is primarily an accounting service. The tax pool analysis may also be considered an accounting service since it is often performed by accountants. Nevertheless, we would be reluctant to hold that a lawyer's analysis of the soft spots in a tax return and his judgments on the outcome of litigation on it are not legal advice. We need not decide this issue, however, because we believe that El Paso's attempt to claim the privilege fails on other grounds.

To retain the attorney-client privilege, the confidentiality surrounding the communications made in that relationship must be preserved. The purpose of the privilege is to foster full client disclosure to the lawyer; the privilege exists to assure the client that his private disclosures will not become common knowledge. The need to cloak these communications with secrecy, however, ends when the secrets pass through the client's lips to others. Thus, a breach of confidentiality forfeits the client's right to claim the privilege. *Permian Corp. v. United States,* 665 F.2d 1214, 1219 (D.C.Cir.1981).

The district court found in this case that El Paso discussed "some of the information and many of the potential tax liability issues" in its tax pool analysis with the independent auditors who certify the corporation's books. This finding is not clearly erroneous. *Pullman–Standard v. Swint,* [456] U.S. [273], 102 S.Ct. 1781, 72 L.Ed.2d 66 (1982). The evidence showed that in the course of the audit, the accountants determine whether the company has set aside an adequate reserve for contingent taxes. This task carries the auditors into the tax pool analysis and into at least some of the supporting memoranda. Confidentiality as to these documents is neither expected nor preserved, for they are created with the knowledge that independent accountants may need access to them to complete the audit. *See United States v. Pipkins,* 528 F.2d at 563.

El Paso generates the tax pool analysis to portray its financial condition accurately. As the securities laws require, independent accountants then verify the financial statements by probing the corporation's reasons for allocating a given amount to its noncurrent tax account. In El Paso's case, the tax pool analysis is revealed to the independent accountants as part of their audit. Our Circuit does not recognize an accountant-client communications privilege, and, as the Supreme Court has acknowledged, neither does any other federal court. *Couch v. United States,* 409 U.S. 322, 335 (1973). Under these circumstances, El Paso's disclosure of the tax pool analysis to the auditors destroys confidentiality with respect to it. With the destruction of confidentiality goes as well the right to claim the attorney-client privilege.

We believe that El Paso may not withdraw behind the shield of the attorney-client privilege for an additional reason. El Paso failed to particularize its assertion of the privilege and prove its case with respect to any specific document. El Paso made only a blanket assertion of the privilege as to all documents in, or backing up, its tax pool analysis. Such a showing is simply inadequate.

The reasons for refusing to tolerate blanket assertions of the privilege apply fully to this case. El Paso's tax department employs eighty accountants and ten attorneys. The tax department as a whole has responsibility for preparing the various memoranda that underpin the tax pool analysis. Both the head of the tax department and the general counsel testified at the enforcement hearing, but neither witness had reviewed the backup memoranda prior to testifying. As a result, neither was able to state how many or which memoranda were prepared by attorneys rather than by accountants.

El Paso's failure to prove which documents were prepared by attorneys considerably undermines its claim to the attorney-client privilege. Because the privilege does not attach to tax work prepared by accountants unless the accountant is translating complex tax terms into a form intelligible to a lawyer at the lawyer's behest, *United States v. Kovel,* 296 F.2d at 922, the memoranda prepared by accountants do not qualify for the privilege. We cannot say that any single memorandum in the El Paso's tax department is stamped with an attorney's seal. A general claim that the tax department funnels tax work through its attorneys will not do, and El Paso's proof amounted to little more.

We hold, therefore, that El Paso has breached the confidentiality needed to shield its attorney-client communications, and in any event, has failed to meet its burden to assert the privilege specifically. The attorney-client privilege does not protect El Paso against disclosing the documents that the IRS seeks.

VI.

El Paso next contends that the work product doctrine immunizes the tax pool analysis from production. It is settled, of course, that a work product defense may be asserted against enforcement of an IRS summons. Upjohn Co. v. United States, 101 S.Ct. at 686.

The work product doctrine is not an umbrella that shades all materials prepared by a lawyer, however. The work product doctrine focuses only on materials assembled and brought into being in anticipation of litigation. Excluded from work product materials, as the advisory committee notes to Rule 26(b)(3) make clear, are "[m]aterials assembled in the ordinary course of business, or pursuant to public requirements unrelated to litigation * * *." 48 F.R.D. at 501.

Even assuming that El Paso's tax pool analysis otherwise qualifies for work product protection, we hold the doctrine unavailable here because the tax pool analysis is not prepared "in anticipation of litigation." But in doing so we concede that determining whether a document is prepared in anticipation of litigation is a slippery task. In *United States v. Davis* we phrased the test in the following terms: "[L]itigation need not be imminent * * * as long as the primary motivating purpose behind the creation of the document was to aid in possible future litigation." 636 F.2d at 1040. *Davis* held that an attorney's work in preparing a tax return did not fall under the work product doctrine because the work was not primarily motivated to assist in future litigation over the return. We reach a similar conclusion with respect to El Paso's tax pool analysis.

El Paso establishes its non-current tax account to bring its financial books into conformity with generally accepted auditing principles. The desire to please the accountants, in turn, is compelled by the securities laws. The primary motivating force behind the tax pool analysis, therefore, is not to ready El Paso for litigation over its tax returns. Rather, the primary motivation is to anticipate, for financial reporting purposes, what the impact of litigation might be on the company's tax liability. El Paso thus creates the tax pool analysis with an eye on its business needs, not on its legal ones.

We recognize that the tax pool analysis involves weighing legal arguments, predicting the stance of the IRS, and forecasting the ultimate likelihood of sustaining El Paso's position in court. Nevertheless, this analysis (assuming it is legal rather than accounting work) is only a means to a business end. The legal analysis is not an end in itself: the memoranda underlying the tax pool analysis do not map out El Paso's actual litigating strategy, should litigation occur. In fact, no single item in the tax pool analysis is specifically under scrutiny by the IRS when the memoranda are drafted. Business imperatives, not the press of litigation, call these documents into being.

Moreover, El Paso's tax litigation is handled by outside counsel. Although an attorney from El Paso's tax department serves as co-counsel, outside counsel takes the lead in directing the conduct of El Paso's tax suits. There is no evidence in the record that the tax pool analysis or underlying memoranda are referred to outside counsel or used by El Paso's attorneys to prepare for trial or negotiations.

In sum, we believe that the tax pool analysis does not contemplate litigation in the sense required to bring it within the work product doctrine. The tax pool analysis concocts theories about the results of possible litigation; such analyses are not designed to prepare a specific case for trial or negotiation. Their sole function, from all that appears in the record, is to back up a figure on a financial balance sheet. Written ultimately to comply with SEC regulations, the tax pool analysis carries much more the aura of daily business than it does of courtroom combat. We hold, therefore, that the tax pool analysis and backup memoranda are not protected work product materials.

VII.
CONCLUSION

Our tax collection system depends primarily on the voluntary compliance of taxpayers acting in good faith. Congress has chosen to enforce this system of self-assessment through an agency vested with broad investigatory powers. Because we find the summons here to be authorized by Congress and not otherwise prohibited, we enforce the tax pool analysis summons.

We restate our holdings. First, we interpret the judgment to extend only to El Paso's tax pool analysis and supporting memoranda in various subject files. Second, we do not find El Paso's tax pool analysis shielded by the attorney-client privilege. Third, the documents in question are not protected work product materials. Fourth, we find a lack of public policy in the securities laws demanding that we deny enforcement. The stay of the district court's judgment is lifted, and the judgment is affirmed.

Notes and Questions

1. The attorney-client privilege is usually waived when the attorney discloses otherwise privileged matters to the government in an effort to avoid prosecution of the client. See United States v. Mierzwicki, 500 F.Supp. 1331 (D.Md.1980). However, effective May 14, 1986, the Tax Division has decided, as a matter of policy, that statements made by attorneys during Justice Department conferences in criminal matters will not be used against the client as a vicarious admission, except to the extent that the attorney authenticates a written instrument. See Tax Division Directive No. 86–58.

2. The courts have recognized an exception to the rule that disclosure to third parties waives the privilege in the case of so-called joint defense disclosures. Thus, where actual or prospective co-defendants in a criminal case or their attorneys confer on matters of mutual interest there is usually no waiver of the privilege. See United States v. McPartlin, 595 F.2d 1321 (7th Cir.1979), cert. denied, 444 U.S. 833, 100 S.Ct. 65, 62 L.Ed.2d 43 (1979); Hunydee v. United States, 355 F.2d 183 (9th Cir.1965). Should the joint defense privilege apply where the attorney is essentially a conduit for information concerning the focus of the investigation?

According to the court in In re Grand Jury Testimony of Attorney X, 621 F.Supp. 590 (E.D.N.Y. 1985), where the information sought is not confidential, the fact that it may incriminate the client is not a valid reason to invoke the attorney-client privilege. In this case, the attorney obtained information about a grand jury investigation from a third person and relayed it to his client. The information was clearly not confidential and the attorney was merely acting as a conduit.

3. Under the Code of Professional Responsibility, Disciplinary Rule 4–101(C), an attorney is entitled to turn over those documents to which the

client asserts an attorney-client privilege in order to protect himself from prosecution. Application of Friend, 411 F.Supp. 776 (S.D.N.Y.1975).

4. Note that communications otherwise protected by the attorney-client privilege lose that protected status if made in furtherance of a crime or fraud. See United States v. Zolin, 491 U.S. 554, 109 S.Ct. 2619, 105 L.Ed.2d 469 (1989); United States v. Hodge and Zweig, 548 F.2d 1347 (9th Cir.1977). The crime/fraud exception can apply to matters covered by the attorney work product doctrine. Where the so-called work product is in aid of a criminal scheme, fear of disclosure may serve a useful deterrent purpose and be the rare occasion on which an attorney's mental processes are not immune from disclosure. See In re John Doe Corp., 675 F.2d 482 (2d Cir.1982). The court in In re Special September 1978 Grand Jury, 640 F.2d 49 (7th Cir.1980), went even further in holding that where there is ongoing crime/fraud, the work product doctrine may be invoked by the law firm, and not the client, to prevent the disclosure of the attorney's mental impressions, conclusions, opinions and legal theories.

B. THE PRIVILEGE AGAINST SELF-INCRIMINATION

BRASWELL v. UNITED STATES

Supreme Court of the United States, 1988.
487 U.S. 99, 108 S.Ct. 2284, 101 L.Ed.2d 98.

CHIEF JUSTICE REHNQUIST delivered the opinion of the Court.

This case presents the question whether the custodian of corporate records may resist a subpoena for such records on the ground that the act of production would incriminate him in violation of the Fifth Amendment. We conclude that he may not.

From 1965 to 1980, petitioner Randy Braswell operated his business—which comprises the sale and purchase of equipment, land, timber, and oil and gas interests—as a sole proprietorship. In 1980, he incorporated Worldwide Machinery Sales, Inc., a Mississippi corporation, and began conducting the business through that entity. In 1981, he formed a second Mississippi corporation, Worldwide Purchasing, Inc., and funded that corporation with the 100 percent interest he held in Worldwide Machinery. Petitioner was and is the sole shareholder of Worldwide Purchasing, Inc.

In compliance with Mississippi law, both corporations have three directors, petitioner, his wife, and his mother. Although his wife and mother are secretary-treasurer and vice-president of the corporations, respectively, neither has any authority over the business affairs of either corporation.

In August 1986, a federal grand jury issued a subpoena to "Randy Braswell, President Worldwide Machinery, Inc. [and] Worldwide Purchasing, Inc.," requiring petitioner to produce the books and records of the two corporations. The subpoena provided that petitioner could deliver the records to the agent serving the subpoena, and did not require petitioner to testify. Petitioner moved to quash the subpoena, arguing that the act of producing the records would incriminate him in violation of his Fifth Amendment privilege against self-incrimination. The District Court denied the motion to quash, ruling that the "collective entity doctrine" prevented petitioner from asserting that his act of producing the corporations' records was protected by the Fifth Amendment. The court rejected petitioner's argument that the collective entity doctrine does not apply when a corporation is so small that it constitutes nothing more than the individual's alter ego.

The United States Court of Appeals for the Fifth Circuit affirmed, citing *Bellis v. United States,* 417 U.S. 85, 88, 94 S.Ct. 2179, 2182, 40 L.Ed.2d 678 (1974), for the proposition that a corporation's records custodian may not claim a Fifth Amendment privilege no matter how small the corporation may be. The Court of Appeals declared that *Bellis* retained vitality following *United States v. Doe,* 465 U.S. 605, 104 S.Ct. 1237, 79 L.Ed.2d 552 (1984), and therefore, "Braswell, as custodian of corporate documents, has no act of production privilege under the fifth amendment regarding corporate documents." *In re Grand Jury Proceedings,* 814 F.2d 190, 193 (CA5 1987). We granted certiorari to resolve a conflict among the Courts of Appeals. 484 U.S. —, 108 S.Ct. 64, 98 L.Ed.2d 28 (1987). We now affirm.

There is no question but that the contents of the subpoenaed business records are not privileged. See *Doe, supra; Fisher v. United States,* 425 U.S. 391, 96 S.Ct. 1569, 48 L.Ed.2d 39 (1976). Similarly, petitioner asserts no self-incrimination claim on behalf of the corporations; it is well established that such artificial entities are not protected by the Fifth Amendment. *Bellis, supra.* Petitioner instead relies solely upon the argument that his act of producing the documents has independent testimonial significance, which would incriminate him individually, and that the Fifth Amendment prohibits government compulsion of that act. The bases for this argument are extrapolated from the decisions of this Court in *Fisher, supra,* and *Doe, supra.*

In *Fisher,* the Court was presented with the question whether an attorney may resist a subpoena demanding that he produce tax records which had been entrusted to him by his client. The records in question had been prepared by the client's accountants. In analyzing the Fifth Amendment claim forwarded by the attorney, the Court considered whether the client-taxpayer would have had a valid Fifth Amendment claim had he retained the records and the subpoena been issued to him. After explaining that the Fifth Amendment prohibits "compelling a person to give 'testimony' that incriminates him," 425 U.S., at 409, 96 S.Ct., at 1580, the Court rejected the argument that the contents of the records were protected. The Court, however, went on to observe:

> "The act of producing evidence in response to a subpoena nevertheless has communicative aspects of its own, wholly aside from the contents of the papers produced. Compliance with the subpoena tacitly concedes the existence of the papers demanded and their possession or control by the taxpayer. It also would indicate the taxpayer's belief that the papers are those described in the subpoena. *Curcio v. United*

States, 354 U.S. 118, 125 [77 S.Ct. 1145, 1150, 1 L.Ed.2d 1225] (1957). The elements of compulsion are clearly present, but the more difficult issues are whether the tacit averments of the taxpayer are both 'testimonial' and 'incriminating' for purposes of applying the Fifth Amendment."

The Court concluded that under the "facts and circumstances" there presented, the act of producing the accountants' papers would not "involve testimonial self-incrimination." *Id.,* at 411, 96 S.Ct., at 1581.

Eight years later, in *United States v. Doe, supra,* the Court revisited the question, this time in the context of a claim by a sole proprietor that the compelled production of business records would run afoul of the Fifth Amendment. After rejecting the contention that the contents of the records were themselves protected, the Court proceeded to address whether respondent's act of producing the records would constitute protected testimonial incrimination. The Court concluded that respondent had established a valid Fifth Amendment claim. It deferred to the lower courts, which had found that enforcing the subpoenas at issue would provide the Government valuable information: By producing the records, respondent would admit that the records existed, were in his possession, and were authentic. 465 U.S., at 613, n. 11, 104 S.Ct. 1242, n. 11.

Had petitioner conducted his business as a sole proprietorship, *Doe* would require that he be provided the opportunity to show that his act of production would entail testimonial self-incrimination. But petitioner has operated his business through the corporate form, and we have long recognized that for purposes of the Fifth Amendment, corporations and other collective entities are treated differently from individuals. This doctrine—known as the collective entity rule—has a lengthy and distinguished pedigree.

The rule was first articulated by the Court in the case of *Hale v. Henkel,* 201 U.S. 43, 26 S.Ct. 370, 50 L.Ed. 652 (1906). Hale, a corporate officer, had been served with a subpoena ordering him to produce corporate records and to testify concerning certain corporate transactions. The Court explained that the corporation "is a creature of the State," *ibid.,* with powers limited by the State. As such, the State may, in the exercise of its right to oversee the corporation, demand the production of corporate records.

The frontiers of the collective entity rule were expanded even further in *Bellis v. United States,* 417 U.S. 85, 94 S.Ct. 2179, 40 L.Ed.2d 678 (1974), in which the Court ruled that a partner in a small partnership could not properly refuse to produce partnership records. Bellis, one of the members of a three-person law firm that had previously been dissolved, was served with a subpoena directing him to produce partnership records he possessed. The District Court held Bellis in contempt when he refused to produce the partnership's financial books and records. We upheld the contempt order.

The plain mandate of these decisions is that without regard to whether the subpoena is addressed to the corporation, or as here, to the individual in his capacity as a custodian, a corporate custodian such as petitioner may not resist a subpoena for corporate records on Fifth Amendment grounds. * * * Artificial entities such as corporations may act only through their agents, *Bellis, supra,* 417 U.S., at 90, 94 S.Ct., at 2184, and a custodian's assumption of his representative capacity leads to certain obligations, including the duty to produce corporate records on proper demand by the Government. Under those circumstances, the custodian's act of production is not deemed a personal act, but rather an act of the corporation. Any claim of Fifth Amendment privilege asserted by the agent would be tantamount to a claim of privilege by the corporation—which of course possesses no such privilege.

We note further that recognizing a Fifth Amendment privilege on behalf of the records custodians of collective entities would have a detrimental impact on the Government's efforts to prosecute "white-collar crime," one of the most serious problems confronting law enforcement authorities. "The greater portion of evidence of wrongdoing by an organization or its representatives is usually found in the official records and documents of that organization. Were the cloak of the privilege to be thrown around these impersonal records and documents, effective enforcement of many federal and state laws would be impossible." *White,* 322 U.S., at 700, 64 S.Ct., at 1252. If custodians could assert a privilege, authorities would be stymied not only in their enforcement efforts against those individuals but also in their prosecutions of organizations. In *Bellis,* the Court observed: "In view of the inescapable fact that an artificial entity can only act to produce its records through its individual officers or agents, recognition of the individual's claim of privilege with respect to the financial records of the organization would substantially undermine the unchallenged rule that the organization itself is not entitled to claim any Fifth Amendment privilege, and largely frustrate legitimate governmental regulation of such organizations." 417 U.S., at 90, 94 S.Ct., at 2184.

Petitioner suggests, however, that these concerns can be minimized by the simple expedient of either granting the custodian statutory immunity as to the act of production, 18 U.S.C. §§ 6002, 6003, or addressing the subpoena to the corporation and allowing it to choose an agent to produce the records who can do so without incriminating himself. We think neither proposal satisfactorily addresses these concerns. Taking the last first, it is no doubt true that if a subpoena is addressed to a corporation, the corporation "must find some means by which to comply because no Fifth Amendment defense is available to it." *In re Sealed Case,* 266 U.S.App.D.C. 30, 44, n. 9, 832 F.2d 1268, 1282, n. 9 (1987). The means most commonly used to comply is the appointment of an alternate custodian. See, *e.g., In re Two Grand Jury Subpoenae Duces Tecum,* 769 F.2d 52, 57 (CA2 1985). But petitioner insists he cannot be required to aid the appointed custodian in his search for the demanded records, for any statement to the surrogate would itself be testimonial and incriminating. If this is correct, then petitioner's "solution" is a chimera. In situations such as this—where the corporate custodian is likely the only person with knowledge about the demanded documents—the appointment of a surrogate will simply not ensure that the documents sought will ever reach the grand jury room; the appointed custodian will essentially be sent on an unguided search.

This problem is eliminated if the Government grants the subpoenaed custodian statutory immunity for the testimonial aspects of his act of production. But that "solution" also entails a significant drawback. All of the evidence obtained under a grant of immunity to the custodian may of course be used freely against the corporation, but if the Government has any thought of prosecuting the custodian, a grant of act of production immunity can have serious consequences. Testimony obtained pursuant to a grant of statutory use immunity may be used neither directly nor derivatively. 18 U.S.C. § 6002; *Kastigar v. United States,* 406 U.S. 441, 92 S.Ct. 1653, 32 L.Ed.2d 212 (1972).

Although a corporate custodian is not entitled to resist a subpoena on the ground that his act of production will be personally incriminating, we do think certain consequences flow from the fact that the custodian's act of production is one in his representative rather than personal capacity. Because the custodian acts as a representative, the act is deemed one of the corporation and not the individual. Therefore, the Government concedes, as it must, that it may make no evidentiary use of the "individual act" against the individual. For example, in a criminal prosecution against the custodian, the Government may not introduce into evidence before the jury the fact that the subpoena was served upon and the corporation's documents were delivered by one particular individual, the custodian. The Government has the right, however, to use the corporation's act of production against the custodian. The Government may offer testimony—for example, from the process server who delivered the subpoena and from the individual who received the records—establishing that the corporation produced the records subpoenaed. The jury may draw from the corporation's act of production the conclusion that the records in question are authentic corporate records, which the corporation possessed, and which it produced in response to the subpoena. And if the defendant held a prominent position within the corporation that produced the records, the jury may, just as it would had someone else produced the documents, reasonably infer that he had possession of the documents or knowledge of their contents. Because the jury is not told that the defendant produced the records, any nexus between the defendant and the documents results solely from the corporation's act of production and other evidence in the case.

Consistent with our precedent, the United States Court of Appeals for the Fifth Circuit ruled that petitioner could not resist the subpoena for corporate documents on the ground that the act of production might tend to incriminate him. The judgment is therefore

Affirmed.

C. THE DEFENSE OF LACK OF POSSESSION

It is settled that the lack of possession of or control over records is a defense to the enforcement of an IRS summons. However, difficult issues arise when the reason that the summoned party does not currently possess the records (or they no longer exist) is incriminating. The complexity in this area is heightened by the Supreme Court's shift in Fifth Amendment analysis from protecting the contents of documents to protecting the testimonial consequences of the act of producing documents.[a]

Before the shift in analysis, the courts assumed that because a corporate custodian could not assert his personal Fifth Amendment privilege to avoid producing corporate documents a custodian who responded to a summons by stating that he did not possess the summoned documents made an adequate response and did not waive his personal privilege not to answer questions about the whereabouts of the documents.[b] Recently, however, some courts have taken the position that a summoned party cannot simply state that he does not possess the records and decline to answer questions concerning the reasons for his nonpossession by invoking the Fifth Amendment. The reasoning of such decisions is that by doing so the summoned party does not carry his burden of proof on the issue of nonpossession, which is an affirmative defense to enforcement.[c] Until the matter is resolved by the Supreme Court, it may be prudent to raise nonpossession issues under the umbrella of the act of production doctrine when the reasons for nonpossession or nonexistence are incriminating.

Once enforcement is ordered, the summoned party cannot defend a subsequent contempt proceeding by claiming that he did not possess the records at the time of the enforcement hearing. The summoned party can, of course, assert his present inability to produce the records as a defense to contempt. However, at the contempt stage, the summoned party does not meet his evidentiary burden of demonstrating nonpossession simply by asserting that his answers might incriminate him.

a. In In re Doe (John) No. 462, 745 F.2d 834 (4th Cir.1984), vacated as moot, 471 U.S. 1001, 105 S.Ct. 1861, 85 L.Ed.2d 155 (1985), the Fourth Circuit held that the contents of personal records—records held in an individual capacity—were protected under the Fifth Amendment. But see In re Grand Jury Subpoenas Served February 27, 1984, 599 F.Supp. 1006 (E.D.Wash. 1984).

b. In United States v. O'Henry's Film Works, Inc., 598 F.2d 313 (2d Cir.1979), the court held that the president of a corporation had not waived his personal Fifth Amendment privilege by stating, in response to a summons: "I am not now, nor was I at the time I was served with the summons in question, in possession or control of the documents called for in the summons."

c. United States v. Huckaby, 776 F.2d 564 (5th Cir.1985). But see United States v. Barth, 745 F.2d 184 (2d Cir.1984).

While he does not have to answer questions if his responses would be incriminating, the assertion of the privilege is not an adequate substitute for evidence of present inability to comply with the summons.ᵈ

SECTION 5. THIRD–PARTY RECORDKEEPER SUMMONSES

In the Tax Reform Act of 1976 Congress provided that certain types of Internal Revenue Service summonses required special safeguards for taxpayers. Essentially, these "third-party recordkeeper" summonses are defined to include summonses issued to specified types of persons who ordinarily keep records of another. Thus, the statute brings within its definition summonses issued to most financial institutions, consumer reporting agencies, persons extending credit through credit cards, brokers, attorneys and accountants. A summons issued to one of these "third-party recordkeepers" for records made or kept for a person identified in the summons is a third-party recordkeeper summons within the meaning of the statute.

Section 331 of TEFRA revised substantially the procedures incident to IRS use of third-party recordkeeper summonses because, in the opinion of Congress, the 1976 Tax Reform Act procedures were "so easy to use that taxpayers * * * frequently delayed enforcement of summonses without considering the merit of any objection they might have." Under the 1976 rules, the service of a summons on a third-party recordkeeper required notice to the taxpayer or other party named in the summons. The person receiving notice then could automatically stay the third-party recordkeeper's compliance simply by providing written notice to the third-party recordkeeper not to comply with the summons. Once such a notice was given to the third-party recordkeeper, no examination of the summoned records could take place absent a court order. The IRS thus was forced to commence a summons enforcement action regardless of the merit of any objection which might have been raised. As was noted by Congress, the Service prevailed in the vast majority of such actions.

Under § 7609, the IRS must give notice of service of a third-party recordkeeper summons to the person identified in the description of the records contained in the summons. The person receiving notice must institute a proceeding to quash the summons within 20 days after the notice is given. Both the IRS and the summoned party must be sent the petition to quash. In any such proceeding the Service may seek to compel compliance with the summons, and the summoned party may intervene in (and in any event will be bound by the decision in) the proceeding. The IRS is prohibited from examining the summoned

---

d. United States v. Rylander, 460 U.S. 752, 103 S.Ct. 1548, 75 L.Ed.2d 521 (1983). See United States v. Rogers Transp., Inc., 793 F.2d 557 (3d Cir.1986) ("We believe that a one person corporation does not demonstrate an inability to comply when it does not prove the non-existence of its duly summoned records or other recognized bases for unavailability and is given the choice of the person to deliver them.").

records until 23 days after notice of the summons is given or, if a proceeding to quash is begun timely, until there is an appropriate order or consent of the party beginning the action. Jurisdiction for the proceeding to quash is in the United States district court in which the person summoned "resides or is found", and an order denying the petition is a final order which may be appealed.

Under the TEFRA provisions, both civil and criminal limitations are suspended as long as an enforcement proceeding is pending if the taxpayer either moves to quash the summons or intervenes in a proceeding between the IRS and the third-party recordkeeper. The Tax Reform Act of 1986 further amended § 7609(e) to provide for the suspension of both civil and criminal limitations periods in the event that a dispute between the IRS and the third-party recordkeeper is not resolved within 6 months after the issuance of the summons.

The third-party recordkeeper, upon receipt of the summons, must proceed to assemble the summoned documents and be prepared to make production on the date specified in the summons. The Service may certify to the third-party recordkeeper that there has been no timely proceeding to quash or that the taxpayer consents to the examination. A person producing documents pursuant to such a certificate (or an order of court requiring production) may not be held liable to any person for such production.

RAPP v. COMMISSIONER
United States Court of Appeals, Ninth Circuit, 1985.
774 F.2d 932.

CANBY, CIRCUIT JUDGE:

Gerald and Mary Rapp appeal a decision of the Tax Court granting the Commissioner's motion for summary judgment on the Rapps' petition for redetermination of tax deficiencies and additions to tax, and denying their motion to suppress notices of deficiency and certificates of assessment. We affirm.

The IRS, pursuant to 26 U.S.C. § 7602, is authorized to examine records and issue summonses for the purpose of determining the tax liability of any individual. When an IRS summons is served on a "third-party record keeper," the taxpayer to whom the records named in the summons relate is entitled to notice of the summons, and may institute a proceeding to quash the summons or intervene in the enforcement proceeding. 26 U.S.C. §§ 7609(a) and (b). The Rapps contend that the Tax Court erred in denying their motion to suppress the notices of deficiency and Certificates of Assessments and Payments because the IRS failed to notify them of the issuance of two of the summonses. The contention is without merit.

"Third-party records" are those containing data about transactions between the taxpayer and parties other than the summoned party. The two summonses in question were issued to Alaska Helicopters Inc., and Ocean Technology Ltd., and sought records pertaining to Gerald Rapp's employment and transactions between him and the summoned parties. These are not "third-party records" within the meaning of section 7609. *See United States v. Income Realty and Mortgage Inc.,* 612 F.2d 1224, 1225–26 (10th Cir.1979), *cert. denied,* 446 U.S. 952, 100 S.Ct. 2918, 64 L.Ed.2d 809 (1980) (forms W–2, W–4 and 1099 and checks paid to and on behalf of taxpayer are not the type of records contemplated by section 7609); *see also United States v. Manchel, Lundy & Lessin,* 477 F.Supp. 326, 328–29 (E.D.Pa.1979) (where records are maintained by the summoned business for its own purposes, even though they relate incidentally to the taxpayer, no third-party record keeper relationship exists and the taxpayer is not entitled to notice of a summons seeking such records); *United States v. Exxon Co. U.S.A.,* 450 F.Supp. 472, 476–77 (D.Md.1978) (records involving contractual relations between taxpayer and summoned corporation are not subject to the notice requirement of section 7609).

Moreover, neither Alaska Helicopters nor Ocean Technology appears to fit within the narrow statutory definition of "third-party recordkeepers" set forth at 26 U.S.C. § 7609(a)(3)(A) through (G).[1] Accordingly, because neither of the summoned parties were "third-party record keepers" within the meaning of section 7609(a)(3), and because the records in question were not the type of records contemplated by that section, the Rapps were not entitled to notice of the summonses.

The Rapps next contend that the Tax Court erred in denying their motion to suppress because, although they were given notice of the summons issued to the First National Bank of Anchorage, they were not informed of the proceeding that the Commissioner instituted to enforce the summons. Title 26 U.S.C. §§ 7609(b)(1) and (2) provide that a party entitled to notice of a third-party summons has the right to institute a proceeding to quash the summons or intervene in the enforcement proceeding. Although their right to intervene could not be exercised if they were not notified of the proceeding, the Rapps have not alleged any concrete prejudice resulting from the failure to receive notice.[2]

1. The Rapps' contention that section 7609 applies because the summons was issued to "C.A. Ellwood, Chief Accountant for Alaska Helicopters," is meritless. The record is devoid of any evidence indicating that either C.A. Ellwood or Alaska Helicopters acted as Gerald Rapp's accountant or was summoned in that capacity. Thus, the notice requirement of section 7609 does not apply. *Cf. United States v. Manchel, Lundy & Lessin,* 477 F.Supp. 326, 328–29 (E.D.Pa.1979) (section 7609 inapplicable where summons directed to law firm sought records pertaining to taxpayer's employment because firm was not summoned as an "attorney" within the contemplation of the definition of third-party recordkeeper).

2. It is likely that even if the IRS had notified the Rapps of the enforcement proceeding, they would have been unable to prevent the bank from complying with the summons because the release of the records in question would not have violated any of the Rapps' constitutional rights. *See United States v. Miller,* 425 U.S. 435, 444, 96 S.Ct. 1619, 1624–25, 48 L.Ed.2d 71 (1976) (depositor has no expectation of privacy in bank records relating to his accounts).

* * *

Notes and Questions

1. What should a taxpayer have to show to obtain relief when the IRS fails to give proper notice under § 7609(a)? What, if any, relief would be appropriate?

2. The 20-day period of § 7609(b) is jurisdictional. The court in Ponsford v. United States, 771 F.2d 1305 (9th Cir.1985) held that the 20-day limit must be strictly construed because it is a condition precedent to the waiver of sovereign immunity. A district court does not have jurisdiction under Section 7609(h)(1) if the plaintiff has failed to comply with the 20-day filing requirement.

Further, the court in Stringer v. United States, 776 F.2d 274 (11th Cir.1985) held that the 20-day limit begins running from the date that notice is given. See § 7609(b)(2)(A). The court held that notice is given on the date it is mailed and not the date it is received by the addressee.

3. Under the plain meaning of § 7609(a), the IRS is only required to give notice to the person or persons "identified" in the summons. See United States v. First Bank, 737 F.2d 269 (2d Cir.1984). Under § 7609 generally, anyone who is not a target of an IRS investigation is not entitled to notice of an administrative summons issued to a third-party recordkeeper which requests production of its financial records, and more importantly, is not entitled to contest the validity of the summons. Vanguard Intern. Mfg., Inc. v. United States, 588 F.Supp. 1229 (S.D.N.Y.1984).

SECTION 6. THE "JOHN DOE" SUMMONS
TIFFANY FINE ARTS, INC. v. UNITED STATES

Supreme Court of the United States, 1985.
469 U.S. 310, 105 S.Ct. 725, 83 L.Ed.2d 678.

JUSTICE MARSHALL delivered the opinion of the Court.

* * *

I

Petitioner Tiffany Fine Arts, Inc., is a holding company for various subsidiaries that promote tax shelters. On October 6, 1981, Revenue Agent Joel Lewis issued four summonses to Tiffany, pursuant to 26 U.S.C. § 7602(a). * * * The summonses requested Tiffany's financial statements for the fiscal years ending October 31, 1979, and October 31, 1980, as well as a list of the names, addresses, social security numbers, and employer identification numbers of persons who had acquired from Tiffany licenses to distribute a medical device known as the "Pedi-Pulsor." Tiffany refused to comply with the summonses, and the Government then brought an enforcement action in the United States District Court for the Southern District of New York, pursuant to 26 U.S.C. §§ 7402(b) and 7604(a).

Tiffany opposed enforcement, principally on the ground that the IRS's request for the names of the licensees indicated clearly that the

IRS's "primary purpose" was to audit the Pedi–Pulsor licensees, not Tiffany itself. Tiffany offered to produce records in which the names of the licensees were redacted. It took the position that, if the IRS were truly interested in only Tiffany's liability, the redacted records would be sufficient for an adequate investigation.

According to Tiffany, if the IRS wanted to go further and obtain the names of all the licensees, it could not proceed solely under § 7602, but would have to comply also with the requirements of § 7609(f), which applies to John Doe summonses. Under § 7609(f), the IRS cannot serve a summons seeking information on the tax liabilities of unnamed taxpayers without obtaining prior judicial approval at an *ex parte* proceeding.

The IRS rejected Tiffany's offer of redacted documents. In an affidavit filed in support of the Government's enforcement petition, Revenue Agent Lewis asserted:

> "I am conducting an investigation, one purpose of which is to ascertain the correctness of the consolidated income tax returns filed by [Tiffany] for the fiscal years ending October 31, 1979, and October 31, 1980. One aspect of my investigation into the correctness of Tiffany's consolidated corporate income tax returns concerns possible underreporting of income received and questionable business deductions claimed by Tiffany and its subsidiaries."

In a supplemental affidavit, Agent Lewis conceded that "[i]t is certainly possible that once the individual [Pedi–Pulsor] licensees are identified further inquiry will be made into whether they correctly reported their income tax liabilities." He reasserted, however, that *one* purpose of his investigation was to audit Tiffany; in particular, he sought to ascertain whether Tiffany had failed to report recourse and nonrecourse notes provided to Tiffany by the Pedi–Pulsor licensees. * * *

* * *

The District Court found that the IRS had made a sufficient showing of its interest in auditing Tiffany's returns and enforced the summonses. The United States Court of Appeals for the Second Circuit affirmed. 718 F.2d 7 (1983). It held that the John Doe provisions of § 7609(f) apply only when "the IRS issue[s] a summons to an identifiable party in whom it ha[s] no interest in order to investigate the potential tax liabilities of unnamed third parties." Given the District Court's finding that one purpose of the summonses was to investigate Tiffany, § 7609(f) was not relevant here "even assuming that the summonses * * * were issued to Tiffany partly for the purpose of investigating Tiffany's customers."

* * *

II

Congress enacted § 7609 in response to two decisions in which we gave a broad construction to the IRS's general summons power under § 7602(a). * * *

In *Donaldson v. United States,* 400 U.S. 517, 91 S.Ct. 534, 27 L.Ed.2d 580 (1971), the IRS issued to an employer a § 7602 summons seeking records prepared by the employer that would be relevant to an investigation of the tax liability of one of its employees. The employee obtained a preliminary injunction restraining his employer from complying with the summons. The Government then moved for enforcement. In response, the employer stated that it would have complied with the summons " 'were it not for' the preliminary injunction." *Id.,* at 521, 91 S.Ct., at 537. The employee, however, filed motions to intervene in the proceedings, * * * in order to oppose enforcement. * * * We held that the employee's interest was not legally protectible and affirmed the denial of the employee's motions for intervention.

Four years later, we decided *United States v. Bisceglia,* 420 U.S. 141, 95 S.Ct. 915, 43 L.Ed.2d 88 (1975). In *Bisceglia,* the IRS issued to a bank a § 7602 summons for the purpose of identifying an unnamed individual who had deposited a large amount of money in severely deteriorated bills. The bills appeared to have been stored for a long period of time under abnormal conditions, and the IRS suspected that they had been hidden to avoid taxes. Although we recognized the danger that the IRS might use its § 7602 summons power to "conduct 'fishing expeditions' into the private affairs of bank depositors," we concluded that, on the facts of the case, the IRS had not abused its power. Thus, we held that the summons was enforceable.

Section 7609, the provision at issue in this case, was clearly a response to these decisions. Both the Senate and the House Reports accompanying the bill that became § 7609 focused exclusively on the problem of "third-party summonses"—that is, summonses served on a party that, like the employer in *Donaldson* and the bank in *Bisceglia,* is not the taxpayer under investigation. In fact, *Donaldson* and *Bisceglia* were the only two cases cited in the texts of the Reports.

* * *

Both Reports asserted that the standards enunciated in *Donaldson* and *Bisceglia* might "unreasonably infringe on the civil rights of taxpayers, including the right to privacy." S.Rep. No. 94–938, at 368; H.R.Rep. No. 94–658, at 307. Section 7609 stems from this concern. To deal with the problem of a third-party summons in a case in which the IRS *knows* the identity of the taxpayer being investigated, Congress enacted §§ 7609(a) and (b); these subsections require that the IRS give notice of the summons to that taxpayer, and give the taxpayer the right "to intervene in any proceeding with respect to the enforcement of such summons." In this provision, Congress overturned the result reached in *Donaldson.*

In the case of a John Doe summons, where the IRS *does not know* the identity of the taxpayer under investigation, advance notice to that taxpayer is, of course, not possible. As a substitute for the procedures of §§ 7609(a) and (b), Congress enacted § 7609(f), which provides:

"Any summons * * * *which does not identify the person with respect to whose liability the summons is issued* may be served only after a court proceeding in which the Secretary establishes that—

"(1) the summons relates to the investigation of a particular person or ascertainable group or class of persons,

"(2) there is a reasonable basis for believing that such person or group or class of persons may fail or may have failed to comply with any provision of any internal revenue law, and

"(3) the information sought to be obtained from the examination of the records (and the identity of the person or persons with respect to whose liability the summons is issued) is not readily available from other sources" (emphasis added).

See also § 7609(h)(2) (providing that these determinations be made *ex parte,* solely on the basis of the IRS's petition and supporting affidavits). Section § 7609(f) was a response to concerns that our decision in *Bisceglia* did not provide sufficient restraints, in the John Doe context, on the IRS's exercise of its summons power. * * *

* * *

III

* * * The District Court found as a matter of fact—and the Court of Appeals affirmed—that the IRS was pursuing a legitimate investigation of Tiffany's tax liability. At the same time, the Court of Appeals assumed, and the Government does not dispute, that the IRS also intended to investigate the tax liabilities of the unnamed Pedi–Pulsor licensees. The question before us, then, is whether the IRS must comply with § 7609(f) in the case of such dual purpose summonses.

This Court has recognized that there is "a formidable line of precedent construing congressional intent to uphold the claimed enforcement authority of the [IRS] if [this] authority is necessary for the effective enforcement of the revenue laws and is not undercut by contrary legislative purposes." *United States v. Euge.* Just last Term, we reemphasized that "restrictions upon the IRS's summons power should be avoided 'absent unambiguous directions from Congress.'" *United States v. Arthur Young & Co.* (quoting *United States v. Bisceglia*). Thus we examine whether the statute and legislative history indicate that Congress expressly considered the problem presented here, and attempt to discern the congressional purposes in enacting § 7609(f).

A

We find that the language of the statute is of little direct help in determining how to treat dual purpose summonses. By their terms, the John Doe provisions of § 7609(f) apply to a summons "which does not identify the person with respect to whose liability the summons is issued." * * *

* * *

The task that the parties ask us to engage in is to determine whether the statutory reference to "the person" should be read as "every person" or whether it should be read as "at least one person." We are reluctant, on the basis of the statutory language alone, to reach even a tentative conclusion about the scope of § 7609(f). * * *

Turning our attention to the legislative history, we note that the facts of this case are different from those of *Donaldson* and *Bisceglia* in one important respect: The summonses here were served on a party that was itself under IRS investigation. Congress did not address this situation in 1976 when it enacted the John Doe provisions. The Reports contain no mention of a summons issued for the dual purpose of investigating both the tax liability of the summoned party and the tax liabilities of unnamed parties. They focus exclusively on summonses issued to parties not themselves under investigation. We conclude that Congress did not expressly consider the problem of dual purpose summonses.

B

We, therefore, turn to consider whether dual purpose summonses give rise to the same concerns that prompted Congress to enact § 7609(f). The Reports discuss only one specific congressional worry: that the party receiving a summons would not have a sufficient interest in protecting the privacy of the records if that party was not itself a target of the summons. Such a taxpayer might have little incentive to oppose enforcement vigorously. Then, with no real adversary, the IRS could use its summons power to engage in "fishing expeditions" that might unnecessarily trample upon taxpayer privacy. Congress determined that when the IRS uses its summons power not to conduct a legitimate investigation of an ascertainable target, but instead to look around for targets to investigate, the privacy rights of taxpayers are infringed unjustifiably.

In response to this concern, §§ 7609(a) and (b) gave the real parties in interest—those actually being investigated—the right to intervene in the enforcement proceedings. Similarly, the John Doe requirements of § 7609(f) were adopted as a substitute for the procedures of §§ 7609(a) and (b). In effect, in the John Doe context, the court takes the place of the affected taxpayer under §§ 7609(a) and (b) and exerts a restraining influence on the IRS. However, § 7609(f) provides no opportunity for the unnamed taxpayers to assert any "personal defenses," such as attorney-client or Fifth Amendment privileges that might be asserted under §§ 7609(a) and (b). What § 7609(f) does is to provide some guarantee that the information that the IRS seeks through a summons is relevant to a legitimate investigation, albeit that of an unknown taxpayer.

When, as in this case, the summoned party is itself under investigation, the interests at stake are very different. First, by definition, the IRS is not engaged in a "fishing expedition" when it seeks information relevant to a legitimate investigation of a particular taxpayer. In such cases, any incidental effect on the privacy rights of unnamed taxpayers is justified by the IRS's interest in enforcing the tax laws. More importantly, the summoned party will have a direct incentive to oppose enforcement. In such circumstances, the vigilance and self-interest of the summoned party—complemented by its right to resist enforcement—will provide some assurance that the IRS will not strike out arbitrarily or seek irrelevant materials. Here, for example, Tiffany argued vigorously—albeit unsuccessfully—against enforcement of the summonses.

This is not to say, of course, that as long as the summoned party is under investigation, the IRS will be guaranteed an adversary. It is possible that the summoned party, even if it is itself being investigated, will not oppose enforcement, and that as a result the IRS might obtain some information that is relevant only to the liabilities of unnamed taxpayers. We recognize that the privacy rights of the unnamed taxpayers might then be unnecessarily trampled upon. Congress, however, did not seek to ensure that the IRS have an adversary in all summons proceedings. All that it did was require that a party with a real interest in the investigation—or the district court in the John Doe context—have standing to challenge the IRS's exercise of its summons authority. It is not up to us, in construing the scope of this authority, to identify a problem that did not trouble Congress, or to attempt to correct it. We therefore conclude that, where the summoned party is itself being investigated, that party's self-interest provides sufficient protection against the evils that Congress sought to remedy when it enacted § 7609(f).

We reject Tiffany's argument that, under the decision below, the IRS can circumvent the requirements of § 7609(f) merely by stating that the summoned party is under investigation. We do not find that argument persuasive for two reasons. First, in such a case, the summoned party would still have a sufficient interest in opposing enforcement, as it would have no way of ascertaining that the IRS was not in fact seeking to investigate it. This party would be an interested adversary, and the concerns to which § 7609(f) was addressed would thus be significantly attenuated. More importantly, if the district court finds in the enforcement proceeding that the IRS does not in fact intend to investigate the summoned party, or that some of the records requested are not relevant to a legitimate investigation of the summoned party, the IRS could not obtain all the information it sought unless it complied with § 7609(f).

Our conclusion that the congressional concerns are adequately met without resort to § 7609(f) when the summoned party is itself under investigation should not be read to imply that the IRS can obtain from that party, without complying with § 7609(f), information that is relevant only to the investigation of unnamed taxpayers. In order to obtain such information, the IRS would have to satisfy the requirements of § 7609(f). Therefore, when the IRS does not comply with § 7609(f), the focus must be on whether the information sought is relevant to the investigation of the summoned party. Thus, we discuss next whether the names of the Pedi–Pulsor licensees were relevant to an investigation of Tiffany's tax liability.

C

During the enforcement proceedings, Tiffany argued that it was possible to perform an investigation of its tax liability without resort to the names of all the Pedi–Pulsor licensees. We have never held, however, that the IRS must conduct its investigations in the least intrusive way possible. Instead, the standard is one of relevance. The Government argues persuasively that contact with the licensees might be necessary to verify that the transactions reported by Tiffany actually occurred. In fact, Tiffany itself acknowledged the relevance of the requested information, as it offered the IRS the names of certain licensees: "They might want to check a number of them at random, and this we are willing to do because we understand that they are entitled to review [Tiffany's] books." Tiffany refused, however, to provide all of the names, as it did not think that in the course of its investigation of Tiffany, the IRS would want to audit "50 out of 50 or 150 out of 150 participants."

On the record before us, we agree with the Government that the names of the licensees "may be relevant" to the legitimate investigation of Tiffany. The decision of how many, and which, licensees to contact is one for the IRS—not Tiffany—to make. Having already found that Congress provided no "unambiguous direction" on the question whether the IRS needs to comply with § 7609(f) in the case of dual purpose summonses, and that the IRS's failure to comply with these requirements when serving such summonses does not undermine the goals that Congress sought to promote through § 7609(f), we conclude that the summonses here were properly enforced.

* * *

Notes and Questions

1. A party summoned under Code Section 7609(f) should be able to challenge the issuance and enforcement of a summons to determine whether the elements of *Powell* have been satisfied. See United States v. Ernst & Whinney, 750 F.2d 516 (6th Cir.1984). Although Ernst & Whinney's challenge of the enforceability of the summons failed, they were successful in convincing the court to place limits on the scope of the summons.

2. In addition to the *Powell* criteria, the attorney-client privilege may be asserted to challenge the enforceability of a "John Doe" summons. United States v. Liebman, 742 F.2d 807 (3d Cir.1984). In *Liebman,* the IRS wanted the names of the law firm's clients who paid fees over a three year period in connection with the acquisition of certain tax shelters. The Service already knew that some had deducted fees illegally and was searching for the names of others. The court held that if they were to deny the attorney-client privilege, the identity, along with the substance of the communication that was already known by the Service, would provide all

there is to know about a confidential communication between a taxpayer/client and his attorney.

3. What practical impact, if any, will the tax shelter registration and customer list requirements of Code § 6111 and § 6112 have on the Service's need to use "John Doe" summonses? See S. Struntz and R. Rubin, Tiffany Fine Arts: Service Need Not Comply With "John Doe" Rules, 62 Journal of Taxation 140 (March 1985).

Chapter IX

FEDERAL TAX CRIMES AND METHODS OF PROOF

Scope Note: The success of the federal system of self-assessment is attributable largely to the existence of a variety of sanctions designed to encourage the highest possible degree of voluntary compliance with the tax laws. Although the civil penalty and interest provisions of the Code may help to encourage such compliance by making non-compliance costly, the deterrent effect of the criminal provisions is the real key to maintaining an effective system of taxation.

This chapter begins with an overview of the basic tax offenses, followed by a discussion of the elements of each offense and the methods used by the government to prove violations.

SECTION 1. THE TAX CRIMES

The Internal Revenue Code contains a number of different criminal provisions.[a] In addition, a wide variety of general criminal offenses defined in Title 18 of the United States Code are pertinent to tax matters. Hence, it would be impractical (if not impossible) to provide a comprehensive discussion of the full range of what might fairly be described as tax crimes. However, the vast majority of criminal tax cases are concerned with four provisions of the Internal Revenue Code (and two related general criminal provisions).

Evasion (or more precisely, attempted evasion)[b] is a felony carrying a maximum penalty of 5 years in prison and/or a $100,000 fine ($500,000 for a corporation), plus the costs of prosecution. The elements of the crime are an attempt to evade or defeat tax (or payment of tax) in any manner, the existence of a tax deficiency (or tax due and owing in an evasion of payment case), an affirmative act of fraud, and willfulness.

a. I.R.C. §§ 7201–7216, 7231, 7232, 7240, 7261, 7262, 7268–7273 and 7275. b. I.R.C. § 7201.

537

The false return charge[c] is a felony carrying a maximum penalty of 3 years in prison and/or a $100,000 fine ($500,000 for a corporation) plus the costs of prosecution. The elements of the offense are the making and subscribing of a return, statement or other document which states that it is signed under penalty of perjury, knowledge that the document is not true as to any material matter, and willfulness.

The charge of aiding or assisting in the preparation of a false return[d] is a felony carrying a maximum penalty of 3 years in prison and/or a $100,000 fine ($500,000 for a corporation), plus the costs of prosecution. The elements of the offense are aiding or assisting in the preparation or presentation of a return or other document which is fraudulent or false as to any material matter, and willfulness.

The "failure to file" charge[e] is a misdemeanor carrying a maximum penalty of 1 year in prison and/or a $25,000 fine ($100,000 for a corporation) plus the costs of prosecution. The elements of the offense are a duty to file a return, supply information or pay any tax or estimated tax, the failure to comply with the duty, and willfulness.

There is also a frequently discussed, but rarely used, misdemeanor charge for delivering or disclosing to the IRS a fraudulent return, statement or other document.[f] This offense carries a maximum penalty of 1 year in prison and/or a $10,000 fine ($50,000 for a corporation) plus the costs of prosecution. The elements of the offense are the delivery or disclosure to the IRS of a return, statement or other document known to be fraudulent or false as to any material matter, and willfulness.

In addition to crimes specified in the Internal Revenue Code, a criminal tax case may be cast in the form of a conspiracy prosecution.[g] A conspiracy conviction carries a maximum penalty of 5 years in prison and/or a $10,000 fine, except where the object of the conspiracy is a misdemeanor. The elements of the crime of conspiracy are an agreement between two or more persons to commit an offense against or to defraud the United States and an overt act in furtherance of the conspiracy.

A criminal tax case may also involve a false statement charge,[h] which carries the possibility of a 5 year prison sentence and/or a $10,000 fine. The elements of the offense are the falsification or concealment of a material fact or the making of a false statement or use of a false document, and willfulness.[i]

Maximum fines. The *actual* fines for criminal violations may exceed maximum amounts specified above. The Criminal Fines Enforcement Act of 1984 establishes maximum fines for crimes committed

c. I.R.C. § 7206(1).
d. I.R.C. § 7206(2).
e. I.R.C. § 7203.
f. I.R.C. § 7207.
g. 18 U.S.C.A. § 371 (West 1966).
h. 18 U.S.C.A. § 1001.
i. Note that a perjury offense, 18 U.S.C.A. §§ 1621, 1623 (West 1984), may exist if the false statement was made under oath.

after 1984. These amounts, now contained in 18 U.S.C.A. § 3571, apply to any offenses not specifically exempted from the new maximum amounts. In addition, for offenses committed after November 1, 1987, the Sentencing Guidelines issued by the United States Sentencing Commission affect the actual fine and term of imprisonment. The current maximum fine is the *greatest of:*

1. The amount specified in the provision establishing the offense; or

2. twice the gross gain or loss (for example, if tax liability was understated and underpaid by $50,000, then the fine could be $100,000); or

3. for felonies, $250,000 for individuals and $500,000 for corporations; or

4. for misdemeanors punishable by more than 6 months' imprisonment, $100,000 for individuals and $200,000 for corporations.

Sentencing guidelines. The United States Sentencing Commission, pursuant to Congressional directive, issued Guidelines for sentencing in cases involving offenses committed after November 1, 1987. The United States Supreme Court upheld the constitutionality of these Guidelines in Mistretta v. United States, 488 U.S. 361, 109 S.Ct. 647, 102 L.Ed.2d 714 (1989). In combination with stated policy of the Justice Department, these Guidelines should increase the number of tax offenders who serve time in prison.

The Justice Department Tax Division's policy is that "the payment of the civil tax liability, plus a fine and suspended sentence, does not constitute a satisfactory disposition of a criminal case." *U.S. Attorneys' Manual* § 6–2.450. Despite this stated policy, criminal tax offenders were able to avoid imprisonment in about 57% of all prosecutions, a percentage the Sentencing Commission found too high in light of the significance of our voluntary compliance system to the functioning of the government. To achieve maximum deterrent effect, the Sentencing Guidelines for tax offenses base the severity of the punishment on the gravity of the offense, both in terms of the type of crime (*i.e.,* felony or misdemeanor) and the amount of tax liability evaded or unpaid. The "offense level" under the Guidelines can be increased if the defendant used "sophisticated means" to impede discovery of the offense, or if he displays lack of remorse or obstructs the proceedings. On the other hand, a defendant's remorse or cooperation can decrease the offense level.

Mail fraud and RICO. The Racketeer Influenced and Corrupt Organizations Act, 18 U.S.C.A. § 1961 *et seq.,* ("RICO") has invaded the province of tax prosecutions, as it has numerous other areas of the law. RICO prosecutions are statutorily authorized only for violation of certain enumerated federal criminal laws. Tax crimes are *not* listed as predicate crimes, but mail fraud and wire fraud violations are predicate crimes for RICO. The federal mail fraud statute, 18 U.S.C.A. § 1341, applies to anyone who devises or intends to devise a scheme to defraud for the purpose of obtaining money or property by false pretense, and who uses the mail to execute the scheme. Wire fraud, 18 U.S.C.A. § 1343, is the transmission across state lines by wire, radio or television any pictures, writings or sounds for the purpose of executing a fraudulent scheme. The mail and wire fraud provisions are both felonies, with maximum jail sentences of five years, and are *in pari materia* so that decisions under one apply equally to the other. United States v. Oren, 893 F.2d 1057, 1060 n. 1 (9th Cir.1990); United States v. Tarnopol, 561 F.2d 466, 475 (3d Cir.1977).

Some courts have found that mailing a fraudulent tax return can be a mail fraud violation and permitted conviction of defendants for both offenses. See United States v. Busher, 817 F.2d 1409 (9th Cir. 1987). Conviction of mail fraud presents fewer proof problems for the government, as it need not prove "willfulness" beyond a reasonable doubt. Because mail fraud is a predicate violation for RICO, if the filing of a fraudulent return violates the mail fraud provision, then RICO prosecutions for tax offenses can occur, notwithstanding that Congress did not list the tax crimes as predicates for RICO. The consequences of a RICO prosecution can be dramatic. The maximum penalties include 20 years' imprisonment, and RICO's broad forfeiture provisions can result in a defendant's forfeiture of all assets from the "enterprise," which could be highly disproportionate to the tax offense involved.

In July of 1989 the Justice Department amended the *U.S. Attorneys' Manual*, section 6–4.211(1), to require prior approval of the Tax Division before charging mail fraud either independently or as a predicate for a RICO charge when the mailing involves a tax return or other document in connection with a tax fraud scheme. The new policy is that authorization will be granted only in "exceptional circumstances." According to the amendment: "It is the position of the Tax Division that Congress intended that tax crimes be charged as tax crimes and that the specific criminal law provisions of the Internal Revenue Code should form the focus of prosecutions when essentially tax law violation motives are involved, even though other crimes may technically have been committed." For a discussion of the tax fraud/mail fraud issue, see Podgor, Tax Fraud–Mail Fraud: Synonymous, Cumulative or Diverse?, 57 U.Cin.L.Rev. 903 (1989).

A. THE BASIC TAX OFFENSES

(1) Sections 7201, 7203 and 7207

SPIES v. UNITED STATES
Supreme Court of the United States, 1943.
317 U.S. 492, 63 S.Ct. 364, 87 L.Ed. 418.

Mr. Justice Jackson delivered the opinion of the Court.

Petitioner has been convicted of attempting to defeat and evade income tax in violation of § 145(b) of * * * the Internal Revenue Code [of 1939].ʲ

Petitioner admitted at the opening of the trial that he had sufficient income during the year in question to place him under a statutory duty to file a return and to pay a tax, and that he failed to do either. The evidence during nearly two weeks of trial was directed principally toward establishing the exact amount of the tax and the manner of receiving and handling income and accounting, which the Government contends shows an intent to evade and defeat tax. Petitioner's testimony related to his good character, his physical illness at the time the return became due, and lack of willfulness in his defaults, chiefly because of a psychological disturbance, amounting to something more than worry but something less than insanity.

Section 145(a)ᵏ makes, among other things, willful failure to pay a tax or make a return by one having petitioner's income at the time or times required by law a misdemeanor. Section 145(b) makes a willful attempt in any manner to evade or defeat any tax such as his a felony. Petitioner was not indicted for either misdemeanor. The indictment contained a single count setting forth the felony charge of willfully attempting to defeat and evade the tax, and recited willful failure to file a return and willful failure to pay the tax as the means to the felonious end.

* * * The Court refused a request to instruct that an affirmative act was necessary to constitute a willful attempt and charged that "Attempt means to try to do or accomplish. In order to find an attempt it is not necessary to find affirmative steps to accomplish the prohibited purpose. An attempt may be found on the basis of inactivity or on refraining to act, as well."

It is the Government's contention that a willful failure to file a return together with a willful failure to pay the tax may, without more, constitute an attempt to defeat or evade a tax within § 145(b). Petitioner claims that such proof establishes only two misdemeanors under § 145(a) and that it takes more than the sum of two such misdemeanors to make the felony under § 145(b). The legislative history of the section contains nothing helpful on the question here at issue, and we must find the answer from the section itself and its context in the revenue laws.

The United States has relied for the collection of its income tax largely upon the taxpayer's own disclosures rather than upon a system of withholding the tax from him by those from whom income may be received. This system can function successfully only if those within and near taxable income keep and render true accounts. In many ways taxpayers' neglect or deceit may prejudice the orderly and punctual administration of the system as well as the revenues themselves. Congress has imposed a variety of sanctions for the protection of the system and the revenues. The relation of the offense of which this

j. The predecessor to § 7201 of the Internal Revenue Code of 1954.

k. The predecessor to § 7203 of the Internal Revenue Code of 1954.

petitioner has been convicted to other and lesser revenue offenses appears more clearly from its position in this structure of sanctions.

The penalties imposed by Congress to enforce the tax laws embrace both civil and criminal sanctions. The former consist of additions to the tax upon determinations of fact made by an administrative agency and with no burden on the Government to prove its case beyond a reasonable doubt. The latter consist of penal offenses enforced by the criminal process in the familiar manner. Invocation of one does not exclude resort to the other.

The failure in a duty to make a timely return, unless it is shown that such failure is due to reasonable cause and not due to willful neglect, is punishable by an addition to the tax of 5 to 25 per cent thereof, depending on the duration of the default. But a duty may exist even when there is no tax liability to serve as a base for application of a percentage delinquency penalty; the default may relate to matters not identifiable with tax for a particular period; and the offense may be more grievous than a case for civil penalty. Hence the willful failure to make a return, keep records, or supply information when required, is made a misdemeanor, without regard to existence of a tax liability. § 145(a). Punctuality is important to the fiscal system, and these are sanctions to assure punctual as well as faithful performance of these duties.

Sanctions to insure payment of the tax are even more varied to meet the variety of causes of default. It is the right as well as the interest of the taxpayer to limit his admission of liability to the amount he actually owes. But the law is complicated, accounting treatment of various items raises problems of great complexity, and innocent errors are numerous, as appear from the number who make overpayments. It is not the purpose of the law to penalize frank difference of opinion or innocent errors made despite the exercise of reasonable care. Such errors are corrected by the assessment of the deficiency of tax and its collection with interest for the delay. If any part of the deficiency is due to negligence or intentional disregard of rules and regulations, but without intent to defraud, five per cent of such deficiency is added thereto; and if any part of any deficiency is due to fraud with intent to evade tax, the addition is 50 per cent thereof. Willful failure to pay the tax when due is punishable as a misdemeanor. § 145(a). The climax of this variety of sanctions is the serious and inclusive felony defined to consist of willful attempt in any manner to evade or defeat the tax. § 145(b). The question here is whether there is a distinction between the acts necessary to make out the felony and those which may make out the misdemeanor.

A felony may, and frequently does, include lesser offenses in combination either with each other or with other elements. We think it clear that this felony may include one or several of the other offenses against the revenue laws. But it would be unusual and we would not readily assume that Congress by the felony defined in § 145(b) meant no more than the same derelictions it had just defined in § 145(a) as a misdemeanor. Such an interpretation becomes even more difficult to accept when we consider this felony as the capstone of a system of sanctions which singly or in combination were calculated to induce prompt and forthright fulfillment of every duty under the income tax law and to provide a penalty suitable to every degree of delinquency.

The difference between willful failure to pay a tax when due, which is made a misdemeanor, and willful attempt to defeat and evade one, which is made a felony, is not easy to detect or define. Both must be willful, and willful, as we have said, is a word of many meanings, its construction often being influenced by its context. It may well mean something more as applied to nonpayment of a tax than when applied to failure to make a return. Mere voluntary and purposeful, as distinguished from accidental, omission to make a timely return might meet the test of willfulness. But in view of our traditional aversion to imprisonment for debt, we would not without the clearest manifestation of Congressional intent assume that mere knowing and intentional default in payment of a tax where there had been no willful failure to disclose the liability is intended to constitute a criminal offense of any degree. We would expect willfulness in such a case to include some element of evil motive and want of justification in view of all the financial circumstances of the taxpayer.

Had § 145(a) not included willful failure to pay a tax, it would have defined as misdemeanors generally a failure to observe statutory duties to make timely returns, keep records, or supply information—duties imposed to facilitate administration of the Act even if, because of insufficient net income, there were no duty to pay a tax. It would then be a permissible and perhaps an appropriate construction of § 145(b) that it made felonies of the same willful omissions when there was the added element of duty to pay a tax. The definition of such nonpayment as a misdemeanor we think argues strongly against such an interpretation.

The difference between the two offenses, it seems to us, is found in the affirmative action implied from the term "attempt," as used in the felony subsection. It is not necessary to involve this subject with the complexities of the common-law "attempt". The attempt made criminal by this statute does not consist of conduct that would culminate in a more serious crime but for some impossibility of completion or interruption or frustration. This is an independent crime, complete in its most serious form when the attempt is complete and nothing is added to its criminality by success or consummation, as would be the case, say, of attempted murder. Although the attempt succeeded in evading tax, there is no criminal offense of that kind, and the prosecution can be only for the attempt. We think that in employing the terminology of attempt to embrace the gravest of offenses against the revenues Congress intended some willful commission in addition to the willful omissions that make up the list of misdemeanors. Willful but passive neglect of the statutory duty may constitute the lesser offense, but to combine with it a willful and positive attempt to evade tax in any manner or to defeat it by any means lifts the offense to the **degree of felony**.

Congress did not define or limit the methods by which a willful attempt to defeat and evade might be accomplished and perhaps did not define lest its effort to do so result in some unexpected limitation. Nor would we by definition constrict the scope of the Congressional provision that it may be accomplished "in any manner". By way of illustration, and not by way of limitation, we would think affirmative willful attempt may be inferred from conduct such as keeping a double set of books, making false entries or alterations, or false invoices or documents, destruction of books or records, concealment of assets or covering up sources of income, handling of one's affairs to avoid making the records usual in transactions of the kind, and any conduct, the likely effect of which would be to mislead or to conceal. If the tax-evasion motive plays any part in such conduct the offense may be made out even though the conduct may also serve other purposes such as concealment of other crime.

In this case there are several items of evidence apart from the default in filing the return and paying the tax which the Government claims will support an inference of willful attempt to evade or defeat the tax. These go to establish that petitioner insisted that certain income be paid to him in cash, transferred it to his own bank by armored car, deposited it, not in his own name but in the names of others of his family, and kept inadequate and misleading records. Petitioner claims other motives animated him in these matters. We intimate no opinion. Such inferences are for the jury. If on proper submission the jury found these acts, taken together with willful failure to file a return and willful failure to pay the tax, to constitute a willful attempt to defeat and evade tax, we would consider conviction of a felony sustainable. But we think a defendant is entitled to a charge which will point out the necessity for such an inference of willful attempt to defeat or evade tax from some proof in the case other than that necessary to make out the misdemeanors; and if the evidence fails to afford such an inference, the defendant should be acquitted.

* * *

Reversed.

SANSONE v. UNITED STATES
Supreme Court of the United States, 1965.
380 U.S. 343, 85 S.Ct. 1004, 13 L.Ed.2d 882.

Mr. Justice Goldberg delivered the opinion of the Court.

Petitioner Sansone was indicted for willfully attempting to evade federal income taxes for the year 1957 in violation of § 7201 of the Internal Revenue Code of 1954. * * *

The following facts were established at trial. In March 1956 petitioner and his wife purchased a tract of land for $22,500 and simultaneously sold a portion of the tract for $20,000. In August 1957 petitioner sold another portion of the tract for $27,000. He did not report the gain on either the 1956 or 1957 sale in his income tax returns for those years. Petitioner conceded that the 1957 transaction was reportable and that, in not reporting it, he understated his tax liability for that year by $2,456.48. He contended, however, that this understatement was not willful since he believed at the time that extensive repairs on a creek adjoining a portion of the tract he retained might be necessary and that the cost of these repairs might wipe out his profit on the 1957 sale.

To counter this defense, the Government introduced the following signed statement made by petitioner during the Treasury investigation of his tax return:

"I did not report the 1957 sale in our joint income tax return for 1957 because I was burdened with a number of financial obligations and did not feel I could raise the money to pay any tax due. It was my intention to report all sales in a future year and pay the tax due. I knew that I should have reported the 1957 sale, but my wife did not know that it should have been reported. It was not my intention to evade the payment of our proper taxes and I intended to pay any additional taxes due when I was financially able to do so."

At the conclusion of the trial, petitioner requested that the jury be instructed that it could acquit him of the charged offense of willfully attempting to evade or defeat taxes in violation of § 7201, but still convict him of either or both of the asserted lesser-included offenses of willfully filing a fraudulent or false return, in violation of § 7207, or willfully failing to pay his taxes at the time required by law, in violation of § 7203. * * *

* * *

We are faced with the threshold question as to whether or not § 7207, which proscribes the willful filing with a Treasury official of any known false or fraudulent "return," applies to the filing of an income tax return. If § 7207 does not apply to income tax returns, it is obvious that the defendant was not here entitled to a lesser-included offense charge based on that section. [The Court determined, however, that § 7207 would apply to the filing of a false income tax return.]

* * *

* * * Since there is no doubt that §§ 7201 and 7203 also apply to income tax violations, with obvious overlapping among them, there can be no doubt that the lesser-included offense doctrine applies to these statutes in an appropriate case.

The basic principles controlling whether or not a lesser-included offense charge should be given in a particular case have been settled by this Court. Rule 31(c) of the Federal Rules of Criminal Procedure provides in relevant part, that the "defendant may be found guilty of an offense necessarily included in the offense charged." Thus, "[i]n a case where some of the elements of the crime charged themselves constitute a lesser crime, the defendant, if the evidence justifie[s] it * * * [is] entitled to an instruction which would permit a finding of guilt of the lesser offense." Berra v. United States, 351 U.S. 131, 134, 76 S.Ct. 685, 688, 100 L.Ed. 1013 (1956). But a lesser-offense charge is not proper where, on the evidence presented, the factual issues to be resolved by the jury are the same as to both the lesser and greater offenses. In other words, the lesser offense must be included within but not, on the facts of the case, be completely encompassed by the greater. A lesser-included offense instruction is only proper where the charged greater offense requires the jury to find a disputed factual element which is not required for conviction of the lesser-included offense. We now apply the principles declared in these cases to the instant case.

The offense here charged was a violation of § 7201, which proscribes willfully attempting in any manner to evade or defeat any tax imposed by the Internal Revenue Code. * * * [Section] 7201 necessarily includes among its elements actions which, if isolated from the others, constitute lesser offenses in this hierarchical system of sanctions. Therefore, if on the facts of a given case there are disputed issues of fact which would enable the jury rationally to find that, although all the elements of § 7201 have not been proved, all the elements of one or more lesser offenses have been, it is clear that the defendant is entitled to a lesser-included offense charge as to such lesser offenses.

As has been held by this Court, the elements of § 7201 are willfulness; the existence of a tax deficiency; and an affirmative act constituting an evasion or attempted evasion of the tax. In comparison, § 7203 makes it a misdemeanor willfully to fail to perform a number of specified acts at the time required by law—the one here relevant being the failure to pay a tax when due. This misdemeanor requires only willfulness and the omission of the required act—here the payment of the tax when due. As recognized by this Court in Spies v. United States, 317 U.S. at 499, 63 S.Ct. at 368, the difference between a mere willful failure to pay a tax (or perform other enumerated actions) when due under § 7203 and a willful attempt to evade or defeat taxes under § 7201 is that the latter felony involves "some willful commission in addition to the willful omissions that make up the list of misdemeanors." Where there is, in a § 7201 prosecution, a disputed issue of fact as to the existence of the requisite affirmative commission in addition to the § 7203 omission, a defendant would, of course, be entitled to a lesser-included offense charge based on § 7203. In this case, however, it is undisputed that petitioner filed a tax return and that the petitioner's filing of a false tax return constituted a sufficient affirmative commission to satisfy that requirement of § 7201. The only issue at trial was whether petitioner's act was willful. Given this affirmative commission and the conceded tax deficiency, if petitioner's act was willful, that is, if the jury believed, as it obviously did, that he knew that the capital gain on the sale of the property was reportable in

1957, he was guilty of violating both §§ 7201 and 7203. If his act was not willful, he was not guilty of violating either § 7201 or § 7203. Thus on the facts of this case, §§ 7201 and 7203 "covered precisely the same ground." Berra v. United States, supra, 351 U.S. at 134, 76 S.Ct. at 688. This being so, on the authorities cited, it is clear that petitioner was not entitled to a lesser-included offense charge based on § 7203.

Section 7207 requires the willful filing of a document known to be false or fraudulent in any material manner. The elements here involved are willfulness and the commission of the prohibited act. Section 7207 does not, however, require that the act be done as an attempt to evade or defeat taxes. Conduct could therefore violate § 7207 without violating § 7201 where the false statement, though material, does not constitute an attempt to evade or defeat taxation because it does not have the requisite effect of reducing the stated tax liability. This may be the case, for example, where a taxpayer understates his gross receipts and he offsets this by also understating his deductible expenses. In this example, if the Government in a § 7201 case charged tax evasion on the grounds that the defendant had understated his tax by understating his gross receipts, and the defendant contended that this was not so, as the misstatement of gross receipts had been offset by an understatement of deductible expenses, the defendant would be entitled to a lesser-included offense charge based on § 7207, there being this relevant disputed issue of fact. This would be so, for in such a case, if the jury believed that an understatement of deductible expenses had offset the understatement of gross receipts, while the defendant would have violated § 7207 by willfully making a material false and fraudulent statement on his return, he would not have violated § 7201 as there would not have been the requisite § 7201 element of a tax deficiency. Here, however, there is no dispute that petitioner's material misstatement resulted in a tax deficiency. Thus there is no disputed issue of fact concerning the existence of an element required for conviction of § 7201 but not required for conviction of § 7207. Given petitioner's material misstatement which resulted in a tax deficiency, if, as the jury obviously found, petitioner's act was willful in the sense that he knew that he should have reported more income than he did for the year 1957, he was guilty of violating both §§ 7201 and 7207. If his action was not willful, he was guilty of violating neither. As was true with § 7203, on the facts of this case §§ 7201 and 7207 "covered precisely the same ground," Berra v. United States, supra, and thus petitioner was not entitled to a lesser-included offense charge based on § 7207.

Petitioner makes one final contention. He argues that he could have been acquitted of attempting to evade or defeat his 1957 taxes, in violation of § 7201, but still have been convicted for willfully failing to pay his tax when due in violation of § 7203 or willfully filing a fraudulent return in violation of § 7207, if the jury believed his statement contained in the government-introduced affidavit, that, although he knew that profit on the sale in question was reportable for

1957 and that tax was due thereon, he intended to report the sale and pay the 1957 tax at some unspecified future date. The basic premise of this argument is that, although all three sections require willfulness, on the facts here, the contents of these willfulness requirements differ. The argument is made that while an intent to report and pay the tax in the future does not vitiate the willfulness requirements of §§ 7203 and 7207, it does constitute a defense to a willful attempt "in any manner to evade or defeat any tax imposed by" the Internal Revenue Code, in violation of § 7201. While we agree that the intent to report the income and pay the tax sometime in the future does not vitiate the willfulness required by §§ 7203 and 7207, we cannot agree that it vitiates the willfulness requirement of § 7201.

No defense to a § 7201 evasion charge is made out by showing that the defendant willfully and fraudulently understated his tax liability for the year involved but intended to report the income and pay the tax at some later time. As this Court has recognized, § 7201 includes the offense of willfully attempting to evade or defeat the *assessment* of a tax as well as the offense of willfully attempting to evade or defeat the *payment* of a tax. The indictment here charged an attempt to evade income taxes by defeating the assessment for 1957. The fact that petitioner stated to a revenue agent that he intended to report his 1957 income in some later year, even if taken at face value, would not detract from the criminality of his willful act defeating the 1957 assessment. That crime was complete as soon as the false and fraudulent understatement of taxes (assuming, of course, that there was in fact a deficiency) was filed.

In sum, it is clear here that there were no disputed issues of fact which would justify instructing the jury that it could find that petitioner had committed all the elements of either or both of the §§ 7203 and 7207 misdemeanors without having committed a violation of the § 7201 felony. This being the case, the petitioner was not entitled to a lesser-included offense charge and the judgment of the Court of Appeals is Affirmed.

Notes

1. The courts have been liberal in defining the conduct that satisfies the affirmative act of evasion requirement of *Spies*. For example, in United States v. Copeland, 786 F.2d 768 (7th Cir.1985), the court held that supplying false withholding certificates to an employer in violation of § 7205 (a misdemeanor offense) were sufficient affirmative acts to elevate the defendant's willful failure to file returns in 1980 and 1981 to the crime of attempted evasion. Similarly, in United States v. Goodyear, 649 F.2d 226 (4th Cir.1981), the court held that a false statement made to a Revenue Agent in 1974 concerning why no return was filed for 1971 was a sufficient affirmative act to sustain the defendant's conviction for attempted evasion for the taxes due in 1971.

2. If a taxpayer files a tax return but fails to file with the return schedules required by the Treasury Regulations, he can be convicted of the

offense defined in § 7203. See Pappas v. United States, 216 F.2d 515 (10th Cir.1954).

(2) Sections 7206(1) and 7206(2)

The essence of the charge under § 7206(1) is that there is a false tax return. Typically, but not exclusively, the statute is applied in cases where there has been a false entry on the return which results in an understatement of tax liability. However, as noted below, § 7206(1) may also be utilized in cases in which a false item on the tax return does not materially affect tax liability or, perhaps, where the falsity lies in an omission.

UNITED STATES v. GREENBERG
United States Court of Appeals, Second Circuit, 1984.
735 F.2d 29.

KEARSE, CIRCUIT JUDGE:

Defendant Jack Greenberg appeals from a judgment entered in the United States District Court for the Eastern District of New York after a jury trial before Jacob Mishler, *Judge,* convicting him on one count of filing a materially false corporate income tax return, in violation of 26 U.S.C. § 7206(1) (1982); two counts of filing materially false personal income tax returns, in violation of § 7206(1); and one count of willfully failing to file a federal income tax return, in violation of 26 U.S.C. § 7203 (1982). Greenberg was sentenced to a prison term of a year and a day. On appeal, he contends that his convictions should be reversed because the issue of materiality should have been submitted to the jury rather than decided by the court as a matter of law, and because in any event his misstatements were not material. Finding no merit in his contentions, we affirm.

BACKGROUND

The sufficiency of the government's evidence to prove that Greenberg filed, and assisted in filing, false income tax returns is not disputed. Greenberg was an accountant who was also a participant in a joint venture called P.R.P. Industries, Inc. ("PRP"). With respect to the charge that Greenberg aided and abetted the filing of a false corporate income tax return for PRP's 1978 fiscal year, in violation of § 7206(1), government witnesses testified that Greenberg had instructed them, *inter alia,* to classify as PRP business expenses expenditures that were solely for the personal benefit of Greenberg's co-venturer, and to classify as loans payments that in fact were investments in other businesses or were compensation to the co-venturers. Notwithstanding these misallocations, PRP reported more income than it should have for that fiscal year, and its net taxable income was stated in the proper amount.

With respect to the charges that Greenberg filed, jointly with his wife, false personal income tax returns for the years 1976 and 1977, in violation of § 7206(1), the evidence was that for each of those years, Greenberg overreported his wife's income and underreported his own. For 1976, Mrs. Greenberg was reported to have had a gross income of some $32,000, when in fact she had none; Greenberg was reported to have had earnings of some $4400, when in fact his earnings were approximately $25,000. For 1977, Mrs. Greenberg was reported to have had gross income of some $35,000, when in fact she had none; Greenberg was reported to have had gross receipts of some $66,000, when in fact his gross receipts were more than $100,000. Greenberg testified that the purpose of these false allocations was to present a picture that would enable Mrs. Greenberg to obtain credit in her own name despite having no occupation. Notwithstanding these misallocations, the variance between the taxes paid by the Greenbergs and the taxes actually owing under a proper allocation was $48.

In its charge with respect to the counts alleging violations of § 7206(1), the court instructed the jury that there could be no violation unless the false statements were material and that the court had found as a matter of law that the misstatements were material. Greenberg contends that the court erred in not submitting the materiality question to the jury and in not finding the misstatements immaterial. We disagree with both contentions.

Discussion

Section 7206(1) of 26 U.S.C. makes it unlawful for a person to "[w]illfully make[ ] and subscribe[ ] any return * * * under the penalties of perjury * * * which he does not believe to be true and correct as to every material matter." The cardinal question in this case is the meaning of the term "material."

Where a false statement is made to a public body or its representative, materiality refers to the impact that the statement may reasonably have on the ability of that agency to perform the functions assigned to it by law. The question is not what effect the statement actually had; its actual effect would plainly present an issue of fact. The question is rather whether the statement had the potential for an obstructive or inhibitive effect. A consideration of this potential requires an analysis of the responsibilities of the public agency—responsibilities that are assigned by law—and analysis of the relevance of the statement to those responsibilities. Both relevance and the nature of a duty are traditionally questions of law to be decided by the court. Perforce the interrelationship of these two legal questions is a question of law.

The question of the nature of materiality in the context of a prosecution under § 7206(1) has not previously been decided by this Court. When confronted with this issue in the context of false statements alleged to violate the perjury-type provisions of title 18, however, we have uniformly concluded that materiality was a question of law to be decided by the court. We see no basis for reaching a different conclusion with respect to 26 U.S.C. § 7206(1).

We note that our conclusion that materiality under § 7206(1) is a question of law is consistent with virtually all of the decisions of our Sister Circuits. We are aware of only one court of appeals case, *United States v. Null*, 415 F.2d 1178, 1181 (4th Cir.1969), that has stated that materiality in a § 7206(1) prosecution was an issue for the jury, and since that court did not state its analysis of the question, we find its ruling unpersuasive.

Finally, we are not persuaded that the court erred in concluding that the misstatements in the PRP return and in Greenberg's personal income tax returns were material. The purpose of § 7206(1) is not simply to ensure that the taxpayer pay the proper amount of taxes—though that is surely one of its goals. Rather, that section is intended to ensure also that the taxpayer not make misstatements that could hinder the Internal Revenue Service ("IRS") in carrying out such functions as the verification of the accuracy of that return or a related tax return.

Greenberg's argument that the misstatements were not material because they resulted in, at most, minimal underpayments of taxes ignores the potential of the misstatements for impeding the IRS's performance of its responsibilities. The fraudulent description of PRP's payment of its owners' personal expenses as business expenses, for example, presented a distorted picture of both PRP's expenses and the owners' income. The fraudulent allocation of income to Mrs. Greenberg on the joint personal returns, with the corresponding underreporting of Greenberg's own income, gave a similar distorted view. All of these distortions had the potential for hindering the IRS's efforts to monitor and verify the tax liability of PRP and the Greenbergs.

In short, the district court correctly determined that the false statements made and assisted by Greenberg were material.

CONCLUSION

The judgment of conviction is affirmed.

UNITED STATES v. DiVARCO

United States District Court, Northern District of Illinois, 1972.
343 F.Supp. 101, affirmed, 484 F.2d 670 (7th Cir.1973).

WILL, DISTRICT JUDGE.

The government is prosecuting the defendants in this case pursuant to an indictment which charges each of them with having made "a false statement as to a material matter on their respective 1965 United States Individual Income Tax Return," in violation of 26 U.S.C. § 7206(1), in that each reported income from commissions paid them by Chemical Mortgage & Investment Corporation never having received any income from such a source, thereby falsely stating the source of their reported income. * * * The defendants have moved to dismiss the indictment on the ground that the source of one's income as distinguished from the amount of one's income is not a material matter which can be falsely stated within the meaning of 26 U.S.C. § 7206(1). Defendants' motion is denied inasmuch as we find the source of income to be such a material matter.

* * *

Defendants' essential argument is that the source of one's income is not a material matter within the meaning of 26 U.S.C. § 7206(1), and that a false statement of the source of income on one's tax return is not an indictable offense. They contend that the only material matter on a tax return that is indictable is the amount of one's taxable income. They continue that, since an overstatement of taxable income is not an indictable offense, citing Poonian v. United States, 294 F.2d 74 (9th Cir.1961), no valid prosecution can be maintained under 26 U.S.C. § 7206(1) without a showing of understatement of the defendants' taxable income.

The question whether misstatement of the source of one's income alone without a misstatement of the amount of one's income is indictable under 26 U.S.C. § 7206(1) is one of first impression. The government has cited a number of cases in support of their position that an indictment for the misstatement of source of income alone is valid. See Gaunt v. United States, 184 F.2d 284 (1st Cir.1950), cert. denied 340 U.S. 917, 71 S.Ct. 350, 95 L.Ed. 662 (1951); United States v. Null, 415 F.2d 1178 (4th Cir.1969); United States v. Rayor, 204 F.Supp. 486 (S.D.Cal.1962). The defendants have correctly noted that none of these cases involved an indictment solely for the false statement of the source of income. Technically, not one of the cases proffered by the government holds that a false statement as to the source of income alone is an indictable offense under 26 U.S.C. § 7206(1). Most of the government cases involved prosecution for the understatement of taxable income. In a few of the cases, it is unclear what material matter was falsely misstated.

The mere fact that the government cases are not strict precedents for the indictment in the instant case does not, however, render them useless in our analysis. Defendants' historical position that there have been no reported prosecutions under § 7206(1) for false statement as to source of income alone is not dispositive of the issue whether source of income is a material matter under the statute, the false statement of which is indictable. The reported cases, while involving fact patterns where there had been understatement of the amount of income, did not focus on the particular material matter which had been misstated. Rather, these courts found a more general rationale underlying the section.

One of the more basic tenets running through all the cases is that the purpose behind the statute is to prosecute those who intentionally falsify their tax returns regardless of the precise ultimate effect that such falsification may have. In the early and oft-cited *Gaunt* case, it was stated:

> It seems to us clear that the latter subsection [§ 145(c) of the 1939 Code, which is virtually identical to its successor § 7206(1)] makes it a felony merely to make and subscribe a tax return without believing it to be true and correct as to every material matter, whether or not the purpose in so doing was to evade or defeat the payment of taxes. That is to say, it seems to us that the subsection's purpose is to impose the penalties for perjury upon those who willfully falsify their returns regardless of the tax consequences of the falsehood. 184 F.2d at 288.

* * *

Another basic rationale for prohibiting any falsity on the return is that without truthful representation as to all matters it becomes administratively more difficult, if not impossible, for the Internal Revenue Service (IRS) to compute the amount of tax due or to check on the accuracy of returns. In *Rayor,* the court borrowed a test for materiality from the D.C. Circuit in Weinstock v. United States, 97 U.S.App.D.C. 365, 231 F.2d 699 (1956), a prosecution under the federal false statement statute, 18 U.S.C. § 1001, for submitting an allegedly false affidavit to the Subversive Activities Control Board, where the D.C. Circuit stated:

> The test [for materiality] is whether the false statement has a natural tendency to influence, or was capable of influencing, the decision of the tribunal in making a determination required to be made. 231 F.2d at 701–702.

The idea that a matter is material under § 7206(1) if it would have a tendency to influence the IRS in its normal processing of tax returns was reiterated in *Null,* supra.

Each of these analyses of the statute and its purpose argues for validating the indictment in the instant case. It is alleged in the indictment that the defendants willfully falsified their tax returns. So under *Gaunt* and its progeny, the indictment is valid. In addition, the indictment envisions no mere oversight or mistake. The W-2 forms defendants attached to their tax returns were allegedly fabricated. Certainly, such a scheme would impede the IRS in its quite proper role of auditing and investigating returns and would be material under *Rayor* and *Null.*

Even defendants' argument that there can be no prosecution except for understatement of income reflects the importance and *materiality* of the source of one's income as reported on the tax return. Without truthful representation of the source of income, it is impossible for the government to determine whether the amount paid is in fact understated, overstated, or correct. Surely, save the amount, there is no more material matter on the tax return than the source of income.

Moreover, the consequence of accepting defendants' position would be to open one of the widest loopholes in the tax structure. To allow taxpayers to willfully misstate and fabricate the source of their income would thereby render virtually impossible the task of ascertaining whether the amount of income as reported is accurate. Evasion of income tax would become much easier. It is inconceivable that Congress could have intended that this statute be construed in a manner that would make it impossible for the IRS to verify and check the accuracy of the amounts reported.

In summary, we hold that the source of one's income as stated on the federal income tax return is a material matter within the meaning of 26 U.S.C. § 7206(1), and that, as such, the government may properly prosecute a taxpayer for falsely stating the source of his income on his federal income tax return. Accordingly, defendants' motion to dismiss the indictment is denied.

An appropriate order will enter.

UNITED STATES v. SHORTT ACCOUNTANCY CORP.

United States Court of Appeals, Ninth Circuit, 1986.
785 F.2d 1448.

DUNIWAY, CIRCUIT JUDGE:

Shortt Accountancy Corporation appeals from its conviction on seven counts of making and subscribing false tax returns in violation of § 7206(1) of the Internal Revenue Code of 1954. We affirm.

FACTS

Appellant Shortt Accountancy Corporation (SAC) is a CPA firm that performs accounting services, prepares tax returns and gives tax planning advice to its clients. Ronald Ashida was its chief operating officer and ran its day-to-day activities in 1981–82.

In the fall of 1981, Clifford Wilson contacted SAC for tax planning advice and services. In late December 1981, Ashida told Wilson that he could invest through SAC in a "straddle" position in government securities that would enable Wilson to claim a sizable deduction on his 1981 federal income tax return. A straddle is the simultaneous holding of a contract to purchase and a contract to sell a specific commodity at some time in the future. It is used to minimize risks by offsetting losses and gains. In order to claim the deduction, however, Wilson would have to backdate a promissory note so that the investment would appear to have been made in May, 1981, rather than December. The backdating was necessary, said Ashida, because Congress had changed the law to disallow deductions to taxpayers who purchased a straddle investment after June 23, 1981. Wilson agreed to consider the investment, but made no decision before the end of the year.

In early January 1982, Wilson told an Assistant U.S. Attorney about Ashida's investment advice. The Attorney put him in touch with the IRS, which proposed that Wilson cooperate with it in building a criminal case against SAC. He agreed upon the condition that the IRS reimburse him for the purchase price of the straddle position and for any fees charged him by SAC. He also understood that if SAC eventually prepared a tax return for him, the IRS would audit it and disallow any improper deductions claimed by SAC on his behalf. In that case, the IRS would assess Wilson for additional taxes owed, but would not require him to pay interest or penalties resulting from the improper deductions.

Wilson ultimately purchased a straddle position from SAC in April 1982. In addition to the purchase price of $3400, SAC charged Wilson interest calculated from May 1, 1981, so that it appeared that the transaction had occurred before the June 1981 cutoff date. No backdated documents were ultimately used in the transaction.

SAC completed preparation of Wilson's 1981 tax return in January 1983. In it, the firm claimed a $23,024 deduction for Wilson relating to his April 1982 straddle investment. Paul Whatley, who supervised the actual preparation of the return and subscribed to its correctness on behalf of SAC, based this figure on information provided to him by Ashida. Whatley did not know, when he signed the return, that the straddle investment was improperly claimed.

After receiving his 1981 return from SAC, Wilson delivered it to an IRS special agent who immediately filed it with the IRS District Director. He forwarded it to a processing center in October 1983 and Wilson has since received the tax refund claimed, plus applicable interest. He has not filed any other 1981 federal income tax return.

In the subsequent investigation of SAC's preparation of Wilson's 1981 return, the grand jury determined that SAC had prepared tax returns for at least six additional clients in which it improperly claimed deductions for straddle investments. In each case, the straddle position at issue was originally owned by other SAC clients who had purchased their interests from SAC before Congress' disallowance of the deduction in June 1981. Although these clients incurred straddle losses in May 1981 that properly could have been claimed on their 1981 tax returns, SAC determined that the original owners were oversheltered for the year and did not need the deductions. As a result, SAC, which was authorized to sell the client's interest in the straddle should it deem it to be in the client's best interest, sold their straddle positions and resulting losses to Wilson and the other new clients. Each sale occurred after the change in the law disallowing straddle deductions and each was structured to appear that it had occurred before the cutoff date.

In June 1984, the grand jury issued a fourteen count indictment charging SAC, Shortt and Ashida with violations of 18 U.S.C. § 371, conspiracy to commit an offense against or to defraud the United States, and 26 U.S.C. §§ 7206(1), false declaration under penalty of perjury, and (2), aiding preparation or presentation of false documents, under the internal revenue laws. The indictment's basis was SAC's alleged sale of interests in straddle positions after Congress disallowed deductions from such investments and its knowing preparation of tax returns claiming improper straddle deductions.

In August 1984, the defendants filed a joint motion for an evidentiary hearing on their motion to dismiss the counts relating to Wilson's return. They claimed that Wilson never intended the document prepared by SAC to represent his true 1981 federal income tax return and that his return was not, therefore, filed as required by *United States v. Dahlstrom*, 9 Cir., 1983, 713 F.2d 1423. The court denied the motion, holding that the issue was one for the jury.

At trial, defendants moved for judgment of acquittal following the opening statement and again at the close of the government's case. They claimed that a preparer of tax returns cannot be charged under § 7206(1), which proscribes making and subscribing a false return, because it cannot "make" a return within the meaning of the statute. Defendants also argued that a corporation cannot be guilty of an offense under § 7206(1) when the person who actually subscribes the false return believes it to be true and correct. The district court denied the motions.

One of defendant's defense theories at trial was that the returns it prepared were not false because Ashida had established a new partnership before the June 23, 1981 change in the law. This new partnership allegedly acquired the interests of the original straddle owners before May 4, 1981, the date when the straddle losses later sold to Wilson and the others actually occurred. Defendant claimed that Wilson and the other new SAC clients subsequently became partners in the new partnership and thus could properly deduct the straddle losses on their 1981 returns.

In charging the jury on SAC's partnership defense theory, the trial judge included the statement that "some act must have occurred creating this parent partnership on or before May 4, 1981, in order for this theory to apply." Defendants objected to the instruction on the grounds that it was erroneous as a matter of law and deprived them of their partnership defense theory. Their objection was overruled.

The jury ultimately convicted SAC on seven counts of willfully making and subscribing as preparer false income tax returns in violation of 26 U.S.C. § 7206(1). SAC timely appeals.

* * *

II. *Denial of Judgment of Acquittal on Count Five.*

SAC next argues that the district court erred as a matter of law in denying its motion for judgment of acquittal on Count Five of the indictment. The basis of the motion, as with SAC's pretrial motion to dismiss, was that Wilson had never intended his SAC-prepared return to be his "true" return for 1981 and that the return could not, therefore, serve as the basis for conviction under 26 U.S.C. § 7206(1). This court must affirm the district court if it applied the correct standard of law and if "after viewing the evidence in the light most favorable to the prosecution, *any* rational trier of fact could have found the essential elements of the crime beyond a reasonable doubt." *Jackson v. Virginia,* 1979, 443 U.S. 307, 319, 99 S.Ct. 2781, 2789, 61 L.Ed.2d 560 (emphasis in original).

SAC bases this argument on our decision in *United States v. Dahlstrom,* 9 Cir., 1983, 713 F.2d 1423. In *Dahlstrom,* we held that the filing of a return is an element of a section 7206(2) violation (assisting in the preparation of a false return) and implied that a completed filing requires that the taxpayer intend the return to represent his "true return" with the IRS. *Id.* at 1429. The taxpayer in *Dahlstrom,* who cooperated with the IRS in gathering evidence against a tax adviser, was told by his IRS contact that the fraudulent return did not represent his true return. *Id.* at 1426. The taxpayer also prepared and filed a second return that served as his actual return for the year in question. Here, but one return was filed by Wilson and acted upon by the IRS. Even assuming, therefore, that *Dahlstrom*'s "true return" requirement extends to offenses charged under section 7206(1), a question we do not decide, there is sufficient evidence in the record to permit a rational finder of fact to conclude that Wilson's return meets that requirement.

SAC concedes the differences between the handling of the returns in this case and in *Dahlstrom,* but argues that they are insignificant in light of Wilson's agreement with the IRS that he would be audited at the close of the case, but would not be assessed the usual penalties and interests on any additional taxes owed. The problem with SAC's analysis is that it implies that the only "true return" filed by a taxpayer-informant is one in which he bears the full cost of all improprieties he helps to reveal. Such a result would unfairly penalize honest taxpayers for cooperating with the IRS and would undoubtedly undermine their willingness to come forward at all. We decline to adopt so restrictive a view. Thus, the differences between *Dahlstrom* and this case are significant and support a finding that Wilson's SAC-prepared return was his "true return" for 1981.

III. *"Making" a Return Under Section 7206(1).*

SAC claims that its convictions on seven counts of violating section 7206(1) should be reversed as a matter of law because a tax return preparer cannot "make" a return within the meaning of the statute. 26 U.S.C. § 7206(1). While SAC does not deny its participation in preparing the false returns, it claims that it could only be charged under section 7206(2) for *assisting* in the preparation of a false return. 26 U.S.C. § 7206(2). It bases its distinction on the fact that the taxpayer alone has the statutory duty to file a federal income tax return.

Nothing in the statute or case law indicates that a charge under section 7206(1) for making and subscribing a false return is based on the taxpayer's duty to file or "make" an income tax return. Instead, sections 7206(1) and 7206(2) are "closely related companion provisions" that differ in emphasis more than in substance. *United States v.*

Haynes, 5 Cir., 1978, 573 F.2d 236, 240. Section 7206(1) is a perjury statute, making any person who knowingly makes and subscribes a false statement on any return criminally liable. *Id.;* 26 U.S.C. § 7206(1). Section 7206(2) has a broader sweep, making all forms of willful assistance in preparing a false return an offense. 26 U.S.C. § 7206(2). Perjury in connection with the preparation of a federal tax return is chargeable under either section. *Haynes,* 573 F.2d at 240; *see United States v. Miller,* 5 Cir., 1974, 491 F.2d 638, 649. The Fifth Circuit has considered the exact issue of whether a tax preparer can be charged under section 7206(1) rather than 7206(2) and held that he could. *Miller,* 5 Cir., 491 F.2d at 649; *see Haynes,* 573 F.2d at 240. We are persuaded to do the same.

SAC argues that our decision in another *United States v. Miller,* 9 Cir., 1976, 545 F.2d 1204, recognizes the exclusivity of sections 7206(1) and (2). We disagree. In *Miller,* we commented *sua sponte* in a footnote that the defendant, who had prepared a false return for his wife, should have been charged under section 7206(2) for assisting in the preparation of the return, rather than under section 7206(1) for subscribing the return. *Id.* at 1216 n. 16. It is not clear from the opinion whether the defendant actually committed perjury by subscribing his wife's false return or whether he merely prepared it in advance of her subscription. *Id.* In either case, we went on to hold that the possible error was not fatal because indictment under section 7206(1) contains the elements of the section 7206(2) offense sufficiently to apprise the defendant of what he has to be prepared to meet at trial and is detailed enough to assure against double jeopardy. *Id.* See also *Miller,* 5 Cir., 491 F.2d at 649. This holding does not conflict with our conclusion here that a tax return preparer can properly be charged under section 7206(1) for willfully making and subscribing a false return.

IV. *Collective Intent in Subscribing the Returns.*

SAC also claims that six of its convictions under section 7206(1) should be reversed because Paul Whatley, the corporate agent who actually subscribed six of the seven contested returns on behalf of SAC, did not have the requisite intent of willfully making and subscribing a false return. While it acknowledges that Ashida, who supplied Whatley with all of his information regarding the straddle losses, did have the requisite intent, it contends that his intent is irrelevant to a section 7206(1) charge because he did not physically subscribe the return. SAC concludes that if the government wanted to charge SAC for Ashida's admittedly illegal conduct and intent, it should have drawn up the indictment under section 7206(2) or some other statute, and not under section 7206(1).

SAC's argument is completely meritless. If it were accepted by the courts, any tax return preparer could escape prosecution for perjury by arranging for an innocent employee to complete the proscribed act of subscribing a false return. This interpretation of section 7206(1) defies logic and has no support in the case law. A corporation will be held liable under section 7206(1) when its agent deliberately causes it to make and subscribe to a false income tax return.

* * *

Affirmed.

UNITED STATES v. REYNOLDS
United States Court of Appeals, Seventh Circuit, 1990.
919 F.2d 435.

EASTERBROOK, CIRCUIT JUDGE.

For more than a decade Milwaukee has participated in the community development block grant program administered by the Department of Housing and Urban Development. The City selects urban projects that meet federal criteria and pays a contractor to do the work; the federal government reimburses the City on certification that the work has been done according to the federal standards. A pot of money attracts many people, not all of them interested in fulfilling the statutory objectives. David Reynolds was one such person.

Reynolds formed the Phoenix Redevelopment Project, Inc., ostensibly to renovate housing in the 10th Aldermanic District of Milwaukee. That the extent of a federal redevelopment project should be limited by political boundaries in Milwaukee—boundaries having nothing to do with housing that could benefit from rehabilitation—seems to have drawn little attention at Milwaukee's Community Development Agency or at HUD. The link between Phoenix and the 10th District reflects the link between Reynolds and Michael McGee, the Alderman of the 10th District. Reynolds was one of McGee's confidants, able to induce action on applications for liquor licenses in his district (in exchange for baksheesh). Phoenix may have been another vehicle to send money in McGee's direction.

Reynolds arranged for two of Phoenix's suppliers to submit false invoices for supplies. Reynolds also forged some invoices on letterheads he obtained from these two suppliers. He submitted both the fraudulent and the forged invoices to the City for payment. Reynolds and his suppliers arranged to split the proceeds 50–50, but Reynolds reneged, paying them only ⅓ of the takings on the explanation that he needed a larger share to take care of someone from the City. The skimming led to four kinds of charges, in addition to the drearily inevitable yet pointless conspiracy charge: making false claims against the government, in violation of 18 U.S.C. § 287; embezzling federal funds, in violation of 18 U.S.C. § 641; theft from a governmental program, in violation of 18 U.S.C. § 666; and filing false income tax returns, in violation of 26 U.S.C. § 7206(1) (Reynolds, not content to rob a fund designed to assist the neediest in society, neglected to pay taxes on the booty). He was charged with and acquitted of three counts of extortion. The 42 counts on which he was convicted produced a term of four years' imprisonment, plus restitution of $52,219 and special assessments of $2,100.

The tax counts are the most problematic. Reynolds filed IRS form 1040EZ for each of tax years 1986 and 1987. Line 1 of this form says: "Total wages, salaries, and tips. This should be shown in Box 10 of your W–2 form(s). (Attach your W–2 form(s).)" Reynolds inserted in the space provided the amount shown on his W–2 forms, which he dutifully attached. The only other line on form 1040EZ calling for income is line 2, which reads: "Interest income of $400 or less. If the total is more than $400, you cannot use Form 1040EZ." Reynolds performed the additions and subtractions called for on the other lines, filling in the total on line 7, which reads: "Subtract line 6 from line 5. If line 6 is larger than line 5, enter 0 on line 7. This is your taxable income."

> The indictment charged Reynolds with filing a return,

which said income tax return he did not believe to be true and correct as to every material matter in that on line 7 of the return, the defendant's taxable income was represented as being $12,743.00 [in 1986; $16,185 in 1987], whereas, as he then and there well knew and believed, he had taxable income in 1986 [or 1987] in excess of that heretofore stated.

Line 7 did not call for anything other than the difference between line 6 (the personal exemption, preprinted on the form) and line 5. Line 5 came from lines 1 and 2 (added to yield line 3), from which Reynolds subtracted charitable contributions (line 4). The veracity of Reynolds' verification (by signing the return) that line 7 is "true, correct, and complete" therefore depends on the accuracy of his entry on line 1. He contends that the entry on line 1 is literally correct: he wrote down everything he had received as "wages, salaries, and tips", exactly as it appeared on the forms W–2.

To this the prosecutor has two replies. One is that by filing form 1040EZ, Reynolds represented that he had no income not called for on lines 1 and 2. The other is that, according to expert testimony, Reynolds could have put his illegal income on line 1. Only one of these can be true. If income that is not reflected on a W–2 disqualifies someone from filing form 1040EZ, then illegal income may *not* be included on line 1 of that form. And the existence of such income indeed disqualifies a taxpayer from using form 1040EZ. It is designed for persons whose entire income appears on W–2s, plus interest income that financial institutions report on forms 1099. Anything more complex requires the taxpayer to use form 1040.

The prosecutor's argument that by filing form 1040EZ a taxpayer implicitly represents that he has no additional income has more substance, but this is not the theory in the indictment. It charged that line 7, specifically, was false, and line 7 is derived arithmetically from other lines. Section 7206(1) is a perjury statute, and literal truth is a defense to perjury, even if the answer is highly misleading. *Bronston v. United States*, 409 U.S. 352, 93 S.Ct. 595, 34 L.Ed.2d 568 (1973). Using the wrong form does not violate § 7206(1). *Hartford–Connecticut Trust Co. v. Eaton,* 34 F.2d 128, 130 (2d Cir.1929). If the form has an open-ended line calling for § 61 income, and the taxpayer leaves some income out, § 7206(1) applies. *United States v. Young,* 804 F.2d 116, 119 (8th Cir.1986). Form 1040EZ is anything but open-ended, however. The right charges are tax evasion (26 U.S.C. § 7201) and failure to supply information required by law (26 U.S.C. § 7203). Reynolds did not reveal his complete income (§ 7203) and evaded taxation on that income (§ 7201). Neither the indictment nor the charge to the jury set out the elements of these offenses, so the problem is deeper than a citation to the wrong statute in the indictment. We vacate Reynolds' tax convictions, without foreclosing indictment and trial for the offenses that match the prosecution's theory of the case.[1]

UNITED STATES v. CRUM
United States Court of Appeals, Ninth Circuit, 1976.
529 F.2d 1380.

WRIGHT, CIRCUIT JUDGE.

Crum was convicted on four counts of aiding and assisting in the preparation of false income tax returns [26 U.S.C. § 7206(2)] and on this appeal argues that (a) the indictment is infirm because Section 7206(2) is inapplicable to those not preparers of tax returns, [and] (b) the evidence was insufficient to sustain the verdict * * *. There being no merit to any contention, we affirm the conviction on all counts.

An attorney, Galas, devised a scheme of enticing high income taxpayers and physicians in particular to invest in domesticated beavers as a tax shelter device. Galas solicited the aid of Monroe, an accountant, and Crum, who bred and sold beavers. The scheme employed the fraudulent use of depreciation deductions by backdating beaver purchase contracts. As purchasers became involved, Galas and Monroe participated by preparing the doctors' income tax returns.

All three schemers were indicted. Their usual procedure was to visit a prospect, ask for his income figures for his yet unfiled tax return, then suggest how many beavers he would need to reduce his income tax by use of the depreciation deduction. Crum admits that he attended two such meetings with Drs. McAdams and Harris.

Crum advised Dr. McAdams that investment in beavers would provide a good depreciation deduction and Crum heard Galas and Monroe tell the doctor how much deduction would be needed. A backdated beaver purchase contract was then signed by Crum and McAdams.

Some months later, when an IRS agent was in Dr. McAdams' waiting room with an appointment to discuss the doctor's tax return, Galas, Monroe and Crum entered through a rear door and persuaded

---

1. The portion of the opinion dealing with conspiracy is at p. 611.

McAdams to sign a new backdated contract which could be exhibited to the agent. Crum also signed it.

We reject Crum's contention that Section 7206(2) applies only to preparers of tax returns. In United States v. Johnson, 319 U.S. 503, 518, 63 S.Ct. 1233, 1240, 87 L.Ed. 1546 (1943), the Court said: [1]

> The nub of the matter is that they aided and abetted if they consciously were parties to the concealment of [a taxable business] interest * * *.

In United States v. Maius, 378 F.2d 716, 718 (6th Cir.1967), the court sustained a conviction under Section 7206(2) even though defendant was not a preparer. The court reasoned:

> There was sufficient evidence to support the conclusion of the jury that appellant was a party to the scheme of concealing the receipt of income and not reporting it on the corporate records, and this [sic] his knowledge of the use of such records in preparing the tax returns is sufficient * * *.

Since the reach of Section 7206(2) is clearly not limited to acts of tax return "preparers," the indictment in this case encompasses Crum's conduct.

As for the sufficiency of the evidence argument, we view the evidence in a light most favorable to the government. The facts as we have outlined them amply support the jury's conclusion that Crum fraudulently backdated the purchase contracts, knowing that the false information would be used in the preparation of tax returns. His complicity is beyond dispute.

We reject as frivolous Crum's argument that the evidence failed to show that the information on the returns was false as to any material matter under Section 7206(2). We can scarcely imagine anything more material than a false schedule designed to induce allowance of a wholly unwarranted depreciation deduction.

* * *

Affirmed.

B. THE WILLFULNESS ELEMENT

(1) *Willfulness Defined*

UNITED STATES v. BISHOP
Supreme Court of the United States, 1973.
412 U.S. 346, 93 S.Ct. 2008, 36 L.Ed.2d 941.

Mr. Justice Blackmun delivered the opinion of the Court.

---

1. The court in *Johnson* was construing then 26 U.S.C. § 145(b) (53 Stat. 63, 1939 Code) (making it a felony for any person who, being subject to tax, "willfully attempts in any manner to evade or defeat any tax imposed by this chapter or the payment thereof"), together with then 18 U.S.C. § 550 (Section 332 of the Criminal Code) (the general aiding and abetting statute).

* * *

Mr. Bishop is a lawyer who has practiced his profession in Sacramento, California, since 1951. During that period, he owned an interest in a walnut ranch he and his father operated. In 1960 his secretary, Louise, married his father. The father died, and thereafter respondent's stepmother managed the ranch.

Respondent periodically sent checks to Louise. These were used to run the ranch, to pay principal on loans, and to make improvements.

Louise maintained a record of ranch expenditures and submitted an itemized list of these disbursements to respondent at the end of each calendar year. In his 1963 return respondent asserted as business deductions all amounts paid to Louise and, in addition, all the expenses Louise listed. This necessarily resulted in a double deduction for all ranch expenditures in 1963. Moreover, some of these expenditures were for repayment of loans and for other personal items that did not qualify as income tax deductions. In his 1964 and 1965 returns respondent similarly included nondeductible amounts among the ranch figures that were deducted.

[Bishop was charged with felony violations of § 7206(1) with respect to his 1963, 1964 and 1965 returns. At trial he requested lesser-included offense instructions based on the misdemeanor statute, § 7207. This tax misdemeanor is committed by one "who willfully delivers or discloses" to the IRS any return or document "known by him to be fraudulent or to be false as to any material matter." Bishop argued that the word "willfully" in the misdemeanor statute should be construed to require less scienter than the same word in the felony statute. With the state of the defendant's guilty knowledge in dispute, Bishop's proposed instructions would have allowed the jury to choose between a misdemeanor based on caprice or careless disregard and a felony requiring evil purpose. The trial judge declined to give the requested instructions and, instead, gave an instruction only on the felony, requiring a finding by the jury that the defendant intended "with evil motive or bad purpose either to disobey or to disregard the law." The jury convicted Bishop, but the Court of Appeals reversed the judgment of the District Court and remanded the case for a new trial. The Supreme Court granted certiorari in order to resolve a division in the circuits concerning the meaning of "willfully" as used in the tax crime statutes.]

The Court of Appeals relied upon and followed a series of its own cases, particularly Abdul v. United States, 9 Cir., 254 F.2d 292 (1958), enunciating the proposition that the word "willfully" has a meaning in tax felony statutes that is more stringent than its meaning in tax misdemeanor statutes. * * *

* * *

In the present case the Court of Appeals continued this *Abdul* distinction between willfulness in tax misdemeanor charges and willfulness in tax felony charges. Section 7207, it was said, requires only a showing of "unreasonable, capricious, or careless disregard for the truth or falsity of income tax returns filed," whereas § 7206(1) "requires proof of an evil motive and bad faith." The level of willfulness, thus, would create a disputed factual element that made appropriate a lesser-included-offense instruction.

The decisions of this Court do not support the holding in *Abdul,* and implicitly they reject the approach taken by the Court of Appeals. In *Spies* the Court speculated that Congress could have distinguished between the regulatory aspects of the tax system, which call for compliance regardless of financial status, and the revenue-collecting aspects, which may place demands on a taxpayer he cannot meet. Since the antecedent of § 7203 (as does that section itself today) punished both failure to file and failure to pay as misdemeanors, the Court concluded that Congress had not drawn the line between felonies and misdemeanors on the basis of distinctions between the system's regulatory aspects and its revenue-collecting aspects. The reliance in *Abdul* on that hypothetical statutory scheme, discussed by this Court in *Spies* but found not in line with what Congress had actually done, was misplaced. Utilizing the unsupported *Abdul* distinction as a foundation, the Court of Appeals constructed the further general distinction between tax felonies and tax misdemeanors, a distinction also inconsistent with prior decisions of this Court.

* * *

It would be possible, of course, that the word "willfully" was intended by Congress to have a meaning in § 7206(1) different from its meaning in § 7207, and we turn now to that possibility.

We continue to recognize that context is important in the quest for the word's meaning. See United States v. Murdock, 290 U.S. 389, 394–395, 54 S.Ct. 223, 225, 78 L.Ed. 381 (1933). Here, as in *Spies,* the "legislative history of the section[s] contains nothing helpful on the question here at issue, and we must find the answer from the [sections themselves] and [their] context in the revenue laws." 317 U.S., at 495, 63 S.Ct., at 366. We consider first, then, the sections themselves.

A. Respondent argues that both §§ 7206(1) and 7207 apply to a fraudulent "return" and cover the same ground if the word "willfully" has the same meaning in both sections. Since "it would be unusual and we would not readily assume that Congress by the felony * * * meant no more than the same derelictions it had just defined * * * as a misdemeanor," 317 U.S., at 497, 63 S.Ct., at 367, respondent concludes that Congress must have intended to require a more willful violation for the felony than for the misdemeanor.

The critical difficulty for respondent is that the two sections have substantially different express terms. The most obvious difference is that § 7206(1) applies only if the document "contains or is verified by a written declaration that it is made under the penalties of perjury." No equivalent requirement is present in § 7207. Respondent recognizes this but then relies on the presence of perjury declarations on all federal income tax returns, a fact that effectively equalizes the sections where a federal tax return is at issue. See 26 U.S.C. § 6065(a).

This approach, however, is not persuasive for two reasons. First, the Secretary or his delegate has the power under § 6065(a) to provide that no perjury declaration is required. If he does so provide, then § 7207 immediately becomes operative in the area theretofore covered by § 7206(1). Second, the term "return" is not necessarily limited to a federal income tax return. A state or other nonfederal return could be intended and might not contain a perjury warning. If this type of return were submitted in support of a federal return, or in the course of a tax audit, § 7207 could apply even if § 7206(1) could not.

There are other distinctions. The felony applies to a document that a taxpayer "[w]illfully makes and subscribes * * * and which he does not believe to be true and correct as to every material matter," whereas the misdemeanor applies to a document that a taxpayer "willfully delivers or discloses to the Secretary or his delegate * * * known by him * * * to be false as to any material matter." In the felony, then, the taxpayer must verify the return or document in writing, and he is liable if he does not affirmatively believe that the material statements are true. For the misdemeanor, however, a document prepared by another could give rise to liability on the part of the taxpayer if he delivered or disclosed it to the Service; additional protection is given to the taxpayer in this situation because the document must be known by him to be fraudulent or to be false.

These differences in the respective applications of §§ 7206(1) and 7207 provide solid evidence that Congress distinguished the statutes in ways that do not turn on the meaning of the word "willfully."

* * *

Thus the word "willfully" may have a uniform meaning in the several statutes without rendering any one of them surplusage. We next turn to context.

B. The hierarchy of tax offenses set forth in §§ 7201–7207, inclusive, utilizes the mental state of the offender as a guide in establishing the penalty. Section 7201, relating to attempts to evade or defeat tax, has been described and recognized by the Court as the "climax of this variety of sanctions" and as the "capstone of a system of sanctions which singly or in combination were calculated to induce prompt and forthright fulfillment of every duty under the income tax law and to provide a penalty suitable to every degree of delinquency." *Spies*, 317 U.S., at 497, 63 S.Ct. 367; *Sansone*, 380 U.S., at 350–351, 85 S.Ct. at 1009. The actor's mental state is described both by the requirement that acts be done "willfully" and by the designation of certain express elements of the offenses. In § 7201, for example, the Court has held that, by requiring an attempt to evade, "Congress intended some willful commission in addition to the willful omissions that make up the list of misdemeanors." *Spies*, 317 U.S., at 499, 63 S.Ct. at 368. Similarly, in

§ 7207, the Government must show that the document was known by the taxpayer to be fraudulent or to be false as to a material matter.

All these offenses, except two subsections of § 7206, viz., subsections (3) and (4), require that acts be done "willfully." Although the described states of mind might be included in the normal meaning of the word "willfully," the presence of both an express designation and the simultaneous requirement that a violation be committed "willfully" is strong evidence that Congress used the word "willfully" to describe a constant rather than a variable in the tax penalty formula.

The Court, in fact, has recognized that the word "willfully" in these statutes generally connotes a voluntary, intentional violation of a known legal duty. It has formulated the requirement of willfulness as "bad faith or evil intent," *Murdock* 290 U.S., at 398, 54 S.Ct. at 226, or "evil motive and want of justification in view of all the financial circumstances of the taxpayer," *Spies,* 317 U.S., at 498, 63 S.Ct. at 368, or knowledge that the taxpayer "should have reported more income than he did." *Sansone,* 380 U.S., at 353, 85 S.Ct. at 1011.

This longstanding interpretation of the purpose of the recurring word "willfully" promotes coherence in the group of tax crimes. In our complex tax system, uncertainty often arises even among taxpayers who earnestly wish to follow the law. The Court has said, "It is not the purpose of the law to penalize frank difference of opinion or innocent errors made despite the exercise of reasonable care." *Spies,* 317 U.S., at 496, 63 S.Ct. at 367. Degrees of negligence give rise in the tax system to civil penalties. The requirement of an offense committed "willfully" is not met, therefore, if a taxpayer has relied in good faith on a prior decision of this Court. The Court's consistent interpretation of the word "willfully" to require an element of *mens rea* implements the pervasive intent of Congress to construct penalties that separate the purposeful tax violator from the well-meaning, but easily confused, mass of taxpayers.

Until Congress speaks otherwise, we therefore shall continue to require, in both tax felonies and tax misdemeanors that must be done "willfully," the bad purpose or evil motive described in *Murdock,* supra. We hold, consequently, that the word "willfully" has the same meaning in § 7207 that it has in § 7206(1). Since the only issue in dispute in this case centered on willfulness, it follows that a conviction of the misdemeanor would clearly support a conviction for the felony. Under these circumstances a lesser-included-offense instruction was not required or proper, for in the federal system it is not the function of the jury to set the penalty.

The judgment of the Court of Appeals is reversed, and the case is remanded for further proceedings. It is so ordered.

def.

UNITED STATES v. POMPONIO
Supreme Court of the United States, 1976.
429 U.S. 10, 97 S.Ct. 22, 50 L.Ed.2d 12.

PER CURIAM.

After a jury trial, respondents were convicted of willfully filing false income tax returns in violation of 26 U.S.C. § 7206(1). Based on its reading of United States v. Bishop, the Court of Appeals held that the jury was incorrectly instructed concerning willfulness, and remanded for a new trial. The United States petitioned for certiorari. We reverse.

* * *

The jury was instructed that respondents were not guilty of violating § 7206(1) unless they had signed the tax returns knowing them to be false, and had done so willfully. A willful act was defined in the instructions as one done "voluntarily and intentionally and with the specific intent to do something which the law forbids, that is to say with [the] bad purpose either to disobey or to disregard the law." Finally, the jury was instructed that "[g]ood motive alone is never a defense where the act done or omitted is a crime," and that consequently motive was irrelevant except as it bore on intent. The Court of Appeals held this final instruction improper because "the statute at hand requires a finding of a bad purpose or evil motive." In so holding, the Court of Appeals incorrectly assumed that the reference to an "evil motive" in United States v. Bishop and prior cases meant something more than the specific intent to violate the law described in the trial judge's instruction.

In *Bishop* we held that the term "willfully" has the same meaning in the misdemeanor and felony sections of the Revenue Code, and that it requires more than a showing of careless disregard for the truth. We did not, however, hold that the term requires proof of any motive other than an intentional violation of a known legal duty. We explained the meaning of willfulness in § 7206 and related statutes:

> "The Court, in fact, has recognized that the word 'willfully' in these statutes generally connotes a voluntary, intentional violation of a known legal duty. It has formulated the requirement of willfulness as 'bad faith or evil intent,' *Murdock,* 290 U.S. 398, 54 S.Ct. at 226, or 'evil motive and want of justification in view of all the financial circumstances of the taxpayer,' *Spies,* 317 U.S. 498, 63 S.Ct. at 368, or knowledge that the taxpayer 'should have reported more income than he did.' *Sansone,* 380 U.S. 353, 85 S.Ct. at 1011."

Our references to other formulations of the standard did not modify the standard set forth in the first sentence of the quoted paragraph. On the contrary, as the other Courts of Appeals that have considered the question have recognized, willfulness in this context simply means a voluntary, intentional violation of a known legal duty. The trial judge

568   FEDERAL TAX CRIMES AND METHODS OF PROOF   Ch. 9

in the instant case adequately instructed the jury on willfulness. An additional instruction on good faith was unnecessary.

* * *

(2) Willfulness Applied

CHEEK v. UNITED STATES
United States Court of Appeals, Seventh Circuit, 1991.
___ U.S. ___, 111 S.Ct. 604, 112 L.Ed.2d 617.

JUSTICE WHITE delivered the opinion of the Court.

Title 26, § 7201 of the United States Code provides that any person "who willfully attempts in any manner to evade or defeat any tax imposed by this title or the payment thereof" shall be guilty of a felony. Under 26 U.S.C. § 7203, "[a]ny person required under this title * * * or by regulations made under authority thereof to make a return * * * who willfully fails to * * * make such return" shall be guilty of a misdemeanor. This case turns on the meaning of the word "willfully" as used in §§ 7201 and 7203.

I

Petitioner John L. Cheek has been a pilot for American Airlines since 1973. He filed federal income tax returns through 1979 but thereafter ceased to file returns.[1] He also claimed an increasing number of withholding allowances—eventually claiming 60 allowances by mid-1980—and for the years 1981 to 1984 indicated on his W-4 forms that he was exempt from federal income taxes. In 1983, petitioner unsuccessfully sought a refund of all tax withheld by his employer in 1982. Petitioner's income during this period at all times far exceeded the minimum necessary to trigger the statutory filing requirement.

As a result of his activities, petitioner was indicted for 10 violations of federal law. He was charged with six counts of willfully failing to file a federal income tax return for the years 1980, 1981, and 1983 through 1986, in violation of 26 U.S.C. § 7203. He was further charged with three counts of willfully attempting to evade his income taxes for the years 1980, 1981, and 1983 in violation of 26 U.S.C. § 7201. In those years, American Airlines withheld substantially less than the amount of tax petitioner owed because of the numerous allowances and exempt status he claimed on his W-4 forms.[2] The tax offenses with which petitioner was charged are specific intent crimes that require the defendant to have acted willfully.

At trial, the evidence established that between 1982 and 1986, petitioner was involved in at least four civil cases that challenged

---

1. Cheek did file what the Court of Appeals described as a frivolous return in 1982.
2. Because petitioner filed a refund claim for the entire amount withheld by his employer in 1982, petitioner was also charged under 18 U.S.C. § 287 with one count of presenting a claim to an agency of the United States knowing the claim to be false and fraudulent.

various aspects of the federal income tax system.³ In all four of those cases, the plaintiffs were informed by the courts that many of their arguments, including that they were not taxpayers within the meaning of the tax laws, that wages are not income, that the Sixteenth Amendment does not authorize the imposition of an income tax on individuals, and that the Sixteenth Amendment is unenforceable, were frivolous or had been repeatedly rejected by the courts. During this time period, petitioner also attended at least two criminal trials of persons charged with tax offenses. In addition, there was evidence that in 1980 or 1981 an attorney had advised Cheek that the courts had rejected as frivolous the claim that wages are not income.⁴

Cheek represented himself at trial and testified in his defense. He admitted that he had not filed personal income tax returns during the years in question. He testified that as early as 1978, he had begun attending seminars sponsored by, and following the advice of, a group that believes, among other things, that the federal tax system is unconstitutional. Some of the speakers at these meetings were lawyers who purported to give professional opinions about the invalidity of the federal income tax laws. Cheek produced a letter from an attorney stating that the Sixteenth Amendment did not authorize a tax on wages and salaries but only on gain or profit. Petitioner's defense was that, based on the indoctrination he received from this group and from his own study, he sincerely believed that the tax laws were being unconstitutionally enforced and that his actions during the 1980–1986 period were lawful. He therefore argued that he had acted without the willfulness required for conviction of the various offenses with which he was charged.

In the course of its instructions, the trial court advised the jury that to prove "willfulness" the Government must prove the voluntary and intentional violation of a known legal duty, a burden that could not be proved by showing mistake, ignorance, or negligence. The court further advised the jury that an objectively reasonable good-faith misunderstanding of the law would negate willfulness but mere disagree-

---

3. In March 1982, Cheek and another employee of the company sued American Airlines to challenge the withholding of federal income taxes. In April 1982, Cheek sued the IRS in the United States Tax Court, asserting that he was not a taxpayer or a person for purposes of the Internal Revenue Code, that his wages were not income, and making several other related claims. Cheek and four others also filed an action against the United States and the CIR in Federal District Court, claiming that withholding taxes from their wages violated the Sixteenth Amendment. Finally, in 1985 Cheek filed claims with the IRS seeking to have refunded the taxes withheld from his wages in 1983 and 1984. When these claims were not allowed, he brought suit in the District Court claiming that the withholding was an unconstitutional taking of his property and that his wages were not income. In dismissing this action as frivolous, the District Court imposed costs and attorneys fees of $1,500 and a sanction under Rule 11 in the amount of $10,000. The Court of Appeals agreed that Cheek's claims were frivolous, reduced the District Court sanction to $5,000 and imposed an additional sanction of $1,500 for bringing a frivolous appeal.

4. The attorney also advised that despite the Fifth Amendment, the filing of a tax return was required and that a person could challenge the constitutionality of the system by suing for a refund after the taxes had been withheld, or by putting himself "at risk of criminal prosecution."

ment with the law would not. The court described Cheek's beliefs about the income tax system [5] and instructed the jury that if it found that Cheek "honestly and reasonably believed that he was not required to pay income taxes or to file tax returns," App. 81, a not guilty verdict should be returned.

After several hours of deliberation, the jury sent a note to the judge that stated in part:

"We have a basic disagreement between some of us as to if Mr. Cheek honestly & reasonably believed that he was not required to pay income taxes.

* * *

"'Page 32 [the relevant jury instruction] discusses good faith misunderstanding & disagreement. Is there any additional clarification you can give us on this point?'" *Id.,* at 85.

The District Judge responded with a supplemental instruction containing the following statements:

"[A] person's opinion that the tax laws violate his constitutional rights does not constitute a good faith misunderstanding of the law. Furthermore, a person's disagreement with the government's tax collection systems and policies does not constitute a good faith misunderstanding of the law." *Id.,* at 86.

At the end of the first day of deliberation, the jury sent out another note saying that it still could not reach a verdict because "'[w]e are divided on the issue as to if Mr. Cheek honestly & reasonably believed that he was not required to pay income tax.'" *Id.,* at 87. When the jury resumed its deliberations, the District Judge gave the jury an additional instruction. This instruction stated in part that "[a]n honest but unreasonable belief is not a defense and does not negate willfulness," *id.,* at 88, and that "[a]dvice or research resulting in the conclusion that wages of a privately employed person are not income or that the tax laws are unconstitutional is not objectively reasonable and cannot serve as the basis for a good faith misunderstanding of the law defense." *Ibid.* The court also instructed the jury that "[p]ersistent refusal to acknowledge the law does not constitute a good faith misunderstanding of the law." *Ibid.* Approximately two hours later, the

---

5. "The defendant has testified as to what he states are his interpretations of the United States Constitution, court opinions, common law and other materials he has reviewed. * * * He has also introduced materials which contain references to quotations from the United States Constitution, court opinions, statutes, and other sources.

"He testified he relied on his interpretations and on these materials in concluding that he was not a person required to file income tax returns for the year or years charged, was not required to pay income taxes and that he could claim exempt status on his W-4 forms, and that he could claim refunds of all moneys withheld." App. 75–76.

"Among other things, Mr. Cheek contends that his wages from a private employer, American Airlines, does not constitute income under the Internal Revenue Service laws." *Id.,* at 81.

jury returned a verdict finding petitioner guilty on all counts.[6]

Petitioner appealed his convictions, arguing that the District Court erred by instructing the jury that only an objectively reasonable misunderstanding of the law negates the statutory willfulness requirement. The United States Court of Appeals for the Seventh Circuit rejected that contention and affirmed the convictions. 882 F.2d 1263 (1989). In prior cases, the Seventh Circuit had made clear that good-faith misunderstanding of the law negates willfulness only if the defendant's beliefs are objectively reasonable; in the Seventh Circuit, even actual ignorance is not a defense unless the defendant's ignorance was itself objectively reasonable. See, *e.g., United States v. Buckner,* 830 F.2d 102 (1987). In its opinion in this case, the court noted that several specified beliefs, including the beliefs that the tax laws are unconstitutional and that wages are not income, would not be objectively reasonable.[7] Because the Seventh Circuit's interpretation of "willfully" as used in these statutes conflicts with the decisions of several other Courts of Appeals, see, *e.g., United States v. Whiteside,* 810 F.2d 1306, 1310–1311 (CA5 1987); *United States v. Phillips,* 775 F.2d 262, 263–264 (CA10 1985); *United States v. Aitken,* 755 F.2d 188, 191–193 (CA1 1985), we granted certiorari, 493 U.S. ___ (1990).

II

The general rule that ignorance of the law or a mistake of law is no defense to criminal prosecution is deeply rooted in the American legal system. See, *e.g., United States v. Smith,* 5 Wheat. 153, 182 (1820) (Livingston, J., dissenting); *Barlow v. United States,* 7 Pet. 404, 411 (1833); *Reynolds v. United States,* 98 U.S. 145, 167 (1879); *Shevlin–Carpenter Co. v. Minnesota,* 218 U.S. 57, 68 (1910); *Lambert v. Califor-*

---

6. A note signed by all 12 jurors also informed the judge that although the jury found petitioner guilty, several jurors wanted to express their personal opinions of the case and that notes from these individual jurors to the court were "a complaint against the narrow & hard expression under the constraints of the law." *Id.,* at 90. At least two notes from individual jurors expressed the opinion that petitioner sincerely believed in his cause even though his beliefs might have been unreasonable.

7. The opinion stated, 882 F.2d 1263, 1268–1269, n. 2 (CA7 1989), as follows:

"For the record, we note that the following beliefs, which are stock arguments of the tax protester movement, have not been, nor ever will be, considered 'objectively reasonable' in this circuit:

"(1) the belief that the sixteenth amendment to the constitution was improperly ratified and therefore never came into being;

"(2) the belief that the sixteenth amendment is unconstitutional generally;

"(3) the belief that the income tax violates the takings clause of the fifth amendment;

"(4) the belief that the tax laws are unconstitutional;

"(5) the belief that wages are not income and therefore are not subject to federal income tax laws;

"(6) the belief that filing a tax return violates the privilege against self-incrimination; and

"(7) the belief that Federal Reserve Notes do not constitute cash or income.

"*Miller v. United States,* 868 F.2d 236, 239–41 (7th Cir.1989); *Buckner,* 830 F.2d at 102; *United States v. Dube,* 820 F.2d 886, 891 (7th Cir.1987); *Coleman v. Comm'r,* 791 F.2d 68, 70–71 (7th Cir. 1986); *Moore,* 627 F.2d at 833. We have no doubt that this list will increase with time."

nia, 355 U.S. 225, 228 (1957); *Liparota v. United States*, 471 U.S. 419, 441 (1985) (White, J., dissenting); O. Holmes, The Common Law 47–48 (1881). Based on the notion that the law is definite and knowable, the common law presumed that every person knew the law. This common-law rule has been applied by the Court in numerous cases construing criminal statutes. See, *e.g., United States v. International Minerals & Chemical Corp.*, 402 U.S. 558 (1971); *Hamling v. United States*, 418 U.S. 87, 119–124 (1974); *Boyce Motor Lines, Inc. v. United States*, 342 U.S. 337 (1952).

The proliferation of statutes and regulations has sometimes made it difficult for the average citizen to know and comprehend the extent of the duties and obligations imposed by the tax laws. Congress has accordingly softened the impact of the common-law presumption by making specific intent to violate the law an element of certain federal criminal tax offenses. Thus, the Court almost 60 years ago interpreted the statutory term "willfully" as used in the federal criminal tax statutes as carving out an exception to the traditional rule. This special treatment of criminal tax offenses is largely due to the complexity of the tax laws. In *United States v. Murdock*, 290 U.S. 389 (1933), the Court recognized that:

> "Congress did not intend that a person, by reason of a bona fide misunderstanding as to his liability for the tax, as to his duty to make a return, or as to the adequacy of the records he maintained, should become a criminal by his mere failure to measure up to the prescribed standard of conduct." *Id.*, at 396.

The Court held that the defendant was entitled to an instruction with respect to whether he acted in good faith based on his actual belief. In *Murdock*, the Court interpreted the term "willfully" as used in the criminal tax statutes generally to mean "an act done with a bad purpose," *id.*, at 394, or with "an evil motive." *Id.*, at 395.

Subsequent decisions have refined this proposition. In *United States v. Bishop*, 412 U.S. 346 (1973), we described the term "willfully" as connoting "a voluntary, intentional violation of a known legal duty," *id.*, at 360, and did so with specific reference to the "bad faith or evil intent" language employed in *Murdock*. Still later, *United States v. Pomponio*, 429 U.S. 10 (1976) (*per curiam*), addressed a situation in which several defendants had been charged with willfully filing false tax returns. The jury was given an instruction on willfulness similar to the standard set forth in *Bishop*. In addition, it was instructed that " '[g]ood motive alone is never a defense where the act done or omitted is a crime.' " *Id.*, at 11. The defendants were convicted but the Court of Appeals reversed, concluding that the latter instruction was improper because the statute required a finding of bad purpose or evil motive. *Ibid.*

We reversed the Court of Appeals, stating that "the Court of Appeals incorrectly assumed that the reference to an 'evil motive' in *United States v. Bishop, supra,* and prior cases," *ibid.*, "requires proof of any motive other than an intentional violation of a known legal duty." *Id.,* at 12. As "the other Courts of Appeals that have considered the question have recognized, willfulness in this context simply means a voluntary, intentional violation of a known legal duty." *Ibid.* We concluded that after instructing the jury on willfulness, "[a]n additional instruction on good faith was unnecessary." *Id.,* at 13. Taken together, *Bishop* and *Pomponio* conclusively establish that the standard for the statutory willfulness requirement is the "voluntary, intentional violation of a known legal duty."

III

Cheek accepts the *Pomponio* definition of willfulness, Brief for Petitioner 5, and n. 4, 13, 36; Reply Brief for Petitioner 4, 6–7, 11, 13, but asserts that the District Court's instructions and the Court of Appeals' opinion departed from that definition. In particular, he challenges the ruling that a good-faith misunderstanding of the law or a good-faith belief that one is not violating the law, if it is to negate willfulness, must be objectively reasonable. We agree that the Court of Appeals and the District Court erred in this respect.

A

Willfulness, as construed by our prior decisions in criminal tax cases, requires the Government to prove that the law imposed a duty on the defendant, that the defendant knew of this duty, and that he voluntarily and intentionally violated that duty. We deal first with the case where the issue is whether the defendant knew of the duty purportedly imposed by the provision of the statute or regulation he is accused of violating, a case in which there is no claim that the provision at issue is invalid. In such a case, if the Government proves actual knowledge of the pertinent legal duty, the prosecution, without more, has satisfied the knowledge component of the willfulness requirement. But carrying this burden requires negating a defendant's claim of ignorance of the law or a claim that because of a misunderstanding of the law, he had a good-faith belief that he was not violating any of the provisions of the tax laws. This is so because one cannot be aware that the law imposes a duty upon him and yet be ignorant of it, misunderstand the law, or believe that the duty does not exist. In the end, the issue is whether, based on all the evidence, the Government has proved that the defendant was aware of the duty at issue, which cannot be true if the jury credits a good-faith misunderstanding and belief submission, whether or not the claimed belief or misunderstanding is objectively reasonable.

In this case, if Cheek asserted that he truly believed that the Internal Revenue Code did not purport to treat wages as income, and the jury believed him, the Government would not have carried its burden to prove willfulness, however unreasonable a court might deem such a belief. Of course, in deciding whether to credit Cheek's good-faith belief claim, the jury would be free to consider any admissible evidence from any source showing that Cheek was aware of his duty to file a return and to treat wages as income, including evidence showing his awareness of the relevant provisions of the Code or regulations, of court decisions rejecting his interpretation of the tax law, of authoritative rulings of the Internal Revenue Service, or of any contents of the personal income tax return forms and accompanying instructions that made it plain that wages should be returned as income.[8]

We thus disagree with the Court of Appeals' requirement that a claimed good-faith belief must be objectively reasonable if it is to be considered as possibly negating the Government's evidence purporting to show a defendant's awareness of the legal duty at issue. Knowledge and belief are characteristically questions for the factfinder, in this case the jury. Characterizing a particular belief as not objectively reasonable transforms the inquiry into a legal one and would prevent the jury from considering it. It would of course be proper to exclude evidence having no relevance or probative value with respect to willfulness; but it is not contrary to common sense, let alone impossible, for a defendant to be ignorant of his duty based on an irrational belief that he has no duty, and forbidding the jury to consider evidence that might negate willfulness would raise a serious question under the Sixth Amendment's jury trial provision. Cf. *Francis v. Franklin,* 471 U.S. 307 (1985); *Sandstrom v. Montana,* 442 U.S. 510 (1979); *Morissette v. United States,* 342 U.S. 246 (1952). It is common ground that this Court, where possible, interprets congressional enactments so as to avoid raising serious constitutional questions. See, *e.g., Edward J. DeBartolo Corp. v. Florida Gulf Coast Building and Construction Trades Council,* 485 U.S. 568, 575 (1988); *Crowell v. Benson,* 285 U.S. 22, 62, and n. 30 (1932); *Public Citizen v. United States Dept. of Justice,* 491 U.S. [440], [465] (1989) (slip op., at 24–25).

It was therefore error to instruct the jury to disregard evidence of Cheek's understanding that, within the meaning of the tax laws, he was not a person required to file a return or to pay income taxes and that wages are not taxable income, as incredible as such misunderstandings of and beliefs about the law might be. Of course, the more unreasonable the asserted beliefs or misunderstandings are, the more likely the jury will consider them to be nothing more than simple disagreement with known legal duties imposed by the tax laws and will find that the Government has carried its burden of proving knowledge.

B

Cheek asserted in the trial court that he should be acquitted because he believed in good faith that the income tax law is unconstitu-

---

8. Cheek recognizes that a "defendant who knows what the law is and who disagrees with it * * * does not have a bona fide misunderstanding defense" but asserts that "a defendant who has a bona fide misunderstanding of [the law] does not 'know' his legal duty and lacks willfulness." Brief for Petitioner 29, and n. 13. The Reply Brief for Petitioner, at 13, states: "We are in no way suggesting that Cheek or anyone else is immune from criminal prosecution if he knows what the law is, but believes it should be otherwise, and therefore violates it." See also Tr. of Oral Arg. 9, 11, 12, 15, 17.

tional as applied to him and thus could not legally impose any duty upon him of which he should have been aware.⁹ Such a submission is unsound, not because Cheek's constitutional arguments are not objectively reasonable or frivolous, which they surely are, but because the *Murdock–Pomponio* line of cases does not support such a position. Those cases construed the willfulness requirement in the criminal provisions of the Internal Revenue Code to require proof of knowledge of the law. This was because in "our complex tax system, uncertainty often arises even among taxpayers who earnestly wish to follow the law" and " '[i]t is not the purpose of the law to penalize frank difference of opinion or innocent errors made despite the exercise of reasonable care.' " *United States v. Bishop*, 412 U.S. 346, 360–361 (1973), (quoting *Spies v. United States*, 317 U.S. 492, 496 (1943)).

Claims that some of the provisions of the tax code are unconstitutional are submissions of a different order.¹⁰ They do not arise from innocent mistakes caused by the complexity of the Internal Revenue

---

9. In his opening and reply briefs and at oral argument, Cheek asserts that this case does not present the issue of whether a claim of unconstitutionality would serve to negate willfulness and that we need not address the issue. Brief for Petitioner 13; Reply Brief for Petitioner 5, 11, 12; Tr. of Oral Arg. 6, 13. Cheek testified at trial, however, that "[i]t is my belief that the law is being enforced unconstitutionally." App. 60. He also produced a letter from counsel advising him that " 'Finally you make a valid contention * * * that Congress' power to tax comes from Article I, Section 8, Clause 1 of the U.S. Constitution, and not from the Sixteenth Amendment and that the [latter], construed with Article I, Section 2, Clause 3, never authorized a tax on wages and salaries, but only on gain and profit." *Id.*, at 57. We note also that the jury asked for "the portion [of the transcript] wherein Mr. Cheek stated he was attempting to test the constitutionality of the income tax laws," Tr. 1704, and that the trial judge later instructed the jury that an opinion that the tax laws violate a person's constitutional rights does not constitute a good faith misunderstanding of the law. We also note that at oral argument Cheek's counsel observed that "personal belief that a known statute is unconstitutional smacks of knowledge with [sic] [of] existing law, but disagreement with it." Tr. of Oral Arg. 5. He also opined that:

"If the person believes as a personal belief that known—law known to them [sic] is unconstitutional, I submit that that would not be a defense, because what the person is really saying is I know what the law is, for constitutional reasons I have made my own determination that it is invalid. I am not suggesting that that is a defense.

"However, if the person was told by a lawyer or by an accountant erroneously that the statute is unconstitutional, and it's my professional advice to you that you don't have to follow it, then you have got a little different situation. This is not that case." *Id.*, at 6.

Given this posture of the case, we perceive no reason not to address the significance of Cheek's constitutional claims to the issue of willfulness.

10. In *United States v. Murdock*, 290 U.S. 389 (1933), discussed *supra*, at 7–8, the defendant Murdock was summoned to appear before a revenue agent for examination. Questions were put to him, which he refused to answer for fear of self-incrimination under state law. He was indicted for refusing to give testimony and supply information contrary to the pertinent provisions of the Internal Revenue Code. This Court affirmed the reversal of Murdock's conviction, holding that the trial court erred in refusing to give an instruction directing the jury to consider Murdock's asserted claim of a good-faith, actual belief that because of the Fifth Amendment he was privileged not to answer the questions put to him. It is thus the case that Murdock's asserted belief was grounded in the Constitution, but it was a claim of privilege not to answer, not a claim that any provision of the tax laws were unconstitutional, and not a claim for which the tax laws provided procedures to entertain and resolve. Cheek's position at trial, in contrast, was that the tax laws were unconstitutional as applied to him.

Code. Rather, they reveal full knowledge of the provisions at issue and a studied conclusion, however wrong, that those provisions are invalid and unenforceable. Thus in this case, Cheek paid his taxes for years, but after attending various seminars and based on his own study, he concluded that the income tax laws could not constitutionally require him to pay a tax.

We do not believe that Congress contemplated that such a taxpayer, without risking criminal prosecution, could ignore the duties imposed upon him by the Internal Revenue Code and refuse to utilize the mechanisms provided by Congress to present his claims of invalidity to the courts and to abide by their decisions. There is no doubt that Cheek, from year to year, was free to pay the tax that the law purported to require, file for a refund and, if denied, present his claims of invalidity, constitutional or otherwise, to the courts. See 26 U.S.C. § 7422. Also, without paying the tax, he could have challenged claims of tax deficiencies in the Tax Court, 26 U.S.C. § 6213, with the right to appeal to a higher court if unsuccessful. § 7482(a)(1). Cheek took neither course in some years, and when he did was unwilling to accept the outcome. As we see it, he is in no position to claim that his good-faith belief about the validity of the Internal Revenue Code negates willfulness or provides a defense to criminal prosecution under §§ 7201 and 7203. Of course, Cheek was free in this very case to present his claims of invalidity and have them adjudicated, but like defendants in criminal cases in other contexts, who "willfully" refuse to comply with the duties placed upon them by the law, he must take the risk of being wrong.

We thus hold that in a case like this, a defendant's views about the validity of the tax statutes are irrelevant to the issue of willfulness, need not be heard by the jury, and if they are, an instruction to disregard them would be proper. For this purpose, it makes no difference whether the claims of invalidity are frivolous or have substance. It was therefore not error in this case for the District Judge to instruct the jury not to consider Cheek's claims that the tax laws were unconstitutional. However, it was error for the court to instruct the jury that petitioner's asserted beliefs that wages are not income and that he was not a taxpayer within the meaning of the Internal Revenue Code should not be considered by the jury in determining whether Cheek had acted willfully.[11]

IV

For the reasons set forth in the opinion above, the judgment of the Court of Appeals is vacated, and the case is remanded for further proceedings consistent with this opinion.

It is so ordered.

---

11. Cheek argues that applying to him the Court of Appeals' standard of objective reasonableness violates his rights under the First, Fifth, and Sixth Amendments of the Constitution. Since we have invalidated the challenged standard on statutory grounds, we need not address these submissions.

JUSTICE SOUTER took no part in the consideration or decision of this case.

* * *

JUSTICE SCALIA, concurring in the judgment.

I concur in the judgment of Court because our cases have consistently held that the failure to pay a tax in the good-faith belief that it is not legally owing is not "willful." I do not join the Court's opinion because I do not agree with the test for willfulness that it directs the Court of Appeals to apply on remand.

As the Court acknowledges, our opinions from the 1930s to the 1970s have interpreted the word "willfully" in the criminal tax statutes as requiring the "bad purpose" or "evil motive" of "intentional[ly] violat[ing] a known legal duty." See, *e.g.*, *United States v. Pomponio*, 429 U.S. 10, 12 (1976); *United States v. Murdock*, 290 U.S. 389, 394–395 (1933). It seems to me that today's opinion squarely reverses that long-established statutory construction when it says that a good-faith erroneous belief in the unconstitutionality of a tax law is no defense. It is quite impossible to say that a statute which one believes unconstitutional represents a "known legal duty." See *Marbury v. Madison*, 1 Cranch 137, 177–178 (1803).

Although the facts of the present case involve erroneous reliance upon the Constitution in ignoring the otherwise "known legal duty" imposed by the tax statutes, the Court's new interpretation applies also to erroneous reliance upon a tax statute in ignoring the otherwise "known legal duty" of a regulation, and to erroneous reliance upon a regulation in ignoring the otherwise "known legal duty" of a tax assessment. These situations as well meet the opinion's crucial test of "reveal[ing] full knowledge of the provisions at issue and a studied conclusion, however wrong, that those provisions are invalid and unenforceable," *ante*, at 13. There is, moreover, no rational basis for saying that a "willful" violation is established by full knowledge of a statutory requirement, but is not established by full knowledge of a requirement explicitly imposed by regulation or order. Thus, today's opinion works a revolution in past practice, subjecting to criminal penalties taxpayers who do not comply with Treasury Regulations that are in their view contrary to the Internal Revenue Code, Treasury Rulings that are in their view contrary to the regulations, and even IRS auditor pronouncements that are in their view contrary to Treasury Rulings. The law already provides considerable incentive for taxpayers to be careful in ignoring any official assertion of tax liability, since it contains civil penalties that apply even in the event of a good-faith mistake, see, *e.g.*, 26 U.S.C. §§ 6651, 6653. To impose in addition *criminal* penalties for misinterpretation of such a complex body of law is a startling innovation indeed.

I find it impossible to understand how one can derive from the lonesome word "willfully" the proposition that belief in the nonexistence of a textual prohibition excuses liability, but belief in the invalidity (*i.e.,* the legal nonexistence) of a textual prohibition does not. One may say, as the law does in many contexts, that "willfully" refers to consciousness of the act but not to consciousness that the act is unlawful. See, *e.g., American Surety Co. of New York v. Sullivan,* 7 F.2d 605, 606 (CA2 1925) (L. Hand, J.); cf. *United States v. International Minerals and Chemical Co.,* 402 U.S. 558, 563–565 (1971). Or alternatively, one may say, as we have said until today with respect to the tax statutes, that "willfully" refers to consciousness of both the act *and* its illegality. But it seems to me impossible to say that the word refers to consciousness that some legal text exists, without consciousness that that legal text is binding, *i.e.,* with the good-faith belief that it is not a valid law. Perhaps such a test for criminal liability would make sense (though in a field as complicated as federal tax law, I doubt it), but some text other than the mere word "willfully" would have to be employed to describe it—and that text is not ours to write.

Because today's opinion abandons clear and long-standing precedent to impose criminal liability where taxpayers have had no reason to expect it, because the new contours of criminal liability have no basis in the statutory text, and because I strongly suspect that those new contours make no sense even as a policy matter, I concur only in the judgment of the Court.

* * *

JUSTICE BLACKMUN, with whom JUSTICE MARSHALL joins, dissenting.

It seems to me that we are concerned in this case not with "the complexity of the tax laws," *ante,* at 7, but with the income tax law in its most elementary and basic aspect: Is a wage earner a taxpayer and are wages income?

The Court acknowledges that the conclusively established standard for willfulness under the applicable statutes is the "voluntary, intentional violation of a known legal duty." *Ante,* at 8. See *United States v. Bishop,* 412 U.S. 346, 360 (1963), and *United States v. Pomponio,* 429 U.S. 10, 12 (1976). That being so, it is incomprehensible to me how, in this day, more than 70 years after the institution of our present federal income tax system with the passage of the Revenue Act of 1913, 38 Stat. 166, any taxpayer of competent mentality can assert as his defense to charges of statutory willfulness the proposition that the wage he receives for his labor is not income, irrespective of a cult that says otherwise and advises the gullible to resist income tax collections. One might note in passing that this particular taxpayer, after all, was a licensed pilot for one of our major commercial airlines; he presumably was a person of at least minimum intellectual competence.

The District Court's instruction that an objectively reasonable and good faith misunderstanding of the law negates willfulness lends further, rather than less, protection to this defendant, for it added an additional hurdle for the prosecution to overcome. Petitioner should be grateful for this further protection, rather than be opposed to it.

This Court's opinion today, I fear, will encourage taxpayers to cling to frivolous views of the law in the hope of convincing a jury of their sincerity. If that ensues, I suspect we have gone beyond the limits of common sense.

While I may not agree with every word the Court of Appeals has enunciated in its opinion, I would affirm its judgment in this case. I therefore dissent.

UNITED STATES v. JALBERT
United States Court of Appeals, First Circuit, 1974.
504 F.2d 892.

ALDRICH, SENIOR CIRCUIT JUDGE.

Defendant Jalbert, a college graduate who had also had one year in law school and had been a special agent of the F.B.I., became a Dover, New Hampshire businessman with interests in several enterprises. He was convicted, after a jury trial, of filing false income tax returns in violation of 26 U.S.C. § 7201 for the years 1968, 1969 and 1970. Substantial unreported items were fully established, largely by direct evidence. The returns, signed by the defendant, were prepared by others on the basis of information supplied by defendant, and the omissions in the returns were, or could be found to be, due to defendant, not to any error by the preparers. Defendant's "basic defense," to quote his brief, was that "during the years in question he was a 'chronic alcoholic' and unable to form the requisite criminal intent." *Cf.* Hopt v. People, 1881, 104 U.S. 631, 634, 26 L.Ed. 873; Kane v. United States, 9 Cir., 1968, 399 F.2d 730, 736, cert. denied, 393 U.S. 1057, 89 S.Ct. 698, 21 L.Ed.2d 699; Tao, Alcoholism as a Defense to Crime, 1969, 45 Notre Dame L. 68, 72–74.

Defense witnesses offered extensive evidence, including medical testimony, of defendant's drinking, and of its incapacitating effect upon his ability to manage his business affairs. In addition, defendant's medical expert testified that alcoholics do things without knowledge, and without recollection afterwards. "I don't believe they can have criminal intent." In rebuttal, the government did not deny defendant's heavy drinking, but did introduce substantial evidence that contradicted his assertion that he lacked business acumen.

Defendant's contention that this testimony was not proper rebuttal, but should have been offered in chief to counter an anticipated defense, is too frivolous to require comment. *Cf.* Goldsby v. United States, 1895, 160 U.S. 70, 74, 76–77, 16 S.Ct. 216, 40 L.Ed. 343; United States v. Fench, 1972, 152 U.S.App.D.C. 325, 470 F.2d 1234, 1240–1241, cert. denied sub nom. Blackwell v. United States, 410 U.S. 909, 93 S.Ct. 964, 35 L.Ed.2d 271. Even if the question were closer, we would defer to the discretion of the trial court. *See* Goldsby, ante, 160 U.S. at 74, 16 S.Ct. 216; United States v. Montgomery, 3 Cir., 1942, 126 F.2d 151, 153, cert. denied, 316 U.S. 681, 62 S.Ct. 1268, 86 L.Ed. 1754. It is of no consequence that the government produced some of its rebuttal evidence by recalling its original witnesses.

Equally frivolous is defendant's claim that the evidence did not warrant a conviction. It is true that the government offered no medical expert to contradict defendant's expert. However, the testimony of defendant's expert itself admits of the possibility that even a chronic alcoholic may function well at times. And far more persuasive in this context than expert testimony, *cf.* Dusky v. United States, 8 Cir., 1961, 295 F.2d 743, 754, cert. denied, 368 U.S. 998, 82 S.Ct. 625, 7 L.Ed.2d 536, were the witnesses who observed defendant's actual conduct. They amply supported a jury finding that defendant was capable of conducting his business affairs despite his alcoholic condition. *Cf.* United States v. Bishop, 1 Cir., 1972, 469 F.2d 1337, 1347.

* * *

BURSTEN v. UNITED STATES
United States Court of Appeals Fifth Circuit, 1968.
395 F.2d 976.

BEN C. DAWKINS, JR., DISTRICT JUDGE:

This appeal is from a conviction for willful income tax evasion. 26 U.S.C. § 7201. For the reasons hereinafter indicated, we reverse and remand for a new trial.

Appellant, Bursten, a non-Florida lawyer, but who engaged in legal and financial activities there, and was apparently quite a "wheeler-and-dealer," was indicted for evading federal income taxes for 1957. Specifically, the indictment charged him with reporting he had no taxable income in 1957, when in fact he knew that his income for that year was $152,767.14. Income tax which would have been due on this amount would have been $93,093.40.

After a one-week trial, defendant was found guilty as charged. He was sentenced to eighteen months (fifteen months of which was suspended) and fined $5,000. In this appeal Bursten complains of various errors, said to have been committed by the trial court, which will be discussed hereinafter.

Appellant's financial transactions, as detailed in the record, were somewhat complicated.

* * *

Bursten further stated that he claimed this loss in 1957 because he was specifically advised to do so by his tax counsel, William J. Goldworn. Goldworn, accepted by the Court as an expert in income tax matters, testified that he had represented both Mr. and Mrs. Bursten in their tax affairs through 1957, and in some instances thereafter. He further declared that Mrs. Bursten initially came to him because she was unhappy with what had happened to the East Corporation stock.

Sec. 1 THE TAX CRIMES 581

Concerning the 1957 return, Goldworn testified that Bursten brought to him several contracts dealing with his various land transactions. They then discussed the propriety of appellant's reporting certain of these transactions as gains and losses on his 1957 income tax return. Goldworn said that, since the purchase price of the land from the Lightseys was $220,000, and "since his [Bursten's] wife had a two-thirds interest in it which had been—he had purchased certain stock from her for that interest—then the value of the stock would be what he [Bursten] paid her for it if it was an arm's length transaction and that, therefore, two-thirds of $220,000 was approximately $140,000." (Tr. 676) Goldworn then stated that, in his opinion, the transaction was indeed an arm's length transaction.

The Government countered by asking Goldworn whether he knew such losses were not deductible under Section 267 of the Internal Revenue Code of 1954. Goldworn replied that in his opinion such an "arm's length transaction" as the one he had described was not within the reach of Section 267.

As noted, at the close of the evidence and after the jury was charged by the Court as to the law, appellant was convicted of willful evasion of income tax due in 1957. We now proceed to consideration of the specific issues presented by this appeal. While appellant has set forth a nine-point argument in brief, we find it necessary to rule upon only three of these, which are definitely dispositive of the appeal.[3]

* * *

II.

Appellant further contends that the trial judge committed reversible error in refusing to give to the jury the following specially requested instruction:

"If you find that the defendant had discussed this matter with competent tax counsel and that the tax return herein was prepared pursuant to that advice, then you must find that the defendant did not willfully file a false return or make a false statement, and you should bring in a verdict of not guilty." (Tr. 859)

We agree that there is substantial merit in this contention for the following reasons:

In Perez v. United States, 297 F.2d 12 (5 Cir.1961), we held:

"It is elementary law that the defendant in a criminal case is entitled to have presented instructions relating to a theory of defense for which there is any foundation in the evidence. * * * A charge is erroneous which ignores a claimed defense with such a foundation. * * * The charge to which he is entitled, upon proper request, in such circumstances is one which precisely and specifically, rather than merely generally or abstractly, points to his theory of defense, * * * and one

---

3. We seriously doubt whether there is any validity to these other arguments by appellant.

which does not unduly emphasize the theory of the prosecution, thereby de-emphasizing proportionally the defendant's theory." (Citations omitted) (297 F.2d at 12, 15, 16)

Our recent ruling in Strauss v. United States, 376 F.2d 416 (5 Cir.1967) also involved an appeal from a conviction of willful tax evasion. Coincidentally, that case also was tried before the same District Court in Florida. In reversing the conviction and sentence for failure of the Trial Court properly to instruct the jury, we noted:

" * * * If the trial judge evaluates or screens the evidence supporting a proposed defense, and upon such evaluation declines to charge on that defense, he dilutes the defendant's jury trial by removing the issue from the jury's consideration. In effect, the trial judge directs a verdict on that issue against the defendant. This is impermissible. Bryan v. United States, 5 Cir.1967, 373 F.2d 403." (376 F.2d 416, 419)

Review of the record here leaves little or no doubt as to why appellant requested the quoted instruction. One of the essential elements to be proved by the Government here was that he, appellant, willfully evaded the federal income tax laws. To have been successful, the Government must have proved, beyond a reasonable doubt, that appellant willfully filed a false income tax return with intent to defraud the Government. Thus, if the jury believed that appellant honestly relied on the advice of his tax counsel, Goldworn, it might have found that the element of willfulness was lacking and have acquitted. Moreover, there is no doubt that there was adequate basis in the record for this requested instruction.

Careful review of this quite lengthy record reveals why this instruction was refused by the District Judge:

"Mr. Booth: Which one are you refusing?

The Court: *Well, that 'advice'; that's no excuse at all for a lawyer, particularly. It's no excuse at all.* (Emphasis added.)

[We must note here, as a matter of judicial knowledge, that most lawyers have only scant knowledge of the tax laws.]

Mr. Osman: I give this to the Court and ask him if he is going to have a charge on that?

The Court: If this were the law, then I could get advice from anybody.

Mr. Soltz: Well, it says, 'competent'.

The Court: Well, that's silly. You can always find a crook that will give you any advice that you don't owe any tax."

(Tr. 725, 726)

Moreover, we note from the Charge Conference, this:

"Mr. Booth: Your Honor, it certainly goes on the question of what the intent was from what he was advised and what he believed.

The Court: Well, I'm not saying intent—

Mr. Booth: Whether it's the law or not.

The Court: That's a matter of argument. I agree with you that he may have been foolish enough to believe that so-called professor we had here—

Mr. Booth: He teaches at the graduate school.

The Court: I don't care what school he teaches in, *he is not a good tax man*. (Emphasis added)

Mr. Booth: Well, on the question of intent, that really doesn't make much difference.

The Court: No, he may have given that advice. I don't say he didn't; and if he did, I don't say that this man is guilty in this case if he believed him.

Mr. Booth: That's what the testimony shows.

The Court: That's up to the jury. I'm not going to decide that."

(Tr. 729, 730)

This clearly establishes that this instruction was refused because the trial judge thought "he [Goldworn] [was] not a good tax man." In the very same colloquy with defense counsel, the trial judge also noted that whether appellant relied upon advice given by Goldworn was up to the jury. As was stated in Strauss v. United States, supra:

" * * * We agree that the substance (though not necessarily the wording) of these charges should have been given. Defendant's dissatisfaction here is not pettifoggery over nuances of words. His objections go to the refusal to submit substantive defenses." (376 F.2d 416, 418–419)

While the record reveals (Tr. 795–798) that the trial judge gave a *general* instruction to the jury on the element of intent, the authorities cited and quoted from conclusively hold that appellant was entitled to a more specific charge in light of his contention that he relied on advice of his tax counsel. This failure to give such a specific charge, even though it should have been reworded, so as to indicate that, to rely on this defense, appellant should have been found to have given *all* the facts to his advisor, was reversible error.

* * *

Reversed and remanded.

SIMPSON, CIRCUIT JUDGE (concurring specially):

I concur in the result, on the basis of the matters discussed in Part III of the opinion, even though a number of the prejudicial remarks of the trial court were elicited by the conduct of defense counsel.

I disagree with Part II of the opinion. The requested instruction was deficient in at least two respects: (1) it speaks in terms of the defendant discussing the matter with tax counsel, rather than in terms of a full disclosure to such counsel, and (2) the necessary element of reliance upon counsel's advice is omitted. Under these circumstances, I am not persuaded that it was error to refuse the charge or to fail to edit it and give it in amended form.

Note

As indicated in Judge Simpson's concurring opinion, the reliance defense to willfulness is not available to a taxpayer who is less than candid with the professional upon whom he purportedly relied. Thus, the following instruction to the jury was approved in United States v. Cox, 348 F.2d 294, 296 (6th Cir.1965):

> However, effectiveness of [the reliance] defense requires not only that the advice be sought from a person believed to be competent to give advice, but also that the taxpayer make full disclosure to that person of all pertinent facts, in order that the advice given may be in response to the true situation and not to one from which material facts have been withheld.

UNITED STATES v. AUSMUS
United States Court of Appeals, Sixth Circuit, 1985.
774 F.2d 722.

CORNELIA G. KENNEDY, CIRCUIT JUDGE.

Defendant-appellant, James C. Ausmus, Jr., appeals from his convictions on three counts of violating 26 U.S.C. § 7203 by willfully and knowingly failing to pay federal income taxes for calendar years 1978, 1979, and 1980. Defendant filed federal tax returns reporting taxable income of $23,260, $39,328, and $42,365 for the respective years, but did not pay the taxes due, $6,732, $13,211, and $15,401, respectively.

* * *

The United States introduced evidence that the defendant had disposable income of $7,876.40 in 1978, $23,790.22 in 1979, and $23,567.72 in 1980, which defendant could have used to pay his federal income taxes. On cross-examination, defendant admitted that since 1967 he had not paid any income taxes voluntarily. Defendant admitted that he had spent his money on other things, such as rent, new suits, entertainment, going out to dinner, tires, flowers, supporting his fiancee, and sending one of his sons to college, rather than pay his income taxes. Defendant testified that he kept very little money in the bank to prevent the Internal Revenue Service from seizing it. Defendant admitted his failure to pay the taxes was not an accident, negligence or inadvertence, but he stated that he intended to pay the taxes when he got the money.

The jury convicted the defendant on all charges. * * *

* * *

Defendant argues that the District Court incorrectly instructed the jury regarding the defense of financial inability to pay federal income taxes. Defendant contends that the challenged instruction eliminated the requirement that the government prove that the defendant had the necessary specific intent to commit the offense. The District Court instructed the jury:

The defendant asserts that his failure to pay his taxes for the years 1978, 1979 and 1980, was not willful because he did not have enough money to pay them. However, every United States citizen has an obligation to pay his income tax when it comes due. A taxpayer is obligated to conduct his financial affairs in such a way that he has cash available to satisfy his tax obligations on time. As a general rule, financial inability to pay the tax when it comes due is not a defense to criminal liability for willfully failing to pay income taxes.

* * *

* * * The language in the instruction came from *United States v. Tucker*, 686 F.2d 230, 233 (5th Cir.), cert. denied, 459 U.S. 1071, 103 S.Ct. 492, 74 L.Ed.2d 634 (1982). In *Tucker*, the appellant regularly filed his income tax returns but consistently failed to pay the disclosed tax liability. Tucker, however, spent considerable sums of money on luxuries including two trips to the Virgin Islands, a trip to Guadalajara, Mexico, jewelry, a new pleasure boat, a new car for his son, and club dues. Tucker also made payments totaling more than $2,000 to a woman he was dating. The court stated that Tucker's defense that he did not have the liquid assets to pay his taxes "borders on the ridiculous." The court concluded that, absent exceptional circumstances, mere unavailability of liquid assets does not excuse criminal liability under 26 U.S.C. § 7203.

Defendant asserts that *Tucker* was an incorrect statement of the law and that the United States must prove that, at the time defendant filed the returns, defendant possessed readily available funds so that he could pay his taxes. Defendant relies on *United States v. Andros*, 484 F.2d 531, 533–34 (9th Cir.1973), and *United States v. Goodman*, 190 F.Supp. 847 (N.D.Ill.1961), for the proposition that the prosecution must prove that the defendant was financially able to pay his taxes to establish a 26 U.S.C. § 7203 violation. The *Tucker* court specifically rejected those cases and refused to follow them.

In *United States v. Andros, supra,* the court stated, in dicta, that to establish a willful failure to pay taxes under 26 U.S.C. § 7203, the government must prove that the taxpayer possessed sufficient funds to meet his obligations to the government and that the taxpayer voluntarily and intentionally did not pay the tax due. The court, however, affirmed the defendant's conviction concluding that the taxpayer had the financial resources to pay his taxes when they were due. In *United States v. Goodman, supra,* defendant contended that his failure to pay income taxes was not willful but was caused by his financial inability to pay. The court stated that a taxpayer does not have any obligation to prefer the government as a creditor. Likewise, the court took the position that the taxpayer had no obligation to borrow money or agree to an assignment of wages so that the taxpayer could pay his taxes on time.

We adopt the rationale of the *Tucker* court and reject the language in *Andros* and *Goodman.* Otherwise, a recalcitrant taxpayer could spend his money as fast as he earns it and evade criminal liability while not paying taxes as long as his bank balance is zero when the taxpayer's taxes are due. We note that the Ninth Circuit appears to have retreated from its dicta in *Andros*.[3] In this case, defendant admitted that he spent money on luxuries including entertainment, new clothes, and support for his fiancee. Furthermore, the United States introduced evidence that defendant earned sufficient disposable income in the respective years so that defendant could have paid his taxes. Defendant, however, chose to spend his disposable income on other things. * * * the District Court did not err in giving the instruction.

* * *

UNITED STATES v. GARBER

United States Court of Appeals, Fifth Circuit, 1979.
607 F.2d 92.

Appeal from the United States District Court for the Southern District of Florida.

Before BROWN, CHIEF JUDGE, and COLEMAN, GOLDBERG, AINSWORTH, GODBOLD, CHARLES CLARK, RONEY, GEE, TJOFLAT, HILL, FAY, RUBIN, VANCE and KRAVITCH, CIRCUIT JUDGES.

CHARLES CLARK, CIRCUIT JUDGE:

Dorothy Clark Garber was indicted for willfully and knowingly attempting to evade a portion of her income tax liability for the years 1970, 1971, and 1972 by filing a false and fraudulent income tax return on behalf of herself and her husband. A jury found her innocent of the charges for 1970 and 1971 but convicted her under 26 U.S.C.A. § 7201 for knowingly misstating her income on her 1972 tax return. She was sentenced to 18 months imprisonment—all but 60 days of which was suspended—placed on probation for 21 months, and fined $5,000 exclusive of any civil tax liability. The taxability of the money received by Garber presents a unique legal question. Because of trial errors which deprived defendant of her defense on the element of willfulness, we reverse the conviction.

Some time in the late 1960's after the birth of her third child, Dorothy Garber was told that her blood contained a rare antibody

---

3. In *United States v. Poll*, 521 F.2d 329, 333 (9th Cir.1975), after citing *Andros*, the court reversed appellant's conviction under 26 U.S.C. § 7202 because the district court excluded evidence that the corporation lacked the liquid resources to pay the full amounts of federal income withholding taxes and social security taxes due and that appellant intended to make up the deficiencies later. Appellant offered the evidence to rebut the presence of willfulness. The court held that:

[T]o establish willfulness the Government must establish beyond a reasonable doubt that at the time payment was due the taxpayer possessed sufficient funds to enable him to meet his obligation or that the lack of sufficient funds on such date was created by (or was the result of) a voluntary and intentional act without justification in view of all the financial circumstances of the taxpayer.

useful in the production of blood group typing serum. Dade Reagents, Inc. (Dade Reagents), a manufacturer of diagnostic reagents used in clinical laboratories and blood banks, had made the discovery and in 1967 induced her to enter into a contract for the sale of her blood plasma. By a technique called plasmapheresis, a pint of whole blood was extracted from her arm, plasma was centrifugally separated, and the red cells were returned to her body. The process was then repeated. The two bleeds produced one pint of plasma from two pints of blood, and took a total of from one and a half to two and a half hours.

Plasmapheresis is often preceded by a stimulation of the donor whereby the titre or concentration of the desired antibody in the blood is artificially increased by an injection of an incompatible blood type. Both stimulation and plasmapheresis are accompanied by pain and discomfort and carry the risks of hepatitis and blood clotting.

In exchange for Garber's blood plasma, Dade Reagents agreed to pay her for each bleed on a sliding scale dependent on the titre or strength of the plasma obtained. Dade Reagents then marketed the substance for the production of blood group typing serum.

Because Garber's blood is so rare—she is one of only two or three known persons in the world with this antibody—she was approached by other laboratories which lured her away from Dade Reagents by offering an increasingly attractive price for her plasma. By 1970, 1971, and 1972, the three years covered in the indictment, she was receiving substantial sums of money in exchange for her plasma.[1] For two of those years she was selling her blood under separate contract to Associated Biologicals, Inc. (Associated) and to Biomedical Industries, Inc. (Biomedical), in both cases receiving in exchange a sum of money dependent on the strength of the antibody in each unit sold. In addition, Biomedical offered a weekly salary of $200, provided a leased automobile, and in 1972 added a $25,000 bonus. In that last year Garber sold her plasma to Biomedical exclusively, producing the coveted body fluid as often as six times a month.

For all three years involved, Biomedical had treated the regular $200 weekly payments as a salary subject to withholding taxes and provided Garber with a yearly W-2 form noting the taxes withheld. Every year, Garber attached those W-2 forms to her income tax return (which was filed jointly with her husband whom she has since divorced), declared the $200 per week as income, and paid the taxes due. All other payments, both from Biomedical and from Associated, had been paid directly to defendant by check. No income taxes were withheld by the companies; she received no W-2 forms, and paid no taxes on the money received. Biomedical did, however, file a Form 1099 Information Return with the IRS which showed a portion of Garber's donor fees not subject to withholding. Garber was provided a copy of each 1099,

1. Sale of her plasma allegedly brought her $80,200 in 1970, $71,400 in 1971, and $87,200 in 1972.

which plainly states that it is for information only and is not to be attached to the income tax return. She had never before received Information Returns, and, while she was receiving checks from both Biomedical and Associated, only Biomedical provided this information.

In this prosecution for the felony of willful evasion of income taxes the government had the burden of proving every element of the crime beyond a reasonable doubt. This required proof of a tax deficiency, an affirmative act constituting evasion or attempted evasion of the tax due, and willfulness. The element we find lacking here was willfulness.

At trial, outside the presence of the jury, the government proffered the testimony of Jacquin Bierman, a professor of law and practicing attorney in the City of New York, who stated his opinion that Garber had made available her bodily functions or products for a consideration which constituted taxable gross income. His conclusion was based on section 61(a) of the Internal Revenue Code (Code) which defines gross income as

> all income from whatever source derived, including (but not limited to) the following items:
>
> > (1) Compensation for services, including fees, commissions, and similar items;
>
> * * *
>
> > (3) Gains derived from dealings in property;

While admitting that this case is the first of its kind, Bierman opined that if the exchanges were considered the sale of a product, there would be no tax basis or original cost for the product sold, and the entire sales price would constitute gain subject to tax under section 61(a)(3). Alternatively, he considered categorizing the transactions as the rendition of a service, in which case he was of the opinion that the entire sales price similarly would be fully taxable under section 61(a)(1).

The defense proffered to the court the testimony of Daniel Nall, a Certified Public Accountant and former revenue agent, who concluded that the money received by Garber was not within the legal definition of income in section 61(a) and that she had therefore participated in tax-free exchanges. He patterned his reasoning on early case law resting on *Doyle v. Mitchell Brothers,* 247 U.S. 179, 38 S.Ct. 467, 62 L.Ed. 1054 (1918), which held that funds obtained by the conversion of capital assets and which represented only the actual value of such assets was not taxable income. According to Nall, the Attorney General in a 1918 opinion considered the human body a kind of capital asset. Following the reasoning in *Doyle,* the opinion held that the proceeds of an accident insurance policy were not subject to tax because the proceeds of the insurance policy represented a conversion of the capital loss which the injured taxpayer had suffered. Nall mentioned similar opinions finding settlements received for personal injury not taxable income. Eventually the Code was amended to include a specific provision covering the tax consequences of compensation for injuries or sickness.[2] Nevertheless, Nall explained, the theory has reappeared in situations involving the exchange of something so personal that its value is not susceptible to measurement. In these transactions—such as property settlements in divorce actions or damage awards for alienation of affection or for defamation of character—the value received is deemed equal to the value given, resulting in no taxable gain. Nall compared blood plasma, a part of the body which no one can value, and concluded that it too must be worth its market value. He therefore reasoned that its exchange produces no gain.

The district court heard the testimony of these two experts but refused to admit either opinion in the evidence which went to the jury because it considered the question of taxability to be one of law for the court and not the jury to decide. However, the court did permit the government to introduce testimony by an Internal Revenue Service agent who qualified as an expert in the field of accounting and taxation. This agent offered his opinion that additional taxable income was due but not reported in the years in question. His testimony was received over defense objection that it was based on his conclusion that the compensation received was income and taxable. During cross examination, the witness conceded that the taxability of money received for giving up a part of one's body is a unique and undecided question in tax law. He also agreed that money received as a return on a capital product is not subject to tax. Yet, he based his calculations on his opinion that the blood plasma donations here were taxable personal services. His view was, in turn, based solely on a Revenue Ruling which declared donations of whole blood to be a service for purposes of determining the deductibility of a charitable contribution. The court sustained objections to the relevancy of further inquiry regarding the nature or value of blood plasma.

The defense argued to the court that the expert testimony of Daniel Nall should be presented to the jury to rebut the government's expert IRS agent, to show that doubt existed as to whether a tax was due because it was incapable of being computed, and to demonstrate the vagueness of the law, which would preclude a willful intent to violate it. The court recognized that Nall's theory could be relevant to its judicial resolution of the legal conflict. It ruled however that since Nall had never discussed his opinion of the law with the defendant, it had no

---

2. Section 104 of the Code, 26 U.S.C.A. § 104, now expressly excludes from taxable income certain insurance proceeds and

(2) the amount of any damages received (whether by suit or agreement) on account of personal injuries or sickness; 26 U.S.C.A. § 104(a)(2).

The defendant has alternatively argued that the payments here in question fall within this exclusion from taxable income. Section 104(a)(2) has consistently been applied only to payments resulting from the settlement or prosecution of a tort claim. *Knuckles v. CIR*, 349 F.2d 610 (10th Cir. 1965); *Starrels v. CIR*, 304 F.2d 574 (9th Cir.1962); *Agar v. CIR*, 290 F.2d 283 (2d Cir.1961). The only evidence in the record which could possibly support a claim that the payments to Garber were in settlement of a tort liability were medical release of liability forms she signed. We express no opinion on the ultimate merits of this contention.

relevancy to the fact issue of Garber's intent. The jury never heard the testimony. It did, however, hear considerable factual evidence relating to Garber's actual intent.[3]

After hearing all the evidence, the court ruled as a matter of law that the moneys Garber received for her blood plasma, whether considered a personal service or a product, were income subject to federal income taxation. Consistent with that ruling the jury was instructed that the funds Garber received from the sale of her blood plasma were taxable income. The court also instructed the jury extensively on good faith and willfulness but refused the instructions requested by defense to the effect that a misunderstanding as to defendant's liability for the tax is a valid defense to the charge of income tax evasion, saying:

> I have said over and over again [to the jury] that she must act willfully, knowingly and willfully, in an effort to evade and defeat a tax by filing a false return, and that tells it all as far as I am concerned. This business about doubt and all these debatable things I have listened to around here for several days, and I'm not going to charge the jury that way, so as to confuse them. I think that would do more harm than good, and I think it would be error.

We hold that the combined effect of the trial court's evidentiary rulings excluding defendant's proffered expert testimony and its requested jury charge prejudicially deprived the defendant of a valid theory of her defense. No court has yet determined whether payments received by a donor of blood or blood components are taxable as income. If, as the government contends, by subjecting herself to the plasmapheresis process Garber has performed a service, her compensation would be

---

[3] To prove that Garber had to have been actually aware of her tax liability, the government offered testimony from an employee of Dade Reagents, contradicted by defendant's own statements, that in Garber's early dealings with that company not only had she been advised of the taxable element of her payments but the company had also opened a savings account in her name and regularly deposited a portion of her earnings allegedly for income tax purposes. The IRS agent who first investigated the Garbers took the stand and testified that, in his initial interview with both Mr. and Mrs. Garber concerning their 1971 joint return, defendant denied having received any income other than the reported $200 per week salary from Biomedical. However, that same afternoon following the interview, defendant called the agent, explained that she and her husband were about to be divorced, and arranged a second interview in which she discussed her plasma donations and disclosed all monies received. The agent admitted that Garber was cooperative in the absence of her husband; she produced all relevant records including the 1099 forms received from Biomedical.

The defense offered affirmative evidence to show that Garber did not willfully misstate her income. An accountant had prepared all three joint returns from information supplied by Mr. Garber, who was not indicted, without consulting with defendant. Furthermore, it was undisputed that all payments to defendant were made by check, payable to her, and deposited in her bank account. Payments were never made in cash; there was no duplicative bookkeeping or other clandestine financial dealings indicative of an attempt to secrete earnings. Her returns for the years in question disclosed Biomedical as a source of income. In addition, Garber produced a copy of her 1969 tax return on which she declared no taxable income but noted "I have no W-2 forms as my income was made up entirely from donating blood plasma from various blood banks." The defendant herself testified that she thought, after speaking with other blood donors, that because she was selling a part of her body the money received was not taxable.

taxable under section 61(a)(1) of the Code. In some ways, Garber's activity does resemble work: artificial stimulation, which is not a necessary prerequisite to plasma extraction, causes nausea and dizziness; the ordeal of plasmapheresis can be extremely painful if a nerve is struck, can cause nausea, blackouts, dizziness and scarring, and increases the risks of blood clotting and hepatitis. These efforts of production may logically compare to the performance of a service.

On the other hand, blood plasma, like a chicken's eggs, a sheep's wool, or like any salable part of the human body, is tangible property which in this case commanded a selling price dependent on its value. The amount of Garber's compensation for any given pint of plasma was directly related to the strength of the desired antibodies. The greater their concentration, the more she was paid; her earnings were in no way related to the amount of work done, pain incurred, or time spent producing one pint of plasma.

Of course, the product/service distinction is relevant only if the sale of the product results in no taxable gain. The experts testifying for both parties here concede that section 61(a)(3) includes in income only the profit gained through the sale or conversion of capital assets. They do not, however, agree on the computation of gain, because they differ in their theories as to how the value of the product before its sale is to be established. The cost of Garber's blood plasma, containing its rare antibody, cannot be mathematically computed by aggregating the market cost of its components such as salt and water. That would be equivalent to calculating the basis in a master artist's portrait by costing the canvas and paints. No evidence of any original cost exists in the case of Garber's unusual natural body fluid.

In such a situation it may well be that its value should be deemed equal to the price a willing buyer would pay a willing seller on the open market. If this were the proper basis, the exchange would be a wash resulting in no tax consequences. However, we need not and do not undertake the complex task of resolving what the law should be, nor is it necessary to decide whether, as the trial court concluded, the question is purely one of law for the court and not the jury to resolve. Rather, because the district court refused to permit Bierman, the expert for the government, and Nall, the expert for the defense, to testify and because it reserved to itself the job of unriddling the tax law, thus completely obscuring from the jury the most important theory of Garber's defense—that she could not have willfully evaded a tax if there existed a reasonable doubt in the law that a tax was due— her trial was rendered fundamentally unfair.

A tax return is not criminally fraudulent simply because it is erroneous. Willfulness is an essential element of the crime charged. As such, the government must prove beyond a reasonable doubt that the defendant willfully and intentionally attempted to evade and defeat income taxes for each year in question by filing with the IRS tax returns which she knew were false. It is not enough to show merely that a lesser tax was paid than was due. Nor is a negligent, careless, or unintentional understatement of income sufficient. The government must demonstrate that the defendant willfully concealed and omitted from her return income which she knew was taxable.

When the taxability of unreported income is problematical as a matter of law, the unresolved nature of the law is relevant to show that defendant may not have been aware of a tax liability or may have simply made an error in judgment. Furthermore, the relevance of a dispute in the law does not depend on whether the defendant actually knew of the conflict. In *United States v. Critzer*, 498 F.2d 1160 (4th Cir.1974), the Fourth Circuit reversed a criminal tax fraud conviction against an Eastern Cherokee Indian who failed to report a portion of her income derived from land held by the United States in trust for the Eastern Cherokee Band. The evidence clearly established that the underreporting was intentional. Whether the income was taxable, however, was a disputed question dependent on the interpretation of certain land allotment statutes, which the court did not resolve. Instead, it reversed the conviction because of the absence of authority definitively governing the situation. The court's language is particularly apt here:

> As a matter of law, defendant cannot be guilty of willfully evading and defeating income taxes on income, the taxability of which is so uncertain that even co-ordinate branches of the United States Government plausibly reach directly opposing conclusions. As a matter of law, the requisite intent to evade and defeat income taxes is missing. *The obligation to pay is so problematical that defendant's actual intent is irrelevant. Even if she had consulted the law and sought to guide herself accordingly, she could have had no certainty as to what the law required.*

498 F.2d at 1162 (emphasis added).

Critzer differs from this case in that the defendant there had been advised by the Bureau of Indian Affairs that the income received from the transactions on the Reservation was exempt from taxation. The fact that Garber did not have the benefit of such official advice does not persuade us that the result here should be different. The *Critzer* court did not so limit its holding:

> It is settled that when the law is vague or highly debatable, a defendant—actually or imputedly—lacks the requisite intent to violate it.

498 F.2d at 1162. To hold otherwise would advocate convicting an unsophisticated taxpayer who failed to seek expert advice as to whether certain income was taxable while setting free a wise taxpayer who could find advice that taxes were not due on the identical type of debatably taxable income.

That *Critzer* was not decided on the basis of the defendant's actual intent is further evidenced by the reasoning of the court and its reliance on *James v. United States*, 366 U.S. 213, 81 S.Ct. 1052, 6 L.Ed.2d 246 (1961). In *James,* the Supreme Court put to rest a dispute over the taxability of embezzled funds. Fifteen years before *James,* the Court had held such funds non-taxable. *CIR v. Wilcox,* 327 U.S. 404, 66 S.Ct. 546, 90 L.Ed. 752 (1946). Subsequently a realigned Court undermined the viability of *Wilcox* by deciding that extortion money was taxable, distinguishing *Wilcox* on tenuous grounds. *Rutkin v. United States,* 343 U.S. 130, 72 S.Ct. 571, 96 L.Ed. 833 (1952). When the taxability of embezzled funds again reached the Court in *James,* it decided that *Rutkin* had in effect overruled *Wilcox* and that embezzled monies were taxable. Nevertheless, the court reversed James' conviction for willfully failing to report embezzled funds in violation of section 7201 because of the uncertainty of the law created by *Wilcox.* Significantly, neither *James* nor the cases following *James* required actual reliance on *Wilcox* to negate willful intent.[4] As noted in *Critzer*:

> the uncertainty created by *Wilcox* as a matter of law precluded a demonstration of "willfulness," without regard to the defendant's actual state of mind with respect to his knowledge or reliance on *Wilcox.*

498 F.2d at 1163.

Both *Critzer* and *James* involved disagreements among recognized authorities which were more clearly documented than the theories presented here. *James* involved conflicting Supreme Court decisions, and in *Critzer* the Bureau of Indian Affairs and the Internal Revenue Service strongly disagreed on the taxability of the income. In the case presently before us, as conceded by all the experts who testified, there is a dearth of authority directly supporting either argument. However, the fact that the question has never before evoked anything more than theories on either side adds to rather than detracts from the critical conflict upon which defendant's criminal liability hinges. Neither position is frivolous, and the fact that both are urged without clear precedential support in law demonstrates that the court should not have restricted the evidence or instructed as it did.

The tax treatment of earnings from the sale of blood plasma or other parts of the human body is an uncharted area in tax law. The parties in this case presented divergent opinions as to the ultimate

---

4. The plurality opinion in *James* stated:

> We believe that the element of willfulness could not be proven in a criminal prosecution for failing to include embezzled funds in gross income in the year of misappropriation so long as the statute contained the gloss placed upon it by *Wilcox* at the time the alleged crime was committed. Therefore, we feel that petitioner's conviction may not stand and that the indictment against him must be dismissed. 366 U.S. at 221–222, 81 S.Ct. at 1057.

Justices Black and Douglas were of the opinion that *Wilcox* still represented the controlling law, but agreed with the plurality that the new determination finding embezzled funds taxable should not be applied to past conduct:

> [A] criminal statute that is so ambiguous in scope that an interpretation of it brings about totally unexpected results, thereby subjecting people to penalties and punishments for conduct which they could not know was criminal under existing law, raises serious questions of unconstitutional vagueness. 366 U.S. at 224, 81 S.Ct. at 1058.

The two dissenting Justices argued that a remand was necessary for a jury to determine the factual question of actual reliance on *Wilcox.*

taxability by analogy to two legitimate theories in tax law. The trial court should not have withheld this fact, and its powerful impact on the issue of Garber's willfulness, from the jury. *Morissette v. United States,* 342 U.S. 246, 72 S.Ct. 240, 96 L.Ed. 288 (1952); *United States v. Pomponio,* 563 F.2d 659 (4th Cir.1977). In a case such as this where the element of willfulness is critical to the defense, the defendant is entitled to wide latitude in the introduction of evidence tending to show lack of intent. *United States v. Brown,* 411 F.2d 1134 (10th Cir.1969); *Petersen v. United States,* 268 F.2d 87 (10th Cir.1959); *Miller v. United States,* 120 F.2d 968 (10th Cir.1941). The defendant testified that she subjectively thought that proceeds from the sale of part of her body were not taxable. By disallowing Nall's testimony that a recognized theory of tax law supports Garber's feelings, the court deprived the defendant of evidence showing her state of mind to be reasonable.

This error was compounded by the court's instructions to the jury which took from them the question of the validity of the tax. In effect, the court adopted the government's position that a tax was owing as a matter of law. Garber admitted receiving unreported money and disclosed its source; the defense in this case rested entirely on a denial of the necessary criminal intent to evade taxes. The court erred by refusing to instruct the jury that a reasonable misconception of the tax law on her part would negate the necessary intent. By withholding this theory, the court left the jury with the impression that a tax was clearly due and that Garber simply refused to pay it.[5] A panel of this court in *United States v. McClain,* 593 F.2d 658 (5th Cir.1979), recently reached a similar conclusion when criminal liability for importing stolen Mexican artifacts depended on an interpretation of complicated, uncertain, and changing Mexican law declaring national ownership of artifacts. At the first trial, the district court heard *in camera* expert testimony interpreting the Mexican Constitution and relevant statutes, and instructed the jury on its determination of the foreign law. On appeal this was held to be error and the case remanded:

> The court's instruction that the Mexican government had owned the artifacts for over seventy-five years was highly prejudicial to the defendants. It could have been the decisive factor in the jury's inferring that the defendants must have known that the artifacts in question were stolen.

United States v. McClain, 545 F.2d 988, 1000 (5th Cir.1977). The second trial was replete with historians, professors, and others expressing their views on the changing Mexican laws, based for the most part on independent review of the Mexican Constitution and relevant statutes. After hearing all the experts, the jury was given the task of first deciding whether and when Mexico actually enacted national ownership of the artifacts, and then determining the defendants' guilt based

---

5. During its deliberations, the jury asked the court whether any effort was made by the government to settle the case in any other way previous to filing an indictment. Obviously they were not aware that the taxability of the sums was still a disputed question.

on that law. The defendants were convicted. Despite the "near overwhelming" evidence of guilt and intent to violate the law, the panel reversed the substantive convictions

> because the most likely jury construction of Mexican law upon the evidence at trial is that Mexico declared itself owner of all artifacts at least as early as 1897. And under this view of Mexican law, we believe the defendants may have suffered the prejudice of being convicted pursuant to laws that were too vague to be a predicate for criminal liability under our jurisprudential standards.

593 F.2d at 670.

Similarly in the case before us, the government presented persuasive evidence showing that the defendant knowingly and willfully evaded her taxes. She received a significant amount of money over a three year period, but reported none of it. The proof also showed that those with whom she dealt advised her that they thought the proceeds were taxable. Nevertheless, the tax question was completely novel and unsettled by any clearly relevant precedent. A criminal proceeding pursuant to section 7201 is an inappropriate vehicle for pioneering interpretations of tax law. The conviction is reversed and the cause is remanded for retrial.

Reversed and Remanded.

JAMES C. HILL, CIRCUIT JUDGE, specially concurring:

Because I conclude that the transactions under investigation constituted services and the income derived therefrom taxable under 61(a)(1), I should have preferred that the court say so in positive terms. The question would thus cease to be a novel one for those considering it in the future.

It was a novel question when it arose here, however, and the defendant should have been permitted to demonstrate its novelty, not so that the jury could pass upon the tax consequences of the transactions, but so that the jurors could better determine the question of willfulness. The case should be sent back for retrial with the willfulness issue determined upon consideration of all the evidence.

I take it that, at some length, the majority winds up by doing just that. So, I concur.

AINSWORTH, CIRCUIT JUDGE, with whom GODBOLD, TJOFLAT and ALVIN B. RUBIN, CIRCUIT JUDGES, join, dissenting:

This dissent to the majority opinion is made on the basis of two principal issues involved in the trial in district court. The first of these follows.

> 1) Did the trial judge err in ruling, as a matter of law, that the income derived by defendant Garber was taxable?

* * *

It is our view that defendant Garber's income was taxable and that Judge Fulton correctly ruled, as a matter of law, that it was. Further, his instruction to the jury that the income was taxable and withdrawal of that issue from the jury was a correct trial ruling.

Unfortunately, under the majority opinion, when the case goes back to Judge Fulton for retrial, he will be unable to tell from the majority opinion whether he correctly ruled that defendant Garber's income was taxable. The trial court should not be left in such a dilemma.

* * *

The second principal issue follows.

2) Did the trial judge properly submit the question of willfulness to the jury?

On the issue of willfulness, we first consider whether the trial judge erred in declining to permit the proffered testimony of defendant Garber's so-called expert Nall to go to the jury. The majority argues strenuously that this was probably the most serious of the errors committed in the trial since Nall's testimony would have shown that the law was so uncertain as to whether defendant Garber's income was taxable that she could not have had criminal intent to evade payment of taxes.

Our view is that receipt of opinion testimony of this kind as to pure issues of law invades the province of the district court. It is the trial judge who must make rulings on the law involved in the case, and boilerplate jury instructions have since time immemorial stated that the jury takes the law only from the court. Now a new rule is attempted by the majority which in effect states that the jury must take its instructions on the law from expert witnesses as well as the trial judge.

* * *

Indeed, other precedent directly supports the inadmissibility of the expert's testimony on the law. The question should be controlled by this court's decision in *White v. United States*, 5 Cir., 1954, 216 F.2d 1. In *White*, the trial judge refused to allow the defendant's experts to testify that certain funds should be treated as capital gains rather than ordinary income as the Government argued. On appeal, the court held that the testimony was properly excluded since the defendant had not relied upon the expert's opinion. "[T]he defendant not having acted in accordance with the witness' opinion and hence that opinion not being relevant on the question of intention, we think that the opinion of the witness as to the law of the case could not be substituted for that of the court * * *." *Id.* at 5. *Cf. United States v. Caserta*, 3 Cir., 1952, 199 F.2d 905, 909 (where the purpose of expert testimony is "criticism of the government's legal theory," such evidence should be excluded).

* * *

We next point out that the majority's view concerning the supposed impropriety of the judge's instruction on willfulness is similarly mistaken. An examination of the relevant authority relied upon by the majority demonstrates that those cases are not applicable in the circumstances here. *Morissette v. United States,* 342 U.S. 246, 72 S.Ct. 240, 96 L.Ed. 288 (1952), involved a defendant who had taken bomb casings from government property thinking that they were abandoned scrap. The trial court ruled that the defendant had conclusively demonstrated the requisite intent merely by taking the casings. Thus, the defendant was unable to argue that he had a good faith belief that the casings were abandoned by the Government and the question of intent was taken away from the jury. In reversing the conviction, the Supreme Court held that the matter of intent was a question of fact which must be submitted to the jury. Similarly, in Mann v. United States, 5 Cir., 1963, 319 F.2d 404, cert. denied, 375 U.S. 986, 84 S.Ct. 520, 11 L.Ed.2d 474 (1964), the trial judge instructed the jury that an actor intends the natural and probable consequences of his acts. The court held that the result of this instruction was that the jury was essentially told that it could presume intent from the mere fact that an incorrect tax return had been filed. We held that it was "error to give a charge in a criminal case of this nature, the overall effect of which is to place a burden upon the defendant to produce evidence to overcome a presumption of guilt." 319 F.2d at 410. * * * In summary, the cases cited by the majority stand for the proposition that the trial judge may not refuse the defense of lack of intent or hinder its usefulness by creating a presumption which lowers the Government's burden of proof. The jury must be instructed that it is a defense to the charge if the defendant acted with a good faith belief in the propriety of his or her conduct.

The district judge in this case did not hamper appellant's right to a defense based upon her lack of criminal intent and he properly stated the applicable law. The judge made clear that it was the jury's responsibility to determine intent from its consideration of all the evidence. He instructed that the appellant could not be convicted if her actions were "not voluntary and intentional on her part but [were] the result of a mistake or inadvertence or some other innocent reason. * * *" Thus, the good faith defense was not taken from the appellant as in *Morissette.* Furthermore, the judge did not create any presumptions which lowered the Government's burden of proof. *Cf. Mann v. United States, supra,* 319 F.2d 404. On the crucial issue of the relationship between the taxability of the income and the issue of appellant's willfulness, the trial judge made it absolutely clear that his ruling that the income was taxable in no way affected the jury's responsibility for determining intent.

* * *

We believe the original panel opinion in this case which affirmed defendant Garber's conviction was correct and for the reasons there expressed and expanded here. No valid reason has been shown to change that result.

TJOFLAT, CIRCUIT JUDGE, with whom AINSWORTH and ALVIN B. RUBIN, CIRCUIT JUDGES, join, dissenting:

I would affirm the conviction of defendant Garber for essentially the reasons stated by Judge Ainsworth. The majority opinion disturbs me more by its analysis than by its result, however. The majority says that the Government should never have prosecuted Garber for tax evasion. The criminal proceedings were "inappropriate," the majority intimates, because it is an open question whether the proceeds of her blood plasma constituted taxable income and because even if they were taxable, the doubt surrounding the taxability issue suggests that Garber could not have had the willfulness that is an essential element of the crime of tax evasion. Notwithstanding the majority's belief that the prosecution was a mistake, it apparently feels trapped by an assumption that the Government is *entitled* to prosecute Garber. The majority's response is to manufacture a rule of evidence that might permit Garber to extricate herself.

The new rule of evidence embraces *any* case where someone is charged with an offense involving willfulness. If the defendant avers that the requirements of the law were too vague to give adequate notice, the trial court must permit the parties to call to the stand "experts" to give their opinions about the state of the law. I have no doubt that this innovation in trial procedure, by allowing the jury to consider matters irrelevant to factual issues, will spawn unfair convictions and acquittals. In addition, the rule will inevitably lead to a protracted and unmanageable sequence of impeachment and rehabilitation of every expert allowed to present such testimony. My intention is first to demonstrate that this new rule springs from the majority's failure to confront straightforwardly certain legal questions that this court has the responsibility to resolve and second to define exactly why I think the majority's holding will have such a pernicious effect.

The case before us involves three distinct issues that are present in every tax evasion prosecution. The threshold issue is whether the "income" in question is subject to federal income taxation. If the "income" is taxable, the trial court next must determine whether the civil obligation to pay taxes was sufficiently clear to support a criminal prosecution for tax evasion. Finally there arises the factual issue whether the defendant acted with the willfulness that is an essential element of the crime. The majority's analysis goes astray, in my view, by confusing the legal issues of taxability and sufficiency of notice with the factual issue of intent. For the court to dispose of this appeal properly, it is essential that these three issues be sorted out and considered individually.

I

Dorothy Garber was charged under section 7201 of the Internal Revenue Code with willfully attempting to evade her obligation to pay taxes on "income" she received for her blood plasma. This allegation is premised on the notion that Garber actually had such an obligation.

Of course, section 7201 does not itself create any duty to pay taxes; it merely sets out criminal sanctions that enforce the tax liability imposed by other sections of the Internal Revenue Code. Whether Garber was actually liable for taxes on the sums in question depends on whether those sums are a part of her "gross income" within the meaning of section 61(a) of the Internal Revenue Code. This question of the meaning of "gross income" is purely a legal one, a matter of statutory construction. Such a question of law is for the court alone, *United States v. Seaboard Coast Line Railroad,* 368 F.Supp. 1079, 1083 (M.D.Fla.1973), although the court would certainly be free to consider the opinions of the parties' experts or any other sources of authority in making this threshold determination.

* * *

I believe Judge Ainsworth's analysis conclusively shows that this ruling was correct. The majority casts doubt on the ruling but purportedly declines to settle the issue. Nevertheless, the majority apparently *assumes* that the sales proceeds are taxable income and that the indictment is sufficient, for the opinion hinges on an evidentiary question that would otherwise never arise. If the court really believes that the monies are not taxable, it is unfortunate that it does not so hold and avoid an unnecessary retrial.

II

After ruling on the taxability issue, the district court was confronted with a second question of law: whether, at the time of the alleged tax evasions, the taxability of the monies was so uncertain as to make it fundamentally unfair to prosecute Garber. Due process requires that the language of a criminal statute convey "sufficiently definite warning as to the proscribed conduct when measured by common understanding and practices." *Jordan v. De George,* 341 U.S. 223, 231–32, 71 S.Ct. 703, 708, 95 L.Ed. 886 (1951). At the commencement of trial, Garber's attorney argued to the court that the taxability of the monies is "so uncertain" that "defendant cannot be guilty of willfully evading and defeating taxes on income." Record, vol. 2, at 16. This argument contained the essential elements of the vagueness challenge, although it was not put squarely in those terms or in the form of a motion to dismiss the indictment.[2] Here the vagueness issue is whether the obligation to pay taxes on monies received for plasmapheresis was too uncertain to give notice that a taxpayer who willfully evaded such taxes would be subject to prosecution under section 7201. The question narrows to the consideration whether it was or should have been reasonably clear to Garber that those monies were a part of her "gross income" within the meaning of section 61(a). Although "common understanding and practices" are the standards by which the adequacy

---

2. Whether or not the question was properly raised below, this court may consider the sufficiency of the indictment on appeal. *United States v. Seuss,* 474 F.2d 385, 387 n. 2 (1st Cir.) *cert. denied,* 412 U.S. 928, 93 S.Ct. 2751, 37 L.Ed.2d 155 (1973); 8 Moore's Federal Practice ¶ 12.03[1], at 12–16 & n. 9 (2d ed. 1978).

of the notice given by a criminal statute is to be measured, it is settled that the question of vagueness is for the court rather than the jury. The question is separate from the court's threshold inquiry whether the monies are taxable at all. The court might well have held that although the monies are taxable, their taxability was so uncertain at the times when Garber filed her returns that she did not have constitutionally sufficient notice of the conduct proscribed by section 7201. If this had been the court's conclusion, the proper disposition of the case would, again, have been to have dismissed the indictment under rule 12(b)(2). Whereas the trial judge did not rule specifically that the obligation to pay taxes was not unconstitutionally vague, he effectively rejected any vagueness challenge when he sent the case to the jury.

United States v. Critzer, 498 F.2d 1160 (4th Cir.1974), relied on by the majority, suggests what is essentially another approach to the vagueness issue. *Critzer* is premised on the proposition that "when the law is vague or highly debatable, a defendant—actually or imputedly—lacks the requisite intent to violate it." *Id.* at 1162. The court held that "willfulness" could not be shown in a prosecution under section 7201 given the uncertainty concerning whether the sums in question were taxable:

> *As a matter of law,* defendant cannot be guilty of willfully evading and defeating income taxes on income, the taxability of which is so uncertain that even co-ordinate branches of the United States Government plausibly reach directly opposing conclusions. *As a matter of law,* the requisite intent to evade and defeat income taxes is missing.

Id. (emphasis added). As under the conventional "vagueness" analysis, the inquiry focuses on the certainty of the obligation to pay taxes at the time the tax return was filed. *Id.* at 1164. Under either approach, if the obligation was unclear, the defendant *cannot be guilty as a matter of law,* so the indictment should be dismissed for failure to charge an offense.

Just after discussing *Critzer,* the majority opinion says:

> The tax treatment of earnings from the sale of blood plasma or other parts of the human body is an unchartered area in tax law. The parties in this case presented divergent opinions as to the ultimate taxability by analogy to two legitimate theories in tax law. The trial court should not have withheld this fact, and its powerful impact on the issue of Garber's willfulness, from the jury.

Ante at 99. While I agree that *Critzer* says that the clarity of the law has an impact on Garber's willfulness, *Critzer* does not support the suggestion that confusion in the tax laws is a "defense" that should be considered by the jury. The *Critzer* court reiterates that the impact of any vagueness of the law on the defendant's intent is a matter of law—a determination to be made by the court alone.

Under either the conventional vagueness analysis or the *Critzer* analysis, the question on appeal is whether Judge Fulton *should* have dismissed the indictment on the ground that the taxability of the monies was too unclear to support criminal liability. My view is that the monies were so clearly a part of Garber's "gross income" that no reasonable person could have supposed otherwise. The majority, on the other hand, appears to give much credence to Garber's contention that she reasonably supposed the monies to be nontaxable.[3] If this is the majority's persuasion, the proper resolution of the case would be to dismiss the charges as the court did in *Critzer,* not to remand for a new trial. Since the certainty of the law would be assessed as of a past date, a dismissal on this ground would be perfectly consistent with a ruling that money received for blood plasma is indeed taxable. Thus, no future defendant in Garber's position could escape under the same vagueness challenge.

The majority's mysterious refusal to follow the logic of its reasoning and dismiss the indictment leads to certain inconsistencies. The opinion, like the opinion in the *Critzer* case, ends with the observation that "[a] criminal proceeding pursuant to section 7201 is an inappropriate vehicle for pioneering interpretations of tax law." *Ante* at 100. This conclusion makes sense in *Critzer,* but in the present case it is blatantly inconsistent with the court's decision that there should be a *new* "criminal proceeding" that will allow the jury to hear evidence concerning the certainty of the tax laws.

III

The court need consider the propriety of Judge Fulton's refusal to admit the testimony of Nall, Garber's expert, only if we find that Judge Fulton correctly declined to dismiss the indictment. Assuming that the indictment *is* sufficient, the critical issue in the case becomes a factual one: whether Garber acted with the requisite willfulness in failing to pay taxes on the sums in question. To be admissible, the proffered testimony must be relevant to this issue, Fed.R.Evid. 402,[4] and its probative value must outweigh the danger of unfair prejudice, confusion of the issues, or misleading the jury. Fed.R.Evid. 403.[5] I conclude that Nall's testimony is not relevant to Garber's intent, and that it certainly fails the weighing test. I would hold, therefore, that Judge Fulton properly excluded the evidence.[6] It is necessary to examine

---

3. For example, at the conclusion of the opinion the court states that "the tax question was completely novel and unsettled by any clearly relevant precedent" and suggests that the case involves "pioneering interpretations of tax law." *Ante* at 100.

4. Rule 402 states:

All relevant evidence is admissible, except as otherwise provided by the Constitution of the United States, by Act of Congress, by these rules, or by other rules prescribed by the Supreme Court pursuant to statutory authority. Evidence which is not relevant is not admissible.

5. Rule 403 provides that:

Although relevant, evidence may be excluded if its probative value is substantially outweighed by the danger of unfair prejudice, confusion of the issues, or misleading the jury, or by considerations of undue delay, waste of time, or needless presentation of cumulative evidence.

6. This court has sometimes made the distinction between "logical relevance" and "legal relevance." *See, e.g., Rozier v. Ford Motor Co.,* 573 F.2d 1332, 1347 (5th Cir. 1978). Evidence is said to be "logically relevant" if it has any probative value and "legally relevant" if that probative value outweighs the counter factors of prejudice, confusion, and repetition. In this discus-

closely this relevance issue to show the dangers created by the majority opinion.

* * *

Because I conclude that the district court correctly decided the issues of law before it and properly excluded "expert" testimony concerning the state of the law, I would affirm Garber's conviction.

UNITED STATES v. CURTIS
United States Court of Appeals, Sixth Circuit, 1986.
782 F.2d 593.

* * *

The charges against defendant arise from his operation of the Meat Shop, a wholesale meat retailer. Curtis is the president and sole shareholder of the business. Most of the Meat Shop's revenue comes from its sales of meat to the Fayette County Detention Center, which paid for its purchases by issuing monthly checks to the Meat Shop.

This case concerns portions of thirty-five checks from the Detention Center to the Meat Shop that Curtis deposited in his personal checking and savings accounts during 1978, 1979, and 1980.

* * *

Curtis maintains that the amounts that were transferred to his personal accounts were interest-free loans to him from the Meat Shop. He contends that the money he paid to the Meat Shop was in partial repayment of these loans. The government disagrees, arguing that Curtis received income from the corporation. According to the government, the checks Curtis wrote to the Meat Shop were initial loans from him to the corporation.

At the trial the government produced the relevant corporate and individual tax returns, and established the flow of money from the Detention Center to the Meat Shop and Curtis. The government called as its final witness an Internal Revenue Service field auditor who testified that in his opinion the money that Curtis received from the Meat Shop was taxable income.

The defendant called only one witness, a C.P.A. named David Wilkerson. He stated that the money that Curtis transferred to his personal accounts from the corporation "should have been accounted for as loans" which are not deductible by the corporation or taxable as income to the recipient. Wilkerson reasoned that the money could not be regarded as salary, for the corporation did not take a tax deduction for the amounts received by Curtis. The money also could not be deemed a dividend, for the corporation had no retained earnings and its

---

sion I have adopted Professor McCormick's view that it makes for clearer thinking to discard the term "legal relevancy" altogether and use "relevancy" to refer to what has been called "logical relevancy." *See* McCormick, Evidence § 185, at 441 (2d ed. 1972).

balance sheet reflected no dividend payments. Wilkerson then stated that he could only conclude that the money was a loan from the Meat Shop to Curtis. He testified that such tax-free loans were common, and that they represented a tax planning opportunity.

The trial court submitted all of these matters as a part of the case to the jury, which convicted Curtis on all three counts. Curtis now appeals his conviction on the several grounds indicated above.

* * *

III. THE LAW AS UNSETTLED OR COMPLEX

At the close of the government's case, it moved *in limine* to exclude the testimony of a defense witness who was proferred to testify that the area of tax law governing the treatment of corporation distributions to shareholders was unsettled and complex. The trial court granted the motion, holding that defendant could not present this evidence unless he could establish that he was confused or had relied on the expert's advice. The defense acknowledged that it could not make this showing. Curtis now complains that the trial court's ruling unjustifiably deprived him of a defense on the issue of the willfulness of his conduct.

Defendant also objects to the trial court's refusal to give his proposed instruction number 13–B. This instruction tells the jury that it may consider the unresolved nature of the tax law in determining whether defendant willfully evaded taxation. The instruction also states that if the jury finds the law to be unsettled or complex, then defendant lacked the requisite intent to violate the law, regardless of whether or not defendant knew of the legal uncertainty.[3]

Curtis' objections to the trial court's granting of the motion *in limine* and to its refusal to give proposed instruction 13–B are based primarily on *United States v. Garber*, 607 F.2d 92 (5th Cir.1979). The defendant in *Garber* received over $200,000 for allowing medical suppliers to extract rare antibodies from her blood. Mrs. Garber failed to report the payments she received for her blood components, and she was convicted for willfully attempting to evade federal income tax for 1970, 1971, and 1972.

---

3. Defendant's proposed instruction 13–B reads as follows:

There has been testimony relating to the unsettled nature of the law pertaining to those transactions which are nontaxable events, such as loans and repayments of loans, returns of capital, and those transactions which are taxable events and comprise forms of income such as salary or constructive dividends.

I instruct you that when the characterization of such amounts is problematical, as a matter of law, the unresolved nature of the law is relevant to show that the Defendant may not have been aware of the responsibility to report an item or may simply have made an error in judgment. Furthermore, the relevance of a dispute in the law does not depend on whether the Defendant knew of the conflict. If you determine that this area of the tax law relating to loans, returns of capital, and constructive dividends is vague, unsettled, complex or debatable, then, as a matter of law, the Defendant lacks the requisite intent to violate the law and therefore cannot be found guilty of willfully underreporting such items, the taxability of which is so uncertain and problematical.

At the time Mrs. Garber was prosecuted, no court or agency had ever decided whether payments for blood donations are income that is subject to taxation. Mrs. Garber argued in the trial court that she could not have willfully evaded the tax because the law was unsettled. She offered to call an expert witness to testify that the tax treatment of the blood sale proceeds was a novel and uncertain question. The trial judge refused to allow this testimony, describing the issue of taxability and legal uncertainty as matters of law for the judge. Based on the extensive evidence taken on Mrs. Garber's state of mind, other than evidence concerning the status of the tax law, the jury convicted her.

The Fifth Circuit reversed Mrs. Garber's conviction, finding that the trial court mistakenly "reserved to itself the job of unriddling the tax law." 607 F.2d at 97. The court held that a jury deciding whether a defendant acted willfully may consider the uncertain state of the law, as revealed by expert testimony, as evidence of the defendant's state of mind. Moreover, the court declared that "the relevance of a dispute in the law does not depend on whether the defendant actually knew of the conflict." *Id.* at 98. It reasoned that even if defendant had consulted the law, she would not and could not have discovered how to comply with it. *Id.* The court concluded with the observation that "[a] criminal proceeding pursuant to section 7201 is an inappropriate vehicle for pioneering interpretations of tax law." *Id.* at 100.[4]

After carefully reviewing *Garber* and other cases, this court declines to follow and rejects *Garber* for several important reasons. First, *Garber* allows juries to find that uncertainty in the law negates willfulness even when the defendant is unaware of that uncertainty. This contradicts the prior cases on willfulness, which "consistently require factual evidence of the defendants' state of mind to negate willfulness under any theory." *United States v. Ingredient Technology Corp.*, 698 F.2d 88, 97 (2d Cir.1983), *cert. denied*, 462 U.S. 1131, 103 S.Ct. 3111, 77 L.Ed.2d 1366 (1983); Note, *Criminal Liability for Willful Evasion of an Uncertain Tax*, 81 Colum.L.Rev. 1348, 1357 (1981). Willfulness is personal. It relates to the defendant's state of mind. It does not exist in the abstract. Unless there is a connection between the external facts and the defendant's state of mind, the evidence of the external facts is not relevant.

Second, the *Garber* approach distorts the role of expert witnesses and the purpose of their testimony. Expert testimony is intended to

---

4. The Fifth Circuit appears to have retreated from the sweeping language used in *Garber*, however. In *United States v. Burton*, 737 F.2d 439 (5th Cir.1984), the court affirmed the lower court's refusal to allow testimony from a tax professor that defendant's theory of taxation was plausible but not legally accepted. The Fifth Circuit found that evidence of legal uncertainty need not generally be received in cases where the defendant was unaware of the law. Such evidence is admissible only in cases involving a level of uncertainty "approaching legal vagueness," or in cases addressing a "novel or unusual application of the law." 737 F.2d at 444. The court summarized its reading of *Garber* as follows: "In short, we read *Garber* no more broadly than its facts in deciding that in other cases the judge will ordinarily be the sole source of the law." *Id.*

"assist the trier of fact to understand the evidence or to determine a fact in issue * * * " Fed.R.Evid. 702. *See also Garber, supra,* at 106 (Ainsworth, J., dissenting). Experts are supposed to interpret and analyze factual evidence. They do not testify about the law because the judge's special legal knowledge is presumed to be sufficient, and it is the judge's duty to inform the jury about the law that is relevant to their deliberations. *See Marx & Co. v. Diners' Club,* 550 F.2d 505, 509–10 (2d Cir.1977), *cert. denied,* 434 U.S. 861, 98 S.Ct. 188, 54 L.Ed.2d 134 (1977); Note, *supra,* at 1362. The *Garber* approach also creates problems for the jurors listening to expert testimony. Jurors might be confused by opposing opinions of law offered by different experts. *See United States v. Ingredient Technology Corp.,* 698 F.2d at 97. *Garber* would also force jurors to take their instructions on the law from expert witnesses as well as from the trial judge. Any differences in the legal rules given by the expert and the judge would be another potential source of confusion.

Finally, and perhaps most significantly, *Garber* requires the jury to assume part of the judge's responsibility to rule on questions of law. *Garber* asks the jury to read and interpret statutes to determine whether or not the governing law is uncertain or debatable. This function has traditionally belonged to the judge, as:

> The jury is not composed of lawyers; the typical juror is untrained in legal affairs. To attempt to explain the myriad rules of judicial construction, the complexity of legal principles, or the function of precedent would hopelessly divert the jury from their preeminent duty of assessing appellant's guilt.

Garber, supra, 607 F.2d at 105 (Ainsworth J., dissenting). *See also United States v. Mallas,* 762 F.2d 361, 364 n. 4 (4th Cir.1985).

The trial court in the present case properly granted the government's motion *in limine* and properly refused to give defendant's proposed instruction 13–B. For each of the reasons set out earlier in this case, evidence of the unsettled or complex nature of the law is irrelevant, and instructions to the jury on this subject are not proper.

Defendant's conviction is affirmed.

UNITED STATES v. MONTALVO
United States Court of Appeals, 5th Circuit, 1987.
820 F.2d 686.

Before CLARK, CHIEF JUDGE, BROWN, and JOHNSON, CIRCUIT JUDGES.

CLARK, CHIEF JUDGE: Dr. Jose M. Montalvo appeals from his conviction for conspiracy to defraud the United States by impeding the functioning of the Internal Revenue Service (IRS). 18 U.S.C. § 371.[1]

---

1. The statute provides in relevant part: If two or more persons conspire either to commit any offense against the United States, or to defraud the United States, or

His primary challenge is to the sufficiency of the evidence showing his intent to impede the IRS. We find the evidence sufficient to support his conviction, reject his other challenges, and affirm.

I.

Montalvo, a doctor at the University of Mississippi Medical Center, was arrested following an undercover operation investigating marijuana trafficking in Mississippi. Agent Robert M. Turner of the Mississippi Bureau of Narcotics, acting under cover, arranged a purchase of 600 pounds of marijuana from Junious C. Morgan. The marijuana, which actually weighed 427 pounds, was delivered by Linda Hawkins on April 15, 1985. Turner then negotiated with Morgan for the purchase of a larger quantity of marijuana. On May 2, 1985, during negotiations, Turner asked Morgan if he had a way to "clean up" the proceeds of the drug sales. Morgan responded that he, his wife, and Montalvo had a foreign corporation that Morgan used to "move his money around." Morgan explained that the corporation would issue fictitious loan papers, and that when Turner paid Morgan for the marijuana Morgan would wire the money out of the country disguised as a payment on a loan.

Turner agreed to pay Morgan $50,000 as partial payment for the marijuana previously delivered. They set up a meeting on May 29, 1985. Morgan also contacted Montalvo to bring documents for the foreign corporation to the May 29th meeting. Neither Turner nor Montalvo knew the other would be at the meeting. The meeting was recorded by a hidden microphone. For fifteen minutes the three discussed the possibility of setting up a foreign subsidiary for Turner's use. Montalvo assured Turner he could handle at least $250,000 in any denomination bills. At the end of the meeting Morgan and Montalvo were arrested and various documents were seized, including the ones brought by Montalvo as well as others Morgan had brought. The documents were a corporate charter for a Panamanian company named Montmor International, S.A., a power of attorney authorizing Montalvo to do business for the company, a business agreement by which Montalvo appointed Morgan and his wife equal partners in Montmor, stationery listing Morgan as president and Montalvo as vice president, a joint venture agreement signed by Montalvo on behalf of Montmor purporting to show a $500,000 loan by Montmor to Morgan, a letter to a third party stating that Montmor had loaned Morgan $50,000, and another letter purporting to evidence a $1,000,000 loan from Montmor to Morgan.

Montalvo was indicted on three counts of an eighteen-count federal indictment. Count I charged Montalvo with conspiracy to possess marijuana with intent to distribute. Count II charged Montalvo with conspiracy to import marijuana. Montalvo was alleged to have joined any agency thereof in any manner or for any purpose, and one or more of such persons do any act to effect the object of the conspiracy, each shall be fined not more than $10,000 or imprisoned not more than five years, or both.

the conspiracies by providing a money laundering service to disguise the illegal source of the income. Count VI charged Montalvo with conspiracy to defraud the United States by impeding the IRS in the ascertainment and collection of revenue by disguising the true source of United States currency. Co-defendant Morgan was indicted on sixteen counts of various drug and currency violations. Co-defendant Hawkins was indicted on five drug counts and pleaded guilty before trial.

Montalvo testified at trial in his own defense. His story was that Montmor was established to help refugees from Latin American nations get their wealth out of the currency of those nations and into American currency. Montmor is an acronym for "movimientos nacionales de transacciones monetarios para refugiados," which translates roughly as "national movements of monetary transactions for refugees." According to Montalvo, he attempted to arrange various business ventures that would allow the refugees to invest using foreign currency and be repaid in American currency. Those ventures included a commercial fishing enterprise, a shrimp farm deal, and a hot sauce deal. Montalvo testified that he thought Turner was a Haitian trying to get his money out of Haiti. Montalvo admitted, however, that none of his deals had been successful. Morgan's testimony generally supported Montalvo's story, although it was internally inconsistent in other ways. Morgan's wife, however, testified that the name Montmor was derived from Montalvo and Morgan. In addition, the one person whom Montalvo specifically claimed to have aided denied having any such dealings with him.

The jury acquitted Montalvo on counts I and II, related to conspiracies to possess and to import marijuana, but found him guilty on count VI, the conspiracy to impede the IRS. Morgan was convicted on all fourteen counts; he fled the country before the jury returned its verdict. Montalvo was sentenced to five years imprisonment and fined $10,000. He now appeals.

II.

Montalvo's primary argument is that the evidence is insufficient to support his conviction. We will uphold the jury's verdict unless "it is found that upon the record evidence adduced at the trial no rational trier of fact could have found proof of guilt beyond a reasonable doubt." *Jackson v. Virginia*, 443 U.S. 307, 324, 99 S.Ct. 2781, 2791–92, 61 L.Ed.2d 560 (1979); *United States v. Basey*, 816 F.2d 980, 1000–02 (5th Cir.1987). All inferences from the evidence and all credibility determinations must be viewed in the light most favorable to the verdict. *Basey*, 816 F.2d at 1000–02; *see Glasser v. United States*, 315 U.S. 60, 80, 62 S.Ct. 457, 469, 86 L.Ed. 680 (1942).

Montalvo does not challenge the sufficiency of the evidence linking him to Montmor or demonstrating the use of Montmor to conceal the source of currency. Indeed, the evidence is more than sufficient to show that Montalvo used Montmor to help Morgan surreptitiously get money out of the United States. The documents seized at the time of arrest list Montalvo as a vice president of Montmor or at least as having power of attorney for the company. And Morgan's wife testified at trial that Montmor stood for *Mont*alvo and *Mor*gan. Moreover, Morgan and Montalvo explained to Turner at the May 29th meeting that they were wiring money out of the United States disguised as loan repayments. The jury was entitled to disbelieve Montalvo's story about aiding refugees. The one person Montalvo claimed to have helped testified that she had never discussed the matter with him. Montalvo himself admitted at trial that his various deals had never gone through.

Instead, Montalvo contends that merely concealing or disguising the source of currency is insufficient to support a conviction for conspiracy to obstruct the IRS. He relies on *United States v. Enstam*, 622 F.2d 857 (5th Cir.1980), *cert. denied*, 450 U.S. 912, 101 S.Ct. 1351, 67 L.Ed.2d 336 (1981), and *United States v. Browning*, 723 F.2d 1544 (11th Cir. 1984). In *Enstam*, the Fifth Circuit reviewed a conviction for conspiracy to impede the IRS through use of a scheme similar to the one involved in the present case. Enstam and his associates sent drug money out of the country and returned it to the United States in the form of fictitious loans. Enstam contended that the object of the conspiracy was only to hide the source of the money and not to impede the assessment and collection of taxes. The court expressed concern about the sufficiency of the evidence but reserved the question whether merely concealing the source of income is illegal after finding substantial evidence of intent to impede the IRS. 622 F.2d at 863 & n. 5. That evidence consisted of statements by the conspirators that the scheme was designed to conceal information in the event of an IRS audit and advice to undercover agents that they could avoid taxes by reporting bogus business expenses and deducting fictitious interest payments. *Id.* at 861–62.

In *Browning,* the Eleventh Circuit dealt with the same issue in a case involving a money laundering scheme identical to the one in *Enstam.* Again the court did not decide whether merely concealing the source of income would be enough to support the conviction because the court found sufficient evidence of intent to obstruct the IRS. The conspirators in *Browning* expressed fear of an IRS audit and stated a desire to avoid paying any more taxes. 723 F.2d at 1548. One conspirator also bragged that he had bribed an IRS agent who was auditing him. *Id.*

Montalvo argues that the evidence present in *Enstam* and *Browning* showing an intent to obstruct the IRS is lacking in this case. The evidence, Montalvo submits, shows that he did not know Morgan's money came from the sale of illegal drugs. He finds support in Morgan's warning to Turner not to discuss drugs in front of Montalvo and in Morgan's statement that Montalvo knows "where [the money] goes" and "that's all." Montalvo also points to his acquittal on counts I and II, which charged him with conspiracy to disguise the "illegal source" of drug money, as the jury's finding that he did not know the money was drug money. Montalvo asserts that in fact he told Turner to pay taxes. As a result, according to Montalvo, this court must reach the question reserved in *Enstam* and *Browning* and should hold that concealing the source of money alone is insufficient to support his conviction.

On the facts of this case, we find no need to reach the question reserved in *Enstam* and *Browning*. This fact situation is controlled by the holding rather than the dicta in those cases. The evidence in this case was sufficient to permit a reasonable jury to conclude that Montalvo intended to participate in a conspiracy to launder money, meaning that he agreed to a procedure that would disguise the true source of the money, with the obvious intent and purpose of impeding and obstructing the IRS in the collection of revenue and the performance of its duties.

First, the evidence was sufficient for the jury to find Montalvo's knowing participation in a scheme to launder untaxed money. The evidence showing Montalvo's involvement with Montmor was discussed earlier. In addition, at the May 29th meeting, Morgan assured Turner that Montalvo knew what was "going on." Morgan did tell Turner not to discuss drugs in front of Montalvo, but then he reassured Turner that Montalvo knew "pretty much what the deal [wa]s" so that there was no need to discuss it. A reasonable jury could infer that Montalvo knew Morgan's money was obtained in a way that no taxes had been paid on it.

Montalvo's acquittal on counts I and II does not require a different conclusion. Inconsistent verdicts do not require reversal. *United States v. Powell,* 469 U.S. 57, 105 S.Ct. 471, 476–77, 83 L.Ed.2d 461 (1984). The purportedly inconsistent verdict may merely reflect the jury's leniency, not that it was unconvinced of the defendant's guilt. *Id.* at 477. The defendant's protection lies in sufficiency of the evidence review, and that review is to be "independent of the jury's determination that evidence on another count was insufficient." *Id.* at 478. Thus, our review of the sufficiency of the evidence supporting Montalvo's conviction must be uncolored by his acquittal on the other counts.

Second, the evidence is also sufficient for the jury to find that one purpose of the conspiracy was to impede the IRS. In Montalvo's presence, Morgan assured Turner that the money laundering transaction was structured so that the average American could not understand it. Montmor's documents were kept in Spanish "in case anybody wants to get the IRS on us." Similarly, Montalvo gave Morgan the fictitious loan papers so that "the minute somebody looks at [the money] it's a loan." These statements are similar to the statements made by the defendants in *Enstam* and *Browning*.

Montalvo contends that he told Turner he would have to pay taxes. Montalvo is referring to the following exchange:

> TURNER: And that's a, well let me ask you this, the, the, uh, the loans supposedly that we're doing from this corporation in Panama,

they're, they'll be, uh, uh, tax free as far as in the United States, isn't that right?

MORGAN: Yea, it's

MONTALVO: Well it depends on what you do with the money.

TURNER: Uh huh.

MONTALVO: They don't tax the loan. They tax what you do with the money.

TURNER: What, what you do with the money.

MONTALVO: If, if you make, if you invest it let's say if you put it in a, on a, uh, uh, other company or CD

MORGAN: CD's

MONTALVO: CD's you have to pay the interest.

MORGAN: Interest, yea.

TURNER: Well won't, won't

MONTALVO: You pay tax on the interest but you won't pay tax on the, uh

TURNER: Well what if, what if you, what if you draw me up a loan agreement say for two hundred and fifty thousand dollars

MONTALVO: Uh huh.

TURNER: To just, well can I, can I spend that though as I wish or, you know, uh, uh

MORGAN: Oh, yea (unintelligible)

TURNER: I'm talking about to get around the tax situation. See what

MONTALVO: Well

TURNER: I'm saying?

MONTALVO: Yea. Well the, the, uh, the 'cause what you do with the money is whether they decide to tax you or not.

In fact, the exchange further demonstrates the tax avoidance purpose of the conspiracy. Morgan agrees that the money that supposedly was a loan would be tax free. Montalvo does warn Turner he will have to pay taxes, but only on interest earned on the money, not on the untaxed money itself. The evidence before the jury, taken in the light most favorable to the verdict, shows that a purpose of the conspiracy was to impede the IRS in the collection of revenue and demonstrates Montalvo's knowing involvement in that conspiracy. That is sufficient to sustain his conviction.

Montalvo also challenges the sufficiency of the evidence supporting the three overt acts alleged in the indictment. The three overt acts alleged were that Morgan arranged a meeting among himself, Montalvo, and others to discuss the conspiracy; that Morgan and Montalvo met with others to discuss the formation of a fictitious or "shell" corporation and the use of foreign bank accounts to conceal United

States currency; and that Montalvo gave Morgan documents pertaining to that "shell" corporation. Montalvo contends that the evidence was insufficient because Montalvo and Turner did not know the other would be at the meeting and because they discussed forming a subsidiary, not a shell corporation. These arguments are meritless. The fact that Montalvo and Turner did not collectively participate in planning the meeting has nothing to do with the fact that a meeting was arranged to discuss the conspiracy. That they discussed forming a subsidiary rather than a "shell" corporation is immaterial to the overt act charged. Even though a subsidiary is a true corporation, it can still be a shell if it had no valid business purpose. Montalvo attended the meeting, discussed Montmor, and provided documents dealing with Montmor. Montmor was used to launder money. The evidence was sufficient to establish the overt acts in furtherance of the conspiracy to impede the IRS.

* * *

The evidence was sufficient to support Montalvo's conviction and his other contentions of error are meritless. The judgment of conviction is affirmed.

* * *

Notes and Questions

1. Would the failure to record certain sales on the books of a company, or the falsification of those records, be sufficient evidence to convict a taxpayer under the "conspiracy to defraud" clause of § 371? See United States v. Tarnopol, 561 F.2d 466 (3d Cir.1977), in which the court overturned the convictions.

2. The boundaries between lawful tax planning and tax evasion are often vague. Is it illegal to use corporations and partnerships to control the timing of income and the amounts that are ultimately received by the individual taxpayers? See United States v. Klein, 139 F.Supp. 135 (S.D.N.Y.1955), affirmed, 247 F.2d 908 (2d Cir.1957). See generally Sisson, The Sandman Cometh: Conspiracy Prosecutions and Tax Practitioners, 31 Tax Lawyer 805 (1978).

3. In United States v. Reynolds, p. 559 and below, the court also addressed the conspiracy conviction:

UNITED STATES v. REYNOLDS
United States Court of Appeals, Seventh Circuit, 1990.
919 F.2d 435.

A third line of attack goes to the conspiracy conviction. The indictment charged Reynolds with conspiring to defraud the United States, in violation of 18 U.S.C. § 371. Section 371 makes it a crime for "two or more persons [to] conspire either to commit any offense against the United States, or to defraud the United States". Reynolds contends that when the prosecutor challenges conduct that violates a specific statute (such as § 287 or § 641), the indictment must charge a conspiracy "to commit [that] offense against the United States", rather than a generic conspiracy to defraud. Reynolds invokes *United States v. Minarik,* 875 F.2d 1186 (6th Cir.1989), in support of this conclusion.

Stated the way Reynolds frames it, the argument cannot be right. There are no common law federal crimes. Thus there will *always* be a specific substantive offense that the defendants conspired to commit. If the prosecutor must charge a conspiracy to commit the specific crime, there can never be a charge of conspiracy to defraud the United States. Some statutory language is redundant, but we hesitate to read out of § 371 the language that has been the foundation for so many convictions. Moreover, reading § 371 this way would do defendants no favors. If agreement to violate each specific statute is a distinct offense, then Reynolds should have been charged with *three* conspiracies rather than just one, for his acts transgressed §§ 287, 641, and 666. Why would defendants be better off facing three conspiracy charges rather than one generic charge of conspiring to defraud?

Although some language in *Minarik* suggests that the sixth circuit thought it better practice to charge a conspiracy to violate a particular statute, the *holding* of that case is only that the prosecution's theory changed so often that the defendant lacked notice of the charge against which he had to defend. Reynolds had plenty of notice. The conspiracy charge and the prosecution's theory were stable from indictment through conviction; the 39 specific charges laid under §§ 287, 641, and 666 gave Reynolds ample notice of the facts that the prosecution would contend constituted the fraud. Reynolds had adequate notice, and an alteration in the phraseology of the conspiracy charge could not have assisted his defense.

When listing the charges against Reynolds we called the conspiracy charge inevitable yet pointless. It is inevitable because prosecutors seem to have conspiracy on their word processors as Count I; rare is the case omitting such a charge. It is pointless because, under the Sentencing Guidelines, the conspiracy is grouped with the substantive offense for the purpose of computing the offense level. U.S.S.G. § 3D1.2(b) and Application Note 4. Although the existence of a conspiracy allows the prosecution to use co-conspirator statements that would otherwise be hearsay, it is not necessary to *charge* a conspiracy in order to take advantage of Fed.R.Evid. 801(d)(2)(E); it is enough to show that a criminal venture existed and that statements took place during and in furtherance of that scheme. Conspiracy, once a formidable weapon in the prosecutor's arsenal, has become a distraction, useful only to obtain an extra $50 special assessment and to generate complex issues for appeal. The $50 hardly compensates for the costs the allegation imposes on the parties and the judicial system. Our portfolio does not include making prosecutorial decisions, however, and we are satisfied that the conspiracy as charged comports with the United States Code.

None of Reynolds' other arguments requires extended comment. He contends, for example, that the court should have "struck the jury panel" because of pretrial publicity. His scam was front-page news in Milwaukee, apparently because of the potential role of Alderman McGee. Yet Reynolds does not contend that the jurors actually seated were unable to decide the case fairly on the record. There is no principle that high-visibility cases are untriable or must be tried in another state. See *Patton v. Yount,* 467 U.S. 1025, 104 S.Ct. 2885, 81 L.Ed.2d 847 (1984); *Murphy v. Florida,* 421 U.S. 794, 95 S.Ct. 2031, 44 L.Ed.2d 589 (1975). Anyway, Reynolds did not request a change of venue. He had a fair trial.

The tax convictions are reversed. The remaining convictions are affirmed. The sentences are vacated, and the case is remanded for resentencing in accordance with our policy of giving the judge an opportunity to reformulate the sentencing package knowing which charges held up.

D. STATUTE OF LIMITATIONS

For most tax prosecutions there is a six-year statute of limitations, although a three-year limitations period is applicable to certain offenses.[m] The period of limitations commences with the date of commission of the charged offense—a date which is frequently, but not always, the due date of the relevant tax return. The running of the statute of limitations is suspended for any period during which the accused is outside the United States or is a fugitive from justice.

UNITED STATES v. HABIG
Supreme Court of the United States, 1968.
390 U.S. 222, 88 S.Ct. 926, 19 L.Ed.2d 1055.

MR. JUSTICE FORTAS delivered the opinion of the Court.

Appellees were indicted for crimes relating to allegedly false income tax returns. The District Court dismissed Counts 4 and 6 of the indictment, charging an attempt to evade taxes by filing of a false return (26 U.S.C. § 7201) and aiding in the preparation and presentation of a false return (26 U.S.C. § 7206(2)), on the ground that the six-year statute of limitations, 26 U.S.C. § 6531, barred prosecution under those counts. * * *

The question presented is the construction of §§ 6531 and 6513(a) of the Internal Revenue Code of 1954. It is squarely raised by the facts of this case. The indictment was filed on August 12, 1966. The income tax returns involved in Counts 4 and 6 were filed on August 12, and 15, 1960. Section 6531 limits the time when indictments may be filed for the charged offenses to six years "next after the commission of the offense."

---

m. I.R.C. § 6531.

The offenses involved in Counts 4 and 6 are committed at the time the return is filed. Six years had not quite elapsed from the commission of the crimes in the present case to the filing of the indictment. Appellees do not contest the chronological calculation. But because of § 6513(a) of the Code, they say that the critical date here is not the date when the returns were actually filed but the date when they were initially due to be filed, *viz.,* May 15, and not August 15, 1960.

The basis for this contention is as follows: Section 6531, which prescribes the six-year period of limitations, also says that "[f]or the purpose of determining [such] periods of limitation * * * the rules of section 6513 shall be applicable." Instead of filing on the due date of May 15, 1960, the corporations obtained extensions of time to August 15, 1960. Accordingly, if the six-year period of limitations runs not from the date of actual filing (August 12 and 15, 1960) but from the original due date of the returns (May 15, 1960), the indictment, having been filed on August 12, 1966, was several months too late.

Section 6513(a) reads as follows:

"SECTION 6513. TIME RETURNED DEEMED AND TAX CONSIDERED PAID.

"(a) *Early Return or Advance Payment of Tax.*—For purposes of section 6511 [relating to claims for credit or refund], any return filed before the last day prescribed for the filing thereof shall be considered as filed on such last day. For purposes of section 6511(b)(2) and (c) and section 6512 [relating to suits in the Tax Court], payment of any portion of the tax made before the last day prescribed for the payment of the tax shall be considered made on such last day. For purposes of this subsection, the last day prescribed for filing the return or paying the tax shall be determined without regard to any extension of time granted the taxpayer and without regard to any election to pay the tax in installments."

Appellees' argument is that by reason of the third sentence of § 6513(a), the starting date for computing the six-year limitations period is to be determined by the original due date of the return, May 15, 1960, "without regard to any extension of time granted the taxpayer." The District Court agreed. * * *

On the other hand, the Government argues that appellees' contention, despite its support in the decisions of several courts, is necessarily based upon the surprising assertion that Congress intended the limitations period to begin to run before appellees committed the acts upon which the crimes were based. It argues that this result cannot be squared with the language of the Code or the intent of Congress. We perforce agree with the Government's analysis.

Section 6513(a), as its title clearly indicates, was designed to apply when a return is filed or a tax is paid before the statutory deadline. The first two sentences provide that the limitations periods on claims for refunds and tax suits (26 U.S.C. §§ 6511, 6512), when the return has been filed or payment made in advance of the date "prescribed" therefor, shall not begin to run on the early date, but on the "prescribed" date. The third sentence states that, for "purposes of [the] subsection," the date "prescribed" for filing or payment shall be determined on the basis fixed by statute or regulations, without regard to any extension of time. The net effect of the language is to prolong the limitations period when, and only when, a return is filed or tax paid in advance of the statutory deadline.

There is no reason to believe that § 6531, by reference to the "rules of section 6513" expands the effect and operation of the latter beyond its own terms so as to make it applicable to situations other than those involving early filing or advance payment. The reference to § 6513 in § 6531 extends the period within which criminal prosecution may be begun only when the limitations period would also be extended for the refunds and tax suits expressly dealt with in § 6513—only when there has been early filing or advance payment. In other words, if a taxpayer anticipates the April 15 filing date by filing his return on January 15, the six-year limitations period for prosecutions under § 6531 commences to run on April 15. Practically, the effect of the reference to § 6513 in § 6531 is to give the Government the administrative assistance, for purposes of its criminal tax investigations, of a uniform expiration date for most taxpayers, despite variations in the dates of actual filing.

The legislative history supports this reading. The first predecessor of § 6513(a) was enacted in 1942. See § 332(b)(4) of the 1939 Code. This section applied only to civil income tax refund proceedings. The Report of the House Ways and Means Committee (H.R.Rep. No. 2333, 77th Cong., 2d Sess., 119) states:

> "If the taxpayer files his return before the last day on which it is due, the period in which he can file a claim for refund under the provisions of section 322(b)(1), measured from the date the return was filed, will expire sooner than would be the case if he waited until such last day. Section 150 of the bill adds paragraph (4) to section 322(b) to provide that the period of limitations with respect to credit or refund is measured from the last day prescribed for the filing of the return in cases where the return is filed before such last day. *This provision does not apply to taxpayers who are given the benefit of an extension of time in which to file their returns, and file the return before the last day of the extended period * * * "* (Emphasis added.)

Then, in adopting the 1954 Code, the contested reference to § 6513 was added to § 6531. The House and Senate Reports expressly confirmed that § 6513 still encompassed "the existing * * * rule *as to early returns and advance payment.*" H.R.Rep. No. 1337, 83d Cong., 2d Sess., A. 416; S.Rep. No. 1622, 83d Cong., 2d Sess., 587. (Emphasis added.)

The language of § 6513(a) does not purport to apply when a return is filed during an extension of time. The legislative history is to the same effect. Accordingly, although we reiterate the principle that criminal limitations statutes are "to be liberally interpreted in favor of repose," United States v. Scharton, 285 U.S. 518, 522, 52 S.Ct. 416, 417, 76 L.Ed. 917 (1932), we cannot read the statute as appellees urge.

The judgment of the District Court is reversed and the case is remanded for further proceedings.

Reversed and remanded.

UNITED STATES v. SHORTER
United States District Court, District of Columbia, 1985.
608 F.Supp. 871.

HAROLD H. GREENE, DISTRICT JUDGE.

Defendant was indicted in one felony count of willful attempt to evade the payment of income taxes due for the years 1972 through 1983, in violation of 26 U.S.C. § 7201, and in six misdemeanor counts of willful failure to pay income tax for each of the years 1978 through 1983, in violation of 26 U.S.C. § 7203. Presently pending before the Court is defendant's motion to dismiss the tax evasion count. * * *

The statute of limitations for tax evasion is six years. 26 U.S.C. § 6531. Since the indictment in this case was returned in 1984, it bars prosecution for offenses committed before 1978. However, the statute of limitations does not *ipso facto* rule out prosecution with respect to taxes owing prior to 1978, for the offense of tax evasion is not necessarily committed only in the year when the tax was due and payable. That is so because the existence of a tax deficiency is but one of the two essential elements of the crime, the other being an affirmative act of willful evasion. An act constituting evasion which occurs during the limitations period brings the prosecution within the statute of limitations even if the taxes being evaded were due and payable prior thereto.

It follows that the indictment in this case is not subject to dismissal even with respect to the evasion of taxes due prior to 1978 if it is supported by proof of one or more affirmative acts of evasion committed by the defendant within the past six years if these acts relate to taxes due in earlier years.

The government claims that it will prove acts of evasion occurring within the limitations period which relate to the nonpayment of taxes during the years prior to that period. It is clear that, on this basis, the statute of limitations as such is not a bar.

* * *

[The court next concluded that joining all of the tax years in a single evasion count did not render the indictment impermissibly duplicitous.]

* * *

Initially, the Court expects to instruct the jury that, while it may consider both evidence of a failure to pay taxes and evidence of tax evasion occurring prior to 1978, it may not convict the defendant unless it finds that he took affirmative steps to evade income taxes after 1978, and further that it may not return a guilty verdict unless there is unanimity with respect to at least one act of evasion since that year.

More specifically, the Court intends to instruct the jury that, to return a verdict of guilty on the felony count, it must agree unanimously (1) that during one or more specific years since 1972 the defendant failed to pay his federal income taxes, (2) that after 1978 he willfully committed one or more particular acts which constituted evasion, such as concealing the existence and location of assets, placing assets beyond service of process, or making false statements to agents of the Internal Revenue Service, and (3) that these acts of evasion were part of a course of conduct which had as its purpose the willful evasion of the payment of such taxes.[27] The Court further expects the jury to return, in addition to its verdict on the felony count, answers to specific questions regarding these elements of the offense.

For the reasons stated, the motion to dismiss Count I of the indictment is hereby denied.

Notes and Questions

1. The *Shorter* case involved a charge of attempted evasion of payment of taxes in violation of § 7201. Can an argument be made that attempted evasion of *payment* of taxes is not a "continuing offense," at least where the taxpayer files nonfraudulent returns. See United States v. Hook, 781 F.2d 1166, 1175 (6th Cir.1986) (Merritt, J., dissenting).

> ("It seems more consistent with Congressional intent and good policy in tax cases to run the statute of limitations from the date of the commission of the offense, as the traditional rule requires, rather than the date of the last act related to the offense. Otherwise acts of concealment of assets or willfulness committed decades after the first wrongful tax acts would revive or extend criminal liability.").

2. The crime of willfully failing to file a return, § 7203, is committed when the required return is not filed on the due date. Assuming continued willfulness, however, is the crime also committed on each day thereafter that the failure to file continues. What about the misdemeanor offense of willful failure to pay?

SECTION 2. METHODS OF PROOF OF INCOME

A. DIRECT PROOF: THE SPECIFIC ITEMS METHOD

In most tax prosecutions the government will be required to prove the taxpayer's income for the years in issue. Proof of income, like proof of any other ultimate fact, may be presented by direct or circum-

---

27. Although the existence of a course of conduct is not an element of the offense as such, it would be unfair to the defendant and inconsistent with the prosecution's theory to permit it to rely on the existence of such a course to defeat the duplicity claim (as augmented by the statute of limitations defense), but then to have this factor ignored when the jury is called upon to make its decision.

stantial evidence. In the jargon of tax fraud, direct evidence of income is presented by what is known as the "specific items" method. Circumstantial proof of income may be accomplished through what are commonly referred to as the "indirect" methods of proof, such as the net worth, cash expenditures, bank deposits, percentage mark-up or other methods.

The specific items method of proof of income is simple to describe. In brief, the prosecution will establish the taxpayer's income by proof of every item of income which the taxpayer realized (or, more accurately, which the IRS could find) for the period in issue. The specific items method is useful only to the extent that there are provable income producing transactions. For example, this method frequently is used in cases in which the taxpayer failed to report interest or dividend income or the income arising from specific provable transactions. In such a case the prosecution would introduce the tax returns (with supporting evidence) to prove the income reported thereon, and establish through the payors of interests or dividends, or other persons, the specific items of income received but not reported.

The specific items method is available, of course, only in a case in which the taxpayer's precise sources of income can be located by an investigating agent. The method is of little, if any, use in the investigation and prosecution of a taxpayer engaged in a cash business (i.e., one in which there are substantial receipts in currency). Imagine, for example, a specific items investigation of a gambler, a bartender, a cab driver or a drug dealer. The specific items method is also of limited value in cases in which a taxpayer has a substantial number of customers, clients or patients.

In view of the difficulty (and frequent impossibility) of proving income through the specific items method, the IRS will often utilize indirect methods of proof of income. As discussed more fully below, the indirect methods are inherently less precise than the specific items method. However, when the pertinent standards are met, the indirect methods can result in the requisite proof of income beyond a reasonable doubt.

B. INDIRECT PROOF

(1) *The Net Worth Method*

HOLLAND v. UNITED STATES
Supreme Court of the United States, 1954.
348 U.S. 121, 75 S.Ct. 127, 99 L.Ed. 150.

Mr. Justice Clark delivered the opinion of the Court.

Petitioners, husband and wife, stand convicted under § 145 of the Internal Revenue Code of an attempt to evade and defeat their income taxes for the year 1948. The prosecution was based on the net worth method of proof * * *.

In recent years, * * * tax-evasion convictions obtained under the net worth theory have come here with increasing frequency and left impressions beyond those of the previously unrelated petitions. We concluded that the method involved something more than the ordinary use of circumstantial evidence in the usual criminal case. Its bearing, therefore, on the safeguards traditionally provided in the administration of criminal justice called for a consideration of the entire theory. * * *

In a typical net worth prosecution, the Government, having concluded that the taxpayer's records are inadequate as a basis for determining income tax liability, attempts to establish an "opening net worth" or total net value of the taxpayer's assets at the beginning of a given year. It then proves increases in the taxpayer's net worth for each succeeding year during the period under examination and calculates the difference between the adjusted net values of the taxpayer's assets at the beginning and end of each of the years involved. The taxpayer's nondeductible expenditures, including living expenses, are added to these increases, and if the resulting figure for any year is substantially greater than the taxable income reported by the taxpayer for that year, the Government claims the excess represents unreported taxable income. In addition, it asks the jury to infer willfulness from this understatement, when taken in connection with direct evidence of "conduct, the likely effect of which would be to mislead or to conceal." Spies v. United States, 317 U.S. 492, 499, 63 S.Ct. 364, 368, 87 L.Ed. 418.

Before proceeding with a discussion of these cases, we believe it important to outline the general problems implicit in this type of litigation. In this consideration we assume, as we must in view of its widespread use, that the Government deems the net worth method useful in the enforcement of the criminal sanctions of our income tax laws. Nevertheless, careful study indicates that it is so fraught with danger for the innocent that the courts must closely scrutinize its use.

One basic assumption in establishing guilt by this method is that most assets derive from a taxable source, and that when this is not true the taxpayer is in a position to explain the discrepancy. The application of such an assumption raises serious legal problems in the administration of the criminal law. Unlike civil actions for the recovery of deficiencies, where the determinations of the Commissioner have *prima facie* validity, the prosecution must always prove the criminal charge beyond a reasonable doubt. This has led many of our courts to be disturbed by the use of the net worth method, particularly in its scope and the latitude which it allows prosecutors.

But the net worth method has not grown up overnight. It was first utilized in such cases as Capone v. United States, 7 Cir., 1931, 51 F.2d 609 and Guzik v. United States, 7 Cir., 1931, 54 F.2d 618, to corroborate direct proof of specific unreported income. In United States v. Johnson, [319 U.S. 503, 63 S.Ct. 1233, 87 L.Ed. 1546 (1943)] this Court approved of its use to support the inference that the taxpayer, owner of a vast and elaborately concealed network of gambling houses upon which he declared no income, had indeed received unreported income in a "substantial amount." It was a potent weapon in establishing taxable income from undisclosed sources when all other efforts failed. Since the *Johnson* case, however, its horizons have been widened until now it is used in run-of-the-mine cases, regardless of the amount of tax deficiency involved. In each of the four cases decided today the allegedly unreported income comes from the same disclosed sources as produced the taxpayer's reported income and in none is the tax deficiency anything like the deficiencies in *Johnson, Capone* or *Guzik*. The net worth method, it seems, has evolved from the final volley to the first shot in the Government's battle for revenue, and its use in the ordinary income-bracket cases greatly increases the chances for error. This leads us to point out the dangers that must be consciously kept in mind in order to assure adequate appraisal of the specific facts in individual cases.

1. Among the defenses often asserted is the taxpayer's claim that the net worth increase shown by the Government's statement is in reality not an increase at all because of the existence of substantial cash on hand at the starting point. This favorite defense asserts that the cache is made up of many years' savings which for various reasons were hidden and not expended until the prosecution period. Obviously, the Government has great difficulty in refuting such a contention. However, taxpayers too encounter many obstacles in convincing the jury of the existence of such hoards. This is particularly so when the emergence of the hidden savings also uncovers a fraud on the taxpayer's creditors.

In this connection, the taxpayer frequently gives "leads" to the Government agents indicating the specific sources from which his cash on hand has come, such as prior earnings, stock transactions, real estate profits, inheritances, gifts, etc. Sometimes these "leads" point back to old transactions far removed from the prosecution period. Were the Government required to run down all such leads it would face grave investigative difficulties; still its failure to do so might jeopardize the position of the taxpayer.

2. As we have said, the method requires assumptions, among which is the equation of unexplained increases in net worth with unreported taxable income. Obviously such an assumption has many weaknesses. It may be that gifts, inheritances, loans and the like account for the newly acquired wealth. There is great danger that the jury may assume that once the Government has established the figures in its net worth computations, the crime of tax evasion automatically follows. The possibility of this increases where the jury, without guarding instructions, is allowed to take into the jury room the various charts summarizing the computations; bare figures have a way of acquiring an existence of their own, independent of the evidence which gave rise to them.

3. Although it may sound fair to say that the taxpayer can explain the "bulge" in his net worth, he may be entirely honest and yet unable to recount his financial history. In addition, such a rule would tend to shift the burden of proof. Were the taxpayer compelled to come forward with evidence, he might risk lending support to the Government's case by showing loose business methods or losing the jury through his apparent evasiveness. Of course, in other criminal prosecutions juries may disbelieve and convict the innocent. But the courts must minimize this danger.

4. When there are no books and records, willfulness may be inferred by the jury from that fact coupled with proof of an understatement of income. But when the Government uses the net worth method, and the books and records of the taxpayer appear correct on their face, an inference of willfulness from net worth increases alone might be unjustified, especially where the circumstances surrounding the deficiency are as consistent with innocent mistake as with willful violation. On the other hand, the very failure of the books to disclose a proved deficiency might indicate deliberate falsification.

5. In many cases of this type, the prosecution relies on the taxpayer's statements, made to revenue agents in the course of their investigation, to establish vital links in the Government's proof. But when a revenue agent confronts the taxpayer with an apparent deficiency, the latter may be more concerned with a quick settlement than an honest search for the truth. Moreover, the prosecution may pick and choose from the taxpayer's statement, relying on the favorable portion and throwing aside that which does not bolster its position. The problem of corroboration * * * therefore becomes crucial.

6. The statute defines the offense here involved by individual years. While the Government may be able to prove with reasonable accuracy an increase in net worth over a period of years, it often has great difficulty in relating that income sufficiently to any specific prosecution year. While a steadily increasing net worth may justify an inference of additional earnings, unless that increase can be reasonably allocated to the appropriate tax year the taxpayer may be convicted on counts of which he is innocent.

While we cannot say that these pitfalls inherent in the net worth method foreclose its use, they do require the exercise of great care and restraint. The complexity of the problem is such that it cannot be met merely by the application of general rules. Trial courts should approach these cases in the full realization that the taxpayer may be ensnared in a system which, though difficult for the prosecution to utilize, is equally hard for the defendant to refute. Charges should be especially clear, including, in addition to the formal instructions, a summary of the nature of the net worth method, the assumptions on which it rests, and the inferences available both for and against the accused. Appellate courts should review the cases, bearing constantly in mind the difficulties that arise when circumstantial evidence as to guilt is the chief weapon of a method that is itself only an approximation.

With these considerations as a guide, we turn to the facts.

The indictment returned against the Hollands embraced three counts. The first two charged Marion L. Holland, the husband, with attempted evasion of his income tax for the years 1946 and 1947. He was found not guilty by the jury on both of these counts. The third count charged Holland and his wife with attempted evasion in 1948 of the tax on $19,736.74 not reported by them in their joint return. The jury found both of them guilty. Mrs. Holland was fined $5,000, while her husband was sentenced to two years' imprisonment and fined $10,000.

The Government's opening net worth computation shows defendants with a net worth of $19,152.59 at the beginning of the indictment period. Shortly thereafter, defendants purchased a hotel, bar and restaurant, and began operating them as the Holland House. Within three years during which they reported $31,265.92 in taxable income, their apparent net worth increased by $113,185.32. The Government's evidence indicated that, during 1948, the year for which defendants were convicted, their net worth increased by some $32,000, while the amount of taxable income reported by them totaled less than one-third that sum.

USE OF NET WORTH METHOD WHERE BOOKS ARE APPARENTLY ADEQUATE

As we have previously noted, this is not the first net worth case to reach this Court. In United States v. Johnson, supra, the Court affirmed a tax-evasion conviction on evidence showing that the taxpayer's expenditures had exceeded his "available declared resources." Since Johnson and his concealed establishments had destroyed the few records they had, the Government was forced to resort to the net worth method of proof. This Court approved on the ground that "To require more * * * would be tantamount to holding that skilful concealment is an invincible barrier to proof", 319 U.S. at 517–518, 63 S.Ct. at 1240. Petitioners ask that we restrict the *Johnson* case to situations where the taxpayer has kept no books. They claim that § 41 of the Internal Revenue Code, expressly limiting the authority of the Government to deviate from the taxpayer's method of accounting, confines the net worth method to situations where the taxpayer has no books or where his books are inadequate. Despite some support for this view among the lower courts, we conclude that this argument must fail. The provision that the "net income shall be computed * * * in accordance with the method of accounting regularly employed in keeping the books of such taxpayer", refers to methods such as the cash receipts or the accrual method, which allocate income and expenses between years. The net worth technique, as used in this case, is not a method of accounting different from the one employed by defendants. It is not a method of accounting at all, except insofar as it calls upon taxpayers to account for their unexplained income. Petitioners' accounting system was appropriate for their business purposes; and, admittedly, the Government did not detect any specific false entries therein. Nevertheless, if we believe the Government's evidence, as the jury did, we must conclude that the defendants' books were more consistent than truthful, and that many items of income had disappeared before they had even reached the recording stage. Certainly Congress never intended to make § 41 a set of blinders which prevents the Government from looking beyond the self-serving declarations in a taxpayer's books. "The United States has relied for the collection of its income tax largely upon the taxpayer's own disclosures * * *. This system can function successfully only if those within and near taxable income keep and render true accounts." Spies v. United States, 317 U.S. 495, 63 S.Ct. 366. To protect the revenue from those who do not "render true accounts", the Government must be free to use all legal evidence available to it in determining whether the story told by the taxpayer's books accurately reflects his financial history.

Establishing a Definite Opening Net Worth

We agree with petitioners that an essential condition in cases of this type is the establishment, with reasonable certainty, of an opening net worth, to serve as a starting point from which to calculate future increases in the taxpayer's assets. The importance of accuracy in this figure is immediately apparent, as the correctness of the result depends entirely upon the inclusion in this sum of all assets on hand at the outset. The Government's net worth statement included as assets at the starting point stock costing $29,650 and $2,153.09 in cash. The Hollands claim that the Government failed to include in its opening net worth figure an accumulation of $113,000 in currency and "hundreds and possibly thousands of shares of stock" which they owned at the beginning of the prosecution period. They asserted that the cash had been accumulated prior to the opening date, $104,000 of it before 1933, and the balance between 1933 and 1945. They had kept the money, they claimed, mostly in $100 bills and at various times in a canvas bag, a suitcase, and a metal box. They had never dipped into it until 1946, when it became the source of the apparent increase in wealth which the Government later found in the form of a home, a ranch, a hotel and other properties. This was the main issue presented to the jury. The Government did not introduce any direct evidence to dispute this claim. Rather it relied on the inference that anyone who had had $104,000 in cash would not have undergone the hardship and privation endured by the Hollands all during the late 20's and throughout the 30's. During this period they lost their cafe business; accumulated $35,000 in debts which were never paid; lost their household furniture because of an unpaid balance of $92.20; suffered a default judgment for $506.66; and were forced to separate for some eight years because it was to their "economical advantage." During the latter part of this period, Mrs. Holland was obliged to support herself and their son by working at a motion picture house in Denver while her husband was in Wyoming. The evidence further indicated that improvements to the hotel, and other assets acquired during the prosecution years, were bought in installments and with bills of small denominations, as if out of earnings rather than from an accumulation of $100 bills. The Government also negatived the possibility of petitioners' accumulating such a sum by checking Mr. Holland's income tax returns as far back as 1913, showing that the income declared in previous years was insufficient to enable defendants to save any appreciable amount of money. The jury resolved this question of the existence of a cache of cash against the Hollands, and we believe the verdict was fully supported.

* * *

The Government's Investigation of Leads

So overwhelming, indeed, was the Government's proof on the issue of cash on hand that the Government agents did not bother to check petitioners' story that some of the cash represented proceeds from the sales of two cafes in the 20's; and that in 1933 an additional portion of this $113,000 in currency was obtained by exchanging some $12,000 in gold at a named bank. While sound administration of the criminal law requires that the net worth approach—a powerful method of proving otherwise undetectable offenses—should not be denied the Government, its failure to investigate leads furnished by the taxpayer might result in serious injustice. It is, of course, not for us to prescribe investigative procedures, but it is within the province of the courts to pass upon the sufficiency of the evidence to convict. When the Government rests its case solely on the approximations and circumstantial inferences of a net worth computation, the cogency of its proof depends upon its effective negation of reasonable explanations by the taxpayer inconsistent with guilt. Such refutation might fail when the Government does not track down relevant leads furnished by the taxpayer—leads reasonably susceptible of being checked, which, if true, would establish the taxpayer's innocence. When the Government fails to show an investigation into the validity of such leads, the trial judge may consider them as true and the Government's case insufficient to go to the jury. This should aid in forestalling unjust prosecutions, and have the practical advantage of eliminating the dilemma, especially serious in this type of case, of the accused's being forced by the risk of an adverse verdict to come forward to substantiate leads which he had previously furnished the Government. * * *

In this case, the Government's detailed investigation was a complete answer to the petitioners' explanations. Admitting that in cases of this kind it "would be desirable to track to its conclusion every conceivable line of inquiry," the Government centered its inquiry on the explanations of the Hollands and entered upon a detailed investigation of their lives covering several states and over a score of years. The jury could have believed that Mr. Holland had received moneys from the sale of cafes in the twenties and that he had turned in gold in 1933 and still it could reasonably have concluded that the Hollands lacked the claimed cache of currency in 1946, the crucial year. Even if these leads were assumed to be true, the Government's evidence was sufficient to convict. The distant incidents relied on by petitioners were so remote in time and in their connection with subsequent events proved by the Government that, whatever petitioners' net worth in 1933, it appears by convincing evidence that on January 1, 1946, they had only such assets as the Government credited to them in its opening net worth statement.

NET WORTH INCREASES MUST BE ATTRIBUTABLE TO TAXABLE INCOME

Also requisite to the use of the net worth method is evidence supporting the inference that the defendant's net worth increases are attributable to currently taxable income.

The Government introduced evidence tending to show that although the business of the hotel apparently increased during the years in question, the reported profits fell to approximately one-quarter of the amount declared by the previous management in a comparable period; that the cash register tapes, on which the books were based, were destroyed by the petitioners; and that the books did not reflect the receipt of money later withdrawn from the hotel's cash register for the personal living expenses of the petitioners and for payments made for restaurant supplies. The unrecorded items in this latter category totaled over $12,500 for 1948. Thus there was ample evidence that not all the income from the hotel had been included in its books and records. In fact, the net worth increase claimed by the Government for 1948 could have come entirely from the unreported income of the hotel and still the hotel's total earnings for the year would have been only 73% of the sum reported by the previous owner for the comparable period in 1945.

But petitioners claim the Government failed to adduce adequate proof because it did not negative all the possible nontaxable sources of the alleged net worth increases—gifts, loans, inheritances, etc. We cannot agree. The Government's proof, in our view, carried with it the negations the petitioners urge. Increases in net worth, standing alone, cannot be assumed to be attributable to currently taxable income. But proof of a likely source, from which the jury could reasonably find that the net worth increases sprang, is sufficient. In the *Johnson* case, where there was no direct evidence of the source of the taxpayer's income, this Court's conclusion that the taxpayer "had large, unreported income was reinforced by proof * * * that [for certain years his] private expenditures * * * exceeded his available declared resources." This was sufficient to support "the finding that he had some unreported income which was properly attributable to his earnings * * *." There the taxpayer was the owner of an undisclosed business capable of producing taxable income; here the disclosed business of the petitioners was proven to be capable of producing much more income than was reported and in a quantity sufficient to account for the net worth increases. Any other rule would burden the Government with investigating the many possible nontaxable sources of income, each of which is as unlikely as it is difficult to disprove. This is not to say that the Government may disregard explanations of the defendant reasonably susceptible of being checked. But where relevant leads are not forthcoming, the Government is not required to negate every possible source of nontaxable income, a matter peculiarly within the knowledge of the defendant.

THE BURDEN OF PROOF REMAINS ON THE GOVERNMENT

Nor does this rule shift the burden of proof. The Government must still prove every element of the offense beyond a reasonable doubt though not to a mathematical certainty. The settled standards of the criminal law are applicable to net worth cases just as to prosecutions for other crimes. Once the Government has established its case, the defendant remains quiet at his peril. The practical disadvantages to the taxpayer are lessened by the pressures on the Government to check and negate relevant leads.

WILLFULNESS MUST BE PRESENT

A final element necessary for conviction is willfulness. The petitioners contend that willfulness "involves a specific intent which must be proven by independent evidence and which cannot be inferred from the mere understatement of income." This is a fair statement of the rule. Here, however, there was evidence of a consistent pattern of underreporting large amounts of income, and of the failure on petitioners' part to include all of their income in their books and records. Since, on proper submission, the jury could have found that these acts supported an inference of willfulness, their verdict must stand. * * *

In the light of these considerations the judgment is affirmed.

(2) The Cash Expenditures Method

TAGLIANETTI v. UNITED STATES
United States Court of Appeals, First Circuit, 1968.
398 F.2d 558.

COFFIN, CIRCUIT JUDGE.

* * *

Appellant filed joint tax returns with his wife for the years in prosecution, showing income from two sources: his employment as a "locations" man for a cigarette vending machine company and his net winnings from parimutuel betting. * * * The government's evidence at trial showed substantially larger amounts of income and tax due.

The government proceeded on a "cash expenditure" theory. This is a variant of the net worth method of establishing unreported taxable income. Both proceed by indirection to overcome the absence of direct proof. The net worth method involves the ascertaining of a taxpayer's net worth positions at the beginning and end of a tax period, and deriving that part of any increase not attributable to reported income.

This method, while effective against taxpayers who channel their income into investment or durable property, is unavailing against the taxpayer who consumes his self-determined tax free dollars during the year and winds up no wealthier than before. The cash expenditure method is devised to reach such a taxpayer by establishing the amount of his purchases of goods and services which are not attributable to the resources at hand at the beginning of the year or to non-taxable receipts during the year. The beginning and ending net worth positions must be identified with sufficient particularity to rule out or account for the use of a taxpayer's capital to pay for his purchases. If the end-of-year net worth position is equal to that at the beginning of the year, and if there are no non-taxable sources of income during the year, such as gifts or inheritances, the totality of the year's expenditures reflects total taxable income. If ending net worth shows an increase, the increase reflects an added component of income. If ending net worth shows a diminution, the decrease reduces pro tanto the extent to which expenditures reflect income.

* * *

Appellant's contention that there was a failure of proof in the government's case is, to follow his position as stated in his brief, "* * * that even assuming, *arguendo,* that the evidence adduced shows he spent more money during the indictment years than his reported gross income, there is not one scintilla of evidence to show that said expenditures came out of current receipts *only* and not out of available assets acquired in prior years. This is so because there is absolutely no competent evidence which, in any way suffices to clearly and accurately establish the extent of defendant's prior assets at the beginning of any or all the indictment years; i.e., there is no opening net worth for January 1, 1956, 1957 or 1958."

Appellant mistakes form for substance. In this case, the prosecution presented evidence to support the conclusion that the assets owned by appellant and his wife either remained at a static level, or instead increased over the taxable years, and in any event made no contribution to the expenditures shown. The jury was entitled to accept appellant's statement that he did not touch his loan proceeds for other than betting and to reject the testimony of payments received from Merola. There is no suggestion that cars, boats, furniture, jewels, or other property were disposed of to finance current purchases. The expense items excluded by appellant's accountant presented issues of fact which the jury obviously resolved against appellant.

This state of the proof fully satisfies the requirement in Holland v. United States of "the establishment, with reasonable certainty, of an opening net worth, to serve as a starting point from which to calculate future increases in the taxpayer's assets." In a typical net worth case, as *Holland,* precise figures would have to be attached to opening and closing net worth positions for each of the taxable years to provide a basis for the critical subtraction. In a cash expenditures case reasonable certainty may be established without such a presentation, as long as the proof—as in this case—makes clear the extent of any contribution which beginning resources or a diminution of resources over time could have made to expenditures. We recognize that courts occasionally blur the distinction between the two approaches and use language implying that they are subject not only to the same principle of excluding the availability of nontaxable resources but also to the same method of implementing that principle, i.e., establishing net worth figures. Appellant has cited several cash expenditure cases for the latter proposition. A careful review of the language used and the problems addressed in these opinions indicates that they cannot be fairly read as embracing such an inflexible formal requirement.

In the case at bar it is apparent that while the jury may not have been apprised of the dollar value of each of the assets comprising appellant's opening net worth, it was so informed as to his cash on hand and the few non-liquid items which were disposed of or acquired during the course of each prosecution year. A running series of net worth statements would not have added to the jury's understanding. We therefore hold that the proof adduced here was sufficient to allow the jury an intelligent determination of the single relevant issue; whether any expenditures found to be in excess of reported income can be accounted for by assets available at the outset of the prosecution period or non-taxable receipts during the period.

* * *

Affirmed.

(3) *The Bank Deposits Method*
UNITED STATES v. ESSER
United States Court of Appeals, Seventh Circuit, 1975.
520 F.2d 213.

BAUER, CIRCUIT JUDGE.

Appellant-defendant, Dr. Charles Esser, a veterinarian, was indicted on three counts of willful evasion of income taxes for the years 1967, 1968 and 1969 in violation of 26 U.S.C. § 7201.

* * *

Appellant argues that the trial court should have granted motions for judgment of acquittal based upon the government's failure to conduct a thorough examination and analysis of defendant's bank deposits. We do not accept appellant's argument and find that the trial judge had sufficient grounds for denial of the motion for acquittal.

I.R.S. Agent Hoak testified that deposit slips and underlying items of deposit are customarily introduced to demonstrate the nature of the deposits. However, in this instance it was virtually impossible to introduce the deposit slips due to their poor quality, unreliability, and unavailability. The government introduced the bank statements and pass books as the most reliable evidence available. Though appellant attempted on cross-examination to establish that the slips and items were capable of retrieval, the question was left as one of fact for the jury.

Defendant argues also that the bank deposits theory requires an analysis of the bank deposit items themselves. He contends that the government's duty to specifically identify and analyze the defendant's deposit slips and the underlying items is mandated by the "bank deposits cases"; and that failure to do so is fatal to the government's case. On examination the authorities reveal no such duty.

These cases establish that the bank deposits theory requires the government to prove that the defendant was engaged in an income producing business and that regular deposits of funds having the appearance of income were in fact made to bank accounts during the course of business. The total deposits figure serves as the starting point for further analysis of the taxpayer's accounts. The government must do everything that is reasonable and fair under the circumstances to identify any non-income transactions and deduct them from total deposits. Further, all proper deductions and credits must be subtracted. However, the government's investigators are not obliged to track down every conceivable lead offered by the taxpayer to justify the non-income designation of a particular item.

After the government proves that deposits having the appearance of income were made the defendant has the burden to explain as far as possible the deposits. With this done the jury is entitled to infer that the difference between the balance of deposited items and reported income constitutes unreported income.[2]

* * *

In short, the government proved by clear, reliable evidence that defendant had enormous bank deposits and that after deducting all non-income sources of deposits, the business receipts far exceeded the amounts shown on his income tax returns. This evidence was more than sufficient to support the jury verdict below.

* * *

Accordingly it is the decision of this Court that the conviction should be affirmed.

Affirmed.

(4) The Percentage Mark-Up Method

The percentage mark-up method of proof of income is rarely used as the principal method in a criminal prosecution. However, this

---

2. The government explained in detail the method employed to analyze the defendant's bank deposits during the years in question. Total deposits were determined by examination of the defendant's bank statements. From that total, all interbank deposits, re-deposits of cash, proceeds of inheritance and gifts and all other nontaxable sources of income were deducted.

method may be utilized to support or corroborate proof of income by another indirect method.

In essence, under the percentage mark-up method, the taxpayer's cost of goods sold or merchandise purchases are "marked up" to establish gross profit. The method is useful in cases in which the taxpayer has one (or only a few) sources of supply, and the taxpayer's mark-up can be established to a reasonable degree of certainty. The method is most accurately applied in those industries in which pricing is regulated, as is the liquor industry in certain states. The percentage mark-up method is typically attacked on the basis of the inaccuracy of the percentage used due to the taxpayer's deviation from the comparable operations used by the investigating agent. The defense also frequently argues that the Service has failed properly to take into account such factors as spillage, breakage and theft. Hence, as noted above, one will rarely, if ever, see a criminal tax prosecution based solely upon this method of proof.

Chapter X

CRIMINAL TAX INVESTIGATIONS AND PROSECUTIONS

Scope Note: This chapter covers some of the recurring issues involved in the representation of taxpayers who are suspected of criminal tax violations, and a number of features peculiar to the prosecution of a criminal tax case. Section 2 discusses the relatively new (but highly significant) cash transaction reporting requirements and the civil and criminal forfeiture laws. Also discussed is the problem of when may a taxpayer "take the Fifth" on a tax return.

SECTION 1. CRIMINAL TAX INVESTIGATIONS

A criminal tax case usually develops from an investigation by the Criminal Investigation Division (CID) of the Internal Revenue Service. The investigation itself can be triggered in many different ways. A large number of criminal tax investigations result from referrals from the civil (particularly Examination and Collection) divisions of the Service upon the suspicion of fraud in matters within their jurisdiction. However, the Service's informant [a] and information gathering system, other law enforcement agencies, the daily newspapers and countless other sources all yield "information items" which can result in a criminal tax investigation.

The criminal tax investigation, conducted by a Special Agent of the CID (often with the assistance of a civil agent and advice from IRS counsel), will result in either the referral of the case for civil disposition or a recommendation for prosecution. Should the Special Agent recommend prosecution, the taxpayer under investigation is entitled, upon request, to a conference at the CID level,[b] with the Chief of the pertinent section of the Division.

[a.] I.R.C. § 7623 authorizes (but does not require) the payment of rewards to informants at the discretion of the Service. See also Reg. § 301.7623–1.

[b.] Proc.Rules § 601.107(b)(2). See also

These conferences normally (if not invariably) are followed by the referral of a recommendation for prosecution [c] to a division of the Office of Chief Counsel, IRS, usually the District Counsel for the district in which the investigation was conducted. The precise review steps prior to an indictment vary depending upon the characteristics of the case.[d] Hence, a definitive and universally applicable "flow chart" of the progress of a criminal tax case cannot be provided without extensive and detailed discussion. However, it should be noted that there will be a review of the case by an IRS attorney, often one in the office of the District Counsel. The taxpayer usually will be afforded a conference at this level, if one is requested, and will have the opportunity at the conference to present reasons why prosecution is not appropriate. The IRS attorney's consideration (and internal review) will conclude with either a termination of the criminal case and a referral for civil disposition, a referral back to the Criminal Investigation Division for further investigation, or a referral to the Department of Justice with a recommendation for prosecution.

At the Department of Justice, criminal tax cases are referred to the Criminal Section of the Tax Division. The Tax Division, in some cases, may refer the matter to a United States Attorney without further review. However, in many cases a substantive review will take place at the Tax Division. Under certain circumstances, the Tax Division usually will provide the taxpayer the opportunity for a conference in Washington, D.C., if one is requested. At the conference, the taxpayer can attempt to persuade the Justice Department attorney assigned to the case that prosecution is not appropriate. If a conference at the Justice Department is desired, it is important to request the conference promptly upon learning that the case has been forwarded to the Justice Department. Cases classified as "noncomplex" (because they involve straightforward facts or legal issues) are simply forwarded by the Justice Department to the U.S. Attorney for prosecution. "Complex" cases (those involving indirect methods of proving income or complex legal issues) are retained for consideration at the Justice Department. Significantly, in non-complex cases for which there is a conference request on file, the case will be reclassified as "complex" and a conference usually will be granted. The Tax Division's consideration of a criminal tax case can result in a declination of prosecution and a referral back to the IRS or a referral to a United States Attorney. The referral to the United States Attorney can be with an authorization and direction to prosecute, with discretion to prosecute or decline and refer

---

Short v. Murphy, 512 F.2d 374 (6th Cir. 1975) (taxpayer cannot compel IRS to disclose specifics of its case at CID conference); United States v. Goldstein, 342 F.Supp. 661 (E.D.N.Y.1972) (conference opportunity is for benefit of Service, cannot be demanded as a matter of right by taxpayer).

c. Since they are provided after the Special Agent's decision to recommend prosecution has been reached, a decision which has doubtlessly been cleared with his Chief, it is most unlikely that a taxpayer will be able to stop a criminal case at the CID conference level.

d. See Internal Revenue Manual—Administration § 9600 et seq.

for civil disposition, or with directions to conduct further investigation through a grand jury.[e]

The United States Attorney, upon receipt of a criminal tax case, normally will afford a pre-indictment conference to the taxpayer. The taxpayer may be able to persuade the United States Attorney to decline prosecution (in those cases in which he has the discretion to do so) or to refer the case back to the Justice Department for reconsideration. On the other hand, the taxpayer may be able only to obtain a "plea bargain" for consideration in lieu of proceeding to trial on the charges.

Especially in the recent past, many criminal tax cases arise out of an investigation conducted by a grand jury assisted by IRS agents. In such a case, there will be IRS and Tax Division review of the use of the agents in the grand jury investigation and of any charges prior to indictment. The taxpayer's ability to have conferences with the Service and the Tax Division may be limited (or perhaps even nonexistent) in the context of a grand jury investigation.[f]

A. DEFENSE CONCERNS AT THE EARLY STAGES OF THE INVESTIGATION

Defense concerns at the early stages center around "damage control" and gathering evidence. Both are critical in thwarting prosecution, because of the importance to the government of not losing any criminal tax prosecution it pursues. The Justice Department Tax Division's policy is to recommend prosecution if there is a "reasonable probability of conviction."[g] In the recent past, the government's success rate in tax prosecutions has exceeded 90%. From the defense standpoint, this means that weaknesses in the defense case must be minimized and proof problems with the prosecution emphasized. In practice, this usually requires that the taxpayer remain silent (despite his or her wishes to cooperate with the investigator to dispel the idea that he or she might actually be a tax evader) and scrupulously adhere to the advice of counsel. For many reasons, however, this does not usually happen.

First, the taxpayer is often surprised to find himself the subject of a criminal investigation. Special agents of the CID may appear at the taxpayer's residence very early in the morning or late at night and warn the taxpayer that they are conducting a criminal investigation. Despite the partial *Miranda* warnings the special agent should give (discussed in the next section), the taxpayer's first impulse may be to try to convince the agent that a mistake has been made. Any statements made by the target, or answers the target supplies to questions,

e. A referral back to the IRS for further investigation is theoretically possible. However, there is some question as to the propriety of utilizing an IRS summons once a case has been referred to Justice. See § 7602(c).

f. See Internal Revenue Manual—Administration § 9267, for the internal IRS procedures incident to the use of IRS agents in a grand jury investigation.

g. U.S. Attorneys' Manual § 6–2.213.

are likely to be harmful. Therefore, the taxpayer should remain silent, but his impulses often compel him to make statements that may be damaging. This may be true even if the taxpayer suspects a criminal investigation may occur or even if the taxpayer is not a novice to this process.

The client should be told to say nothing to the special agent and to notify his lawyer immediately. The lawyer should then contact the agent and attempt to determine the nature of the investigation and the specific transactions or issues under investigation. The taxpayer need not meet with or talk with the special agent. The goal at this stage is to identify the focus of the investigation and to narrow the focus, if possible.

The importance of narrowing the focus can be seen in comparing the tax fraud investigation to other types of criminal investigations. Unlike a murder investigation, for example, the inquiry does not begin with a known crime and proceed to identifying possible suspects. Quite the contrary, in fact: the investigation begins with a known suspect and proceeds to identifying possible crimes.[h] Significantly, the emphasis is not on the accuracy of the return, but instead on gathering evidence that will help establish or defeat the elements of a tax crime, most importantly the "willfulness" element. Thus, once the CID has become involved, the nature of the audit or examination of the taxpayer's returns has shifted: the government is no longer interested in proving that the taxpayer's position is incorrect, but instead that it is knowingly and intentionally incorrect. In aid of this goal, any "badges of fraud" identified at earlier stages of the investigation (which, in fact, may have spurred the criminal investigation) will take on new significance.

The defense strategy at this stage is clear: to show that no reasonable probability of conviction exists. To accomplish this, the attorney should carefully examine the taxpayer's returns and learn as much as possible about the taxpayer and any statements he may have made to investigators or documents he may have turned over to them. Having assessed the potential damage that has already been done, the attorney should concentrate on preventing further damage by discouraging cooperation by the taxpayer with investigators. Aside from "damage control," the goal at this stage is to gather sufficient evidence to make a convincing case that there is no "reasonable probability of conviction."

UNITED STATES v. RICHARD HEBEL
United States Court of Appeals, Eighth Circuit, 1982.
668 F.2d 995.

PER CURIAM.

Carlyle Merritt and Richard Hebel appeal from single-count convictions for criminal violation of the income tax laws. In a bench trial on

---

[h]. See Crowley & Manning, Criminal Tax Fraud—Representing the Taxpayer Before Trial, Practising Law Institute (1976).

stipulated facts the district court found Merritt guilty of knowingly and willfully subscribing his 1975 income tax return which failed to report his true income. The court convicted Merritt of violating 26 U.S.C. § 7206(1), and fined him $5,000. At the same bench trial, the district court found Hebel guilty of income tax evasion for calendar year 1975, in violation of 26 U.S.C. § 7201, and fined him $10,000. We affirm.

Merritt and Hebel do not dispute these violations on appeal. Each taxpayer voluntarily disclosed his filing of a false return to the Internal Revenue Service, corrected the tax discrepancies in an amended return, and paid the appropriate tax due. They contend, however, that an IRS practice of not prosecuting persons who make such voluntary disclosures bars their prosecution.

Based on this alleged practice of the IRS, appellants assert the following issues on appeal:

1) That the trial court erred in finding that defendants had not established a governmental practice not to prosecute voluntary disclosure tax cases and therefore erred in denying the motions to enjoin their indictments, and motions to dismiss and suppress;

2) That the trial court erred in denying dismissal on grounds of selective prosecution; and

3) That these prosecutions violated due process and denied taxpayers effective assistance of counsel because their attorneys counseled them to make disclosure of the facts concerning their tax delinquencies in reliance upon the policy and practice of the Government not to prosecute taxpayers who voluntarily disclose tax falsifications.

The district court initially referred these matters to Magistrate James D. Hodges, Jr., to hear and make recommendations concerning defendants' motions to suppress evidence and to dismiss the prosecutions. After an evidentiary hearing, the magistrate made the following findings:

8. Messrs. Smith and Brown [experienced tax lawyers] advised defendants that based upon their experience in the tax area that while the Internal Revenue Service and Justice Department had publicly stated in 1952 that they would no longer assure taxpayers of nonprosecution where a voluntary disclosure of previous tax errors was made, that it had been counsels' experience that prosecution would not result where a true voluntary disclosure was made.

9. Based upon this advice defendants requested counsel to disclose to the Internal Revenue Service that apparently errors existed in their income tax returns. Pursuant to these instructions counsel informed the Internal Revenue Service on December 2, 1976 of the defendants' identities and that there appeared to be substantial tax deficiencies on defendants' individual returns as well as those of Hebel Fertilizer & Chemical, Inc. for the years at issue. At this time neither

defendants nor counsel was aware of any pending investigations involving defendants.

10. At the time the disclosure was made to Robert J. Moeller, acting Chief of the Internal Revenue Service Audit Division, and Jack L. Schroeder, Chief of Internal Revenue Service Branch I counsel were advised that defendants' returns had previously been referred to a Revenue Agent for audit.

11. Defendants provided a complete and absolute disclosure of any and all transactions which may have had tax ramifications for the years at issue to his counsel and to the CPAs engaged by counsel. At the conclusion of the independent audit defendants caused amended individual and corporate tax returns to be prepared. These amended returns were filed on December 27, 1976 and the tax due of approximately $200,000 was paid.

12. Subsequent to filing the amended returns, defendants supplied the IRS with detailed identification of the location, amounts, time periods and occasions of the then determined inaccuracies in defendants' tax returns by allowing the IRS to examine and make copies of extensive accounting workpapers and produced by the accounting firm working for defendants' counsel. Defendants also provided access to their original records and were interviewed by the IRS regarding their tax returns.

13. Defendants were indicted on February 24, 1981.

* * *

15. Defendants' disclosures were voluntarily made in reliance upon the advice of counsel but with knowledge that, while it was counsel's belief that they would not be prosecuted, there was no absolute grant of immunity from prosecution.

[*United States v. Hebel and Merritt,* No. CR 81–3001 (N.D.Ia. May 5, 1981 at 2–4) (magistrate's report and recommendation).]

In considering the motions to suppress and dismiss, Magistrate Hodges reviewed the same factual matters asserted in this appeal. His opinion stated in part:

In light of the fact that the IRS publicly abandoned its voluntary disclosure policy in 1952 and defendants and their counsel were aware of this, the court is of the view that defendants' disclosures were knowingly and voluntarily made and accordingly all motions should be denied, alternatively, if a voluntary disclosure policy should be found to exist there appears to be a serious question as to whether defendants' disclosure was in fact a true voluntary disclosure.

Specifically, defendants have moved to dismiss the indictment against them under the due process clause of the fifth amendment to the United States Constitution based upon lack of notice, failure to comply with the Administrative Procedure Act, equitable estoppel and selective prosecution.

The record appears to be relatively clear that the IRS and Department of Justice followed a written policy of not prosecuting criminally, taxpayers who made voluntary disclosures of irregularities in their tax returns during the period between 1934 and 1952. However, this policy was abandoned in 1952 and from that time until the present it has been the announced policy of the IRS that a voluntary disclosure would be considered along with all other facts and circumstances of a case in determining whether or not criminal charges would be filed. See generally, *United States v. Shotwell Mfg. Co.,* 355 U.S. 233, 235 n. 2, 78 S.Ct. 245, 248, 2 L.Ed.2d 234 (1957); *United States v. Choate,* 619 F.2d 21 (9th Cir.1980). Since counsel was aware of this change in policy and advised defendants of the change, defendants' arguments based upon lack of notice and under the APA must fail. In this regard, defendants argue that while no written policy existed there was an unwritten practice of not prosecuting taxpayers who made a voluntary disclosure. The simple answer to this is defendants have failed to establish the existence of such a practice. While there appears to have been few, if any, prosecutions of true voluntary disclosures the IRS has consistently reserved the right to do so. Indeed, the position is recognized by the legal publications submitted by the government and at best there appears to be disagreement among the bar as to the possibility of prosecution.

* * *

Further, defendants' motion based upon selection [sic] prosecution is without merit. To prevail on this motion defendants must show both that he was singled out for prosecution and that the prosecution was based upon impermissible grounds. *See e.g., United States v. Larson,* 612 F.2d 1301 (8th Cir.1980); *United States v. Catlett,* 584 F.2d 864 (8th Cir.1978); *United States v. Alarik,* 439 F.2d 1349 (8th Cir. 1971)[.] Here, defendants have failed to meet either prong of the test. In light of the amount of tax due and the status of the IRS's investigation at the time of disclosure, the record shows ample reason for prosecuting defendants. Further, defendants have been unable to raise any colorable claim of improper motive.

Finally, defendants' motion to suppress must likewise be denied. It is well recognized that the government must establish guilt by evidence independently secured and not by evidence obtained as a result of trickery or coercion from defendants, *Rogers v. Richmond,* 365 U.S. 534, 81 S.Ct. 735, 5 L.Ed.2d 760 (1960). Further, this principal clearly includes evidence induced from a person under a governmental promise, either direct or implied, of immunity, *Bram v. United States,* 168 U.S. 532, 18 S.Ct. 183, 42 L.Ed. 568 (1857). Here, however, the record does not support a finding that defendants' disclosures were brought about as a result of any government conduct. Rather, it does support a finding that all disclosures were freely made by defendants in hope that they would not be prosecuted rather than in reliance upon any governmental promise of immunity.

Indeed, as noted above, the government has withdrawn its policy of non-prosecution of voluntary disclosures and this fact was known to counsel and related to defendants. Further, there is no evidence of any acts on the part of the government which could be considered calculated to lead defendants to believe that the practice was any different from the stated policy. Indeed, this record reveals that the IRS and its officials have consistently maintained that prosecution was a possibility in voluntary disclosure cases. Finally, defendants have produced no evidence of direct promises or inducements made to defendants or counsel during the proceedings.

[*United States v. Hebel and Merritt, supra* at 4–7 (magistrate's report and recommendation).]

The magistrate recommended denial of the motions, and the district court accepted that recommendation. Thereafter, the trial proceeded before the district court upon facts stipulated by the parties subject to reserved objections. The district court found each defendant guilty on one count of a multiple indictment. On appeal, the defendants attack the findings and rulings denying dismissal of the indictments and suppression of the evidence.

We agree with the district court. The magistrate's findings, which are supported by the evidence, demonstrate that no governmental policy or practice on voluntary disclosure relating to false tax returns necessarily relieves taxpayers who file false tax returns from criminal prosecution. The prior existence of that policy and its abandonment came to the attention of the Supreme Court in *United States v. Shotwell Manufacturing Co.*, 355 U.S. 233, 78 S.Ct. 245, 2 L.Ed.2d 234 (1957). The Court noted:

> Under that policy, first announced by the Treasury Department in 1945, the Department did not refer to the Department of Justice for prosecution cases of intentional income tax evasion where the taxpayers had made a clean breast of things to the Treasury before any investigation had been initiated by the Revenue Service. This policy was set forth in various informal announcements by Treasury officials, but was never formalized by statute or regulation. The policy was abandoned in January 1952. [*Id.* at 235 n. 2, 78 S.Ct. at 247 n. 2.]

As of 1973, the Treasury Department's "voluntary disclosure policy" read as follows:

> The Treasury Department on January 10, 1952, formally abandoned its longstanding "voluntary disclosure policy". Treasury Department Information Release, No. S–2930; 1955 P–H, par. 18, 604–A. It is, therefore, no longer an administrative basis for declining prosecution in the Revenue Service that a prospective defendant voluntarily revealed his tax fraud to an appropriate official of that Service before any investigation of his affairs had begun. * * * Now the fact that a taxpayer seeks voluntarily to rectify a false return without prodding by investigators or the threat of investigation is given some weight in determining whether to prosecute but is not conclusive of the issue. [U.S. Department of Justice Manual for Criminal Tax Trials, Ch. 1, p. 5.]

In an earlier civil case brought by Hebel to enjoin his prosecution, the same district court noted the Treasury Department's 1973 position.

Hebel v. United States Department of Justice, Nos. C 80–155, C 80–156 (N.D.Ia. Feb. 18, 1981). *See also United States v. Choate,* 619 F.2d 21, 23 (9th Cir.1980).

In this case, taxpayers Hebel and Merritt received a substantial benefit from disclosing and rectifying past errors. The indictment consisted of seven counts, three counts each charging Hebel and Merritt individually, and one count charging them both. Each defendant was convicted on only one count, and neither received a sentence of imprisonment.

Regardless of whether a taxpayer actually benefits or suffers detriment from voluntarily disclosing and rectifying faulty tax returns, that disclosure itself does not insulate the taxpayer from prosecution under any administrative policy or practice recognized by this court. Taxpayers and their attorneys cannot rely on a long-since abandoned policy of non-prosecution when a taxpayer voluntarily discloses violation of the tax laws. Accordingly, we affirm the convictions of Hebel and Merritt on the basis of the magistrate's findings and opinion, adopted by the district court.

B. MIRANDA–TYPE WARNINGS

MATHIS v. UNITED STATES
Supreme Court of the United States, 1968.
391 U.S. 1, 88 S.Ct. 1503, 20 L.Ed.2d 381.

MR. JUSTICE BLACK delivered the opinion of the Court.

Petitioner was convicted by a jury in a United States District Court on two counts charging that he knowingly filed false claims against the Government in violation of 18 U.S.C. § 287 and sentenced to 30 months' imprisonment on each count, the sentences to run concurrently. The frauds charged were claims for tax refunds growing out of petitioner's individual income taxes for 1960 and 1961. * * * A part of the evidence on which the conviction rested consisted of documents and oral statements obtained from petitioner by a government agent while petitioner was in prison serving a state sentence. Before eliciting this information, the government agent did not warn petitioner that any evidence he gave the Government could be used against him, and that he had a right to remain silent if he desired as well as a right to the presence of counsel and that if he was unable to afford counsel one would be appointed for him. At trial petitioner sought several times without success to have the judge hold hearings out of the presence of the jury to prove that his statements to the revenue agent were given without these warnings and should therefore not be used as evidence against him. For this contention he relied exclusively on our case of Miranda v. State of Arizona, 384 U.S. 436, 86 S.Ct. 1602, 16 L.Ed.2d 694 (1966). * * *

* * * The Government here seeks to escape application of the *Miranda* warnings on two arguments: (1) that these questions were

asked as a part of a routine tax investigation where no criminal proceedings might even be brought, and (2) that the petitioner had not been put in jail by the officers questioning him, but was there for an entirely separate offense. These differences are too minor and shadowy to justify a departure from the well-considered conclusions of *Miranda* with reference to warnings to be given to a person held in custody.

It is true that a "routine tax investigation" may be initiated for the purpose of a civil action rather than criminal prosecution. To this extent tax investigations differ from investigations of murder, robbery, and other crimes. But tax investigations frequently lead to criminal prosecutions, just as the one here did. In fact, the last visit of the revenue agent to the jail to question petitioner took place only eight days before the full-fledged criminal investigation concededly began. And as the investigating revenue agent was compelled to admit, there was always the possibility during his investigation that his work would end up in a criminal prosecution. We reject the contention that tax investigations are immune from the *Miranda* requirements for warnings to be given a person in custody.

The Government also seeks to narrow the scope of the *Miranda* holding by making it applicable only to questioning one who is "in custody" in connection with the very case under investigation. There is no substance to such a distinction, and in effect it goes against the whole purpose of the *Miranda* decision which was designed to give meaningful protection to Fifth Amendment rights. We find nothing in the *Miranda* opinion which calls for a curtailment of the warnings to be given persons under interrogation by officers based on the reason why the person is in custody. In speaking of "custody" the language of the *Miranda* opinion is clear and unequivocal:

> "To summarize, we hold that when an individual is taken into custody or otherwise deprived of his freedom by the authorities in any significant way and is subjected to questioning, the privilege against self-incrimination is jeopardized." 384 U.S., at 478, 86 S.Ct., at 1630.

And the opinion goes on to say that the person so held must be given the warnings about his right to be silent and his right to have a lawyer.

Thus, the courts below were wrong in permitting the introduction of petitioner's self-incriminating evidence given without warning of his right to be silent and right to counsel. The cause is reversed and remanded for further proceedings consistent with this opinion. It is so ordered.

Reversed and remanded.

MR. JUSTICE WHITE, with whom MR. JUSTICE HARLAN and MR. JUSTICE STEWART join, dissenting.

* * *

* * * Although petitioner was confined, he was at the time of interrogation in familiar surroundings. Neither the record nor the Court suggests reasons why petitioner was "coerced" into answering

Lawless' questions any more than is the citizen interviewed at home by a revenue agent or interviewed in a Revenue Service office to which citizens are requested to come for interviews. * * *

C. SEARCHES AND SEIZURES
VOSS v. BERGSGAARD
United States Court of Appeals, Tenth Circuit, 1985.
774 F.2d 402.

McKAY, CIRCUIT JUDGE.

* * *

On April 5, 1985, a United States Magistrate authorized the issuance of search warrants presented to him by agents of the Internal Revenue Service, authorizing the search of three locations. Each was supported by the same affidavit of a special agent of the IRS.

The affidavit detailed an investigation of the National Commodities and Barter Association (NCBA) and its National Commodities Exchange (NCE). It described meetings between IRS undercover agents and NCBA officials in which those officials allegedly described how their organization was designed to conduct financial transactions on behalf of its clients in a manner designed to avoid detection by the IRS. * * * The affidavit further described the use of an NCBA account by an IRS agent to convert into cash sums of money payable to assumed names.

A large volume of documents was seized at each search site. Shortly thereafter, appellees, members of the NCBA, filed a complaint pursuant to Rule 41(e) of the Federal Rules of Criminal Procedure, seeking the return of all documents and other evidence seized. Appellees alleged, among other things, that the warrants were not supported by sufficient probable cause, and that they failed to describe with sufficient particularity the property to be seized.

After an evidentiary hearing, the district court held that the affidavit set forth sufficient probable cause, but that the warrants were nevertheless invalid on particularity grounds. Subsequently, the government filed with this court an emergency motion for stay pending appeal, which was granted.

* * *

[The court first held that although an order denying a Rule 41(e) motion was not appealable under Di Bella v. United States, 369 U.S. 121, 82 S.Ct. 654, 7 L.Ed.2d 614 (1962), an order granting such a motion was immediately appealable by the government.]

* * *

On the merits the government claims that the district court erred in finding the search warrants to be insufficiently particular in their description of the items to be seized. The warrants authorized the seizure of all books, records or documents relating to the following: NCBA/NCE customer accounts; financial transactions; financial services; the purchase, sale, or storage of precious metals; employees; and marketing and promotions. They further authorized the seizure of books, literature and tapes advocating nonpayment of federal income taxes; publications of tax protestor organizations; and literature relating to communications between persons conspiring to defraud the IRS, or to conceal such fraud.

The district court, in holding that the warrant amounted to an illegal writ of assistance, found that:

> It is so pervasive that I think it's invalid, and I so hold. If, indeed, the description of the items to be seized were set forth with particularity, and only with particularity, there would be nothing wrong with this warrant, but what it gave was carte blanche for government agents to take anything that they saw, whether it was nailed down or otherwise, and, indeed, as best I can find from the returns and the pleadings, that's precisely what did happen.

Record, vol. 3, at 68.

The fourth amendment requires that a search warrant describe the things to be seized with sufficient particularity to prevent a "general, exploratory rummaging in a person's belongings." *Coolidge v. New Hampshire,* 403 U.S. 443, 467, 91 S.Ct. 2022, 2038, 29 L.Ed.2d 564 (1971). * * *

The particularity requirement ensures that a search is confined in scope to particularly described evidence relating to a specific crime for which there is demonstrated probable cause. The government affidavit supporting the warrants at issue alleged a scheme of tax fraud, and the district court found that probable cause existed. The bulk of the warrant was not restricted to evidence relating to tax fraud, however. It authorized government agents to rummage through all of the NCBA's customer files, bank records, employee records, precious metal records, marketing and promotional literature, and more, seeking any information pertaining to any federal crime. Even to describe the warrant as limited to evidence relating to federal crimes is an interpretation generous to the government. The concluding sentence in the warrant refers to the general conspiracy statute, but is not couched in terms that clearly restrict seizure to evidence relevant to the violation of the statute. The sentence simply reads: "All of which are evidence of violations of Title 18, United States Code, Section 371." Even if the reference to section 371 is construed as a limitation, it does not constitute a constitutionally adequate particularization of the items to be seized.

* * *

The insufficient particularity of the warrants is further illustrated by some of the items actually seized under their terms, including copies of the Internal Revenue Code, the Federal Rules of Criminal and Civil Procedure, and *The Federalist Papers.* The warrants allowed precisely the kind of rummaging through a person's belongings, in search of evidence of even previously unsuspected crimes or of no crime at all, that the fourth amendment proscribes.

* * *

The government argues, however, that where there is probable cause to believe that an enterprise has engaged in a pervasive scheme to defraud, all of its business records may be seized. In the case at hand, however, while the district court found probable cause for the issuance of a properly restricted warrant, it did not find probable cause to believe that fraud pervaded every aspect of the NCBA. Indeed, while the government's affidavit pointed to evidence in support of a substantial tax fraud scheme, it did not even purport to support the proposition that fraud pervaded every aspect of the NCBA. Certainly, the organization's advocation of modifying or abolishing our country's tax system is a legitimate activity. Indeed, it is an activity protected by the first amendment. Thus, the case at hand is distinguishable from those cited by the government in that probable cause to believe that fraud pervaded every aspect of the NCBA was not shown, and first amendment rights are implicated.

Even if the allegedly fraudulent activity constitutes a large portion, or even the bulk, of the NCBA's activities, there is no justification for seizing records and documents relating to its legitimate activities. At least one of the circuits which has allowed the seizure of all of an organization's records where there is probable cause to believe the organization is pervaded by fraud has refused to allow such a broad seizure when the fraudulent activity, though substantial, could be segregated from other legitimate activities of the organization. *United States v. Roche,* 614 F.2d 6 (1st Cir.1980).[2]

Moreover, to the extent that the above cases can be read as allowing the seizure of all of an organization's records when there is probable cause to believe the organization is pervasively criminal, whether or not those records are relevant to an alleged crime, we decline to follow them. This is not to say that a search may never properly result in the seizure of all of an organization's records. Where a warrant authorizes the seizure of particularly described records relevant to a specific crime and all of an organization's records, in fact, fall into that category, they may all lawfully be seized. However, a warrant that simply authorizes the seizure of all files, whether or not relevant to a specified crime, is insufficiently particular.

* * * The government argues that it should be allowed to retain evidence seized under sufficiently particular provisions [of the warrant] even if other provisions are overly broad. The bulk of the warrant's

---

2. The warrants at issue in *Roche* authorized the search of various insurance agencies, which the government had probable cause to believe were engaged in a fraud scheme involving motor vehicle insurance. Because the warrant allowed the seizure of documents relating to all types of insurance carried by the companies, the court found the warrants overly broad.

provisions, however, simply allow for the seizure of evidence, whether or not related to tax fraud, and largely subsume those provisions that would have been adequate standing alone. Accordingly, we affirm the trial court's decision to require the return of all evidence seized pursuant to the warrants.

* * *

LOGAN, CIRCUIT JUDGE, concurring:

I arrive at the same conclusion as my colleagues, but by a different route and apparently with more difficulty. This warrant, in its first eight paragraphs, allowed the seizure of all the business records of the National Commodity Barter Exchange (NCBE). I would hold that, under proper circumstances, an "all business records" search warrant is legally permissible.

* * *

My problem with this seizure concerns the probable cause element. The breadth of a warrant must be justified by the breadth of the probable cause.

* * *

As the majority opinion notes, the government does not charge *any* specific substantive crime. It relies instead on the general conspiracy statute, 18 U.S.C. § 371. All of the cases that have approved an "all business records" search, however, have identified concrete statutory violations that supposedly permeated the entire suspect business. They did not involve organizations that had other legitimate activities.

* * *

I thus cannot support an "all business records" search in this case. The government has neither demonstrated that virtually all of the NCBE's activities are illegal nor pinpointed the statutes that the business allegedly has violated. The purpose of an "all records" search cannot be to find out what crime a person or entity might have committed.

Note

Although the court in *Voss* held the search invalid and ordered the IRS to return the seized records, would information learned by the IRS as a result of the search necessarily be excluded from evidence in a subsequent criminal prosecution? There were two 1984 Supreme Court decisions that dealt with this issue. In United States v. Leon, 468 U.S. 897, 104 S.Ct. 3405, 82 L.Ed.2d 677 (1984), the Court held that suppression of evidence in a criminal prosecution that was produced by an invalid search is appropriate only if the police officers were dishonest or reckless in preparing their affidavit or could not have harbored an objectively reasonable belief in the existence of probable cause. See also Massachusetts v. Sheppard, 468 U.S. 981, 104 S.Ct. 3424, 82 L.Ed.2d 737 (1984).

Sec. 1 CRIMINAL TAX INVESTIGATIONS 645

UNITED STATES v. CACERES
Supreme Court of the United States, 1979.
440 U.S. 741, 99 S.Ct. 1465, 59 L.Ed.2d 733.

Mr. Justice Stevens delivered the opinion of the Court.

The question we granted certiorari to decide is whether evidence obtained in violation of Internal Revenue Service (IRS) regulations may be admitted at the criminal trial of a taxpayer accused of bribing an IRS agent.

* * *

I

Neither the Constitution nor any Act of Congress requires that official approval be secured before conversations are overheard or recorded by Government agents with the consent of one of the conversants. Such "consensual electronic surveillance" between taxpayers and IRS agents is, however, prohibited by Internal Revenue Service regulations unless appropriate prior authorization is obtained.

The Internal Revenue Service Manual sets forth in detail the procedures to be followed in obtaining such approvals. * * *

II

[On March 14, 1974, Agent Yee, auditing the Caceres' 1971 income tax returns, was offered a bribe by Mr. Caceres, reported the offer to his superiors, and prepared an affidavit describing it. In a further audit session on January 27, 1975, the bribe offer was repeated. Subsequent telephone conversations (properly monitored) led to a meeting on January 31, 1975. The IRS obtained "emergency approval" under its regulations to monitor that meeting. Similarly, on February 5, 1975, "emergency approval" was obtained to monitor a February 6, 1975 meeting. On February 11, 1975, the IRS obtained approval to monitor conversations for thirty days, which covered a meeting of that date. The District Court and the Court of Appeals both held that the two earlier meetings had not been monitored in accordance with IRS regulations.]

The Government does not challenge that conclusion. We are therefore presented with the question whether the tape recordings, and the testimony of the agents who monitored the January 31st and February 6th conversations, should be excluded because of the violation of the IRS regulations.

III

A court's duty to enforce an agency regulation is most evident when compliance with the regulation is mandated by the Constitution or federal law. In Bridges v. Wixon, 326 U.S. 135, 152–153, 65 S.Ct. 1443, 1451–1452, 89 L.Ed. 2103, for example, this Court held invalid a deportation ordered on the basis of statements which did not comply with the Immigration Service's rules requiring signatures and oaths, finding that the rules were designed "to afford [the alien] due process of law" by providing "safeguards against essentially unfair procedures."

In this case, however, unlike Bridges v. Wixon, the agency was not required by the Constitution or by statute to adopt any particular procedures or rules before engaging in consensual monitoring and recording. While Title III of the Omnibus Crime Control and Safe Streets Act of 1968, 18 U.S.C. § 2510 et seq., regulates electronic surveillance conducted without the consent of either party to a conversation, federal statutes impose no restrictions on recording a conversation with the consent of one of the conversants.

Nor does the Constitution protect the privacy of individuals in respondent's position. In Lopez v. United States, 373 U.S. 427, 439, 83 S.Ct. 1381, 1388, 10 L.Ed.2d 462, we held that the Fourth Amendment provided no protection to an individual against the recording of his statements by the IRS agent to whom he was speaking. In doing so, we repudiated any suggestion that the defendant had a "constitutional right to rely on possible flaws in the agent's memory, or to challenge the agent's credibility without being beset by corroborating evidence that is not susceptible of impeachment," concluding instead that "the risk that the petitioner took in offering a bribe to [the IRS agent] fairly included the risk that the offer would be accurately reproduced in court, whether by faultless memory or mechanical recording." The same analysis was applied in United States v. White, 401 U.S. 745, 91 S.Ct. 1122, 28 L.Ed.2d 453, to consensual monitoring and recording by means of a transmitter concealed on an informant's person, even though the defendant did not know that he was speaking with a government agent * * *.

Our decisions in Lopez and White demonstrate that the IRS was not required by the Constitution to adopt these regulations.[14] It is equally clear that the violations of agency regulations disclosed by this record do not raise any constitutional questions.

---

14. It does not necessarily follow, however, as a matter of either logic or law, that the agency had no duty to obey them. "Where the rights of individuals are affected, it is incumbent upon agencies to follow their own procedures. This is so even where the internal procedures are possibly more rigorous than otherwise would be required." Morton v. Ruiz, 415 U.S. 199, 235, 94 S.Ct. 1055, 1074, 39 L.Ed.2d 270. See, e.g., United States ex rel. Accardi v. Shaughnessy, 347 U.S. 260, 74 S.Ct. 499, 98 L.Ed. 681 (holding habeas corpus relief proper where government regulations "with the force and effect of law" governing the procedure to be followed in processing and passing upon an alien's application for suspension of deportation were not followed); Service v. Dulles, 354 U.S. 363, 77 S.Ct. 1152, 1 L.Ed.2d 1403 (invalidating Secretary of State's dismissal of an employee where regulations requiring approval of the Deputy Undersecretary and consultation of full record were not satisfied); Vitarelli v. Seaton, 359 U.S. 535, 79 S.Ct. 968, 3 L.Ed.2d 1012 (invalidating dismissal of Interior Department employee where regulations governing hearing procedures for national security dismissals were not followed). See also Yellin v. United States, 374 U.S. 109, 83 S.Ct. 1828, 10 L.Ed.2d 778 (reversing contempt conviction where congressional committee had not complied with its rules requiring it to consider a witness' request to be heard in executive session).

[The Court stated that there was no denial of equal protection just because others would be monitored only in compliance with the regulations. Moreover, the IRS officials' erroneous interpretation of the regulations in this case was not obviously wrong, so that there was no error of constitutional dimension.]

Nor is this a case in which the Due Process Clause is implicated because an individual has reasonably relied on agency regulations promulgated for his guidance or benefit and has suffered substantially because of their violation by the agency. Respondent cannot reasonably contend that he relied on the regulation, or that its breach had any effect on his conduct. He did not know that his conversations with Yee was being recorded without proper authority. He was, of course, prejudiced in the sense that he would be better off if all monitoring had been postponed until after the Deputy Assistant Attorney General's approval was obtained on February 11, 1975, but precisely the same prejudice would have ensued if the approval had been issued more promptly. For the record makes it perfectly clear that a delay in processing the request, rather than any doubt about its propriety or sufficiency, was the sole reason why advance authorization was not obtained before February 11.

* * *

IV

Respondent argues that the regulations concerning electronic eavesdropping, even though not required by the Constitution or by statute, are of such importance in safeguarding the privacy of the citizenry that a rigid exclusionary rule should be applied to all evidence obtained in violation of any of their provisions. We do not doubt the importance of these rules. Nevertheless, without pausing to evaluate the Government's challenge to our power to do so, we decline to adopt any rigid rule requiring federal courts to exclude any evidence obtained as a result of a violation of these rules.

* * * In the long run, it is far better to have rules like those contained in the IRS Manual, and to tolerate occasional erroneous administration of the kind displayed by this record, than either to have no rules except those mandated by statute, or to have them framed in a mere precatory form.

Nor can we accept respondent's further argument that even without a rigid rule of exclusion, his is a case in which evidence secured in violation of the agency regulation should be excluded on the basis of a more limited, individualized approach. Quite the contrary, this case exemplifies those situations in which evidence would *not* be excluded if a case-by-case approach were applied. The two conversations at issue here were recorded with the approval of the IRS officials in San Francisco and Washington. In an emergency situation, which the agents thought was present, this approval would have been sufficient. The agency action, while later found to be in violation of the regulations, nonetheless reflected a reasonable, good-faith attempt to comply in a situation in which no one questions that monitoring was appropriate and would have certainly received Justice Department authorization, had the request been received more promptly. In these circumstances, there is simply no reason why a court should exercise whatever discretion it may have to exclude evidence obtained in violation of the regulations.

The judgment of the Court of Appeals is reversed.

UNITED STATES v. PAYNER
Supreme Court of the United States, 1980.
447 U.S. 727, 100 S.Ct. 2439, 65 L.Ed.2d 468.

MR. JUSTICE POWELL delivered the opinion of the Court.

The question is whether the District Court properly suppressed the fruits of an unlawful search that did not invade the respondent's Fourth Amendment rights.

I

Respondent Jack Payner was indicted in September 1976 on a charge of falsifying his 1972 federal income tax return in violation of 18 U.S.C. § 1001. The indictment alleged that respondent denied maintaining a foreign bank account at a time when he knew that he had such an account at the Castle Bank and Trust Company of Nassau, Bahama Islands. The Government's case rested heavily on a loan guarantee agreement dated April 28, 1972, in which respondent pledged the funds in his Castle Bank account as security for a $100,000 loan.

Respondent waived his right to jury trial and moved to suppress the guarantee agreement. With the consent of the parties, the United States District Court for the Northern District of Ohio took evidence on the motion at a hearing consolidated with the trial on the merits. The court found respondent guilty as charged on the basis of all the evidence. The court also found, however, that the Government discovered the guarantee agreement by exploiting a flagrantly illegal search that occurred on January 15, 1973. The court therefore suppressed "all evidence introduced in the case by the Government with the exception of Jack Payner's 1972 tax return * * * and the related testimony." As the tax return alone was insufficient to demonstrate knowing falsification, the District Court set aside respondent's conviction.

The events leading up to the 1973 search are not in dispute. In 1965, the Internal Revenue Service launched an investigation into the financial activities of American citizens in the Bahamas. The project, known as "Operation Trade Winds," was headquartered in Jacksonville, Fla. Suspicion focused on the Castle Bank in 1972, when investigators learned that a suspected narcotics trafficker had an account there. Special Agent Richard Jaffe of the Jacksonville office asked Norman Casper, a private investigator and occasional informant, to learn what he could about the Castle Bank and its depositors. To that end, Casper cultivated his friendship with Castle Bank vice-president Michael Wolstencroft. Casper introduced Wolstencroft to Sybol Kennedy, a private investigator and former employee. When Casper discovered that the banker intended to spend a few days in Miami in January of 1973, he devised a scheme to gain access to the bank records he knew Wolstencroft would be carrying in his briefcase. Agent Jaffe approved the basic outline of the plan.

Wolstencroft arrived in Miami on January 15 and went directly to Kennedy's apartment. At about 7:30 p.m., the two left for dinner at a Key Biscayne restaurant. Shortly thereafter, Casper entered the apartment using a key supplied by Kennedy. He removed the briefcase and delivered it to Jaffe. While the agent supervised the copying of approximately 400 documents taken from the briefcase, a "lookout" observed Kennedy and Wolstencroft at dinner. The observer notified Casper when the pair left the restaurant, and the briefcase was replaced. The documents photographed that evening included papers evidencing a close working relationship between the Castle Bank and the Bank of Perrine, Fla. Subpoenas issued to the Bank of Perrine ultimately uncovered the loan guarantee agreement at issue in this case.

The District Court found that the United States, acting through Jaffe, "knowingly and willfully participated in the unlawful seizure of Michael Wolstencroft's briefcase. * * * " According to that court, "the Government affirmatively counsels its agents that the Fourth Amendment standing limitation permits them to purposefully conduct an unconstitutional search and seizure of one individual in order to obtain evidence against third parties * * *." The District Court also found that the documents seized from Wolstencroft provided the leads that ultimately led to the discovery of the critical loan guarantee agreement. Although the search did not impinge upon the respondent's Fourth Amendment rights, the District Court believed that the Due Process Clause of the Fifth Amendment and the inherent supervisory power of the federal courts required it to exclude evidence tainted by the Government's "knowing and purposeful *bad faith hostility* to any person's fundamental constitutional rights."

The Court of Appeals for the Sixth Circuit affirmed in a brief order endorsing the District Court's use of its supervisory power. The Court of Appeals did not decide the due process question. We granted certiorari, and we now reverse.

II

This Court discussed the doctrine of "standing to invoke the [Fourth Amendment] exclusionary rule" in some detail last Term. Rakas v. Illinois, 439 U.S. 128, 138, 99 S.Ct. 421, 427–28, 58 L.Ed.2d 387 (1978). We reaffirmed the established rule that a court may not exclude evidence under the Fourth Amendment unless it finds that an unlawful search or seizure violated the defendant's own constitutional rights. And the defendant's Fourth Amendment rights are violated only when the challenged conduct invaded *his* legitimate expectation of privacy rather than that of a third party.

The foregoing authorities establish, as the District Court recognized, that respondent lacks standing under the Fourth Amendment to suppress the documents illegally seized from Wolstencroft. The Court of Appeals did not disturb the District Court's conclusion that "Jack Payner possessed no privacy interest in the Castle Bank documents that were seized from Wolstencroft." Nor do we. United States v. Miller, 425 U.S. 435, 96 S.Ct. 1619, 48 L.Ed.2d 71 (1976), established that a depositor has no expectation of privacy and thus no "protectable Fourth Amendment interest" in copies of checks and deposit slips retained by his bank. Nothing in the record supports a contrary conclusion in this case.[4]

The District Court and the Court of Appeals believed, however, that a federal court should use its supervisory power to suppress evidence tainted by gross illegalities that did not infringe the defendant's constitutional rights. The United States contends that this approach—as applied in this case—upsets the careful balance of interests embodied in the Fourth Amendment decisions of this Court. In the Government's view, such an extension of the supervisory power would enable federal courts to exercise a standardless discretion in their application of the exclusionary rule to enforce the Fourth Amendment. We agree with the Government.

III

We certainly can understand the District Court's commendable desire to deter deliberate intrusions into the privacy of persons who are unlikely to become defendants in a criminal prosecution. No court should condone the unconstitutional and possibly criminal behavior of those who planned and executed this "briefcase caper." Indeed, the decisions of this Court are replete with denunciations of willfully lawless activities undertaken in the name of law enforcement. But our cases also show that these unexceptional principles do not command the exclusion of evidence in every case of illegality. Instead, they must be weighed against the considerable harm that would flow from indiscriminate application of an exclusionary rule.

Thus, the exclusionary rule "has been restricted to those areas where its remedial objectives are most efficaciously served." United States v. Calandra, 414 U.S. 338, 348, 94 S.Ct. 613, 620, 38 L.Ed.2d 561 (1974). The Court has acknowledged that the suppression of probative but tainted evidence exacts a costly toll upon the ability of courts to ascertain the truth in a criminal case. E.g., Rakas v. Illinois, supra, 439 U.S., at 137–138, 99 S.Ct., at 427–28; Stone v. Powell, 428 U.S. 465, 489–491, 96 S.Ct. 3037, 3050–51, 49 L.Ed.2d 1067 (1976). Our cases have consistently recognized that unbending application of the exclu-

---

4. We are not persuaded by respondent's suggestion that the Bahamian law of bank secrecy creates an expectation of privacy not present in United States v. Miller, 425 U.S. 435, 96 S.Ct. 1619, 48 L.Ed.2d 71 (1976). * * *

sionary sanction to enforce ideals of governmental rectitude would impede unacceptably the truth-finding functions of judge and jury. E.g., Stone v. Powell, supra, 428 U.S., at 485–489, 96 S.Ct., at 3048–3050. After all, it is the defendant, and not the constable, who stands trial.

The same societal interests are at risk when a criminal defendant invokes the supervisory power to suppress evidence seized in violation of a third party's constitutional rights. The supervisory power is applied with some caution even when the defendant asserts a violation of his own rights.[7] In United States v. Caceres, 440 U.S. 741, 754–757, 99 S.Ct. 1465, 1473–74, 59 L.Ed.2d 733 (1979), we refused to exclude all evidence tainted by violations of an executive department's rules. And in Elkins v. United States, 364 U.S. 206, 216, 80 S.Ct. 1437, 1443, 4 L.Ed.2d 1669 (1960), the Court called for a restrained application of the supervisory power.

> "[A]ny apparent limitation upon the process of discovering truth in a federal trial ought to be imposed only upon the basis of considerations which outweigh the general need for untrammeled disclosure of competent and relevant evidence in a court of justice." 364 U.S., at 216, 80 S.Ct., at 1443.

We conclude that the supervisory power does not authorize a federal court to suppress otherwise admissible evidence on the ground that it was seized unlawfully from a third party not before the court. Our Fourth Amendment decisions have established beyond any doubt that the interest in deterring illegal searches does not justify the exclusion of tainted evidence at the instance of a party who was not the victim of the challenged practices. Rakas v. Illinois, supra, 439 U.S., at 137, 99 S.Ct., at 427. The values assigned to the competing interests do not change because a court has elected to analyze the question under the supervisory power instead of the Fourth Amendment. In either case, the need to deter the underlying conduct and the detrimental impact of excluding the evidence remain precisely the same.

The District Court erred, therefore, when it concluded that "society's interest in deterring [bad faith] conduct by exclusion outweigh[s] society's interest in furnishing the trier of fact with all relevant evidence." This reasoning, which the Court of Appeals affirmed, amounts to a substitution of individual judgment for the controlling decisions of this Court. Were we to accept this use of the supervisory power, we would confer on the judiciary discretionary power to disregard the considered limitations of the law it is charged with enforcing. We hold that the supervisory power does not extend so far.

---

7. Federal courts may use their supervisory power in some circumstances to exclude evidence taken from the *defendant* by "willful disobedience of law." McNabb v. United States, 318 U.S. 332, 345, 63 S.Ct. 608, 615, 87 L.Ed. 819 (1943). This Court has never held, however, that the supervisory power authorizes suppression of evidence obtained from third parties in violation of Constitution, statute or rule. The supervisory power merely permits federal courts to supervise "the administration of criminal justice" among the parties before the bar. McNabb v. United States, supra, 318 U.S., at 340, 63 S.Ct. 612.

The judgment of the Court of Appeals is reversed.

WEISS v. COMMISSIONER
United States Court of Appeals, Ninth Circuit, 1990.
919 F.2d 115.

REINHARDT, CIRCUIT JUDGE: In April 1984, the IRS determined deficiencies in Eric and Mary Weiss's income tax and assessed additional taxes for 1976, 1977, and 1978. The Weisses petitioned the Tax Court for a redetermination and moved the Tax Court to suppress evidence derived from the IRS's exercise of "institutional bad faith." This institutional bad faith, which was found to exist by a district judge in a prior criminal prosecution based on the same facts, consisted at least in part of violations of internal agency regulations. However, IRS regulatory violations do not require the suppression of evidence. *United States v. Caceres* [79–1 USTC ¶ 9294], 440 U.S. 741 (1979). On the other hand, it is not clear whether evidence must be suppressed when statutory violations are involved, see *Caceres* [79–1 USTC ¶ 9294], 440 U.S. at 755 & n. 21; *United States v. Appoloney*, 761 F.2d 520, 522–23 (9th Cir.), *cert. denied*, 474 U.S. 949 (1985); *United States v. Snowadzki* [84–1 USTC ¶ 9157], 723 F.2d 1427, 1430–31 (9th Cir.), *cert. denied*, 469 U.S. 839 (1984), and the parties are in disagreement on whether the district court found that the IRS had committed statutory as well as regulatory violations by issuing civil summonses for a criminal investigation. See 26 U.S.C. § 7602 (1976) (amended 1982).[1]

The Tax Court denied the Weisses' motion to suppress and upheld the IRS's assessment. The Weisses argue that the Tax Court wrongly ignored the IRS's statutory violations and that, because of these violations, the Tax Court should have suppressed the evidence. We need not decide whether in the earlier criminal case the district court made a finding of statutory violations, nor under what circumstances a finding

---

1. Prior to 1982, the IRS was authorized to issue summonses for civil investigations only. See 26 U.S.C. § 7602 (1976). The Supreme Court recognized, however, that "[f]or a fraud investigation to be solely criminal in nature would require an extraordinary departure from the normally inseparable goals of examining whether the basis exists for criminal charges and for the assessment of civil penalties." *United States v. LaSalle Nat'l Bank* [78–2 USTC ¶ 9501], 437 U.S. 298, 314 (1978). Therefore, as long as the IRS had not institutionally abandoned its goal of civil enforcement of the tax laws at the time the summonses were issued, the summonses were valid. *Id.* at 316.

In 1982, Congress eliminated the requirement that, for a summons to be valid, the IRS investigation must have a civil component. Today, the IRS may issue summonses not only for the purpose of civil enforcement, but also for "the purpose of inquiring into *any offense* connected with the administration or enforcement of the internal revenue laws." 26 U.S.C. § 7602(b) (1988) (emphasis added). The amendments make clear that the IRS may issue summonses unless a case is under referral to the Justice Department for criminal enforcement. *Id.* § 7602(c). Thus, the conduct that the Weisses challenge would not today violate any statutory provision. See *United States v. Millman* [87–2 USTC ¶ 9397], 822 F.2d 305, 308 (2d Cir.1987) (dictum); *Groder v. United States* [87–1 USTC ¶ 9259], 816 F.2d 139, 144 (4th Cir. 1987) (dictum); *LaMura v. United States* [85–2 USTC ¶ 9548], 765 F.2d 974, 980 n. 9 (11th Cir.1985); *Pickel v. United States* [84–2 USTC ¶ 9934], 746 F.2d 176, 183–85 (3d Cir.1984).

of a statutory violation would require application of the exclusionary rule in a civil case. We conclude, instead, that regardless of whether statutory violations took place, this is not an appropriate case in which to apply the exclusionary rule. We affirm.

I.

This civil case follows an earlier criminal prosecution of Eric Weiss for tax evasion, based on the same facts. See *United States v. Weiss* [83-2 USTC ¶ 9479], 566 F.Supp. 1452 (C.D.Cal.1983) ("*Weiss I*"), *appeal dismissed*, 730 F.2d 772 (9th Cir.1984). The district court dismissed the criminal prosecution *sua sponte,* with prejudice, because it found evidence that the IRS had acted with institutional bad faith in gathering evidence for the prosecution. Specifically, the court found that the IRS had failed to comply with its Internal Revenue Manual ("IRM")[2] procedures. The court also found evidence that the IRS had improperly issued civil summonses for a solely criminal investigation.

The *Weiss I* court made the following findings: Although the Civil Audit Division used the proper form to refer the investigation to the Criminal Intelligence Division, the Criminal Intelligence Division did not return the referral report within the fifteen work-day deadline. The Criminal Intelligence Division did not inform the Civil Audit Division that it had accepted the referral until twenty-six work days had passed, and it failed to check a box on the notification form requesting that a cooperating civil officer be assigned to the investigation. Instead, the Criminal Intelligence Division improperly used a separate form to request a cooperating civil officer and did not make this request until October 9, 1979. The Civil Audit Division did not act on the request until October 10, 1979, when it assigned civil officer Floyd Krietz to the investigation.

Meanwhile, the Criminal Intelligence Division had begun its investigation. Krietz unofficially participated in the investigation before his assignment. On October 1 and October 4, Krietz and a criminal officer interviewed Weiss and demanded records. At some point, the IRS issued fifteen summonses pursuant to 26 U.S.C. § 7602 (1976) (amended 1982).[3] This statute, prior to its 1982 amendments, authorized the IRS

---

2. For the Internal Revenue Manual in effect during the time in question, see Internal Revenue Manual (C.C.H.1979).

3. This statute, as it existed at the time of the IRS investigation of Weiss, stated in its entirety:

§ 7602. Examination of books and witnesses. For the purpose of ascertaining the correctness of any return, making a return where none has been made, determining the liability of any person for any internal revenue tax or the liability at law or in equity of any transferee or fiduciary of any person in respect of any internal revenue tax, or collecting any such liability, the Secretary is authorized—

(1) To examine any books, papers, records, or other data which may be relevant or material to such inquiry;

(2) To summon the person liable for tax or required to perform the act, or any officer or employee of such person, or any person having possession, custody, or care of books of account containing entries relating to the business of the person liable for tax or required to perform the act, or any other person the Secretary may deem proper, to appear before the Secretary at a time and place

to issue summonses for civil investigations but not for criminal ones. See *United States v. LaSalle Nat'l Bank* [78–2 USTC ¶ 9501], 437 U.S. 298 (1978). Because the Assistant United States Attorney did not comply with the district court's repeated requests to supply copies of those summonses, or even a list of dates when they were issued, the court could not determine whether any were issued prior to Krietz's assignment. It therefore concluded that "the Court cannot assume anything except that it was possible, if not probable, that at least some of these Civil Summonses were utilized by the Criminal Special Agent or the Civil Revenue Agent in support of an investigation wholly criminal in nature." *Weiss I* [83–2 USTC ¶ 9479], 566 F.Supp. at 1455.

The *Weiss I* court stated that the judiciary could not sanction the wholly criminal use of a civil summons. See *Weiss I* [83–2 USTC ¶ 9479], 566 F.Supp. at 1455 (citing *LaSalle*). The court then compared the situation to a precedent in which the IRS had improperly issued civil summonses for a criminal investigation. See *United States v. Dahlstrum* [80–2 USTC ¶ 9562], 493 F.Supp. 966 (C.D.Cal.1980), *appeal dismissed*, [81–2 USTC ¶ 9810], 655 F.2d 971 (9th Cir.1981), *cert. denied*, 455 U.S. 928 (1982). Stating that "[t]he *Dahlstrum* factual situation is virtually identical to the facts found here, which compels the Court to conclude that the present case is legally undistinguishable [sic] from *Dahlstrum*," the court dismissed the indictment. *Weiss I* [83–2 USTC ¶ 9479], 566 F.Supp. at 1455. Because jeopardy had attached, this court dismissed the government's appeal. *United States v. Weiss*, No. 83–5198 (9th Cir. Jan. 30, 1984) (unpublished memorandum disposition).

Following the termination of its criminal action against Eric Weiss, the IRS proceeded civilly against Eric and Mary Weiss, determining deficiencies and additions to their taxes for 1976, 1977, and 1978. The Weisses filed this present action in the Tax Court to seek a redetermination. *Weiss v. Commissioner of Internal Revenue* [CCH Dec. 45,240(M)], T.C.M. (P–H) ¶ 88,586 (Dec. 27, 1988) ("*Weiss II*"). They also filed a motion to suppress all evidence derived from the IRS's exercise of institutional bad faith, as determined by the district court in *Weiss I*. The parties stipulated to alternative tax liabilities, depending on whether the Tax Court granted or denied the Weisses' motion to suppress. They also stipulated to the facts and holdings of the district court in *Weiss I*. Because the only issue remaining in the case was the motion to suppress, the Tax Court treated the motion as a motion for summary judgment. *Id.* at 88–3033.

The Tax Court refused to suppress the evidence. In determining the basis for the *Weiss I* court's finding of institutional bad faith, the Tax Court focused on the IRS's failure to comply with the IRM procedures. It found that the *Weiss I* court had been conditional in its

named in the summons and to produce such books, papers, records, or other data, and to give such testimony, under oath, as may be relevant or material to such inquiry; and

(3) To take such testimony of the person concerned, under oath, as may be relevant or material to such inquiry.

26 U.S.C. § 7602 (1976) (amended 1982).

finding of additional violations. *Id.* at 88–3037. Stating that the dismissal of the criminal case had been a sufficient deterrent, the Tax Court then entered judgment in accordance with the parties' stipulation. *Id.* at 88–3037 to 88–3038.

The Weisses appeal from the Tax Court's ruling. They argue that the district court made a finding of statutory violations which the Tax Court wrongly ignored, and that, because of res judicata,[4] we should accept the conclusion that the IRS's institutional bad faith rested in part on statutory violations. They urge us to suppress all evidence derived from the IRS's exercise of institutional bad faith.

We need not resolve whether the district court's finding of statutory violations was conditional. Even assuming that the IRS did, if fact, improperly issue civil summonses to further a criminal investigation, the acts of misconduct relied upon by the district court were not egregious. This case does not present an appropriate situation for us to apply the exclusionary rule. Therefore, we need not decide under what circumstances the violation of a statute might make the exclusionary rule applicable in a civil case.

II.

Prior to 1982, the IRS was not authorized to issue summonses for wholly criminal investigations.[5] See *LaSalle* [78–2 USTC ¶ 9501], 437 U.S. at 316 n. 18. As the Supreme Court stated: "Congress * * * intended the summons authority to be used to aid the determination and collection of taxes. These purposes d[id] not include the goal of filing criminal charges against citizens." *Id.* The reason for this limitation was that "[n]othing in § 7602 or its legislative history suggests that Congress intended the summons authority to broaden the Justice Department's right of criminal litigation discovery or to infringe on the role of the grand jury as a principal tool of criminal accusation." *Id.* at 312.

We are willing to assume for purposes of this case that the district court in *Weiss I* made a finding of a statutory violation. In light of *LaSalle*, this finding would mean that the IRS issued summonses to aid an investigation which, from an institutional perspective, was wholly criminal in nature.[6] See *id.* at 316–17. This single-minded pursuit of a

---

4. We assume that the Weisses intended to raise the issue of collateral estoppel, not res judicata. Our disposition of this case does not require us to reach issues regarding the law of prior adjudication.

5. Under the new law, the IRS may issue summonses in a wholly criminal investigation before it refers a case to the Justice Department for investigation. 26 U.S.C. § 7602(b) (1988). However, the agency still may not issue summonses after it has made a Justice Department referral. *Id.* § 7602(c).

6. We note that the same district judge decided both *Dahlstrum*, the case on which *Weiss I* relied, and *Weiss I*. The appeals from both cases were dismissed for reasons of double jeopardy. Therefore, this court has neither approved nor disapproved the interpretation of *LaSalle* contained in those cases. Notwithstanding Congress's amendment of § 7602 to authorize the IRS to issue summonses for a wholly criminal investigation, see 26 U.S.C., § 7602(b) (1988), the law applicable to this case is that which was in effect at the time the summonses in question were issued. Be-

criminal conviction by the IRS is precisely the situation which Congress sought to avoid; § 7602 required that a case which was being considered only for criminal prosecution be referred to the Justice Department. See *id.* By suppressing the evidence obtained through use of the unlawful subpoena and dismissing the criminal case, the district court in *Weiss I* punished this illegal government conduct and precluded the IRS from circumventing the requirements of § 7602.

Although the facts of *Weiss II* are the same, the circumstances are entirely different. The material subpoenaed is now being used for the fundamental purpose for which the IRS has always been authorized to obtain materials: the civil enforcement of the tax laws. The congressional intent behind limiting the IRS's summons authority to civil investigations—disallowing the Justice Department a basis for expanded discovery in a criminal prosecution—does not apply in this civil proceeding. Congress never intended to deny the IRS the civil discovery that is necessary for civil enforcement of the tax laws. Here, the fruit of the civil summonses in question is being used for a strictly civil purpose.

The IRS has already been penalized for its wrongdoing through the dismissal of the criminal case. We see no justification for also suppressing evidence in this civil case. We therefore hold that the Tax Court properly refused to apply the exclusionary rule to the facts of this case.

Affirmed.

Notes and Questions

1. Under Tax Division Directive No. 49, effective October 1, 1984, the authority to approve search warrants in tax investigations was delegated to local United States Attorneys, except in situations such as searches directed at the premises of lawyers, accountants, physicians, and public officials. Why should lawyers and accountants be accorded special treatment?

2. Before the decision in *Caceres,* the federal courts had excluded evidence in criminal cases, principally under a due process rationale, when the IRS violated its regulations in conducting a tax investigation. See United States v. Leahey, 434 F.2d 7 (1st Cir.1970); United States v. Heffner, 420 F.2d 809 (4th Cir.1969). After *Caceres,* however, the federal courts have generally rejected defense attempts to obtain exclusion or some other remedy based on the IRS' violation of its own regulations. See United States v. Irvine, 699 F.2d 43 (1st Cir.1983); United States v. Nuth, 605 F.2d 229 (6th Cir.1979). What should be the result if the defendant could demonstrate that he relied on the regulation that was violated?

3. In view of the *Payner* and *Caceres* decisions, it is difficult to imagine what type of IRS conduct would be sufficiently egregious, short of

cause the parties before us today have stipulated to the *Weiss I* court's findings of fact and conclusions of law, for purposes of this appeal we accept that court's interpretation of *LaSalle* as correct. We need not decide whether we would have affirmed or reversed if faced with a direct appeal from such an interpretation in which we had jurisdiction to review the merits.

a clear violation of a defendant's constitutional rights, to warrant a remedy in a criminal case. However, one such case of egregious conduct was presented in United States v. Omni Intern. Corp., 634 F. Supp. 1414 (D.Md. 1986). In this case the court found that the Service had altered pre-existing documents and produced them to defense counsel without a representation that alterations had been made, presented untrue and incorrect testimony before the court, and that Government personnel created typewritten interview memoranda. In light of such outrageous conduct by the IRS, the court held that it was compelled to dismiss the indictment against the corporation.

4. In view of the decision in *Payner*, is it clear that a criminal defendant would have standing to seek suppression of information improperly obtained by summons from a third party recordkeeper? In United States v. Beacon Federal Savings & Loan, 718 F.2d 49 (2d Cir. 1983), the court held that the very purpose of Section 7609 is to put the taxpayer "in the shoes of the third-party recordkeeper." Congress intended to confer on the taxpayer standing to assert the recordkeeper's rights vis-a-vis the summons. The court held that the purpose behind section 7609 is to avoid the standing problem a defendant faces in such a situation. See also United States v. McMullen, 755 F.2d 65 (6th Cir. 1984), where the court's determination fell on whether the Service had decided to prosecute at the time the summonses were issued. If they had, this would not be a good faith use of civil authority.

5. At first glance, one might think that suppression would be appropriate if the IRS had obtained the information from the defendant after there had been a referral for prosecution to the Justice Department. However, the real answer is that so long as a summons was issued prior to referral, any information obtained from the defendant either through voluntary compliance or enforcement proceedings need not be suppressed. If courts were to hold otherwise, it would encourage litigants to purposefully delay compliance with a summons in order to use the Justice Department referral as a defense. See United States v. Picciandra, 788 F.2d 39 (1st Cir.1986).

The situation could be different if the IRS had obtained the information by means of an affirmative misrepresentation to the defendant. In United States v. Tweel, 550 F.2d 297 (5th Cir. 1977), the IRS agent's failure to apprise the appellant of the obvious criminal nature of the investigation was held to be a sneaky deliberate deception by the agent and a flagrant disregard for appellant's rights. Therefore, evidence was suppressed because it was derived from an illegal Fourth Amendment search and seizure. However, courts are very cautious in suppressing evidence and suggest it is only appropriate where there are fairly serious affirmative misrepresentations made to a defendant. See United States v. Irvine, 699 F.2d 43 (1st Cir.1983).

D. GRAND JURY PROCEEDINGS

The federal grand jury, composed of 23 individuals, has an accusatory role in all felony tax prosecutions since, absent a waiver, the

United States may prosecute a felony charge only upon an indictment returned by a grand jury.[i] The accusatory function of the grand jury in a tax case takes place at the termination of the investigation and after the various review procedures are concluded with a decision to prosecute. The grand jury may, however, have a material role during the investigative phase of a tax case.

A grand jury is utilized to investigate criminal tax offenses in essentially three categories of situations:

(1) Where the government attorney conducting a grand jury investigation of non-tax criminal violations uncovers during the course of that investigation evidence indicating that tax violations may also have been committed. The government attorney thus seeks to investigate jointly, through the grand jury, these alleged tax offenses, together with the non-tax violations that initially gave rise to the grand jury inquiry.

(2) Where the IRS has reached an impasse in its administrative investigation and recommends that a tax grand jury investigation be undertaken to develop evidence regarding the alleged criminal tax violations.

(3) Where the IRS has referred a case to the Department of Justice recommending prosecution and the Tax Division's evaluation affirms prosecution potential, but discloses the need for additional investigation.

When a tax investigation is conducted by a grand jury, IRS personnel act as "agents of the grand jury" in connection with the investigation. There will then be imposed upon the IRS personnel various safeguards to separate the Service (in its civil capacity) from the grand jury (a purely criminal investigatory body). The procedural safeguards imposed include the following:[j]

(1) IRS personnel assisting in the investigation may not use administrative summonses.

(2) If a revenue agent is assigned to assist the government attorney conducting the grand jury investigation, he has no civil tax function. Neither special agents nor revenue agents may seek information for other than criminal purposes while assisting the grand jury.

(3) No disclosure may be made of information gathered during the grand jury process by IRS personnel for other than criminal purposes, and then only to IRS personnel who are assisting the government attorney conducting the grand jury investigation.

(4) All information gathered during the course of the grand jury investigation remains under the custody and control of the grand jury, the United States Attorney's Office (or Strike Force office) or the Tax Division—including, for example, documentary evidence and copies,

---

i. I.e., voted for by at least twelve grand jurors.

j. See Internal Revenue Manual—Administration § 9267.3.

information obtained from witnesses, and information gathered from discussions with the government attorney conducting the investigation.

(5) All IRS personnel—even those on the highest management levels—who have had access to information obtained through the grand jury process must exclude themselves from involvement in non-grand jury matters concerning the individuals, entities, and subject matter of the grand jury investigation.

(6) Information gathered during the grand jury investigation may not be used for civil purposes without a court order pursuant to Rule 6(e) of the Federal Rules of Criminal Procedure specifically authorizing such civil use.

The procedures incident to a grand jury investigation are far more efficient for the prosecution and far more burdensome for the defense than those incident to an IRS investigation. There is no requirement that notice of any grand jury subpoena be provided to the subject of the investigation.[k] Witnesses must testify before the grand jury without the presence of their attorney and can consult with counsel only by leaving the room for this purpose. Objections to subpoenas and to questions asked of witnesses can be brought immediately to the attention of a district judge for prompt ruling, rather than made the subject of a separately instituted summons enforcement action. The investigation is controlled directly by government counsel rather than by agents of the IRS.

Because of the procedural differences, and because of the generally greater intensity and impact of a grand jury investigation, taxpayers frequently consider the possibility of objecting to the use of a grand jury to conduct what they argue is an administrative investigation. However, there is little that the subject of an investigation can do to tell the government how it must investigate his allegedly criminal activities.

UNITED STATES v. BAGGOT
Supreme Court of the United States, 1983.
463 U.S. 476, 103 S.Ct. 3164, 77 L.Ed.2d 785.

JUSTICE BRENNAN delivered the opinion of the Court.

In United States v. Sells Engineering, Inc.,[l] we decide today that in some circumstances the Government may obtain disclosure of grand jury materials for civil uses under Federal Rule of Criminal Procedure 6(e)(3)(C)(i) (hereinafter sometimes referred to as "(C)(i)"). The question in this case is whether an Internal Revenue Service investigation to determine a taxpayer's civil tax liability is "preliminar[y] to or in connection with a judicial proceeding" within the meaning of that Rule. We agree with the Court of Appeals that it is not.

---

k. Compare I.R.C. § 7609 regarding third-party recordkeeper summonses.

l. In United States v. Sells Engineering, Inc., 463 U.S. 418, 103 S.Ct. 3133, 77 L.Ed.2d 743 (1983), the Court held that the government was not automatically entitled under Rule 6(e) to use grand jury materials for civil purposes and, like private litigants, must first obtain a court order after demonstrating "particularized need" for the information.

In May 1976, a special grand jury began investigating certain commodity futures transactions on the Chicago Board of Trade. Respondent James E. Baggot became a target of the investigation. He was never indicted; instead, after interviews with IRS agents and plea negotiations with the Government, he pleaded guilty to two misdemeanor counts of violating the Commodities Exchange Act. The substance of Baggot's crime was a scheme to use sham commodities transactions to create paper losses, which he deducted on his tax returns. A fraction of the "losses" was then recovered in cash kickbacks which were not reported as income.

About eight months after Baggot's plea, the Government filed a (C)(i) motion for disclosure of grand jury transcripts and documents to the IRS, for its use in an audit to determine Baggot's civil income tax liability. At first the District Court denied the request. After two renewed motions, however, the Court granted disclosure. It held that some of the materials sought are not "matters occurring before the grand jury," and therefore not subject to Rule 6(e)'s requirement of secrecy. With respect to the remainder of the materials, the Court concluded that disclosure is not authorized by (C)(i) because the IRS's proposed civil tax investigation is not "preliminar[y] to or in connection with a judicial proceeding." Nevertheless, the Court allowed disclosure under its "general supervisory powers over the grand jury."

The Court of Appeals reversed. It held that all the materials sought, with one possible exception, are "matters occurring before the grand jury" and therefore subject to Rule 6(e). It agreed with the District Court that no disclosure is available under (C)(i), but it held that the District Court erred in granting disclosure under "general supervisory powers." It remanded the case for further consideration concerning the material that might not be "matters occurring before the grand jury." The Government sought certiorari, limited to the question of whether the IRS's civil tax audit is "preliminar[y] to or in connection with a judicial proceeding" under (C)(i). We granted certiorari.

The IRS is charged with responsibility to determine the civil tax liability of taxpayers. To this end, it conducts examinations or audits of taxpayers' returns and affairs. If, after the conclusion of the audit and any internal administrative appeals, the IRS concludes that the taxpayer owes a deficiency, it issues a formal notice of deficiency as prescribed by 26 U.S.C. § 6212. Upon receiving a notice of deficiency, the taxpayer has, broadly speaking, four options: (1) he can accept the IRS's ruling and pay the amount of the deficiency; (2) he can petition the Tax Court for a redetermination of the deficiency; (3) he can pay the amount of the deficiency and, after exhausting an administrative claim, bring suit for a refund in the Claims Court or in district court; or (4) he can do nothing and await steps by the IRS or the Government to collect the tax.

Certain propositions are common ground between the parties. Both sides, sensibly, understand the term "in connection with," in (C)(i), to refer to a judicial proceeding already pending, while "preliminarily to" refers to one not yet initiated. The Government concedes that an IRS audit, including its informal internal appeal component, is not itself a "judicial proceeding" within the meaning of the Rule. Conversely, Baggot agrees that either a Tax Court petition for redetermination or a suit for refund would be a "judicial proceeding." The issue, then, is whether disclosure for use in an IRS civil audit is "preliminar[y] to" a redetermination proceeding or a refund suit within the meaning of (C)(i). We conclude that it is not.

The provision in (C)(i) that disclosure may be made "preliminarily to or in connection with a judicial proceeding" is, on its face, an affirmative limitation on the availability of court-ordered disclosure of grand jury materials. In our previous cases under Rule 6(e), we have not had occasion to address this requirement in detail, focusing instead on the requirement that the moving party show particularized need for access to grand jury materials. See *Sells,* ante. The two requirements, though related in some ways, are independent prerequisites to (C)(i) disclosure. The particularized need test is a criterion of *degree;* the "judicial proceeding" language of (C)(i) imposes an additional criterion governing the *kind* of need that must be shown. It reflects a judgment that not every beneficial purpose, or even every valid governmental purpose, is an appropriate reason for breaching grand jury secrecy. Rather, the Rule contemplates only uses related fairly directly to some identifiable litigation, pending or anticipated. Thus, it is not enough to show that some litigation may emerge from the matter in which the material is to be used, or even that litigation is factually likely to emerge. The focus is on the *actual use* to be made of the material. If the primary purpose of disclosure is not to assist in preparation or conduct of a judicial proceeding, disclosure under (C)(i) is not permitted.

It follows that disclosure is not appropriate for use in an IRS audit of civil tax liability, because the purpose of the audit is not to prepare for or conduct litigation, but to assess the amount of tax liability through administrative channels. Assuming *arguendo* that this audit will inevitably disclose a deficiency on Baggot's part, there is no particular reason why that must lead to litigation, at least from the IRS's point of view. The IRS's decision is largely self-executing, in the sense that it has independent legal force of its own, without requiring prior validation or enforcement by a court. The IRS need never go into court to assess and collect the amount owed; it is empowered to collect the tax by non-judicial means (such as levy on property or salary, 26 U.S.C. §§ 6331, 6332), without having to prove to a court the validity of the underlying tax liability. Of course, the matter may end up in court if Baggot chooses to take it there, but that possibility does not negate the fact that the primary use to which the IRS proposes to put the materials it seeks is an extrajudicial one—the assessment of a tax deficiency by the IRS. The Government takes countless actions that affected citizens are permitted to resist or challenge in court. The fact that judicial redress may be sought, without more, does not mean that the Government's action is "preliminar[y] to a judicial proceeding." Of course, it may often be loosely said that the Government is "preparing for litigation," in the sense that frequently it will be wise for an agency to anticipate the chance that it may be called upon to defend its actions in court. That, however, is not alone enough to bring an administrative action within (C)(i). Where an agency's action does not require resort to litigation to accomplish the agency's present goal, the action is not preliminary to a judicial proceeding for purposes of (C)(i).

We need not decide whether an agency's action would always be preliminary to litigation if it arose under an administrative scheme that does require resort to courts—one in which, for example, the agency, when it found a probable violation of law, was required to bring a civil suit or criminal prosecution to vindicate the law and obtain compliance.[6] We also do not hold that the Government (or, for that matter, a private party who anticipates a suit or prosecution against him) may never obtain (C)(i) disclosure of grand jury materials any time the initiative for litigating lies elsewhere.[7] Nor do we hold that such a party must always await the actual commencement of litigation before obtaining disclosure. In In re Grand Jury Proceedings (Miller Brewing Co.), 687 F.2d 1079 (CA7 1982), rehearing pending, for example, the IRS had closed its audit and issued a notice of deficiency, and the taxpayer had clearly expressed its intention to seek redetermination of the deficiency in the Tax Court. The same Court that denied disclosure in this case correctly held in *Miller Brewing* that the IRS may seek (C)(i) disclosure. In such a case, the Government's primary purpose is

---

6. In particular, we find it unnecessary to address the complex contentions of the parties as to the level of likelihood of litigation that must exist before an administrative action is preliminary to litigation. Baggot points out that the purpose of an audit is to determine whether *or not* he owes any tax deficiency. Thus, he argues, the occurrence of litigation is contingent not only on his decision to contest an assessment, but on the outcome of the audit itself. He concludes that administrative investigations of this kind can never qualify as "preliminar[y] to a judicial proceeding," since to posit a judicial proceeding is to prejudge the very question supposedly being decided in the investigation. The Government counters that when the taxpayer has already pleaded guilty to a tax scam, the prospect of exoneration from civil liability is more theoretical than real. As a general matter, many an investigation, begun to determine *whether* there has been a violation of law, reaches a tentative affirmative conclusion on that question; at that point, the focus of the investigation commonly shifts to ascertaining the scope and details of the violation and building a case in support of any necessary enforcement action. We decline in this case to address how firm the agency's decision to litigate must be before its investigation can be characterized as "preliminar[y] to a judicial proceeding," or whether it can ever be so regarded before the conclusion of a formal preliminary administrative investigation.

7. We reject Baggot's argument that litigation is a remote contingency because, if a deficiency is assessed against him, he may simply choose to pay it, or to negotiate some settlement with the Government. The Government correctly points out that settlement (including settlement by surrender) is almost always a possibility. If some chance of settlement were enough to disqualify a case from eligibility for (C)(i) disclosure, there would be nothing left of the "preliminarily to" language of the Rule. There may conceivably be instances in which the chances of litigation are so low that it cannot be considered a realistic possibility, but this case at least is not such an instance.

plainly to use the materials sought to defend the Tax Court litigation, rather than to conduct the administrative inquiry that preceded it. There may be other situations in which disclosure is proper; we need not canvass the possibilities here. In this case, however, it is clear that the IRS's proposed use of the materials is to perform the non-litigative function of assessing taxes rather than to prepare for or to conduct litigation. Hence, no disclosure is available under (C)(i).

The judgment of the Court of Appeals is Affirmed.

Notes and Questions

1. Under the Supreme Court's decisions in *Baggot* and *Sells Engineering*, is the IRS precluded from using for civil purposes information the IRS developed before the beginning of a grand jury investigation but which was eventually presented to the grand jury during the criminal investigation? According to the court's holding in Sisk v. Commissioner, 791 F.2d 58 (6th Cir.1986), *Baggot* and *Sells Engineering* are not applicable in such a situation where the evidence was presented only to a grand jury and not at trial. In *Sisk*, the evidence brought before the grand jury was the IRS agent's report. The report was in the possession of the IRS before the grand jury investigation, and therefore, it was not derived from grand jury materials.

Additionally, the IRS is not prohibited from using information disclosed in a grand jury proceeding in connection with a guilty plea. In United States v. Manglitz, 773 F.2d 1463 (4th Cir.1985), the court held that *Sells* and *Baggot* do not require a blanket rule of secrecy regarding grand jury proceedings. The district court is not required to seal the record after every guilty plea in which a prosecutor discloses grand jury material, unless the prosecutor abuses his discretion. There are also exceptions under Rule 6(e) which permit disclosure of grand jury material both with and without court approval.

2. There are certain factual showings the IRS must make in order to obtain grand jury materials for use in a civil matter. First, the material sought is needed to avoid a possible injustice in another judicial proceeding; second, the need for disclosure is greater than the need for continued secrecy; and third, the request is structured to cover only material necessary. See In re Sealed Case, 801 F.2d 1379 (D.C.Cir.1986).

Where there has been unlimited release of grand jury information to one party in litigation, disclosure to the other party is in order not merely to assure the accuracy of the testimony but also to equalize the access to relevant facts which each side possesses and to eliminate the obvious unfair advantage.

SECTION 2. CASH TRANSACTION REPORTING AND ASSET FORFEITURE

Various criminal activities that have been resistant to traditional law enforcement techniques, especially drug trafficking, have spawned extensive statutory regulation in the past two decades. Perhaps the most famous of these is RICO, which is discussed in Chapter 9. Many of these illegal activities are currently identified and prosecuted under federal tax laws. As discussed below, enforcement of the cash transaction reporting requirements of the Code and the asset forfeiture laws affects not only the perpetrator of the alleged crimes, but also third parties who deal with the defendant, including bankers, lawyers, accountants and salesmen.

Although few would disagree with the need to wage a serious war on drugs, some observers fear the impact and sweep of the recent legislation and the courts' interpretations and applications of it. As the Eleventh Circuit observed, "at the core of [our system of government] lies the Constitution, with its guaranties of individuals' rights. We cannot permit these rights to become fatalities of the government's war on drugs." United States v. $38,000, 816 F.2d 1538, 1548–49 (11th Cir.1987).

Consider the following questions in connection with your study of the materials in this section.

Questions

A potential client visits Attorney Harper's office to discuss possible representation. The client states that he has not filed federal income tax returns for several years and that he fears possible indictment on drug trafficking and racketeering charges. He requests absolute secrecy regarding Harper's representation of him. The fee arrangement agreed upon is that the client will deed to Harper a condominium on the beach near Harper's residence and will immediately give Harper $11,000 in cash. The client hands over $6,000 in cash and promises the balance that afternoon. Harper sends the $6,000 cash to the firm's bank account that morning by messenger. Later in the day, the remaining $5,000 is delivered to Harper, who again sends it for deposit by messenger.

1. Are there any potential problems with this fee arrangement?
2. Can Harper keep the identity of the client totally secret?

A. MONEY LAUNDERING AND CASH TRANSACTION REPORTING

Broadly speaking, money laundering is the "sanitizing" of cash obtained from illegal activities. Money laundering allows the illegally obtained funds to enter the financial system without payment of tax on their receipt or identifying the owner. Although the asset forfeiture laws discussed later in this chapter are a formidable weapon in forcing illegally earned income to be disgorged, these laws operate "after the fact" in the sense that they permit seizure of the fruits of the crimes. In contrast, the money laundering and cash transaction reporting laws are designed to identify potential criminal activity as well as the fruits of actual criminal activity.

The basic thrust of the various money laundering and cash transaction reporting requirements is to destroy the secrecy of the identity of the participants, thus exposing them to potential criminal investigation to determine the source of the cash. Congress first addressed money laundering in 1970 when it enacted legislation that authorized the Treasury Department to issue regulations requiring financial institutions or others involved in a cash transaction exceeding $10,000 to file a currency transaction report ("CTR"). The regulations required only financial institutions to file CTRs. Shortly there developed numerous methods of circumventing the reporting requirements, such as the use of aliases, the use of numerous financial institutions each of which would receive less than $10,000, and the "structuring" of transactions within a single institution so that each single deposit was less than $10,000.

Courts struggled with the various loopholes that had developed but that were not clearly covered either by the Act or by the regulations. Congress responded with the Money Laundering Control Act of 1986, which made money laundering a crime and closed many of the loopholes that had been plaguing the courts.

On a separate front, Congress amended the Code in 1984 by adding section 6050I, which requires "any person" engaged in a "trade or business" to report receipts of more than $10,000 in "cash" in a transaction or a series of related transactions. The report is to be made on a Form 8300 and filed with the IRS Service Center in Detroit. A copy of the Form 8300 is in Appendix E.

Penalties for failure to comply with section 6050I. There are both civil and criminal penalties for failure to comply with section 6050I. The civil penalty is $50 per failure, up to an annual maximum of $250,000. For intentional failure to comply, the penalty was 10% of the aggregate of the items required to be reported with no maximum amount. In 1990, as part of the Omnibus Budget Reconciliation Act of 1990 ("OBRA 1990") Congress increased the civil penalty for intentional disregard of the section 6050I reporting requirement to mirror the civil penalty for failure to comply with Bank Secrecy Act reporting requirements. Thus, the penalty for intentional failures after October of 1990 is the greater of $25,000 or the amount of cash received in the transaction (but not to exceed $100,000).

The criminal penalties for failure to comply with section 6050I are quite stiff. Failure to file a Form 8300 is punishable as a felony under section 7203, with a maximum imprisonment of five years and a maximum fine of $25,000 ($100,000 for corporations). Recall that section 7203 is normally a misdemeanor statute, but an exception is made for failures to comply with section 6050I. Filing a false Form 8300 is a felony under section 7206(1).

"Cash" defined. Regulations issued under section 6050I defined "cash" as including both domestic and foreign coin and currency, but excluded such items as money orders, traveller's checks or other cash equivalents. In OBRA 1990 Congress directed the Treasury Department to issue new regulations not later than June 1, 1991 specifying

the types of cash equivalents that will henceforth be treated as "cash" for purposes of section 6050I. Personal checks with a face amount of less than $10,000 are not to be treated as "cash."

"Related transactions." According to Reg. § 1.6050I–1(c)(3)(ii), a "related transaction" that must be aggregated with another is one that occurs between a payer (or its agent) and the recipient within a 24-hour period. Both the statute and the regulations thereunder specifically prohibit "structuring" transactions to avoid aggregation, however. The same section of the regulations provides that "transactions conducted between a payer (or its agent) and a cash recipient during a period of more than 24 hours are related if the recipient knows or has reason to know that each transaction is one of a series of related transactions."

Information disclosed on Form 8300. The regulations require that the Form 8300 be used to comply with section 6050I. The information that must be disclosed by the cash recipient includes the name, address, and taxpayer identification number of the payer, the amount of cash received, the date and nature of the transaction, and any other information required to be furnished by instructions on the form. Reg. § 1.6050I–1(e). The Form 8300 must be filed by the 15th day after the cash is received. *Id.*

Notes

Returning to the question posed at the beginning of this section, can the attorney ensure that the client's identity is kept secret, or must the attorney comply with section 6050I and file a Form 8300 identifying the client? As of this writing, the answer to that question is unclear. Clearly the attorney received more than $10,000 in cash in related transactions in connection with the lawyer's trade or business. Should the "last link doctrine" of *Baird v. Koerner,* discussed in the following case, insulate the lawyer in a summons enforcement action (as opposed to a situation involving a grand jury subpoena)? If it does not apply, and the attorney must disclose the client's identity to the IRS, has the attorney become a government informant for her own client? At a minimum, a complete Form 8300 filed by a criminal defense lawyer indicates that the client thinks he has a legal problem and is paying the attorney in cash. Under these circumstances, an immediate investigation of the client, resulting in potential prosecution for tax evasion as well as other crimes, is a distinct possibility.

Some attorneys have filed incomplete Forms 8300, reporting the receipt of cash but omitting client identifying information. In a summons enforcement action brought to compel attorneys to disclose client identifying information in connection with incomplete Forms 8300, a case of first impression, one court held that the attorney-client privilege did *not* protect disclosure of the client identifying information. United States v. Goldberger & Dubin, 935 F.2d 501 (2d Cir.1991). Similarly, the Seventh Circuit held that neither the attorney-client privilege nor the Sixth Amendment prohibits the Service from issuing a summons to the taxpayer's lawyer seeking fee information, and that the lawyer must comply with the summons unless he can establish on a document-by-document basis why the requested information is privileged. Holifield v. United States, 909 F.2d 201 (7th Cir.1990).

In re GRAND JURY PROCEEDINGS 88–9 (MIA)
United States Court of Appeals, Eleventh Circuit, 1990.
899 F.2d 1039.

HATCHETT, CIRCUIT JUDGE:

In this recalcitrant witness case, we affirm, in part, the district court's finding of contempt of court against a lawyer who refused to testify, as ordered, before a grand jury seeking information regarding the identity of the lawyer's client and the receipt of fees.[1]

FACTS

On July 19, 1989, a federal grand jury in the Southern District of Florida issued a *subpoena duces tecum* ordering Jerald W. Newton, a lawyer, to appear before the grand jury and bring the financial documents related to an unidentified client, "John Doe." The government requested "[a]ny and all documents and records relating to the delivery, receipt and disbursement of cashier's check number 668917 in the amount of $30,200 dated 10/7/87, payable to [J]erald W. Newton, including but not limited to, cash receipts journal, cash disbursements journal, general ledger, invoices or other books of original entry."

Newton moved to quash the subpoena claiming that the subpoena sought information protected by the attorney-client privilege and the work product doctrine. John Doe, the client, moved to intervene and to quash the grand jury subpoena citing similar grounds and alleging that the subpoena violated his sixth amendment right to assistance of counsel.

In response to the motions, the government filed two sealed evidentiary submissions containing grand jury evidence protected from disclosure under Federal Rule of Criminal Procedure 6(e). The district court conducted an evidentiary hearing on the motions to quash, including an *in camera* presentation to determine the existence of the attorney-client relationship and to establish the confidential nature of the communications between Newton and John Doe. The government responded by

---

1. The government requested information along the following lines:

    1. Who gave the $30,200 cashier's check to Mr. Newton and with what services was this payment in connection?

    2. What is Newton's relationship with the remitter on the check, the third party beneficiary of the check, or the distributor of the check?

    3. How were the funds derived from the check subsequently disbursed and to whom and for what reason?

    4. What is the source of the $30,200 in funds as disclosed to Newton by any party?

    5. Did Mr. Newton handle any financial, business and/or loan transactions for any and all parties connected to the check?

    6. Questions related to the delivery of the check to Newton and whether Newton traveled to Florida to receive or transport funds on behalf of any party connected to the check.

presenting testimony *in camera* to establish the applicability of the crime-fraud exception.

On December 11, 1989, the district court denied the motions to quash the subpoena, ruling that the "necessary particularized showing of the asserted attorney-client privilege" had not been established. The district court further found that even if the attorney-client privilege existed, the government "fulfilled its consequent burden of making the requisite showings pursuant to the two-pronged test establishing the 'crime-fraud' exception." (Citing *In re Grand Jury Investigation (Schroeder)*, 842 F.2d 1223 (11th Cir.1987)). The district court granted John Doe's motion to intervene and denied his motion to quash the subpoena.

Procedural History

On March 7, 1990, the district court granted Newton use immunity and ordered him to testify and produce documents under the terms of 18 U.S.C. §§ 6002–6003. Later that day, Newton appeared before the grand jury in his personal capacity and as custodian of records for Jerald W. Newton, P.A. Newton refused to answer certain questions or to produce subpoenaed documents, claiming the attorney-client privilege. The government subsequently filed a motion requesting that the district court issue an order to show cause why Newton should not be held in contempt of court.

At a compulsion hearing on March 8, 1990, the district court ordered Newton to appear before the grand jury and provide complete answers to the questions and to produce the subpoenaed documents ruled on in the December 11, 1989 order on the motions to quash. When Newton stated that he would continue to refuse to answer those questions or provide the requested documents, the district court adjudged Newton to be in direct and continuing contempt for failure to obey the compulsion order. By agreement of the parties, the district court stayed execution of the contempt order pending the determination of this appeal. Newton filed a notice of appeal from the contempt order, and John Doe filed a notice of appeal from the compulsion order. This consolidated appeal follows.[2]

Contentions of the Parties

Newton contends that the identity of John Doe falls within the attorney-client privilege, pursuant to the "last link" doctrine. Because the government is unaware of the identity of John Doe, the issuer of the check, and unaware of the identity of the third party who sent the check, Newton argues that the government cannot establish the existence of the crime-fraud exception to the attorney-client privilege. According to Newton, the identity of his client is further protected by his obligation under the California Business and Professions Code,

---

2. For simplicity, we refer only to Newton as the appellant. Newton's client did not submit a separate brief.

§ 6068(e) to maintain the confidences and secrets of his client. Relying upon the ninth and tenth amendments reserving certain powers to the people and to the states, Newton, a member of the California bar, argues that the federal government may not interfere with the regulation of lawyers in California by requiring him to disclose information that the state of California deems privileged. Newton also contends that his refusal to testify is supported by the sixth amendment to the Constitution because the government was required to offer evidence of the necessity of obtaining the information requested and because the subpoena places Newton in an adversarial position against his client.

The government contends that the attorney-client privilege does not protect the information it seeks from Newton. The government contends that even if the attorney-client privilege applies, the district court properly found that the crime-fraud exception negates the privilege. The government also contends that the remaining constitutional claims are insufficient as a matter of law.

ISSUES

The issues in this case are (1) whether the district court properly ruled that the attorney-client privilege does not protect the information sought, and (2) whether the information sought is otherwise protected under either the sixth, ninth, or tenth amendments.

DISCUSSION

Because it involves a mixed question of law and fact, our standard of review for the district court's determination of the applicability of the attorney-client privilege is plenary. *See United States v. McConney,* 728 F.2d 1195, 1202 (9th Cir.) (*in banc*), *cert. denied,* 469 U.S. 824, 105 S.Ct. 101, 83 L.Ed.2d 46 (1984).

Attorney–Client Privilege

"The attorney-client privilege exists to protect confidential communications between client and lawyer made for the purpose of securing legal advice * * *." *In re Grand Jury Subpoena of Slaughter,* 694 F.2d 1258, 1260 (11th Cir.1982). This court's leading case on the attorney-client privilege is *United States v. Jones,* 517 F.2d 666 (5th Cir.1975).[3] *Jones* holds that a claim of attorney-client privilege requires proof of the following elements:

> (1) the asserted holder of the privilege is or sought to become a client; (2) the person to whom the communication was made (a) is [the] member of a bar of a court, or his subordinate and (b) in connection with this communication is acting as a lawyer; (3) the communication relates to a fact of which the attorney was informed (a) by his client (b) without the presence of strangers (c) for the purpose of securing primarily either (i) an opinion on law or (ii) legal services or (iii) assistance in some legal proceeding, and not (d) for the purpose of

---

3. In *Bonner v. City of Prichard,* 661 F.2d 1206 (11th Cir.1981) (in banc), the court adopted as precedent all decisions of the former Fifth Circuit Court of Appeals decided prior to October 1, 1981.

committing a crime or tort; and (4) the privilege has been (a) claimed and (b) not waived by the client.

Jones, 517 F.2d at 670 (quoting *United States v. United Shoe Machinery Corp.*, 89 F.Supp. 357, 358–59 (D.Mass.1950)).

The identity of a client and the receipt of fees from a client normally are not privileged. *Jones*, 517 F.2d at 671. In *Jones*, the court held that the identity of an unknown client is protected by the attorney-client privilege where disclosure of the identity would also reveal the privileged motive for the client to seek legal advice. *Jones*, 517 F.2d at 674–75. The government sought the names of unidentified clients who had paid substantial attorney's fees for certain *known* clients. Because the large amounts of the fee payments might incriminate the unidentified clients, the court found that "the income tax aspects of the government's inquiry demonstrate a strong independent motive for why the unidentified clients could be expected to (1) seek legal advice, and (2) reasonably anticipate that their names would be kept confidential." *Jones*, 517 F.2d at 674. *See Baird v. Koerner*, 279 F.2d at 633 (client identities not discoverable where disclosure of names would disclose motive [advice regarding underpayment of taxes] for retaining counsel). *See also United States v. Hodge and Zweig*, 548 F.2d 1347, 1353 (9th Cir.1977) (privilege exists "where the person invoking the privilege can show that a strong probability exists that disclosure of such information would implicate that client in the very criminal activity for which legal advice was sought.").

This exception to the normal rule that a client's identity is not privileged falls within what is known as the "last link" doctrine. Under the "last link" doctrine, the identity of a client may become privileged because "it may well be the link that could form the chain of testimony necessary to convict an individual of a federal crime." *Baird v. Koerner*, 279 F.2d 623, 633 (9th Cir.1960). Since *Jones*, this court has consistently held that the "last link" doctrine is only applicable to rare situations "where the disclosure of fee information would give the identity of a previously undisclosed client/suspect." *In re Grand Jury Subpoena of Slaughter*, 694 F.2d 1258, 1260 (11th Cir.1982). In essence, the last link doctrine extends the protection of the attorney-client privilege to nonprivileged information—the identity of the client—when "disclosure of that identity would disclose *other*, privileged communications (e.g., motive or strategy) and when the incriminating nature of the privileged communications has created in the client a reasonable expectation that the information would be kept confidential." *Rabin v. United States*, 896 F.2d 1267, 1273 (11th Cir.1990) (emphasis original).

The government is unaware of the identity of Newton's client and the third-party issuer of the $30,200 cashier's check. In addition to requesting the name of the unidentified client, the government seeks the name of the third-party check issuer, any information the client communicated to the lawyer concerning payment of the cashier's check, and any information the client communicated to the lawyer concerning two "other" individuals. Newton argues that his client's identity will provide the last link necessary to indict the client. According to Newton, disclosure of the client's name will provide additional privileged information about the client's relationship with the third-party issuer of the check, and possibly the client's relationship with the target of the government's money laundering investigation.

We hold that the district court properly ruled that the attorney-client privilege does not protect information concerning the client's name and the fees paid. On this record, we are not persuaded that disclosure of this usually nonprivileged information will reveal other privileged information. In fact, the appellant raises interesting legal arguments, but failed to establish in the district court the necessary facts to support the arguments. Because we hold that the attorney-client privilege does not apply to the information regarding client identity and fees, we do not reach the crime-fraud exception issue.

According to Newton, his client hired him in 1987 in connection with the client's indictment in a separate criminal matter. Thus, the client did not seek Newton's legal advice reasonably anticipating that his name would be kept confidential. In this case, disclosure of the client's identity will also reveal the fact of prior indictments or criminal record. Such records are public documents and thus not privileged. Disclosure of the client's identity also will link the client to the still unidentified third person who arranged for the payment of the attorney's fees.[4] The mere fact that "John Doe's" attorney's fees were paid by an unidentified third person, however, does not disclose privileged communications, motive, or strategy. On the record in this case, disclosure of the client's identity will merely reveal the client's name, and thus the identity is not protected by the attorney-client privilege.

Similarly, this circuit has consistently held that information concerning payment of attorney's fees is not generally privileged. Such information is privileged only if "more than simple fee information will necessarily come to light by compliance with the order, thereby uncovering privileged information." *Slaughter,* 694 F.2d at 1260. We therefore hold that Newton's client's name and the fees paid are not protected by the attorney-client privilege.

II. Ninth and Tenth Amendment Claims

Newton argues that disclosure of the information regarding client identity and fees would also breach the California state bar rules of confidentiality in violation of the ninth and tenth amendments to the United States Constitution. This argument fails because questions of attorney-client privilege in this circuit are governed by federal common law. "Under F.R.Crim.P. 26, the principles of the common law, 'as they may be interpreted by the courts of the United States in the light of

---

4. Before the grand jury, Newton testified that he did not know the name of the third person who called to ascertain whether the cashier's check had arrived.

reason and experience,' govern over state law in matters of evidence, which includes privileges." *Jones,* 517 F.2d at 670. A state's attorney-client privilege rules cannot prevent compelled disclosure where federal law precludes applicability of the common law privilege.

III. Sixth Amendment Claims

Newton also argues that the order to compel his testimony violates his client's sixth amendment right to counsel. He argues that the sixth amendment compels the government to make a preliminary showing that the information is essential and cannot be acquired through another source. This court has repeatedly rejected the argument that the sixth amendment requires the government to make a preliminary showing of relevance and need before a lawyer can be compelled to appear before a grand jury. We again decline to do so, despite contrary rulings in other circuits. *See, e.g., In re Special Grand Jury Number 81-1 (Harvey),* 676 F.2d 1005, *vacated* 697 F.2d 112, 113 (4th Cir.1982) (opinion vacated because Harvey became a fugitive).

Newton also argues that requiring disclosure in this case would violate his client's sixth amendment right to counsel of choice. Doe, however, has counsel at this time. Furthermore, nothing in the record indicates that, should disclosure be required, the relationship between Doe and Newton would be severed. Nor can we conclude from the record that, should the relationship be severed, Doe will be unable to secure other counsel. In virtually identical circumstances, this court held that such a sixth amendment claim was not ripe for adjudication. *See Rabin v. United States (In re Grand Jury Proceedings),* 896 F.2d 1267, 1277 (11th Cir.1990). We therefore hold that Newton's "sixth amendment right to counsel of choice" claim is not yet ripe for adjudication.

CONCLUSION

The district court properly found that the attorney-client privilege does not protect the client's identity or the fees paid—information which is generally nonprivileged—unless such information will reveal other, privileged information. Likewise, such information is not protected from disclosure under the sixth, ninth, or tenth amendments to the United States Constitution.

Having found that the district court properly ruled on the issues regarding client identity and fees, we remand this case to the district court to allow it to fully and separately address issues regarding other questions and documents.

Accordingly, we affirm the district court's finding of contempt and remand for further proceedings consistent with this opinion.

Affirmed and Remanded.

B. ASSET FORFEITURE

As discussed above, the money laundering and cash transaction reporting statutes are an important tool for the government's efforts to detect and punish those involved in such criminal activities as drug trafficking and gambling. Furthermore, as *Jones v. Commissioner* (Chapter 7, p. 337) illustrates, civil tax deficiencies and penalties for underreporting income are an almost inevitable result of investigations and prosecutions concerning illegal-source income. As the following materials demonstrate, a lawyer who represents a client under investigation for such activities may not be able to collect or retain the fees owed by such clients.

CAPLIN & DRYSDALE, CHARTERED v. UNITED STATES
Supreme Court of the United States, 1989.
491 U.S. 617, 109 S.Ct. 2646, 105 L.Ed.2d 528.

JUSTICE WHITE delivered the opinion of the Court.

We are called on to determine whether the federal drug forfeiture statute includes an exemption for assets that a defendant wishes to use to pay an attorney who conducted his defense in the criminal case where forfeiture was sought. Because we determine that no such exemption exists, we must decide whether that statute, so interpreted, is consistent with the Fifth and Sixth Amendments. We hold that it is.

I

In January 1985, Christopher Reckmeyer was charged in a multi-count indictment with running a massive drug importation and distribution scheme. The scheme was alleged to be a continuing criminal enterprise (CCE), in violation of 84 Stat. 1265, as amended, 21 U.S.C. § 848 (1982 ed., Supp. V). Relying on a portion of the CCE statute that authorizes forfeiture to the government of "property constituting, or derived from * * * proceeds * * * obtained" from drug-law violations, 21 U.S.C. § 853(a) (1982 ed., Supp. V),[1] the indictment sought forfeiture of specified assets in Reckmeyer's possession. At this time, the District Court, acting pursuant to 21 U.S.C. § 853(e)(1)(A),[2] entered a restrain-

---

1. The forfeiture statute provides, in relevant part, that any person convicted of a particular class of criminal offenses:

"shall forfeit to the United States, irrespective of any provision of State law—

"(1) any property constituting, or derived from, any proceeds the person obtained, directly or indirectly, as the result of such violation;

* * *

"The court, in imposing sentence on such person, shall order, in addition to any other sentence imposed * * * that the person forfeit to the United States all property described in this subsection." 21 U.S.C. § 853 (1982 ed., Supp. V).

There is no question here that the offenses respondent was accused of in the indictment fell within the class of crimes triggering this forfeiture provision.

2. The pretrial restraining order provision states that

"[u]pon application of the United States, the court may enter a restraining order or injunction * * * or take any other action to preserve the availability of property described in subsection (a) of [§ 853] for forfeiture under this section—

"(A) upon the filing of an indictment or information charging a violation * * * for which criminal forfeiture may be ordered under [§ 853] and alleging that the property with respect to which the order

ing order forbidding Reckmeyer to transfer any of the listed assets that were potentially forfeitable.

Sometime earlier, Reckmeyer had retained petitioner, a law firm, to represent him in the ongoing grand jury investigation which resulted in the January 1985 indictments. Notwithstanding the restraining order, Reckmeyer paid the firm $25,000 for preindictment legal services a few days after the indictment was handed down; this sum was placed by petitioner in an escrow account. Petitioner continued to represent Reckmeyer following the indictment.

On March 7, 1985, Reckmeyer moved to modify the District Court's earlier restraining order to permit him to use some of the restrained assets to pay petitioner's fees; Reckmeyer also sought to exempt from any postconviction forfeiture order the assets that he intended to use to pay petitioner. However, one week later, before the District Court could conduct a hearing on this motion, Reckmeyer entered a plea agreement with the Government. Under the agreement, Reckmeyer pleaded guilty to the drug-related CCE charge, and agreed to forfeit all of the specified assets listed in the indictment. The day after the Reckmeyer's plea was entered, the District Court denied his earlier motion to modify the restraining order, concluding that the plea and forfeiture agreement rendered irrelevant any further consideration of the propriety of the court's pretrial restraints. Subsequently, an order forfeiting virtually all of the assets in Reckmeyer's possession was entered by the District Court in conjunction with his sentencing.

After this order was entered, petitioner filed a petition under 21 U.S.C. § 853(n) (1982 ed., Supp. V), which permits third parties with an interest in forfeited property to ask the sentencing court for an adjudication of their rights to that property; specifically, § 853(n)(6)(B) gives a third party who entered into a bona fide transaction with a defendant a right to make claims against forfeited property, if that third party was "at the time of [the transaction] reasonably without cause to believe that the [defendant's assets were] subject to forfeiture." See also 21 U.S.C. § 853(c) (1982 ed., Supp. V). Petitioner claimed an interest in $170,000 of Reckmeyer's assets, for services it had provided Reckmeyer in conducting his defense; petitioner also sought the $25,000 being held in the escrow account, as payment for preindictment legal services. Petitioner argued alternatively that assets used to pay an attorney were exempt from forfeiture under § 853, and if not, the failure of the statute to provide such an exemption rendered it unconstitutional. The District Court granted petitioner's claim for a share of the forfeited assets.

A panel of the Fourth Circuit affirmed, finding that—while § 853 contained no statutory provision authorizing the payment of attorneys' fees out of forfeited assets—the statute's failure to do so impermissibly infringed a defendant's Sixth Amendment right to the counsel of his

is sought would, in the event of conviction, be subject to forfeiture under this section." 21 U.S.C. § 853(e)(1) (1982 ed., Supp. V).

choice. *United States v. Harvey,* 814 F.2d 905 (4th Cir.1987). The Court of Appeals agreed to hear the case en banc, and reversed. *In re Forfeiture Hearing as to Caplin & Drysdale, Chartered,* 837 F.2d 637 (4th Cir.1988). All the judges of the Fourth Circuit agreed that the language of the CCE statute acknowledged no exception to its forfeiture requirement that would recognize petitioner's claim to the forfeited assets. A majority found this statutory scheme constitutional, 837 F.2d, at 642–648; four dissenting judges, however, agreed with the panel's view that the statute so-construed violated the Sixth Amendment, *id.,* at 651–653 (Phillips, J., dissenting).

Petitioner sought review of the statutory and constitutional issues raised by the Court of Appeals' holding. We granted certiorari, 488 U.S. [940], 109 S.Ct. 363, 102 L.Ed.2d 352 (1988), and now affirm.

II

Petitioner's first submission is that the statutory provision that authorizes pretrial restraining orders on potentially forfeitable assets in a defendant's possession, 21 U.S.C. § 853(e), grants district courts equitable discretion to determine when such orders should be imposed. This discretion should be exercised under "traditional equitable standards," petitioner urges, including a "weigh[ing] of the equities and competing hardships on the parties"; under this approach, a court "must invariably strike the balance so as to allow a defendant [to pay] * * * for *bona fide* attorneys fees," petitioner argues. Brief for Petitioner 8. Petitioner further submits that once a district court so exercises its discretion, and fails to freeze assets that a defendant then uses to pay an attorney, the statute's provision for recapture of forfeitable assets transferred to third parties, 21 U.S.C. § 853(c), may not operate on such sums.

Petitioner's argument, as it acknowledges, is based on the view of the statute expounded by Judge Winter of the Second Circuit in his concurring opinion in that Court of Appeals' en banc decision, *United States v. Monsanto,* 852 F.2d 1400, 1405–1411 (2nd Cir.1988). We reject this interpretation of the statute today in our decision in *United States v. Monsanto, ante,* ___ U.S., at ___, 109 S.Ct., at ___, which reverses the Second Circuit's holding in that case. As we explain in our *Monsanto* decision, *ante,* at _____, 109 S.Ct., at _____ whatever discretion § 853(e) provides district court judges to refuse to enter pretrial restraining orders, it does not extend as far as petitioner urges—nor does the exercise of that discretion "immunize" nonrestrained assets from subsequent forfeiture under § 853(c), if they are transferred to an attorney to pay legal fees. Thus, for the reasons provided in our opinion in *Monsanto,* we reject petitioner's statutory claim.

III

We therefore address petitioner's constitutional challenges to the forfeiture law.[3] Petitioner contends that the statute infringes on crimi-

---

3. The Solicitor General argues that petitioner lacks *jus tertii* standing to advance Reckmeyer's Sixth Amendment rights. See Brief for United States 35, and n. 17.

nal defendants' Sixth Amendment right to counsel of choice, and upsets the "balance of power" between the government and the accused in a manner contrary to the Due Process Clause of the Fifth Amendment. We consider these contentions in turn.

A

Petitioner's first claim is that the forfeiture law makes impossible, or at least impermissibly burdens, a defendant's right "to select and be represented by one's preferred attorney." *Wheat v. United States,* 486 U.S. 153, 159, 108 S.Ct. 1692, 1697, 100 L.Ed.2d 140 (1988). Petitioner does not, nor could it defensibly do so, assert that impecunious defendants have a Sixth Amendment right to choose their counsel. The amendment guarantees defendants in criminal cases the right to adequate representation, but those who do not have the means to hire their own lawyers have no cognizable complaint so long as they are adequately represented by attorneys appointed by the courts. "[A] defendant may not insist on representation by an attorney he cannot afford." *Wheat, supra,* at 159, 108 S.Ct., at 1697. Petitioner does not dispute these propositions. Nor does the Government deny that the Sixth Amendment guarantees a defendant the right to be represented by an otherwise qualified attorney whom that defendant can afford to hire, or who is willing to represent the defendant even though he is without funds. Applying these principles to the statute in question here, we observe that nothing in § 853 prevents a defendant from hiring the attorney of his choice, or disqualifies any attorney from serving as a defendant's counsel. Thus, unlike *Wheat,* this case does not involve a

Though the argument is not without force, we conclude that petitioner has the requisite standing.

When a person or entity seeks standing to advance the constitutional rights of others, we ask two questions: first, has the litigant suffered some injury in fact, adequate to satisfy Article III's case-or-controversy requirement; and second, do prudential considerations which we have identified in our prior cases point to permitting the litigant to advance the claim? See *Singleton v. Wulff,* 428 U.S. 106, 112, 96 S.Ct. 2868, 2873, 49 L.Ed.2d 826 (1976). As to the first inquiry, there can be little doubt that petitioner's stake in $170,000 of the forfeited assets—which it would almost certainly receive if the Sixth Amendment claim it advances here were vindicated—is adequate injury-in-fact to meet the constitutional minimum of Article III standing.

The second inquiry—the prudential one—is more difficult. To answer this question, our cases have looked at three factors: the relationship of the litigant to the person whose rights are being asserted; the ability of the person to advance his own rights; and the impact of the litigation on third-party interests. See, *e.g., Craig v. Boren,* 429 U.S. 190, 196, 97 S.Ct. 451, 456, 50 L.Ed.2d 397 (1976); *Singleton v. Wulff, supra,* 428 U.S., at 113–118, 96 S.Ct., at 2873–2876; *Eisenstadt v. Baird,* 405 U.S. 438, 443–446, 92 S.Ct. 1029, 1033–1035, 31 L.Ed.2d 349 (1972). The second of these three factors counsels against review here: as *Monsanto, ante,* ___ U.S., at ___, 109 S.Ct., at ___, illustrates, a criminal defendant suffers none of the obstacles discussed in *Wulff, supra,* 428 U.S., at 116–117, 96 S.Ct., at 2875–2876, to advancing his own constitutional claim. We think that the first and third factors, however, clearly weigh in petitioner's favor. The attorney-client relationship between petitioner and Reckmeyer, like the doctor-patient relationship in *Baird,* is one of special consequence; and like *Baird,* it is credibly alleged that the statute at issue here may "materially impair the ability of" third persons in Reckmeyer's position to exercise their constitutional rights. See *Baird, supra,* 405 U.S., at 445, 92 S.Ct., at 1034. Petitioner therefore satisfies our requirements for *jus tertii* standing.

situation where the Government has asked a court to prevent a defendant's chosen counsel from representing the accused. Instead, petitioner urges that a violation of the Sixth Amendment arises here because of the forfeiture, at the instance of the Government, of assets that defendants intend to use to pay their attorneys.

Even in this sense, of course, the burden the forfeiture law imposes on a criminal defendant is limited. The forfeiture statute does not prevent a defendant who has nonforfeitable assets from retaining any attorney of his choosing. Nor is it necessarily the case that a defendant who possesses nothing but assets the Government seeks to have forfeited will be prevented from retaining counsel of choice. Defendants like Reckmeyer may be able to find lawyers willing to represent them, hoping that their fees will be paid in the event of acquittal, or via some other means that a defendant might come by in the future. The burden placed on defendants by the forfeiture law is therefore a limited one.

Nonetheless, there will be cases where a defendant will be unable to retain the attorney of his choice, when that defendant would have been able to hire that lawyer if he had access to forfeitable assets, and if there was no risk that fees paid by the defendant to his counsel would later be recouped under § 853(c).[4] It is in these cases, petitioner argues, that the Sixth Amendment puts limits on the forfeiture statute.

This submission is untenable. Whatever the full extent of the Sixth Amendment's protection of one's right to retain counsel of his choosing, that protection does not go beyond "the individual's right to spend his own money to obtain the advice and assistance of * * * counsel." Cf. *Walters' v. National Assn. of Radiation Survivors*, 473 U.S. 305, 370, 105 S.Ct. 3180, 3215, 87 L.Ed.2d 220 (1985) (Stevens, J., dissenting). A defendant has no Sixth Amendment right to spend another person's money for services rendered by an attorney, even if those funds are the only way that that defendant will be able to retain the attorney of his choice. A robbery suspect, for example, has no Sixth Amendment right to use funds he has stolen from a bank to retain an attorney to defend him if he is apprehended. The money, though in his possession, is not rightfully his; the government does not violate the Sixth Amendment if it seizes the robbery proceeds, and refuses to permit the defendant to use them to pay for his defense. "[N]o lawyer, in any case, * * * has the right to accept stolen property, or * * * ransom money, in payment of a fee * * *. The privilege to practice law is not a license to steal." *Laska v. United States*, 82 F.2d

---

4. That section of the statute, which includes the so-called "relation back" provision, states:

"All right, title, and interest in property described in [§ 853] vests in the United States upon the commission of the act giving rise to forfeiture under this section. Any such property that is subsequently transferred to a person other than the defendant may be the subject of a special verdict of forfeiture and thereafter shall be forfeited to the United States, unless the transferee [establishes his entitlement to such property pursuant to § 853(n) (discussed *supra*)]." 21 U.S.C. § 853(c) (1982 ed., Supp. V).

672, 677 (CA10 1936). Petitioner appears to concede as much, see Brief for Petitioner 40, n. 25, as respondent in *Monsanto* clearly does, see Brief for Respondent in No. 88–454, pp. 36–37.

Petitioner seeks to distinguish such cases for Sixth Amendment purposes by arguing that the bank's claim to robbery proceeds rests on "pre-existing property rights," while the Government's claim to forfeitable assets rests on a "penal statute" which embodies the "fictive property-law concept of * * * relation-back" and is merely "a mechanism for preventing fraudulent conveyances of the defendant's assets, not ... a device for determining true title to property." Brief for Petitioner 40–41. In light of this, petitioner contends, the burden placed on defendant's Sixth Amendment rights by the forfeiture statute outweighs the Government's interest in forfeiture. *Ibid.*

The premises of petitioner's constitutional analysis are unsound in several respects. First, the property rights given the Government by virtue of the forfeiture statute are more substantial than petitioner acknowledges. In § 853(c), the so-called "relation-back" provision, Congress dictated that "[a]ll right, title and interest in property" obtained by criminals via the illicit means described in the statute "vests in the United States upon the commission of the act giving rise to forfeiture." 21 U.S.C. § 853(c) (1982 ed., Supp. V). As Congress observed when the provision was adopted, this approach, known as the "taint theory," is one that "has long been recognized in forfeiture cases," including the decision in *United States v. Stowell*, 133 U.S. 1, 10 S.Ct. 244, 33 L.Ed. 555 (1890). See S.Rep. No. 98–225, p. 200, and n. 27 (1983). In *Stowell*, the Court explained the operation of a similar forfeiture provision (for violations of the Internal Revenue Code) as follows:

> "As soon [the possessor of the forfeitable asset committed the violation] of the internal revenue laws, the forfeiture under those laws took effect, and (though needing judicial condemnation to perfect it) operated from that time as a statutory conveyance to the United States of all the right, title, and interest then remaining in the [possessor]; and was as valid and effectual, against all the world, as a recorded deed. The right so vested in the United States could not be defeated or impaired by any subsequent dealings of the * * * [possessor]." *Stowell, supra*, at 19, 10 S.Ct., at 248.

In sum, § 853(c) reflects the application of the long-recognized and lawful practice of vesting title to any forfeitable assets, in the United States, at the time of the criminal act giving rise to forfeiture. Concluding that Reckmeyer cannot give good title to such property to petitioner because he did not hold good title is neither extraordinary or novel. Nor does petitioner claim, as a general proposition that the relation-back provision is unconstitutional, or that Congress cannot, as a general matter, vest title to assets derived from the crime in the Government, as of the date of the criminal act in question. Petitioner's claim is that whatever part of the assets that is necessary to pay attorney's fees cannot be subjected to forfeiture. But given the Government's title to Reckmeyer's assets upon conviction, to hold that the

Sixth Amendment creates some right in Reckmeyer to alienate such assets, or creates a right on petitioner's part to receive these assets, would be peculiar.

There is no constitutional principle that gives one person the right to give another's property to a third party, even where the person seeking to complete the exchange wishes to do so in order to exercise a constitutionally protected right. While petitioner and its supporting *amici* attempt to distinguish between the expenditure of forfeitable assets to exercise one's Sixth Amendment rights, and expenditures in the pursuit of other constitutionally protected freedoms, see, *e.g.,* Brief for the American Bar Association as *Amicus Curiae* 6, there is no such distinction between, or hierarchy among, constitutional rights. If defendants have a right to spend forfeitable assets on attorney's fees, why not on exercises of the right to speak, practice one's religion, or travel? The full exercise of these rights, too, depends in part on one's financial wherewithal; and forfeiture, or even the threat of forfeiture, may similarly prevent a defendant from enjoying these rights as fully as he might otherwise. Nonetheless, we are not about to recognize an antiforfeiture exception for the exercise of each such right; nor does one exist for the exercise of Sixth Amendment rights, either.[5]

Petitioner's "balancing analysis" to the contrary rests substantially on the view that the Government has only a modest interest in forfeitable assets that may be used to retain an attorney. Petitioner takes the position that, in large part, once assets have been paid over from client to attorney, the principal ends of forfeiture have been achieved: dispossessing a drug dealer or racketeer of the proceeds of his wrong-doing. See Brief for Petitioner 39; see also 814 F.2d, at 924–925. We think that this view misses the mark for three reasons.

First, the Government has a pecuniary interest in forfeiture that goes beyond merely separating a criminal from his illgotten gains; that legitimate interest extends to recovering *all* forfeitable assets, for such assets are deposited in a Fund that supports law-enforcement efforts in a variety of important and useful ways. See 28 U.S.C. § 524(c), which establishes the Department of Justice Assets Forfeiture Fund. The sums of money that can be raised for law-enforcement activities this way are substantial,[6] and the Government's interest in using the profits of crime to fund these activities should not be discounted.

---

5. It would be particularly odd to recognize the Sixth Amendment as a defense to forfeiture, because forfeiture is a substantive charge in the indictment against a defendant. Thus, petitioner asks us to take the Sixth Amendment's guarantee of counsel "for his defense," and make that guarantee *petitioner's defense* to the indictment. We doubt that the Amendment's guarantees, which are procedural in nature, cf. *Faretta v. California,* 422 U.S. 806, 818, 95 S.Ct. 2525, 2532, 45 L.Ed.2d 562 (1975), provide such a substantive defense to charges against an accused.

6. For example, just one of the assets which Reckmeyer agreed to forfeit, a parcel of land known as "Shelburne Glebe," see App. 57 (forfeiture order), was recently sold by federal authorities for $5.3 million. Washington Post, May 10, 1989, p. D1, cols. 1–4. The proceeds of the sale will fund federal, state, and local law enforcement activities. *Ibid.*

Second, the statute permits "rightful owners" of forfeited assets to make claims for forfeited assets before they are retained by the government. See 21 U.S.C. § 853(n)(6)(A). The Government's interest in winning undiminished forfeiture thus includes the objective of returning property, in full, to those wrongfully deprived or defrauded of it. Where the Government pursues this restitutionary end, the government's interest in forfeiture is virtually indistinguishable from its interest in returning to a bank the proceeds of a bank robbery; and a forfeiture-defendant's claim of right to use such assets to hire an attorney, instead of having them returned to their rightful owners, is no more persuasive than a bank robber's similar claim.

Finally, as we have recognized previously, a major purpose motivating congressional adoption and continued refinement of the RICO and CCE forfeiture provisions has been the desire to lessen the economic power of organized crime and drug enterprises. See *Russello v. United States,* 464 U.S. 16, 27–28, 104 S.Ct. 296, 302–303, 78 L.Ed.2d 17 (1983). This includes the use of such economic power to retain private counsel. As the Court of Appeals put it: "Congress has already underscored the compelling public interest in stripping criminals such as Reckmeyer of their undeserved economic power, and part of that undeserved power may be the ability to command high-priced legal talent." 837 F.2d, at 649. The notion that the government has a legitimate interest in depriving criminals of economic power, even in so far as that power is used to retain counsel of choice, may be somewhat unsettling. But when a defendant claims that he has suffered some substantial impairment of his Sixth Amendment rights by virtue of the seizure or forfeiture of assets in his possession, such a complaint is no more than the reflection of "the harsh reality that the quality of a criminal defendant's representation frequently may turn on his ability to retain the best counsel money can buy." *Morris v. Slappy,* 461 U.S. 1, 23, 103 S.Ct. 1610, 1622, 75 L.Ed.2d 610 (1983) (Brennan, J., concurring in result). Again, the Court of Appeals put it aptly: "The modern day Jean Valjean must be satisfied with appointed counsel. Yet the drug merchant claims that his possession of huge sums of money * * * entitles him to something more. We reject this contention, and any notion of a constitutional right to use the proceeds of crime to finance an expensive defense." 837 F.2d, at 649.[7]

---

7. We also reject the contention, advanced by amici, see, *e.g.,* Brief for Amicus Curiae of the American Bar Association as *Amicus Curiae* 20–22, and accepted by some courts considering claims like petitioner's, see, *e.g., United States v. Rogers,* 602 F.Supp. 1332, 1349–1350 (Col.1985), that a type of *"per se"* ineffective assistance of counsel results—due to the particular complexity of RICO or drug-enterprise cases—when a defendant is not permitted to use assets in his possession to retain counsel of choice, and instead must rely on appointed counsel. If such an argument were accepted, it would bar the trial of indigents charged with such offenses, because those persons would have to rely on appointed counsel—which this view considers *per se* ineffective.

If appointed counsel is ineffective in a particular case, a defendant has resort to the remedies discussed in *Strickland v. Washington,* 466 U.S. 668, 104 S.Ct. 2052, 80 L.Ed.2d 674 (1984). But we cannot say that the Sixth Amendment's guarantee of effective assistance of counsel is a guarantee of a privately-retained counsel in every

It is our view that there is a strong governmental interest in obtaining full recovery of all forfeitable assets, an interest that overrides any Sixth Amendment interest in permitting criminals to use assets adjudged forfeitable to pay for their defense. Otherwise, there would be an interference with a defendant's Sixth Amendment rights whenever the government freezes or takes some property in a defendant's possession before, during or after a criminal trial. So-called "jeopardy assessments"—IRS seizures of assets to secure potential tax liabilities, see 26 U.S.C. § 6861—may impair a defendant's ability to retain counsel in a way similar to that complained of here. Yet these assessments have been upheld against constitutional attack,[8] and we note that the respondent in Monsanto concedes their constitutionality. Moreover, petitioner's claim to a share of the forfeited assets postconviction would suggest that the government could never impose a burden on assets within a defendant's control that could be used to pay a lawyer.[9] Criminal defendants, however, are not exempted from federal, state, and local taxation simply because these financial levies may deprive them of resources that could be used to hire an attorney.

We therefore reject petitioner's claim of a Sixth Amendment right of criminal defendants to use assets that are the government's—assets adjudged forfeitable, as Reckmeyer's were—to pay attorneys' fees, merely because those assets are in their possession.[10] See also *Monsan-*

---

complex case, irrespective of a defendant's ability to pay.

8. See, *e.g., Avco Delta Corporation Canada Ltd. v. United States,* 484 F.2d 692 (CA7 1973); *Summers v. United States,* 250 F.2d 132, 133–135 (CA9 1957); *United States v. Brodson,* 241 F.2d 107, 109–111 (CA7 1957) (en banc).

9. A myriad of other law-enforcement mechanisms operate in a manner similar to IRS jeopardy assessments, and might also be subjected to Sixth Amendment invalidation if petitioner's claim were accepted. See Brickey, Attorneys' Fee Forfeitures, 36 Emory L.J. 761, 770–772 (1987).

10. Petitioner advances three additional reasons for invalidating the forfeiture statute, all of which concern possible ethical conflicts created for lawyers defending persons facing forfeiture of assets in their possession. See Brief for Petitioner 35–37; see also Brief for the American Bar Association as *Amicus Curiae* 17–22.

Petitioner first notes the statute's exemption from forfeiture of property transferred to a bona fide purchaser who was "reasonably without cause to believe that the property was subject to forfeiture." 21 U.S.C. § 853(n)(6)(B). This provision, it is said, might give an attorney an incentive not to investigate a defendant's case as fully as possible, so that the lawyer can invoke it to protect from forfeiture any fees he has received. Yet given the requirement that any assets which the Government wishes to have forfeited must be specified in the indictment, see Fed.Rule Crim. Proc. 7(c)(2), the only way a lawyer could be a beneficiary of § 853(n)(6)(B) would be to fail to read the indictment of his client. In this light, the prospect that a lawyer might find himself in conflict with his client, by seeking to take advantage of § 853(n)(6)(B), amounts to very little. Petitioner itself concedes that such a conflict will, as a practical matter, never arise: a defendant's "lawyer * * * could not demonstrate that he was 'reasonably without cause to believe that the property was subject to forfeiture,' " petitioner concludes at one point. Brief for Petitioner 31.

The second possible conflict arises in plea bargaining: petitioner posits that a lawyer may advise a client to accept an agreement entailing a more harsh prison sentence but no forfeiture—even where contrary to the client's interests—in an effort to preserve the lawyer's fee. Following such a strategy, however, would surely constitute ineffective assistance of counsel. We see no reason why our cases such as *Strickland v. Washington,* 466 U.S. 668, 104 S.Ct. 2052, 80 L.Ed.2d 674 (1984), are inadequate to deal with any such ineffectiveness where it arises. In any event,

to, ante, [491] U.S., at [616], 109 S.Ct., at [2666], which rejects a similar claim with respect to pretrial orders and assets not yet judged forfeitable.

B

Petitioner's second constitutional claim is that the forfeiture statute is invalid under the Due Process Clause of the Fifth Amendment because it permits the Government to upset the "balance of forces between the accused and his accuser." *Wardius v. Oregon,* 412 U.S. 470, 474, 93 S.Ct. 2208, 2212, 37 L.Ed.2d 82 (1973). We are not sure that this contention adds anything to petitioner's Sixth Amendment claim, because, while "[t]he Constitution guarantees a fair trial through the Due Process Clauses * * * it defines the basic elements of a fair trial largely through the several provisions of the Sixth Amendment," *Strickland v. Washington,* 466 U.S. 668, 684–685, 104 S.Ct. 2052, 2062–2063, 80 L.Ed.2d 674 (1984). We have concluded above that the Sixth Amendment is not offended by the forfeiture provisions at issue here. Even if, however, the Fifth Amendment provides some added protection not encompassed in the Sixth Amendment's more specific provisions, we find petitioner's claim based on the Fifth Amendment unavailing.

Forfeiture provisions are powerful weapons in the war on crime; like any such weapons, their impact can be devastating when used unjustly. But due process claims alleging such abuses are cognizable only in specific cases of prosecutorial misconduct (and petitioner has made no such allegation here) or when directed to a rule that is inherently unconstitutional. "The fact that the * * * Act might operate unconstitutionally under some conceivable set of circumstances is insufficient to render it * * * invalid," *United States v. Salerno,* 481 U.S. 739, 745, 107 S.Ct. 2095, 2100, 95 L.Ed.2d 697 (1987). Petitioner's claim—that the power available to prosecutors under the statute *could* be abused—proves too much, for many tools available to prosecutors can be misused in a way that violates the rights of innocent persons. As the Court of Appeals put it, in rejecting this claim when advanced below: "Every criminal law carries with it the potential for abuse, but there is no claim that such conduct occurred here, nor could there be, as Reckmeyer's plea agreement included forfeiture of virtually every asset in his possession. Moreover, we rejected a claim similar to this one in *Evans v. Jeff D.,* 475 U.S. 717, 727–728, 106 S.Ct. 1531, 1537–1538, 89 L.Ed.2d 747 (1986).

Finally, petitioner argues that the forfeiture statute, in operation, will create a system akin to "contingency fees" for defense lawyers: only a defense lawyer who wins acquittal for his client will be able to collect his fees, and contingent fees in criminal cases are generally considered unethical. See ABA Model Rules of Professional Conduct, Rule 1.5(d)(2) (1983); ABA Model Code of Professional Responsibility DR 2-106(C) (1979). But there is no indication here that petitioner, or any other firm, has actually sought to charge a defendant on a contingency basis; rather the claim is that a law firm's prospect of collecting its fee may turn on the outcome at trial. This, however, may often be the case in criminal defense work. Nor is it clear why permitting contingent fees in criminal cases—if that is what the forfeiture statute does—violates a criminal defendant's Sixth Amendment rights. The fact that a federal statutory scheme authorizing contingency fees—again, if that is what Congress has created in § 853 (a premise we doubt)—is at odds with model disciplinary rules or state disciplinary codes hardly renders the federal statute invalid.

a potential for abuse does not require a finding of facial invalidity." 837 F.2d, at 648.

We rejected a claim similar to petitioner's last Term, in *Wheat v. United States,* 486 U.S. 153, 108 S.Ct. 1692, 100 L.Ed.2d 140 (1988). In *Wheat,* the petitioner argued that permitting a court to disqualify a defendant's chosen counsel because of conflicts of interest—over that defendant's objection to the disqualification—would encourage the government to "manufacture" such conflicts to deprive a defendant of his chosen attorney. *Wheat, supra,* at 163, 108 S.Ct. at 1699. While acknowledging that this was possible, we declined to fashion the *per se* constitutional rule petitioner sought in *Wheat,* instead observing that "trial courts are undoubtedly aware of [the] possibility" of abuse, and would have to "take it into consideration," when dealing with disqualification motions.

A similar approach should be taken here. The Constitution does not forbid the imposition of an otherwise permissible criminal sanction, such as forfeiture, merely because in some cases prosecutors may abuse the processes available to them, *e.g.,* by attempting to impose them on persons who should not be subjected to that punishment. Cf. *Brady v. United States,* 397 U.S. 742, 751, and n. 8, 90 S.Ct. 1463, 1470, and n. 8, 25 L.Ed.2d 747 (1970). Cases involving particular abuses can be dealt with individually by the lower courts, when (and if) any such cases arise.

IV

For the reasons given above, we find that petitioner's statutory and constitutional challenges to the forfeiture imposed here are without merit. The judgment of the Court of Appeals is therefore *affirmed.*

JUSTICE BLACKMUN, with whom JUSTICE BRENNAN, JUSTICE MARSHALL, and JUSTICE STEVENS join, dissenting.*

Those jurists who have held forth against the result the majority reaches in these cases have been guided by one core insight: that it is unseemly and unjust for the Government to beggar those it prosecutes in order to disable their defense at trial. The majority trivializes "the burden the forfeiture law imposes on a criminal defendant." Instead, it should heed the warnings of our district court judges, whose day-to-day exposure to the criminal-trial process enables them to understand, perhaps far better than we, the devastating consequences of attorney's fee forfeiture for the integrity of our adversarial system of justice.

The criminal-forfeiture statute we consider today could have been interpreted to avoid depriving defendants of the ability to retain private counsel—and should have been so interpreted, given the grave "constitutional and ethical problems" raised by the forfeiture of funds used to pay legitimate counsel fees. *United States v. Badalamenti,* 614 F.Supp.

* This dissent is to both *Caplin & Drysdale* and its companion case, *United States v. Monsanto.*

194, 196 (SDNY 1985). But even if Congress in fact required this substantial incursion on the defendant's choice of counsel, the Court should have recognized that the Framers stripped Congress of the power to do so when they added the Sixth Amendment to our Constitution.

I

The majority acknowledges, as it must, that *no* language in the Comprehensive Forfeiture Act of 1984 expressly provides for the forfeiture of attorney's fees, and that the legislative history contains no substantive discussion of the question.[2] The fact that "the legislative history and congressional debates are similarly silent on the use of forfeitable assets to pay stockbroker's fees, laundry bills, or country club memberships," 109 S.Ct., at 2663, means nothing, for one cannot believe that Congress was unaware that interference with the payment of attorney's fees, unlike interference with these other expenditures, would raise Sixth Amendment concerns.

Despite the absence of any indication that Congress intended to use the forfeiture weapon against legitimate attorney's fees, the majority—all the while purporting to "respect" the established practice of construing a statute to avoid constitutional problems, contends that it is constrained to conclude that the Act reaches attorney's fees. The Court cannot follow its usual practice here, we are told, because this is not a "close cas[e]" in which "statutory language is ambiguous." *Ibid.* The majority finds unambiguous language in § 853(a) of the Act, which provides that when a defendant is convicted of certain crimes, the defendant "shall forfeit to the United States" any property derived from proceeds of the crime or used to facilitate the crime. I agree that § 853(a) is broad in language and is cast in mandatory terms.[3] But I do not agree with the majority's conclusion that the lack of an express exemption for attorney's fees in § 853(a) makes the Act *as a whole* unambiguous.

The majority succeeds in portraying the Act as "unambiguous" by making light of its most relevant provisions. As Judge Winter observed, the broad mandatory language of § 853(a) applies by its terms only to "'any person convicted' of the referenced crimes." *United States v. Monsanto,* 852 F.2d 1400, 1410 (CA2 1988). Because third parties to whom assets have been transferred in return for services

---

2. Indeed, the strongest statement on the question is the comment in the House Report: "Nothing in this section is intended to interfere with a person's Sixth Amendment right to counsel." H.R.Rep. No. 98-845, pt. 1, p. 19, n. 1 (1984). Even if the majority were correct that this statement is "nothing more than an exhortation for the courts to tread carefully in this delicate area," *United States v. Monsanto, ante,* [491] U.S., at [608], n. 8, 109 S.Ct., at 2662, n. 8, the majority does not explain why it proceeds to ignore Congress' exhortation to construe the statute to avoid implicating Sixth Amendment concerns.

3. As the majority acknowledges, so did Judge Winter, whose interpretation of the Act Caplin & Drysdale and Monsanto adopt in their briefs to this Court. See *Monsanto, ante,* 491 U.S., at 608, 109 S.Ct., at 2662; *United States v. Monsanto,* 852 F.2d 1400, 1409–1410 (CA2 1988) (en banc) (Winter, J., concurring).

rendered are not "persons convicted," however, forfeiture of property in *their* possession is controlled by § 853(c) rather than by § 853(a). Section 853(c) provides: "Any such property that is subsequently transferred to a person other than the defendant *may be the subject of a special verdict of forfeiture* and thereafter shall be ordered forfeited to the United States" (emphasis added) if the third party fails to satisfy certain requirements for exemption. Thus, § 853(c) does not, like § 853(a), provide that all property defined as forfeitable under § 853 "must" or "shall" be forfeited: forfeitable property held by a third party presumptively "shall be ordered forfeited" only if it is included in the special verdict, and its inclusion in the verdict is discretionary.[5]

There is also considerable room for discretion in the language of § 853(e)(1), which controls the Government's use of post-indictment protective orders to prevent the pre-conviction transfer of potentially forfeitable assets to third parties. That section provides:

> "Upon application of the United States, the court *may enter a restraining order or injunction* * * * or take any other action to preserve the availability of property * * * for forfeiture under this section * * * upon the filing of an indictment or information charging a violation * * * for which criminal forfeiture may be ordered * * * and alleging the property with respect to which the order is sought would, in the event of conviction, be subject to forfeiture under this section" (emphasis added).

The Senate Report makes clear that a district court may hold a hearing to "consider factors bearing on the reasonableness of the order sought." S.Rep. No. 98–225, p. 202 (1983), 1984 U.S.Code Cong. & Admin.News pp. 3182, 3385. Even if the court chooses to enter an order *ex parte* at the Government's request, it may "modify the order" if it later proves to be unreasonable. *Id.,* at 203, 1984 U.S.Code Cong. & Admin.News at 3386. In the course of this process, the court may also consider the circumstances of any third party whose interests are implicated by the restraining order. Thus, the Government does not have an absolute right to an order preserving the availability of property by barring its transfer to third parties. Pre-conviction injunctive relief is available, but at the discretion of the district court.

---

5. That the Act is mandatory in its treatment of forfeiture of property in the defendant's hands, but not in its treatment of property transferred to third parties, is consistent with the distinction between civil forfeiture and criminal forfeiture. The theory (or, more properly, the fiction) underlying civil forfeiture is that the property subject to forfeiture is itself tainted by having been used in an unlawful manner. The right of the Government to take possession does not depend on the Government's ultimately convicting the person who used the property in an unlawful way, nor is it diminished by the innocence or bona fides of the party into whose hands the property falls. See *United States v. Stowell,* 133 U.S. 1, 10 S.Ct. 244, 33 L.Ed. 555 (1890). Criminal forfeiture, in contrast, is penal in nature: it is predicated on the adjudicated guilt of the defendant, and has punishment of the defendant as its express purpose. See generally Cloud, Forfeiting Defense Attorneys' Fees: Applying an Institutional Role Theory to Define Individual Constitutional Rights, 1987 Wis. L.Rev. 1, 18–19 (Forfeiting Fees). Where the purpose of forfeiture is to punish the defendant, the Government's penal interests are weakest when the punishment also burdens third parties.

The majority does not deny that §§ 853(c) and 853(e)(1) contain discretionary language. It argues, however, that the exercise of discretion must be "cabined by the purposes" of the Act. *Monsanto,* ante, 109 S.Ct., at 2665. That proposition, of course, is unassailable: I agree that discretion created by the Act cannot be used to defeat the purposes of the Act. The majority errs, however, in taking an overly broad view of the Act's purposes.

Under the majority's view, the Act aims to preserve the availability of *all* potentially forfeitable property during the pre-conviction period, and to achieve the forfeiture of *all* such property upon conviction. *Monsanto,* ante, 109 S.Ct., at 2665. This view of the Act's purposes effectively writes all discretion out of §§ 853(c) and 853(e)(1), because any exercise of discretion will diminish the Government's post-conviction "take." But a review of the legislative history of the Act demonstrates that the Act does not seek forfeiture of property for its own sake merely to maximize the amount of money the Government collects.[6] The central purposes of the Act, properly understood, are fully served by an approach to forfeiture that leaves ample room for the exercise of statutory discretion.

Congress' most systemic goal for criminal forfeiture was to prevent the profits of criminal activity from being poured into future such activity, for "it is through economic power that [criminal activity] is sustained and grows." Senate Report, at 191. "Congress recognized in its enactment of statutes specifically addressing organized crime and illegal drugs that the conviction of individual racketeers and drug dealers would be of only limited effectiveness if the economic power bases of criminal organizations or enterprises were left intact, and so included forfeiture authority designed to strip these offenders and organizations of their economic power." *Ibid.;* see also H.R.Rep. No. 98–845, pt. 1, p. 6 (1984) (criminal forfeiture statutes are "a bold attempt to attack the economic base of the criminal activity").[7]

---

6. In adopting this view of the Act, the majority ignores the Government's concession at oral argument before the en banc Second Circuit Court of Appeals that the Act was not enacted as a revenue-raising measure. See *United States v. Monsanto,* 852 F.2d, at 1407 and n. 1 (Winter, J., concurring). Thus, although the Government's interest in "using the profits of crime to fund [law-enforcement] activities" should perhaps not be "discounted," *Caplin & Drysdale,* ante, [491] U.S., at [631], 109 S.Ct., at 2654, it is not dispositive. Nor does Congress' willingness to return forfeited funds to victims of crime instead of using them for law-enforcement purposes indicate that restitution is a primary goal of the Act. See *ibid.* Restitution, in any event, is not a likely result in the typical case for which the Act was designed: one in which the property forfeited consists of derivative proceeds of illegal activity, rather than of stolen property that is readily traceable to a particular victim. See Forfeiting Fees, 1987 Wis.L.Rev., at 20.

7. The majority contends that "the desire to lessen the economic power of organized crime and drug-enterprises * * * includes the use of such economic power to retain private counsel." *Caplin & Drysdale,* ante, [491] U.S., at [630], 109 S.Ct., at 2654-2655. "The notion that the Government has a legitimate interest in depriving criminals"—*before they are convicted*—"of economic power, even in so far as that power is used to retain counsel of choice" is more than just "somewhat unsettling," as the majority suggests. *Ibid.* That notion is constitutionally suspect, and—equally important for present purposes—completely foreign to Congress' stated goals. The purpose of the relation-back

Congress also had a more traditional punitive goal in mind: to strip convicted criminals of all assets purchased with the proceeds of their criminal activities. Particularly in the area of drug trafficking, Congress concluded that crime had become too lucrative for criminals to be deterred by conventional punishments. "Drug dealers have been able to accumulate huge fortunes as a result of their illegal activities. The sad truth is that the financial penalties for drug dealing are frequently only seen by dealers as a cost of doing business." House Report, at 2. The image of convicted drug dealers returning home from their prison terms to all the comforts their criminal activity can buy is one Congress could not abide.[8]

Finally, Congress was acutely aware that defendants, if unhindered, routinely would defeat the purposes of the Act by sheltering their assets in order to preserve them for their own future use and for the continued use of their criminal organizations. The purpose of § 853(c) is to "to permit the voiding of certain pre-conviction transfers and so close a potential loophole in current law whereby the criminal forfeiture sanction could be avoided by transfers that were not 'arms' length' transactions." Senate Report, at 200–201, 1984 U.S.Code Cong. & Admin.News at 3383–3384.

With these purposes in mind, it becomes clear that a district court acts within the bounds of its statutory discretion when it exempts from pre-conviction restraint and post-conviction forfeiture those assets a defendant needs to retain private counsel for his criminal trial. Assets used to retain counsel by definition will be unavailable to the defendant or his criminal organization after trial, even if the defendant is eventually acquitted. See Cloud, Government Intrusions Into the Attorney–Client Relationship: The Impact of Fee Forfeitures on the Balance of Power in the Adversary System of Criminal Justice, 36 Emory L.J. 817, 832 (1987) (*Intrusions*). Thus, no important and legitimate purpose is served by employing § 853(c) to require post-conviction forfeiture of funds used for legitimate attorney's fees, or by employing § 853(e)(1) to bar pre-conviction payment of fees. The Government's interests are adequately protected so long as the district court supervises transfers to the attorney to make sure they are made in good faith.[9] See Comment,

provision is to assure that assets *proved at trial* to be the product of criminal activity cannot be channeled into further criminal activity—not to strip defendants of their assets on no more than a showing of probable cause that they are "tainted." See *United States v. Bassett*, 632 F.Supp., at 1316; Comment, 61 N.Y.U.L.Rev. 124, 139 (1986). For its contrary view, the majority relies on nothing more than the rhetoric of the en banc Court of Appeals' majority opinion in *Caplin & Drysdale*.

8. Congress' desire to maximize punishment, however, cannot be viewed as a blanket authorization of government action that punishes the defendant before he is proved guilty.

9. Judge Winter noted that the same logic suggests that the forfeiture of assets the defendant uses to support himself and his family is unduly harsh and is not necessary to achieve the goals of the Act. *United States v. Monsanto*, 852 F.2d, at 1405. The majority chides Judge Winter for suggesting that, once it is established that there is discretion to exclude assets used to pay attorney's fees and normal living expenses from forfeiture, the necessary result is that such assets *must* be excluded. *Monsanto, ante,* ___ U.S., at ___–___, 109 S.Ct., at 2664–2665. I find it

61 N.Y.U.L.Rev. 124, 138–139 (1986). All that is lost is the Government's power to punish the defendant before he is convicted. That power is not one the Act intended to grant.[10]

A careful analysis of the language of the Act and its legislative history thus proves that "a construction of the statute is fairly possible by which the [constitutional] question may be avoided." *Crowell v. Benson*, 285 U.S. 22, 62, 52 S.Ct. 285, 297, 76 L.Ed. 598 (1932).[11] Indeed, the prudentially preferable construction is also the only one that gives full effect to the discretionary language in §§ 853(c) and 853(e)(1). Thus, "if anything remains of the canon that statutes capable of differing interpretations should be construed to avoid constitutional issues * * * it surely applies here." *United States v. Monsanto*, 852 F.2d, at 1409.

II

The majority has decided otherwise, however, and for that reason is compelled to reach the constitutional issue it could have avoided. But the majority pauses hardly long enough to acknowledge "the Sixth Amendment's protection of one's right to retain counsel of his choos-

---

exceedingly unlikely that a district court, instructed that it had the discretion to permit a defendant to retain counsel, would ever choose not to do so. Normal equitable considerations, combined with a proper regard for Sixth Amendment interests, would weigh so strongly in favor of that result that any "slippage" from permissive to mandatory language on Judge Winter's part seems to me entirely accurate as a predictive matter.

10. The majority states in *Monsanto, ante,* ___ U.S., at ___-___, 109 S.Ct., at 2664, that another forfeiture statute contemporaneous with the Act contains "the *precise* exemption from forfeiture which respondent asks us to imply into § 853," and suggests that this is evidence that "Congress understood what it was doing in omitting such an exemption" from the Act. This argument is makeweight. The express exemption to which the majority refers involves the use of proceeds from publications and other accounts of a crime to:

"(i) satisfy a money judgment rendered in any court in favor of a victim of any offense for which such defendant has been convicted, or a legal representative of such victim; and

(ii) pay for legal representation of the defendant in matters *arising from the offense for which such defendant has been convicted,* but no more than 20 percent of the total proceeds may be so used." Pub.L. 98–473, § 1406(a), 98 Stat. 2175, codified as 18 U.S.C. § 3681 (1982 ed., Supp. V) (emphasis added).

When this provision is read in context, it is clear that it concerns payment of attorney's fees related to post-conviction civil suits brought against convicted defendants by their victims. It does not, therefore, constitute the "*precise* exemption" sought in these cases. Indeed, the provision cuts against the result the majority reaches. In light of Congress' decision to permit a convicted criminal to use wealth he has obtained by publicizing his crime to hire counsel to resist his victim's damages claims, it would be bizarre to think that Congress intended to be *more* punitive when it comes to a defendant's need for counsel *prior* to conviction, when the defendant's own liberty is at stake.

11. For this reason, I need not rely on *NLRB v. Catholic Bishop of Chicago,* 440 U.S. 490, 500, 99 S.Ct. 1313, 1318, 59 L.Ed.2d 533 (1979), in which the Court held that even the broadest statutory language may be interpreted as excluding cases that would raise serious constitutional questions, absent a clear expression of an affirmative intention of Congress to include those cases. See also *Edward J. DeBartolo Corp. v. Florida Gulf Coast Building & Construction Trades Council,* 485 U.S. 568, 108 S.Ct. 1392, 99 L.Ed.2d 645 (1988). Under the *Catholic Bishop* approach, however, there could be no doubt that "the required 'clearest indication in the legislative history'" or statutory language is absent here. 485 U.S., at 579, 108 S.Ct. at [1399].

ing," let alone to explore its "full extent." *Caplin & Drysdale, ante,* 109 S.Ct., at 2652. Instead, *ante,* 109 S.Ct., at 2651–2652, it moves rapidly from the observation that "a defendant may not insist on representation by an attorney he cannot afford," *Wheat v. United States,* 486 U.S. 153, 161, 108 S.Ct. 1692, [1698], 100 L.Ed.2d 140 (1988), to the conclusion that the Government is free to deem the defendant indigent by declaring his assets "tainted" by criminal activity the Government has yet to prove. That the majority implicitly finds the Sixth Amendment right to counsel of choice so insubstantial that it can be outweighed by a legal fiction demonstrates, still once again, its " 'apparent unawareness of the function of the independent lawyer as a guardian of our freedom.' " See *id.,* at [172], 108 S.Ct., at 1704 (Stevens, J., dissenting).

A

Over 50 years ago, this Court observed: "It is hardly necessary to say that the right to counsel being conceded, a defendant should be afforded a fair opportunity to secure counsel of his own choice." *Powell v. Alabama,* 287 U.S. 45, 53, 53 S.Ct. 55, 58, 77 L.Ed. 158 (1932). For years, that proposition was settled; the controversial question was whether the defendant's right to use his own funds to retain his chosen counsel was the outer limit of the right protected by the Sixth Amendment. See, *e.g., Chandler v. Fretag,* 348 U.S. 3, 9, 75 S.Ct. 1, 4, 99 L.Ed. 4 (1954). The Court's subsequent decisions have made clear that an indigent defendant has the right to appointed counsel, see, *e.g., Gideon v. Wainwright,* 372 U.S. 335, 83 S.Ct. 792, 9 L.Ed.2d 799 (1963), and that the Sixth Amendment guarantees at least minimally effective assistance of counsel, see, *e.g., Strickland v. Washington,* 466 U.S. 668, 104 S.Ct. 2052, 80 L.Ed.2d 674 (1984). But while court appointment of effective counsel plays a crucial role in safeguarding the fairness of criminal trials, it has never defined the outer limits of the Sixth Amendment's demands. The majority's decision in this case reveals that it has lost track of the distinct role of the right to counsel of choice in protecting the integrity of the judicial process, a role that makes "the right to be represented by privately retained counsel * * * the primary, preferred component of the basic right" protected by the Sixth Amendment. *United States v. Harvey,* 814 F.2d 905, 923 (CA4 1987), rev'd *sub nom. In re Forfeiture Hearing as to Caplin & Drysdale,* 837 F.2d 637 (CA4 1988) (en banc).

The right to retain private counsel serves to foster the trust between attorney and client that is necessary for the attorney to be a truly effective advocate. See ABA Standards for Criminal Justice 4–3.1, p. 4–29 (commentary) (2d ed. 1980). Not only are decisions crucial to the defendant's liberty placed in counsel's hands, see *Faretta v. California,* 422 U.S. 806, 95 S.Ct. 2525, 45 L.Ed.2d 562 (1975), but the defendant's perception of the fairness of the process, and his willingness to acquiesce in its results, depend upon his confidence in his counsel's dedication, loyalty, and ability. When the Government insists upon the right to choose the defendant's counsel for him, that relationship of trust is undermined: counsel is too readily perceived as the Government's agent rather than his own. Indeed, when the Court in *Faretta* held that the Sixth Amendment prohibits a court from imposing appointed counsel on a defendant who prefers to represent himself, its decision was predicated on the insight that "[t]o force a lawyer on a defendant can only lead him to believe that the law contrives against him." 422 U.S., at 834, 95 S.Ct., at 2540.

The right to retain private counsel also serves to assure some modicum of equality between the Government and those it chooses to prosecute. The Government can be expected to "spend vast sums of money * * * to try defendants accused of crime," *Gideon v. Wainwright,* 372 U.S., at 344, 83 S.Ct., at 796, and of course will devote greater resources to complex cases in which the punitive stakes are high. Precisely for this reason, "there are few defendants charged with crime, few indeed, who fail to hire the best lawyers they can get to prepare and present their defenses." *Ibid.* But when the Government provides for appointed counsel, there is no guarantee that levels of compensation and staffing will be even average.[12] Where cases are complex, trials long, and stakes high, that problem is exacerbated. "Despite the legal profession's commitment to *pro bono* work," *United States v. Bassett,* 632 F.Supp. 1308, 1316 (Md.1986), aff'd on other grounds *sub nom. United States v. Harvey,* 814 F.2d 905 (CA4 1987), even the best-intentioned of attorneys may have no choice but to decline the task of representing defendants in cases for which they will not receive adequate compensation. See, *e.g., United States v. Rogers,* 602 F.Supp. 1332, 1349 (Colo.1985). Over the long haul, the result of lowered compensation levels will be that talented attorneys will "decline to enter criminal practice * * * This exodus of talented attorneys could devastate the criminal defense bar." Winick, Forfeiture of Attorneys' Fees under RICO and CCE and the Right to Counsel of Choice: The Constitutional Dilemma and How to Avoid It, 43 U.Miami L.Rev. 765, 781 (1989). Without the defendant's right to retain private counsel, the Government too readily could defeat its adversaries simply by outspending them.[13]

The right to privately chosen and compensated counsel also serves broader institutional interests. The "virtual socialization of criminal defense work in this country" that would be the result of a widespread

---

12. "Even in the federal courts under the Criminal Justice Act of 1964, 18 U.S.C. § 3006A, which provides one of the most generous compensation plans, the rates for appointed counsel * * * are low by American standards. Consequently, the majority of persons willing to accept appointments are the young and inexperienced." *Argersinger v. Hamlin,* 407 U.S. 25, 57, n. 21, 92 S.Ct. 2006, 2022, n. 21, 32 L.Ed.2d 530 (1972) (Powell, J., concurring in result). Indeed, there is evidence that "Congress did not design [the Criminal Justice Act] to be compensatory, but merely to reduce financial burdens on assigned counsel." See Winick, Forfeiture of Attorneys' Fees under RICO and CCE and the Right to Counsel of Choice: The Constitutional Dilemma and How to Avoid It, 43 U.Miami L.Rev. 765, 773 and n. 40 (1989).

13. That the Government has this power when the defendant is indigent is unfortunate, but "[i]t is an irrelevancy once recognized." *United States v. Harvey,* 814 F.2d, at 923.

abandonment of the right to retain chosen counsel, too readily would standardize the provision of criminal-defense services and diminish defense counsel's independence. There is a place in our system of criminal justice for the maverick and the risk-taker, for approaches that might not fit into the structured environment of a public defender's office, or that might displease a judge whose preference for nonconfrontational styles of advocacy might influence the judge's appointment decisions. There is also a place for the employment of "specialized defense counsel" for technical and complex cases. The choice of counsel is the primary means for the defendant to establish the kind of defense he will put forward. Only a healthy, independent defense bar can be expected to meet the demands of the varied circumstances faced by criminal defendants, and assure that the interests of the individual defendant are not unduly "subordinat[ed] * * * to the needs of the system."

In sum, our chosen system of criminal justice is built upon a truly equal and adversarial presentation of the case, and upon the trust that can exist only when counsel is independent of the Government. Without the right, reasonably exercised, to counsel of choice, the effectiveness of that system is imperilled.

B

Had it been Congress' express aim to undermine the adversary system as we know it, it could hardly have found a better engine of destruction than attorney's-fee forfeiture. The main effect of forfeitures under the Act, of course, will be to deny the defendant the right to retain counsel, and therefore the right to have his defense designed and presented by an attorney he has chosen and trusts.[14] If the Government restrains the defendant's assets before trial, private counsel will be unwilling to continue or to take on the defense. Even if no restraining order is entered, the possibility of forfeiture after conviction will itself substantially diminish the likelihood that private counsel will agree to take the case. The "message [to private counsel] is 'Do not represent this defendant or you will lose your fee.' That being the kind of message lawyers are likely to take seriously, the defendant will find it difficult or impossible to secure representation." *United States v. Badalamenti,* 614 F.Supp., at 196.

* * *

14. There is reason to fear that, in addition to depriving a defendant of counsel of choice, there will be circumstances in which the threat of forfeiture will deprive the defendant of *any* counsel. If the Government chooses not to restrain transfers by employing § 853(e)(1), it is likely that the defendant will not qualify as "indigent" under the Criminal Justice Act. Potential private counsel will be aware of the threat of forfeiture, and, as a result, will likely refuse to take the case. Although it is to be hoped that a solution will be developed for a defendant who "falls between the cracks" in this manner, there is no guarantee that accommodation will be made in an orderly fashion, and that trial preparation will not be substantially delayed because of the difficulties in securing counsel. For discussions of this problem, see *United States v. Ianniello,* 644 F.Supp., at 456–457; *United States v. Badalamenti,* 614 F.Supp., at 197.

Even if the defendant finds a private attorney who is "so foolish, ignorant, beholden or idealistic as to take the business," *id.*, at 196, the attorney-client relationship will be undermined by the forfeiture statute. Perhaps the attorney will be willing to violate ethical norms by working on a contingent fee basis in a criminal case. See *Caplin & Drysdale, ante,* 109 S.Ct., at 2656, n. 10. But if he is not—and we should question the integrity of any criminal-defense attorney who would violate the ethical norms of the profession by doing so—the attorney's own interests will dictate that he remain ignorant of the source of the assets from which he is paid. Under § 853(c), a third-party transferee may keep assets if "the transferee establishes . . . that he is a bona fide purchaser for value of such property who at the time of purchase was reasonably without cause to believe that the property was subject to forfeiture under this section." The less an attorney knows, the greater the likelihood that he can claim to have been an "innocent" third party. The attorney's interest in knowing nothing is directly adverse to his client's interest in full disclosure. The result of the conflict may be a less vigorous investigation of the defendant's circumstances, leading in turn to a failure to recognize or pursue avenues of inquiry necessary to the defense. Other conflicts of interest are also likely to develop. The attorney who fears for his fee will be tempted to make the Government's waiver of fee-forfeiture the *sine qua non* for any plea agreement, a position which conflicts with his client's best interests.

Perhaps most troubling is the fact that forfeiture statutes place the Government in the position to exercise an intolerable degree of power over any private attorney who takes on the task of representing a defendant in a forfeiture case. The decision whether to seek a restraining order rests with the prosecution, as does the decision whether to waive forfeiture upon a plea of guilty or a conviction at trial. The Government will be ever tempted to use the forfeiture weapon against a defense attorney who is particularly talented or aggressive on the client's behalf—the attorney who is better than what, in the Government's view, the defendant deserves. The spectre of the Government's selectively excluding only the most talented defense counsel is a serious threat to the equality of forces necessary for the adversarial system to perform at its best. An attorney whose fees are potentially subject to forfeiture will be forced to operate in an environment in which the Government is not only the defendant's adversary, but also his own.

The long-term effects of the fee-forfeiture practice will be to decimate the private criminal-defense bar. As the use of the forfeiture mechanism expands to new categories of federal crimes and spreads to the States, only one class of defendants will be free routinely to retain private counsel: the affluent defendant accused of a crime that generates no economic gain. As the number of private clients diminishes, only the most idealistic and the least skilled of young lawyers will be attracted to the field, while the remainder seek greener pastures elsewhere.

Sec. 2   CASH TRANSACTION & ASSET FORFEITURE   693

In short, attorney's-fee forfeiture substantially undermines every interest served by the Sixth Amendment right to chosen counsel, on the individual and institutional levels, over the short term and the long haul.

C

We have recognized that although there is a "presumption in favor of [the defendant's] counsel of choice," the right to counsel of choice is not absolute. Some substantial and legitimate governmental interests may require the courts to disturb the defendant's choice of counsel, as "[w]hen a defendant's selection of counsel, under the particular facts and circumstances of a case, gravely imperils the prospect of a fair trial," or threatens to undermine the orderly disposition of the case. But never before today has the Court suggested that the Government's naked desire to deprive a defendant of "the best counsel money can buy," *Caplin & Drysdale, ante,* 109 S.Ct., at 2655, is itself a legitimate government interest that can justify the Government's interference with the defendant's right to chosen counsel—and for good reason. "[W]eakening the ability of an accused to defend himself at trial is an advantage for the government. But it is not a legitimate government interest that can be used to justify invasion of a constitutional right." *United States v. Monsanto,* 852 F.2d, at 1403 (Feinberg, C.J., concurring). And the *legitimate* interests the Government asserts are extremely weak, far too weak to justify the Act's substantial erosion of the defendant's Sixth Amendment rights.

The Government claims a property interest in forfeitable assets, predicated on the relation-back provision, § 853(c), which employs a legal fiction to grant the Government title in all forfeitable property as of the date of the crime. The majority states: "Permitting a defendant to use assets for his private purposes that, under this provision, will become the property of the United States if conviction occurs, cannot be sanctioned." *Monsanto, ante,* [491] U.S., at [613], 109 S.Ct., at 2665. But the Government's insistence that it has a paramount interest in the defendant's resources "simply begs the constitutional question rather than answering it. Indeed, the ultimate constitutional issue might well be framed precisely as whether Congress may use this wholly fictive device of property law to cut off this fundamental right of the accused in a criminal case. If the right must yield here to countervailing governmental interests, the relation-back device undoubtedly could be used to implement the governmental interests, but surely it cannot serve as a substitute for them." *In re Forfeiture Hearing as to Caplin & Drysdale,* 837 F.2d 637, 652 (CA4 1988) (en banc) (dissenting opinion).

Furthermore, the relation-back fiction gives the Government no property interest whatsoever in the defendant's assets before the defendant is convicted. In most instances, the assets the Government attempts to reach by using the forfeiture provisions of the Act are derivative proceeds of crime, property that was not itself acquired illegally, but was purchased with the profits of criminal activity. Prior to conviction, sole title to such assets—not merely possession, as is the case in the majority's bank robbery example, *Caplin & Drysdale,* 109 S.Ct., at 2652–2653—rests in the defendant; no other party has any present legal claim to them.[15] Yet it is in the preconviction period that the forfeiture threat (or the force of a § 853(e)(1) restraining order) deprives the defendant of use of the assets to retain counsel. The Government's interest in the assets at the time of their restraint is no more than an interest in safeguarding fictive property rights, one which hardly weighs at all against the defendant's formidable Sixth Amendment right to retain counsel for his defense.

Finally, even if the Government's asserted interests were entitled to some weight, the manner in which the Government has chosen to protect them undercuts its position. Under § 853(c), a third-party transferee may keep assets if he was "reasonably without cause to believe that the property was subject to forfeiture." Most legitimate providers of services will meet the requirements for this statutory exemption. The exception is the defendant's attorney, who cannot do his job (or at least cannot do his job well) without asking questions that will reveal the source of the defendant's assets. It is difficult to put great weight on the Government's interest in increasing the amount of property available for forfeiture when the means chosen are so starkly underinclusive, and the burdens fall almost exclusively upon the exercise of a constitutional right.[16]

---

15. Other analogies the majority and the Government have drawn are also inapt. We do not deal with contraband, which the Government is free to seize because the law recognizes no right to possess it. See *One 1958 Plymouth Sedan v. Pennsylvania,* 380 U.S. 693, 699, 85 S.Ct. 1246, 1250, 14 L.Ed.2d 170 (1965). Nor do we deal with instrumentalities of crime, which may have evidentiary value, and may also traditionally be seized by the Government and retained even if the defendant is not proved guilty, unless a party with a rightful claim to the property comes forward to refute the Government's contention that the property was put to an unlawful use. See *Calero–Toledo v. Pearson Yacht Leasing Co.,* 416 U.S. 663, 679, 94 S.Ct. 2080, 2089, 40 L.Ed.2d 452 (1974); Comment, 48 U.Chi.L.Rev. 960, 963–964 (1981). As to the analogy to "jeopardy assessments" under the Internal Revenue Code, the IRS in that situation has a legal claim to the sums at issue at the time of the assessment, based upon substantive provisions of the Code. Here, in contrast, the Government's claim will not arise until after conviction. In addition, even if a jeopardy assessment were to deprive a taxpayer of the funds necessary to file a challenge to the assessment in the Tax Court, the proceeding in that court is civil, and the Sixth Amendment therefore does not apply. I agree with Judge Phillips when he observes that the constitutionality of a jeopardy assessment that deprived the defendant of the funds necessary to hire counsel to ward off a criminal challenge is not to be assumed. See *United States v. Harvey,* 814 F.2d, at 926.

16. Certainly criminal defendants "are not exempted from federal, state, and local taxation simply because these financial levies may deprive them of resources that could be used to hire an attorney." *Caplin & Drysdale, ante,* [491] U.S., at [631], 109 S.Ct., at 2655. The Government's interest in raising revenue need not stand aside merely because the individual being taxed would rather spend the money by participating in a constitutionally protected activity. But I doubt that we would hesitate to reject as an undue burden on the exercise of a constitutional right a system that generally exempted personal-service transactions from taxation, but taxed payments to criminal-defense attorneys. In such circumstances, a clear-headed analysis of the Government's action would likely reveal that burdening the exercise of the defendant's Sixth Amendment right was not the

Interests as ephemeral as these should not be permitted to defeat the defendant's right to the assistance of his chosen counsel.

III

In my view, the Act as interpreted by the majority is inconsistent with the intent of Congress, and seriously undermines the basic fairness of our criminal-justice system. That a majority of this Court has upheld the constitutionality of the Act as so interpreted will not deter Congress, I hope, from amending the Act to make clear that Congress did not intend this result. This Court has the power to declare the Act constitutional, but it cannot thereby make it wise.

I dissent.

Notes

1. Defense counsel in *Caplin & Drysdale* argued that allowing forfeiture of attorney's fees would impede defendants' ability to hire defense counsel. As of this writing, former Panamanian dictator General Manuel Noriega, imprisoned in the United States awaiting trial on numerous drug trafficking and money laundering offenses, continues to be affected by the asset forfeiture rules. According to the National Law Journal (June 25, 1990, p. 13):

> The four lawyers defending General Manuel Noriega recently asked to be allowed to resign from the defense. According to their statement, the case was threatening to bankrupt them. The government had claimed that all of Mr. Noriega's assets were derived from illegal activities and, under federal law, could be frozen before the trial or, if not frozen before the trial, could be seized by the government after the trial if Mr. Noriega was convicted. The defense lawyers negotiated with the government lawyers in the hope that they would allow some of Mr. Noriega's wealth to be used to pay for his defense. When the negotiations failed, the defense lawyers asked the Court either to free some of the money or free them.

2. Until relatively recently, forfeiture in this country was an *in rem* civil action against the property. Today, however, civil actions relating to drug enforcement are governed by the Controlled Substances Act, which is frequently used to bring civil forfeiture actions against money, vehicles, real property and other fruits of drug proceeds. In civil forfeiture actions, seizure occurs at the beginning of the proceeding, rather than after an adjudication on the merits of the government's case. Criminal conviction is not a prerequisite, and acquittal in a criminal case will not necessarily prevent a civil forfeiture.

In civil forfeiture actions, the government need only show probable cause to believe that the property in question is related to the illegal activity. Once probable cause has been shown, the defendant must then establish the inappropriateness of allowing seizure of the property. Suppose that the alleged illegal activity was the sale of $500 of illegal drugs and that the government brings a civil forfeiture action against property

unfortunate consequence of the Government's action, but its very purpose.

worth $50,000. Can the defense prevail on a claim that the proposed seizure would violate the Eighth Amendment's "proportionality of punishment" requirement? *See* United States v. Tax Lot 1500, 861 F.2d 232 (9th Cir.1988) (holding that the Eighth Amendment provided no defense).

3. The government is currently using the civil forfeiture laws to thwart the operations of the Colombian drug trafficking network known as the Medellin Cartel. The following discussion is based on Claimants' Omnibus Memorandum of Law in Support of Motions to Dismiss, filed on May 30, 1990, in United States v. Eighty-Eight Accounts, 740 F.Supp. 842 (S.D.Fla.1990) (referred to as the "Omnibus Memorandum").

In 1989 the government obtained indictments against members of the Cartel and a Panamanian financial institution, charging the defendants with various drug and money laundering offenses. As part of the indictment the government sought forfeiture of hundreds of specified bank accounts that were allegedly owned or controlled by the defendants. More than a year later, the government brought a massive civil forfeiture action seeking the freezing of approximately 690 accounts and an unspecified number of related accounts, all of which were in addition to the accounts identified in the indictment. According to the Omnibus Memorandum, "the accounts ultimately frozen pursuant to this motion included the primary operating accounts of both the Republic of China and Merrill Lynch, Pierce, Fenner & Smith, Inc. * * * "

Although the motion was granted, it was later amended based on the court's finding that the government, pursuant to a portion of the order requiring the financial institutions involved to supply the government with all information in their custody concerning such accounts, was using the order solely for discovery purposes. Finding such use of the restraining order improper, the order was dissolved as to the accounts not named in the indictment.

Later the government instituted a civil forfeiture action in Florida seeking seizure of 72 of the accounts named in the indictment plus an unspecified number of "related" accounts. In support of its efforts to seize these accounts, the government submitted the same affidavits it had submitted in connection with the earlier proceedings, but which by this time were at least partially discredited. Three weeks after it filed the civil forfeiture application in Florida, the government amended its complaint to seek seizure of 88 designated accounts, including the 72 accounts named in the indictment and 16 accounts that were designated as "related." Counsel for the account owners moved to dismiss, alleging *inter alia* prosecutorial misconduct, abuse of process and failure to establish probable cause linking the accounts to the alleged illegal activity. The court denied the motion to dismiss, finding that the skeletal facts alleged by the government were sufficient to establish probable cause to support any legal theory of forfeiture, which was all it was required to do.

SECTION 3. CRIMINAL TAX PROSECUTIONS

A criminal tax prosecution is neither more nor less than a federal criminal case in which the alleged violation happens to pertain to the internal revenue laws. There are, nevertheless, a number of aspects of federal criminal practice which are of particular interest in the context of tax prosecutions. In this section, a sampling of these subjects is provided.

A. VENUE

The basic rule is that venue for a federal criminal prosecution lies in the district in which the offense was committed.[m] Hence, when the prosecution is for a failure to file returns, the prosecution may be brought in the district in which the return should have been filed. This could be either the district in which the legal residence or principal place of business of the taxpayer was located, or the district in which the IRS service center serving the accused taxpayer was located.[n] When the offense is attempted evasion, the filing of a false return or conspiracy, there may be more than one district in which the prosecution may be brought. Thus, in an evasion case, the prosecution might properly be brought in the district in which the false return was filed, signed or prepared, or in which some other affirmative act of fraud was committed.[o] Moreover, in a conspiracy prosecution, proper venue lies in any district in which any overt act in furtherance of the conspiracy was committed.

Once a prosecution is brought in a district of proper venue, the defendant may seek to transfer the case to another district. As in all federal criminal cases, transfer in a tax case can be sought for plea and sentencing,[p] for prejudice in the district,[q] or "for the convenience of parties and witnesses, and in the interest of justice."[r] However, in certain tax prosecutions there is a special statutory provision which gives the defendant the right to have the case transferred to the district in which he was residing at the time the alleged offense was committed.[s] In cases in which the statute is applicable, the defendant's right to transfer is absolute.

UNITED STATES v. UNITED STATES DISTRICT COURT
United States Court of Appeals, Ninth Circuit, 1982.
693 F.2d 68.

PER CURIAM.

The government petitions for a writ of mandamus, seeking to overturn a district court order transferring certain counts of a tax evasion indictment to the district where some of the defendants reside. The wording of 18 U.S.C. § 3237(b) compels us to deny the petition.

m. Fed.R.Crim.P. 18.
n. See I.R.C. § 6091. See United States v. Garman, 748 F.2d 218 (4th Cir.1984).
o. 18 U.S.C.A. § 3237(a) (West 1985). See United States v. Marchant, 774 F.2d 888 (8th Cir.1985).

p. Fed.R.Crim.P. 20(a).
q. Fed.R.Crim.P. 21(a).
r. Fed.R.Crim.P. 21(b).
s. 18 U.S.C.A. § 3237(b) (West 1985).

In May 1982, the government filed an 89-count indictment in the Southern District of California (San Diego), charging five defendants with a conspiracy to defraud the United States. In addition, the indictment raised numerous substantive tax evasion counts against the defendants individually. The indictment described a continuing program of tax evasion devised by the defendants, organized and operated from San Diego.

Virtually all the alleged activity connected with the scheme took place in or around San Diego. Tax returns of the defendants and the other individuals investing in the "tax shelters" established by the defendants were mailed to the Internal Revenue Service (IRS) Center in Fresno, which is in the Eastern District of California. Two of the defendants, Nicoladze and De Julio, resided in the San Francisco Bay Area, in the Northern District of California.

These two defendants filed a timely motion under 18 U.S.C. § 3237(b) to transfer venue as to them to the Northern District of California because of their residence therein. After extensive briefing and argument, the district court granted the change of venue as to the substantive counts against them, while retaining the conspiracy count in San Diego. The government then conditionally stipulated to the transfer of additional counts against two other defendants to the Northern District. The charges against the remaining defendant, a resident of San Diego, and conspiracy charges against another were kept in the Southern District.

Faced with the prospect of conducting two potentially lengthy trials instead of one, the government then petitioned this Court for a writ of mandamus to review the order granting the transfer as to Nicoladze and De Julio.

Our disposition turns on the interpretation of 18 U.S.C. § 3237(b) (1976), which provides in pertinent part:

> Notwithstanding subsection (a), * * * where an offense involves use of the mails and is an offense described in section 7201 or 7206(1), (2), or (5) of * * * [the Internal Revenue] Code * * * and prosecution is begun in a judicial district other than the district in which the defendant resides, he may upon motion filed in the district in which the prosecution is begun, elect to be tried in the district in which he was residing at the time the alleged offense was committed * * *.

The principal inquiry concerns the meaning of the phrase "involves use of the mails". It is undisputed that all the various tax returns encompassed by the indictment in this case were mailed to the IRS Center in Fresno. The defendants argued that this fact was literally sufficient to bring the case within § 3237(b). The government, however, urges a much more restrictive reading of the phrase.

The government contends that the phrase should be confined to situations where the prosecution relies upon the fact of mailing to lay venue in a particular district. In support of its theory, the government invites us to examine the legislative history of the statute, and in particular certain remarks made by Congressman Preston of Georgia, the sponsor of the bill that ultimately became § 3237(b).[2]

Under prior law, where tax evasion events took place in one district ("District A"), and the tax returns were mailed to an IRS office in another district ("District B"), the government had the option of bringing the prosecution in either District A or B. Congressman Preston introduced H.R. 8252, 85th Cong., 2d Sess. (1958) to prevent government abuse of such situations, where the prosecution was brought in a district far from the taxpayer's home simply because of the location of the IRS office.

The original motivation behind 18 U.S.C. § 3237(b) seems clear enough. However, Congress may not have considered, in drafting the statute, the situation where the alleged tax evasion took place in District A, the tax returns were mailed to the IRS office in District B, but some of the defendants happen to reside in District C. If the government attempted to bring the prosecution in District B, based on a mailing to the IRS office located there, § 3237(b) would apply, as Congress intended. In this case, however, venue was laid in District A, the location of the alleged criminal activity.

The government relies heavily on the majority opinion in *In re United States (Clemente)*, to support its narrow reading of § 3237(b). There the court, finding a legislative intent only to prevent a limited type of abuse, held that the "home venue option" was not available where no such abuse was present. Thus, where the government relied on independent facts of tax evasion to lay venue in one district, the Second Circuit held that the prosecution did not "involve use of the mails". *Id.* at 80. Accordingly, the transfer option was not allowed.

There is much to be said for the government's position. It does not appear that the sponsors of H.R. 8252 actually considered the type of situation presented in this case when the statute was drafted. Indeed, the Senate Report stated that any additional costs of prosecution to the government under this new law would be "inconsequential." Application of the law to this case, however, would require the government to conduct two lengthy and similar trials at considerable expense and inconvenience. One of these trials would be in a remote district with no connection with the crime except for the fortuity of the defendants' residence there. On the other hand, there are balancing considerations of the expense and inconvenience of defendants, who are presumed to be innocent.

Despite the practical advantages in avoiding duplicate effort, we find ourselves compelled by the plain language of the statute to reject the positions taken by the government and the Second Circuit. Whatever may have been the original intent of the bill's sponsors, the language adopted to accomplish those goals is much broader than that

---

2. The historical references are thoroughly explored in both the majority and minority opinions in *In re United States (Clemente)*, 608 F.2d 76 (2d Cir.1979), *cert. denied,* 446 U.S. 908, 100 S.Ct. 1834, 64 L.Ed.2d 260 (1980).

which would have covered the situations actually considered by Congress. We are drawn to this conclusion for the reasons outlined in the dissenting opinion by Judge Kearse in *Clemente,* 608 F.2d at 81–86.

As noted by Judge Kearse, the legislative history can be read to support the view that Congress intended *all* tax evasion defendants to have the "home venue option" where returns were mailed to the IRS. Further, the plain language of the statute does apply to the facts of this case because the defendants did use the mails to send in the tax returns at issue. Finally, the overwhelming weight of judicial authority prior to *Clemente* held that the option was available to defendants whether or not the government relied upon mailing to establish venue.

We also note that Congress amended § 3237(b) in 1966, to add willful failure to file tax returns as a crime for which the transfer option would be available. At that time, several courts had reached the conclusion that transfer would be allowed whether or not the government relied upon mailing to lay venue. Not only did Congress fail to address this problem, but the Senate Report stated broadly, "to be sure that the taxpayer has the right to be tried in the district in which he resides, the bill amends present law to provide that he may elect to remove his trial to the judicial district of his residence." S.Rep. No. 1625, 89th Cong., 2d Sess. 3, *reprinted in* 1966 U.S.Code Cong. & Ad.News 3676, 3681.

We find ourselves obliged to accord to § 3237(b) the plain meaning of its rather broad language. If the result in this case is disturbing on the grounds of judicial efficiency, application for the amendment of the statute must be made to Congress, not to this Court. Accordingly, the government's petition for a writ of mandamus is

Denied.

Notes and Questions

1. The judicial debate over the proper application of Section 3237 continues on. Section 3237 gives a defendant in certain prosecutions for a criminal violation of the Internal Revenue Code the option to have the case transferred from a district in which he is not a resident to the district of his residence. Among them is a charged violation of section 7206(2), where the "offense involved use of the mails." The Court of Appeals for the Fourth Circuit in In re United States (Nardone), 706 F.2d 494 (4th Cir.1983), construed the language of § 7206(2) narrowly to deny taxpayer/defendant a transfer of venue. The words were construed to be applicable only when the use of the mails was the basis upon which the United States based venue in a district other than that of the taxpayer's residence. This interpretation first came to light in In re United States (Clemente), 608 F.2d 76 (2d Cir.1979), cert. denied, 446 U.S. 908, 100 S.Ct. 1834, 64 L.Ed.2d 260 (1980). See also, Use of the Mails Requirement, 53 Fordham L.Rev. 937 (1985).

2. A defendant can also invoke § 3237(b) where the tax offense is brought by way of a conspiracy charge under 18 U.S.C.A. § 371. United States v. Ostrer, 458 F. Supp. 540 (S.D.N.Y.1978). A defendant has an

absolute right to use § 3237(b) when charged with an enumerated offense; however, a conflict exists when the defendant is charged with an offense *based* upon an enumerated offense. The district court held that the better view is to leave to the trial judge's discretion the decision whether or not to transfer the charges. This affords the court an opportunity to balance the interests to be served by a transfer, with those militating in favor of retaining the conspiracy counts. *Id.,* at 542. See also United States v. DeMarco, 394 F.Supp. 611 (D.D.C.1975), where the court held that the test is to examine the *nature and effect* of the acts alleged in determining whether a defendant has the right to invoke Section 3237(b).

B. THE USE OF SUMMARY WITNESSES AND CHARTS

A criminal tax trial is, or should be, both a criminal and a tax trial. In many ways, however, the trial of a criminal tax charge is different from the run of the mill federal case. For example, there usually is no issue as to "who did it," or even as to what the defendant did or failed to do. Rather, the focus is normally upon the intention of the defendant in performing or failing to perform the acts in question. Moreover, the issue as to the defendant's state of mind frequently is directed to a broad period of time (usually years) rather than to a specific time and place.

While a criminal tax trial presents many (if not potentially all) of the situations which can arise in any complex criminal case, there is perhaps one circumstance which is characteristic of tax prosecutions. That is the appearance (generally at the conclusion of the government's case) of the summary expert witness and the summary charts.

UNITED STATES v. CITRON
United States Court of Appeals, Second Circuit, 1986.
783 F.2d 307.

MANSFIELD, CIRCUIT JUDGE:

Ira Paul Citron appeals a judgment, entered in the Eastern District of New York after a jury trial before Judge Leonard D. Wexler, convicting him of income tax evasion and filing false income tax returns.

* * *

Appellant contends that the government failed as a matter of law to establish that he underreported his income for the years in question. The § 7201 conviction (Count Two) must be sustained if the proof, viewed in the light most favorable to the government, "is such that a jury, drawing reasonable inferences therefrom, may fairly and logically have concluded that the defendant was guilty beyond a reasonable doubt." *United States v. Barnes,* 604 F.2d 121, 157 (2d Cir.1979), *cert. denied,* 446 U.S. 907, 100 S.Ct. 1833, 64 L.Ed.2d 260 (1980). We find that the evidence supporting the conviction may well have been sufficient, but that it must be vacated because of the improper admission of a summary chart placed before the jury.

Under the cash expenditure method the government bears the burden of demonstrating "to a reasonable certainty" (i) expenditures during the period in question and (ii) the opening net worth of the taxpayer, including cash on hand.

* * *

Appellant argues that the government failed to meet these burdens in several respects. First, he maintains that the government failed to prove net worth adequately, particularly cash on hand, for each of the years in question. In advancing this claim, he argues that the district court erred in admitting in evidence the government's summary chart specifying his alleged cash on hand. Absent this chart, appellant asserts, the government's case was fatally flawed by a failure to establish cash on hand.

* * *

The government prepared a summary chart which listed Citron's cash on hand as $24,412.27 and identified government exhibits * * * as the source of this figure.

At trial the government sought to introduce the summary chart containing and based on the $24,412.27 cash-on-hand figure without providing testimony explaining how cash on hand was calculated from the grab-bag of documents listed above. When defense counsel objected to the lack of foundation for the figure, the district court agreed, stating "I have never seen such playing with numbers and doubletalk and triple talk, which no one understands." Nonetheless, Judge Wexler admitted the chart in evidence on the theory that "if it is weak, cross examination will destroy it totally."

Although reliance on cross-examination may be appropriate in other contexts, the defendant here was entitled to greater protection. Summary charts should not be admitted unless a proper foundation is established connecting the numbers on the chart with the underlying evidence. Courts have long required that district courts ascertain that summary charts "fairly represent and summarize the evidence upon which they are based." *United States v. O'Connor,* 237 F.2d 466, 475 (2d Cir.1956). Unless this requirement is met, the chart is more likely to confuse or mislead the jury than it is to assist it. In this case, the summary chart contained a figure for cash on hand that was obviously the product of calculation. Yet the government provided no explanation, either in the form of worksheets, testimony, or other methods of elucidation, showing how it derived the figure. The district court did not consider whether the chart was based on the evidence but instead noted that the chart was "doubletalk" and admitted it. In this respect the court abused its discretion.

Our ruling that the chart was inadmissible does not mean that the government must provide detailed testimony stating the basis of each calculation undertaken when a summary chart is prepared. All that is required is enough explanation to allow the jury to see how the numbers on a chart were derived from the underlying evidence put before it. The adequacy of the explanation requires the court to exercise practical judgment in recognition of the fact that a jury usually consists of laymen, not mathematicians.

We cannot label the error as harmless. *Kotteakos v. United States,* 328 U.S. 750, 764–65, 66 S.Ct. 1239, 1247–48, 90 L.Ed. 1557 (1946). The jury's acquittal of Ira on six of the nine counts in the indictment does not indicate that it rejected the figures in the summary chart offered by the government. A higher cash-on-hand figure would have directly reduced the amount of income alleged to have been underreported and a lower figure would have had the opposite effect. Thus the seemingly arbitrary figures used in the government's chart were an important link in its case. Because the chart was the only computation of Ira's opening cash provided by the government, its absence would have rendered proof of underreporting less certain and may well have altered the jury's calculation of the resources he received prior to the years in which his taxable income was in dispute.

Nor was the error adequately alleviated by Judge Wexler's instructions to the jury.[10] * * *

When the figures on a summary chart are properly established, a cautionary instruction that the chart itself is not evidence may be sufficient to head off any misimpression by the jury. But when the figures on the chart have not been properly established and keyed to the chart, as was the case here, a cautionary instruction is inadequate.

* * *

* * * the admission into evidence of the summary chart prepared by the government, which contained and relied on a seemingly arbitrary figure of $24,412.27 for cash on hand, constituted prejudicial error requiring a reversal of the conviction and a retrial of Count 2.

* * *

---

10. Judge Wexler instructed the jury that

"[a]ny chart or schedule presented to you by the prosecution or defense was prepared solely for the purpose of summarizing the facts claimed by the lawyers to have been proved by testimony, books, records and other documents which are in evidence. In other words, such a chart or schedule merely is the lawyer's pictoral summary of what he contends the evidence shows and is no better than the evidence on which it is based.

"Such charts and schedules, however, are not in and of themselves evidence or proof of any facts. They were used only as a matter of convenience. Under no circumstances may you consider them as independent evidence of anything.

"If you find that any chart or schedule does not correctly reflect facts shown by the evidence in the case, you should disregard it entirely."

SECTION 4. THE FIFTH AMENDMENT CLAIM ON TAX RETURNS

UNITED STATES v. SULLIVAN
Supreme Court of the United States, 1927.
274 U.S. 259, 47 S.Ct. 607, 71 L.Ed. 1037.

MR. JUSTICE HOLMES delivered the opinion of the Court.

The defendant in error was convicted of willfully refusing to make a return of his net income as required by the Revenue Act of 1921. The judgment was reversed by the Circuit Court of Appeals. A writ of certiorari was granted by this Court.

We may take it that the defendant had sufficient gross income to require a return under the statute unless he was exonerated by the fact that the whole or a large part of it was derived from business in violation of the National Prohibition Act (Comp.St. § 10138¼ et seq.). The Circuit Court of Appeals held that gains from illicit traffic in liquor were subject to the income tax, but that the Fifth Amendment to the Constitution protected the defendant from the requirement of a return.

The Court below was right in holding that the defendant's gains were subject to the tax. By section 213(a), gross income includes "gains, profits, and income derived from * * * the transaction of any business carried on for gain or profit, or gains or profits and income derived from any source whatever." * * * We see no reason to doubt the interpretation of the Act, or any reason why the fact that a business is unlawful should exempt it from paying the taxes that if lawful it would have to pay.

As the defendant's income was taxed, the statute of course required a return. In the decisions that this was contrary to the Constitution we are of opinion that the protection of the Fifth Amendment was pressed too far. If the form of return provided called for answers that the defendant was privileged from making he could have raised the objection in the return, but could not on that account refuse to make any return at all. We are not called on to decide what, if anything, he might have withheld. Most of the items warranted no complaint. It would be an extreme if not an extravagant application of the Fifth Amendment to say that it authorized a man to refuse to state the amount of his income because it had been made in crime. But if the defendant desired to test that or any other point he should have tested it in the return so that it could be passed upon. He could not draw a conjurer's circle around the whole matter by his own declaration that to write any word upon the government blank would bring him into danger of the law. In this case the defendant did not even make a declaration, he simply abstained from making a return.

* * *

Judgment reversed.

GARNER v. UNITED STATES
Supreme Court of the United States, 1976.
424 U.S. 648, 96 S.Ct. 1178, 47 L.Ed.2d 370.

MR. JUSTICE POWELL delivered the opinion of the Court.

This case involves a nontax criminal prosecution in which the Government introduced petitioner's income tax returns to prove the offense against him. The question is whether the introduction of this evidence, over petitioner's Fifth Amendment objection, violated the privilege against compulsory self-incrimination when petitioner made the incriminating disclosures on his returns instead of then claiming the privilege.

* * *

II

In United States v. Sullivan, 274 U.S. 259, 47 S.Ct. 607, 71 L.Ed. 1037 (1927), the Court held that the privilege against compulsory self-incrimination is not a defense to prosecution for failing to file a return at all. But the Court indicated that the privilege could be claimed against specific disclosures sought on a return * * *.

Had Garner invoked the privilege against compulsory self-incrimination on his tax returns in lieu of supplying the information used against him, the Internal Revenue Service could have proceeded in either or both of two ways. First, the Service could have sought to have Garner criminally prosecuted under § 7203 of the Internal Revenue Code of 1954 (Code), 26 U.S.C. § 7203, which proscribes, among other things, the willful failure to make a return. Second, the Service could have sought to complete Garner's returns administratively "from [its] own knowledge and from such information as [it could] obtain through testimony or otherwise." 26 U.S.C. § 6020(b)(1). Section 7602(2) of the Code authorizes the Service in such circumstances to summon the taxpayer to appear and to produce records or give testimony. 26 U.S.C. § 7602(2). If Garner had persisted in his claim when summoned, the Service could have sued for enforcement in district court, subjecting Garner to the threat of the court's contempt power. 26 U.S.C. § 7604.

Given *Sullivan*, it cannot fairly be said that taxpayers are "volunteers" when they file their tax returns. The Government compels the filing of a return much as it compels, for example, the appearance of a "witness"[7] before a grand jury. The availability to the Service of § 7203 prosecutions and the summons procedure also induces taxpayers to disclose unprivileged information on their returns. The question,

---

7. The term "witness" is used herein to identify one who, at the time disclosures are sought from him, is not a defendant in a criminal proceeding. The more frequent situations in which a witness' disclosures are compelled, subject to Fifth Amendment rights, include testimony before a grand jury, in a civil or criminal case or proceeding, or before a legislative or administrative body possessing subpoena power.

however, is whether the Government can be said to have compelled Garner to incriminate himself with regard to specific disclosures made on his return when he could have claimed the Fifth Amendment privilege instead.

III

We start from the fundamental proposition:

"[A] witness protected by the privilege may rightfully refuse to answer unless and until he is protected at least against the use of his compelled answers and evidence derived therefrom in any subsequent criminal case in which he is a defendant. * * * Absent such protection, if he is nevertheless compelled to answer, his answers are inadmissible against him in a later criminal prosecution. * * *" Lefkowitz v. Turley, 414 U.S. 70, 78, 94 S.Ct. 316, 322, 38 L.Ed.2d 274, 282 (1973).

Because the privilege protects against the use of compelled statements as well as guarantees the right to remain silent absent immunity, the inquiry in a Fifth Amendment case is not ended when an incriminating statement is made in lieu of a claim of privilege. Nor, however, is failure to claim the privilege irrelevant.

* * *

* * * Despite its cherished position, the Fifth Amendment addresses only a relatively narrow scope of inquiries. Unless the government seeks testimony that will subject its giver to criminal liability, the constitutional right to remain silent absent immunity does not arise. An individual therefore properly may be compelled to give testimony, for example, in a noncriminal investigation of himself. Unless a witness objects, a government ordinarily may assume that its compulsory processes are not eliciting testimony that he deems to be incriminating. Only the witness knows whether the apparently innocent disclosure sought may incriminate him, and the burden appropriately lies with him to make a timely assertion of the privilege. If, instead, he discloses the information sought, any incriminations properly are viewed as not compelled.

* * *

IV

The information revealed in the preparation and filing of an income tax return is, for purposes of Fifth Amendment analysis, the testimony of a "witness," as that term is used herein. Since Garner disclosed information on his returns instead of objecting, his Fifth Amendment claim would be defeated by an application of the general requirement that witnesses must claim the privilege. Garner, however, resists the application of that requirement, arguing that incriminating disclosures made in lieu of objection are "compelled" in the tax-return context. He relies specifically on three situations in which incriminatory disclosures have been considered compelled despite a failure to claim the privilege. * * *

A

Garner relies first on cases dealing with coerced confessions, e.g., Miranda v. Arizona, 384 U.S. 436, 86 S.Ct. 1602, 16 L.Ed.2d 694 (1966) * * *.

It is evident that these cases have little to do with disclosures on a tax return. The coerced-confession cases present the entirely different situation of custodial interrogation. It is presumed that without proper safeguards the circumstances of custodial interrogation deny an individual the ability freely to choose to remain silent. * * * Nothing in this case suggests the need for a similar presumption that a taxpayer makes disclosures on his return rather than claims the privilege because his will is overborne. In fact, a taxpayer, who can complete his return at leisure and with legal assistance, is even less subject to the psychological pressures at issue in *Miranda* than a witness who has been called to testify in judicial proceedings.

B

Garner relies next on Mackey v. United States, 401 U.S. 667, 91 S.Ct. 1160, 28 L.Ed.2d 404 (1971), the relevance of which can be understood only in light of Marchetti v. United States, 390 U.S. 39, 88 S.Ct. 697, 19 L.Ed.2d 889 (1968), and Grosso v. United States, 390 U.S. 62, 88 S.Ct. 709, 19 L.Ed.2d 906 (1968). In the latter cases the Court considered whether the Fifth Amendment was a defense in prosecutions for failure to file the returns required of gamblers in connection with the federal occupational and excise taxes on gambling. The Court found that any disclosures made in connection with the payment of those taxes tended to incriminate because of the pervasive criminal regulation of gambling activities. Since submitting a claim of privilege in lieu of the returns also would incriminate, the Court held that the privilege could be exercised by simply failing to file.

In *Mackey,* the disclosures required in connection with the gambling excise tax had been made before *Marchetti* and *Grosso* were decided. Mackey's returns were introduced in a criminal prosecution for income tax evasion. Although a majority of the Court considered the disclosures on the returns to have been compelled incriminations, Mackey was not immunized against their use because *Marchetti* and *Grosso* were held nonretroactive. Garner assumes that if Mackey had made his disclosures after *Marchetti* and *Grosso,* they could not have been used against him. He then concludes that since Mackey would have been privileged to file no returns at all, *Mackey* stands for the proposition that an objection at trial always suffices to preserve the privilege even if disclosures have been made previously.

Assuming that Garner otherwise reads *Mackey* correctly, we do not think that case should be applied in this context. The basis for the holdings in *Marchetti* and *Grosso* was that the occupational and excise taxes on gambling required disclosures only of gamblers, the great majority of whom were likely to incriminate themselves by responding.

Therefore, as in the coerced-confession cases, any compulsion to disclose was likely to compel self-incrimination. Garner is differently situated. Although he disclosed himself to be a gambler, federal income tax returns are not directed at those "'inherently suspect of criminal activities.'" *Marchetti*, supra, 390 U.S. at 52, 88 S.Ct., at 704, 19 L.Ed.2d, at 900. As noted in Albertson v. SACB, 382 U.S. 70, 79, 86 S.Ct. 194, 199, 15 L.Ed.2d 165, 172 (1965), "the questions in [an] income tax return [are] neutral on their face and directed at the public at large." The great majority of persons who file income tax returns do not incriminate themselves by disclosing their occupation. The requirement that such returns be completed and filed simply does not involve the compulsion to incriminate considered in *Mackey*.

C

Garner's final argument relies on Garrity v. New Jersey, 385 U.S. 493, 87 S.Ct. 616, 17 L.Ed.2d 562 (1967). There policemen summoned during an investigation of police corruption were informed that they could claim the privilege but that they would be discharged for doing so. The disclosures they made were introduced against them in subsequent criminal prosecutions. The Court held that the penalty of discharge for reliance on the privilege foreclosed a free choice to remain silent, and therefore had the effect of compelling the incriminating testimony given by the policemen. Garner notes that a taxpayer who claims the privilege on his return faces the possibility of a criminal prosecution under § 7203 for failure to make a return. He argues that the possibility of prosecution, like the threat of discharge in *Garrity*, compels a taxpayer to make incriminating disclosures rather than claim the privilege. This contention is not entirely without force, but we find it unpersuasive.

The policemen in *Garrity* were threatened with punishment for a concededly valid exercise of the privilege, but one in Garner's situation is at no such disadvantage. A § 7203 conviction cannot be based on a valid exercise of the privilege. This is implicit in the dictum of United States v. Sullivan, 274 U.S. 259, 47 S.Ct. 607, 71 L.Ed. 1037 (1927), that the privilege may be claimed on a return. Furthermore, the Court has held that an individual summoned by the Service to provide documents or testimony can rely on the privilege to defend against a § 7203 prosecution for failure to "supply any information." See United States v. Murdock, 284 U.S. 141, 52 S.Ct. 63, 76 L.Ed. 210 (1931) (*Murdock I*), disapproved on other grounds, Murphy v. Waterfront Comm'n, 378 U.S. 52, 84 S.Ct. 1594, 12 L.Ed.2d 678 (1964). The Fifth Amendment itself guarantees the taxpayer's insulation against liability imposed on the basis of a valid and timely claim of privilege, a protection broadened by § 7203's statutory standard of "willfulness." [18]

---

18. Because § 7203 proscribes "willful" failures to make returns, a taxpayer is not at peril for every erroneous claim of privilege. The Government recognizes that a defendant could not properly be convicted for an erroneous claim of privilege asserted in good faith. * * *

See *United States v. Bishop*, 412 U.S. 346, 93 S.Ct. 2008, 36 L.Ed.2d 941 (1973).

Since a valid claim of privilege cannot be the basis for a § 7203 conviction, Garner can prevail only if the possibility that a claim made on the return will be tested in a criminal prosecution suffices in itself to deny him freedom to claim the privilege. He argues that it does so, noting that because of the threat of prosecution under § 7203 a taxpayer contemplating a claim of privilege on his return faces a more difficult choice than does a witness contemplating a claim of privilege in a judicial proceeding. If the latter claims the protection of the Fifth Amendment, he receives a judicial ruling at that time on the validity of his claim, and he has an opportunity to reconsider it before being held in contempt for refusal to answer. A § 7203 prosecution, however, may be brought without a preliminary judicial ruling on a claim of privilege that would allow the taxpayer to reconsider.

In essence, Garner contends that the Fifth Amendment guarantee requires such a preliminary-ruling procedure for testing the validity of an asserted privilege. It may be that such a procedure would serve the best interests of the Government as well as of the taxpayer, but we certainly cannot say that the Constitution requires it. The Court previously has considered Fifth Amendment claims in the context of a criminal prosecution where the defendant did not have the benefit of a preliminary judicial ruling on a claim of privilege. It has never intimated that such a procedure is other than permissible. Indeed, the Court has given some measure of endorsement to it. In *Murdock I*, supra, an individual was prosecuted under predecessors of § 7203 for refusing to make disclosures after being summoned by the Bureau of Internal Revenue. In this Court he contended, apparently on statutory grounds, that there could be no prosecution without a prior judicial enforcement suit to allow presentation of his claim of privilege to a court for a preliminary ruling. The Court said:

> "While undoubtedly the right of a witness to refuse to answer lest he incriminate himself may be tested in proceedings to compel answer, there is no support for the contention that there must be such a determination of that question before prosecution for the willful failure so denounced." 284 U.S., at 148, 52 S.Ct., at 64, 76 L.Ed., at 213.

We are satisfied that *Murdock I* states the constitutional standard.

What is at issue here is principally a matter of timing and procedure. As long as a valid and timely claim of privilege is available as a defense to a taxpayer prosecuted for failure to make a return, the taxpayer has not been denied a free choice to remain silent merely because of the absence of a preliminary judicial ruling on his claim. We therefore do not agree that Garner was deterred from claiming the privilege in the sense that was true of the policemen in *Garrity*.

In this respect, the protection for the taxpayer in a § 7203 prosecution is broader than that for a witness who risks contempt to challenge a judicial order to disclose. In the latter case, a mere erroneous refusal to disclose warrants a sanction. See *Maness v. Meyers*, 419 U.S. 449, 460–461, 95 S.Ct. 584, 592–593, 42 L.Ed.2d 574, 584–585 (1975).

V

In summary, we conclude that since Garner made disclosures instead of claiming the privilege on his tax returns his disclosures were not compelled incriminations.[21] He therefore was foreclosed from invoking the privilege when such information was later introduced as evidence against him in a criminal prosecution.

The judgment is

Affirmed.

MR. JUSTICE MARSHALL, with whom MR. JUSTICE BRENNAN joins, concurring in the judgment.

* * *

I accept the proposition that a preliminary ruling is not a prerequisite to a § 7203 prosecution. But it does not follow, and *Murdock I* does not hold, that the absence of a preliminary ruling is of no import in considering whether a defense of good-faith assertion of the privilege is constitutionally required. It is one thing to deny a good-faith defense to a witness who is given a prompt ruling on the validity of his claim of privilege and an opportunity to reconsider his refusal to testify before subjecting himself to possible punishment for contempt. It would be quite another to deny a good-faith defense to someone like petitioner, who may be denied a ruling on the validity of his claim of privilege until his criminal prosecution, when it is too late to reconsider. If, contrary to the undisputed fact, a taxpayer had no assurance of either a preliminary ruling or a defense of good-faith assertion of the privilege, he could claim the privilege only at the risk that an erroneous assessment of the law of self-incrimination would subject him to criminal liability. In that event, I would consider the taxpayer to have been denied the free choice to claim the privilege, and would view any incriminating disclosures on his tax return as "compelled" within the meaning of the Fifth Amendment. Only because a good-faith erroneous claim of privilege entitles a taxpayer to acquittal under § 7203 can I conclude that petitioner's disclosures are admissible against him.

Question

Under what circumstances, if any, could you advise a client to claim the privilege against self-incrimination with regard to the amount of income reported on a federal tax return?

---

21. No language in this opinion is to be read as allowing a taxpayer desiring the protection of the privilege to make disclosures concurrently with a claim of privilege and thereby to immunize himself against the use of such disclosures. If a taxpayer desires the protection of the privilege, he must claim it instead of making disclosures. Any other rule would deprive the Government of its choice between compelling the evidence from the claimant in exchange for immunity and avoiding the burdens of immunization by obtaining the evidence elsewhere.

UNITED STATES v. CARLSON
United States Court of Appeals, Ninth Circuit, 1980.
617 F.2d 518.

WALLACE, CIRCUIT JUDGE.

Carlson was convicted of willful failure to file income tax returns in violation of 26 U.S.C. § 7203. On appeal he seeks reversal by claiming that his failure to file proper returns constituted a valid exercise of his Fifth Amendment privilege against self-incrimination. We affirm the conviction.

I

Carlson, a factory worker, earned $9,346.21 in 1974 and $13,053.53 in 1975. Although he had filed complete tax returns for previous years, Carlson did not do so for 1974 and 1975. Instead, as part of a tax protest movement, he utilized the following tax-evasion scheme for each of those years. In 1974, Carlson claimed 99 withholding exemptions on the withholding tax form (form W-4) that he submitted to his employer, although he was not married and had no dependents. This form W-4 remained effective through 1975, and resulted in no federal income taxes being withheld from Carlson's wages in either 1974 or 1975. Carlson thereafter asserted the Fifth Amendment in his 1974 and 1975 year-end tax returns (form 1040) in lieu of providing any information from which his tax liability could be calculated. He appended to the 1974 return tax protest material claiming that federal reserve notes were unconstitutional, that he therefore had not received enough constitutionally valid money to require filing a tax return, and that all rules promulgated by the Secretary of the Treasury were also unconstitutional.

The result of Carlson's submission of the false withholding form and his subsequent assertion of the Fifth Amendment in his year-end returns was that Carlson paid no federal income taxes for 1974 or 1975. Carlson claims that he validly asserted the Fifth Amendment to avoid incriminating himself for having previously filed the false withholding forms. After hearing all of the evidence, however, the district judge, sitting without a jury, found that Carlson "did not have a good-faith claim or reasonable ground for [asserting the] privilege, as he was a tax protestor and his activities and his actions and methods of submitting his returns were those of a tax protestor only." He held, therefore, that Carlson's Fifth Amendment claim did not constitute defense to his prosecution, pursuant to section 7203, for failure to file a tax return.

II

This case presents a question of first impression: can the privilege against self-incrimination constitute a defense to a section 7203 prosecution when it is asserted to avoid incrimination for a past violation of income tax laws? * * *

* * *

An examination of the facts of this case reveals that Carlson did assert the privilege at the time he filed his return, and did so while facing a real and appreciable hazard of prosecution for having previously filed a false withholding form. In addition, there is little doubt that a truthfully completed tax return, stating his gross income, the lack of federal income taxes actually withheld, and the true number of available deductions would have provided " 'a lead or clue' to evidence having a tendency to incriminate" Carlson. It is equally certain that a trial judge examining these facts would find a substantial threat of incrimination. Thus, it appears that Carlson satisfies those indicia of validity previously considered by us in cases where the privilege has been asserted to avoid self-incrimination other than under the tax laws.

When the privilege is asserted to avoid incrimination for past tax crimes, however, additional complications arise. If Carlson's assertion of the privilege were valid, it would license a form of conduct that would undermine the entire system of personal income tax collection. The essence of Carlson's plan was to claim 99 withholding exemptions so that no federal income tax would be withheld by his employer, and then to assert the Fifth Amendment privilege in lieu of a properly completed tax return, thus attempting to avoid both prosecution for the false withholding claim and payment of required income taxes. The widespread use of such a scheme would emasculate the present system of revenue collection which, by virtue of its scope alone, necessarily depends upon personal reporting by wage earners. We are thus confronted with the collision of two critical interests: the privilege against self-incrimination, and the need for public revenue collection by a process necessarily reliant on self-reporting.

To decide which of these two interests prevails, we follow Supreme Court guidance:

> Tension between the State's demand for disclosures and the protection of the right against self-incrimination is likely to give rise to serious questions. Inevitably these must be resolved in terms of balancing the public need on the one hand, and the individual claim to constitutional protections on the other; neither interest can be treated lightly.

California v. Byers, 402 U.S. 424, 427, 91 S.Ct. 1535, 1537, 29 L.Ed.2d 9 (1971). * * *

* * *

In the case before us, Carlson has attempted to take advantage of the privilege's protective capacity to further a calculated effort to avoid the payment of taxes. Although it is true that Carlson actually seeks protection against self-incrimination for his prior tax crime, he does so only as part of an overall plan to evade taxes. The first step of that plan—submitting a false withholding form to his employer—was concealed from the Service by assertion of the Fifth Amendment on Carlson's year-end returns; and the very act of asserting the Fifth Amendment also effectuated the second step of the plan—failing to file meaningful returns that would divulge both his prior misstatement and his overall year-end tax liabilities. In other words, the Fifth Amendment was the linchpin of Carlson's plan to evade the payment of taxes. He used the privilege more as a sword than as a shield. The history and purpose of the privilege do not, in light of such circumstances, weigh heavily in favor of extending its coverage to Carlson.

At the same time, the character and urgency of the public interest in raising revenue through self-reporting weighs heavily against affording the privilege to Carlson. The federal government's power to raise revenue is its lifeblood. Were taxpayers permitted to employ Carlson's scheme, they could avoid filing completed tax returns and thereby severely impair the government's ability to determine tax liability.
* * *

Another factor in our weighing process is that the requirement of filing an annual income tax return is primarily designed to facilitate revenue collection, not criminal prosecution. "[T]he questions in the income tax return [are] neutral on their face and directed at the public at large." Albertson v. SACB, 382 U.S. 70, 79, 86 S.Ct. 194, 199, 15 L.Ed.2d 165 (1965). * * *

After weighing the appropriate factors, we conclude that the purpose and history of the privilege against self-incrimination do not compel protection of Carlson's actions, and that the character and urgency of the opposing revenue interests require that his scheme not be permitted. We therefore hold that an individual who seeks to frustrate the tax laws by claiming too many withholding exemptions, with an eye to covering that crime and evading the tax return requirement by assertion of the Fifth Amendment, is not entitled to the amendment's protection.

III

In spite of our holding that Carlson is not entitled to protection of the Fifth Amendment, we still must review the district court's finding that Carlson did not assert his claim in "good faith." * * * In prosecutions of the kind before us, * * * a defendant's assertion of even an invalid Fifth Amendment claim in "good faith" would defeat the section 7203 requirement that a failure to file income tax returns be "willful." Someone who thinks he is complying with the law cannot be said to be "willfully" violating it. Therefore, we must review the trial court's finding that Carlson did not make his claim in good faith.

The trial judge's determination was a finding of fact. "[U]pon appeal of a conviction in a criminal case the evidence must be considered in a light most favorable to the government and the findings of fact of a trial judge (or jury) may not be set aside unless clearly erroneous." United States v. Glover, 514 F.2d 390, 391 (9th Cir.), cert. denied, 423 U.S. 857, 96 S.Ct. 108, 46 L.Ed.2d 83 (1975). The record clearly discloses that Carlson was a tax protestor who attempted to frustrate the tax laws by use of the Fifth Amendment. We cannot say that the trial judge's conclusion that Carlson failed to assert the privilege in good faith was clearly erroneous.

Affirmed.

UNITED STATES v. NEFF
United States Court of Appeals, Ninth Circuit, 1980.
615 F.2d 1235.

WALLACE, CIRCUIT JUDGE:

* * *

I

During 1974 and 1975, Neff was employed as a police officer and received wages from the City of San Jose, California. During 1974 he also received capital gains from dealings in gold and silver coins. His community property share of income from employment and investments exceeded $14,000 in 1974 and $8,500 in 1975. During each of these years, Neff, who had previously filed proper returns, submitted to the IRS a standard individual income tax return form (form 1040) on which Neff provided no financial information from which his tax liabilities could be calculated. As returned by Neff, the forms contained only essential identification information and Neff's signature. In response to more than 25 questions about his financial and tax status, Neff had printed the words "Object: Self–Incrimination." Remaining questions had been answered either "None" or "Unknown." Neff also appended to the forms, in each of these years, over 100 pages of general protest material challenging, among other things, the national monetary system, government spending, and federal reserve notes.

The Internal Revenue Service (IRS) responded by letter to Neff, explaining that the forms as he filled them out were not acceptable tax returns and providing additional blank forms for proper completion. Neff refused to comply, claiming that by doing so he would waive his Fifth Amendment privilege against self-incrimination. The government filed an information charging Neff with two counts of willful failure to file income tax returns, and a jury found him guilty of both counts.

* * *

We are here faced with a case in which the taxpayer did assert his privilege in response to specific questions in the tax return form, but did so on such a wholesale basis as to deny the IRS any useful financial or tax information. Other circuits, faced with similar wholesale assertions of the privilege against self-incrimination, have concluded that a tax return form which contains no information from which tax liability can be calculated does not constitute a tax return within the meaning of the IRS laws. Once these courts determine that the taxpayer has filed no return, simple application of the *Sullivan* precedent, [United States v. Sullivan, 274 U.S. 259, 47 S.Ct. 607, 71 L.Ed. 1037 (1927),] which states that the Fifth Amendment will never justify a complete failure to file a return, invalidates the Fifth Amendment defense.

Although we recognize the ease with which the logic used in these cases would resolve the issue before us, we conclude that such reliance upon the definition of a tax return is inappropriate, because it lacks independent Fifth Amendment analysis. Moreover, the usefulness of this definitional approach is too limited because it is confined to facts such as those presented here: the wholesale assertion, albeit in response to specific questions, of the privilege against self-incrimination. In settings in which the Fifth Amendment right has been more discretely asserted, it would be difficult to conclude that no return has been filed, and, therefore, inappropriate to apply this definitional analysis. We therefore choose not to follow the lead of the cited cases. We believe that the better approach to this and future Fifth Amendment tax return cases is to apply more traditional Fifth Amendment analysis.

* * *

To claim the privilege validly a defendant must be faced with " 'substantial hazards of self-incrimination,' " California v. Byers, 402 U.S. at 429, 90 S.Ct. at 1538, that are " 'real and appreciable' and not merely 'imaginary and unsubstantial.' " Marchetti v. United States, 390 U.S. at 48, 88 S.Ct. at 702. Moreover, he must have "reasonable cause to apprehend [such] danger from a direct answer" to questions posed to him. Hoffman v. United States, 341 U.S. 479, 486, 71 S.Ct. 814, 818, 95 L.Ed. 1118 (1951). The information that would be revealed by direct answer need not be such as would itself support a criminal conviction, however, but must simply "furnish a link in the chain of evidence needed to prosecute the claimant for a federal crime." Id. Indeed, it is enough if the responses would merely "provide a lead or clue" to evidence having a tendency to incriminate. Id. at 348.

* * *

Applying these principles to the facts before us, we conclude that the trial judge correctly decided that Neff had no valid Fifth Amendment defense to the section 7203 prosecution. The questions asked of Neff on the income tax form did not, of themselves, suggest that the response would be incriminating; nor did the setting in which they were asked—a general inquiry about Neff's financial and tax status, to be completed in the privacy of his own home—alter the non-incriminatory nature of those questions. Moreover, the peculiarities of the case did not strengthen Neff's claim. If anything, the tax protest nature of defense witness Holmes' testimony and of the materials that Neff appended to his returns suggest that Neff's refusal to complete the forms was motivated by a desire to protest taxes, rather than a fear of self-incrimination. In short, the whole circumstance was "innocuous and thus unprotected absent some positive disclosure by the witness of its hidden dangers * * *." Hashagen v. United States, supra, 283 F.2d at 350. Neff made no such disclosure. At no point during the trial, including when Neff testified, was the district judge presented with any indicia of potential incrimination. On the contrary, Neff's counsel argued that Neff's sincerity of belief was sufficient to validate his assertion of the privilege, and that Neff alone should be the final arbiter of the assertion's validity. As we have seen, that is not the law. Neff did not show that his response to the tax form questions would have been self-incriminating. He cannot, therefore, prevail on his Fifth Amendment claim.

* * *

Affirmed.

Notes and Questions

1. A client has failed to report income taxable to him derived from annual payments into a foreign bank account of the receipts from his sale, three years earlier, of property located offshore. He is under a criminal tax investigation with regard to the failure to report this income. He seeks your advice as to the reporting of these continuing payments on his income tax return for the current year. In light of the decisions in *Carlson* and *Neff*, what can you advise him to do?

2. Assume that a defendant improperly claims the Fifth Amendment on a return so that he does not have an absolute defense to the prosecution. Is it proper for the court to instruct the jury that the returns filed by the defendant were not income tax returns, within the meaning of § 7203, as a matter of law? Such was the case in United States v. Malquist, 791 F.2d 1399 (9th Cir.1986). In *Malquist,* the trial judge instructed the jury that, as a matter of law, the documents submitted by defendant were not income tax returns within the meaning of Section 7203 since they did not contain sufficient information from which a tax could be computed.

The issue of whether a return is valid for Section 7203 purposes is a question of law for the court to decide. United States v. Grabinski, 727 F.2d 681, 686 (8th Cir.1984). In United States v. Goetz, 746 F.2d 705, 707–08 (11th Cir.1984), the court also held that returns containing no financial information are not "returns" under Section 7203.

In *Malquist,* the trial judge merely instructed the jury that the information Malquist submitted was not a valid return, which was correct for him to decide, as a matter of law.

Chapter XI

COLLECTION OF THE TAX

Scope Note: The final step in the administration of the federal tax laws is collection of the tax determined to be due by the Service or the courts. This Chapter contains a general discussion of the broad powers of the IRS Collection Division, and the means available to the Service to assist it in the collection of the tax, including the federal tax lien and jeopardy and termination assessments. The materials that follow also cover some recurring problems relating to collection of taxes from persons who might be described as "secondarily liable" for the taxes of another, including liability for withholding taxes by responsible persons, lenders and providers of wages; transferee and fiduciary liability; and the "innocent spouse" provisions of the Code. Sections 7 and 8 are devoted to a discussion of the means available to taxpayers and others, in appropriate cases, to prevent the Service from assessing or collecting taxes alleged to be due; and the final section contains a brief description of the rules applicable to administration of the tax laws in the context of a proceeding under the federal Bankruptcy Code.

SECTION 1. OVERVIEW

The Collection Division of the IRS enjoys broad statutory authority to support its mission of collecting taxes. Unpaid taxes are a debt to the government, but the Internal Revenue Code alters the normal debt-collection rules by permitting seizure of the taxpayer's property without judicial intervention or supervision. Inevitably, stories of abuse by IRS employees receive considerable attention in the press, as all taxpayers can sympathize with those unfortunate individuals who have been treated unfairly by the federal tax authorities. In 1988 Congress enacted the Omnibus Taxpayer Bill of Rights [a] as part of the Technical and Miscellaneous Revenue Act of 1988. One of the goals of the Taxpayer Bill of Rights was to prevent the use of "strong-arm tactics" against taxpayers during the tax collection process and to provide remedies for those who are victims of collection abuses.

a. Pub.L. 100–647, §§ 6226–6247, 102 Stat. 3730–3751 (1988).

In hearings held before passage of the legislation, IRS collection agents and "victimized" taxpayers testified before Congressional committees about IRS collection misconduct. One taxpayer testified that he discovered his own error and voluntarily reported the error to the IRS. Rather than cooperating with the taxpayer, the IRS "seized" the taxpayer's bank account just hours after the taxpayer's first meeting with an IRS revenue officer. The IRS action resulted in the taxpayer and 31 employees being put out of their business of restoring slum housing.[b]

Another taxpayer testified at the same hearing that he also encountered problems with IRS tax collectors after he discovered his own error and reported the error to the IRS. This taxpayer was only given ten days to pay off the entire amount of his tax bill. Unable to pay the bill in the time afforded, this taxpayer was forced into bankruptcy to protect his family restaurant business from seizure by the IRS. Although the business was eventually saved, the taxpayer's credit rating was damaged.[c]

The Taxpayers Bill of Rights was designed to provide basic protection to taxpayers who are willing to pay taxes owed. The legislation was not designed to stymie IRS collection activities or to hinder the government from collecting any taxes owed.[d] Previous egregious conduct of IRS collection activity employees may have been encouraged by criteria used in job performance evaluations. Prior to passage of the Taxpayer Bill of Rights, promotions and pay raises were sometimes directly connected with seizures made and cases closed. The attitude of some collection employees was captured in a poster in one IRS office that read: "Seizure fever. Catch it."[e] The Taxpayer Bill of Rights prohibits use of records of tax enforcement results in evaluation of either IRS employees who are directly involved in collection activities or their immediate supervisors.[f]

The Taxpayer Bill of Rights attempted to render more fair and understandable the often harsh and complex process of tax collection and to reduce the intimidation involved in taxpayer contacts with the Collection Division. The first section of the Taxpayer Bill of Rights requires the IRS to disclose to the taxpayer his rights in clear and understandable language.[g] As a result, the IRS revised its publication that explains taxpayer rights and IRS obligations during an audit, taxpayer appeal procedures regarding adverse IRS decisions, procedures for prosecuting refund claims and taxpayer complaints, and IRS procedures in enforcing internal revenue laws (such as assessment, enforcement of liens, levy, and jeopardy assessment).[h]

[b.] 133 Cong.Rec. S11,399 (daily ed. Aug. 6, 1987) (statement of Sen. Pryor).
[c.] Id.
[d.] Id.
[e.] Id. at S11,397.
[f.] Pub.L. 100–647, Sec. 6231(a), 102 Stat. 3734 (1988).
[g.] See I.R.C. § 7521(b).
[h.] See Your Rights as a Taxpayer, IRS Publication 1 (revised June 1989).

Prior to passage of the Taxpayer Bill of Rights, the IRS could seize a taxpayer's property if the tax liability was not paid within ten days from the date notice of intent to levy was made. To afford taxpayers a more realistic opportunity to marshall the funds to pay the tax bill, the Taxpayer Bill of Rights increased the "grace period" from ten to 30 days.[i]

A taxpayer who will have difficulty in timely acquiring sufficient funds to pay a tax liability has several options in the collection process. The options include extending the time to pay tax, paying the tax in installments, and offering a compromise amount in satisfaction of the tax liability. Code sections 6161 to 6166 provide for extensions of time for payment of taxes. A reasonable extension period between six months and ten years is allowed. An extension may be granted only upon a showing of undue hardship that is more than just a mere inconvenience to the taxpayer.[j] Form 1127 (Application for Extension of Time for Payment of Tax) is used for extending the time for payment of income tax.

A delinquent taxpayer may also enter into an installment payment agreement if the IRS determines that such an agreement will facilitate collection of the tax liability.[k] Installment payment agreements are appropriate for taxpayers who are able to pay the full amount of the tax due over a reasonable time.[l] On the other hand, installment agreements are not appropriate for taxpayers who will be unable to pay the full amount of the tax due. Such taxpayers should investigate the use of an offer in compromise. The IRS has authority to accept a taxpayer's offer in compromise which provides for payment by the taxpayer of an amount that is less than the tax liability in satisfaction of the full tax liability.[m] A taxpayer who seeks the protection of bankruptcy laws should consider the use of an offer in compromise as an alternative to bankruptcy. According to the IRS:

> A compromise may be made on one or both of two grounds—(1) doubt as to the liability for the amount owed or (2) doubt as to your ability to make full payment on the amount owed. The doubt as to the liability for the amount owed must be supported by the evidence and the amount acceptable will depend on the degree of doubt found in the particular case. In the case of inability to pay, the amount offered must exceed the total value of your equity in all your assets. The amount must also give sufficient consideration to your present and future earning capacity. If your offer is acceptable, we may require a written agreement to pay a percentage of future earnings as part of the

---

i. I.R.C. § 6331(d). Note that this 30-day period is in addition to the the notice and demand period of section 6303.

j. Reg. § 1.6161–1(b).

k. I.R.C. § 6159.

l. Installment agreements are entered into on Form 433–D, and can be supplemented by an agreement permitting the liability to be paid by automatic deduction from the taxpayer's wages (Form 2159—Payroll Deduction Agreement). An installment agreement authorizing payment via automatic debit from the taxpayer's bank account is entered into on Form 433–G.

m. I.R.C. § 7122.

offer. A written agreement may also be required to relinquish certain present or potential tax benefits.

Submission of an offer in compromise does not automatically suspend collection of an account. If there is any indication that the filing of the offer is solely for the purpose of delaying collection of the tax or that delay would negatively affect collection of the tax, we will continue collection efforts."

Finally, if the taxpayer is in danger of enforced collection activities that are inappropriate (because, for example, payment has been made but not acknowledged by the IRS computers), the IRS Problem Resolution Program may be able to resolve the problem. Section 7811, as amended by the Taxpayer Bill of Rights, authorizes the Taxpayer Ombudsman in the National Office or his delegate ° to issue Taxpayer Assistance Orders (staying collection activities or ordering remedial actions such as release of liens) if "the taxpayer is suffering or about to suffer significant hardship as a result of the manner in which the internal revenue laws are being administered * * *." The Service has issued Form 911, Application for Taxpayer Assistance Order to Relieve Hardship, for use in seeking relief under section 7811.

A. ASSESSMENT, NOTICE AND DEMAND

Enforced collection activity generally may not begin until the taxpayer has been given notice of the assessment of the tax liability and demand for its payment. Recall from Chapter 5 that assessment is merely the recording of the liability on a special form and the signing of the form by an assessment officer. I.R.C. § 6203. Notice of the assessment and demand for payment should be made "as soon as practicable" and in no event more than 60 days after the date of assessment. I.R.C. § 6303(a). The notice should be delivered to the taxpayer's residence or usual place of business or mailed to the taxpayer's last known address. *Id.* (See Section 1 of Chapter 7 for rules concerning the "last known address.") The taxpayer is then given a grace period of at least ten days in which to make payment. If the tax is not paid within ten days, the Service may then send notice of intent to levy, and if the tax is not paid within 30 days of this notice, it may begin enforced collection activity by "levying" on the taxpayer's property that is subject to the federal tax lien. I.R.C. § 6331(d).

B. THE FEDERAL TAX LIEN

Scope of the lien. The federal tax lien arises automatically upon the occurrence of the events described above. When assessment has been made, notice and demand delivered or mailed, and payment has not been made in 10 days, the federal tax lien arises automatically against "all property and rights to property, whether real or personal,

n. The Collection Process (Income Tax Accounts), IRS Pub. 586A, Rev. July 1989.

o. Each district office has a problems resolution office.

Sec. 1 OVERVIEW 721

belonging to" the taxpayer. I.R.C. § 6321. The lien attaches to property owned by the taxpayer at any time during the life of the lien, including property acquired by the taxpayer after the lien arises. Reg. § 301.6321-1. Whether the taxpayer owns property or has an interest in property to which the lien can attach is subject to state law. See United States v. Rodgers, at page 722 of this Chapter. The Service may levy on all property to which the lien attaches, except types of property exempt from levy under section 6334.

Duration of the lien. Section 6502 requires the Service to institute collection activities (whether by administrative levy or by suit) within ten years from the date the lien arises. Prior to its amendment in 1990, the statute of limitations under section 6502 was six years. If the Service brings suit to collect a tax, then the limitations period on issuing levies is suspended until the liability is satisfied or becomes unenforceable. I.R.C. § 6502(a) (as amended in 1988). The limitations period on enforced collection activity can be extended by written agreement. *Id.*

Recording the lien. A delinquent taxpayer is usually also delinquent on other debts, and the courts are constantly called upon to determine the priority of the various creditors, including the IRS. One way the IRS can obtain an advantage over certain other creditors is to file notice of the existence of the tax lien. The Service must exercise some caution in filing notice of the existence of the federal tax lien, however, because filing such a notice could destroy the taxpayer's credit and jeopardize collection of the tax. The Service's policy on filing notices of liens is as follows:

> A notice of lien shall not be filed, except in jeopardy assessment cases, until reasonable efforts have been made to contact the taxpayer in person, by telephone or by a notice sent by certified mail, delivered in person or left at the taxpayer's last known address, to afford him/her the opportunity to make payment. All pertinent facts must be carefully considered as the filing of the notice of lien may adversely affect the taxpayer's ability to pay and thereby hamper or retard the collection process.[p]

Once the federal tax lien is recorded, it takes priority over other creditors' interests, except for the so-called "superpriorities" identified in section 6323(b).[q] A federal tax lien that has not been recorded does not take priority over claims of purchasers, holders of security interests, mechanic's lienors or judgment creditors, but a recorded tax lien is superior to each of these interests. See I.R.C. § 6323(a).

Releasing the lien. Section 6325 requires the Service to release a federal tax lien within 30 days of the date when the underlying tax has been paid or bonded or has become uncollectible, or the taxpayer has

---

p. Internal Revenue Manual, Policies of the IRS Handbook, P-5-47.

q. In addition to the superpriorities of section 6323(b), special protection is given to holders of security interests in commercial transaction financing agreements and other specified creditors under certain circumstances. See section 6323(c), (d) and (e).

requested release on the basis that the liability has been paid or was unenforceable. When one of these circumstances exists, the Service must issue a certificate evidencing the release of the lien within 30 days. Prior to passage in 1988 of the Taxpayer Bill of Rights, the Code contained no means of compelling the Service to comply with section 6325. Now, however, the taxpayer may sue under section 7432 for damages for the Service's negligent or intentional violation of section 6325. Damages that can be awarded are the "actual, direct economic damages sustained," plus "the costs of the action," less the amount (if any) by which the taxpayer reasonably could have mitigated the damages.

The Taxpayer Bill of Rights also added section 6326, which provides for administrative appeal of erroneously recorded liens. Section 6326 requires the Service to release an erroneously recorded lien and issue a certificate of release (reflecting that the lien was erroneously recorded) within 14 days. Damages for failure to comply with section 6326 are recoverable under section 7433, which authorizes suit against the government for damages resulting from reckless or intentional disregard by IRS employees of any federal tax statute or regulation. Sections 7432 and 7433 are discussed in Miklautsch v. Commissioner, at page 847.

SECTION 2. JUDICIAL AND ADMINISTRATIVE COLLECTION PROCEDURES

Once the lien has attached, the IRS can begin enforced collection activities of two types. First, it can bring any type of civil action appropriate under the circumstances. For example, it can sue to foreclose the federal tax lien, to reduce the tax assessment to judgment, or to enter the taxpayer's property to seize property subject to the lien. United States v. Rodgers, below, is an example of a civil suit brought by the IRS to foreclose a tax lien. The other avenue available to the IRS is to levy on the taxpayer's property under authority of section 6331. United States v. National Bank of Commerce, page 740 below, discusses the administrative levy process. Section 6502 of the Code was amended in 1990 to extend the statute of limitations on enforced collection activities from six years after assessment to ten years after assessment.

UNITED STATES v. RODGERS
Supreme Court of the United States, 1983.
461 U.S. 677, 103 S.Ct. 2132, 76 L.Ed.2d 236.

JUSTICE BRENNAN delivered the opinion of the Court.

These consolidated cases involve the relationship between the imperatives of federal tax collection and rights accorded by state property laws. Section 7403 of the Internal Revenue Code of 1954 authorizes the judicial sale of certain properties to satisfy the tax indebtedness of delinquent taxpayers. The issue in both cases is whether § 7403 empowers a federal district court to order the sale of a family home in which a delinquent taxpayer had an interest at the time he incurred his indebtedness, but in which the taxpayer's spouse, who does not owe any of that indebtedness, also has a separate "homestead" right as defined by Texas law. We hold that the statute does grant power to order the sale, but that its exercise is limited to some degree by equitable discretion. We also hold that, if the home is sold, the nondelinquent spouse is entitled, as part of the distribution of proceeds required under § 7403, to so much of the proceeds as represents complete compensation for the loss of the homestead estate.

I

A

Section 7403 provides in full as follows:

"(a) Filing.—In any case where there has been a refusal or neglect to pay any tax, or to discharge any liability in respect thereof, whether or not levy has been made, the Attorney General or his delegate, at the request of the Secretary [of the Treasury], may direct a civil action to be filed in a district court of the United States to enforce the lien of the United States under this title with respect to such tax or liability or to subject any property, [of] whatever nature, of the delinquent, or in which he has any right, title, or interest, to the payment of such tax or liability. For purposes of the preceding sentence, any acceleration of payment under section 6166(g) or 6166A(h) shall be treated as a neglect to pay tax.

"(b) Parties.—All persons having liens upon or claiming any interest in the property involved in such action shall be made parties thereto.

"(c) Adjudication and decree.—The court shall, after the parties have been duly notified of the action, proceed to adjudicate all matters involved therein and finally determine the merits of all claims to and liens upon the property, and, in all cases where a claim or interest of the United States therein is established, may decree a sale of such property, by the proper officer of the court, and a distribution of the proceeds of such sale according to the findings of the court in respect to the interests of the parties and of the United States. If the property is sold to satisfy a first lien held by the United States, the United States may bid at the sale such sum, not exceeding the amount of such lien with expenses of sale, as the Secretary directs.

"(d) Receivership.—In any such proceeding, at the instance of the United States, the court may appoint a receiver to enforce the lien, or, upon certification by the Secretary during the pendency of such proceedings that it is in the public interest, may appoint a receiver with all the powers of a receiver in equity."

As a general matter, the "lien of the United States" referred to in § 7403(a) is that created by 26 U.S.C. § 6321, which provides:

"If any person liable to pay any tax neglects or refuses to pay the same after demand, the amount (including any interest, additional amount, addition to tax, or assessable penalty, together with any costs that may accrue in addition thereto) shall be a lien in favor of the United States upon all property and rights to property, whether real or personal, belonging to such person."

Section 7403 * * * is one of a number of distinct enforcement tools available to the United States for the collection of delinquent taxes. The Government may, for example, simply sue for the unpaid amount, and, on getting a judgment, exercise the usual rights of a judgment creditor. See 26 U.S.C. §§ 6502(a), 7401, 7402(a). Yet a third route is administrative levy under 26 U.S.C. § 6331, which provides:

"If any person liable to pay any tax neglects or refuses to pay the same within 10 days after notice and demand, it shall be lawful for the Secretary or his delegate to collect such tax (and such further sum as shall be sufficient to cover the expenses of the levy) by levy upon all property and rights to property (except such property as is exempt under section 6334) belonging to such person or on which there is a lien provided in this chapter for the payment of such tax. * * *"

Administrative levy, unlike an ordinary lawsuit, and unlike the procedure described in § 7403, does not require any judicial intervention, and it is up to the taxpayer, if he so chooses, to go to court if he claims that the assessed amount was not legally owing.

The common purpose of this formidable arsenal of collection tools is to ensure the prompt and certain enforcement of the tax laws in a system relying primarily on self-reporting. Moreover, it has long been an axiom of our tax collection scheme that, although the definition of underlying property interests is left to state law, the consequences that attach to those interests is a matter left to federal law. See * * * Aquilino v. United States, 363 U.S. 509, 513–515, 80 S.Ct. 1277, 1280–1281, 4 L.Ed.2d 1365 (1960), and cases cited (attachment of federal lien depends on whether "property" or "rights to property" exist under state law; priority of federal lien depends on federal law) * * *.

B

The substance of Texas law related to the homestead right may usefully be divided into two categories. First, in common with a large number of States, Texas establishes the family home or place of business as an enclave exempted from the reach of most creditors. Thus, under Tex. Const., Art. 16, § 50,

"The homestead of a family, or of a single adult person, shall be, and is hereby protected from forced sale, for the payment of all debts except for [certain exceptions not relevant here] * * * No mortgage, trust deed, or other lien on the homestead shall ever be valid, except for [certain exceptions not relevant here] * * *."

Second, in common with a somewhat smaller number of states, Texas gives members of the family unit additional rights in the homestead property itself. Thus, in a clause not included in the above quotation, Tex. Const., Art. 16, § 50, also provides that "the owner or claimant of the property claimed as a homestead [may not], if married, sell or abandon the homestead without the consent of the other spouse, given in such manner as may be prescribed by law." Equally important, Art. 16, § 52, provides that:

> "On the death of the husband or wife, or both, the homestead shall descend and vest in like manner as other real property of the deceased, and shall be governed by the same laws of descent and distribution, but it shall not be partitioned among the heirs of the deceased during the lifetime of the surviving husband or wife, or so long as the survivor may elect to use or occupy the same as a homestead, or so long as the guardian of the minor children of the deceased may be permitted, under the order of the proper court having the jurisdiction to use and occupy the same."

The effect of these provisions in the Texas Constitution is to give each spouse in a marriage a separate and undivided possessory interest in the homestead, which is only lost by death or abandonment, and which may not be compromised either by the other spouse or by his or her heirs. It bears emphasis that the rights accorded by the homestead laws vest independently in each spouse regardless of whether one spouse, or both, actually owns the fee interest in the homestead. Thus, although analogy is somewhat hazardous in this area, it may be said that the homestead laws have the effect of reducing the underlying ownership rights in a homestead property to something akin to remainder interests and vesting in each spouse an interest akin to undivided life estate in the property. This analogy, although it does some injustice to the nuances present in the Texas homestead statute, also serves to bring to the fore something that has been repeatedly emphasized by the Texas courts, and which was reaffirmed by the Court of Appeals in these cases: that the Texas homestead right is not a mere statutory entitlement, but a vested property right. As the Supreme Court of Texas has put it, a spouse "has a vested estate in the land of which she cannot be divested during her life except by abandonment or a voluntary conveyance in the manner prescribed by law." Paddock v. Siemoneit, supra, 147 Tex., at 585, 218 S.W.2d at 436; see United States v. Rogers, 649 F.2d 1117, 1127 (CA5 1981), and cases cited.

II

The two cases before us were consolidated for oral argument before the United States Court of Appeals for the Fifth Circuit, and resulted in opinions issued on the same day. United States v. Rogers, supra,[13] Ingram v. Dallas Department of Housing & Urban Rehabilitation, 649 F.2d 1128 (1981). They arise out of legally comparable, but quite distinct, sets of facts.

---

13. Mrs. Rodgers's name was misspelled in the complaint filed by the Government. See 649 F.2d at 1119, n. 1.

A

Lucille Mitzi Bosco Rodgers is the widow of Philip S. Bosco, whom she married in 1937. She and Mr. Bosco acquired, as community property, a residence in Dallas, Texas, and occupied it as their homestead. Subsequently, in 1971 and 1972, the Internal Revenue Service issued assessments totalling more than $900,000.00 for federal wagering taxes, penalties, and interest, against Philip for the taxable years 1966 through 1971. These taxes remained unpaid at the time of Philip's death in 1974. Since Philip's death, Lucille has continued to occupy the property as her homestead, and now lives there with her present husband.

On September 23, 1977, the Government filed suit under 26 U.S.C. §§ 7402 and 7403 in the United States District Court for the Northern District of Texas against Mrs. Rodgers and Philip's son, daughter, and executor. The suit sought to reduce to judgment the assessments against Philip, to enforce the Government's tax liens, including the one that had attached to Philip's interest in the residence, and to obtain a deficiency judgment in the amount of any unsatisfied part of the liability. On cross-motions for summary judgment, the District Court granted partial summary judgment on, among other things, the defendants' claim that the federal tax liens could not defeat Mrs. Rodgers's state-created right not to have her homestead subjected to a forced sale.

The Court of Appeals affirmed on the homestead issue, holding that if "a homestead interest is, under state law, a property right, possessed by the nontaxpayer spouse at the time the lien attaches to the taxpayer spouse's interest, then the federal tax lien may not be foreclosed against the homestead property for as long as the nontaxpayer spouse maintains his or her homestead interest under state law." The court implied that the Government had the choice of either waiting until Mrs. Rodgers's homestead interest lapsed, or satisfying itself with a forced sale of only Philip Bosco's interest in the property.

B

Joerene Ingram is the divorced wife of Donald Ingram. During their marriage, Joerene and Donald acquired, as community property, a residence in Dallas, Texas, and occupied it as their homestead. Subsequently, in 1972 and 1973, the Internal Revenue Service issued assessments against Donald Ingram relating to unpaid taxes withheld from wages of employees of a company of which he was president. Deducting payments made on account of these liabilities, there remains unpaid approximately $9,000, plus interest. In addition, in 1973, the Service made an assessment against both Donald and Joerene in the amount of $283.33, plus interest, relating to their joint income tax liability for 1971. These amounts also remain unpaid.

In March 1975, at about the time the Ingrams were seeking a divorce, their residence was destroyed by fire. In September 1975, the Ingrams obtained a divorce. In connection with the divorce, they entered into a property settlement agreement, one provision of which was that Donald would convey to Joerene his interest in the real property involved in this case in exchange for $1,500, to be paid from the proceeds of the sale of the property. Joerene tried to sell the property, through a trustee, but was unsuccessful in those efforts, apparently because of the federal tax liens encumbering the property. To make matters worse, she then received notice from the City of Dallas Department of Housing and Urban Rehabilitation (Department) that unless she complied with local ordinances, the remains of the fire-damaged residence would be demolished. Following a hearing, the Department issued a final notice and a work order to demolish. Joerene Ingram and the trustee then filed suit in Texas state court to quiet title to the property, to remove the federal tax liens, and to enjoin demolition. The defendants were the United States, the Department, and several creditors claiming an interest in the property.

The United States removed the suit to the District Court for the Northern District of Texas. It then filed a counterclaim against Joerene Ingram and Donald Ingram (who was added as a defendant on the counterclaim) for both the unpaid withholding taxes and the joint liability for unpaid income taxes. In its prayer for relief, the Government sought, among other things, judicial sale of the property under § 7403. Pursuant to a stipulation of the parties, the property was sold unencumbered and the proceeds (approximately $16,250) were deposited into the registry of the District Court pending the outcome of the suit. The parties agreed that their rights, claims, and priorities would be determined as if the sale had not taken place, and that the proceeds would be divided according to their respective interests. On cross-motions for summary judgment, the District Court granted summary judgment on the Government's counterclaims.

The Court of Appeals affirmed in part, and reversed and remanded in part. It agreed that the Government could foreclose its lien on the proceeds from the sale of the property to collect the $283.33, plus interest, for the unpaid income tax owed by Joerene and Donald Ingram jointly. Applying its decision in Rodgers, however, it also held that the Government could not reach the proceeds of the sale of the property to collect the individual liability of Donald Ingram, assuming Joerene Ingram had maintained her homestead interest in the property. The court remanded, however, for a factual determination of whether Joerene had "abandoned" the homestead by dividing the insurance proceeds with Donald and by attempting—even before the stipulation entered into with the Government—to sell the property and divide the proceeds of that sale with Donald.

C

The Government filed a single petition for certiorari in both these cases. We granted certiorari in order to resolve a conflict among the Courts of Appeals as to the proper interpretation of § 7403.

III

A

The basic holding underlying the Court of Appeals's view that the Government was not authorized to seek a sale of the homes in which respondents held a homestead interest is that "when a delinquent taxpayer shares his ownership interest in property jointly with other persons, rather than being the sole owner, his 'property' and 'rights to property' to which the federal tax lien attaches under 26 U.S.C. § 6321, and on which federal levy may be had under 26 U.S.C. § 7403(a), involve only his *interest* in the property, and not the entire property." According to the Court of Appeals, this principle applies, not only in the homestead context, but in any cotenancy in which unindebted third parties share an ownership interest with a delinquent taxpayer.

We agree with the Court of Appeals that the Government's lien under § 6321 cannot extend beyond the property interests held by the delinquent taxpayer. We also agree that the Government may not ultimately collect, as satisfaction for the indebtedness owed to it more than the value of the property interests that are actually liable for that debt. But, in this context at least, the right to collect and the right to seek a forced sale are two quite different things.

The Court of Appeals for the Fifth Circuit recognized that it was the only Court of Appeals that had adopted the view that the Government could seek the sale, under § 7403, of only the delinquent taxpayer's "interest in the property, and not the entire property." We agree with the prevailing view that such a restrictive reading of § 7403 flies in the face of the plain meaning of the statute. See, e.g., United States v. Overman, 424 F.2d 1142, 1146 (CA9 1970).

Section 7403(a) provides, not only that the Government may "enforce [its] lien," but also that it may seek to "subject *any property,* [of] whatever nature, of the delinquent, or *in which he has any right, title, or interest* to the payment of such tax or liability" (emphasis added). This clause in and of itself defeats the reading proposed by the Court of Appeals. Section 7403(b) then provides that "[a]ll persons having liens upon *or claiming any interest in the property involved in such action* shall be made parties thereto" (emphasis added). Obviously, no joinder of persons claiming independent interests in the property would be necessary if the Government were only authorized to seek the sale of the delinquent taxpayer's own interests. Finally, § 7403(c) provides that the district court should "determine the merits of all claims to and liens upon the property, and, in all cases where a claim or interest of the United States therein is established, may decree a sale *of such property * * * and a proper distribution of the proceeds of such sale according to the findings of the court in respect to the interests of the parties and of the United States.*" (emphasis added). Again, we must read the statute to contemplate, not merely the sale of the delinquent taxpayer's own interest, but the sale of the entire property (as long as the United States has any "claim or interest" in it), and the recognition of third-party interests through the mechanism of judicial valuation and distribution.

Our reading of § 7403 is consistent with the policy inherent in the tax statutes in favor of the prompt and certain collection of delinquent taxes. It requires no citation to point out that interests in property, when sold separately, may be worth either significantly more or significantly less than the sum of their parts. When the latter is the case, it makes considerable sense to allow the Government to seek the sale of the whole, and obtain its fair share of the proceeds, rather than satisfy itself with a mere sale of the part.

Our reading is also supported by an examination of the historical background against which the predecessor statute to § 7403 was enacted. In 1868, as today, state taxation consisted in large part of ad valorem taxation on real property. In enforcing such taxes against delinquent taxpayers, one usual remedy was a sale by the State of the assessed property. The prevailing—although admittedly not universal—view was that such sales were in rem proceedings, and that the title that was created in the sale extinguished not only the interests of the person liable to pay the tax, but also any other interests that had attached to the property, even if the owners of such interests could not otherwise be held liable for the tax. Where in rem proceedings were the rule, they were generally held to cut off as well dower or homestead rights possessed by the delinquent taxpayer's spouse.

One evident purpose of the federal judicial sale provision enacted in 1868 was to obtain for the federal tax collector some of the advantages that many States enjoyed through in rem tax enforcement. * * *

Even as it gave the Government the right to seek an undivided sale in an in rem proceeding, however, the predecessor to § 7403 departed quite sharply from the model provided by the States by guaranteeing that third parties with an interest in the property receive a share of the proceeds commensurate with the value of their interests. This apparently unique provision was prompted, we can assume, by the sense that, precisely because the federal taxes involved were not taxes on the real property being sold, simple justice required significantly greater solicitude for third parties than was generally available in state in rem proceedings.

Finally, our reading of the statute is significantly bolstered by a comparison with the statutory language setting out the administrative levy remedy also available to the Government. Under 26 U.S.C. § 6331, the Government may sell for the collection of unpaid taxes all non-exempt "property and rights to property * * * *belonging to such person* [i.e., the delinquent taxpayer] or on which there is a lien provided in this chapter for the payment of such tax" (emphasis added). This language clearly embodies the limitation that the Court of Appeals thought was present in § 7403, and it has been so interpreted by the courts. Section 6331, unlike § 7403, does not require notice and hearing for third parties, because no rights of third parties are intended to be implicated by § 6331. Indeed, third parties whose property or interests in property have been seized inadvertently are entitled to claim that the property has been "wrongfully levied upon," and may apply for its return either through administrative channels, 26 U.S.C. § 6343(b), or through a civil action filed in a federal district court, § 7426(a)(1); see §§ 7426(b)(1), 7426(b)(2)(A). In the absence of such "wrongful levy," the entire proceeds of a sale conducted pursuant to administrative levy may be applied, without any prior distribution of the sort required by § 7403, to the expenses of the levy and sale, the specific tax liability on the seized property, and the general tax liability of the delinquent taxpayer. 26 U.S.C. § 6342.

We are not entirely unmoved by the force of the basic intuition underlying the Court of Appeals's view of § 7403—that the Government, though it has the "right to pursue the property of the [delinquent] taxpayer with all the force and fury at its command," should not have any right, superior to that of other creditors, to disturb the settled expectations of innocent third parties. In fact, however, the Government's right to seek a forced sale of the entire property in which a delinquent taxpayer had an interest does not arise out of its privileges as an ordinary creditor, but out of the express terms of § 7403. Moreover, the use of the power granted by § 7403 is not the act of an ordinary creditor, but the exercise of a sovereign prerogative, incident to the power to enforce the obligations of the delinquent taxpayer himself, and ultimately grounded in the constitutional mandate to "lay and collect taxes."

Admittedly, if § 7403 allowed for the gratuitous confiscation of one person's property interests in order to satisfy another person's tax indebtedness, such a provision might pose significant difficulties under the Due Process Clause of the Fifth Amendment. But, as we have already indicated, § 7403 makes no further use of third-party property interests than to facilitate the extraction of value from those concurrent property interests that *are* properly liable for the taxpayer's debt. To the extent that third-party property interests are "taken" in the process, § 7403 provides compensation for that "taking" by requiring that the court distribute the proceeds of the sale "according to the findings of the court in respect to the interests of the parties and of the United States." Cf. United States v. Overman, 424 F.2d, at 1146. Moreover, we hold, on the basis of what we are informed about the nature of the homestead estate in Texas, that it is the sort of property interest for whose loss an innocent third-party must be compensated under § 7403.[25] We therefore see no contradiction, at least at the level

25. We therefore reject the Government's contention at oral argument, that the homestead estate would be irrelevant to a distribution under § 7403, and that, assuming that the entire underlying ownership interest is liable for the delinquent taxes, the Government would be entitled to the entire proceeds of the sale.

We also reject the Government's suggestion that the homestead estate held by respondent Rodgers was only contingent at the time that the federal tax lien attached to her husband's interests in her home, and is therefore subordinate to the tax lien. The "probate homestead" provided

of basic principle, between the enforcement powers granted to the Government under § 7403 and the recognition of vested property interests granted to innocent third parties under state law.

The exact method for the distribution required by § 7403 is not before us at this time. But we can get a rough idea of the practical consequences of the principles we have just set out. For example, if we assume, *only for the sake of illustration,* that a homestead estate is the exact economic equivalent of a life estate, and that the use of a standard statutory or commercial table and an 8% discount rate is appropriate in calculating the value of that estate, then three non-delinquent surviving or remaining spouses, aged 30, 50, and 70 years, each holding a homestead estate, would be entitled to approximately 97%, 89%, and 64%, respectively, of the proceeds of the sale of their homes as compensation for that estate. In addition, if we assume that each of these hypothetical non-delinquent spouses also has a protected half-interest in the underlying ownership rights to the property being sold,[27] then their total compensation would be approximately 99%, 95%, and 82%, respectively, of the proceeds from such sale.

In sum, the Internal Revenue Code, seen as a whole, contains a number of cumulative collection devices, each with its own advantages and disadvantages for the tax collector. Among the advantages of administrative levy is that it is quick and relatively inexpensive. Among the advantages of a § 7403 proceeding is that it gives the Federal Government the opportunity to seek the highest return possible on the forced sale of property interests liable for the payment of federal taxes. The provisions of § 7403 are broad and profound. Nevertheless, § 7403 is punctilious in protecting the vested rights of third parties caught in the Government's collection effort, and in ensuring that the Government not receive out of the proceeds of the sale any more than that to which it is properly entitled. Of course, the exercise in any particular case of the power granted under § 7403 to seek the forced sale of property interests other than those of the delinquent taxpayer is left in the first instance to the good sense and common decency of the collecting authorities. 26 U.S.C. § 7403(a). We also explore in Part IV of this opinion the nature of the limited discretion left to the courts in proceedings brought under § 7403. But that the power exists, and that it is necessary to the prompt and certain enforcement of the tax laws, we have no doubt.

B

There is another, intermeshed but analytically distinguishable, ground advanced by the Court of Appeals and the respondents—and

for in Tex.Const., Art. 16, § 52, is clearly, with respect to outside creditors, only a continuation of the separate homestead rights vested in each spouse by Tex.Const., Art. 16, § 50.

27. In the cases before us, the Government argues that, under Texas law, the entire community property (*i.e.,* the underlying ownership interest that we have analogized to a remainder interest), rather than merely the delinquent spouse's half-interest in it, is liable for the indebtedness of the delinquent spouse. The Court of Appeals did not address this issue, and we leave it open for determination on remand.

reiterated by the dissent—for denying the Government the right to seek the forced sale of property held as a homestead by a non-delinquent third party. Taken in itself, this view would hold that, even if § 7403 normally allows for the forced sale of property interests other than those directly liable for the indebtedness of the delinquent taxpayer, the special protections accorded by the exemption aspect of Texas homestead law should immunize it from the reach of § 7403.

The Court of Appeals conceded that "the homestead interest of a *taxpayer* spouse, i.e., that of one who himself has tax liability, clearly cannot by itself defeat [the enforcement under § 7403 of] a federal tax lien." * * * This proposition, although not explicit in the Code, is clearly implicit in 26 U.S.C. § 6334(c) (relating to exemptions from levy) [28] * * *. The Court of Appeals also held that, if the homestead interest under Texas law were "merely an exemption" without accompanying vested property rights, it would not be effective against the Federal Government in a § 7403 proceeding, even in the case of a non-delinquent spouse. Nevertheless, the court concluded that, if the homestead estate both was claimed by a non-delinquent spouse and constituted a property right under state law then it would bar the federal Government from pursuing a forced sale of the entire property.

We disagree. If § 7403 is intended, as we believe it is, to reach the entire property in which a delinquent taxpayer has or had any "right, title, or interest," then state-created exemptions against forced sale should be no more effective with regard to the entire property than with regard to the "right, title, or interest" itself. No exception of the sort carved out by the Court of Appeals appears on the face of the statute, and we decline to frustrate the policy of the statute by reading such an exception into it. Moreover, the Supremacy Clause—which provides the underpinning for the Federal Government's right to sweep aside state-created exemptions in the first place—is as potent in its application to innocent bystanders as in its application to delinquent debtors. Whatever property rights attach to a homestead under Texas law are adequately discharged by the payment of compensation, and no further deference to state law is required, either by § 7403 or by the Constitution.

The dissent urges us to carve out an exception from the plain language of § 7403 in that "small number of joint-ownership situations * * * [in which] the delinquent taxpayer has no right to force partition or otherwise to alienate the entire property without the consent of the co-owner." Its primary argument in favor of such an exception is that it would be consistent with traditional limitations on the rights of a lienholder. * * * [W]e believe that the better analogy in this case is not to the traditional rights of lienholders, but to the traditional powers

---

28. Section 6334(c) provides, "Notwithstanding any other law of the United States, no property or rights to property shall be exempt from levy other than the property specifically made exempt by [§ 6334(a).]"

of a taxing authority in an in rem enforcement proceeding.[31]

IV
A

Although we have held that the Supremacy Clause allows the federal tax collector to convert a non-delinquent spouse's homestead estate into its fair cash value, and that such a conversion satisfies the requirements of due process, we are not blind to the fact that in practical terms financial compensation may not always be a completely adequate substitute for a roof over one's head. This problem seems particularly acute in the case of a homestead interest. First, the nature of the market for life estates or the market for rental property may be such that the value of a homestead interest, calculated as some fraction of the total value of a home, would be less than the price demanded by the market for a lifetime's interest in an equivalent home. Second, any calculation of the cash value of a homestead interest must of necessity be based on actuarial statistics, and will unavoidably undercompensate persons who end up living longer than the average. * * *

If the sale and distribution provided for in § 7403 were mandatory, the practical problems we have just described would be of little legal consequence. The statute provides, however, that the court in a § 7403 proceeding "*shall* * * * proceed to adjudicate all matters involved therein and finally determine the merits of all claims to and liens upon the property, and, in all cases where a claim or interest of the United

---

31. In addition to its reliance on the traditional limitations imposed on lienholders * * * the dissent makes a number of additional arguments which require at least a brief response. First, it claims that the weight of authority is on its side. The dissent's use of sources largely overlooks, however, the important distinction between the power of sale under § 7403 on the one hand and the extent of the underlying lien and the power of administrative levy on the other.

Second, the dissent relies on a piece of 1954 legislative history concerning the application of the federal tax lien to interests in tenancies by the entirety. Quite apart from the fact that the dissent's argument depends on events taking place almost a century after enactment of the statute at issue, it suffers from * * * serious flaws.

(1) The question at issue in 1954 bears only the most tangential relationship to that at issue here. The amendments at issue in 1954 did not concern § 7403. More important, tenancies by the entirety pose a problem quite distinct from that at issue in the case of homestead rights. The basic holding of the line of cases mentioned by the dissent was, not merely that interests in a tenancy by the entirety could not be sold to satisfy a tax debt of one spouse, but that, as a result of the peculiar legal fiction governing tenancies by the entirety in some States, no tax lien could attach in the first place because neither spouse possessed an independent interest in the property. Indeed, in most of the cases in this line, the Government was *not* trying to sell the property out from under the nondelinquent spouse, but was merely trying to exercise one of the more benign rights of a lienholder to which the dissent would automatically relegate the Government in this case. In the homestead context, by contrast, there is no doubt, even under state law, that not only do *both* spouses (rather than neither) have an independent interest in the homestead property, but that a federal tax lien can at least *attach* to each of those interests. Thus, *if* the tenancy by the entirety cases are correct, they do no more than illustrate the proposition that, in the tax enforcement context, federal law governs the consequences that attach to property interests, but state law governs whether any property interests exist in the first place.

* * *

States therein is established, *may* decree a sale of such property * * * " (emphasis added), and respondents argue that this language allows a district court hearing a § 7403 proceeding to exercise a degree of equitable discretion and refuse to authorize a forced sale in a particular case. The Court of Appeals agreed with this interpretation of the statute, although it does not appear to have relied on it, and in any event neither it nor the District Court undertook any particularized equitable assessment of the cases now before us. We find the question to be close, but on balance, we too conclude that § 7403 does not require a district court to authorize a forced sale under absolutely all circumstances, and that some limited room is left in the statute for the exercise of reasoned discretion.

* * *

C

To say that district courts need not always go ahead with a forced sale authorized by § 7403 is not to say that they have unbridled discretion. We can think of virtually no circumstances, for example, in which it would be permissible to refuse to authorize a sale simply to protect the interests of the delinquent taxpayer himself or herself. And even when the interests of third parties are involved, we think that a certain fairly limited set of considerations will almost always be paramount.

First, a court should consider the extent to which the Government's financial interests would be prejudiced if it were relegated to a forced sale of the partial interest actually liable for the delinquent taxes. Even the Government seems to concede that, if such a partial sale would not prejudice it at all (because the separate market value of the partial interest is likely to be equal to or greater than its value as a fraction of the total value of the entire property) then there would be no reason at all to authorize a sale of the entire property. We think that a natural extension of this principle, however, is that, even when the partial interest would be worth *less* sold separately than sold as part of the entire property, the possibility of prejudice to the Government can still be measured as a matter of degree. Simply put, the higher the expected market price, the less the prejudice, and the less weighty the Government's interest in going ahead with a sale of the entire property.

Second, a court should consider whether the third party with a non-liable separate interest in the property would, in the normal course of events (leaving aside § 7403 and eminent domain proceedings, of course), have a legally recognized expectation that that separate property would not be subject to forced sale by the delinquent taxpayer or his or her creditors. If there is no such expectation, then there would seem to be little reason not to authorize the sale. Again, however, this factor is amenable to considerations of degree. The Texas homestead laws are almost absolute in their protections against forced sale. The usual cotenancy arrangement, which allows any cotenant to seek a judicial sale of the property and distribution of the proceeds, but which also allows the other cotenants to resist the sale and apply instead for a partition in kind, is further along the continuum. And a host of other types of property interests are arrayed between and beyond.

Third, a court should consider the likely prejudice to the third party, both in personal dislocation costs and in the sort of practical undercompensation described supra.

Fourth, a court should consider the relative character and value of the non-liable and liable interests held in the property: if, for example, in the case of real property, the third party has no present possessory interest or fee interest in the property, there may be little reason not to allow the sale; if, on the other hand, the third party not only has a possessory interest or fee interest, but that interest is worth 99% of the value of the property, then there might well be virtually no reason to allow the sale to proceed.

We do not pretend that the factors we have just outlined constitute an exhaustive list; we certainly do not contemplate that they be used as a "mechanical checklist" to the exclusion of common sense and consideration of special circumstances. We do emphasize, however, that the limited discretion accorded by § 7403 should be exercised rigorously and sparingly, keeping in mind the Government's paramount interest in prompt and certain collection of delinquent taxes.

V

In these cases, no individualized equitable balance of the sort we have just outlined has yet been attempted. In the Rodgers case, the record before us, although it is quite clear as to the legal issues relevant to the second consideration noted above, affords us little guidance otherwise. In any event, we think that the task of exercising equitable discretion should be left to the District Court in the first instance.

The Ingram case is a bit more complicated, even leaving aside the fact of the stipulated sale by which we are constrained to treat the escrow fund now sitting in the registry of the District Court as if it were a house. First, as the Court of Appeals pointed out, there remains a question under Texas law as to whether Joerene Ingram abandoned the homestead by the time of the stipulated sale. Second, the Government, in addition to its lien for the individual debt of Donald Ingram, has a further lien for $283.33, plus interest, on the house, representing the joint liability of Donald and Joerene Ingram. Because Joerene Ingram is not a "third party" as to that joint liability, we can see no reason, as long as that amount remains unpaid, not to allow a "sale" of the "house" (i.e., a levy on the proceeds of the stipulated sale) for satisfaction of the debt. Moreover, once the dam is broken, there is no reason, under our interpretation of § 7403, not to allow the Government also to collect on the individual debt of Donald Ingram *out of that portion of the proceeds of the sale representing property interests properly liable for the debt.* On the other hand, it would certainly be to Mrs. Ingram's advantage to discharge her personal liability before the Government can proceed with its "sale," in which event, assuming that she has not abandoned the homestead, the District Court will be obliged to strike an equitable balance on the same general principles as those that govern the Rodgers case.

The judgment of the Court of Appeals in Rodgers is reversed, its judgment in Ingram is vacated, and both cases are remanded with directions that they be remanded to the District Court for further proceedings consistent with this opinion.

So ordered.

JUSTICE BLACKMUN, with whom JUSTICE REHNQUIST, JUSTICE STEVENS, and JUSTICE O'CONNOR join, concurring in part and dissenting in part.

The Court today properly rejects the broad legal principle concerning 26 U.S.C. § 7403 that was announced by the Court of Appeals. I agree that, in some situations, § 7403 gives the Government the power to sell property not belonging to the taxpayer. Our task, however, is to ascertain how far Congress intended that power to extend. In my view, § 7403 confers on the Government the power to sell or force the sale of jointly-owned property only insofar as the *tax debtor's* interest in that property would permit *him* to do so; it does not confer on the Government the power to sell jointly-owned property if an unindebted co-owner enjoys an *indestructible* right to bar a sale and to continue in possession. Because Mrs. Rodgers had such a right, and because she is not herself indebted to the Government, I dissent from the Court's disposition of her case.

I

It is basic in the common law that a lienholder enjoys rights in property no greater than those of the debtor himself; that is, the lienholder does no more than step into the debtor's shoes. * * *

In a small number of joint-ownership situations * * * the delinquent taxpayer has no right to force partition or otherwise to alienate the entire property without the consent of the co-owner. These include tenancies by the entirety and certain homestead estates. In this case, the homestead estate owned by the delinquent taxpayer—Mrs. Rodgers' deceased husband—did not include the right to sell or force the sale of the homestead during Mrs. Rodgers' lifetime without her consent. Mrs. Rodgers had, and still has, an indefeasible right to possession, an interest, as the Court recognizes, "akin to an undivided life estate." A lienholder stepping into the shoes of the delinquent taxpayer would not be able to force a sale.

II

By holding that the District Court has the discretion to order a sale of Mrs. Rodgers' property, the Court necessarily finds in the general language of § 7403 a congressional intent to abrogate the rule that the tax collector's lien does not afford him rights in property in excess of the rights of the delinquent taxpayer. I do not dispute that the general language of § 7403, standing alone, is subject to the interpretation the Court gives it. From its enactment in 1868 to the present day, the language of this statute has been sweeping; read literally, it admits of no exceptions. But when broadly worded statutes, particularly those of some antiquity, are in derogation of common-law principles, this Court has hesitated to heed arguments that they should be applied literally. In such cases, the Court has presumed in the absence of a clear indication to the contrary that Congress did not mean by its use of general language to contravene fundamental precepts of the common law.

* * *

III

Without direct evidence of congressional intent to contravene the traditional—and sensible—common-law rule, the Court advances three arguments purporting to lend indirect support for its construction of § 7403.

A

First, the Court claims that its construction is consistent with the policy favoring "the prompt and certain collection of delinquent taxes." This rationale would support any exercise of governmental power to secure tax payments. Were there two equally plausible suppositions of congressional intent, the policy might counsel in favor of choosing the construction more favorable to the Government. But when one interpretation contravenes both traditional rules of law and the common sense and common values on which they are built, the fact that it favors the Government's interests cannot be dispositive.

Moreover, the Government's interest would not be compromised substantially by a rule permitting it to sell property only when the delinquent taxpayer could have done so. In this case, the delinquent taxpayer's homestead interest, it is assumed, gave him a "half-interest in the underlying ownership rights to the property being sold." An immediate forced sale of the entire property would yield for the Government no more than half the present value of the remainder interest, the residue left after the present values of the nondelinquent spouse's life estate and half-interest in the remainder are subtracted. As the Court notes, the Government can expect to receive only a small fraction of the proceeds. An immediate sale of the delinquent taxpayer's future interest in the property might well command a commensurate price.

Alternatively, the Government could maintain its lien on the property until Mrs. Rodgers dies and then could force a sale. Because the delinquent taxpayer's estate retains a half interest in the remainder, the Government would be entitled to half the proceeds at that time. The Government's yield from this future sale, discounted to its present value, should not differ significantly from its yield under the

Court's approach. The principal difference is that, following the common-law rule, Mrs. Rodgers' entitlement to live out her life on her homestead would be respected.

An approach consistent with the common law need not prejudice the Government's interest in the "certain" collection of taxes. Under § 7403(d), the District Court has the power to appoint a receiver, who could supervise the property to protect the Government's interests while respecting Mrs. Rodgers' rights to possession and enjoyment.
* * *

B

The Court also would support its construction by contrasting § 7403 with the more restrictive language of § 6331, the administrative tax levy provision. It is true that § 6331 permits the sale only of "property and rights to property * * * belonging to" the taxpayer, while § 7403 generally authorizes the sale of property in which the taxpayer has an interest. But the greater power conferred by § 7403 is needed to enable the Government to seek the sale of jointly-owned property whenever the tax debtor's rights in the property would have permitted *him* to seek a forced sale. Section 7403 certainly permits the Government, in such circumstances, to seek partition of the property in federal, rather than state, court, to seek authority to sell the tax debtor's part or the whole, and, in the same proceeding, to have determined the entitlements of the various claimants, including competing lienholders, to the proceeds of the property sold. Absent the more expansive language of § 7403, this would not be possible. That language, however, does not manifest congressional intent to produce the extraordinary consequences yielded by the Court's interpretation.

C

The Court also asserts that its construction of § 7403 is consistent with "the traditional powers of a taxing authority in an in rem enforcement proceeding," even if it is not consistent with the traditional rights of lienholders. This, with all respect, is not so. In rem tax-enforcement proceedings never have been used to sell property belonging to unindebted third parties in order to satisfy a tax delinquency unrelated to the property sold. * * * [S]uch proceedings are brought to sell land in order to satisfy delinquent ad valorem taxes assessed on the land itself. It is said that the land itself is liable for such taxes, and that conflicting ownership rights thus do not bar its sale. The cases relied upon by the Court for the proposition that in rem tax proceedings extinguish the homestead rights of an unindebted spouse merely applied this rule.

On the other hand, if the tax is assessed on an individual's separate interest in the land, rather than on the land itself, the tax debt is personal to the individual and "[n]othing more [than the individual's interest] * * * can become delinquent; nothing more can be sold." The real property interests of third parties cannot be sold through an in rem proceeding to satisfy a personal tax liability. The "traditional powers of a taxing authority" to sell the entire property and extinguish the interests of unindebted third parties thus are limited to collection of taxes assessed on the land itself, and have no application to delinquent taxes, like those at issue in these cases, assessed personally against one joint owner.

Some States, it is true, have authorized by statute the sale of real property to satisfy the owner's tax debts, even where the delinquent taxes are unrelated to the property. The Court does not suggest, however, that jointly-owned real property ever has been sold pursuant to such a statute when an unindebted co-owner has indefeasible rights therein. Indeed, the traditional distinction between taxes for which the land is liable and tax liabilities personal to the taxpayer would preclude such a sale. Thus, even if one purpose of § 7403's predecessor statute "was to obtain for the federal tax collector some of the advantages that many States enjoyed through in rem tax enforcement," Congress would not have intended the result the Court reaches today. A state tax collector could not confiscate the indefeasible real property interests of a nondelinquent third party to satisfy the personal tax liability of a co-owner.

IV

The Court recognizes that Mrs. Rodgers has an indestructible property right under Texas law to use, possess, and enjoy her homestead during her lifetime, and that the delinquent taxpayer's property interests would not have enabled him to disturb that right against her will. The Court recognizes that Mrs. Rodgers has no outstanding tax liability and that the Government has no lien on Mrs. Rodgers' property or property rights. Because I conclude that Congress did not intend § 7403 to permit federal courts to grant property rights to the Government greater than those enjoyed by the tax debtor, I would hold that the Government may not sell Mrs. Rodgers' homestead without her consent. To the extent the Court holds to the contrary, I respectfully dissent.

V

Mrs. Ingram's case, however, is materially different. Like her husband, Mrs. Ingram was liable for back taxes, and consequently the Government had a lien on her interests in property as well as on her husband's interests. Exercising both spouses' rights in the homestead, the Government is entitled to force a sale, subject only to the discretion of the District Court. Second, when Mrs. Ingram and her former husband were divorced, the homestead became subject to partition under Texas law. In Mrs. Ingram's case, therefore, I concur in the result.

UNITED STATES v. NATIONAL BANK OF COMMERCE
Supreme Court of the United States, 1985.
472 U.S. 713, 105 S.Ct. 2919, 86 L.Ed.2d 565.

JUSTICE BLACKMUN delivered the opinion of the Court.

* * *

The controversy in this case concerns two joint accounts in a bank in Arkansas. The issue is whether the Internal Revenue Service (IRS) has a right to levy on those accounts for delinquent federal income taxes owed by only one of the persons in whose names the joint accounts stand in order that the IRS may obtain provisional control over the amount in question.

I

A

The relevant facts are stipulated. On December 10, 1979, the IRS assessed against Roy J. Reeves federal income taxes, penalties, and interest for the taxable year 1977 in the total amount of $3,607.45. As a result of payments and credits, the amount owing on the assessment was reduced to $856.61.

On June 13, 1980, there were on deposit with respondent National Bank of Commerce, at Pine Bluff, Ark., the sum of $321.66 in a checking account and the sum of $1,241.60 in a savings account, each in the names of "Roy Reeves or Ruby Reeves or Neva R. Reeves." Each of the persons named, Roy Reeves, Ruby Reeves, and Neva R. Reeves, was authorized by contract with the bank to make withdrawals from each of these joint accounts.

On the same date, that is, on June 13, 1980, a notice of levy was served on the respondent bank pursuant to § 6331(d) of the Code, 26 U.S.C. § 6331(d), demanding that the bank pay over to the United States all sums the bank owed to Roy J. Reeves up to a total of $1,302.56. Subsequently, there was a Partial Release of Levy for the amount in excess of $856.61. On October 10, a final demand for payment was served on the bank.

The bank, contending that it did not know how much of the money on deposit belonged to Roy as opposed to Ruby and Neva, refused to comply with the levy. The United States thereupon instituted this action in the United States District Court for the Eastern District of Arkansas, pursuant to § 6332(c)(1) of the Code, 26 U.S.C. § 6332(c)(1), seeking judgment against the bank in the amount of $856.61.

By way of a supplement to the stipulation of facts, it was agreed that "[n]o further evidence as to the ownership of the monies in the subject bank accounts will be submitted." As a consequence, we do not know which of the three codepositors, as a matter of state law, owned the funds in the two accounts, or in what proportion. * * *

B

The case was submitted to the District Court on cross motions for summary judgment and on the respondent bank's motion to dismiss the complaint. The District Court granted the motion to dismiss, holding the case procedurally "immature." The court concluded that due process mandates "something more than the post-seizure lawsuit allowed" by the Code's levy procedures. In its view, "the minimum due process required in distraint actions against joint bank accounts," compelled the IRS to identify the codepositors of the delinquent taxpayer and to provide them with notice and an opportunity to be heard.

* * *

The United States Court of Appeals for the Eighth Circuit affirmed. It expressed no opinion on the District Court's constitutional analysis. It reached essentially the same result, however, as a matter of statutory construction. It ruled that the IRS, when levying on a joint bank account, has the burden of proving "the actual value of the delinquent taxpayer's interest in jointly owned property." It observed that here "the rights of the various parties," had not been determined. Therefore, the Government had not shown the bank to be in possession of property or rights to property belonging to the delinquent taxpayer, Roy J. Reeves, as § 6331(a) required.

* * *

II

A

Section 6321 of the Code, 26 U.S.C. § 6321, provides: "If any person liable to pay any tax neglects or refuses to pay the same after demand, the amount * * * shall be a lien in favor of the United States upon all property and rights to property, whether real or personal, belonging to such person." Under the succeeding § 6322, the lien generally arises when an assessment is made, and it continues until the taxpayer's liability "is satisfied or becomes unenforceable by reason of lapse of time."

The statutory language "all property and rights to property," appearing in § 6321 (and, as well, in §§ 6331(a) and 6332(a)), is broad and reveals on its face that Congress meant to reach every interest in property that a taxpayer might have. See 4 B. Bittker, Federal Taxation of Income, Estates and Gifts ¶ 111.5.4, p. 111–100 (1981) (Bittker). * * *

A federal tax lien, however, is not self-executing. Affirmative action by the IRS is required to enforce collection of the unpaid taxes. The Internal Revenue Code provides two principal tools for that purpose. The first is the lien-foreclosure suit. Section 7403(a) authorizes the institution of a civil action in federal district court to enforce a lien "to subject any property, of whatever nature, of the delinquent, or in which he has any right, title, or interest, to the payment of such tax." Section 7403(b) provides: "All persons having liens upon or claiming any interest in the property involved in such action shall be made parties thereto." The suit is a plenary action in which the court "shall * * * adjudicate all matters involved therein and finally determine the merits of all claims to and liens upon the property." § 7403(c). See generally *United States v. Rodgers,* 461 U.S. 677, 680–682, 103 S.Ct. 2132, 2136–2137, 76 L.Ed.2d 236 (1983). The second tool is the collection of the unpaid tax by administrative levy. The levy is a provisional remedy and typically "does not require any judicial intervention." The governing statute is § 6331(a). It authorizes collection of the tax by levy which, by § 6331(b), "includes the power of distraint and seizure by any means."

In the situation where a taxpayer's property is held by another, a notice of levy upon the custodian is customarily served pursuant to § 6332(a). This notice gives the IRS the right to all property levied upon, and creates a custodial relationship between the person holding the property and the IRS so that the property comes into the constructive possession of the Government. If the custodian honors the levy, he is "discharged from any obligation or liability to the delinquent taxpayer with respect to such property or rights to property arising from such surrender or payment." § 6332(d). If, on the other hand, the custodian refuses to honor a levy, he incurs liability to the Government for his refusal. § 6332(c)(1).

The administrative levy has been aptly described as a "provisional remedy." 4 Bittker, at ¶ 111.5.5, p. 111–108. In contrast to the lien-foreclosure suit, the levy does not determine whether the Government's rights to the seized property are superior to those of other claimants; it, however, does protect the Government against diversion or loss while such claims are being resolved. "The underlying principle" justifying the administrative levy is "the need of the government promptly to secure its revenues." *Phillips v. Commissioner,* 283 U.S. 589, 596, 51 S.Ct. 608, 611, 75 L.Ed. 1289 (1931). "Indeed, one may readily acknowledge that the existence of the levy power is an essential part of our self-assessment tax system," for it "enhances voluntary compliance in the collection of taxes." *G.M. Leasing Corp. v. United States,* 429 U.S. 338, 350, 97 S.Ct. 619, 627, 50 L.Ed.2d 530 (1977). "Among the advantages of administrative levy is that it is quick and relatively inexpensive." *United States v. Rodgers,* 461 U.S., at 699, 103 S.Ct., at 2145.

The constitutionality of the levy procedure, of course, "has long been settled." *Phillips v. Commissioner,* 283 U.S., at 595, 51 S.Ct., at 611.

B

It is well established that a bank account is a species of property "subject to levy," within the meaning of §§ 6331 and 6332. * * *

The courts uniformly have held that a bank served with an IRS notice of levy "has only two defenses for a failure to comply with the demand." *United States v. Sterling National Bank & Trust Co. of New*

York, 494 F.2d 919, 921 (CA2 1974), and cases cited. One defense is that the bank, in the words of § 6332(a), is neither "in possession of" nor "obligated with respect to" property or rights to property belonging to the delinquent taxpayer. The other defense, again with reference to § 6332(a), is that the taxpayer's property is "subject to a prior judicial attachment or execution." 494 F.2d, at 921.

There is no suggestion here that the Reeves' accounts were subject to a prior judicial attachment or execution. Nor is there any doubt that the bank was "obligated with respect to" the accounts because, as it concedes, "Roy Reeves did have a right under Arkansas law to make withdrawals from the bank accounts in question." Brief for Respondent 2. The bank's only defense, therefore, is that the joint accounts did not constitute "property or rights to property" of Roy J. Reeves. See § 6331(a).

C

" '[I]n the application of a federal revenue act, state law controls in determining the nature of the legal interest which the taxpayer had in the property.' " *Aquilino v. United States,* 363 U.S. 509, 513, 80 S.Ct. 1277, 1280, 4 L.Ed.2d 1365 (1960), quoting *Morgan v. Commissioner,* 309 U.S. 78, 82, 60 S.Ct. 424, 426, 84 L.Ed. 585 (1940). This follows from the fact that the federal statute "creates no property rights but merely attaches consequences, federally defined, to rights created under state law." *United States v. Bess,* 357 U.S. 51, 55, 78 S.Ct. 1054, 1057, 2 L.Ed.2d 1135 (1958). And those consequences are "a matter left to federal law." *United States v. Rodgers,* 461 U.S., at 683, 103 S.Ct., at 2137. "[O]nce it has been determined that state law creates sufficient interests in the [taxpayer] to satisfy the requirements of [the statute], state law is inoperative," and the tax consequences thenceforth are dictated by federal law. *United States v. Bess,* 357 U.S., at 56–57, 78 S.Ct., at 1057–1058.

In the *Bess* case, the Court held that a delinquent taxpayer, who had purchased life insurance policies, did not have "property or rights to property" in the death proceeds of the policies, but that he did have such rights in their cash surrender value. The latter conclusion, it was said, followed from the fact that the taxpayer insured had "the right under the policy contract to compel the insurer to pay him this sum." *Id.,* at 56, 78 S.Ct., at 1058. Thus, the insured's interest in the cash surrender value was subject to the federal tax lien. The fact that "under State law the insured's property right represented by the cash surrender value is not subject to creditors' liens" was irrelevant. *Id.,* at 56–57, 78 S.Ct., at 1057–1058. State law defined the nature of the taxpayer's interest in the property, but the state law consequences of that definition are of no concern to the operation of the federal tax law.

As noted above, it is stipulated that Roy J. Reeves had the unqualified right to withdraw the full amounts on deposit in the joint accounts without notice to his codepositors. In any event, wholly apart from the stipulation, Roy's right of withdrawal is secured by his contract with the bank, as well as by the relevant Arkansas statutory provisions. See Ark.Stat.Ann. §§ 67–521 and 67–552 (1980). On its part, the bank was obligated to honor any withdrawal requests Roy might make, even up to the full amounts of the accounts. The Court of Appeals thus correctly concluded that, under Arkansas law, "Roy could have withdrawn any amount he wished from the account and used it to pay his debts, including federal income taxes, and his co-owners would have had no lawful complaint against the bank." 726 F.2d, at 1295.

Roy, then, had the absolute right under state law and under his contract with the bank to compel the payment of the outstanding balances in the two accounts. This, it seems to us, should have been an end to the case, for we agree with the Government that such a state-law right constituted "property [or] rights to property * * * belonging to" Roy, within the meaning of § 6331(a). The bank, in its turn, was "obligated with respect to" Roy's right to that property, § 6332(a), since state law required it to honor any withdrawal request he might make. The bank had no basis for refusing to honor the levy.

The overwhelming majority of courts that have considered the issue has held that a delinquent taxpayer's unrestricted right to withdraw constitutes "property" or "rights to property" subject to provisional IRS levy, regardless of the facts that other claims to the funds may exist and that the question of ultimate ownership may be unresolved at the time. * * * And the Eighth Circuit itself has observed that the "unqualified contractual right to receive property is itself a property right subject to seizure by levy." *St. Louis Union Trust Co. v. United States*, 617 F.2d 1293, 1302 (1980).[9]

Common sense dictates that a right to withdraw qualifies as a right to property for purposes of §§ 6331 and 6332. In a levy proceeding, the IRS " 'steps into the taxpayer's shoes,' " *United States v. Rodgers*, 461 U.S., at 691, n. 16, 103 S.Ct., at 2141, n. 16, quoting 4 Bittker, at ¶ 111.5.4, p. 111–102; M. Saltzman, IRS Practice and Procedure ¶ 14.08, p. 14–32 (1981). The IRS acquires whatever rights the taxpayer himself possesses. And in such circumstances, where, under state law, a taxpayer has the unrestricted right to withdraw funds from the account, "it is inconceivable that Congress * * * intended to prohibit the Government from levying on that which is plainly accessible to the delinquent taxpayer-depositor." *United States v. First National Bank of Arizona*, 348 F.Supp., at 389. Accord, *United States v. Citizens & Southern National Bank*, 538 F.2d, at 1107.[10] The taxpayer's right to

9. The dissent's suggestion that these cases are "irrelevant," stems from its erroneous assumption that state law dictates the extent of the Government's power to levy. It does not, and these cases all stand for the proposition that a delinquent's state-law right to withdraw funds from the joint bank account is a property interest sufficient for purposes of federal law for the Government to levy the account, notwithstanding the fact that questions as to the ultimate ownership of the funds may be unresolved.

10. We stress the narrow nature of our holding. By finding that the right to withdraw funds from a joint bank account is a right to property subject to administrative levy under § 6331, we express no opinion concerning the federal characterization of

withdraw is analogous in this sense to the IRS' right to levy on the property and secure the funds. Both actions are similarly provisional and subject to a later claim by a codepositor that the money in fact belongs to him or her.

III

The Court of Appeals, however, applied state law beyond the point of that law's specification of the nature of the property right, and bound the IRS to certain consequences of state property law. Because under Arkansas garnishment law, a creditor of a depositor is not subrogated to the depositor's power to withdraw the account, the court reasoned that the IRS, too, could not stand in the depositor's shoes. This gloss, it seems to us, is contrary to the analysis and holding in *United States v. Bess, supra.* * * *

* * *

In its understandable concern for Ruby's and Neva's property interests, the Court of Appeals has ignored the statutory scheme established by Congress to protect those rights. Crucially, the administrative levy, as has been noted, is only a provisional remedy. Other claimants, if they have rights, may assert them. Congress recognized this when the Code's summary-collection procedures were enacted, S.Rep. No. 1708, 89th Cong., 2nd Sess., 29 (1966), U.S.Code Cong. & Admin.News 1966, p. 3722, and when it provided in § 7426 of the Code, 26 U.S.C. § 7426, that one claiming an interest in property seized for another's taxes may bring a civil action against the United States to have the property or the proceeds of its sale returned.[11] Congress also has provided, by § 6343(b), an effective and inexpensive administrative remedy for the return of the property. See Treas.Reg. § 301.6343–1(b)(2), 26 CFR § 301.6343–1(b)(2) (1984).[12]

other kinds of state-law created forms of joint ownership. This case concerns the right to levy only upon joint bank accounts.

11. The dissent would find support in *United States v. Stock Yards Bank of Louisville,* 231 F.2d 628 (CA6 1956), and *Raffaele v. Granger,* 196 F.2d 620 (CA3 1952). Both cases are clearly distinguishable. *Stock Yards Bank* concerned an attempted levy upon United States Savings Bonds, held in the names of husband and wife, to satisfy the husband's tax liability. Savings bonds, however, are different from joint bank accounts and possess "limitations and conditions * * * which are delineated by the terms of the contract and by federal law." 231 F.2d, at 630. Furthermore, the case was decided prior to the enactment of § 7426, which was added to the Internal Revenue Code by the Federal Tax Lien Act of 1966, § 110(a), 80 Stat. 1142.

Raffaele v. Granger is even less on point. The decision there did not concern the propriety of a provisional remedy, but the final ownership of the property in question. * * *

12. We do not pass upon the constitutional questions that were addressed by the District Court, but not by the Court of Appeals, concerning the adequacy of the notice provided by § 6343(b) and § 7426 to persons with competing claims to the levied property. There is nothing in the sparse record in this case to indicate whether Ruby and Neva Reeves were on notice as to the levy, or as to what the Government's practice is concerning the notification of codepositors in this context. As the parties are free to address this issue on remand, the dissent's concerns on this score * * * are decidedly premature.

Congress thus balanced the interest of the Government in the speedy collection of taxes against the interests of any claimants to the property, and reconciled those interests by permitting the IRS to levy on the assets at once, leaving ownership disputes to be resolved in a post-seizure administrative or judicial proceeding. Its decision that certain property rights must yield provisionally to governmental need should not have been disregarded by the Court of Appeals. Nor would the bank be exposed to double liability were it to honor the IRS levy. The Code provides administrative and judicial remedies for codepositors against the Government, and any attempt to secure payment in this situation from the bank itself would be contrary to the federal enforcement scheme.[13]

* * *

Rodgers held that § 7403 empowers a District Court to order the sale of a family house in which a delinquent taxpayer has an interest, even though a nondelinquent spouse also has a homestead interest in the house under state law. In so ruling, the Court contrasted the operation of § 7403 with that of § 6331. The Court noted that § 6331, unlike § 7403, does not "implicate the rights of third parties," because an administrative levy, unlike a judicial lien-foreclosure action, does not determine the ownership rights to the property. Instead, third parties whose property is seized in an administrative levy "are entitled to claim that the property has been 'wrongfully levied upon,' and may apply for its return either through administrative channels * * * or through a civil action." *Id.*, at 696, 103 S.Ct., at 2144. The Court, in other words, recognized what we now make explicit: that § 6331 is a *provisional* remedy, which does not determine the rights of third parties until *after* the levy is made, in postseizure administrative or judicial hearings.[15]

13. As a result, it may well be that any attempt to recover against the bank under state law would be pre-empted. We need not resolve that question, however, for, under Arkansas law, the bank's payment to one depositor was a complete defense against suit on a codepositor's claim. * * *

15. The dissent's misreading of *Rodgers* is of a piece with its misunderstanding of the Government's use of § 6331 as a provisional remedy to seize property. The reason that § 6331 is not itself "punctilious in protecting the vested rights of third parties caught in the Government's collection effort," *Rodgers*, 461 U.S., at 699, 103 S.Ct., at 2145 is that the levy does not purport to determine any rights to the property. It merely protects the Government's interests so that rights to the property may be determined in a postseizure proceeding. It is in those proceedings that the rights of any who claim an interest to the property are punctiliously protected. In comparing § 6331 to § 7403 in this manner, the dissent compares apples and oranges. A more telling comparison to the lien-foreclosure proceeding of § 7403 would be with the administrative and judicial remedies for third parties whose property has been subject to wrongful levy, that is, with §§ 7343(b) and 7426(a)(1). It was just such a comparison that was made in this context by the Court in *Rodgers*.

Nor is *Mansfield v. Excelsior Refining Co.*, 135 U.S. 326, 10 S.Ct. 825, 34 L.Ed. 162 (1890) * * * in any way related to our holding today. That case involved provisions of the 1868 tax code that required a distiller who rented the property upon which it ran its distillery to obtain a "waiver" from the fee holder stipulating that a lien of the United States on the property for taxes owed by the distiller shall have priority over any mortgage held by the person executing the waiver, and giving the Government the rightful title to the

The Court of Appeals' result would force the IRS, if it wished to pursue a delinquent taxpayer's interest in a joint bank account, to institute a lien-foreclosure suit under § 7403, joining all codepositors as defendants. The practical effect of this would be to eliminate the alternative procedure for administrative levy under §§ 6331 and 6332. We do not lightly discard this alternative relief that Congress so clearly has provided for the Government. If the IRS were required to bring a lien-foreclosure suit each time it wished to execute a tax lien on funds in a joint bank account, it would be uneconomical, as a practical matter, to do so on small sums of money such as those at issue here. And it would be easy for a delinquent taxpayer to evade, or at least defer, his obligations by placing his funds in joint bank accounts. * * *

The judgment of the Court of Appeals is reversed.

It is so ordered.

JUSTICE POWELL, with whom JUSTICE BRENNAN, JUSTICE MARSHALL, and JUSTICE STEVENS join, dissenting.

The issue presented is whether the Internal Revenue Service (IRS) may lawfully seize a joint bank account for payment of a single codepositor's delinquent taxes when it does not know how much, if any, of the account belongs to the delinquent. As it seems to me that the Court today misreads the relevant statutory language, in effect overrules prior decisions of this Court, and substantially ignores the property rights of nondelinquent taxpayers, I dissent.

* * *

The Court today * * * ignores the property rights of nondelinquents. It holds that a delinquent's right to compel payment from a bank of balances in a joint account entitles the Government to levy on all of those funds—even when it is stipulated, as in this case, that the Government does not know that *any* of the money in the account actually belongs to the delinquent. By so holding, the Court disregards both the plain language and structure of the statute, ignores this Court's century-long interpretation of the Code (effectively overruling *Mansfield v. Excelsior Refining Co.*, and part of *United States v. Bess*), and disregards the fact that under Arkansas law a codepositor may have no property interest in funds that he may withdraw from the joint account.

III

Administrative levy under 26 U.S.C. § 6331 is the more drastic of the Government's two primary collection procedures. By allowing the Government summarily to seize and sell "all property or rights to

property in case of forfeiture. The Court held that this waiver did not entitle the Government to treat the property as if it belonged to the distiller for purposes of the then tax code's levy provisions. The waiver, the Court held, did not give the distiller a fee interest in the premises, nor did it give the Government the right to anything more than a first or prior lien.

That holding is irrelevant to the present controversy. * * *

property * * * belonging to [the delinquent]," 26 U.S.C. § 6331(a), administrative levy permits the IRS to collect unpaid taxes without judicial intervention. * * * It provides no notice to third parties that property in which they may have an interest has been seized. If an individual discovers a levy and believes that it was wrongful, his or her only recourse is to seek administrative review under 26 U.S.C. § 6343(b) within nine months or file suit in federal district court under 26 U.S.C. § 7426(a)(1) within the same amount of time.

Section 7403 provides a quite different method for collecting delinquent taxes. Under § 7403, the Attorney General, at the request of the Secretary of the Treasury, institutes a civil action in federal district court "to subject any property * * * in which [the delinquent] has any right, title, or interest, to the payment of such tax." All persons "claiming any interest in the property" must be joined as parties, and "duly notified of the action". Unlike a § 6331 levy, a § 7403 suit is a plenary action in which the court "adjudicate[s] all matters involved" and "finally determine[s] the merits of all claims to and liens upon the property." The district court may decree the sale of the property and distribution of the proceeds "according to the findings of the court in respect to the interests of the parties and of the United States."

The language of these two provisions reveals the central difference between them. While § 6331 applies to "property and rights to property * * * belonging to [the delinquent]," § 7403 applies to "property * * * in which [the delinquent] has any right, title, or interest * * *,". In other words, § 6331 permits seizure and sale of property or property rights *belonging to* the delinquent, while § 7403 allows the Government to seize and sell any property right in which the delinquent has an interest—even a *partial* interest. In many cases, of course, this difference is unimportant. Both procedures, for example, apply to any property interest that belongs completely to the delinquent, for it is necessarily true that any right to property "belonging to" the delinquent is also property in which he "has a[n] * * * interest." In general, however, the opposite is not always true. A property right in which the delinquent has only a partial interest does not "belon[g] to" the delinquent and hence is not susceptible to levy.

Until today, this Court has followed this interpretation of the levy and foreclosure provisions for the past century. In *Mansfield v. Excelsior Refining Co.*, the Court held that the Government could not levy on property rights in which a delinquent had less than a complete interest. * * *

* * *

* * * [T]he Government could have either levied administratively only on the leasehold or proceeded in equity (the forerunner of § 7403) to condemn the entire freehold interest. Under the former approach, it could take only the interest that completely "belong[ed] to" the delin-

quent, while under the latter, it could take property interests of which the delinquent owned only a part.⁵

In *United States v. Rodgers,* 461 U.S. 677, 103 S.Ct. 2132, 76 L.Ed.2d 236 (1983), we recently reaffirmed this understanding of the statutory scheme. * * * The Court * * * described the various advantages of each method of tax collection as follows:

> "Among the advantages of administrative levy is that it is quick and relatively inexpensive. Among the advantages of a § 7403 proceeding is that it gives the Federal Government the opportunity to seek the highest return possible on the forced sale of property interests liable for the payment of federal taxes. The provisions of § 7403 are broad and profound. *Nevertheless, § 7403 is punctilious in protecting the vested rights of third parties caught in the Government's collection effort,* and in ensuring that the Government not receive out of the proceeds of the sale any more than that to which it is properly entitled." Id., at 699, 103 S.Ct., at 2145 (emphasis added).⁶

As *Mansfield* and *Rodgers* make clear, this Court long has interpreted "property and rights to property *belonging to* the delinquent" to mean exactly that. Section 6331's reach extends only to property rights completely belonging to the delinquent.

IV

The narrow question presented, then, is whether the Government levied upon property or rights to property belonging only to Roy Reeves. The Court holds that the Government did so because it levied on Roy Reeves's right under state law to require the bank to pay over to

---

5. The Court argues that *Mansfield* is irrelevant to today's decision because it stands for the unremarkable proposition that "the Government cannot levy upon a leasehold interest and then turn around and sell a fee interest—an entirely different kind of interest." It bases this reading of *Mansfield* on the presence of a waiver from the feeholder, which was in fact tangential to the Court's holding in that case. The Court in *Mansfield* discussed the feeholder's waiver only in order to determine whether it gave the Government an interest in the fee. If it did, it was clear that the Government could sell the fee. The Court, however, concluded that the waiver gave the Government no such interest. Thus, the Court had to consider whether the levy on the property could *by itself* effectively transfer more than the delinquent's leasehold interest. Justice Harlan, writing for the *Mansfield* Court, found that the levy could not, and it is in this respect that *Mansfield* is a highly pertinent—if not a controlling—authority.

6. The Court attempts to minimize the conflict between its holding today and the holding in *Rodgers* by mischaracterizing that case. The Court states that "[t]he [*Rodgers*] Court noted that § 6331, unlike § 7403, does not 'implicate the rights of third parties,' because an administrative levy, unlike a judicial lien-foreclosure action, does not determine the ownership rights to the property." Nothing in *Rodgers*, however, suggests that § 6331 is not intended to implicate third-party rights for this reason. * * *

The Court also argues that comparing § 6331 and § 7403 is like comparing "apples and oranges." It suffices to say that this Court always has relied on comparison of these two provisions. Furthermore, the "more telling" comparison that the Court believes *Rodgers* made between § 7403 and a wrongful levy action, actually works against today's result. By stating that wrongful levy actions can be pursued when "property ha[s] been seized inadvertently," 461 U.S., at 696, 103 S.Ct., at 2144, the *Rodgers* Court makes clear its assumption that the Government cannot levy on property it knows may belong to third parties. The reasoning of the Court today, however, would allow exactly this result.

him the outstanding balances in the accounts. This right unquestionably belonged to Roy Reeves, as it did to each of the other codepositors. They all had the same right to withdraw. But the right to withdraw funds was no more than that. It was a right accorded parties to joint accounts as a matter of mutual convenience and it was independent of any right *to* or *in* the property. It encompassed no right of possession, use, or ownership over the funds when withdrawn. * * *

The Government, however, is not levying on the mere right to withdraw, which is of little value without any right of ownership. The levy at issue reaches the underlying funds in the accounts—no matter whom they belong to. Roy Reeves could, as the Court argues, have withdrawn all the joint funds, but, if under state law he had no independent right in the property itself, he could not legally possess the funds of the others, let alone use them to pay *his* taxes. That the delinquent might unlawfully convert the money of others to pay his taxes does not give the Government the right to do so. The Government cannot "ste[p] into the taxpayer's shoes," *ante,* at 2927, quoting *United States v. Rodgers,* 461 U.S., at 691, n. 16, 103 S.Ct., at 2141, n. 16, in this sense. It hardly comports with the "[c]ommon sense" the Court relies on, *ante,* at 2927, to hold that the Government may seize and sell property belonging only to third parties to pay taxes owed by the delinquent.[8]

The Court nevertheless holds that the right to withdraw all of a joint account is determinative because " 'it is inconceivable that Congress * * * intended to prohibit the Government from levying on that which is plainly *accessible* to the delinquent taxpayer-depositor.' "[9] By

8. The Courts of Appeals that have considered whether the IRS can levy on jointly held property to pay a co-owner's taxes have held that it cannot when it does not know how much of the property actually belongs to the delinquent. In *United States v. Stock Yards Bank of Louisville,* 231 F.2d 628 (CA6 1956), Justice (then Judge) Stewart, writing for the court, held that a joint bondholder's right to present a bond for redemption, receive payment in full, and thereby eliminate completely the other co-owner's interest as far as the issuer was concerned did not give the IRS the right to levy on the entire bond to pay one co-owner's taxes. "Proof of the actual value of the taxpayer's interest was an essential element of the government's case under the statute, and for lack of such proof the case falls." The Court attempts to distinguish this case on the ground that "[s]avings bonds * * * are different from joint bank accounts * * *." In *Stock Yards Bank,* however, the Court of Appeals expressly analogized savings bonds to joint bank accounts, and the Court today points to no relevant distinguishing feature. It merely creates a distinction without a difference.

Likewise, in *Raffaele v. Granger,* 196 F.2d 620 (CA3 1952), the Court of Appeals rejected the IRS's view that it could levy on joint bank accounts held as tenancies by the entirety when "either spouse may draw upon them." The court found that the "power of each spouse to withdraw funds," which the IRS argued was determinative, *ibid.,* was actually irrelevant because under state law "the ownership of both [spouses] attaches to funds withdrawn by either,". "The United States," it held, "has no power to take property from one person, the innocent spouse, to satisfy the obligation of another." * * *

9. The Court today states that "[t]he overwhelming majority of courts that have considered the issue has held that a delinquent taxpayer's unrestricted right to withdraw constitutes 'property' or 'rights to property' subject to provisional IRS levy, regardless of the facts that other claims to the funds may exist and that the question of ultimate ownership may be unresolved at the time." *Ante,* at 2927. Insofar as

holding that mere accessibility controls, the Court simply ignores the plain language of § 6331. It also effectively overrides state law that "controls in determining the nature of the legal interest which the taxpayer ha[s] in the property." [10] *Aquilino v. United States,* 363 U.S. 509, 513, 80 S.Ct. 1277, 1280, 4 L.Ed.2d 1365 (1960), quoting *Morgan v. Commissioner,* 309 U.S. 78, 82, 60 S.Ct. 424, 426, 84 L.Ed. 585 (1940). Under the Court's reasoning, for example, a codepositor's right to withdraw would allow the Government to levy on a joint account even if the Government knew that under state law none of the funds in the joint account "belonged to" the delinquent codepositor, *i.e.,* the delinquent had *no* property interest in the funds themselves. Such a position exceeds even the IRS's own interpretation of its levy powers. Rev.Ruling 55–187 ("A joint checking account is subject to levy only to the extent of a taxpayer's interest therein, which will be determined from the facts in each case."). This position, moreover, effectively overrules not only *Mansfield* but also part of *United States v. Bess, supra,* a case in which this Court held that a delinquent could have no "property or right to property" in funds over which he had no right of possession. 357 U.S., at 55–56, 78 S.Ct., at 1057–1058.

The Court also disregards the statutory language and its prior cases when it argues that the levy authorized by § 6331 is only a "provisional" remedy. Third parties who have their property taken may pursue—if they know about the taking—either administrative or judicial relief. But one would hardly characterize as "provisional" the Government's taking of an innocent party's property without notice,

the Court states that the IRS can levy on the right to withdraw, one can assume, without deciding, that it is correct, because the statement is irrelevant. In the present case, the IRS is not levying on the right to withdraw, but on the underlying right in the property, which may well belong to innocent third parties. On the other hand, insofar as the Court states that "these cases all stand for the proposition that a delinquent's state law right to withdraw funds from [a] joint bank account is a property interest sufficient for purposes of federal law for the Government to levy the account * * *," it is simply mistaken. *Not one, let alone "all," of these cases stand for this proposition.* * * *

Nothing in my opinion suggests that under existing federal law the IRS can *never* levy on a joint bank account. As the cited cases make clear, many, if not most, States give codepositors property rights in *all* the funds in a joint account. As long as state law grants such a right—which Arkansas law does not—levy on all the funds to pay a single codepositor's taxes is proper. It is only when state law does not grant such a right that the IRS should not be allowed to levy under § 6331 without first determining that the funds "belong to" the delinquent. The Court's position, however, would permit levies even when the IRS knows that none of the funds in the account belongs to the delinquent taxpayer.

10. At several points, the Court mischaracterizes my reliance on state law. * * * Like the Court, I would follow the statement in *Bess* that § 6331 "creates no property rights but merely attaches consequences, federally defined, *to rights created under state law* * * *." *Id.,* at 55, 78 S.Ct., at 1057 (emphasis added). * * * Here, however, the delinquent taxpayer may have *no* legal interest in the property. All that is known is that he has a right of withdrawal that is completely independent of the funds themselves. Nevertheless, the Court attaches "federal consequences" sufficient to levy on the accounts. In effect, what the Court holds today is that the delinquent's right against the bank creates "federal consequences" that attach to the completely different right to the funds themselves. By so construing the "federal consequences" of *Bess,* the Court does nothing less than rewrite § 6331, a provision that authorizes levy *only* on "property and rights to property belonging to" the delinquent.

especially when, even if the taking is discovered, the burden is then on the innocent party to institute recovery proceedings.[12] Furthermore, absent notice of any kind, the nine months that the administrative, 26 U.S.C. § 6343(b), and judicial, 26 U.S.C. § 6532(c)(1), remedies ordinarily give third parties to contest a levy is a short time indeed. There is no certainty that within this time they will discover that their property has been used to pay someone else's taxes. This may be particularly true as to the owners of joint *savings* accounts, owners in common of unimproved real estate, and owners in other situations where there may be little occasion to know that one's property has been seized by an IRS levy. In short, the Court's decision often will place the property rights of third parties in serious jeopardy.[13]

* * *

I accordingly dissent, and would affirm the judgment of the Court of Appeals.

Notes and Questions

1. Under the *Rodgers* decision a court has limited discretion not to order a sale after engaging in an individualized, equitable balancing of the interests of the government and the nondelinquent spouse. Compare United States v. Garsky, 57 AFTR 2d 86–1413 (E.D.Wis.1986) (sale refused) with Indiana Nat. Bank v. Gamble, 612 F.Supp. 1272 (N.D.Ill.1984) (sale ordered). How should the nondelinquent spouse's interest be valued? See Harris v. United States, 764 F.2d 1126 (5th Cir.1985).

2. The decision in United States v. Cache Valley Bank, 866 F.2d 1242 (10th Cir.1989) explains that a bank's right to setoff is subject to a federal tax lien if the tax lien attached to the taxpayer's account before the bank exercised its right.

3. The case law is unsettled regarding the applicability of state statutes of limitations to judgments obtained by the Service against delinquent taxpayers. The decisions in United States v. Overman, 424 F.2d 1142 (9th Cir.1970) and United States v. Ettelson, 159 F.2d 193 (7th Cir.1947), are cited for the proposition that as long as the court proceeding

---

12. The Court also argues that a levy on third-party property may be justified because "[the levy] merely protects the Government's interests so that rights to the property may be determined in a post-seizure proceeding." This statement incorrectly states the law. Under the levy statute, the IRS has the power not only to seize but also to sell property. 26 U.S.C. § 6331(b). A co-owner of a house seized and sold to pay a delinquent's taxes would indeed be surprised to discover that the IRS's levy "merely protects the Government's interests * * *." Assuming that the co-owner discovered within nine months that the IRS had levied on the property (for no notice to him is required), he could recover in a wrongful levy action at most some of the proceeds from the sale. * * *

13. The Court also emphasizes that administrative levy is justified because, like the delinquent's right to withdraw, it is "subject to a later claim by a codepositor that the money in fact belongs to him or her." This statement proves too much. Under the Court's reasoning, the IRS could levy on anyone's property to pay anyone else's taxes because such wrongful seizures are nearly always "subject to a later claim by [the owner] that the [property] in fact belongs to him or her." The fact that every wrongful taking is subject to a subsequent claim for conversion does not justify the taking.

reducing the assessment lien to judgment is commenced within six years of the date of assessment (pursuant to IRC § 6502(a)), the resulting judgment can be enforced at any time. However, a contrary result was reached in the case of United States v. Home Beneficial Life Ins. Co., Inc., 31 AFTR 2d 73–1085 (E.D.Tenn.1973). In that case, the court held that the government was barred from enforcing a judgment against the taxpayer's estate where the enforcement proceeding was commenced after the running of both the six-year period under § 6502(a) and the ten-year period of limitations applicable to judgments of the state courts of Tennessee. Which view is best supported by the language of §§ 6322 and 6502? Would the applicability of a state statute of limitations depend upon whether the judgment sought to be enforced was rendered by a federal district court instead of by a state court? See 28 U.S.C.A. § 1962 (West 1982 & Supp. 1991).

SECTION 3. JEOPARDY AND TERMINATION ASSESSMENTS

The Internal Revenue Service must be able to prevent a taxpayer from rendering his tax liabilities uncollectable by dissipating, hiding or removing his assets from the country. Once the subject tax has been assessed there is, as discussed above, ample power to accomplish this objective. However, a taxpayer may seek to place assets outside the reach of the Service prior to the conclusion of the administrative and/or judicial proceedings which normally must precede the assessment of a tax liability. Therefore, the Internal Revenue Code (sections 6861–6867, 6867) consistently has permitted the IRS to make an immediate assessment of tax in "jeopardy" situations, so that the collection powers can be utilized to secure the payment of taxes without delay.

Collection of taxes is considered to be in jeopardy if any one of the following conditions exist: (1) the taxpayer is or appears to be designing quickly to depart from the United States or to conceal himself or herself; (2) the taxpayer is or appears to be designing quickly to place property beyond government reach either by removing it from the United States, by concealing it, by dissipating it, or by transferring it to other persons; or, (3) the taxpayer's financial solvency is or appears to be imperiled. Reg. § 1.6851–1(a)(i)–(iii). Does the third condition strike you as quite broad?

As discussed in the following cases, the Service is permitted to make a jeopardy assessment for a tax period for which a tax return has been filed or is due. I.R.C. §§ 6861, 6862. In addition, for a taxable period which is not yet completed, or for which a return is not yet due, the Service is permitted to terminate the taxable period or accelerate the due date of the return and make a jeopardy assessment. I.R.C. § 6851. The *Laing* case was the last of a series of decisions questioning the long-standing provisions of the Code relating to termination assessments. As a reaction to this litigation, and to concomitant concerns regarding the effectively unrestricted discretion of the Service in the jeopardy area, the jeopardy and termination provisions were revised by the Tax Reform Act of 1976.

LAING v. UNITED STATES
Supreme Court of the United States, 1976.
423 U.S. 161, 96 S.Ct. 473, 46 L.Ed.2d 416.

MR. JUSTICE MARSHALL delivered the opinion of the Court.

These companion cases involve two taxpayers whose taxable years were terminated by the Internal Revenue Service (IRS) prior to their normal expiration date pursuant to the jeopardy termination provisions of § 6851(a)(1) of the Internal Revenue Code of 1954 (Code). Section 6851(a)(1) allows the IRS immediately to terminate a taxpayer's taxable period when it finds that the taxpayer intends to do any act tending to prejudice or render ineffectual the collection of his income tax for the current or preceding taxable year. Upon termination the tax is immediately owing and, after notice, the IRS may, and usually does, levy upon the taxpayer's property under § 6331(a) of the Code to assure payment.

We must decide whether the IRS, when assessing and collecting the unreported tax due after the termination of a taxpayer's taxable period, must follow the procedures mandated by § 6861 et seq. of the Code for the assessment and collection of a deficiency whose collection is in jeopardy. The answer, as we shall see, depends on whether the unreported tax due upon such a termination is a "deficiency" as defined in § 6211(a) of the Code. The Government argues that the tax liability that arises after a § 6851 termination cannot be a "deficiency," and that the procedures for the assessment and collection of deficiencies in jeopardy are therefore inapplicable. We reject this argument. We agree with the taxpayers that any tax owing, but unreported, after a § 6851 termination is a deficiency, and that the assessment of that deficiency is subject to the provisions of § 6861 et seq. * * *

I

[In the *Laing* case, customs officials in Vermont searched a car in which Mr. Laing and three other persons were traveling. They found over $300,000 in currency and notified the IRS, which "orally asserted" a termination deficiency of $310,000 against each of the individuals and seized the cash. The assessment against Mr. Laing subsequently was abated to $195,985.55 when a formal letter-notice of termination and demand for payment and the filing of a tax return were sent. In the companion case, United States v. Hall, the Respondent-taxpayer's husband was arrested on drug-related charges and the Respondent's house subsequently was searched by state police, who found controlled substances there. The next day, Mrs. Hall received notice from the IRS that a termination assessment of $52,680.25 had been made against her. In neither case was the taxpayer provided with a deficiency notice under § 6861(b), or otherwise given any specific information as to how the tax was determined.]

II

In these cases, the taxpayers seek the protection of certain procedural safeguards that the Government claims were not intended to apply to jeopardy terminations. Specifically, the taxpayers argue that the procedures mandated by § 6861 et seq. for assessing and collecting deficiencies whose collection is in jeopardy also govern assessments of taxes owing, but not reported, after the termination of a taxpayer's taxable period under § 6851. Resolution of this claim requires analysis of the interplay between these two basic jeopardy provisions—§ 6851, the jeopardy-termination provision, and § 6861, the jeopardy-assessment provision.

The initial workings of the jeopardy-termination provision, which essentially permits the shortening of a taxable year, are not in dispute. When the District Director determines that the conditions of § 6851(a) are met—generally, that the taxpayer is preparing to do something that will endanger the collection of his taxes—the District Director may declare the taxpayer's current tax year terminated. The tax for the shortened period and any unpaid tax for the preceding year become due and payable immediately, § 6851(a), and the taxpayer must file a return for the shortened year. § 443(a)(3).

The disagreement between the taxpayers and the Government focuses on the applicability of the jeopardy-assessment procedures of § 6861 et seq. to the assessment and collection of taxes that become due upon a § 6851 termination. Section 6861(a) provides for the immediate assessment of a deficiency, as defined in § 6211(a), whenever the assessment or collection of the deficiency would be "jeopardized by delay." By allowing an immediate assessment, § 6861(a) provides an exception to the general rule barring an assessment until the taxpayer has been sent a notice of deficiency and has been afforded an opportunity to seek resolution of his tax liability in the Tax Court. Certain procedural safeguards are provided, however, to the taxpayer whose deficiency is assessed immediately under § 6861(a). Within 60 days after the jeopardy assessment, the District Director must send the taxpayer a notice of deficiency, § 6861(b), which enables the taxpayer to file a petition with the Tax Court for a redetermination of the deficiency. The taxpayer can stay the collection of the amount assessed by posting an equivalent bond, § 6863(a). Any property seized for the collection of the tax cannot be sold until a notice of deficiency is issued and the taxpayer is afforded an opportunity to file a petition in the Tax Court. If the taxpayer does seek a redetermination of the deficiency in the Tax Court, the prohibition against sale extends until the Tax Court decision becomes final. § 6863(b)(3)(A).

The taxpayers view the provisions of § 6861 et seq. as complementary to those of § 6851. They contend that to the extent the tax owing upon a jeopardy termination has not been reported, it is a "deficiency" as that term is defined in § 6211(a) and used in § 6861(a), and that the deficiency, being of necessity one whose assessment or collection is in jeopardy, must be assessed and collected in accordance with the procedures of § 6861 et seq.

* * *

* * * [U]nder the Government's reading of the Code, the procedures for assessment and collection of a tax owing, but not reported, after the termination of a taxable period are not governed by § 6861 et seq. The Government argues that, with the single exception of the bond provision of § 6851(e), the taxpayer's only remedy upon a jeopardy termination is to pay the tax, file for a refund, and, if the refund is refused, bring suit in the district court or the Court of Claims. Since the IRS has up to six months to act on a request for a refund, the taxpayer, under the Government's theory, may have to wait up to half a year before gaining access to any judicial forum.

The Government does not seriously challenge the taxpayers' conclusion that if the termination of their taxable periods created a deficiency whose assessment or collection was in jeopardy, the assessments and collections in these cases should have been pursuant to the procedures of § 6861 et seq. The question, then, is whether the tax owing, but not reported, upon a jeopardy termination is a deficiency within the meaning of § 6211(a).

III

In essence, a deficiency as defined in the Code is the amount of tax imposed less any amount that may have been reported by the taxpayer on his return. § 6211(a). Where there has been no tax return filed, the deficiency is the amount of tax due. Treas.Reg. § 301.6211–1(a). As we have seen, upon terminating a taxpayer's taxable year under § 6851, the District Director makes a demand for the payment of the unpaid tax for the terminated period and for the preceding taxable year. The taxpayer is then required to file a return for the truncated taxable year. § 443(a)(3). The amount due, of course, must be determined according to ordinary tax principles, as applied to the abbreviated reporting period. The amount properly assessed upon a § 6851 termination is thus the amount of tax imposed under the Code for the preceding year and the terminated short year, less any amount that may already have been paid. To the extent this sum has not been reported by the taxpayer on a return, it fits precisely the statutory definition of a deficiency.

The Government resists this conclusion by reading the definition of "deficiency" restrictively to include only those taxes due at the end of a full taxable year when a return has been or should have been made. It argues that a "deficiency" cannot be determined before the close of a taxable year. Of course, we agree with the Government that a deficiency does not arise until the tax is actually due and the taxable year is complete. The fact is, however, that under § 6851 the tax is due immediately upon termination. Moreover, upon a § 6851 termination, the taxpayer's taxable year has come to a close. Section 441(b)(3) defines as a "taxable year" the terminated taxable period on which a return is due under § 443(a)(3). See also § 7701(a)(23). Under the statutory definition of § 6211(a), the tax owing and unreported after a jeopardy termination, which in these cases and in most § 6851 terminations is the full tax due, is clearly a deficiency. We see nothing in the definition to suggest that a deficiency can arise only at the conclusion of a 12–month taxable year; it is sufficient that the taxable period in question has come to an end and the tax in question is due and unreported.

Besides conflicting with the plain language of the Code provisions directly before us, the Government's position in these cases would, for no discernible purpose, isolate the taxpayer subjected to a jeopardy termination from most other income-tax payers. If the unreported tax due after a jeopardy termination is not a deficiency, the IRS need not issue the taxpayer a deficiency notice and accord him access to the Tax Court for a redetermination of his tax. Denial of an opportunity to litigate in the Tax Court is out of keeping with the thrust of the Code, which generally allows income-tax payers access to that court. Where exceptions are intended, the Code is explicit on the matter. See, e.g., § 6871(b). Denying a Tax Court forum to a particular class of taxpayers is sufficiently anomalous that an intention to do so should not be imputed to Congress when the statute does not expressly so provide. This is particularly so in view of the Government's concession that the jeopardy-assessment procedures of § 6861 et seq. are sufficient to protect its interests, and that providing taxpayers with the limited protections of those procedures would not impair the collection of the revenues.

IV

While the plain language of the provisions at issue here and their place in the legislative scheme suggest that the unreported tax due upon a § 6851 termination is a deficiency and that the deficiency, its collection being in jeopardy, must be assessed and collected according to the procedures of § 6861 et seq., the Government attempts to undercut this conclusion by pointing to the legislative history of the several provisions at issue in this case. We are unpersuaded. The jeopardy-assessment and jeopardy-termination provisions have long been treated in a closely parallel fashion, and nothing that the Government points to in the early codification suggests the contrary.

* * *

V

Based on the plain language of the statutory provisions, their place in the legislative scheme, and the legislative history, we agree with the taxpayers' reading of the pertinent sections of the Code.[26] Under that

---

26. As a final reason for adopting their construction of the Code, the taxpayers argue that the Government's reading would violate the Due Process Clause of the Fifth

reading, the tax owing, but not reported, at the time of a § 6851 termination is a deficiency whose assessment and collection are subject to the procedures of § 6861 et seq. Section 6861(b) requires a notice of deficiency to be mailed to a taxpayer within 60 days after the jeopardy assessment. Section 6863 bars the offering for sale of property seized until the taxpayer has had an opportunity to litigate in the Tax Court. Because the District Director failed to comply with these requirements in these cases, the taxpayers' suits were not barred by the Anti-Injunction Act, § 7421(a) of the Code. The judgment of the United States Court of Appeals for the Sixth Circuit in No. 74-75 is affirmed. The judgment of the United States Court of Appeals for the Second Circuit in No. 73-1808 is reversed, and the case is remanded to that court for further proceedings consistent with this opinion.

It is so ordered.

MR. JUSTICE BRENNAN, concurring.

I join the Court's opinion, and the statutory construction that makes unnecessary the Court's addressing the claims of Mr. Laing and Mrs. Hall that they were denied procedural due process secured by the Fifth Amendment. Decision of that question is therefore expressly reserved, ante, at n. 26. I write only to state my views of the considerations raised by the due process claim.

The Court's construction of the relevant statutes permits the IRS to seize a taxpayer's assets upon a finding by the Commissioner in compliance with § 6851(a)(1). No hearing is required, judicial or administrative, prior to the seizure. But it cannot be gainsaid that the risk of erroneous determinations by the Commissioner with consequent possibility of irreparable injury to a taxpayer is very real. This suffices to bring due process requirements into play.

The "root requirement" of the Due Process Clause is "that an individual be given an opportunity for a hearing before he is deprived of any significant property interest, except for extraordinary situations where some valid governmental interest is at stake that justifies postponing the hearing until after the event." Boddie v. Connecticut, 401 U.S. 371, 379, 91 S.Ct. 780, 786, 28 L.Ed.2d 113 (1971) (emphasis in

Amendment. The basis for this claim is that under the assessment procedures of § 6861 et seq. the taxpayer is guaranteed access to the Tax Court within 60 days, while under the procedures suggested by the Government the taxpayer in a termination case could be denied access to a judicial forum for up to six months. Moreover, the taxpayers argue, under the procedures of § 6861 et seq. the property seized may not be sold until after a final determination by the Tax Court, § 6863, while under the Government's theory the property seized in a jeopardy termination may be immediately subject to sale. Because we agree with the taxpayers' construction of the Code, we need not decide whether the procedures available under the Government's theory would, in fact, violate the Constitution.

The taxpayers do not question here, and we do not consider whether, even if the jeopardy-assessment procedures of § 6861 et seq. are followed, due process demands that the taxpayer in a jeopardy-assessment situation be afforded a prompt post-assessment hearing at which the Government must make some preliminary showing in support of the assessment.

original). The precise timing and attributes of the due process requirement, however, depend upon accommodating the competing interests involved.

Governmental seizures without a prior hearing have been sustained where (1) the seizure is necessary to protect an important governmental or public interest, (2) there is a "special need for very prompt action," and (3) "the standards of a narrowly drawn statute" require that an official determine that the particular seizure is both necessary and justified. See Fuentes v. Shevin, 407 U.S. 67, 91, 92 S.Ct. 1983, 2000, 32 L.Ed.2d 556 (1972). Seizures pursuant to jeopardy assessments are clearly necessary to protect important governmental interests and there is a "special need for very prompt action." But § 6851(a)(1), although requiring an official determination that the particular seizure is both necessary and justified, nevertheless falls short, in my view, of meeting due process requirements. This is because present law denies an affected taxpayer access to any forum for review of jeopardy assessments for up to 60 days.

* * *

* * * However expeditiously the Tax Court handles the claim, that court is not required to decide the merits within any specified time, and no provision is made for a prompt preliminary evaluation of the basis for the assessment. In my view, such delay would be constitutionally permissible only if there were some overriding governmental interest at stake, and the IRS suggested none in either of these cases. But even if delay in judicial review on the merits were justifiable, due process would at least require some supporting rationale for denying taxpayers the opportunity for a prompt preliminary determination by an unbiased tribunal on the validity of the basis for the assessment. Again, none was offered in either of these cases.

Congress sought to remedy the issues identified in *Laing* by enactment of section 7429. In addition to providing for expedited administrative and judicial review of the *propriety* of jeopardy and termination assessments (as discussed in the following case), section 7429 also explicitly provides a *prepayment forum* for those who received termination assessments. To solve the problems recognized in *Laing,* Congress provided that if a termination assessment is made, the IRS must issue a statutory notice of deficiency for the full taxable year with respect to which the termination assessment was made. This notice must be issued within 60 days after the later of the due date of the taxpayer's return for the full taxable year or the date the return is actually filed. IRC § 6851(b). Thus, a taxpayer receiving a terminated year assessment, in addition to his rights to immediate review under § 7429, will have the opportunity to petition the Tax Court for a determination of the merits of the assessment relatively promptly.

Nevertheless, there remains a difference (perhaps unavoidable) between the two types of assessments. The jeopardy assessment made under § 6861 requires a notice and opportunity to petition the Tax Court *within 60 days of the assessment.* The delay between a termination assessment under § 6851 and the required issuance of a deficiency notice, on the other hand, will be 60 days plus the time between the assessment and the due date or filing of the return for the full taxable year. The delay could thus extend for as long as seventeen and one-half months (or more, if the return for the full taxable year is not filed on time). Assuming a termination assessment on January 2, 1991, the deficiency notice would be due on June 15, 1992, i.e., 60 days after April 15, 1992 (the due date for the full year return for 1991).

FIDELITY EQUIPMENT LEASING CORP. v. UNITED STATES

United States District Court, Northern District of Georgia, 1978.
462 F.Supp. 845.

HAROLD L. MURPHY, DISTRICT JUDGE.

On October 23, 1978, the plaintiffs filed a complaint to determine the reasonableness and appropriateness of two jeopardy assessments for income tax levied against them by the Internal Revenue Service on August 9, 1978. Jurisdiction of the Court was invoked pursuant to 26 U.S.C. § 7429(b).

* * *

1. Section 7429(a)(1) of the Internal Revenue Code requires that within 5 days after an assessment is made pursuant to 26 U.S.C. § 6861(a), "the Secretary shall provide the taxpayer with a written statement of the information upon which the Secretary relies in making such assessment." Apparently attempting to comply with this notice requirement the defendant included the following paragraph in the letters of August 11, 1978, notifying the plaintiffs of the jeopardy assessment:

> Under section 6861 of the Internal Revenue Code, you are notified that I have found you to be designing quickly to place your property beyond the reach of the Government either by removing it from the United States, by concealing it, by transferring it to other persons, or by dissipating it, thereby tending to prejudice or render ineffectual collection of income tax for the taxable years ended as shown below. Accordingly, based on information available at this time, I have approved assessment of tax and additional amounts determined to be due as reflected in the attached computations:

The plaintiff correctly argues that such conclusionary statements do not fulfill the requirements of the statute. * * *

However, the Government's failure to satisfy the notice requirement of section 7429 will not serve to invalidate these proceedings. The legislative history of this section indicates that both the notice and administrative review requirements were included simply to facilitate the subsequent Court proceedings. Through the process of discovery the taxpayers have been informed of the information relied upon by the Government. Any deficiency in the notice issued by the Government is now immaterial. The plaintiffs were not prejudiced by the lack of information contained in the notification letters.

2. The plaintiffs contend that this proceeding should be declared illegal and void because of inadequate administrative review. The only deficiency raised by the plaintiffs is again the Government's failure to supply adequate information. Without determining the adequacy of the administrative review, the Court holds that any possible inadequacy has been corrected through full use of the discovery process and the *de novo* review of plaintiffs' claims provided by this Court.

3. In order to support its determination of a jeopardy assessment the Government must show that the assessment is "reasonable under the circumstances * * * " 26 U.S.C. § 7429(b)(2). The burden of proof in such a showing rests upon the Government. 26 U.S.C. § 7429(g)(1). In determining the reasonableness of the assessment, this Court is not limited to information available to the IRS at the time of the assessment, but may also consider relevant information gathered after that date.

In determining "reasonableness" the Court is given little guidance by the statute. A jeopardy assessment may be levied by the IRS if it believes that the collection of a deficiency will be "jeopardized by delay". 26 U.S.C. § 6861(a). The Internal Revenue Manual suggests that a jeopardy assessment should not be made unless one of the following three conditions is met:

> (1) The taxpayer is or appears to be designing quickly to depart from the United States or to conceal himself;

> (2) The taxpayer is or appears to be designing quickly to place his property beyond the reach of the Government either by removing it from the United States, or by concealing it, or by transferring it to other persons, or by dissipating it; or

> (3) The taxpayer's financial solvency appears to be imperiled.

The legislative history of section 7429 indicates Congressional approval of the standards set forth in the IRS manual. The Court agrees that a finding of any one of the three conditions listed would support the Government's determination. However, the Court's consideration is in no way limited to the factors delineated in the IRS manual.

[The Government's evidence established that the corporate taxpayer was attempting to liquidate its real estate holdings, was engaging in "skimming" operations, and was insolvent.]

The factors outlined above support the Government's decision to seek a jeopardy assessment. The apparent attempt to sell substantial amounts of real property, the evidence of past skimming of income and the likelihood of its continuation, and the significant evidence of plaintiffs' insolvency make the assessment rendered pursuant to 26 U.S.C. § 6861, reasonable under the circumstances.

* * *

5. The plaintiffs argue that the statutory scheme enacted in 26 U.S.C. §§ 6861 and 7429 is unconstitutional because it does not provide for adequate post-seizure review as required by the Fifth Amendment to the Constitution. The Court does not agree. The statutory scheme provides a taxpayer with notice of the governmental action. The judicial review afforded allows the taxpayer to examine witnesses, present evidence and receive a *de novo* review from an uninterested impartial party.

The jeopardy assessment procedures can be used only in circumstances which indicate that the collection of taxes would be adversely affected by the delay inherent in normal deficiency collection procedures. The collection of tax is of the very highest priority to any government. The importance of revenue collection justifies the extraordinary procedures Congress has provided for in sections 6861 and 7429 of the Internal Revenue Code. The statutory procedures available in the case of a jeopardy assessment are constitutionally valid.

6. The final question to be passed on by the Court concerns the propriety of the amount of the assessment. 26 U.S.C. § 7429(b)(2)(B). The taxpayer bears the burden of proving that the amount assessed is not appropriate. 26 U.S.C. § 7429(g)(2).

The assessment against Fidelity Equipment Leasing Corporation and its subsidiaries for the taxable year ending November 30, 1975, equaled $1,207,405.12. * * * The total amount assessed against [co-plaintiff] Global equaled $10,718,553.07. The amounts assessed against the plaintiffs included substantial penalties levied pursuant to 26 U.S.C. § 6653(b) and interest.

While it is unable to specify any incorrect determination by the Government, the Court cannot hold that the amount assessed is appropriate under the circumstances. The Internal Revenue Service, in determining the assessed deficiencies, relied on findings that this Court, with the evidence now before it, cannot uphold nor deny. For example, while the Court has before it copies of the sales agreement and promissory notes executed between Fidelity and Michael G. Thevis, the Internal Revenue Service determined that the transaction was a sham and disallowed deductions for interest paid on the notes. Further, a substantial portion of the assessment constituted addition to the tax, under 26 U.S.C. § 6653(b), as a result of the Government's decision that the underpayment resulted from fraud. This Court is not able to presently make such a finding. While the IRS apparently used the best available means of determining the deficiency, the unreliability of its methods combined with the Government's other holdings, compels this Court to deny the Government's request for a finding that the amount of liability assessed was appropriate.

Pursuant to 26 U.S.C. § 7429(b)(3), when the Court finds that the amount assessed is inappropriate, authority is granted to take such action, "as the court finds appropriate." Accordingly, the Court will fashion a remedy which protects the Government's ability to collect its revenue, allows an accurate determination of the plaintiffs' deficiency and does not subject the plaintiffs to irreparable injury. The Court orders the following:

1. The liens imposed by the IRS as a result of their jeopardy assessment will be allowed to stay in effect, however the enforcement of those liens by seizure or sale is stayed until such time as the actual deficiencies owed by the plaintiffs may be determined by the Tax Court.

2. The plaintiffs are ordered to immediately retain the services of a reputable accounting firm (the choice will be subject to this Court's approval). This firm will be retained in order to establish an acceptable method of business procedures for the accounting and bookkeeping obligations of the plaintiffs. The large daily flow of cash now a part of plaintiffs' operation must be stopped. All of plaintiffs' dealings must be by check, draft, or other documentary means. Each of plaintiffs' subsidiaries must strictly maintain accurate records of all sales, purchases, or other transactions. All "peep shows" or theaters must maintain accurate meter or ticket readings, which are to be recorded and stored. Any operation which is not susceptible to some reliable method of record keeping will be halted immediately. All procedures for documenting income and expenses must have the approval of the retained accounting firm.

Upon completion of procedures to assure accurate bookkeeping and accounting procedures for plaintiffs, the accounting firm instituting such procedures shall file a report with this Court as to the methods and procedures utilized to assure accuracy of the plaintiffs' records, and complete reporting as to all income and expenses, with a copy of such report being furnished to the Internal Revenue Service.

All of this action shall be taken at plaintiffs' expense and plaintiffs must commence implementing this order immediately.

Additionally, Agents of the Internal Revenue Service shall be allowed continuing reasonable access to the current books and records of plaintiffs to assure compliance with this order and to determine if plaintiffs are maintaining correct records of all income and expenses and are otherwise complying with this order.

In order to facilitate any future interpretations of this order, the Court notes that the collection of revenue by the Government is the primary purpose of this order. If at any time the plaintiffs jeopardize that purpose through skimming, dissipation of assets, inadequate or inaccurate record keeping, the Government may seek an immediate lifting of the stay and execution of their liens. The Court retains jurisdiction of the present action in order to insure compliance with these instructions and for such other action as may hereafter be appropriate.

So ordered, this the 20th day of December, 1978.

WILLIAMS v. COMMISSIONER
Tax Court of the United States, 1989.
92 T.C. 920.

COLVIN, JUDGE: This case of first impression is before the Court on petitioners' motion to review the respondent's determination to sell seized property. The issue for decision is the propriety of respondent's determination to sell jewelry and furs previously seized from petitioners. This is the first motion received by the Tax Court to stay the sale of seized property under section 6863(b)(3)(C),[1] enacted November 10, 1988, effective February 8, 1989.

As discussed below, if a motion to review respondent's decision to sell is granted, the Court may enter an order to stay the sale by the Internal Revenue Service (IRS). An order to stay the sale may by its terms bar or delay the sale, and can be compared to an injunction. See Rule 65, Federal Rules of Civil Procedure.

FINDINGS OF FACT

1. Petitioners' Pending Tax Court Cases

Petitioners filed joint tax returns for taxable years 1980–1984.

By notices dated May 22, 1987, respondent determined deficiencies and additions to petitioners' joint Federal income taxes as follows:

TYE	Deficiency	Additions to tax Sec. 6653(b)(1), (b)(2)*	Sec. 6661
Docket No. 28141–87:			
Dec. 31, 1981	$ 70,410.73	$36,098.36	
Dec. 31, 1982	58,258.27	29,129.13	$14,654.57
Dec. 31, 1983	114,944.19	57,472.10	28,736.05
Docket No. 28142–87:			
Dec. 31, 1980	6,075.49	3,037.74	
Dec. 31, 1984	126,565.53	62,282.76	31,641.38

*Respondent failed to distinguish between the secs. 6653(b), 6653(b)(1) and (b)(2) additions.

Docket Nos. 28141–87 and 28142–87 have been consolidated by separate order for purposes of trial, briefing, and opinion, including for purposes of this motion. Rule 141(a).

At the time the petitions were filed, petitioner Melvin Williams was an inmate at the Federal penitentiary at Lewisburg, Pennsylvania, and petitioner Mary Williams resided in Baltimore, Maryland.

Petitioner Melvin Williams filed a motion to proceed in forma pauperis on October 24, 1988, in which he stated that neither he nor his

---

1. All section references are to the Internal Revenue Code of 1986 as amended, unless otherwise indicated. All Rule references are to the Tax Court Rules of Practice and Procedure unless otherwise indicated.

family have sufficient funds to pay the cost (approximately $3,000) of his transportation and housing to return him to Baltimore, Maryland, for trial.

2. *Seizure of and Determination to Sell Petitioners' Property*

On December 5, 1984, the Drug Enforcement Administration (DEA) seized various items of personal property belonging to petitioners. The principal items seized were furs and jewelry. The furs and jewelry were appraised in January, 1985.

In 1987, the IRS made a jeopardy assessment under section 6861 against petitioners and subsequently served a levy on DEA for any of petitioners' assets. On September 29, 1987, DEA gave numerous pieces of jewelry and furs to the IRS which they had previously seized from petitioners. The items were appraised at the request of the Government. As a result of the jeopardy assessment, two statutory notices of deficiency were issued to petitioners on May 22, 1987. Petitioners filed two timely petitions with the Tax Court.

Respondent sent petitioners a letter, dated February 2, 1989, and an IRS Form 4585, Minimum Bid Worksheet (worksheet). The letter included a discussion of the minimum bid price "of property seized from you," and advised petitioners that they could request a professional appraiser to reevaluate the price if petitioners disagreed with the minimum bid price. The "Remarks" section of the worksheet provided, "The jewerly [sic] have been depreciating in value everyday. Some of the jewerly [sic] are the gaudy type and persinalize [sic]." The worksheet did not mention furs. The worksheet stated that the estimated expenses of the sale are $7,000.

The letter also stated, "If we do not hear from you within 5 days from the date shown above (February 2), we will assume you agree with the established minimum bid price." The envelope in which the letter and worksheet were mailed bore a postmark date of February 7, 1989. The postal claim check attached to the envelope indicates first notice on February 9, second notice on February 14, and return on February 24. In their memorandum in support of their motion for review, petitioners allege that actual delivery was made on February 10, 1989. There is no indication that petitioners submitted any appraisals to respondent at that time.

Apparently sometime in late January or early February, 1989, the IRS scheduled a sale by auction of the jewelry and furs. The auction was scheduled for 7:00 p.m. on March 1, 1989.

Respondent's memorandum, which we treat as a response to petitioners' motion, states that the property was scheduled for sale because of the "continuous and substantial decline in value" shown by respondent's appraisals. We infer from this that respondent determined that the property is liable to become greatly reduced in price or value. There is no indication that respondent determined that the property was liable to perish or could not be kept without great expense.

3. *Petitioners' Motion to Review the Determination to Sell Seized Property*

Late on Tuesday afternoon, February 28, 1989, the day before the scheduled sale, counsel for petitioners delivered to the Tax Court and to respondent's counsel a motion to review respondent's determination to sell the seized property. Petitioners asserted that the jewelry and furs were not wasting assets and that there would be no reduction in value of the seized property if this Court were to grant petitioners' motion.

Petitioners' motion included the following allegations and points:

1. The motion was brought under section 6863(b)(3)(C).

2. Property had been seized from petitioners on December 5, 1984, and has been in the Government's possession since then.

3. The property seized was furs and jewelry.

4. Grounds for the motion were that none of the exceptions of section 6863(b)(3)(B) are applicable.

5. Further grounds for the motion are that the jewelry and furs are not losing value.

6. This Court has jurisdiction in that petitioners filed timely petitions with the Tax Court with respect to two notices of deficiency.

7. The seized property was the subject of a jeopardy assessment.

The motion also alleged that petitioners' counsel had advised respondent's officer of petitioners' "wishing to find some way to have a family member or friend redeem the property" at the minimum bid price, but that "This the officer refused to do." Petitioners' counsel did not allege that he had offered payment or a bond.

The motion also included a certificate of service to respondent's counsel, and the address and phone number of petitioners' counsel.

On Wednesday, March 1, 1989, the Court held two conference calls with counsel for petitioners and respondent. In the first conference call, at 11:00 a.m., petitioners' counsel stated arguments for granting the motion and respondent's counsel stated arguments for denying the motion.

In the second conference call, at 2:00 p.m., the Court indicated the terms of the Court order that was issued in response to petitioners' motion.

The order issued by the Court on March 1, 1989, provided as follows:

> Upon due consideration of petitioners' motion for stay of sale of seized property and pursuant to the conference call between the Court and the parties on this date, the Court has concluded that the motion raises several legal and factual questions in dispute between the parties. The Court believes a 30–day stay would enable the Court to properly consider whether the stay should extend beyond April 1, 1989. Accordingly, it is

ORDERED that petitioners' motion is granted in that the sale of petitioners' property in the possession of respondent, scheduled for March 1, 1989, is stayed until not before April 1, 1989. It is further

ORDERED that the parties shall provide, on or before March 15, 1989, written memoranda with respect to whether the stay should be extended by this Court's order beyond April 1, 1989.

The Court later extended the temporary stay through May 31, 1989.[2]

The auction previously scheduled for that evening was cancelled as a result of the Court order.

The parties filed written memoranda with the Court. Both parties attached copies of appraisals as exhibits to their respective memoranda. Neither party requested a hearing.

4. *The Appraisals*

* * *

c. *Summary of Appraisals*

d. *Storage and Maintenance Costs*

Respondent made no claim in its memorandum that storage or maintenance costs were a factor in its determination to sell the property.

OPINION

1. *Introduction*

The Tax Court's jurisdiction to stay sales of seized property became effective on February 8, 1989. This is the first motion received by the Tax Court in which a party seeks review of respondent's determination to sell seized property under section 6863(b)(3)(C).

The Technical and Miscellaneous Revenue Act of 1988 (TAMRA), 102 Stat. 3750, was enacted on November 10, 1988. Section 6245 of TAMRA amended section 6863(b) and granted jurisdiction to the Tax Court to review determinations by the IRS to sell property under section 6863(b)(3)(B) if a Tax Court petition has been filed under section 6213(a) to redetermine a deficiency the collection of which is otherwise stayed by virtue of section 6863(b)(3)(A).

Section 6863(b)(3)(C), as added by TAMRA, sec. 6245(a), provides as follows:

SEC. 6863. STAY OF COLLECTION OF JEOPARDY ASSESSMENTS.

* * * * * * * * *

(b) FURTHER CONDITIONS IN CASE OF INCOME, ESTATE, OR GIFT TAXES.—In the case of taxes subject to the jurisdiction of the Tax Court—

---

2. By separate order, the temporary stay expires May 9, 1989, the filing date of this opinion.

On Apr. 27, 1989, respondent filed a motion for order on petitioners' motion for stay of sale of seized property. The motion is mooted by release of this opinion. Although the motion included further argument for respondent's position, we did not consider it, nor did we order a response thereto from petitioners.

* * * * * * * * *

(3) STAY OF SALE OF SEIZED PROPERTY PENDING TAX COURT DECISION—

* * * * * * * * *

(C) REVIEW BY TAX COURT.—If, but for the application of subparagraph (B), a sale would be prohibited by subparagraph (A)(iii), then the Tax Court shall have jurisdiction to review the Secretary's determination under subparagraph (B) that the property may be sold. Such review may be commenced upon motion by either the Secretary or the taxpayer. An order of the Tax Court disposing of a motion under this paragraph shall be reviewable in the same manner as a decision of the Tax Court.

The House version of TAMRA included no provisions for Tax Court review under section 6863. The Conference Committee Report adopted the Senate Finance Committee Report which stated:

The Tax Court is granted jurisdiction during the pendency of proceedings before it to review the IRS's determination to sell seized property under one of the present-law exceptions to the stay of sale.

The provision is effective on the 90th day after the date of enactment. [H.Rept. 100–1104, at 232 (Conf.)(1988).]

The Conference Agreement further provides:

The conference agreement follows the Senate Amendment. [H.Rept. 100–1104, at 232 (Conf.)(1988).]

The amendment to section 6863(b) became effective 90 days after the enactment of TAMRA, on February 8, 1989.

2. Stay of Sales of Seized Property Seized Pursuant to a Jeopardy or Termination Assessment

If a statutory notice of deficiency has been sent to a taxpayer and a timely petition is filed with the Tax Court, no assessment of a deficiency may be made until the decision of the Tax Court becomes final. Sec. 6213(a).

Sections 6851, 6852, and 6861 provide exceptions to the nonassessment rule and authorize respondent to make termination and jeopardy assessments before or during the pendency of a case in the Tax Court if it finds that ordinary assessment or collection is threatened.

Respondent may determine to sell property seized because of a jeopardy or termination assessment. Secs. 6335 and 6336.

Under section 6335(b), respondent must give notice of a proposed sale in at least two newspapers published or circulated in the county where the seizure was made. The sale must be held not less than 10 nor more than 40 days after public notice is given. Sec. 6335(d). Respondent must also establish the minimum bid price. Sec. 6335(e).

Under section 6337, the property must be returned to the taxpayer if the taxpayer pays the amounts determined to be owing.

The Secretary has general authority to collect taxes after assessment. Sec. 6331.

Under section 6863(a), collection of a jeopardy or termination assessment may be stayed by filing a bond with respondent. Collection will be stayed up to the amount of the bond.

Under section 6863(b)(3)(A), property seized under a jeopardy or termination assessment generally may not be sold pending Court review (until the decision of the Tax Court becomes final, or until the expiration of time under section 6213 to file a petition).

Section 6863(b)(3)(B) provides several exceptions to the rule barring sale:

a. If the taxpayer consents;

b. If the Secretary determines that the expenses of conservation and maintenance will greatly reduce the net proceeds; or

c. If the property is of the type described in section 6336.[3] Property described in section 6336 is property which—

1. Is liable to perish or to become greatly reduced in price or value by keeping, or

2. Cannot be kept without great expense.

Section 6336 also requires respondent—

1. To appraise the property; and

2. If the owner can be readily found, to notify him of the appraised value, and to give him an opportunity to reclaim or post bond for the property based on the appraised price.

Property shall be returned to its owner if, within the time specified in the notice, the owner pays the appraised amount or furnishes an acceptable bond. Section 6336 also authorizes respondent to immediately make public sale of the property if the owner fails to pay the amount or furnish a bond as required in the notice of sale.

As discussed above, section 6863(b)(3)(C) gives jurisdiction to this Court to review determinations by the Secretary to sell seized property under the exceptions described in section 6336. A motion to review a determination may be made by the taxpayer or respondent. Sec. 6863(b)(3)(C).

---

3. Sec. 6336 provides, in part:

If the Secretary determines that any property seized is liable to perish or become greatly reduced in price or value by keeping or that such property cannot be kept without great expense, he shall appraise the value of such property and—

(1) RETURN TO OWNER.—If the owner of the property can be readily found, the Secretary shall give him notice of such determination of the appraised value of the property. The property shall be returned to the owner if, within such time as may be specified in the notice the owner—

(A) Pays to the Secretary an amount equal to the appraised value, or

* * *

(2) IMMEDIATE SALE.—If the owner does not pay such amount * * *, the Secretary shall as soon as practicable make public sale of the property.

Except for "extraordinary and exceptional circumstances," judicial review in other courts under section 6336 has been negligible due to the anti-injunction provisions of section 7421(a). See, e.g., *Miller v. Standard Nut Margarine Co.,* 284 U.S. 498, 509 (1932); *Hill v. Wallace,* 259 U.S. 44, 62 (1922); *Smith v. Flinn,* 261 F.2d 781, 784 (8th Cir.1958), modified and rehearing denied 264 F.2d 523 (8th Cir.1959).

3. The Court Has Jurisdiction to Act on the Motion

Petitioners alleged that the Court had jurisdiction over the motion brought under section 6863(b)(3)(C) in their original submission to the Court. Respondent does not object to the Court's jurisdiction.

There are five requirements for jurisdiction:

a. An assessment must have been made under section 6851 (Termination Assessments), section 6852 (Termination Assessments in Case of Flagrant Political Expenditures of Section 501(c)(3) Organizations), or section 6861 (Jeopardy Assessments of Income, Estate, Gift, and Certain Excise Taxes) and property seized, section 6863(b)(3)(A).

b. A timely petition must have been filed with the Tax Court (whether before or after the making of such assessment), section 6863(b)(3)(A)(iii), before the expiration of the period during which the assessment of the deficiency would be prohibited if neither sections 6851(a), 6852(a), nor 6861(a) were applicable.

c. Respondent has determined that one of the exceptions to the general prohibition against sale provided in section 6863(b)(3)(B) applies, i.e., (1) the taxpayer consents to the sale, or (2) respondent determines that the expenses of conservation and maintenance will greatly reduce the net proceeds, or (3) the property is of the type described in section 6336 (Sale of Perishable Goods). * * *

d. A proper motion must be filed. And,

e. A proper party must file the motion, i.e., the taxpayer or respondent.

In the present case, an assessment was made under section 6861, timely petitions were filed, respondent determined that the property is of the type described in section 6336, and the matter was brought before the Court on motion by petitioners. Thus, we have jurisdiction to review respondent's determination to sell the property.

4. Special Circumstances Warrant That We Consider Petitioners' Motion

Petitioners' motion to stay the sale of seized property was filed 1 day before the scheduled sale. We believe the newness of the law justified our consideration of petitioners' last-minute filing in this case.

However, last-minute filing effectively prevents orderly review of legal and factual issues raised by the parties unless a temporary stay is ordered. Accordingly, eleventh-hour filing will not be allowed by the

Court in the future absent special circumstances, such as late notice to petitioner.

   5. The Court May Issue a Temporary Stay if Appropriate

When petitioners' motion was filed, the Court believed it merited consideration. However, there was not time to properly consider it before the scheduled sale. Thus, the Court considered use of a temporary stay. A temporary stay would preserve the rights of the parties so that the merits could be properly presented to and reviewed by the Court.

We hold that the Court has authority to issue a temporary stay in appropriate cases, and that this is an appropriate case.

Section 6863(b)(3)(C) grants the Tax Court jurisdiction during the pendency of proceedings before it to review the IRS's determination to sell property seized pursuant to a jeopardy or termination assessment. We believe this necessarily includes the authority to issue a temporary stay if appropriate. It is essential to the exercise of our authority to review a determination to sell seized property that we be able to stay a sale temporarily.

We believe the authority to order a temporary stay pending review was important to the exercise of our jurisdiction here because it enabled the parties to present appraisals and written arguments on factual or legal issues presented by the motion to stay.

Courts have the inherent authority to issue such orders as they deem necessary and prudent to achieve the "orderly and expeditious disposition of cases" in their jurisdiction. *Roadway Express, Inc. v. Piper,* 447 U.S. 752, 764–765 (1980); *Link v. Wabash Railroad Co.,* 370 U.S. 626, 630–631 (1962). For example, the Tax Court has the power to impose a variety of sanctions on both litigants and attorneys in order to regulate their docket, promote judicial efficiency, and deter frivolous filings. This Court's powers also include, for example, the power: (1) To consider new issues and new theories in support of an adjustment; (2) to appoint a tax matters partner; (3) to vacate a void decision; and (4) generally to protect its own process from abuse, oppression, and injustice and to enforce and vindicate its lawful process. Accordingly, we hold that the granting of the temporary stay of sale here was a proper exercise of this Court's jurisdiction.

We next turn to whether issuance of a temporary stay was appropriate under these circumstances.

Circumstances require that the Court has broad discretion in deciding whether to stay sales temporarily. The purpose of a temporary stay is not to resolve the matter on the merits. Instead it is to preserve the issue so it can be properly reviewed.

Temporary stays will not be granted automatically. We will be selective as warranted by the circumstances. To do otherwise would fail to recognize that delayed sales would sometimes cost the public or the taxpayer significantly, either because the property is losing value or is expensive to maintain.

Neither party submitted affidavits or appraisals in connection with consideration of this temporary stay. We recognize that it was not possible for the parties to provide affidavits or other documentation in the time available before deciding whether to grant a temporary stay. Thus, we decided whether it was appropriate to grant this temporary stay based on the information reasonably available to the Court.

The temporary stay was granted here because the Court believed that the motion was sufficiently justified to warrant preserving the rights of the parties. This gave the parties more time to prepare the merits of the motion. Based on the conference call with both counsel on March 1, we believed petitioners' claim that the jewelry and furs would not become greatly reduced in value during the period of the temporary stay more likely to be true than respondent's claim to the contrary. We were also influenced by the substantial length of time the property had been held by respondent (and DEA previously) prior to the determination to sell.

6. Burden of Proof

Introduction

Section 6863(b)(3)(C) is silent as to the burden of proof for a motion to stay sales of seized property. At present, there is no Tax Court Rule that specifically addresses a proceeding brought under section 6863(b)(3)(C). Under section 7453, the Tax Court is given the power to establish rules of practice and procedure for its proceedings. Tax Court Rule 142(a) provides that petitioner generally bears the burden of proof, except as otherwise provided by statute or determined by the Court.

Here, we must decide whether to follow the usual rule that petitioners bear the burden of proof, or whether special circumstances warrant that we provide otherwise.

At the outset, we note that a decision on a motion to stay a sale of seized property does not decide tax liability. Instead, it decides whether respondent can sell property which petitioner continues to own. The property is held by respondent as security for payment of tax which will be owing if respondent prevails in the pending litigation.

A proceeding to review respondent's determination to sell seized property has many unique characteristics. Among these are:

(1) The motions will usually arise in a time-sensitive environment.

(2) Respondent has physical possession or control of the property.

(3) Respondent initiates the sale of the property.

(4) Respondent controls the scheduling and conditions of the sale.

(5) Respondent has had the opportunity to develop documentation to support the determination to sell the property.

(6) Petitioner may have had very little opportunity to develop evidence.[4]

We recognize that there is significant public interest in permitting sales in appropriate circumstances. That is, if the property loses value, or if maintenance expenses of the property are large in relation to its value, the public interest in collecting tax is frustrated. Further, we believe that respondent's role as property manager is entitled to some deference.

In light of these circumstances, we hold that—

(1) If movant seeks a stay, movant must first request a stay on grounds that are plausible and believable.

(2) If movant does this, respondent must bear the burden of proving by a preponderance of the evidence that the determination to sell seized property was correct.

Initial Showing By Movant

The movant must first make a request for a stay on grounds that are plausible and believable. Frivolous or dilatory motions will not be considered.

Here we conclude that petitioners successfully made this initial showing.

Burden of Proof on Respondent

If movant meets this preliminary requirement, respondent must bear the burden of proving by a preponderance of the evidence that the determination to sell seized property was correct. We believe the special circumstances present with motions to review a determination to sell seized property make this appropriate.

We recognize that, in many proposed sales of seized property, respondent may have had little time to determine to sell the property. In these instances evidence available to both parties may be significantly restricted compared to what would be available if there were more time. The Court is aware of the obstacles facing parties in these cases and will decide motions to stay sales of seized property based on the facts and record reasonably available to it at the time. However, if respondent has unreasonably delayed scheduling or giving petitioner notice of the sale, it can thwart the parties' opportunity to adequately prepare for the motion. If this occurs, we will not allow respondent to claim lack of opportunity to develop its case. Similarly, the movant may not profit from its own delay. That is, where there is significant advance notice of the sale but movant unreasonably delays seeking a stay, the Court will not excuse lack of support for movant's position.

Next, we discuss why we place on respondent the burden of showing why the determination to sell seized property is correct.

---

4. See, e.g., *Omnibus Financial Corp. v. United States*, 566 F.2d 1097 (9th Cir.1977) (notice provided 1 day before sale).

Generally, a notice of deficiency is presumed correct, and petitioner bears the burden of disproving respondent's determination of his tax liability, *Welch v. Helvering,* 290 U.S. 111 (1933). We believe placing the burden on respondent for motions to stay sales of seized property is fully consistent with this.

One reason given for placing the burden of proof on petitioner is that the facts and figures on which tax liability rests are peculiarly within the taxpayer's knowledge. The opposite is true in the instant situation. Here, respondent has possession of the property, and the greater ability to make a showing as to the correctness of a determination to sell it. Respondent also controls the timing and conditions of the sale.

Another reason given for petitioner's bearing the burden of proof for tax deficiencies is that "taxes are the life-blood of government, and their prompt and certain availability is an imperious need." *Bull v. United States,* 295 U.S. 247, 259 (1935). But here, respondent is already holding property as security for a tax liability determined to be owing. The issue is whether respondent may sell petitioners' property.

In deciding that respondent must show that the determination was correct, we do not believe we are limited to acting only where there was abuse of discretion by respondent.

In adding section 6863(b)(3)(C) to the Code, Congress specifically called on this Court to consider taxpayers' motions to review respondent's determination to sell seized property. Congress did not impose a restrictive standard of review in the statute. Rather, the Court was simply authorized to "review" the Commissioner's determination to sell seized property.

In determining whether to sell seized property, the Commissioner is provided little discretion, but rather a specific, objective standard under section 6863(b)(3)(B). A determination that this standard is met lends itself to Court review.

Section 6863(b)(3)(C) imposes no limitations on the standard of review of determinations by respondent to sell property, and it does not limit the Court to a review of the correctness of respondent's determination, unlike section 7429(b)(3)(A)(i) (review of Jeopardy Levy or Assessment Procedures) and former section 7477 (repealed by section 131(e)(1) of the Tax Reform Act of 1984, Pub.L. 98–369, 98 Stat. 664) (declarations as to whether a determination by respondent regarding a section 367(a) exchange was reasonable). See *Dittler Bros., Inc. v. Commissioner,* 72 T.C. 896, 908–909 (1979).

7. *Court Not Limited to Review of the Administrative Record*

The facts before the Court consist primarily of various appraisals. We must decide whether we may properly consider petitioners' appraisal which was attached to their written memoranda filed in response to the temporary stay order. We hold we can also consider affidavits, appraisals, or other appropriate information. Accordingly, we choose to consider petitioners' appraisal of the jewelry. Petitioners did not provide an appraisal of the furs.

8. Relevance and Weight of Appraisals Stating Past and Current Values

We next consider whether the Government's appraisals of the fur and jewelry, taken between 1985 and 1989, are relevant in determining under section 6336 whether the value of the property is "liable to become greatly reduced in value." If the appraisals are relevant, a related issue for decision is what weight they should have.

> Rule 401, Federal Rules of Evidence, applicable in the Court pursuant to Rule 143 * * *, and section 7453, defines relevant evidence as "evidence having any tendency to make the existence of any fact that is of consequence to the determination of the action more probable or less probable than it would be without the evidence." [*Armco, Inc. v. Commissioner*, 87 T.C. 865, 867 (1986).]

The courts have interpreted the language "liable to become greatly reduced in value" to mean "likely" to become greatly reduced in value. See, e.g., *United States v. Mellon Bank*, 521 F.2d 708, 712 n. 15 (3d Cir.1975); *Hohman v. United States*, 535 F.Supp. 1218, 1219 n. 6 (D.D.C.1982). We take this to mean that a great loss in value is likely to occur in the foreseeable future. Thus, likelihood that property is liable to become greatly reduced in value is not necessarily established by appraisals of value from earlier dates. Estimates which provide reasonable grounds for predicting future value would mean much more in determining if the property is liable to become greatly reduced in value. No such evidence or data was provided by respondent. However, the appraisals offered by respondent in this case may be given some weight in determining whether the property is likely to become greatly reduced in value.

9. Stay of Sales of Some Property

We believe that inherent in our authority to administer our jurisdiction under section 6863(b)(3)(C) is the authority to stay the sale of some assets but not others if the record so indicates. In this case we stay the sale of the jewelry to the extent discussed below, but we do not further stay the sale of the furs.

10. Stay of Sale of Jewelry for 6 Months

Petitioners' appraisal included the best information of prospective value of the jewelry in that it estimated that the jewelry will not decrease in value for at least 6 months. We are unconvinced that respondent appropriately determined that the future value of the jewelry is likely to become greatly diminished. We believe it appropriate to tailor the order to the information available to the Court. Accordingly, we will order a stay in the sale of the jewelry for approximately 6 months.

11. Stay of Sale of Furs Denied

Respondent submitted a 1987 appraisal of the furs indicating a replacement cost [5] of $31,900 and a 1989 appraisal showing a resale value [6] of $13,000. Respondent did not explain the difference between the two different methods of valuing [7] the furs, i.e., the replacement cost method and the resale value method. Replacement cost is generally not favored for tax purposes in arriving at fair market valuations. *Ingram–Richardson, Inc. v. Commissioner*, T.C.Memo. 1972–157; *National Packing Corp. v. Commissioner*, 24 B.T.A. 952, 956 (1931); and *Berg v. United States*, 167 F.Supp. 756 (W.D.Wis.1958). Indeed, in a case to determine the fair market value of automotive equipment distributed in a corporate liquidation to the taxpayers, this Court noted that replacement cost while "some indication of fair market value, is by no means conclusive" and has been held to be "of questionable weight as valuation evidence." *Carty v. Commissioner*, 38 T.C. 46, 66 (1962). In *Carty*, the taxpayers valued the automotive equipment using a current replacement cost adjusted by actual depreciation and failed to carry their burden of showing that the equipment had a value in excess of that determined by respondent. See *Philadelphia Steel and Iron Corp. v. Commissioner*, T.C.Memo. 1964–93, affd. per curiam 344 F.2d 964 (3d Cir.1965); and *National Packing Corp. v. Commissioner*, 24 B.T.A. 952, 956 (1931). In all of these cases the taxpayers used replacement cost but failed to carry their burden of overcoming the "presumptive correctness of the Commissioner's determination" of value. Nonetheless, the Court in each case apparently gave some weight to an appraisal based on replacement cost.

Petitioners did not provide any evidence regarding the furs. They evidently could have done so, as shown by their submission of a jewelry appraisal.

On balance, we find that respondent has borne the burden of proving that the determination to sell the seized furs was correct. We do not further stay the sale of the furs.

For the foregoing reasons,

---

5. The replacement cost value of an item of property is equal to the cost that would be incurred in acquiring an acceptable substitute property. 1 J. Bonbright, Valuation of Property, 152 (1937). The replacement cost of used property, such as petitioners' jewelry, is the cost of replacing such used property with identical or equivalent property which is in substantially the same condition as the original. Equivalent property is that which has the same value as the original, or gives the same benefits of ownership, but which is not identical with it. A general principle of valuation states that the cost of replacement equals the upper limit of value of the property. H. Babcock, Appraisal Principles and Procedures, pars. 541, 750, 752 (1980).

6. Respondent's memorandum uses this term interchangeably with fair market value.

7. Sales need not achieve a fair market value price for property, but the sale price may not be unreasonably low. *Citibank, N.A. v. Data Lease Financial Corp.*, 645 F.2d 333 (5th Cir.1981); *Smith v. Juhan*, 311 F.2d 670, 672 (10th Cir.1962); *Ringer v. Basile*, 645 F.Supp. 1517 (D.Colo.1986); *Crump v. United States*, 66–1 USTC par. 9308, 17 AFTR 2d 637 (N.D.Ga.1966); *Miracle–Span Corp. v. United States*, 82–1 USTC par. 9365, 50 AFTR 2d 82–5334 (D.S.D.1982).

An appropriate order will be issued.

Reviewed by the Court.

NIMS, CHABOT, PARKER, KORNER, HAMBLEN, COHEN, SWIFT, JACOBS, GERBER, WRIGHT, PARR, WILLIAMS, WELLS, RUWE, and WHALEN, JJ., agree with this opinion.

Notes

1. In the case of an assessment under I.R.C. §§ 6851, 6861 or 6862, the Service may levy immediately upon the taxpayer's property, without regard to the 10-day notice period provided by § 6331(a). I.R.C. § 6331(a). In addition to the preliminary review procedure provided by § 7429, the taxpayer may wish to stay collection of the assessment by filing a bond pursuant to I.R.C. § 6863. This section provides that "[w]hen an assessment has been made under section 6851, 6861 or 6862 * * * the collection of the whole or any amount of such assessment may be stayed by filing with the Secretary * * * a bond in an amount equal to the amount as to which the stay is desired * * *." It is a rare case, however, in which the taxpayer against whom a jeopardy assessment has been made will be able to file a bond to secure the payment of the *full* asserted liability.

2. Prior to 1982, it was unclear whether the jeopardy and termination procedures were available in cases in which the IRS had reason to believe that a tax was owing with respect to cash, but could not determine the proper owner of the cash. Section 330 of TEFRA added section 6867 to the Code, effective September 4, 1982. Under section 6867, the Service can presume that the collection of an amount of income tax will be jeopardized by delay where an individual in physical possession of more than $10,000 in cash or its equivalent denies ownership of the cash and does not claim that it belongs to another person whose identity is readily ascertainable by the Service (and who acknowledges ownership). I.R.C. § 6867(a).

In such a case, the IRS may presume, for purposes of the jeopardy and termination provisions, that such cash represents gross income of a single individual for the year of possession, and that such income is taxable at the highest rate for individuals. I.R.C. § 6867(b)(1), (2). Notice with respect to the jeopardy or termination assessment is given to, and the right to contest the assessment is vested in, the person found in possession of the cash. I.R.C. § 6867(b)(3). However, the true owner of the cash can come forward and challenge the assessment and will be retroactively substituted for the possessor for all purposes as of the date of the original assessment. I.R.C. § 6867(c). See Matut v. Commissioner, 858 F.2d 683 (11th Cir.1988).

The terms "cash" and "cash equivalent" include cash, foreign currency, any bearer obligation and any other medium of exchange which is a type used frequently in illegal activities and specified as a cash equivalent by the IRS in regulations. I.R.C. § 6867(d)(1), (2). Bearer obligations are to be valued at face value, but other cash equivalents are to be valued at fair market value. I.R.C. § 6867(d)(3).

SECTION 4. TRUST FUND TAXES (WITHHOLDINGS)

There is no area of tax practice more depressing to the practitioner and client than the problem of unpaid withholding taxes. The business entity involved is invariably in the process of failing or (worse yet) has collapsed already, owing substantial amounts in withholding taxes. The Internal Revenue Service, armed with the ability to seek payment from any "responsible person" and certain others, stands ready to unleash the full force of its collection arsenal to recoup the taxes owed by the business.

A. RESPONSIBLE PERSONS' LIABILITY

(1) *The Basic Tests*

SLODOV v. UNITED STATES
Supreme Court of the United States, 1978.
436 U.S. 238, 98 S.Ct. 1778, 56 L.Ed.2d 251.

MR. JUSTICE BRENNAN delivered the opinion of the Court.

Petitioner, an orthodontist by profession, on January 31, 1969, purchased the stock and assumed the management of three corporations engaged in the food vending business. The corporations were indebted at the time of the purchase for approximately $250,000 of taxes, including federal wage and Federal Insurance Contribution Act (FICA) taxes withheld from employees' wages prior to January 31. The sums withheld had not been paid over when due, however, but had been dissipated by the previous management before petitioner acquired the businesses. After petitioner assumed control, the corporations acquired funds sufficient to pay the taxes, but petitioner used the funds to pay employees' wages, rent, suppliers and other creditors, and to meet other day-to-day expenses incurred in operating the businesses. * * *

I

* * * When he bought the stock, petitioner understood, and the purchase agreement reflected, that the corporations had an outstanding obligation for taxes in the amount of $250,000 due for payment on January 31, including withheld employee wage and FICA taxes (hereinafter trust-fund taxes). During the purchase negotiations, the sellers represented to petitioner that balances in the various corporate checking accounts were sufficient to pay these taxes as well as bills due other creditors. Relying on the representation, petitioner, on Saturday, February 1, sent four checks to the IRS in payment of the taxes. On Monday, February 3, petitioner discovered that the accounts were overdrawn and stopped payment on the checks. Thus, at the time that petitioner assumed control, the corporations had no liquid assets, and whatever trust-fund taxes had been collected prior to petitioner's assumption of control had been dissipated.

Petitioner immediately advised the IRS that the corporations had no funds with which to pay the taxes, and solicited guidance concerning how the corporations should proceed. There was evidence that IRS officials advised petitioner that they had no objection to his continuing operations so long as current tax obligations were met, and that petitioner agreed to do so and to endeavor to pay the arrearages as soon as possible. The IRS never represented that it would hold petitioner harmless under § 6672 for the back taxes, however.

To continue operations, petitioner deposited personal funds in the corporate account, and, to obtain inventory, agreed with certain suppliers to pay cash upon delivery. During petitioner's tenure, from January 31 to July 15, 1969, the corporations' gross receipts approximated $130,000 per week for the first few months but declined thereafter. The corporations "established a system of segregating funds for payment of withheld taxes and did, in fact, pay withheld taxes during the period February 1, 1969, to July 15, 1969." The bankruptcy judge found, and the IRS concedes, that the $249,212 in taxes paid during this period was approximately sufficient to defray current tax obligations. No taxes owing for periods prior to February 1, were paid, however, and in July 1969 the corporations terminated operations and filed for bankruptcy.

II

Several provisions of the Internal Revenue Code require third persons to collect taxes from the taxpayer. Among the more important are 26 U.S.C. §§ 3102(a) and 3402(a) which respectively require deduction from wages paid to employees of the employees' share of FICA taxes, and the withholding tax on wages applicable to individual income taxes. The withheld sums are commonly referred to as "trust fund taxes," reflecting the Code's provision that such withholdings or collections are deemed to be a "special fund in trust for the United States." 26 U.S.C. § 7501(a). There is no general requirement that the withheld sums be segregated from the employer's general funds, however, or that they be deposited in a separate bank account until required to be paid to the Treasury. Because the Code requires the employer to collect taxes as wages are paid, § 3102(a), while requiring payment of such taxes only quarterly, the funds accumulated during the quarter can be a tempting source of ready cash to a failing corporation beleaguered by creditors. Once net wages are paid to the employee, the taxes withheld are credited to the employee regardless of whether they are paid by the employer, so that the IRS has recourse only against the employer for their payment.

An employer who fails to pay taxes withheld from its employees' wages is, of course, liable for the taxes which should have been paid, §§ 3102(b) and 3403. The IRS has several means at its disposal to effect payment of the taxes so withheld. First, once it has been determined that an employer has been inexcusably delinquent, the IRS, upon giving hand-delivered notice, may require the employer, thereafter, and until further notice, to deposit withheld taxes in a special bank trust account within two banking days after collection, to be retained there until required to be paid to the Treasury at the quarter's end. § 7512. Second, with respect to trust funds past due prior to any such notification, the amount collected or withheld "shall be held to be a special fund in trust for the United States [and] [t]he amount of such fund shall be assessed, collected, and paid in the same manner and subject to the same provisions and limitations (including penalties) as are applicable with respect to the taxes from which such fund arose." 26 U.S.C. § 7501. Thus there is made applicable to employment taxes withheld but not paid the full range of collection methods available for the collection of taxes generally. After assessment, notice, and demand, the IRS may, therefore, create a lien upon the property of the employer, § 6321, and levy, distrain, and sell the employer's property in satisfaction. §§ 6331 to 6344.

Third, penalties may be assessed against the delinquent employer. Section 6656 of the Code imposes a penalty of 5% of the underpayment of any tax required to be deposited, and 26 U.S.C. §§ 7202 and 7215 provide criminal penalties respectively for willful failure to "collect or truthfully account for and pay over" trust-fund taxes, and for failure to comply with the requirements of § 7512, discussed *supra,* regarding special accounting requirements upon notice by the Secretary.

Finally, as in this case, the officers or employees of the employer responsible for effectuating the collection and payment of trust-fund taxes who willfully fail to do so are made personally liable to a "penalty" equal to the amount of the delinquent taxes. Section 6672 provides, *inter alia:*

> "Any person required to collect, truthfully account for, and pay over any tax imposed by this title who willfully fails to collect such tax, or truthfully account for and pay over such tax, or willfully attempts in any manner to evade or defeat any such tax or the payment thereof, shall, in addition to other penalties provided by law, be liable to a penalty equal to the total amount of the tax evaded, or not collected, or not accounted for and paid over * * *."

Section 6671(b) defines "person," for purposes of § 6672, as including "an officer or employee of a corporation, or a member or employee of a partnership, who as such officer, employee, or member is under a duty to perform the act in respect of which the violation occurs." Also, § 7202 of the Code, which tracks the wording of § 6672, makes a violation punishable as a felony subject to a fine of $10,000, and imprisonment for 5 years. Thus, an employer-official or other employee responsible for collecting and paying taxes who willfully fails to do so is subject to both a civil penalty equivalent to 100% of the taxes not collected or paid, and to a felony conviction. Only the application to petitioner of the civil penalty provision, § 6672, is at issue in this case.

III

When the same individual or individuals who caused the delinquency in any tax quarter are also the "responsible persons" at the time the Government's efforts to collect from the employer have failed, and it seeks recourse against the "responsible employees," there is no question that § 6672 is applicable to them. It is the situation that arises when there has been a change of control of the employer enterprise, here corporations, prior to the expiration of a tax quarter, or at a time when a tax delinquency for past quarters already exists that creates the question for our decision. In this case, petitioner assumed control at a time when a delinquency existed for unpaid trust-fund taxes, while the specific funds withheld but not paid had been dissipated by predecessor officers and when the corporations had no liquid assets with which to pay the overdue taxes.

A

Petitioner concedes that he was subject to personal liability under § 6672 as a person responsible for the collection, accounting, and payment of employment taxes required to be withheld between January 31, 1969, when he assumed control of the corporations and July 15, 1969, when he resigned. His contention is that he was not, however, a responsible person within § 6672 with respect to taxes withheld prior to his assumption of control and that § 6672 consequently imposed no duty upon him to pay the taxes collected by his predecessors. Petitioner argues that this construction of § 6672 follows necessarily from the statute's limitation of personal liability to "[a]ny person required to collect, truthfully account for *and* pay over any tax imposed by this title," who willfully fails to discharge those responsibilities (emphasis added). He argues that since the obligations are phrased in the conjunctive, a person can be subject to the section only if all three duties—(1) to collect, (2) truthfully account for, *and* (3) pay over—were applicable to him with respect to the tax dollars in question. On the other hand, as the Government argues, the language could be construed as describing, in terms of their general responsibilities, the persons potentially liable under the statute, without regard to whether those persons were in a position to perform all of the duties with respect to the specific tax dollars in question. Although neither construction is inconsistent with the language of the statute, we reject petitioner's as inconsistent with its purpose.

Sections 6672 and 7202 were designed to assure compliance by the employer with its obligation to withhold and pay the sums withheld, by subjecting the employer's officials responsible for the employer's decisions regarding withholding and payment to civil and criminal penalties for the employer's delinquency. If § 6672 were given petitioner's construction, the penalties easily could be evaded by changes in officials' responsibilities prior to the expiration of any quarter. Because the duty to *pay over* the tax arises only at the quarter's end, a "responsible person" who willfully failed to *collect* taxes would escape personal liability for that failure simply by resigning his position, and transferring to another the decisionmaking responsibility prior to the quarter's end. Obversely, a "responsible person" assuming control prior to the quarter's end could, without incurring personal liability under § 6672, willfully dissipate the trust funds collected and segregated by his predecessor.

That this result, obviously at odds with the statute's purpose to assure payment of withheld taxes, was not intended is buttressed by the history of the provision. * * *

We conclude therefore that the phrase "[a]ny person required to collect, truthfully account for, and pay over any tax imposed by this title" was meant to limit § 6672 to persons responsible for collection of third-party taxes and not to limit it to those persons in a position to perform all three of the enumerated duties with respect to the tax dollars in question.

We turn then to the Government's contention that petitioner was subject to personal liability under § 6672 when during the period in which he was a responsible person, the corporations generated gross receipts sufficient to pay the back taxes, but used the funds for other purposes.

B

Although at the time petitioner became a responsible person the trust-fund taxes had been dissipated and the corporations had no liquid assets, the Government contends that § 6672 imposed civil liability upon petitioner because sums received from sales in carrying on the businesses after January 31, 1969, were impressed with a trust in favor of the United States for the satisfaction of overdue employment taxes, and petitioner's willful use of those funds to pay creditors other than the United States, violated the obligation to "pay over" imposed by § 6672. The Government does not argue that the statute requires a "responsible person," to liquidate corporate assets to pay the back taxes upon assuming control, however; it argues only that a trust was impressed on all cash received by the corporations. We think that that construction of § 6672 would not advance the statute's purpose and, moreover, is inconsistent with the context and legislative history of the provision and its relation to the Code's priority rule applicable to collection of back taxes.

(1)

The Government argues that its construction of the statute is necessary to effectuate the congressional purpose to assure collection and payment of taxes. Although that construction might in this case garner tax dollars otherwise uncollectable, its long-term effect arguably would more likely frustrate than aid the IRS's collection efforts.

At the time petitioner assumed control, the corporations owed back taxes, were overdue on their supplier accounts, and had no cash. To the extent that the corporations had assets unencumbered by liens superior to a tax lien, the IRS could satisfy its claim by levy and sale. But as will often be the case, the corporations here apparently did not have such assets. The Government admits that in such circumstances, the IRS's practice is to be "flexible," and does not insist that the corporation discontinue operations, thereby substituting for certain loss at least the potential of recovering back taxes if the corporation makes a financial recovery. It argues nevertheless that the "responsible person" renders himself personally liable to the § 6672 penalty by using gross receipts to purchase inventory or pay wages, or even by using personal funds for those purposes, so long as any third-party employment tax bill remains unpaid.

Thus, although it is in the IRS's interest to encourage the responsible person to continue operation with the hope of receiving payment of the back taxes, if the attempt fails and the taxes remain unpaid, the IRS insists that the § 6672 personal-liability penalty attached upon payment of the first dollar to a supplier. The practical effect of that construction of the statute would be that a well-counseled person contemplating assuming control of a financially beleaguered corporation owing back employment taxes would recognize that he could do so without incurring personal civil and criminal penalties only if there were available sufficient borrowed or personal funds fully to pay all back employment taxes before doing *any* business. If that course is unattractive or unavailable to the corporation, the Government will be remitted to its claim in bankruptcy. When an immediate filing for bankruptcy means a total loss, the Government understandably, as it did here, does not discourage the corporation from continuing to operate so long as current taxes are paid. As soon as the corporation embarks upon that course, however, the "responsible person" is potentially liable to heavy civil and criminal penalties not for doing anything which compromised the Government's collection efforts, but for doing what the Government regards as maximizing its chances for recovery. As construed by the Government, § 6672 would merely discourage changes of ownership and management of financially troubled corporations and the infusion of equity or debt funding which might accompany it without encouraging employer compliance with tax obligations or facilitating collection of back taxes. Thus, recovery of employer taxes would likely be limited to the situation in which the prospective purchaser or management official is ignorant of § 6672.

(2)

As noted in the previous section, § 6672 as construed by the Government would, in effect, make the responsible person assuming control of a business a guarantor for payment of the delinquent taxes simply by undertaking to continue operation of the business. That construction is precluded by the history and context of § 6672 and cognate provisions of the Code.

Section 6672 cannot be read as imposing upon the responsible person an absolute duty to "pay over" amounts which should have been collected and withheld. The fact that the provision imposes a "penalty" and is violated only by a "willful failure" is itself strong evidence that it was not intended to impose liability without personal fault. Congress, moreover, has not made corporate officers personally liable for the corporation's tax obligations generally, and § 6672 therefore should be construed in a way which respects that policy choice. The Government's concession—that § 6672 does not impose a duty on the responsible officer to use personal funds or even to liquidate corporate assets to satisfy the tax obligations—recognizes that the "pay over" requirement does not impose an absolute duty on the responsible person to pay back taxes.

Recognizing that the statute cannot be construed to impose liability without fault, the Government characterizes petitioner's use of gross receipts for payment of operating expenses as a breach of trust, arguing that a trust was impressed on all after-acquired cash. Nothing whatever in § 6672 or its legislative history suggests that the effect of the requirement to "pay over" was to impress a trust on the corporation's after-acquired cash, however. Moreover, the history of a related section, 26 U.S.C. § 7501, makes clear that it was not. Section 7501 of the Code provides, *inter alia,* that the "amount of tax * * * collected or withheld shall be held to be a special fund in trust for the United States [which] shall be assessed, collected, and paid in the same manner and subject to the same provisions and limitations (including penalties) as are applicable with respect to the taxes from which such fund arose." This section was enacted in 1934. The provision was added to H.R. 7835, 73d Cong., 2d Sess., by the Senate Finance Committee, which explained:

> "Under existing law the liability of the person collecting and withholding the taxes to pay over the amount is merely a debt, and he cannot be treated as a trustee or proceeded against by distraint. Section [607] of the bill as reported impresses the amount of taxes withheld or collected with a trust and makes applicable for the enforcement of the Government's claim the administrative provisions for assessment and collection of taxes." S.Rep. No. 558, 73d Cong., 2d Sess., 53 (1934).

Since the very reason for adding § 7501 was, as the Senate Report states, that "the liability of the person collecting and withholding the taxes * * * is *merely a debt*" (emphasis added), § 6672, whose predecessor section was enacted in 1919 while the *debt* concept prevailed, hardly could have been intended to impose a *trust* on after-acquired cash.

We further reject the argument that § 7501, whose trust concept may be viewed as having modified the duty imposed under § 6672, can be construed as establishing a fiduciary obligation to pay over after-acquired cash unrelated to the withholding taxes. The language of § 7501 limits the trust to "the amount of the taxes *withheld* or *collected.*" (Emphasis added.) Comparing that language with § 6672, which imposes liability for a willful failure to *collect* as well as failure to pay over, makes clear that under § 7501 there must be a nexus between the funds collected and the trust created. That construction is consistent with the accepted principle of trust law requiring tracing of misappropriated trust funds into the trustee's estate in order for an impressed trust to arise. Finally, for the reasons discussed in the next section, a construction of § 7501 or § 6672 as imposing a trust on all after-acquired corporate funds without regard to the interests of others in those funds would conflict with the priority rules applicable to the collection of back taxes.

(3)

We developed in Part II, *supra,* that the Code affords the IRS several means to collect back taxes, including levy, distraint, and sale. But the IRS is not given the power to levy on property in the hands of the taxpayer beyond the extent of the taxpayer's interest in the property, and the Code specifically subordinates tax liens to the interests of certain others in the property, generally including those with a perfected security interest in the property. * * * As a consequence, secured parties often will have interests in certain proceeds superior to the tax lien, and it is unlikely, moreover, that corporations in the position of those involved here could continue in operation without making some payments to secured creditors under the terms of security agreements. Those payments may well take the form of cash or accounts receivable, which like other property may be subject to a security interest, * * *. Thus, although the IRS is powerless to attach assets in which a secured party has a superior interest, it would impose a penalty under § 6672 if the responsible person fails to divert the secured party's proceeds to the Treasury without regard to whether the secured party's interests are superior to those of the Government. Surely Congress did not intend § 6672 to hammer the responsible person with the threat of heavy civil and criminal penalties to pay over proceeds in which the Code does not assert a priority interest.

IV

We hold that a "responsible person" under § 6672 may violate the "pay over" requirement of that statute by willfully failing to pay over trust funds collected prior to his accession to control when at the time he assumed control the corporation has funds impressed with a trust under § 7501, but that § 7501 does not impress a trust on after-acquired funds, and that the responsible person consequently does not violate § 6672 by willfully using employer funds for purposes other than satisfaction of the trust-fund tax claims of the United States when at the time he assumed control there were no funds with which to satisfy the tax obligation and the funds thereafter generated are not directly traceable to collected taxes referred to by that statute. * * *

Mr. Justice White, with whom The Chief Justice and Mr. Justice Blackmun join, dissenting.

* * *

* * * The Court holds that a person who assumes control must satisfy the business' pre-existing trust-fund tax obligations if the concern has funds available at the time he assumes control. Apparently, neither it nor the IRS would require the sale of the business' assets in order to meet such obligations. It is clear, however, that there will be a great number of companies which do not have cash available at the time of a change in ownership and management but are nevertheless viable, ongoing enterprises not in need of Government subsidization. Furthermore, any businessman with a minimum of acumen could in most circumstances make sure that the financial affairs of the company are so arranged that there are no uncommitted funds available at the moment of his accession to control. Finally, there can be little doubt that the Court's ruling today will result in changes in management and ownership which are in fact nothing but subterfuges to avoid using the company's funds to pay outstanding trust-fund tax obligations. The investors in any corporation seriously in arrears will also have a strong incentive to arrange changes of management, whether sham or real, in order to permit funds acquired by the corporation to be used for purposes other than satisfying its tax obligations without exposing its managers to personal liability. In addition, changes of ownership, often more formal than real, will frequently be arranged for no purpose other than to permit the concern to use future funds without regard to its pre-existing tax obligations.

* * *

Because I believe that the Court has without justification, created yet another means of impeding the collection of taxes for purposes designated by Congress, I dissent from Parts III–B and IV of the Court's opinion.

ROTH v. UNITED STATES
United States Court of Appeals, Eleventh Circuit, 1986.
779 F.2d 1567.

TUTTLE, SENIOR CIRCUIT JUDGE:

This is an appeal by the United States from a denial by the trial court of a motion for j.n.o.v. after a jury had found that the appellee, Roth, was not a "responsible person" within the meaning of Section 6672 of the Internal Revenue Code of 1954 who would be required "to collect such tax, and truthfully account for and pay over such tax" to the United States government.

I. STATEMENT OF THE CASE

Taxpayer, Charles Richard Roth, filed this suit to recover $200.00 which he had paid on a penalty of $22,805.26 imposed against him pursuant to Section 6672 of the Internal Revenue Code of 1954,[1] for

---

1. Section 6672(a) provides:
SEC. 6672. FAILURE TO COLLECT AND PAY OVER TAX, OR ATTEMPT TO EVADE OR DEFEAT TAX.

(a) [as amended by Sec. 9(a), Act of November 10, 1978, Pub.L. No. 95–628, 92 Stat. 3627] *General Rule.* Any person required to collect, truthfully account

failure to collect and pay over federal employment taxes withheld from the wages of the employees of Leewood Development Corp. (later Leewood, Inc.) for the last two quarters of 1977. The United States filed a counterclaim against taxpayer for the unpaid balance of the assessment amounting to $22,637.89 plus interest. The case was tried to a jury which returned a verdict that taxpayer was not a person responsible for the unpaid employment taxes with respect to the stated quarters. The government, having moved for directed verdict, thereafter moved for judgment notwithstanding the verdict which was denied in an opinion and order entered on January 9, 1985.

II. STATEMENT OF FACTS

With a single exception, the facts that went to the jury were undisputed. The one exception is the conflict in testimony between the plaintiff, Roth, and Dobbins, the chief executive officer and president and majority owner of the corporation. Roth testified that he was instructed by Dobbins in August of 1977 not to pay the withheld employees' taxes, but to pay other creditors and the salaries of the employees. Dobbins denied that he gave such instructions and denied that he knew the taxes were unpaid. Thus, the only issue presented to the jury was that presented by a charge to the jury, duly objected to by the United States, as follows:

> Even if you, the jury, find that plaintiff is otherwise a responsible person within the meaning of the statute, but also find that the plaintiff was prevented from paying the payroll taxes by specific instructions by the president of the company, then you must find that plaintiff did not willfully fail to pay the payroll taxes and plaintiff must be relieved of liability.

As we have stated above, the evidence which would establish the fact that the "plaintiff is otherwise a responsible person within the meaning of the statute" is undisputed. Essentially, it is as follows.

Roth was offered an opportunity to participate in a small corporation to be organized by Dobbins who was a real estate developer and who was a beneficiary of a trust which owned the majority stock in a number of other real estate corporations. After incorporation of Leewood Development Corporation ("LDC"), whose name was later changed to Leewood, Inc., Roth was named executive vice president and Dobbins became president and chairman of the board. Roth was not a director. LDC was engaged in contracting with builders for performing part of construction projects, such as putting sheet rock in buildings

---

for, and pay over any tax imposed by this title who willfully fails to collect such tax, or truthfully account for and pay over such tax, or willfully attempts in any manner to evade or defeat any such tax or the payment thereof, shall, in addition to other penalties provided by law, be liable to a penalty equal to the total amount of the tax evaded, or not collected, or not accounted for and paid over. No penalty shall be imposed under section 6653 for any offense to which this section is applicable.

under construction. Initially, LDC and Roth and his secretary and bookkeeper had offices in the same complex as Dobbins and his other companies. Within a year, however, Leewood moved away into a warehouse which was used for the storing of material used in its construction work. At all times, Roth hired office employees and signed checks for the payrolls, including his salary of $700.00 a week. He paid substantially all bills for supplies and signed the checks paying to the United States the amount deducted from the employees as payroll deductions, so long as these were paid. Roth had signature authority on all of the company's checking accounts and he drew most of the checks, including those for his weekly salary until he resigned towards the end of the second quarter of 1977. He signed as the officer of the company a mortgage for $115,000.00 secured by property belonging to Dobbins and which was also endorsed by Dobbins. Roth was given an option to buy up to 50 percent of LDC's corporation stock which he never exercised. Taxpayer made the contracts which the company performed and, according to his testimony, he handled "the day to day operations of Leewood Development Corporation." From the middle of August, 1977, taxpayer was aware of the fact that the payroll taxes were not being remitted to the United States although he had at all times known of the obligation of the company to transfer them. During the period involved, the company had more than sufficient funds to have paid all of the withheld taxes.

According to the verdict of the jury, it must have believed Roth's testimony that he told Dobbins in August, 1977, that the company did not have the funds necessary to pay the payroll taxes.

The jury must also have accepted the following testimony by Roth:

BY MR. SMITH:

Q. Let me ask it this way, then, Rick. Were you aware that the payroll taxes had not been paid?

A. Yes, sir.

Q. When were you made aware of that?

A. Approximately the middle of August of '77.

Q. Okay. Who made it aware to you?

A. Kathy Hosmar [the company's bookkeeper].

Q. Okay. What did you do when you were aware that Leighwood didn't have sufficient funds to pay the payroll taxes?

A. I contacted Mr. Dobbins to see what would be done at that point.

Q. Did you have a conversation?

A. Yes, sir.

Q. What was that conversation?

A. The conversation was that what was we going to do in getting the money to the company to pay the taxes and when would it be in there and how was we going to pay it.

Q. And what did he tell you?

A. He came over to the office—

MS. PRIVETT: I'm going to object, Your Honor, again, on the same purposes.

THE COURT: Overruled. This goes to the authority and it goes to the issue of wilfulness.

BY MR. SMITH:

Q. Okay. What did Mr. Dobbins tell you, Rick?

A. He came to the office and he looked at the amount of taxes that was owed and we had a discussion on where we could come up with the money.

And his conversation with me was that he had some apartments that would be sold and, upon the sale of those apartments, he would put the necessary funds in the company to pay the taxes.

Q. Did he give you any instructions—

A. At that time—

Q. About who to pay and who not to pay?

A. At that time, he was thinking that the apartments would close very soon. So his instructions to me was to be sure to make the payroll and pay the creditors so we could stay in business, that these apartments could close and he could pay the taxes and not to pay the taxes, and it would put the company in bankruptcy.

Q. What did you do?

A. I done what Mr. Dobbins told me to do. I made the payroll and paid the creditors that was necessary to keep getting the material, waiting for the apartments to close so that we might be able to pay the taxes.

Q. And this was in August of '77, you say?

A. Yes, sir.

Q. Did you talk to him at any time subsequent to August of '77 about payroll taxes?

A. Not to my knowledge, because it was August before I was aware that the taxes was—

Q. After August, did you talk to him about these payroll taxes?

A. Almost weekly.

Q. What was his response?

A. Well, the response that I got was that whatever the problem was, it was a problem with closing on the apartments due to some zoning laws in Vestavia, and it was going to take longer than he first anticipated to close the apartments and come up with case.

Q. What instructions, if any, did he give you?

A. To continue to keep the company going until he could close those apartments and pay those taxes.

R., Vol. II, p. 79.

Thus, it is plain that we have a case in which it is clear that Roth was a responsible person within the contemplation of the Act, unless he was removed from that status by the instructions given him by Dobbins. Although Dobbins testified that he did not give Roth any such instructions, because he did not even know that the payments on the 941 forms were past due until the end of November, 1977, we must treat the case as if the jury believed Roth's testimony with respect to this rather than that of Dobbins.

III. Discussion

The sole issue before the Court is whether it is true that an otherwise responsible person under the Act sheds that status if, after the taxes are withheld, and while they are being continually withheld, such responsible person is directed by an officer with authority to control his actions as to corporate affairs not to pay the government's trust funds to the Internal Revenue Service. Initially, we must consider the nature of the funds we are talking about. They are amounts which LDC deducted from the payroll checks given to its employees for the payment of the employee's income tax and Social Security taxes, together with the amount that LDS itself owed as Social Security taxes for the employees. Next, we must realize that the statute that requires these funds to be withheld by an employer makes these trust funds of the United States. Also, such withholding is treated by the IRS as payment by the employees of their taxes.

Section 7501 of the Internal Revenue Code provides:

A. *Liability for taxes withheld or collected.*

(a) *General rule.*—Whenever any person is required to collect or withhold any internal revenue tax from any other person and to pay over such tax to the United States, the amount of tax so collected or withheld shall be held to be a special fund in trust for the United States. The amount of such fund shall be assessed, collected, and paid in the same manner and subject to the same provisions and limitations (including penalties) as are applicable with respect to the taxes from which such fund arose.

We must bear in mind that, even after he was instructed by Dobbins not to pay the government its withheld funds, taxpayer as manager of the day to day affairs of the company, caused deductions to continue to be made from the weekly pay checks given to the company's employees, fully knowing that he would not transmit such funds to the government. We must also remember that it was not until the middle of August, or the middle of the third quarter of 1977, that Roth was instructed by Dobbins not to pay the withheld funds to the IRS. Since Roth knew that payments were required at least biweekly, according to his testimony, he was certainly the responsible officer up until the time he was told by Dobbins to stop making such payments, even on the assumption that he lost such status after having been so instructed.

There is no dispute between the parties about the fact that more than one person may be a "responsible person" for an employer. *Mazo v. United States*, 591 F.2d 1151 (5th Cir.1979); [2] *Moore v. United States*, 465 F.2d 514 (5th Cir.1972).

The Court of Appeals for the Fifth Circuit has held that "responsibility" in this context is "status, duty, and authority not knowledge." *Mazo, supra*, at 1156. Most of the cases cited by appellee deal with decisions as to what constitutes a "responsible person" without any reference to directions given by a superior officer. *Neckles v. United States*, 579 F.2d 938 (5th Cir.1978); *Brown v. United States*, 464 F.2d 590 (5th Cir.1972); *Liddon v. United States*, 448 F.2d 509 (5th Cir.1971). However, the government cites one case which deals with the same problem that is presented here. In *Howard v. United States*, 711 F.2d 729 (5th Cir.1983) (a case which is not a binding precedent for us), the Court held that a person who was otherwise a "responsible person" within the contemplation of the statute remained liable for failure to pay over the withheld funds to the United States in spite of the fact that he had been instructed by the CEO of the corporation not to pay the IRS anything. The Court stated:

> The fact that Jennings (the CEO) might well have fired Howard had he disobeyed Jennings' instructions and paid the taxes does not make Howard any less responsible for their payment. *See Brown*, 464 F.2d [590] at 591, n. 1 (5th Cir.1972) ("responsible person" need not have final word on payment of bills and taxes). Howard had the status, duty and authority to pay the taxes owed, and would only have lost that authority after he had paid them. Authority to pay in this context means effective *power* to pay. That Howard had this authority is demonstrated by the fact that he did issue small checks without Jennings' approval on a number of occasions. *Commonwealth National Bank [v. U.S.]*, 665 F.2d [743] at 752 [(5th Cir.1982)]. Had Jennings fired Howard for paying the taxes, Howard would at least have fulfilled his legal obligations. Faced with the possibility of leaving the frying pan with only minor burns, Howard chose instead to stay on in the vain hope of avoiding the fire. While we appreciate the difficulty of his position, we cannot condone his abdication of the responsibility imposed upon him by law. *See Moore*, 465 F.2d at 517 (corporate officers who merely followed their superiors' instructions in issuing checks to creditors were nevertheless "responsible persons").

Id. at 734–35 (footnote omitted.)

2. In *Bonner v. City of Prichard*, 661 F.2d 1206 (11th Cir.1981) (en banc), the court adopted as binding precedent all of the decisions of the former Fifth Circuit handed down prior to the close of business on September 30, 1981. *Id.* at 1209.

The trial court in the instant case noted the *Howard* decision but expressly declined to follow it, stating that to follow the precept of *Howard* would be to condone the corporation's vice president's using corporation money contrary to the instructions of the president and that this would be equated with embezzlement.

We perceive a reason, beyond that stated in *Howard* for rejecting Roth's argument here. That is, that the funds which accumulated in the bank account of LDC by reason of withholding the Social Security taxes and income taxes owed by the employees to the federal government became trust funds of the United States. With respect to those funds, the federal statute created a distinct and definite obligation on every responsible officer. That obligation was to remit such funds to the Internal Revenue Service. In our view, no instruction by the president or the majority owner of LDC could effectively bar an otherwise responsible officer from paying these funds in accordance with the law. Although in the company's bank accounts, the company was in effect an interloper with respect to that part of the bank account that represented the trust funds accumulated because of the payment by the employees of their federal taxes. Roth once having become an "otherwise responsible person" to pay over the taxes became obligated by statute to pay these funds to the Internal Revenue Service. He was under no obligations to obey instructions from his corporate supervisor not to do so. Moreover, it should be borne in mind as noted above, that during the second half of 1977, Roth received over $8,000 by checks signed by him knowing that the corporation was obligated to use these funds to pay the debt to the government.

We conclude that the result in *Howard* was correct for the reasons stated there and in light of the additional considerations which we have stated here.

The judgment is Reversed and the case is Remanded to the district court with directions that it enter a judgment for the defendant and cross-appellant j.n.o.v.

GODBOLD, CHIEF JUDGE, concurring in part and dissenting in part:

I concur in the holding that the government was entitled to judgment n.o.v. for the statutory penalty arising out of failure of the corporation to pay over withheld taxes for the third quarter of 1977. I cannot agree that judgment n.o.v. was properly granted based upon failure to pay for the fourth quarter of 1977. Whether Roth is liable for the corporation's failure to pay in the fourth quarter is an issue to be decided by a properly instructed jury.

The jury found, in response to interrogatories, that Roth was not "a person responsible to collect, truthfully account for and pay over income taxes and social security taxes withheld from the wages of the Corporation's employees ending for the third quarter of 1977", and made the same finding with respect to the fourth quarter. This court concludes, as a matter of law, that under the evidence Roth was a "person responsible" with respect to both quarters, and implicitly holds that the jury instruction quoted in its opinion concerning the effect of specific instructions given Roth by the president of the company was erroneous.

I. Was Roth a person responsible for payment of withheld taxes and for what period?

Roth was a corporate employee employed at will and charged with day-to-day operation of a small corporation engaged mostly in installing dry walls in construction jobs. He found work, supervised work, purchased materials, and paid for materials. The corporate bookkeeper kept him informed. He signed most checks, including salary checks. He signed the quarterly tax withholding forms (941's) for the last two quarters of 1977.

Roth was not a director of the corporation but was designated as executive vice president. He was not even a stockholder. Dobbins, the president and chairman of the board, and his family owned all the stock. The by-laws vested management of the corporation in the board of directors, who must be stockholders, and general supervision of the business in the president. No one suggests that Roth was an alter ego. There is no proof that under the by-laws of the corporation the executive vice president had authority to handle or disburse funds. In short, Roth had authority to handle corporate funds because the corporation, through president Dobbins, conferred it upon him. He did not, either expressly or by implication, otherwise possess the authority to handle money.

The government has not even made an assessment against Dobbins.

Whether one is the person responsible so as to fall within § 6672 "is a matter of status, duty and authority, not knowledge." *Mazo v. U.S.*, 591 F.2d 1151, 1156 (5th Cir.), *cert. denied sub nom., Lattimore v. U.S.*, 444 U.S. 842, 100 S.Ct. 82, 62 L.Ed.2d 54 (1979). Roth enjoyed status and authority until late August, when—the jury necessarily found—he was instructed by president Dobbins, who was in sole control of the corporation, not to pay out of corporate funds the corporation's obligation for withheld taxes. To be a responsible person for a tax quarter, one need not be a responsible person at the end of the quarter so long as responsible during the quarter. *Brown v. U.S.*, 591 F.2d 1136, 1140 (5th Cir.1979). Thus because Roth was a responsible person until late July, he is obligated for all of the July–September 1977 quarter.[1] This continuation of authority to the end of the quarter, whether or not actually possessed to that time, vindicates the interest of the government that responsibility for a quarter may not be avoided by an intra-quarter shift of authority.[2]

---

1. Under Roth's own testimony neither willfulness nor "reasonable cause" for the period July 1 to late August was an issue. See Part II, below.

2. Thus, under *Brown*, Roth would be liable for the third quarter even if Dobbins had fired him in August.

Responsibility to pay the taxes for the October-December quarter presents a number of issues. Arguably, as a matter of law, a mere employee authorized to handle corporate funds by delegation from the president, and not otherwise authorized, ceases to be a responsible person once his delegated authority is removed (subject to his being responsible to the end of the quarter, pursuant to *Brown*). At a minimum, stripping such an employee of his authority to pay taxes before a quarter commences creates a jury issue of whether he continues to be a responsible person for the new quarter during which he had no actual authority to pay taxes. This court does not hold that Roth's partial loss of authority was a sham. Rather it seems to say that, because he once had unlimited authority to disburse corporate funds, a limitation by the corporation, as a matter of law, could not relieve him of the responsibility imposed by the statute.

In applying § 6672 some recognition must be given to the law governing corporate affairs. The status and authority of a corporate employee can be withdrawn: if derived from the by-laws, by amendment; if implied from office, by removal; and if conferred through delegation, by withdrawal. Presumably if the president had fired Roth in August, this court would not have held that he was a responsible person for the October-December quarter. Presumably, also, the same result would be reached if in August the corporation removed Roth's authority to handle corporate funds in any respect. The corporation employee cannot do more than he can do, and § 6672 is not intended to hold him liable for failure to exercise authority he does not have, or, even if he has it, when his failure is not willful. Roth had authority to sign checks. This is a "significant factor because it generally comes with the ability to choose which creditors will be paid." *Burack v. U.S.*, 461 F.2d 1282, 198 Ct.Cl. 855 (1972). In this case, after late August, Roth did not have the ability to choose.

The majority rely upon *Howard v. U.S.*, 711 F.2d 729 (5th Cir.1983) (not binding). But Howard had "status, duty and authority," because he was a director, minority stockholder, treasurer, and executive vice president of the corporation, in addition to running its day-to-day operations. The status, duty and authority he possessed as treasurer and executive vice president continued during the periods in question. Presumably the chief executive officer had no authority to tell Howard as treasurer not to perform his duties as treasurer. The Fifth Circuit found: "Howard had the status, duty and authority to pay the taxes owed, and would only have lost that authority after he paid them."[3] In this case, a jury can find that Roth had no authority to pay taxes once that authority was withdrawn.

Two other Fifth Circuit cases emphasized by the government also are distinguishable. In *Mazo, supra*, the taxpayer was the general

---

3. Footnote 4 in *Howard* recognizes that a responsible person can have his authority removed. 711 F.2d at 734 n. 4.

manager of the corporation, and his authority to sign checks or to use corporate funds to pay taxes was never removed. His defense was that he thought the controller was paying the taxes. In *Moore v. U.S.*, 465 F.2d 514 (5th Cir.), *cert. denied,* 409 U.S. 1108, 93 S.Ct. 907, 34 L.Ed.2d 688 (1973), taxpayers were corporate officers and a majority of the board of directors who, the court held, had ultimate authority over the expenditure of funds.

There is not a dearth of authority on the specific point that the court recognizes is presented by this case—the extent to which corporate employees who are under the direction of corporate officers are responsible persons. In *Geiger v. U.S.*, 583 F.Supp. 1166 (D.Ariz.1984), Geiger was a consultant who exercised an unusual degree of influence and control over a corporate business. Also, though he was not a shareholder, officer or director, he was authorized to sign checks, and did so, and assigned accounts receivable to a bank using the title of acting president. After a non-jury trial, the court found that he was not a responsible person. It distinguished *Howard:*

> Although defendant maintains that plaintiff was in a position of responsibility for the acts giving rise to the violation in the instant case, in the recent decision of *Howard v. United States,* 711 F.2d 729 (5th Cir.1983), where a "subservient" person was held to have a duty to pay withheld taxes, the "person" there was a substantial shareholder, director, and executive vice president of the corporation. This Court is convinced that plaintiff has shown that although he signed the checks he did so only at the behest and direction of Mr. Kennelly, in the latter's capacity as president of Standard, and therefore, plaintiff lacked the "final word" as defined in *United States v. Graham* [309 F.2d 210 (9th Cir.1962)], *supra,* and in *Pacific National Insurance v. United States,* 422 F.2d 26 (9th Cir.1970).

Id. at 1168–69.

Klotz v. U.S., 602 F.2d 920 (9th Cir.1979) is similar to the present case. Klotz was director, secretary-treasurer, and purchasing agent for a corporation and one of two joint signatories required for corporate checks. The corporation failed to pay its withholding taxes for the third and fourth quarters of 1969 and collapsed in January 1970. Persons who lent money to the corporation began to take over its affairs, and their representative was added as a signatory to the bank account. Klotz fell out with the president, Howe. In mid-August 1969 his authority to sign checks was removed. He was "effectively" out of the corporation by the end of August and resigned in late October. The district court held that the lenders entirely controlled the corporation's finances, that neither Howe nor Klotz was a responsible person and that neither was willful. On appeal the Ninth Circuit found it unnecessary to reach the responsible person issue but affirmed on the ground that neither Klotz nor Howe was willful because under the facts neither was any more than negligent.

In the present case, the reasoning of the court is essentially circular and stands the statutory scheme on its head: "Because Roth has status and authority he is a responsible person and therefore bound to pay; his status and authority cannot be terminated because as a responsible person he is bound to pay." Responsibility to pay during the fourth quarter is an inference that must be drawn from status and authority, not the contrary. The "burdened with a trust" rationale is likewise circular: "For the fourth quarter the corporation held funds impressed with a trust in favor of the government; therefore Roth is a person responsible because he failed to carry out the trust obligations." Again, responsibility to pay must derive from status and authority, not status and authority from responsibility to pay.

Roth's lack of authority during the last quarter is demonstrated by the evidence that in October Dobbins took over in toto the affairs of the corporation.[4] Roth's pay stopped in late November, although he performed some duties for the corporation until early 1978.

II. Willfulness and "reasonable cause"

Willfulness is a required element for liability for the § 6672 penalty. Once one is found to be a responsible person, the burden of proving lack of willfulness is on him. *Mazo,* 591 F.2d at 1155. For this statute, willfulness is a voluntary, conscious and intentional act, or acting with a reckless regard of a known or obvious risk. *Id.* at 1154. It is "the state of the responsible person's mind, a subjective determination," *Id.* at 1157. Roth came forward with evidence to create a jury issue. Even if he continued to enjoy corporate status and authority to pay taxes during the fourth quarter despite the instructions of the president, it is for a properly instructed jury to decide whether—bearing in mind what Dobbins told him—Roth's failure to exercise his status and authority was willful. There was no separate jury instruction on willfulness because, as was recognized during the charge conferences, the instruction given on the effect of directions to Roth from president Dobbins contained its own instruction on willfulness.[5]

Cellura v. U.S., 245 F.Supp. 379 (N.D.Ohio 1965) is parallel to the present case. Plaintiff was hired as manager of a restaurant. It was in serious financial difficulty and operating on a cash basis. As soon as funds were deposited in its bank account they were withdrawn so that they could not be attached. The sole stockholder and president of the corporation gave plaintiff instructions on the priority of creditors to be paid. He told her that her prime concern was to keep the restaurant operating and pay trade creditors ahead of all others. Tax liabilities were to be paid when there was money available to do so. Plaintiff carried out these instructions. Some funds were available for payment to the government, plaintiff paid the available funds over and they

---

4. I have not been able to find in the record support for the majority's statement that he resigned toward the end of the second quarter.

5. See also, comment of the court in overruling objection, recognizing that willfulness was an issue. Majority opinion, 779 F.2d at 1569.

were applied against delinquent withholding obligations. The district court found that plaintiff was not liable under § 6672 because she did not act willfully:

> On the state of this record the Court finds that plaintiff does not come within the scope of 26 U.S.C. §§ 6671(b) and 6672. Plaintiff's authority was limited to paying bills under the general instructions of her employer. While plaintiff did not have to check with her employer as to payment of a particular bill, she had instructions as to the priorities of classes of creditors, and under such instructions the Internal Revenue was at the end of the list.
>
> The Court finds that plaintiff had no authority to pay taxes ahead of trade creditors, and the decision to prefer trade creditors over Internal Revenue originated with her employer, and not with the plaintiff. The Court further finds that there is no evidence that plaintiff on her own accord failed to pay taxes to the Internal Revenue when excess funds were available.

Id. at 382. A jury could reach a similar conclusion here. *See also, Klotz v. U.S., supra,* distinguishing negligence from willfulness.

As the case stands the government has a judgment for the fourth quarter without determination by a factfinder that Roth acted willfully with respect to that quarter. Failure to exercise authority is not necessarily willful when one has no express or implied authority from the corporation other than by direction of the president and thinks that his authority has been circumscribed. A jury might find that Roth's "subjective determination," *see Mazo,* was that he could not pay the taxes.

Finally, no factfinder has addressed the issue of "reasonable cause," which may excuse a failure to collect, account for, or pay over withholding taxes. *Mazo,* 591 F.2d at 1155; *Newsome v. U.S.,* 431 F.2d 742, 746 (5th Cir.1970). Under the circumstances of this case, reasonable cause is a jury issue. No instruction on reasonable cause was given or asked, presumably for the same reason set out above, that is, the plenary instruction that the jury "must find" that Roth was relieved of liability if he was prevented from paying taxes by specific instructions from the president of the company pretermitted the necessity for it.

I respectfully dissent.

REV.RUL. 84–83

ISSUE

Can a volunteer member of a board of trustees of organizations referred to in section 501(a) of the Code be considered a responsible person and liable for the penalty under section 6672?

LAW AND ANALYSIS

Under section 6672(a) of the Code any person required to collect, truthfully account for, and pay over any internal revenue tax who willfully fails to collect such tax, or truthfully account for and pay over such tax, or willfully attempts in any manner to evade or defeat such tax or the payment thereof, shall, in addition to other penalties, be liable to a penalty equal to the total amount of the tax evaded, or not collected, or not accounted for and paid over. No penalty will be imposed under section 6653 for any offense to which this section is applicable.

Section 6671(b) of the Code defines the term person to include an officer or employee of a corporation, or a member or employee of a partnership, who as such officer, employee, or member is under a duty to perform the act in respect of which the violation occurs.

The determination of who is the person under a duty to collect, account for, and pay over the employment and withholding taxes for wages paid to employees is especially dependent upon the facts of the case. See *United States v. Graham*, 309 F.2d 210 (9th Cir.1962); *Bauer v. United States*, 543 F.2d 142 (Ct.Cl.1976); *Feist v. United States*, 607 F.2d 954 (Ct.Cl.1979).

The term "person" includes an officer or employee, but does not exclude others. Its scope is illustrated rather than limited by the examples in section 6671(b) of the Code. Section 6672(a) is addressed to those persons who have responsibility for payment of the withheld taxes, who have knowledge of the tax delinquency and who have authority over the decision to pay or not to pay the taxes, not necessarily persons who have the duty of filling out the forms. Trustees can have this responsibility, knowledge and authority.

HOLDING

The trustee can be liable for unpaid employment and withholding taxes. The fact that a trustee is a volunteer member of the board of trustees does not in and of itself mean the trustee will or will not be deemed liable. The trustee's liability depends on whether he or she is found to meet the tests of responsibility and willfulness under section 6672 of the Code.

Notes and Questions

1. What are the obligations of a responsible person of a business who discovers, just prior to the sale of the company, that there are withholding taxes owed to the government? Generally, the responsible person's liability would continue despite the subsequent sale of the business. In Feist v. United States, 607 F.2d 954 (Ct.Cl.1979), however, a rather extreme set of circumstances led the Court of Claims to a different conclusion. The responsible person in *Feist* discovered, on the day of the planned sale of the business, that the company's taxes for its most recent quarter were delinquent. Rather than postpone the sale and gather the cash necessary to pay

the tax from the company's several hundred cash registers scattered throughout various retail outlets, the responsible person elected to proceed with the sale after receiving oral assurances from the buyer that it would pay the tax immediately after the sale. However, just after the sale one of the principals of the buyer illegally appropriated the company's funds and two weeks later the company was adjudicated bankrupt. In an action against the responsible person/seller for payment of the tax, the court seized upon the Supreme Court's statement in *Slodov,* that section 6672 "was not intended to impose liability without personal fault," and found the failure to pay the tax not willful, as the seller had taken reasonable precautions to see that the tax was paid, given the nature of the surrounding circumstances.

2. The willfulness requirement in a section 6672 case is satisfied by "showing that the responsible person recklessly disregarded his duty to collect, account for, and pay over the trust fund taxes or by showing that the responsible person ignored an obvious and known risk that the trust fund might not be remitted." Feist v. United States, 607 F.2d 954, 961 (Ct.Cl.1979); see also Teel v. United States, 529 F.2d 903, 905–906 (9th Cir.1976). However, "[m]ere negligence in failing to ascertain facts regarding a tax delinquency is insufficient to constitute willfulness under the code." Bauer v. United States, 543 F.2d 142 (Ct.Cl.1976). The burden of proving a lack of willfulness is on the responsible person. Anderson v. United States, 561 F.2d 162, 165 (8th Cir.1977).

3. Section 6672(b), added to the Code in 1979 by P.L. 95–628 and effective with respect to penalties assessed after January 9, 1979, permits an individual to stay collection of the 100% penalty if, within 30 days of the date on which notice and demand for payment of the penalty is made, he pays the minimum amount necessary to invoke the jurisdiction of a court in a refund suit, files a claim for refund of the amount paid, and posts a bond equal to one and one-half times the amount of the balance of the unpaid assessment. The stay of collection expires automatically, however, if the alleged responsible person fails to file suit in a district court or the Claims Court within 30 days after the date on which his claim for refund is denied.

Prior to the enactment of section 6672(b) there was no statutory provision for obtaining a stay of collection of the 100% penalty. The Service could institute collection proceedings 10 days after notice and demand for payment was made, and any stay had to be worked out with the Collection Division on an informal basis. Although section 6672(b) now makes a stay a matter of statutory right if a bond is posted, the provision is not intended to *require* an individual to post a bond in order to have his liability adjudicated in a district court or the Claims Court prior to collection. Thus, in appropriate cases, the IRS and the taxpayer can agree to an informal stay pending a court decision on the taxpayer's liability for the penalty. In such a case, the alleged responsible person still would have to pay the minimum jurisdictional amount and file a claim for refund before instituting proceedings in a district court or the Claims Court.

(2) Joint and Several Liability
USLIFE TITLE INSURANCE CO. v. HARBISON
United States Court of Appeals, Fifth Circuit, 1986.
784 F.2d 1238.

GOLDBERG, CIRCUIT JUDGE.

An old saying has it that the art of taxation consists in so plucking the goose as to get the most feathers with the least hissing. The practice of taxation, however, is seldom pretty. In this case, appellee's hissing roused the district court to condemn the Internal Revenue Service for overzealous plucking. This condemnation took the form of an award of attorneys' fees against the Government based on the finding that the Government's zealousness was not substantially justified within the meaning of the Equal Access to Justice Act.

* * *

A person whom the IRS determines to be responsible has two years from the date she pays the tax in which to file for a refund and thereby challenge her liability.[6] The burden is on the taxpayer to rebut the Commissioner's determination. *Brown [v. United States,* 591 F.2d 1136 (5th Cir.1970)]. Moreover, responsible persons under Section 6672 are held jointly and severally liable for the underlying withholding tax delinquency. *Brown, supra,* 591 F.2d at 1142. Therefore, the fact that more than one person is responsible for a particular delinquency does not relieve another responsible person of her personal liability, nor can a responsible person avoid collection against herself on the ground that the Government should first collect the tax from someone else. *Hornsby v. United States,* 588 F.2d 952, 954 (5th Cir.1979).

Although nothing in the language of Section 6672 explicitly prevents the Government from collecting and retaining from each responsible person a full satisfaction, this court has construed it to bring to the Government "only the same amount to which it was entitled by the way of tax." *Newsome v. United States,* 431 F.2d 742, 745 (5th Cir. 1970). "Double recovery by the government is not necessary to fulfill § 6672's primary purpose—protection of government revenues." *Brown, supra,* 591 F.2d at 1143. The Government acknowledges this fact and states that its policy is

> to use assessments pursuant to Section 6672 solely as a collection device. Any excess amounts that are temporarily collected are refunded upon expiration of the statutory period for filing a refund claim

---

6. As relevant here, 26 U.S.C. § 6511(a) provides that a claim for refund can be filed within three years of the date the return is filed (and the taxes paid) or two years from the date the taxes were paid, whichever is later. Since no returns are filed in the case of Section 6672 liabilities, only the two-year rule has significance here. Moreover, a Section 6672 liability is a divisible liability. *See Steele v. United States,* 280 F.2d 89 (9th Cir.1960). Accordingly, a responsible person need only pay the tax attributable to one employee for one quarter in order to maintain a claim for refund. * * *

* * *. Thus, the Government does not seek more than one full satisfaction of delinquent withholding taxes, but takes action to protect the revenue by assuring that one satisfaction of the withholding taxes ultimately will be retained.

Appellant's Brief at 24–25.[7]

It should be noted that the problem involved here is not present when each responsible person has litigated her liability under Section 6672. When a person against whom an assessment has been made contests her liability by instituting a refund suit, the Government joins the other persons against whom Section 6672 assessments have been made. See Rev.Proc. 69–26, 1969–2 Cum.Bull. 308. This procedure resolves doubts as to whom the Government may look to for payment of the withholding tax delinquency.

By contrast, where one or more of the allegedly responsible persons chooses not to contest her liability within a short time after the assessments are made, protection of the revenue becomes a more complicated matter. Until the limitations period for seeking a refund expires, it cannot be determined with certainty whether the Government will be entitled to retain the funds it has collected. The six-year period for collecting the liabilities assessed against the remaining responsible persons, see 26 U.S.C. § 6502(a), could expire while the first responsible person's refund claim is still pending. In such circumstances, if the Government were prohibited from pursuing collection activities against the other responsible persons, a successful claim for refund by one of the responsible persons would have the effect of defeating collection of the full amount of the underlying taxes. In this case, a premature cessation of collection efforts against Harbison would have forced the Government to rely on payments made by Walker to satisfy the delinquency, despite the possibility—albeit in hindsight nonexistent—that it might later be called upon to refund Walker's payments.

The Government's position also finds ample support in *Gens v. United States,* 615 F.2d 1335 (Ct.Cl.1980). In that case, the taxpayer, a person against whom an assessment had been made pursuant to Section 6672, contended that the Government was required to abate the assessment against him to the extent that it had already collected assessments arising from the same withholding tax liabilities from two other

---

7. In this regard, the Internal Revenue Service has stated in its Policies of the IRS Handbook, P–5–60 (Approved 5–30–84), reprinted in 1 Administration, CCH Internal Revenue Manual 1305–15:

The withheld income and employment taxes or collected excise taxes will be collected only once, whether from the corporation, from one or more of its responsible persons, or from the corporation and one or more of its responsible persons. Collection of the withheld income and employment taxes or collected excise taxes is achieved when the Service's right to retain the amount collected is established. An abatement of the tax assessment against the corporation will be made to the extent that the related 100–percent penalty assessment is paid, after expiration of the period for filing a claim by the person(s) from whom the 100–percent penalty was collected.

See generally 2 Administration, CCH Internal Revenue Manual, para. 5548.3–5548.4, at 7317–3–7318.

responsible persons. Although the Government had in fact collected some funds, one of the business associates had filed a suit for refund which was still pending, while the other associate had entered into a settlement of his liability with the Government. The court held that since the Government did not have an established right to retain the funds it had collected, the taxpayer was not entitled to an abatement at that time.

* * *

In this case, the Government's decision to continue to collect from both Harbison and Walker and to defend this suit as part of that effort was clearly reasonable in both law and fact. To uphold the award of fees in this case would penalize the IRS for doing nothing more than carrying out its statutory mandate. As such, the Government's position was more than substantially justified under the Equal Access to Justice Act, and the award of fees must fall.

Reversed.

---

(3) Designation of Payments

Section 6672 provides for the assessment against a responsible person of the *tax* not withheld or collected and paid over. The assessment is limited to this tax and is not coextensive with the tax obligation of the business entity with respect to which it is assessed. In common parlance, the responsible person is held liable for the "trust fund" portion of the business liability, *i.e.*, the employees' share of FICA taxes and the withholding tax on wages applicable to individual income taxes.

By way of example, assume that Ajax, Inc. has failed to meet its full obligations for the relevant quarters, and that Mr. A is a responsible person of Ajax, Inc. The corporation owes the following amounts as of the date the responsible person assessment is made:

Withholding Tax on Wages	$10,000 (Balance)
Late Filing Penalty	5,000
Employer's Share FICA	1,000
Employees' Share FICA	1,000
Interest	3,000
	$20,000

The section 6672 assessment against Mr. A will be in the amount of $11,000, consisting of the withholding tax of $10,000 and the employees' share of FICA (withheld), but will exclude the penalty, the employer's share of FICA and the interest due from the corporation. Interest (and a late payment penalty) due from Mr. A will accrue on *his* liability only after an assessment is made against him.

In light of Mr. A's exposure for the trust fund portion only of the liabilities of Ajax, Inc., there is great significance to the precise application of any corporate funds collected by the IRS. Assume, for example, that $5,000 of Ajax funds are paid to the Service or collected by means of a levy or seizure and sale of corporate assets. If the funds are allocated to the corporate late filing penalty, the total corporate obligation would be reduced by $5,000, but the liability of Mr. A would remain the full $11,000. On the other hand, if the funds were allocated to withholding taxes, the corporation would still owe $15,000, but Mr. A's liability also would be reduced to $6,000.

It is well established that the IRS must allocate a payment as directed by the payor.[r] Therefore, if Ajax, Inc. submits a check to the Service and designates the payment "to be applied to the trust fund portion of Form 941 liability" for the relevant period, Mr. A will receive the maximum personal benefit. In the absence of a specific direction, the Service can allocate the payment as it sees fit—generally not to maximize the benefit to a responsible person. Moreover, where a payment is effected involuntarily (by levy or seizure and sale) the Service does not consider itself obligated to apply the collection as designated by the taxpayer.

In view of the foregoing, it greatly behooves a potential (or assessed) responsible person who has control over corporate assets to see to it that payments are made to the Service on the corporation's tax liabilities and that the payments are appropriately designated. It should also be noted that the designation of payments as among several taxable periods may also be important. For example, one usually would wish to designate payments to a period for which he is clearly liable, rather than to a period for which he may have a defense to responsibility.

The key point to be considered in the context of any payments to the Internal Revenue Service is that one should always precisely designate the application of a payment so as to maximize the benefit of the payment to the client.

Cases concerning "trust fund taxes" in the bankruptcy context are considered in Section 9 of this Chapter.

B. LIABILITY OF PROVIDERS OF WAGES

UNITED STATES v. FRED A. ARNOLD, INC.
United States Court of Appeals, Ninth Circuit, 1978.
573 F.2d 605.

PER CURIAM:

The United States brought this action under § 3505(a) of the Internal Revenue Code, seeking to collect from Fred A. Arnold, Inc., a general contractor, the withholding and F.I.C.A. taxes which its subcontractor, Pannell Brothers Construction Co., failed to pay on behalf of its employees. Arnold appeals from the district court's grant of the

---

r. Rev.Rul. 79–284, 1979–2 C.B. 83, modifying Rev.Rul. 73–305, 1973–2 C.B. 43.

government's motion for summary judgment. This court has jurisdiction under 28 U.S.C. § 1291.

* * *

We question whether this case was an appropriate one for summary judgment. * * *

* * *

This case presents a situation surely not uncommon in the construction industry. On a contract for the United States Navy, Arnold subcontracted the framing work to Pannell. Pannell eventually requested that progress payments be made weekly so as to alleviate cash flow problems, rather than biweekly or monthly, as had been the case up to that point. Arnold agreed to the proposed payment schedule, provided the funds were expended on Arnold's project rather than on other Pannell jobs. A special checking account was set up in the name of Pannell Brothers. The funds advanced were to be deposited to this account and an Arnold supervisor was to cosign all withdrawals to ensure that the funds were not diverted to other Pannell jobs. Arnold paid amounts sufficient to cover more than the net payroll. Pannell drew on the account for purposes other than payroll, including the partnership draw. Arnold's supervisors apparently never refused to countersign a withdrawal.

Eventually, Pannell defaulted on the contract and went into bankruptcy. At that point Arnold learned that the bank signature card permitted funds to be withdrawn on the signature of the two Arnold supervisors. They withdrew $4,400, using it to pay wages to Pannell employees for the payroll period ending on the day of default. The taxes owing on those wages were paid, and from that point on, Arnold paid workers to finish the subcontract work, remitting withholding and F.I.C.A. taxes to the government on the wages it paid. The only taxes in question are those related to the wages paid out of the special account prior to Pannell's default.

Before 1966 only "employers" were liable for withholding taxes. This lead to problems, especially in the construction industry. A financially-strapped subcontractor would go to a lender, often his general contractor, for interim financing. The lender, wishing to minimize costs, would supply only the net payroll funds. The employees received credit as if the withholding taxes had been paid. The subcontractor-employer remained liable under 26 U.S.C. §§ 3102(b) and 3402, but recourse against him frequently proved fruitless.

In 1966, Congress enacted § 3505 of the Code.[2] It provides that a surety, lender, or other person who directly or indirectly pays another's employees is secondarily liable for F.I.C.A. and withholding taxes.

---

2. "(a) Direct payment by third parties—For purposes of sections 3102, 3202, 3402, and 3403, if a lender, surety, or other person, who is not an employer under such sections with respect to any employee or group of employees, pays wages directly to such an employee or group of employees, employed by one or more employers, or to

Under § 3505(b), when a surety, lender, or other person advances funds to the employer, he is liable for the employer's withholding taxes if he knows that the funds are to be used specifically for the payment of wages and if he has actual notice or knowledge that the employer does not intend to, or will not be able to, make payment of the withholding taxes.

In contrast, under § 3505(a), a person is automatically liable, whatever his knowledge or notice, if he "directly" pays the employees. The intention of Congress was to prevent sureties, lenders, or other persons from assuming responsibility for net wages, excluding taxes. If payroll responsibility is assumed, it must include responsibility for the taxes tied to the wages.

To decide this appeal we must determine what constitutes "direct payment" for the purposes of § 3505(a). In our opinion, in order to be direct payment the payor must have (1) the ability to control the funds, and (2) the right and legal authority to exercise that control.

With respect to the first prong: "the ability to control the funds", the inferences which might be drawn from the evidence are conflicting. It is not clear whether Arnold sent checks to Pannell Brothers, and left it to the good faith of the payee to deposit the checks in the restricted account, or whether Arnold itself deposited the checks. The depositions indicate that the deposit books were kept in the Arnold field office, an assertion which finds support in the defendant's admission that, at the time the plaintiff's interrogatories were propounded, it had possession of the deposit books. This fact alone is not dispositive, because Pannell Brothers did not maintain an office at the worksite, but worked out of the Arnold field office there. Nor are the deposit slips, reproduced in Exhibit 11 to the deposition of Fred A. Arnold, particularly helpful. Most were standard slips, bearing the printed name of Pannell Brothers Construction Co. One was a counter-deposit slip which bears the name of "Fred A. Arnold" as the depositor, rather than the usual Pannell Brothers designation. Of the seventeen Arnold checks deposited, only three appear to have been endorsed by a Pannell Brothers' representative. In addition, the depositions of John and Jesse Pannell both intimate that Arnold employees were the ones who carried the checks

---

an agent on behalf of such employee or employees, such lender, surety, or other person shall be liable in his own person and estate to the United States in a sum equal to the taxes (together with interest) required to be deducted and withheld from such wages by such employer."

"(b) Personal liability where funds are supplied.—If a lender, surety, or other person supplies funds to or for the account of an employer for the specific purpose of paying wages of the employees of such employer, with actual notice or knowledge (within the meaning of section 6323(i)(*l*)) that such employer does not intend to or will not be able to make timely payment or deposit of the amounts of tax required by this subtitle to be deducted and withheld by such employer from such wages, such lender, surety, or other person shall be liable in his own person and estate to the United States in a sum equal to the taxes (together with interest) which are not paid over to the United States by such employer with respect to such wages. However, the liability of such lender, surety, or other person shall be limited to an amount equal to 25 percent of the amount so supplied to or for the account of such employer for such purpose."

to the bank. Each check also carries a typewritten "for deposit only Account # 011183" (number of Del Monte account) notation on its back. Nowhere in the depositions or the record have the parties developed the information of who placed this endorsement on the checks. The typeface appears to be the same as that which appears on the face of the checks. A disputed issue of material fact thus exists with respect to whether Arnold retained and maintained the ability to control the funds.

Also disputed is whether Arnold had "the right and legal authority to exercise that control." At the time Arnold took over the work and the bank account it learned that under the bank signature card funds could be withdrawn under the signature of two Arnold employees without Pannell participation. It is important to a proper disposition of the case to know whether the agreement between Arnold and Pannell did require both an Arnold and a Pannell signature for withdrawals. Also, the exact purpose of the restricted account under the agreement of the parties is important. If it was contemplated that Arnold signatories would "rubber stamp" checks prepared by Pannell which on their face were for job connected expenses, that is one thing, but if it was contemplated that Arnold would have a more pervasive control of the disbursements, albeit by the reservation of a veto power, the situation would be different.

The action is remanded for trial.

C. LENDERS' LIABILITY

JERSEY SHORE STATE BANK v. UNITED STATES

Supreme Court of the United States, 1987.
479 U.S. 442, 107 S.Ct. 782, 93 L.Ed.2d 800.

CHIEF JUSTICE REHNQUIST delivered the opinion of the Court.

Subtitle C of the Internal Revenue Code of 1954, 26 U.S.C. § 3101 *et seq.* (Code), imposes a number of employment taxes, among which are the income tax withheld from an employee's wages and the Social Security tax. The Code divides the burden of the Social Security tax between the employer and the employee, but imposes the income tax on the employee alone. The employer has responsibility, however, for both paying its share of the Social Security tax and withholding from the employee's wages the income tax and the employee's share of the Social Security tax. If the employer fails to pay over the withheld Social Security and income taxes to the Government, the employer is liable for their payment. Within 60 days of making an assessment of unpaid taxes against an employer, the Government is required, under § 6303(a) of the Code, to provide the employer with notice of the assessment and demand for payment. In some instances, a person other than the employer, such as a lender, may directly or indirectly pay the employee's wages. Section 3505 of the Code provides that such a person may be personally liable if the employee's Social Security and income taxes are not withheld and paid to the Government. This case presents the question whether § 6303(a) requires the Government to provide notice and demand for payment to a lender before bringing a civil suit against the lender to collect sums for which it is liable under § 3505. We hold that it does not.

The United States brought the present action against Jersey Shore State Bank in the United States District Court for the Middle District of Pennsylvania, seeking a determination that Jersey Shore was personally liable under § 3505 for amounts reflecting unpaid taxes required to be withheld from the wages of the employees of Pennmount Industries. The Government claimed that Jersey Shore paid wages directly to Pennmount employees during the fourth quarter of 1977 through the first quarter of 1980, thereby making it liable under § 3505(a) for a sum equal to the full amount of the unpaid withholding taxes for that period.[1] In the alternative, the complaint alleged that, for the same period, Jersey Shore supplied funds to Pennmount for the wages of Pennmount employees "with actual notice and knowledge" that Pennmount "did not intend or would not be able to make timely payment or desposits [sic] of the * * * taxes required to be deducted and withheld" from the wages. App. to Pet. for Cert. 40a–41a. Based on this latter allegation, the Government asserted that Jersey Shore was liable under § 3505(b) for 25 percent of the amount of funds supplied to Pennmount.[2]

The District Court granted summary judgment in favor of Jersey Shore, holding that § 6303(a)[3] requires the Government to send notice of an assessment against an employer to a third-party lender liable under § 3505. 628 F.Supp. 15 (MD Pa.1985). Because the United States conceded that it had not provided Jersey Shore with notice of the assessments against Pennmount pursuant to § 6303(a), the court concluded that the suit against Jersey Shore was barred. The Court of

---

1. Section 3505(a) provides, in pertinent part:

"[I]f a lender, surety, or other person, who is not an employer * * * with respect to an employee, * * * pays wages directly to such an employee * * *, such lender, surety, or other person shall be liable in his own person and estate to the United States in a sum equal to the taxes (together with interest) required to be deducted and withheld * * *."

2. Section 3505(b) provides, in pertinent part:

"If a lender, surety, or other person supplies funds to * * * an employer for the specific purpose of paying wages of the employees of such employer, with actual notice or knowledge * * * that such employer does not intend to or will not be able to make timely payment or deposit of the amounts of tax required * * * to be deducted and withheld by such employer * * *, such lender, surety, or other person shall be liable in his own person and estate to the United States in a sum equal to the taxes (together with interest) which are not paid over to the United States by such employer. However, * * * the liability of such lender, surety, or other person shall be limited to an amount equal to 25 percent of the amount so supplied to * * * such employer for such purpose."

3. Section 6303(a) provides, in pertinent part:

"Where it is not otherwise provided by this title, the Secretary shall, as soon as practicable, and within 60 days, after the making of an assessment of a tax pursuant to section 6203, give notice to each person liable for the unpaid tax, stating the amount and demanding payment thereof."

Appeals for the Third Circuit reversed. 781 F.2d 974 (1986).[4] We granted certiorari to resolve the intercircuit conflict over the issue decided by the Court of Appeals.[5] 476 U.S. 1157 (1986). We now affirm.

Section 6303(a) requires notice of an assessment to "each person liable for the unpaid tax." According to Jersey Shore, this phrase clearly describes a third-party lender liable under § 3505 for unpaid withholding taxes assessed against an employer. The relationship between § 3505 and § 6303(a), however, is not as clear as Jersey Shore maintains. Section 3505 does not declare that a lender is "liable for the unpaid tax." Instead, the section imposes liability on the lender for all or part of "a sum equal to the taxes." § 3505(a), (b).

Other portions of the text of § 6303(a) further demonstrate a lack of connection between that section and § 3505. Section 6303(a) not only provides that the Government shall give notice of an assessment "to each person liable for the unpaid tax," but it also requires notice "stating the amount" assessed and "demanding payment thereof." § 6303(a). Notice complying with these latter two requirements may have little meaning for a third-party lender. In the first place, the assessment against the employer may include the employer's share of unpaid Social Security taxes for which the lender is not liable. See § 3505; H.R.Rep. No. 1884, 89th Cong., 2d Sess., 21 (1966) (a lender "is not liable for the employer's portion of payroll taxes"); S.Rep. No. 1708, 89th Cong., 2d Sess., 23 (1966) (same). Even where the assessment does not include such taxes, the lender's liability could equal the amount stated in the notice only if the lender provided payroll financing throughout the time period reflected in the assessment. Moreover, the chances are slim that the notice amount would be accurate for lenders liable only under § 3505(b), which limits a lender's exposure to 25 percent of the funds supplied to the employer. Accordingly, if sent to a lender, the notice required under § 6303(a) is likely to demand payment of an amount different from that for which the lender is liable. We find it improbable that Congress intended such a result. Reading the two sections together, we agree with the Court of Appeals that § 6303(a) is most logically read not to apply where the Government seeks to collect from a lender under § 3505.

---

4. One judge dissented from the majority opinion, arguing that the plain language of § 6303(a) required that the Government provide notice to the lender.

5. In addition to the Court of Appeals for the Third Circuit, four other Circuits have addressed whether the Government must provide § 6303(a) notice to third parties liable under § 3505. See *United States v. Messina Builders & Contractors Co.*, 801 F.2d 1029 (CA8 1986) (§ 6303(a) notice required), cert. pending, No. 86–1007; *United States v. Hunter Engineers & Constructors, Inc.*, 789 F.2d 1436 (CA9 1986) (§ 6303(a) notice not required), cert. pending, No. 86–209; *United States v. Merchants National Bank of Mobile*, 772 F.2d 1522 (CA11 1985) (§ 6303(a) notice not required), cert. pending, No. 85–1480; *United States v. Associates Commercial Corp.*, 721 F.2d 1094 (CA7 1983) (§ 6303(a) notice required); see also *United States v. Friedman*, 739 F.2d 252 (CA7 1984) (failure to provide notice within 60 days of assessment will not bar suit where Government has provided notice before assessment to person liable under § 3505).

In arguing to the contrary, Jersey Shore urges that it would be fundamentally unfair not to require the Government to provide lenders with § 6303(a) notice. Jersey Shore first maintains that, because employers and lenders are similarly situated under the Code, the procedural requirements applicable to employers also must be accorded to lenders. But even assuming that § 6303(a) notice would provide lenders with meaningful information, we are unpersuaded by this contention. Under the collection mechanisms established by the Code, employers and lenders are in very different positions. While employers are subject to the Government's summary collection procedures soon after unpaid employment taxes are assessed, see, *e.g.*, §§ 6321, 6322, 6331, 6335, the legislative history of § 3505 makes clear that the Government may forcibly collect against a lender only by filing a civil suit. See H.R.Rep. No. 1884, 89th Cong., 2d Sess., 66 (1966) (where a third-party does not voluntarily satisfy the liability imposed by § 3505, "the United States may collect such liability by appropriate civil proceeding"). An employer therefore has a far greater need for an assessment notice than third-party lenders, who are not subject to summary collection procedures.

We also reject Jersey Shore's related contention that a third-party lender is unfairly prejudiced by lack of an assessment notice because of the effect of an assessment on the statute of limitations for collection suits. Under the general rule set forth in § 6501(a), "the amount of any tax imposed * * * shall be assessed within 3 years after the return was filed * * * and no proceeding in court without assessment for the collection of such tax shall be begun after the expiration of such period." Nevertheless, where a proper assessment has been made, the unpaid tax generally "may be collected by levy or by a proceeding in court * * * begun * * * within 6 years after the assessment." § 6502(a)(1). Under Jersey Shore's reading of these provisions, the Government enjoys an additional 6–year limitations period for collecting against a lender if it makes an assessment against the employer within three years after the corresponding employment tax return is filed. Jersey Shore submits that Congress could not have intended the Government to benefit from this longer statute of limitations when it seeks to collect against a lender without also requiring the Government to provide the lender with notice of the assessment against the employer.

Assuming, without deciding, that Jersey Shore's reading of the statute of limitations provisions is correct, we are not convinced that they render our construction of § 6303(a) implausible. A lender is not liable under § 3505 unless it either "pays wages directly" to an employee or supplies funds for the wages with "actual notice or knowledge" that the employer is either unable to make timely payment of the required withholding taxes or has no intention of doing so. The lender is deemed to have such actual notice or knowledge from the time the lender, in the exercise of due diligence, would have been aware that the employer would not or could not make timely payment. § 6323(i)(1).

Accordingly, a prudent lender could be alerted to its liability under § 3505 at the time it engaged in what the Government describes as "net payroll financing," a practice whereby the lender provides funds for payment of employees' net wages, but not funds for payment of withholding taxes. Thus, even without § 6303(a) notice, such a lender could take steps to protect itself against the possibility of a future § 3505 suit. The Committee Reports concerning § 3505 demonstrate that Congress considered precautions third parties could take to protect themselves:

> "[S]ureties can protect themselves against any losses attributable to withholding taxes by including this risk of liability in establishing their premiums, and lenders by including the amounts in their loans and taking adequate security." S.Rep. No. 1708, 89th Cong., 2d Sess., 23 (1966); H.R.Rep. No. 1884, 89th Cong., 2d Sess., 22 (1966).[6]

As the Court of Appeals recognized, this passage suggests that "Congress envisioned a system in which third parties would take their potential liability under section 3505 into consideration at the time they entered into the transaction exposing them to liability under the statute." 781 F.2d, at 982.

For the foregoing reasons, we conclude that Congress did not intend to require the Government to provide a lender with notice under § 6303(a) before bringing a civil suit to collect under § 3505. The judgment of the Court of Appeals for the Third Circuit is therefore affirmed.

SECTION 5. TRANSFEREE AND FIDUCIARY LIABILITY

HUNT v. COMMISSIONER
Tax Court of the United States, 1988.
T.C.Memo. 1988–360.

NIMS, CHIEF JUDGE: Respondent assessed deficiencies in income taxes and additions to tax against James P. Powers III as follows:

Year	Deficiency	Addition to Tax Section 6654[1]
1976	$1,113	$ 42
1977	7,478	266
1978	3,964	128

---

6. Jersey Shore argues that this passage does not relate to § 3505, but instead refers only to an amendment to the Miller Act concerning the requirements for performance bonds on public works. It is true that the passage appears in each Committee Report under subheadings referencing the Miller Act. In both Reports, however, the passage immediately follows a discussion of lenders, sureties, and other persons liable under § 3505 and is prefaced with the phrase "[i]n the cases discussed above." Thus, the context of the passage makes clear that it relates to § 3505.

1. Except as otherwise indicated, all section references are to sections of the Internal Revenue Code as in effect at the time of the transfer involved herein. All Rule references are to the Tax Court Rules of Practice and Procedure.

The issue for decision is whether petitioner is liable as a transferee of assets of James Powers III for the deficiencies in tax and additions to tax as determined above.

FINDINGS OF FACT

Petitioner resided in Stone Mountain, Georgia, and James P. Powers III (hereinafter referred to as James) resided in Buford, Georgia, at the time the petition in this case was filed. Petitioner and James are sister and brother, and Ruby Powers is their mother.

At least as early as August, 1964, James was married to Marie Powers (hereinafter referred to as Marie). On August 28, 1964, James purchased a three-bedroom house and lot located at 1187 Robin Road, Conyers, Georgia (hereinafter sometimes referred to as the Robin Road property). The deed was recorded on September 4, 1964. On August 27, 1964, petitioner loaned James $1,200 from her insurance proceeds for the down payment on the purchase of the Robin Road property.

In 1968 James and Marie were divorced. Although James kept the house on Robin Road for himself after the divorce, he moved in with petitioner and lived with her in her rental home from 1968 until 1969.

In 1969 petitioner and James moved into the house on Robin Road. At that time petitioner paid $3,400 for furnishings for the house which she obtained from a settlement of a tort claim. Petitioner paid $105.99 a month for the mortgage on the Robin Road property from the time James moved in with her in 1968 until she moved out of the Robin Road house in 1971 to get married. When petitioner moved out, she left all of the furniture in the Robin Road house with James. During the time they lived together, petitioner supported James and also paid $60 a month for his child support payments.

James operated an ambulance service in Rockdale County, Georgia, from the years 1976 through 1982. The ambulance service operated by James received an annual subsidy from Rockdale County, Georgia, in the amount of $300,000 and derived additional income from independent billing. As of December 31, 1979, James owed approximately $101,000 in Federal employment taxes. The Federal employment taxes were James' personal obligation.

As of December 31, 1979, James owed the State of Georgia $19,654.74 in unemployment insurance taxes and $9,554.04 in employment taxes in connection with his ambulance service. The unemployment insurance taxes James owed to the State of Georgia were paid on July 30, 1984, and the employment taxes were paid on July 10, 1980.

During the period from 1971 through 1979, James continually lacked sufficient cash to pay his bills. Petitioner added money to James' checking account to help him pay his bills during this period.

In late 1979 petitioner asked James to return some of her money. He replied that he did not have cash because all his money was tied up in his ambulance service. In response to petitioner's request for money, James transferred the Robin Road property by warranty deed to her on December 24, 1979. The deed recites that the property was transferred for a consideration of "Ten Dollars and other valuable considerations," and reflects a payment of $29 in real estate transfer tax. Market data showed that the price for a home from January, 1977, to November, 1979, in the immediate neighborhood in which the Robin Road property was located ranged between $32,900 and $42,500.

When she received the Robin Road property, petitioner borrowed approximately $5,000 from her mother, Ruby Powers, to pay off the principal balance on an existing mortgage on the property. In September, 1982, petitioner sold the Robin Road property to her mother for cancellation of $28,000 in loans made to her by her mother, including the $5,000 loan to pay off the mortgage in December, 1979. In March, 1985, Ruby Powers sold the Robin Road property to Emma Janet Stanton for approximately $43,000.

James continued to operate his ambulance service until 1982. In 1982 James transferred three ambulances to his mother, Ruby Powers.

Federal income tax returns for the years 1976, 1977 and 1978 were filed for James on October 28, 1982. On November 26, 1982, Federal income taxes in the amounts of $1,113, $7,478 and $3,964 were assessed against James for the respective years 1976, 1977 and 1978. When James transferred the Robin Road property to petitioner in December, 1979, petitioner had no knowledge of the financial status of James' ambulance service, nor did she know that James had failed to file income tax returns or to pay taxes for the years in issue.

OPINION

Respondent determined that petitioner was liable as a transferee of assets for the deficiencies in James' income tax and additions to tax as determined above. Under section 6901(a),[2] the liability of a transferee may be assessed, paid and collected in the same manner and subject to the same provisions and limitations as in the case of the taxes with respect to which the liabilities were incurred. Section 6901(h) includes

---

2. Section 6901 provides in pertinent part:

(a) METHOD OF COLLECTION.—The amounts of the following liabilities shall, except as hereinafter in this section provided, be assessed, paid, and collected in the same manner and subject to the same provisions and limitations as in the case of the taxes with respect to which the liabilities were incurred:

(1) INCOME, ESTATE, AND GIFT TAXES.—

(A) TRANSFEREES.—The liability, at law or in equity, of a transferee of property—

(i) of a taxpayer in the case of a tax imposed by subtitle A (relating to income taxes),

* * *

in respect of the tax imposed by subtitle A or B.

(b) LIABILITY.—Any liability referred to in subsection (a) may be either as to the amount of tax shown on a return or as to any deficiency or underpayment of any tax.

* * *

(h) DEFINITION OF TRANSFEREE.—As used in this section, the term "transferee" includes donee, heir, legatee, devisee, and distributee * * *.

in the classification of a transferee, a "donee, heir, legatee, devisee and distributee." Courts have defined a transferee as one who takes or receives property of another without full, fair and adequate consideration to the prejudice of creditors.[3]

A transferee is liable retroactively for the transferor's taxes and additions to tax in the year of the transfer. Transferee liability subjects the property in the hands of the transferee to the debts of the transferor. The transferee's liability is limited to the fair market value of the property received from the transferor.

Respondent bears the burden of proving, by a preponderance of the evidence, that petitioner is liable as a transferee of property of James, but not that James was liable for the tax. Section 6902(a); Rule 142(d); *C.B.C. Super Markets, Inc. v. Commissioner* [Dec. 30,081], 54 T.C. 882, 898 (1970).

The provisions of section 6901 are merely procedural; the existence and extent of a transferee's liability for the unpaid tax liability of the transferor is determined under state law. *Commissioner v. Stern* [58-2 USTC ¶ 9594], 357 U.S. 39, 45 (1958). Accordingly, we must decide the issue in this case under the law of Georgia.

The applicable statute in this case is Ga.Code Ann. section 18-2-22 (hereinafter cited as section 18-2-22), which sets forth the rights of creditors to pursue property transfers as follows:

> The following acts by debtors shall be fraudulent in law against creditors and others and as to them shall be null and void:
>
> (1) Every assignment or transfer by a debtor, insolvent at the time, of real or personal property or choses in action of any description to any person, either in trust or for the benefit of or on behalf of creditors, where any trust or benefit is reserved to the assignor or any person for him;
>
> (2) Every conveyance of real or personal estate, by writing or otherwise, and every bond, suit, judgment and execution, or contract of any description had or made with intention to delay or defraud creditors, where such intention is known to the taking party; a bona fide transaction on a valuable consideration, where the taking party is without notice or ground for reasonable suspicion of said intent of the creditor, shall be valid; and
>
> (3) Every voluntary deed or conveyance, not for a valuable consideration, made by a debtor who is insolvent at the time of the conveyance.

---

3. We note that the Supreme Court has held that the existence and extent of transferee liability is determined under state law. *Commissioner v. Stern* [58-2 USTC ¶ 9594], 357 U.S. 39, 45 (1958). Bittker has observed that transferee liability can arise under a state creditor protection statute even though the transferee has paid full value for the transferred property, i.e., if the procedural requirements of the statute were not satisfied. Thus, the definition of transferee in the text, while usually accurate, may be too restrictive. See 4 Bittker, Federal Taxation of Income, Estates and Gifts, par. 111.5.7, pp. 111-119 (1981).

The parties agree that paragraphs (1) and (2) of section 18-2-22 do not apply in this case. To prove that the transfer of the Robin Road property was fraudulent under paragraph (3) of section 18-2-22, respondent must show the indebtedness, the insolvency of the debtor and that the deed was voluntary. It is not necessary for respondent to show fraudulent intent under paragraph (3) of section 18-2-22.

The evidence shows that James did not pay his taxes for the years 1976, 1977 and 1978 when they were due. James transferred the Robin Road property to petitioner on December 24, 1979, after he incurred the tax liabilities for the years in issue. Accordingly, respondent has established James' indebtedness.

However, respondent has failed to prove that the deed transferring the Robin Road property to petitioner was voluntary. Nor has respondent proved that James was insolvent at the time of the transfer.

Under Georgia law a voluntary deed is one without any valuable consideration. Stokes v. McRae, 247 Ga. 658, 278 S.E.2d 393, 395 (1981). A valuable consideration is founded on money, or something convertible into money or having a value in money. Stokes v. McRae, supra.

In Georgia, a conveyance of property between related parties in payment of a pre-existing indebtedness is based on valuable consideration and is not a voluntary conveyance. However, a transfer by a debtor to a related party of property of a value that is grossly in excess of the amount owed to the related party will be set aside as a fraud upon the other creditors of the debtor.

The evidence supports petitioner's testimony that she received the Robin Road property from James in cancellation of $29,000 in debts that James owed her. The face of the deed under which the Robin Road property was transferred to petitioner reflects the payment of a real estate transfer tax of $29, which is the tax due on a conveyance of property for a consideration of $29,000. See Ga.Code Ann. section 48-6-1 (imposing a tax at the rate of $1 for the first $1,000 or fractional part of $1,000 and 10 cents for each additional $100 or fractional part of $100 on a deed by which realty is transferred to a purchaser or purchasers when the consideration or value of the property conveyed exceeds $100.)

Petitioner testified that in 1964 she loaned James $1,200 for a down payment for the Robin Road property, that from 1968 through 1971 she made mortgage payments in the amount of $105.99 per month on the Robin property and paid $60 per month in child support to James' former wife, that she loaned James approximately $7,000 for his maintenance and support from 1968 through 1969 and approximately $5,000 for his maintenance and support from 1971 through 1979. In addition, petitioner loaned James $3,400 in 1969 to purchase furnishings for the house on Robin Road. Petitioner borrowed $5,000 from her mother in 1979 to pay off the mortgage on the Robin Road property. In

1979 petitioner and James added all the loans she advanced to him and determined that he owed her $29,000 which included interest.

Respondent argues that petitioner could not have earned enough from 1968 through 1979 to have advanced so much money to James. Of the amounts petitioner loaned to James, petitioner's uncontroverted testimony establishes that she obtained $1,200 for the down payment on the Robin Road property from insurance proceeds, $3,400 to purchase furnishings for the house from a settlement of a tort claim and $5,000 as a loan from her mother to pay off the mortgage on the Robin Road property.

In 1967 petitioner began working for Western Electric which was part of AT & T. Petitioner has been employed by AT & T since 1967 and continued to work there as of the time this case was tried. Petitioner could not remember how much she earned at AT & T from 1968 through 1979. However, she testified that when she began working at Western Electric on March 14, 1967, she earned $88.50 a week and that at the time of trial she was earning $36,000 per year at AT & T. Although we cannot find that petitioner loaned James $7,000 from the wages she earned at AT & T from 1968 to 1969, we believe that she loaned him at least $5,000 generated essentially from this source during the period from 1971 through 1979.

Having heard petitioner's testimony, we believe that the sums she testified to were basically rough estimates. Petitioner's uncontroverted testimony established that she and James determined that he owed her $29,000 in loans extended to him during the period from 1964 through 1979. The amount of real estate transfer tax recited on the deed corroborates that the debt was $29,000. The testimony of Ruby Powers supports a finding that petitioner loaned money to James and paid off the mortgage on the Robin Road property. Accordingly, we find that James transferred the Robin Road property to petitioner for consideration of $29,000.

In an attempt to establish that $29,000 was grossly inadequate consideration for the Robin Road property, respondent offered the testimony and a report of an expert witness who determined that the property was worth approximately $40,000 in 1979.

We find petitioner's testimony credible and therefore do not believe that the Robin Road property was worth $40,000 when James transferred it to petitioner in December, 1979. Accordingly, the consideration petitioner paid for the property was not grossly inadequate and the deed was not voluntary.

Even if the deed in this case were voluntary, respondent has failed to prove that James was insolvent at the time he transferred the Robin Road property to petitioner. A debtor is insolvent within the meaning of section 18-2-22(3) if after the voluntary deed or conveyance, the value of his remaining property is not sufficient to pay in full all of his debts. *Goodman v. Lewis,* 247 Ga. 605, 277 S.E.2d 908, 909-910 n. 1 (1981). The value of the debtor's remaining property must be determined as of the date the conveyance sought to be set aside was made. *Goodman v. Lewis, supra.*

Although petitioner testified that James "was forever running short of money," during the years 1971 through 1979, her statement only shows that James suffered from a lack of liquid funds. Respondent has established that at the time of the transfer to petitioner of the Robin Road property James owed the State of Georgia $9,554.04 in employment taxes and $19,654.74 in unemployment insurance taxes and that he owed the Federal Government approximately $12,991 in Federal income taxes and additions to tax and approximately $101,000 in Federal employment taxes, or a total of $143,199.78.

However, the evidence shows that James was operating an ambulance service at the time he transferred the Robin Road property to petitioner and that, in addition to a $300,000 annual subsidy from Rockdale County, James' ambulance service received income from independent billings. The ambulance service operated by James continued as an ongoing business after the December 24, 1979, transfer of the property to petitioner.

Respondent offered the testimony of Revenue Officer Kenneth Thompson to show that James was insolvent at the time of the transfer of the Robin Road property to petitioner. Thompson testified that in 1983 and 1984 he searched the public records for property belonging to James and found three ambulances registered in James' name. Later, Thompson learned that James had transferred the ambulances to his mother, Ruby Powers, in 1982. The ambulance service operated by James closed in 1982. We conclude that in December, 1979, James owned three ambulances for use in his business. Respondent has failed his burden of proving the value of the ambulances which James owned in 1979 and that James did not possess sufficient property to pay his state and Federal tax liabilities when he transferred the Robin Road property to petitioner. Accordingly, respondent has failed his burden of proving that petitioner was liable as a transferee under section 6901.[4]

To reflect the foregoing,

Decision will be entered for the petitioner.

GRIEB v. COMMISSIONER
Tax Court of the United States, 1961.
36 T.C. 156.

FISHER, JUDGE.

Respondent determined a fiduciary liability against petitioner under section 311(a)(2)[s] of the 1939 Code resulting from the distribution to him of the assets of Victory Builders, Inc., upon its liquidation, and the

---

4. Because we hold for petitioner on this ground, we need not address petitioner's other arguments.

s. The predecessor to § 6901(a)(1)(B) of the 1986 Code.

Sec. 5   TRANSFEREE & FIDUCIARY LIABILITY   817

subsequent payment of some of its debts without first satisfying a liability of that company for unpaid income taxes of $560.37 for the year 1949. Respondent has also determined against petitioner an addition to tax in the amount of $61.88 under section 293(a), I.R.C.1939, and $177.75 for interest which was also determined against the company.

Petitioner, having failed to contest the propriety of the determination of the tax liability against Victory, either in pleading or on brief, has apparently conceded the corporate liability. The significant question for our determination is whether petitioner is liable as a fiduciary of the company for its tax liability, any transferee liability being barred by limitations.

* * *

OPINION

Pursuant to the provisions of section 311(a)(2) of the Internal Revenue Code of 1939, which provides for enforcement of Government priority and fiduciary liability imposed under sections 3466 and 3467 of the Revised Statutes,[t] the respondent has determined that petitioner was a fiduciary of the company and, as such, is liable for the unpaid balance of the deficiency in income tax determined against the company for the year 1949, additions to tax, and interest.

Section 311 of the 1939 Code provides for two separate liabilities, one against a transferee, and another against a fiduciary. A transferee is defined in section 311(f) as an "heir, legatee, devisee, and distributee." The regulation under this section also includes the shareholder of a dissolved corporation, the assignee or donee of an insolvent person, and the successor of a corporation. A transferee may be liable to the full amount which he received from the debtor irrespective of any payments of debts he made on behalf of the debtor transferor. It is a defense, however, if any of the debts so paid, or his own debt, had priority over that of the Government.

Transferee liability covers the situation where one takes complete title to property from an insolvent debtor without full, fair, and adequate consideration to the prejudice of the rights of the creditors of the transferor. The transfer is void against existing creditors. The rights and priorities of the Government, however, as any other creditor, against the transferee is determined under State law. The rationale for this liability is that a transferee, not having priority over the Government, holds the property in trust for the Government. Commissioner v. Stern, 357 U.S. 39.

A fiduciary, on the other hand, is defined in the Code as "a guardian, trustee, executor, administrator, receiver, conservator, or any person acting in any fiduciary capacity for any person." Sec. 3797(a)(6), I.R.C. 1939.[u] Unlike a transferee, a fiduciary can be liable under the

---

t. 31 U.S.C.A. §§ 191 and 192 (West 1983).

u. See § 7701(a)(6) of the 1954 Code.

provisions of Revised Statutes, section 3467, supra, only to the extent of debts he pays on behalf of the debtor which do not have priority over the Government. Thus, when a fiduciary retains assets for himself absolutely or distributes them to persons not creditors of the transferor, although he may be subject to transferee liability, he is not subject to fiduciary liability within the meaning of section 3467.

The basis of fiduciary liability in the Code rests solely upon the provisions of sections 3466 and 3467 of the Revised Statutes. It is not a liability attaching to one receiving funds without fair consideration which is based upon any equitable principles of constructive trust, but rather a liability to enforce the prior claim of the Government to the fund he so received over general creditors of the debtor.

Fiduciary liability has been summarized in Bush v. United States, 14 F. 321, 323 (D.Ore.1882), as follows:

> The latter [sec. 3467] is only applicable to cases where the debtor's estate, either by his death, legal bankruptcy, or insolvency, has passed into the hands of an administrator or assignee for the benefit of his creditors, or where the debtor himself has voluntarily made such disposition of it. It does not apply, then, to a conveyance, assignment, or transfer, by whatever means accomplished, to a real or pretended creditor or creditors in payment or satisfaction of a debt or claim. There must be in some way an assignment of the debtor's property to a third person for distribution among his creditors before the statute can be invoked, and then it operates directly upon the assignee by requiring him to pay the claim of the United States first, and making him personally liable therefor if he does not. * * *

The payments made by the fiduciary to creditors not having priority over the Government are not avoided or set aside. Unlike the transferee's liability which is limited to the value of the property which he has unjustly received, the fiduciary may be liable to the full extent of debts he paid for the transferor, irrespective of any benefit, and notwithstanding that he has received none.

* * *

From the above analysis it is clear that transferee and fiduciary liability attaches to persons holding different interests in property for different purposes, and imposes different standards of liability. While we have seen that one person may hold the same property in both capacities at different times, and one person may hold different properties in both capacities at the same time, from the very nature of the two capacities, one person may not hold the same property in both capacities at the same time.

It has long been established that stockholders receiving the assets of a corporation upon liquidation are liable to the Government for unpaid taxes of the corporation under the broader transferee liability section of the Code, since it is presumed that they received them absolutely for their own benefit. This liability is imposed even in situations when a stockholder in fact subsequently distributes all of the proceeds to liquidate corporate debts. We find no authority for the view that a stockholder, receiving the assets of his liquidated corporation, is liable as a fiduciary rather than a transferee.

* * *

Petitioner, as sole stockholder, received all of the assets of the company at a time when it was liable for income taxes. These facts would indicate liability as a transferee rather than as a fiduciary. The respondent, conceding that the burden lies with him to go forward with the evidence in this respect, maintains that petitioner took the assets of the company under an express trust for the benefit of creditors. If such a trust was, in fact, created, petitioner would be a fiduciary under the Code.

* * *

Respondent has offered no evidence of an express trust created over all of the assets of the company. On the basis of what we have before us, we are unable to find as a fact that any such express trust was ever created between petitioner and the company.

We next must see whether petitioner is included under section 311(a)(2) in a capacity other than an express trustee. From the definition of "fiduciary" we must eliminate, as not applying to petitioner, a guardian, trustee, executor, administrator, receiver, or conservator. The only remaining position is "any person acting in any fiduciary capacity for any person."

The word "fiduciary" used in the Internal Revenue Code is not mentioned in the Revised Statutes. It is, however, descriptive of the types of persons intended to be covered under the statute. The statute provides that the person covered is executor, administrator, assignee, or other person who pays a debt due by the person "for whom or for which he acts."

The mere payment of a debt for another person will not automatically cause one to be included under this section. The crucial test, therefore, looking at both the Internal Revenue Code and the Revised Statutes, is whether the payment of the debts were made by one who is acting for the debtor in a fiduciary or representative capacity.

Petitioner can only be liable as a fiduciary if he, in fact, received the assets from the company as an officer or director for the purpose of liquidating the corporate debts rather than as a stockholder, and that he paid these debts in his capacity as a representative of the company.

* * *

A stockholder receiving all of the assets of a corporation is one of the clearest cases of one receiving assets in his own behalf, and he will be presumed to be acting on his own behalf as a transferee unless there is a clear showing to the contrary. In the absence of such proof, we cannot find that petitioner was acting as a fiduciary upon receipt and distribution of the corporate assets.

* * *

The sole basis for transferee liability is that the recipient of the funds is, under certain circumstances, deemed to hold them in constructive trust for certain creditors. If everyone who is held to hold funds in trust for another is deemed to be a fiduciary under the Code, as respondent contends, it would completely eliminate the basis for the distinction between the two liabilities. Respondent has failed to recognize that in order to be a fiduciary, petitioner must have, in fact, *acted* as such, rather than on his own behalf.

The existence of an *actual* fiduciary relationship is indispensable in placing one within the provisions of fiduciary liability. This fiduciary capacity must be established from the very nature of the transaction rather than through the equitable "trust fund" doctrine. This distinction was well illustrated in the case of *Jessie Smith, Executrix,* [24 B.T.A. 807 (1931)]. In this case a wife, upon the death of her husband, received the assets of her husband's estate as executrix, and she received complete title to real estate which was held jointly by her husband and herself. It was held that since the real estate was not a part of the estate she did not receive it as executrix and, therefore, she did not hold it in a fiduciary capacity. Section 3467 was held to relate only to the payment of debts out of the funds or assets *coming into her hands as executrix* and not to the real estate. It was added that if it were found that the real estate was burdened with the tax liability of the decedent, under the *trust fund* doctrine, she would be liable as a transferee of the real estate, albeit not as a fiduciary.

The mere finding of a "trust fund," then, is insufficient to deem the holder a fiduciary under the statute. If a trust is created out of the nature of the transfer, such as the transfer of assets for the benefit of another, then the holder is a fiduciary. On the other hand, if a trust arises because the person receiving the assets was not rightfully entitled to them, he is a transferee. In the latter situation, the debtor has divested himself completely of the assets to another and this transfer, if prejudicial to other creditors, can be avoided. In the former situation, on the other hand, the debtor by placing his assets with a representative has not divested himself completely of the assets to defraud creditors, inasmuch as his creditors have a beneficial interest in them pursuant to the very nature of the assignment. The transfer to a fiduciary cannot be avoided, and liability attaches to the fiduciary only if he fails to recognize legal priorities in discharging his obligation under the trust.

The distinction between the two different types of trusts was also recognized in Hollins v. Brierfield Coal & Iron Co., 150 U.S. 371, 378 (1893), where it was said (p. 383):

> Becoming insolvent, the equitable interest of the stockholders in the property, together with their conditional liability to the creditors, places the property in a condition of trust, first, for the creditors, and then for the stockholders. Whatever of trust there is arises from the

peculiar and diverse equitable rights of the stockholders as against the corporation in its property and their conditional liability to its creditors. It is rather a trust in the administration of the assets after possession by a court of equity than a trust attaching to the property, as such, for the direct benefit of either creditor or stockholder.

* * *

* * * The sole basis for transferee liability is that a trust is created in equity for the benefit of creditors. Wherein would lie the distinction if we were to hold that such equitable trustees were fiduciaries rather than transferees? This would completely nullify the difference between the two liabilities, and, indeed, eliminate transferee liability.

* * *

One of the main objectives of the provisions for transferee liability in the Code is to provide an effective remedy for such a situation as that presented in the instant case. To accept respondent's contention that such persons are fiduciaries rather than transferees would create the anomalous result of providing a statutory remedy only to the extent of the corporate debts they pay with the corporate assets but providing no statutory remedy for recovery of the assets they retain for themselves.

* * *

We have not closed our eyes to the obvious fact that the company was liquidated with the full knowledge on the part of petitioner of the pending tax liability, but this is clearly one of the situations sought to be remedied by proceeding on the basis of transferee liability.

The statute of limitations has obviously barred transferee liability which appears to be the reason why respondent relies solely on a claim of fiduciary liability because, if his contention were well grounded, he would get the benefit of a longer period of limitations. Since we have held that the provisions of section 311(a)(2) relating to fiduciary liability do not apply upon the record before us, we must hold for petitioner.

Decision will be entered for the petitioner.

SECTION 6. THE INNOCENT SPOUSE PROVISIONS

PURCELL v. COMMISSIONER
Tax Court of the United States, 1986.
86 T.C. 228 (affirmed 826 F.2d 470 (6th Cir.1987)).

SCOTT, JUDGE: Respondent determined deficiencies in petitioner's income tax for the calendar years 1977 and 1978 in the amounts of $82,955.89 and $49,749.21, respectively. The issue for decision is whether petitioner is relieved from liability under section 6013(e) with respect to the income tax resulting from (1) the inclusion in the income of petitioner and her then husband of (a) dividends resulting from amounts paid by a corporation of which they were stockholders for personal travel and entertainment expenses, and (b) a portion of the sales price of petitioner's stock in another corporation allocated to a covenant not to compete; and (2) the disallowance of claimed bad debt and worthless stock deductions with respect to a third corporation in which both petitioner and her then husband owned stock.

* * *

Section 6013(e), as amended by the Tax Reform Act of 1984, Pub.L. 98–369, sec. 424(a), 98 Stat. 801 (1984–3 C.B. 309),[2] provides that a spouse is relieved of liability under regulations prescribed by the Commissioner where a joint return has been made for a taxable year and on that return there is a substantial understatement of tax attributable to grossly erroneous items of one spouse, if the other spouse establishes that in signing the return she did not know, and had no reason to know, that there was such substantial understatement, and taking into account all the facts and circumstances, it is inequitable to hold the other spouse liable for the deficiency in tax for the taxable year attributable to such substantial understatement.

2. Sec. 6013(e), as amended by the Tax Reform Act of 1984, provides as follows:

(e) Spouse Relieved of Liability in Certain Cases.—

(1) In general.—Under regulations prescribed by the Secretary, if—

(A) a joint return has been made under this section for a taxable year,

(B) on such return there is a substantial understatement of tax attributable to grossly erroneous items of one spouse,

(C) the other spouse establishes that in signing the return he or she did not know, and had no reason to know, that there was such substantial understatement, and

(D) taking into account all the facts and circumstances, it is inequitable to hold the other spouse liable for the deficiency in tax for such taxable year attributable to such substantial understatement, then the other spouse shall be relieved of liability for tax (including interest, penalties, and other amounts) for such taxable year to the extent such liability is attributable to such substantial understatement.

(2) Grossly erroneous items.—For purposes of this subsection, the term "grossly erroneous items" means, with respect to any spouse—

(A) any item of gross income attributable to such spouse which is omitted from gross income, and

(B) any claim of a deduction, credit, or basis by such spouse in an amount for which there is no basis in fact or law.

(3) Substantial understatement.—For purposes of this subsection, the term "substantial understatement" means any understatement (as defined in section 6661(b)(2)(A)) which exceeds $500.

(4) Understatement must exceed specified percentage of spouse's income.—

(A) Adjusted gross income of $20,000 or less.—If the spouse's adjusted gross income for the preadjustment year is $20,000 or less, this subsection shall apply only if the liability described in paragraph (1) is greater than 10 percent of such adjusted gross income.

(B) Adjusted gross income of more than $20,000.—If the spouse's adjusted gross income for the preadjustment year is more than $20,000, subparagraph (A) shall be applied by substituting "25 percent" for "10 percent."

(C) Preadjustment year.—For purposes of this paragraph, the term "preadjustment year" means the most recent taxable year of the spouse ending before the date the deficiency notice is mailed.

Grossly erroneous items are defined to mean "any item of gross income attributable to such spouse which is omitted from gross income" and "any claim of a deduction, credit, or basis by such spouse in an amount for which there is no basis in fact or law." Section 6013(e)(2)(A) and (B). Substantial understatement "means any understatement * * * which exceeds $500." Section 6013(e)(3).

* * *

Respondent apparently admits that petitioner has met the requirements of section 6013(e), as amended, with respect to omission of income resulting from the determination of a dividend to petitioner's former husband because of personal use of an aircraft, although he argues generally that petitioner has failed to show that it would be inequitable to hold her liable for the total deficiency in this case. Also, respondent does not claim that the items on which petitioner claims relief as grossly erroneous items were not items of Mr. Purcell. Respondent contends that petitioner either knew, or had reason to know, that Purcell Enterprises, Inc., was paying personal expenses of petitioner and her then husband. Respondent contends that petitioner did in fact know that there had been a covenant not to compete signed with respect to the sale of the stock of Reese Tires, Inc., and that all petitioner has shown with respect to the income allocable to the covenant not to compete is that she did not know the tax effect of such a covenant being part of a contract for the sale of stock.

* * *

In our view, petitioner did not know or have reason to know that personal expenses and personal travel were being paid for by Purcell Enterprises, Inc. and therefore did not know, or have reason to know, of the omission of these items from the joint tax returns she filed with her then husband. The record shows that petitioner had an American Express Card of Purcell Enterprises, Inc., which she used to pay travel expenses for herself and her husband when her husband was on a business trip. The record also shows that she used this card for certain personal items. However, the testimony shows that her husband represented to her that amounts charged on the American Express Card of Purcell Enterprises, Inc., had to be justified as company expenses in order to be paid by the company and that any personal expenses which petitioner put on the card were being paid by him personally and not by the company. In fact, the company comptroller testified that charges on the company's American Express Card were required to be justified in order for him to authorize payment by the company and in connection with charges involving the Purcells, he looked to Mr. Purcell for justification. Under the circumstances, we conclude that petitioner did not in fact know that the personal charges she put on the Purcell Enterprises, Inc., American Express Card were being paid for by the company rather than by her then husband and did not know that he was charging personal items to the company credit card.

In our view, petitioner must have known in connection with the sale of the Reese Tires, Inc., stock that the contract of sale contained a covenant not to compete. Although she did not assist in negotiating the sale, she was the owner of the stock and a signatory to the contract. One of the persons to whom the noncompete provision applied was petitioner and another was her then husband, Mr. Purcell. Not only did petitioner sign the contract, she initialed a change in the years for which the covenant not to compete was effective. Petitioner never specifically testified that she did not read the agreement with respect to the sale of stock that she signed, although she testified that her husband did all the negotiating. In our view, the evidence here does not support lack of knowledge on the part of petitioner with respect to the terms of the contract for the sale of the stock of Reese Tires, Inc. Certainly petitioner did not know the legal effect of the provision with respect to a covenant not to compete. However, the cases are clear that the spouse claiming to be relieved from liability for omission from income of an item must be unaware of the circumstances which give rise to that omission and not merely to the tax consequences of the facts. As we pointed out in the Smith case, it is immaterial that both spouses were unaware of the tax liability created by the transactions of which they were aware. * * *

The record is clear that petitioner did know of loans made by her then husband to International Demolition. From the evidence we conclude that she did not examine the returns sufficiently to know that these amounts had been deducted in 1977 and 1978 as worthless debts on the joint returns she filed with her then husband. We also conclude that she did not examine the returns sufficiently to know that there had been a deduction for worthless stock of International Demolition taken as a deduction on the returns. However, petitioner has made no showing as to the circumstances which caused these items to be deducted. * * * In our view, petitioner's conceding that respondent's adjustments with respect to the worthless stock and bad debt deductions are correct is not sufficient to establish that the claimed deductions were in an amount for which there was no basis in fact or law. If the statute had intended that a mere concession that respondent was not in error in disallowing a claimed deduction was sufficient to cause the item to be grossly erroneous as having no basis in fact or law, it would have so provided.

Prior to the amendment of section 6013(e) by Pub.L. 98–369 in 1984, no relief was granted where the deficiency was because of the disallowance of claimed deductions. In explaining the reason for the change in the law with respect to disallowed deductions made by Pub.L. 98–369, in 1984, the House Committee Report states that—

> The Committee believes that the present law rules relieving innocent spouses from liability for tax on a joint return are not sufficiently broad to encompass many cases where the innocent spouse deserves relief. Relief may be desirable, for example, where one spouse claims phony business deductions in order to avoid paying tax and the other

spouse has no reason to know that the deductions are phony and may be unaware that there are untaxed profits from the business which the other spouse has squandered. [Supplemental Report of Comm. on Ways and Means, H.Rept. 98–432 (Pt. 2), on H.R. 4170 (Tax Reform Act of 1984), at 1502 (1984).]

* * *

It is clear from the statute itself, and made even clearer by the committee reports, that whereas any omission of income resulting in an understatement of tax in excess of $500 is to be considered a grossly erroneous item, only deductions without a basis in fact or law are to be considered grossly erroneous. Therefore, in order to be relieved from tax resulting from a disallowed deduction, it is incumbent on a taxpayer to prove that the claimed deduction not only is not properly allowable but that it has no basis in fact or law. * * *

Here, petitioner has made no showing that the bad debt deductions which were disallowed by respondent and the worthless stock deduction that was disallowed had no basis in fact or law. All that has been shown is that she did not contest the adjustments as made by respondent. In fact, the evidence that is in the record with respect to these items indicates that they were not "grossly erroneous" from the standpoint of being "phony" deductions. The record shows that loans had been made by petitioner's husband to International Demolition and that that company was in bad financial condition in 1977 and 1978. The accountant who prepared the joint returns of petitioner and her then husband testified that he thought he had sufficient information to justify the items shown on the returns, and the comptroller of Purcell Enterprises, Inc., who also handled the books of International Demolition, testified that he had furnished information to the accountant.

Under the facts of this case, there has been no showing that the claimed deductions had no basis in fact or law. They were not "phony" deductions as referred to in the committee report. We therefore conclude that petitioner is not an innocent spouse with respect to the claimed bad debts and worthless stock deductions.

Since respondent has conceded that petitioner is an "innocent spouse" with respect to the constructive dividends received by her husband from the private use of the airplane owned by Purcell Enterprises, Inc., and we have concluded that petitioner did not know, or have reason to know, of the constructive dividends from the payments by that corporation of personal bills and travel, it is necessary for us to determine whether it would be inequitable to hold petitioner liable for the deficiency in tax attributable to these understatements of income.

Whereas the law prior to the 1984 amendment specifically referred to whether the spouse claiming relief from tax significantly benefitted from the omissions from income, the present law does not specifically contain this provision. However, even though the present statute does not specifically refer to the other spouse receiving substantial benefits from the omissions or wrongfully claimed deductions, in our view it would not be inequitable to hold the other spouse liable for the deficiency if such substantial benefits were received. Therefore, we deem it necessary to determine whether petitioner received substantial benefits from the omission of the constructive dividends from the income reported on the returns.

The record shows no benefit to petitioner from her husband's use of the company plane and only very minor benefits received by petitioner from the payment by Purcell Enterprises, Inc., for a few meals and some lodging she charged to the American Express Card issued in her name. Certainly these benefits were not substantial. * * *

Since we have held that petitioner is not entitled to relief under section 6013(e) for the omitted income from the covenant not to compete or from the disallowance of the deductions for bad debts and worthless stock, we need only consider whether it would be inequitable to hold petitioner liable for the tax on the omitted income from constructive dividends. The regulation in effect with respect to the prior law provided, in section 1.6013–5(b), Income Tax Regs., that whether it is inequitable to hold a person liable for the deficiency in tax is to be determined on the basis of all the facts and circumstances. This section of the regulations states that in making the determination a factor to be considered is whether the person seeking relief significantly benefitted, directly or indirectly, "from the items omitted from gross income." This regulation goes on to say that normal support is not to be considered a significant benefit. It further refers to a person seeking relief receiving from his spouse "an inheritance of property or life insurance proceeds which are traceable to items omitted from gross income by his spouse."

Here, the record shows that the property received by petitioner in the divorce proceeding had been acquired in years prior to the years here in issue. Petitioner had paid the insurance premiums prior to her divorce from Mr. Purcell. The omitted income was from personal items paid by Purcell Enterprises, Inc. Clearly, the use of the airplane by Mr. Purcell for personal purposes in no way benefitted petitioner and the Government apparently does not contend to the contrary. Although petitioner may have received some small benefit from the payment of travel and entertainment expenses by the corporation, from her testimony it is reasonably clear that whatever benefit she received was not significant. * * *

Based on the record as a whole, we conclude that petitioner did not significantly benefit from the constructive dividends received by Mr. Purcell from Purcell Enterprises, Inc., because of the payment by that corporation of personal expenses for meals, travel and entertainment for Mr. Purcell and, to some extent, for petitioner. We therefore conclude that with respect to the entire constructive dividends from Purcell Enterprises, Inc., in each of the years here in issue, petitioner is entitled to relief under section 6013(e).

Decision will be entered under Rule 155.

PRICE v. COMMISSIONER OF INTERNAL REVENUE
United States Court of Appeals, Ninth Circuit, 1989.
887 F.2d 959.

O'SCANNLAIN, CIRCUIT JUDGE:

This appeal turns on interpretation of the defense to joint federal income tax liability known as the "innocent spouse" provision of the Internal Revenue Code. The wife-taxpayer asserts that the tax court erred by applying an incorrect standard in determining that she was ineligible for relief under this provision. She claims that she was "innocent" within the meaning of the provision at the time she signed the return, and thus should be shielded from liability as to the tax deficiency arising from a deduction as to which her husband-taxpayer had superior knowledge. We agree and reverse the judgment of the tax court.[1]

I

Patricia Price ("Patricia") married Charles Price ("Charles") in 1969. During the marriage, which ended in divorce in 1986, Charles handled all of the family's investment decisions and maintained a separate checking account for investments. Patricia and Charles also held a joint account that consisted primarily of Patricia's earnings and was used to pay for household expenses as well as the mortgage on the Prices' home. Patricia had to ask Charles for money when she needed to cover expenses exceeding her earnings and the amount in their joint checking account.

In 1976, Patricia, who had studied as a sociology major at a junior college for two years, became part of the "office staff" at Commuter Transportation Services, a car pooling agency. Within five years, she had become a branch manager with the agency. Around the same time, Charles, who had been a stockbroker when the couple wed, was working as an investment broker, and he began to sell shares in a venture known as Cal–Colombian Mines, Ltd. ("CCM"), a Colombian gold mining operation. Patricia was aware of Charles's involvement in the venture. More specifically, Charles informed her that he had acquired several shares of CCM, that he had flown to Colombia to check on the mine's development, that the mining operation was a viable investment, and that two persons Patricia knew, a pharmacy owner and a local developer, had invested in CCM. Patricia also saw photos that Charles stated were taken on the mining operation site which showed heavy equipment.

Other than the above details, Patricia knew virtually nothing else about CCM. For example, she had not seen a CCM offering circular or any other CCM document, and did not know the purchase price of a

---

[1] Because the record before us is sufficiently complete to allow us to resolve the issue as to whether Patricia qualifies as an "innocent spouse," we conclude that a remand to allow the tax court to find further facts is unnecessary.

CCM share or of the existence or the value of any mineral interest. Nevertheless, she stated that she trusted Charles in financial matters, including the CCM investment, because of what she perceived to be his "excellent" business reputation and experience.

Patricia and Charles filed a joint federal income tax return for 1981 which was prepared by a local CPA firm familiar to Patricia. Patricia's only participation in the execution of the return was to provide Charles with her W-2 form, which indicated that Patricia earned approximately $23,000 during 1981. The return reported this income and also recorded Charles's net income as approximately $80,000. On one of the schedules attached to the return, the Prices claimed a $90,000 deduction for the exploration and development expenses allegedly incurred while mining ore in the CCM mine. The Prices offset this deduction against their income from other sources to lessen their total federal income tax liability for 1981 to $391 in self-employment tax.

On the filing deadline day, Charles presented the completed 1981 joint return to Patricia for her signature. Patricia reviewed the return "cursorily," and noticed the $90,000 deduction taken for the mining expenses, which she testified she "thought * * * was a bit much." When she asked Charles about the deduction, she testified that he assured her that "if there had been any problems [the CPA] would * * * never have drawn the papers for us and put his name on them." After Charles's assurances, Patricia signed the return.

Several years later, the Commissioner issued a joint notice of deficiency to Patricia and Charles, asserting an original deficiency of $40,120 on their 1981 return and assessing an additional five percent fee under Internal Revenue Code § 6653(a)(1) for the Prices' negligent disregard of tax rules and regulations.[2] The Commissioner bases the deficiency claim on his assertion that the $90,000 deduction for the CCM exploration and development expenses is invalid. In support of this assertion, he alleges that the Prices failed to establish that they had paid or incurred any bona fide mine development expenses, that the alleged CCM mining activity had any economic substance, or that the mining was pursued for profit.

In June 1985, Charles filed a joint petition in the tax court seeking redeterminations of the deficiency and the additions to tax. *See* 26 U.S.C. § 6213 (1982 & Supp. V 1987). Although Charles included Patricia's name on the petition, she did not learn of the notice of deficiency and the petition until sometime later. She eventually obtained her own counsel and filed an amended petition in the tax court asserting that she is not liable for the tax deficiency because she is an "innocent spouse" under the Internal Revenue Code. *See* 26 U.S.C. § 6013(e) (Supp. V 1987).

---

2. The Commissioner eventually conceded that Patricia is not liable for any addition to tax under section 6653(a) for negligent disregard of tax rules and regulations; she in turn conceded that the deficiency is correct.

The "innocent spouse provision" exempts a spouse from joint federal income tax liability [3] if she can establish for the taxable year in question that: (1) she and her spouse filed a joint return, 26 U.S.C. § 6013(e)(1)(A); (2) the return contained a "substantial understatement of tax" attributable to errors the other spouse committed, 26 U.S.C. § 6013(e)(1)(B); (3) in signing the return she did not know or have reason to know of the substantial understatement, 26 U.S.C. § 6013(e)(1)(C); and (4) it would be inequitable to hold her liable for the deficiency in question, 26 U.S.C. § 6013(e)(1)(D).[4] The person seeking relief from liability carries the burden of proving each element of section 6013(e)(1). *Shea v. Commissioner,* 780 F.2d 561, 565 (6th Cir. 1986); *Sonnenborn v. Commissioner,* 57 T.C. 373, 381 (1971).

The tax court denied Patricia innocent spouse protection based on its specific ruling that she failed to carry her burden as to the third element of section 6013(e)(1),[5] which requires a spouse to establish that

---

3. Ordinarily, when a husband and wife file a joint federal income tax return, they are jointly and severally liable for any tax due. 26 U.S.C. § 6013(d)(3) (1982). Congress first implemented an exception to joint and several liability for certain spouses who file joint returns in the form of an innocent spouse provision in 1971. *See* Act of Jan. 12, 1971, § 1, Pub.L. No. 91–679, 84 Stat. 2063. The original provision provided relief only to those innocent spouses who were otherwise subject to liability because of an understatement due to an omission of taxable income. In 1984, Congress expanded the scope of the provision, bringing within its ambit deficiencies arising from invalid deductions or credits. *See* Tax Reform Act of 1984, Pub.L. No. 98–369, § 424, 98 Stat. 494, 801–803 (1984).

4. Section 6013(e), as amended in 1984, reads as follows:

(e) Spouse relieved of liability in certain cases.—

(1) In general.—Under regulations prescribed by the Secretary, if—

(A) a joint return has been made under this section for a taxable year,

(B) on such return there is a substantial understatement of tax attributable to grossly erroneous items of one spouse,

(C) the other spouse establishes that in signing the return he or she did not know, and had no reason to know, that there was such substantial understatement, and

(D) taking into account all the facts and circumstances, it is inequitable to hold the other spouse liable for the deficiency in tax for such taxable year attributable to such substantial understatement,

then the other spouse shall be relieved of liability for tax (including interest, penalties, and other amounts) for such taxable year to the extent such liability is attributable to such substantial understatement.

(2) Grossly erroneous items.—For purposes of this subsection, the term "grossly erroneous items" means, with respect to any spouse—

(A) any item of gross income attributable to such spouse which is omitted from gross income, and

(B) any claim of a deduction, credit, or basis by such spouse in an amount for which there is no basis in fact or law.

Tax Reform Act of 1984, Pub.L. No. 98–369, § 424(a), 98 Stat. 494, 801–02 (1984) (current version at 26 U.S.C. § 6013(e) (Supp. V 1987)).

This amended version of the innocent spouse provision, although not enacted until 1984, applies to Patricia nonetheless because section 424(c) of the Act provides for retroactive operation of the amendments to all open tax years to which the Internal Revenue Code of 1954 applies. H.R.Rep. No. 432, 98th Cong., 2d Sess., pt. 2, at 1502, *reprinted in* 1984 U.S.Code Cong. & Admin.News 697, 1144.

5. The Commissioner conceded by way of pre-trial stipulations that Patricia had satisfied the first and part of the second of these four criteria; *i.e.,* the parties stipulated to the facts that the Prices filed a joint return for 1981, and that the return reflected a substantial understatement of tax that was solely attributable to "a de-

"in signing the return he or she did not know, and had no reason to know, that there was such substantial understatement * * *." 26 U.S.C. § 6013(e)(1)(C).[6] The court read this subsection as requiring a taxpayer seeking innocent spouse protection to establish that she did not know of the transaction underlying the deduction. Because it found that Patricia knew about the CCM investment, the court rejected her defense and ruled that both she and Charles were liable for the deficiency arising from the CCM deduction.

In accordance with this ruling, the court entered a final judgment upholding both the Commissioner's assessment of income tax deficiency and his determination that the Prices should be subjected to an additional interest penalty on the deficiency under 26 U.S.C. § 6621(c) (Supp. V 1987).[7] Patricia appeals,[8] alleging that the tax court erroneously interpreted section 6013(e)(1)(C) in ruling that she does not qualify as an innocent spouse under the Code.

II

In construing a statute, we look first to its plain meaning. *United States v. 594,464 Pounds of Salmon*, 871 F.2d 824, 825–26 (9th Cir.1989). Section 6013(e)(1)(C) states that to qualify for the shield of innocent spouse protection, a spouse must establish that "in signing the return he or she did not know, and had no reason to know, that there was such substantial understatement * * *." 26 U.S.C. § 6013(e)(1)(C). The plain meaning of the section is clear. It requires a spouse seeking relief to establish that she did not know and did not have reason to know that the deduction would give rise to a substantial understatement.[9] *See Stevens v. Commissioner*, 872 F.2d 1499, 1505 (11th Cir.1989).

duction which has no basis in fact or law, as defined by I.R.C. § 6013(e)(2)(B)." The court then found that the invalid deduction was "attributable to Charles Price," thereby completing satisfaction of the second "innocent spouse" criterion, a finding not challenged on appeal. Thus, the third criterion is the focus of our inquiry.

Because the tax court found that Patricia failed to satisfy section 6013(e)(1)(C), it declined to resolve whether Patricia had satisfied the section's fourth criterion relating to the inequity of holding her liable under the totality of circumstances. 26 U.S.C. § 6013(e)(1)(D).

6. "Substantial understatement" is defined within subsection (e) as "any understatement (as defined in section 6661(b)(2)(A)) which exceeds $500." 26 U.S.C. § 6013(e)(3). "Understatement" in turn is defined as "(i) the amount of the tax required to be shown on the return for the taxable year, over (ii) the amount of the tax imposed which is shown on the return" reduced by any rebate not applicable here.

The invalid mining expense deduction easily fits within this definition. First, the invalid $90,000 deduction led to the Prices recording an amount on their 1981 joint return that was below what they legally owed. Second, the amount by which the deduction caused the Prices' assessment of tax liability to be deficient by $40,120, which far exceeds the $500 threshold of section 6013(e)(3).

7. Section 6621(c) of the Code provides that an additional interest penalty is to be assessed if a taxpayer's underpayment is attributable to a tax-motivated transaction. Under the penalty, the interest rate is 120 percent of the normal underpayment rate.

8. The court granted the Commissioner's motion to dismiss Charles's case for want of proper prosecution after he failed to appear at trial. Charles did not appeal from the tax court's decision dismissing his petition.

9. This differs from the interpretation the tax court gave section 6013(e)(1)(C), but as even it conceded, its interpretation does not comport with a fair reading of the

If the statutory language is unambiguous, its plain meaning controls unless Congress has "clearly expressed" a contrary legislative intention. *594,464 Pounds of Salmon,* 871 F.2d at 826. Here, far from conflicting with congressional intent, the plain meaning squares with one of the few glimpses the sparse legislative history of the 1984 Amendments provides. In discussing the 1984 Amendments, the House Ways and Means Committee stated that it:

> believes that the present law rules relieving innocent spouses from liability for tax on a joint return are not sufficiently broad to encompass many cases where the innocent spouse deserves relief. Relief may be desirable, for example, where one spouse claims a phony business

plain meaning of the statute. *See Sanders v. United States,* 509 F.2d 162, 169 n. 14 (5th Cir.1975) (noting that a virtually identical legal standard "is difficult to square with a literal reading of the statutory language" of section 6013(e)). The tax court, borrowing language from cases involving deficiencies caused by omissions of income, read section 6013(e)(1)(C) to require a spouse to establish that she did not know of *the transaction* underlying the deduction. *See, e.g., Quinn v. Commissioner,* 524 F.2d 617, 626 (7th Cir.1975); *Mayworm v. Commissioner,* 54 T.C.M. (CCH) 941, 944 (1987); *McCoy v. Commissioner,* 57 T.C. 732 (1972).

We decline to follow the tax court's literal superimposition of the legal standard developed in omission cases onto deduction cases in part because to do so would for the most part wipe out innocent spouse protection in the latter category. Such a standard may be workable in omission cases simply because the understatement is caused by includable income being left off a return. Therefore, it is considerably easier for a spouse to show that she was unaware of the transaction giving rise to the omission, and thus to qualify for relief. *See* Borison, Innocent Spouse Relief: A Call for Legislative & Judicial Liberalization, 40 Tax Law. 819, 836-37 (1988). But because deductions are necessarily recorded, any spouse who at least reads the joint return will be put on notice that *some* transaction allegedly has occurred to give rise to the deduction. As a result, if knowledge of the transaction, operating of itself, were to bar relief, a spouse would be extremely hard-pressed ever to be able to satisfy the lack of actual and constructive knowledge element of section 6013(e)(1) in a deduction case.

Thus, adoption of such an interpretation would do violence to the intent Congress clearly expressed when it expanded coverage of the provision to include relief for spouses from deficiencies caused by deductions for which there is no basis in fact or law. Tax Reform Act of 1984, Pub.L. No. 98–369, § 424(a), 98 Stat. 494, 801–02 (1984); H.R.Rep. No. 98–432, Pt. 2, 98th Cong., 2d Sess. 1502, *reprinted in* 1984 U.S.Code Cong. & Admin.News 697, 1143. It would also hinder Congress's broader purpose in enacting section 6013(e)—that of seeking to remedy an injustice—by giving the section an unduly narrow and restrictive reading. *See Allen v. Commissioner,* 514 F.2d 908, 915 (5th Cir.1975); *Estate of Killian,* 53 T.C.M. (CCH) 1438, 1441 (1987).

While we do not embrace the tax court's construction of section 6013(e)(1)(C), we do not mean to say that a spouse's knowledge of the transaction underlying the deduction is irrelevant. Obviously, the more a spouse knows about a transaction, *ceteris paribus,* the more likely it is that she will know or have reason to know that the deduction arising from that transaction may not be valid. We merely conclude that standing by itself, such knowledge does not preclude relief.

In addition, when we look beyond the *language* courts have used in omission cases to the *function* such a standard has served, we see that it represents merely a different way of approaching what is the same inquiry as the one we announce today. *See Purcell v. Commissioner,* 826 F.2d 470, 474 (6th Cir.1987). That is, in income omission cases, knowledge of the transaction is virtually equivalent to knowledge of the understatement because if a spouse knows of a transaction which generated income that the return does not report, then it is extremely likely that she will know that the return does not report all income (unless she merely lacks knowledge of tax consequences). Thus, the omission cases that have examined whether a spouse had knowledge of the transaction in a sense really have been looking to discern whether she knew or had reason to know of the substantial understatement.

deduction in order to avoid paying tax and the other spouse has no reason to know *that* the deductions are phony and may be unaware that there are untaxed profits from the business which the other spouse has squandered.

Supplemental Report of Comm. on Ways & Means, H.R.Rep. 98–432 (Pt. 2), on Tax Reform Act of 1984, H.R. 4170, at 1502 (1984), 1984 U.S.Code Cong. & Admin.News 1143 (emphasis supplied).

Initially, we note that the tax court correctly found that Patricia did not know the legal consequences of the deduction, which, while not sufficient, is obviously necessary to entitle her to relief. Moreover, the record contains no evidence to suggest that Patricia *knew* upon signing the return that it contained a substantial understatement for any reason. Thus, our focus must turn toward whether Patricia *had reason to know* of the substantial understatement. *Lessinger v. Commissioner,* 85 T.C. 824, 838 (1985), *rev'd on other grounds,* 872 F.2d 519 (2d Cir.1989).

Of itself, ignorance of the attendant legal or tax consequences of an item which gives rise to a deficiency is no defense for one seeking to obtain innocent spouse relief. *McCoy v. Commissioner,* 57 T.C. 732, 734 (1972); *Mayworm v. Commissioner,* 54 T.C.M. (CCH) 941, 944 (1987); *Price v. Commissioner,* 53 T.C.M. (CCH) 1414 (1987); *see also Sanders v. United States,* 509 F.2d 162, 169 (5th Cir.1975). In *Price* for example, the tax court denied "innocent spouse" protection to a joint return taxpayer who admitted she knew about unreported funds her husband had embezzled despite the fact she did not know that embezzled funds constitute taxable income. *Price,* 53 T.C.M. at 1416. Thus, if a spouse knows virtually all of the facts pertaining to the transaction which underlies the substantial understatement, her defense in essence is premised solely on ignorance of law. *Id.* In such a scenario, regardless of whether the spouse possesses knowledge of the tax consequences of the item at issue, she is considered as a matter of law to have reason to know of the substantial understatement and thereby is effectively precluded from establishing to the contrary. *See Stevens,* 872 F.2d at 1505 & n. 8; *Quinn v. Commissioner,* 62 T.C. 223, 231 (1974), *aff'd,* 524 F.2d 617 (7th Cir.1975); *Mayworm,* 54 T.C.M. at 944 (although spouse did not know legal consequences of transaction, because she "had actual knowledge of the basic structure of the transaction *and* of her ex-husband's receipt of the additional funds she is *not eligible* for relief under section 6013(e)") (emphasis supplied).

Here, while the tax court properly concluded that Patricia knew certain facts about the CCM investment, it cannot be said that Patricia was so intimately involved with the investment such that she knew virtually all of the facts of the transaction underlying the deduction, leaving her no option but to rely solely upon ignorance of law as a defense and therefore leaving us no option but to conclude that she had reason to know of the understatement. *See* Borison, Innocent Spouse Relief: A Call for Legislative and Judicial Liberalization, 40 Tax Law.

819, 834 (1987). Because Patricia's ignorance extends beyond the legal consequences of the deduction, we proceed to determine on the facts before us whether Patricia had reason to know that the return contained a substantial understatement.

A spouse has "reason to know" of the substantial understatement if a reasonably prudent taxpayer in her position at the time she signed the return could be expected to know that the return contained the substantial understatement. *Stevens*, 872 F.2d at 1505 (citing *Sanders*, 509 F.2d at 167); *Hinds v. Commissioner*, T.C.M. 1988–426; *Estate of Killian*, 53 T.C.M. 1438, 1441 (1987). Factors to consider in analyzing whether the alleged innocent spouse had "reason to know" of the substantial understatement include: (1) the spouse's level of education; (2) the spouse's involvement in the family's business and financial affairs; (3) the presence of expenditures that appear lavish or unusual when compared to the family's past levels of income, standard of living, and spending patterns; and (4) the culpable spouse's evasiveness and deceit concerning the couple's finances. *Stevens*, 872 F.2d at 1505; Borison, 40 Tax Law. at 831–32.[10]

In applying these factors, we note that Patricia had limited involvement in the financial affairs of her marriage with Charles in general and none whatsoever in the CCM investment in particular. *See Mysse v. Commissioner*, 57 T.C. 680 (1972). Indeed, Charles held a separate checking account for his investments, while Patricia's participation in the couple's money matters apparently was limited to paying household expenses and the mortgage on their home. *See Hinds*, T.C.M. 1988–426.[11] Further, the Commissioner points to no unusually lavish expenditures the couple made during this time period when compared to their past levels of income, standard of living, and spending patterns. Finally, the record indicates Charles took advantage of Patricia's lack of understanding of their financial affairs and misled her. Given these facts, we conclude that a reasonably prudent person in Patricia's position at the time she signed the return could not be expected to know that the return contained a substantial understatement. Thus, Patricia has satisfied her burden to establish that she did not have reason to know that the CCM deduction would give rise to a substantial understatement.

---

10. The fact that these comport with factors courts have used in omission cases further bolsters our assertion that the legal standard we announce today is in essence no different functionally than the one used in omission cases. *See, e.g., Sanders*, 509 F.2d at 167–68.

11. The similarity between the facts here and the facts of *Hinds* is striking. In *Hinds*, in finding a taxpayer eligible for innocent spouse relief, the tax court found that:

[the culpable spouse] exerted near total control over the couple's financial affairs. The extent of petitioner's participation in their financial affairs was to accept money from him to use to pay household expenses and to purchase the family's food and clothing. She relied on her husband to ensure that their Federal income tax returns were properly completed. She undoubtedly presumed that the returns were proper as they had been prepared by certified public accountants.

Hinds v. Commissioner, T.C.M. 1988–426.

Even if a spouse is not aware of sufficient facts to give her *reason to know* of the substantial understatement, she nevertheless may know enough facts to put her *on notice* that such an understatement exists. *Cf. Stevens*, 872 F.2d at 1505. Such notice is provided if the spouse knows sufficient facts such that a reasonably prudent taxpayer in her position would be led to question the legitimacy of the deduction. *See Mysse*, 57 T.C. at 698–99; *see also Stevens*, 872 F.2d at 1505. In such a scenario, a duty of inquiry arises, which, if not satisfied by the spouse, may result in constructive knowledge of the understatement being imputed to her. *Levin v. Commissioner*, 53 T.C.M. (CCH) 6, 8–9 (1987) (spouse cannot obtain benefits of innocent spouse protection in deduction case "by simply turning a blind eye to—by preferring not to know of—facts fully disclosed on a return, of such a large nature as would reasonably put such spouse on notice that further inquiry would need to be made").

We agree with the Commissioner that the size of the deduction ($90,000) viz-a-viz the total income reported on the return (just more than $100,000), when considered in light of the fact that Patricia knew of the existence of the CCM investment and its rather unusual nature (Colombian gold mining), was enough to put Patricia on notice. We disagree with the Commissioner, however, in his insistence that Patricia did not satisfy the resultant duty to inquire.

Patricia did not ignore the deduction, but instead questioned Charles about it. We therefore distinguish this case from one in which the tax court denied relief to a spouse seeking relief who simply ignored a large deduction and who refused to make inquiries. *Levin*, 53 T.C.M. at 8. In addition, Patricia agreed to sign the return only after Charles had assured her that a putatively reputable CPA had prepared it. *See Killian*, 53 T.C.M. at 1441 (spouse "took reasonable steps to determine the accuracy of the return" in agreeing to sign return only after having questioned husband about sham loss claimed on return and having received assurances that loss was due to investment that had been recommended by CPA who prepared return). Thus, especially given her relative lack of experience in and understanding of financial affairs, *see Mysse*, 57 T.C. 680; *Hinds*, T.C.M. 1988–426, we conclude that Patricia satisfied her duty of inquiry.

The tax court stated that it was not necessary for it to make an official finding as to whether Patricia satisfied the fourth criterion of section 6013(e)(1) concerning the inequity of holding her liable for the deficiency under the totality of circumstances. Nevertheless, it "conclude(d) that * * * it would be inequitable to hold her liable".[12] The record supports the tax court's conclusion. Accordingly, we hold that Patricia has also satisfied the fourth element of section 6013(e)(1), thereby entitling her to relief as an innocent spouse.

---

12. The tax court specifically ruled "[s]pecifically, the Court concludes that Petitioner did not benefit from the item in question, and that taking all of the other circumstances into account it would be inequitable to hold her liable." Tax Court Bench Opinion, Docket No. 15475–85, December 16, 1987 at RT 69.

III

For the reasons set forth herein, the judgment of the tax court is REVERSED.

Notes and Questions

1. The Tax Court has rejected the Ninth Circuit's approach in *Price* in a case that was appealable to the Eleventh Circuit, the court that decided *Stevens v. Commissioner,* 872 F.2d 1499 (11th Cir.1989), which the *Price* court discusses. Bokum v. Commissioner, 94 T.C. 126 (1990) (reviewed).

2. If the understatement on the joint return results from claiming improper deductions, § 6013(e)(4) requires that the spouse's adjusted gross income for the preadjustment year (i.e. the most recent taxable year ending before the deficiency notice was mailed) must exceed 10% of adjusted gross income where his adjusted gross income is $20,000 or less, or 25% if it is more than $20,000. In calculating the understatement, are interest and penalties to be included? At what time is the understatement to be determined—when the notice of deficiency is mailed, when any amounts due are actually paid, some other time? See Farmer v. United States, 794 F.2d 1163 (6th Cir.1986), holding that penalties asserted in the deficiency notice plus interest accrued to the date of the deficiency notice should be included in calculating the "understatement."

3. Should the innocent spouse defense be available when neither spouse actually signed the purportedly joint returns prepared by a return preparer? Is some other defense available? See Shea v. Commissioner, 780 F.2d 561 (6th Cir.1986), holding the return "invalid" as to the purported innocent spouse.

SECTION 7. RESTRAINING TAX COLLECTION

The Anti-Injunction Act, § 7421 of the Internal Revenue Code, provides that " * * * no suit for the purpose of restraining the assessment or collection of any tax shall be maintained in any court by any person * * *." There are, however, limited exceptions to the general prohibition against injunctions. The Code itself expressly permits injunctions to restrain assessment and/or collection in the following circumstances:

1. When deficiency notice requirements have not been met or a prohibited deficiency notice is issued.[v]

2. When a responsible person assessment has been made and an appropriate bond is furnished to secure collection pending litigation of the liability.[w]

3. When certain penalties have been assessed, 15% of the amount of the assessment is paid and the payor pursues litigation to determine liability.[x]

v. I.R.C. §§ 6212(a) and (c); 6213(a).   x. I.R.C. §§ 6694(c); 6703(c)(1).
w. I.R.C. § 6672(b).

4. When there has been a wrongful levy.ʸ

5. When there has been an improper termination or jeopardy assessment.ᶻ

There is also a judicially recognized exception to the general prohibition against injunctions to restrain assessment or collection. In this section the scope of the non-statutory exception to the Anti-Injunction is examined, as well as the statutory exceptions for failure to comply with deficiency notice requirements and for wrongful levy.

Note

Congress has provided that most types of tax penalties shall be assessed and collected "in the same manner as taxes." I.R.C. §§ 6659(a) and 6671. Thus, the Anti–Injunction Act applies to bar taxpayer suits to restrain the assessment or collection of such penalties. See, e.g., Crouch v. Commissioner, 447 F.Supp. 385 (N.D.Cal.1978) (tax return preparer penalty imposed under § 6695(c) for failure to include preparer's social security number on return held "tax" within meaning of Anti–Injunction Act). Sections 6659(a) and 6671 render inapplicable an old line of cases holding that the Anti–Injunction Act does not bar suits to restrain the assessment or collection of tax penalties which are truly penal in nature. See, e.g., Pool v. Walsh, 282 Fed. 620 (9th Cir.1922); Tovar v. Jarecki, 173 F.2d 449 (7th Cir.1949).

ENOCHS v. WILLIAMS PACKING & NAVIGATION CO.
Supreme Court of the United States, 1962.
370 U.S. 1, 82 S.Ct. 1125, 8 L.Ed.2d 292.

Mr. Chief Justice Warren delivered the opinion of the Court.

Fearing that the District Director of Internal Revenue for Mississippi would attempt to collect allegedly past due social security and unemployment taxes for the years 1953, 1954 and 1955, respondent, in late 1957, brought suit in the District Court, maintaining that it was not liable for the exactions and seeking an injunction prohibiting their collection. The District Director, petitioner herein, made no objection to the issuance of a preliminary restraining order but resisted a permanent injunction, asserting that the provisions of § 7421(a) of the Internal Revenue Code of 1954 barred any such injunctive proceeding. * * * The exception for Tax Court proceedings created by §§ 6212(a) and (c) and 6213(a), 26 U.S.C.A. §§ 6212(a, c), 6213(a) was not applicable because that body is without jurisdiction over taxes of the sort here in issue. Nevertheless, on July 14, 1959, the court, relying upon Miller v. Standard Nut Margarine Co., 284 U.S. 498, 52 S.Ct. 260, 76 L.Ed. 422, permanently enjoined collection of the taxes on the ground that they were not, in fact, payable and because collection would destroy respondent's business. On June 14, 1961, the Court of Appeals for the Fifth Circuit affirmed, one judge dissenting. We granted certiorari to deter-

---

y. I.R.C. §§ 7426(a) and (b)(1).   z. I.R.C. § 7429(b).

mine whether the case came within the scope of this Court's holding in *Nut Margarine* which indicated that § 7421(a) was not, in the "special and extraordinary facts and circumstances" of that case, intended to apply.

Respondent corporation (hereinafter referred to as Williams) is engaged in the business of providing trawlers to fishermen who take shrimp, oysters and fish off the Louisiana and Mississippi coasts. It is the Government's position that these fishermen are the corporation's employees * * *. If, under the involved circumstances of this case, the fishermen were employees, respondent Williams is admittedly liable for social security and unemployment taxes for the years in question.

* * *

The object of § 7421(a) is to withdraw jurisdiction from the state and federal courts to entertain suits seeking injunctions prohibiting the collection of federal taxes. In Miller v. Standard Nut Margarine Co., supra, this Court was confronted with the question whether a manufacturer of "Southern Nut Product" could enjoin the collection of federal oleomargarine taxes on its goods. Prior to the assessment in issue three lower federal court cases had held that similar products were nontaxable and, by letter, the collector had informed the manufacturer that "Southern Nut Product" was not subject to the tax. This Court found that "[a] valid oleomargarine tax could by no legal possibility have been assessed against [the manufacturer], and therefore the reasons underlying [§ 7421(a)] apply, if at all, with little force." Noting that collection of the tax "would destroy its business, ruin it financially and inflict loss for which it would have no remedy at law," the Court held that an injunction could properly issue. The courts below seem to have found that *Nut Margarine* decides that § 7421(a) does not bar suit for an injunction against the collection of taxes not due if the legal remedy is inadequate. We cannot agree.

The enactment of the comparable Tax Injunction Act of 1937, 50 Stat. 738, now, as amended, 28 U.S.C.A. § 1341, forbidding the federal courts to entertain suits to enjoin collection of state taxes "where a plain, speedy, and efficient remedy may be had at law or in equity in the courts of such State," throws light on the proper construction to be given § 7421(a). It indicates that if Congress had desired to make the availability of the injunctive remedy against the collection of federal taxes not lawfully due depend upon the adequacy of the legal remedy, it would have said so explicitly. Its failure to do so shows that such a suit may not be entertained merely because collection would cause an irreparable injury, such as the ruination of the taxpayer's enterprise. This is not to say, of course, that inadequacy of the legal remedy need not be established if § 7421(a) is inapplicable; indeed, the contrary rule is well established. However, since we conclude that § 7421 bars any suit for an injunction in this case, we need not determine whether the taxpayer would suffer irreparable injury if collection were effected.

The manifest purpose of § 7421(a) is to permit the United States to assess and collect taxes alleged to be due without judicial intervention, and to require that the legal right to the disputed sums be determined in a suit for refund. In this manner the United States is assured of prompt collection of its lawful revenue. Nevertheless, if it is clear that under no circumstances could the Government ultimately prevail, the central purpose of the Act is inapplicable and, under the *Nut Margarine* case, the attempted collection may be enjoined if equity jurisdiction otherwise exists. In such a situation the exaction is merely in "the guise of a tax."

We believe that the question of whether the Government has a chance of ultimately prevailing is to be determined on the basis of the information available to it at the time of suit. Only if it is then apparent that, under the most liberal view of the law and the facts, the United States cannot establish its claim, may the suit for an injunction be maintained. Otherwise, the District Court is without jurisdiction, and the complaint must be dismissed. To require more than good faith on the part of the Government would unduly interfere with a collateral objective of the Act—protection of the collector from litigation pending a suit for refund. And to permit even the maintenance of a suit in which an injunction could issue only after the taxpayer's nonliability had been conclusively established might "in every practical sense operate to suspend collection of the * * * taxes until the litigation is ended." Great Lakes Dredge & Dock Co. v. Huffman, 319 U.S. 293, 299, 63 S.Ct. 1070, 1073, 87 L.Ed. 1407. Thus, in general, the Act prohibits suits for injunctions barring the collection of federal taxes when the collecting officers have made the assessment and claim that it is valid.

The record before us clearly reveals that the Government's claim of liability was not without foundation. Therefore, we reverse the judgment of the Court of Appeals and remand the case to the District Court with directions to dismiss the complaint.

Reversed.

Note

In Bob Jones Univ. v. Simon, 416 U.S. 725, 94 S.Ct. 2038, 40 L.Ed.2d 496 (1974), the taxpayer sought an order enjoining the IRS from revoking a ruling letter which stated that the university qualified for tax-exempt status. The IRS had proposed taking this action because of the school's racially discriminatory admissions policy. The Supreme Court, applying the *Williams Packing* standard, which it described as the "capstone of judicial construction of the Act", refused to grant the injunction. The Court held that the test for issuance of an injunction is two-pronged—in addition to proving that equity jurisdiction exists, (i.e., the taxpayer, threatened with irreparable injury, has no adequate remedy at law), the taxpayer must also establish that the Service's action is clearly without legal basis. See also Alexander v. "Americans United" Inc., 416 U.S. 752, 758–759, 94 S.Ct. 2053, 2057–2058, 40 L.Ed.2d 518 (1974) ("the constitutional nature of a taxpayer's claim, as distinct from its probability of success," is of no consequence in overcoming the barrier of § 7421(a)). Note that much of the hardship inherent in situations involving the revocation of an organization's tax-exempt status has been eliminated by the enactment of I.R.C. § 7428(a), which authorizes the Tax Court, the Claims Court and the United States District Court for the District of Columbia to issue declaratory judgments relating to an organization's qualification for tax-exempt treatment.

COMMISSIONER v. SHAPIRO
Supreme Court of the United States, 1976.
424 U.S. 614, 96 S.Ct. 1062, 47 L.Ed.2d 278.

MR. JUSTICE WHITE delivered the opinion of the Court.

* * *

Normally, the Internal Revenue Service may not "assess" a tax or collect it, by levying on or otherwise seizing a taxpayer's assets, until the taxpayer has had an opportunity to exhaust his administrative remedies, which include an opportunity to litigate his tax liability fully in the Tax Court, 26 U.S.C. §§ 6212, 6213; and if the Internal Revenue Service does attempt to collect the tax by levy or otherwise, before such exhaustion of remedies in violation of § 6213, the collection is not protected by the Anti–Injunction Act and may be restrained by a United States district court at the instance of the taxpayer. §§ 6213(a), 7421(a). The rule is otherwise when the Commissioner proceeds under § 6861 and finds that collection of a tax due and owing from a taxpayer will be "jeopardized by delay" in collection. * * * When the Commissioner follows this procedure, the Anti–Injunction Act applies in full force and "no suit for the purpose of restraining the assessment or collection of any tax shall be maintained in any court by any person." § 7421(a).

In this case, the Commissioner found, on December 6, 1973, that the imminent departure of respondent Samuel Shapiro (hereinafter Shapiro or respondent) for Israel and the probable departure with him of the assets in his New York bank accounts and safe-deposit boxes jeopardized the collection of income taxes claimed to be due and owing by him for the tax years 1970 and 1971. Accordingly, he assessed income taxes against respondent in the amount of $92,726.41 for the tax years 1970 and 1971. On the same day, he filed liens against respondent and served notices of levy upon various banks in New York State in which respondent maintained accounts or had safe-deposit boxes. These notices of levy effectively froze the money in the accounts—totaling about $35,000—and the contents of the safe-deposit boxes.

At that time respondent Shapiro was under a final order of extradition to Israel, for trial on criminal fraud charges * * *.

Upon learning of the notices of levy, respondent obtained the consent of the State of Israel to postpone his extradition date until December 16, 1973; and then on December 13, 1973, he initiated the instant lawsuit. Claiming that he owed no taxes; that he could not litigate the issue with the Internal Revenue Service while in jail in Israel; that he would be in jail in Israel, unless he could use the frozen $35,000 as bail money; and that the Internal Revenue Service had deliberately and in bad faith waited until December 6, 1973, before filing its notices of levy precisely in order to place him in this predicament, respondent requested in his complaint an order enjoining his extradition until he had an opportunity to litigate the question whether he owed the Internal Revenue Service any taxes or, in the alternative, an order directing the Internal Revenue Service to lift the notices of levy.

[The District Court dismissed the complaint on the ground of the Anti–Injunction Act. The Court of Appeals] concluded that the District Court should not have dismissed the complaint without further inquiry into the factual foundation for the jeopardy assessment and that further proceedings were necessary before finally determining whether upon viewing the law and the facts most favorably to the Government there was "no factual foundation" for the Government's claim that Shapiro was a tax-delinquent narcotics dealer during 1971 and thus no basis for the assessment. Accordingly, the court remanded in order to "allow the District Court * * * to develop a record" and to determine in light of it whether the asserted deficiency was "so arbitrary and excessive" as to be an exaction in the guise of a tax.

* * *

In Enochs v. Williams Packing Co., the Court held that an injunction may be obtained against the collection of any tax if (1) it is "clear that under no circumstances could the government ultimately prevail" and (2) "equity jurisdiction" otherwise exists, i.e., the taxpayer shows that he would otherwise suffer irreparable injury, 370 U.S. at 7, 82 S.Ct. at 1129, 8 L.Ed.2d at 296. The Court also said that "the question of whether the Government has a chance of ultimately prevailing is to be determined on the basis of the information available to it at the time of the suit," ibid. The Government's claim that the Court of Appeals placed on it the burden of justifying its assessment and thereby erroneously applied the *Williams Packing* rule is wrong. *Williams Packing* did not hold that the taxpayer's burden of persuading the District Court that the Government will under no circumstances prevail must be accomplished without any disclosure of information by the Government. It says instead that the question will be resolved on the basis of the information available to the Government at the time of the suit. Since it is absolutely impossible to determine what information is available to the Government at the time of the suit, unless the Government discloses such information in the District Court pursuant to appropriate procedures, it is obvious that the Court in *Williams Packing* intended some disclosure by the Government. Although the

Government casts its argument in terms of "burden of proof," the Court of Appeals did not place any technical burden of producing evidence on the Government and it would appear to matter little whether the Government discloses such information because it is said to have the burden of producing evidence on the question or whether it discloses such evidence by responding to a discovery motion made or interrogatories served by the taxpayer—in which case the burden of producing evidence may be said to have rested with the taxpayer. Thus the Court of Appeals cannot be said to have erred in declining to specify the precise manner in which the relevant facts would be revealed on remand. In either event, under *Williams Packing* the relevant facts are those in the Government's possession and they must somehow be obtainable from the Government.[10]

* * *

Our conclusion that the Court of Appeals correctly reversed the judgment of the District Court and remanded for further proceedings is fortified by the fact that construing the Act to permit the Government to seize and hold property on the mere good-faith allegation of an unpaid tax would raise serious constitutional problems in cases, such as this one, where it is asserted that seizure of assets pursuant to a jeopardy assessment is causing irreparable injury. * * * Here the Government seized respondent's property and contends that it has absolutely no obligation to prove that the seizure has any basis in fact no matter how severe or irreparable the injury to the taxpayer and no matter how inadequate his eventual remedy in the Tax Court.

* * *

* * * At the time the District Court dismissed the complaint, the Government had done little more than assert that respondent owed taxes in an amount greater than the value of the property levied—it had alleged that respondent had made an unexplained bank deposit of $18,000 in 1970 and, in a wholly conclusory fashion, that he had received $137,280 in income from selling hashish. Before the taxpayer had an opportunity to inquire into the factual basis for this conclusory allegation, it was not possible to tell whether the Government had any chance of ultimately prevailing. Accordingly, the Court of Appeals properly concluded that the Anti-Injunction Act did not require dismissal of the taxpayer's complaint.

* * *

The Government may defeat a claim by the taxpayer that its assessment has no basis in fact—and therefore render applicable the Anti-Injunction Act—without resort to oral testimony and cross-exami-

---

10. We believe that it is consistent with *Williams Packing* to place the burden of producing evidence with the taxpayer, and to require, if the Government insists, that facts in its sole possession be obtained through discovery. However, nothing we say here should prevent the Government from voluntarily and immediately disclosing the basis for its assessment, which, if sufficient, would terminate discovery proceedings and justify judgment for the Government.

nation. Affidavits are sufficient so long as they disclose basic facts from which it appears that the Government may prevail. The Constitution does not invariably require more and we would not hold that it does where collection of the revenues is involved.

* * *

The judgment of the Court of Appeals is Affirmed.

Notes and Questions

1. The Anti-Injunction Act was amended by the Tax Reform Act of 1976 to provide an explicit exception to the general prohibition against injunctions in cases falling under § 7429(b) of the Code, which provides taxpayers with the right to a prompt judicial determination of (1) whether an assessment under §§ 6851, 6861 or 6862 is reasonable under the circumstances, and (2) whether the amount so assessed is appropriate under the circumstances. Section 7429(a) also requires the Service, within 5 days after such an assessment is made, to "provide the taxpayer with a written statement of the information upon which the Secretary relies in making such assessment." Do the provisions of § 7429 address adequately the constitutional problems in the jeopardy and termination assessment area which the Supreme Court perceived in the *Shapiro* case? What additional reforms do you think may be necessary?

2. If a taxpayer timely pays 15% of a penalty under § 6700 or § 6701, can he enjoin the IRS from collecting the balance pending a determination of his refund claim? See § 6703.

FLYNN v. UNITED STATES
United States Court of Appeals, Third Circuit, 1986.
786 F.2d 586.

OPINION OF THE COURT

STAPLETON, CIRCUIT JUDGE:

M. Rutledge Flynn ("Taxpayer") brought this suit in the district court to enjoin collection by the Internal Revenue Service ("The Service") of federal income taxes, penalties, and interest purportedly owed for the taxable years 1974, 1975 and 1976. Jurisdiction was predicated on 28 U.S.C. § 1340. The district court dismissed the complaint and Flynn appealed. * * *

I

Taxpayer and his wife filed joint federal income tax returns for 1974, 1975 and 1976. Thereafter they were divorced. In August, 1981, the Service proposed certain adjustments to Taxpayer's tax liabilities for those years. He objected to the proposal and began negotiating with the Service in an attempt to reach a settlement. During the negotiations Taxpayer and his former spouse executed extensions of the limitations period for assessment of the taxes. The last of these extensions apparently expired on June 30, 1982.

The Taxpayer and a Service representative tentatively arrived at a satisfactory settlement, memorialized on Service Form 870–AD, which the Taxpayer signed. * * *

* * *

Taxpayer's former spouse refused to sign the form. Nonetheless, Taxpayer mailed the form to the Service in June, 1983, allegedly to show his good faith. The Service signed it on September 8, 1983, but it is not clear when the Taxpayer was informed of this acceptance. Subsequently, the Service, without first issuing a formal notice of deficiency to Taxpayer, began to collect taxes, penalties and interest for years 1974, 1975 and 1976.

II

Before the district court, Taxpayer argued that the assessments should be restrained because he was not first issued a notice of deficiency as required by 26 U.S.C. Section 6213(a). Taxpayer further argued, citing *Accardi v. Shaughnessy,* 347 U.S. 260, 74 S.Ct. 499, 98 L.Ed. 681 (1954), that he was entitled to an injunction because the Service conduct violated its own procedural rules. Finally, Taxpayer argued that injunctive relief was justified under *Enochs v. Williams Packing and Navigation Company,* 370 U.S. 1, 82 S.Ct. 1125, 8 L.Ed.2d 292 (1962), because the statute of limitations absolutely bars the assessments.

The district court ruled only on the *Williams Packing* claim, which it decided in favor of the Service. * * *

III

A. THE ANTI-INJUNCTION ACT

The government argues that the Anti–Injunction Act, Section 7421(a), which proscribes most suits instituted to enjoin the collection of taxes, bars the instant suit. * * *

* * *

The prohibition against injunctions is not, however, absolute. In certain circumstances, the Internal Revenue Code provides for the issuance of an injunction, notwithstanding Section 7421(a). Taxpayer claims that one such statutory exception, Section 6213(a), applies here.[2]

2. Section 6213(a) states:
Within 90 days * * * after the notice of deficiency authorized in section 6212 is mailed * * * the taxpayer may file a petition with the Tax Court for a redetermination of the deficiency. Except as otherwise provided * * * no assessment of a deficiency in respect of any tax imposed by subtitle A or B, chapter 41, 42, 43, 44 or 45 and no levy or proceeding in court for its collection shall be made, begun, or prosecuted until such notice has been mailed to the taxpayer, nor until the expiration of such 90-day or 150-day period, as the case may be, nor, if a petition has been filed with the Tax Court, until the decision of the Tax Court has become final. Notwithstanding the provisions of section 7421(a), the making of such assessment or the beginning of such proceeding or levy during the time such prohibition is in force may be enjoined by a proceeding in the proper court.

Under Section 6213(a), if the Service discovers a tax deficiency, it must give notice to the taxpayer before it can initiate collection proceedings. The taxpayer may, within ninety days after mailing of the notice, petition the Tax Court for redetermination of the deficiency. During the ninety day period, and if the taxpayer seeks redetermination, until the final decision of the Tax Court, no assessment, levy or court proceeding for the collection of the deficiency may be made or brought. A suit to enjoin the assessment of a deficiency is permissible if the taxpayer has not been mailed a notice of deficiency and afforded the opportunity for review in the Tax Court. * * *

A separate, judicially-created exception to Section 7421(a) was formulated by the Supreme Court in *Williams Packing:*

* * *

Taxpayers must meet two independent requirements before *Williams Packing* will support a claim for injunctive relief. First, when the facts and law are examined in the light most favorable to the government, it must appear that the government cannot prevail on the merits. Second, because *Williams Packing* did not alter the long-established prerequisites for equitable relief, there must also be an independent basis for the court to exercise its equitable jurisdiction.

The *Williams Packing* exception to the Anti–Injunction Act is distinct from and in addition to those exceptions contained in the text of Section 7421(a) itself. *Williams Packing* recognized that where there is no basis for the government position, the government exaction is merely in the "guise of a tax." The exceptions listed in Section 7421(a), e.g., Section 6213(a), address the obverse situation where the government attempts to collect what admittedly is a tax. Thus, a taxpayer proceeding under Section 6213(a) need not satisfy *Williams Packing* in addition to the requirements imposed by Section 6213(a).

Thus, contrary to the government's position in this litigation, the *Williams Packing* prerequisite—that under the most liberal view of the law and the facts, it is apparent that the Service cannot justify its position—only applies to the judicially-crafted exception and *need not* be met when a taxpayer is proceeding under one of the statutory exceptions to Section 7421(a). Accordingly, a court, when assessing a Section 6213(a) claim, may not view the facts and law in the light most favorable to the Service, as required when reviewing a *Williams Packing* claim. Rather, the court is required to make findings of facts and law.

Finally, Taxpayer argues that there is a third relevant exception to the Anti–Injunction Act. He cites *Accardi v. Shaughnessy,* 347 U.S. 260, 74 S.Ct. 499, 98 L.Ed. 681 (1954), for the proposition that an administrative agency's failure to adhere to its own internal operating procedures may justify injunctive relief to prevent injury to one who has relied on those procedures. While the teaching of the *Accardi* case provides a basis for injunctive relief in some circumstances, it does not address the issue of whether the Anti–Injunction Act may be circumvented by pointing to procedural errors in the Service's collection efforts. We find it unnecessary to resolve that issue in this case. * * *

B. SECTION 6213(A)

The Service did not contend in the court below that it had issued a notice of deficiency. Its defense to Taxpayer's Section 6213(a) claim was that the executed Form 870–AD constituted a waiver of the Taxpayer's right to such a notice. In response, Taxpayer sought to introduce parol evidence to prove that the form was *nullius juris*. Indeed, he claims that the Service knew that the form was not meant to have any legal effect. However, the district court, relying on the parol evidence rule, refused to admit evidence relevant to these factual issues. For this reason, the trial judge failed to engage in the fact-finding necessary to resolve the issue of whether Taxpayer, by signing and submitting Form 870–AD, waived notice of deficiency as permitted by Section 6213(d).[4]

Form 870–AD, which is an offer to settle, is properly treated according to principles of contract law. Although parol evidence is usually inadmissible to alter or modify an existing contract, it is admissible to demonstrate the complete absence of agreement. This is precisely Taxpayer's claim; he asserts that the excluded evidence conclusively demonstrates that the Form 870–AD never had any legal effect. Therefore, the district court should have admitted the Taxpayer's evidence and resolved the disputed issues of fact relating to the waiver issue.

Contrary to Taxpayer's suggestion, however, waiver is not the only issue that the trial court will have to address on remand in connection with Taxpayer's Section 6213(a) claim. Even if the Taxpayer can show that his signing Form 870–AD did not waive his rights to notice and an opportunity to file a petition with the Tax Court, as provided for by Section 6213(a), he nonetheless cannot obtain injunctive relief unless he makes the kind of showing traditionally required as a prerequisite to equitable relief. Congress, in enacting Section 6213(a), did not repudiate the principle that injunctive relief is an extraordinary remedy which is unavailable absent a showing of irreparable injury and no adequate remedy at law. The Supreme Court made this clear in the *Williams Packing* case. After noting that the Anti–Injunction Act, where applicable, bars injunctive relief even in the face of a showing of irreparable injury, the Court added:

> "This is not to say, of course, that inadequacy of the legal remedy need not be established if Section 7421(a) is inapplicable; indeed, the contrary rule is well established." 370 U.S. at 6, 82 S.Ct. at 1129. (citations omitted).

---

4. Section 6213(d) reads: "The taxpayer shall * * * have the right * * * to waive the restrictions provided in subsection (a) * * *." The Service does not argue that the Taxpayer received his deficiency notice. Thus, it is necessary to determine whether Taxpayer waived notice by signing Form 870–AD.

By its own terms, Section 7421(a) does not apply to a suit for injunctive relief based on Section 6213(a). Therefore, the Taxpayer must establish the "inadequacy of the legal remedy" to prevent an irreparable injury. *See Bob Jones University,* 416 U.S. at 742 n. 16, 94 S.Ct. at 2048 n. 16; *Sherman v. Nash,* 488 F.2d 1081, 1085 (3d Cir.1973) (action to restrain assessment under Section 6213(a) is an action seeking equitable relief).[6]

* * * Section 6213(a) states that a court "may" grant injunctive relief. Congress's use of the conditional suggests that such relief is not mandatory in every case where the Service fails to honor the notice provisions. If equitable relief is not mandatory in all such cases, but instead lies within the discretion of the court, there is no reason to cast off those principles that traditionally have informed the exercise of a court's broad equity powers.

C. THE WILLIAMS PACKING CLAIM

The Taxpayer also argues that he is entitled to relief based on the judicially-crafted exception to the Anti-Injunction Act of *Williams Packing*. He argues that the relevant statute of limitations and all extensions thereto expired before the Service began its assessments, completely barring the Service from recovering the disputed amounts. *See* Section 6501(a). In response, the Service says that it was proceeding in good faith because Taxpayer waived the defense of limitations by executing Form 870–AD. Alternatively, the Service asserts that because Taxpayer's tax returns were fraudulent, the statute of limitations remains open. *See* Section 6501(c)(1).

While we have considerable doubt whether Taxpayer will be able to satisfy the requirements of *Williams Packing*, we cannot rule out that possibility without knowledge of the evidence which the trial court declined to consider. We emphasize again, however, that a Taxpayer's burden under *Williams Packing* is very substantial; he must show that, when the facts and law are viewed in the light most favorable to the Service, it is clear that the Service will be unable to prevail in its contentions. Moreover, he must also show that equitable relief is appropriate.

* * *

The judgment below will be vacated and this case will be remanded for further proceedings consistent with this opinion.

Notes and Questions

1. The court in *Flynn* held that the taxpayer would not necessarily be entitled to an injunction to restrain collection even if he proved that the IRS did not provide him with the deficiency notice required by § 6213(a). Indeed, in footnote 8 the court stated that economic harm is usually

---

6. Although economic harm is usually insufficient to establish irreparable injury, in some cases, e.g., ruination or forced sale of a taxpayer's business, it will provide grounds for the exercise of a court's equity powers. *Williams Packing,* 370 U.S. at 6, 82 S.Ct. at 1128.

insufficient to warrant equitable relief. Can this holding be correct? Under *Flynn,* are not the settled concepts that jeopardy and termination assessments are the only exceptions to the requirement of a deficiency notice rendered meaningless?

2. Can the holding of *Flynn* be squared with the Supreme Court's landmark decision in *Flora,* page 400 above, which discusses the rationale behind the prepayment remedy of the Tax Court? Can there be irreparable harm as long as the taxpayer can bring suit for a refund?

MIKLAUTSCH v. GIBBS

(D.Alaska 1990) (unreported opinion).

FACTS

The underlying facts of this case are not without dispute, but as presently briefed they appear to the court as follows:

During the mid-1970's, plaintiffs engaged in a series of transactions which could best be described as placing plaintiffs in an "aggressive" tax position. Plaintiffs were investing in exotic tax shelters. In 1975 and 1976, plaintiffs invested in what have become known as "London Options". These transactions were designed to create short-term losses which would then be recouped over subsequent years as long-term gains. Plaintiffs also purchased video tapes from Metro Productions, Inc. These purchases gave the plaintiffs depreciation and interest deductions, in essence creating another tax shelter.

Thereafter, the IRS began auditing the plaintiffs, taking the position that the above transactions were a sham. The claimed deductions for 1975 were disallowed and a deficiency was assessed.

Plaintiffs, along with several other taxpayers, challenged the IRS's determinations in *Glass v. Commissioner,* 87 T.C. 1087 (1986).[1] In November of 1986, the tax court held that the London Options transactions lacked economic substance and were therefore a sham. Hence, the tax court entered a finding that no gain or loss should be recognized from those transactions. Plaintiffs chose not to appeal the tax court's decision.[2]

Apparently, there would be no problem today if plaintiffs' liability for the 1975 tax year had been determined in 1986 when the tax court entered its findings. Unfortunately, that did not occur. The tax court case remained open pending a final resolution of the total amount of plaintiffs' deficiency for 1975. The IRS was thereby precluded from collecting on the 1975 liability. Not to be dissuaded, the IRS then assessed taxes on gains from the London Options for tax years subse-

---

1. The video tape transactions were not made a part of the tax court case. Plaintiffs had executed a closing agreement with the IRS settling the dispute as to those transactions.

2. Others did appeal. Defendant (IRS) prevailed. *Keane v. Commissioner,* 865 F.2d 1088 (9th Cir.1988); *Yosha v. Commissioner,* 861 F.2d 494 (7th Cir.1988).

quent to 1975. It is these assessments and the resulting collection activities which resulted in the instant lawsuit.

In September of 1987 the IRS issued a deficiency notice claiming that plaintiffs owed well over $1 million for tax years 1974, 1977, 1979, 1982, 1983, and 1984. These figures were arrived at primarily by recognizing the gains from the London Options transactions in apparent contravention of the tax court's holding. To use plaintiffs' words, the IRS was "having its cake and eating it too". Plaintiffs did not challenge this deficiency notice, and the deficiencies were assessed and liens were filed.

Plaintiffs appear to have been unable to pay the assessments and collection proceedings were commenced. The IRS seized three properties owned by plaintiffs, including their personal residence. The IRS also levied upon plaintiffs' bank accounts and upon their grandchildren's trust accounts.

On May 24, 1988, plaintiffs' accountant, Gary Johanson, wrote to Byron Broda, the IRS collection agent handling plaintiffs' case. In that letter, Mr. Johanson explained that the assessments were in error since they recognized gains from the London Options. Unable to convince Mr. Broda, Mr. Johanson then contacted Arthur Wadekamper, an IRS appeals officer in Seattle. On October 18, 1988, Mr. Wadekamper wrote back to Mr. Johanson, agreeing with the substance of Mr. Johanson's claim that the assessments were in error. Mr. Wadekamper also forwarded a copy of his letter to Mr. Broda.[3] Two days later, plaintiffs' residence was sold at auction for $8,600.

Plaintiffs subsequently filed the instant lawsuit. The IRS filed the first motion to dismiss which was denied on November 1, 1989. Since that initial motion to dismiss, the IRS has abated its assessments for 1974, 1977, 1979, 1982, 1983, and 1984; applied the amounts collected to plaintiffs' admitted tax liability for 1975,[4] and returned the seized properties (except of course the house which had been sold). The tax liens for these years were released on March 27, 1990.[5]

Plaintiffs' amended complaint asserts causes of action for injunctive relief, for refund pursuant to 26 U.S.C. § 7422, for damages under the Federal Tort Claims Act,[6] for damages resulting from unconstitutional acts by federal officers,[7] for damages under 26 U.S.C. §§ 7432 and 7433, and for damages against Byron Broda under the Racketeer Influenced and Corrupt Organizations Act (RICO).

3. Actually, Mr. Wadekamper's letter purports to be forwarded to "Steven" Broda. Mr. Broda's correct name is apparently *Byron* Broda.

4. The amount that plaintiffs owe for 1975 is not in dispute. The assessed deficiency for 1975 is in excess of $700,000. Although unclear, it appears that the amount applied to the 1975 liability was approximately $50,000.

5. This release document does not cover tax year 1974, but the status of the 1974 tax lien has no bearing on this decision.

6. 28 U.S.C. §§ 2671–2680.

7. *See Bivens v. Six Unknown Federal Narcotics Agents*, 403 U.S. 388 (1971).

The IRS again seeks to have plaintiffs' complaint dismissed, this time arguing: (1) plaintiffs' claims for injunctive relief are moot; (2) plaintiffs' claims for a refund for tax years other than 1975 are moot; (3) this court lacks jurisdiction to hear a refund suit regarding the 1975 tax year; (4) plaintiffs cannot make out a claim under the Federal Tort Claims Act, RICO, or sections 7432 and 7433 of the tax code; and (5) plaintiffs cannot make out a claim under *Bivens*.

The instant motion was originally fashioned as a motion to dismiss pursuant to Rule 12(b)(6).[8] However, both parties have submitted affidavits and exhibits which are indeed necessary for a fair resolution of the motion. Where matters outside the pleadings are presented to the court, Rule 12(b) provides that a motion to dismiss should be treated as a motion for summary judgment under Rule 56. Moreover, both parties have requested that this motion be treated as a summary judgment motion.[9] Therefore the instant motion shall be treated as one for summary judgment.

It is the court's function in ruling on a motion for summary judgment to determine whether genuine issues exist for trial, but not to resolve those issues. *Winzeler Excavating Co. v. Brock*, 694 F.Supp. 362 (N.D.Ohio 1988). The standard on a summary judgment mirrors the standard for a directed verdict under Rule 50(a). *Anderson v. Liberty Lobby, Inc.*, 477 U.S. 242, 250. Summary judgment must be granted, after a sufficient time for discovery, against a party who has failed to produce sufficient evidence to establish an element of that party's case upon which that party bears the burden of proof. *Celotex Corp. v. Catrett*, 477 U.S. 317, 322 (1986). Thus, summary judgment should be granted unless there is sufficient evidence upon which a reasonable fact finder could find for plaintiffs. *Anderson*, 477 U.S. at 252.

Discussion
Injunctive Relief

The IRS argues that plaintiffs' claims seeking injunctive relief are moot because the IRS has abated its assessments regarding tax years 1974, 1977, 1979, 1982, 1983, and 1984. The court agrees that there no longer exists a reasonable possibility that the IRS will attempt to collect for those years. However, such does not support a finding that plaintiffs' injunction claims are now moot. Plaintiffs' claims are not limited to those particular tax years. Rather, plaintiffs seek to enjoin the IRS from attempting to collect on any tax year until their rights to any refund or damages can be determined. In particular, plaintiffs seek to enjoin the IRS from collecting on their 1975 tax liability. Plaintiffs' whole point is that, because of the damage the IRS has wrought upon them, they are no longer capable of paying their tax liability for 1975, and any attempt to collect thereon will only further

---

8. All references herein to a "rule" are in reference to the Federal Rules of Civil Procedure.

9. Plaintiffs' opposition memorandum at 3, defendants' reply memorandum at 6 n. 1.

the damage already done. Such is clearly not moot since the IRS is presently attempting to collect for the 1975 deficiency.

However, while plaintiffs' claims for injunctive relief are not moot, it is barred by the Anti-Injunction Act, 26 U.S.C. § 7421(a). The Anti-Injunction Act bars any suit to restrain the collection or assessment of a tax unless it is shown that: (1) under no circumstances could the Government ultimately prevail, and (2) equity jurisdiction otherwise exists. *Enochs v. William Packing & Navigation Co.,* 370 U.S. 1 (1962).

The purpose of the act is to permit the United States to assess and collect taxes without judicial intervention, and to require that all rights to a disputed sum be litigated in a refund suit. *Id.* at 7. Ordinarily, the purpose of a preliminary injunction is to maintain the *status quo* pending an ultimate resolution of the parties' rights. *Los Angeles Memorial Coliseum Commission v. National Football League,* 634 F.2d 1197 (9th Cir.1980). Yet such is precisely what section 7421 is designed to prevent by forcing taxpayers to pay first, then sue for a refund.

In the instant case, plaintiffs argue that—because of the IRS's unlawful collections for tax years 1974, 1977, 1979, 1982, 1983, and 1984—any collection for the 1975 tax year will ruin them and exacerbate the damage already done. Plaintiffs do not contend that the 1975 assessment is in error. Rather, they assert that until their damage claims can be resolved, the IRS should be prevented from further harming them. Again, as stated above, maintaining the *status quo* pending litigation is exactly what section 7421 was enacted to prevent.

In denying the IRS's earlier motion to dismiss, this court stated that it felt plaintiffs had made out a *prima facie* case for injunctive relief. When that motion was decided, the IRS had not yet abated its assessments for 1974, 1977, 1979, 1982, 1983, and 1984. Any further collections on those tax years may very well have been subject to injunction. Those claims, however, are now moot. Plaintiffs' motion for a preliminary injunction must therefore be denied.

Refund Claim

The question of whether plaintiffs' suit for a refund under 26 U.S.C. § 7422[10] is moot depends not so much on traditional mootness analysis, but rather on what relief is available under 26 U.S.C. § 7422. The IRS claims that since it has credited the amounts that were collected against plaintiffs' 1975 tax liability, plaintiffs have been made whole and their refund suit is therefore moot.

> In the case of any *overpayment,* the Secretary, within the applicable period of limitations, may credit the amount of such overpayment, including any interest allowed thereon, against any liability in respect of an internal revenue tax on the part of the person who made the overpayment and shall * * * refund any balance to such person.

26 U.S.C. § 6402(a) (emphasis added).

---

10. At oral argument, plaintiffs in substance conceded this aspect of their motion.

Contrary to the IRS's assertions, plaintiffs have been anything but made whole. Yet, plaintiffs are entitled to a refund only for the amount "overpaid" in excess of the amount credited to their 1975 tax liability. Thus, if the amount credited represents the total "overpayment", then indeed the claim is now moot.

Therefore the essential question is what constitutes an "overpayment"? Plaintiffs infer that the term overpayment should include the fair market value of their residence, as well as the rental value of the other seized properties up until the time they were returned.[11]

With regard to the properties which were seized but later returned, the determinative question is whether or not the seizure of plaintiffs' properties constituted a "payment" of the fair rental value. Where ownership of property is not transferred to the IRS, it is impossible for a seizure to constitute a payment. *Sly v. United States*, 836 F.2d 1310 (11th Cir.1988). In *United States v. Whiting Pools, Inc.*, 462 U.S. 198 (1983), the Court held that a seizure of property by the IRS did not result in a change in ownership, and the property could be made part of the bankruptcy estate. Therefore, the seizure of property alone does not constitute payment. *Sly*, 836 F.2d at 1312. Under this reasoning, plaintiffs are not entitled to any refund stemming from the seizure of their properties since such did not constitute a payment.

In a refund suit, the taxpayer bears the burden of proving the existence of an overpayment. *Miller v. United States*, 155 F.Supp. 767 (D.Ky.1957), *aff'd* 262 F.2d 584 (6th Cir.1958). There having been a reasonable time for discovery, there presently exists no evidence before the court that the IRS did anything beyond seize the property in question. Hence, plaintiffs have failed to establish that a triable issue exists.

Therefore, with respect to the properties that were returned to plaintiffs, there has never been a payment which could be refunded.

With regard to plaintiffs' residence, it is clear that there was a payment since the property was in fact sold. The dispute lies in determining the amount of that payment—specifically, whether or not such should include the fair market value of the residence.[12]

26 U.S.C. § 6343(b) provides:

If the Secretary determines that property has been wrongfully levied upon, it shall be lawful for the Secretary to return—

    (1) the specific property levied upon,

    (2) an amount of money equal to the amount of money levied upon, or

    (3) an amount of money equal to the amount of money received by the United States from the sale of such property.

---

11. At oral argument, plaintiffs' counsel admitted that he felt such was probably not recoverable in a refund suit but that he had not fully researched the question.

12. See footnote 11, *ante*.

Therefore, where the IRS has sold property that was wrongfully seized, section 6343(b)(3) authorizes a refund only of the amount received in the sale. Hence, it is that amount which has been "paid" to the IRS. If Congress had intended the term "overpayment" to include the fair market value of the property rather than what it was actually sold for, section 6343 would have authorized the repayment of that amount. Otherwise, every time the IRS were to make a repayment under section 6343(b)(3), it would immediately be faced with a refund suit for the balance of the fair market value. This is because property will almost invariably be sold at a tax sale for a price substantially below its fair market value.

Girard Bank Trust v. United States, 643 F.2d 725 (Ct.Cl.1981), provides some authority for awarding the fair market value of property in a refund action. In *Girard,* the taxpayer had redeemed "flower bonds" in payment of a tax later found to have been wrongfully assessed. The issue was, for purposes of calculating interest pursuant to 26 U.S.C. § 6621, whether the court should use the face value or the fair market value of the bonds. The court held that the purpose of section 6621 was to compensate for the loss of control of the property; thus, the interest should be calculated from the bonds' fair market value. However, in so holding, the court recognized that it was dealing with a specialized form of tax liability satisfaction. Those same concerns are not present where the IRS has sold property and received a cash payment therefor.

It appears on the present briefing that all the plaintiffs could hope to gain in a refund action under 26 U.S.C. § 7422 has in fact been credited to their 1975 tax liability.[13] Accordingly, those claims are moot.

Damages under 26 U.S.C. § 7433

Plaintiffs' claim for damages under 26 U.S.C. § 7433 presents an entirely different matter. Section 7433(a) provides:

> If, in connection with any collection of Federal tax with respect to a taxpayer, any officer or employee of the Internal Revenue Service recklessly or intentionally disregards any provision of this title, or any regulation promulgated under this title, such taxpayer may bring a civil action for damages against the United States in a district court of the United States. Except as provided in section 7432, such civil action shall be the exclusive remedy for recovering damages resulting from such actions.

---

13. Plaintiffs apparently do not now challenge the validity of the IRS simply treating the amounts collected as an overpayment. However, there seems to be a split of authority where the collections were made pursuant to a wholly invalid and arbitrary assessment. *See, e.g., Kabbaby v. Richardson,* 520 F.2d 334 (5th Cir. 1975) (holding that where a jeopardy assessment was excessive, arbitrary, capricious, and wholly without foundation, collections made thereunder could not constitute a payment under section 6402; thus, the IRS could not validly apply the amounts collected to the taxpayer's outstanding liability, and the taxpayer was entitled to a refund of the total amount collected); *cf., Boyd v. United States,* 439 F.Supp. 907 (E.D.Pa.1977).

Section 7433(b) limits any recovery under this section to $100,000.

This section was added to the tax code in 1988 as a part of the "Taxpayers' Bill of Rights" because, as Congress saw it, "[t]axpayers [did] not have a specific right to bring an action against the Government for damage sustained due to unreasonable actions taken by an IRS employee." [14]

The IRS here contends that because section 7433 authorizes suits only for wrongful conduct in connection with the "collection" of a tax, section 7433 is inapplicable where the IRS employs procedurally correct collection methods to collect on a tax that was wrongfully [15] assessed. This interpretation would clearly thwart Congress's intent in passing section 7433. Under the IRS's view, the IRS could arbitrarily—and without any justification whatsoever—assess a tax, and then collect on that tax with impunity so long as procedurally proper methods were employed. It was the intent of Congress to protect taxpayers, not to allow the IRS to wrongfully bring a person to financial ruin so long as its collection methods were procedurally correct.

The IRS's argument is also contrary to the plain meaning of section 7433. The statute is not limited only to acts in disregard of proper collection procedures. Rather, the statute refers to any act in disregard of *any* provision in the tax code, which is connected with the eventual "collection" of a tax.

Under a proper interpretation of section 7433, where a tax has been wrongfully assessed, and the IRS goes ahead and enforces collection on the tax, an action shall lie. It is true Congress chose not to extend section 7433 to damages arising from the wrongful determination of a tax alone. Yet, all this means is that where a tax is wrongfully assessed but the taxpayer voluntarily remits payment, there is no action for damages because there has been no enforced collection. The distinction between enforced collection and voluntary payment is sensible in that a taxpayer who has voluntarily paid is not likely to suffer the severe damage that occurs when the IRS brings its full collection powers to bear. Moreover, a taxpayer who voluntarily makes payments usually does so in cash which can easily be recouped by way of a refund. When the IRS collects an outstanding tax, it does so by seizures and levies on property, creating losses that (as this case demonstrates) cannot be recovered in an ordinary refund action.

This interpretation is further bolstered by Congress's clear intent to limit the Government's potential liability in cases such as this. As stated above, section 7433(b) limits a plaintiff's potential recovery to $100,000. Moreover, section 7433(a) states that it and section 7432 shall be the exclusive remedy for "such actions." Under the IRS's interpretation, however, a capricious and arbitrary assessment would

14. H.R.Conf.Rep. No. 1104, 100th Cong., 3d Sess. 228.

15. The use of the term "wrongful" in this context is intended to mean wrongful under section 7433, that is, an assessment that was made in intentional or reckless disregard of the tax code.

not be within "such actions", thereby opening the door to whatever causes of action creative lawyers could conjure up. In this case alone, plaintiffs have asserted causes of action under RICO, *Bivens,* and the Federal Tort Claims Act. Under any one of these theories, the damages could well exceed $100,000. Under this view, the Government becomes exposed to potential liability far in excess of $100,000. Such is a result Congress sought to avoid. Therefore, a cause of action does exist under section 7433 where there has been a wrongful assessment upon which the IRS made collections.[16] The next question is whether or not plaintiffs have made out such an action.

It appears from the evidence presented to the court that there exists a triable issue as to whether IRS agents intentionally or recklessly disregarded the tax code in wrongfully assessing and then collecting taxes from plaintiffs. The IRS admits that it disallowed losses from the 1975 transactions, but went ahead and recognized gains from those same transactions in subsequent years. Worse, the tax court in *Glass* held that *no gain* or loss should be recognized from those transactions. Plaintiffs accepted this finding by not appealing. Yet a litany of IRS employees chose to ignore this holding and assessments were made on those gains. At one point an IRS official, Arthur Wadekamper, at least saw the light and apparently attempted to inform the collecting agent of the problem. Despite this, Agent Broda went ahead and further collected on the invalid assessments.

The IRS's only defense is that it was attempting to "protect itself" from an appeal that plaintiffs were not even part of. The IRS has also asserted at various times that it was protecting itself from inconsistent positions taken by plaintiffs. The court is not aware of any code provision or regulation that allows the IRS simply to ignore a tax court's holding in order to "protect itself". Moreover, the court can not find any inconsistency in plaintiffs' position.

Plaintiffs' claims under 26 U.S.C. § 7433 are not subject to dismissal or summary judgment in defendants' favor.

Damages under 26 U.S.C. § 7432

Plaintiffs' claim under section 7432 presents a slightly different problem. Section 7432(a), also passed as part of the "Taxpayers' Bill of Rights", provides:

---

16. The court is not unmindful that this result may seem inconsistent with an earlier position stated herein. On page 11 of this order, it was stated that if the term "payment" were to include the fair market value of properties levied and sold by the IRS, any return of the amount received would always be followed by a refund suit. The same might be argued here. However, in a refund suit there is no requirement that the IRS agents be shown to have acted intentionally or recklessly. All that is required in a refund suit is that an overpayment was made for which the taxpayer has received no credit.

Under the court's interpretation of section 7433, the code can be read consistently. If no intentional or reckless conduct exists, then the taxpayer is only entitled to a refund as discussed above. Where the taxpayer has been wronged by intentional or reckless conduct on the part of the IRS, then the code allows for damages.

If any officer or employee of the Internal Revenue Service knowingly, or by reason of negligence, fails to release a lien under section 6325 on property of the taxpayer, such taxpayer may bring a civil action for damages against the United States in a district court of the United States.

Section 6325(a) requires the Secretary to release a lien within thirty days after the Secretary finds that the amount assessed has been satisfied or has become legally unenforceable.

In this case, on October 18, 1988, Mr. Wadekamper agreed with the plaintiffs' accountant that the assessments for tax years other than 1975 were not legally enforceable. Mr. Wadekamper is an appeals officer with the IRS, and appears to have the authority to make such a determination. Therefore, as of October 18, 1988, there had been a determination that the assessments were not legally enforceable. The IRS's failure to release the liens within thirty days gives rise to an action under section 7432.

The IRS argues that section 6325 only mandates that a lien be released if the Secretary finds that the assessment became unenforceable subsequent to its inception, but not if the finding is that it had always been unenforceable. This argument is untenable. Section 6325(a)(1) reads: "[t]he Secretary finds that the liability for the amount assessed * * * has become legally unenforceable." A literal reading of the words "has become legally unenforceable" can be construed as the IRS contends, yet, to do so would make the statute quite ridiculous. A court may depart from a statute's literal meaning in cases of gross absurdity and contrary congressional intent. *Ink v. Commissioner*, No. 89-70328, slip op. (9th Cir.1990) (citing, *Watt v. Alaska*, 451 U.S. 259, 266 (1981)). It is highly doubtful that Congress intended to allow a lien to stand even after the Secretary had determined that the assessment upon which it was based was never valid. Such would be an absurd result indeed.

Therefore, it appears on this briefing that there does exist a triable issue.[17]

Other Claims

Finding in favor of plaintiffs on their section 7433 claim mandates that plaintiffs' damage claims under *Bivens*, RICO, and the Federal Tort Claims Act be dismissed. As stated above, section 7433 clearly states that, except for claims under section 7432, section 7433 states the exclusive remedy. The court recognizes that this is a hollow victory for plaintiffs, but Congress was very careful to limit the Government's potential liability. This court cannot ignore a clear congressional mandate. Accordingly, this court concludes that plaintiffs' claims

---

17. This order should not be construed as expressing an opinion as to whether Arthur Wadekamper's letter of October 18, 1988, constitutes a "finding of the Secretary"—for purposes of 26 U.S.C. § 6321(a)(1)—that the liens herein involved are legally unenforceable. As presently briefed, the court considers this an open issue.

under *Bivens*, RICO, and the Federal Tort Claims act must be dismissed.

CONCLUSION

For the reasons stated above, defendants' motion to dismiss is denied with respect to plaintiffs' claims for damages under 26 U.S.C. §§ 7432 and 7433. With respect to all other claims, defendants' motion is granted. Plaintiffs' motion for a preliminary injunction is denied.

DATED at Anchorage, Alaska, this 6 day of November, 1990.

SECTION 8. WRONGFUL LEVY

Section 7426 provides a mechanism for third parties (that is, not the delinquent taxpayer) to recover for wrongful levies against property in which the third party has an interest. Section 7426 authorizes a civil suit in a United States district court against the United States for any of the following: to recover property improperly seized by the government under a wrongful levy (section 7426(a)(1)); to establish that the third party's interest in the property entitles him to an interest in the surplus proceeds from sale of the property (section 7426(a)(2)); or to enforce an interest in substituted sales proceeds (section 7426(a)(3)). The latter type of action may be brought by the delinquent taxpayer, as well as by a third party.

Under section 6532(c)(1), suit under section 7426 must be brought within nine months following the levy. The burdens of proof in an action under section 7426 are as follows: "[T]here is an initial burden on the plaintiff to prove it has an interest in the property and that the government levied on the property because of tax assessments against another person, a taxpayer. The burden then shifts to the government to prove the nexus between the property and the taxpayer by substantial evidence. The plaintiff has the ultimate burden of proving that the levy was wrongful and should be overturned." Xemas, Inc. v. United States, 689 F.Supp. 917 (D.Minn.1988).

As the following case illustrates, wily taxpayers and their lawyers can pay a steep price for attempting to insulate assets from seizure by transfer to a third party, followed by a suit under section 7426.

LEMASTER v. UNITED STATES
United States Court of Appeals, Sixth Circuit, 1989.
891 F.2d 115.

PER CURIAM: Both plaintiffs and their attorney appeal from an award of sanctions under Federal Rules of Civil Procedure 11 and 28 U.S.C. § 1927. Plaintiffs filed suit against the United States and a revenue officer of the Internal Revenue Service after the officer (Webb) seized property ostensibly owned by Stephen Lemaster to pay the tax liabilities owed by his parents, James and Barbara Lemaster. The district court granted the defendants' motion for summary judgment as to all plaintiffs' claims except Stephen's claim under section 7426 of the Internal Revenue Code (26 U.S.C.), which was dismissed after a two-day trial. The court subsequently awarded the government sanctions against both the attorney (Kingsley) and the three plaintiffs, and all four persons now appeal. While Kingsley and the Lemasters raise a number of points on appeal, their basic argument is that this was not an appropriate case for sanctions and that, even if sanctions were allowable, the court did not compute the amount of the sanctions properly. Finding no abuse of discretion by the district court, we affirm the award of sanctions.

I.

The events relevant to this case began in 1980. At that time, the IRS determined that Barbara and James Lemaster owed substantial taxes, and the IRS commenced making assessments. Also in 1980, James and Barbara began transferring property to their son, Stephen, apparently in order to insulate the property from creditors. James and Barbara transferred their house, worth over $60,000, to Stephen in 1980, although Stephen was then a senior in high school with little or no money. The title was transferred to Stephen and there was a claim made that the purchase price was subsequently forgiven over three years as a gift, but James and Barbara continued to reside in the home, and James indicated in subsequent, unrelated legal proceedings that he, James, was the owner of the house.

Since the 1970s, James had operated a trucking business, B & L Leasing. In the 1980s, as a result of the IRS assessments and assorted other legal problems, James was forced to shut down his operation. At approximately the same time as B & L was encountering difficulties, the Lemaster family began operating a new trucking business. All of the property and assets of the new business, "S. Lemaster Trucking," were in Stephen's name. When B & L ceased operations, S. Lemaster Trucking acquired all of B & L's property by assuming B & L's mortgage obligations. As soon as S. Lemaster Trucking commenced operations, Stephen signed a form granting James his power of attorney. Thus, while all business was conducted in Stephen's or the company's name, James controlled all aspects of S. Lemaster Trucking's day-to-day operations. In fact, Stephen soon moved to Florida to pursue his own career as a hairdresser. While he was in Florida, Stephen rarely was consulted about the trucking business, and his approval was not required for major purchases. Stephen did receive some revenues from the trucking operation over the years. However, it is also clear that Barbara and James regarded the S. Lemaster Trucking checking account as their own personal checking account, using it to pay all of their household expenses.

In 1985, after years of unsuccessful collection attempts, the delinquent tax liabilities of Barbara and James were assigned to Agent Webb for collection. Webb was unable to locate any seizable assets in the name of Barbara or James, but he did discover that James was operating a trucking business with assets listed in Stephen's name. After an investigation, which included an interview with Stephen in Florida in which Stephen demonstrated almost no familiarity with the trucking business, Webb became convinced that Stephen Lemaster was simply a nominee for, or alter ego of, James Lemaster.

On August 14 and 15, 1986, Webb served notices of levy on a number of individuals and institutions doing business with S. Lemaster Trucking or with Stephen Lemaster. These levies produced little money, so on September 4, 1986, Webb and a number of other government officials seized a 1984 Lincoln Continental from the driveway of the house owned by Stephen but inhabited by Barbara and James. The agents also seized a number of items—trucks, engines, automobile parts, a forklift—from the business premises of S. Lemaster Trucking.

On the very day that the seizures occurred, James Lemaster tendered to Webb a check for $9,000 of the $25,820.18 tax liability. All property but the Lincoln was returned. One month later James presented Webb with a check for the balance of his outstanding tax obligation, and the Lincoln was returned.

On August 26, 1986, after the levies on individuals and institutions dealing with Stephen Lemaster, but before the seizure of the car and business properties, all three Lemasters filed suit against the United States and against Agent Webb personally. All three plaintiffs sought an injunction under 26 U.S.C. § 7426,[1] alleging that the government should be prevented from illegally seizing property titled in the name of Stephen Lemaster to pay the tax debt of James and Barbara Lemaster. James Lemaster also sought to enjoin the government from interfering with the power of attorney granted him by Stephen. Finally, Stephen sued Agent Webb, seeking damages of one billion dollars for lost property and emotional distress.

After discovery proceeded, the government moved for summary judgment as to all claims. The court granted the motion as to the claims brought by James and Barbara. As taxpayers owing money they did not have standing under section 7426 to contest the seizures. James' power of attorney claim was likewise dismissed. However, the court refused to accept the government's position in respect to Stephen's section 7426 complaint, finding that the material question of whether James Lemaster was acting as a bona fide agent of Stephen (making the government's alter ego theory improper) or actually was the owner of the property could not be conclusively resolved before trial.

The case proceeded to trial and, after a two-day bench trial, the court ruled in favor of the government. The district court found that Stephen's ownership of the property was undoubtedly a "sham" de-

---

1. What was formerly the "Internal Revenue Code of 1954" has been substantially amended and redesignated as the "Internal Revenue Code of 1986." However, this case relates to tax years predating the amendments, so all references to sections of the Internal Revenue Code refer to the Internal Revenue Code of 1954.

signed to insulate assets from the reach of James' and Barbara's creditors. In such a situation, the court ruled that the government had the right to seize assets held in the name of Stephen Lemaster or S. Lemaster Trucking to satisfy the tax obligations of the real owner, James Lemaster.

After announcing its decision, the court notified the parties that it was considering an award of sanctions. After both sides submitted materials relevant to the sanctions question, the court issued a memorandum opinion and order awarding the government $17,653.21 in attorney's fees and $1,919.50 in costs, for a total award of $19,572.71. The sanctions were awarded under both Fed.R.Civ.P. 11 and 28 U.S.C. § 1927. Of the total award, $4,893.17 was assessed against the attorney, Kingsley, while the three plaintiffs were made jointly and severally liable for the remainder. Plaintiffs and their counsel appeal solely from the awarding of sanctions.[2]

II.

While the district court stated that its award was based upon violations of both Fed.R.Civ.P. 11 and 28 U.S.C. § 1927, the district court memorandum opinion only discusses standards applicable to Rule 11 questions. Following this lead, the plaintiffs and Kingsley (hereinafter referred to collectively as "plaintiffs") do not even discuss 28 U.S.C. § 1927 in their brief on appeal. It is thus clear that we are faced primarily with a dispute involving the appropriateness of sanctions issued under Rule 11.

Since the amendment of Rule 11 in 1983, this court has addressed an increasing number of appeals from Rule 11 sanctions. A set of clear standards to guide our review has thus developed:

> [T]he test for the imposition of Rule 11 sanctions in this circuit, inspired by the Advisory Committee's Note to the 1983 Amendment, is whether the individual's conduct was reasonable under the circumstances. *INVST [Financial Group, Inc. v. Chem-Nuclear Systems, Inc.],* 815 F.2d [391] at 401-02; *Albright [v. Upjohn Co.],* 788 F.2d [1217] at 1221. The question of whether an individual's conduct was reasonable under the circumstances is a mixed question of law and fact. In light of the district court's more intimate knowledge of the facts of these cases, this court has determined that an abuse of discretion standard of review of the district court's decision to grant Rule 11 sanctions is proper. *INVST,* 815 F.2d at 401-02; *Albright,* 788 F.2d at 1221.

Century Prods., Inc. v. Sutter, 837 F.2d 247, 253 (6th Cir.1988). On appeal, we look to see whether the district court judge abused his discretion in finding plaintiffs' conduct to have been unreasonable under the circumstances.

---

2. In their brief on appeal, plaintiffs also attempt to argue that the district court erred in ruling that their first amended complaint did not relate back. This is an issue relating to the trial of the case, and not to the decision on the sanctions question. The appeal, which was filed 22 days after the decision on the motion for sanctions, but 90 days after entry of judgment in the plaintiffs' case, was timely only as to the sanctions order. Fed.R.App.P. 4(a).

Plaintiffs suggest that their decision to push ahead with their case was not at all unreasonable under the circumstances. They maintain that the law relating to seizure under an alter ego theory was unsettled at the time they filed suit, and that their claim based on the impropriety of governmental seizure of property from the transferee of a taxpayer was well-founded. The plaintiffs assert that the district court simply failed to consider all relevant factors in deciding to award sanctions.

We do not find the plaintiffs' arguments to be convincing. The flaw in plaintiffs' argument lies in the misguided notion that the issue of transferee rights is somehow involved in this dispute. The plaintiffs expend a great deal of energy arguing that, according to statute and law, the government must pursue all possible direct means of satisfying a taxpayer's debt and provide some form of pre-seizure procedure before it may seize a transferee's assets to satisfy the tax debts of the transferor. 26 U.S.C. § 6901. Whether or not this is an accurate statement of the law we do not address, as it is wholly irrelevant to the case before us. Here, the government nowhere suggested that it was seizing the assets of Stephen Lemaster because he was a transferee of James Lemaster. Rather, the government made clear from the outset that it was proceeding under 26 U.S.C. § 6331, treating Stephen Lemaster as an alter ego of James Lemaster, making James Lemaster the true owner of the assets and the assets properly seizable. Under the circumstances, the district court correctly noted that counsel should have recognized that transferee and beneficial ownership principles under section 6901 are of no consequence, and that the only possible way for plaintiffs to succeed in an action for wrongful seizure would be if the government erred in treating James as the actual owner.

In dealing with the reasonableness of their actions, assuming that the government acted to pursue funds from an alter ego under section 6331, plaintiffs attempt to claim that their challenge to the government's actions was reasonable because, at the time the suit was filed, the legality of seizures from nominees without pre-seizure hearings was uncertain. We disagree. The Supreme Court resolved the alter ego seizure question, in the government's favor, in *G.M. Leasing Corp. v. United States* [77-1 USTC ¶ 9140], 429 U.S. 338 (1977).[3] The tactic of

---

3. Plaintiffs attempt to support their assertion that the *G.M. Leasing* case is not dispositive by referring us to the language in that opinion stating:

Our grant of certiorari was limited to the Fourth Amendment issue, and we declined to review petitioner's and Norman's son's claims that the assessments and levies should have been voided and that petitioner was not Norman's alter ego. * * * We therefore approach this case accepting the Court of Appeals' determinations that the assessments and levies were valid and that petitioner was Norman's alter ego.

G.M. Leasing, 429 U.S. at 351. However, this statement merely indicates that the Court did not consider the factual question of whether alter ego status was proved. As to the more basic question—whether the government may properly proceed against property titled to one other than the taxpayer under an alter ego theory—the Court makes patently clear that such actions are permissible. The Court states that "[i]f petitioner was Norman's alter ego * * * the Service could properly regard petitioner's assets as Norman's property * * * and the Service would be empowered, under § 6331, to levy upon assets held in petitioner's name in satisfaction of Norman's income tax liability." *G.M. Leasing*, 429 U.S. at 351.

proceeding against the nominee of a taxpayer for the purpose of satisfying the taxpayer's tax obligations had also been upheld by post-*G.M. Leasing* circuit court decisions. *Loving Saviour Church v. United States* [84–1 USTC ¶ 9261], 728 F.2d 1085 (8th Cir.1984); *Valley Finance, Inc. v. United States* [80–2 USTC ¶ 9554], 629 F.2d 162, 171–73 (D.C.Cir.1980), *cert. denied,* 451 U.S. 1018 (1981). Given these facts, it was unreasonable to believe that doubt existed as to the legality of the government's theory.

Plaintiffs also argue that the district court abused its discretion in finding that plaintiffs could not have reasonably believed there was a chance of success on the pivotal, factual question of whether Stephen Lemaster was the alter ego of James Lemaster. Upon review we conclude that the district court was correct in ruling that there is no reasonable way the Lemasters or Kingsley could have doubted that James was the true owner of all contested assets. All four individuals knew that James' transfer of assets to Stephen began at approximately the same time as the government began pursuing James for back taxes, that Stephen knew or cared little about the trucking industry, that Stephen spent four years in Florida while "his" company was operating in Ohio, that Stephen made no significant contributions to the management of the trucking company while James ran the business, and that the Lemaster family in Ohio used a transferred house as a residence and used the trucking company checking account for personal business. The district court noted that, by any standard of proof, Stephen Lemaster's ownership of the assets of the trucking company was a sham. This sham ownership was so inartful and the scheme so transparent that neither the Lemasters nor Kingsley could reasonably have thought the district court might find the seizures to have been improper.

* * *

Finally, the plaintiffs argue that, if the sanctions are found to be proper, this court should hold that all sanctions should be assessed solely against James Lemaster as the main violator. The plaintiffs argue that James committed the only wrongs because it was he who constructed the elaborate scheme to hide his assets from the IRS. However, Rule 11 sanctions do not attempt to punish anyone for conduct involved in concealing assets from the IRS. Rather, the purpose of Rule 11 sanctions is to serve to deter potential litigants from filing groundless lawsuits. Here, the relevant conduct was the filing of the suit against the United States and Agent Webb, and all three members of the Lemaster family, on the advice of their attorney, engaged in the filing of groundless lawsuits. This is the conduct for which sanctions issued, and the conduct of all three Lemasters and their attorney is equally sanctionable.

The decision of the district court is Affirmed.

Notes

1. Can a third party bring suit to restrain a threatened wrongful levy? See American Pacific Inv. Corp. v. Nash, 342 F.Supp. 797 (D.N.J.1972), holding § 7426 does not authorize such suits.

2. Suppose that property is wrongfully levied on but the levy is released prior to the institution of a suit. Would the court have jurisdiction to entertain the claim? See Three "M" Investments, Inc. v. United States, 781 F.2d 352 (10th Cir.1986), holding that the court lacked jurisdiction.

3. Is the nine month limitations period for a wrongful levy suit jurisdictional? Would forebearance from filing suit upon the assurances of an IRS collections officer that the levy would be released permit the application of equitable estoppel? Compare O'Neal v. United States, 57 AFTR 2d 86–1040 (M.D.N.C.1986) (holding the action barred as untimely) with Belton v. Commissioner, 562 F.Supp. 30 (D.D.C.1982) (allowing the suit and holding the IRS estopped to rely on the statute of limitations as a defense).

4. A spouse who signs a joint return with respect to which a tax liability is asserted is not a third party within the meaning of § 7426 and cannot enjoin the Service from collecting upon separately owned property. Moreover, the innocent spouse provision of § 6013(e) provides no independent source of jurisdiction for such action. Kirtley v. Bickerstaff, 488 F.2d 768 (10th Cir.1973), cert. denied, 419 U.S. 828, 95 S.Ct. 47, 42 L.Ed.2d 52 (1974).

SECTION 9. BANKRUPTCY

Bankruptcy cases commenced after September 30, 1979 are governed by the provisions of the Bankruptcy Reform Act of 1978, P.L. 95–598 (commonly referred to as the Bankruptcy Code) and the Bankruptcy Tax Act of 1980, P.L. 96–589 (which is intended to coordinate the provisions of the Internal Revenue Code of 1954 with those of the Bankruptcy Code). Bankruptcy cases pending and filed after July 10, 1984 are subject to most of the 1984 amendments relating to jurisdiction; those filed after October 7, 1984 are subject to the 1984 substantive changes in bankruptcy law of the Bankruptcy Amendments and Federal Judgeship Act of 1984.

Automatic Stay of Assessment and Collection Activity. The Bankruptcy Code provides for an automatic stay of the assessment and/or collection of any taxes owed by the debtor.[z] It prohibits the commencement or continuation of both judicial and administrative proceedings (including collection activities) against the debtor or with respect to property of the debtor or property of the estate.[a] The Bankruptcy Code

---

[z] 11 U.S.C.A. § 362(a)(6).

[a] 11 U.S.C.A. § 362(a)(1)–(a)(5). Thus, the IRS may not set off an overpayment of taxes from one year against the delinquent tax liability in another year. E.g., United States v. Reynolds, 764 F.2d 1004 (4th Cir. 1985); United States v. Norton, 717 F.2d 767 (3d Cir.1983).

does not, however, stay the commencement or continuation of any criminal proceedings,[b] or any proceedings over which the Bankruptcy Court has jurisdiction, or issuance of a notice of deficiency.[c]

The running of the limitations period for the assessment and collection of tax is suspended for the time during which the stay is in effect, plus (i) for assessments, 60 days thereafter, and (ii) for collection, 6 months thereafter.[d] This rule provides the IRS adequate time to collect nondischargeable taxes following the close of Title 11 cases.

Judicial Resolution of Tax Claims During Bankruptcy. Once a bankruptcy case has been instituted, the Bankruptcy Court has jurisdiction over any new tax claim arising against the individual debtor or the bankruptcy estate involving unpaid taxes, fines, penalties or additions to tax, whether or not previously assessed,[e] and upon a determination by the Bankruptcy Court, the Service may assess the tax immediately.[f] The Bankruptcy Court will not have jurisdiction to rule on the merits of any tax claim which has been previously adjudicated in a contested proceeding before a court of competent jurisdiction.[g] For this purpose, a proceeding in the Tax Court is to be considered "contested" if the debtor filed a petition in the Tax Court and the IRS answered the petition by the time of the commencement of the bankruptcy case. The Bankruptcy Court can, under certain conditions, determine the amount of a tax refund claim by the trustee. If the refund results from an offset or counterclaim to a claim or request for payment by the IRS, the trustee would not first have to file an administrative claim for refund with the Service. However, if the trustee requests a refund in other situations, he would first have to submit an administrative claim for the refund. If the IRS does not rule on the refund claim within 120 days (rather than the usual six months), then the Bankruptcy Court may rule on the merits of the refund claim.[h]

If there is no proceeding pending in the Tax Court at the time the bankruptcy petition is filed, the Service has two procedural options in asserting a pre-petition deficiency. It may file a claim against the bankruptcy estate,[i] in which case the claim will be adjudicated in Bankruptcy Court and the taxpayer will not be allowed to petition the Tax Court. If the Service fails to present the claim to the Bankruptcy Court, the debtor or trustee may file the claim on the Service's behalf. Note, however, that jurisdiction in the Bankruptcy Court is discretionary with respect to the tax issues.[j] Alternatively, the Service may follow regular procedures by issuing a notice of deficiency. Recall that the issuance of a notice of deficiency does not violate the automatic stay. (The stay applies, however, if a deficiency notice issued prior to the bankruptcy proceeding had not yet been petitioned to the Tax

b. 11 U.S.C.A. § 362(b)(1).
c. 11 U.S.C.A. § 362(b)(9).
d. I.R.C. § 6503(i); 11 U.S.C.A. § 108(c).
e. 11 U.S.C.A. § 505(a)(1).
f. 11 U.S.C.A. § 505(c); I.R.C. § 6871(b).
g. 11 U.S.C.A. § 505(a)(2)(A).
h. 11 U.S.C.A. § 505(a)(2)(B).
i. I.R.C. § 6871(c)(1).
j. 28 U.S.C.A. § 1471(d).

Court, and the time for filing a petition had not expired at the commencement of the bankruptcy case.)[k]

If a proceeding is pending in the Tax Court at the time the bankruptcy petition is filed, further action by the Service or the Tax Court is stayed unless the stay is lifted by order of the Bankruptcy Court. The stay may be lifted at the request of the trustee, who may wish to intervene in the Tax Court action on behalf of the bankruptcy estate,[l] or at the request of either the individual debtor or the Service, in which case the decision of the Tax Court will be res judicata for purposes of the bankruptcy action. If the stay is not lifted, the Tax Court will determine the debtor's liability for any nondischargeable taxes at the close of the bankruptcy case.

Provisions for Accelerating Determination of the Tax Liability of the Bankruptcy Estate. The Bankruptcy Code accelerates the procedures for determining the bankruptcy estate's tax liability so that the trustee may distribute expeditiously the assets of the estate. The trustee may request a prompt determination of the estate's liability for any tax incurred during the administration of the estate by submitting a tax return and a request for a determination of the tax.[m] The IRS must notify the trustee within sixty days after the request if it intends to audit any return filed by the trustee with respect to the estate's tax liability.[n] Furthermore, the examination must be completed and the trustee notified of any tax deficiency within 180 days of the request for determination.[o] If the Service fails either to notify the trustee of its intention to audit, or to complete the audit, within the required time, the trustee, the debtor, and any successor to the debtor are discharged from any liability for the tax upon payment of the amount shown due on the return (unless the return filed by the trustee was materially false or fraudulent).[p] Otherwise, the trustee and the debtor receive such a discharge upon payment of the tax as determined by the Bankruptcy Court after notice and a hearing on the correctness of the determination made by the Service.[q]

As noted above, if the trustee files a claim for refund he need wait only 120 days for IRS approval or disapproval of the claim before submitting the claim for refund for adjudication by the Bankruptcy Court.

k. I.R.C. § 6213(f) provides that the running of the normal 90 or 150 day period for filing a petition in the Tax Court under § 6213(a) is suspended during the period the bankruptcy stay is in effect and for 60 days thereafter. Note, also, that the Bankruptcy Tax Act of 1980 amended I.R.C. § 6871 to delete language which previously had prevented taxpayers from filing Tax Court petitions during the pendency of bankruptcy proceedings.

l. Pursuant to I.R.C. § 7464, added to the Code by the Bankruptcy Tax Act of 1980.

m. 11 U.S.C.A. § 505(b).

n. 11 U.S.C.A. § 505(b)(1)(A).

o. 11 U.S.C.A. § 505(b)(1)(B).

p. 11 U.S.C.A. § 505(b)(1).

q. 11 U.S.C.A. § 505(b)(2).

Sec. 9 BANKRUPTCY 865

Priorities of Tax Claims in Bankruptcy. Tax liabilities incurred during the administration of the bankruptcy estate are given first priority, along with other administrative expenses of the estate.[r] The bulk of the remaining federal, state and local tax liabilities are accorded seventh level priority behind administrative expenses, certain claims arising in the ordinary course of the debtor's business, wages, contributions to employee benefit plans, and certain narrowly defined unsecured claims.[s] The seventh level priority claims include:

1. Income taxes for which the due date of the return, including any extensions, occurred within three years preceding the filing of the bankruptcy petition.[t]

2. Income taxes assessed within 240 days preceding the filing of the petition, except that a submission of an offer in compromise for payment of the assessed amount may toll the running of the 240-day period.[u]

3. Income taxes not assessed prior to the filing of the bankruptcy petition, but which may be assessed under applicable law or by agreement after the commencement of the case.[v]

4. Taxes required to be collected or withheld and for which the debtor is liable in any capacity.[w] This would include taxes for which the debtor is liable as an employer, as a responsible person under § 6672 of the Code, or as a lender or provider of wages under § 3505 of the Code.

5. The employer's share of employment taxes for returns due within three years preceding the filing of the petition.[x]

6. Excise taxes for returns due or transactions occurring within three years preceding the filing of the petition.[y]

Discharge of Tax Liabilities. The Bankruptcy Code provides that no individual debtor shall be discharged from any of the taxes accorded seventh level priority under section 507.[z] Also excepted from discharge are taxes from any period in which the debtor willfully attempted to evade or defeat tax, subscribed to a false return, or failed to file a return.[a] Penalties which are punitive in nature and which relate to a nondischargeable tax liability are similarly excepted from discharge.[b]

A plan of reorganization under Chapter 13 of the Bankruptcy Code (Adjustment of Debts of an Individual with Regular Income) must provide for full payment of all § 507 priority debts, but can do so over

---

r. 11 U.S.C.A. § 507(a)(1).
s. See generally 11 U.S.C.A. § 507(a).
t. 11 U.S.C.A. § 507(a)(7)(A)(i).
u. 11 U.S.C.A. § 507(a)(7)(A)(ii).
v. 11 U.S.C.A. § 507(a)(7)(A)(iii).
w. 11 U.S.C.A. § 507(a)(7)(C).
x. 11 U.S.C.A. § 507(a)(7)(D).
y. 11 U.S.C.A. § 507(a)(7)(E).

z. 11 U.S.C.A. § 523(a)(1)(A). Thus, as under the former Bankruptcy Act, the liability of a "responsible person" is not dischargeable. See United States v. Sotelo, 436 U.S. 268, 98 S.Ct. 1795, 56 L.Ed.2d 275 (1978).

a. 11 'J.S.C.A. § 523(a)(1)(B) and (C).
b. 11 U.S.C.A. § 523(a)(7).

the term of the plan.ᶜ Thus, tax liabilities incurred within the three years preceding the petition generally may not be discharged in any bankruptcy case.ᵈ

Tax Liens and Bankruptcy. As a general rule, taxes will be accorded their seventh level priority in liquidation proceedings regardless of whether the government perfects its tax lien by filing. Payment of the debt secured by a perfected tax lien is effectively postponed until the first through sixth priorities have been satisfied, without prejudice to other parties having an interest in the assets.ᵉ Thus, perfecting a tax lien would merely give the tax lien priority over other seventh level claims.

A tax lien which has not been perfected by filing prior to bankruptcy may be voidable, under certain circumstances, by the trustee.ᶠ It is, however, merely the lien which may be extinguished, and not the underlying tax liability. The liability would remain as an unsecured claim which would be entitled to general seventh level priority.

Miscellaneous Provisions of the Bankruptcy Tax Act of 1980. The Bankruptcy Tax Act of 1980 is concerned with the application of the internal revenue laws to bankruptcy and insolvency proceedings. The Act sets forth the permissible means of accounting for any discharged debt.ᵍ The Act also gives an individual debtor the option of terminating his or her taxable year on the day before Chapter 7 or 11 cases are filed.ʰ The debtor's taxable year can thus be split into two "short" taxable years, with the tax liability for the first period becoming an allowable claim against the bankruptcy estate. If this election is made, the debtor is required to annualize his or her taxable income in accordance with IRC § 1398(d)(2)(F). This election is not available to a debtor filing under Chapter 13.

Anglemyer v. United States
United States District Court, District of Maryland, 1990.
115 B.R. 510.

GARBIS, DISTRICT JUDGE.

There is before the Court the Plaintiffs' Motion for Summary Judgment.

During 1980, Jim S. and Agnes B. Anglemyer (who were husband and wife at all times here relevant) operated Anglemyer Construction Company, Inc. The corporation did not comply with its withholding

---

c. 11 U.S.C.A. § 1322(a)(2).

d. Note, however, that the section 523 exceptions from discharge do not apply to a discharge under § 1328(a) of the Bankruptcy Code. Thus, under 11 U.S.C.A. § 1328(a), a Chapter 13 debtor will receive a discharge "as soon as practicable after completion * * * of all payments under the plan" for taxes and penalties, even if incurred in connection with the filing of fraudulent returns or the failure to file returns.

e. 11 U.S.C.A. § 724(b).

f. 11 U.S.C.A. § 544(a)(1).

g. See I.R.C. § 108.

h. I.R.C. § 1398(d).

tax obligations. Unfortunately, this resulted because the corporation found itself in financial difficulties and those in control made the all too common mistake of utilizing payroll withholdings to finance the business. It is assumed for purposes of the pending motion that both Mr. and Mrs. Anglemyer participated in the use of withholding tax trust funds to finance corporate operations. Therefore, both Mr. and Mrs. Anglemyer would be persons "required to collect * * * and pay over [a] tax * * * who willfully fail[ed] to collect such tax or truthfully account for and pay over said tax * * *." 26 U.S.C. § 6672(a).[2] Accordingly, both would be liable for the "responsible person" penalty,[3] i.e. an amount equal to the total amount of tax not collected or not paid over.

On June 30, 1981, Mr. and Mrs. Anglemyer filed a joint petition in bankruptcy pursuant to Chapter 7 of the United States Bankruptcy Code (11 U.S.C. §§ 701-66) in the United States Bankruptcy Court for the District of Maryland (Case No. 80-1-0651). The filing of the bankruptcy petition triggered the automatic stay imposed by Section 362 of the Bankruptcy Code. The Government contends, and the Court assumes for purposes of this Motion, that the Internal Revenue Service did not have actual notice of the filing of the bankruptcy petition until September 21, 1981.

On September 14, 1981, the Internal Revenue Service made § 6672 assessments against Mr. and Mrs. Anglemyer with regard to the unpaid withholding tax liability of Anglemyer Construction Co. for the four quarters[4] of the calendar year 1980. Thereafter the Internal Revenue Service filed a proof of claim for the amount of the assessment in the pending bankruptcy proceeding. The Service did not then, or at any time, seek to lift the automatic stay under 11 U.S.C. § 362(d).

On April 22, 1983, the Anglemyers were discharged from bankruptcy. The bankruptcy discharge did not purport to, and could not, discharge any liability of Mr. and Mrs. Anglemyer for the Section 6672 liability in issue herein. 11 U.S.C. § 507(a)(7)(C), 523(a)(1)(A). The discharge did, however, terminate the automatic stay. 11 U.S.C. § 362(c).

Although the Internal Revenue Service did file tax liens, no collection on the subject assessments was effected until 1987. Hence, interest compounded relentlessly and late payment penalties accumulated. By early 1987, Mr. and Mrs. Anglemyer's liability for an initial assessment of $163,809.99 had grown to some $320,000.00 with interest

---

2. Since each of the Anglemyers was a responsible person, each was jointly and severally liable for the full amount assessed.

3. As stated in M. Saltzman, IRS Practice and Procedure (1981) Para. 17.07 at 17-31:

"The term penalty is somewhat misleading. The amount of the liability imposed by Section 6672 is equal to the amount of the delinquent trust fund taxes and is not in addition to those taxes. Consequently, the "penalty" is actually a collection device designed for the purpose of collecting the taxes the employer should have paid over."

4. Withholding taxes are reported on Forms 941 for each calendar quarter.

continuing to accrue. On January 2, 1987, the Internal Revenue Service levied on the Anglemyers' bank account at Citizens Bank and Trust of Maryland and collected $2,206.15. On January 29, 1987, the Internal Revenue Service levied upon Mr. Anglemyer's wages due from his employer and collected $1,220.31. On February 20, 1987, the Anglemyers filed a timely [5] claim seeking a refund of the total of $3,426.36 which had been collected.

The claim for refund filed by Mr. Anglemyer asserted that the purported assessment of September 14, 1981 was void and without effect by virtue of the automatic stay provision, Section 362(a) of the Bankruptcy Code. The claim for refund filed by Mrs. Anglemyer was based on that ground as well as the contention that she was not, in fact, a responsible person within the meaning of Section 6672 of the Internal Revenue Code.

On April 8, 1988, Mr. and Mrs. Anglemyer timely [6] filed suit for refund of the amount claimed. The Court has jurisdiction of the tax refund suit despite the failure of the plaintiffs to make a full payment of the total amount assessed because the Section 6672 penalty is considered to be a "divisible" tax. M. Garbis, P. Junghans, S. Struntz, Federal Tax Litigation, Para. 15.02(2) (1985); *Jones v. Fox*, 162 F.Supp. 449 (D.Md.1957). Hence, jurisdiction for a tax refund suit may be obtained by paying only the liability with regard to any divisible part of the total assessment. *Flora v. United States*, 362 U.S. 145, 171 n. 37, 80 S.Ct. 630, 644 n. 37, 4 L.Ed.2d 623 (1960). There is no contention by the Government that the Plaintiffs failed to meet the jurisdictional standards to bring this suit. In June of 1988, the Government filed its counterclaim against Mr. and Mrs. Anglemyer for the unpaid balance of the assessment (plus interest). Accordingly, this Court has jurisdiction with respect to the entire assessment against Mr. and Mrs. Anglemyer.

There is no doubt that the action of the Internal Revenue Service in making the September 14, 1981 assessment was in violation of the automatic stay provision. 11 U.S.C. § 362(a). Hence, the assessment was improper. *In re Coleman American Companies, Inc.*, 26 B.R. 825 (Bankr.D.Kans.1983). Moreover, the Internal Revenue Service did not make a proper assessment of this tax following the Anglemyers' discharge from bankruptcy in April of 1983.

It should be noted that the Internal Revenue Service had ample time to make a proper assessment. The responsible person penalty at issue in this case relates to the 1980 withholding tax liability of Anglemyer Construction Company, Inc. Hence, the statute of limitations on assessment would have expired no earlier than April 15, 1984.

---

5. A claim for refund may be filed within two years of the date of the payment sought to be refunded. 26 U.S.C. Sec. 6511(a).

6. A tax refund suit is mature if filed after the earlier of six months from the date of filing the claim in issue or the date on which the Internal Revenue Service disallows the claim. 26 U.S.C. Sec. 6532(a)(1). The period of limitations for filing a tax refund suit expires two years after formal notice of disallowance of the claim. *Id.*

However, by virtue of the Anglemyers' filing in bankruptcy, there was a suspension of the running of limitations during the entire pendency of the bankruptcy proceeding, and for six months thereafter. 26 U.S.C. Sec. 6503(b). Thus, the running of the period of limitations was suspended from June 30, 1981 to at least October 22, 1983 (six months after the April 22, 1983 discharge), a period of almost 28 months. Hence, the Internal Revenue Service could have made a proper assessment of the tax liability in question until early August of 1986. The Service, for whatever reason, did not do so.

The Government argues that there was only a "technical" violation of the automatic stay provision because the Internal Revenue Service did not have actual notice of the filing of the petition at the time that it made the assessments in question. At the hearing on the Summary Judgment Motion, Government counsel conceded that if the Internal Revenue Service had actual notice of the bankruptcy filing the Government would have no basis to contend that the September 14, 1981 assessment was valid for any purpose. For purposes of this Motion, the Court assumes that the Service was totally unaware of the bankruptcy filing by the Anglemyers. However, the absence of notice on the part of the Internal Revenue Service would be relevant only to the question whether Service should have, in the bankruptcy proceeding, been held in contempt of court for a knowing violation of the automatic stay. See *In re Santa Rosa Truck Stop, Inc.,* 74 B.R. 641 (Bankr.N.D.Fla.1987). No contempt issue is presented in the case before this Court and the absence of actual notice is totally irrelevant.

The Government argues that the assessment in question should be held to be "voidable rather than void." Therefore, it is contended, the assessment somehow should be considered sufficiently valid to have enabled the Internal Revenue Service to have met the statute of limitations on assessments but insufficiently valid to provide a presumption of correctness. In support of this contention, the Government cites the case of *In re Twomey,* 24 B.R. 799 (Bankr.W.D.N.Y.1982). However, the *Twomey* decision does not support the Government's position and, instead, indicates the correctness of the taxpayers' position.

In *Twomey,* the taxpayer operated a business during the year 1979 and, like Mr. and Mrs. Anglemyer, utilized withheld trust funds to finance the business rather than meet the corporate payroll tax obligations. In 1981, Twomey filed a petition in bankruptcy. During the existence of the automatic stay which arose by virtue of the filing of the bankruptcy, the Internal Revenue Service made an assessment in violation of the stay, filed a proof of claim and filed an action in the bankruptcy proceeding to lift the automatic stay and approve, *nunc pro tunc,* the prior assessment and an additional assessment. The Internal Revenue Service also sought a judgment for the full amount of the Section 6672 penalty. The bankruptcy court decided that the assessment made in violation of the automatic stay was null and void. However, since the Internal Revenue Service had properly and, it must be emphasized, *timely, filed an action to seek a judgment on the Section 6672 penalty liability,* the bankruptcy court in *Twomey* was able to consider the merits of the liability.[7] The Internal Revenue Service is free to sue to obtain a judgment for a tax liability even without an assessment. However, in such a suit, since there is no valid assessment the Internal Revenue Service does not have the benefit of a presumption of correctness and must bear the burden of proof of establishing liability. That is exactly what happened in the *Twomey* case. The Court held that the assessment was null and void and of no effect. Thus, the Internal Revenue Service had a valid and timely case against the taxpayer but one in which they did not have the benefit of an assessment and had to carry the burden of proof. In the *Twomey* case, the Internal Revenue Service did carry the burden of proof and prevailed.

In the case at bar, the situation is critically different. The Internal Revenue Service needs to have the September 14, 1981 assessment held valid in order to meet the statute of limitations.[8] However, the assessment is null and void *ab initio* and has no validity for any purpose.

The Government has chosen to rely on the case of *In re Abt,* 2 B.R. 323 (Bankr.E.D.Pa.1980). I find the *Abt* decision an inapt precedent on which to rely. In *Abt,* a lender had no actual notice of the filing of a bankruptcy petition and, hence, of the existence of the automatic stay. In "innocent" violation of the automatic stay, the lender seized the debtor's car. After it had actual notice of the existence of the automatic stay, the lender refused to return the vehicle. The bankruptcy court in *Abt* correctly held that the lender would not be found in contempt for having repossessed the car in violation of a stay in which it was unaware. The Court also held, incorrectly in the view of this Court, that since the initial possession of the car had been obtained in a noncontemptuous manner, the lender would not be required to return the car even after it knew of the automatic stay. Thus the *Abt* case allowed the creditor to benefit from the violation of the automatic stay to the extent of keeping possession of the automobile.

The rationale of the erroneous holding in the *Abt* decision has been soundly rejected by every Court that has considered the decision, including the Bankruptcy Court for the District of Maryland. *E.g., In re Miller,* 22 B.R. 479 (D.Md.1982); *In re LaTempa,* 58 B.R. 538

---

7. The suit was filed timely because the underlying penalty involved a responsible person assessment with regard to the four quarters of 1979. The statute of limitations on the assessment of this liability would have expired no earlier than April 15, 1983. It is apparent from the opinion (which was issued in November of 1982) that the Internal Revenue Service acted well within the period of limitations on assessment in order to seek to reduce the liability to judgment.

8. The Government is quick to say that it will assume the burden of proof on the merits of this case. However, that is only what it would have had to do had it timely filed a suit or counterclaim with respect to the liability in issue. The assumption of the burden of proof does not render timely the Government's late action in enforcing the liabilities in issue.

(Bankr.W.D.Va.1986); *In re Holman,* 92 B.R. 764 (Bankr.S.D.Ohio 1988). Even more significantly, the very court that issued the *Abt* decision in the first place has ruled that the case was erroneously decided. *In re McLaughlin,* 96 B.R. 554 (Bankr.E.D.Pa.1989). Hence, the *Abt* decision is totally unpersuasive.

In sum, the Internal Revenue Service's purported assessment of September 14, 1981 was in direct violation of the automatic stay which was in effect by virtue of the bankruptcy filing in June of 1981. Thus, the September 14, 1981 assessment is null and void *ab initio.* In view of this, the collection which was effected in 1987 was based upon an illegal assessment and the plaintiffs' motion for summary judgment on their suit for refund shall be granted by separate Order. The Government's counterclaim was barred by the statute of limitations when filed. Accordingly, the Anglemyers will be awarded summary judgment with regard to the counterclaim, as well, by separate Order.

Finally, I note that the plaintiffs have substantially prevailed with respect to the amount in controversy and with respect to all issues and, further, that the position of the United States was not substantially justified. Accordingly, as indicated at the hearing on the summary judgment motion, a motion for an award of reasonable litigation costs pursuant to Section 7430 of the Internal Revenue Code will, if timely filed by the Plaintiffs, be granted.

In accordance with the foregoing, by July 15, 1990 the parties shall provide the Court with an agreed Judgment Order to be entered in this matter, or, absent agreement, with separate proposed Judgment Orders.

BEGIER v. IRS
Supreme Court of the United States, 1990.
___ U.S. ___, 110 S.Ct. 2258, 110 L.Ed.2d 46.

JUSTICE MARSHALL delivered the opinion of the Court.

This case presents the question whether a trustee in bankruptcy may "avoid" (*i.e.,* recover) from the Internal Revenue Service payments of certain withholding and excise taxes that the debtor made before it filed for bankruptcy. We hold that the funds paid here were not the property of the debtor prior to payment; instead, they were held in trust by the debtor for the IRS. We accordingly conclude that the trustee may not recover the funds.

I

American International Airways, Inc., was a commercial airline. As an employer, AIA was required to withhold federal income taxes and to collect Federal Insurance Contributions Act taxes from its employees' wages. 26 U.S.C. § 3402(a) (income taxes); § 3102(a) (FICA taxes). As an airline, it was required to collect excise taxes from its customers for payment to the IRS. § 4291. Because the amount of these taxes is "held to be a special fund in trust for the United States," § 7501, they are often called "trust-fund taxes." See, *e.g., Slodov v.*

United States, 436 U.S. 238, 241 (1978). By early 1984, AIA had fallen behind in its payments of its trust-fund taxes to the Government. In February of that year, the IRS ordered AIA to deposit all trust-fund taxes it collected thereafter into a separate bank account. AIA established the account, but did not deposit funds sufficient to cover the entire amount of its trust-fund tax obligations. It nonetheless remained current on these obligations through June 1984, paying the IRS $695,000 from the separate bank account and $946,434 from its general operating funds. AIA and the IRS agreed that all of these payments would be allocated to specific trust-fund tax obligations.

On July 19, 1984, AIA petitioned for relief from its creditors under Chapter 11 of the Bankruptcy Code, 11 U.S.C. § 1101 *et seq.* (1982 ed.). AIA unsuccessfully operated as a debtor in possession for three months. Accordingly, on September 19, the Bankruptcy Court appointed petitioner Harry P. Begier trustee and converted the case to a Chapter 7 liquidation. 11 U.S.C. § 701 *et seq.* (1982 ed.). Among the powers of a Chapter 7 trustee is the power under § 547(b)[1] to avoid certain payments made by the debtor that would "enabl[e] a creditor to receive payment of a greater percentage of his claim against the debtor than he would have received if the transfer had not been made and he had participated in the distribution of the assets of the bankrupt estate." H.R.Rep. No. 95–595, p. 177 (1977). Seeking to exercise his avoidance power, Begier filed an adversary action against the Government to recover the entire amount that AIA had paid the IRS for trust-fund taxes during the 90 days before the bankruptcy filing.

The Bankruptcy Court found for the Government in part and for the trustee in part. *In re American International Airways, Inc.,* 83 B.R. 324 (ED Pa.1988). It refused to permit the trustee to recover any of the money AIA had paid out of the separate account on the theory that AIA had held that money in trust for the IRS. *Id.,* at 327. It allowed

---

1. This case is governed by 11 U.S.C. § 547(b) (1982 ed.), which reads:

"Except as provided in subsection (c) of this section, the trustee may avoid any transfer of property of the debtor—

"(1) to or for the benefit of a creditor;

"(2) for or on account of an antecedent debt owed by the debtor before such transfer was made;

"(3) made while the debtor was insolvent;

"(4) made—

"(A) on or within 90 days before the date of the filing of the petition; or

"(B) between 90 days and one year before the date of the filing of the petition, if such creditor, at the time of such transfer—

"(i) was an insider; and

"(ii) had reasonable cause to believe the debtor was insolvent at the time of such transfer; and

"(5) that enables such creditor to receive more than such creditor would receive if—

"(A) the case were a case under chapter 7 of this title;

"(B) the transfer had not been made; and

"(C) such creditor received payment of such debt to the extent provided by the provisions of this title."

The statute has been amended to replace "property of the debtor" with "an interest of the debtor in property." See n. 3, *infra.* The old version of § 547(b) applies to this case, however, because AIA filed its bankruptcy petition before the effective date of the amendment.

the trustee to avoid most of the payments that AIA had made out of its general accounts, however, holding that "only where a tax trust fund is actually established by the debtor and the taxing authority is able to trace funds segregated by the debtor in a trust account established for the purpose of paying the taxes in question would we conclude that such funds are not property of the debtor's estate." *Id.,* at 329. The District Court affirmed. App. to Pet. for Cert. A–22–A–26. On appeal by the Government, the Third Circuit reversed, holding that *any* prepetition payment of trust-fund taxes is a payment of funds that are not the debtor's property and that such a payment is therefore not an avoidable preference. 878 F.2d 762 (1989).[2] We affirm.

II

A

Equality of distribution among creditors is a central policy of the Bankruptcy Code. According to that policy, creditors of equal priority should receive pro rata shares of the debtor's property. See, *e.g.,* 11 U.S.C. § 726(b) (1982 ed.); H.R.Rep. No. 95–595, *supra,* at 177–178. Section 547(b) furthers this policy by permitting a trustee in bankruptcy to avoid certain preferential payments made before the debtor files for bankruptcy. This mechanism prevents the debtor from favoring one creditor over others by transferring property shortly before filing for bankruptcy. Of course, if the debtor transfers property that would not have been available for distribution to his creditors in a bankruptcy proceeding, the policy behind the avoidance power is not implicated. The reach of § 547(b)'s avoidance power is therefore limited to transfers of "property of the debtor."

The Bankruptcy Code does not define "property of the debtor." Because the purpose of the avoidance provision is to preserve the property includable within the bankruptcy estate—the property available for distribution to creditors—"property of the debtor" subject to the preferential transfer provision is best understood as that property that would have been part of the estate had it not been transferred before the commencement of bankruptcy proceedings. For guidance, then, we must turn to § 541, which delineates the scope of "property of the estate" and serves as the postpetition analog to § 547(b)'s "property of the debtor." [3]

2. No other Court of Appeals has decided a case that presents the precise issue we decide here. The Ninth and District of Columbia Circuits have, however, resolved against the taxing authorities cases presenting related issues. See *In re R & T Roofing Structures & Commercial Framing, Inc.,* 887 F.2d 981, 987 (CA9 1989) (rejecting the Government's argument that assets the IRS seized from a debtor to satisfy a trust-fund tax obligation before the debtor filed its bankruptcy petition were assets held in trust for the Government under 26 U.S.C. § 7501, and therefore deciding that the transfer effected by the seizure involved "property of the debtor" and was not exempt from avoidance); *Drabkin v. District of Columbia,* 263 U.S.App.D.C. 122, 125, 824 F.2d 1102, 1105 (1987) (reaching a similar conclusion with respect to a voluntary payment of withheld District of Columbia employee income taxes in a case governed by a provision of local law that "essentially mirror[ed]" § 7501).

3. To the extent the 1984 amendments to § 547(b) are relevant, they confirm our view that § 541 guides our analysis of

Section 541(a)(1) provides that the "property of the estate" includes "all legal or equitable interests of the debtor in property as of the commencement of the case." Section 541(d) provides:

> "Property in which the debtor holds, as of the commencement of the case, only legal title and not an equitable interest * * * becomes property of the estate under subsection (a) of this section only to the extent of the debtor's legal title to such property, but not to the extent of any equitable interest in such property that the debtor does not hold."

Because the debtor does not own an equitable interest in property he holds in trust for another, that interest is not "property of the estate." Nor is such an equitable interest "property of the debtor" for purposes of § 547(b).⁵ As the parties agree, then, the issue in this case is whether the money AIA transferred from its general operating accounts to the IRS was property that AIA had held in trust for the IRS.

B

We begin with the language of 26 U.S.C. § 7501, the Internal Revenue Code's trust-fund tax provision: "Whenever any person is required to collect or withhold any internal revenue tax from any other person and to pay over such tax to the United States, the amount of tax so collected or withheld shall be held to be a special fund in trust for the United States." The statutory trust extends, then, only to "the amount of tax so collected or withheld." Begier argues that a trust-fund tax is not "collected or withheld" until specific funds are either sent to the IRS with the relevant return or placed in a segregated fund. AIA neither put the funds paid from its general operating accounts in a separate account nor paid them to the IRS before the beginning of the preference period. Begier therefore contends that no trust was ever created with respect to those funds and that the funds paid to the IRS were therefore property of the debtor.

We disagree. The Internal Revenue Code directs "every person receiving any payment for facilities or services" subject to excise taxes to "collect the amount of the tax from the person making such payment." § 4291. It also requires that an employer "collec[t]" FICA taxes from its employees "by deducting the amount of the tax from the wages *as and when paid*." § 3102(a) (emphasis added). Both provisions make clear that the act of "collecting" occurs at the time of payment—the recipient's payment for the service in the case of excise taxes and the employer's payment of wages in the case of FICA taxes.

---

what property is "property of the debtor" for purposes of § 547(b). Among the changes was the substitution of "an interest of the debtor in property" for "property of the debtor." 11 U.S.C. § 547(b). Section 547(b) thus now mirrors § 541's definition of "property of the estate" as certain "interests of the debtor in property." § 541(a)(1). The Senate Report introducing a predecessor to the bill that amended § 547(b) described the new language as a "clarifying change." S.Rep. No. 98–65, p. 81 (1983). We therefore read both the older language ("property of the debtor") and the current language ("an interest of the debtor in property") as coextensive with "interests of the debtor in property" as that term is used in § 541(a)(1).

The mere fact that AIA neither placed the taxes it collected in a segregated fund nor paid them to the IRS does not somehow mean that AIA never collected the taxes in the first place.

The same analysis applies to taxes the Internal Revenue Code requires that employers "withhold." Section 3402(a)(1) requires that "every employer making payment of wages shall deduct and withhold *upon such wages* [the employee's federal income tax]." (Emphasis added.) Withholding thus occurs at the time of payment to the employee of his net wages. S.Rep. No. 95–1106, p. 33 (1978) ("[A]ssume that a debtor owes an employee $100 for salary on which there is required withholding of $20. If the debtor paid the employee $80, there has been $20 withheld. If, instead, the debtor paid the employee $85, there has been withholding of $15 (which is not property of the debtor's estate in bankruptcy)"). See *Slodov,* 436 U.S., at 243 (stating that "[t]here is no general requirement that the withheld sums be segregated from the employer's general funds," and thereby necessarily implying that the sums are "withheld" whether or not segregated). The common meaning of "withholding" supports our interpretation. See Webster's Third New International Dictionary 2627 (1981) (defining "withholding" to mean "the act or procedure of deducting a tax payment from income *at the source* ") (emphasis added).

Our reading of § 7501 is reinforced by § 7512, which permits the IRS, upon proper notice, to require a taxpayer who has failed timely "to collect, truthfully account for, or pay over [trust-fund taxes]", or who has failed timely "to make deposits, payments, or returns of such tax," § 7512(a)(1), to "deposit such amount in a separate account in a bank * * * and * * * keep the amount of such taxes in such account until payment over to the United States," § 7512(b). If we were to read § 7501 to mandate segregation as a prerequisite to the creation of the trust, § 7512's requirement that funds be segregated in special and limited circumstances would become superfluous. Moreover, petitioner's suggestion that we read a segregation requirement into § 7501 would mean that an employer could avoid the creation of a trust simply by refusing to segregate. Nothing in § 7501 indicates, however, that Congress wanted the IRS to be protected only insofar as dictated by the debtor's whim. We conclude, therefore, that AIA created a trust within the meaning of § 7501 at the moment the relevant payments (from customers to AIA for excise taxes and from AIA to its employees for FICA and income taxes) were made.

C

Our holding that a trust for the benefit of the IRS existed is not alone sufficient to answer the question presented by this case: whether the *particular dollars* that AIA paid to the IRS from its general operating accounts were "property of the debtor." Only if those particular funds were held in trust for the IRS do they escape characterization as "property of the debtor." All § 7501 reveals is that AIA at one point created a trust for the IRS; that section provides no rule by which we can decide whether the assets AIA used to pay the IRS were assets belonging to that trust.

In the absence of specific statutory guidance on how we are to determine whether the assets transferred to the IRS were trust property, we might naturally begin with the commonlaw rules that have been created to answer such questions about other varieties of trusts. Unfortunately, such rules are of limited utility in the context of the trust created by § 7501. Under common-law principles, a trust is created *in property;* a trust therefore does not come into existence until the settlor identifies an ascertainable interest in property to be the trust res. G. Bogert, Law of Trusts and Trustees § 111 (rev. 2d ed. 1984); 1A W. Fratcher, Scott on Trusts § 76 (4th ed. 1987). A § 7501 trust is radically different from the common-law paradigm, however. That provision states that "the *amount* of [trust-fund] tax * * * collected or withheld shall be held to be a special fund in trust for the United States." (Emphasis added.) Unlike a common-law trust, in which the settlor sets aside particular *property* as the trust res, § 7501 creates a trust in an abstract "amount"—a dollar *figure* not tied to any particular assets—rather than in the actual dollars withheld.[4] Common-law tracing rules, designed for a system in which particular property is identified as the trust res, are thus unhelpful in this special context.

Federal law delineating the nature of the relationship between the § 7501 trust and preferential transfer rules is limited. The only case in which we have explored that topic at any length is *United States v. Randall,* 401 U.S. 513 (1971), a case dealing with a postpetition transfer of property to discharge trust-fund tax obligations that the debtor had accrued pre-petition. There, a court had ordered a debtor in possession to maintain a separate account for its withheld federal income and FICA taxes, but the debtor did not comply. When the debtor was subsequently adjudicated a bankrupt, the United States sought to recover from the debtor's general assets the amount of withheld taxes ahead of the expenses of the bankruptcy proceeding. The Government argued that the debtor held the amount of taxes due in trust for the IRS and that this amount could be traced to the funds the debtor had in its accounts when the bankruptcy petition was filed. The trustee maintained that no trust had been created because the debtor had not segregated the funds. The Court declined directly to address either of these contentions. *Id.,* at 515. Rather, the Court simply refused to permit the IRS to recover the taxes ahead of administrative expenses, stating that "the statutory policy of subordinating taxes to costs and expenses of administration would not be served by creating or enforcing trusts which eat up an estate, leaving little or nothing for creditors and court officers whose goods and services created the assets." *Id.,* at 517.

In 1978, Congress fundamentally restructured bankruptcy law by passing the new Bankruptcy Code. Among the changes Congress

---

4. The general common-law rule that a trust is not created absent a designation of particular property obviously does not invalidate § 7501's creation of a trust in the "amount" of withheld taxes. The common law of trusts is not binding on Congress.

decided to make was a modification of the rule this Court had enunciated in *Randall* under the old Bankruptcy Act. The Senate bill attacked *Randall* directly, providing in § 541 that trust-fund taxes withheld or collected prior to the filing of the bankruptcy petition were not "property of the estate." See S.Rep. No. 95–1106, p. 33 (1978). See also *ibid.* ("These amounts will not be property of the estate regardless of whether such amounts have been segregated from other assets of the debtor by way of a special account, fund, or otherwise, or are deemed to be a special fund in trust pursuant to provisions of applicable tax law") (footnote omitted). The House bill did not deal explicitly with the problem of trust-fund taxes, but the House Report stated that "property of the estate" would not include property held in trust for another. See H.R.Rep. No. 95–595, p. 368 (1977). Congress was unable to hold a conference, so the Senate and House floor managers met to reach compromises on the differences between the two bills. See 124 Cong. Rec. 32392 (1978) (remarks of Rep. Edwards); Klee, Legislative History of the New Bankruptcy Law, 28 DePaul L.Rev. 941, 953–954 (1979). The compromise reached with respect to the relevant portion of § 541, which applies to postpetition transfers, was embodied in the eventually-enacted House amendment and explicitly provided that "in the case of property held in trust, the property of the estate includes the legal title, but not the beneficial interest in the property." 124 Cong.Rec., at 32417 (remarks of Rep. Edwards). Compare *id.*, at 32363 (text of House amendment). Accordingly, the Senate language specifying that withheld or collected trust-fund taxes are not part of the bankruptcy estate was deleted as "unnecessary since property of the estate does not include the beneficial interest in property held by the debtor as a trustee. Under [§ 7051], the amounts of withheld taxes are held to be a special fund in trust for the United States." *Id.*, at 32417 (remarks of Rep. Edwards).[5]

Representative Edwards discussed the effects of the House language on the rule established by *Randall*, indicating that the House amendment would supplant that rule:

> "[A] serious problem exists where 'trust fund taxes' withheld from others are held to be property of the estate where the withheld amounts are commingled with other assets of the debtor. The courts should permit the use of reasonable assumptions under which the Internal Revenue Service, and other tax authorities, can demonstrate that amounts of withheld taxes are still in the possession of the debtor at the commencement of the case." *Ibid.*

The context of Representative Edwards' comment makes plain that he was discussing whether a *post*petition payment of trust-fund taxes

---

5. Because of the absence of a conference and the key roles played by Representative Edwards and his counterpart floor manager Senator DeConcini, we have treated their floor statements on the Bankruptcy Reform Act of 1978 as persuasive evidence of congressional intent. See, *e.g., CFTC v. Weintraub,* 471 U.S. 343, 351 (1985). Cf. 124 Cong.Rec. 32391 (1978) (remarks of Rep. Rousselot) (expressing view that remarks of floor manager of the Act have "the effect of being a conference report").

involved "property of the estate." This focus is not surprising given that *Randall*, the case Congress was addressing, involved a postpetition demand for payment by the IRS. But Representative Edwards' discussion also applies to the question whether a *pre*petition payment is made from "property of the debtor." We have explained that "property of the debtor" is that property that would have been part of the estate had it not been transferred before the commencement of bankruptcy proceedings. *Supra*, at 4–5. The same "reasonable assumptions" therefore apply in both contexts.

The strict rule of *Randall* thus did not survive the adoption of the new Bankruptcy Code. But by requiring the IRS to "demonstrate that amounts of withheld taxes are still in the possession of the debtor at the commencement of the case [*i.e.*, at the filing of the petition]," 124 Cong.Rec., at 32417 (remarks of Rep. Edwards), Congress expected that the IRS would have to show *some* connection between the § 7501 trust and the assets sought to be applied to a debtor's trust-fund tax obligations. See *United States v. Whiting Pools, Inc.*, 462 U.S. 198, 205, n. 10 (1983) (IRS cannot exclude funds from the estate if it cannot trace them to § 7501 trust property). The question in this case is how extensive the required nexus must be. The Bankruptcy Code provides no explicit answer, and Representative Edwards' admonition that courts should "permit the use of reasonable assumptions" does not add much. The House Report does, however, give sufficient guidance regarding those assumptions to permit us to conclude that the nexus requirement is satisfied here. That Report states:

> "A payment of withholding taxes constitutes a payment of money held in trust under Internal Revenue Code § 7501(a), and thus will not be a preference because the beneficiary of the trust, the taxing authority, is in a separate class with respect to those taxes, if they have been properly held for payment, as they will have been if the debtor is able to make the payments." H.R.Rep. No. 95–595, *supra*, at 373.[6]

Under a literal reading of the above passage, the bankruptcy trustee could not avoid *any* voluntary prepetition payment of trust-fund taxes, regardless of the source of the funds. As the House Report expressly states, the limitation that the funds must "have been properly held for payment" is satisfied "if the debtor is able to make the payments." The debtor's act of voluntarily paying its trust-fund tax obligation therefore is alone sufficient to establish the required nexus between the "amount" held in trust and the funds paid.

We adopt this literal reading. In the absence of any suggestion in the Bankruptcy Code about what tracing rules to apply, we are rele-

---

6. Petitioner's claim that this legislative history is irrelevant because the House Bill was not enacted is in error. The exact language to which the quoted portion of the House Report refers was enacted into law. Compare § 547(b) with H.R. 8200, 95th Cong., 1st Sess., § 547(b) (1977). The version of § 541 that was eventually enacted *is* different than the original House bill, but only in that it makes explicit rather than implicit that "property of the estate" does not include the beneficiary's equitable interest in property held in trust by the debtor. Compare § 541(d) with H.R. 8200, *supra*, § 541(a)(1).

gated to the legislative history. The courts are directed to apply "reasonable assumptions" to govern the tracing of funds, and the House Report identifies one such assumption to be that any voluntary prepetition payment of trust-fund taxes out of the debtor's assets is not a transfer of the debtor's property. Nothing in the Bankruptcy Code or its legislative history casts doubt on the reasonableness of that assumption. Other rules might be reasonable, too, but the only evidence we have suggests that Congress preferred this one. We see no reason to disregard that evidence.

III

We hold that AIA's payments of trust-fund taxes to the IRS from its general accounts were not transfers of "property of the debtor," but were instead transfers of property held in trust for the Government pursuant to § 7501. Such payments therefore cannot be avoided as preferences. The judgment of the Court of Appeals is *affirmed.*

JUSTICE SCALIA, concurring in the judgment.

Representative Edwards, the House floor manager for the bill that enacted the Bankruptcy Code, said on the floor that "[t]he courts should permit the use of reasonable assumptions" regarding the tracing of tax trust funds. 124 Cong.Rec. 32417 (1978). We do not know that anyone except the presiding officer was present to hear Representative Edwards. Indeed, we do not know for sure that Representative Edwards' words were even uttered on the floor rather than inserted into the Congressional Record afterwards. If Representative Edwards did speak these words, and if there were others present, they must have been surprised to hear him talking about the tracing of 26 U.S.C. § 7501 tax trust funds, inasmuch as the bill under consideration did not relate to the Internal Revenue Code but the Bankruptcy Code, and contained no provision even mentioning trust-fund taxes. Only the Senate bill, and not the House proposal, had mentioned trust-fund taxes—and even the former had said nothing whatever about the *tracing* of tax trust funds. See S. 2266, 95th Cong., 2d Sess., § 541 (1978). Only the Senate *Committee Report* on the *unenacted* provision of the Senate bill had discussed that subject. See S.Rep. No. 95–1106, p. 33 (1978).

Nonetheless, on the basis of Representative Edwards' statement today's opinion concludes that "[t]he courts are *directed* " (presumably it means directed by the entire Congress, and not just Representative Edwards) "to apply 'reasonable assumptions' to govern the tracing of funds." *Ante,* at 12 (emphasis added). I do not agree. Congress conveys its directions in the Statutes at Large, not in excerpts from the Congressional Record, much less in excerpts from the Congressional Record that do not clarify the text of any pending legislative proposal.

Even in the absence of direction to do so, however, I certainly think we should apply reasonable assumptions to govern the tracing of funds. Unfortunately, that still does not answer the question before us here. One "traces" a fund only after one identifies the fund in the first place.

The problem here is not "following the res" of the tax trust, but identifying the res to begin with. Seeking to come to grips with this point, the Court once again resorts to legislative history, this time even farther afield. It relies upon the House Report on what later became 11 U.S.C. § 547, which says:

> "A payment of withholding taxes constitutes a payment of money held in trust under Internal Revenue Code § 7501(a), and thus will not be a preference because the beneficiary of the trust, the taxing authority, is in a separate class with respect to those taxes, if they have been properly held for payment, as they will have been if the debtor is able to make the payments." H.R.Rep. No. 95–595, p. 373 (1977).

The Court decides this case by "adopting" "a literal reading" of the above language. *Ante*, at 12. I think it both demeaning and unproductive for us to ponder whether to adopt literal or not-so-literal readings of Committee Reports, as though they were controlling statutory text. Moreover, even applying the lax legislative-history standards of recent years, this Committee Report should not be considered relevant. If a welfare bill conditioned benefits upon a certain maximum level of "income," courts might well (regrettably) regard as authoritative the Committee Report's statement that "income" means "income as computed under the Internal Revenue Code"; but surely they would not regard as authoritative its statement that a particular class of receipt *constitutes* income under the Internal Revenue Code. Authoritativeness on the latter sort of point is what the Court accepts here. The proposed (and ultimately enacted) provision of law to which this Committee Report pertained was the general provision of the Bankruptcy Code setting forth the five conditions for a voidable preference, reading in part as follows:

> "Except as provided in subsection (c) of this section, the trustee may avoid any transfer of property of the debtor—
>
> "(1) to or for the benefit of a creditor;
>
> "(2) for or on account of an antecedent debt owed by the debtor before such transfer was made;
>
> "(3) made while the debtor was insolvent;
>
> "(4) made * * * on or within 90 days before the date of the filing of the petition * * *; and
>
> "(5) that enables such creditor to receive more than such creditor would receive [under a chapter 7 bankruptcy distribution]." H.R. 8200, 95th Cong., 2d Sess., § 547(b) (1977); see 11 U.S.C. § 547(b).

The Committee Report's discussion of withholding taxes paid during the preference period presumably clarifies the meaning of the phrase "property of the debtor" in this text. If that is authoritative concerning the construction and effect of § 7501, imagine what other laws concerning "property of the debtor" could also have been enacted through discussion in this Committee Report. The matter seems to me plainly too far beyond the immediate focus of the legislation to be deemed resolved by the accompanying Committee Report. It was certainly thoughtful of whoever drafted the report to try to clear up the issue of what kind of an estate, legal or equitable, the debtor possesses in trust-fund taxes that are paid, but that discussion is a kind of legislative-history "rider" that even the most ardent devotees of legislative history should ignore.

If the Court had applied to the text of the statute the standard tools of legal reasoning, instead of scouring the legislative history for some scrap that is on point (and therefore *ipso facto* relevant, no matter how unlikely a source of congressional reliance or attention), it would have reached the same result it does today, as follows: Section 7501 obviously intends to give the United States the advantages of a trust beneficiary with respect to collected and withheld taxes. Unfortunately, it does not always succeed in doing so. A trust without a res can no more be created by legislative decree than can a pink rock-candy mountain. In the nature of things no trust exists until a res is identified. Ordinarily the res is identified by the settlor of the trust; in the case of § 7501 it is initially identified (if at all) by the statute, subject (as I shall discuss) to later reidentification by the taxpayer. Where the taxes subject to the trust-fund provision of § 7501 are *collected* taxes, the statute plainly identifies the res: it is the collections. There may be difficulty in tracing them, but there is no doubt that they exist. Where, however, the taxes subject to the trust-fund provision are *withheld* taxes, the statute provides no clear identification. When I pay a worker $90 there is no clearly identifiable locus of the $10 in withheld taxes that I do *not* pay him. Indeed, if my total assets at the time of the payment are $90 there is no conceivable locus.

We may have to grapple at some later date with the question whether the lack of immediate identification means that no trust arises, or rather that § 7501 creates some hitherto unheard-of floating trust in an unidentified portion of the taxpayer's current or later-acquired assets. We do not have to reach that question today, because even though identification was not made by the statute immediately, it *was* made by the taxpayer when it wrote a check upon a portion of a designated fund to the Government. (It is clear from the statutory scheme that the taxpayer has the power to identify which portion of its assets constitutes the trust fund; indeed, 26 U.S.C. § 7512 permits the government to compel such identification where it has not been made.) Even if no trust existed before that check was written, it is clear that a trust existed then. See 1 W. Fratcher, Scott on Trusts § 26.5 (4th ed. 1987) (promise to create trust becomes effective when settlor transfers or otherwise designates res as trust property).

The designation here, however, occurred within the 90-day preference period. Ordinarily, the debtor's alienation of his equitable interest by declaring a trust would constitute a preference. It seems to me, however, that one must at least give this effect to § 7501's clearly expressed but sometimes ineffectual intent to create an *immediate* trust: if and when the trust res is identified from otherwise unencumbered assets, the trust should be deemed to have been in existence from the time of the collection or withholding. Thus, the designation of res does not constitute a preference, and the funds paid were not part of the debtor's estate.

For these reasons, I concur in the judgment of the Court.

UNITED STATES v. ENERGY RESOURCES CO.
Supreme Court of the United States, 1990.
__ U.S. __, 110 S.Ct. 2139, 109 L.Ed.2d 580.

JUSTICE WHITE delivered the opinion of the Court.

In this case, we decide that a bankruptcy court has the authority to order the Internal Revenue Service (IRS) to treat tax payments made by Chapter 11 debtor corporations as trust fund payments where the bankruptcy court determines that this designation is necessary for the success of a reorganization plan.

I

The Internal Revenue Code requires employers to withhold from their employees' paychecks money representing employees' personal income taxes, and social security taxes. 26 U.S.C. §§ 3012(a), 3402(a). Because federal law requires employers to hold these funds in "trust for the United States," 26 U.S.C. § 7501(a), these taxes are commonly referred to as "trust fund" taxes. *Slodov v. United States*, 436 U.S. 238, 242–243 (1978). Should employers fail to pay trust fund taxes, the Government may collect an equivalent sum directly from the officers or employees of the employer who are responsible for collecting the tax. 26 U.S.C. § 6672. These individuals are commonly referred to as "responsible" individuals. *Slodov, supra*, at 244–245.

This case involves corporations that have filed petitions for reorganization under Chapter 11 of the Bankruptcy Code, 11 U.S.C. §§ 1101–1174. Newport Offshore, Ltd., filed a petition for reorganization on November 13, 1985; the Bankruptcy Court approved a reorganization plan in June 1986, creating Newport Oil Offshore, Inc. Over the IRS's objection, that plan included a provision stating that the reorganized Newport Offshore would pay its tax debts (totaling about $300,000) over a period of about six years and that the payments would be applied to extinguish all trust fund tax debts "'prior to the commencement of payment of the non-trust fund portion'" of the tax debts owed. *In re Energy Resources Co., Inc.*, 871 F.2d 223, 226 (CA1 1989). The IRS appealed to the United States District Court for the District of Rhode Island, which reversed in an unpublished opinion. The debtor then sought review in the Court of Appeals for the First Circuit.

Energy Resources Co., Inc., petitioned for reorganization under Chapter 11 in January 1983. In September 1984, the Bankruptcy Court confirmed a reorganization plan that created a special trust which, among other things, was to pay Energy Resources' federal tax debt of approximately $1,000,000 over roughly five years. In November

1985, the trustee of the special trust sent approximately $358,000 in payment to the IRS. The trustee asked the IRS to apply the money to Energy Resources' trust fund tax debt. After the IRS refused to do so, the trustee successfully petitioned the Bankruptcy Court to order the IRS to apply the money to the trust fund tax liabilities. *Id.*, at 226–227. The IRS appealed this order to the United States District Court for the District of Massachusetts which affirmed the Bankruptcy Court in an oral opinion. The Government then appealed to the First Circuit.

Consolidating the two cases, the First Circuit reversed in *In re Newport Offshore Ltd.* and affirmed in *In re Energy Resources Co. Id.*, at 234. The court first considered whether a tax payment made pursuant to a Chapter 11 reorganization plan is "voluntary" or "involuntary" as those terms are used in the IRS's own rules. IRS policy permits taxpayers who "voluntarily" submit payments to the IRS to designate the tax liability to which the payment will apply. See *id.*, at 227, citing Rev.Rul. 79–284, 1979–2 Cum.Bull. 83, modifying Rev.Rul. 73–305, 1973–2 Cum.Bull. 43, superseding Rev.Rul. 58–239, 1958–1 Cum.Bull. 94. The taxpayer corporations argued that tax payments within a Chapter 11 reorganization are best characterized as "voluntary" and therefore that the IRS's own rules bind the agency to respect the debtors' designation of the tax payments. Granting deference to the agency's interpretation of its own rules, the First Circuit accepted the IRS's view that payments made pursuant to the Chapter 11 plan are involuntary for purposes of the IRS's rules. 871 F.2d, at 230. The First Circuit concluded, however, that even if the payments were properly characterized as involuntary under the IRS's regulations, the Bankruptcy Court nevertheless had the authority to order the IRS to apply an "involuntary" payment made by a Chapter 11 debtor to trust fund tax liabilities if the Bankruptcy Court concluded that this designation was necessary to ensure the success of the reorganization. *Id.*, at 230–234.

We granted certiorari because the First Circuit's conclusion on this issue conflicts with decisions in other circuits. 493 U.S. ___; see *e.g.*, *In re Ribs–R–Us, Inc.*, 828 F.2d 199 (CA3 1987). We affirm the judgment below, for whether or not the payments at issue are rightfully considered to be involuntary, the bankruptcy court has the authority to order the IRS to apply the payments to trust fund liabilities if the bankruptcy court determines that this designation is necessary to the success of a reorganization plan.

II

The Bankruptcy Code does not explicitly authorize the bankruptcy courts to approve reorganization plans designating tax payments as either trust fund or nontrust fund. The Code, however, grants the bankruptcy courts residual authority to approve reorganization plans including "any * * * appropriate provision not inconsistent with the applicable provisions of this title." 11 U.S.C. § 1123(b)(5); see also § 1129. The Code also states that bankruptcy courts may "issue any order, process, or judgment that is necessary or appropriate to carry out the provisions" of the Act. § 105. These statutory directives are consistent with the traditional understanding that bankruptcy courts, as courts of equity, have broad authority to modify creditor-debtor relationships. See *Pepper v. Litton,* 308 U.S. 295, 303–304 (1939); *United States National Bank v. Chase National Bank,* 331 U.S. 28, 36 (1947); *Katchen v. Landy,* 382 U.S. 323, 327 (1966).

The Government suggests that, in this case, the Bankruptcy Court has transgressed one of the limitations on its equitable power. Specifically, the Government contends that the orders conflict with the Code's provisions protecting the Government's ability to collect delinquent taxes. As the Government points out, the Code provides a priority for specified tax claims, including those at issue in this case, and makes those tax debts nondischargeable. See 11 U.S.C. §§ 507(a)(7), 523(a)(1)(A). The Code, moreover, requires the bankruptcy court to assure itself that reorganization will succeed, § 1129(a)(11), and therefore that the IRS, in all likelihood, will collect the tax debt owed. The tax debt must be paid off within six years. § 1129(a)(9)(C).

It is evident that these restrictions on the bankruptcy court's authority do not preclude the court from issuing orders of the type at issue here, for those restrictions do not address the bankruptcy court's ability to designate whether tax payments are to be applied to trust fund or nontrust fund tax liabilities. The Government is correct that, if it can apply a debtor corporation's tax payments to nontrust fund liability before trust fund liability, it stands a better chance of debt discharge because the debt that is not guaranteed will be paid off before the guaranteed debt. While this result might be desirable from the Government's standpoint, it is an added protection not specified in the Code itself: whereas the Code gives it the right to be assured that its taxes will be paid in six years, the Government wants an assurance that its taxes will be paid even if the reorganization fails—*i.e.,* even if the bankruptcy court is incorrect in its judgment that the reorganization plan will succeed.

Even if consistent with the Code, however, a bankruptcy court order might be inappropriate if it conflicted with another law that should have been taken into consideration in the exercise of the court's discretion. The Government maintains that the orders at issue here contravene § 6672 of the Internal Revenue Code, the provision permitting the IRS to collect unpaid trust fund taxes directly from the personal assets of "responsible" individuals. The Government contends that § 6672 reflects a congressional decision to protect the Government's tax revenues by ensuring an additional source from which trust fund taxes might be collected. It is true that § 6672 provides that, if the Government is unable to collect trust fund taxes from a corporate taxpayer, the Government has an alternative source for this revenue. Here, however, the Bankruptcy Courts' orders do not prevent the Government from collecting trust fund revenue; to the contrary, the orders require the Government to collect trust fund payments before collecting nontrust fund payments. As the Government concedes, § 6672 remains both during and after the corporate Chapter 11 filing as an alternative collection source for trust fund taxes.

The Government nevertheless contends that the Bankruptcy Court's orders contravene § 6672 because, if the IRS cannot designate a debtor corporation's tax payments as nontrust fund, the debtor might be able to pay only the guaranteed debt, leaving the Government at risk for nontrust fund taxes. This may be the case, but § 6672, by its terms, does not protect against this eventuality. That section plainly does not require us to hold that the orders at issue here, otherwise wholly consistent with the bankruptcy court's authority under the Bankruptcy Code, were nonetheless improvident.

III

In this case, the Bankruptcy Court has not transgressed any limitation on its broad power. We therefore hold that it may order the IRS to apply tax payments to offset trust fund obligations where it concludes that this action is necessary for a reorganization's success. The judgment of the Court of Appeals is therefore *affirmed.*

JUSTICE BLACKMUN dissents.

Appendix A

POWER OF ATTORNEY (FORM 2848) AND TAX INFORMATION AUTHORIZATION (FORM 8821)

App. A   TAX INFORMATION AUTHORIZATION   **887**

Form **2848** (Rev. March 1991) Department of the Treasury Internal Revenue Service	**Power of Attorney and Declaration of Representative** ▶ For Paperwork Reduction and Privacy Act Notice, see the instructions.	OMB No 1545-0150 Expires 5-31-93

Part I   Power of Attorney

1 Taxpayer Information

Taxpayer name(s) and address (**Please type or print.**)	Social security number(s)	Employer identification number
	Daytime telephone number ( )	Plan number (if applicable)

hereby appoint(s) the following representative(s) as attorney(s)-in-fact:

2 Representative(s) (Please type or print.)

Name and address	CAF No. .... Telephone No. ( ) .... Fax No. ( ) .... Check if new: Address ... ☐ Telephone No. ☐
Name and address	CAF No. .... Telephone No. ( ) .... Fax No. ( ) .... Check if new: Address ... ☐ Telephone No. ☐
Name and address	CAF No. .... Telephone No. ( ) .... Fax No. ( ) .... Check if new: Address ... ☐ Telephone No. ☐

to represent the taxpayer(s) before the Internal Revenue Service for the following tax matters:

3 Tax Matters

Type of Tax (Income, Employment, Excise, etc.)	Tax Form Number (1040, 941, 720, etc.)	Year(s) or Period(s)

4 Specific Use Not Recorded on Centralized Authorization File (CAF).—If the power of attorney is for a specific use not recorded on CAF, please check this box. (See the instructions for *Specific Use Not Recorded on CAF* on page 4.) . . . . ▶ ☐

5 Acts Authorized.—The representatives are authorized to receive and inspect confidential tax information and to perform any and all acts that I can perform with respect to the tax matters described in line 3, for example, the authority to sign any agreements, consents, or other documents. The authority does not include the power to receive refund checks or the power to sign certain returns. (See instructions.)
List any specific additions or deletions to the acts otherwise authorized in this power of attorney: ....
....
....

Note: *In general, an unenrolled preparer of tax returns cannot sign any document for a taxpayer. See Revenue Procedure 81-38, printed as Pub. 470, for more information.*

Note: *The tax matters partner/person of a partnership or S corporation is not permitted to authorize representatives to perform certain acts. See the instructions for more information.*

6 Receipt of Refund Checks.—If you want to authorize a representative named in line 2 to receive, **BUT NOT TO ENDORSE OR CASH,** refund checks, initial here _____ and list the name of that representative below.

Name of representative to receive refund check(s) ▶

Cat. No. 11980J   Form **2848** (Rev. 3-91) [G5399]

POWER OF ATTORNEY

Form 2848 (Rev. 3-91)   Page **2**

7 Notices and Communications.—Notices and other written communications will be sent to the first representative listed in line 2.
   a If you want the second representative listed to receive such notices and communications, check this box . . . . ▶ ☐
   b If you do not want any notices or communications sent to your representative, check this box . . . . ▶ ☐

8 Retention/Revocation of Prior Power(s) of Attorney.—The filing of this power of attorney automatically revokes all earlier power(s) of attorney on file with the Internal Revenue Service for the **same** tax matters and years or periods covered by this document. If you do not want to revoke a prior power of attorney, check here . . . . ▶ ☐
   YOU MUST ATTACH A COPY OF ANY POWER OF ATTORNEY YOU WANT TO REMAIN IN EFFECT.

9 Signature of Taxpayer(s).—If a tax matter concerns a joint return, **both** husband and wife must sign if joint representation is requested, otherwise, see the instructions. If signed by a corporate officer, partner, guardian, tax matters partner/person, executor, receiver, administrator, or trustee on behalf of the taxpayer, I certify that I have the authority to execute this form on behalf of the taxpayer.
   ▶ **If this power of attorney is not signed, it will be returned.**

Signature	Date	Title (if applicable)
Print Name		
Signature	Date	Title (if applicable)
Print Name		

Part II Declaration of Representative

Under penalties of perjury, I declare that:
- I am not currently under suspension or disbarment from practice before the Internal Revenue Service;
- I am aware of regulations contained in Treasury Department Circular No. 230 (31 CFR, Part 10), as amended, concerning the practice of attorneys, certified public accountants, enrolled agents, enrolled actuaries, and others;
- I am authorized to represent the taxpayer(s) identified in Part I for the tax matter(s) specified there; and
- I am one of the following:
   a Attorney—a member in good standing of the bar of the highest court of the jurisdiction shown below.
   b Certified Public Accountant—duly qualified to practice as a certified public accountant in the jurisdiction shown below.
   c Enrolled Agent—enrolled as an agent under the requirements of Treasury Department Circular No. 230.
   d Officer—a bona fide officer of the taxpayer organization.
   e Full-Time Employee—a full-time employee of the taxpayer.
   f Family Member—a member of the taxpayer's immediate family (*i.e.*, spouse, parent, child, brother, or sister).
   g Enrolled Actuary—enrolled as an actuary by the Joint Board for the Enrollment of Actuaries under 29 U.S.C. 1242 (the authority to practice before the Service is limited by section 10.3(d)(1) of Treasury Department Circular No. 230).
   h Unenrolled Return Preparer—an unenrolled return preparer under section 10.7(a)(7) of Treasury Department Circular No. 230.

▶ **If this power of attorney is not signed, it will be returned.**

Designation —Insert above letter (a–h)	Jurisdiction (state) or Enrollment Card No.	Signature	Date

[G5400]

App. A — TAX INFORMATION AUTHORIZATION

Form 2848 (Rev. 3-91) — Page 3

Paperwork Reduction and Privacy Act Notice.—We ask for the information on this form to carry out the Internal Revenue laws of the United States. Form 2848 is provided by the IRS for your convenience and its use is voluntary. If you choose to designate a representative to act on your behalf, under section 6109 you must disclose your social security number or your employer identification number. The principal purpose of this disclosure is to secure proper identification of the taxpayer. We also need this information to gain access to your tax information in our files and properly respond to your request. If you do not disclose this information, the IRS may suspend processing the power of attorney and may not be able to fill your request until you provide the number.

The time needed to complete and file this form will vary depending on individual circumstances. The estimated average time is: **Recordkeeping,** 20 minutes; **Learning about the law or the form,** 29 minutes; **Preparing the form,** 29 minutes; **Copying, assembling, and sending the form to IRS,** 35 minutes.

If you have comments concerning the accuracy of these time estimates or suggestions for making this form more simple, we would be happy to hear from you. You can write to both the **Internal Revenue Service,** Washington, DC 20224, Attention: IRS Reports Clearance Officer, T:FP; and the **Office of Management and Budget,** Paperwork Reduction Project (1545-0150), Washington, DC 20503. DO NOT send this tax form to either of these offices. Instead, see the instructions below for information on where to file.

Changes You Should Note.—Form 2848, Power of Attorney and Declaration of Representative, and **Form 2848-D,** Tax Information Authorization and Declaration of Representative, have been combined into one form, Form 2848. Form 2848-D is now obsolete and should no longer be used. Unenrolled return preparers may now use Form 2848; however, their practice before the IRS is limited. See the instructions for line 5 below. New **Form 8821,** Tax Information Authorization, should be used instead of Form 2848 to allow only disclosure of tax information to a third party.

General Instructions

(Section references are to the Internal Revenue Code unless otherwise noted.)

Purpose of Form.—Form 2848 may be used to grant authority to an individual to represent you before the IRS and to receive tax information. You may file this form ONLY if you want to name a person(s) to represent you and that person is a "person recognized to practice before the Service." Persons recognized to practice before the Service are listed in Part II, Declaration of Representative, items **a-h.** Any person who is not listed in **a-h** of Part II is not authorized to practice before the IRS under the provisions of Treasury Department Circular No. 230 and therefore cannot act as your representative. However, you can use Form 8821 to authorize any person (or an organization) to receive and inspect confidential tax return information under the provisions of section 6103. For additional information about this or any other matter concerning practice before the IRS, please see **Pub. 216,** Conference and Practice Requirements.

Fiduciaries.—A fiduciary (trustee, executor, administrator, receiver, or guardian) stands in the position of a taxpayer and acts as the taxpayer. Therefore, a fiduciary does not act as a representative and should not file a power of attorney to act as a representative. **Form 56,** Notice Concerning Fiduciary Relationship, should be filed to notify the IRS of the existence of a fiduciary relationship. If a fiduciary wishes to authorize an individual to represent or perform certain acts on behalf of the entity, a power of attorney must be filed and signed by the fiduciary acting in the position of the taxpayer.

Authority Granted.—This power of attorney authorizes the individual(s) named to perform any and all acts you can perform, such as signing consents extending the time to assess tax, recording the interview, or executing waivers agreeing to a tax adjustment. Delegating authority or substituting another representative must be specifically stated on line 5. However, the authority granted to an unenrolled preparer may not exceed that allowed under Revenue Procedure 81-38. See **Pub. 470,** Limited Practice Without Enrollment.

The power to sign tax returns can only be granted in limited situations. See Regulations section 1.6012-1(a)(5). The power to receive refund checks must be specified separately on line 6 of the form. Additions or deletions to the authority to perform any acts must be indicated on line 5 of the form.

Filing the Power of Attorney.—File the original, photocopy, or facsimile transmission (fax) of the power of attorney with each IRS office with which you deal. If you choose to file a power of attorney by fax, you must first be sure that the appropriate IRS office is equipped to accept fax transmissions. If the power of attorney is filed for a matter currently pending before an office of the IRS, such as an examination, file the power of attorney with that office. Otherwise, file it with the service center where the related return was, or will be, filed. Refer to the instructions for the related tax return for the service center addresses.

Line-by-Line Instructions

Part I—Power of Attorney

Line 1—Taxpayer Information.—

Individuals.—Enter your name, social security number (and/or employer identification number, if applicable), and street address in the space provided. If a joint return is used, and you and your spouse are designating the same representative(s), also enter your spouse's name and social security number, and your spouse's address if different from yours.

Corporations, partnerships, or associations.—Enter the name, employer identification number, and business address. If this form is being prepared for corporations filing a consolidated tax return (Form 1120), do not attach a list of subsidiaries to this form. Only the parent corporation information is required in line 1. Also, line 3 should only list Form 1120 in the Tax Form Number column. A subsidiary must file its own Form 2848 for returns that are required to be filed separately from the consolidated return, such as **Form 720,** Quarterly Federal Excise Tax Return, and **Form 941,** Employer's Quarterly Federal Tax Return.

Employee plan.—Enter the plan name, employer identification number of the plan sponsor, three-digit plan number, and business address of the plan sponsor.

Trust.—Enter the name, title, and address of the trustee, and the name and employer identification number of the trust.

Estate.—Enter the name, title, and address of the decedent's executor/personal representative, and the name and identification number of the estate. The identification number for an estate includes both the employer identification number, if the estate has one, and the decedent's social security number.

Line 2—Representative(s).—Enter the name of your representative(s). Only individuals may be named as representatives. Please use the identical name on all submissions. If you want to name more than three representatives, indicate so on this line and attach a list of additional representatives to the form.

Enter the nine-digit Centralized Authorization File (CAF) number for each representative. If a CAF number has not been assigned, enter "None," and IRS will issue one directly to your representative. The CAF number is a unique nine-digit identification number (not the social security number, employer identification number, or enrollment card number) that the IRS assigns to representatives. The CAF number is not an indication of authority to practice. The representative should use the assigned CAF number on all future powers of attorney. CAF numbers will not be assigned for employee plans and exempt organizations application requests (EP/EO).

Check the appropriate box to indicate if either the address or telephone number is new since a CAF number was assigned. Enter your representative's fax telephone number, if available.

If the representative is a former employee of the Federal Government, he or she must be aware of the post-employment restrictions contained in 18 U.S.C., section 207 and in Treasury Department Circular No. 230, section 10.26. Criminal penalties are provided for violation of the statutory restrictions, and the Director of Practice is authorized to take disciplinary action against the practitioner.

Line 3—Tax Matters.—Enter the type of tax, the tax form number, and the year(s) or period(s) (not to exceed 5 years). For example, you may list "Income tax, Form 1040" for calendar year "1990" and "Excise tax, Form 720" for the "1st, 2nd, 3rd, and 4th quarters of 1990." A general reference to "All years," "All periods," or "All taxes" is not acceptable. Any power of attorney with such general reference will be

[G6754]

returned. You may list any tax years or periods that have already ended as of the date you sign the power of attorney. However, the number of future tax periods is limited to returns with due dates within 3 years of your signature on Form 2848. If the matter relates to estate tax, enter the date of the taxpayer's death instead of the year or period. If the type of tax, tax form number, or years or periods does not apply to the matter (i.e., representation for a penalty or filing a ruling request or determination), specifically describe on this line the matter to which the power of attorney pertains and enter "Not Applicable" in the appropriate column(s).

Line 4—Specific Uses Not Recorded on CAF.—Generally, IRS records all powers of attorney on the CAF system. However, a power of attorney will not be recorded on CAF if it does not relate to a specific tax period or it is for a specific issue. Examples of specific issues include but are not limited to the following: (1) civil penalty issues, (2) 100% penalty, (3) request for a private letter ruling, (4) application for an employer identification number, (5) claims filed on **Form 843**, Claim for Refund and Request for Abatement, (6) corporate dissolutions, (7) a request to change accounting methods, and (8) a request to change accounting periods. Check the specific use box on line 4 if the power of attorney is for a use that will not be listed on CAF. If the box on line 4 is checked, the representative should bring a copy of the power of attorney to each meeting with IRS. A specific use power of attorney will not automatically revoke any prior powers of attorney.

Line 5—Acts Authorized.—If you want to modify the acts that your named representative(s) can perform, you should describe any specific additions or deletions in the space provided. The authority to substitute another representative or delegate authority must be specifically stated on line 5.

If you want to authorize your representative to sign an income tax return, this authorization must be specifically listed and the requirements of Regulations section 1.6012-1(a)(5) must be satisfied. In general, this regulation only permits a representative to sign your return if you are unable to make the return by reason of: **(a)** disease or injury, **(b)** continuous absence from the U.S. (including Puerto Rico) for a period of at least 60 days prior to the date required by law for filing the return, or **(c)** specific permission is requested of and granted by the district director for other good cause.

If any representative you name is an unenrolled return preparer, the acts that person can perform on your behalf are limited by Revenue Procedure 81-38 (Pub. 470). In general, an unenrolled return preparer is permitted to appear as your representative only before revenue agents and examining officers of the Examination Division and the EP/EO Division and is not permitted to represent you before other offices (i.e., Collection Division or Appeals Division) of the IRS. Also, an unenrolled return preparer is not permitted to extend the statutory period, execute waivers, delegate authority, or substitute another representative.

Tax Matters Partner/Person.—The tax matters partner/person (TMP)(as defined in sections 6231(a)(7) and 6244) is authorized to perform various acts on behalf of the partnership or S corporation. The following are examples of acts performed by the TMP that **cannot** be delegated to the representative: (1) binding nonnotice partners to a settlement agreement under section 6224 and, under certain circumstances, binding all partners or shareholders to a **settlement agreement** under Tax Court Rule 248; (2) filing a petition for readjustment of partnership or subchapter S items in the Tax Court, District Court, or Claims Court, under sections 6226 and 6244, based on the issuance of a notice of final partnership administrative adjustment or notice of final S corporation administrative adjustment by the IRS; (3) filing a request for administrative adjustment on behalf of the partnership or S corporation under sections 6227 and 6244; (4) filing a petition for adjustment of partnership items with respect to an administrative request in the Tax Court, District Court, or Claims Court, under sections 6228 and 6244; and (5) extending the statute of limitations on assessment of any tax attributable to partnership or subchapter S items (and affected items) under sections 6229 and 6244.

Line 6—Receipt of Refund Checks.—If you want to authorize your representative to receive, but not endorse, refund checks on your behalf, you must initial and enter the name of that person in the space provided. Section 10.31 of Treasury Department Circular No. 230 prohibits an attorney, CPA, or enrolled agent, any of whom is an income tax return preparer, from endorsing or otherwise negotiating a tax refund check.

Line 7—Notices and Communications.—Notices and other written communications will be sent to the first representative listed. Also, if you want the second representative listed to receive such communications, check box **(a)** on line 7. IRS will send notices only to two representatives.

However, if you do not want any notices or communications sent to your representative, you must check box **(b)** on line 7.

Line 8—Retention/Revocation of Prior Power(s) of Attorney.—If there is any existing power(s) of attorney you do not want to revoke, check the box on this line and attach a copy of the power(s) of attorney.

If you want to revoke an existing power of attorney and do not want to name a new representative, send a copy of the previously executed power of attorney to each IRS office where the power of attorney was filed. The copy of the power of attorney must have a current signature of the taxpayer under the signature already on line 9. Write "REVOKE" across the top of the form. If you do not have a copy of the power of attorney you want to revoke, send a statement to each IRS office where you filed the power of attorney. The statement of revocation must indicate that the authority of the power of attorney is revoked and must be signed by the taxpayer. Also, the name and address of each recognized representative whose authority is revoked must be listed.

★ U.S GPO 1991-0-265-313

The filing of a Form 2848 will not revoke any Form 8821 that is in effect.

Line 9—Signature of Taxpayer(s).—

Individuals.—You must sign and date the power of attorney. If a joint return is used and both husband and wife will be represented by the same individual(s), both must sign the power of attorney unless one spouse authorizes the other, in writing, to sign for both. In that case, attach a copy of the authorization. However, if a joint return is used and husband and wife will be represented by different individuals, each taxpayer must execute his or her own power of attorney on a separate Form 2848.

Corporations or associations.—An officer having authority to bind the taxpayer must sign. However, the tax matters person may sign on behalf of an S corporation.

Partnerships.—All partners must sign unless one partner is authorized to act in the name of the partnership. A partner is authorized to act in the name of the partnership if, under state law, the partner has authority to bind the partnership. A copy of such authorization must be attached. For purposes of executing Form 2848, the tax matters partner is authorized to act in the name of the partnership. For dissolved partnerships, see Regulations section 601.503(c)(6).

Other.—If the taxpayer is: (1) a dissolved corporation, (2) deceased, (3) insolvent, or (4) a person for whom or by whom a fiduciary (a trustee, guarantor, receiver, executor, or administrator) has been appointed, see Regulations section 601.503(d).

Part II—Declaration of Representative

The representative(s) you name must sign this declaration and enter the designation (i.e., items **a-h**) under which he or she is authorized to practice before the IRS. In addition, the representative(s) must list the following in the "Jurisdiction" column:

a Attorney—Enter the two-letter abbreviation for the state (e.g., "NY" for New York) in which admitted to practice.

b Certified Public Accountant— Enter the two-letter abbreviation for the state (e.g., "CA" for California) in which licensed to practice.

c Enrolled Agent—Enter the enrollment card number issued by the Director of Practice.

d Officer—Enter the title of the officer (i.e., President, Vice President, or Secretary).

e Full-Time Employee—Enter title or position (e.g., Comptroller or Accountant).

f Family Member—Enter the relationship to taxpayer (i.e., spouse, parent, child, brother, or sister).

g Enrolled Actuary—Enter the enrollment card number issued by the Joint Board for the Enrollment of Actuaries.

h Unenrolled Return Preparer— Enter the two-letter abbreviation for the state (e.g., "KY" for Kentucky) in which the return was prepared.

[G6755]

App. A TAX INFORMATION AUTHORIZATION

Form 8821
(March 1991)
Department of the Treasury
Internal Revenue Service

Tax Information Authorization

OMB No 1545-1165
Expires 5-31-93

1 Taxpayer Information

Taxpayer name(s) and address (**Please type or print.**)

Social security number(s)

Employer identification number

Daytime telephone number ( )

Plan number (if applicable)

2 Appointee (Please type or print.)

Name and address

CAF No. ....
Telephone No. ( ) ....
Fax No. ( ) ....
Check if new: Address ☐ Telephone No. ☐

is authorized to inspect and/or receive confidential tax information in any office of the Internal Revenue Service for the following tax matters:

3 Tax Matters

Type of Tax (Income, Employment, Excise, etc.)	Tax Form Number (1040, 941, 720, etc.)	Year(s) or Period(s)

4 Specific Use Not Recorded on Centralized Authorization File (CAF).—If the tax information authorization is for a specific use not recorded on CAF, please check this box. (See the instructions for **Specific Use Not Recorded on CAF** on page 2.) ▶ ☐
Do not use lines 5 and 6 if the box on line 4 is checked.

5 DISCLOSURE OF TAX INFORMATION (check only one of the following):
  a If you want tax information, notices, and other written communications sent to the appointee on an ongoing basis, check this box ▶ ☐
  b If you do not want any notices or communications sent to your appointee, check this box ▶ ☐

6 Retention/Revocation of Tax Information Authorization.—This tax information authorization automatically revokes all earlier tax information authorizations on file with the Internal Revenue Service for the **same** tax matters and years or periods covered by this document. If you do not want to revoke a prior tax information authorization, check this box ▶ ☐
  YOU MUST ATTACH A COPY OF ANY TAX INFORMATION AUTHORIZATION YOU WANT TO REMAIN IN EFFECT.

7 Signature of Taxpayer(s).—If a tax matter concerns a joint return, **either** husband or wife must sign. If signed by a corporate officer, partner, guardian, executor, receiver, administrator, trustee, or party other than the taxpayer, I certify that I have the authority to execute this form with respect to the tax matters/periods covered.

▶ If this tax information authorization is not signed, it will be returned.

....
Signature   Date   Title (if applicable)

....
Print Name

....
Signature   Date   Title (if applicable)

....
Print Name

Privacy Act and Paperwork Reduction Act Notice.—We ask for the information on this form to carry out the Internal Revenue laws of the United States. Form 8821 is provided by the IRS for your convenience and its use is voluntary. If you choose to designate an appointee to inspect and/or receive confidential information, under section 6109 you must disclose your social security number or your employer identification number. The principal purpose of this disclosure is to secure proper identification of the taxpayer. We also need this information to gain access to your tax information in our files and properly respond to your request. If you do not disclose this information, the IRS may suspend processing the tax information authorization and may not be able to fill your request until you provide the number.

The time needed to complete and file this form will vary depending on individual circumstances. The estimated average time is: **Recordkeeping,** 7 min.; **Learning about the law or the form,** 11 min.; **Preparing the form,** 22 min.; **Copying, assembling, and sending the form to IRS,** 20 min.

If you have comments concerning the accuracy of these time estimates or suggestions for making this form more simple, we would be happy to hear from you. You can write to both the **Internal Revenue Service,** Washington, DC 20224, Attention: IRS Reports Clearance Officer, T:FP; and the **Office of Management and Budget,** Paperwork Reduction Project (1545-1165), Washington, DC 20503. DO NOT send

Form **8821** (3-91)

Form 8821 (3-91)

Form 8821 to either of these offices. Instead, see the instructions below for information on where to file.

Changes You Should Note.—Form 8821 replaces **Form 2848-D**, Tax Information Authorization and Declaration of Representative. Form 2848-D should not be used. This form will no longer be accepted for Centralized Authorization File (CAF) processing. Obsolete Form 2848-D acted as an authorization for either (1) representation of a taxpayer before the Internal Revenue Service (i.e., a power of attorney), or (2) disclosure of confidential tax information (i.e., a disclosure authorization). Use of the new Form 8821 is limited to the disclosure of confidential tax information. However, if a taxpayer wants to authorize an individual to represent his or her interests before the IRS (and not just to inspect and/or receive confidential tax information), **Form 2848**, Power of Attorney and Declaration of Representative, must be used.

General Instructions

(Section references are to the Internal Revenue Code unless otherwise noted.)

Purpose of the Form.—Form 8821 authorizes any individual, corporation, firm, organization, or partnership you designate to inspect and/or receive confidential information in any office of the IRS for the type of tax and the years or periods you list on this form. You may file a tax information authorization without using Form 8821, but it must reflect all information that is required on Form 8821.

If you want an individual to have the authority to represent you and/or perform other acts on your behalf, such as the execution of waivers, consents, closing agreements, signing returns, or receiving refund checks, use Form 2848 instead of Form 8821.

Fiduciaries.— A fiduciary (trustee, executor, administrator, receiver, or guardian) stands in the position of a taxpayer and acts as the taxpayer. Therefore, a fiduciary does not act as an appointee and should not file a tax information authorization to act as an appointee. **Form 56**, Notice Concerning Fiduciary Relationship, should be filed to notify the IRS of the existence of a fiduciary relationship. If a fiduciary wishes to authorize an appointee to inspect and/or receive confidential tax information on behalf of the entity, a tax information authorization must be filed and signed by the fiduciary acting in the position of the taxpayer.

Partnership/Subchapter S Items.— Sections 6221-6231 and 6241-6245 authorize a Tax Matters Partner or Tax Matters Person to perform certain acts on behalf of an affected partnership or S corporation. Rules governing the use of Form 8821 do not supersede any provisions of the above referenced sections.

Filing the Tax Information Authorization.— File the original, photocopy, or facsimile transmission (fax) of the tax information authorization with each IRS office in which you want your appointee to inspect and/or receive confidential tax information on your behalf. If you choose to file a tax information authorization by fax, you must first be sure that the appropriate IRS office is equipped to accept fax transmissions. If the tax information authorization is filed for a matter currently pending before an office of the IRS, such as an examination, file the tax information authorization with that office. Otherwise, file the tax information authorization with the service center where

the related return was, or will be, filed. Refer to the instructions for the related tax return for the service center addresses. Form 8821 must be received by the IRS within 60 days of the date it was signed and dated by the taxpayer.

Line-by-Line Instructions

Line 1—Taxpayer Information.—

Individuals.—Enter your name, social security number (and/or employer identification number, if applicable), and street address in the space provided. If a joint return is used, enter your spouse's name and social security number also.

Corporations, partnerships, or associations.—Enter the name, employer identification number, and business address.

Employee plan.—Enter the plan name, employer identification number of the plan sponsor, three-digit plan number, and business address of the plan sponsor.

Trust.—Enter the name, title, and address of the trustee, and the name and employer identification number of the trust.

Estate.—Enter the name, title, and address of the decedent's executor/personal representative, and the name and identification number of the estate. The identification number for an estate includes both the employer identification number, if the estate has one, and the decedent's social security number.

Line 2—Appointee.—Enter the name of your appointee. Please use the identical name on all submissions. If you wish to name more than one appointee, indicate so on this line and attach a list to the form. Enter the nine-digit CAF number for each appointee. If an appointee has been issued a CAF number for any previously filed tax information authorization (Form 8821 or obsolete Form 2848-D) or power of attorney (Form 2848), that number should be used. If a CAF number has not been assigned, enter "NONE," and IRS will issue one directly to your appointee.

The CAF number is a unique nine-digit identification number (not the social security number or employer identification number) that the IRS assigns to appointees. The CAF number is not an indication of authority to practice. The appointee should use the assigned CAF number on all future tax information authorizations. CAF numbers will not be assigned for employee plans and exempt organization application requests.

Check the appropriate box to indicate if either the address or telephone number is new since the date a CAF number was originally assigned. Enter your fax telephone number, if available.

Line 3—Tax Matter(s).—Enter the type of tax, the tax form number, and the years or periods (not to exceed 5 years). For example, you may list "Income tax Form 1040" for calendar year "1990" and "Excise tax Form 720" for the "1st, 2nd, 3rd, and 4th quarters of 1990." A general reference to "All years," "All periods," or "All taxes" is not acceptable. Any tax information authorization with such general reference will be returned. You may list any tax years or periods already ended as of the date you sign the tax information authorization. However, the number of future periods is limited to returns with due dates within 3 years of your signature on Form 8821. If the matter relates to estate tax, enter the date of the taxpayer's death instead of the year or period. If either the type of tax, tax form number, or years or periods do not apply to the matter, specifically describe on this line the matter to which the tax information authorization pertains and enter "Not Applicable" in the appropriate column(s).

Line 4—Specific Use Not Recorded on CAF.—Generally, IRS records all tax information authorizations on the CAF system. However, a tax information authorization will not be recorded on CAF if it relates to a specific issue. Examples of specific issues include but are not limited to: (1) requests to disclose information to loan companies or educational institutions, (2) requests to disclose information to Federal or state agency investigators for background checks, (3) civil penalty issues, (4) 100% penalty, (5) application for employer identification number, and (6) claims filed on **Form 843**, Claim for Refund and Request for Abatement. Check the specific use box on line 4 if the tax information authorization is for a use that will not be listed on CAF. If the box on line 4 is checked, the appointee should bring a copy of the tax information authorization to each meeting with IRS. A specific use tax information authorization will not automatically revoke any prior tax information authorizations.

Line 6—Retention/Revocation of Prior Tax Information Authorizations.—If there is any existing tax information authorization you do not want to revoke, check the box on this line and attach a copy of the tax information authorization.

If you want to revoke an existing tax information authorization and do not want to name a new appointee, send a copy of the previously executed tax information authorization to each IRS office where the tax information authorization was filed. The copy of the tax information authorization must have a current signature of the taxpayer under the signature already on line 7. Write "REVOKE" across the top of the form. If you do not have a copy of the tax information authorization you want to revoke, send a statement to each IRS office where you filed the tax information authorization. The statement of revocation must indicate that the authority of the tax information authorization is revoked and must be signed by the taxpayer. Also, the name and address of each recognized appointee whose authority is revoked must be listed.

The filing of a Form 8821 will not revoke any Form 2848 that is in effect.

Line 7—Signature of Taxpayer(s).—

Individuals.—You must sign and date the tax information authorization. If a joint return is used, **either** husband or wife must sign. Signatures of both husband and wife are not required.

Corporations.—Generally, Form 8821 can be signed by: (1) an officer having legal authority to bind the corporation, (2) any person designated by the board of directors or other governing body, (3) any officer or employee upon written request signed by any principal officer and attested by the secretary or other officer, and (4) any other person authorized to access information under section 6103(e). (For shareholders in S corporations not excepted and provided for under sections 6241-6245, see **Partnership/Subchapter S Items** under **General Instructions.**)

Partnerships.— Generally, Form 8821 can be signed by any person who was a member of the partnership during any part of the tax period covered by Form 8821. (For partners in partnerships provided for and defined by sections 6221-6231, see **Partnership/Subchapter S Items** under **General Instructions.**)

Other.—If the taxpayer has died, is insolvent, is a dissolved corporation, or if a trustee, guardian, executor, receiver, or administrator is acting for the taxpayer, see section 6103(e).

☆ U.S.GPO:1991-0-521-804/20516

[G6757]

Appendix B

WAIVER OF RESTRICTIONS ON ASSESSMENT AND COLLECTION OF DEFICIENCY IN TAX AND ACCEPTANCE OF OVERASSESSMENT (FORM 870), OFFER OF WAIVER OF ASSESSMENT AND COLLECTION OF DEFICIENCY IN TAX AND ACCEPTANCE OF OVERASSESSMENT (FORM 870–AD), AGREEMENT AS TO FINAL DETERMINATION OF TAX LIABILITY (FORM 866), CLOSING AGREEMENT ON FINAL DETERMINATION COVERING SPECIFIC MATTERS (FORM 906)

WAIVER OF RESTRICTIONS

[Form 870]

Form 870
(Rev. February 1986)

Department of the Treasury — Internal Revenue Service

Waiver of Restrictions on Assessment and Collection of Deficiency in Tax and Acceptance of Overassessment

Date received by Internal Revenue Service

Names and address of taxpayers *(Number, street, city or town, State, ZIP code)*

Social security or employer identification number

Increase (Decrease) in Tax and Penalties

Tax year ended	Tax	Penalties			
	$	$	$	$	$
	$	$	$	$	$
	$	$	$	$	$
	$	$	$	$	$
	$	$	$	$	$
	$	$	$	$	$
	$	$	$	$	$

(For instructions, see back of form)

Consent to Assessment and Collection

I consent to the immediate assessment and collection of any deficiencies *(increase in tax and penalties)* and accept any overassessment *(decrease in tax and penalties)* shown above, plus any interest provided by law. I understand that by signing this waiver, I will not be able to contest these years in the United States Tax Court, unless additional deficiencies are determined for these years.

Signatures

		Date
		Date
By	Title	Date

Form 870 (Rev. 2-86)

[Form 870]

Instructions

General Information

If you consent to the assessment of the deficiencies shown in this waiver, please sign and return the form in order to limit any interest charge and expedite the adjustment to your account. Your consent will not prevent you from filing a claim for refund *(after you have paid the tax)* if you later believe you are so entitled. It will not prevent us from later determining, if necessary, that you owe additional tax; nor extend the time provided by law for either action.

We have agreements with State tax agencies under which information about Federal tax, including increases or decreases, is exchanged with the States. If this change affects the amount of your State income tax, you should file the required State form.

If you later file a claim and the Service disallows it, you may file suit for refund in a district court or in the United States Claims Court, but you may not file a petition with the United States Tax Court.

We will consider this waiver a valid claim for refund or credit of any overpayment due you resulting from any decrease in tax and penalties shown above, provided you sign and file it within the period established by law for making such a claim.

Who Must Sign

If you filed jointly, both you and your spouse must sign. If this waiver is for a corporation, it should be signed with the corporation name, followed by the signatures and titles of the corporate officers authorized to sign. An attorney or agent may sign this waiver provided such action is specifically authorized by a power of attorney which, if not previously filed, must accompany this form.

If this waiver is signed by a person acting in a fiduciary capacity *(for example, an executor, administrator, or a trustee)* Form 56, Notice Concerning Fiduciary Relationship, should, unless previously filed, accompany this form.

[¶ 174]

[G6759]

WAIVER OF RESTRICTIONS

App. B

[¶175] 257 2-87   [FORM 870-AD]   1135

Form 870-AD
(Rev. December 1986)

DEPARTMENT OF THE TREASURY — INTERNAL REVENUE SERVICE
OFFER OF WAIVER OF RESTRICTIONS ON ASSESSMENT AND COLLECTION OF DEFICIENCY IN TAX AND OF ACCEPTANCE OF OVERASSESSMENT

SYMBOLS	NAME OF TAXPAYER	SSN or EIN

Pursuant to the provisions of section 6213(d) of the Internal Revenue Code of 1986, or corresponding provisions of prior internal revenue laws, the undersigned offers to waive the restrictions provided in section 6213(a) of the Internal Revenue Code of 1986, or corresponding provisions of prior internal revenue laws, and to consent to the assessment and collection of the following deficiencies with interest as provided by law. The undersigned offers also to accept the following overassessments as correct:

DEFICIENCIES (OVERASSESSMENTS)

YEAR ENDED	KIND OF TAX	TAX				
		$	$	$		
		$	$	$		
		$	$	$		
		$	$	$		
		$	$	$		
		$	$	$		

SIGNATURE OF TAXPAYER		DATE
SIGNATURE OF TAXPAYER		DATE
BY	TITLE	DATE

FOR INTERNAL REVENUE USE ONLY	DATE ACCEPTED FOR COMMISSIONER	SIGNATURE
	OFFICE	TITLE

(SEE REVERSE SIDE)   [¶175] Form 870-AD (Rev. 12-86)
[G6760]

OFFER OF WAIVER OF ASSESSMENT

[FORM 870-AD]

This offer is subject to acceptance for the Commissioner of Internal Revenue. It shall take effect as a waiver of restrictions on the date it is accepted. Unless and until it is accepted, it shall have no force or effect.

If this offer is accepted for the Commissioner, the case shall not be reopened in the absence of fraud, malfeasance, concealment or misrepresentation of material fact, an important mistake in mathematical calculation, deficiencies or overassessments resulting from adjustments made under Subchapters C and D of Chapter 63 concerning the tax treatment of partnership and subchapter S items determined at the partnership and corporate level, or excessive tentative allowances of carrybacks provided by law; and no claim for refund or credit shall be filed or prosecuted for the year(s) stated above other than for amounts attributed to carrybacks provided by law.

NOTE.—The execution and filing of this offer will expedite the above adjustment of tax liability. This offer, when executed and timely submitted, will be considered a claim for refund for the above overassessments, as provided in Revenue Ruling 68-65, C.B. 1968-1, 555. It will not, however, constitute a closing agreement under section 7121 of the Internal Revenue Code.

If this offer is executed with respect to a year for which a JOINT RETURN OF A HUSBAND AND WIFE was filed, it must be signed by both spouses unless one spouse, acting under a power of attorney, signs as agent for the other.

If the taxpayer is a corporation, the offer shall be signed with the corporate name followed by the signature and title of the officers authorized to sign.

This offer may be executed by the taxpayer's attorney or agent provided this action is specifically authorized by a power of attorney which, if not previously filed, must accompany the form.

WAIVER OF RESTRICTIONS

[Form 866]

Form 866
(Rev. July 1981)

Department of the Treasury — Internal Revenue Service

Agreement as to Final Determination of Tax Liability

(Complete three copies of this form)

Under Section 7121 of the Internal Revenue Code, _____
(Taxpayer's name, address, and identifying number)

_____

_____

and the Commissioner of Internal Revenue agree that the liability of the above taxpayer for the taxable periods and kinds of tax listed in this agreement is as follows: (The applicability or inapplicability of interest or penalties, including additions to tax or additional amounts authorized by Subchapter A of Chapter 68 of the Code, is not determined except as provided in this agreement.)

Taxable Period	Kind of Tax or Penalty	Chapter Number and Subchapter Letter of Internal Revenue Code	Total Tax Liability for Period

This agreement is final and conclusive except:

   (1) the liability it relates to may be reopened in the event of fraud, malfeasance, or misrepresentation of material fact and

   (2) it is subject to the Internal Revenue Code sections that expressly provide that effect be given to their provisions notwithstanding any other law or rule of law except Code section 7122.

By signing this agreement, the above parties certify they have read and agreed to its terms.

Your signature _____ Date signed _____

Spouse's signature (If a joint return was filed) _____ Date signed _____

_____

Signature of taxpayer's representative _____ Date signed _____

Taxpayer (other than individual) _____

   By _____ Date signed _____

   Title _____

Commissioner of Internal Revenue

   By _____ Date signed _____

   Title _____

Part 3 — District Copy   (See back)   [¶ 173]   Form 866 (Rev. 7-81)
[G6762]

OFFER OF WAIVER OF ASSESSMENT

[Form 866]

Instructions

This agreement must be signed and filed in triplicate. If more than one taxpayer (party) enters into and signs this closing agreement, two additional copies of the agreement are required for each additional party. *(All copies must have original signatures.)*

The original and copies of the agreement must be identical.

The name of the taxpayer must be stated accurately.

The agreement may relate to one or more taxable periods.

The liability must be separately stated as to taxable periods and kinds of taxes. Each kind of tax or penalty must reflect the Chapter Number and Subchapter Letter of the Internal Revenue Code under which each tax was levied, as shown in the following examples:

Taxable Period	Kind of Tax or Penalty	Chapter Number and Subchapter Letter of Internal Revenue Code	Total Tax Liability for Period
Calendar Year 1978	Income	1A	$ 3,000.00
Calendar Year 1978	Personal Holding Co.	1G	6,000.00
Date of Death, March 1, 1978	Estate	11A	100,000.00
Fiscal Year Ending March 31, 1978	Income	1A	9,000.00

If an attorney or agent signs the agreement for the taxpayer, the power of attorney *(or a copy)* authorizing that person to sign must be attached to the agreement. If the agreement is made for a year in which a joint income tax return was filed by a husband and wife, it should be signed by or for both. One spouse may sign as agent for the other if the document *(or a copy)* specifically authorizing that spouse to sign is attached to the agreement.

If the fiduciary signs the agreement for a decedent or an estate, an attested copy of the letters testamentary or the court order authorizing the fiduciary to sign, and a recently dated certificate that the authority remains in effect must be attached to the agreement. If a trustee signs, a certified copy of the trust instrument or a certified copy of extracts from the instrument must be attached showing:

(1) the date of the instrument;

(2) that it is or is not of record in any court;

(3) the names of the beneficiaries;

(4) the appointment of the trustee, the authority granted, and other information necessary to show that the authority extends to Federal tax matters; and

(5) that the trust has not been terminated and the trustee appointed is still acting.

If a fiduciary is a party, Form 56, Notice Concerning Fiduciary Relationship, is usually required.

If the taxpayer is a corporation, the agreement must be dated and signed with the name of the corporation, followed by the signature and title of an authorized officer, or officers, or the signature of an authorized attorney or agent. It is not necessary that a copy of an enabling corporate resolution be attached. See 26 C.F.R. 601.504(b)(2)(ii) as to dissolved corporations.

Use additional pages if necessary, and identify them as part of this agreement.

Please see Revenue Procedure 68-16, 1968-1 C.B. 770, for a detailed description of practices and procedures applicable to most closing agreements.

Form 906
(Rev. December 1983)

Department of the Treasury—Internal Revenue Service

Closing Agreement On Final Determination Covering Specific Matters

Under section 7121 of the Internal Revenue Code ....

....
(Taxpayer's name, address, and identifying number)

....

and the Commissioner of Internal Revenue make the following closing agreement:

OFFER OF WAIVER OF ASSESSMENT

[Form 906]

Instructions

This agreement must be signed and filed in triplicate. (All copies must have original signatures.)

The original and copies of the agreement must be identical.

The name of the taxpayer must be stated accurately.

The agreement may relate to one or more years.

If an attorney or agent signs the agreement for the taxpayer, the power of attorney (or a copy) authorizing that person to sign must be attached to the agreement. If the agreement is made for a year when a joint income tax return was filed by a husband and wife, it should be signed by or for both spouses. One spouse may sign as agent for the other if the document (or a copy) specifically authorizing that spouse to sign is attached to the agreement.

If the fiduciary signs the agreement for a decedent or an estate, an attested copy of the letters testamentary or the court order authorizing the fiduciary to sign, and a certificate of recent date that the authority remains in full force and effect must be attached to the agreement. If a trustee signs, a certified copy of the trust instrument or a certified copy of extracts from that instrument must be attached showing:

(1) the date of the instrument;

(2) that it is or is not of record in any court;

(3) the names of the beneficiaries;

(4) the appointment of the trustee, the authority granted, and other information necessary to show that the authority extends to Federal tax matters; and

(5) that the trust has not been terminated, and that the trustee appointed is still acting. If a fiduciary is a party, Form 56, Notice Concerning Fiduciary Relationship, is ordinarily required.

If the taxpayer is a corporation, the agreement must be dated and signed with the name of the corporation, the signature and title of an authorized officer or officers, or the signature of an authorized attorney or agent. It is not necessary that a copy of an enabling corporate resolution be attached. See 26 C.F.R. 601.504(b)(2)(ii) as to dissolved corporations.

Use additional pages if necessary, and identify them as part of this agreement.

Please see Revenue Procedure 68–16, C.B. 1968–1, page 770, for a detailed description of practices and procedures applicable to most closing agreements.

WAIVER OF RESTRICTIONS — App. B

[Form 906]

I have examined the specific matters involved and recommend the acceptance of the proposed agreement.

_____
(Receiving Officer)   (Date)

_____
(Title)

I have reviewed the specific matters involved and recommend approval of the proposed agreement.

_____
(Reviewing Officer)   (Date)

_____
(Title)

[The next page is 1161.]

[193]

Form 906 (Rev. 12-33)
[G6766]

App. B — OFFER OF WAIVER OF ASSESSMENT

[Form 906]

This agreement is final and conclusive except:

(1) the matter it relates to may be reopened in the event of fraud, malfeasance, or misrepresentation of material fact;
(2) it is subject to the Internal Revenue Code sections that expressly provide that effect be given to their provisions notwithstanding any other law or rule of law except Code section 7122; and
(3) if it relates to a tax period ending after the date of this agreement, it is subject to any law, enacted after the agreement date, that applies to that tax period.

By signing, the above parties certify that they have read and agreed to the terms of this document.

Your signature .... Date Signed ....

Spouse's signature (if a joint return was filed) .... Date Signed ....

Taxpayer's representative .... Date Signed ....

Taxpayer (other than individual)..

    By .... Date Signed ....

    Title ....

Commissioner of Internal Revenue

    By .... Date Signed ....

    Title ....

[¶ 193]

Appendix C

CONSENT TO EXTEND THE TIME TO ASSESS INCOME TAX (FORM 872), SPECIAL CONSENT TO EXTEND THE TIME TO ASSESS TAX (FORM 872–A), NOTICE OF TERMINATION OF SPECIAL CONSENT TO EXTEND THE TIME TO ASSESS TAX (FORM 872–T)

App. C SPECIAL CONSENT TO EXTEND TIME

[¶ 177A]

Form **872** OIO MODIFICATION (Rev. Jan. 1979)	Department of the Treasury — Internal Revenue Service **Consent to Extend the Time to Assess Income Tax**	In Reply Refer To:

_____
(Name(s))

taxpayer(s) of _____
(Number, Street, City or Town, State, ZIP Code)

and the Director of International Operations consent and agree to the following:

(1) The amount(s) of any Federal income tax due on any return(s) made by or for the above taxpayer(s) for the tax year(s) ended _____

may be assessed at any time on or before _____
(Expiration date)

However, if a notice of deficiency in tax for any such period(s) is sent to the taxpayer(s) on or before that date, then the time for assessing the tax will be further extended by the number of days the assessment was previously prohibited, plus 60 days.

(2) This agreement ends on the earlier of the above expiration date or the assessment date of an increase in the above tax that reflects the final determination of tax and the final administrative appeals consideration. An assessment for one period covered by this agreement will not end this agreement for any other period it covers. Some assessments do not reflect a final determination and appeals consideration and therefore will not terminate the agreement before the expiration date. Examples are assessments of: (a) tax under a partial agreement; (b) tax in jeopardy; (c) tax to correct mathematical or clerical errors; (d) tax reported on amended returns; and (e) advance payments. In addition, unassessed payments, such as amounts treated by the Service as cash bonds and advance payments not assessed by the Service, will not terminate this agreement before the expiration date.

This agreement ends on the above expiration date regardless of any assessment for any period includible in a report to the Joint Committee on Taxation submitted under section 6405 of the Internal Revenue Code.

(3) The taxpayer(s) may file a claim for credit or refund and the Service may credit or refund the tax within 6 months after this agreement ends.

(SIGNATURE INSTRUCTIONS AND SPACE FOR SIGNATURE ARE ON THE BACK OF THIS FORM.)

[¶ 177A] Form **872** (OIO MODIFICATION) (Rev. 1-79)

906 CONSENT TO EXTEND TIME App. C

1140

MAKING THIS CONSENT WILL NOT DEPRIVE THE TAXPAYER(S) OF ANY APPEAL RIGHTS TO WHICH THEY WOULD OTHERWISE BE ENTITLED.

YOUR SIGNATURE HERE ⟶ .... (Date signed)

SPOUSE'S SIGNATURE ⟶ .... (Date signed)

TAXPAYER'S REPRESENTATIVE
SIGN HERE ⟶ .... (Date signed)

CORPORATE
NAME ⟶ .... (Date signed)

CORPORATE
OFFICERS
SIGN
HERE
.... (Date signed)
(Signature and Title)

.... (Date signed)
(Signature and Title)

DIRECTOR OF INTERNATIONAL OPERATIONS

BY .... (Date signed)
(Signature and Title)

Instructions

If this consent is made for any year(s) for which a joint return was filed, both husband and wife must sign the original and copy of this form unless one, acting under a power of attorney, signs as agent for the other. The signatures should match the names as they appear on the front of this form.

If this consent is for a partnership return, only one authorized partner need sign.

If you are an attorney or agent of the taxpayer(s), you may sign this consent provided the action is specifically authorized by a power of attorney. If the power of attorney was not previously filed, please include it with this form.

If you are acting as a fiduciary (such as executor, administrator, trustee, etc.) and you sign this consent, attach Form 56, Notice of Fiduciary Relationship, unless it was previously filed.

If the taxpayer is a corporation, sign this consent with the corporate name followed by the signature and title of the officer(s) authorized to sign.

Form **872** (OIO MODIFICATION) (Rev. 1-79)
IG67691

App. C SPECIAL CONSENT TO EXTEND TIME 907

Form **872-A** (Rev October 1987)	Department of the Treasury – Internal Revenue Service **Special Consent to Extend the Time to Assess Tax**	In reply refer to: SSN or EIN

_____
(Name(s))

taxpayer(s) of _____
(Number, Street, City or Town, State, ZIP Code)

and the District Director of Internal Revenue or Regional Director of Appeals consent and agree as follows:

(1) The amount(s) of any Federal _____ tax due on any return(s) made by or
(Kind of tax)
for the above taxpayer(s) for the period(s) ended _____
may be assessed on or before the 90th (ninetieth) day after: (a) the Internal Revenue Service office considering the case receives Form 872-T, Notice of Termination of Special Consent to Extend the Time to Assess Tax, from the taxpayer(s); or (b) the Internal Revenue Service mails Form 872-T to the taxpayer(s); or (c) the Internal Revenue Service mails a notice of deficiency for such period(s); except that if a notice of deficiency is sent to the taxpayer(s), the time for assessing the tax for the period(s) stated in the notice of deficiency will end 60 days after the period during which the making of an assessment is prohibited. A final adverse determination subject to declaratory judgment under sections 7428, 7476, or 7477 of the Internal Revenue Code will not terminate this agreement.

(2) This agreement ends on the earlier of the above expiration date or the assessment date of an increase in the above tax or the overassessment date of a decrease in the above tax that reflects the final determination of tax and the final administrative appeals consideration. An assessment or overassessment for one period covered by this agreement will not end this agreement for any other period it covers. Some assessments do not reflect a final determination and appeals consideration and therefore will not terminate the agreement before the expiration date. Examples are assessments of: (a) tax under a partial agreement; (b) tax in jeopardy; (c) tax to correct mathematical or clerical errors; (d) tax reported on amended returns; and (e) advance payments. In addition, unassessed payments, such as amounts treated by the Service as cash bonds and advance payments not assessed by the Service, will not terminate this agreement before the expiration date determined in (1) above. This agreement ends on the date determined in (1) above regardless of any assessment for any period includible in a report to the Joint Committee on Taxation submitted under section 6405 of the Internal Revenue Code.

(3) This agreement will not reduce the period of time otherwise provided by law for making such assessment.

(4) The taxpayer(s) may file a claim for credit or refund and the Service may credit or refund the tax within 6 (six) months after this agreement ends.

(Signature instructions and space for signature are on the back of this form)

Form 872-A (Rev 10-87)
[G6770]

MAKING THIS CONSENT WILL NOT DEPRIVE THE TAXPAYER(S) OF ANY APPEAL RIGHTS TO WHICH THEY WOULD OTHERWISE BE ENTITLED.

YOUR SIGNATURE HERE ▶ _____   _____
                                                                (Date signed)

SPOUSE'S SIGNATURE ▶ _____   _____
                                                                (Date signed)

TAXPAYER'S REPRESENTATIVE
SIGN HERE ▶ _____   _____
                                                       (Date signed)

CORPORATE
NAME ▶ _____

CORPORATE   _____   _____
OFFICER(S)   (Title)   (Date signed)
SIGN HERE
                   _____   _____
                             (Title)   (Date signed)

_____   _____
DISTRICT DIRECTOR OF INTERNAL REVENUE   REGIONAL DIRECTOR OF APPEALS

BY _____   _____
         (Signature and Title)   (Date signed)

Instructions

If this consent is for income tax, self-employment tax, or FICA tax on tips and is made for any year(s) for which a joint return was filed, both husband and wife must sign the original and copy of this form unless one, acting under a power of attorney, signs as agent for the other. The signatures must match the names as they appear on the front of this form.

If this consent is for gift tax and the donor and the donor's spouse elected to have gifts to third persons considered as made one-half by each, both husband and wife must sign the original and copy of this form unless one, acting under a power of attorney, signs as agent for the other. The signatures must match the names as they appear on the front of this form.

If this consent is for Chapter 41, 42, or 43 taxes involving a partnership, only one authorized partner need sign.

If you are an attorney or agent of the taxpayer(s), you may sign this consent provided the action is specifically authorized by a power of attorney. If the power of attorney was not previously filed, you must include it with this form.

If you are acting as a fiduciary (such as executor, administrator, trustee, etc.) and you sign this consent, attach Form 56, Notice Concerning Fiduciary Relationship, unless it was previously filed.

If the taxpayer is a corporation, sign this consent with the corporate name followed by the signature and title of the officer(s) authorized to sign.

If this consent is for Chapter 42 taxes, a separate Form 872-A should be completed for each potential disqualified person or entity that may have been involved in a taxable transaction during the related tax year. See Revenue Ruling 75-391, 1975-2 C.B. 446.

Form 872-A (Rev 10-87)
[G6771]

App. C — SPECIAL CONSENT TO EXTEND TIME

[¶ 181] [Form 872-T] 1143-13

Form 872-T (Rev. June 1986)	Department of the Treasury — Internal Revenue Service **Notice of Termination of Special Consent to Extend the Time to Assess Tax**	In reply refer to:
Taxpayer(s) Name(s)		Termination By: ☐ Taxpayer ☐ IRS
Taxpayer(s) Address		Taxpayer Identifying Number
Kind of Tax	Tax Period(s) Covered by this Notice	Issuing Office Code
		Service Center Code

Under the agreement dated _____, between the above taxpayer(s) and the Internal Revenue Service, this form is written notification of termination of Form 872-A, Special Consent to Extend the Time to Assess Tax, for the kind of tax and tax period(s) indicated above.

Signature and mailing instructions are on the back of this form.
Signing this notice will not deprive the taxpayer(s) of any appeal rights to which they would otherwise be entitled.

YOUR SIGNATURE HERE ▶ _____ _____
                                                      (Date signed)

SPOUSE'S SIGNATURE ▶ _____ _____
                                                      (Date signed)

TAXPAYER'S REPRESENTATIVE
SIGN HERE ▶ _____ _____
                                                      (Date signed)

CORPORATE
NAME ▶ _____

CORPORATE   ▶ _____ _____
OFFICER(S)   (Title)   (Date signed)
SIGN HERE   ▶ _____ _____
                         (Title)   (Date signed)

_____   _____
DISTRICT DIRECTOR OF INTERNAL REVENUE   REGIONAL DIRECTOR OF APPEALS

BY _____   _____
         (Signature and Title)   (Date signed)

[¶ 181]   Form 872-T (Rev. 6-86)
                         [G6772]

[Form 872-T]

Instructions

This notice may be made by either the taxpayer(s) or the Internal Revenue Service.

Please enter, in the space provided on the front of this form, the date Form 872-A was signed for the Internal Revenue Service.

If this notice is for income tax, self-employment tax, or FICA tax on tips and is made for any year(s) for which a joint return was filed, both husband and wife must sign this form unless one, acting under a power of attorney, signs as agent for the other. The signatures must match the names as they appear on the Form 872-A.

If this notice is for gift tax and the donor and the donor's spouse elected to have gifts to third persons considered as made one-half by each, both husband and wife must sign this form unless one, acting under a power of attorney, signs as agent for the other. The signatures must match the names as they appear on the Form 872-A.

If this notice is for Chapter 41, 42, or 43 taxes involving a partnership, only one authorized partner need sign.

If you are an attorney or agent of the taxpayer(s), you may sign this notice provided the action is specifically authorized by a power of attorney. If the power of attorney was not previously filed, you must include it with this form.

If you are acting as a fiduciary (such as executor, administrator, trustee, etc.) and you sign this notice, attach Form 56, Notice Concerning Fiduciary Relationship, unless it was previously filed.

If the taxpayer is a corporation, sign this notice with the corporate name followed by the signature and title of the officer(s) authorized to sign.

If the tax return(s) to which this notice applies is under consideration by the Examination Division, mail this notice to the District Director of Internal Revenue having jurisdiction over the return(s), Attention: Chief, Examination Division.

If the tax return(s) to which this notice applies is under consideration by the Employee Plans and Exempt Organizations Division, mail this notice to the District Director of Internal Revenue for the key district having jurisdiction over the return(s), Attention: Chief, EP/EO Division. See Rev. Proc. 85-32, 1985-2 C.B. 414, for a listing of the key district offices and the districts covered by each.

If the tax return(s) to which this notice applies is under consideration by Appeals, mail this notice to the Chief, Appeals Office, having jurisdiction over the return(s).

Form 872-T (Rev. 6-86)

Appendix D

TAX COURT PETITION FORMS
FORM 1—PETITION (OTHER THAN IN SMALL TAX CASE)
FORM 2—PETITION (SMALL TAX CASE)

FORM 1

PETITION (Other Than In Small Tax Case)

(See Rules 30 through 34)

UNITED STATES TAX COURT

....
Petitioner(s)
v.
COMMISSIONER OF INTERNAL REVENUE,
Respondent

Docket No.

PETITION

The petitioner hereby petitions for a redetermination of the deficiency (or liability) set forth by the Commissioner of Internal Revenue in his notice of deficiency (or liability) [Service symbols] dated ...., 19 ..., and as the basis for his case alleges as follows:

1. The petitioner is [set forth whether an individual, fiduciary, corporation, etc., as provided in Rule 60] with legal residence (or principal office) now at

....
Street   City   State   Zip Code

Petitioner's taxpayer identification number (e.g., Social Security or employer identification number) is

The return for the period here involved was filed with the Office of the Internal Revenue Service at ....
City   State

2. The notice of deficiency (or liability) (a copy of which, including so much of the statement and schedules accompanying the notice as is material, is attached and marked Exhibit A) was mailed to the petitioner on ...., 19 ..., and was issued by the Office of the Internal Revenue Service at ....
City   State

3. The deficiencies (or liabilities) as determined by the Commissioner are in income (estate, gift, or certain excise) taxes for the calendar (or fiscal) year 19 ..., in the amount of $ ...., of which $ ...., is in dispute.

4. The determination of tax set forth in the said notice of deficiency (or liability) is based upon the following errors: [Here set forth specifically in lettered subparagraphs the assignments of error in a concise manner and avoid pleading facts which properly belong in the succeeding paragraph.]

5. The facts upon which the petitioner relies, as the basis of his case, are as follows: [Here set forth allegations of fact, but not the evidence, sufficient to inform the Court and the Commissioner of the positions taken and the bases therefor, in orderly and logical sequence, with subparagraphs lettered, so as to enable the Commissioner to admit or deny each allegation. See Rules 31(a) and 34(b)(5).]

WHEREFORE, petitioner prays that [here set forth the relief desired].

(Signed) ....
Petitioner or Counsel

....
Post office address

Dated: ...., 19 ...

....
Telephone (include area code)

[G6774]

FORM 2

PETITION (Small Tax Case)

(Available—Ask for Form 2)

(See Rules 170 through 179)

UNITED STATES TAX COURT

....
Petitioner(s)
v.
COMMISSIONER OF INTERNAL REVENUE,
Respondent

Docket No.

PETITION

1. Petitioner(s) request(s) the Court to redetermine the tax deficiency(ies) for the year(s) ....,......., as set forth in the notice of deficiency dated ...., A COPY OF WHICH IS ATTACHED. The notice was issued by the Office of the Internal Revenue Service at ....
City   State

2. Petitioner(s) taxpayer identification (e.g., Social Security) number(s) is(are) ....

3. Petitioner(s) make(s) the following claims as to his tax liability:

Year	Amount of deficiency disputed	Addition to tax (penalty), if any, disputed	Amount of overpayment claimed
......	....	....	....
......	....	....	....

4. Set forth those adjustments, i.e., changes, in the notice of deficiency with which you disagree and why you disagree.

....
....
....
....
....

Petitioner(s) request(s) that the proceedings in this case be conducted as a "Small Tax Case" under section 7463 of the Internal Revenue Code of 1954, as amended, and Rule 172 of the Rules of Practice and Procedure of the United States Tax Court.*(See page 8 of the enclosed booklet.) A decision in a "Small Tax Case" is final and cannot be appealed by either party.

....
Signature of Petitioner

Present Address—Street, City, State, Zip Code, Telephone (include area code)

....
Signature of Petitioner (Spouse)

Present Address—Street, City, State, Zip Code, Telephone (include area code)

....
Signature and address of counsel, if retained by petitioner(s)

*If you do not want to make this request, you should place an "X" in the following box. ☐

[G6775]

Appendix E

REPORT OF CASH PAYMENTS OVER $10,000 RECEIVED IN A TRADE OR BUSINESS (FORM 8300)

App. E CASH PAYMENTS OVER $10,000 915

Form 8300
(Rev. January 1990)
Department of the Treasury
Internal Revenue Service

Report of Cash Payments Over $10,000 Received in a Trade or Business

Failure to file this form or filing a false form may result in imprisonment.
▶ See instructions on back.
Please type or print.

OMB No. 1545-0892
Expires 10-31-92

1 Check appropriate boxes if: a ☐ amends prior report;   b ☐ suspicious transaction.

Part I — Identity of Individual From Whom the Cash Was Received

2 If more than one individual is involved, see instructions and check here . . . . ▶ ☐

3 Last name   4 First name   5 Middle initial   6 Social security number

7 Address (number and street)   8 Occupation, profession, or business

9 City   10 State   11 ZIP code   12 Country (if not U.S.)   13 Date of birth (see instructions)

14 Method used to verify identity: a Describe identification ▶
    b Issued by   c Number

Part II — Person (See Definitions) on Whose Behalf This Transaction Was Conducted

15 If this transaction was conducted on behalf of more than one person, see instructions and check here . . . . ▶ ☐

16 This person is an: ☐ individual or ☐ organization   17 If funded by another party, see instructions and check here . . ▶ ☐

18 Individual's last name or Organization's name   19 First name   20 Middle initial   21 Social security number

22 Alien identification: a Describe identification ▶   Employer identification number
    b Issued by   c Number

23 Address (number and street)   24 Occupation, profession, or business

25 City   26 State   27 ZIP code   28 Country (if not U.S.)   29 Date of birth (see instructions)

Part III — Description of Transaction and Method of Payment

30 a ☐ personal property purchased   d ☐ business services provided   g ☐ exchange of cash
    b ☐ real property purchased   e ☐ intangible property purchased   h ☐ escrow or trust funds
    c ☐ personal services provided   f ☐ debt obligations paid   i ☐ other (specify) ▶

31 Specific description of property or service purchased. Give serial or registration number of car, boat, airplane, etc., address of real estate, etc.

32 Total price $ _____ .00   33 Amount of cash received $ _____ .00   34 Amount in $100 bills or larger $ _____ .00

35 If part of an installment sale, give information below and check box . . . . ▶ ☐   36 Date of transaction
   a Number of payments _____   b Amount of each payment $ _____ .00
   c Frequency: ☐ monthly ☐ other (describe)   d Balloon payment (amount) $ _____ .00

37 ☐ Paid with U.S. currency   ☐ Paid with foreign currency (country) _____   Amount (U.S. dollar equivalent) $ _____ .00

Part IV — Business Reporting This Transaction

38 Name of reporting business   39 Employer identification number

40 Street address where transaction occurred   Social security number

41 City   42 State   43 ZIP code   44 Nature of your business

45 Under penalties of perjury, I declare that to the best of my knowledge the information I have furnished above is true, correct, and complete.

Sign Here
(Authorized signature—See Instructions)   (Title)   (Date signed)   (Telephone number)

Paperwork Reduction Act Notice.—The requested information is useful in criminal, tax, and regulatory investigations, for instance by directing the Federal Government's attention to unusual or questionable transactions. Trades or businesses are required to provide the information under 26 U.S.C. 6050I.

The time needed to complete this form will vary depending on individual circumstances. The estimated average time is 18 minutes. If you have comments concerning the accuracy of this time estimate or suggestions for making this form more simple, you can write to the **Internal Revenue Service**, Washington, DC 20224, Attention: IRS Reports Clearance Officer T:FP; or the **Office of Management and Budget**, Paperwork Reduction Project (1545-0892), Washington, DC 20503.

Form **8300** (Rev. 1-90)
[G6776]

General Instructions

Who Must File.—Each person engaged in a trade or business who, in the course of such trade or business, receives more than $10,000 in cash in one transaction or two or more related transactions must file Form 8300. Any transactions conducted between a payer (or its agent) and the recipient in a 24-hour period are related transactions and must be aggregated and reported as a single transaction if the total amount exceeds $10,000. Also, a transaction is related even though it occurs during a period of more than 24 hours if the recipient knows, or has reason to know, that each transaction is one of a series of connected transactions. In addition, this form may voluntarily be filed for any suspicious transaction, even if it does not exceed $10,000.

Multiple Payments.—How and when you must report receipt of cash deposits, cash installment payments, or other similar payments or prepayments depend upon the dollar amounts of the initial and subsequent payments.

If the initial payment exceeds $10,000, it must be reported within 15 days. If the initial payment does not exceed $10,000, the recipient must add together the initial payment and subsequent payments made within one year until the total exceeds $10,000, at which time the report must be filed within 15 days. If subsequent payments, singly or in the aggregate, received within any one-year period exceed $10,000, they must be reported separately within 15 days of the date they exceed $10,000 if they have not been previously reported. (If two or more separately reportable payments are received less than 15 days apart, they may be filed on a single report. In this case, the report is due within 15 days of receipt of the first payment.) If subsequent payments, singly or in the aggregate, received within one year do not exceed $10,000, they need not be reported.

Exceptions.—Section 1.6050I-1 of the Treasury Regulations provides for exceptions to the reporting requirements, including:

(1) Financial institutions required to file **Form 4789**, Currency Transaction Report, are exempted from filing Form 8300 for the same transaction.

(2) Casinos required to file (or excepted from filing) **Form 8362** are exempted from filing Form 8300 for the same transaction. However, nongaming businesses (such as shops, restaurants, and hotels) at the casinos must report on Form 8300 receipt of cash in excess of $10,000.

(3) Cash received by a person other than in the person's trade or business is not reportable.

(4) Cash transactions that occur entirely outside the United States are generally exempt from the reporting requirements. The United States includes the 50 states and the District of Columbia. However, if any part of the transaction occurs in Puerto Rico, or a possession or territory of the United States, and the recipient is subject to the general jurisdiction of the IRS under the Internal Revenue Code, the transaction must be reported by the recipient.

(5) An agent who: (a) receives cash from a principal, (b) uses all of the cash within 15 days in a cash transaction that is reportable on Form 8300 or 4789, and (c) discloses all of the information necessary to complete Part II of Form 8300 to the recipient of the cash in the second transaction does not have to file Form 8300 for the initial receipt of the cash.

When and Where To File.—File this form by the 15th day after the date of the transaction with the Internal Revenue Service, Detroit Computing Center, P.O. Box 32621, Detroit, MI 48232, or with your local IRS office. Keep a copy of each Form 8300 for 5 years from the date you file it.

Penalties.—Civil and criminal penalties including up to 5 years imprisonment are provided for failure (or causing the failure) to file a report, for filing (or causing the filing) of a false or fraudulent report, and for structuring a transaction.

Statement To Be Provided.—A written statement must be provided to each person named in this form on or before January 31 of the year following the calendar year in which this report is made. The statement must show the name and address of the business, the total amount of reportable cash received, and that the information was furnished to the IRS. Keep a copy for your records.

Specific Instructions

Item 1.—If you are reporting a suspicious transaction (see *Definitions*), check Box 1b. For a suspicious transaction, you are also encouraged to telephone the local Internal Revenue Service Criminal Investigation Division. If you do not know the number, please call toll-free 1-800-BSA-CTRS.

Part I.—This part must always be completed.

Item 2.—Check the box if two or more individuals conducted the transaction you are reporting. Enter identifying information in Part I for one of the individuals. Provide information on the other individual(s) on additional sheets of paper and attach them to this report.

Item 6.—Enter the social security number of the individual named in Part I. If the individual has no number, enter "None."

Item 8.—In identifying the occupation, profession, or business of the individual named in Part I, use fully descriptive terms such as plumber, attorney, etc., and not nondescriptive terms such as merchant, businessman, self-employed, etc.

Item 13.—Enter six numerals for the date of birth of the individual named in Part I. For example, if the individual's birth date was July 6, 1960, enter 07 06 60.

Item 14.—You must verify the name and address of the individual identified in Part I. Verification must be made by examination of a document normally acceptable as a means of identification when cashing checks (for example, a driver's license, passport, or other official document). In Item 14a, enter the type of document used to verify the identification. In Item 14b, identify the issuer of that document. In Item 14c, enter the document's number. For example, if the individual has a Utah driver's license, enter "driver's license" in Item 14a, "Utah" in Item 14b, and its number in Item 14c.

Part II.—If the individual in Part I is conducting the transaction for himself or herself only, do not complete Part II. In all other cases, complete Part II.

Item 15.—If the transaction is being conducted on behalf of more than one person (e.g., 2 persons are jointly purchasing a vehicle), check the box and complete Part II on any one of the persons. Provide the same information requested in Part II on the other person(s) on additional sheets of paper and attach them to this report.

Item 16.—If the person identified in Part II is an individual, check the "individual" box. For any person other than an individual, check the "organization" box. Check both boxes if the transaction is on behalf of both an individual and an organization.

Item 17.—Check the box if any of the cash received is from a party or parties not identified in Part I or II. Provide the same information requested in Part II on that party or parties on additional sheets of paper and attach them to this report.

Items 18, 19, and 20.—If the person on whose behalf the transaction was conducted was an individual, put his or her last name in Item 18, first name in Item 19, and middle initial in Item 20. If the person is an organization, put its name in Item 18 and leave Items 19 and 20 blank.

Item 21.—If the person is an individual, enter his or her social security number; if not an individual, enter its employer identification number. If the person does not have a social security or employer identification number, enter "None."

Item 22.—If the person is an alien without a social security number, complete this item. Enter a general description of the type of official document issued to that person in Item 22a (e.g., "passport"), the country that issued the document in Item 22b, and the document's number in Item 22c.

Item 29.—Refer to Item 13.

Part III.—This part must always be completed.

Item 30.—Check the appropriate box(es) that describe the transaction. If the transaction is not specified in Boxes a – h, check Box i and briefly describe it (e.g., car lease).

Items 32, 33, and 34.—Provide the total price of the goods purchased, services provided, amount of cash exchanged, etc. (e.g., the total cost of a vehicle purchased, cost of catering service, exchange of currency) in Item 32. Enter the total amount of cash received reportable on this return (see *Multiple Payments* for reporting requirements) in Item 33 and the amount of $100 (and larger) bills in Item 34. Show only nearest dollar amounts. Round 50 cents or more to the next whole dollar.

Item 35.—If the transaction is part of an installment sale, check the box. In Item 35a, enter the number of payments agreed upon; in Item 35b, enter the amount of each installment payment; in Item 35c, check the "monthly" box if the payments are to be made monthly, or the "other" box if the payments are made at any other intervals and describe the intervals (e.g., weekly, semi-annually, etc.). If the installments are for different amounts, attach a schedule.

Item 36.—If the aggregate amount of cash received in two or more installment payments exceeds $10,000, enter the payment date that causes the aggregate amount to exceed $10,000. Also, see *Multiple Payments*.

Item 37.—Check the appropriate box(es). If foreign currency is used, provide the country of issuance and the amount (in U.S. dollar equivalent) in the spaces provided. If currency of more than one foreign country is used, enter the information required by Item 37 on an additional sheet of paper and attach it to this report.

Part IV.—This part must always be completed.

Item 39.—Enter the employer identification number (EIN) of the reporting business. Enter the owner's social security number only if the business has no EIN.

Item 44.—Describe the nature of the business filing the report. Use descriptive terms (auto dealer, jewelry dealer) rather than nondescriptive terms (business, store).

Item 45.—This report must be signed by an authorized individual. Also type or print the name of the signer below the signature.

Definitions

Person.—An individual, corporation, partnership, trust or estate, joint stock company, association, syndicate, joint venture, or other unincorporated organization or group, and all entities treated as legal personalities, including organizations that are exempt from tax.

Cash.—The coin and currency of the United States or of any other country, which circulate in and are customarily used and accepted as money in the country in which issued. It includes United States notes and Federal Reserve notes, but does not include bank checks or drafts, travelers checks, wire transfers, or other negotiable or monetary instruments not customarily accepted as money.

Suspicious Transaction.—A transaction in which it appears that a person is attempting to cause this report not to be filed or a false or incomplete report to be filed; or where there is an indication of possible illegal activity.

Transaction.—It includes (but is not limited to) the purchase of goods, services, personal or real property, and intangible property by a customer; a debt obligation paid for with cash; the receipt and conversion of cash to a negotiable instrument (e.g., a receipt of cash from a person in exchange for a check); and the receipt of cash to be held in escrow or trust.

☆ U.S. Government Printing Office: 1989-261-151/00024

[G6777]

Index

References are to Pages

ACCOUNT STATED, SUIT ON, 420–421

ACCOUNTANT–CLIENT PRIVILEGE
See Evidence

ACCOUNTANTS
Practice before IRS, 42–46

ACQUIESCENCE BY COMMISSIONER
See also, Rulings Program
Generally, 70–71

ADMINISTRATIVE PROCEDURE ACT
Rulemaking procedures, 56–68

ADMISSION TO PRACTICE, 36

ANTI–ASSIGNMENT STATUTE, 417–420

ANTI–INJUNCTION ACT
See Injunctions

APPEALS
See also, Appeals Office; Thirty-Day Letter
Administrative,
Generally, 131–139
Judicial, see Forum Selection

APPEALS OFFICE
See also, Technical Advice
Generally, 134–136
Function, 134–135
Jurisdiction, 135
Request for Appeals Office conference, 134
Restrictions, 135
Settlement rates, 135

ASSESSMENT OF DEFICIENCIES
Assessment defined, 163
Jeopardy assessment, see Jeopardy and Termination Assessments
Limitations period,
Generally, 161–162
Agreement extending, 178–184
Commencement of running of period, 167–171
Failure to file return, 162
Fraud,
Generally, 162, 277
Amended non-fraudulent returns affecting, 171–177

ASSESSMENT OF DEFICIENCIES—Cont'd
Limitations period—Cont'd
Fraud—Cont'd
Omission of 25% gross income, 162, 176–178
Reopening of closed periods, 162–163

ASSIGNMENT OF CLAIMS
See Anti–Assignment Statute

ASSISTANT SECRETARY FOR TAX POLICY
See Department of the Treasury

ATTORNEY–CLIENT PRIVILEGE
See Evidence

ATTORNEYS' FEES, RECOVERY OF, 457–459

ATTORNEYS IN TAX PRACTICE
Generally, 16–52
Ethics in tax practice, 17–36
Multiple representation, 48–52
Treasury department standards, 36–48

AUDIT
See Examination of Returns

BANKRUPTCY
Generally, 862–866
Accelerating determinations of tax liability, 864
Automatic stay of assessment and collection, 862–863
Discharge of tax liability, 865
Judicial resolution of tax claim, 863–864
Priorities of tax claims, 865
Resolution of tax claims pending, 863–864

BOARD OF TAX APPEALS (TAX COURT)
See Tax Court

CASH TRANSACTION REPORTING, 664–672

CHIEF COUNSEL, OFFICE OF
See Internal Revenue Service

CHOICE OF FORUM
See Forum Selection

INDEX
References are to Pages

CIVIL PENALTIES
See Penalties, Civil

CLAIM FOR REFUND
See Refund Litigation

CLAIMS COURT
See Forum Selection

CLOSED CASES
See Second Inspections

CLOSING AGREEMENTS
See Settlement and Closing Agreements

COLLATERAL AGREEMENT, 150–151

COLLATERAL ESTOPPEL
    See also, Res Judicata
Fraud cases, 271–276
Government a party in first case, 432–443
Government not a party in first case, 443–453
Negligence cases, 442
Nolo contendere plea, effect of, 442

COLLECTION OF TAX
    See also, Fiduciary Liability; Jeopardy and Termination Assessments; Liens; Transferee Liability; Trust Fund Taxes
Fourth Amendment protections, applicability of, 497
Power of IRS,
    Judicial proceedings to collect, 722
    Levy, 722, 777
    Lien, see Liens
    Set off, 752

COMPLIANCE WITH TAX LAWS, 12–15

CONFIDENTIALITY AND DISCLOSURE
    See also, Ethical Considerations; Evidence; Freedom of Information Act; Privacy Act of 1974
Generally, 85–120
Provisions of the Internal Revenue Code, 103–120
Relationship to FOIA, 85–102

CONFLICT OF INTEREST
See Multiple Representation

CONGRESS
See Legislation Process

CONSPIRACY
See Criminal Charges

CONSTITUTIONAL RIGHTS
    See also, Evidence
Generally, 703–716
Miranda-type warnings, 639–641
Searches and seizures, 641–657

CRIMINAL CHARGES
Aiding or assisting in false return (IRC § 7206(2)), 538, 549
Civil penalties, comparison to, 220
Conspiracy (18 U.S.C.A. § 371), 538
Evasion (IRC § 7201), 537, 540, 548
Failure to file or pay tax (IRC § 7203), 538
False return (IRC § 7206(1)), 538, 549
False statement (18 U.S.C.A. § 1001), 538
Limitations periods,
    Generally, 613
    Commencement of running of period, 613
    Continuing offense theory, 617

CRIMINAL TAX INVESTIGATIONS
    See also, Constitutional Rights; Forfeiture; Grand Jury Proceedings; Summons Power of IRS
Generally, 631–663
Conference opportunities during, 631–633
Information sources triggering, 631
Justice Department's role, 632
Representation of taxpayer during, 633–639

CRIMINAL TAX PROSECUTIONS
See Evidence; Proof of Income; Summary Witness; Venue

DECLARATORY JUDGMENTS, 397–400

DEFICIENCY
See Assessment of Deficiencies; Deficiency Notice; Penalties, Civil

DEFICIENCY NOTICE (90–day letter)
Function of, 162
Prerequisite to assessment and collection of tax, 162

DEPARTMENT OF JUSTICE, 7–8
See also, Criminal Tax Investigations

DEPARTMENT OF TREASURY
    See also, Internal Revenue Service
Generally, 1–7
Assistant Secretary for Tax Policy, 7

DETERMINATION LETTER, 191–193

DISCLOSURE ACTIONS
See Declaratory Judgments

DISTRICT COURTS
See Forum Selection

EQUITABLE RECOUPMENT AND STATUTORY MITIGATION, 189–216

ETHICAL CONSIDERATIONS
    See also, Practice before the IRS
Aiding and abetting understatement of tax liability, 303–306
Conflict of interest, see Multiple Representation

ETHICAL CONSIDERATIONS—Cont'd
Disclosures to IRS,
    Generally, 18–22
Opinion, 19–21
Tax shelter opinions, 22

EVASION OF TAXES
See Criminal Charges; Willfulness

EVIDENCE
    See also, Constitutional Rights; Proof of Income; Summary Chart; Summary Witness
Attorney-client,
    Crime/fraud exception, 520
    Specific disclosures discussed,
        Client's identity, 535–536
        Documents in attorney's possession, 519–520
        Joint-defense, 519
    Proof of income, 617–630
Self-incrimination,
    Waiver of privilege, 519
    Work-product doctrine, 513–514
        Applicability to summons enforcement, 520
Suppression,
    Civil proceedings, use in, 453–457
    Summons power, 520

EXAMINATION OF RETURNS
    See also, Second Inspections; Settlement and Closing Agreements
Examination procedures, 123–128
Selection for audit, 121–123
Settlement, 140
Special partnership procedures, 151–160
Thirty-day letter, 131–134

FIDUCIARY LIABILITY, 273, 810–821

FIFTH AMENDMENT CLAIM ON TAX RETURN
See Evidence

FORFEITURE
Asset, 672–696

FORUM SELECTION
Available Forums,
    Claims Court, 325–326
    District Court, 323–325
    Tax Court, 322–323, 334–342
New Issues, government's ability to assert, 329–330
Partnership proceedings, 330–331
Precedents applied, 328–329
Restrictions on choice, 326–327

FRAUD
See Criminal Charges; Collateral Estoppel; Penalties, Civil

FREEDOM OF INFORMATION ACT (FOIA)
    See also, Confidentiality and Disclosure; Privacy Act of 1974

FREEDOM OF INFORMATION ACT (FOIA)
—Cont'd
    Generally, 85–90
Disclosable information, 85–86
Exempt information, 86–89

GRAND JURY PROCEEDINGS, 657–663

IMPROVED PENALTY ADMINISTRATION AND COMPLIANCE TAX ACT ("IMPACT")
See Penalties, Civil

INCOME TAX RETURN PREPARER REGULATIONS
    Generally, 36–48
Disclosure and recordkeeping requirements, 54–55
Income tax return preparer, defined, 52–53
Penalties, 53–54, 277–297

INJUNCTIONS
Anti-Injunction Act, 835–836
Jeopardy and termination assessments, 847
Wrongful levy, 856–862

INNOCENT SPOUSE, 821–835

INTEREST
Deductibility, 320
Deficiencies, 318
Rate of, 319
Tax motivated transactions, 319–320

INTERNAL REVENUE SERVICE
    See also, Collection of Tax; Criminal Tax Investigations; Department of Treasury; Examination of Returns
Assistant Commissioner (International), 5
Chief Counsel, Office of, 5–6
District offices, 4–5
National Office, 3
Regional offices, 3–4
Service centers, 4

INTERVIEW ("Q & A")
See Summons Power of IRS

JEOPARDY AND TERMINATION ASSESSMENTS, 753

LEGISLATION PROCESS, 8–12

LENDERS' LIABILITY
See Trust Fund Taxes

LEVY
See Collection of Tax

LIENS
    See also, Collection of Tax
Bankruptcy, 866
Federal tax lien,
    Creation, 720–721
    Duration, 721
    Release, 721–722

LIMITATIONS
See Assessment of Deficiencies; Collection of Tax; Criminal Charges; Refund Litigation

MIRANDA-TYPE WARNINGS
See Constitutional Rights

MONEY LAUNDERING AND CASH TRANSACTION REPORTING, 664–672

MULTIPLE REPRESENTATION
IRS Guidelines, 51
Witness and target, 51–52

NOTICE OF DEFICIENCY
See Deficiency Notice

PENALTIES, CIVIL
  Generally, 217–220
Assessment of, see Assessment of Deficiencies
Criminal, comparison to, 220
Delinquency penalties, 310–318
Fraud,
  Generally, 253–277
  Burden of proof, 276
  Computation of penalty, 276–277
  Defined, 253–276
Frivolous income tax return, 306–308
IMPACT, 218–220, 223, 240–241, 251–253, 302–303, 310–312, 317–318
Negligence, 224–231
Substantial understatement, 231–244
Tax shelter penalties, 297–303
Understatement of liability, aiding and abetting, 303–306

PENALTIES, CRIMINAL
See Criminal Charges

POWER OF ATTORNEY, 39

PRACTICE BEFORE IRS, 36

PRIVACY ACT OF 1974, 102–103
See also, Confidentiality and Disclosure; Freedom of Information Act

PRIVILEGES
See Evidence

PROOF OF INCOME
Direct proof (specific items method), 617–618
Indirect proof,
  Bank deposits method, 628–629
  Cash expenditures method, 626–628
  Net worth method, 618–626
  Percentage mark-up method, 629–630

PROTEST
See Thirty-Day Letter.

PROVIDERS OF WAGES, LIABILITY OF
See Trust Fund Taxes

Q & A (Formal Interview)
See Summons Power of IRS

REFUND LITIGATION
  See also, Account Stated, Suit On; Equitable Recoupment and Statutory Mitigation; Forum Selection
Anti-assignment statute, 417–420
Burden of proof, 331–342
Jurisdictional prerequisites,
  Generally, 400
  Claim for refund, 400–416
  Divisible taxes, 409–410
  Full payment rule, 400–409
  Payment on an assessment, 410
Limitations, 185–188
Nature of refund suit, 332–334
Timely filing, 188, 416–417

REGULATIONS
See Treasury Regulations

REOPENING OF CLOSED CASES
See Second Inspections

RES JUDICATA
See Collateral Estoppel

RESPONSIBLE PERSONS' LIABILITY
See Trust Fund Taxes

RETURN PREPARERS
See Income Tax Return Preparer Regulations

RULINGS PROGRAM
  See also, Acquiescence by Commissioner; Declaratory Judgments; Treasury Regulations
Comfort Rulings, 68
Definitions,
  Actions on Decision, 71
  Determination letter, 70
  Letter ruling, 66–69
  Revenue procedures, 67
  Revenue ruling, 66–67
  Ruling, 66
  Technical Advice, 70
Discriminatory treatment by IRS, 79–85
Reliance, effect of, 71–72
Requests for rulings,
  Generally, 66–85
  Considerations involved, 68–69
  Procedure, 69
  Withdrawal of request, 68
Revocation of rulings, 71–79
"User fee" program, 68

SEARCHES AND SEIZURES
See Constitutional Rights

SECOND INSPECTIONS, 129–131
Closed case, 131
Continuing investigations, 513
Notice requirement, 513

SETTLEMENT AND CLOSING AGREEMENTS
  See also, Collateral Agreement
Consent to assessment (Form 870), 140–143

SETTLEMENT AND CLOSING AGREEMENTS—Cont'd
Informal settlement agreements,
    Generally, 140
    Agreement to assessment (Form 870–AD), 143–149
Statutory closing agreements (Forms 866 and 906), 149–150

SMALL TAX CASES
See Tax Court

SUMMARY CHART, 701–703

SUMMARY WITNESS, 701–703

SUMMONS POWER OF IRS
See also, Evidence
Defenses to compliance,
    Improper purpose (bad faith), 494–506
    Information not within IRS possession, 509
    Lack of possession, 525
Enforcement proceedings, 491
Handwriting exemplars, 491
Interview, formal ("Q & A"), 483–486
John Doe summons, 529–536
"Powell" standard, 491–494
Relevance, 506
Second inspections, 511
Third party recordkeeper summons, 491, 526–527

SUPPRESSION OF EVIDENCE
See Constitutional Rights; Evidence

TAX COURT
See also, Forum Selection
Decision-making authority, 378–383
Described, 322–323
Discovery, 384
Jurisdiction,
    Irrevocability of, 377–378
    Prerequisites to, 347–377
Sanctions, 389–392
Settlement, 392–396

TAX COURT—Cont'd
Small cases, 396–397

TAX SHELTERS
Penalty provisions, 242–244, 297–303

TECHNICAL ADVICE, 139–140

TERMINATION ASSESSMENTS
See Jeopardy and Termination Assessments

THIRTY-DAY LETTER
Generally, 131–134
Responses to,
    Generally, 131–134
    Protest, 132, 134

TRANSFEREE LIABILITY
See Fiduciary Liability

TREASURY REGULATIONS
Interpretative regulations, 56–57
Judicial review, 62–66
Legislative reenactment doctrine, 61–62
Legislative regulations, 57
Procedural regulations, 62
Retroactive effect, 57–62
Temporary regulations, 57
Validity of, 56–57

TRUST FUND TAXES (Withholdings)
Generally, 806–810
Providers of wages, liability of, 803–806
Responsible person's liability,
    Designation of payments, 802–803
    Joint and several liability, 800–802
    Responsible person, 778–798
    Willfulness requirement, 799

VENUE (Criminal), 697–701

WILLFULNESS, 562

WITHHOLDING TAXES
See Trust Fund Taxes